Department of Economic and Social Affairs
Département des affaires économiques et sociales

DÉPÔT
DEPOSIT

2001

Demographic Yearbook

Annuaire démographique

Fifty-third issue/Cinquante-troisième édition

Université d'Ottawa
BIBLIOTHEQUES

LIBRARIES
University of Ottawa

United Nations/Nations Unies
New York, 2003

NOTE

Symbols of United Nations documents are composed of capital letters combined with figures. Mention of such a symbol indicates a reference to a United Nations document.

The designations used in this publication have been provided by the competent authorities. Those designations and the presentation of material in this publication do not imply the expression of any opinion whatsoever on the part of the Secretariat of the United Nations concerning the legal status of any country, territory, city or area or of its authorities, or concerning the delimitation of its frontiers or boundaries.

Where the designation "country or area" appears in the headings of tables, it covers countries, territories, cities or areas.

NOTE

Les cotes des documents de l'Organisation des Nations Unies se composent de lettres majuscules et de chiffres. La simple mention d'une cote dans un texte signifie qu'il s'agit d'un document de l'Organisation.

Les appellations employées dans cette publication ont été fournies par les autorités compétentes. Ces appellations et la présentation des données qui figurent dans cette publication n'impliquent, de la part du Secrétariat de l'Organisation des Nations Unies, aucune prise de position quant au statut juridique des pays, territoires, villes ou zones, ou de leurs autorités, ni quant au tracé de leurs frontières ou limites.

L'appellation « pays ou zone » figurant dans les titres des rubriques des tableaux désigne des pays, des territoires, des villes ou des zones.

ST/ESA/STAT/SER.R/32

UNITED NATIONS PUBLICATION
Sales No. E/F.03.XIII.1

PUBLICATION DES NATIONS UNIES
Numéro de vente : E/F.03.XIII.1

Enquiries should be directed to:
PUBLISHING DIVISION
UNITED NATIONS
NEW YORK, NY 10017

Adresser toutes demandes de renseignements à la :
DIVISION DES PUBLICATIONS
NATIONS UNIES
NEW YORK, NY 10017

ISBN 92-1-051094-1

Copyright © United Nations, 2003
All rights reserved

Copyright © Nations Unies, 2003
Tous droits réservés

The Department of Economic and Social Affairs of the United Nations Secretariat is a vital interface between global policies in the economic, social and environmental spheres and national action. The Department works in three main interlinked areas: (i) it compiles, generates and analyses a wide range of economic, social and environmental data and information on which States Members of the United Nations draw to review common problems and to take stock of policy options; (ii) it facilitates the negotiations of Member States in many intergovernmental bodies on joint courses of action to address ongoing or emerging global challenges; and (iii) it advises interested Governments on the ways and means of translating policy frameworks developed in United Nations conferences and summits into programmes at the country level and, through technical assistance, helps build national capacities.

Le Département des affaires économiques et sociales du Secrétariat de l'Organisation des Nations Unies sert de relais entre les orientations arrêtées au niveau international dans les domaines économiques, sociaux et environnementaux et les politiques exécutées à l'échelon national. Il intervient dans trois grands domaines liés les uns aux autres : i) il compile, produit et analyse une vaste gamme de données et d'éléments d'information sur des questions économiques, sociales et environnementales dont les États Membres de l'Organisation se servent pour examiner des problèmes communs et évaluer les options qui s'offrent à eux; ii) il facilite les négociations entre les États Membres dans de nombreux organes intergouvernementaux sur les orientations à suivre de façon collective afin de faire face aux problèmes mondiaux existants ou en voie d'apparition; iii) il conseille les gouvernements intéressés sur la façon de transposer les orientations politiques arrêtées à l'occasion des conférences et sommets des Nations Unies en programmes exécutables au niveau national et aide à renforcer les capacités nationales au moyen de programmes d'assistance technique.

NOTE

Symbols of United Nations documents are composed of capital letters combined with figures. Mention of such a symbol indicates a reference to a United Nations document.

The designations used in this publication have been provided by the competent authorities. Those designations and the presentation of material in this publication do not imply the expression of any opinion whatsoever on the part of the Secretariat of the United Nations concerning the legal status of any country, territory, city or area or of its authorities, or concerning the delimitation of its frontiers or boundaries.

Where the designation "country or area" appears in the headings of tables, it covers countries, territories, cities or areas.

NOTE

Les cotes des documents de l'Organisation des Nations Unies se composent de lettres majuscules et de chiffres. La simple mention d'une cote dans un texte signifie qu'il s'agit d'un document de l'Organisation.

Les appellations utilisées dans cette publication ont été fournies par les autorités compétentes. Ces appellations et la présentation des données qui figurent dans cette publication n'impliquent de la part du Secrétariat de l'Organisation des Nations Unies aucune prise de position quant au statut juridique des pays, territoires, villes ou zones, ou de leurs autorités, ni quant au trace de leurs frontières ou limites.

L'appellation « pays ou zone» figurant dans les titres des rubriques des tableaux désigne des pays, des territoires, des villes ou des zones.

ST/ESA/STAT/SER.R/32

UNITED NATIONS PUBLICATION
Sales No. E/F.03.XIII.1

PUBLICATION DES NATIONS UNIES
Numéro de vente: E/F.03.XIII.1

Inquiries should be directed to:
PUBLISHING DIVISION
UNITED NATIONS
NEW YORK, NY 10017

Adresser toutes demandes de renseignements à la
DIVISION DES PUBLICATIONS
NATIONS UNIES
NEW YORK, NY 10017

ISBN 92-1-051094-1

Copyright © United Nations, 2003
All rights reserved

Copyright © Nations Unies, 2003
Tous droits réservé

Topics of the Demographic Yearbook series: 1948 - 2001

Sujets des diverses éditions de l'Annuaire démographique: 1948 - 2001

Year Année	Sales No. - Numéro de vente	Issue - Edition	Special topic - Sujet spécial
1948	49.XIII.1	First-Première	General demography-Démographie générale
1949-50	51.XIII.1	Second-Deuxième	Natality statistics-Statistiques de la natalité
1951	52.XIII.1	Third-Trosième	Mortality statistics-Statistiques de la mortalité
1952	53.XIII.1	Fourth-Quatrième	Population distribution-Répartition de la population
1953	54.XIII.1	Fifth-Cinquième	General demography-Démographie générale
1954	55.XIII.1	Sixth-Sixième	Natality statistics -Statistiques de la natalité
1955	56.XIII.1	Seventh-Septième	Population censuses-Recensement de population
1956	57.XIII.1	Eighth-Huitième	Ethnic and economic characteristics of population-Caractéristiques ethniques et économiques de la population
1957	58.XIII.1	Ninth-Neuvième	Mortality statistics- Statistiques de la mortalité
1958	59.XIII.1	Tenth-Dixième	Marriage and divorce statistics- Statistiques de la nuptialitè et de la divortialité
1959	60.XIII.1	Eleventh-Onzième	Natality statistics- Statistiques de la natalité
1960	61.XIII.1	Twelfth-Douzième	Population trends- l' évolution de la population
1961	62.XIII.1	Thirteenth-Treizième	Mortality Statistics- Statistiques de la mortalité
1962	63.XIII.1	Fourteenth-Quatorzième	Population census statistics I- Statistiques des recensements de population I
1963	64.XIII.1	Fifteenth-Quinzième	Population census statistics II- Statistiques des recensements de population II
1964	65.XIII.1	Sixteenth-Seizième	Population census statistics III- Statistiques des recensements de population III
1965	66.XIII.1	Seventeenth-Dix-septième	Natality statistics- Statistiques de la natalité
1966	67.XIII.1	Eighteenth-Dix-huitième	Mortality statistics I- Statistiques de la mortalité I
1967	E/F.68.XIII.1	Nineteenth-Dix-neuvième	Mortality statistics II - Statistiques de la mortalité II
1968	E/F.69.XIII.1	Twentieth-Vingtième	Marriage and divorce statistics-Statistiques de la nuptialité et de la divortialité
1969	E/F.70.XIII.1	Twenty-first-Vingt et unième	Natality statistics-Statistiques de la natalité
1970	E/F.71.XIII.1	Twenty-second-Vingt-deuxième	Population trends-l' évolution de la population
1971	E/F.72.XIII.1	Twenty-third-Vingh-troisième	Population census statistics I- Statistiques de recensements de population I
1972	E/F.73.XIII.1	Twenty-fourth-Vingt-quatrième	Population census statistics II- Statistiques des recensements de population II
1973	E/F.74.XIII.1	Twenty-fifth-Vingt-cinquième	Population census statistics III- Statistiques des recensements de population III
1974	E/F.75.XIII.1	Twenty-sixth-Vingt-sixième	Mortality statistics - Statistiques de la mortalité
1975	E/F.76.XIII.1	Twenty-seventh-Vingt-septième	Natality statistics- Statistiques de la natalité
1976	E/F.77.XIII.1	Twenty-eighth-Vingt-huitième	Marriage and divorce statistics- Statistiques de la nuptialité et de la divortialité
1977	E/F.78.XIII.1	Twenty-ninth-Vingt-neuvième	International Migration Statistics- internationales
1978	E/F.79.XIII.1	Thirtieth-Trentième	General tables- Tableaux de caractère général
1978	E/F.79.XIII.8	Special issue-Edition spéciale	Historical supplement-Supplément rétrospectif
1979	E/F.80.XIII.1	Thirty-first-Trente et unième	Population census statistics-Statistiques des recensements de population

Topics of the Demographic Yearbook series: 1948 - 2001

Sujets des diverses éditions de l'Annuaire démographique: 1948 - 2001

Year Année	Sales No. - Numéro de vente	Issue - Edition	Special topic - Sujet spécial
1980	E/F.81.XIII.1	Thirty-second- Trente-deuxième	Mortality statistics- Statistiques de la mortalité
1981	E/F.82.XIII.1	Thirty-third- Trente-troisième	Natality statistics- Statistiques de la natalité
1982	E/F.83.XIII.1	Thirty-fourth- Trente-quatrième	Marriage and divorce statistics- Statistiques de la nuptialité et de la divortialité
1983	E/F.84.XIII.1	Thirty fifth- Trente-cinquième	Population census statistics I- Statistiques des recensements de population I
1984	E/F.85.XIII.1	Thirty-sixth- Trente-sixième	Population census statistics II- Statistiques des recensements de population II
1985	E/F.86.XIII.1	Thirty-seventh- Trente-septième	Mortality statistics- Statistiques de la mortalité
1986	E/F.87.XIII.1	Thirty-eightth- Trente-Hiutième	Natality statistics- Statistiques de la natalité
1987	E/F.88.XIII.1	Thirty-ninth- Trente-neuvième	Household composition- Les éléments du ménage
1988	E/F.89.XIII.1	Fortieth- Quarantième	Population census statistics- Statistiques des recensements de population
1989	E/F.90.XIII.1	Forty-first- Quarante-et-unième	International Migration Statistics- Statistiques des migration internationales
1990	E/F.91.XIII.1	Forty-second- Quarante-deuxième	Marriage and divorce statistics- Statistiques de la nuptialité et de la divortialité
1991	E/F.92.XIII.1	Forty-third- Quarante-troisième	General tables- Tableaux de caractère général
1991	E/F.92.XIII.8	Special issue- Edition spéciale	Population ageing and the situation of elderly persons- Vieillissement de la population et situation des personnes agées
1992	E/F.94.XIII.1	Forty-forth- Quarante-quatrième	Fertility and mortality statistics- Statistiques de la fecondité et de la mortalité
1993	E/F.95.XIII.1	Forty-fifth- Quarante-cinquième	Population census statistics I- Statistiques des recensements de population I
1994	E/F.96.XIII.1	Forty-sixth- Quarante-sixième	Population census statistics II- Statistiques des recensements de population II
1995	E/F.97.XIII.1	Forty-seventh- Quarante-septième	Household composition-Les éléments du ménage
1996	E/F.98.XIII.1	Forty-eighth- Quarante-hutième	Mortality statistics- Statistiques de la mortalité
1997	E/F.99.XIII.1	Forty-ninth- Quarante-neuvième	General tables- Tableaux de caractère général
1997	E/F.99.XIII.12	Special issue- Edition spéciale (CD)	Historical supplement- Supplément rétrospectif
1998	E/F.00.XIII.1	Fiftieth- Cinquantième	General tables- Tableaux de caractère général
1999	E/F.01.XIII.1	Fifty-first- Cinquante-et-unième	General tables- Tableaux de caractère général
1999	E/F.02.XIII.6	Special issue- Edition spéciale (CD)	Natality Statistics- Statistiques de la natalité
2000	E/F.02.XIII.1	Fifty-second- Cinquante-deuxième	General tables- Tableaux de caractère général
2001	E/F.03.XIII.1	Fifty-third- Cinquante- troisième	General tables- Tableaux de caractère général

CONTENTS - TABLE DES MATIERES

vii

EXPLANATIONS OF SYMBOLS

Category not applicable	..
Data not available	...
Magnitude zero	-
Magnitude not zero, but less than half of unit employed	0 and/or 0.0
Provisional	*
Data tabulated by year of registration rather than occurrence	+
Based on less than specified minimum	◆
Relatively reliable data	Roman type
Data of lesser reliability	*Italics*

EXPLICATION DES SIGNES

Sans objet	..
Données non disponibles	...
Néant	-
Chiffre inférieur à la moitié de l'unité employée	0 et/ou 0.0
Données provisoires	*
Donnée exploitées selon l'année de l'enregistrement et non l'année de l'événement	+
Rapport fondé sur un nombre inférieur à celui spécifié	◆
Données relativement sûres	Charactères romains
Données dont l'exactitude est moindre	*Italiques*

INTRODUCTION

The *Demographic Yearbook* is an international collection of national demographic statistics, provided by national statistical authorities to the Statistics Division of the United Nations Department of Economic and Social Affairs. The *Yearbook* is in the set of coordinated and interrelated publications issued by the United Nations and its specialized agencies,[1] designed to supply basic statistical data for such users as demographers, economists, public-health workers and sociologists. Under the coordinated plan, the *Demographic Yearbook* is the source of national demographic statistics. Through the co-operation of national statistical services, official demographic statistics are compiled in the *Yearbook*, as available, for over 230 countries or areas throughout the world.

The *Demographic Yearbook 2001* is the fifty-third in a series published by the United Nations, since 1948. It contains general tables including a world summary of selected demographic statistics, statistics on the size, distribution and trends in national populations, natality, foetal mortality, infant and maternal mortality, general mortality, nuptiality and divorce. Data are shown by urban/rural residence, as available. In addition, the volume provides Technical Notes, a cumulative index and a listing of the issues of the *Yearbook* published to date.

The Technical Notes on the Statistical Tables are provided to assist the reader in using the tables. The cumulative historical index, at the end of the *Yearbook*, is a guide on content and coverage of all fifty-three issues, and indicates for each of the topics that have been published, the issues in which they are presented and the years covered. A list of the *Demographic Yearbook* issues, with their corresponding sales number and the special topics featured in each issue are shown on pages iii and iv.

Until the 1996 issue (i.e., the 48th issue), each Issue consisted of two parts, the general tables and special topic tables, published in the same volume with the regular topics.[2] Beginning with the 1997 issue (49th issue), the special topic tables are being disseminated on CD-ROMs as supplements to the regular issues. Two CD-ROMs have so far been issued: the *Demographic Yearbook Historical Supplement*, which presents a wide panorama of basic demographic statistics for the period 1948 to 1997, and the *Demographic Yearbook: Natality Statistics*, which contains a series of detailed tables dedicated to natality and covering the period from 1980 to 1998.

The first issue of the CD-ROMs contains historical demographic statistics and presents time series of population size, by age, sex and urban/rural residence; natality; mortality; and nuptiality, as well as selected derived measures on these vital events and of population change for a 50-year period, 1948-1997. It complements the *Demographic Yearbook: Historical Supplement*, issued in 1979, which presents time series on the same topics over a 30-year time period, 1948-1978.

The second CD-ROM issue serves to update the statistics presented in the 1986 issue. It contains summary tables on natality and natality data classified by characteristics such as, age of mother, birth order, by age of father and type of birth, and birth-weight and gestational age. Other tables include fertility of mothers in wedlock by duration of married life, and deaths. The first issue of the *Yearbook*, the *Demographic Yearbook 1948*, included many of the same tables, showing annual data for the period 1932 to 1947. Therefore, the above-mentioned historical supplements jointly present a wealth of historical demographic data for international analyses.

Population statistics are not available for all the countries or areas, for a variety of reasons. In an effort to provide estimates of mid-year population and of selected vital statistics for all countries and areas, two annexes have been introduced in this issue of the *Demographic Yearbook*. Annex 1 presents United Nations population estimates for the period 1992-2001 and the second presents average crude birth and death rates, infant mortality and total fertility rates, as well as expectation of life at birth over the period 2000-2005. These data are produced by the United Nations Population Division and published in the *World Population Prospects - The 2002 Revision*.[3]

Demographic statistics shown in this issue of the *Yearbook* are available in electronic format, for further analysis by users, by contacting the Statistics Division of the United Nations Secretariat, at demostat@un.org. Information about the Statistics Division's data collection and dissemination programme is also available on website at http://unstats.un.org/unsd/demographic/workshop/EGM_dyb/index.htm.

TECHNICAL NOTES ON THE STATISTICAL TABLES

1. GENERAL REMARKS

1.1 Arrangement of Technical Notes

These Technical Notes are designed to provide the reader with relevant information for using the statistical tables. Information pertaining to the *Yearbook* in general is presented in the sections dealing with geographical aspects, population and vital statistics. In addition, preceding each table are notes describing the variables, remarks on the reliability and limitation of the data, countries covered, and information on the presentation of earlier data. When appropriate, details on computation of rates, ratios or percentages are presented.

1.2 Arrangement of tables

This issue contains general tables only. Since the numbering of the tables does not correspond exactly to those in previous issues, the reader is advised to use the historical index that appears at the end of this book to find the reference to data in earlier issues.

1.3 Source of data

The statistics presented in the *Demographic Yearbook* are official national data unless otherwise indicated. The primary source of data for the *Yearbook* is a set of questionnaires sent annually by the United Nations Statistics Division to over 230 national statistical services and other appropriate government offices. Data reported on these questionnaires are supplemented, to the extent possible, with data taken from official national publications, official websites and through correspondence with national statistical services. In the interest of comparability, rates, ratios and percentages have been calculated by the Statistics Division of the United Nations, except for the life table functions, and total fertility rate, and also crude birth rate and crude death rate for some countries or areas, in table 4, as appropriately noted. The methods used by the Statistics Division to calculate these rates and ratios are described in the Technical Notes for each table. The population figures used for these computations are those pertaining to the corresponding years published in this or previous issues of the *Yearbook*.

In cases when data in this issue of the *Demographic Yearbook* differ from those published in earlier issues or related publications, statistics in this issue may be assumed to reflect revisions to these data received by August 2003. In particular, data shown as provisional are generally subject to further revision by national offices.

2. GEOGRAPHICAL ASPECTS

2.1 Coverage

Data are shown for as many individual countries or areas as provided the information. Table 3 is the most comprehensive in geographical coverage, presenting data on population and surface area for all countries and areas with a population of at least 50 persons. Not all of these countries or areas appear in subsequent tables. In many cases the data required for a particular table are not available. In general, the more detailed the data required for a table, the fewer the number of countries or areas that can provide them.

In addition, with one exception, rates and ratios are presented only for countries or areas reporting at least a minimum number of relevant events. The minimums are stated in the Technical Notes to individual tables. The exception, in which rates for countries or areas are shown regardless of the number of events on which they were based, is table 4, presenting a summary of vital statistics rates, crude birth rates and crude death rates respectively.

Except for summary data shown for the world and by major areas and regions in tables 1 and 2, all data are presented at the national level. The number of countries shown in each table is given in the table specific technical notes, and a table at the end of these Technical notes indicates which countries are covered in each of the tables.

2.2 Territorial composition

To the extent possible, all data, including time series data, relate to the territory within 2001 boundaries, when the data were requested from the countries or areas. Exceptions to this are footnoted in individual tables. Additionally, in table 3, recent changes and other relevant clarifications are specified.

Data relating to the People's Republic of China generally include those for Taiwan Province for statistics relating to population, surface area, natural resources, natural conditions such as climate, etc. Therefore in this publication, the data published under the heading "China" include those for Taiwan Province. In other fields of statistics, they may not include Taiwan Province.

Through accession of the German Democratic Republic to the Federal Republic of Germany, as of 3 October 1990, the two German States have united to form one sovereign State — Germany. Data pertaining to Germany prior to 3

October 1990 are indicated separately for the Federal Republic of Germany and the former German Democratic Republic based on their respective boundaries at the time indicated; they are otherwise presented jointly under "Germany".

In 1991, the Union of Soviet Socialist Republics formally dissolved into fifteen individual countries (Armenia, Azerbaijan, Belarus, Estonia, Georgia, Kazakhstan, Kyrgyzstan, Latvia, Lithuania, Republic of Moldova, Russian Federation, Tajikistan, Turkmenistan, Ukraine and Uzbekistan). Data for the period after 1991 are shown for each of these individual countries.

2.3 Nomenclature

Because of space limitations, the country or area names listed in the tables are generally the commonly employed short titles in use in the United Nations as of March 2004[4], the full titles being used only when a short form is not available. The latest version of the *Standard Country or Area Codes for Statistics Use* can be accessed at http://unstats.un.org/unsd/methods/m49/m49.htm.

2.3.1 Order of presentation

Countries or areas are listed in English alphabetical order within the following continents: Africa, North America, South America, Asia, Europe and Oceania.

The designations and presentation of the material in this publication were adopted solely for the purpose of providing a convenient geographical basis for the accompanying statistical series. The same qualification applies to all notes and explanations concerning the geographical units for which data are presented.

2.4 Surface area data

Surface area data, shown in tables 1 and 3, represent the total surface area, comprising land area and inland waters (assumed to consist of major rivers and lakes) and excluding only Polar Regions and uninhabited islands. The surface area given is the most recent estimate available. They are presented in square kilometres, a conversion factor of 2.589988 having been applied to surface areas originally reported in square miles.

2.4.1 Comparability over time

Comparability over time in surface area estimates for any given country or area may be affected by changes in the surface area estimation procedures, increases in actual land surface by reclamation, boundary changes, changes in the concept of "land surface area" used or a change in the unit of measurement used. In most cases it was possible to ascertain the reason for a revision; otherwise, the latest figures have generally been accepted as correct and substituted for those previously on file.

2.4.2 International comparability

Lack of international comparability between surface area estimates arises primarily from differences in definition. In particular, there is considerable variation in the treatment of coastal bays, inlets and gulfs, rivers and lakes. International comparability is also impaired by the variation in methods employed to estimate surface area. These range from surveys based on modern scientific methods to conjectures based on diverse types of information. Some estimates are recent while others may not be. Since neither the exact method of determining the surface area nor the precise definition of its composition and time reference is known for all countries or areas, the estimates in table 3 should not be considered strictly comparable from one country or area to another.

3. POPULATION

Population statistics, that is, those pertaining to the size, geographical distribution and demographic characteristics of the population, are presented in a number of tables of the *Demographic Yearbook*.

Data for countries or areas include population census figures, estimates based on results of sample surveys (in the absence of a census), postcensal or intercensal estimates and those derived from continuous population registers. In the present issue of the *Yearbook*, the latest available census figure of the total population of each country or area and mid-year estimates for 1995 and 2001 are presented in table 3. Mid-year estimates of total population for 10 years (1992-2001) are shown in table 5 and mid-year estimates of urban and total population by sex for 10 years (1992-2001) are shown in table 6. The latest available data on population by age, sex and urban/rural residence are given in table 7. The latest available figures on the population of capital cities and of cities or urban agglomerations of 100,000 or more inhabitants are presented in table 8.

Summary estimates of the mid-year population of the world, major areas and regions for selected years and of its age and sex distribution in 2001 are set forth in tables 1 and 2, respectively.

The statistics on total population, population by age, sex and urban/rural distribution are used in the calculation of rates in the *Yearbook*. Vital rates by age and sex were calculated using data that appear in table 7 in this issue or the corresponding tables of previous issues of the *Demographic Yearbook*.

3.1 Sources of variation of data

The comparability of data is affected by several factors, including (1) the definition of total population; (2) the definition used to classify the population into its urban/rural components; (3) the accuracy of age reporting; (4) the extent of over-enumeration or under-enumeration in the most recent census or other source of bench-mark population statistics; and (5) the quality of population estimates. These five factors will be discussed in some detail in sections 3.1.1 to 3.2.2 below. Other relevant problems are discussed in the technical notes to the individual tables. Readers interested in more detail, relating in particular to the basic concepts of population size, distribution and characteristics as elaborated by the United Nations, should consult the *Principles and Recommendations for Population and Housing Censuses, Revision 1.*[5]

3.1.1 Total population

The most important impediment to comparability of total populations is the difference between the concept of a de facto and de jure population. A de facto population should include all persons physically present in the country or area at the reference date. The de jure population, by contrast, should include all usual residents of the given country or area, whether or not they were physically present in the area at the reference date. By definition, therefore, a de facto total and a de jure total are not entirely comparable.

Comparability of even two de facto or de jure totals is often affected by the fact that strict conformity to either of these concepts is rare. For example, some so-called de facto counts do not include foreign military, naval and diplomatic personnel present in the country or area on official duty, and their accompanying family members and servants; some do not include foreign visitors in transit through the country or area or transients on ships in the harbour. On the other hand, they may include such persons as merchant seamen and fishermen who are temporarily out of the country or area working at their trade.

The de jure population figure presents even greater variations in comparability, in part because it depends in the first place on the concept of "usual residence", which varies from one country or area to another and is difficult to apply consistently in a census or survey enumeration. For example, non-national civilian temporarily in a country or area as short-term workers may officially be considered residents after a stay of a specified period of time or they may be considered as non-residents throughout the duration of their stay; at the same time, these individuals may be officially considered as residents or non-residents of the country or area from which they came, depending on the duration and/or purpose of their absence. Furthermore, regardless of the official treatment, individual respondents may apply their own interpretation of residence in responding to the inquiry. In addition, there may be considerable differences in the accuracy with which countries or areas are informed about the number of their residents temporarily out of the country or area.

As far as possible, the population statistics presented in the tables of the *Yearbook* refer to the de facto population. Those reported to have been based on the de jure concept are identified as such. Figures not otherwise qualified may, therefore, be assumed to have been reported by countries or areas as being based on a de facto definition of the population. In an effort to overcome, to the extent possible, the effect of the lack of strict conformity to either the de facto or the de jure concept given above, significant exceptions with respect to inclusions and exclusions of specific population groups, are footnoted when they are known.

It should be remembered, however, that the necessary detailed information has not been available in many cases. It cannot, therefore, be assumed that figures not thus qualified reflect strict de facto or de jure definitions.

A possible source of variation within the statistics of a single country or area may arise from the fact that some countries or areas collect information on both the de facto and the de jure population in, for example, a census, but prepare detailed tabulations for only the de jure population. Hence, even though the total population shown in table 3 is de facto, the figures shown in the tables presenting various characteristics of the population, for example, urban/rural distribution, age and sex distribution, may be de jure. These de jure figures are footnoted when known.

3.1.2 Urban/rural classification

International comparability of urban/rural distributions is seriously impaired by the wide variation among national definitions of the concept of "urban". The definitions used by individual countries or areas and their implications are shown at the end of technical notes for table 6.

3.1.3 Age distribution

The classification of population by age is a core element of most analyses, estimation and projection of population statistics. Unfortunately, age data are subject to a number of sources of error and non-comparability. Accordingly, the reliability of age data should be of concern to users of these statistics.

3.1.3.1 Collection and compilation of age data

Age is the estimated or calculated interval of time between the date of birth and the date of the census or survey, expressed in completed solar years.[3] There are two methods of collecting information on age. The first is to obtain the date of birth for each member of the population in a census or survey and then to calculate the completed age of the individual by subtracting the date of birth from the date of enumeration.[6] The second method is to record the individual's completed age at the time of the census or survey, that is to say, age at last birthday.

The recommended method is to calculate age at last birthday by subtracting the exact date of birth from the date of the census. Some practices, however, do not use this method but instead calculate the difference between the year of birth and the year of the census. Classifications of this type are footnoted whenever possible. They can be identified to a certain extent by a smaller than expected population under one year of age. However, an irregular number of births from one year to the next or age selective omission of infants may also obscure the expected population under one year of age.

3.1.3.2 Errors in age data

Errors in age data may be due to a variety of causes, including ignorance of the correct age; reporting years of age in terms of a calendar concept other than completed solar years since birth,[7] carelessness in reporting and recording age; a general tendency to state age in figures ending in certain digits (such as zero, two, five and eight); a tendency to exaggerate length of life at advanced ages; a subconscious aversion to certain numbers; and wilful misrepresentations.

These reasons for errors in reported age data are common to most investigations of age and to most countries or areas, and they may significantly impair comparability of the data.

As a result of the above-mentioned difficulties, the age-sex distribution of population in many countries or areas shows irregularities which may be summarized as follows: (1) a deficiency in the number of infants and young children; (2) a concentration at ages ending with zero and five (that is, 5, 10, 15, 20...); (3) heaping at even ages (for example, 10, 12, 14...) relative to odd ages (for example, 11, 13, 15...); (4) unexpectedly large differences between the frequency of males and females at certain ages; and (5) unaccountably large differences between the frequencies in adjacent age groups. Comparing of identical age-sex cohorts from successive censuses, as well as studying the age-sex composition of each census, may reveal these and other inconsistencies, some of which in varying degree are characteristic of even the most modern censuses.

3.1.3.3 Evaluation of accuracy

To measure the accuracy of data by age, based on the evidence of irregularities in 5-year groups, an index was devised for presentation in the *Demographic Yearbook 1949-1950*[8]. Although this index was sensitive to various sources of inaccuracy in the data, it could also be affected considerably by real fluctuations in past demographic processes. It could not, therefore, be applied indiscriminately to all types of statistics, unless certain adjustments were made and caution used in the interpretation of results.

The publication of population statistics by single years of age in the *Demographic Yearbook 1955* made it possible to apply a simple, yet highly sensitive, index known as Whipple's Index, or the Index of Concentration,[9] the interpretation of which is relatively free from consideration of factors not connected with the accuracy of age reporting. More refined methods for the measurement of accuracy of distributions by single year of age have been devised, but this particular index was selected for presentation in the *Demographic Yearbook* for its simplicity and the wide use it has already found in other sources.

Whipple's Index is obtained by summing the age returns between 23 and 62 years inclusive and finding what percentage is borne by the sum of the returns of years ending with 5 and 0 to one-fifth of the total sum.

The results would vary between a minimum of 100, representing no concentration at all, and a maximum of 500, if no returns were recorded with any digits other than the two mentioned.[10]

The index is applicable to all age distributions for which single years are given at least to the age of 62, with the following exceptions: (1) where the data presented are the result of graduation, no irregularity is scored by Whipple's Index, even though the graduated data may still be affected by inaccuracies of a different type; and (2) where statistics on age have been derived by reference to the year of birth, and tendencies to round off the birth year would result in an excessive number of ages ending in odd numbers, the frequency of age reporting with terminal digits 5 and 0 is not an adequate measure of their accuracy.

Using statistics for both sexes combined, the index has now been computed for all the single-year age distributions in table 26 of the 1993 *Yearbook* from censuses held between 1985 and 1993, with the exception of those excluded on the criteria set forth above. The ratings achieved by such distributions can be found on pages 19 to 20 of the *Demographic Yearbook 1993*.[11] The present issue of the *Demographic Yearbook* does not display the population by single years of age; the Index and the ratings are planned to be included in the next special issue of the *Demographic Yearbook* focusing on population censuses.

Although Whipple's Index measures only the effects of preferences for ages ending in 5 and 0, it can be assumed that such digit preference is usually connected with other sources of inaccuracy in age statements and the index can be accepted as a fair measure of the general reliability of the age distribution.

3.2 Methods used to indicate quality of published statistics

To the extent possible, efforts have been made to give the reader an indication of reliability of the statistics published in the *Demographic Yearbook*. This has been approached in several ways. Any information regarding a possible under-enumeration or over-enumeration, coming from a postcensal survey, for example, has been noted in the footnotes to table 3.[12] Any deviation from full national coverage, as explained in section 2.1 under Geographical Aspects, has also been noted. In addition, national statistical offices have been asked to evaluate the estimates of total population they submit to the Statistics Division of the United Nations.

3.2.1 Treatment of time series of population estimates

When a series of mid-year population estimates are presented, the same indication of quality is shown for the entire series as was determined for the latest estimate. The quality is indicated by the type face employed.

No attempt has been made to split the series even though it is evident that in cases where the data are now considered reliable, in earlier years, many may have been considerably less reliable than the current classification implies. Thus it will be evident that this method overstates the probable reliability of the time series in many cases. It may also understate the reliability of estimates for years immediately preceding or following a census enumeration.

3.2.2 Treatment of estimated distributions by age and other demographic characteristics

Estimates of the age-sex distribution of population may be constructed by two major methods: (1) by applying the specific components of population change to each age-sex group of the population as enumerated at the time of the census, and (2) by distributing the total estimated for a postcensal year proportionately according to the age-sex structure at the time of the census. Estimates constructed by the latter method are not published in the *Demographic Yearbook*.

Estimated age-sex distributions are categorized as "reliable" or otherwise, according to the method of construction established for the latest estimate of total mid-year population. Hence, the quality designation of the total figure, as indicated by the code, is considered to apply also to the whole distribution by age and sex, and the data are set in *italic* or roman type, as appropriate, on this basis alone. Further evaluation of detailed age structure data has not been undertaken to date.

4. VITAL STATISTICS

For purposes of the *Demographic Yearbook*, vital statistics have been defined as statistics of live birth, death, foetal death, marriage and divorce.

This volume of the *Yearbook* presents general tables on natality, nuptiality and divorce as well as tables on mortality referring to: foetal mortality, infant and maternal mortality and general mortality.

4.1 Sources of variation of data

Most of the vital statistics data published in this *Yearbook* come from national civil registration systems. The completeness and the accuracy of the data which these systems produce vary from one country or area to another.[13]

The provision for a national civil registration system is not universal, and in some cases, the registration system covers only certain vital events. For example, in some countries or areas only births and deaths are registered. There are also differences in the effectiveness with which national laws pertaining to civil registration operate in the various countries or areas. The manner in which the law is implemented and the degree to which the public complies with the legislation determine the reliability of the vital statistics obtained from the civil registers.

It should be noted that some statistics on marriage and divorce are obtained from sources other than civil registers. For example, in some countries or areas, the only source for data on marriages is church registers. Divorce statistics, on the other hand, are obtained from court records and/or civil registers according to national practice. The actual compilation of these statistics may be the responsibility of the civil registrar, the national statistical office or other government offices.

Other factors affecting international comparability of vital statistics are much the same as those that must be considered in evaluating the variations in other population statistics. Differences in statistical definitions of vital events, differences in geographical and ethnic coverage of the data and diverse tabulation procedures may also influence comparability.

In addition to vital statistics from civil registers, some vital statistics published in the *Yearbook* are official estimates. These estimates are frequently from sample surveys. As such, their comparability may be affected by the national completeness of reporting in household surveys, non-sampling and sampling errors and other sources of bias.

Readers interested in more detailed information on standards for vital statistics should consult the *Principles and Recommendations for a Vital Statistics System Revision 2*;[14] *Handbook of vital statistics systems and Methods Volume 1, Legal, Organizational and Technical Aspects*;[13] *Handbook of Vital Statistics Systems and Methods, Volume 2, Review of national practices*;[15] *Handbook on Civil Registration and Vital Statistics Systems: Management, Operation and*

Maintenance;[16] *Handbook on Civil Registration and Vital Statistics Systems: Preparation of a Legal Framework;*[17] *Handbook on Civil Registration and Vital Statistics Systems: Developing Information, Education and Communication;*[18] *Handbook on Civil Registration and Vital Statistics Systems: Policies and Protocols for the Release and Archiving of Individual Records;*[19] and *Handbook on Civil Registration and Vital Statistics Systems: Computerization*[20]. The *Handbook of Household Surveys*[21] provides information in collection and evaluation of data on fertility, mortality and other vital events collected in household surveys. These publications are also available on the website at http://unstats.un.org/unsd/demographic/vital_statistics/index.htm.

4.1.1 Statistical definition of events

An important source of variation lies in the statistical definition of each vital event. The *Demographic Yearbook* attempts to collect data on vital events, using the standard definitions put forth in paragraph 57 of *Principles and Recommendations for a Vital Statistics System Revision 2.*[14] These are as follows:

LIVE BIRTH *is the complete expulsion or extraction from its mother of a product of conception, irrespective of the duration of pregnancy, which after such separation breathes or shows any other evidence of life such as beating of the heart, pulsation of the umbilical cord, or definite movement of voluntary muscles, whether or not the umbilical cord has been cut or the placenta is attached; each product of such a birth is considered live-born regardless of gestational age.*

DEATH *is the permanent disappearance of all evidence of life at any time after live birth has taken place (postnatal cessation of vital functions without capability of resuscitation). This definition therefore excludes foetal deaths.*

FOETAL DEATH *is death prior to the complete expulsion or extraction from its mother of a product of conception, irrespective of the duration of pregnancy; the death is indicated by the fact that after such separation the foetus does not breathe or show any other evidence of life, such as beating of the heart, pulsation of the umbilical cord, or definite movement of voluntary muscles. Late foetal deaths are those of twenty-eight or more completed weeks of gestation. These are synonymous with the events reported under the pre-1950 term stillbirth*[22].

MARRIAGE *is an act, ceremony or process by which the legal relationship of husband and wife is constituted. The legality of the union may be established by civil, religious or other means as recognized by the laws of each country or area.*

DIVORCE *is a final legal dissolution of a marriage, that is, that separation of husband and wife which confers on the parties the right to remarriage under civil, religious and/or other provisions, according to the laws of each country.*

In addition to these recommended definitions, the *Demographic Yearbook* collects and presents data on abortions, defined as:

ABORTION *is defined, with reference to the woman, as any interruption of pregnancy before 28 weeks of gestation with a dead foetus. There are two major categories of abortion: spontaneous and induced. Induced abortions are those initiated by deliberate action undertaken with the intention of terminating pregnancy; all other abortions are considered as spontaneous.*

4.1.2 Problems relating to standard definitions

A basic problem affecting international comparability of vital statistics is deviations from the standard definitions of vital events. An example of this can be seen in the cases of live births and foetal deaths.[23] In some countries or areas, an infant must survive for at least 24 hours, to be inscribed in the live-birth register. Infants who die before the expiration of the 24-hour period are classified as late foetal deaths and, barring special tabulation procedures, they would not be counted either as live births or as deaths. Similarly, in several other countries or areas, those infants who are born alive but who die before registration of their birth, are also considered as late foetal deaths.

Unless special tabulation procedures are adopted in such cases, the live-birth and death statistics will both be deficient by the number of these infants, while the incidence of late foetal deaths will be increased by the same amount. Hence the infant mortality rate is underestimated. Although both components (infant deaths and live births) are deficient by the same absolute amount, the deficiency is proportionally greater in relation to the infant deaths, causing greater errors in the infant mortality rate than in the birth rate.

Moreover, the practice exaggerates the late foetal death ratios. Some countries or areas make provision for correcting this deficiency (at least in the total frequencies) at the tabulation stage. Data for which the correction has not been made are indicated by footnote whenever possible.

The definitions used for marriage and divorce also present problems for international comparability. Unlike birth and death, which are biological events, marriage and divorce are defined only in terms of law and custom and as such are less amenable to universally applicable statistical definitions. They have therefore been defined for statistical purposes in general terms referring to the laws of individual countries or areas. Laws pertaining to marriage and particularly to divorce, vary from one country or area to another. With respect to marriage, the most widespread requirement relates to the minimum age at which persons may marry but frequently other requirements are specified.

When known the minimum legal age of men and women at which marriage can occur with (or in some cases without) parental consent is presented in table 24 showing marriages by age of groom and age of bride. Laws and regulations relating to the dissolution of marriage by divorce range from total prohibition, through a wide range of grounds upon which divorces may be granted, to the granting of divorce in response to a simple statement of desire or intention by husbands.

4.1.3 Fragmentary geographical or ethnic coverage

Ideally, vital statistics for any given country or area should cover the entire geographical area and include all ethnic groups. Fragmentary coverage is, however, not uncommon. In some countries or areas, registration is compulsory for only a small part of the population, limited to certain ethnic groups, for example. In other places there is no national provision for compulsory registration, but only municipal or state ordinances that do not cover the entire geographical area. Still others have developed a registration area that comprises only a part of the country or area, the remainder being excluded because of inaccessibility or for economic and cultural considerations that make regular registration practically impossible.

4.1.4 Tabulation procedures

4.1.4.1 By place of occurrence

Vital statistics presented on the national level relate to the de facto, that is, the present-in-area population. Thus, unless otherwise noted, vital statistics for a given country or area cover all the events which occur within its present boundaries and among all segments of the population therein. They may be presumed to include events among nomadic tribes and indigenous peoples, and among nationals and foreigners. When known, deviations from the de facto concept are footnoted.

Urban/rural differentials in vital rates for some countries may vary considerably depending on whether the relevant vital events were tabulated on the basis of place of occurrence or place of usual residence. For example, if a substantial number of women residing in rural areas near major urban centres travel to hospitals or maternity homes located in a city to give birth, urban fertility and neo-natal and infant mortality rates will usually be higher (and the corresponding rural rates will usually be lower) if the events are tabulated on the basis of place of occurrence rather than on the basis of place of usual residence. A similar process will affect general mortality differentials if substantial numbers of persons residing in rural areas use urban health facilities when seriously ill.

4.1.4.2 By date of occurrence versus by date of registration

To the extent possible, the vital statistics presented in the *Demographic Yearbook* refer to events that occurred during the specified year, rather than to those that were registered during that period. However, a considerable number of countries or areas tabulate their vital statistics not by date of occurrence, but by date of registration. Because such statistics can be very misleading, the countries or areas known to tabulate vital statistics by date of registration are identified in the tables by a plus sign (+). Since information on the method of tabulating vital statistics is not available for all countries and areas, tabulation by date of registration may be more prevalent than the symbols on the vital statistics tables would indicate.

Because quality of data is inextricably related to the timeliness of registration, this must always be considered in conjunction with the quality code description in section 4.2.1 below. If registration of births is complete and timely (code C), the ill effects of tabulating by date of registration, are, for all practical purposes, nullified. Similarly, with respect to death statistics, the effect of tabulating events by date of registration may be minimized in many countries or areas in which the sanitary code requires that a death must be registered before a burial permit can be issued, and this regulation tends to make registration prompt. With respect to foetal death, registration is usually done right away or not at all. Therefore, if registration is prompt, the difference between statistics tabulated by date of occurrence and those tabulated by date of registration may be negligible. In many cases, the length of the statutory time period allowed for registering various vital events plays an important part in determining the effects of tabulation by date of registration on comparability of data.

With respect to marriage and divorce, the practice of tabulating data by date of registration does not generally pose serious problems. In many countries or areas marriage is a civil legal contract which, to establish its legality, must be celebrated before a civil officer. It follows that for these countries or areas registration would tend to be almost automatic at the time of, or immediately following, the marriage ceremony. Because the registration of a divorce in many countries or areas is the responsibility solely of the court or the authority which granted it, and since the registration record in such cases is part of the records of the court proceedings, it follows that divorces are likely to be registered soon after the decree is granted.

On the other hand, if registration is not prompt, vital statistics by date of registration will not produce internationally comparable data. Under the best circumstances, statistics by date of registration will include primarily events that occurred in the immediately preceding year; in countries or areas with less developed systems, tabulations will include some events that occurred many years in the past. Examination of available information reveals that delays of many years are not uncommon for birth registration, though the majority is recorded between two to four years after birth.

As long as registration is not prompt, statistics by date of registration will not be internationally comparable either among themselves or with statistics by date of occurrence.

It should also be mentioned that lack of international comparability is not the only limitation introduced by date-of-registration tabulation. Even within the same country or area, comparability over time may be lost by the practice of counting registrations rather than occurrences. If the number of events registered from year to year fluctuates because of ad hoc incentives to stimulate registration, or to the sudden need, for example, for proof of (unregistered) birth or death to meet certain requirements, vital statistics tabulated by date of registration are not useful in measuring and analyzing demographic levels and trends. All they can give is an indication of the fluctuations in the need for a birth, death or marriage certificate and the work-load of the registrars. Therefore statistics tabulated by date of registration may be of very limited use for either national or international studies.

4.2 Methods used to indicate quality of published vital statistics

The quality of vital statistics can be assessed in terms of a number of factors. Most fundamental is the completeness of the civil registration system on which the statistics are based. In some cases, the incompleteness of the data obtained from civil registration systems is revealed when these events are used to compute rates. However, this technique applies only where the data are markedly deficient, where they are tabulated by date of occurrence and where the population base is correctly estimated. Tabulation by date of registration will often produce rates which appear correct, simply because the numerator is artificially inflated by the inclusion of delayed registrations and, conversely, rates may be of credible magnitude because the population at risk has been underestimated. Moreover, it should be remembered that knowledge of what is credible in regard to levels of fertility, mortality and nuptiality is extremely scanty for many parts of the world, and borderline cases, which are the most difficult to appraise, are frequent.

4.2.1 Quality code for vital statistics from registers.

In the *Demographic Yearbook* annual "Questionnaire on vital statistics" national statistical offices are asked to provide their own estimates of the completeness of the births, deaths, late foetal deaths, marriages and divorces recorded in their civil registers.

On the basis of information from the questionnaires, from direct correspondence and from relevant official publications, it has been possible to classify current national statistics from civil registers of birth, death, infant death, late foetal death, marriage and divorce into three broad quality categories, as follows:

C: Data estimated to be virtually complete, that is, representing at least 90 per cent of the events occurring each year.

U: Data estimated to be incomplete, that is representing less than 90 per cent of the events occurring each year.

...: Data for which no specific information is available regarding completeness.

These quality codes appear in the first column of the tables which show total frequencies and crude rates (or ratios) over a period of years for live births (table 9), late foetal deaths (table 12), infant deaths (table 15), deaths (table 18), marriages (table 23), and divorces (table 25).

The classification of countries and areas in terms of these quality codes may not be uniform. Nevertheless, it was felt that national statistical offices were in the best position to judge the quality of their data. It was considered that even the very broad categories that could be established on the basis of the available information would provide useful indicators of the quality of the vital statistics presented in this *Yearbook*.

In the past, the bases of the national estimates of completeness were usually not available. In connection with the *Demographic Yearbook 1977*, countries were asked, for the first time, to provide some indication of the basis of their completeness estimates. They were requested to indicate whether the completeness estimates reported for registered live births, deaths, and infant deaths were prepared on the basis of demographic analysis, dual record checks or some other specified method. Relatively few countries or areas have responded to this new question; therefore, no attempt has been made to revise the system of quality codes used in connection with the vital statistics data presented in the *Yearbook*. It is hoped that, in the future, more countries will be able to provide this information so that the system of quality codes used in connection with the vital statistics data presented in the *Yearbook* may be revised.

Among the countries or areas indicating that the registration of live births was estimated to be 90 per cent or more complete (and hence classified as C in table 9), the following countries or areas provided information on the basis of this completeness estimate:

(a) Demographic analysis -- Argentina, Australia, Canada, Chile, Cuba, Egypt, French Guiana, Guadeloupe, Guernsey, Iceland, Ireland, Israel, Kuwait, Latvia, Mauritius, Puerto Rico, Romania, San Marino, Singapore, Switzerland and United States.

(b) Dual record check -- Bahamas, Barbados, Bulgaria, Cook Islands, Cuba, Cyprus, Denmark, Fiji, Finland, France, French Guiana, Greece, Guam, Guadeloupe, Guernsey, Iceland, Isle of Man, Japan, Maldives, New Zealand, Peninsular Malaysia, Romania, Saint Kitts and Nevis, Saint Lucia, Singapore, Sri Lanka, Sweden, Switzerland, Tokelau, Uruguay and Venezuela.

(c) Other specified methods -- Belgium, Bermuda, Cayman Islands, Germany, Greenland, Hong Kong SAR, Iceland, Japan, Luxembourg, Netherlands, Norway, Poland, Singapore and Slovenia.

Among the countries or areas indicating that the registration of deaths was estimated to be 90 per cent or more complete (and hence classified as C in table 18), the following countries or areas provided information on the basis of this completeness estimate:

(a) Demographic analysis -- Argentina, Australia, Canada, Chile, Cuba, Egypt, French Guiana, Guadeloupe, Guernsey, Iceland, Ireland, Israel, Kuwait, Latvia, Mauritius, Puerto Rico, Romania, San Marino, Singapore, Switzerland and United States.

(b) Dual record check -- Bahamas, Bulgaria, Cook Islands, Cuba, Denmark, Fiji, Finland, France, Greece, Greenland, Guam, Guernsey, Iceland, Isle of Man, Maldives, New Zealand, Romania, Saint Kitts and Nevis, Saint Lucia, Singapore, Sri Lanka, Sweden, Switzerland, Tokelau and Uruguay.

(c) Other specified methods -- Belgium, Bermuda, Cayman Islands, Germany, Hong Kong SAR, Iceland, Ireland, Japan, Luxembourg, Netherlands, Norway, Poland, Singapore and Slovenia.

Among the countries or areas indicating that the registration of infant deaths was estimated to be 90 per cent or more complete (and hence classified as C in table 15), the following countries or areas provided information on the basis of this completeness estimate:

(a) Demographic analysis -- Argentina, Australia, Canada, Chile, Cuba, Egypt, Iceland, Ireland, Israel, Kuwait, Latvia, Mauritius, Puerto Rico, Romania, San Marino, Singapore, Sri Lanka, Switzerland and United States.

(b) Dual record check -- Bahamas, Bulgaria, Cook Islands, Cuba, Denmark, Fiji, Finland, France, Greece, Greenland, Guam, Guernsey, Iceland, Isle of Man, Japan, Maldives, New Zealand, Romania, Saint Kitts and Nevis, Saint Lucia, Singapore, Sweden, Switzerland, Tokelau and Uruguay.

(c) Other specified methods -- Belgium, Bermuda, Cayman Islands, Germany, Hong Kong SAR, Iceland, Japan, Luxembourg, Netherlands, Norway, Poland, Singapore and Slovenia.

4.2.2 Treatment of vital statistics from registers

On the basis of the quality code described above, the vital statistics shown in all tables of the *Yearbook* are treated as either reliable or unreliable. Data coded C are considered reliable and appear in roman type. Data coded U or ... are considered unreliable and appear in *italics*. Although the quality code itself appears only in certain tables, the indication of reliability (that is, the use of *italics* to indicate unreliable data) is shown in all tables presenting vital statistics data.

In general, the quality code for deaths shown in table 18 is used to determine whether data on deaths in other tables appear in roman or *italic* type. However, for some of the maternal deaths data shown in *italics* in table 17, the known quality code differs from that ascribed on the basis of the completeness of registration of the total number of deaths. In cases where the quality code in table 18 does not correspond with the quality level implied by the typeface used in table 17, relevant information regarding the completeness of maternal mortality is given in a footnote.

The same indication of reliability used in connection with tables showing the frequencies of vital events is also used in connection with tables showing the corresponding vital rates. For example, death rates computed using deaths from a register that is incomplete or of unknown completeness are considered unreliable and appear in *italics*. Strictly speaking, to evaluate vital rates more precisely, one would have to also take into account the accuracy of population data used in the denominator of these rates. The quality of population data is discussed in section 3.2 of the Technical Notes.

It should be noted that the indications of reliability used for infant mortality rates, maternal mortality rates and late foetal death ratios (all of which are calculated using the number of live births in the denominator) are determined on the basis of the quality codes for infant deaths, deaths and late foetal deaths respectively. To evaluate these rates and ratios more precisely, one would have to take into account the quality of the live-birth data used in the denominator of these rates and ratios. The quality codes for live births are shown in table 9 and described more fully in the text of the technical notes for that table.

4.2.3 Treatment of time series of vital statistics from registers

The quality of a time series of vital statistics is more difficult to determine than the quality of data for a single year. Since a time series of vital statistics is usually generated only by a system of continuous civil registration, it was assumed that the quality of the entire series was the same as that for the latest year's data obtained from the civil register. The entire series is treated as described in section 4.2.2 above. That is, if the quality code for the latest registered data is C, the frequencies and rates for earlier years are also considered reliable and appear in roman type. Conversely, if the latest registered data are coded as U or ... then data for earlier years are considered unreliable and appear in *italics*. It is recognized that this method is not entirely satisfactory because it is known that data from earlier years in many of the series were considerably less reliable than the current code implies.

4.2.4 Treatment of estimated vital statistics

In addition to data from vital registration systems, estimated frequencies and rates of the events, usually ad hoc official estimates which have been derived either from the results of a sample survey or by demographic analyses, also appear in the *Demographic Yearbook*. Estimated frequencies and rates have been included in the tables because it is assumed that they provide information which is more accurate than that from existing civil registration systems. By implication, therefore, they are also assumed to be reliable and as such they are not set in italics. Estimated frequencies and rates continue to be treated in this manner even when they are interspersed in a time series with data from civil registers.

In tables showing the quality code, the code applies only to data from civil registers. If a series of data for a country or area contains both data from a civil register and estimated data, the code applies only to the registered data; if only estimated data are shown, the symbol (|) is shown.

4.3 Cause of death

World Health Organization (WHO) Member States are bound by the International Nomenclature Regulations to provide the Organization with cause of death data coded in accordance with the current revision of the International Statistical Classification of Diseases and Related Health Problems (ICD) as adopted from time to time by the World Health Assembly[24]. The data are collected by the WHO using the ICD. In order to promote international comparability of cause of death statistics, the World Health Organization organizes and conducts an international Conference for the revision of the ICD on a regular basis in order to insure that the Classification is kept current with the most recent clinical and statistical concepts. The data are now usually submitted to WHO at the full four-character level of detail provided by the ICD and are stored in the WHO Mortality Database at the level of detail as provided by the country. For earlier versions, however, the data are only available according to the ICD's list of 150 causes. Data from the WHO Mortality Database are available in electronic format at http://www3.who.int/whosis/menu.cfm.

Although revisions provide an up-to-date version of the ICD, such revisions create several problems related to the comparability of cause of death statistics. The first is the lack of comparability over time that inevitably accompanies the use of a new classification. The second problem affects comparability between countries and areas because they may adopt the new classification at different times. The more refined the classification becomes the greater is the need for expert clinical diagnosis of cause of death. In many countries or areas, few of the deaths occur in the presence of an attendant, who is medically trained, i.e., most deaths are certified by a lay attendant. Because the ICD contains many diagnoses that cannot be identified by a non-medical person, the ICD does not always promote international comparability particularly between countries and areas where the level of medical services differ widely.

The chapters of the tenth revision[25], the latest revision of the ICD, consist of an alphanumeric coding scheme of one letter followed by three numbers at the four-character level. Chapter one contains infectious and parasitic diseases, chapter two refers to all neoplasms, chapter three to disorders of the immune mechanism including diseases of the blood and blood-forming organs; and chapter four to endocrine, nutritional and metabolic diseases. The remaining chapters group diseases according to the anatomical site affected, except for chapters that refer to mental disorders; complications of pregnancy, childbirth and the puerperium; congenital malformations; and conditions originating in the perinatal period. Finally, an entire chapter is devoted to symptoms, signs, and abnormal findings.

4.3.1 Maternal mortality

According to the tenth revision of the ICD, "Maternal death" is defined as the death of a woman while pregnant or within 42 days of termination of pregnancy, irrespective of the duration and the site of the pregnancy, from any cause related to or aggravated by the pregnancy or its management but not from accidental or incidental causes.

"Maternal deaths should be subdivided into direct and indirect obstetric deaths. Direct obstetric deaths are those resulting from obstetric complications of the pregnant state (pregnancy, labour and puerperium), from interventions, omissions, incorrect treatment, or from a chain of events resulting from any of the above. Indirect obstetric deaths are those resulting from previous existing disease or disease that developed during pregnancy and which was not due to direct obstetric causes, but which was aggravated by physiologic effects of pregnancy".

While the denominator maternal rate should be the number of pregnant women, it is impossible to determine the number of pregnant women. A further recommendation by the tenth revision conference is therefore that maternal mortality rates be expressed per 100,000 live births or per 100,000 total births (live births and foetal deaths).[26] The maternal mortality rate calculated here is expressed per 100,000 live births. Although live births do not represent an unbiased estimate of pregnant women, this figure is more reliable than other estimates in particular, live births are more accurately registered than live births plus foetal deaths.

4.3.2 Perinatal mortality

The definition of perinatal death was recommended by the Study Group on Perinatal Mortality set up by the World Health Organization. The International Conference for the Eighth Revision of the International Classification of Diseases adopted the recommendation that the perinatal period be defined "as extending from the 28th week of gestation to the seventh day of life". Noting that several countries considered as late foetal deaths any foetal death of 20 weeks or longer gestation, the Conference agreed to accept a broader definition of perinatal death that extends from the 20th week of gestation to the 28th day of life. This alternative definition was believed to promote more complete registration of events between 28 weeks of gestation and the end of the first 6 days of life. In 1975, the Ninth Revision Conference recommended the collection of perinatal mortality statistics by use of a standard perinatal death certificate according to a definition which not only includes a minimum length of gestation but also minimum weight and length criteria.

In table 19 of the *Demographic Yearbook 1996* and previous issues of the Yearbook that included perinatal mortality statistics, the definition of perinatal deaths used is the sum of late foetal deaths (foetal deaths of 28 or more weeks of gestation) and infant deaths within the first week of life. In addition, in order to standardize the definition and eliminate differences due to national practice, the figures on perinatal death are calculated by the Statistics Division for inclusion in the *Demographic Yearbook*. Following the recommendations of the Tenth Revision Conference, the perinatal mortality rate is calculated per 1,000 live births in order to minimize the effect of limited foetal death registration on the magnitude of the denominator. [25]

NOTES

[1] The data on maternal mortality are from the World Health Organization, and are available at http://www3.who.int/whosis/menu.cfm, as one data on cause of death. The table on cause of death, which has been published regularly in previous issues of the *Demographic Yearbook*, are not presented in this issue.

[2] There are two exceptions – the 1978 and 1991 issues, which were disseminated in separate volumes from the respective regular issues.

[3] Sales No. E/03.XIII.6, New York, 2003.

[4] ST/ESA/STAT/SER.M/49/Rev.4/WWW ; http://unstats.un.org/unsd/methods/m49/m49.htm; see also Standard Country or Area Codes for Statistical Use, Sales No. M.98.XVII.9, United Nations, New York, 1999.

[5] Sales No. E.98.XVII.8, United Nations, New York, 1998.

[6] Alternatively, if a population register is used, completed ages are calculated by subtracting the date of birth of individuals listed in the register from a reference date to which the age data pertain.

[7] A source of non-comparability may result from differences in the method of reckoning age, is for example, the Western versus the Eastern or, as it is usually known, the English versus the Chinese system. By the latter, a child is considered one year old at birth and advances an additional year at each Chinese New Year. The effect of this system is most obvious at the beginning of the age span, where the frequencies in the under-one-year category are markedly understated. The effect on higher age groups is not so apparent. Distributions constructed on this basis are often adjusted before publication, but the possibility of such aberrations should not be excluded when census data by age are compared.

[8] In this index, differences were scored from expected values of ratios between numbers of either sex in the same age group, and numbers of the same sex in adjoining age group. In compounding the score, allowance had to be made for certain factors such as the effects of past fluctuations in birth rates, of heavy war casualties, and of the smallness of the population itself. A detailed description of the index, with results from its application to the data presented in the 1949-1950 and 1951 issues of the *Demographic Yearbook*, is furnished in *Population Bulletin, No. 2* (United Nations publication, Sales No. 52.XIII.4), pp. 59-79. The scores obtained from statistics presented in *Demographic Yearbook 1952* are presented in that issue, and the index has also been briefly explained in that issue, as well as those of 1953 and 1954.

[9] United States, Bureau of the Census, Thirteenth Census, Vol. I (Washington, D.C., U.S. Government Printing Office), pp. 291-292.

[10] J. T. Marten, Census of India, 1921, vol. I, part I (Calcutta, 1924), pp. 126-127.

[11] *Demographic Yearbook 1993*, Sales No. E/F.95.XIII.1, United Nations, New York, 1995.

[12] For further discussion, see Chapter 1 of *Demographic Yearbook 1962*, Sales No. 63.XIII.1, United Nations, New York, 1963.

[13] Sales No. E.91.XVII.5, United Nations, New York, 1991; and *Handbook on Civil Registration and Vital Statistics Systems: Preparation of a Legal Framework* , Sales No. E98.XVII.7, United Nations, 1998; http://unstats.un.org/unsd/demographic/vital_statistics/index.htm.

[14] Sales No. E. 01.XVII.10, United Nations, New York, 2001; http://unstats.un.org/unsd/demographic/vital_statistics/index.htm.

[15] Sales No. E.84.XVII.11, United Nations, New York, 1985; http://unstats.un.org/unsd/demographic/vital_statistics/index.htm.

[16] *Handbook on Civil Registration and Vital Statistics Systems: Management, Operation and Maintenance*, Sales No. E.98.XVII.11, United Nations, New York, 1998. http://unstats.un.org/unsd/demographic/vital_statistics/index.htm.

[17] Sales No. E. 98.XVII.7, United Nations, New York, 1998; http://unstats.un.org/unsd/demographic/vital_statistics/index.htm.

[18] Sales No. E.98.XVII.4, United Nations, New York, 1998; http://unstats.un.org/unsd/demographic/vital_statistics/index.htm.

[19] Sales No. E.98.XVII.6, United Nations, New York, 1998; http://unstats.un.org/unsd/demographic/vital_statistics/index.htm.

NOTES (Continued)

[20]   Sales No. E.98.XVII.10, United Nations, New York, 1998; http://unstats.un.org/unsd/demographic/vital_statistics/index.htm.

[21]   *Handbook of Household Surveys*, Sales No. E.83.XVII.13, United Nations, New York, 1984.

[22]   For more detailed discussion on this issue, refer to *Principles and Recommendations for a Vital Statistics System Revision 2,* Sales No. E. 01.XVII.10, United Nations, New York, 2001, para 57.

[23]   For more information on historical and legal background on the use of differing definitions of live births and foetal deaths, comparisons of definitions used as of 1 January 1950, and evaluation of the effects of these differences on the calculation of various rates, see *Handbook of Vital Statistics Systems and Methods Volume 2, Review of National Practices*, Sales No. E.84.XVII.11, United Nations, New York, 1985, Chapter IV.

[24]   The World Health Assembly is the annual meeting of the Member States of the World Health Organization and its highest governing body.

[25]   *International Statistical Classification of Diseases and Related Health Problems*, Tenth Revision, Volume 2, World Health Organization, Geneva, 1992.

[26]   *International Statistical Classification of Diseases and Related Health Problems*, Tenth Revision, Volume 2, World Health Organization, Geneva, 1992, pp. 129-136.

INTRODUCTION

L'*Annuaire démographique* est un recueil de statistiques démographiques internationales qui est établi par la Division de statistique du Département des Affaires Economiques et Sociales de l'Organisation des Nations Unies. L'*Annuaire démographique* s'intègre dans un ensemble de publications complémentaires publiées par l'Organisation des Nations Unies et les institutions spécialisées et qui ont pour objet de fournir des statistiques de base aux démographes, aux économistes, aux spécialistes de la santé publique et aux sociologues. Conformément au plan de coordination, l'*Annuaire démographique* constitue la source internationale des statistiques démographiques nationales. Grâce à la coopération des services nationaux de statistique, il a été possible de faire figurer dans la présente édition des statistiques démographiques officielles pour environ 230 pays ou zones du monde entier.

L'*Annuaire démographique 2001* est le cinquante-troisième d'une série que publie l'ONU depuis 1948. Le présent volume contient des tableaux de caractère général y compris un aperçu mondial des statistiques démographiques de base, des tableaux qui présentent des statistiques sur la dimension, la répartition et les tendances de la population, la natalité, la mortalité fœtale, la mortalité infantile et la mortalité liée à la maternité, la mortalité générale, la nuptialité et la divortialité. Dans l' ensemble de l' Annuaire, des donnée classées selon la résidence (urbaine/rurale) sont présentées dans un grand nombre de tableaux. En outre, l' Annuaire contient des Notes Techniques, un index cumulatif et une liste des éditions de l'Annuaire publiées jusqu'à présent.

Les Notes techniques sur les tableaux statistiques sont destinées à aider le lecteur. A la fin de l'Annuaire, un index cumulatif donne des renseignements sur les matières traitées dans chacune des cinquante-trois éditions et sur les années sur lesquelles portent les données. Les numéros de vente des éditions antérieures et une liste des sujets spéciaux traités dans les différentes éditions apparaissent en page iii et iv.

Jusqu'à l'édition de 1996 (i.e., la 48ème édition), chaque édition été composée de deux parties : les tableaux générales et ceux sur des sujets spéciaux. A partir de l'édition de 1997 (49ème édition), les tableaux sur les sujets spéciaux ont été publiés sur support électronique (CD-ROM) comme suppléments aux éditions régulières de l'Annuaire. Jusqu'à maintenant, deux CD-ROM ont été produits : l'*Annuaire démographique: Supplément rétrospectif* qui présent un grand nombre de statistiques démographiques pour la période de 1948 à 1997 et l'*Annuaire démographique : Statistiques de la Natalité* qui contient des tableaux détaillés sur la natalité pour la période de 1980 à 1998.

La première édition de l'*Annuaire démographique* sur support électronique (cédérom) contient statistiques démographiques historiques pour des séries chronologiques sur la dimension de la population, l'âge, le sexe et la résidence urbaine/rurale, la natalité, la mortalité et la nuptialité ainsi que quelques mesures indirectes concernant les changements de population sur une période de 50 années, 1948-1997. Il compléments l'*Annuaire démographique: Supplément rétrospectif* qui a été publiée en 1979 et qui présente des séries chronologiques sur les mêmes sujets pour une période de 30 années (1948-1978).

La deuxième édition de l'Annuaire sur support électronique (CD-ROM) a été publiée pour mettre à jour l'information sur la natalité depuis 1986. Le CD-ROM contient des tableaux de synthèse sur la natalité selon l'âge de la mère, le rang de naissance, l'âge du père et le type de naissance, le poids à la naissance et la durée de gestation. En suite, sont présentés des tableaux sur les naissances selon la légitimité, la durée de mariage, et les morts fœtales. L'*Annuaire démographique 1948*, qui était la première édition, comprenait beaucoup de tableaux semblables présentant des données annuelles couvrant la période 1932-1947. De ce fait, le sus mentionné, Supplément rétrospectif, utilisé conjointement avec l'Annuaire de 1948, pourra fournir des données démographiques internationales de grande valeur historique.

Les statistiques sur la population ne sont pas disponibles pour tous les pays et zones pour plusieurs raisons. Dans un effort d'offrir une information élémentaire sur la population mondiale, cette édition de l'*Annuaire démographique* contient deux annexes. Le premier présente les estimations de la population pour chaque pays ou zones pour la période 1992-2001. Le second présente les taux bruts sur les naissances vivantes, la mortalité, la mortalité infantile et les indicateurs synthétiques de fécondité; aussi sont présentés l'espérance de vie à la naissance pour la période 2000-2005. Ces données ont été produites par la Division de la population de l'ONU et son publiés dans *World Population Prospects - The 2002 Revision.*[1]

Les statistiques démographiques publiées dans cette édition de l'Annuaire, sont disponibles en format magnétique, pour l'analyse des utilisateurs en contactant la Division de Statistique des Nations Unies à l'adresse suivante : demostat@un.org . Plus d'information sur le programme de collecte et diffusion de données officielles par la Division de Statistique des Nation Unies et aussi disponible sur le site suivant : http://unstats.un.org/demographic/workshop/EGM_dyb/index.htm .

NOTES TECHNIQUES SUR LES TABLEAUX STATISTIQUES

1. REMARQUES D'ORDRE GENERAL

1.1 Ordonnance des Notes techniques

Les Notes techniques ont pour but de donner au lecteur tous les renseignements dont il a besoin pour se servir des tableaux statistiques. Les renseignements qui concernent l'Annuaire en général sont présentés dans des sections portant sur diverses considérations géographiques, sur la population et sur les statistiques de natalité et de mortalité. Dans la section suivante, les tableaux sont commentés chacun séparément et, après chacun d'entre eux, on trouvera une description des variables ainsi que des indications sur la fiabilité, les insuffisances et la portée des données, et sur les données publiées antérieurement. Des détails sont fournis également, le cas échéant, sur le mode de calcul des taux, quotients ou pourcentages.

1.2 Ordonnance des tableaux

La présente édition contient seulement des tableaux généraux. Comme la numérotation des tableaux ne correspond pas exactement à celle des éditions précédentes, il est recommandé au lecteur de se reporter à l'index qui figure à la fin du présent ouvrage pour trouver les données publiées dans les précédentes éditions.

1.3 Origine des données

Sauf indication contraire, les statistiques présentés dans *l'Annuaire démographique* sont des données officielles. Elles sont fournies essentiellement par des questionnaires qui sont envoyés, annuellement ou mensuellement, à environ 229 services nationaux de statistique et autres services gouvernementaux compétents. Les données communiquées en réponse à ces questionnaires sont complétées, dans toute la mesure possible, par des données tirées de publications nationales officielles et des renseignements communiqués par les services nationaux de statistique dans leur correspondance avec l'ONU. Pour que les données soient comparables, les taux, rapports et pourcentages ont été calculés par la Division de statistique de l'ONU, excepté les paramètres des tables de mortalité et quelques cas dans les tableaux relatifs aux taux, qui ont été dûment signalés en note. Les méthodes suivies par la Division pour le calcul des taux et rapports sont décrites dans les Notes techniques relatives à chaque tableau. Les chiffres de population utilisés pour ces calculs sont ceux, qui figurent dans la présente édition de l'Annuaire ou qui ont paru dans des éditions antérieures.

Chaque fois que l'on constatera des différences entre les données du présent volume et celles des éditions antérieures de *l'Annuaire démographique*, ou de certaines publications apparentées, on pourra en conclure que les statistiques publiées cette année sont des chiffres révisés communiqués a la Division de statistique avant Août 2003. On notera en particulier que les chiffres présentés comme provisoires pourront être révisés eux aussi.

2. CONSIDERATIONS GEOGRAPHIQUES

2.1 Portée

La portée géographique des tableaux du présent Annuaire est aussi complète que possible. Des données sont présentées sur tous les pays ou zones qui en ont communiqué. Le tableau 3, le plus complet, contient des données sur la population et la superficie de chaque pays ou zone ayant une population d'au moins 50 habitants. Ces pays ou zones ne figurent pas tous dans les tableaux suivants. Dans bien des cas, les données requises pour un tableau particulier n'étaient pas disponibles. En général, le nombre de pays ou zones qui peuvent fournir des données est d'autant plus petit que les données demandées sont plus détaillées.

De plus, sauf dans trois tableaux, les taux et rapports ne sont présentés que pour les pays ou zones ayant communiqué des chiffres correspondant à un nombre minimal de faits considérés. Les minimums sont indiqués dans les Notes techniques relatives à chacun des tableaux. Les trois tableaux faisant exception, où les taux pour les pays ou zones sont présentés quel que soit le nombre de faits sur lequel ils se fondent, sont les tableaux 4, 9 et 18, où figurent respectivement des données récapitulatives sur les taux démographiques, les taux bruts de natalité et les taux bruts de mortalité.

A l'exception des données récapitulatives présentées dans les tableaux 1 et 2 pour le monde, les grandes régions et les régions, toutes les données se rapportent aux pays.

2.2 Composition territoriale

Autant que possible, toutes les données, y compris les séries chronologiques, se rapportent au territoire de 2001. Les exceptions à cette règle sont signalées en note au bas des tableaux. De plus, les changements intervenus récemment et d'autres précisions intéressantes figurent au tableau 3.

Les données relatives à la République populaire de Chine comprennent en général celles de la province de Taiwan concernant la population, la superficie, les ressources naturelles, les conditions naturelles telles que le climat, etc. Dans d'autres domaines statistiques, elles ne comprennent pas les données relatives à la province de Taiwan. Dans la présente publication, les données figurant sous la rubrique "Chine" comprennent donc les données relatives à la province de Taiwan.

En vertu de l'adhésion de la République démocratique allemande à la République fédérale d'Allemagne, prenant effet le 3 octobre 1990, les deux Etats allemands se sont unis pour former un seul Etat souverain. A compter de la date de l'unification, la République fédérale d'Allemagne est désigné a l'ONU sous le nom d'Allemagne. Toutes les données se rapportant à l'Allemagne avant le 3 octobre figurent dans deux rubriques séparées basées sur les territoires respectifs de la République fédérale d'Allemagne et l'ancienne République démocratique allemande selon la période indiquée.

En 1991, l'Union des républiques socialistes soviétiques s'est séparée en 15 pays distincts (Arménie, Azerbaïdjan, Bélarus, Estonie, Géorgie, Kazakhstan, Kirghizstan, Lettonie, Lituanie, la République de Moldavie, Fédération Russe, Tadjikistan, Turkménistan, Ukraine, Ouzbékistan). Les données sont présentées pour ces pays pris séparément quand cela est possible.

2.3 Nomenclature

Pour gagner de la place, on a jugé commode de nommer en général dans les tableaux les pays ou zones par les désignations abrégées couramment utilisées par les Nations Unies en Mars 2004[2], les désignations complètes n'étant utilisées que lors qu'il n'existait pas de forme abrégée. La liste des désignations des pays ou zones est disponible sur le site : http://unstats.un.org/unsd/methods/m49/m49.htm.

2.3.1 Ordre de présentation

Les pays ou zones sont classés dans l'ordre alphabétique anglais et regroupés par continent comme ci-après : Afrique, Amérique du Nord, Amérique du Sud, Asie, Europe et Océanie.

Les appellations employées dans la présente édition et la présentation des données qui y figurent n'ont d'autre objet que de donner un cadre géographique commode aux séries statistiques. La même observation vaut pour toutes les notes et précisions fournies sur les unités géographiques pour lesquelles des données sont présentées.

2.4 Superficie

Les données relatives à la superficie qui figurent dans les tableaux 1 et 3 représentent la superficie totale, c'est-à-dire qu'elles englobent les terres émergées et les eaux intérieures (qui sont censées comprendre les principaux lacs et cours d'eau) à la seule exception des régions polaires et des îles inhabitées. Les données relatives à la superficie correspondent aux chiffres estimatifs les plus récents. Les superficies sont toutes exprimées en kilomètres carrés; les chiffres qui avaient été communiqués en miles carrés ont été convertis à l'aide d'un coefficient de 2,589988.

2.4.1 Comparabilité dans le temps

La comparabilité dans le temps des estimations relatives à la superficie d'un pays ou d'une zone donnés peut être affectée par la révision des estimations antérieures de la superficie, par des augmentations effectives de la superficie terrestre dues par exemple à des travaux d'assèchement, par des rectifications de frontières, par des changements d'interprétation du concept de "terres émergées", ou par l'utilisation de nouvelles unités de mesure. Dans la plupart des cas, il a été possible de déterminer la raison de ces révisions; toutefois, lors qu'on n'a pas pu le faire, on a néanmoins remplacé les anciens chiffres par les nouveaux et on a généralement admis que ce sont ces derniers qui sont exacts.

2.4.2 Comparabilité internationale

Le défaut de comparabilité internationale entre les données relatives à la superficie est dû essentiellement à des différences de définition. En particulier, la définition des golfes, baies et criques, lacs et cours d'eau varie sensiblement d'un pays à l'autre. La diversité des méthodes employées pour estimer les superficies nuit-elle aussi à la comparabilité internationale. Certaines données proviennent de levés effectués selon des méthodes scientifiques modernes; d'autres ne représentent que des conjectures reposant sur diverses catégories de renseignements. Certains chiffres sont récents, d'autres pas. Comme ni la méthode de calcul de la superficie ni la composition du territoire et la date à laquelle se rapportent les données ne sont connues avec précision pour tous les pays ou zones, les estimations figurant au tableau 3 ne doivent pas être considérées comme rigoureusement comparables d'un pays ou d'une zone à l'autre.

3. POPULATION

Les statistiques de la population, c'est-à-dire celles qui se rapportent à la dimension, à la répartition géographique et aux caractéristiques démographiques de la population, sont présentées dans un certain nombre de tableaux de l'Annuaire démographique.

Les données concernant les pays ou les zones représentent les résultats de recensements de population, des estimations fondées sur les résultats d'enquêtes par sondage (s'il n'y a pas eu recensement), des estimations postcensitaires ou intercensitaires, ou des estimations établies à partir de données tirées des registres de population permanents. Dans la présente édition de l'Annuaire, le tableau 3 présente pour chaque pays ou zone le chiffre le plus récent de la population totale au dernier recensement et des estimations établies au milieu de l'année 1995 et de l'année 2001. Le tableau 5 contient des estimations de la population totale au milieu de chaque année pendant 10 ans, et le tableau 6 des estimations de la population urbaine et de la population totale, par sexe, au milieu de chaque année pendant 10 ans. Les dernières données disponibles sur la répartition de la population selon l'âge, le sexe et la résidence (urbaine/rurale) sont présentées dans le tableau 7. Les derniers chiffres disponibles sur la population des capitales et des villes de 100 000 habitants ou plus sont présentés dans le tableau 8.

Les tableaux 1 et 2 présentent respectivement des estimations récapitulatives de la population du monde, des grandes régions et des régions en milieu d'année, pour diverses années, ainsi que des estimations récapitulatives, pour 2001, de cette population répartie selon l'âge et le sexe. La source pour ces donnés est la publication de la Division de population de l'ONU *World Population Prospects, The 2002 Revision, United nations publcation, sales no. E.03.XIII.6.*

On a utilisé pour le calcul des taux les statistiques de la population totale et de la population répartie selon l'âge, le sexe et la résidence (urbaine/rurale). Les taux démographiques selon l'âge et le sexe ont été calculés à partir des données qui figurent dans le tableau 7 de la présente édition ou dans les tableaux correspondants de précédentes éditions de *l'Annuaire démographique.*

3.1 Sources de variation des données

Plusieurs facteurs influent sur la comparabilité des données : 1) la définition de la population totale, 2) les définitions utilisées pour distinguer entre population urbaine et population rurale, 3) les difficultés liées aux déclarations d'âge, 4) l'étendue du sur-dénombrement ou du sous-dénombrement dans le recensement le plus récent ou dans une autre source de statistiques de référence sur la population, et 5) la qualité des estimations relatives à la population. Ces cinq facteurs sont analysés en quelques détails dans les sections 3.1.1 à 3.2.2 ci-après. D'autres questions seront traitées dans les Notes techniques relatives à chaque tableau. Pour plus de précisions concernant, notamment, les concepts fondamentaux de dimension, de répartition et de caractéristiques de la population qui ont été élaborés par les Nations Unies, le lecteur est prié de se reporter aux Principes et recommandations concernant les recensements de la population et l'habitation[3].

3.1.1 Population totale

Le facteur qui fait le plus obstacle à la comparabilité des données relatives à la population totale est la différence qui existe entre population de fait et population de droit. La population de fait comprend toutes les personnes présentes dans le pays ou la zone à la date de référence, tandis que la population de droit comprend toutes les personnes qui résident habituellement dans le pays ou la zone, qu'elles y aient été ou non présentes à la date de référence. La population totale de fait et la population totale de droit ne sont donc pas rigoureusement comparables entre elles par définition.

Même lorsqu'on veut comparer deux totaux qui se rapportent manifestement à des populations de fait ou deux totaux qui se rapportent manifestement à des populations de droit, on risque souvent de faire des erreurs pour cette raison que, aussi simples que ces concepts puissent paraître, il est rare qu'ils soient appliqués strictement. Pour citer quelques exemples, certains comptages qui sont censés porter sur la population de fait ne tiennent pas compte du personnel militaire, naval et diplomatique étranger en fonction dans le pays ou la zone, ni des membres de leurs familles et de leurs domestiques les accompagnant; certains autres ne comprennent pas les visiteurs étrangers de passage dans le pays ou la zone ni les personnes à bord de navires ancrés dans les ports. En revanche, il arrive que l'on compte des personnes, inscrits maritimes et marins pêcheurs par exemple, qui, en raison de leur activité professionnelle, se trouvent hors du pays ou de la zone de recensement.

Les risques de disparités sont encore plus grands quand il s'agit de comparer des populations de droit, car ces comparaisons dépendent au premier chef de la définition de la "résidence habituelle", qui varie d'un pays ou d'une zone à l'autre et qu'il est, de toute façon, difficile d'appliquer uniformément pour le dénombrement lors d'un recensement ou d'une enquête. Par exemple, les civils étrangers qui se trouvent temporairement dans un pays ou une zone comme travailleurs à court terme peuvent officiellement être considérés comme résidents après un séjour d'une durée déterminée, mais ils peuvent aussi être considérés comme non-résidents pendant toute la durée de leur séjour; ailleurs, ces mêmes personnes peuvent être considérées officiellement comme résidents ou comme non-résidents du pays ou de la zone d'où ils viennent, selon la durée et, éventuellement, la raison de leur absence. Qui plus est, quel que soit son statut officiel, chacun des recensés peut, au moment de l'enquête, interpréter à sa façon la notion de résidence. De plus, les autorités nationales ou de zones ne savent pas toutes avec la même précision combien de leurs résidents se trouvent temporairement à l'étranger.

Les chiffres de population présentés dans les tableaux de l'Annuaire représentent, autant qu'il a été possible, la population de fait. Sauf indication contraire, on peut supposer que les chiffres présentés ont été communiqués par les pays ou les zones comme se rapportant à la population de fait. Les chiffres qui ont été communiqués comme se rapportant à la population de droit sont identifiés comme tels. Lorsqu'on savait que les données avaient été recueillies selon une définition de la population de fait ou de la population de droit qui s'écartait sensiblement de celle indiquée plus haut, on l'a signalé en note, de manière à compenser dans toute la mesure possible les conséquences de cette divergence.

Il ne faut pas oublier néanmoins qu'on ne disposait pas toujours de renseignements détaillés à ce sujet. On ne peut donc partir du principe que les chiffres qui ne sont pas accompagnés d'une note signalant une divergence correspondent exactement aux définitions de la population de fait ou de la population de droit.

Il peut y avoir hétérogénéité dans les statistiques d'un même pays ou d'une même zone dans le cas des pays ou zones qui, bien qu'ils recueillent des données sur la population de droit et sur la population de fait à l'occasion d'un recensement, par exemple, ne font une exploitation statistique détaillée des données que pour la population de droit. Ainsi, tandis que les chiffres relatifs à la population totale qui figurent au tableau 3 se rapportent à la population de fait, ceux des tableaux qui présentent des données sur diverses caractéristiques de la population résidence (urbaine/rurale), âge et sexe, par exemple peuvent ne se rapporter qu'à la population de droit. Lorsqu'on savait que les chiffres se rapportaient à la population de droit, on l'a signalé en note.

3.1.2 Résidence (urbaine/rurale)

L'hétérogénéité des définitions nationales du terme "urbain" nuit sérieusement à la comparabilité internationale des données concernant la répartition selon la résidence. Les définitions utilisées par les différents pays ou zones et leurs implications, sont reproduites à la fin des notes techniques pour le tableau 6,.

3.1.3 Répartition par âge

La répartition de la population selon l'âge est un paramètre fondamental de la plupart des analyses, estimations et projections relatives aux statistiques de la population. Malheureusement, ces données sont sujettes à un certain nombre d'erreurs et difficilement comparables. C'est pourquoi pratiquement tous les utilisateurs de ces statistiques doivent considérer ces répartitions avec la plus grande circonspection.

3.1.3.1 Collecte et exploitation des données sur l'âge

L'âge est l'intervalle de temps déterminé par calcul ou par estimation qui sépare la date de naissance de la date du recensement et qui est exprimé en années solaires révolues.[2] Les données sur l'âge peuvent être recueillies selon deux méthodes: la première consiste à obtenir la date de naissance de chaque personne à l'occasion d'un recensement ou d'un sondage, puis à calculer l'âge en années révolues en soustrayant la date de naissance de celle du dénombrement[4]. La seconde consiste à enregistrer l'âge en années révolues au moment du recensement, c'est-à-dire l'âge au dernier anniversaire.

La méthode recommandée consiste à calculer l'âge au dernier anniversaire en soustrayant la date exacte de la naissance de la date du recensement. Toutefois, on n'a pas toujours recours à cette méthode; certains pays ou zones calculent l'âge en faisant la différence entre l'année du recensement et l'année de la naissance. Lorsque les données sur l'âge ont été établies de cette façon, on l'a signalé chaque fois si possible en note au bas des tableaux. On peut d'ailleurs s'en rendre compte dans une certaine mesure, car les chiffres dans la catégorie des moins d'un an sont plus faibles qu'ils ne devraient l'être. Cependant, un nombre irrégulier de naissances d'une année à l'autre ou l'omission de certains âges parmi les moins d'un an peut fausser les chiffres de la population de moins d'un an.

3.1.3.2 Erreurs dans les données sur l'âge

Les causes d'erreurs dans les données sur l'âge sont diverses: on peut citer notamment l'ignorance de l'âge exact, la déclaration d'années d'âge correspondant à un calendrier différent de celui des années solaires révolues depuis la naissance[5], la négligence dans les déclarations et dans la façon dont elles sont consignées, la tendance générale à déclarer des âges se terminant par certains chiffres tels que 0, 2, 5 ou 8, la tendance, pour les personnes âgées, à exagérer leur âge, une aversion subconsciente pour certains nombres, et les fausses déclarations faites délibérément pour des motifs d'ordre économique, social, politique ou simplement personnel.

Les causes d'erreurs mentionnées ci-dessus, communes à la plupart des enquêtes sur l'âge et à la plupart des pays ou zones, peuvent nuire sensiblement à la comparabilité.

A cause des difficultés indiquées ci-dessus, les répartitions par âge et par sexe de la population d'un grand nombre de pays ou de zones comportent des irrégularités qui sont notamment les suivantes : 1) erreurs par défaut dans les groupes d'âge correspondant aux enfants de moins d'un an et aux jeunes enfants; 2) polarisation des déclarations sur les âges se terminant par les chiffres 0 ou 5 (c'est-à-dire 5, 10,15, 20...); 3) prépondérance des âges pairs (par exemple 10, 12, 14...) au détriment des âges impairs (par exemple 11, 13, 15...); 4) écart considérable et surprenant entre le rapport masculin/féminin à certains âges; 5) différences importantes et difficilement explicables entre les données concernant des groupes d'âge voisins. En comparant les statistiques fournies par des recensements successifs pour des cohortes identiques d'âge et de sexe et en étudiant la répartition par âge et par sexe de la population à chaque recensement, on peut déceler l'existence de ces incohérences et de quelques autres, un certain nombre d'entre elles se retrouvant à des degrés divers même dans les recensements les plus modernes.

3.1.3.3 Evaluation de l'exactitude

Pour déterminer, sur la base des anomalies relevées dans les groupes d'âge quinquennaux, le degré d'exactitude des statistiques par âge, on avait mis au point un indice spécial[6] pour *l'Annuaire démographique 1949-1950*. Cet indice était sensible à l'influence des différents facteurs qui limitent l'exactitude des données et il n'échappait pas non plus à celle des véritables fluctuations démographiques du passé. On ne pouvait donc l'appliquer indistinctement à tous les types de données à moins d'effectuer les ajustements nécessaires et de faire preuve de prudence dans l'interprétation des résultats.

La publication dans *l'Annuaire démographique 1955* de statistiques de la population par année d'âge a permis d'utiliser un indice simple, mais très sensible, connu sous le nom d'indice de Whipple ou indice de concentration[7], dont l'interprétation échappe pratiquement à l'influence des facteurs sans rapport avec l'exactitude des déclarations d'âge. Il existe des méthodes plus perfectionnées pour évaluer l'exactitude des répartitions de population par année d'âge, mais on a décidé de se servir ici de cet indice à cause de sa simplicité et de la large utilisation dont il a déjà fait l'objet dans d'autres publications.

L'indice de Whipple s'obtient en additionnant les déclarations d'âge comprises entre 23 et 62 ans inclusivement et en calculant le pourcentage des âges déclarés se terminant par 0 ou 5 par rapport au cinquième du nombre total de déclarations.

Les résultats varient entre un minimum de 100, s'il n'y a aucune concentration, et un maximum de 500, si aucun âge déclaré ne se termine par un chiffre autre que 0 et 5[8].

Cet indice est applicable à toutes les répartitions par âge pour lesquelles les années d'âge sont données au moins jusqu'à 62 ans, sauf dans les cas suivants : 1) lorsque les données présentées ont déjà fait l'objet d'un ajustement, l'indice de Whipple ne révèle aucune irrégularité bien que des inexactitudes d'un type différent puissent fausser ces données; 2) lorsque les statistiques relatives à l'âge sont établies sur la base de l'année de naissance et que la tendance à arrondir l'année de naissance se traduit par une fréquence excessive des âges impairs, on ne peut utiliser la méthode reposant sur les déclarations d'âge se terminant par 5 et 0 pour évaluer l'exactitude des données recueillies.

A partir de chiffres relatifs à l'ensemble des deux sexes, on a calculé cet indice pour toutes les répartitions par année d'âge du tableau de l'édition de 1993 de *l'Annuaire démographique* sur la base des recensements effectués entre 1985 et 1993, à l'exception de celles que l'on a écartées pour les motifs indiqués plus haut. L'édition de 1993 de *l'Annuaire démographique* (p. 19 à 20) donne une évaluation de l'exactitude des déclarations d'âge pour les distributions données[9].

Bien que l'indice de Whipple ne mesure que les effets de la préférence pour les âges se terminant par 5 et 0, il semble que l'on puisse admettre qu'il existe généralement certains liens entre préférence et d'autres sources d'inexactitudes dans les déclarations d'âge, de telle sorte que l'on peut dire qu'il donne une assez bonne idée de l'exactitude de la répartition par âge en général, non seulement dans les données de recensements.

3.2 Méthodes utilisées pour indiquer la qualité des statistiques publiées

On a cherché dans toute la mesure possible à donner au lecteur une indication du degré de fiabilité des statistiques publiées dans *l'Annuaire démographique*. On a, pour ce faire, procédé de diverses façons. Chaque fois que l'on savait, grâce par exemple à une enquête post censitaire, qu'il y avait eu sous-dénombrement ou surdénombrement, on l'a signalé en note au bas du tableau 3[10]. Ainsi qu'on l'a indiqué dans la section 2.1 sous la rubrique "Considérations géographiques", chaque fois que les données ne portaient pas sur la totalité du pays, on l'a également signalé en note. De plus, les services nationaux de statistique ont été priés de fournir une évaluation des estimations de la population totale qu'ils communiquaient à la Division de statistique de l'ONU.

3.2.1 Traitement des séries chronologiques d'estimations de la population

En ce qui concerne les séries d'estimations de la population en milieu d'année, on considère que la qualité de la série tout entière est la même que celle de la dernière estimation. La qualité de la série est indiquée par le caractère d'imprimerie utilisé.

On n'a pas cherché à subdiviser les séries, mais il est évident que les données qui sont jugées sûres actuellement n'ont pas toutes le même degré de fiabilité et que, pour les premières années, nombre d'entre elles étaient peut-être bien moins sûres que la classification actuelle ne semble l'indiquer. Ainsi, il apparaît clairement que cette méthode tend, dans bien des cas, à surestimer la fiabilité probable des séries chronologiques. Elle peut aussi sous-estimer la fiabilité des estimations pour les années qui précèdent ou qui suivent immédiatement un recensement.

3.2.2 Traitement des séries estimatives selon l'âge et d'autres caractéristiques démographiques

Des estimations de la répartition de la population par âge et par sexe peuvent être obtenues selon deux méthodes principales : 1) en appliquant les composantes spécifiques du mouvement de la population, pour chaque groupe d'âge et pour chaque sexe, à la population dénombrée lors du recensement; et 2) en répartissant proportionnellement le chiffre total estimé pour une année postcensitaire d'après la composition par âge et par sexe au moment du recensement. Les estimations obtenues par la seconde méthode ne sont pas publiées dans *l'Annuaire démographique*.

Les séries estimatives selon l'âge et le sexe qui sont publiées sont classées en deux catégories, "sûres" ou "moins sûres", selon la méthode retenue pour le plus récent calcul estimatif de la population totale en milieu d'année. Ainsi, l'appréciation de la qualité du chiffre total, telle qu'elle ressort des signes de code, est censée s'appliquer aussi à l'ensemble de la répartition par âge et par sexe, et c'est sur cette seule base que l'on décide si les données figureront en caractères italiques ou romains. On n'a pas encore procédé à une évaluation plus poussée des données détaillées concernant la composition par âge.

4. STATISTIQUES DE L'ETAT CIVIL

Aux fins de *l'Annuaire démographique*, on entend par statistiques de l'état civil les statistiques des naissances vivantes, des décès, des morts fœtales, des mariages et des divorces.

Dans le présent volume de l'Annuaire 2000, on n'a présenté que les tableaux généraux sur la natalité, la mortalité, la nuptialité et la divortialité. Les tableaux consacrés à la mortalité sont groupés sous les trois rubriques suivantes: mortalité fœtale, mortalité infantile et mortalité liée à la maternité, et mortalité générale.

4.1 Sources de variations des données

La plupart des statistiques de l'état civil publiées dans le présent Annuaire sont fournies par les systèmes nationaux d'enregistrement des faits d'état civil. Le degré d'exhaustivité et d'exactitude de ces données varie d'un pays ou d'une zone à l'autre.

Il n'existe pas partout de système national d'enregistrement des faits d'état civil et, dans quelques cas, seuls certains faits sont enregistrés. Par exemple, dans certains pays ou zones, seuls les naissances et les décès sont enregistrés. Il existe également des différences quant au degré d'efficacité avec lequel les lois relatives à l'enregistrement des faits d'état civil sont appliquées dans les divers pays ou zones. La fiabilité des statistiques tirées des registres d'état civil dépend des modalités d'application de la loi et de la mesure dans laquelle le public s'y soumet.

Il est à signaler qu'en certains cas les statistiques de la nuptialité et de la divortialité sont tirées d'autres sources que les registres d'état civil. Dans certains pays ou zones, par exemple, les seules données disponibles sur la nuptialité sont tirées des registres des églises. Les statistiques de la divortialité sont en outre, suivant la pratique suivie par chaque pays, tirées des actes des tribunaux et/ou des registres d'état civil. L'officier de l'état civil, le service national de statistique ou d'autres administrations publiques peuvent être chargés d'établir ces statistiques.

Les autres facteurs qui influent sur la comparabilité internationale des statistiques de l'état civil sont à peu près les mêmes que ceux qu'il convient de prendre en considération pour interpréter les variations observées dans les statistiques de la population. La définition des faits d'état civil aux fins de statistique, la portée des données du point de vue géographique et ethnique ainsi que les méthodes d'exploitation des données sont autant d'éléments qui peuvent influer sur la comparabilité.

En plus des statistiques tirées des registres d'état civil, l'Annuaire présente des statistiques de l'état civil qui sont des estimations officielles nationales, fondés souvent sur les résultats de sondages. Aussi leur comparabilité varie-t-elle en fonction du degré d'exhaustivité des déclarations recueillies lors d'enquêtes sur les ménages, des erreurs d'échantillonnage ou autres, et des distorsions d'origines diverses. Dans certains cas, les données officielles ont été complétées par des estimations établies par la Division de la population du Secrétariat de l'Organisation des Nations Unies. Les estimations officielles nationales et celles établies par l'ONU sont signalées en note au bas des tableaux où elles figurent.

Pour plus de détails au sujet des pratiques nationales dans le rassemblement des statistiques d'état civil[11], le lecteur pourra se reporter aux : Principes et Recommandations pour un Système de statistiques de l'état civil, révision 2[12]; Manuel de statistique de l'état civil Volume I: Aspects légaux, d'organisation et techniques[13] ; Manuel des systèmes d'enregistrement des faits d'état civil et de statistiques de l'état civil: Gestion, Fonctionnement et tenue[14]; Manuel des systèmes d'enregistrement des faits d'état civil et de statistiques de l'état civil : Elaboration d'un cadre juridique[15] ; Manuel des systèmes d'enregistrement des faits d'état civil et de statistiques de l'état civil : Elaboration de programmes d'information, d'éducation et de communication[16] ; Manuel des systèmes d'enregistrement des faits d'état civil et de statistiques de l'état civil : Principes et protocoles concernant la communication et l'archivage des documents individuels[17]; Manuel des systèmes d'enregistrement des faits d'état civil et de statistiques de l'état civil : Informatisation[18].

Le Manuel des méthodes d'enquêtes sur les ménages[19] fournit des informations sur la collecte et sur l'évaluation des données sur la fécondité, mortalité et sur d'autres faits d'état civil, recueillies au cours des enquêtes sur les familles.

4.1.1 Définition des faits d'état civil aux fins de la statistique

Une cause importante d'hétérogénéité dans les données est le manque d'uniformité des définitions des différents faits d'état civil. Aux fins de *l'Annuaire démographique*, il est recommandé de recueillir les données relatives aux faits d'état civil en utilisant les définitions établies au paragraphe 46 des Principes et recommandations pour un système de statistiques de l'état civil, révision 2[10]. Ces définitions sont les suivantes :

La NAISSANCE VIVANTE est l'expulsion ou l'extraction complète du corps de la mère, indépendamment de la durée de la gestation, d'un produit de la conception qui, après cette séparation, respire ou manifeste tout autre signe de vie, tel que battement de cœur, pulsation du cordon ombilical ou contraction effective d'un muscle soumis à l'action de la volonté, que le cordon ombilical ait été coupé ou non et que le placenta soit ou non demeuré attaché; tout produit d'une telle naissance est considéré comme "enfant né vivant".

Le DECES est la disparition permanente de tout signe de vie à un moment quelconque postérieur à la naissance vivante (cessation des fonctions vitales après la naissance sans possibilité de réanimation). Cette définition ne comprend donc pas les morts fœtales.

La MORT FŒTALE est le décès d'un produit de la conception lorsque ce décès est survenu avant l'expulsion ou l'extraction complète du corps de la mère, indépendamment de la durée de la gestation; le décès est indiqué par le fait qu'après cette séparation le fœtus ne respire ni ne manifeste aucun signe de vie, tel que battement de cœur, pulsation du cordon ombilical ou contraction effective d'un muscle soumis à l'action de la volonté. Les morts fœtales tardives sont celles qui sont survenues après 28 semaines de gestation ou plus. Il n'y a aucune différence entre ces "morts fœtales tardives" et les faits désignés, avant 1950, par le terme mortinatalité[20].

Par référence à la femme, l'AVORTEMENT se définit comme "toute interruption de grossesse qui est survenue avant 28 semaines de gestation et dont le produit est un fœtus mort". Il existe deux grandes catégories d'avortement : l'avortement spontané et l'avortement provoqué. L'avortement provoqué a pour origine une action délibérée entreprise dans le but d'interrompre une grossesse. Tout autre avortement est considéré comme spontané[19].

Le MARIAGE est l'acte, la cérémonie ou la procédure qui établit un rapport légal entre mari et femme. L'union peut être rendue légale par une procédure civile ou religieuse, ou par toute autre procédure, conformément à la législation du pays.

Le DIVORCE est la dissolution légale et définitive des liens du mariage, c'est-à-dire la séparation de l'époux et de l'épouse qui confère aux parties le droit de se remarier civilement ou religieusement, ou selon toute autre procédure, conformément à la législation du pays.

4.1.2 Problèmes posés par les définitions établies

Les variations par rapport aux définitions établies des faits d'état civil sont le facteur essentiel qui nuit à la comparabilité internationale des statistiques de l'état civil. Un exemple en est fourni par le cas des naissances vivantes et celui des morts fœtales[21]. Dans certains pays ou zones, il faut que le nouveau-né ait vécu 24 heures pour pouvoir être inscrit sur le registre des naissances vivantes. Les décès d'enfants qui surviennent avant l'expiration des 24 heures sont classés parmi les morts fœtales tardives et, en l'absence de méthodes spéciales d'exploitation des données, ne sont comptés ni dans les naissances vivantes ni dans les décès. De même, dans plusieurs autres pays ou zones, les décès d'enfants nés vivants et décédés avant l'enregistrement de leur naissance sont également comptés dans les morts fœtales et tardives.

A moins que des méthodes spéciales aient été adoptées pour l'exploitation de ces données, les statistiques des naissances vivantes et des décès ne tiendront pas compte de ces cas, qui viendront en revanche accroître d'autant le nombre des morts fœtales tardives.   Le résultat le plus important est que le taux de mortalité infantile s'en trouvera sous-estimé.   Bien que les éléments constitutifs du taux (décès d'enfants de moins d'un an et naissances vivantes) accusent exactement la même insuffisance en valeur absolue, les lacunes sont proportionnellement plus fortes pour les décès de moins d'un an, ce qui cause des erreurs plus importantes dans les taux de mortalité infantile.

En plus cette pratique augmente les rapports de mortinatalité. Quelques pays ou zones effectuent, au stade de la mise en tableau, les ajustements nécessaires pour corriger ce défaut (du moins dans les fréquences totales). Lorsqu'il n'a pas été effectué d'ajustement, les notes l'indiquent chaque fois que possible.

Les définitions du mariage et du divorce posent aussi un problème du point de vue de la comparabilité internationale. Contrairement à la naissance et au décès, qui sont des faits biologiques, le mariage et le divorce sont uniquement déterminés par la législation et la coutume et, de ce fait, il est moins facile d'en donner une définition statistique qui ait une application universelle. A des fins statistiques, ces concepts ont donc été définis de manière générale par référence à la législation de chaque pays ou zone. La législation relative au mariage, et en particulier au divorce, varie d'un pays ou d'une zone à l'autre. En ce qui concerne le mariage, l'âge de nubilité est la condition la plus fréquemment requise mais il arrive souvent que d'autres conditions soient exigées.

Lorsqu'il est connu, l'âge minimum auquel le mariage peut avoir lieu avec le consentement des parents est indiqué au tableau 24, où sont présentés les mariages selon l'âge de l'époux et de l'épouse.   Les lois et règlements relatifs à la dissolution du mariage par le divorce vont de l'interdiction absolue, en passant par diverses conditions requises pour l'obtention du divorce, jusqu'à la simple déclaration, par l'époux, de son désir ou de son intention de divorcer requise par la loi islamique en vigueur dans certains pays ou zones.

4.1.3 Portée géographique ou ethnique restreinte

En principe, les statistiques de l'état civil devraient s'étendre à l'ensemble du pays ou de la zone auxquels elles se rapportent et englober tous les groupes ethniques. En fait, il n'est pas rare que les données soient fragmentaires. Dans certains pays ou zones, l'enregistrement n'est obligatoire que pour une petite partie de la population, certains groupes ethniques seulement, par exemple. Dans d'autres, il n'existe pas de disposition qui prescrive l'enregistrement obligatoire sur le plan national, mais seulement des règlements ou décrets des municipalités ou des Etats, qui ne s'appliquent pas à l'ensemble du territoire. Il en est encore autrement dans d'autres pays ou zones où les autorités ont institué une zone d'enregistrement comprenant seulement une partie du territoire, le reste étant exclu en raison des difficultés d'accès ou parce qu'il est pratiquement impossible, pour des raisons d'ordre économique ou culturel, d'y procéder à un enregistrement régulier.

4.1.4 Exploitation des données

4.1.4.1 Selon le lieu de l'événement

Les statistiques de l'état civil qui sont présentées pour l'ensemble du territoire national se rapportent à la population de fait ou population présente. En conséquence, sauf indication contraire, les statistiques de l'état civil relatives à un pays ou zone donné portent sur tous les faits survenus dans l'ensemble de la population, à l'intérieur des frontières actuelles du pays ou de la zone en cause. On peut donc considérer qu'elles englobent les faits d'état civil survenus dans les tribus nomades et parmi les aborigènes ainsi que parmi les ressortissants du pays et les étrangers. Des notes signalent les exceptions lorsque celles-ci sont connues.

Pour certains pays, les écarts entre les taux démographiques pour les zones urbaines et pour les zones rurales peuvent varier très sensiblement selon que les faits d'état civil ont été exploités sur la base du lieu de l'événement ou du lieu de résidence habituelle. Par exemple, si un nombre appréciable de femmes résidant dans des zones rurales à de grands centres urbains vont accoucher dans les hôpitaux ou maternités d'une ville, les taux de fécondité ainsi que les taux de mortalité néo-natale et infantile seront généralement plus élevés pour les zones urbaines (et par conséquent plus faibles pour les zones rurales) si les faits sont exploités sur la base du lieu de l'événement et non du lieu de résidence habituelle. Le phénomène sera le même dans le cas de la mortalité générale si un bon nombre de personnes résidant dans des zones rurales font appel aux services de santé des villes lorsqu'elles sont gravement malades.

4.1.4.2 Selon la date de l'événement ou la date de l'enregistrement

Autant que possible, les statistiques de l'état civil figurant dans l'Annuaire démographique se rapportent aux faits survenus pendant l'année considérée et non aux faits enregistrés au cours de ladite année. Bon nombre de pays ou zones, toutefois, exploitent leurs statistiques de l'état civil selon la date de l'enregistrement et non selon la date de l'événement. Comme ces statistiques risquent d'induire gravement en erreur, les pays ou zones dont on sait qu'ils établissent leurs statistiques d'après la date de l'enregistrement sont identifiés dans les tableaux par un signe (+). On ne dispose toutefois pas pour tous les pays ou zones de renseignements complets sur la méthode d'exploitation des statistiques de l'état civil et les données sont peut-être exploitées selon la date de l'enregistrement plus souvent que ne le laisserait supposer l'emploi des signes.

Etant donné que la qualité des données est inextricablement liée aux retards dans l'enregistrement, il faudra toujours considérer en même temps le code de qualité qui est décrit à la section 4.2.1 ci-après. Evidemment, si l'enregistrement des naissances est complet et effectué en temps voulu (code C), les effets perturbateurs de cette méthode seront pratiquement annulés. De même, en ce qui concerne les statistiques des décès, les effets de cette méthode pourront bien souvent être réduits au minimum dans les pays ou zones où le code sanitaire subordonne la délivrance du permis d'inhumer à l'enregistrement du décès, ce qui tend à hâter l'enregistrement. Quant aux morts fœtales, elles sont généralement déclarées immédiatement ou ne sont pas déclarées du tout. En conséquence, si l'enregistrement se fait dans un délai très court, la différence entre les statistiques établies selon la date de l'événement et celles qui sont établies selon la date de l'enregistrement peut être négligeable. Dans bien des cas, la durée des délais légaux accordés pour l'enregistrement des faits d'état civil est un facteur dont dépend dans une large mesure l'incidence sur la comparabilité de l'exploitation des données selon la date de l'enregistrement.

En ce qui concerne le mariage et le divorce, la pratique consistant à exploiter les statistiques selon la date de l'enregistrement ne pose généralement pas de graves problèmes. Le mariage étant, dans de nombreux pays ou zones, un contrat juridique civil qui, pour être légal, doit être conclu devant un officier de l'état civil, il s'ensuit que dans ces pays ou zones l'enregistrement se fait à peu près automatiquement au moment de la cérémonie ou immédiatement après. Comme dans de nombreux pays ou zones le tribunal ou l'autorité qui a prononcé le divorce est seul habilité à enregistrer cet acte, et comme l'acte d'enregistrement figure alors sur les registres du tribunal l'enregistrement suit généralement de peu le jugement.

En revanche, si l'enregistrement n'a lieu qu'avec un certain retard, les statistiques de l'état civil établies selon la date de l'enregistrement ne sont pas comparables sur le plan international. Au mieux, les statistiques par date de l'enregistrement prendront surtout en considération des faits survenus au cours de l'année précédente; dans les pays ou zones où le système d'enregistrement n'est pas très développé, il y entrera des faits datant de plusieurs années. Il ressort des documents dont on dispose que des retards de plusieurs années dans l'enregistrement des naissances ne sont pas rares, encore que, dans la majorité des cas, les retards ne dépassent pas deux à quatre ans.

Tant que l'enregistrement se fera avec retard, les statistiques fondées sur la date d'enregistrement ne seront comparables sur le plan international ni entre elles ni avec les statistiques établies selon la date de fait d'état civil.

Il convient également de noter que l'exploitation des données selon la date de l'enregistrement ne nuit pas seulement à la comparabilité internationale le des statistiques. Même à l'intérieur d'un pays ou d'une zone, le procédé qui consiste à compter les enregistrements et non les faits peut compromettre la comparabilité des chiffres sur une longue période. Si le nombre des faits d'état civil enregistrés varie d'une année à l'autre (par suite de l'application de mesures destinées spécialement à encourager l'enregistrement ou par suite du fait que, tout d'un coup, il est devenu nécessaire, par exemple, de produire le certificat d'une naissance ou décès non enregistré pour l'accomplissement de certaines formalités), les statistiques de l'état civil établies d'après la date de l'enregistrement ne permettent pas de quantifier ni d'analyser l'état et l'évolution de la population. Tout au plus peuvent-elles montrer les fluctuations qui se sont produites dans les conditions d'exigibilité du certificat de naissance, de décès ou de mariage et dans le volume de travail des bureaux d'état civil. Les statistiques établies selon la date de l'enregistrement peuvent donc ne présenter qu'une utilité très réduite pour des études nationales ou internationales.

4.2 Méthodes utilisées pour indiquer la qualité des statistiques de l'état civil qui sont publiés

La qualité des statistiques de l'état civil peut être évaluée sur la base de plusieurs facteurs. Le facteur essentiel est la complétude du système d'enregistrement des faits d'état civil d'après lequel les statistiques sont établies. Dans certains cas, on constate que les données tirées de l'enregistrement ne sont pas complètes lorsqu'on les utilise pour le calcul des taux. Toutefois, cette observation est valable uniquement lorsque les statistiques présentent des lacunes évidentes, qu'elles sont exploitées d'après la date de l'événement et que l'estimation du chiffre de population pris pour base est exacte. L'exploitation des données d'après la date de l'enregistrement donne souvent des taux qui paraissent exacts, tout simplement parce que le numérateur est artificiellement gonflé par suite de l'inclusion d'un grand nombre d'enregistrements tardifs; inversement, il arrive que des taux paraissent vraisemblables parce que l'on a sous-évalué la population exposée au risque. Il ne faut pas oublier, en outre, que les renseignements dont on dispose sur les taux de fécondité, de mortalité et de nuptialité normaux dans un grand nombre de régions du monde sont extrêmement sommaires et que les cas limites, qui sont les plus difficiles à évaluer, sont fréquents.

4.2.1 Codage qualitatif des statistiques tirées des registres de l'état civil

Dans le "Questionnaire relatif au mouvement de la population" de l'Annuaire démographique qui leur est présenté chaque année, les services nationaux de statistique sont priés de donner leur propre évaluation du degré de complétude des données sur les naissances, les décès, les décès d'enfants de moins d'un an, les morts fœtales tardives, les mariages et les divorces figurant dans leurs registres d'état civil.

D'après les renseignements directement fournis par les gouvernements ou tirés des questionnaires ou de publications officielles pertinentes, il été possible de classer les statistiques courantes de l'enregistrement des faits d'état civil (naissances, décès, décès d'enfants de moins d'un an, morts fœtales tardives, mariages et divorces) en trois grandes catégories, selon leur qualité :

C : Données jugées pratiquement complètes, c"est-à-dire représentant au moins 90 p. 100 des faits d'état civil survenant chaque année.

U : Données jugées incomplètes, c'est-à-dire représentant moins de 90 p. 100 des faits survenant chaque année.

... : Données dont le degré de complétude ne fait pas l'objet de renseignements précis.

Ces codes de qualité figurent dans la première colonne des tableaux qui présentent, pour un nombre d'années déterminé les chiffres absolus et les taux (ou rapports) bruts concernant les décès naissances vivantes (tableau 9), les morts fœtales tardives (tableau 12), décès d'enfants de moins d' un an (tableau 15), les décès (tableau 18), les mariages (tableau 23) et les divorces (tableau 25).

La classification des pays ou zones selon ces codes de qualité peut ne pas être uniforme. On a estimé néanmoins que les services nationaux de statistique étaient les mieux placés pour juger de la qualité de leurs données. On a pensé que les catégories que l'on pouvait distinguer sur la base des renseignements disponibles, bien que très larges, donnent cependant une indication utile de la qualité des statistiques de l'état civil publiées dans l'Annuaire.

Dans le passé, les bases sur lesquelles les pays évaluaient l'exhaustivité de leurs données n'étaient généralement pas connues. Pour l'Annuaire démographique 1977, les pays ont été priés, pour la première fois, de donner des indications à ce sujet. On leur a demandé d'indiquer si leurs estimations du degré d'exhaustivité des données d'enregistrement des naissances vivantes, des décès et de la mortalité infantile reposaient sur une analyse démographique, un double contrôle des registres ou d'autres méthodes qu'ils devaient spécifier. Relativement peu de pays ou zones ont jusqu'à présent répondu à cette nouvelle question; on n'a donc pas cherché à réviser le système de codage qualitatif utilisé pour les statistiques de l'état civil présentées dans l'Annuaire. Il faut espérer qu'à l'avenir davantage de pays pourront fournir ces renseignements afin que le système de codage qualitatif employé pour les statistiques de l'état civil présentées dans l'Annuaire puisse être révisé.

Sur les pays ou zones qui ont estimé à 90 p. 100 ou plus le degré d'exhaustivité de leur enregistrement des naissances vivantes (classé C dans le tableau 9), les pays ou zones suivants ont fourni les indications ci-après touchant les bases sur lesquelles leur estimation reposait :

(a) Analyse démographique Argentine, Australie, Canada, Chili, Cuba, Egypte, Etats-Unis, Guadeloupe, Guernesey, Guyane française, Irlande, Islande, Israël, Koweït, Lettonie, Maurice, Porto Rico, Roumanie, Saint-Marin, Singapour, et Suisse.

(b) Double contrôle des registres, Bahamas, Barbade, Bulgarie, Chypre, Cuba, Danemark, Fidji, Finlande, France, Guadeloupe, Guernesey, Guyane française,Grèce, Guam, Ile de Man, Iles Cook, Islande, Malaisie péninsulaire, Maldives,

Nouvelle-Zélande, Saint-Kitts-et-Nevis, Sainte-Lucie, Romanie, Singapour, Sri Lanka, Suède, Suisse , Tokélaou, Uruguay et Venezuela.

(c) Autre méthode spécifiée , Allemagne, Belgique, Bermudes, Groenland, Hong-kong RAS, Iles Caîmanes, Islande, Japon, Luxembourg, Norvège, Pays-Bas, Pologne, Singapour et Slovénie.

Sur les pays ou zones qui ont estimé à 90 p. 100 ou plus le degré d'exhaustivité de leur enregistrement des décès (classé C dans le tableau 18), les pays ou zones suivants donné des indications touchant la base de cette estimation:

(a) Analyse démographique - Argentine, Australie, Canada, Chili, Cuba, Egypte, Etats-Unis, Guadeloupe, Guernesey, Guyane française, Islande, Israël, Koweît, Lettonie, Maurice, Porto Rico, Roumanie, Saint-Marin, Singapour, et Suisse.

(b) Double contrôle des registres -- Bahamas, Bulgarie, Cuba, Danemark, Fidji, Finlande,   France, Grèce, Groenland, Guadeloupe, Guam, Guernesey, Guyane française, Ile de Man, Islande, Maldives, Nouvelle Zélande, Saint-Kitts-et-Nevis, Saint-Lucie, Roumanie, Singapour, Sri Lanka, Suède, Suisse, Tokélaou et Uruguay.

(c) Autre méthode spécifiée -- Allemagne, Belgique, Bermudes, Hong Kong RAS, Iles Caîmanes, Islande, Japon, Luxembourg, Norvège, Pays-Bas, Pologne, Singapour et Slovénie.

Sur les pays ou zones qui ont estimé à 90 p. 100 ou plus le degré d'exhaustivité de leur enregistrement des décès à moins d'un an classé C dans le tableau 15, les pays ou zones suivant ont donné des indications touchant la base de cette estimation :

(a) Analyse démographique -- Argentine, Australie, Canada, Chili, Cuba, Egypte, Etats-Unis, Irlande, Islande, Israël, Koweît, Lettonie, Maurice, Porto Rico, Roumanie, Saint-Marin, Singapour, Sri Lanka et Suisse.

(b) Double contrôle des registres -- Bahamas, Bulgarie, Cuba, Danemark, Fidji, Finlande, France, Grèce, Gröenlandie, Guam, Guernesey, Ile de Man, Iles Cook, Islande, Japon, Maldives, Nouvelle-Zélande, Roumanie, Saint-Kitts-et-Nevis, Saint-Lucie, Singapour, Suède, Suisse, Tokélaou, et Uruguay.

(c) Autre méthode spécifiée -- Allemagne, Belgique, Bermudes, Hong-kong RAS, Iles Caîmanes, Islande, Japon, Luxembourg, Norvège, Pays-Bas, Pologne, Singapour et Slovénie.

4.2.2 Traitement des statistiques tirées des registres d'état civil

Dans tous les tableaux de l'Annuaire, on a indiqué le degré de fiabilité des statistiques de l'état civil en se fondant sur le codage qualitatif décrit ci-dessus. Les statistiques codées C, jugées sûres, sont imprimées en caractères romains. Celles qui sont codées U ou ..., jugées douteuses, sont reproduites en *italique*. Bien que le codage qualitatif proprement dit n'apparaisse que dans certains tableaux, l'indication du degré de fiabilité (c'est-à-dire l'emploi des italiques pour désigner les données douteuses) se retrouve dans tous les tableaux présentant des statistiques de l'état civil.

En général, le code de qualité pour les décès indiqué au tableau 18 sert à déterminer si, dans les autres tableaux, les données relatives aux décès apparaissent en caractères romains ou en italique. Toutefois, certaines données sur les décès selon la cause figurent en italique dans les tableaux 17 et 21 lorsqu'on sait que leur degré d'exhaustivité diffère grandement de celui du nombre total des décès.

Dans les cas où le code de qualité du tableau 18 ne correspond pas aux caractères utilisés dans les tableaux 17 et 21, les renseignements concernant l'exhaustivité des statistiques des décès selon la cause sont indiqués en note à la fin du tableau.

On a utilisé la même indication de fiabilité dans les tableaux des taux démographiques et dans ceux des fréquences correspondantes. Par exemple, les taux de mortalité calculés d'après les décès figurant sur un registre incomplet ou d'exhaustivité indéterminée sont jugés douteux et apparaissent en *italique*. Au sens strict, pour évaluer de façon plus précise les taux démographiques, il faudrait tenir compte de la précision des données sur la population figurant au dénominateur dans les taux. La qualité des données sur la population est étudiée à la section 3.2 des Notes techniques.

Il convient de noter que, pour les taux de mortalité infantile, les taux de mortalité liée à la maternité et les rapports de morts fœtales tardives (calculées en utilisant au dénominateur le nombre de naissances vivantes), les indications relatives à la fiabilité sont déterminées sur la base des codes de qualité utilisés pour les décès d'enfants de moins d'un an, les décès totaux et les morts fœtales tardives, respectivement. Pour évaluer ces taux et rapports de façon plus précise, il faudrait tenir compte de la qualité des données relatives aux naissances vivantes, utilisées au dénominateur dans leur calcul. Les codes de qualité pour les naissances vivantes figurent au tableau 9 et sont décrits plus en détail dans les Notes techniques se rapportant à ce tableau.

4.2.3 Traitement des séries chronologiques de statistiques tirées des registres d'état civil

Il est plus difficile de déterminer la qualité des séries chronologiques de statistiques de l'état civil que celle des données pour une seule année. Etant donné qu'une série chronologique de statistiques de l'état civil ne peut généralement avoir pour source qu'un système permanent d'enregistrement des faits d'état civil, on a arbitrairement supposé que le degré d'exactitude de la série tout entière était le même que celui de la dernière tranche annuelle de données tirées du registre d'état civil. La série tout entière est traitée de la manière décrite à la section 4.2.2 ci-dessus : lorsque le code de qualité relatif aux données d'enregistrement les plus récentes est C, les fréquences et les taux relatifs aux années antérieures sont eux aussi considérés comme sûrs et figurent en caractères romains. Inversement, si les données d'enregistrement les plus récentes sont codées U ou ..., les données des années antérieures sont jugées douteuses et figurent en italique. Cette méthode n'est certes pas entièrement satisfaisante, car les données des premières années de la série sont souvent beaucoup moins sûres que le code actuel ne l'indique.

4.2.4 Traitement des estimations fondées sur les statistiques de l'état civil

En plus des données provenant des systèmes d'enregistrement des faits d'état civil, *l'Annuaire démographique* contient aussi des estimations fréquences et taux. Les taux estimés sont soit officiels, soit calculés par la Division de la population du Secrétariat de l'ONU. Ils sont en général calculés spécialement à partir des résultats d'un sondage ou par analyse démographique. Si des estimations fréquences et taux figurent dans les tableaux, c'est parce que l'on considère qu'elles fournissent des renseignements plus exacts que les systèmes existants d'enregistrement des faits d'état civil. En conséquence, elles sont également jugées sûres et ne sont donc pas indiquées en italique, et cela même si elles sont entrecoupées, dans une série chronologique de données tirées des registres d'état civil.

Dans les tableaux qui indiquent le code de qualité, ce code ne s'applique qu'aux données tirées des registres d'état civil. Si une série pour un pays ou une zone renferme à la fois des données tirées d'un registre d'état civil et des données estimatives, le code ne s'applique qu'aux données d'enregistrement. Si seules des données estimatives apparaissent, le symbole '|' est utilisé.

4.3 Causes de décès

Les données sont recueillies par l'Organisation Mondiale de la Santé. Les Etats membres de l'OMS sont tenus à fournir à l'Organisation les données sur les causes de décès codifiées selon la révision courante de la Classification internationale des maladies (CIM) adoptée par l'Assemblé Mondiale de la Sante[22]. Pour assurer la comparabilité internationale des statistiques des causes de décès, l'Organisation mondiale de la santé organise régulièrement des conférences internationales de révision de la Classification internationale des maladies (CIM) et veille ainsi à l'aligner, au fur et à mesure, sur les progrès les plus récents de la médecine clinique et de la statistique. Les données sont généralement envoyées à l'OMS au niveau de 4 caractères de détail en suivant la CIM et sont archivées dans la base de données sur la mortalité de l'OMS au niveau de détail fourni par le pays. Pour les versions antérieures, par contre, les données sont disponibles seulement selon la liste A de 150 causes de la CIM. Les données de l'OMS sont disponibles sur le site Internet suivant: http://www3.who.int/whosis/menu.cfm.

Bien que ces révisions aboutissent à l'élaboration d'une version actualisée de la CIM, elle pose plusieurs problèmes de comparabilité des statistiques des causes de décès. Le premier de ces problèmes tient au manque de comparabilité dans le temps, qui accompagne inévitablement la mise en oeuvre d'une classification nouvelle. Le deuxième est celui de la comparabilité entre pays ou zones, car les différents pays peuvent adopter la classification nouvelle à des époques différentes. Plus la classification se précise, plus il faut s'appuyer sur un diagnostic clinique compétent des causes de décès. Dans beaucoup de pays ou zones, il est rare que les décès se produisent en présence d'un témoin possédant une formation médicale, c'est-à-dire que le certificat de décès est le plus souvent établi par un témoin non qualifié médicalement. Comme la CIM offre de nombreux diagnostics qu'il est impossible d'établir si l'on n'a pas de formation en médecine, elle ne favorise pas toujours la comparabilité internationale, notamment entre pays ou zones où la qualité des services médicaux est très différente.

La dixième révision[23], est la dernière qu'ait connue la CIM. Les chapitres de la dixième révision se fondent sur un système de codification alphanumérique à une lettre suivie de trois chiffres par les catégories à quatre caractères. Le chapitre 1 concerne les maladies infectieuses et parasitaires, le chapitre 2 l'ensemble des néoplasmes, le chapitre 3 les troubles du système immunitaire ont été rattachés aux maladies du sang et des organes hématopoïétiques; et chapitre 4 les maladies du système endocrinien, de la nutrition et du métabolisme, les affections immunitaires. Enfin, les autres chapitres groupent les maladies selon leur site anatomique, à l'exception des qui concernent les affections mentales, les complications de la grossesse, de l'accouchement et des suites de couches; les malformations congénitales et les affections de la période périnatale. Enfin, un chapitre entier est consacré aux symptômes, manifestations, et résultats anormaux.

4.3.1 Mortalité maternelle

D'après la dixième révision de la CIM, "la mortalité maternelle se définit comme le décès d'une femme survenu au cours de la grossesse ou dans une délai de 42 jours après sa terminaison, quelle qu'en soit la durée et la localisation, pour une cause quelconque déterminée ou aggravée par la grossesse ou les soins qu'elle a motivés, mais ni accidentelle ni fortuite".

Les morts maternelles se répartissent en deux groupes:

1)   Décès par cause obstétricale directe ... qui résultent de complications obstétricales (grossesse, travail et suites de couches), d'interventions, d'omissions, d'un traitement incorrect ou d'un enchaînement d'événements de l'un quelconque des facteurs ci-dessus.

2) Décès par cause obstétricale indirecte ... qui résultent d'une maladie préexistante ou d'une affection apparue au cours de la grossesse, sans qu'elles soit due à des causes obstétricales directes, mais qui a été aggravée par les effets physiologiques de la grossesse.

La dixième révision recommande également que les taux de mortalité maternelle soient exprimés sur la base de 10 000 naissances vivantes ou 100 000 naissances totales (naissances vivantes et morts fœtales)[24]. Le taux de mortalité maternelle est ici calculé par 100 000 naissances vivantes. Bien que les naissances vivantes ne permettent pas d'évaluer sans distorsion le nombre des femmes enceintes, leur nombre est plus sûr que d'autres estimations car il est impossible d'évaluer le nombre des femmes enceintes, et le nombre des naissances vivantes est plus exactement enregistré que celui des naissances vivantes et des morts fœtales.

4.3.2 Mortalité périnatale

La définition de la mortalité périnatale a été recommandée par le Groupe d'étude sur la mortalité périnatale, constitué par l'Organisation mondiale de la santé. La Conférence internationale pour la huitième révision de la Classification internationale des maladies a adopté la recommandation selon laquelle la période périnatale devait être définie comme suit : "période comprise entre la vingt-huitième semaine de gestation et la septième journée de vie". Considérant que plusieurs pays comptaient comme mort fœtale tardive toute mort fœtale intervenu 20 semaines ou plus après le début de la gestation, la Conférence a décidé d'accepter aussi une définitions plus large de la mortalité périnatale qui s'étend de la vingtième semaine de la gestation à la vingt-huitième journée de vie. Cette deuxième définition devait en principe permettre l'enregistrement plus complet des morts fœtales intervenues entre la vingt-huitième semaine de gestation et la fin des six premières journées de la vie. En 1975, la Conférence chargée de la neuvième révision a recommandé que les statistiques de la mortalité périnatale s'appuient sur un certificat de mortalité périnatale standardisé, fondé sur une définition qui prévoit non seulement une durée minimale de gestation, mais également un minimum de poids et de taille.

Dans le tableau 19 de l'Annuaire démographique 1996 et dans les éditions antérieures de l'Annuaire où figuraient des statistiques sur la mortalité périnatale, la définition de mortalité périnatale s'appuie sur la somme des morts fœtales tardives (mortalité fœtale au terme de 28 semaines de gestation ou plus) et de la mortalité infantile dans la première semaine de vie. De plus, afin de normaliser la définition et d'éliminer les différences dues aux pratiques nationales, les chiffres de la mortalité périnatale sont calculés par la Division de statistique aux fins d'inclusion dans l'Annuaire démographique. Contrairement aux recommandations de la dixième conférence de révision, le taux de mortalité périnatale avait été calculé sur 1,000 naissances vivantes, afin de minimiser l'effet des insuffisances d'enregistrement des morts fœtales sur le dénominateur de la fraction[25].

NOTES

[1] United Nations publication, Sales No. E/03.XIII.6, New York, 2003

[2] Standard Country or Area Codes for Statistical Use, Sales No. M.98.XVII.9, United Nations, New York, 1999.

3 Principes et recommandations concernant les recensements de la population et de l'habitat, Première révision, numéro de vente : F.98.XVII.8, Nations Unis, 1998.

[4] Lorsqu'on utilise un registre de la population, on peut également calculer l'âge en années révolues en soustrayant la date de naissance de chaque personne inscrite sur le registre de la date de référence à laquelle se rapportent les données sur l'âge.

[5] L'emploi de méthodes différentes de calcul de l'âge, par exemple la méthode occidentale et la méthode orientale, ou, comme on les désigne plus communément, la méthode anglaise et la méthode chinoise, représente une cause de non-comparabilité. Selon la méthode chinoise, on considère que l'enfant est âgé d'un an à sa naissance et qu'il avance d'un an à chaque nouvelle année chinoise. Les répercussions de cette méthode sont très apparentes dans les données pour le premier âge : les données concernant les enfants de moins d'un an sont nettement inférieures à la réalité. Les effets sur les chiffres relatifs aux groupes d'âge suivants sont moins visibles. Les séries ainsi établies sont souvent ajustées avant d'être publiées, mais il ne faut pas exclure la possibilité d'aberrations de ce genre lorsqu'on compare des données censitaires sur l'âge.

[6] Dans cet indice, on déterminait les différences à partir des rapports prévus de masculinité dans un groupe d'âge et dans les groupes d'âge adjacents. Il fallait pour cela tenir compte de l'influence de facteurs tels que les mouvements passés des taux de natalité, les pertes de guerre élevées et, le cas échéant, le faible effectif de la population. On trouvera dans le Bulletin démographique, no. 2 (publication des Nations Unies, numéro de vente : 52.XIII.4), p. 64 à 87, un exposé détaillé sur cet indice ainsi que les résultats de son application aux données présentées dans les éditions de 1949-1950 et de 1951 de l'Annuaire démographique. On a fait les mêmes calculs sur les statistiques publiées dans l'Annuaire démographique 1952 et les résultats obtenus sont indiqués dans cette édition de l'Annuaire, qui, comme celles de 1953 et de 1954, donne de brèves explications sur l'indice en question.

[7] United States Bureau of the Census, Thirteenth Census, vol. I (Washington, D.C., U.S. Government Printing Office), page 291 et 292.

[8] J.T. Marten, Census of India, 1921, vol. I, partie I (Calcutta, 1924), p. 126 et 127.

[9] Annuaire démographique 1993, numéro de vente : E/F.95.XIII.1. Nations Unies, New York, 1995.

[10] Pour plus de détails, voir le premier chapitre de l'Annuaire démographique 1962, numéro de vente : 63.XIII.1. Nations Unies, New York, 1963.

[11] Numéro de vente F.84.XVII.11, Nations Unies, New York, 1985.

[12] Sales No. E. 01.XVII.10, United Nations, New York, 2001.

[13] Numéro de vente F.91.XVII.5, Nations Unies, New York, 1991.

[14] Numéro de vente F.98.XVII.11, Nations Unies, New York, 1998.

[15] Numéro de vente F. 98.XVII.7, Nations Unies, New York, 1998.

[16] Numéro de vente F.98.XVII.4, Nations Unies, New York, 1998.

[17] Numéro de vente F.98.XVII.6, Nations Unies, New York, 1998.

[18] Numéro de vente F.98.XVII.10, Nations Unies, New York, 1998.

[19] Numéro de vente F.83.XVII.13, Nation Unis, New York, 1984.

[20] Pour plus de précisions au sujet, voir les *Principles and Recommendations for a Vital Statistics System Revision 2*, numéro de vente E. 01.XVII.10, United Nations, New York, 2001, para 57.

[21] Pour plus de précisions au sujet des considérations historiques et juridiques auxquelles se rattachent les différentes définitions utilisées des naissances vivantes et des morts fœtales, pour une comparaison des définitions utilisées depuis le 1er janvier 1950 et pour une évaluation des effets de ces différences de définition sur le calcul de divers taux, voir le *Manuel de statistique de l'état civil, Volume II, Etude des pratiques nationales* numéro de vente E.84.XVII.11, United Nations, New York, 1985, chap. IV.

[22] L'Assemblé Mondiale de la santé est la réunion annuelle des Pays Membres de l'Organisation mondiale de la santé et des ses plus hauts fonctionnaires.

[23] Organisation mondiale de la santé, *Classification statistique internationale des maladies et problèmes de santé connexes.* Dixième Révision, vol. I Genève, 1992.

[24] Organisation mondiale de la santé, *Classification statistique internationale des maladies et problèmes de santé connexes.* Dixième Révision, vol. II Genève, 1992. Pages 129-136.

Table A. *Demographic Yearbook 2001* synoptic table: Availability of data by country/area, table and urban/rural areas, where applicable
Tableau A. Tableau synoptique de l'*Annuaire démographique 2001:* Disponibilité des données par pays ou zone, tableau et zones urbaines/rurales, si disponible

(See notes at end of table. — Voir notes à la fin du tableau.)

Continent, country or area / Continent, pays ou zone	Table totals	General topic and table number[1] - Suject général et numéro de tableau[1]															
		Summary - Apercu		Population						Natality - Natalité						Foetal mortality - Mortalité foetale			
		3	4	5	6	7 Total	7 U/R	8	9 Total	9 U/R	10 Total	10 U/R	11 Total	11 U/R	12 Total	12 U/R	13	14
Total number of countries or areas - Total des pays ou zones	..	230	166	200	138	174	79	228	157	59	130	52	92	30	78	40	52	39
AFRICA — AFRIQUE																		
Algeria - Algérie	13	•	•	•	–	•	–	•	•	–	–	–	–	–	•	–	–	–
Angola	3	•	–	•	–	–	–	•	–	–	–	–	–	–	–	–	–	–
Benin - Bénin	16	•	•	•	•	•	–	•	•	–	•	•	•	•	–	–	–	–
Botswana	11	•	•	•	•	•	–	•	•	–	–	–	–	–	–	–	–	–
Burkina Faso	5	•	–	•	•	•	–	•	•	–	–	–	–	–	–	–	–	–
Burundi	10	•	•	•	•	•	•	•	•	–	–	–	–	–	–	–	–	–
Cameroon - Cameroun	4	•	–	•	•	–	–	•	•	–	–	–	–	–	–	–	–	–
Cape Verde - Cap-Vert	7	•	–	•	–	–	–	•	•	–	–	–	–	–	–	–	–	–
Central African Republic - République centrafricaine	3	•	–	•	–	–	–	•	–	–	–	–	–	–	–	–	–	–
Chad - Tchad	8	•	•	•	•	–	–	•	–	–	–	–	–	–	–	–	–	–
Comoros - Comores	2	•	–	•	–	–	–	•	–	–	–	–	–	–	–	–	–	–
Congo	2	•	–	•	–	–	–	•	–	–	–	–	–	–	–	–	–	–
Côte d'Ivoire	9	•	•	•	•	–	–	•	•	–	–	–	–	–	–	–	–	–
Democratic Republic of the Congo - République démocratique du Congo	2	•	–	–	–	–	–	•	–	–	–	–	–	–	–	–	–	–
Djibouti	3	•	–	–	–	–	–	•	–	–	–	–	–	–	–	–	–	–
Egypt - Égypte	29	•	•	•	•	•	•	•	•	•	•	•	•	•	–	–	–	–
Equatorial Guinea - Guinée équatoriale	2	•	–	–	–	–	–	•	–	–	–	–	–	–	–	–	–	–
Eritrea - Érythrée	2	•	–	–	–	–	–	•	–	–	–	–	–	–	–	–	–	–
Ethiopia - Éthiopie	15	•	•	•	•	•	–	•	•	•	–	–	–	–	–	–	–	–
Gabon	6	•	•	•	•	–	–	•	–	–	–	–	–	–	–	–	–	–
Gambia - Gambie	5	•	–	•	•	•	–	•	–	–	–	–	–	–	–	–	–	–
Ghana	5	•	•	•	•	–	–	•	–	–	–	–	–	–	–	–	–	–
Guinea - Guinée	2	•	–	–	–	–	–	•	–	–	–	–	–	–	–	–	–	–
Guinea-Bissau - Guinée-Bissau	2	•	–	–	–	–	–	•	–	–	–	–	–	–	–	–	–	–
Kenya	3	•	–	•	–	–	–	•	–	–	–	–	–	–	–	–	–	–
Lesotho	5	•	–	•	•	–	–	•	–	–	–	–	–	–	–	–	–	–
Liberia - Libéria	4	•	–	•	•	–	–	•	–	–	–	–	–	–	–	–	–	–
Libyan Arab Jamahiriya - Jamahiriya arabe libyenne	11	•	•	•	–	–	–	•	•	–	•	–	•	–	–	–	–	–
Madagascar	2	•	–	–	–	–	–	•	–	–	–	–	–	–	–	–	–	–
Malawi	16	•	•	•	•	•	•	•	•	–	–	–	–	–	–	–	–	–
Mali	6	•	•	•	–	–	–	•	•	–	–	–	–	–	–	–	–	–
Mauritania - Mauritanie	4	•	–	•	–	–	–	•	–	–	–	–	–	–	–	–	–	–
Mauritius - Maurice	26	•	•	•	•	•	–	•	•	•	•	–	•	–	•	•	–	–
Morocco - Maroc	20	•	•	•	•	•	–	•	•	•	•	•	•	–	–	–	–	–
Mozambique	14	•	•	•	•	•	•	•	•	–	–	–	–	–	–	–	–	–
Namibia - Namibie	4	•	–	•	–	–	–	•	–	–	–	–	–	–	–	–	–	–
Niger	2	•	–	–	–	–	–	•	–	–	–	–	–	–	–	–	–	–
Nigeria - Nigéria	4	•	–	•	–	–	–	•	–	–	–	–	–	–	–	–	–	–
Réunion	15	•	•	•	•	•	–	•	•	–	•	–	•	–	–	–	–	–
Rwanda	2	•	–	–	–	–	–	•	–	–	–	–	–	–	–	–	–	–
Saint Helena - Sainte-Hélène	15	•	•	•	•	•	–	•	•	–	•	–	•	–	–	–	–	–
Sao Tome and Principe - Sao Tomé-et-Principe	3	•	–	•	–	–	–	•	–	–	–	–	–	–	–	–	–	–
Senegal - Sénégal	5	–	–	•	•	•	–	•	–	–	–	–	–	–	–	–	–	–
Seychelles	14	•	•	•	•	–	–	•	•	–	•	–	•	–	–	–	–	–
Sierra Leone	2	•	–	–	–	–	–	•	–	–	–	–	–	–	–	–	–	–
Somalia - Somalie	2	•	–	–	–	–	–	•	–	–	–	–	–	–	–	–	–	–
South Africa - Afrique du Sud	17	•	•	•	•	•	•	•	•	•	•	–	–	–	–	–	•	–

Table A. *Demographic Yearbook 2001* synoptic table: Availability of data by country/area, table and urban/rural areas, where applicable
Tableau A. Tableau synoptique de l'*Annuaire démographique 2001:* Disponibilité des données par pays ou zone, tableau et zones urbaines/rurales, si disponible (continued — suite)

(See notes at end of table. — Voir notes à la fin du tableau.)

Continent, country or area / Continent, pays ou zone	Infant mortality - Mortalité infantile				General mortality - Mortalité générale								Nuptiality and divorces - Nuptialité et divortialité			
	15		16	17	18		19		20		21	22	23		24	25
	Total	U/R			Total	U/R	Total	U/R	Total	U/R			Total	U/R		
Total number of countries or areas - Total des pays ou zones	143	53	113	76	157	60	132	62	81	34	131	108	129	43	90	115
AFRICA — AFRIQUE																
Algeria - Algérie	•	–	–	–	•	–	•	–	–	–	•	•	•	–	–	–
Angola	–	–	–	–	–	–	–	–	–	–	–	–	–	–	–	–
Benin - Bénin	•	•	–	–	•	–	–	–	–	–	–	•	–	–	–	–
Botswana	•	–	–	–	•	–	–	–	–	–	•	•	–	–	–	–
Burkina Faso	•	–	–	–	–	–	–	–	–	–	–	–	–	–	–	–
Burundi	•	–	–	–	•	–	–	–	–	–	–	–	–	–	–	–
Cameroon - Cameroun	–	–	–	–	–	–	–	–	–	–	–	–	–	–	–	–
Cape Verde - Cap-Vert	–	–	–	–	–	–	–	–	–	–	•	•	–	–	–	–
Central African Republic - République centrafricaine	–	–	–	–	–	–	–	–	–	–	–	–	–	–	–	–
Chad - Tchad	–	–	–	–	•	–	–	–	–	–	–	–	–	–	–	–
Comoros - Comores	–	–	–	–	–	–	–	–	–	–	–	–	–	–	–	–
Congo	–	–	–	–	–	–	–	–	–	–	–	–	–	–	–	–
Côte d'Ivoire	•	–	–	–	•	–	–	–	–	–	–	–	–	–	–	•
Democratic Republic of the Congo - République démocratique du Congo	–	–	–	–	–	–	–	–	–	–	–	–	–	–	–	–
Djibouti	–	–	–	–	–	–	–	–	–	–	–	–	–	–	–	•
Egypt - Égypte	•	•	•	–	•	•	•	•	–	•	•	•	•	•	•	–
Equatorial Guinea - Guinée équatoriale	–	–	–	–	–	–	–	–	–	–	–	–	–	–	–	–
Eritrea - Érythrée	–	–	–	–	–	–	–	–	–	–	–	–	–	–	–	–
Ethiopia - Éthiopie	•	–	–	–	•	–	•	–	–	–	–	–	•	–	•	–
Gabon	–	–	–	–	–	–	–	–	–	–	–	–	–	–	–	–
Gambia - Gambie	–	–	–	–	–	–	–	–	–	–	–	–	–	–	–	–
Ghana	–	–	–	–	–	–	–	–	–	–	–	–	–	–	–	–
Guinea - Guinée	–	–	–	–	–	–	–	–	–	–	–	–	–	–	–	–
Guinea-Bissau - Guinée-Bissau	–	–	–	–	–	–	–	–	–	–	–	–	–	–	–	–
Kenya	–	–	–	–	–	–	–	–	–	–	–	–	–	–	–	–
Lesotho	–	–	–	–	–	–	–	–	–	–	–	–	–	–	–	–
Liberia - Libéria	–	–	–	–	–	–	–	–	–	–	–	–	–	–	–	–
Libyan Arab Jamahiriya - Jamahiriya arabe libyenne	•	–	–	–	•	–	•	–	–	–	–	–	•	–	–	•
Madagascar	–	–	–	–	–	–	–	–	–	–	–	–	–	–	–	–
Malawi	–	–	–	–	–	–	–	–	–	–	–	–	–	–	–	–
Mali	–	–	–	–	–	–	–	–	–	–	•	–	–	–	–	–
Mauritania - Mauritanie	–	–	–	–	–	–	–	–	–	–	–	–	–	–	–	–
Mauritius - Maurice	•	•	•	•	•	–	•	–	•	–	•	•	•	•	•	•
Morocco - Maroc	•	•	•	–	•	–	•	•	–	–	–	–	–	–	–	–
Mozambique	•	–	–	–	–	–	–	–	–	–	–	–	–	–	–	–
Namibia - Namibie	–	–	–	–	–	–	–	–	–	–	–	–	–	–	–	–
Niger	–	–	–	–	–	–	–	–	–	–	–	–	–	–	–	–
Nigeria - Nigéria	–	–	–	–	–	–	–	–	–	–	–	–	–	–	–	–
Réunion	•	–	•	–	•	–	•	–	•	–	•	–	•	–	–	•
Rwanda	–	–	–	–	–	–	–	–	–	–	–	–	–	–	–	•
Saint Helena - Sainte-Hélène	•	–	–	–	•	–	•	–	–	–	–	•	•	–	•	–
Sao Tome and Principe - Sao Tomé-et-Principe	–	–	–	–	–	–	–	–	–	–	–	–	–	–	–	–
Senegal - Sénégal	–	–	–	–	–	–	–	–	–	–	–	–	–	–	–	–
Seychelles	•	–	–	–	•	–	•	–	–	–	•	–	•	–	•	•
Sierra Leone	–	–	–	–	–	–	–	–	–	–	–	–	–	–	–	–
Somalia - Somalie	–	–	–	–	–	–	–	–	–	–	–	–	–	–	–	–
South Africa - Afrique du Sud	–	–	•	•	–	–	•	–	–	–	•	–	•	–	•	•

29

Table A. *Demographic Yearbook 2001* synoptic table: Availability of data by country/area, table and urban/rural areas, where applicable

Tableau A. Tableau synoptique de l'*Annuaire démographique 2001:* Disponibilité des données par pays ou zone, tableau et zones urbaines/rurales, si disponible (continued — suite)

(See notes at end of table. — Voir notes à la fin du tableau.)

Continent, country or area / Continent, pays ou zone	Table totals	3	4	5	6	7 Total	7 U/R	8	9 Total	9 U/R	10 Total	10 U/R	11 Total	11 U/R	12 Total	12 U/R	13	14
AFRICA — AFRIQUE																		
Sudan - Soudan	5	•	–	•	•	•	–	•	–	–	–	–	–	–	–	–	–	–
Swaziland	22	•	•	•	•	•	•	•	•	•	•	•	•	•	–	–	–	–
Togo	3	•	–	•	–	•	–	•	–	–	–	–	–	–	–	–	–	–
Tunisia - Tunisie	21	•	•	•	•	•	–	•	•	–	•	–	•	–	•	–	–	–
Uganda - Ouganda	4	•	–	•	•	•	–	•	–	–	–	–	–	–	–	–	–	–
United Republic of Tanzania - République Unie de Tanzanie	3	•	–	•	–	–	–	•	–	–	–	–	–	–	–	–	–	–
Western Sahara - Sahara occidental	2	•	–	–	–	–	–	•	–	–	–	–	–	–	–	–	–	–
Zambia - Zambie	5	•	–	•	•	•	–	•	–	–	–	–	–	–	–	–	–	–
Zimbabwe	11	•	–	•	•	•	•	•	–	–	•	–	•	–	–	–	–	–
AMERICA, NORTH — AMERIQUE DU NORD																		
Anguilla	12	•	•	•	•	–	–	•	–	•	–	•	–	–	–	–	–	–
Antigua and Barbuda - Antigua-et-Barbuda	10	•	•	•	–	•	–	•	–	•	–	•	–	–	–	–	–	–
Aruba	12	•	•	•	–	•	–	•	–	•	–	•	–	–	–	–	–	–
Bahamas	12	•	•	•	•	–	–	•	–	•	–	•	–	–	–	–	–	–
Barbados - Barbade	12	•	•	•	–	•	–	•	–	•	–	•	–	–	–	–	–	–
Belize	16	•	•	•	•	•	–	•	–	•	–	•	–	–	–	–	–	–
Bermuda - Bermudes	18	•	•	•	–	•	–	•	–	•	–	•	–	•	–	•	–	–
British Virgin Islands - Îles Vierges britanniques	8	•	•	•	–	•	–	•	–	•	–	•	–	–	–	–	–	–
Canada	23	•	•	•	•	•	–	•	–	•	–	•	–	•	–	•	–	•	•
Cayman Islands - Îles Caïmanes	12	•	•	•	–	•	–	•	–	•	–	•	–	–	–	–	–	–
Costa Rica	22	•	•	•	–	•	–	•	•	–	•	–	•	–	•	–	–	–
Cuba	32	•	•	•	•	•	–	•	•	•	•	•	•	•	•	–	•	–
Dominica - Dominique	9	•	•	•	–	•	–	•	–	•	–	•	–	–	–	–	–	–
Dominican Republic - République dominicaine	17	•	•	•	•	•	–	•	•	–	•	–	•	–	–	–	–	–
El Salvador	31	•	•	•	•	•	•	•	•	•	•	•	•	•	•	–	•	–
Greenland - Groenland	25	•	•	•	–	•	•	•	–	•	–	•	–	•	–	•	–	–
Grenada - Grenade	14	•	•	•	–	•	–	•	–	•	–	•	–	•	–	–	–	–
Guadeloupe	6	•	–	•	–	•	–	•	–	–	–	–	–	–	–	–	–	–
Guatemala	22	•	•	•	–	•	–	•	•	–	•	–	•	–	•	–	–	–
Haiti - Haïti	6	•	–	•	–	•	–	•	–	–	–	–	–	–	–	–	–	–
Honduras	4	•	–	•	•	•	–	•	–	–	–	–	–	–	–	–	–	–
Jamaica - Jamaïque	13	•	–	•	–	•	–	•	–	•	–	•	–	•	–	–	–	–
Martinique	10	•	–	•	–	•	–	•	–	•	–	•	–	•	–	–	–	–
Mexico - Mexique	29	•	•	•	•	•	–	•	•	–	•	–	•	–	•	–	•	•
Montserrat	4	•	–	•	–	–	–	•	–	–	–	–	–	–	–	–	–	–
Netherlands Antilles - Antilles néerlandaises	11	•	•	•	–	•	–	•	–	•	–	•	–	–	–	–	–	–
Nicaragua	22	•	•	•	•	•	–	•	•	•	•	•	•	–	–	–	–	–
Panama	30	•	•	•	•	•	–	•	•	•	•	•	•	–	•	–	–	–
Puerto Rico - Porto Rico	27	•	•	•	•	•	–	•	•	–	•	–	•	–	•	–	•	–
Saint Kitts and Nevis - Saint-Kitts-et-Nevis	14	•	•	•	–	•	–	•	–	•	–	•	–	•	–	–	–	–
Saint Lucia - Sainte-Lucie	23	•	•	•	•	•	–	•	•	–	•	–	•	–	•	–	–	–
Saint Pierre and Miquelon - Saint Pierre-et-Miquelon	3	•	–	•	–	–	–	•	–	–	–	–	–	–	–	–	–	–
Saint Vincent and the Grenadines - Saint Vincent-et-les Grenadines	18	•	•	•	•	•	–	•	–	•	–	•	–	•	–	•	–	–
Trinidad and Tobago - Trinité-et-Tobago	19	•	•	•	–	•	–	•	•	–	•	–	•	–	•	–	–	–
Turks Caicos Islands - Îles Turques et Caïques	3	•	–	–	–	–	–	•	–	–	–	–	–	–	–	–	–	–
United States - États-Unis	20	•	•	•	•	•	–	•	–	•	–	•	–	•	–	•	–	–
United States Virgin Islands - Îles Vierges américaines	7	•	–	–	–	•	–	•	–	–	•	–	•	–	–	–	–	–

Table A. *Demographic Yearbook 2001* synoptic table: Availability of data by country/area, table and urban/rural areas, where applicable
Tableau A. Tableau synoptique de l'*Annuaire démographique 2001*: Disponibilité des données par pays ou zone, tableau et zones urbaines/rurales, si disponible (continued — suite)

(See notes at end of table. — Voir notes à la fin du tableau.)

Continent, country or area / Continent, pays ou zone	Infant mortality - Mortalité infantile 15 Total	15 U/R	16	17	General mortality - Mortalité générale 18 Total	18 U/R	19 Total	19 U/R	20 Total	20 U/R	21	22	Nuptiality and divorces - Nuptialité et divortialité 23 Total	23 U/R	24	25
AFRICA — AFRIQUE																
Sudan - Soudan	–	–	–	–	–	–	–	–	–	–	–	–	–	–	–	–
Swaziland	•	•	–	–	•	•	•	•	•	•	–	•	–	–	–	–
Togo	–	–	–	–	–	–	–	–	–	–	–	–	–	–	–	–
Tunisia - Tunisie	•	–	•	–	•	–	•	–	–	–	•	•	•	–	•	•
Uganda - Ouganda	–	–	–	–	–	–	–	–	–	–	–	–	–	–	–	–
United Republic of Tanzania - République Unie de Tanzanie	–	–	–	–	–	–	–	–	–	–	–	–	–	–	–	–
Western Sahara - Sahara occidental	–	–	–	–	–	–	–	–	–	–	–	–	–	–	–	–
Zambia - Zambie	–	–	–	–	–	–	–	–	–	–	–	–	–	–	–	–
Zimbabwe	–	–	–	–	–	–	–	–	–	–	–	•	–	–	–	–
AMERICA, NORTH — AMERIQUE DU NORD																
Anguilla	•	–	–	–	•	–	•	–	–	–	–	–	•	–	–	•
Antigua and Barbuda - Antigua-et-Barbuda	–	–	•	–	•	–	•	–	–	–	–	–	–	–	–	–
Aruba	•	–	–	–	•	–	•	–	–	–	–	–	•	–	–	•
Bahamas	•	–	–	–	•	–	•	–	–	–	–	–	•	–	–	–
Barbados - Barbade	•	–	–	•	•	–	•	–	–	–	–	–	•	–	•	•
Belize	•	–	–	•	•	–	•	–	–	–	•	–	•	–	•	•
Bermuda - Bermudes	•	–	–	•	•	–	•	–	–	–	•	–	•	–	•	•
British Virgin Islands - Îles Vierges britanniques	•	–	–	–	•	–	•	–	–	–	•	–	•	–	–	•
Canada	•	–	•	•	•	–	•	•	•	•	•	•	•	•	•	•
Cayman Islands - Îles Caïmanes	–	–	•	–	•	–	•	–	–	–	•	–	•	–	–	•
Costa Rica	•	–	–	•	•	–	•	–	•	–	•	•	•	–	•	•
Cuba	•	•	–	•	•	•	•	•	•	•	•	•	•	–	•	•
Dominica - Dominique	•	–	–	–	•	–	•	–	–	–	–	–	•	–	–	•
Dominican Republic - République dominicaine	•	–	–	–	•	–	•	–	•	–	•	•	•	•	–	•
El Salvador	•	•	•	•	•	–	•	–	•	•	•	•	•	•	–	•
Greenland - Groenland	•	–	–	•	•	–	•	–	•	–	•	•	•	–	–	–
Grenada - Grenade	•	–	–	•	•	–	•	–	–	–	•	–	•	–	•	•
Guadeloupe	–	–	•	–	•	–	•	–	•	–	•	–	•	–	–	•
Guatemala	•	–	–	•	•	–	•	–	•	–	•	•	•	–	–	•
Haiti - Haïti	–	–	–	–	–	–	–	–	–	–	–	–	–	–	–	–
Honduras	–	–	–	–	•	–	–	–	–	–	–	–	–	–	–	–
Jamaica - Jamaïque	•	–	–	–	•	–	–	–	–	–	–	–	–	–	–	–
Martinique	–	–	•	–	•	–	•	–	•	–	•	–	•	–	–	•
Mexico - Mexique	•	•	•	•	•	•	•	–	•	•	•	•	–	–	–	•
Montserrat	–	–	–	–	–	–	–	–	–	–	•	–	–	–	–	–
Netherlands Antilles - Antilles néerlandaises	–	–	–	•	•	–	•	–	•	–	–	–	•	–	–	•
Nicaragua	•	•	•	•	•	–	•	–	•	–	•	•	•	–	–	•
Panama	•	–	•	•	•	•	•	•	•	•	•	•	•	•	–	•
Puerto Rico - Porto Rico	•	•	•	•	•	•	•	–	•	•	•	•	•	•	–	•
Saint Kitts and Nevis - Saint-Kitts-et-Nevis	•	–	•	–	•	–	–	–	•	–	•	•	•	•	•	•
Saint Lucia - Sainte-Lucie	•	•	•	–	•	–	•	–	–	–	•	•	•	•	•	•
Saint Pierre and Miquelon - Saint Pierre-et-Miquelon	··	–	–	–	–	–	–	–	–	–	–	–	–	–	–	–
Saint Vincent and the Grenadines - Saint Vincent-et-les Grenadines	•	–	•	–	•	–	•	–	–	–	•	–	•	–	–	•
Trinidad and Tobago - Trinité-et-Tobago	•	–	•	•	•	–	•	–	•	–	•	•	•	–	•	•
Turks Caicos Islands - Îles Turques et Caïques	–	–	–	–	–	–	–	–	–	–	•	–	–	–	–	–
United States - États-Unis	•	–	•	•	•	–	•	–	•	–	•	•	•	–	–	•
United States Virgin Islands - Îles Vierges américaines	–	–	•	–	•	–	•	–	–	–	•	–	–	–	–	–

Table A. *Demographic Yearbook 2001* synoptic table: Availability of data by country/area, table and urban/rural areas, where applicable

Tableau A. Tableau synoptique de l'*Annuaire démographique 2001:* Disponibilité des données par pays ou zone, tableau et zones urbaines/rurales, si disponible (continued — suite)

(See notes at end of table. — Voir notes à la fin du tableau.)

Continent, country or area / Continent, pays ou zone	Table totals	Summary - Apercu 3	4	Population 5	6	7 Total	7 U/R	8	Natality - Natalité 9 Total	9 U/R	10 Total	10 U/R	11 Total	11 U/R	Foetal mortality - Mortalité foetale 12 Total	12 U/R	13	14
AMERICA, SOUTH — AMERIQUE DU SUD																		
Argentina - Argentine	19	•	•	•	•	•	•	•	•	–	•	–	•	–	•	–	–	–
Bolivia - Bolivie	11	•	•	•	•	•	•	•	•	–	•	–	•	–	–	–	–	–
Brazil - Brésil	19	•	•	•	•	•	•	•	•	–	•	–	•	–	•	–	–	–
Chile - Chili	29	•	•	•	•	•	•	•	•	–	•	–	•	–	•	–	•	–
Colombia - Colombie	23	•	•	•	•	•	•	•	•	•	•	•	•	–	•	–	–	–
Ecuador - Équateur	26	•	•	•	•	•	•	•	•	•	•	•	•	–	•	–	•	–
Falkland Islands (Malvinas) - Îles Falkland (Malvinas)	10	•	•	–	–	•	•	•	•	–	•	–	•	–	–	–	–	–
French Guiana - Guyane française	16	•	•	•	–	•	•	•	•	–	•	–	•	–	•	–	–	–
Guyana	6	•	•	•	–	–	•	–	•	–	•	–	•	–	–	–	–	–
Paraguay	12	•	•	•	•	•	•	•	•	–	•	–	•	–	–	–	–	–
Peru - Pérou	13	•	•	•	•	•	•	•	•	–	•	–	•	–	–	–	–	–
Suriname	23	•	•	•	•	•	•	•	•	•	•	–	•	–	•	–	–	–
Uruguay	21	•	•	•	•	•	•	•	•	–	•	–	•	–	•	–	–	–
Venezuela	22	•	•	•	•	•	•	•	•	–	•	–	•	–	•	–	–	–
ASIA — ASIE																		
Afghanistan	2	•	–	–	–	–	•	–	–	–	–	–	–	–	–	–	–	–
Armenia - Arménie	32	•	•	•	•	•	•	•	•	•	•	•	•	•	•	–	•	•
Azerbaijan - Azerbaïdjan	32	•	•	•	•	•	•	•	•	•	•	•	•	•	•	–	•	–
Bahrain - Bahreïn	14	•	•	•	–	•	•	•	•	–	•	–	•	–	–	–	–	–
Bangladesh	10	•	•	•	•	•	•	•	•	–	•	–	•	–	–	–	–	–
Bhutan - Bhoutan	5	•	–	•	•	•	•	•	–	–	–	–	–	–	–	–	–	–
Brunei Darussalam - Brunéi Darussalam	16	•	•	•	–	•	•	•	•	–	•	–	•	–	•	–	–	–
Cambodia - Cambodge	6	•	–	•	•	•	•	•	–	–	–	–	–	–	–	–	–	–
China - Chine[2]	14	•	•	•	•	•	•	•	•	–	•	–	•	–	•	–	–	–
China: Hong Kong SAR - Chine: Hong Kong RAS	31	•	•	•	9	•	–	•	•	–	•	–	•	–	•	–	•	•
China: Macao SAR - Chine: Macao RAS	28	•	•	•	9	•	–	•	•	–	•	–	•	–	•	–	•	–
Cyprus - Chypre	20	•	•	•	•	•	•	•	•	–	•	–	•	–	•	–	–	–
Georgia - Géorgie	32	•	•	•	•	•	•	•	•	•	•	•	•	•	•	–	•	•
India - Inde[3]	7	•	•	•	•	•	•	•	–	–	–	–	–	–	–	–	–	–
Indonesia - Indonésie	8	•	•	•	•	•	•	•	•	–	–	–	–	–	–	–	–	–
Iran (Islamic Republic of) - Iran (République islamique d')	18	•	•	•	•	•	•	•	•	•	•	•	•	–	–	–	–	–
Iraq	13	•	•	•	•	•	•	•	•	–	•	–	•	–	–	–	–	–
Israel - Israël[4]	29	•	•	•	•	•	•	•	•	–	•	–	•	–	•	–	•	•
Japan - Japon	29	•	•	•	•	•	•	•	•	–	•	–	•	–	•	–	•	•
Jordan - Jordanie	14	•	•	•	•	•	•	•	•	–	•	–	•	–	•	–	•	•
Kazakhstan	32	•	•	•	•	•	•	•	•	•	•	•	•	•	•	–	•	–
Korea (Dem. People's Republic of) - Corée (Rép. populaire dém. de)	10	•	•	–	–	•	•	•	•	–	•	–	•	–	–	–	–	–
Korea (Republic of) - Corée (République de)	23	•	•	•	•	•	•	•	•	–	•	–	•	–	•	–	•	–
Kuwait - Koweït	20	•	•	•	–	•	•	•	•	–	•	–	•	–	•	–	•	–
Kyrgyzstan - Kirghizistan	32	•	•	•	•	•	•	•	•	•	•	•	•	•	•	–	•	–
Lao People's Democratic Republic - République démocratique populaire lao	6	•	•	•	•	•	•	•	–	–	–	–	–	–	–	–	–	–
Lebanon - Liban	7	•	•	–	•	•	•	•	–	–	–	–	–	–	–	–	–	–
Malaysia - Malaisie	18	•	•	•	•	•	•	•	•	–	•	–	•	–	•	–	•	–
Maldives	23	•	•	•	•	•	•	•	•	–	•	–	•	–	•	–	•	–
Mongolia - Mongolie	28	•	•	•	•	•	•	•	•	–	•	–	•	–	•	–	•	–
Myanmar	9	•	–	•	•	•	•	•	•	–	–	–	–	–	–	–	–	–
Nepal - Népal	9	•	•	•	•	•	•	•	–	–	–	–	–	–	–	–	–	–

32

Table A. *Demographic Yearbook 2001* synoptic table: Availability of data by country/area, table and urban/rural areas, where applicable
Tableau A. Tableau synoptique de l'*Annuaire démographique 2001:* Disponibilité des données par pays ou zone, tableau et zones urbaines/rurales, si disponible (continued — suite)

(See notes at end of table. — Voir notes à la fin du tableau.)

Continent, country or area / Continent, pays ou zone	Infant mortality - Mortalité infantile				General mortality - Mortalité générale								Nuptiality and divorces - Nuptialité et divortialité			
	15		16	17	18		19		20		21	22	23		24	25
	Total	U/R			Total	U/R	Total	U/R	Total	U/R			Total	U/R		
AMERICA, SOUTH — AMERIQUE DU SUD																
Argentina - Argentine	•	–	•	•	•	–	•	–	•	–	•	•	•	•	–	–
Bolivia - Bolivie	•	–	•	•	•	–	•	–	•	–	–	•	–	–	–	–
Brazil - Brésil	•	–	•	•	•	–	•	–	•	–	•	•	–	–	•	•
Chile - Chili	•	•	•	•	•	•	•	•	•	•	•	•	•	•	–	–
Colombia - Colombie	•	•	•	•	•	•	•	•	–	•	•	•	–	•	–	–
Ecuador - Équateur	•	•	•	•	•	•	•	–	•	–	•	•	•	•	–	–
Falkland Islands (Malvinas) - Îles Falkland (Malvinas)	–	–	–	–	•	–	•	–	•	–	–	–	•	–	–	–
French Guiana - Guyane française	•	–	•	–	•	–	•	–	•	–	•	•	•	•	–	•
Guyana	–	–	•	–	•	–	•	–	•	–	•	•	–	–	–	–
Paraguay	–	–	•	–	•	–	•	–	•	–	•	•	–	–	–	–
Peru - Pérou	•	–	•	–	•	–	•	–	•	–	•	•	–	–	–	–
Suriname	•	–	•	•	•	–	•	–	•	–	•	•	•	–	•	•
Uruguay	•	–	•	–	•	–	•	–	•	–	•	•	•	•	•	•
Venezuela	•	–	•	–	•	–	•	–	•	–	•	•	•	•	•	•
ASIA — ASIE																
Afghanistan	–	–	–	–	–	–	–	–	–	–	–	–	–	–	–	–
Armenia - Arménie	•	•	•	•	•	•	•	•	•	•	•	•	•	•	•	•
Azerbaijan - Azerbaïdjan	•	•	•	•	•	•	•	•	•	•	•	•	•	•	•	•
Bahrain - Bahreïn	•	–	•	•	•	–	•	–	•	–	•	•	•	•	–	–
Bangladesh	•	–	–	–	–	–	–	–	–	–	•	•	–	–	–	–
Bhutan - Bhoutan	–	–	–	–	–	–	–	–	–	–	•	•	–	–	–	–
Brunei Darussalam - Brunéi Darussalam	•	–	•	•	•	–	•	–	•	–	•	•	•	•	–	–
Cambodia - Cambodge	–	–	–	–	–	–	–	–	–	–	•	•	–	–	–	–
China - Chine[2]	•	–	•	–	•	–	•	–	•	–	•	•	•	–	–	–
China: Hong Kong SAR - Chine: Hong Kong RAS	•	–	•	•	•	–	•	–	•	–	•	•	•	•	•	•
China: Macao SAR - Chine: Macao RAS	•	–	•	–	•	–	•	–	•	–	•	•	•	•	•	•
Cyprus - Chypre	•	–	•	•	•	–	•	–	•	–	•	•	•	•	•	•
Georgia - Géorgie	•	•	•	•	•	•	•	•	•	•	•	–	•	•	•	•
India - Inde[3]	•	–	•	•	•	–	•	–	•	–	•	•	•	•	–	–
Indonesia - Indonésie											•	•				
Iran (Islamic Republic of) - Iran (République islamique d')	–	–	–	–	•	–	•	–	•	–	•	•	•	•	•	•
Iraq	–	–	–	–	•	–	•	–	•	–	•	•	•	•	–	–
Israel - Israël[4]	•	•	•	•	•	•	•	•	•	•	•	•	•	•	•	•
Japan - Japon	•	•	•	•	•	•	•	•	•	•	•	•	•	•	•	•
Jordan - Jordanie	•	•	•	•	•	•	•	•	•	•	•	•	•	•	•	•
Kazakhstan	•	•	•	•	•	•	•	•	•	•	•	•	•	•	•	•
Korea (Dem. People's Republic of) - Corée (Rép. populaire dém. de)	–	–	–	–	–	–	•	–	–	–	–	–	–	–	–	–
Korea (Republic of) - Corée (République de)	•	–	–	•	•	–	•	–	•	–	•	•	•	•	–	•
Kuwait - Koweït	•	–	•	•	•	–	•	–	•	–	•	•	•	•	–	–
Kyrgyzstan - Kirghizistan	•	•	•	•	•	•	•	•	•	•	•	•	•	•	•	•
Lao People's Democratic Republic - République démocratique populaire lao	–	–	–	•	–	–	–	–	–	–	–	–	•	•	–	•
Lebanon - Liban	–	–	–	•	–	–	–	–	–	–	–	–	•	•	–	–
Malaysia - Malaisie	•	–	•	•	•	–	•	–	•	–	•	•	•	•	–	–
Maldives	•	•	•	•	•	•	•	•	•	•	•	•	•	–	–	–
Mongolia - Mongolie	•	–	•	•	•	–	•	–	•	–	•	•	•	•	–	–
Myanmar	•	–	–	–	•	–	–	–	–	–	–	–	–	–	–	–
Nepal - Népal	•	–	–	–	•	–	–	–	–	–	–	–	–	–	–	–

Table A. *Demographic Yearbook 2001* synoptic table: Availability of data by country/area, table and urban/rural areas, where applicable

Tableau A. Tableau synoptique de l'*Annuaire démographique 2001:* Disponibilité des données par pays ou zone, tableau et zones urbaines/rurales, si disponible (continued — suite)

(See notes at end of table. — Voir notes à la fin du tableau.)

Continent, country or area / Continent, pays ou zone	Table totals	Summary - Aperçu 3	4	Population 5	6	7 Total	7 U/R	8	Natality - Natalité 9 Total	9 U/R	10 Total	10 U/R	11 Total	11 U/R	Foetal mortality 12 Total	12 U/R	13	14
ASIA — ASIE																		
Occupied Palestinian Territory - Territoire palestinien occupé	15	•	•	•	•	•	–	•	•	–	•	–	•	–	•	–	–	–
Oman	9	•	•	•	–	•	–	•	–	–	•	–	•	–	•	–	–	–
Pakistan[5]	23	•	•	•	•	•	•	•	•	–	•	•	•	–	•	–	–	–
Philippines	17	•	•	•	–	•	–	•	–	–	•	–	•	–	•	–	–	–
Qatar	15	•	•	•	–	•	–	•	•	–	•	–	•	–	•	–	–	–
Saudi Arabia - Arabie saoudite	11	•	•	•	–	•	–	•	•	–	•	–	•	–	•	–	–	–
Singapore - Singapour	22	•	•	•	–	•	–	•	–	–	•	–	•	–	•	–	•	•
Sri Lanka	17	•	•	•	•	•	–	•	•	–	•	–	•	–	•	–	–	–
Syrian Arab Republic - République arabe syrienne	12	•	•	•	•	•	–	•	•	–	•	–	•	–	•	–	–	–
Tajikistan - Tadjikistan	24	•	•	•	•	•	–	•	•	–	•	–	•	•	•	–	•	–
Thailand - Thaïlande	20	•	•	•	•	•	•	•	•	•	•	–	•	–	•	–	–	–
Timor-Leste	2	•	–	–	–	•	–	–	–	–	–	–	–	–	–	–	–	–
Turkey - Turquie	20	•	•	•	–	•	–	•	•	–	•	–	•	–	•	–	–	–
Turkmenistan - Turkménistan	11	•	•	•	–	•	–	•	•	–	•	–	•	–	•	–	–	–
United Arab Emirates - Émirats arabes unis	3	•	–	–	–	•	–	•	–	–	–	–	–	–	–	–	–	–
Uzbekistan - Ouzbékistan	31	•	•	•	•	•	–	•	•	•	•	•	•	•	•	–	•	–
Viet Nam	6	•	–	•	•	•	•	•	–	–	–	–	–	–	–	–	–	–
Yemen - Yémen	6	•	–	•	•	•	•	•	–	–	–	–	–	–	–	–	–	–
EUROPE																		
Albania - Albanie	12	•	•	•	•	•	–	•	•	–	–	–	–	–	–	–	–	–
Andorra - Andorre	11	•	•	•	•	•	–	•	•	–	•	–	•	–	–	–	–	–
Austria - Autriche	24	•	•	•	•	•	–	•	•	–	•	–	•	–	•	–	•	–
Belarus - Bélarus	31	•	•	•	•	•	–	•	•	–	•	–	•	–	•	–	•	•
Belgium - Belgique	22	•	•	•	–	•	–	•	•	–	•	–	•	–	•	–	•	•
Bosnia and Herzegovina - Bosnie-Herzégovine	13	•	•	•	–	•	–	•	•	–	•	–	•	–	–	–	–	–
Bulgaria - Bulgarie	33	•	•	•	•	•	–	•	•	•	•	•	•	•	•	•	•	•
Channel Islands - Îles Anglo-Normandes	1	–	–	•	–	–	–	–	–	–	–	–	–	–	–	–	–	–
Channel Islands: Guernsey - Îles Anglo-Normandes: Guernesey	16	•	•	–	–	•	–	•	–	–	•	–	•	–	–	–	–	–
Channel Islands: Jersey - Îles Anglo-Normandes: Jersey	7	–	–	–	–	•	–	•	–	–	•	–	•	–	•	–	•	–
Croatia - Croatie	28	•	•	•	–	•	–	•	•	–	•	–	•	–	•	–	•	•
Czech Republic - République tchèque	32	•	•	•	•	•	–	•	•	–	•	–	•	–	•	–	•	•
Denmark - Danemark	21	•	•	•	–	•	–	•	•	–	•	–	•	–	•	–	•	•
Estonia - Estonie	32	•	•	•	•	•	–	•	•	–	•	–	•	–	•	–	•	•
Faeroe Islands - Îles Féroé	5	•	–	–	–	•	–	•	–	–	–	–	–	–	–	–	–	–
Finland - Finlande	32	•	•	•	•	•	•	•	•	–	•	–	•	–	•	–	•	•
France	29	•	•	•	–	•	–	•	•	–	•	–	•	–	•	•	•	–
Germany - Allemagne	22	•	•	•	–	•	–	•	•	–	•	–	•	–	•	–	•	•
Gibraltar	9	•	•	•	–	•	–	•	•	–	•	–	•	–	–	–	–	–
Greece - Grèce	28	•	•	•	–	•	–	•	•	–	•	–	•	–	•	–	•	•
Holy See - Saint-Siège	5	•	•	•	–	–	–	•	–	–	–	–	–	–	–	–	–	–
Hungary - Hongrie	33	•	•	•	•	•	–	•	•	–	•	–	•	–	•	–	•	•
Iceland - Islande	31	•	•	•	–	•	–	•	•	•	•	•	•	•	•	•	•	•
Ireland - Irlande	27	•	•	•	•	•	–	•	•	–	•	–	•	–	–	–	•	•
Isle of Man - Îles de Man	16	•	•	•	–	•	–	•	•	–	•	–	•	–	–	–	–	–
Italy - Italie	23	•	•	•	•	•	–	•	•	–	•	–	•	–	•	–	•	•
Latvia - Lettonie	33	•	•	•	•	•	–	•	•	–	•	–	•	–	•	–	•	•
Liechtenstein	15	•	•	•	–	•	–	•	•	–	•	–	•	–	–	–	–	–
Lithuania - Lituanie	33	•	•	•	•	•	–	•	•	–	•	•	•	•	•	–	•	•

Table A. *Demographic Yearbook 2001* synoptic table: Availability of data by country/area, table and urban/rural areas, where applicable

Tableau A. Tableau synoptique de l'*Annuaire démographique 2001*: Disponibilité des données par pays ou zone, tableau et zones urbaines/rurales, si disponible (continued — suite)

(See notes at end of table. — Voir notes à la fin du tableau.)

Continent, country or area / Continent, pays ou zone	Infant mortality - Mortalité infantile 15 Total	15 U/R	16	17	General mortality - Mortalité générale 18 Total	18 U/R	19 Total	19 U/R	20 Total	20 U/R	21	22	Nuptiality and divorces - Nuptialité et divortialité 23 Total	23 U/R	24	25
ASIA — ASIE																
Occupied Palestinian Territory - Territoire palestinien occupé	•	–	•	–	•	–	•	–	–	–	–	•	•	–	•	•
Oman	•	–	–	–	•	–	•	–	–	–	–	–	•	–	•	•
Pakistan[5]	•	•	–	–	•	–	•	–	•	–	•	–	•	–	•	–
Philippines	•	–	•	•	•	–	•	–	–	–	•	•	•	–	•	•
Qatar	•	–	–	–	•	–	•	–	–	–	–	•	•	–	•	•
Saudi Arabia - Arabie saoudite	•	–	–	–	•	–	•	–	–	–	–	•	•	–	•	•
Singapore - Singapour	•	–	•	•	•	–	•	–	•	–	•	•	•	–	•	•
Sri Lanka	•	–	•	–	•	–	•	•	•	–	•	–	–	–	•	–
Syrian Arab Republic - République arabe syrienne	–	–	–	–	•	–	•	–	•	–	•	–	•	–	•	•
Tajikistan - Tadjikistan	•	–	•	–	•	•	•	•	•	•	•	–	•	–	•	•
Thailand - Thaïlande	•	•	•	–	•	–	•	–	•	–	•	–	•	–	•	–
Timor-Leste	–	–	–	–	–	–	–	–	–	–	–	–	–	–	–	–
Turkey - Turquie	•	•	•	–	•	•	•	–	–	–	•	•	•	•	–	•
Turkmenistan - Turkménistan	•	–	–	–	•	–	•	–	•	–	•	–	•	–	•	–
United Arab Emirates - Émirats arabes unis	–	–	–	–	–	–	–	–	–	–	–	–	–	–	–	–
Uzbekistan - Ouzbékistan	•	•	•	•	•	•	•	•	•	•	•	–	•	–	•	•
Viet Nam	–	–	–	–	–	–	–	–	–	–	–	–	–	–	–	–
Yemen - Yémen	–	–	–	–	–	–	–	–	–	–	–	–	–	–	–	–
EUROPE																
Albania - Albanie	•	–	•	–	•	–	–	–	–	–	•	–	•	–	–	–
Andorra - Andorre	•	–	–	–	•	–	•	–	–	–	•	–	•	–	–	–
Austria - Autriche	•	–	•	–	•	–	•	–	•	–	•	•	•	–	•	•
Belarus - Bélarus	•	•	•	•	•	•	•	•	•	•	•	•	•	–	•	•
Belgium - Belgique	•	–	•	–	•	–	•	–	•	–	•	–	•	–	•	•
Bosnia and Herzegovina - Bosnie-Herzégovine	•	–	•	–	•	–	•	–	–	–	•	–	•	–	–	–
Bulgaria - Bulgarie	•	•	•	•	•	•	•	•	•	•	•	•	•	•	•	•
Channel Islands - Îles Anglo-Normandes	–	–	–	–	–	–	–	–	–	–	–	–	–	–	–	–
Channel Islands: Guernsey - Îles Anglo-Normandes: Guernesey	•	–	•	–	•	–	•	–	–	–	•	–	•	–	•	–
Channel Islands: Jersey - Îles Anglo-Normandes: Jersey	–	–	•	–	–	–	•	–	–	–	•	–	–	–	–	–
Croatia - Croatie	•	–	•	–	•	–	•	–	–	–	–	–	–	•	•	•
Czech Republic - République tchèque	•	•	•	•	•	•	•	•	•	•	•	•	•	•	•	•
Denmark - Danemark	•	–	•	•	•	–	•	–	•	–	•	–	•	–	•	•
Estonia - Estonie	•	•	•	•	•	•	•	•	•	•	•	•	•	–	•	•
Faeroe Islands - Îles Féroé	–	–	•	–	–	–	–	–	–	–	•	–	–	–	–	–
Finland - Finlande	•	•	•	•	•	•	•	•	•	•	•	•	•	•	•	•
France	•	–	•	•	•	–	•	–	•	–	–	–	•	–	•	•
Germany - Allemagne	•	–	•	•	•	–	•	–	•	–	•	–	•	•	•	•
Gibraltar	–	–	•	–	•	–	•	–	–	–	–	–	•	–	–	–
Greece - Grèce	•	–	•	–	•	–	•	–	•	–	•	–	•	–	•	•
Holy See - Saint-Siège	–	–	–	–	•	–	•	–	•	–	–	–	–	–	–	–
Hungary - Hongrie	•	•	•	–	•	–	•	–	•	–	•	•	•	–	•	•
Iceland - Islande	•	–	•	–	•	–	•	–	•	–	•	–	•	–	•	•
Ireland - Irlande	•	•	•	–	•	–	•	–	•	–	•	–	•	–	•	•
Isle of Man - Îles de Man	•	–	•	–	•	–	•	–	–	–	•	–	•	–	•	•
Italy - Italie	•	–	•	–	•	–	•	–	•	–	•	–	•	–	•	•
Latvia - Lettonie	•	•	•	•	•	–	•	–	•	–	•	–	•	–	•	•
Liechtenstein	•	–	•	–	•	–	•	–	•	–	•	–	•	–	•	•
Lithuania - Lituanie	•	•	•	•	•	•	•	•	•	•	•	•	•	•	•	•

(See notes at end of table. — Voir notes à la fin du tableau.)

Table A. *Demographic Yearbook 2001* synoptic table: Availability of data by country/area, table and urban/rural areas, where applicable
Tableau A. Tableau synoptique de l'*Annuaire démographique 2001*: Disponibilité des données par pays ou zone, tableau et zones urbaines/rurales, si disponible (continued — suite)

Continent, country or area / Continent, pays ou zone	Table totals	Summary - Aperçu		Population					Natality - Natalité						Foetal mortality - Mortalité foetale			
		3	4	5	6	7 Total	7 U/R	8	9 Total	9 U/R	10 Total	10 U/R	11 Total	11 U/R	12 Total	12 U/R	13	14
EUROPE																		
Luxembourg	20	•	•	•	–	•	–	•	•	–	•	–	•	–	•	–	–	–
Malta - Malte	18	•	•	•	–	•	–	•	•	–	•	–	•	–	•	–	–	–
Monaco	9	•	•	•	–	•	–	•	•	–	•	–	•	–	•	–	–	–
Netherlands - Pays-Bas	31	•	•	•	•	•	•	•	•	–	•	–	•	–	•	•	•	•
Norway - Norvège	22	•	•	•	•	•	•	•	•	–	•	–	•	–	•	•	•	•
Poland - Pologne	30	•	•	•	•	•	–	•	•	–	•	–	•	–	•	•	•	•
Portugal	21	•	•	•	–	•	–	•	•	–	•	–	•	–	•	•	–	–
Republic of Moldova - République de Moldova	31	•	•	•	•	•	•	•	•	•	•	•	•	–	•	•	•	•
Romania - Roumanie	33	•	•	•	•	•	•	•	•	•	•	•	•	•	•	•	•	•
Russian Federation - Fédération de Russie	32	•	•	•	•	•	•	•	•	•	•	•	•	•	•	•	•	•
San Marino - Saint-Marin	22	•	•	•	•	•	•	•	•	•	•	•	•	•	•	•	•	•
Serbia and Montenegro - Serbie-et-Montenegro	31	•	•	•	•	•	•	•	•	•	•	•	•	•	•	•	•	•
Slovakia - Slovaquie	30	•	•	•	–	•	•	•	•	•	•	•	•	•	•	•	•	•
Slovenia - Slovénie	32	•	•	•	•	•	•	•	•	•	•	•	•	•	•	•	•	•
Spain - Espagne	22	•	•	•	•	•	•	•	•	•	•	•	•	•	•	•	•	•
Svalbard and Jan Mayen Islands - Îles Svalbard et Jan-Mayen	1	•	–	–	–	–	–	–	–	–	–	–	–	–	–	–	–	–
Sweden - Suède	22	•	•	•	–	•	–	•	•	–	•	–	•	–	•	•	•	•
Switzerland - Suisse	28	•	•	•	•	•	–	•	•	•	•	•	•	•	•	•	–	–
The Former Yugoslav Rep. of Macedonia - L'ex-République yougoslave de Macédoine	30	•	•	•	•	•	•	•	•	•	•	•	•	•	•	•	•	•
Ukraine	30	•	•	•	•	•	•	•	•	•	•	•	•	•	•	•	•	•
United Kingdom - Royaume-Uni	22	•	•	•	–	•	–	•	•	–	•	–	•	–	•	•	•	•
OCEANIA — OCEANIE																		
American Samoa - Samoas américaines	10	•	•	•	–	•	–	•	•	–	•	–	–	–	–	–	–	–
Australia - Australie	20	•	•	•	–	•	–	•	•	–	•	–	•	–	•	–	•	–
Cook Islands - Îles Cook	11	•	•	•	•	•	•	•	•	–	–	–	–	–	–	–	–	–
Fiji - Fidji	12	•	•	•	•	•	•	•	•	–	–	–	–	–	–	–	–	–
French Polynesia - Polynésie française	10	•	•	•	•	•	•	•	•	–	–	–	–	–	–	–	–	–
Guam	16	•	•	•	•	•	•	•	•	•	•	•	–	–	–	–	–	–
Kiribati	3	•	–	•	–	–	–	•	–	–	–	–	–	–	–	–	–	–
Marshall Islands - Îles Marshall	10	•	•	•	•	•	•	•	•	–	–	–	–	–	–	–	–	–
Micronesia, Federated States of - Micronésie (États fédérés de)	9	•	•	•	–	•	–	•	•	–	–	–	–	–	–	–	–	–
Nauru	3	•	–	•	–	–	–	•	–	–	–	–	–	–	–	–	–	–
New Caledonia - Nouvelle-Calédonie	21	•	•	•	•	•	•	•	•	–	•	–	•	–	•	–	•	–
New Zealand - Nouvelle-Zélande	31	•	•	•	•	•	•	•	•	–	•	–	•	–	•	•	•	•
Niue - Nioué	4	•	–	•	–	•	–	•	–	–	–	–	–	–	–	–	–	–
Norfolk Island - Île Norfolk	2	•	–	–	–	–	–	•	–	–	–	–	–	–	–	–	–	–
Northern Mariana Islands - Îles Mariannes septentrionales	10	•	•	•	•	•	•	•	•	–	–	–	–	–	–	–	–	–
Palau - Palaos	11	•	•	•	•	•	•	•	•	•	–	–	–	–	–	–	–	–
Papua New Guinea - Papouasie-Nouvelle-Guinée	3	•	–	–	–	•	–	•	–	–	–	–	–	–	–	–	–	–
Pitcairn	3	•	–	–	–	•	–	•	–	–	–	–	–	–	–	–	–	–
Samoa	7	•	•	•	–	•	–	•	•	–	–	–	–	–	–	–	–	–
Solomon Islands - Îles Salomon	2	•	–	–	–	•	–	•	–	–	–	–	–	–	–	–	–	–
Tokelau - Tokélaou	1	•	–	–	–	–	–	•	–	–	–	–	–	–	–	–	–	–
Tonga	18	•	•	•	•	•	•	•	•	–	•	–	•	–	•	–	–	–
Tuvalu	2	•	–	–	–	–	–	•	–	–	•	–	–	–	–	–	–	–
Vanuatu	4	•	–	•	•	–	–	•	–	–	–	–	–	–	–	–	–	–
Wallis and Futuna Islands - Îles Wallis et Futuna	2	•	–	–	–	–	–	•	–	–	–	–	–	–	–	–	–	–

Table A. *Demographic Yearbook 2001* synoptic table: Availability of data by country/area, table and urban/rural areas, where applicable
Tableau A. Tableau synoptique de l'*Annuaire démographique 2001:* Disponibilité des données par pays ou zone, tableau et zones urbaines/rurales, si disponible (continued — suite)

(See notes at end of table. — Voir notes à la fin du tableau.)

Continent, country or area / Continent, pays ou zone	Infant mortality - Mortalité infantile				General mortality - Mortalité générale								Nuptiality and divorces - Nuptialité et divortialité			
	15 Total	15 U/R	16	17	18 Total	18 U/R	19 Total	19 U/R	20 Total	20 U/R	21	22	23 Total	23 U/R	24	25
EUROPE																
Luxembourg	•	–	•	•	•	–	•	–	•	–	•	•	•	–	•	•
Malta - Malte	•	–	•	•	•	–	•	–	•	–	•	•	•	–	•	•
Monaco	–	–	–	–	•	–	–	–	–	–	–	–	•	–	–	•
Netherlands - Pays-Bas	•	–	•	•	•	–	•	•	•	•	•	•	•	•	•	•
Norway - Norvège	•	–	•	•	•	•	•	•	•	•	•	•	•	•	•	•
Poland - Pologne	•	•	•	•	•	•	•	•	•	•	•	•	•	•	•	•
Portugal	–	–	•	•	•	–	•	–	•	–	•	•	•	–	•	•
Republic of Moldova - République de Moldova	•	•	•	•	•	•	•	•	•	•	•	•	•	•	•	•
Romania - Roumanie	•	•	•	•	•	•	•	•	•	•	•	•	•	•	•	•
Russian Federation - Fédération de Russie	•	•	•	•	•	•	•	•	•	•	•	•	•	•	•	•
San Marino - Saint-Marin	•	–	•	–	•	–	•	–	•	–	•	•	•	–	•	•
Serbia and Montenegro - Serbie-et-Montenegro	•	•	•	–	•	•	•	•	•	•	•	•	•	•	•	•
Slovakia - Slovaquie	•	•	•	•	•	•	•	•	•	–	•	•	•	•	•	•
Slovenia - Slovénie	•	•	•	•	•	•	•	•	•	•	•	•	•	•	•	•
Spain - Espagne	•	–	•	•	•	–	•	–	•	–	•	•	•	–	•	•
Svalbard and Jan Mayen Islands - Îles Svalbard et Jan-Mayen	–	–	–	–	–	–	–	–	–	–	–	–	–	–	–	–
Sweden - Suède	•	•	•	•	•	–	•	–	•	–	•	•	•	•	•	•
Switzerland - Suisse	•	•	•	•	•	•	•	•	•	•	•	•	•	•	•	•
The Former Yugoslav Rep. of Macedonia - L'ex-République yougoslave de Macédoine	•	•	•	•	•	•	•	•	•	•	•	•	•	•	•	•
Ukraine	•	•	•	•	•	•	•	•	•	•	•	•	•	•	•	•
United Kingdom - Royaume-Uni	•	–	•	•	•	–	•	–	•	–	•	•	•	–	•	•
OCEANIA — OCEANIE																
American Samoa - Samoas américaines	•	–	–	–	–	–	•	–	–	–	•	–	–	–	–	–
Australia - Australie	•	–	•	–	•	–	•	–	•	–	•	•	•	–	•	•
Cook Islands - Îles Cook	•	–	•	–	•	–	•	–	•	–	•	–	•	–	–	–
Fiji - Fidji	•	–	•	–	•	–	•	–	•	–	•	–	•	–	–	–
French Polynesia - Polynésie française	•	–	•	–	•	–	•	–	•	–	•	–	•	–	–	–
Guam	•	–	•	–	•	–	•	–	•	–	•	–	•	–	–	–
Kiribati	–	–	–	–	–	–	–	–	–	–	–	–	–	–	–	–
Marshall Islands - Îles Marshall	•	–	–	–	•	–	–	–	–	–	•	–	–	–	–	–
Micronesia, Federated States of - Micronésie (États fédérés de)	•	–	–	–	•	–	–	–	–	–	•	–	•	–	–	–
Nauru	–	–	–	–	–	–	–	–	–	–	–	–	–	–	–	–
New Caledonia - Nouvelle-Calédonie	•	–	•	–	•	–	•	–	•	–	•	•	•	–	•	•
New Zealand - Nouvelle-Zélande	•	•	•	•	•	–	•	–	•	–	•	•	•	–	•	•
Niue - Nioué	–	–	–	–	–	–	–	–	–	–	–	–	–	–	–	–
Norfolk Island - Île Norfolk	–	–	–	–	–	–	–	–	–	–	•	–	–	–	–	–
Northern Mariana Islands - Îles Mariannes septentrionales	•	–	–	–	•	–	•	–	•	–	–	–	–	–	–	–
Palau - Palaos	•	–	–	–	•	–	•	–	•	–	–	–	–	–	–	–
Papua New Guinea - Papouasie-Nouvelle-Guinée	–	–	–	–	–	–	–	–	–	–	–	–	–	–	–	–
Pitcairn	–	–	–	–	–	–	–	–	–	–	–	–	–	–	–	–
Samoa	•	–	–	–	•	–	–	–	–	–	•	–	•	–	–	–
Solomon Islands - Îles Salomon	–	–	–	–	–	–	–	–	–	–	–	–	–	–	–	–
Tokelau - Tokélaou	–	–	–	–	–	–	–	–	–	–	–	–	–	–	–	–
Tonga	•	–	•	–	•	–	•	–	•	–	•	•	•	•	•	•
Tuvalu	–	–	–	–	–	–	–	–	–	–	–	–	–	–	–	–
Vanuatu	–	–	–	–	–	–	–	–	–	–	–	–	–	–	–	–
Wallis and Futuna Islands - Îles Wallis et Futuna	–	–	–	–	–	–	–	–	–	–	–	–	–	–	–	–

FOOTNOTES - NOTES

• Data presented in the table - Les données présentées dans le tableau.

– Data not available - Données pas disponibles.

[2] For statistical purposes, the data for China do not include those for the Hong Kong Special Administrative Region (Hong Kong SAR), Macao special Administrative Region (Macao SAR) and Taiwan province of China. - Pour la présentation des statistiques, les données pour Chine ne comprend pas la Région Administrative Spéciale de Hong Kong (Hong Kong RAS), la Région Administrative Spéciale de Macao (Macao RAS) et Taïwan province de Chine.
[3] Including data for the Indian-held part of Jammu and Kashmir, the final status of which has not yet been determined. - Y compris les données pour la partie du Jammu et du Cachemire occupée par l'Inde dont le statut définitif n'a pas encore été déterminé.
[4] Including data for East Jerusalem and Israeli residents in certain other territories under occupation by Israeli military forces since June 1967. - Y compris les données pour Jérusalem-Est et les résidents israéliens dans certains autres territoires occupés depuis 1967 par les forces armées israéliennes.
[5] Excluding data for the Pakistan-held part of Jammu and Kashmir, the final status of which has not yet been determined. - Non compris les données concernant la partie du Jammu et Cachemire occupée par le Pakistan dont le statut définitif n'a pas été déterminé.

Table 1

Table 1 presents for the world, major areas and regions estimates of the order of magnitude of population size, rates of population increase, crude birth and death rates, surface area and population density.

Description of variables: Estimates of world population by major areas and by regions are presented for 1950, 1960, 1970, 1980, 1990, 2000 and 2001. Average annual percentage rates of population growth, the crude birth and crude death rates are shown for the period 2000 to 2005. Surface area in square kilometers and population density estimates relate to 2001.

All population estimates and rates presented in this table were prepared by the Population Division of the United Nations Secretariat, Department of Economic and Social Affairs, and have been published in *World Population Prospects: The 2002 Revision. Volume 1: Comprehensive Tables*[1].

The scheme of regionalization used for the purpose of making these estimates is described below. Although some continental totals are given, and all can be derived, the basic scheme presents major areas that are so drawn as to obtain greater homogeneity in sizes of population, types of demographic circumstances and accuracy of demographic statistics.

Five of the major areas are further subdivided into 20 regions. These are arranged within major areas; these together with Northern America, which is not subdivided, make a total of 21 regions.

The major areas of Northern America and Latin America were distinguished, rather than the conventional continents of North America and South America, because population trends in the middle American mainland and the Caribbean region more closely resemble those of South America than those of America north of Mexico. Data for the traditional continents of North and South America can be obtained by adding Central America and Caribbean region to Northern America and deducting from Latin America. Latin America, as defined here, has somewhat wider limits than it would be if defined only to include the Spanish-speaking, French-speaking and Portuguese-speaking countries.

The average annual percentage rates of population growth were calculated by the Population Division, United Nations Department of Economic and Social Affairs, using an exponential rate of increase.

Crude birth and crude death rates are expressed in terms of the average annual number of births and deaths, respectively, per 1 000 mid-year population. These rates are estimated.

Surface area totals were obtained by summing the figures for individual countries or areas shown in table 3.

Computation: Density, calculated by the Statistics Division of the United Nations Department of Social and Economic Affairs, is the number of persons in the 2001 total population per square kilometer of total surface area.

Reliability of data: With the exception of surface area, all data are set in *italic* type to indicate their conjectural quality.

Limitations: The estimated orders of magnitude of population and surface area are subject to all the basic limitations set forth in connection with table 3, and to the same qualifications set forth for population and surface area statistics in sections 3 and 2.4 of the Technical Notes, respectively.

Likewise, the rates of population increase and density indexes are affected by the limitations of the original figures. However, it may be noted that, in compiling data for regional and major areas totals, errors in the components may tend to compensate each other and the resulting aggregates may be somewhat more reliable than the quality of the individual components would imply.

Because of their estimated character, many of the birth and death rates shown should also be considered only as orders of magnitude, and not as measures of the true level of natality or mortality. Rates for 2000-2005 are based on the data available as of 2002, the time when the estimates were prepared, and much new information has been taken into account in constructing these new estimates. As a result they may differ from earlier estimates prepared for the same years and published in previous issues of the Yearbook.

Because surface area totals were obtained by summing the figures for individual countries or areas shown in table 3, they exclude places with a population of less than 50, for example, uninhabited polar areas.

In interpreting the population densities, one should consider that some of the regions include large segments of land that are uninhabitable or barely habitable, and density values calculated as described make no allowance for this, nor for differences in patterns of land settlement.

Coverage: Data for 21 regions are presented.

Composition of macro geographical regions and sub-regions

AFRICA-AFRIQUE

Eastern Africa
Burundi
Comoros
Djibouti
Eritrea
Ethiopia
Kenya
Madagascar
Malawi
Mauritius
Mozambique
Réunion
Rwanda
Seychelles
Somalia
Uganda
United Republic of Tanzania
Zambia
Zimbabwe

Middle Africa
Angola
Cameroon
Central African Republic
Chad
Congo
Democratic Republic of the Congo
Equatorial Guinea
Gabon
Sao Tome and Principe

Northern Africa
Algeria
Egypt
Libyan Arab Jamahiriya
Morocco
Sudan
Tunisia
Western Sahara

Southern Africa
Botswana
Lesotho
Namibia
South Africa
Swaziland

Western Africa
Benin
Burkina Faso
Cape Verde
Côte d'Ivoire
Gambia
Ghana
Guinea
Guinea-Bissau
Liberia
Mali
Mauritania
Niger
Nigeria
Saint Helena
Senegal
Sierra Leone
Togo

LATIN AMERICA

Caribbean
Anguilla
Antigua and Barbuda
Aruba
Bahamas
Barbados
British Virgin Islands
Cayman Islands
Cuba
Dominica
Dominican Republic
Grenada
Guadaloupe
Haiti
Jamaica
Martinique
Montserrat
Netherlands Antilles
Puerto Rico
Saint Kitts and Nevis
Saint Lucia
Saint Vincent and the
  Grenadines
Trinidad and Tobago
Turks and Caicos Islands
United States Virgin
  Islands

Central America
Belize
Costa Rica
El Salvador
Guatemala
Honduras
Mexico
Nicaragua
Panama

South America
Argentina
Bolivia
Brazil
Chile
Colombia
Ecuador
Falkland Islands (Malvinas)
French Guiana
Guyana
Paraguay
Peru
Suriname
Uruguay
Venezuela

NORTHERN AMERICA
Bermuda
Canada
Greenland
Saint Pierre and Miquelon
United States of America

ASIA-ASIE

Eastern Asia
China
China - Hong Kong SAR
China - Macao SAR
Japan
Korea, Democratic People's Republic of
Korea, Republic of
Mongolia

South-central Asia
Afghanistan
Bangladesh
Bhutan
India
Iran (Islamic Republic of)
Kazakhstan
Kyrgyzstan
Maldives
Nepal
Pakistan
Sri Lanka
Tajikistan
Turkmenistan
Uzbekistan

South-eastern Asia
Brunei Darussalam
Cambodia
Indonesia
Lao People's Democratic Republic
Malaysia
Myanmar
Philippines
Singapore
Thailand
Timor Leste
Viet Nam

Western Asia
Armenia
Azerbaijan
Bahrain
Cyprus
Georgia
Iraq
Israel
Jordan
Kuwait
Lebanon
Occupied Palestinian Territory
Oman
Qatar
Saudi Arabia
Syrian Arab Republic
Turkey
United Arab Emirates
Yemen

EUROPE

Eastern Europe
Belarus
Bulgaria

Czech Republic
Hungary
Poland
Republic of Moldova
Romania
Russian Federation
Slovakia
Ukraine

Northern Europe
Channel Islands
Denmark
Estonia
Faeroe Islands
Finland
Iceland
Ireland
Isle of Man
Latvia
Lithuania
Norway
Sweden
United Kingdom of Great Britain and
    Northern Ireland

Southern Europe
Albania
Andorra
Bosnia and Herzegovina
Croatia

Gibraltar
Greece
Holy See
Italy
Malta
Portugal
San Marino
Serbia and Montenegro
Slovenia
Spain
The former Yugoslav Republic of
    Macedonia

Western Europe
Austria
Belgium
France
Germany
Liechtenstein
Luxembourg
Monaco
Netherlands
Switzerland

OCEANIA

Australia and New Zealand
Australia

New Zealand
Norfolk Island

Melanesia
Fiji
New Caledonia
Papua New Guinea
Solomon Islands
Vanuatu

Micronesia
Guam
Kiribati
Marshall Islands
Micronesia (Federated States of)
Nauru
Northern Mariana Islands
Palau

Polynesia
American Samoa
Cook Islands
French Polynesia
Niue
Pitcairn
Samoa
Tokelau
Tonga
Tuvalu
Wallis and Futuna Islands

NOTES

[1] *World Population Prospects, the 2002 Revision, Volume 1: Comprehensive Tables,* United Nations publication Sales No. E.03.XIII.6, United Nations, New York, 2003.

Tableau 1

Le tableau 1 présente, pour l'ensemble du monde et les régions macro géographiques, des estimations de l'ordre de grandeur de la population, les taux d'accroissement démographique, les taux bruts de natalité et de mortalité, la superficie et la densité de peuplement.

Description des variables : Des estimations de la population mondiale par les régions macro géographiques et par les composantes géographiques des régions sont présentées pour 1950, 1960, 1970, 1980, 1990, 2000 ainsi que pour 2001. Les taux annuels moyens d'accroissement de la population et les taux bruts de natalité et de mortalité portent sur la période 2000 à 2005. Les indications concernant la superficie exprimée en kilomètres carrés et les estimations de la densité de population se rapportent à 2001.

Toutes les estimations de population et les taux de natalité, taux de mortalité et taux annuels d'accroissement de la population qui sont présentés dans ce tableau ont été établis par la Division de la population du Département des affaires économiques et sociales du Secrétariat de l'Organisation des Nations Unies, et ont été publiés dans World Population Prospects: The 2002 Revision, Volume 1: Comprehensive tables[1].

Bien que l'on ait donné certains totaux pour les continents (tous les autres pouvant être calculés), on a réparti le monde en huit régions macro géographique qui ont été découpées de manière à obtenir une plus grande homogénéité du point de vue des dimensions de population, des types de situation démographique et de l'exactitude des statistiques démographiques.

Cinq de ces huit régions macro géographique ont été subdivisées en 20 composantes. Celles-ci ont été classées à l'intérieur de chaque région macro géographique. Avec l'Amérique septentrionale, qui n'est pas subdivisée, on arrive à un total de 21composantes (voir au-dessus.)

On présente l'Amérique septentrionale et l'Amérique latine, au lieu des continents classiques (Amérique du Nord et Amérique du Sud), parce que les tendances démographiques dans la partie continentale de l'Amérique centrale et dans la région des Caraïbes se rapprochent davantage de celles de l'Amérique du Sud que de celles de l'Amérique au nord du Mexique. On obtient les données pour les continents traditionnels de l'Amérique du Nord et de l'Amérique du Sud en extrayant des données relatives à l'Amérique latine, les données concernant l'Amérique centrale et les Caraïbes, et les regroupant avec celles relatives à l'Amérique septentrionale. L'Amérique latine ainsi définie a par conséquent des limites plus larges que celles des pays ou zones de langues espagnoles, portugaise et française qui constituent l'Amérique latine au sens le plus strict du terme.

Les taux annuels moyens d'accroissement de la population ont été calculés par la Division de la population, en appliquant un taux d'accroissement exponentiel.

Les taux bruts de natalité et de mortalité représentent respectivement le nombre annuel moyen de naissances et de décès par millier d'habitants en milieu d'année. Ces taux sont estimatifs.

La superficie totale a été obtenue en faisant la somme des superficies des pays ou zones du tableau 3.

Calculs : La densité, calculée par la Division de statistique du Département des affaires économiques et sociales du Secrétariat de l'Organisation des Nations Unies, est égale au rapport entre l'effectif total de la population en 2001 et la superficie totale exprimée en kilomètres carrés.

Fiabilité des données : A l'exception des données concernant la superficie, toutes les données sont reproduites en *italique* pour en faire ressortir le caractère conjectural.

Insuffisance des données: Les estimations concernant l'ordre de grandeur de la population et la superficie reposent en partie sur les données du tableau 3; elles appellent donc toutes les réserves fondamentales formulées à propos de ce tableau, et celles qui ont été respectivement formulées aux sections 3 et 2.4 des Notes techniques à l'égard des statistiques relatives à la population et à la superficie.

Les taux d'accroissement et les indices de densité de la population se ressentent eux aussi des insuffisances inhérentes aux données de base. Toutefois, il est à noter que, lorsqu'on additionne des données par territoire pour obtenir des totaux régionaux et par grandes régions, les erreurs qu'elles comportent arrivent parfois à s'équilibrer, de sorte que les agrégats obtenus peuvent être un peu plus exacts que chacun des éléments dont on est parti.

Vu leur caractère estimatif, un grand nombre des taux de natalité et de mortalité du tableau 1 doivent être considérés uniquement comme des ordres de grandeur et ne sont pas censés mesurer exactement le niveau de la natalité ou de la mortalité. On s'est fondé pour établir les taux de 2000-2005 sur les données dont on disposait en 2002, date à laquelle les nouvelles estimations ont été établies, et beaucoup d'éléments nouveaux sont alors intervenus dans le calcul de celles-ci. C'est pourquoi il se peut qu'elles s'écartent d'estimations antérieures portant sur ces mêmes années et publiées dans de précédentes éditions de l'Annuaire.

Parce que les totaux des superficies ont été obtenus en additionnant les chiffres pour chaque pays ou zones, qui apparaissent dans le tableau 3, ils ne comprennent pas les lieux où la population est de moins de 50 personnes, tels que les régions polaires inhabitées.

Pour interpréter les valeurs de la densité de population, il faut tenir compte du fait qu'il existe dans certaines des régions de vastes étendues de terres inhabitables ou à peine habitable, et que les chiffres calculés selon la méthode indiquée ne tiennent compte ni de ce fait ni des différences de dispersion de la population selon le mode d'habitat.

Portée : Les données présentées concernent 21 régions macro géographiques.

Composition des régions macro géographique et composantes géographique

AFRICA-AFRIQUE

Afrique orientale
Burundi
Comores
Djibouti
Érythrée
Éthiopie
Kenya
Madagascar
Malawi
Maurice
Mozambique
Ouganda
République-Unie de Tanzanie
Réunion
Rwanda
Seychelles
Somalie
Zambie
Zimbabwe

Afrique centrale
Angola
Cameroun
Congo
Gabon
Guinée équatoriale
République centrafricaine
République démocratique du Congo
Sao Tomé-et-Principe
Tchad

Afrique septentrionale
Algérie
Égypte
Jamahiriya arabe libyenne
Maroc
Sahara Occidental
Soudan
Tunisie

Afrique australe
Afrique du Sud
Botswana
Lesotho
Namibie
Swaziland

Afrique occidentale
Bénin
Burkina Faso
Cap-Vert
Côte d'Ivoire
Gambie

Ghana
Guinée
Guinée-Bissau
Libéria
Mali
Mauritanie
Niger
Nigéria
Sainte-Hélène
Sénégal
Sierra Leone
Togo

AMERIQUE LATINE

Caraïbes
Anguilla
Antigua-et-Barbuda
Antilles néerlandaises
Aruba
Bahamas
Barbade
Cuba
Dominique
Grenade
Guadeloupe
Haïti
Îles Caïmanes
Îles Turques et Caïques
Îles Vierges américaines
Îles Vierges britanniques
Jamaïque
Martinique
Montserrat
Porto Rico
République dominicaine
Saint-Kitts-et-Nevis
Sainte-Lucie
Saint Vincent-et-les Grenadines
Trinité-et-Tobago

Amérique centrale
Belize
Costa Rica
El Salvador
Guatemala
Honduras
Mexique
Nicaragua
Panama

Amérique du Sud
Argentine
Bolivie
Brésil

Chili
Colombie
Équateur
Guyana
Guyane française
Îles Falkland (Malvinas)
Paraguay
Pérou
Suriname
Uruguay
Venezuela

AMERIQUE SEPTENTRIONALE

Bermudes
Canada
États-Unis de l'Amérique
Groenland
Saint-Pierre-et-Miquelon

ASIA-ASIE

Asie orientale
Chine
Chine - Hong Kong RAS
Chine - Macao RAS
Japon
Mongolie
République de Corée
République populaire démocratique de Corée

Asie centrale et de Sud
Afghanistan
Bangladesh
Bhoutan
Inde
Iran (République Islamique d')
Kazakhstan
Kirghizistan
Maldives
Népal
Ouzbékistan
Pakistan
Sri Lanka
Tadjikistan
Turkménistan

Asie du Sud-Est
Brunéi Darussalam
Cambodge
Indonésie
Malaisie
Myanmar
Philippines
République démocratique populaire lao

Singapour
Thaïlande
Timor-Leste
Viet Nam

Asie occidentale
Arabie saoudite
Arménie
Azerbaïdjan
Bahreïn
Chypre
Émirats arabes unis
Géorgie
Iraq
Israël
Jordanie
Koweït
Liban
Oman
Qatar
République arabe syrienne
Territoire palestinien occupé
Turquie
Yémen

EUROPE

Europe orientale
Bélarus
Bulgarie
Fédération de Russie
Hongrie
Pologne
République de Moldova
République tchèque
Roumanie
Slovaquie

Ukraine

Europe septentrionale
Danemark
Estonie
Finlande
Île de Man
Îles Anglo-Normandes
Îles Féroé
Îles Svalbard et Jan Mayen
Irlande
Islande
Lettonie
Lituanie
Norvège
Royaume-Uni de Grande-
    Bretagne et d'Irlande du Nord
Suède

Europe méridionale
Albanie
Andorre
Bosnie-Herzégovine
Croatie
Espagne
Ex-République yougoslave de
    Macédoine
Gibraltar
Grèce
Italie
Malte
Portugal
Saint-Marin
Saint-Siège
Serbie-et-Montenegro
Slovénie

Europe occidentale
Allemagne
Autriche
Belgique
France

Liechtenstein
Luxembourg
Monaco
Pays-Bas
Suisse

OCEANIE

Australie et Nouvelle-Zélande
Australie
Île Norfolk
Nouvelle-Zélande

Mélanésie
Fidji
Îles Salomon
Nouvelle Calédonie
Papouasie-Nouvelle-Guinée
Vanuatu

Micronésie
Guam
Îles Mariannes septentrionales
Îles Marshall
Kiribati
Micronésie (États fédérés de)
Nauru
Palaos

Polynésie
Îles Cook
Îles Wallis et Futuna
Nioué
Pitcairn
Polynésie française
Samoa
Samoas américaines
Tokélaou
Tonga
Tuvalu

NOTES

[1] *World Population Prospects, The 2002 Revision, Volume 1: Comprehensive Tables,* Sales No. E.03.XIII.6, United Nations, New York, 2003.

1. Population, rate of increase, birth and death rates, surface area and density for the world, major areas and regions: selected years
Population, taux d'accroissement, taux de natalité et taux de mortalité, superficie et densité pour l'ensemble du monde, les régions macro géographiques et les composantes géographiques: diverses années

(See notes at end of table. — Voir notes à la fin du tableau.)

Major areas and regions Régions macro géographiques et composantes	Mid-year population estimates - Estimations de population au milieu de l'année (millions)							Annual rate of increase - Taux d'accroissement annuel (%)	Crude birth rate - Taux bruts de natalité	Crude death rate - Taux bruts de mortalité	Surface area (km2) - Superficie (km2) (000s)	Density - Densité[1]
	1950	1960	1970	1980	1990	2000	2001	2000 - 2005			2001	2001
WORLD TOTAL - ENSEMBLE DU MONDE	2 519	3 021	3 692	4 435	5 264	6 071	6 148	1.2	21	9	136 056	45
AFRICA - AFRIQUE	221	277	357	470	622	796	814	2.2	37	15	30 250	27
Eastern Africa - Afrique orientale	66	83	108	144	195	253	259	2.2	41	19	6 300	41
Middle Africa - Afrique centrale	26	32	41	53	71	93	95	2.7	47	20	6 613	14
Northern Africa - Afrique septentrionale	53	67	86	111	143	174	177	1.9	26	7	8 525	21
Southern Africa- Afrique méridionale	16	20	26	33	42	50	51	0.6	24	18	2 675	19
Western Africa - Afrique occidentale	60	76	97	128	172	226	232	2.6	41	15	6 138	38
LATIN AMERICA AND CARIBBEAN - AMERIQUE LATINE ET CARAIBES	167	218	285	361	442	520	528	1.4	22	6	20 546	26
Caribbean - Caraïbes	17	20	25	29	34	38	38	0.9	20	9	234	162
Central America - Amérique centrale	37	49	68	90	111	135	138	1.7	24	5	2 480	56
South America - Amérique du Sud	112	148	192	242	296	347	352	1.4	21	7	17 832	20
NORTHERN AMERICA - AMERIQUE SEPTENTRIONALE[2]	172	204	232	256	284	316	319	1.0	14	8	21 776	15
ASIA - ASIE[3]	1 398	1 701	2 143	2 632	3 168	3 680	3 728	1.3	20	8	31 870	117
Eastern Asia - Asie orientale	671	792	987	1 178	1 350	1 481	1 492	0.7	14	7	11 763	127
South Central Asia-Asie centrale méridionale	499	620	783	981	1 225	1 486	1 512	1.7	26	9	10 791	140
South Eastern Asia - Asie méridionale orientale	178	223	286	358	440	520	528	1.4	22	7	4 495	117
Western Asia - Asie occidentale[3]	51	67	87	115	153	192	196	2.1	27	6	4 822	41
EUROPE[3]	547	604	656	692	721	728	728	-0.1	10	12	22 050	33
Eastern Europe - Europe orientale	220	253	276	295	311	305	303	-0.5	11	13	18 814	16
Northern Europe - Europe septentrionale	77	81	87	89	92	94	94	0.2	11	10	1 748	54
Southern Europe - Europe méridionale	109	118	127	138	143	146	146	0.1	10	10	1 317	111
Western Europe - Europe occidentale	141	152	166	170	176	184	184	0.2	10	10	1 108	166
OCEANIA - OCEANIE[2]	12.8	15.9	19.4	22.8	26.7	31.0	31.0	1.2	17	8	8 564	4
Australia and New Zealand - Australie et Nouvelle-Zélande	10.1	12.6	15.4	17.7	20.2	22.9	23.1	0.9	13	7	8 012	3
Melanesia - Melanésie	2.3	2.7	3.4	4.4	5.5	7.0	7.1	2.1	30	8	541	13
Micronesia - Micronésie	0.2	0.2	0.2	0.3	0.4	0.5	0.5	1.7	25	5	3	167
Polynesia - Polynésie	0.2	0.3	0.4	0.5	0.5	0.6	0.6	1.3	24	6	8	75

GENERAL NOTES - NOTES GENERALES

Unless otherwise specified all figures are estimates of the order of magnitude and are subject to substantial margin of error; all data except for surface area are therefore set in italics. For composition of major areas and regions and for method of construction of estimates, see Technical Notes for this table. — Sauf indication contraire, tous les chiffres sont des estimations de l'ordre de grandeur comportant une assez grande marge d'erreur; toutes les données à l' exception de celles relatives à la 'superficie', sont de ce fait en italique. Pour la composition des régions macro géographiques et la méthode utilisée afin d'établir les estimations, voir Notes tecniques pour ce tableau.

FOOTNOTES - NOTES

[1] Population per square kilometre of surface area. Figures are estimated of population divided by surface area and are not to be considered as either reflecting density in the urban sense or as indicating the supporting power of a territory's land and resources. — Habitants per kilomèter corré. Il s'agit simplement du quotient calculé en divisant la population par la superficie et n'est par considéré comme indiquant la densité au sens urbain du mot ni l'effectif de population que les terres et les ressources du territoire sont capables de nourrir.

[2] Hawaii, a state of the United States of America, is included in Northern America rather than in Oceania. — Hawaii, un Etat des Etats-Unis d'Amérique, est compris en Amérique septentrionale plutôt qu'en Océanie.

[3] The European portion of Turkey is included in Western Asia rather than Europe. — La partie européenne de la Turquie est comprise en Asie Occidentale plutôt qu'en Europe.

Table 2

Table 2 presents estimates of population and the percentage distribution, by age and sex and sex ratio for all ages, for the world, major areas and regions for 2001.

Description of variables: All population estimates presented in this table were prepared by the Population Division of the United Nations Department for Economic and Social Affairs. These estimates have been published (using more detailed age groups) in the *World Population Prospects: The 2002 Revision, Volume II, Sex and Age Distribution of Populations*[1].

The scheme of regionalization used for the purpose of making these estimates is described and discussed in detail in the technical notes for table 1. Age groups presented in this table are: under 15 years, 15-64 years and 65 years and over. Sex ratio refers to the number of males per 100 females of all ages.

Using the Population Division estimates, the percentage distributions and the sex ratios that appear in this table have been calculated by the Statistics Division of the United Nations.

Reliability of data: All data are set in *italic* type to indicate their conjectural quality.

Limitations: The data presented in this table are from the same series of estimates, prepared by the Population Division of the United Nations Secretariat, presented in table 1. The estimated orders of magnitude of population are subject to all the basic limitations set forth for population statistics in section 3 of the Technical Notes.

In brief, because they are estimates, these distributions by broad age groups and sex should be considered only as orders of magnitude. However, it may be noted that, in compiling data for regional and macro region totals, errors in the components may tend to compensate each other and the resulting aggregates may be somewhat more reliable than the quality of the individual components would imply.

In addition, data in this table are limited by factors affecting data by age. These factors are described in the technical notes for table 7. Because the age groups presented in this table are so broad, these problems are minimized.

Coverage: Data for 21 regions are presented.

NOTES

[1] *United Nations publication, Sales No. E.03.XIII.7, United Nations, New York, 2003.*

Tableau 2

Le tableau 2 fournit, pour l'ensemble du monde, les régions macro géographique et les composantes géographique, des estimations de la population pour 2001 ainsi que sa répartition en pourcentage selon l'âge et le sexe, et le rapport de masculinité tous âges.

Description des variables : Toutes les données figurant dans ce tableau ont été établies par la Division de la population du Département des affaires économiques et sociales du Secrétariat de l'Organisation des Nations Unies et ont été publiées dans *le World Population Prospects: The 2002 Revision.Volume II : Sex and Age Distribution of Populations*[1].

La classification géographique utilisée pour établir ces estimations est exposée et analysée en détail dans les notes techniques relatives au tableau 1. Les groupes d'âge présentés dans ce tableau sont définis comme suit : moins de 15 ans, de 15 à 64 ans et 65 ans et plus. Le rapport de masculinité représente le nombre d'individus de sexe masculin pour 100 individus de sexe féminin sans considération d'âge.

Les pourcentages et les rapports de masculinité qui sont présentés dans ce tableau ont été calculés par la Division de statistique de l'ONU d'après des estimations établies par la Division de la population.

Fiabilité des données : Toutes les données figurant dans ce tableau sont reproduites en *italique* pour en faire ressortir le caractère conjectural.

Insuffisance des données : Les données de ce tableau appartiennent à la même série d'estimations, établie par la Division de la population du Secrétariat de l'ONU, que celles qui figurent au tableau 1. Les estimations concernant l'ordre de grandeur de la population appellent donc toutes les réserves fondamentales qui ont été formulées à la section 3 des Notes techniques à l'égard des statistiques relatives à la population.

Sans entrer dans le détail, il convient de préciser que les données relatives à la répartition par grand groupe d'âge et par sexe doivent, en raison de leur caractère estimatif, être considérées uniquement comme des ordres de grandeur. Toutefois, il est à noter que, lorsqu'on additionne des données par territoire pour obtenir des totaux régionaux et par grandes régions, les erreurs qu'elles comportent arrivent parfois à s'équilibrer, de sorte que les agrégats obtenus peuvent être un peu plus exacts que chacun des éléments dont on est parti.

En outre, les donnés figurant dans ce tableau présentent un caractère d'insuffisance en raison des facteurs influant sur les données par âge. Ces facteurs sont décrits dans les notes techniques relatives au tableau 7. Ces problèmes sont cependant minimisés du fait de l'étendue des groupes d'âge présentés dans ce tableau.

Portée : Les données présentées concernent 21 régions.

NOTES

[1] *United Nations publication, Sales No. E.03.XIII.7, United Nations, New York, 2003.*

2. Estimates of population and its percentage distribution, by age and sex and sex ratio for all ages for the world, major areas and regions: 2001
Estimations de la population et pourcentage de répartition selon l'âge et le sexe et rapport de masculinité pour l'ensemble du monde, les grandes regions et les régions géographiques: 2001

(See notes at end of table. — Voir notes à la fin du tableau.)

Major areas and regions Grandes régions et régions	Population (millions)											
	Both sexes - Les deux sexes				Male - Masculin				Female - Féminin			
	All ages - Tous âges	-15	15-64	65+	All ages - Tous âges	-15	15-64	65+	All ages - Tous âges	-15	15-64	65+
WORLD TOTAL - ENSEMBLE DU MONDE	6 148	1 830	3 888	430	3 093	940	1 966	186	3 055	890	1 922	243
AFRICA - AFRIQUE	814	345	442	26	405	174	219	12	409	171	223	15
Eastern Africa - Afrique orientale	259	118	134	7	128	59	65	3	131	59	68	4
Middle Africa - Afrique centrale	95	44	49	3	47	22	24	1	48	22	25	2
Northern Africa - Afrique septentrionale	177	62	107	8	89	32	54	3	88	30	53	4
Southern Africa- Afrique méridionale	51	18	31	2	25	9	15	1	26	9	16	1
Western Africa - Afrique occidentale	232	104	121	7	116	53	60	3	116	51	61	4
LATIN AMERICA AND CARIBBEAN - AMERIQUE LATINE ET CARAIBES	528	166	333	29	261	85	164	13	267	81	169	17
Caribbean - Caraïbes	38	11	24	3	19	6	12	1	19	5	12	1
Central America - Amérique centrale	138	48	83	6	68	24	41	3	70	24	43	4
South America - Amérique du Sud	352	107	225	20	174	54	111	9	178	53	114	12
NORTHERN AMERICA - AMERIQUE SEPTENTRIONALE[1]	319	68	212	39	157	35	105	17	162	33	106	23
ASIA - ASIE[2]	3 728	1 118	2 388	223	1 903	578	1 224	102	1 825	540	1 164	121
Eastern Asia - Asie orientale	1 492	348	1 026	118	763	183	527	53	729	165	499	65
South Central Asia-Asie centrale méridionale	1 512	531	910	70	777	274	469	33	735	257	441	37
South Eastern Asia - Asie méridionale orientale	528	168	334	25	263	86	166	11	265	83	168	14
Western Asia - Asie occidentale	196	70	118	9	101	36	61	4	96	34	57	5
EUROPE[2]	728	125	494	109	351	64	245	42	377	61	249	67
Eastern Europe - Europe orientale	303	53	210	40	143	27	103	14	160	26	108	26
Northern Europe - Europe septentrionale	94	18	62	15	46	9	31	6	48	9	31	9
Southern Europe - Europe méridionale	146	23	99	24	71	12	50	10	75	11	49	14
Western Europe - Europe occidentale	184	31	123	30	90	16	62	12	94	15	61	18
OCEANIA - OCEANIE[1]	31.45	8.07	20.29	3.09	15.79	4.16	10.25	1.38	15.66	3.91	10.04	1.71
Australia and New Zealand - Australie et Nouvelle Zélande	23.17	4.80	15.52	2.85	11.52	2.46	7.80	1.26	11.65	2.33	7.72	1.59
Melanesia - Melanésie	7.15	2.87	4.09	0.19	3.68	1.49	2.09	0.10	3.47	1.38	2.00	0.09
Micronesia - Micronésie	0.51	0.18	0.30	0.02	0.26	0.09	0.16	0.01	0.24	0.09	0.14	0.01
Polynesia - Polynésie	0.62	0.22	0.37	0.03	0.32	0.11	0.19	0.01	0.30	0.10	0.18	0.02

2. Estimates of population and its percentage distribution, by age and sex and sex ratio for all ages for the world, major areas and regions: 2001
Estimations de la population et pourcentage de répartition selon l'âge et le sexe et rapport de masculinité pour l'ensemble du monde, les grandes regions et les régions géographiques: 2001 (continued — suite)

(See notes at end of table. — Voir notes à la fin du tableau.)

Major areas and regions / Grandes régions et régions	Percent - Pourcentage												Sex ratio (Males per 100 females of all ages) - Rapport de masculinité (Hommes pour 100 femmes de tous âges)
	Both sexes - Les deux sexes				Male - Masculin				Female - Féminin				
	All ages - Tous âges	-15	15-64	65+	All ages - Tous âges	-15	15-64	65+	All ages - Tous âges	-15	15-64	65+	
WORLD TOTAL - ENSEMBLE DU MONDE	100.0	29.8	63.2	7.0	100.0	30.4	63.6	6.0	100.0	29.1	62.9	8.0	101
AFRICA - AFRIQUE	100.0	42.5	54.3	3.2	100.0	43.1	54.0	2.9	100.0	41.8	54.6	3.6	99
Eastern Africa - Afrique orientale	100.0	45.5	51.7	2.8	100.0	46.2	51.2	2.6	100.0	44.7	52.2	3.1	98
Middle Africa - Afrique centrale	100.0	45.9	51.1	2.9	100.0	46.5	50.9	2.6	100.0	45.4	51.3	3.3	98
Northern Africa - Afrique septentrionale	100.0	35.2	60.5	4.3	100.0	35.8	60.3	3.9	100.0	34.6	60.7	4.7	101
Southern Africa- Afrique méridionale	100.0	34.6	61.6	3.8	100.0	35.6	61.4	3.0	100.0	33.7	61.8	4.5	96
Western Africa - Afrique occidentale	100.0	44.9	52.2	2.9	100.0	45.4	51.9	2.7	100.0	44.4	52.4	3.2	100
LATIN AMERICA AND CARIBBEAN - AMERIQUE LATINE ET CARAIBES	100.0	31.4	63.0	5.6	100.0	32.4	62.7	4.9	100.0	30.6	63.3	6.2	98
Caribbean - Caraïbes	100.0	29.0	63.8	7.2	100.0	29.7	63.6	6.6	100.0	28.3	64.0	7.7	99
Central America - Amérique centrale	100.0	34.9	60.4	4.7	100.0	36.0	59.7	4.3	100.0	33.8	61.1	5.1	98
South America - Amérique du Sud	100.0	30.4	63.9	5.7	100.0	31.2	63.8	5.0	100.0	29.5	64.0	6.5	98
NORTHERN AMERICA - AMERIQUE SEPTENTRIONALE[1]	100.0	21.4	66.3	12.3	100.0	22.3	67.1	10.6	100.0	20.5	65.5	14.0	97
ASIA - ASIE[2]	100.0	30.0	64.0	6.0	100.0	30.4	64.3	5.4	100.0	29.6	63.8	6.6	104
Eastern Asia - Asie orientale	100.0	23.3	68.7	7.9	100.0	24.0	69.0	7.0	100.0	22.7	68.4	8.9	105
South Central Asia-Asie centrale méridionale	100.0	35.1	60.2	4.7	100.0	35.2	60.4	4.3	100.0	35.0	60.0	5.0	106
South Eastern Asia - Asie méridionale orientale	100.0	31.9	63.3	4.8	100.0	32.5	63.2	4.3	100.0	31.3	63.4	5.3	100
Western Asia - Asie occidentale	100.0	35.6	59.9	4.5	100.0	35.4	60.6	4.0	100.0	35.7	59.3	5.0	105
EUROPE[2]	100.0	17.1	67.9	14.9	100.0	18.2	69.9	11.9	100.0	16.1	66.1	17.8	93
Eastern Europe - Europe orientale	100.0	17.4	69.4	13.2	100.0	18.9	71.5	9.6	100.0	16.1	67.5	16.4	90
Northern Europe - Europe septentrionale	100.0	18.9	65.5	15.6	100.0	19.9	66.9	13.2	100.0	17.9	64.2	17.9	95
Southern Europe - Europe méridionale	100.0	15.5	67.8	16.6	100.0	16.3	69.5	14.2	100.0	14.8	66.3	19.0	96
Western Europe - Europe occidentale	100.0	16.9	66.9	16.2	100.0	17.8	69.1	13.2	100.0	16.2	64.7	19.1	96
OCEANIA - OCEANIE[1]	100.0	25.7	64.5	9.8	100.0	26.3	64.9	8.8	100.0	25.0	64.1	10.9	101
Australia and New Zealand - Australie et Nouvelle Zélande	100.0	20.7	67.0	12.3	100.0	21.4	67.7	10.9	100.0	20.0	66.3	13.7	99
Melanesia - Melanésie	100.0	40.2	57.2	2.6	100.0	40.5	56.8	2.7	100.0	39.9	57.6	2.6	106
Micronesia - Micronésie	100.0	36.0	59.2	4.7	100.0	35.8	59.8	4.4	100.0	36.3	58.6	5.1	108
Polynesia - Polynésie	100.0	35.1	60.3	4.6	100.0	35.1	60.7	4.2	100.0	35.1	59.8	5.1	107

GENERAL NOTES - NOTES GENERALES

All figures are estimates of the order of magnitude and are subject to a substantial margin of error; all data are therefore set in italics. For composition of major areas and regions and for method of construction of estimates, see Technical Notes for this table. — Tous les chiffres sont des estimations de grandeur comportant une assez grande marge d'erreur, toutes les données sont de ce fait en italique. Pour le composition des grandes régions et la méthode utilisée afin d'établir les estimations, voir

Notes techniques pour ce tableau.

FOOTNOTES - NOTES

[1] Hawaii, a state of the United States of America, is included in Northern America rather than in Oceania. — Hawaii, un Etat des Etats-Unis d'Amérique, est compris en Amérique septentrionale plutôt qu'en Océanie.

[2] The European portion of Turkey is included in Western Asia rather than Europe. — La partie européenne de la Turquie est comprise en Asie Occidentale plutôt qu'en Europe.

Table 3

Table 3 presents for each country or area of the world the total, male and female population enumerated at the latest population census, estimates of the mid-year total population for 1995 and 2001, the average annual exponential rate of increase (or decrease) for the period 1995 to 2001, and the surface area and the population density for 2001.

Description of variables: The total, male and female population is, unless otherwise indicated, the de facto (present-in-area) population enumerated at the most recent census for which data are available. The date of this census is given. Unless otherwise indicated, population census data are the results of a nation-wide enumeration. If, however, a nation-wide enumeration has not taken place, the results of a sample survey, essentially national in character, may be presented. Results of surveys referring to less than 50 percent of the total territory or population are not included.

Mid-year population estimates refer to the population on 1 July. Otherwise, a footnote is appended.

Mid-year estimates of the total population are those provided by national statistical offices, unless otherwise indicated.

Surface area, expressed in square kilometres, refers to the total surface area, comprising land area and inland waters (assumed to consist of major rivers and lakes) and excluding only Polar Regions and uninhabited islands. Exceptions to this are noted. Surface areas, originally reported in square miles, have been converted to square kilometres using a conversion factor of 2.589988.

Computation: The annual rate of increase is the average annual percentage rate of population growth between 1995 and 2001, computed by the Statistics Division of the United Nations Department for Economic and Social Affairs using the mid-year estimates (unrounded) presented in this table applying an exponential rate of increase.

Density is the number of persons in the 2001 total population per square kilometre of total surface area.

Reliability of data: Reliable mid-year population estimates are those which are based on a complete census (or a sample survey) and have been adjusted by a continuous population register or adjusted on the basis of the calculated balance of births, deaths and migration. Mid-year estimates of this type are considered reliable and appear in roman type. Mid-year estimates not calculated on this basis are considered less reliable and are shown in italics. Estimates for years prior to 2001 are considered reliable or less reliable on the basis of the 2001 quality code and appear in roman type or in *italics*, accordingly.

In addition, census data and sample survey results are considered reliable and, therefore, appear in roman type.

Rates of population increase that were calculated using population estimates considered less reliable, as described above, are set in italics rather than roman type.

All surface area data are assumed to be reliable and therefore appear in roman type. Population density data, however, are considered reliable or less reliable on the basis of the reliability of the 2001 population estimates used as the numerator.

Limitations: Statistics on the total population enumerated at the time of the census, estimates of the mid-year total population and surface area data are subject to the same qualifications as have been set forth for population and surface area statistics in sections 3 and 2.4 of the Technical Notes, respectively.

Regarding the limitations of census data, it should be noted that although census data are considered reliable, and therefore appear in roman type, the actual quality of census data varies widely from one country or area to another. When known, an estimate of the extent of over-enumeration or under-enumeration is given in footnotes. In the case of sample surveys, a description is given of the population covered.

Because the reliability of the population estimates for any given country or area is based on the quality of the 2001 estimate, the reliability of estimates prior to 2001 may be overstated.

Percentage rates of population growth are subject to all the qualifications of the population estimates mentioned above. In some cases, they simply reflect the rate calculated or assumed in constructing the estimates themselves when adequate measures of natural increase and net migration were not available. For small populations, an error up to approximately 0.5 may be introduced by chance alone. Despite their shortcomings, these rates do provide a useful index for studying population change and, used with proper precautions, they can be useful also in evaluating the accuracy of vital and migration statistics.

Because no indication is given in the table to show which of the mid-year estimates are rounded and which are not, the rates calculated on the basis of these estimates may be much more precise in some cases than in others.

With respect to data on population density, it should be emphasized that density values are very rough indexes, inasmuch as they do not take account of the dispersion or concentration of population within countries or areas nor the proportion of habitable land. They should not be interpreted as reflecting density in the urban sense nor as indicating the supporting power of a territory's land and resources.

Coverage: Population by sex, rate of population increase, surface area and density are shown for 230 countries or areas with a population of 50 or more.

Tableau 3

Le tableau 3 indique pour chaque pays ou zone du monde la population totale selon le sexe d'après les derniers recensements effectués, les estimations concernant la population totale au milieu de l'année 1995 et de l'année 2001, le taux moyen d'accroissement annuel exponentiel positif ou négatif pour la période allant de 1995 à 2001, ainsi que la superficie et la densité de population en 2001.

Description des variables : Sauf indication contraire, la population masculine et féminine totale est la population de fait ou population présente dénombrée lors du dernier recensement dont les résultats sont disponibles. La date de ce recensement est indiquée. Sauf indication contraire, les données de recensement fournies résultent d'un dénombrement de population nationale. S'il n'y a jamais eu de dénombrement général, ce sont les résultats d'une enquête par sondage à caractère essentiellement national qui sont indiqués. Il n'est pas présenté de résultats d'enquêtes portant sur moins de 50 p. 100 de l'ensemble du territoire ou de la population.

Les estimations de la population en milieu d'année sont celles de la population au 1er juillet. Dans les cas ou la date est différente, une note est attachée.

Les estimations de la population totale en milieu d'année sont celles qui ont été communiquées par les services nationaux de statistique.

La superficie -- exprimée en kilomètres carrés -- représente la superficie totale, c'est-à-dire qu'elle englobe les terres émergées et les eaux intérieures (qui sont censées comprendre les principaux lacs et cours d'eau) à la seule exception des régions polaires et de certaines îles inhabitées. Les exceptions à cette règle sont signalées en note. Les indications de superficie initialement fournies en milles carrés ont été transformées en kilomètres carrés au moyen d'un coefficient de conversion de 2,589988.

Calculs : Le taux d'accroissement annuel est le taux annuel moyen de variation (en pourcentage) de la population entre 1995 et 2001, calculé par la Division de Statistique du Département des Affaires Economiques et Sociales du Secrétariat de l'Organisation des Nations Unies à partir des estimations en milieu d'année (non arrondies) qui figurent dans le tableau utilisant le taux exponentiel d'accroissement.

La densité est égale au rapport de l'effectif total de la population en 2001 à la superficie totale, exprimée en kilomètres carrés.

Fiabilité des données: Les estimations en milieu d'année qui sont considérées sûres sont fondées sur un recensement complet (ou sur une enquête par sondage) et ont été ajustées en fonction des données fournies par un registre de population permanent ou en fonction de la balance établie par le calcul des naissances, des décès et des migrations. Les estimations de ce type sont considérées comme sûres et apparaissent en caractères romains. Les estimations en milieu d'année dont le calcul n'a pas été effectué sur cette base sont considérées comme moins sûres et apparaissent en italique. Les estimations relatives aux années antérieures à 2001 sont jugées plus ou moins sûres en fonction du codage qualitatif de 2001 et indiquées, selon le cas, en caractères romains ou en italique.

En outre, les données de recensements ou les résultats d'enquêtes par sondage sont considérés comme sûrs et apparaissent par conséquent en caractères romains.

Les taux d'accroissement de la population, calculés à partir d'estimations jugées moins sûres d'après les normes décrites ci-dessus, sont indiqués en italique plutôt qu'en caractères romains.

Toutes les données de superficie sont présumées sûres et apparaissent par conséquent en caractères romains. En revanche, les données relatives à la densité de la population sont considérées plus ou moins sûres en fonction de la fiabilité des estimations de la population en 2001 ayant servi de numérateur.

Insuffisance des données : Les statistiques portant sur la population totale dénombrée lors d'un recensement, les estimations de la population totale en milieu d'année et les données de superficie appellent les mêmes réserves que celles qui ont été respectivement formulées aux sections 3 et 2.4 des Notes techniques à l'égard des statistiques relatives à la population et à la superficie.

S'agissant de l'insuffisance des données obtenues par recensement, il convient d'indiquer que, bien que ces données soient considérées comme sûres et apparaissent par conséquent en caractères romains, leur qualité réelle varie considérablement d'un pays ou d'une région à l'autre. Lorsqu'on possédait les renseignements voulus, on a donné une estimation du degré de surdénombrement ou de sous-dénombrement. Dans le cas des enquêtes par sondage, une description de la population considérée est fournie.

La fiabilité des estimations de la population d'un pays ou zone quelconque reposant sur le qualitatif des estimations de 2001, il se peut que la fiabilité des estimations antérieures à 2001 soit surévaluée.

Les taux d'accroissement en pourcentage appellent toutes les réserves mentionnées plus haut à propos des estimations concernant la population. Dans certains cas, ils représentent seulement le taux qu'il a fallu calculer ou présumer pour établir les estimations elles-mêmes lorsqu'on ne disposait pas de mesures appropriées de l'accroissement naturel et des migrations nettes. Lorsqu'il s'agit de populations peu nombreuses, l'erreur fortuite peut atteindre à elle seule jusqu'à plus ou moins 0,5. Malgré leurs imperfections, ces taux fournissent des indications intéressantes pour l'étude du mouvement de la population et, utilisés avec les précautions nécessaires, ils peuvent également servir à évaluer l'exactitude des statistiques de l'état civil et des migrations.

Rien dans le tableau ne permettant de déterminer si telle ou telle estimation en milieu d'année a été arrondie ou non, il se peut que les taux calculés à partir de ces estimations soient beaucoup plus précis dans certains cas que dans d'autres.

En ce qui concerne les données relatives à la densité de population, il convient de souligner que les valeurs de cette densité ne constituent que des indices très approximatifs, car elles ne tiennent compte ni de la dispersion ou de la concentration de la population à l'intérieur des pays ou zones, ni de la proportion du territoire qui est habitable. Il ne faut donc y voir d'indication ni de la densité au sens urbain du terme ni du chiffre de population que seraient capables de supporter les terres et les ressources naturelles du territoire considéré.

Portée : L'effectif de la population par sexe, le taux d'accroissement de la population, la superficie et la densité de population sont indiqués pour 230 pays ou zones ayant une population de 50 habitants au moins.

3. Population by sex, rate of population increase, surface area and density
Population selon le sexe, taux d'accroissement de la population, superficie et densité

(See notes at end of table. — Voir notes à la fin du tableau.)

Continent, country or area and census date / Continent, pays ou zone et date du recensement	Census type[a]	Latest available census — Dernier recensement disponible (in units — en unités)			Mid-year estimates Estimations au milieu de l'année (in thousands — en milliers)		Estimate type	Annual rate of increase Taux d'accrois sement annuel 1995-01	Surface area Superficie (km²) 2001	Density Densité 2001[1]
		Both sexes Les deux sexes	Male Masculin	Female Feminin	1995	2001				
AFRICA — AFRIQUE										
Algeria - Algérie										
25 VI 1998	DJ	29 100 867	14 698 589	14 402 278	*28 060*	**30 836*	DJ	1.6	2 381 741	13
Angola[2]										
15 XII 1970	DF	5 646 166	2 943 974	2 702 192	...	...	...	...	1 246 700	...
Benin - Bénin										
11 II 2002	DJ	*6 752 569	...	...	*5 412*	**6 417*	DF	2.8	112 622	57
Botswana										
17 VIII 2001	DF	*1 680 863	*813 488	*867 375	...	...	...	...	581 730	...
Burkina Faso										
10 XII 1996	DF	10 312 609	4 970 882	5 341 727	...	...	...	...	274 000	...
Burundi										
16 VIII 1990	DF	5 139 073	2 473 599	2 665 474	...	...	...	...	27 834	...
Cameroon - Cameroun										
10 IV 1987	DF	10 493 655	...	...	...	...	...	...	475 442	...
Cape Verde - Cap-Vert										
16 VI 2000	DF	*434 812	...	...	*386*	**442*	DF	2.3	4 033	110
Central African Republic - République centrafricaine										
8 XII 1988	DF	2 463 616	1 210 734	1 252 882	...	...	...	...	622 984	...
Chad - Tchad[3]										
8 IV 1993	DF	6 279 931	...	...	...	...	...	...	1 284 000	...
Comoros - Comores[4]										
15 IX 1991	DF	446 817	221 152	225 665	...	...	...	...	2 235	...
Congo										
22 XII 1984	DF	1 843 421	...	...	...	...	...	...	342 000	...
Côte d'Ivoire										
1 III 1988	DF	10 815 694	5 527 343	5 288 351	*14 230*	**16 939*	DF	2.9	322 463	53
Democratic Republic of the Congo - République démocratique du Congo										
1 VII 1984	DF	29 916 800	14 543 800	15 373 000	...	...	...	...	2 344 858	...
Djibouti										
11 XII 1960	DF	81 200	...	...	...	...	...	...	23 200	...
Egypt - Égypte										
19 XI 1996	DF	59 312 914	30 351 390	28 961 524	*57 510*	**67 886*	DF	2.8	1 001 449	68
Equatorial Guinea - Guinée équatoriale[5]										
4 VII 1994	DF	*406 151	...	...	...	...	...	...	28 051	...
Eritrea - Érythrée										
9 V 1984	DF	2 748 304	1 374 452	1 373 852	...	...	...	...	117 600	...
Ethiopia - Éthiopie										
11 X 1994	DF	53 477 265	26 910 698	26 566 567	*54 649*	**65 374*	DF	3.0	1 104 300	59
Gabon										
31 VII 1993	DF	1 014 976	501 784	513 192	*1 066*	**1 237*	DF	2.5	267 668	5
Gambia - Gambie										
15 IV 2003	DF	*1 364 507	*687 781	*676 726	...	...	...	...	11 295	...
Ghana										
26 III 2000	DF	18 912 079	9 357 382	9 554 697	...	...	...	...	238 533	...
Guinea - Guinée										
1 XII 1996	DF	*7 156 406	...	...	...	...	...	...	245 857	...
Guinea-Bissau - Guinée-Bissau										
1 XII 1991	DF	983 367	476 210	507 157	...	...	...	...	36 125	...

3. Population by sex, rate of population increase, surface area and density
Population selon le sexe, taux d'accroissement de la population, superficie et densité
(continued — suite)

(See notes at end of table. — Voir notes à la fin du tableau.)

Continent, country or area and census date / Continent, pays ou zone et date du recensement	Census type[a]	Latest available census — Dernier recensement disponible (in units — en unités)			Mid-year estimates Estimations au milieu de l'année (in thousands — en milliers)		Estima-te type	Annual rate of increase Taux d' accrois sement annuel 1995-01	Surface area Superficie (km²) 2001	Density Densité 2001[1]
		Both sexes Les deux sexes	Male Masculin	Female Feminin	1995	2001				
AFRICA — AFRIQUE										
Kenya										
24 VIII 1999	DF	28 686 607	14 205 589	14 481 018	...	...	...	...	580 367	...
Lesotho										
14 IV 1996	DF	1 862 275	312 444	1 549 831	...	...	...	...	30 355	...
Liberia - Libéria										
1 II 1984	DF	2 101 628	1 063 127	1 038 501	...	...	...	...	111 369	...
Libyan Arab Jamahiriya - Jamahiriya arabe libyenne[6]										
11 VIII 1995	DF	4 404 986	2 236 943	2 168 043	4 395	*5 299	DF	3.1	1 759 540	3
Madagascar										
1 VIII 1993	DF	12 092 157	5 991 171	6 100 986	...	...	...	...	587 041	...
Malawi										
1 IX 1998	DF	9 933 868	4 867 563	5 066 305	9 788	*11 140	DF	2.2	118 484	94
Mali										
1 IV 1998	DJ	9 790 492	4 847 436	4 943 056	...	...	...	...	1 240 192	...
Mauritania - Mauritanie										
1 XI 2000	DF	2 548 157	1 240 414	1 307 743	2 284	*2 724	DF	2.9	1 025 520	3
Mauritius - Maurice										
2 VII 2000	DJ	1 178 848	583 756	595 092	1 122	*1 200	DJ	1.1	2 040	588
Morocco - Maroc										
2 IX 1994	DF	26 019 280	12 944 517	13 074 763	26 386	29 170	DF	1.7	446 550	65
Mozambique[7,8]										
1 VIII 1997	DF	16 099 246	7 714 306	8 384 940	15 820	*17 656	DF	1.8	801 590	22
Namibia - Namibie										
27 VIII 2001	DF	1 826 854	936 718	890 136	...	...	...	...	824 292	...
Niger										
20 V 1988	DF	7 248 100	3 590 070	3 658 030	...	...	...	...	1 267 000	...
Nigeria - Nigéria										
26 XI 1991	DF	88 992 220	44 529 608	44 462 612	99 210	118 801	DF	3.0	923 768	129
Réunion										
8 III 1999	DJ	706 180	347 076	359 104	...	...	...	...	2 510	...
Rwanda										
16 VIII 2002	DF	*8 128 553	*3 879 448	*4 249 105	...	...	...	...	26 338	...
Saint Helena ex. dep. - Sainte-Hélène sans dép.										
8 III 1998	DF	5 157	2 612	2 545	...	...	...	...	122	...
Saint Helena: Ascension - Sainte-Hélène: Ascension										
31 XII 1978	DF	849	608	241	...	...	...	...	88	...
Saint Helena: Tristan da Cunha - Sainte-Hélène: Tristan da Cunha										
31 XII 1988	DF	296	139	157	...	...	...	...	...	...
Sao Tome and Principe - Sao Tomé-et-Principe										
4 VIII 1991	DF	116 998	57 837	59 161	...	...	...	...	964	...
Senegal - Sénégal										
27 V 1988	DJ	6 896 808	3 353 599	3 543 209	8 347	*9 803	DF	2.7	196 722	50
Seychelles										
29 VIII 1997	DF	75 876	37 589	38 287	75	81	DF	1.3	455	178

3. Population by sex, rate of population increase, surface area and density
Population selon le sexe, taux d'accroissement de la population, superficie et densité
(continued — suite)

(See notes at end of table. — Voir notes à la fin du tableau.)

Continent, country or area and census date / Continent, pays ou zone et date du recensement	Census type[a]	Latest available census — Dernier recensement disponible (in units — en unités)			Mid-year estimates Estimations au milieu de l'année (in thousands — en milliers)		Estimate type	Annual rate of increase Taux d'accroissement annuel 1995-01	Surface area Superficie (km²) 2001	Density Densité 2001[1]
		Both sexes Les deux sexes	Male Masculin	Female Feminin	1995	2001				
AFRICA — AFRIQUE										
Sierra Leone[9] 15 XII 1985	DF	3 515 812	1 746 055	1 769 757	...	...	...	...	71 740	...
Somalia - Somalie 15 II 1987	DF	7 114 431	3 741 664	3 372 767	...	...	...	...	637 657	...
South Africa - Afrique du Sud 10 X 2001	DF	*44 819 778	*21 434 041	*23 385 737	39 477	*44 328	DF	1.9	1 221 037	36
Sudan - Soudan 15 IV 1993	DF	24 940 683	12 518 638	12 422 045	27 008	*31 627	DF	2.6	2 505 813	13
Swaziland 11 V 1997	DF	929 718	440 154	489 564	...	...	...	...	17 364	...
Togo 22 XI 1981	DF	2 703 250	...	...	...	...	...	...	56 785	...
Tunisia - Tunisie 20 IV 1994	DF	8 785 711	4 439 289	4 346 422	8 958	*9 674	DF	1.3	163 610	59
Uganda - Ouganda 12 IX 2002	DF	*24 748 977	*12 124 761	*12 624 216	19 263	*22 788	DF	2.8	241 038	95
United Republic of Tanzania - République-Unie de Tanzanie 24 VIII 2002	DF	*34 569 232	*16 910 321	*17 658 911	...	...	...	...	883 749	...
Western Sahara - Sahara occidental[10] 31 XII 1970	DF	76 425	43 981	32 444	...	...	...	...	266 000	...
Zambia - Zambie 25 X 2000	DF	10 285 631	5 070 891	5 214 740	...	...	...	...	752 618	...
Zimbabwe 17 VIII 2002	DF	*11 634 663	...	...	11 526	*12 960	DF	2.0	390 757	33
AMERICA, NORTH — AMERIQUE DU NORD										
Anguilla 9 V 2001	DF	11 430	5 628	5 802	10	*12	DF	2.7	96	120
Antigua and Barbuda - Antigua-et-Barbuda 28 V 2001	DF	77 426	37 002	40 424	...	...	...	...	442	...
Aruba 14 X 2000	DJ	90 508	43 435	47 073	80	92	DJ	2.3	193	476
Bahamas 1 V 2000	DF	303 611	147 715	155 896	...	...	...	...	13 878	...
Barbados - Barbade 1 V 2000	DF	250 010	119 926	130 084	...	...	...	...	430	...
Belize 12 V 2000	DF	240 204	121 278	118 926	216	*257	DF	2.9	22 966	11
Bermuda - Bermudes[11] 20 V 2000	DJ	*62 059	*29 802	*32 257	60	*62	DJ	0.6	53	1 169
British Virgin Islands - Îles Vierges britanniques 12 V 1991	DF	17 809	...	...	...	...	...	...	151	...
Canada[12] 15 V 2001	DJ	*30 007 090	*14 706 850	*15 300 240	29 302	*31 021	DJ	1.0	9 970 610	3
Cayman Islands - Îles Caïmanes 10 X 1999	DF	39 410	...	...	33	*41	DJ	3.9	264	157

3. Population by sex, rate of population increase, surface area and density
Population selon le sexe, taux d'accroissement de la population, superficie et densité
(continued — suite)

(See notes at end of table. — Voir notes à la fin du tableau.)

Continent, country or area and census date / Continent, pays ou zone et date du recensement	Census type[a]	Latest available census — Dernier recensement disponible (in units — en unités)			Mid-year estimates Estimations au milieu de l'année (in thousands — en milliers)		Estima-te type	Annual rate of increase Taux d' accrois sement annuel 1995-01	Surface area Superficie (km²) 2001	Density Densité 2001[1]
		Both sexes Les deux sexes	Male Masculin	Female Feminin	1995	2001				
AMERICA, NORTH — AMERIQUE DU NORD										
Costa Rica										
26 VI 2000	DJ	3 810 179	1 902 614	1 907 565	3 333	*3 873	DJ	2.5	51 100	76
Cuba										
6 IX 2002	DJ	11 177 743	5 597 233	5 580 510	10 978	*11 230	DF	0.4	110 861	101
Dominica - Dominique										
12 V 2001	DF	*71 239	*36 313	*34 926	...	...	...	...	751	...
Dominican Republic - République dominicaine										
18 X 2002	DF	*8 230 722	*4 102 880	*4 127 842	7 705	*8 528	DF	1.7	48 511	176
El Salvador										
27 IX 1992	DF	5 118 599	2 485 613	2 632 986	5 669	6 397	DF	2.0	21 041	304
Greenland - Groenland[13]										
26 X 1976	DJ	49 630	26 856	22 774	...	...	...	...	2 175 600	-
Grenada - Grenade[14]										
25 V 2001	DF	102 632	50 798	51 834	98	101	DF	0.4	344	293
Guadeloupe[15]										
8 III 1999	DJ	422 222	203 146	219 076	...	...	...	...	1 705	...
Guatemala[7]										
24 XI 2002	DJ	*11 237 196	...	...	9 976	*11 683	DF	2.6	108 889	107
Haiti - Haïti										
30 VIII 1982	DJ	5 053 792	2 448 370	2 605 422	7 180	*8 132	DJ	2.1	27 750	293
Honduras										
28 VII 2001	DF	*6 071 200	*3 000 530	*3 070 670	...	...	...	...	112 088	...
Jamaica - Jamaïque										
10 IX 2001	DF	*2 607 633	*1 283 547	*1 324 085	2 503	*2 621	DF	0.8	10 991	238
Martinique										
8 III 1999	DJ	381 325	180 910	200 415	...	...	...	...	1 102	...
Mexico - Mexique										
14 II 2000	DJ	97 483 412	47 592 253	49 891 159	91 992	101 754	DJ	1.7	1 958 201	52
Montserrat										
12 V 1991	DF	10 639	5 290	5 349	...	...	...	...	102	...
Netherlands Antilles - Antilles néerlandaises[16]										
29 I 2001	DJ	175 653	82 521	93 132	...	...	...	...	800	...
Nicaragua										
25 IV 1995	DJ	4 357 099	2 147 105	2 209 994	4 427	*5 205	DJ	2.7	130 000	40
Panama										
14 V 2000	DF	2 839 177	1 432 566	1 406 611	2 631	*2 897	DF	1.6	75 517	38
Puerto Rico - Porto Rico[17]										
1 IV 2000	DJ	3 808 610	1 833 577	1 975 033	3 655	3 840	DJ	0.8	8 875	433
Saint Kitts and Nevis - Saint-Kitts-et-Nevis										
14 V 2001	DF	45 841	22 784	23 057	44	*46	DF	1.0	261	177
Saint Lucia - Sainte-Lucie										
22 V 2001	DF	158 147	77 264	80 883	145	*158	DF	1.4	539	293
Saint Pierre and Miquelon - Saint Pierre-et-Miquelon										
8 III 1999	DF	6 316	3 147	3 169	...	...	...	...	242	...

3. Population by sex, rate of population increase, surface area and density
Population selon le sexe, taux d'accroissement de la population, superficie et densité
(continued — suite)

(See notes at end of table. — Voir notes à la fin du tableau.)

Continent, country or area and census date Continent, pays ou zone et date du recensement	Census type[a]	Latest available census — Dernier recensement disponible (in units — en unités)			Mid-year estimates Estimations au milieu de l'année (in thousands — en milliers)		Estima-te type	Annual rate of increase Taux d' accrois sement annuel 1995-01	Surface area Superficie (km²) 2001	Density Densité 2001[1]
		Both sexes Les deux sexes	Male Masculin	Female Feminin	1995	2001				
AMERICA, NORTH — AMERIQUE DU NORD										
Saint Vincent and the Grenadines - Saint Vincent-et-les Grenadines[18]										
14 V 2001	DF	*109 202	...	...	111	*109	DF	-0.3	388	281
Trinidad and Tobago - Trinité-et-Tobago										
15 V 2000	DF	1 262 366	633 051	629 315	...	...	...	...	5 130	...
Turks Caicos Islands - Îles Turques et Caïques										
31 V 1990	DF	12 350	6 289	6 061	...	...	...	...	430	...
United States - États-Unis[19,20]										
1 IV 2000	DJ	*281 421 906	*138 053 563	*143 368 343	263 044	284 797	DJ	1.3	9 629 091	30
United States Virgin Islands - Îles Vierges américaines[17]										
1 IV 2000	DJ	108 612	51 864	56 748	...	...	...	...	347	...
AMERICA, SOUTH — AMERIQUE DU SUD										
Argentina - Argentine										
18 XI 2001	DF	*36 223 947	*17 667 874	*18 556 073	*34 768*	*37 487*	DF	1.3	2 780 400	*13*
Bolivia - Bolivie										
5 IX 2001	DF	*8 274 325	*4 123 850	*4 150 475	...	...	...	...	1 098 581	...
Brazil - Brésil[21]										
1 VIII 2000	DJ	*169 799 170	*83 576 015	*86 223 155	*155 822*	*172 386*	DF	1.7	8 514 047	20
Chile - Chili										
24 IV 2002	DF	*15 116 435	*7 447 695	*7 668 740	14 210	*15 402	DF	1.3	756 626	20
Colombia - Colombie										
24 X 1993	DF	33 109 840	16 296 539	16 813 301	*38 542*	*43 071*	DF	1.9	1 138 914	*38*
Ecuador - Équateur[7,22]										
25 XI 2001	DF	12 156 608	6 018 353	6 138 255	*11 460*	*12 879*	DF	1.9	283 561	*45*
Falkland Islands (Malvinas) - Îles Falkland (Malvinas)[23,24]										
8 IV 2001	DF	2 913	1 598	1 315	...	...	...	...	12 173	-
French Guiana - Guyane française										
8 III 1999	DJ	156 790	78 963	77 827	...	...	...	...	90 000	...
Guyana										
12 V 1991	DF	701 704	344 928	356 776	...	...	...	...	214 969	...
Paraguay										
28 VIII 2002	DF	*5 206 101	*2 640 068	*2 566 033	...	...	...	...	406 752	...
Peru - Pérou[7,25]										
11 VII 1993	DF	22 048 356	10 956 375	11 091 981	*23 532*	*26 347	DF	1.9	1 285 216	20
Suriname										
1 VII 1980	DF	355 240	...	...	...	...	...	...	163 820	...
Uruguay[7]										
22 V 1996	DF	3 163 763	1 532 288	1 631 475	3 218	3 361	DF	0.7	175 016	19
Venezuela[25]										
30 X 2001	DF	*23 054 210	*11 402 869	*11 651 341	21 844	24 630	DF	2.0	912 050	27

3. Population by sex, rate of population increase, surface area and density
Population selon le sexe, taux d'accroissement de la population, superficie et densité
(continued — suite)

(See notes at end of table. — Voir notes à la fin du tableau.)

Continent, country or area and census date / Continent, pays ou zone et date du recensement	Census type[a]	Latest available census — Dernier recensement disponible (in units — en unités) Both sexes Les deux sexes	Male Masculin	Female Feminin	Mid-year estimates Estimations au milieu de l'année (in thousands — en milliers) 1995	2001	Estima-te type	Annual rate of increase Taux d' accrois sement annuel 1995-01	Surface area Superficie (km²) 2001	Density Densité 2001[1]
ASIA — ASIE										
Afghanistan[26]										
23 VI 1979	DF	13 051 358	6 712 377	6 338 981	...	...	...	...	652 090	...
Armenia - Arménie										
10 X 2001	DJ	*3 458 303	...	...	3 760	*3 802	DF	0.2	29 800	128
Azerbaijan - Azerbaïdjan										
27 I 1999	DJ	7 953 438	3 883 155	4 070 283	7 685	8 111	DF	0.9	86 600	94
Bahrain - Bahreïn										
6 IV 2001	DF	650 604	373 649	276 955	578	655	DF	2.1	694	943
Bangladesh										
22 I 2001	DF	*123 151 246	*62 735 988	*60 415 258	...	...	...	...	143 998	...
Bhutan - Bhoutan										
11 XI 1969	DF	1 034 774	...	...	582	699	DF	3.1	47 000	15
Brunei Darussalam - Brunéi Darussalam										
21 VIII 2001	DF	*332 844	...	...	296	344	DF	2.5	5 765	60
Cambodia - Cambodge[27]										
3 III 1998	DF	11 437 656	5 511 408	5 926 248	10 200	13 148	DF	4.2	181 035	73
China - Chine[28,29]										
1 XI 2000	DJ	1242612226	640 275 969	602 336 257	...	...	...	...	9 596 961	...
China: Hong Kong SAR - Chine: Hong Kong RAS[30,31]										
14 III 2001	DJ	6 708 389	3 285 344	3 423 045	6 156	6 725	...	...	1 099	6 119
China: Macao SAR - Chine: Macao RAS										
23 VIII 2001	DJ	435 235	208 865	226 370	409	434	DJ	1.0	26	16 825
Cyprus - Chypre[32,33]										
1 X 2001	DJ	689 565	338 497	351 068	742	789	DJ	1.0	9 251	85
Georgia - Géorgie										
17 I 2002	DJ	4 371 535	2 061 753	2 309 782	5 417	*4 946	DF	-1.5	69 700	71
India - Inde[34]										
1 III 2001	DF	1027015247	531 277 078	495 738 169	923 541	1 033 213	DF	1.9	3 287 263	314
Indonesia - Indonésie[35]										
30 VI 2000	DF	206 264 595	103 417 180	102 847 415	...	...	...	...	1 904 569	...
Iran (Islamic Republic of) - Iran (République islamique d')										
23 X 1996	DJ	60 055 488	30 515 159	29 540 329	59 187	*64 530	DJ	1.4	1 648 195	39
Iraq[36]										
16 X 1997	DF	19 184 543	9 536 570	9 647 973	20 536	24 813	DF	3.2	438 317	57
Israel - Israël[7,37]										
4 XI 1995	DJ	5 548 523	2 738 175	2 810 348	5 545	6 439	DJ	2.5	22 145	291
Japan - Japon[38]										
1 X 2000	DF	126 925 843	62 110 764	64 815 079	125 472	127 130	DF	0.2	377 873	336
Jordan - Jordanie[39]										
10 XII 1994	DF	4 139 458	2 160 725	1 978 733	...	...	...	...	89 342	...
Kazakhstan										
26 II 1999	DJ	14 953 126	7 201 785	7 751 341	16 066	*14 831	DF	-1.3	2 724 900	5
Korea (Dem. People's Republic of) - Corée (Rép. populaire dém. de)										
31 XII 1993	DF	21 213 378	10 329 699	10 883 679	...	...	...	...	120 538	...

3. Population by sex, rate of population increase, surface area and density
Population selon le sexe, taux d'accroissement de la population, superficie et densité
(continued — suite)

(See notes at end of table. — Voir notes à la fin du tableau.)

Continent, country or area and census date / Continent, pays ou zone et date du recensement	Census type[a]	Latest available census — Dernier recensement disponible (in units — en unités)			Mid-year estimates Estimations au milieu de l'année (in thousands — en milliers)		Estima-te type	Annual rate of increase Taux d' accrois sement annuel 1995-01	Surface area Superficie (km²) 2001	Density Densité 2001[1]
		Both sexes Les deux sexes	Male Masculin	Female Feminin	1995	2001				
ASIA — ASIE										
Korea (Republic of) - Corée (République de)[40]										
1 XI 2000	DF	46 136 101	23 158 582	22 977 519	*45 093*	*47 343*	DF	0.8	99 538	*476*
Kuwait - Koweït										
20 IV 1995	DF	1 575 570	913 402	662 168	*1 802*	*2 275*	DF	3.9	17 818	*128*
Kyrgyzstan - Kirghizistan										
24 III 1999	DJ	4 822 938	2 380 465	2 442 473	4 555	4 935	DF	1.3	199 900	25
Lao People's Democratic Republic - République démocratique populaire lao										
1 III 1995	DF	4 574 848	2 260 986	2 313 862	...	...	...	...	236 800	...
Lebanon - Liban[41]										
15 XI 1970	SDF	2 126 325	1 080 015	1 046 310	...	...	...	...	10 400	...
Malaysia - Malaisie[42,43]										
5 VII 2000	DJ	23 274 690	11 853 432	11 421 258	...	...	...	...	329 847	...
Maldives										
31 III 2000	DF	270 101	137 200	132 901	...	...	...	...	298	...
Mongolia - Mongolie										
5 I 2000	DF	2 373 493	1 177 981	1 195 512	*2 299*	*2 425*	DF	0.9	1 566 500	*2*
Myanmar										
31 III 1983	DF	35 307 913	17 518 255	17 789 658	...	...	...	...	676 578	...
Nepal - Népal[44]										
22 VI 2001	DJ	23 151 423	11 563 921	11 587 502	...	...	...	...	147 181	...
Occupied Palestinian Territory - Territoire palestinien occupé [45]										
9 XII 1997	DF	2 601 669	1 322 264	1 279 405	*2 483*	*3 299*	DF	4.7	6 020	*548*
Oman										
1 XII 1993	DF	2 018 074	1 178 005	840 069	*2 131*	**2 478*	DF	2.5	309 500	8
Pakistan[46]										
2 III 1998	DF	130 579 571	67 840 137	62 739 434	*122 360*	**140 470*	DF	2.3	796 095	176
Philippines										
1 V 2000	DJ	76 504 077	38 524 267	37 979 810	*70 267*	*77 926*	DJ	1.7	300 000	*260*
Qatar										
1 III 1997	DF	522 023	342 459	179 564	...	...	...	...	11 000	...
Saudi Arabia - Arabie saoudite										
27 IX 1992	DF	16 948 388	9 479 973	7 468 415	...	...	...	...	2 149 690	...
Singapore - Singapour[47]										
30 VI 2000	DF	4 017 700	2 061 800	1 955 900	3 526	4 131	DF	2.6	683	6 049
Sri Lanka[48]										
17 VII 2001	DF	*16 864 544	*8 343 964	*8 520 580	*18 136*	**18 700*	DF	0.5	65 610	285
Syrian Arab Republic - République arabe syrienne[49]										
3 IX 1994	DF	13 782 315	7 048 906	6 733 409	*14 153*	*16 720*	DF	2.8	185 180	*90*
Tajikistan - Tadjikistan										
20 I 2000	DF	*6 127 000	*3 082 000	*3 045 000	5 836	**6 293*	DF	1.3	143 100	44
Thailand - Thaïlande										
1 IV 2000	DJ	60 617 200	29 850 100	30 767 100	...	...	...	...	513 115	...

3. Population by sex, rate of population increase, surface area and density
Population selon le sexe, taux d'accroissement de la population, superficie et densité
(continued — suite)

(See notes at end of table. — Voir notes à la fin du tableau.)

Continent, country or area and census date / Continent, pays ou zone et date du recensement	Census type[a]	Latest available census — Dernier recensement disponible (in units — en unités)			Mid-year estimates Estimations au milieu de l'année (in thousands — en milliers)		Estimate type	Annual rate of increase Taux d'accrois sement annuel 1995-01	Surface area Superficie (km²) 2001	Density Densité 2001[1]
		Both sexes Les deux sexes	Male Masculin	Female Feminin	1995	2001				
ASIA — ASIE										
Timor-Leste										
31 X 1990	DF	747 750	386 939	360 811	...	...	...	...	14 874	...
Turkey - Turquie										
22 X 2000	DF	67 844 903	...	...	*61 706*	*68 610*	DF	1.8	774 815	*89*
Turkmenistan - Turkménistan										
10 I 1995	DF	4 483 251	2 225 331	2 257 920	...	...	...	...	488 100	...
United Arab Emirates - Émirats arabes unis[50]										
11 XII 1995	DF	2 377 453	1 579 743	797 710	...	...	...	...	83 600	...
Uzbekistan - Ouzbékistan										
12 I 1989	DJ	19 810 077	9 784 156	10 025 921	22 690	*24 964	DF	1.6	447 400	56
Viet Nam										
1 IV 1999	DJ	76 324 753	37 519 754	38 804 999	...	...	...	...	331 689	...
Yemen - Yémen										
16 XII 1994	DF	14 587 807	7 473 540	7 114 267	*15 369*	*18 863	DF	3.4	527 968	36
EUROPE										
Albania - Albanie										
1 IV 2001	DF	*3 069 275	*1 530 443	*1 538 832	...	...	...	...	28 748	...
Andorra - Andorre										
12 VII 1989	DF	46 166	...	...	...	...	...	...	468	...
Austria - Autriche										
15 V 2001	DJ	8 065 465	3 907 244	4 158 221	8 047	8 130	DJ	0.2	83 858	97
Belarus - Bélarus										
16 II 1999	DJ	10 045 237	4 717 621	5 327 616	10 281	*9 973	DF	-0.5	207 600	48
Belgium - Belgique										
1 X 2001	DJ	10 296 350	...	...	10 137	*10 287	DJ	0.2	30 528	337
Bosnia and Herzegovina - Bosnie-Herzégovine										
31 III 1991	DJ	4 377 033	2 183 795	2 193 238	...	...	...	...	51 197	...
Bulgaria - Bulgarie										
1 III 2001	DF	*7 928 901	*3 862 465	*4 066 436	8 406	7 913	DF	-1.0	110 912	71
Channel Islands: Guernsey - Îles Anglo-Normandes: Guernesey										
29 IV 2001	DJ	59 807	29 138	30 669	...	...	...	...	78	...
Channel Islands: Jersey - Îles Anglo-Normandes: Jersey										
11 III 2001	DJ	87 186	42 485	44 701	...	...	...	...	116	...
Croatia - Croatie										
31 III 2001	DJ	4 437 460	2 135 900	2 301 560	4 669	*4 437	DJ	-0.8	56 538	78
Czech Republic - République tchèque										
1 III 2001	DJ	10 292 933	5 019 381	5 273 552	10 331	10 224	DJ	-0.2	78 866	130
Denmark - Danemark[51]										
1 I 1991	DJ	5 146 469	2 536 391	2 610 078	5 228	*5 359	DJ	0.4	43 094	124
Estonia - Estonie										
31 III 2000	DF	*1 370 500	*631 900	*738 600	1 484	1 361	DF	-1.4	45 100	30

3. Population by sex, rate of population increase, surface area and density
Population selon le sexe, taux d'accroissement de la population, superficie et densité
(continued — suite)

(See notes at end of table. — Voir notes à la fin du tableau.)

Continent, country or area and census date / Continent, pays ou zone et date du recensement	Census type[a]	Latest available census — Dernier recensement disponible (in units — en unités)			Mid-year estimates Estimations au milieu de l'année (in thousands — en milliers)		Estimate type	Annual rate of increase Taux d' accrois sement annuel 1995-01	Surface area Superficie (km²) 2001	Density Densité 2001[1]
		Both sexes Les deux sexes	Male Masculin	Female Feminin	1995	2001				
EUROPE										
Faeroe Islands - Îles Féroé										
22 IX 1977	DJ	41 969	21 997	19 972	...	...	...	...	1 399	...
Finland - Finlande										
31 XII 2000	DJ	5 181 115	2 529 341	2 651 774	5 108	5 188	DJ	0.3	338 145	15
France[52]										
8 III 1999	DJ	58 520 688	28 419 419	30 101 269	57 844	59 191	DJ	0.4	551 500	107
Germany - Allemagne										
....	...	...	...	...	81 661	*82 348	DJ	0.1	357 022	231
Germany: Federal Rep. of Germany - Allemagne: République fédérale d'Allemagne[53]										
25 V 1987	DJ	61 077 042	29 322 923	31 754 119	...	...	...	...	248 647	...
Germany: Former German Dem. Rep. - Allemagne: Ancienne république démocratique allema[53]										
31 XII 1981	DJ	16 705 635	7 849 112	8 856 523	...	...	...	...	108 333	...
Gibraltar[54]										
12 XI 2001	DF	27 486	13 639	13 847	27	28	DF	0.6	6	4 707
Greece - Grèce[55,56]										
18 III 2001	DF	10 964 020	5 431 816	5 532 204	10 454	*10 020	DF	-0.7	131 957	76
Holy See - Saint-Siège[13,57]										
30 IV 1948	DF	890	548	342	...	>1	DJ		...	-
Hungary - Hongrie										
1 II 2001	DF	10 198 315	4 850 650	5 347 665	10 229	10 188	DF	-0.1	93 032	110
Iceland - Islande										
1 XII 1970	DJ	204 930	103 621	101 309	267	285	DJ	1.1	103 000	3
Ireland - Irlande										
28 IV 2002	DF	*3 917 336	*1 945 187	*1 972 149	3 601	*3 854	DF	1.1	70 273	55
Isle of Man - Îles de Man										
29 IV 2001	DJ	76 315	37 372	38 943	...	...	...	...	572	...
Italy - Italie										
21 X 2001	DJ	*56 305 568	*27 260 953	*29 044 615	57 301	*57 948	DJ	0.2	301 318	192
Latvia - Lettonie										
31 III 2000	DJ	2 377 383	1 094 964	1 282 419	2 485	2 355	DF	-0.9	64 600	36
Liechtenstein										
2 XII 1980	DF	25 215	...	...	31	*33	DF	1.2	160	207
Lithuania - Lituanie										
6 IV 2001	DJ	3 483 972	1 629 148	1 854 824	3 629	3 481	DF	-0.7	65 300	53
Luxembourg										
15 II 2001	DJ	439 539	216 541	222 998	410	442	DJ	1.3	2 586	171
Malta - Malte[58]										
26 XI 1995	DJ	378 132	186 836	191 296	>378	>395	DJ	0.7	316	1 249
Monaco										
23 VII 1990	DJ	29 972	14 237	15 735	...	...	...	...	1	...
Netherlands - Pays-Bas[59]										
1 I 2002	DJ	16 105 285	7 971 967	8 133 318	15 459	16 046	DJ	0.6	41 526	386
Norway - Norvège[60]										
3 XI 2001	DJ	4 520 947	2 240 281	2 280 666	4 359	4 514	DJ	0.6	385 155	12

3. Population by sex, rate of population increase, surface area and density
Population selon le sexe, taux d'accroissement de la population, superficie et densité
(continued — suite)

(See notes at end of table. — Voir notes à la fin du tableau.)

Continent, country or area and census date Continent, pays ou zone et date du recensement	Census type[a]	Latest available census — Dernier recensement disponible (in units — en unités)			Mid-year estimates Estimations au milieu de l'année (in thousands — en milliers)		Estima-te type	Annual rate of increase Taux d' accrois sement annuel 1995-01	Surface area Superficie (km²) 2001	Density Densité 2001[1]
		Both sexes Les deux sexes	Male Masculin	Female Feminin	1995	2001				
EUROPE										
Poland - Pologne[61]										
20 V 2002	DF	*38 230 000	*18 516 000	*19 714 000	38 588	*38 638	DF	-	323 250	120
Portugal[62]										
12 III 2001	DF	*10 355 824	*4 999 964	*5 355 860	9 916	*10 299	DF	0.6	91 982	112
Republic of Moldova - République de Moldova[63]										
12 I 1989	DF	4 337 592	2 058 160	2 279 432	4 348	3 631	DJ	-3.0	33 851	107
Romania - Roumanie										
18 III 2002	DJ	*21 680 974	*10 568 741	*11 112 233	22 681	22 408	DJ	-0.2	238 391	94
Russian Federation - Fédération de Russie										
9 X 2002	DF	*145 537 200	*67 805 700	*77 731 500	147 774	<143 954	DF	-0.4	17 075 400	8
San Marino - Saint-Marin										
30 XI 1976	DF	19 149	9 654	9 495	...	...	...	...	61	...
Serbia and Montenegro - Serbie-et-Montenegr-o[64]										
31 III 1991	DJ	10 394 026	5 157 120	5 236 906	10 547	10 651	DJ	0.2	102 173	104
Slovakia - Slovaquie										
25 V 2001	DJ	5 379 455	2 612 515	2 766 940	5 364	5 380	DJ	0.1	49 012	110
Slovenia - Slovénie										
31 III 2002	DJ	*1 948 250	*943 994	*1 004 256	1 988	1 992	DJ	-	20 256	98
Spain - Espagne[65]										
1 XI 2001	DF	*40 847 371	...	...	39 223	40 266	DJ	0.4	505 992	80
Svalbard and Jan Mayen Islands - Îles Svalbard et Jan Mayen[66]										
1 XI 1960	DF	3 431	2 545	886	...	...	...	...	62 422	...
Sweden - Suède										
1 XI 1990	DJ	8 587 353	4 242 351	4 345 002	8 827	8 896	DJ	0.1	449 964	20
Switzerland - Suisse										
5 XII 2000	DJ	7 204 055	3 519 698	3 684 357	7 041	7 233	DJ	0.4	41 284	175
The Former Yugoslav Rep. of Macedonia - L'ex-République yougoslave de Macédoine[31]										
1 XI 2002	DJ	*2 038 059	...	...	1 963	2 026	...	...	25 713	79
Ukraine										
5 XII 2001	DJ	48 457 102	22 441 344	26 015 758	51 728	49 037	DF	-0.9	603 700	81
United Kingdom - Royaume-Uni[67]										
29 IV 2001	DF	*58 789 194	...	...	58 612	*59 756	DF	0.3	242 900	246
OCEANIA — OCEANIE										
American Samoa - Samoas américaines[17]										
1 IV 2000	DJ	57 291	29 264	28 027	...	...	...	...	199	...
Australia - Australie										
7 VIII 2001	DF	18 972 350	9 362 021	9 610 329	18 072	19 387	DJ	1.2	7 741 220	3

3. Population by sex, rate of population increase, surface area and density
Population selon le sexe, taux d'accroissement de la population, superficie et densité
(continued — suite)

(See notes at end of table. — Voir notes à la fin du tableau.)

Continent, country or area and census date / Continent, pays ou zone et date du recensement	Census type[a]	Latest available census — Dernier recensement disponible (in units — en unités)			Mid-year estimates Estimations au milieu de l'année (in thousands — en milliers)		Estimate type	Annual rate of increase Taux d'accrois sement annuel 1995-01	Surface area Superficie (km²) 2001	Density Densité 2001[1]
		Both sexes Les deux sexes	Male Masculin	Female Feminin	1995	2001				
OCEANIA — OCEANIE										
Cook Islands - Îles Cook[68,69]										
1 XII 2001	DF	18 027	...	...	19	*18	DF	-1.1	236	77
Fiji - Fidji										
25 VIII 1996	DF	775 077	393 931	381 146	...	...	...	...	18 274	...
French Polynesia - Polynésie française[70]										
7 XI 2002	DF	245 516	...	...	...	...	...	...	4 000	...
Guam[17]										
1 IV 2000	DJ	154 805	79 181	75 624	...	...	...	...	549	...
Kiribati[71]										
7 XI 1995	DF	*77 658	*38 478	*39 180	...	...	...	...	726	...
Marshall Islands - Îles Marshall										
1 VI 1999	DF	50 848	26 034	24 814	56	55	DF	-0.3	181	302
Micronesia, Federated States of - Micronésie, États fédérés de										
1 IV 2000	DJ	107 008	54 191	52 817	107	117	DJ	1.5	702	167
Nauru										
17 IV 1992	DF	9 919	...	...	...	...	...	...	21	...
New Caledonia - Nouvelle-Calédonie[72]										
16 IV 1996	DF	196 836	100 762	96 074	194	214	DF	1.7	18 575	12
New Zealand - Nouvelle-Zélande[73]										
6 III 2001	DJ	3 820 749	1 863 309	1 957 440	3 656	*3 850	DJ	0.9	270 534	14
Niue - Nioué										
7 IX 2001	DF	1 788	897	891	...	...	...	...	260	...
Norfolk Island - Île Norfolk										
7 VIII 2001	DF	2 601	1 257	1 344	...	...	...	...	36	...
Northern Mariana Islands - Îles Mariannes septentrionales										
1 IV 2000	DF	69 221	31 984	37 237	...	...	...	...	464	...
Palau - Palaos										
15 IV 2000	DF	19 129	...	...	17	20	DF	2.2	459	43
Papua New Guinea - Papouasie-Nouvelle-Guinée[74]										
9 VII 2000	DF	5 190 786	2 691 744	2 499 042	...	...	...	...	462 840	...
Pitcairn										
31 XII 1991	DF	66	...	...	...	...	...	...	5	...
Samoa										
5 XI 2001	DF	176 710	92 050	84 660	...	...	...	...	2 831	...
Solomon Islands - Îles Salomon[75]										
21 XI 1999	DF	409 042	211 381	197 661	...	...	...	...	28 896	...
Tokelau - Tokélaou										
11 XII 1991	DF	1 577	...	...	...	...	...	...	12	...
Tonga										
30 XI 1996	DF	97 784	49 615	48 169	>98	>101	DF	0.5	650	155
Tuvalu										
1 XI 2002	DF	9 561	4 729	4 832	...	...	...	...	26	...

3. Population by sex, rate of population increase, surface area and density
Population selon le sexe, taux d'accroissement de la population, superficie et densité
(continued — suite)

(See notes at end of table. — Voir notes à la fin du tableau.)

Continent, country or area and census date Continent, pays ou zone et date du recensement	Census type[a]	Latest available census — Dernier recensement disponible (in units — en unités)			Mid-year estimates Estimations au milieu de l'année (in thousands — en milliers)		Estima-te type	Annual rate of increase Taux d' accrois sement annuel 1995-01	Surface area Superficie (km²) 2001	Density Densité 2001[1]
		Both sexes Les deux sexes	Male Masculin	Female Feminin	1995	2001				
OCEANIA — OCEANIE										
Vanuatu										
16 XI 1999	DJ	186 678	95 682	90 996	...	...	...	...	12 189	...
Wallis and Futuna Islands - Îles Wallis et Futuna										
3 X 1996	DF	14 166	6 984	7 182	...	...	...	...	200	...

GENERAL NOTES - NOTES GENERALES

Surface area estimates include inland waters. For method of evaluation and limitation of data, see Technical Notes for this table. — Pour le méthode d'évaluation et les insuffissances des données, voireNotes techniques, pour ce tableau.

FOOTNOTES - NOTES

* Provisional. — Données provisoires.

< Data refer to the beginning of the year. –- Les donées se raportent au debut de l'année.

> Data refer to the end of the year. — Les donées se raportent au fin de l'année.

[a] 'Code' indicates the source of data, as follows:
DF - De facto
DJ - De jure
SDF - Sample survey, de facto
Le 'Code' indique la source des données, comme suit:
DF - Population de fait
DJ - Population de droit
SDF - Enquête par sondage, population de fait

[1] Population per square kilometre of surface area in 2001. Figures are estimates of population divided by surface area and are not to be considered either as reflecting density in the urban sense or as indicating the supporting power of a territory's land and resources. — Nombre d'habitants au kilomètre carré en 2001. Il s'agit simplement d'éstimations de la population divisé par celui de la superficie: il ne faut pas y voir d'indication de la densité au sens urbain du terme ni de l'effectif de population que les terres et les ressources du territoire sont capables de nourrir.

[2] Including the enclave of Cabinda. — Y compris l'enclave de Cabinda.

[3] Census results have been adjusted for underenumeration, estimated at 1.4 per cent. — Les résultat du recensement ont été ajustées pour compenser les lacunes du dénombrement, estimées à 1,4 p. 100.

[4] Census result, excluding Mayotte. — Les résultat du recensement, non compris Mayotte.

[5] Comprising Bioko (which includes Pagalu) and Rio Muni (which includes Corisco and Elobeys). — Comprend Bioko (qui comprend Pagalu) et Rio Muni (qui comprend Corisco et Elobeys).

[6] For Libyan nationals only. — Pour les nationaux libyens seulement.

[7] Mid-year estimates have been adjusted for underenumeration, at latest census. — Les estimations au millieu de l''année tiennent compte d''une ajustement destiné à compenser les lacunes du dénombrement lors du dernier recensement.

[8] Census results have been adjusted for underenumeration, estimated at 5.1 per cent. — Les résultats du recensement ont été ajustées pour compenser les lacunes du dénombrement, estimées à 5,1 p. 100.

[9] Census results have been adjusted for underenumeration, estimated at 9 per cent. — Les résultat du recensement ont été ajustées pour compenser les lacunes du dénombrement, estimées à 9 p. 100.

[10] Comprising the Northern Region (former Saguia el Hamra) and Southern Region (former Rio de Oro). — Comprend la région septentrionale (ancien Saguia-el-Hamra) et la région méridionale (ancien Rio de Oro).

[11] Excluding institutional population. — Non compris la population dans les institutions.

[12] Revised intercensal estimates adjusted for net undercoverage. — - Estimations inter censitaires corrigées pour tenir en compte du sous dénombrement net.

[13] Population statistics are based on administrative records, not on questionnaire-based population census. — La source de la statistique de la population sont des fichiers administratifs et pas un recensement de population basé sur un questionnaire.

[14] Including Carriacou and other dependencies in the Grenadines. — Y compris Carriacou et les autres dépendances du groupe des îles Grenadines.

[15] Including dependencies: Marie-Galante, la Désirade, les Saintes, Petite-Terre, St. Barthélemy and French part of St. Martin. — Y compris les dépendances: Marie-Galante, la Désirade, les Saintes, Petite-Terre, Saint-Barthélemy et la partie française de Saint-Martin.

[16] Comprising Bonaire, Curaçao, Saba, St. Eustatius and Dutch part of St. Martin. — Comprend Bonaire, Curaçao, Saba, Saint-Eustache et la partie néederlandaise de Saint-Martin.

[17] Including armed forces stationed in the area. — Y compris les militaires en garnison sur le territoire.

[18] Including Bequia and other islands in the Grenadines. — Y compris Bequia et des autres îles dans les Grenadines.

[19] Excluding armed forces overseas and civilian citizens absent from country for an extended period of time. — Non compris les militaires à l'étranger, et les civils hors du pays pendant une période prolongée.

[20] Excluding civilian citizens absent from country for extended periods of time. — Non compris les civils hors du pays pendant une période prolongée.

[21] Data include persons in remote areas, military personnel outside the country, merchant seamen at sea, civilian seasonal workers outside the country, and other civilians outside the country, and exclude nomads, foreign military, civilian aliens temporarily in the country, transients on ships and Indian jungle population. — Y compris les personnes dans des régions éloignées, le personel militaire en dehors du pays, les marins marchands, les ouvriers saisonniers civils de couture en dehors du pays, et autres civils en dehors du pays, et non compris les nomades, les militaires étrangers, les étrangers civils temporairement dans le pays, les transiteurs sur des bateaux et les Indiens de la jungle.

[22] Excluding nomadic Indian tribes. — Non compris les tribus d'Indiens nomades.

[23] Excluding dependencies, of which South Georgia (area 3 755 km2) had an estimated population of 499 in 1964 (494 males, 5 females). The other dependencies namely, the South Sandwich group (surface area 337

km2) and a number of smaller islands, are presumed to be uninhabited. — Non compris les dépendances, parmi lesquelles figure la Georgie du Sud (3 755 km2) avec une population estimée à 499 personnes en 1964 (494 du sexe masculin et 5 du sexe féminin). Les autres dépendances, c'est-à-dire le groupe des Sandwich de Sud (superficie: 337 km2) et certaines petites-îles, sont présumées inhabitées.

24 A dispute exists between the governments of Argentina and the United Kingdom of Great Britain and Northern Ireland concerning sovereignty over the Falkland Islands (Malvinas). — La souveraineté sur les îles Falkland (Malvinas) fait l'objet d'un différend entre le Gouvernement argentin et le Gouvernement du Royaume-Uni de Grande-Bretagne et d'Irlande du Nord.

25 Excluding Indian jungle population. — Non compris les Indiens de la jungle.

26 Census result, excluding nomad population. — Les résultat du recensment, non compris les nomades.

27 Excluding foreign diplomatic personnel and their dependants. — Non compris le personnel diplomatique étranger et les membres de leur famille les accompagnant.

28 For statistical purposes, the data for China do not include those for the Hong Kong Special Administrative Region (Hong Kong SAR), Macao special Adminstrative Region (Macao SAR) and Taiwan province of China. — Pour la présentation des statistiques, les données pour Chine ne comprend pas les Région Administrative Spéciale de Hong Kong (Hong Kong RAS), le Région Administrative Spéciale de Macao (Macao RAS) et Taïwan province de Chine.

29 For the civilian population of 31 provinces, municipalities and autonomous regions. — Pour la population civile seulement de 31 provinces, municipalités et régions autonomes.

30 Data refer to Hong Kong resident population at the census moment, which covers usual residents and mobile residents. Usual residents refer to two categories of people: (1) Hong Kong permanent residents who had stayed in Hong Kong for at least three months during the six months before or for at least three months during the six months after the census moment, regardless of whether they were in Hong Kong or not at the census moment; and (2) Hong Kong non-permanent residents who were in Hong Kong at the census moment. Mobile Residents, they are Hong Kong permanent residents who had stayed in Hong Kong for at least one month but less than three months during the six months before or for at least one month but less than three months during the six months after the census moment, regardless of whether they were in Hong Kong or not at the census moment. — Les données se rapportent à la population résidente à Hong Kong au moment du recensement. Cette population est composée des résidants habituels et des résidants mobiles. La population résidente est partagée en deux catégories: (1) les résidents permanents qui ont habité à Hong Kong au moins trois mois pendant les six mois précédents ou les six mois suivants le recensement; (2) les habitants non-permanents de Hong Kong qui étaient à Hong Kong au moment du recensement. La population mobile se rapporte aux résidents permanents de Hong Kong qui ont habité à Hong Kong pendant les six mois après le recensement pour une période comprise entre un mois et trois mois, indépendamment du fait qu'ils étaient à Hong Kong au moment du recensement au pays.

31 For 2001, de jure population. — Pour 2001, population de droit.

32 Data include all population irrespective of citizenship, who at the time of the census have resided in the country or intended to reside for a period of at least one year. It does not distinguish between those present or absent at the time of census. Data refer to government controlled areas. — Les chiffres comprennent toute la population, quelle que soit la nationalité, qui à l'époque de recensement avait résidé dans le pays, ou avait l'intention de résider, pendant une période de au moins un an. Il n'y a pas de distinction entre les personnes présentes ou absentes au moment du recensement. Les données se raportent aux zones contrôlées par le Gouvernement.

33 Estimates of the number of Turkish Cypriots from 1974 onwards are the result of population projections based on the age and sex structure of the Turkisih Cypriot community at Census 1960 and with assumptions of fertility and mortality similar to the rest of the Cyprus Population. With regard to the migration of Turkish Cypriots after 1974, migration assumptions are based on figures obtained from Turkish Cypriot sources. Settlers from Turkey are not included. — Les estimations du nombre de Chypriotes turcs depuis 1974 résultent des projections de population préparées sur la base de la structure par sexe et age de la communauté chypriote turque au recensement de 1960, et avec des hypothèses de fécondité et de mortalité similaires à celles du reste de la population de Chypre. En ce qui concerne la migration des Chypriotes turcs après 1974, les hypothèses sont basées sur les données obtenues de sources chypriotes turques. Les occupants venus de Turquie ne sont pas inclus.

34 Including data for the Indian-held part of Jammu and Kashmir, the final status of which has not yet been determined. — Y compris les données pour la partie du Jammu et du Cachemire occupée par l'Inde dont le statut définitif n'a pas encore été déterminé.

35 The figure includes an estimated population of 459 557 persons in

urban and 1 857 659 persons in rural areas that were not directly enumerated, and a population of of 566 403 persons in urban and 1 717 578 persons in rural areas that declined participation. Also included are 421 399 non permanent residents (the homeless, the crew of ships carrying national flag, boat/floating house people, remote located tribesmen and refugees.) — Y compris la population estimée a 459 557 personnes dans les zones urbaines et de 1 857 659 personnes dans les zones rurales qui n'ont pas été énumérées directement, aussi que 566 403 personnes qui non pas répondu dans les zones urbaines et de 1 717 578 personnes dans les zones rurales. Y compris 421 399 résidants non permanents (les sans abri, l'équipage des bateaux portant le drapeau national, les habitants des embarcations ou des maisons flottantes, les habitants des tribus isolées et les réfugies.)

36 For the 1997 population census, data exclude population in three autonomous provinces in the north of the country. — Pour le recensement de 1997, la population des trois provinces autonomes dans le nord du pays est exclue.

37 Including data for East Jerusalem and Israeli residents in certain other territories under occupation by Israeli military forces since June 1967. — Y compris les données pour Jérusalem-Est et les résidents israéliens dans certains autres territoires occupés depuis 1967 par les forces armées israéliennes.

38 Excluding diplomatic personnel outside country and foreign military and civilian personnel and their dependants stationed in the area. — Non compris le personnel diplomatique hors du pays ni les militaires et agents civils étrangers en poste sur le territoire et les membres de leur famille les accompagnant.

39 Excluding data for Jordanian territory under occupation since June 1967 by Israeli military forces. Excluding foreigners, including registered Palestinian refugees. — Non compris les données pour le territoire jordanien occupé depuis juin 1967 par les forces armées israéliennes. Non compris les étrangers, mais y compris les réfugiés de Palestine immatriculés.

40 Including diplomats and their families abroad, but excluding foreign diplomats, foreign military personnal, and their families in the country. — Y compris le personnel diplomatique et les membres de leurs familles à l'étranger, mais sans tenir compte du personnel diplomatique et militaire étranger et des membres de leurs familles.

41 Excluding Palestinian refugees in camps. — Non compris les réfugiés de Palestine dans les camps.

42 Excluding Malaysian citizens and permanent residents who were away or intended to be away from the country for more than six months. Excluding Malaysian military, naval and diplomatic personnel and their families outside the country, and tourists, businessman who intended to be in Malaysia for less than six months. — Non compris les citoyens malaisiens et les résidents permanents qui étaient ou qui ont prévu d'être hors du pays pour six mois ou plus. Non compris le personnel militaire Malaisien, le personnel naval ou diplomatique et leurs familles hors du pays, et les touristes et les hommes d'affaires qui avaient l'intention de rester en Malaisie moins de six mois.

43 Data have been adjusted for underenumeration, at 2000 census. — Les données ont été ajustées pour compenser les lacunes du dénombrement recensement de 2000.

44 Data including estimated population from household listing from Village Development Committees and Wards which could not be enumerated at the time of census. — Les données incluent la population estimée par les listes des ménages des comités de développement des villages et des circonscriptions qui n'ont pas pu être énumérée au moment du recensement

45 Total population does not include Palestinian population living in those parts of Jerusalem governorate which were annexed by Israel in 1967, amounting to 210,209 persons. Likewise, the results does not include the estimates of not enumerated population based on the findings of the post enumeration study, i.e 83,805 persons. — Les données relatives à la population totale ne comprennent pas la population palestinienne -équivalent à 210 209 personnes - habitant dans les territoires du gouvernorat de Jérusalem qui ont été annexés par Israël en 1967. Egalement, les données ne tiennent pas compte des estimations de la population calculée sur la base des résultats de l'enquête postcensitaire, équivalent à 83 805 personnes.

46 Excluding data for the Pakistan-held part of Jammu and Kashmir, the final status of which has not yet been determined. — Non compris les données concernant la partie du Jammu et Cachemire occupée par le Pakistan dont le statut définitif n'a pas été déterminé.

47 Census result, excluding transients afloat and non-locally domiciled military and civilian services personnel and their dependants and visitors. — Les résultat du recensment, non compris les personnes de passage à bord de navires ni les militaires et agents civils non-résidents et les membres de leur famille les accompagnant et visiteurs.

48 The Population and Housing Census 2001 did not cover the whole area of the country due to security problems; the Census was complete in

18 districts only; in three districts it was not possible to conduct it; and in four districts it was partially conducted. — Le recensement de la population et de l'habitat en 2001 n'a pas couvert la totalité du pays pour des problèmes de sécurité ; le recensement a été complété seulement en 18 districts ; dans 3 districts ça n'a pas été possible de conduire le recensement et dans 4 districts il a été partialement conduit.

[49] Including Palestinian refugees. — Y compris les réfugiés de Palestine.

[50] Comprising 7 sheikdoms of Abu Dhabi, Dubai, Sharjah, Ajaman, Umm al Qaiwain, Ras al Khaimah and Fujairah, and the area lying within the modified Riyadh line as announced in October 1955. — Comprend les sept cheikhats de Abou Dhabi, Dabai, Ghârdja, Adjmân, Oumm-al-Quiwaïn, Ras al Khaïma et Foudjaïra, ainsi que la zone délimitée par la ligne de Riad modifiée comme il a été annoncé en octobre 1955.

[51] Excluding Faeroe Islands and Greenland. — Non compris les îles Féroé et Gröenland.

[52] Excluding Overseas Departments, namely French Guiana, Guadeloupe, Martinique and Reunion, shown separately. De jure population but excluding diplomatic personnel outside country and including members of alien armed forces not living in military camps and foreign diplomatic personnel not living in embassies or consulates. — Non compris les départements d'outre-mer, c'est-à-dire la Guyane française, la Guadeloupe, la Martinique et la Réunion, qui font l'objet de rubriques distinctes. Population de droit, non compris le personnel diplomatique hors du pays et y compris les militaires étrangers ne vivant pas dans des camps militaires et le personnel diplomatique étranger ne vivant pas dans les ambassades ou les consulats.

[53] All data shown pertaining to Germany prior to 3 October 1990 are indicated separately for the Federal Republic of Germany and the former German Democratic Republic based on their respective territories at the time indicated. — Toutes les données se rapportant à l'Allemagne avant le 3 octobre 1990 figurent dans deux rubriques séparées basées sur les territoires respectifs de la République fédérale de l'Allemagne et l'ancienne République démocratique allemande selon la période.

[54] Excluding armed forces. — Non compris les militaires en garnison.

[55] Census data including armed forces stationed outside the country, but excluding alien armed forces stationed in the area. — Les données de recensement y compris les militaires hors du pays, mais non compris les militaires étrangers en garnison sur le territoire.

[56] Mid-year population excludes armed forces stationed outside the country, but includes alien armed forces stationed in the area. — Les estimations au milieu de l'année non compris les militaires en garnison hors du pays, mais y compris les militaires étrangers en garnison sur le territoire.

[57] Data refer to the Vatican City State. — Les données se rapportent aux Etat du Saint-Siège.

[58] Including foreigners residing in Malta for 12 months before the census date and excluding foreign diplomatic personnel. — Y compris les les étrangers habitant à Malte pour 12 mois avant le recensement et le personnel diplomatique étrangers.

[59] Census result, based on compilation of continuous accounting and sample surveys. — Les résultat du recensement, d'après les résultats des dénombrements et enquêtes par sondage continue.

[60] Including residents temporarily outside the country. — Y compris les résidents se trouvant temporairement hors du pays.

[61] Excluding civilian aliens within country, but including civilian nationals temporarily outside country. — Non compris les civils étrangers dans le pays, mais y compris les civils nationaux temporairement hors du pays.

[62] Including the Azores and Madeira Islands. — Y compris les Açores et Madère.

[63] Data do not include information for Transnistria and the municipality of Bender. — Les données ne tiennent pas compte de l'information sur la Transnistria et la municipalité de Bender.

[64] Beginning with 1998, estimates of Kosovo and Metohia computed on the basis of natural increases from year 1997. — A partir du 1998, les estimations pour le Kosovo et la Metohia ont été calculées sur la base des incréments naturelles depuis 1997.

[65] Including the Balearic and Canary Islands, and Alhucemas, Ceuta, Chafarinas, Melilla and Penon de Vélez de la Gomera. — Y compris les Baléares et les Canaries, Al Hoceima, Ceuta, les îles Zaffarines, Melilla et Penon de Vélez de la Gomera.

[66] Inhabited only during the winter season. Census data are for total population while estimates refer to Norwegian population only. Included also in the de jure population of Norway. — N'est habitée pendant la saison d'hiver. Les données de recensement se rapportent à la population totale, mais les estimations ne concernent que la population norvégienne, comprise également dans la population de droit de la Norvège.

[67] Excluding Channel Islands and Isle of Man, shown separately. — Non compris les îles Anglo-Normandes et l'île de Man, qui font l'objet de rubriques distinctes.

[68] Excluding Niue, shown separately, which is part of Cook Islands, but because of remoteness is administered separately. — Non compris Nioué,

qui fait l'objet d'une rubrique distincte et qui fait partie des îles Cook, mais qui, en raison de son éloignement, est administrée séparément.

[69] The resident population consisted of 14,990 (7,738 males and 7,252 females). — Population résidente de 14 990 (7 738 hommes et 7 252 femmes).

[70] Comprising Austral, Gambier, Marquesas, Rapa, Society and Tuamotu Islands. — Comprend les îles Australes, Gambier, Marquises, Rapa, de la Societé et Tuamotou.

[71] Including Christmas, Fanning, Ocean and Washington Islands. — Y compris les îles Christmas, Fanning, Océan et Washington.

[72] Including the islands of Huon, Chesterfield, Loyalty, Walpole and Belep Archipelago. — Y compris les îles Huon, Chesterfield, Loyauté et Walpole, et l'archipel Belep.

[73] Including Campbell and Kermadec Islands (population 20 in 1961, surface area 148 km2) as well as Antipodes, Auckland, Bounty, Snares, Solander and Three Kings island, all of which are uninhabited. — Y compris les îles Campbell et Kermadec (20 habitants en 1961, superficie: 148 km2) ainsi que les îles Antipodes, Auckland, Bounty, Snares, Solander et Three Kings, qui sont toutes inhabitées.

[74] Comprising eastern part of New Guinea, the Bismarck Archipelago, Bougainville and Buka of Solomon Islands group and about 600 smaller islands. — Comprend l'est de la Nouvelle-Guinée, l'archipel Bismarck, Bougainville et Buka (ces deux dernières du groupe des Salomon) et environ 600 îlots.

[75] Comprising the Solomon Islands group (except Bougainville and Buka which are included with Papua New Guinea shown separately), Ontong, Java, Rennel and Santa Cruz Islands. — Comprend les îles Salomon(à l'exception de Bougainville et de Buka dont la population est comprise dans celle de Papouasie-Nouvelle Guinée qui font l'objet d'une rubrique distincte), ainsi que les îles Ontong, Java, Rennel et Santa Cruz.

Table 4

Table 4 presents, for each country or area of the world, basic vital statistics including in the following order: live births, crude birth rate, deaths, crude death rate and rate of natural increase, infants deaths and infant mortality rate, the expectation of life at birth by sex and the total fertility rate.

Description of variables: The vital events and rates shown in this table are defined as follows[1]:

Live birth is the complete expulsion or extraction from its mother of a product of conception, irrespective of the duration of pregnancy, which after such separation breathes or shows any other evidence of life such as beating of the heart, pulsation of the umbilical cord, of definite movement of voluntary muscles, whether or not the umbilical cord has been cut or the placenta is attached; each product of such a birth is considered live-born regardless of gestational age.

Death is the permanent disappearance of all evidence of life at any time after live birth has taken place (post-natal cessation of vital functions without capability of resuscitation).

Infant deaths are deaths of live-born infants under one year of age.

Expectation of life at birth is defined as the average number of years of life for males and females if they continued to be subject to the same mortality experienced in the year(s) to which these life expectancies refer.

The total fertility rate is the average number of children that would be born alive to a hypothetical cohort of women if, throughout their reproductive years, the age-specific fertility rates for the specified year remained unchanged. The standard method of calculating the total fertility rate is the sum of the age-specific fertility rates.

Crude birth rates and crude death rates presented in this table are calculated using the number of live births and the number of deaths obtained from civil registers. These civil registration data are used only if they are considered reliable (estimated completeness of 90 per cent or more).

Similarly, infant mortality rates presented in this table are calculated using the number of live births and the number of infant deaths obtained from civil registers. If, however, the registration of births or infant deaths for any given country or area is estimated to be less than 90 per cent complete, the rates are not calculated.

The expectation-of-life values are those provided by national statistical offices.

Rate computation: The crude birth and death rates are the annual number of each of these vital events per 1 000 mid-year population.

Infant mortality rate is the annual number of deaths of infants under one year of age per 1 000 live births (presented in table 9) in the same year.

Rates of natural increase are the difference between the crude birth rate and the crude death rate. It should be noted that the rates of natural increase presented here may differ from the population growth rates presented in table 3 as rates of natural increase do not take net international migration into account while the population growth rates do.

Rates that appear in this table have been calculated by the Statistics Division of the United Nations Department for Economic and Social Affairs, unless otherwise noted. The exceptions include official estimated rates, many of which were based on sample surveys.

Rates calculated by the Statistics Division of the United Nations presented in this table have been limited to those countries or areas having a minimum number of 30 events in a given year.

Reliability of data: Rates calculated on the basis of registered vital statistics which are considered unreliable (estimated to be less than 90 per cent complete) are not calculated. Estimated rates, prepared by the individual countries or areas, have been presented whenever applicable.

The designation of vital statistics as being either reliable or unreliable is discussed in general in section 4.2 of the Technical Notes. The technical notes for tables 9, 15 and 18 provide specific information on reliability of statistics on live births, infant deaths and deaths, respectively.

Since the expectation-of-life values shown in this table come either from official life tables they are all considered to be reliable.

Limitations: Statistics on births, deaths and infant deaths are subject to the same qualifications as have been set forth for vital statistics in general in section 4 of the Technical Notes and in the technical notes for individual tables presenting detailed data on these events (table 9, live births; table 15, infant deaths; table 18, deaths).

In assessing comparability it is important to take into account the reliability of the data used to calculate these rates, as discussed above.

It should be noted that the crude rates are particularly affected by the age-sex structure of the population. Infant mortality rates, and to a much lesser extent crude birth rates and crude death rates, are affected by the variation in the definition of a live birth and tabulation procedures.

Coverage: Vital statistics rates, natural increase rates and expectation of life are shown for 166 countries or areas.

_____

NOTES

[1] *Principles and Recommendations for a Vital Statistics System, Revision 2,* United Nations publication, Sales No. E.01.XVII.10, United Nations, New York, 2001.

Tableau 4

Le Tableau 4 présente, pour chaque pays ou zone du monde, des statistiques de base de l'état civil comprenant, dans l'ordre, les naissances vivantes, le taux brut de natalité, les décès, le taux brut de mortalité et le taux d'accroissement naturel de la population, les décès d'enfants de moins d'un an et le taux de mortalité infantile, l'espérance de vie à la naissance par sexe et l'indice synthétique de fécondité.

Description des variables : Les faits d'état civil utilisés aux fins du calcul des taux présentés dans ce tableau sont définis comme suit[1] :

La naissance vivante est l'expulsion ou l'extraction complète du corps de la mère, indépendamment de la duré de la gestation, d'un produit de la conception qui après cette séparation, respire ou manifeste tout autre signe de vie, tel que battement de cœur, pulsation du cordon ombilical ou contraction effective d'un muscle soumis à l'action de la volonté, que le cordon ombilical ait été coupé ou non et que le placenta soit ou non demeuré attaché; tout produit d'une telle naissance est considéré comme 'enfant né vivant'.

Le décès est la disparition permanente de tout signe de vie à un moment quelconque postérieur à la naissance vivante (cessation des fonctions vitales après la naissance sans possibilité de réanimation).

Il convient de préciser que les chiffres relatifs aux décès d'enfants de moins d'un an se rapportent aux naissances vivantes.

L'espérance de vie à la naissance est le nombre moyen d'années de vie que peuvent escompter les individus du sexe masculin et du sexe féminin s'ils continuent d'être soumis aux mêmes conditions de mortalité que celles qui existaient pendant les années auxquelles se rapportent les valeurs indiquées.

L'indice synthétique de fécondité représente le nombre moyen d'enfants que mettrait au monde une cohorte hypothétique de femmes qui seraient soumises, toute au long de leur vie, aux mêmes conditions de fécondité par âge que celles auxquelles sont soumises les femmes, dans chaque groupe d'âge, au cours d'une année ou d'une période donnée. La méthode standard de calculer l'indice synthétique de fécondité est l'addition des taux de fécondité par âge simple.

Les taux bruts de natalité et de mortalité présentés ont été établis sur la base du nombre de naissances vivantes et du nombre de décès inscrits sur les registres de l'état civil. Ces données n'ont été utilisées que lorsqu'elles étaient considérées comme sûres (degré estimatif de complétude égal ou supérieur à 90 p. 100).

De même, les taux de mortalité infantile présentés dans ce tableau ont été établis à partir du nombre de naissances vivantes et du nombre de décès d'enfants de moins d'un an inscrits sur les registres de l'état civil. Toutefois, lorsque les données relatives aux naissances ou aux décès d'enfants de moins d'un an pour un pays ou zone quelconque n'étaient pas considérées complètes à 90 p. 100 au moins, les indices n'ont pas été calculés.

Les valeurs de l'espérance de vie ont été fournies par les services nationaux de statistique.

Calcul des taux : Les taux bruts de natalité et de mortalité, représentent le nombre annuel de chacun de ces faits d'état civil pour 1 000 habitants au milieu de l'année considérée.

Les taux de mortalité infantile représentent le nombre annuel de décès d'enfants de moins d'un an pour 1 000 naissances vivantes (fréquences du tableau 9) survenues pendant la même année.

Le taux d'accroissement naturel est égal à la différence entre le taux brut de natalité et le taux brut de mortalité. Il y a lieu de noter que les taux d'accroissement naturel indiqués dans ce tableau peuvent différer des taux d'accroissement de la population figurant dans le tableau 3, les taux d'accroissement naturel ne tenant pas compte des taux nets de migration internationale, alors que ceux-ci sont inclus dans les taux d'accroissement de la population.

Sauf indication contraire, les taux figurant dans ce tableau ont été calculés par la Division de Statistique du Département des Affaires Economiques et Sociales du Secrétariat de l'Organisation des Nations Unies. Les exceptions comprennent les taux estimatifs officiels, dont bon nombre ont été établis sur la base d'enquêtes par sondage.

Les taux calculés par la Division de Statistique de l'ONU qui sont présentés dans ce tableau se rapportent aux seuls pays ou zones où l'on a enregistré au moins 30 événements au cours d'une année donnée.

Fiabilité des données : Les taux établis sur la base des statistiques de l'état civil obtenues des systèmes d'enregistrement d'état civil qui sont jugés douteux (degré estimatif de complétude inférieur à 90 p.100) n'ont pas été calculés. Au contraire, des taux estimatifs, calculés par les pays ou zones, ont été présentés si disponibles.

Le classement des statistiques de l'état civil en tant que sûres ou douteuses est présenté sur le plan général à la section 4.2 des Notes techniques. Les notes techniques relatives aux tableaux 9, 15 et 18 donnent respectivement des indications spécifiques sur la fiabilité des statistiques des naissances vivantes, décès d'enfants de moins d'un an, et des décès.

Etant donné que les valeurs de l'espérance de vie figurant dans ce tableau proviennent de tables officielles de mortalité, elles sont toutes présumées sûres.

Insuffisance des données: Les statistiques des naissances, décès et décès d'enfants de moins d'un an appellent toutes les réserves qui ont été faites à propos des statistiques de l'état civil en général à la section 4 des Notes techniques et dans les notes techniques relatives aux différents tableaux présentant des données détaillées sur ces événements (tableau 9, naissances vivantes; tableau 15, décès d'enfants de moins d'un an; tableau 18, décès.)

Pour évaluer la comparabilité des divers taux, il importe de tenir compte de la fiabilité des données utilisées pour calculer ces taux, comme il a été indiqué précédemment.

Il y a lieu de noter que la structure par âge et par sexe de la population influe de façon particulière sur les taux bruts. Le manque d'uniformité dans la définition des naissances vivantes et dans les procédures de mise en tableaux influe sur les taux de mortalité infantile et, à moindre degré, sur les taux bruts de natalité et les taux bruts de mortalité.

Portée : Les taux démographiques, les taux d'accroissement naturel et les valeurs de l'espérance de vie sont indiqués pour 166 pays ou zones.

NOTES

[1] *Principles and Recommendations for a Vital Statistics System Revision 2,* Sales No. E. 01.XVII.10, United Nations, New York, 2001.

4. Vital statistics summary and expectation of life at birth: 1997-2001
Aperçu des statistiques de l'état civil et espérance de vie à la naissance: 1997-2001

(See notes at end of table. — Voir notes à la fin du tableau.)

Continent, country or area and year / Continent, pays ou zone et année	Live births / Naissances vivantes			Deaths - Décès			Rate of natural increase / Taux d'accroiss-ement naturel	Infant deaths / Décès d'enfants de moins d'un an			Expectation of life at birth / Espérance de vie à la naissance		Total fertility rate / L'indice synthétique de fécondité
	Code[a]	Number Nombre	Crude birth rate Taux bruts de natalité	Code[a]	Number Nombre	Crude death rate Taux bruts de mortalité		Code[a]	Number Nombre	Rate (per 1000 births) Taux (par 1000 naissances)	Male Masculin	Female Féminin	
AFRICA — AFRIQUE													
Algeria - Algérie[1,2]													
1997	C	628 342	21.6	U	172 431	...	...	U	27 219	...	...	...	..
1998	C	620 322	21.0	U	171 775	...	...	U	33 093	...	...	...	..
1999	C	593 643	19.8	U	129 686	...	...	U	21 798	...	...	...	..
2000	C	588 628	19.4	U	127 951	...	...	U	20 291	...	...	...	..
2001	C	618 380	20.1	U	129 092	...	...	U	21 622	...	...	...	..
Benin - Bénin[3]													
1997	I	255 620	45.3	I	72 520	12.9	32.5	...	...	...	...	...	6.26(
1998	I	260 610	44.8	I	72 130	12.4	32.4	I	24 422	93.7	...	...	..
1999	I	265 980	44.4	I	71 680	12.0	32.4	...	...	...	...	...	..
2000	I	272 640	44.2	I	71 540	11.6	32.6	...	...	...	...	...	..
2001	I	263 726	41.1	I	83 417	13.0	28.1	I	25 001	94.8	...	...	..
Botswana[3]													
1997	I	49 546	32.3	I	10 675	7.0	25.3	...	...	...	65.10	68.60	..
1998	I	50 606	32.2	I	16 244	10.3	21.9	...	...	...	65.40	68.80	..
1999	I	53 407	33.2	I	16 352	10.2	23.0	...	...	...	65.70	69.00	..
2001	I	53 735	32.0	I	16 570	9.9	22.1	I	1 576	29.3	...	...	..
Burundi[3]													
1997	I	284 528	45.9	I	120 145	19.4	26.5	...	...	...	...	...	..
1998	I	290 982	46.2	I	115 693	18.4	27.8	I	45 684	157.0	...	...	..
Cape Verde - Cap-Vert													
1998	C	15 460	37.1	...	...	...	...	...	...	...	...	...	..
Chad - Tchad													
2001	...	397 896	...	...	138 025	...	...	...	...	...	...	...	..
Côte d'Ivoire[3]													
1998	I	614 667	40.0	I	189 010	12.3	27.7	I	44 045	71.7	...	...	..
2000	I	655 904	40.0	I	201 690	12.3	27.7	I	47 000	71.7	...	...	..
Egypt - Égypte													
1997	C	1 654 695	27.5	C	389 301	6.5	21.1	C	50 047	30.2	...	...	..
1998	C	1 687 252	27.5	C	399 772	6.5	21.0	C	49 168	29.1	...	...	..
1999	C	1 693 025	27.0	C	401 433	6.4	20.6	C	49 765	29.4	...	...	..
2001	...	...	...	...	...	...	...	...	...	...	65.63	67.44	..
Ethiopia - Éthiopie													
1999	...	2 186 023	...	...	1 062 114	...	...	...	232 660	...	...	...	..
Gabon													
2000	...	...	...	...	...	...	...	...	...	...	...	...	4.30(
Libyan Arab Jamahiriya - Jamahiriya arabe libyenne													
2000	C	98 752	19.3	U	17 367	...	...	U	2 155	...	...	...	..
2001	C	99 187	18.7	U	18 334	...	...	U	2 568	...	...	...	..
Malawi[4,5]													
1998	I	496 524	...	I	208 040	...	...	I	44 928	90.5	...	...	..
1999	I	531 160	...	I	234 641	...	...	...	...	...	41.06	43.77	..
2000	I	543 654	...	I	228 245	...	...	...	...	...	41.66	44.33	..
2001	I	555 558	49.9	I	221 963	19.9	29.9	...	...	...	42.25	44.90	..
Mali													
2001	U	525 685	...	...	...	...	...	...	...	...	...	...	..
Mauritius - Maurice													
1997	+C	20 012	17.4	+C	7 986	7.0	10.5	+C	406	20.3	66.86	74.47	2.037
1998	+C	19 434	16.7	+C	7 839	6.8	10.0	+C	376	19.3	66.61	74.43	1.960
1999	+C	20 311	17.3	+C	7 944	6.8	10.5	+C	396	19.5	...	...	2.050
2000	+C	20 205	17.0	+C	7 982	6.7	10.3	+C	322	15.9	...	...	1.990
2001	+C	19 696	16.4	+C	7 983	6.7	9.8	+C	282	14.3	...	...	1.930
Morocco - Maroc													
1997	C	552 141	20.2	U	87 225	...	...	U	8 056	...	...	...	..
1998	C	540 907	19.5	U	95 111	...	...	U	9 061	...	...	...	..
1999	C	529 383	18.7	U	98 304	...	...	U	8 885	...	...	...	..

4. Vital statistics summary and expectation of life at birth: 1997-2001
Aperçu des statistiques de l'état civil et espérance de vie à la naissance: 1997-2001 (continued — suite)

(See notes at end of table. — Voir notes à la fin du tableau.)

Continent, country or area and year / Continent, pays ou zone et année	Live births / Naissances vivantes			Deaths - Décès			Rate of natural increase / Taux d'accroiss-ement naturel	Infant deaths / Décès d'enfants de moins d'un an			Expectation of life at birth / Espérance de vie à la naissance		Total fertility rate / L'indice synthétique de fécondité
	Code[a]	Number / Nombre	Crude birth rate / Taux bruts de natalité	Code[a]	Number / Nombre	Crude death rate / Taux bruts de mortalité		Code[a]	Number / Nombre	Rate (per 1000 births) / Taux (par 1000 naiss-ances)	Male / Masculin	Female / Féminin	
AFRICA — AFRIQUE													
Mozambique[3,6]													
1997	...	...	...	I	385 754	23.3	...	...	...	...	...	...	5.900
2000	...	...	...	...	...	...	...	...	...	...	...	...	5.800
2001	I	753 252	42.7	I	331 162	18.8	23.9	I	99 164	131.6	...	...	5.700
Réunion[2]													
1997	C	13 712	20.0	C	3 553	5.2	14.8	C	89	6.5	...	...	...
1998	C	13 538	19.4	C	3 731	5.3	14.1	C	111	8.2	...	...	...
1999	C	14 153	19.9	C	3 825	5.4	14.5	C	84	5.9	...	...	...
2000	C	14 842	20.6	C	3 781	5.2	15.3	C	88	5.9	...	...	...
2001	C	14 541	19.8	C	3 740	5.1	14.7	C	89	6.1	...	...	...
Saint Helena ex. dep. - Sainte-Hélène sans dép.													
1997	C	64	...	C	30	...	...	C	...	...	...	...	...
1998	C	59	...	C	39	...	...	C	1	...	...	...	...
1999	C	52	...	C	45	...	...	C	...	...	...	...	...
2000	C	56	...	C	53	...	...	C	...	...	...	...	...
2001	C	36	...	C	41	...	...	C	...	...	...	...	...
Seychelles													
1997	+C	1 475	19.1	+C	603	7.8	11.3	+C	12	...	...	...	2.140
1998	+C	1 412	17.9	+C	570	7.2	10.7	+C	12	...	...	...	2.040
1999	+C	1 460	18.2	+C	560	7.0	11.2	+C	15	...	...	...	2.040
2000	+C	1 512	18.6	+C	553	6.8	11.8	+C	15	...	...	...	2.080
2001	+C	1 440	17.7	+C	554	6.8	10.9	+C	19	...	...	...	1.980
South Africa - Afrique du Sud													
1997	U	1 046 095	...	...	...	...	...	...	...	...	...	...	...
1998	U	1 216 337	...	...	...	...	...	...	...	...	...	...	...
1999	U	1 363 800	...	...	...	...	...	...	...	...	...	...	...
2000	U	1 407 833	...	...	...	...	...	...	...	...	...	...	...
Swaziland[6]													
1997	I	31 087	33.4	I	8 480	9.1	24.3	I	1 172	37.7	58.00	63.00	4.530
Tunisia - Tunisie													
1997	C	173 757	18.9	U	42 426	...	...	U	3 745	...	...	...	2.380
1998	C	166 718	17.9	U	42 571	...	...	U	3 098	...	...	...	2.230
1999	C	160 169	16.9	U	54 400	...	...	U	4 200	...	...	...	...
2001	C	163 300	16.9	U	53 300	...	...	...	...	...	...	...	...
AMERICA, NORTH — AMERIQUE DU NORD													
Anguilla													
1997	+C	169	16.3	+C	56	5.4	10.9	+C	1	...	...	...	...
1998	+C	155	14.5	+C	62	5.8	8.7	+C	...	...	...	...	...
1999	+C	176	16.1	+C	58	5.3	10.8	+C	1	...	...	...	...
2000	+C	193	17.1	+C	69	6.1	11.0	+C	1	...	...	...	...
2001	+C	183	15.8	+C	66	5.7	10.1	+C	...	...	...	...	...
Antigua and Barbuda - Antigua-et-Barbuda													
1997	+C	1 448	...	+C	468	...	...	...	...	...	...	...	...
1998	+C	1 366	...	+C	456	...	...	...	...	...	...	...	...
1999	+C	1 329	...	+C	508	...	...	...	...	...	...	...	...
2000	+C	1 528	...	+C	451	...	...	...	...	...	...	...	...
Aruba													
1997	+U	1 457	...	+U	497	...	...	...	...	...	...	...	...
1998	+U	1 315	...	+U	505	...	...	...	...	...	...	...	...
1999	+U	1 225	...	+U	554	...	...	...	...	...	...	...	...
2000	+U	1 294	...	+U	531	...	...	...	...	...	...	...	...

4. Vital statistics summary and expectation of life at birth: 1997-2001
Aperçu des statistiques de l'état civil et espérance de vie à la naissance: 1997-2001 (continued — suite)

(See notes at end of table. — Voir notes à la fin du tableau.)

Continent, country or area and year / Continent, pays ou zone et année	Live births — Naissances vivantes			Deaths - Décès			Rate of natural increase — Taux d'accroiss-ement naturel	Infant deaths — Décès d'enfants de moins d'un an			Expectation of life at birth — Espérance de vie à la naissance		Total fertility rate — L'indice synthétiq-ue de fécondité
	Code[a]	Number Nombre	Crude birth rate Taux bruts de natalité	Code[a]	Number Nombre	Crude death rate Taux bruts de mortalité		Code[a]	Number Nombre	Rate (per 1000 births) Taux (par 1000 naiss-ances)	Male Masculin	Female Féminin	
AMERICA, NORTH — AMERIQUE DU NORD													
Aruba													
2001	+U	1 266	...	+U	477	...	...	+U	4	...	...	...	...
Bahamas													
1997	...	...	...	U	1 670	...	...	...	...	...	...	...	...
1998	...	...	...	U	1 725	...	...	...	...	...	...	...	...
1999	U	6 367	...	U	1 567	...	...	U	86	...	...	...	...
Barbados - Barbade													
2000	+U	3 762	...	+U	2 367	...	...	+U	63	...	...	...	...
Belize													
1997	U	7 348	...	U	1 173	...	...	U	168	...	...	...	...
1998	U	5 986	...	U	1 350	...	...	U	144	...	...	...	...
1999	U	6 218	...	U	1 183	...	...	U	116	...	...	...	...
2000	U	7 313	...	U	1 534	...	...	U	155	...	...	...	...
2001	U	7 082	...	U	1 261	...	...	U	120	...	...	...	...
Bermuda - Bermudes													
1997	C	849	14.1	C	437	7.2	6.8	C	4	...	...	...	...
1998	C	825	...	C	505	...	...	C	...	...	...	...	...
2000	C	838	...	C	473	...	...	C	...	...	...	...	...
2001	C	831	13.4	C	442	7.1	6.3	C	3	...	...	...	...
British Virgin Islands - Îles Vierges britanniques													
2000	...	...	...	...	...	...	...	+C	1	...	...	...	...
2001	+C	318	15.4	+C	101	4.9	10.5	...	...	...	...	...	...
Canada[7]													
1997	C	348 598	11.7	C	215 669	7.2	4.4	C	1 928	5.5	...	...	...
1998	C	342 418	11.4	C	218 091	7.2	4.1	C	1 811	5.3	76.10	78.80	...
1999	C	337 249	11.1	C	219 530	7.2	3.9	C	1 776	5.3	76.30	81.70	...
2000	C	327 882	10.7	C	218 062	7.1	3.6	C	1 737	5.3	76.70	82.00	...
2001	C	333 744	10.8	C	219 538	7.1	3.7	C	1 739	5.2	...	...	...
Cayman Islands - Îles Caïmanes													
1997	C	572	15.9	C	123	3.4	12.5	...	...	...	...	...	...
1998	C	545	14.5	C	117	3.1	11.4	...	...	...	...	...	...
1999	C	604	15.5	C	128	3.3	12.2	...	...	...	...	...	...
2000	C	619	15.4	C	137	3.4	12.0	...	...	...	...	...	...
2001	C	622	15.0	C	132	3.2	11.9	...	...	...	...	...	...
Costa Rica													
1997	C	78 018	22.5	C	14 260	4.1	18.4	C	1 108	14.2	...	...	2.680
1998	C	76 982	21.8	C	14 708	4.2	17.7	C	970	12.6	...	...	2.600
1999	C	78 526	21.9	C	15 052	4.2	17.7	C	925	11.8	...	...	2.600
2000	C	78 178	19.9	C	14 944	3.8	16.1	C	798	10.2	...	...	...
2001	C	76 401	19.2	C	15 609	3.9	15.2	C	827	10.8	...	...	...
Cuba													
1997	C	152 681	13.8	C	77 316	7.0	6.8	C	1 098	7.2	...	...	...
1998	C	151 080	13.6	C	77 565	7.0	6.6	C	1 070	7.1	...	...	...
1999	C	150 785	13.5	C	79 499	7.1	6.4	C	977	6.5	...	...	...
2000	C	143 528	12.8	C	76 463	6.8	6.0	C	1 039	7.2	...	...	...
2001	C	138 718	12.4	C	79 395	7.1	5.3	C	861	6.2	...	...	...
Dominica - Dominique													
1997	+C	1 340	17.7	+C	513	6.8	10.9	...	...	...	...	...	...
1998	+C	1 230	16.2	+C	595	7.8	8.4	...	...	...	...	...	...
1999	+C	1 291	...	+C	631	...	...	...	...	...	...	...	...
2000	+C	1 199	16.8	+C	503	7.0	9.7	...	...	...	...	...	...

74

4. Vital statistics summary and expectation of life at birth: 1997-2001
Aperçu des statistiques de l'état civil et espérance de vie à la naissance: 1997-2001 (continued — suite)

(ee notes at end of table. — Voir notes à la fin du tableau.)

Continent, country or area and year / Continent, pays ou zone et année	Live births - Naissances vivantes			Deaths - Décès			Rate of natural increase Taux d'accroiss-ement naturel	Infant deaths - Décès d'enfants de moins d'un an			Expectation of life at birth Espérance de vie à la naissance		Total fertility rate L'indice synthétique de fécondité
	Code[a]	Number Nombre	Crude birth rate Taux bruts de natalité	Code[a]	Number Nombre	Crude death rate Taux bruts de mortalité		Code[a]	Number Nombre	Rate (per 1000 births) Taux (par 1000 naissances)	Male Masculin	Female Féminin	
AMERICA, NORTH — AMERIQUE DU NORD													
Dominican Republic - République dominicaine													
1997	+U	164 556	...	+U	26 301	...	...	+U	1 970	...	...	...	...
1998	+U	179 372	...	+U	25 278	...	...	+U	1 972	...	...	...	...
1999	+U	193 418	...	+U	26 956	...	...	+U	1 966	...	...	...	...
2000	+U	189 332	...	+U	23 776	...	...	+U	2 116	...	...	...	...
El Salvador													
1997	C	164 143	27.8	C	29 118	4.9	22.9	C	2 710	16.5	...	...	...
1998	C	158 350	26.3	C	29 919	5.0	21.3	C	2 380	15.0	...	...	...
1999	C	153 636	25.0	C	28 056	4.6	20.4	C	1 768	11.5	...	...	...
2000	C	150 176	23.9	C	28 154	4.5	19.4	C	1 678	11.2	67.70	73.70	...
2001	C	138 354	21.6	C	29 559	4.6	17.0	C	1 682	12.2			
Greenland - Groenland													
1997	C	1 100	19.5	C	492	8.7	10.8	C	20	...	...	...	2.617
1998	C	986	17.6	C	468	8.3	9.2	C	25	...	...	...	2.393
1999	C	947	16.9	C	482	8.6	8.3	C	16	...	...	...	2.340
Grenada - Grenade													
1997	+C	2 191	22.0	+C	707	7.1	14.9	+C	31	14.1	...	...	...
1998	+C	1 938	19.4	+C	819	8.2	11.2	+C	37	19.1	...	...	...
1999	+C	1 791	17.8	+C	794	7.9	9.9	+C	29	...	...	...	...
2000	+C	1 883	18.6	+C	716	7.1	11.5	+C	27	...	...	...	...
2001	+C	1 899	18.8	+C	727	7.2	11.6	+C	33	17.4	...	...	...
Guatemala													
1997	C	387 862	36.9	C	67 691	6.4	30.4	C	15 413	39.7	...	...	...
1998	C	489 829	45.4	C	70 504	6.5	38.8	C	15 414	31.5	...	...	...
1999	C	360 759	32.5	C	64 563	5.8	26.7	C	13 161	36.5	...	...	...
2000	C	426 346	37.4	C	66 831	5.9	31.6	C	13 247	31.1	...	...	...
2001	C	403 532	34.5	C	69 934	6.0	28.6	...	...	...	...	...	...
Jamaica - Jamaïque													
1997	+C	59 385	23.3	+C	15 087	5.9	17.3	...	...	...	...	...	...
1998	+C	56 937	22.1	+C	18 110	7.0	15.1	+C	480	8.4	...	...	...
1999	+C	56 911	22.0	+C	17 353	6.7	15.3	...	...	...	...	...	...
2000	+C	54 035	20.7	+C	16 338	6.3	14.5	...	...	...	...	...	...
2001	+C	55 270	21.1	+C	17 205	6.6	14.5	...	...	...	...	...	...
Mexico - Mexique													
1997	+U	2 698 425	...	C	440 437	4.6	...	C	44 377	16.4	...	...	...
1998	+U	2 668 428	...	C	444 665	4.6	...	C	42 183	15.8	...	...	...
1999	+U	2 769 089	...	C	443 950	4.5	...	C	40 283	14.5	...	...	...
2000	+U	2 798 339	...	C	437 667	4.4	...	C	38 621	13.8	...	...	...
2001	+U	2 767 610	...	C	443 127	4.4	...	C	35 911	13.0	...	...	...
Netherlands Antilles - Antilles néerlandaises													
1997	C	3 558	17.1	C	1 235	5.9	11.2	...	...	...	...	...	...
1998	C	3 111	15.0	C	1 282	6.2	8.8	...	...	...	...	...	...
1999	C	2 803	13.7	C	1 321	6.4	7.2	...	...	...	...	...	...
Nicaragua													
1997	+U	113 498	...	+U	13 916	...	...	+U	2 474	...	...	...	...
1998	+U	111 154	...	+U	14 804	...	...	+U	2 552	...	...	...	...
1999	+U	91 670	...	+U	13 771	...	...	+U	1 768	...	...	...	...
2000	+U	92 859	...	+U	10 603	...	...	+U	1 649	...	...	...	...
Panama													
1997	C	68 009	25.0	U	12 179	...	...	U	1 170	...	...	...	...
1998	C	62 351	22.6	U	11 824	...	...	U	1 047	...	...	...	...
1999	C	64 248	22.9	U	11 938	...	...	U	1 005	...	...	...	...
2000	C	64 839	22.7	U	11 841	...	...	U	1 081	...	72.19	76.81	...

4. Vital statistics summary and expectation of life at birth: 1997-2001
Aperçu des statistiques de l'état civil et espérance de vie à la naissance: 1997-2001 (continued — suite)

(See notes at end of table. — Voir notes à la fin du tableau.)

Continent, country or area and year / Continent, pays ou zone et année	Live births - Naissances vivantes			Deaths - Décès			Rate of natural increase Taux d'accroiss-ement naturel	Infant deaths - Décès d'enfants de moins d'un an			Expectation of life at birth Espérance de vie à la naissance		Total fertility rate L'indice synthétique de fécondité
	Code[a]	Number Nombre	Crude birth rate Taux bruts de natalité	Code[a]	Number Nombre	Crude death rate Taux bruts de mortalité		Code[a]	Number Nombre	Rate (per 1000 births) Taux (par 1000 naiss-ances)	Male Masculin	Female Féminin	
AMERICA, NORTH — AMERIQUE DU NORD													
Panama													
2001	C	63 900	22.1	U	12 442	...	...	U	1 053	...	...	...	2.4
Puerto Rico - Porto Rico													
1997	C	64 214	17.3	C	29 119	7.8	9.4	C	724	11.3	71.41	79.34	
1998	C	60 518	16.1	C	29 990	8.0	8.1	C	637	10.5	...	...	
1999	C	59 684	15.8	C	29 145	7.7	8.1	C	632	10.6	...	...	
2000	C	59 460	15.6	C	28 550	7.5	8.1	C	589	9.9	...	...	
2001	C	55 982	14.6	C	28 794	7.5	7.1	C	515	9.2	...	...	
Saint Kitts and Nevis - Saint-Kitts-et-Nevis													
1997	+C	875	21.5	+C	393	9.6	11.8	+C	20	...	67.67	71.10	2.6
1998	+C	865	21.6	+C	390	9.7	11.8	+C	24	...	68.21	70.66	2.6
1999	+C	864	20.3	+C	418	9.8	10.5	...	...	...	...	...	
2000	+C	838	20.7	+C	357	8.8	11.9	...	...	...	...	...	
2001	+C	803	17.4	+C	352	7.6	9.8	...	...	...	...	...	
Saint Lucia - Sainte-Lucie[8]													
1997	C	3 303	22.1	C	976	6.5	15.5	C	58	17.6	70.76	72.81	2.5
1998	C	2 950	19.4	C	976	6.4	13.0	C	48	16.3	70.40	72.35	2.5
1999	C	2 997	19.5	C	981	6.4	13.1	C	42	14.0	69.46	73.18	
2000	C	2 840	18.2	C	939	6.0	12.2	C	38	13.4	68.73	73.63	
2001	C	2 919	18.5	C	960	6.1	12.4	C	40	13.7	...	...	
Saint Vincent and the Grenadines - Saint Vincent-et-les Grenadines[8]													
1997	+C	2 311	20.7	+C	736	6.6	14.1	+C	41	17.7	...	...	
1998	+C	2 112	19.0	+C	830	7.5	11.5	+C	47	22.3	...	...	
1999	+C	2 149	19.3	+C	833	7.5	11.8	+C	47	21.9	...	...	
2000	+C	2 171	19.4	+C	697	6.2	13.2	+C	35	16.1	...	...	
2001	+C	1 967	18.0	+C	720	6.6	11.4	+C	38	19.3	...	...	
Trinidad and Tobago - Trinité-et-Tobago													
1997	C	18 452	14.5	C	9 157	7.2	7.3	C	316	17.1	...	...	1.7
United States - États-Unis													
1997	C	3 880 894	14.5	C	2 314 245	8.6	5.8	C	28 045	7.2	73.60	79.20	2.0
1998	C	3 941 553	14.6	C	2 337 256	8.6	5.9	C	28 371	7.2	73.80	79.50	
1999	C	3 959 417	14.5	C	2 391 399	8.8	5.8	C	27 937	7.1	73.90	79.40	
2000	C	4 058 814	14.7	C	2 403 351	8.7	6.0	C	28 035	6.9	74.30	79.70	
2001	C	4 025 933	14.1	C	2 417 762	8.5	5.6	C	27 798	6.9	74.40	79.80	
AMERICA, SOUTH — AMERIQUE DU SUD													
Argentina - Argentine													
1997	C	692 357	19.4	C	270 910	7.6	11.8	C	12 985	18.8	...	...	2.5
1998	C	683 301	18.9	C	280 180	7.8	11.2	C	13 082	19.1	...	...	
1999	C	686 748	18.8	C	289 543	7.9	10.9	C	12 120	17.6	...	...	
2000	C	701 878	19.0	C	277 148	7.5	11.5	C	11 649	16.6	...	...	
2001	C	683 495	18.2	C	285 941	7.6	10.6	C	11 111	16.3	...	...	
Bolivia - Bolivie													
1997	...	...	...	U	71 543	...	...	U	17 324	...	...	...	
1998	...	...	...	U	71 618	...	...	U	16 942	...	...	...	
1999	...	...	...	U	71 680	...	...	U	16 492	...	...	...	
2000	U	264 941	...	U	71 742	...	...	U	16 042	...	...	...	

(See notes at end of table. — Voir notes à la fin du tableau.)

Continent, country or area and year / Continent, pays ou zone et année	Live births - Naissances vivantes			Deaths - Décès			Rate of natural increase - Taux d'accroissement naturel	Infant deaths - Décès d'enfants de moins d'un an			Expectation of life at birth - Espérance de vie à la naissance		Total fertility rate - L'indice synthétique de fécondité
	Code[a]	Number Nombre	Crude birth rate Taux bruts de natalité	Code[a]	Number Nombre	Crude death rate Taux bruts de mortalité		Code[a]	Number Nombre	Rate (per 1000 births) Taux (par 1000 naissances)	Male Masculin	Female Féminin	
AMERICA, SOUTH — AMERIQUE DU SUD													
Brazil - Brésil[8,9]													
1997	...	...	...	...	...	...	...	...	...	...	64.70	70.91	2.286
1998	U	2 459 275	...	U	936 885	...	...	U	64 702	...	64.40	72.00	2.254
1999	U	2 657 613	...	U	943 524	...	...	U	58 767	...	...	...	2.226
2000	U	2 611 422	...	U	927 783	...	...	U	53 097	...	64.77	72.55	2.200
2001	U	2 509 354	...	U	931 017	...	...	U	47 171	...	...	...	2.180
Chile - Chili[8]													
1997	C	259 959	17.8	C	78 472	5.4	12.4	C	2 732	10.5	72.13	78.10	...
1998	C	257 105	17.3	C	80 257	5.4	11.9	C	2 793	10.9	72.28	78.26	...
1999	C	250 674	16.7	C	81 977	5.5	11.2	C	2 651	10.6	72.43	78.42	...
Colombia - Colombie[10]													
1997	+U	990 057	...	+U	170 753	...	...	+U	11 092	...	...	...	2.800
1998	+U	718 880	...	+U	175 442	...	...	+U	14 180	...	...	...	2.760
1999	U	746 194	...	U	183 553	...	...	U	14 621	...	...	...	2.730
2000	U	734 081	...	U	183 865	...	...	U	14 927	...	69.17	75.32	...
2001	...	...	...	...	...	...	...	...	...	...	69.40	75.52	...
Ecuador - Équateur[11]													
1997	U	169 869	...	U	52 089	...	...	U	5 463	...	...	...	...
1998	U	199 079	...	U	54 357	...	...	U	5 186	...	...	...	...
1999	U	218 108	...	U	55 921	...	...	U	5 372	...	...	...	...
2000	U	202 257	...	U	56 420	...	...	U	5 480	...	...	...	...
Falkland Islands (Malvinas) - Îles Falkland (Malvinas)													
1997	+C	29	...	+C	16	...	...	...	...	...	...	...	...
1998	+C	28	...	+C	12	...	...	...	...	...	...	...	...
1999	+C	33	...	+C	20	...	...	...	...	...	...	...	...
2000	+C	27	...	+C	11	...	...	...	...	...	...	...	...
French Guiana - Guyane française[2]													
1997	C	4 453	...	C	562	...	...	C	55	12.4	72.40	78.70	4.000
1998	C	4 696	...	C	614	...	...	C	52	11.1	...	...	...
1999	C	4 907	31.0	...	...	...	...	...	...	...	...	...	...
Guyana													
1997	...	...	...	+C	5 117	6.6	...	...	...	...	...	...	...
1998	...	...	...	+C	4 977	6.4	...	...	...	...	...	...	...
1999	...	...	...	+C	4 197	5.4	...	...	...	...	...	...	...
Paraguay													
2000	...	...	...	...	...	...	...	...	...	...	68.60	73.10	3.800
Peru - Pérou[9,12]													
1997	C	652 467	26.8	C	157 500	6.5	20.3	C	28 252	43.3	...	...	...
1998	C	648 075	26.1	C	158 500	6.4	19.7	C	26 603	41.0	...	...	...
1999	C	642 874	25.5	C	159 900	6.3	19.1	C	25 098	39.0	...	...	...
2000	C	636 064	24.8	C	161 000	6.3	18.5	C	23 681	37.2	...	...	...
2001	C	630 947	23.9	C	164 296	6.2	17.7	C	22 455	35.6	...	...	...
Suriname													
1997	C	10 794	25.8	C	2 878	6.9	18.9	C	237	22.0	...	...	...
1998	C	10 221	24.1	C	2 814	6.6	17.4	C	163	15.9	...	...	...
1999	C	10 144	23.6	C	2 992	7.0	16.6	C	227	22.4	...	...	...
2000	C	9 804	22.5	C	3 090	7.1	15.4	C	156	15.9	...	...	...
Uruguay													
1997	+C	58 032	17.8	C	30 459	9.3	8.4	C	955	16.5	...	...	...
1998	+C	54 127	16.5	C	32 082	9.8	6.7	C	901	16.6	...	...	...
1999	+C	54 004	16.3	C	32 430	9.8	6.5	C	776	14.4	...	...	...
2000	+C	52 770	15.8	C	30 456	9.1	6.7	C	742	14.1	...	...	2.300

4. Vital statistics summary and expectation of life at birth: 1997-2001
Aperçu des statistiques de l'état civil et espérance de vie à la naissance: 1997-2001 (continued — suite)

(See notes at end of table. — Voir notes à la fin du tableau.)

Continent, country or area and year / Continent, pays ou zone et année	Code[a] / Code[a]	Live births - Naissances vivantes		Code[a] / Code[a]	Deaths - Décès		Rate of natural increase / Taux d'accroissement naturel	Code[a] / Code[a]	Infant deaths - Décès d'enfants de moins d'un an		Expectation of life at birth - Espérance de vie à la naissance		Total fertility ra... / L'indice synthétiq ue de féconditi...
		Number / Nombre	Crude birth rate / Taux bruts de natalité		Number / Nombre	Crude death rate / Taux bruts de mortalité			Number / Nombre	Rate (per 1000 births) / Taux (par 1000 naiss-ances)	Male / Masculin	Female / Féminin	
AMERICA, SOUTH — AMERIQUE DU SUD													
Venezuela[9]													
1997	C	516 636	22.7	C	94 334	4.1	18.5	C	9 684	18.7	...	...	3.0...
1998	C	501 808	21.6	C	98 624	4.2	17.3	C	9 871	19.7	...	...	2.9...
1999	C	527 888	22.3	C	101 907	4.3	18.0	...	...	...	...	...	
2000	C	544 416	22.5	C	103 255	4.3	18.3	C	8 524	15.7	...	...	
2001	C	529 552	21.5	C	107 867	4.4	17.1	...					
ASIA — ASIE													
Armenia - Arménie[13]													
1997	C	43 929	11.6	C	23 985	6.3	5.3	C	678	15.4	70.30	77.30	1.4...
1998	C	39 366	10.4	C	23 210	6.1	4.3	C	580	14.7	70.80	78.00	1.2...
1999	C	36 502	9.6	C	24 087	6.3	3.3	C	572	15.7	70.65	75.51	1.1...
2000	C	34 276	9.0	C	24 025	6.3	2.7	C	540	15.8	70.65	75.51	1.1...
2001	C	32 065	8.4	C	24 003	6.3	2.1	C	497	15.5	...	...	
Azerbaijan - Azerbaïdjan[13]													
1997	+C	132 052	16.8	+C	46 962	6.0	10.9	+C	2 589	19.6	67.40	74.60	2.1...
1998	+C	123 996	15.7	+C	46 299	5.9	9.8	+C	2 061	16.6	67.90	75.00	2.0...
1999	+C	117 539	14.7	+C	46 295	5.8	8.9	+C	1 943	16.5	68.10	75.10	2.0...
2000	+C	116 994	14.5	+C	46 701	5.8	8.7	+C	1 501	12.8	68.63	75.10	1.9...
2001	+C	110 356	13.6	+C	45 284	5.6	8.0	+C	1 382	12.5	68.65	75.20	1.8...
Bahrain - Bahreïn													
1997	U	13 382	...	U	1 822	...	...	U	108	...	...	...	2.7...
1998	U	13 381	...	U	1 997	...	...	U	111	...	...	...	2.7...
1999	U	14 280	...	U	1 920	...	...	U	129	...	...	...	2.8...
2000	U	13 947	...	U	2 045	...	...		...	...	...	...	
2001	U	13 468	...	U	1 979	...	...	U	117	...	...	...	
Bangladesh													
1997	U	3 057 000	...	U	958 000	...	...	U	202 000	...	...	...	
Brunei Darussalam - Brunéi Darussalam													
1997	+C	7 459	23.7	+C	883	2.8	20.9	+C	55	7.4	...	...	2.7...
1998	+C	7 411	22.9	+C	928	2.9	20.1	+C	48	6.5	...	...	2.7...
1999	+C	7 408	22.4	+C	905	2.7	19.7	+C	44	5.9	...	...	2.7...
2000	+C	7 481	22.1	+C	965	2.9	19.3	+C	55	7.4	...	...	2.7...
China - Chine[14,15]													
1997	I	20 380 000	16.5	...	8 010 000	...	...	...	...	...	...	...	1.8...
1998	I	19 910 000	16.0	...	8 070 000	...	...	...	...	...	...	...	
1999	I	19 090 000	15.2	...	8 100 000	...	...	...	...	...	...	...	
2000	...	...	12.9	...	...	6.4	...	...	...	...	...	...	
2001	...	...	13.4	...	...	6.4	...	...	...	...	...	...	
China: Hong Kong SAR - Chine: Hong Kong RAS													
1997	C	59 250	9.1	C	31 738	4.9	4.2	C	229	3.9	76.77	82.18	1.0...
1998	C	52 977	8.1	C	32 847	5.0	3.1	C	167	3.2	77.17	82.56	0.9...
1999	C	51 281	7.8	C	33 255	5.0	2.7	C	157	3.1	77.15	82.35	0.9...
2000	C	54 134	8.1	C	33 758	5.1	3.1	C	162	3.0	76.98	82.24	1.0...
2001	C	48 219	7.2	C	33 378	5.0	2.2	C	124	2.6	...	...	
China: Macao SAR - Chine: Macao RAS													
1997	C	5 031	12.1	C	1 293	3.1	9.0	C	27	...	...	...	
1998	C	4 434	10.5	C	1 356	3.2	7.3	C	27	...	...	...	
1999	C	4 148	9.7	C	1 374	3.2	6.5	C	17	...	...	...	
2000	C	3 849	8.9	C	1 338	3.1	5.8	C	11	...	...	...	
2001	C	3 241	7.5	C	1 327	3.1	4.4	C	14	...	...	...	

4. Vital statistics summary and expectation of life at birth: 1997-2001
Aperçu des statistiques de l'état civil et espérance de vie à la naissance: 1997-2001 (continued — suite)

(e notes at end of table. — Voir notes à la fin du tableau.)

tinent, country or area year / tinent, pays ou zone et ée	Live births Naissances vivantes			Deaths - Décès			Rate of natural increase Taux d'accroiss-ement naturel	Infant deaths Décès d'enfants de moins d'un an			Expectation of life at birth Espérance de vie à la naissance		Total fertility rate L'indice synthétiq-ue de fécondité
	Co-de[a]	Number Nombre	Crude birth rate Taux bruts de natalité	Co-de[a]	Number Nombre	Crude death rate Taux bruts de mortalité		Co-de[a]	Number Nombre	Rate (per 1000 births) Taux (par 1000 naiss-ances)	Male Masculin	Female Féminin	
A — ASIE													
Cyprus - Chypre[16]													
1997	C	9 275	12.2	C	5 173	6.8	5.4	C	74	8.0	...	...	2.004
1998	C	8 879	11.6	C	5 432	7.1	4.5	C	62	7.0	75.33	80.37	1.918
1999	C	8 505	11.0	C	5 070	6.5	4.4	C	51	6.0	...	...	1.840
2000	C	8 447	10.8	C	5 355	6.9	4.0	C	47	5.6	...	...	1.835
2001	C	8 167	10.4	C	4 827	6.1	4.2	...	...	...	...	...	...
Georgia - Géorgie[13]													
1997	C	52 000	9.6	C	37 679	6.9	2.6	C	849	16.3	...	...	1.290
1998	C	46 800	8.6	C	39 400	7.2	1.4	C	710	15.2	...	...	1.160
1999	C	40 778	8.9	C	40 378	8.8	0.1	C	714	17.5	...	...	1.070
2000	C	40 392	8.0	C	41 320	8.2	-0.2	C	600	14.9	...	...	1.100
2001	C	40 416	8.2	C	39 339	8.0	0.2	C	478	11.8	...	...	...
India - Inde[17,18]													
1997	...	...	27.2	...	...	8.9	18.3	...	...	71.0	...	...	3.300
1998	...	...	26.4	...	...	9.0	17.4	...	...	72.0	...	...	3.200
1999	...	...	26.0	...	...	8.6	...	...	...	70.0	...	...	3.200
2000	...	...	...	...	...	...	...	...	...	...	...	...	3.200
2001	...	...	25.4	...	...	8.4	17.0	...	...	66.0	...	...	...
Indonesia - Indonésie													
1998	...	...	...	...	...	...	...	...	...	...	...	...	2.676
1999	...	...	...	...	...	...	...	...	...	...	...	...	2.593
2000	...	...	...	...	...	...	...	...	...	...	...	...	2.544
Iran (Islamic Republic of) - Iran (République islamique d')													
1997	C	1 179 260	19.4	...	...	...	...	...	...	...	...	...	...
1998	C	1 185 639	19.2	...	...	...	...	...	...	...	...	...	...
1999	C	1 177 557	18.8	C	374 838	6.0	12.8	C	39 183	33.3	...	...	...
Iraq[19]													
1997	U	520 787	...	U	144 787	...	...	...	...	...	...	...	...
1998	U	519 216	...	U	160 039	...	...	...	...	...	...	...	...
1999	U	532 916	...	U	177 483	...	...	...	...	...	...	...	...
2000	U	471 886	...	U	179 928	...	...	...	...	...	...	...	...
Israel - Israël[20]													
1997	C	124 478	21.4	C	36 124	6.2	15.2	C	802	6.4	76.05	80.44	2.933
1998	C	130 080	21.8	C	36 955	6.2	15.6	C	774	6.0	76.14	80.61	2.982
1999	C	131 936	21.5	C	37 289	6.1	15.5	C	769	5.8	...	...	2.941
2000	C	136 390	21.7	C	37 669	6.0	15.7	C	745	5.5	...	...	2.945
2001	C	136 638	21.2	C	37 162	5.8	15.4	C	694	5.1	...	...	...
Japan - Japon[21]													
1997	C	1 191 665	9.5	C	913 402	7.2	2.2	C	4 403	3.7	77.19	83.82	1.388
1998	C	1 203 147	9.5	C	936 484	7.4	2.1	C	4 380	3.6	77.16	84.01	1.384
1999	C	1 177 669	9.3	C	982 031	7.8	1.5	C	4 010	3.4	77.10	83.99	1.340
2000	C	1 190 547	9.4	C	961 653	7.6	1.8	C	3 830	3.2	77.64	84.62	...
2001	C	1 170 662	9.2	C	970 331	7.6	1.6	C	3 599	3.1	...	...	...
Jordan - Jordanie[22]													
1997	C	130 633	28.4	C	13 190	2.9	25.5	...	...	...	...	...	...
1998	C	133 714	28.1	C	13 552	2.8	25.3	...	...	...	...	...	...
1999	C	135 266	27.6	C	13 936	2.8	24.8	...	...	...	...	...	...
2000	C	143 800	28.5	C	13 339	2.6	25.9	...	...	...	...	...	...
2001	C	143 000	27.6	C	16 200	3.1	24.5	...	...	...	...	...	...
Kazakhstan[13]													
1997	C	232 356	14.8	C	160 138	10.2	4.6	C	5 889	25.3	59.04	70.20	1.863
1998	C	222 380	14.8	C	154 314	10.2	4.5	C	4 843	21.8	...	...	...
1999	C	211 815	14.2	C	145 880	9.8	4.4	C	4 423	20.9	...	...	...
2000	C	217 379	14.6	C	148 834	10.0	4.6	C	4 148	19.1	...	...	...

4. Vital statistics summary and expectation of life at birth: 1997-2001
Aperçu des statistiques de l'état civil et espérance de vie à la naissance: 1997-2001 (continued — suite)

(See notes at end of table. — Voir notes à la fin du tableau.)

Continent, country or area and year / Continent, pays ou zone et année	Code[a]	Live births Naissances vivantes — Number Nombre	Crude birth rate Taux bruts de natalité	Code[a]	Deaths - Décès — Number Nombre	Crude death rate Taux bruts de mortalité	Rate of natural increase Taux d'accroiss-ement naturel	Code[a]	Infant deaths Décès d'enfants de moins d'un an — Number Nombre	Rate (per 1000 births) Taux (par 1000 naiss-ances)	Expectation of life at birth — Male Masculin	Female Féminin	Total fertility rate L'indice synthétique de fécondité
ASIA — ASIE													
Kazakhstan[13]													
2001	C	220 748	14.9	C	147 587	10.0	4.9	C	4 233	19.2	...	...	
Korea (Republic of) - Corée (République de)[23]													
1997	C	675 227	14.7	C	244 763	5.3	9.4	C	1 716	2.5	70.56	78.12	1.54
1998	C	640 126	13.8	C	245 597	5.3	8.5	C	1 460	2.3	...	...	1.46
1999	C	616 322	13.2	C	246 539	5.3	7.9	C	2 776	4.5	71.71	79.22	1.41
2000	C	636 780	13.5	C	247 346	5.3	8.3	C	2 885	4.5	...	...	1.47
2001	C	557 228	11.8	C	242 730	5.1	6.6	C	3 008	5.4			
Kuwait - Koweït													
1997	C	42 815	21.6	C	3 895	2.0	19.7	C	537	12.5	...	...	
1998	C	41 424	20.4	C	4 216	2.1	18.4	C	450	10.9	...	...	4.14
1999	C	41 135	19.5	C	4 187	2.0	17.5	C	386	9.4	...	...	4.16
2000	C	41 843	19.1	C	4 227	1.9	17.2	C	379	9.1	...	...	4.22
2001	C	41 342	18.2	C	4 364	1.9	16.3	C	420	10.2	...	...	
Kyrgyzstan - Kirghizistan[13]													
1997	C	102 050	21.8	C	34 540	7.4	14.4	C	2 920	28.6	62.55	71.35	2.78
1998	C	104 183	21.9	C	34 596	7.3	14.6	C	2 708	26.0	63.14	71.20	2.81
1999	C	104 068	21.5	C	32 850	6.8	14.7	C	2 360	22.7	63.10	71.10	2.62
2000	C	96 770	19.8	C	34 111	7.0	12.8	C	2 225	23.0	64.87	72.40	2.40
2001	C	98 138	19.9	C	32 677	6.6	13.3	C	2 123	21.6			
Lao People's Democratic Republic - République démocratique populaire lao													
2000	...	...	...	...	...	...	...	...	...	...	...	...	4.90
Lebanon - Liban[19]													
1997	U	85 018	...	U	19 884	...	...	...	...	...	...	...	
1998	U	84 250	...	U	20 097	...	...	...	...	...	...	...	
1999	U	85 516	...	U	19 133	...	...	...	...	...	...	...	
2000	U	85 760	...	U	18 756	...	...	...	...	...	...	...	
Malaysia - Malaisie													
1997	C	540 486	24.9	C	97 432	4.5	20.4	C	5 086	9.4	69.58	74.47	3.23
1998	C	524 696	23.7	C	98 219	4.4	19.2	C	4 483	8.5	69.57	74.65	3.29
1999	C	554 200	24.4	C	100 900	4.4	20.0	C	4 400	7.9	...	...	
2000	C	569 500	24.5	C	102 100	4.4	20.1	C	4 500	7.9	...	...	
Maldives													
1997	C	6 184	23.9	C	1 175	4.5	19.4	C	165	26.7	69.20	70.15	
1998	C	5 687	21.3	C	1 130	4.2	17.0	C	115	20.2	...	...	
1999	C	5 226	18.8	C	1 050	3.8	15.0	C	104	19.9	...	...	
2000	C	5 314	19.6	C	1 031	3.8	15.8	C	113	21.3	...	...	
2001	C	4 882	17.7	C	1 081	3.9	13.8	C	85	17.4	...	...	
Mongolia - Mongolie													
1997	C	49 488	21.5	C	16 980	7.4	14.2	C	1 962	39.6	...	...	2.50
1998	C	49 256	21.2	C	15 860	6.8	14.3	C	1 741	35.3	...	...	2.38
1999	C	49 461	21.0	C	16 105	6.8	14.1	C	1 846	37.3	...	...	2.36
2000	C	48 721	20.4	C	15 472	6.5	13.9	C	1 596	32.8	...	...	2.30
2001	C	49 685	20.5	C	15 999	6.6	13.9	C	1 464	29.5	...	...	2.22
Nepal - Népal[24]													
2001	...	...	...	I	106 789	...	...	I	13 037	...	...	...	
Occupied Palestinian Territory - Territoire palestinien occupé													
1997	U	97 473	...	U	8 745	...	...	U	1 353	...	...	...	6.04
1998	U	99 587	...	U	8 540	...	...	U	1 332	...	...	...	
1999	U	96 486	...	U	8 479	...	...	U	1 066	...	...	...	5.93

4. Vital statistics summary and expectation of life at birth: 1997-2001
Aperçu des statistiques de l'état civil et espérance de vie à la naissance: 1997-2001 (continued — suite)

(See notes at end of table. — Voir notes à la fin du tableau.)

Continent, country or area and year / Continent, pays ou zone et année	Live births — Naissances vivantes Code[a]	Number Nombre	Crude birth rate Taux bruts de natalité	Deaths — Décès Code[a]	Number Nombre	Crude death rate Taux bruts de mortalité	Rate of natural increase Taux d'accroiss-ement naturel	Infant deaths — Décès d'enfants de moins d'un an Code[a]	Number Nombre	Rate (per 1000 births) Taux (par 1000 naissances)	Expectation of life at birth — Male Masculin	Female Féminin	Total fertility rate L'indice synthétiq-ue de fécondité
A — ASIE													
Occupied Palestinian Territory - Territoire palestinien occupé													
2000	U	97 529	...	U	8 601	...	...	U	1 033	...	...	...	...
2001	U	93 596	...	U	8 678	...	...	U	1 087	...	70.45	73.59	...
Oman[19]													
1997	...	45 482	...	...	2 354	...	...	...	368	...	...	...	...
1998	...	45 303	...	...	2 297	...	...	...	374	...	...	...	...
1999	...	44 067	...	...	2 440	...	...	...	386	...	...	...	...
Pakistan[25,26]													
1997	I	4 143 507	32.3	I	1 089 595	8.5	23.8	I	349 746	84.4	...	...	5.040
Philippines													
1997	C	1 653 236	23.1	C	339 400	4.7	18.4	C	28 061	17.0	...	...	2.900
1998	C	1 632 859	22.3	C	352 992	4.8	17.5	C	28 196	17.3	...	...	2.800
1999	C	1 613 335	21.6	C	347 989	4.7	16.9	C	25 168	15.6	...	...	...
2000	C	1 766 440	23.1	C	366 931	4.8	18.3	C	27 714	15.7	...	...	...
Qatar													
1997	C	10 447	...	C	1 060	...	...	C	130	12.4	...	...	...
1998	C	10 781	19.8	C	1 157	2.1	17.7	C	141	13.1	...	...	...
1999	C	10 846	...	C	1 148	...	...	C	112	10.3	...	...	...
2000	C	11 250	...	C	1 173	...	...	C	132	11.7	...	...	...
2001	C	12 118	20.3	C	1 210	2.0	18.2	C	111	9.2	...	...	...
Saudi Arabia - Arabie saoudite													
1999	...	509 352	...	...	68 521	...	...	...	11 344	...	...	...	...
2000	...	578 772	...	...	51 614	...	...	...	11 071	...	...	...	...
Singapore - Singapour[27,28]													
1997	C	47 333	12.5	C	15 307	4.0	8.4	+C	179	3.8	75.00	79.20	1.630
1998	C	43 664	11.1	C	15 657	4.0	7.1	+C	183	4.2	75.40	79.50	1.470
1999	C	43 336	11.0	C	15 516	3.9	7.0	+C	150	3.5	75.60	79.70	1.460
2000	C	46 997	11.7	C	15 693	3.9	7.8	C	137	2.9	76.00	80.00	1.580
2001	C	41 451	10.0	C	15 367	3.7	6.3	C	100	2.4	...	...	...
Sri Lanka													
1997	+C	332 626	17.9	+C	113 078	6.1	11.8	...	...	...	...	...	...
1998	+C	329 148	17.5	+C	112 657	6.0	11.5	...	...	...	...	...	...
1999	+C	329 121	17.3	+C	114 392	6.0	11.3	...	...	...	...	...	...
2001	...	...	...	...	...	...	...	+C	4 323	...	...	...	...
Syrian Arab Republic - République arabe syrienne[2,29,30]													
1997	C	496 140	32.9	U	53 366	...	...	...	...	...	...	...	...
1998	C	505 008	32.4	U	57 893	...	...	...	...	...	...	...	...
1999	C	503 473	31.3	U	56 564	...	...	...	...	...	...	...	...
2000	C	505 484	31.0	U	57 759	...	...	...	...	...	...	...	...
2001	C	524 212	31.4	U	60 814	...	...	...	...	...	...	...	...
Tajikistan - Tadjikistan[13]													
1999	C	110 300	17.7	C	24 900	4.0	13.7	C	2 200	19.9	...	...	...
Thailand - Thaïlande													
1997	+U	897 604	...	+U	303 918	...	...	+U	5 172	...	...	...	...
1998	+U	897 495	...	+U	317 793	...	...	+U	4 062	...	...	...	...
1999	+U	772 604	...	+U	362 593	...	...	+U	5 003	...	...	...	...
2000	+U	773 009	...	+U	365 741	...	...	+U	4 822	...	...	...	...
2001	+U	790 425	...	+U	369 493	...	...	+U	5 105	...	...	...	...
Turkey - Turquie[8,31]													
1997	I	1 477 000	23.1	I	424 000	6.6	16.5	I	62 625	42.4	...	...	2.670

4. Vital statistics summary and expectation of life at birth: 1997-2001
Aperçu des statistiques de l'état civil et espérance de vie à la naissance: 1997-2001 (continued — suite)

(See notes at end of table. — Voir notes à la fin du tableau.)

Continent, country or area and year — Continent, pays ou zone et année	Code[a]	Live births — Naissances vivantes Number Nombre	Crude birth rate Taux bruts de natalité	Code[a]	Deaths — Décès Number Nombre	Crude death rate Taux bruts de mortalité	Rate of natural increase Taux d'accroiss-ement naturel	Code[a]	Infant deaths — Décès d'enfants de moins d'un an Number Nombre	Rate (per 1000 births) Taux (par 1000 naiss-ances)	Expectation of life at birth Espérance de vie à la naissance Male Masculin	Female Féminin	Total fertility rate L'indice synthétique de fécondité
ASIA — ASIE													
Turkey - Turquie[8,31]													
1998	i	1 488 000	22.8	i	430 000	6.6	16.2	i	61 347	41.2	...	...	2.63
1999	i	1 498 000	22.6	i	439 000	6.6	16.0	i	60 369	40.3	...	...	2.60
2000	i	1 508 000	22.4	i	453 000	6.7	15.6	i	59 709	39.6	66.40	71.00	2.52
2001	i	1 507 000	22.0	i	463 000	6.7	15.2	i	58 205	38.6	...	...	
Turkmenistan - Turkménistan[13]													
1998	C	98 461	20.3	C	29 628	6.1	14.2	C	3 265	33.2	...	...	
Uzbekistan - Ouzbékistan[13]													
1997	C	602 694	25.6	C	137 331	5.8	19.8	C	13 908	23.1	...	...	
1999	C	553 745	23.1	C	140 526	5.9	17.3	C	12 358	22.3	...	...	
2000	C	527 580	21.4	C	135 598	5.5	15.9	C	10 091	19.1	...	...	
2001	C	512 950	20.5	C	132 542	5.3	15.2	C	9 427	18.4	...	...	
EUROPE													
Albania - Albanie													
1997	C	61 739	16.5	C	18 237	4.9	11.7	C	1 368	22.2	...	...	
1998	C	60 139	15.9	C	18 250	4.8	11.1	C	903	15.0	...	...	
1999	...	...	...	...	...	...	...	...	...	...	...	...	2.10
Andorra - Andorre													
1997	C	730	11.1	C	197	3.0	8.1	C	1	...	...	...	
1998	C	781	11.8	C	235	3.6	8.3	C	5	...	...	...	
1999	C	833	12.6	C	207	3.1	9.5	C	2	...	...	...	
2000	C	747	11.3	C	259	3.9	7.4	C	2	...	...	...	
2001	C	777	11.6	C	237	3.6	8.1	C	3	...	...	...	
Austria - Autriche													
1997	C	84 045	10.4	C	79 432	9.8	0.6	C	398	4.7	74.29	80.64	1.36
1998	C	81 233	10.1	C	78 339	9.7	0.4	C	400	4.9	74.73	80.93	1.34
1999	C	78 138	9.7	C	78 200	9.7	0.0	C	341	4.4	75.10	80.96	1.31
2000	C	78 268	9.7	C	76 780	9.5	0.2	C	378	4.8	75.41	81.21	1.33
2001	C	75 458	9.3	C	74 767	9.2	0.1	C	365	4.8	75.91	81.68	1.31
Belarus - Bélarus[13]													
1997	C	89 586	8.8	C	136 653	13.4	-4.6	C	1 127	12.6	62.88	74.28	1.22
1998	C	92 645	9.1	C	137 296	13.5	-4.4	C	1 041	11.2	62.70	74.40	1.26
1999	C	92 975	9.3	C	142 027	14.2	-4.9	C	1 064	11.4	62.23	73.94	1.30
2000	...	...	...	...	...	...	...	...	...	...	...	...	1.66
2001	...	...	...	...	...	...	...	...	...	...	...	...	1.65
Belgium - Belgique[32]													
1997	C	115 864	11.4	C	103 802	10.2	1.2	C	623	5.4	...	...	
1998	C	114 276	11.2	C	104 583	10.3	1.0	C	591	5.2	...	...	
1999	C	113 469	11.1	C	104 904	10.3	0.8	C	556	4.9	74.87	81.38	1.61
2000	C	114 883	11.2	C	104 903	10.2	1.0	C	554	4.8	...	...	
2001	C	114 014	11.1	C	103 447	10.1	1.0	C	583	5.1	...	...	
Bosnia and Herzegovina - Bosnie-Herzégovine													
1997	C	48 397	12.9	C	27 875	7.5	5.5	C	601	12.4	...	...	
1998	C	45 007	12.3	C	28 679	7.9	4.5	C	494	11.0	...	...	
1999	...	...	...	...	...	...	...	...	...	...	...	...	1.36
Bulgaria - Bulgarie													
1997	C	64 125	7.7	C	121 861	14.7	-6.9	C	1 123	17.5	...	...	1.09
1998	C	65 360	7.9	C	118 193	14.3	-6.4	C	943	14.4	68.15	75.34	
1999	C	72 291	8.8	C	111 786	13.6	-4.8	C	1 057	14.6	68.53	75.23	1.23
2000	C	73 679	9.0	C	115 087	14.1	-5.1	C	981	13.3	68.50	75.10	1.26
2001	C	68 180	8.6	C	112 368	14.2	-5.6	C	982	14.4	...	...	1.24

4. Vital statistics summary and expectation of life at birth: 1997-2001
Aperçu des statistiques de l'état civil et espérance de vie à la naissance: 1997-2001 (continued — suite)

(See notes at end of table. — Voir notes à la fin du tableau.)

Continent, country or area and year / Continent, pays ou zone et année	Code[a]	Live births Naissances vivantes - Number Nombre	Crude birth rate Taux bruts de natalité	Code[a]	Deaths - Décès - Number Nombre	Crude death rate Taux bruts de mortalité	Rate of natural increase Taux d'accroiss-ement naturel	Code[a]	Infant deaths Décès d'enfants de moins d'un an - Number Nombre	Rate (per 1000 births) Taux (par 1000 naiss-ances)	Expectation of life at birth Espérance de vie à la naissance - Male Masculin	Female Féminin	Total fertility rate L'indice synthétiq-ue de fécondité
EUROPE													
Channel Islands: Guernsey - Îles Anglo-Normandes: Guernesey													
1997	c	672	11.4	c	593	10.0	1.3	c	3	...	...	...	...
1998	c	669	11.3	c	540	9.1	2.2	c	2	...	...	...	...
1999	c	672	11.2	c	529	8.8	2.4	c	2	...	...	...	...
2000	c	644	10.7	c	565	9.3	1.3	c	4	...	...	...	...
Croatia - Croatie													
1997	c	55 501	12.1	c	51 964	11.4	0.8	c	457	8.2	...	...	1.690
1998	c	47 068	10.5	c	52 311	11.6	-1.2	c	388	8.2	...	...	1.450
1999	c	45 179	9.9	c	51 953	11.4	-1.5	c	350	7.7	...	...	1.380
2000	c	43 746	10.0	c	50 246	11.5	-1.5	c	324	7.4	...	...	1.390
2001	c	40 993	9.2	c	49 552	11.2	-1.9	c	315	7.7	...	...	1.380
Czech Republic - République tchèque													
1997	c	90 657	8.8	c	112 744	10.9	-2.1	c	531	5.9	70.50	77.49	1.173
1998	c	90 535	8.8	c	109 527	10.6	-1.8	c	472	5.2	71.24	77.93	1.150
1999	c	89 471	8.7	c	109 768	10.7	-2.0	c	413	4.6	71.40	78.13	1.131
2000	c	90 910	8.8	c	109 001	10.6	-1.8	c	373	4.1	71.64	78.35	1.144
2001	c	90 715	8.9	c	107 755	10.5	-1.7	c	360	4.0	72.14	78.45	1.136
Denmark - Danemark[33]													
1997	c	67 636	12.8	c	59 898	11.3	1.5	c	351	5.2	73.68	78.65	...
1998	c	66 170	12.5	c	58 442	11.0	1.5	c	309	4.7	...	...	1.720
1999	c	66 232	12.4	c	59 156	11.1	1.3	c	281	4.2	74.23	78.99	1.733
2000	c	67 081	12.6	c	57 986	10.9	1.7	c	358	5.3	74.50	79.30	1.771
2001	c	65 450	12.2	c	58 338	10.9	1.3	c	320	4.9	...	...	1.740
Estonia - Estonie[13]													
1997	c	12 626	8.7	c	18 566	12.7	-4.1	c	127	10.1	64.78	76.01	1.240
1998	c	12 170	8.4	c	19 440	13.4	-5.0	c	108	8.9	...	...	...
1999	c	12 545	8.7	c	18 455	12.8	-4.1	c	119	9.5	...	...	1.235
2000	c	13 089	9.6	c	18 424	13.5	-3.9	c	110	8.4	65.14	76.17	1.390
2001	c	12 629	9.3	...	...	...	...	c	111	8.8	...	...	1.340
Finland - Finlande[34]													
1997	c	59 329	11.5	c	49 108	9.6	2.0	c	232	3.9	73.43	80.51	1.746
1998	c	57 108	11.1	c	49 262	9.6	1.5	c	239	4.2	73.51	80.83	1.700
1999	c	57 574	11.1	c	49 345	9.6	1.6	c	208	3.6	73.78	80.98	1.735
2000	c	56 742	11.0	c	49 339	9.5	1.4	c	213	3.8	...	...	1.729
2001	c	56 189	10.8	c	48 550	9.4	1.5	c	181	3.2	74.56	81.53	1.726
France[35,36]													
1997	c	726 768	12.4	c	530 319	9.0	3.4	c	3 439	4.7	74.77	82.42	1.726
1998	c	738 080	12.6	c	534 005	9.1	3.5	c	3 399	4.6	74.78	82.37	1.764
1999	c	744 791	12.7	c	537 661	9.2	3.5	c	3 221	4.3	...	...	1.793
2000	c	774 782	13.2	c	536 300	9.1	4.0	c	3 543	4.6	...	...	1.880
2001	c	774 600	13.1	c	530 200	9.0	4.1	c	3 444	4.4	...	...	1.897
Germany - Allemagne													
1997	c	812 173	9.9	c	860 389	10.5	-0.6	c	3 951	4.9	74.44	80.57	1.368
1998	c	797 541	9.7	c	851 412	10.4	-0.7	c	3 667	4.6	...	...	...
1999	c	770 744	9.4	c	846 330	10.3	-0.9	c	3 496	4.5	74.74	80.74	1.360
2000	c	766 999	9.3	c	838 797	10.2	-0.9	c	3 362	4.4	...	...	1.360
2001	c	743 500	9.0	c	823 500	10.0	-1.0	c	3 300	4.4	...	...	1.290
Gibraltar[37]													
1997	c	427	15.7	c	263	9.7	6.0	...	...	...	...	...	...
1998	c	411	15.2	c	267	9.9	5.3	...	...	...	...	...	...
1999	c	381	14.0	c	277	10.2	3.8	...	...	...	...	...	...
2000	c	408	15.1	c	262	9.7	5.4	...	...	...	...	...	...

(See notes at end of table. — Voir notes à la fin du tableau.)

Continent, country or area and year / Continent, pays ou zone et année	Live births - Naissances vivantes			Deaths - Décès			Rate of natural increase Taux d'accroiss-ement naturel	Infant deaths - Décès d'enfants de moins d'un an			Expectation of life at birth Espérance de vie à la naissance		Total fertility rate L'indice synthétique de fécondité
	Code[a]	Number Nombre	Crude birth rate Taux bruts de natalité	Code[a]	Number Nombre	Crude death rate Taux bruts de mortalité		Code[a]	Number Nombre	Rate (per 1000 births) Taux (par 1000 naiss-ances)	Male Masculin	Female Féminin	
EUROPE													
Gibraltar[37]													
2001	C	399	14.1	C	249	8.8	5.3	...	...	...	...	...	...
Greece - Grèce													
1997	C	102 038	9.7	C	99 738	9.5	0.2	C	657	6.4	75.31	80.63	1.311
1998	C	100 894	9.6	C	102 668	9.8	-0.2	C	674	6.7	75.32	80.53	1.292
1999	C	116 038	11.0	C	104 190	9.9	1.1	C	619	5.3	...	...	1.300
2000	C	117 140	11.7	C	105 219	10.5	1.2	C	610	5.2	...	...	1.290
2001	C	102 282	10.2	C	102 559	10.2	0.0	C	522	5.1	...	...	1.290
Holy See - Saint-Siège													
2000	C	1	1.3	C	10	12.5	-11.3	C	...	...	...	...	...
Hungary - Hongrie													
1997	C	100 350	9.9	C	139 434	13.7	-3.8	C	989	9.9	66.35	75.08	1.380
1998	C	97 301	9.6	C	140 870	13.9	-4.3	C	944	9.7	66.14	75.18	1.326
1999	C	94 645	9.4	C	143 210	14.2	-4.8	C	798	8.4	66.32	75.13	1.285
2000	C	97 597	9.7	C	135 601	13.5	-3.8	C	900	9.2	67.11	75.59	1.330
2001	C	97 047	9.5	C	132 183	13.0	-3.4	C	789	8.1	68.15	76.46	1.313
Iceland - Islande													
1997	C	4 151	15.3	C	1 843	6.8	8.5	C	23	...	76.96	81.50	2.040
1998	C	4 178	15.3	C	1 821	6.7	8.6	C	11	...	...	...	2.040
1999	C	4 100	14.8	C	1 901	6.9	7.9	C	10	...	77.80	81.53	1.989
2000	C	4 315	15.3	C	1 828	6.5	8.8	C	13	...	78.00	81.40	2.100
2001	C	4 091	14.4	C	1 725	6.1	8.3	C	11	...	...	...	1.950
Ireland - Irlande[38]													
1997	+C	52 775	14.4	+C	31 581	8.6	5.8	+C	321	6.1	...	...	1.930
1998	+C	53 551	14.5	+C	31 437	8.5	6.0	+C	330	6.2	...	...	1.930
1999	+C	53 354	14.2	+C	31 683	8.5	5.8	+C	293	5.5	73.87	79.07	1.882
2000	+C	54 239	14.3	+C	31 115	8.2	6.1	+C	322	5.9	74.20	79.20	1.890
2001	+C	57 882	15.0	+C	29 812	7.7	7.3	+C	337	5.8	...	...	1.980
Isle of Man - Îles de Man													
1999	+C	894	...	+C	983	...	...	+C	6	...	...	...	...
2000	+C	830	11.1	+C	900	12.0	-0.9	...	...	...	...	...	...
Italy - Italie													
1997	C	534 461	9.3	C	564 679	9.8	-0.5	C	2 973	5.6	...	...	1.210
1998	C	515 439	9.0	C	576 911	10.0	-1.1	C	2 820	5.5	...	...	1.210
1999	C	523 463	9.1	C	571 356	9.9	-0.8	C	2 723	5.2	75.96	82.14	1.222
2000	C	543 039	9.4	C	560 241	9.7	-0.3	C	2 461	4.5	...	...	1.242
2001	C	535 282	9.2	C	555 247	9.6	-0.3	C	2 514	4.7	...	...	1.240
Latvia - Lettonie[13]													
1997	C	18 830	7.7	C	33 533	13.8	-6.0	C	289	15.3	64.21	75.88	1.110
1998	C	18 410	7.6	C	34 200	14.2	-6.6	C	276	15.0	70.49	83.09	1.093
1999	C	19 396	8.1	C	32 844	13.7	-5.6	C	219	11.3	64.89	76.20	1.162
2000	C	20 248	8.5	C	32 205	13.6	-5.0	C	210	10.4	64.93	75.98	1.237
2001	C	19 664	8.3	C	32 991	14.0	-5.7	C	217	11.0	65.18	76.62	1.207
Liechtenstein													
1997	C	435	13.9	C	230	7.4	6.6	C	8	...	...	...	...
Lithuania - Lituanie[13]													
1997	C	37 812	10.6	C	41 143	11.5	-0.9	C	391	10.3	65.90	76.82	1.390
1998	C	37 019	10.4	C	40 757	11.5	-1.1	C	343	9.3	66.50	76.87	1.360
1999	C	36 415	10.3	C	40 003	11.4	-1.0	C	315	8.7	67.07	77.41	1.350
2000	C	34 149	9.8	C	38 919	11.1	-1.4	C	294	8.6	67.62	77.93	1.272
2001	C	31 546	9.1	C	40 399	11.6	-2.5	C	250	7.9	65.88	77.41	1.293
Luxembourg													
1997	C	5 503	13.1	C	3 937	9.4	3.7	C	23	...	...	...	...
1998	C	5 386	12.6	C	3 901	9.1	3.5	C	27	...	...	...	...
1999	C	5 582	12.9	C	3 793	8.8	4.1	C	26	...	74.70	81.23	1.734
2000	C	5 723	13.1	C	3 754	8.6	4.5	C	29	...	74.90	81.30	1.800

4. Vital statistics summary and expectation of life at birth: 1997-2001
Aperçu des statistiques de l'état civil et espérance de vie à la naissance: 1997-2001 (continued — suite)

See notes at end of table. — Voir notes à la fin du tableau.)

continent, country or area and year / continent, pays ou zone et année	Live births Naissances vivantes			Deaths - Décès			Rate of natural increase Taux d'accroiss-ement naturel	Infant deaths Décès d'enfants de moins d'un an			Expectation of life at birth Espérance de vie à la naissance		Total fertility rate L'indice synthétique de fécondité
	Code[a]	Number Nombre	Crude birth rate Taux bruts de natalité	Code[a]	Number Nombre	Crude death rate Taux bruts de mortalité		Code[a]	Number Nombre	Rate (per 1000 births) Taux (par 1000 naiss-ances)	Male Masculin	Female Féminin	
EUROPE													
Luxembourg													
2001	c	5 459	12.4	c	3 719	8.4	3.9	c	32	5.9	...	...	1.700
Malta - Malte[39,40]													
1997	c	4 835	12.6	c	2 888	7.5	5.1	c	31	6.4	74.86	80.09	...
1998	c	4 488	11.6	c	3 044	7.9	3.7	c	24	...	74.40	80.07	...
1999	c	4 308	11.1	c	3 097	8.0	3.1	c	31	7.2	75.06	79.27	...
2000	c	4 255	10.9	c	2 957	7.6	3.3	c	26	...	...	...	...
2001	c	3 859	9.8	c	2 935	7.4	2.3	c	39	10.1	76.07	80.87	1.720
Monaco													
1997	c	713	22.3	c	485	15.2	7.1	...	...	...	...	...	...
1998	c	681	...	c	538	...	...	...	...	...	...	...	...
2000	c	760	22.8	c	547	16.4	6.4	...	...	...	...	...	...
Netherlands - Pays-Bas[41]													
1997	c	192 443	12.3	c	135 783	8.7	3.6	c	968	5.0	75.39	80.71	...
1998	c	199 408	12.7	c	137 482	8.8	3.9	c	1 035	5.2	75.12	80.54	1.628
1999	c	200 445	12.7	c	140 487	8.9	3.8	c	1 048	5.2	75.33	80.46	1.650
2000	c	206 619	13.0	c	140 527	8.8	4.2	c	1 059	5.1	...	...	...
2001	c	202 603	12.6	c	140 377	8.7	3.9	c	1 088	5.4	75.80	80.71	1.710
Norway - Norvège[42]													
1997	c	59 801	13.6	c	44 595	10.1	3.5	c	247	4.1	75.45	80.97	1.857
1998	c	58 352	13.2	c	44 112	10.0	3.2	c	232	4.0	75.54	81.28	1.814
1999	c	59 298	13.3	c	45 170	10.1	3.2	c	232	3.9	75.63	81.14	1.840
2000	c	59 234	13.2	c	44 002	9.8	3.4	c	225	3.8	75.96	81.38	1.851
2001	c	56 696	12.6	c	43 981	9.7	2.8	c	223	3.9	76.21	81.53	1.784
Poland - Pologne													
1997	c	412 635	10.7	c	380 201	9.8	0.8	c	4 194	10.2	68.45	76.99	1.508
1998	c	395 619	10.2	c	375 354	9.7	0.5	c	3 771	9.5	68.87	77.34	1.430
1999	c	382 002	9.9	c	381 415	9.9	0.0	c	3 381	8.9	68.83	77.49	1.360
2000	c	378 700	9.8	c	368 100	9.5	0.3	c	3 068	8.1	69.70	77.90	1.340
2001	c	368 205	9.5	c	363 220	9.4	0.1	c	2 823	7.7	...	...	1.290
Portugal													
1997	c	113 047	11.4	c	105 157	10.6	0.8	c	727	6.4	...	...	1.464
1998	c	113 510	11.4	c	106 382	10.7	0.7	c	950	8.4	...	...	...
1999	c	116 002	11.6	c	107 871	10.8	0.8	c	651	5.6	71.98	79.06	1.489
2000	c	118 551	11.8	c	105 804	10.6	1.3	c	664	5.6	72.70	79.70	1.520
2001	c	112 774	10.9	c	105 092	10.2	0.7	c	567	5.0	...	...	1.420
Republic of Moldova - République de Moldova[13]													
1997	c	49 804	13.6	c	50 614	13.9	-0.2	...	...	...	62.86	70.30	1.216
1998	c	41 332	11.3	c	39 922	10.9	0.4	c	738	17.9	63.74	71.04	1.490
1999	c	38 501	10.6	c	41 315	11.3	-0.8	c	714	18.5	63.74	71.04	1.360
2000	c	36 939	10.2	c	41 224	11.3	-1.2	c	681	18.4	...	...	...
2001	c	36 448	10.0	c	40 075	11.0	-1.0	c	728	20.0	...	...	1.261
Romania - Roumanie													
1997	c	286 891	10.5	c	279 315	12.4	-1.9	c	5 209	22.0	...	...	1.320
1998	c	237 297	10.5	c	269 166	12.0	-1.4	c	4 868	20.5	67.03	74.20	1.316
1999	c	234 600	10.4	c	265 194	11.8	-1.4	c	4 360	18.6	67.69	74.84	1.300
2000	c	234 521	10.5	c	255 820	11.4	-0.9	c	4 370	18.6	67.70	74.60	1.305
2001	c	220 368	9.8	c	259 603	11.6	-1.8	c	4 057	18.4	...	...	1.232
Russian Federation - Fédération de Russie[13]													
1997	c	1 259 943	8.6	c	2 015 779	13.7	-5.1	c	21 735	17.3	...	...	...
1998	c	1 283 292	8.8	c	1 988 744	13.6	-4.8	c	21 097	16.4	...	...	...
1999	c	1 214 689	8.3	c	2 144 316	14.7	-6.4	c	20 731	17.1	59.93	72.38	1.170
2000	c	1 266 800	8.7	c	2 225 332	15.3	-6.6	c	19 286	15.2	...	...	...
2001	c	1 311 604	9.1	c	2 251 814	15.6	-6.5	c	19 124	14.6	...	...	...

4. Vital statistics summary and expectation of life at birth: 1997-2001
Aperçu des statistiques de l'état civil et espérance de vie à la naissance: 1997-2001 (continued — suite)

(See notes at end of table. — Voir notes à la fin du tableau.)

Continent, country or area and year / Continent, pays ou zone et année	Code[a]	Live births - Naissances vivantes — Number Nombre	Crude birth rate Taux bruts de natalité	Code[a]	Deaths - Décès — Number Nombre	Crude death rate Taux bruts de mortalité	Rate of natural increase Taux d'accroiss-ement naturel	Code[a]	Infant deaths - Décès d'enfants de moins d'un an — Number Nombre	Rate (per 1000 births) Taux (par 1000 naiss-ances)	Expectation of life at birth - Espérance de vie à la naissance — Male Masculin	Female Féminin	Total fertility rate L'indice synthétique de fécondité
EUROPE													
San Marino - Saint-Marin													
1997	+C	287	11.1	+C	178	6.9	4.2	+C	...	...	...	...	4.12
1998	+C	285	10.9	+C	190	7.3	3.6	+C	4	...	...	...	4.11
1999	+C	303	11.5	+C	198	7.5	4.0	+C	1	...	...	...	4.37
2000	+C	290	10.8	+C	188	7.0	3.8	+C	...	...	77.43	83.98	4.18
Serbia and Montenegro - Serbie-et-Montenegro													
1997	C	131 394	12.4	C	111 845	10.6	1.8	C	1 876	14.3	69.79	74.65	1.73
1998	C	128 461	12.1	C	113 312	10.7	1.4	C	1 791	13.9	...	...	1.69
1999	C	123 970	11.7	C	115 461	10.9	0.8	C	1 691	13.6	...	...	1.62
2000	C	125 868	11.8	C	118 078	11.1	0.7	C	1 668	13.3	70.10	75.00	1.64
2001	C	131 449	12.3	C	114 881	10.8	1.6	C	1 662	12.6	...	...	1.64
Slovakia - Slovaquie													
1997	C	59 310	11.0	C	52 124	9.7	1.3	C	514	8.7	...	...	
1998	C	57 582	10.7	C	53 156	9.9	0.8	C	506	8.8	68.63	76.74	1.37
1999	C	56 223	10.4	C	52 402	9.7	0.7	C	467	8.3	68.95	77.03	1.33
2000	C	55 103	10.2	C	52 703	9.8	0.4	C	458	8.3	69.20	77.40	
2001	C	51 136	9.5	C	51 980	9.7	-0.2	C	319	6.2	...	...	1.20
Slovenia - Slovénie													
1997	C	18 165	9.1	C	18 928	9.5	-0.4	C	94	5.2	71.05	78.68	.
1998	C	17 856	9.0	C	19 039	9.6	-0.6	C	93	5.2	71.37	78.75	1.23
1999	C	17 533	8.8	C	18 885	9.5	-0.7	C	79	4.5	71.94	79.10	1.21
2000	C	18 180	9.1	C	18 588	9.3	-0.2	C	89	4.9	72.13	79.57	1.26
2001	C	17 477	8.8	C	18 508	9.3	-0.5	C	74	4.2	...	...	1.21
Spain - Espagne													
1997	C	369 035	9.4	C	349 521	8.9	0.5	C	1 856	5.0	...	...	1.18
1998	C	365 193	9.3	C	360 511	9.1	0.1	C	1 774	4.9	75.25	82.16	1.16
1999	C	380 130	9.6	C	371 102	9.4	0.2	C	1 700	4.5	...	...	1.20
2000	C	386 450	9.7	C	360 391	9.0	0.7	C	1 535	4.0	...	...	1.23
2001	C	407 135	10.1	C	351 147	8.7	1.4	C	1 394	3.4	...	...	1.24
Sweden - Suède													
1997	C	90 383	10.2	C	93 278	10.5	-0.3	C	328	3.6	76.70	81.82	1.52
1998	C	89 028	10.1	C	93 271	10.5	-0.5	C	316	3.5	76.87	81.94	1.51
1999	C	88 173	10.0	C	94 726	10.7	-0.7	C	297	3.4	77.06	81.91	1.49
2000	C	90 441	10.2	C	93 285	10.5	-0.3	C	292	3.2	...	...	
2001	C	91 466	10.3	C	93 752	10.5	-0.3	C	334	3.7	77.55	82.07	1.57
Switzerland - Suisse													
1997	C	80 584	11.4	C	62 839	8.9	2.5	C	387	4.8	76.50	82.50	1.79
1998	C	78 949	11.1	C	62 568	8.8	2.3	C	376	4.8	76.70	82.60	1.77
1999	C	78 408	11.0	C	62 503	8.7	2.2	C	361	4.6	76.84	82.55	1.76
2000	C	78 458	10.9	C	62 528	8.7	2.2	C	386	4.9	76.90	82.60	1.49
2001	C	73 509	10.2	C	61 287	8.5	1.7	C	365	5.0	...	...	1.41
The Former Yugoslav Rep. of Macedonia - L'ex-République yougoslave de Macédoine													
1997	C	29 478	14.8	C	16 596	8.3	6.5	C	463	15.7	70.30	74.79	1.75
1998	C	29 244	14.6	C	16 870	8.4	6.2	C	476	16.3	70.48	74.77	.
1999	C	27 309	13.5	C	16 789	8.3	5.2	C	406	14.9	...	...	1.76
2000	C	29 308	...	C	17 253	...	...	C	346	11.8	...	...	1.76
2001	C	27 010	13.3	C	16 919	8.3	5.0	C	321	11.9	...	...	.
Ukraine[13]													
1997	C	442 581	8.7	C	754 151	14.8	-6.1	C	6 282	14.2	62.74	73.50	1.22
1998	C	419 238	8.3	C	719 954	14.3	-6.0	C	5 423	12.9	62.95	73.74	1.15
1999	...	...	...	C	739 170	14.8	...	C	...	...	...	...	.
2000	C	385 126	7.7	C	758 082	15.2	-7.5	C	4 606	12.0	...	...	.

(See notes at end of table. — Voir notes à la fin du tableau.)

Continent, country or area and year / Continent, pays ou zone et année	Code[a]	Live births / Naissances vivantes		Code[a]	Deaths / Décès		Rate of natural increase / Taux d'accroiss-ement naturel	Code[a]	Infant deaths / Décès d'enfants de moins d'un an		Expectation of life at birth / Espérance de vie à la naissance		Total fertility rate / L'indice synthétique de fécondité
		Number / Nombre	Crude birth rate / Taux bruts de natalité		Number / Nombre	Crude death rate / Taux bruts de mortalité			Number / Nombre	Rate (per 1000 births) / Taux (par 1000 naissances)	Male / Masculin	Female / Féminin	
EUROPE													
Ukraine[13]													
2001	C	376 478	7.7	C	745 952	15.2	-7.5	C	4 283	11.4	...	...	...
United Kingdom - Royaume-Uni[43]													
1997	C	726 622	12.3	C	629 746	10.7	1.6	C	4 252	5.9	74.66	79.64	1.720
1998	C	716 888	12.1	C	629 172	10.6	1.5	C	4 079	5.7	...	...	1.713
1999	C	699 976	11.8	C	632 062	10.6	1.1	C	4 045	5.8	74.98	79.78	1.686
2000	C	679 029	11.4	C	608 366	10.2	1.2	C	3 791	5.6	75.40	80.20	1.640
2001	C	668 777	11.2	C	602 268	10.1	1.1	C	3 664	5.5	...	...	1.630
OCEANIA — OCEANIE													
American Samoa - Samoa américaines													
1997	C	1 634	29.7	C	259	4.7	25.0	C	17	...	...	...	...
1998	C	1 688	30.3	C	243	4.4	25.9	C	27	...	...	...	...
1999	C	1 736	30.6	C	249	4.4	26.2	C	22	...	...	...	...
2000	C	1 730	30.0	C	224	3.9	26.1	C	11	...	...	...	...
Australia - Australie													
1997	+C	251 842	13.6	+C	129 350	7.0	6.6	+C	1 341	5.3	76.22	81.77	1.776
1998	+C	249 616	13.3	+C	127 202	6.8	6.5	+C	1 252	5.0	76.56	82.04	1.758
1999	+C	248 870	13.1	+C	128 102	6.8	6.4	+C	1 408	5.7	...	...	1.751
2000	+C	249 636	13.0	+C	128 291	6.7	6.3	+C	1 290	5.2	...	...	1.749
2001	+C	245 759	12.7	+C	128 557	6.6	6.0	+C	1 294	5.3	...	...	...
Cook Islands - Îles Cook													
1997	+C	413	22.6	+C	143	7.8	14.8	+C	15	...	...	...	...
1998	+C	386	22.2	+C	107	6.1	16.0	+C	8	...	...	...	...
1999	+C	346	21.1	+C	96	5.9	15.2	+C	5	...	...	...	...
Fiji - Fidji													
1998	+C	17 944	22.5	+C	5 241	6.6	15.9	+C	212	11.8	...	...	...
1999	+C	16 916	21.0	+C	3 603	4.5	16.5	+C	275	16.3	...	...	...
French Polynesia - Polynésie française													
1997	C	4 702	21.1	U	1 089	...	...	U	36	...	...	...	...
1998	C	4 562	20.2	U	1 114	...	...	U	32	...	...	...	...
1999	C	4 580	20.1	U	1 003	...	...	U	31	...	...	...	...
2000	C	4 900	21.2	U	1 013	...	...	...	...	...	...	...	...
Guam[44]													
1997	C	4 318	27.6	C	639	4.1	23.6	C	37	8.6	...	...	...
1998	C	4 322	29.0	C	651	4.4	24.6	C	34	7.9	...	...	...
1999	C	4 037	26.6	C	724	4.8	21.8	C	35	8.7	...	...	...
2000	C	3 790	24.5	C	667	4.3	20.2	C	24	...	...	...	...
Marshall Islands - Îles Marshall													
1997	+U	1 607	...	+U	243	...	...	+U	49	...	...	...	6.070
1998	+U	1 651	...	...	...	...	...	...	...	...	...	...	5.890
1999	+U	1 478	...	...	...	...	...	...	...	...	...	...	5.710
2001	+U	1 511	...	+U	271	...	...	+U	40	...	...	...	...
Micronesia, Federated States of - Micronésie, États Fédérés de La													
1997	U	2 575	...	U	464	...	...	U	69	...	...	...	...
New Caledonia - Nouvelle-Calédonie													
1997	C	4 490	22.4	C	1 016	5.1	17.3	C	24	...	...	...	2.669
1998	C	4 352	21.3	C	982	4.8	16.5	C	30	6.9	...	...	2.569

4. Vital statistics summary and expectation of life at birth: 1997-2001
Aperçu des statistiques de l'état civil et espérance de vie à la naissance: 1997-2001 (continued — suite)

(See notes at end of table. — Voir notes à la fin du tableau.)

Continent, country or area and year / Continent, pays ou zone et année	Live births - Naissances vivantes			Deaths - Décès			Rate of natural increase Taux d'accroiss-ement naturel	Infant deaths Décès d'enfants de moins d'un an			Expectation of life at birth Espérance de vie à la naissance		Total fertility rate L'indice synthétique de fécondité
	Code^a	Number Nombre	Crude birth rate Taux bruts de natalité	Code^a	Number Nombre	Crude death rate Taux bruts de mortalité		Code^a	Number Nombre	Rate (per 1000 births) Taux (par 1000 naissances)	Male Masculin	Female Féminin	
OCEANIA — OCEANIE													
New Caledonia - Nouvelle-Calédonie													
1999	C	4 316	20.8	C	1 095	5.3	15.5	C	27	...	69.80	75.80	2.52
New Zealand - Nouvelle-Zélande													
1997	+C	57 734	15.4	+C	27 471	7.3	8.0	+C	377	6.5	75.24	80.43	1.97
1998	+C	55 349	14.6	+C	26 206	6.9	7.7	+C	305	5.5	...	...	1.91
1999	+C	57 053	15.0	+C	28 122	7.4	7.6	+C	317	5.6	...	...	1.99
2000	+C	56 605	14.8	+C	26 660	7.0	7.8	+C	346	6.1	...	...	2.00
Northern Mariana Islands - Îles Mariannes septentrionales													
1997	U	1 536	...	U	147	...	...	U	8	...	...	...	...
1998	U	1 421	...	U	180	...	...	U	15	...	...	...	...
1999	U	1 448	...	U	189	...	...	U	11	...	...	...	...
Palau - Palaos													
1997	C	330	18.3	C	121	6.7	11.6	C	4	...	...	...	.
1998	C	280	15.1	C	125	6.8	8.4	C	3	...	...	...	.
1999	C	250	13.2	C	131	6.9	6.3	C	5	...	...	...	.
Samoa													
1998	...	...	...	U	531	...	...	U	17	...	...	...	.
Tonga													
1997	+C	2 700	27.4	+C	467	4.7	22.6	+C	21	...	...	...	3.80
1998	+C	2 737	27.6	+C	498	5.0	22.6	+C	29	...	69.82	71.82	4.04
1999	+C	2 599	26.0	+C	675	6.8	19.3	+C	48	18.5	...	...	3.52
2000	+C	2 471	24.6	+C	653	6.5	18.1	+C	28	...	...	...	3.67

GENERAL NOTES - NOTES GENERALES

Countries or areas not listed may be assumed to lack vital statistics of national scope. Crude birth, death and natural increase rates are computed per 1 000 mid-year population; infant mortality rates per 1 000 live births and total fertility rates are the sum of age-specific fertility rates per woman. For method of evaluation, and limitations of data, see Technical Notes for this table. For more precise information in terms of coverage, basis of tabulation, etc., see Tables 9, 15, 18 and 22. — Les pays et zones ne figurant pas au tableau n'ont vraisemblablement pas de statistiques de l'état civil de portée nationale. Les taux bruts de natalité, de mortalité et d'accroisement naturel sont calculés pour 1 000 personnes au milieu de l'année; les taux de mortalité infantile sont calculés pour 1 000 naissances vivantes et les indices synthétiques de fécondité sont la somme des taux de fécondité par âge par femme. Pour la méthode d'évaluation et les insuffisances des données, voir Notes techniques, pour ces tableaux. Pour plus de détails sur la portée, la base d'exploitation des données, etc., voir tableaux 9, 15, 18 et 22.

Italics: data from civil registers which are incomplete or of unknown completeness. — Italiques: données incomplètes ou dont le degré d'exactitude n'est pas connu provenant des registres de l'état civil.

 ^a 'Code' indicates the source of data, as follows:
C - Civil registration, estimated over 90% complete
U - Civil registration, estimated less than 90% complete
I - Other source, estimated reliable
+ - Indicates that events are counted when registered, not when they occurred.
... - Information not available

Le 'Code' indique la source des données, comme suit:
C - Registres de l'état civil considérés complets à 90 p. 100 au moins.
U - Registres de l'état civil qui ne sont pas considérés complets à 90 p. 100 au moins.
I - Autre source, considéré pas douteuses.
+ - Indique que les statistiques vitales sont comptées au moment de registration, pas au moment de l'évenement.
... - Information pas disponible.

 [1] For Algerian population only. - Pour la population algérienne seulement.
 [2] Excluding live-born infants dying before registration of birth. - Non compris les enfants nés vivants décédés avant l'enregistrement de leur naissance.
 [3] Data refer to national projections. - Les données se referent au projections nationales.
 [4] For 1998, based on the results of the population census. Data for 1999 - 200 refer to national projections. — Pour 1998, d'après les résultats du recensement d la population. Les données pour 1999 - 2001 se referent au projections nationales.
 [5] Data on births refer to the 1998 Population and Housing Census, adjusted for under-enumeration. - Les données sur les naissances referent au Recensement d la population et de l'habitat, ajustés pour compenserles lacunes de dénombremen.
 [6] Data for 1997 refer to last twelve months preceding population and housing census of 1997. - Les données pour 1997 se réfèrent au douze mois précédant le recensement de population et de l'habitat de 1997.
 [7] Including Canadian residents temporarily in the United States, but excluding United States residents temporarily in Canada. - Y compris les résidents canadien se trouvant temporairement aux Etats-Unis, mais ne comprennent pas les résiden des Etats-Unis se trouvant temporairement au Canada.
 [8] Data as reported by national statistical authorities; they may differ from data presented in other tables. This applies to data on live births for Brazil, 1998, St. Lucia and St. Vincent and the Grenadines 2000 and Turkey, 1997; and to data on infant deaths for Chile, 1999. — Les donées comme ils ont été déclarés par l'instit

onal de la statistique; ils peuvent etre different de ceux presentés dans autre
eaux. Cette note se raporte sur les données pour les naissances pour Brazil,
8, pour Saint Lucia and Saint Vincent et les Grenadines, 2000 et la Turquie,
7; aussi pour données sur les décès d'enfants de moins d'un an pour Chile,
9.

Excluding Indian jungle population. - Non compris les Indiens de la jungle.

Data on live births and deaths are based on a civil registration system put in
e in January 1998. - Les données sur les naissances et les décès sont basées
e un système d'enregistrement des faits d'état civil mis en place en janvier 1998.

Excluding nomadic Indian tribes. - Non compris les tribus d'Indiens nomades.

Including an upward adjustment for under-registration. - Y compris un
stement pour sous-enregistrement.

Excluding infants born alive with less than 28 weeks gestation, less than 1
grams in weight and 35 centimeters in length, who die within seven days of
h. - Non compris les enfants nés vivants avant 28 semaines de gestation,
ant moins de 1 000 grammes, mesurant moins de 35 centimètres et décédés
s les sept jours qui ont suivi leur naissance.

For statistical purposes, the data for China do not include those for the Hong
g Special Administrative Region (Hong Kong SAR), Macao special
inistrative Region (Macao SAR) and Taiwan province of China. - Pour la
sentation des statistiques, les données pour Chine ne comprend pas les Région
ninistrative Spéciale de Hong Kong (Hong Kong RAS), le Région Administrative
ciale de Macao (Macao RAS) et Taïwan province de Chine.

Rates for 2000 and 2001 were obtained by the Sample Survey of Population
nge 2002 in China. - Les taux pour 2000 and 2001 ont été obtenus par la 2002
uête de mouvement de la population par échantillon de la Chine.

Data refer to government controlled areas. - Les données se raportent aux
es contrôlées par le Gouvernement.

Including data for the Indian-held part of Jammu and Kashmir, the final status
hich has not yet been determined. - Y compris les données pour la partie du
mu et du Cachemire occupée par l'Inde dont le statut définitif n'a pas encore
déterminé.

Rates were obtained by the Sample Registration System of India, a large
ographic survey. - Les taux ont été obtenus par le Système de l'enregistrement
échantillon de l'Inde qui est au fait une large enquête démographique.

Published by the United Nations Economic and Social Commission for
stern Asia. - Edité par les Nations Unies économiques et la Commission sociale
r l'Asie occidentale.

Including data for East Jerusalem and Israeli residents in certain other
tories under occupation by Israeli military forces since June 1967. - Y compris
données pour Jérusalem-Est et les résidents israéliens dans certains autres
toires occupés depuis 1967 par les forces armées israéliennes.

For Japanese nationals only. - Pour les nationaux japonais seulement.

Excluding data for Jordanian territory under occupation since June 1967 by
eli military forces. Excluding foreigners, including registered Palestinian
gees. - Non compris les données pour le territoire jordanien occupé depuis juin
7 par les forces armées israéliennes. Non compris les étrangers, mais y
pris les réfugiés de Palestine immatriculés.

Excluding alien armed forces, civilian aliens employed by armed forces, and
ign diplomatic personnel and their dependants. - Non compris les militaires
ngers, les civils étrangers employés par les forces armées ni le personnel
matique étranger et les membres de leur famille les accompagnant.

For 2001, data refer to last twelve months preceding census on June 2001. - -
r 2001, les données se rapportent pour la dernière fois à douze mois précédant
censement juin 2001.

Based on the results of the Population Growth Survey. - D'après les résultats
a 'Population Growth Survey.'

Excluding data for the Pakistan-held part of Jammu and Kashmir, the final
us of which has not yet been determined. - Non compris les données
cernant la partie du Jammu et Cachemire occupée par le Pakistan dont le statut
nitif n'a pas été déterminé.

Excluding transients afloat and non-locally domiciled military and civilian
ices personnel and their dependants. - Non compris les personnes de passage
rd de navires, ni les militaires et agents civils domiciliés hors du territoire et les
nbres de leur famille les accompagnant.

Infant deaths prior to 2000 were tabulated by date of registration.
sequently, this should be taken into account when interpreting rates per 1 000
births, tabulated by date of occurence. - Antérieurement à l'année 2000, les
nées sur les décès d'enfants ont été présentées selon la date d'enregistrement.
contre, les données sur les naissances vivantes, qui ont été utilisées pour

calculer les taux de mortalité infantile, sont présentées selon la date de
l'événement. Les lecteurs doivent tenir compte des ces différences dans
l'interprétation des taux de mortalité infantile.

[29] Excluding nomad population and Palestinian refugees. - Non compris la
population nomade et les réfugiés de Palestine.

[30] Including late registered deaths. - Y compris les décès enregistrés
tardivement.

[31] Based on the results of the Population Demographic Survey. - D'après les
résultats de la Population Demographic Survey.

[32] Including armed forces stationed outside the country, but excluding alien
armed forces stationed in the area. - Y compris les militaires nationaux hors du
pays, mais non compris les militaires étrangers en garnison sur le territoire.

[33] Excluding Faeroe Islands and Greenland. - Non compris les îles Féroé et
Gröenland.

[34] Including nationals temporarily outside the country. - Y compris les nationaux
se trouvant temporairement hors du pays.

[35] Including armed forces stationed outside the country. - Y compris les militaires
nationaux hors du pays.

[36] For data on life expectancy, including nationals temporarily outside the
country. - Pour les données sur l'espérance de vie a la naissance, y compris les
nationaux se trouvant temporairement hors du pays.

[37] Excluding armed forces. - Non compris les militaires en garnison.

[38] Events registered within one year of occurrence. - Evénements enregistrés
dans l'année qui suit l'événement.

[39] Rates computed on population including civilian nationals temporarily outside
the country. - Les taux sont calculés sur la base d'un chiffre de population qui
comprend les civils nationaux temporairement hors du pays.

[40] Live births to Maltese parents only. - Naissances vivantes aux parents maltais
seulement.

[41] Including residents outside the country if listed in a Netherlands population
register. - Y compris les résidents hors du pays, s'ils sont inscrits sur un registre de
population néerlandais.

[42] Including residents temporarily outside the country. - Y compris les résidents
se trouvant temporairement hors du pays.

[43] Data revised to exclude births in Northern Ireland to non-residents of Northern
Ireland. - Données révisées non compris des naissances en Irlande du Nord aux
non-résidents de l'Irlande du Nord.

[44] Including United States military personnel, their dependants and contract
employees. - Y compris les militaires des Etats-Unis, les membres de leur famille
les accompagnant et les agents contractuels des Etats-Unis.

Table 5

Table 5 presents national estimates of mid-year population for all available years between 1992 and 2001.

Description of variables: Mid-year estimates of the total population are those provided by national statistical offices. They refer to the *de facto* or *de jure* population on 1 July. In cases where the reference date is not mid-year (1 July) a footnote is appended. The data have been presented in thousands, rounded by the Statistics Division.

Unless otherwise indicated, all estimates relate to the population within present geographical boundaries. Major exceptions to this principle have been explained in footnotes.

Reliability of data: Reliable mid-year population estimates are those which are based on a complete census (or on a sample survey) and have been adjusted on a basis of a continuous population register or on the balance of births, deaths and migration. Reliable mid-year estimates appear in roman type. Mid-year estimates which are not calculated on this basis are considered less reliable and are shown in *italics*.

Limitations: Statistics on estimates of the mid-year total population are subject to the same qualifications as have been set forth for population statistics in general in section 3 of the Technical Notes.

International comparability of mid-year population estimates is also affected by the fact that some of these estimates refer to the *de jure*, and not the *de facto*, population. These are indicated in the column titled "Type". The difference between the *de facto* and the *de jure* population is discussed at length in section 3.1.1 of the Technical Notes.

Coverage: Estimates of the mid-year population are shown for 200 countries or areas, with a population of 1,000 or more.

Earlier data: Estimates of mid-year population have been shown in previous issues of the *Demographic Yearbook*. Information on the years and specific topics covered is presented in the Index.

Tableau 5

Le tableau 5 présente des estimations nationales de la population en milieu d'année pour le plus grand nombre possible d'années entre 1992 et 2001.

Description des variables : Les estimations de la population totale en milieu d'année sont celles qui ont été communiquées par les services nationaux de statistique. Les estimations sont celles de la population de fait ou se réfèrent à la population de droit, au 1er juillet. Dans les cas ou la date est différente, une note est attachée. Sauf indication contraire, tous les chiffres sont exprimés en milliers. Les données ont été arrondies par la Division de statistique de l'ONU.

Sauf indication contraire, toutes les estimations se rapportent à la population présente sur le territoire actuel des pays ou zones considérées. Les principales exceptions à cette règle sont expliquées en note.

Fiabilité des données: Les estimations de la population en milieu d'année sont considérées sûres quand elles sont fondées sur un recensement complet (ou sur une enquête par sondage) qui a été ajusté en fonction des données fournies par un registre de population permanent ou en fonction des naissances, décès et mouvements migratoires qui ont eu lieu dans la période. Les estimations en milieu d'année sont considérées comme sûres et apparaissent en caractères romains. Les estimations en milieu d'année dont le calcul n'a pas été effectué sur cette base sont considérées comme moins sûres et apparaissent en italique. Les estimations relatives aux années antérieures à 2000 sont jugées sûres ou moins sûres en fonction du codage qualitatif de 2000 et indiquées, selon le cas, en caractères romains ou en italique.

Insuffisance des données : Les statistiques concernant les estimations de la population totale en milieu d'année appellent toutes les réserves qui ont été faites à la section 3 des Notes techniques à propos des statistiques de la population en général.

La comparabilité internationale des estimations de la population en milieu d'année est affectée également par le fait que certaines de ces estimations se réfèrent à la population de droit et non à la population de fait. Ces cas ont été signalés dans la colonne 'Type'. La différence entre la population de fait et la population de droit est expliquée en détail dans la section 3.1.1 des Notes techniques.

Portée : Des estimations de la population en milieu d'année sont présentées pour 200 pays ou zones ayant une population de 1000 habitants ou plus.

Données publiées antérieurement : Des estimations de la population en milieu d'année ont été publiées dans des éditions antérieures de l'Annuaire démographique. Pour plus de précisions concernant les années et les sujets spécifiques pour lesquelles des données ont été publiées, se reporter à l'Index.

5. Estimates of mid-year population: 1992 - 2001
Estimations de la population au milieu de l'anneé: 1992 - 2001

(See notes at end of table. — Voir notes à la fin du tableau.)

Continent and country or area Continent et pays ou zone	Ty-pe	Population estimates (in thousands) — Estimations (en milliers)									
		1992	1993	1994	1995	1996	1997	1998	1999	2000	2001
AFRICA — AFRIQUE											
Algeria - Algérie	DJ	26 271	26 894	27 496	28 060	28 566	29 045	29 508	29 950	30 386	30 836
Angola	DF	10 609	...	...	...	...	...	...	...	...	...
Benin - Bénin	DF	5 047	5 075	5 242	5 412	5 594	5 639	5 816	5 990	6 169	6 417
Botswana	DF	1 359	1 391	1 425	1 459	1 496	1 533	1 572	1 611	1 653	...
Burkina Faso	DF	9 433	9 682	9 889	10 200	...	11 087	10 683	...	...	...
Burundi	DF	5 786	5 769	5 875	5 982	6 088	6 194	6 300	6 483	...	...
Cameroon - Cameroun	DF	...	...	...	13 277	...	14 298	14 439	...	...	...
Cape Verde - Cap-Vert	DF	...	...	...	386	396	407	417	428	435	442
Central African Republic - République centrafricaine	DF	...	...	2 998	...	...	3 245	...	...	...	...
Chad - Tchad	DF	5 961	6 098	6 214	...	...	...	...	...	...	8 322
Côte d'Ivoire	DF	12 672	13 175	13 695	14 230	14 781	...	15 367	...	16 398	16 939
Egypt - Égypte	DF	54 082	55 201	56 344	57 510	58 755	60 080	61 341	62 652	63 976	67 886
Ethiopia - Éthiopie	DF	51 570	53 236	...	54 649	56 372	58 117	59 882	61 672	63 495	65 374
Gabon	DF	990	1 015	1 040	1 066	1 093	1 120	1 148	1 177	1 206	1 237
Gambia - Gambie	DF	878	...	...	...	...	...	...	1 385	1 393	1 420
Ghana	DF	...	...	...	...	...	...	...	...	18 412	...
Kenya	DF	...	...	...	...	...	28 414	...	...	...	...
Lesotho	DF	...	...	...	...	...	2 012	2 055	2 100	2 144	...
Liberia - Libéria	DF	2 580	2 640	2 700	2 760	2 820	2 879	...	...	...	...
Libyan Arab Jamahiriya - Jamahiriya arabe libyenne[1]	DF	4 041	4 156	4 274	4 395	4 519	4 648	4 772	4 958	5 125	5 300
Malawi	DF	8 823	9 135	9 461	9 788	10 114	10 441	...	...	...	11 140
Mali	DF	...	...	...	...	...	11 480	...	...	...	10 400
Mauritania - Mauritanie	DF	2 095	2 156	2 211	2 284	2 351	2 421	2 493	2 568	2 645	2 724
Mauritius - Maurice	DJ	1 084	1 097	1 113	1 122	1 134	1 148	1 160	1 175	1 187	1 200
Morocco - Maroc	DF	25 547	26 069	25 926	26 386	26 848	27 310	27 775	28 238	28 705	29 170
Mozambique[2]	DF	14 790	15 583	16 614	15 820	16 177	16 543	16 917	17 299	17 691	17 656
Namibia - Namibie	DF	...	...	...	...	...	...	...	...	1 817	...
Nigeria - Nigéria	DF	...	...	...	99 210	...	...	...	...	115 224	118 801
Réunion	DF	...	632	...	...	669	686	698	710	722	735
Saint Helena ex. dep. - Sainte-Hélène sans dép.	DF	6	6	5	5	5	...	...	...	...	...
Sao Tome and Principe - Sao Tomé-et-Principe	DF	120	122	125	127	...	...	...	...	...	...
Senegal - Sénégal	DF	7 704	7 913	8 127	8 347	8 572	8 802	9 038	9 279	9 524	9 803
Seychelles	DF	71	72	74	75	76	77	79	80	81	81
South Africa - Afrique du Sud[2]	DF	36 992	37 802	38 630	39 477	40 342	41 227	42 130	43 054	43 686	44 328
Sudan - Soudan	DF	27 323	25 588	26 289	27 008	27 747	28 507	29 266	30 046	31 081	31 627
Swaziland	DF	833	851	879	908	938	...	...	...	...	...
Togo	DF	...	...	3 928	...	...	...	...	...	...	...
Tunisia - Tunisie	DF	8 490	8 657	8 815	8 958	9 089	9 215	9 333	9 456	9 564	9 674
Uganda - Ouganda	DF	...	...	...	19 263	19 848	20 752	21 467	22 207	22 972	22 788
United Republic of Tanzania - République Unie de Tanzanie	DF	25 990	26 732	27 495	28 279	29 086	29 984	...	...	...	...
Zambia - Zambie	DF	8 189	8 458	8 764	9 112	9 454	9 780	10 096	10 407	10 723	...
Zimbabwe	DF	10 413	10 779	11 150	11 526	11 908	12 294	12 685	13 079	...	12 960
AMERICA, NORTH — AMERIQUE DU NORD											
Anguilla	DF	9	9	10	10	10	10	11	11	11	12
Antigua and Barbuda - Antigua-et-Barbuda	DF	65	66	66	68	69	...	...	...	...	...
Aruba	DJ	69	74	78	80	83	86	88	90	91	92
Bahamas	DF	264	269	274	279	284	288	293	298	303	...
Barbados - Barbade	DF	263	264	264	264	265	...	266	267	267	...
Belize	DF	199	205	211	216	222	230	238	243	250	257
Bermuda - Bermudes[3]	DJ	59	59	59	60	60	60	...	...	...	62
British Virgin Islands - Îles Vierges britanniques	DF	...	...	...	...	...	...	...	...	...	21

5. Estimates of mid-year population: 1992 - 2001
Estimations de la population au milieu de l'anneé: 1992 - 2001 (continued — suite)

(See notes at end of table. — Voir notes à la fin du tableau.)

Continent and country or area Continent et pays ou zone	Ty-pe	Population estimates (in thousands) — Estimations (en milliers)									
		1992	1993	1994	1995	1996	1997	1998	1999	2000	2001
AMERICA, NORTH — **AMERIQUE DU NORD**											
Canada[4,5,6]	DJ	28 367	28 682	28 999	29 302	29 611	29 907	30 157	30 404	30 689	31 021
Cayman Islands - Îles Caïmanes	DJ	29	31	31	33	34	36	38	39	40	41
Costa Rica	DJ	3 132	3 199	3 266	3 333	3 398	3 464	3 526	3 589	3 925	3 988
Cuba	DF	10 831	10 904	10 950	10 978	11 006	11 066	11 117	11 160	11 199	11 230
Dominica - Dominique	DF	72	73	74	75	75	76	76	...	72	70
Dominican Republic - République dominicaine	DF	*7 471*	*7 620*	*7 769*	*7 705*	*7 833*	*7 966*	*8 105*	*8 325*	*8 396*	*8 528*
El Salvador	DF	5 477	...	...	5 669	5 787	5 908	6 031	6 154	6 276	6 397
Greenland - Groenland	DJ	55	55	56	56	56	56	56	56	...	...
Grenada - Grenade	DF	96	97	98	98	99	100	100	101	101	101
Guadeloupe	DJ	408	...	...	...	...	...	...	424	...	...
Guatemala[2]	DF	9 221	9 466	9 717	9 976	10 243	10 517	10 799	11 088	11 385	11 683
Haiti - Haïti	DJ	*6 764*	*6 903*	*7 041*	*7 180*	*7 336*	*7 492*	*7 647*	*7 803*	*7 959*	*8 132*
Honduras	DF	*5 079*	*5 248*	*5 422*	*5 602*	*5 789*	*5 981*	*6 180*	*6 385*	...	...
Jamaica - Jamaïque	DF	2 424	2 444	2 473	2 503	2 527	2 553	2 572	2 590	2 605	2 621
Martinique	DJ	373	377	...	...	...	...	...	382	...	...
Mexico - Mexique	DJ	*87 114*	*88 755*	*90 386*	*91 992*	*93 572*	*95 127*	*96 649*	*98 132*	*100 249*	*101 754*
Montserrat	DF	...	...	...	...	...	...	...	...	5	...
Netherlands Antilles - Antilles néerlandaises[7]	DJ	*191*	*194*	*198*	*202*	*205*	*208*	*208*	*205*	...	...
Nicaragua	DJ	4 054	4 175	4 299	4 427	4 549	4 674	4 803	4 936	4 957	5 059
Panama	DF	*2 488*	*2 535*	*2 583*	*2 631*	*2 674*	*2 719*	*2 764*	*2 809*	*2 856*	*2 897*
Puerto Rico - Porto Rico[8]	DJ	3 575	3 600	3 627	3 655	3 685	3 716	3 748	3 782	3 818	3 840
Saint Kitts and Nevis - Saint-Kitts-et-Nevis	DF	43	44	43	44	42	41	40	42	40	46
Saint Lucia - Sainte-Lucie	DF	138	140	143	145	147	150	152	154	156	158
Saint Pierre and Miquelon - Saint Pierre-et-Miquelon	DF	6	7	7	7	7	...	...	...	...	...
Saint Vincent and the Grenadines - Saint Vincent-et-les Grenadines	DF	109	110	110	111	111	112	111	112	112	109
Trinidad and Tobago - Trinité-et-Tobago	DF	1 240	1 247	1 250	1 260	1 264	1 275	1 278	...	1 290	...
United States - États-Unis[9]	DJ	255 374	258 083	260 599	263 044	265 463	268 008	270 299	272 691	275 265	284 797
AMERICA, SOUTH — **AMERIQUE DU SUD**											
Argentina - Argentine	DF	*33 421*	*33 869*	*34 318*	*34 768*	*35 220*	*35 672*	*36 125*	*36 578*	*37 032*	*37 487*
Bolivia - Bolivie[2]	DF	*6 897*	*7 065*	*7 237*	*7 414*	*7 588*	*7 767*	*7 950*	*8 137*	*8 329*	...
Brazil - Brésil[10]	DF	*149 358*	*151 572*	*153 726*	*155 822*	*157 872*	*159 636*	*161 790*	*165 371*	*167 724*	*172 386*
Chile - Chili	DF	13 545	13 771	13 994	14 210	14 419	14 622	14 822	15 018	15 211	15 402
Colombia - Colombie	DF	*33 392*	*33 951*	*37 849*	*38 542*	*39 296*	*40 064*	*40 827*	*41 589*	*42 321*	*43 071*
Ecuador - Équateur[2,11]	DF	*10 741*	*10 981*	*11 221*	*11 460*	*11 698*	*11 773*	*11 948*	*12 121*	*12 299*	*12 480*
French Guiana - Guyane française	DJ	...	...	...	...	...	...	...	158	...	...
Guyana	DF	...	...	...	...	...	775	773	771	772	...
Paraguay	DF	*4 453*	*4 575*	*4 700*	*4 828*	*4 955*	*5 085*	*5 219*	*5 356*	...	...
Peru - Pérou[2,12]	DF	*22 454*	...	*23 130*	*23 532*	*23 947*	*24 371*	*24 801*	*25 232*	*25 662*	*26 347*
Suriname	DF	403	404	405	409	413	419	425	430	436	...
Uruguay[2]	DF	3 149	3 172	3 195	3 218	3 242	3 265	3 289	3 313	3 337	3 361
Venezuela[2,12]	DF	20 441	20 910	21 377	21 844	22 311	22 777	23 242	23 707	24 170	24 630
ASIA — ASIE											
Armenia - Arménie	DF	3 686	3 731	3 747	3 760	3 774	3 786	3 795	3 801	3 803	3 802
Azerbaijan - Azerbaïdjan	DF	7 382	7 495	7 597	7 685	7 763	7 838	7 913	7 983	8 049	8 111
Bahrain - Bahreïn	DF	*516*	*530*	*544*	*559*	*574*	*589*	*605*	*621*	*638*	*655*
Bangladesh	DF	...	...	117 700	119 900	122 100	124 300	...	...	...	...
Bhutan - Bhoutan	DF	*533*	*548*	*564*	*582*	*600*	*619*	*638*	*658*	*678*	*699*

5. Estimates of mid-year population: 1992 - 2001
Estimations de la population au milieu de l'anneé: 1992 - 2001 (continued — suite)

(See notes at end of table. — Voir notes à la fin du tableau.)

Continent and country or area / Continent et pays ou zone	Ty-pe	Population estimates (in thousands) — Estimations (en milliers)									
		1992	1993	1994	1995	1996	1997	1998	1999	2000	2001
ASIA — ASIE											
Brunei Darussalam - Brunéi Darussalam	DF	267	274	280	287	294	302	310	317	325	...
Cambodia - Cambodge[13,14]	DF	9 061	9 315	9 869	10 200	10 340	10 368	11 438	12 664	12 825	13 148
China - Chine[15,16]	DF	1 171 710	1 185 170	1 198 500	1 211 210	1 223 890	1 236 260	1 248 100	1 259 090	...	...
China: Hong Kong SAR - Chine: Hong Kong RAS	...	5 800	5 901	6 035	6 156	6 436	6 489	6 544	6 606	6 665	6 725
China: Macao SAR - Chine: Macao RAS	DJ	371	384	397	409	415	417	422	427	431	434
Cyprus - Chypre[17,18]	DJ	706	720	731	742	751	759	767	774	782	789
Georgia - Géorgie	DF	5 455	5 440	5 426	5 417	5 420	5 431	5 441	5 101	5 023	•4 946
India - Inde[19]	DF	869 828	887 566	905 449	923 459	941 579	959 792	978 081	996 430	1 014 825	1 033 248
Indonesia - Indonésie	DF	184 492	187 590	190 676	...	198 320	201 353	204 392	207 440	...	208 437
Iran (Islamic Republic of) - Iran (République islamique d')	DJ	56 656	57 488	58 331	59 187	...	60 939	61 836	62 746	63 664	64 528
Iraq	DF	18 949	19 478	20 007	20 536	21 124	22 046	22 379	22 989	23 577	24 813
Israel - Israël[2,20]	DJ	5 124	5 261	5 399	5 545	5 685	5 829	5 971	6 125	6 289	6 439
Japan - Japon[21]	DF	124 425	124 829	125 178	125 472	125 757	126 057	126 400	126 631	126 843	127 130
Jordan - Jordanie[22]	DF	•3 844	•3 993	...	•4 291	•4 444	•4 600	•4 756	•4 900	•5 039	5 182
Kazakhstan	DF	16 518	16 479	16 297	16 066	15 921	15 751	15 073	14 927	14 896	14 831
Korea (Republic of) - Corée (République de)[23]	DF	43 748	44 195	44 642	45 093	45 546	45 954	46 287	46 617	47 008	47 343
Kuwait - Koweït	DF	1 422	1 461	1 620	1 802	1 894	1 980	2 027	2 107	2 190	2 275
Kyrgyzstan - Kirghizistan	DF	4 534	4 559	4 526	4 555	4 625	4 690	4 760	4 834	4 895	4 935
Lao People's Democratic Republic - République démocratique populaire lao	DF	4 470	...	...	4 536	...	...	...	5 091	5 218	...
Malaysia - Malaisie	DF	19 043	19 564	20 112	20 689	21 169	21 666	22 180	22 712	23 266	...
Maldives	DF	231	238	246	...	251	259	267	278	271	276
Mongolia - Mongolie	DF	2 158	2 172	2 207	2 243	2 276	2 307	2 340	2 373	2 407	2 443
Myanmar	DF	42 333	43 116	43 922	...	...	46 402	...	...	...	...
Nepal - Népal	DJ	18 937	19 394	19 862	20 341	20 832	21 331	21 843	22 367	22 904	...
Occupied Palestinian Territory - Territoire palestinien occupé	DF	...	...	2 317	2 483	2 631	2 783	2 897	3 020	3 150	3 299
Oman	DF	1 882	2 000	2 050	2 131	2 214	2 256	2 288	2 325	2 401	2 478
Pakistan[24]	DF	113 610	116 470	119 390	122 360	125 380	128 420	131 510	134 510	137 510	140 470
Philippines	DJ	68 349	66 982	68 624	70 267	69 952	71 550	73 148	74 746	76 348	77 926
Qatar	DF	533	559	593	...	...	...	544	...	...	598
Saudi Arabia - Arabie saoudite	DF	...	...	...	...	...	...	...	19 895	20 847	...
Singapore - Singapour	...	3 232	3 315	3 421	3 526	...	...	...	...	...	...
Sri Lanka	DF	17 426	17 646	17 891	18 136	18 315	18 552	18 774	19 043	19 359	18 700
Syrian Arab Republic - République arabe syrienne[25]	DF	12 958	13 393	13 844	14 153	14 619	15 100	15 597	16 110	16 320	16 720
Tajikistan - Tadjikistan	DF	5 571	5 638	5 745	5 836	5 919	...	6 103	6 237	6 170	6 293
Thailand - Thaïlande	DJ	57 294	58 010	58 713	59 401	60 003	60 602	61 156	61 564	61 770	...
Turkey - Turquie	DF	58 379	59 478	60 587	61 706	62 841	63 989	65 145	66 304	67 469	68 610
Turkmenistan - Turkménistan	DF	4 032	4 308	4 406	4 509	4 569	...	4 859	...	...	...
United Arab Emirates - Émirats arabes unis	DF	...	...	...	2 314	2 443	2 624	2 776	2 938	...	...
Uzbekistan - Ouzbékistan	DF	21 360	21 852	22 282	22 690	23 130	23 560	24 051	23 954	24 650	24 964
Viet Nam	DF	69 405	71 026	72 510	73 962	75 355	74 346	75 526	76 597	77 686	...
Yemen - Yémen	DF	11 952	12 302	14 859	15 369	15 915	16 484	17 072	17 671	18 261	18 863
EUROPE											
Albania - Albanie	DF	3 363	3 485	3 547	3 609	3 650	3 731	3 791	...	...	...
Andorra - Andorre	DF	60	63	65	...	...	66	66	66	66	67

5. Estimates of mid-year population: 1992 - 2001
Estimations de la population au milieu de l'anneé: 1992 - 2001 (continued — suite)

(See notes at end of table. — Voir notes à la fin du tableau.)

Continent and country or area / Continent et pays ou zone	Ty-pe	Population estimates (in thousands) — Estimations (en milliers)									
		1992	1993	1994	1995	1996	1997	1998	1999	2000	2001
EUROPE											
Austria - Autriche	DJ	7 914	7 991	8 030	8 047	8 059	8 072	8 078	8 092	8 109	8 130
Belarus - Bélarus	DF	10 313	10 356	10 308	10 281	10 250	10 220	10 191	10 035	10 002	9 973
Belgium - Belgique	DJ	10 045	10 084	10 116	10 137	10 157	10 181	10 203	10 226	10 251	10 287
Bosnia and Herzegovina - Bosnie-Herzégovine	DJ	4 409	4 434	4 459	4 180	4 174	3 738	3 653	...	...	...
Bulgaria - Bulgarie	DF	8 540	8 472	8 444	8 406	8 363	8 312	8 257	8 211	8 170	7 913
Channel Islands - Îles Anglo-Normandes	DF	143	142	142	143	...	...	...	...	...	...
Croatia - Croatie	DJ	4 470	4 641	4 649	4 669	4 494	4 572	4 501	4 554	4 381	4 437
Czech Republic - République tchèque	DJ	10 318	10 331	10 336	10 331	10 315	10 304	10 295	10 283	10 273	10 224
Denmark - Danemark[26]	DJ	5 170	5 189	5 205	5 228	5 262	5 284	5 301	5 327	5 319	5 359
Estonia - Estonie	DF	1 544	1 517	1 499	1 484	1 469	1 458	1 450	1 442	1 369	♦1 361
Finland - Finlande	DJ	5 042	5 066	5 088	5 108	5 125	5 140	5 153	5 165	5 176	5 188
France[27]	DJ	57 240	57 467	57 659	57 844	58 026	58 610	58 398	58 623	58 893	59 191
Germany - Allemagne	DJ	80 570	81 187	81 422	81 661	81 896	82 061	82 029	82 057	82 183	82 348
Gibraltar[28]	DF	29	28	27	27	27	27	27	27	27	28
Greece - Grèce[29]	DF	10 322	10 379	10 426	10 454	10 476	10 499	10 516	10 534	10 008	10 020
Holy See - Saint-Siège[30]	DF	...	...	...	...	...	...	1	...	...	...
Hungary - Hongrie	DF	10 324	10 294	10 261	10 229	10 193	10 155	10 114	10 068	10 024	10 188
Iceland - Islande	DJ	261	264	266	267	269	271	274	277	281	285
Ireland - Irlande	DF	3 554	3 574	3 586	3 601	3 626	3 661	3 705	3 745	3 787	3 854
Isle of Man - Îles de Man	DJ	70	71	71	72	71	72	74	...	75	76
Italy - Italie	DJ	56 859	57 049	57 204	57 301	57 380	57 523	57 588	57 646	57 762	57 948
Latvia - Lettonie	DF	2 614	2 563	2 521	2 485	2 457	2 433	2 410	2 390	2 373	2 355
Liechtenstein	DF	30	♦30	30	31	31	31	♦32	♦32	33	33
Lithuania - Lituanie	DF	3 700	3 683	3 657	3 629	3 602	3 575	3 549	3 524	3 500	3 481
Luxembourg	DJ	390	398	404	410	416	421	426	432	436	442
Malta - Malte[31]	DJ	♦369	♦373	♦376	♦378	♦381	♦384	♦386	♦389	♦391	♦395
Monaco	DJ	...	...	...	...	...	32	...	33	33	...
Netherlands - Pays-Bas	DJ	15 184	15 290	15 383	15 459	15 531	15 611	15 707	15 812	15 908	16 046
Norway - Norvège[32]	DJ	4 286	4 312	4 325	4 359	4 381	4 405	4 431	4 462	4 491	4 514
Poland - Pologne[33]	DF	38 365	38 459	38 544	38 588	38 618	38 650	38 666	38 654	38 646	38 638
Portugal[34]	DF	9 867	9 881	9 902	9 916	9 927	9 946	9 968	9 989	10 008	10 299
Republic of Moldova - République de Moldova[35]	DJ	4 348	4 348	4 348	4 348	4 327	3 654	3 652	3 646	3 639	3 631
Romania - Roumanie	DJ	22 789	22 755	22 731	22 681	22 608	22 546	22 503	22 458	22 435	22 408
Russian Federation - Fédération de Russie	DF	148 310	148 146	147 968	147 774	147 739	147 105	146 539	145 943	♦145 559	♦143 954
San Marino - Saint-Marin	DF	24	24	25	25	25	26	26	26	27	...
Serbia and Montenegro - Serbie-et-Montenegro[36]	DJ	10 448	10 482	10 516	10 547	10 577	10 600	10 617	10 629	10 635	10 651
Slovakia - Slovaquie	DJ	5 307	5 325	5 347	5 364	5 374	5 383	5 391	5 395	5 400	5 380
Slovenia - Slovénie	DJ	1 996	1 991	1 989	1 988	1 991	1 987	1 983	1 986	1 990	1 992
Spain - Espagne	DJ	39 011	39 096	39 166	39 223	39 279	39 348	39 453	39 626	39 927	40 266
Sweden - Suède	DJ	8 668	8 719	8 781	8 827	8 841	8 846	8 851	8 861	8 872	8 896
Switzerland - Suisse	DJ	6 875	6 938	6 994	7 041	7 072	7 089	7 110	7 144	7 184	7 233
The Former Yugoslav Rep. of Macedonia - L'ex-République yougoslave de Macédoine	...	2 056	...	...	1 963	1 975	1 997	2 008	2 017	2 024	2 026
Ukraine	DF	52 057	52 244	52 114	51 728	51 334	50 894	50 500	50 106	49 711	♦49 037
United Kingdom - Royaume-Uni[37]	DF	58 013	58 198	58 401	58 612	58 807	59 014	59 237	59 501	59 756	59 756
OCEANIA — OCEANIE											
American Samoa - Samoa américaines[8,38]	DJ	50	52	53	53	54	55	56	57	58	...
Australia - Australie[2]	DJ	17 495	17 667	17 855	18 072	18 311	18 524	18 730	18 937	19 157	19 387
Cook Islands - Îles Cook	DF	...	20	20	19	20	18	17	16	18	18
Fiji - Fidji	DF	746	771	784	796	775	...	797	806	...	...

5. Estimates of mid-year population: 1992 - 2001
Estimations de la population au milieu de l'anneé: 1992 - 2001 (continued — suite)

(See notes at end of table. — Voir notes à la fin du tableau.)

Continent and country or area / Continent et pays ou zone	Ty-pe	Population estimates (in thousands) — Estimations (en milliers)									
		1992	1993	1994	1995	1996	1997	1998	1999	2000	2001
OCEANIA — OCEANIE											
French Polynesia - Polynésie française	DF	205	209	213	216	219	222	226	228	◆231	...
Guam[8]	DJ	139	143	146	149	153	156	149	152	155	158
Kiribati	DF	...	...	...	78	...	83	...	...	...	...
Marshall Islands - Îles Marshall	DF	50	52	54	56	57	61	63	51	53	55
Micronesia, Federated States of - Micronésie, États Fédérés de La	DJ	...	...	104	107	110	110	112	113	119	117
Nauru	DF	...	10	10	11	...	...	...	...	...	...
New Caledonia - Nouvelle-Calédonie	DF	180	184	189	194	197	201	204	208	211	214
New Zealand - Nouvelle-Zélande	DJ	3 514	3 554	3 602	3 656	3 714	3 761	3 792	3 811	3 831	...
Northern Mariana Islands - Îles Mariannes septentrionales	DF	...	...	...	...	61	64	67	69	72	75
Palau - Palaos	DF	16	16	17	17	18	18	18	19	19	20
Papua New Guinea - Papouasie-Nouvelle-Guinée	DF	3 847	3 922	3 997	4 074	...	4 209	4 600	...	5 100	...
Samoa	DF	161	...	164	...	...	...	168	169	171	...
Tonga	DF	•96	•97	•97	•98	...	•99	•99	•100	•100	•101
Vanuatu	DF	154	158	162	166	170	174	...	...	...	...

GENERAL NOTES - NOTES GENERALES

For certain countries or areas, there is a discrepancy between the mid-year population estimates shown in this table and those shown in subsequent tables for the same year. Usually this discrepancy arises because the estimates for a given year are revised, although the remaining tabulations are not. Unless otherwise indicated, data are official estimates of population for 1 July, or averages of end-year estimates. For method of evaluation and limitations of data, see Technical Notes for the present table. — Pour quelques pays ou zones il y a une discordance entres les estimations au milieu de l'année présentées dans ce tableau et celles présentées dans les tableaux suivants pour la même année. Habituellement ces différences apparaîssent lorsque les estimations pour une certaine année ont été révisées; alors que les autres tabulations ne l'ont pas été. Sauf indication contraire, les données sont des estimations officielles de population au 1er juillet ou des moyennes d'estimations de fin d'année. Pour la méthode d'évaluation et les insuffisances des données, voir Notes techniques, pour ce tableau.

DF Estimates of population de facto.
DJ Estimates of population de jure.

Italics: estimates which are less reliable. — Italiques: estimations moins sûres.

FOOTNOTES - NOTES

◆ Data refer to 1 January — Données se raportent au 1 Janvier.
• Data refer to 31 December — Données se raportent au 31 Décembre.
[1] For Libyan nationals only. - Pour les nationaux libyens seulement.
[2] Mid-year estimates have been adjusted for underenumeration, at latest census. - Les estimations au millieu de l'année tiennent compte d'une ajustement destiné à compenser les lacunes du dénombrement lors du dernier recensement.
[3] Excluding institutional population. - Non compris la population dans les institutions.
[4] For 2001, final postcensal estimates. - Pour 2001, évaluations postcensal finales.
[5] From 1996 to 2000, final intercensal estimates. - De 1996 à 2001 estimations inter censitaires finales.

[6] From 1992 to 1995, revised intercensal estimates adjusted for net undercoverage. - De 1992 à 1995, estimations inter censitaires corrigées pour tenir en compte du sous dénombrement net.
[7] Comprising Bonaire, Curaçao, Saba, St. Eustatius and Dutch part of St. Martin. - Comprend Bonaire, Curaçao, Saba, Saint-Eustache et la partie néederlandaise de Saint-Martin.
[8] Including armed forces stationed in the area. - Y compris les militaires en garnison sur le territoire.
[9] Excluding civilian citizens absent from country for extended periods of time. - Non compris les civils hors du pays pendant une période prolongée.
[10] Data include persons in remote areas, military personnel outside the country, merchant seamen at sea, civilian seasonal workers outside the country, and other civilians outside the country, and exclude nomads, foreign military, civilian aliens temporarily in the country, transients on ships and Indian jungle population. - Y compris les personnes dans des régions éloignées, le personnel militaire en dehors du pays, les marins marchands, les ouvriers saisonniers civils de couture en dehors du pays, et autres civils en dehors du pays, et non compris les nomades, les militaires étrangers, les étrangers civils temporairement dans le pays, les transiteurs sur des bateaux et les Indiens de la jungle.
[11] Excluding nomadic Indian tribes. - Non compris les tribus d'Indiens nomades.
[12] Excluding Indian jungle population. - Non compris les Indiens de la jungle.
[13] Excluding foreign diplomatic personnel and their dependants. - Non compris le personnel diplomatique étranger et les membres de leur famille les accompagnant.
[14] For 1996, based on results of a sample survey. - Pour 1996, d'après les résultats d'une enquête par sondage.
[15] For statistical purposes, the data for China do not include those for the Hong Kong Special Administrative Region (Hong Kong SAR), Macao special Adminstrative Region (Macao SAR) and Taiwan province of China. - Pour la présentation des statistiques, les données pour Chine ne comprend pas les Région Administrative Spéciale de Hong Kong (Hong Kong RAS), le Région Administrative Spéciale de Macao (Macao RAS) et Taïwan province de Chine.
[16] Data are estimates on the basis of the annual National Sample Survey on Population changes. - Les données ont été estimées sur la base de l'enquête annuelle "National Sample Survey on Population changes".
[17] Estimates of the number of Turkish Cypriots from 1974 onwards are the result of population projections based on the age and sex structure of the Turkisih Cypriot community as at Census 1960 and with assumptions of fertility and mortality similar to the rest of the Cyprus Population. With regard to the migration of Turkish Cypriots after 1974, migration assumptions are based on figures obtained from Turkish Cypriot sources. Settlers from Turkey are not included. - -

Les estimations du nombre de Chypriotes turcs depuis 1974 résultent des projections de population préparées sur la base de la structure par sexe et age de la communauté chypriote turque au recensement de 1960, et avec des hypothèses de fécondité et de mortalité similaires à celles du reste de la population de Chypre. En ce qui concerne la migration des Chypriotes turcs après 1974, les hypothèses sont basées sur les données obtenues de sources chypriotes turques. Les occupants venus de Turquie ne sont pas inclus.

[18] Data for the period 1993-2000 have been revised on the basis of the Population Census of 2001. - Des données pour 1993 à 2000 ont été calculées sur la base du recensement de population de 2001.

[19] Including data for the Indian-held part of Jammu and Kashmir, the final status of which has not yet been determined. - Y compris les données pour la partie du Jammu et du Cachemire occupée par l'Inde dont le statut définitif n'a pas encore été déterminé.

[20] Including data for East Jerusalem and Israeli residents in certain other territories under occupation by Israeli military forces since June 1967. - Y compris les données pour Jérusalem-Est et les résidents israéliens dans certains autres territoires occupés depuis 1967 par les forces armées israéliennes.

[21] Excluding diplomatic personnel outside country and foreign military and civilian personnel and their dependants stationed in the area. - Non compris le personnel diplomatique hors du pays ni les militaires et agents civils étrangers en poste sur le territoire et les membres de leur famille les accompagnant.

[22] Excluding data for Jordanian territory under occupation since June 1967 by Israeli military forces. Excluding foreigners, including registered Palestinian refugees. - Non compris les données pour le territoire jordanien occupé depuis juin 1967 par les forces armées israéliennes. Non compris les étrangers, mais y compris les réfugiés de Palestine immatriculés.

[23] From 1992 to 1994, excluding alien armed forces, civilian aliens employed by armed forces, foreign diplomatic personnel and their dependants and Korean diplomatic personnel and their dependants outside the country. - De 1992 à 1994, non compris les militaires étrangers, les civils étrangers employés par les forces armées, le personnel diplomatique étranger et les membres de leur famille les accompagnant et le personnel diplomatique coréen hors du pays et les membres de leurs familles les accompagnant.

[24] Excluding data for the Pakistan-held part of Jammu and Kashmir, the final status of which has not yet been determined. - Non compris les données concernant la partie du Jammu et Cachemire occupée par le Pakistan dont le statut définitif n'a pas été déterminé.

[25] Including Palestinian refugees. - Y compris les réfugiés de Palestine.

[26] Excluding Faeroe Islands and Greenland. - Non compris les îles Féroé et Gröenland.

[27] Excluding Overseas Departments, namely French Guiana, Guadeloupe, Martinique and Reunion, shown separately. De jure population but excluding diplomatic personnel outside country and including members of alien armed forces not living in military camps and foreign diplomatic personnel not living in embassies or consulates. - Non compris les départements d'outre-mer, c'est-à-dire la Guyane française, la Guadeloupe, la Martinique et la Réunion, qui font l'objet de rubriques distinctes. Population de droit, non compris le personnel diplomatique hors du pays et y compris les militaires étrangers ne vivant pas dans des camps militaires et le personnel diplomatique étranger ne vivant pas dans les ambassades ou les consulats.

[28] Excluding armed forces. - Non compris les militaires en garnison.

[29] Mid-year population excludes armed forces stationed outside the country, but includes alien armed forces stationed in the area. - Les estimations au millieu de l'année non compris les militaires en garnison hors du pays, mais y compris les militaires étrangers en garnison sur le territoire.

[30] Data refer to the Vatican City State. - Les données se rapportent aux Etat du Saint-Siè-ge.

[31] Including foreigners residing in Malta for 12 months before the census date and excluding foreign diplomatic personnel. - Y compris les les étrangers habitant à Malte pour 12 mois avant le recensement et le personnel diplomatique étrangers.

[32] From 1997, including residents temporarily outside the country. - Après 1997, y compris les résidents se trouvant temporairement hors du pays.

[33] Excluding civilian aliens within country, but including civilian nationals temporarily outside country. - Non compris les civils étrangers dans le pays, mais y compris les civils nationaux temporairement hors du pays.

[34] Including the Azores and Madeira Islands. - Y compris les Açores et Madère.

[35] Figures for 1997-2001 do not include information for Transnistria and the municipality of Bender. - Les données pour 1997-2001 ne tiennent pas compte de l'information sur la Transnistria et la municipalité de Bender.

[36] Beginning with 1998, estimates of Kosovo and Metohia computed on the basis of natural increases from year 1997. - A partir du 1998, les estimations pour le Kosovo et la Metohia ont été calculées sur la base des incréments naturelles depuis 1997.

[37] From 1997 to 2000, data revised to exclude births in Northern Ireland to non-residents of Northern Ireland. - De 1997 à 2000, données révisées non compris des naissances en Irlande du Nord aux non-résidents de l'Irlande du Nord.

[38] Population estimates for the years 1991 to 1999 have been smoothed using the 1995 mid-decade household survey and the year 2000 census. - L'estimation de la population a été lissée pour les années entre 1991 et 1999 en utilisant l'enquête des ménages de 1995 et le recensement de l'année 2000.

Table 6

Table 6 presents urban and total population by sex for as many years as possible between 1992 and 2001.

Description of variables: Data are from nation-wide population censuses or are estimates, some of which are based on sample surveys of population carried out among all segments of the population. The results of censuses are identified by a code following the date in the stub; sample surveys are further identified by footnotes; other data are generally estimates, the characteristics of which (*de jure* or *de facto*) are also indicated with a code.

Estimates of urban population presented in this table have been limited to countries or areas for which estimates have been based on the results of a sample survey or have been constructed by the component method from the results of a population census or sample survey. Distributions which result from the estimated total population being distributed by urban/rural residence according to percentages in each group at the time of a census or sample survey are not acceptable and they have not been included in this table.

Urban is defined according to the national census definition. The definition for each country is set forth at the end of the technical notes to this table.

Percentage computation: Percentages urban are the number of persons residing in an area defined as "urban" per 100 total population. They are calculated by the United Nations Statistics Division.

Reliability of data: Estimates which are believed to be less reliable are set in *italics* rather than in roman type. Classification in terms of reliability is based on the method of construction of the total population estimate as shown in table 3 and discussed in the technical notes for that table.

Limitations: Statistics on urban population by sex are subject to the same qualifications as have been set forth for population statistics in general, as discussed in section 3 of the Technical Notes.

The basic limitations imposed by variations in the definition of the total population and in the degree of under-enumeration are perhaps more important in relation to urban/rural than to any other distributions. The classification by urban and rural is affected by variations in defining usual residence for purposes of sub-national tabulations. Likewise, the geographical differentials in the degree of under-enumeration in censuses affect the comparability of these categories throughout the table. The distinction between *de facto* and *de jure* population is also very important with respect to urban/rural distributions. The difference between the *de facto* and the *de jure* population is discussed at length in section 3.1.1 of the Technical Notes.

A most important and specific limitation, however, lies in the national differences in the definition of urban. Because the distinction between urban and rural areas is made in so many different ways, the definitions have been included at the end of this table. The definitions are necessarily brief and, where the classification as urban involves administrative civil divisions, they are often given in the terminology of the particular country or area. As a result of variations in terminology, it may appear that differences between countries or areas are greater than they actually are. On the other hand, similar or identical terms (for example, town, village, district) as used in different countries or areas may have quite different meanings.

It will be seen from an examination of the definitions that they fall roughly into three major types: (1) classification of localities as urban based on size; (2) classification of administrative centres of minor civil divisions as urban and the remainder of the division as rural; and (3) classification of minor civil divisions on a set of criteria which may include type of local government, number of inhabitants or proportion of population engaged in agriculture.

The designation of areas as urban or rural is so closely bound to historical, political, cultural, and administrative considerations that the process of developing uniform definitions and procedures moves very slowly. Not only do the definitions differ one from the other, but, they may also no longer reflect the original intention for distinguishing urban from rural.

The criteria once established on the basis of administrative subdivisions (as most of these are) become fixed and resistant to change. For this reason, comparisons of time-series data may be severely affected because the definitions used become outdated. Special care must be taken in comparing data from censuses with those from sample surveys because the definitions of urban used may differ.

Despite their shortcomings, however, statistics on urban and rural population are useful in describing the diversity within the population of a country or area.

The definition of urban/rural areas is based on both qualitative and quantitative criteria that may include any combination of the following: size of population, population density, distance between built-up areas, predominant type of economic activity, conformity to legal or administrative status and urban characteristics such as specific services and facilities[1]. Although statistics classified by urban/rural areas are widely available, no international standard definition appears to be possible at this time since the meaning differs from one country or area to another. The urban/rural classification of population used here is reported according to the national definition, as indicated in a footnote to this table and described in detail in the technical notes for table 2 of the Historical Supplement[2].

Coverage: Urban and total population by sex are shown for 120 countries or areas.

Earlier data: Urban and total population by sex have been shown in previous issues of the Demographic Yearbook. For information on specific years covered, readers should consult the Index.

DEFINITION OF "URBAN"

AFRICA

Benin: Not available.
Botswana: Agglomeration of 5 000 or more inhabitants where 75 per cent of the economic activity is non-agricultural.
Burkina Faso: Not available.
Burundi: Commune of Bujumbura.
Cape Verde: Not available.
Comoros: Administrative centres of prefectures and localities of 5 000 or more inhabitants.
Côte d' Ivoire: Not available.
Egypt: Governorates of Cairo, Alexandria, Port Said, Ismailia, Suez, frontier governorates and capitals of other governorates, as well as district capitals (Markaz).
Equatorial Guinea: District centres and localities with 300 dwellings and/or 1 500 inhabitants or more.
Ethiopia: Localities of 2 000 or more inhabitants.
Gabon: Not available.
Liberia: Localities of 2 000 or more inhabitants.
Malawi: All townships and town planning areas and all district centres.
Mauritius: Towns with proclaimed legal limits.
Morocco: Not available.
Namibia: Not available.
Niger: Not available.
Nigeria: Not available.
Rwanda: Not available.
Senegal: Agglomerations of 10 000 or more inhabitants.
South Africa: Places with some form of local authority.
Sudan: Localities of administrative and/or commercial importance or with population of 5 000 or more inhabitants.
Swaziland: Localities proclaimed as urban.
Tunisia: Population living in communes.
Uganda: Not available.
United Republic of Tanzania: 16 gazetted townships.
Zambia: Localities of 5 000 or more inhabitants, the majority of whom all depend on non-agricultural activities.

AMERICA, NORTH

Bahamas: Not available.
Belize: Not available.
Canada: Places of 1 000 or more inhabitants, having a population density of 400 or more per square kilometre.
Costa Rica: Administrative centres of cantons.
Cuba: Population living in a nucleus of 2 000 or more inhabitants.
Dominican Republic: Administrative centres of municipalities and municipal districts, some of which include suburban zones of rural character.
El Salvador: Administrative centres of municipalities.
Greenland: Localities of 200 or more inhabitants.
Guatemala: Municipality of Guatemala Department and officially recognized centres of other departments and municipalities.
Haiti: Administrative centres of communes.
Honduras: Localities of 2 000 or more inhabitants, having essentially urban characteristics.
Jamaica: Not available.
Mexico: Localities of 2 500 or more inhabitants.
Nicaragua: Administrative centres of municipalities and localities of 1 000 or more inhabitants with streets and electric light.
Panama: Localities of 1 500 or more inhabitants having essentially urban characteristics. Beginning 1970, localities of 1 500 or more inhabitants with such urban characteristics as streets, water supply systems, sewerage systems and electric light.
Puerto Rico: Places of 2 500 or more inhabitants and densely settled urban fringes of urbanized areas.
United States: Places of 2 500 or more inhabitants and urbanized areas.

AMERICA, SOUTH

Argentina: Populated centres with 2 000 or more inhabitants.
Bolivia: Localities of 2 000 or more inhabitants.
Brazil: Urban and suburban zones of administrative centres of municipalities and districts.
Chile: Populated centres which have definite urban characteristics such as certain public and municipal services.
Colombia: Not available.
Ecuador: Capitals of provinces and cantons.
Falkland Islands (Malvinas): Town of Stanley.
Paraguay: Cities, towns and administrative centres of departments and districts.
Peru: Populated centres with 100 or more dwellings.
Suriname: Paramaribo town.
Uruguay: Cities.

Venezuela: Centres with a population of 1 000 or more inhabitants.

ASIA

Armenia: Cities and urban-type localities, officially designated as such, usually according to the criteria of number of inhabitants and predominance of agricultural, or number of non-agricultural workers and their families.

Azerbaijan: Cities and urban-type localities, officially designated as such, usually according to the criteria of number of inhabitants and predominance of agricultural, or number of non-agricultural workers and their families.

Bahrain: Communes or villages of 2 500 or more inhabitants.

Brunei Darussalam: Not available.

Cambodia: Towns.

China: Not available.

Cyprus: Municipal areas, suburban areas and some villages.

Georgia: Cities and urban-type localities, officially designated as such, usually according to the criteria of number of inhabitants and predominance of agricultural, or number of non-agricultural workers and their families.

India: Towns (places with municipal corporation, municipal area committee, town committee, notified area committee or cantonment board); also, all places having 5 000 or more inhabitants, a density of not less than 1 000 persons per square mile or 390 per square kilometre, pronounced urban characteristics and at least three fourths of the adult male population employed in pursuits other than agriculture.

Indonesia: Places with urban characteristics.

Iran (Islamic Republic of): All Shahrestan centres, regardless of size, and all places having municipal centres.

Israel: All settlements of more than 2 000 inhabitants, except those where at least one third of households, participating in the civilian labour force, earn their living from agriculture.

Japan: City (shi) having 50 000 or more inhabitants with 60 per cent or more of the houses located in the main built-up areas and 60 per cent or more of the population (including their dependants) engaged in manufacturing, trade or other urban type of business. Alternatively, a shi having urban facilities and conditions as defined by the prefectural order is considered as urban.

Kazakhstan: Cities and urban-type localities, officially designated as such, usually according to the criteria of number of inhabitants and predominance of agricultural, or number of non-agricultural workers and their families.

Korea, Dem. People's Rep. of: Not available.

Korea, Republic of: Population living in cities irrespective of size of population.

Kyrgyzstan: Cities and urban-type localities, officially designated as such, usually according to the criteria of number of inhabitants and predominance of agricultural, or number of non-agricultural workers and their families.

Malaysia: Gazetted areas with population of 10 000 and more.

Maldives: Malé, the capital.

Mongolia: Capital and district centres.

Nepal: Not available.

Pakistan: Places with municipal corporation, town committee or cantonment.

Philippines: Not available.

Syrian Arab Republic: Cities, Mohafaza centres and Mantika centres, and communities with 20 000 or more inhabitants.

Tajikistan: Cities and urban-type localities, officially designated as such, usually according to the criteria of number of inhabitants and predominance of agricultural, or number of non-agricultural workers and their families.

Thailand: Municipal areas.

Turkey: Population of the localities within the municipality limits of administrative centres of provinces and districts.

Turkmenistan: Cities and urban-type localities, officially designated as such, usually according to the criteria of number of inhabitants and predominance of agricultural, or number of non-agricultural workers and their families.

Uzbekistan: Cities and urban-type localities, officially designated as such, usually according to the criteria of number of inhabitants and predominance of agricultural, or number of non-agricultural workers and their families.

Viet Nam: Cities, towns and districts with 2 000 or more inhabitants.

Yemen: Not available.

EUROPE

Albania: Towns and other industrial centres of more than 400 inhabitants.

Austria: Communes of more than 5 000 inhabitants.

Belarus: Cities and urban-type localities, officially designated as such, usually according to the criteria of number of inhabitants and predominance of agricultural, or number of non-agricultural workers and their families.

Bulgaria: Towns, that is, localities legally established as urban.

Croatia: Not available.

Czech Republic: Localities with 2 000 or more inhabitants.

Estonia: Cities and urban-type localities, officially designated as such, usually according to the criteria of number of inhabitants and predominance of agricultural, or number of non-agricultural workers and their families.

Finland: Urban communes. 1970: Localities.

France: Communes containing an agglomeration of more than 2 000 inhabitants living in contiguous houses or with not more than 200 metres between houses, also communes of which the major portion of the population is part of a multicommunal agglomeration of this nature.

Greece: Population of municipalities and communes in which the largest population centre has 10 000 or more inhabitants. Including also the population of the 18 urban agglomerations, as these were defined at the census of 1991, namely: Greater Athens, Thessaloniki, Patra, Iraklio, Volos, Chania, Irannina, Chalkida, Agrinio, Kalamata, Katerini, Kerkyra, Salamina, Chios, Egio, Rethymno, Ermoupolis, and Sparti.

Hungary: Budapest and all legally designated towns.

Iceland: Localities of 200 or more inhabitants.

Ireland: Cities and towns including suburbs of 1 500 or more inhabitants.

Latvia: Cities and urban-type localities, officially designated as such, usually according to the criteria of number of inhabitants and predominance of agricultural, or number of non-agricultural workers and their families.

Lithuania: Cities and urban-type localities, officially designated as such, usually according to the criteria of number of inhabitants and predominance of agricultural, or number of non-agricultural workers and their families.

Netherlands: Urban: Municipalities with a population of 2 000 and more inhabitants. Semi-urban: Municipalities with a population of less than 2 000 but with not more than 20 per cent of their economically active male population engaged in agriculture, and specific residential municipalities of commuters.

Norway: Localities of 200 or more inhabitants.

Poland: Towns and settlements of urban type, e.g. workers' settlements, fishermen's settlements, health resorts.

Portugal: Agglomeration of 10 000 or more inhabitants.

Republic of Moldova: Cities and urban-type localities, officially designated as such, usually according to the criteria of number of inhabitants and predominance of agricultural, or number of non-agricultural workers and their families.

Romania: Cities, municipalities and other towns.

Russian Federation: Cities and urban-type localities, officially designated as such, usually according to the criteria of number of inhabitants and predominance of agricultural, or number of non-agricultural workers and their families.

San Marino: Not available.

Slovakia: 138 cities with 5 000 inhabitants or more.

Slovenia: Not available.

Spain: Localities of 2 000 or more inhabitants.

Sweden: Not available.

Switzerland: Communes of 10 000 or more inhabitants, including suburbs.

The former Yugoslav Rep. of Macedonia: Not available.

Ukraine: Cities and urban-type localities, officially designated as such, usually according to the criteria of number of inhabitants and predominance of agricultural, or number of non-agricultural workers and their families.

Yugoslavia: Not available.

OCEANIA

American Samoa: Places of 2 500 or more inhabitants and urbanized areas.

Guam: Places of 2 500 or more inhabitants and urbanized areas.

New Caledonia: Nouméa and communes of Païta, Nouvel Dumbéa and Mont-Dore.

New Zealand: All cities, plus boroughs, town districts, townships and country towns with a population of 1 000 or more.

Vanuatu: Luganville centre and Vila urban.

NOTES

[1] For further information, see *Social and Demographic Statistics: Classifications of Size and Type of Locality and Urban/Rural Areas.* E/CN.3/551, United Nations, New York, 1980.

[2] *Demographic Yearbook: Historical Supplement 1948-1997, CD-ROM Special Issue*, Sales No. E99.XIII.12, United Nations, 1997.

Tableau 6

Le tableau 6 présente des données sur la population urbaine et la population totale selon le sexe pour le plus grand nombre possible d'années entre 1992 et 2001.

Description des variables : Les données sont tirées de recensements de la population ou sont des estimations fondées, dans certains cas, sur des enquêtes par sondage portant sur tous les secteurs de la population. Les résultats de recensement sont indiqués avec le code placé après la date dans la colonne de gauche du tableau; les enquêtes par sondage sont en outre signalées avec une note en bas de tableau; toutes les autres données sont en général des estimations et sont aussi signalées avec un code.

Les estimations de la population urbaine qui figurent dans ce tableau ne concernent que les pays ou zones pour lesquels les estimations se fondent sur les résultats d'une enquête par sondage ou ont été établies par la méthode des composantes à partir des résultats d'un recensement de la population ou d'une enquête par sondage. Les répartitions selon la résidence (urbaine/rurale) obtenues en appliquant à l'estimation de la population totale les pourcentages enregistrés pour chaque groupe lors d'un recensement ou d'une enquête par sondage ne sont pas acceptables et n'ont pas été reproduites dans ce tableau.

Le sens donné au terme "urbain" est censé être conforme aux définitions utilisées dans les recensements nationaux. La définition pour chaque pays figure à la fin des notes technique du tableau.

Calcul des pourcentages : Les pourcentages urbains représentent le nombre de personnes définies comme vivant dans des "régions urbaines" pour 100 personnes de la population totale. Elles sont calculées par la Division de Statistique des Nations Unies.

Fiabilité des données : Les estimations considérées comme moins sûres sont indiquées en italique plutôt qu'en caractères romains. Le classement du point de vue de la fiabilité est fondé sur la méthode utilisée pour établir l'estimation de la population totale qui figure dans le tableau 3 (voir explications dans les notes techniques relatives à ce même tableau).

Insuffisance des données : Les statistiques de la population urbaine selon le sexe appellent toutes les réserves qui ont été faites à la section 3 des Notes techniques à propos des statistiques de la population en général.

Les limitations fondamentales imposées par les variations de la définition de la population totale et par les lacunes du recensement se font peut-être sentir davantage dans la répartition de la population en urbaine et rurale que dans sa répartition suivant toute autre caractéristique. C'est ainsi que la classification en population urbaine ou population rurale est affectée par des différences de définition de la résidence habituelle utilisée pour l'exploitation des données à l'échelon sous-national. Pareillement, les différences de degré de sous-dénombrement suivant la zone géographique, à l'occasion des recensements, influent sur la comparabilité de ces deux catégories dans l'ensemble du tableau. La distinction entre population de fait et population de droit est également très importante du point de vue de la répartition de la population en urbaine et rurale. Cette distinction est expliquée en détail à la section 3.1.1 des Notes techniques.

Toutefois, la difficulté la plus caractérisée provient du fait que les pays ou zones ne sont pas d'accord sur la définition du terme urbain. La distinction entre les régions urbaines et les régions rurale varie tellement que les définitions utilisées ont été reproduites à la fin de ce tableau. Les définitions sont forcément brèves et, lorsque le classement en "zone urbaine" repose sur des divisions administratives, on a souvent identifié celles-ci par le nom qu'elles portent dans le pays ou zone considéré. Par suite des variations dans la terminologie, les différences entre pays ou zones peuvent sembler plus grandes qu'elles ne le sont réellement. Mais il se peut aussi que des termes similaires ou identiques, tels que ville, village ou district, aient des significations très différentes suivant les pays ou zones.

On constatera, en examinant les définitions adoptées par les différents pays ou zones, qu'elles peuvent être ramenées à trois types principaux: 1) classification des localités de certaines dimensions comme urbaines; 2) classification des centres administratifs de petites circonscriptions administratives comme urbains, le reste de la circonscription étant considéré comme rural; 3) classification des petites divisions administratives selon un critère déterminé, qui peut être soit le type d'administration locale, soit le nombre d'habitants, soit le pourcentage de la population exerçant une activité agricole.

La distinction entre régions urbaines et régions rurales est si étroitement liée à des considérations d'ordre historique, politique, culturel et administratif que l'on ne peut progresser que très lentement vers des définitions et des méthodes uniformes. Non seulement les définitions sont différentes les unes des autres, mais on n'y retrouve parfois même plus l'intention originale de distinguer les régions rurales des régions urbaines.

Lorsque la classification est fondée, en particulier, sur le critère des circonscriptions administratives (comme la plupart le sont), elle a tendance à devenir rigide avec le temps et à décourager toute modification. Pour cette raison, la comparaison des données appartenant à des séries chronologiques risque d'être gravement faussée du fait que les définitions employées sont désormais périmées. Il faut être particulièrement prudent lorsqu'on compare des données de recensements avec des données d'enquêtes par sondage, car il se peut que les définitions du terme urbain auxquelles ces données se réfèrent respectivement soient différentes.

Malgré leurs insuffisances, les statistiques urbaines et rurales permettent de mettre en évidence la diversité de la population d'un pays ou d'une zone.

La distinction urbaine/rurale repose sur une série de critères qualitatifs aussi bien que quantitatifs, dont: l'effectif de la population, la densité de peuplement, la distance entre îlots d'habitations, le type prédominant d'activité économique, le statut juridique ou administratif, et les caractéristiques d'une agglomération urbaine, c'est-à-dire services publics et équipements collectifs[1]. Bien que les statistiques différenciant les zones urbaines des zones rurales soient très généralisées, il ne paraît pas possible pour le moment d'adopter une classification internationale type de ces zones, vu la diversité des interprétations nationales. La classification de la population en urbaine ou rurale retenue ici est celle qui correspond aux définitions nationales, comme l'indique une note au tableau, et selon le détail exposé dans les notes techniques au tableau 2 du Supplément rétrospectif[2].

Portée : Des statistiques de la population urbaine et de la population totale selon le sexe sont présentées pour 120 pays ou zones.

Données publiées antérieurement : Des statistiques de la population urbaine et de la population totale selon le sexe ont été publiées dans des éditions antérieures de l'Annuaire démographique. Pour plus de précisions concernant les années pour lesquelles ces données ont été publiées, se reporter à l'Index.

DEFINITIONS DES "REGIONS URBAINES"

AFRIQUE

Bénin: Définition non communiquée.
Botswana: Agglomération de 5 000 habitants et plus dont 75 p. 100 de l'activité économique n'est pas de type agricole.
Burkina Faso: Définition non communiquée.
Burundi:Commune de Bujumbura.
Cap Vert: Définition non communiquée.
Comores: Chefs-lieux de préfectures et localités de 5 000 habitants et plus.
Côte d'Ivoire: Définition non communiquée.
Egypte: Chefs-lieux de gouvernements du Caire, d'Alexandrie, de Port Saïd, d'Ismaïlia, de Suez; chefs-lieux de gouvernements frontières, autres chefs-lieux de gouvernements et chefs-lieux de district (Markaz).
Guinée équatoriale: Chef-lieux de district et localités avec 300 maisons et/ou 1 500 habitants et plus.
Ethiopie: Localités de 2 000 habitants et plus.
Gabon: Définition non communiquée.
Libéria: Localités de 2 000 habitants et plus.
Malawi: Toutes les villes et zones urbanisées et tous les chefs-lieux de district.
Maurice: Villes ayant des limites officiellement définies.
Maroc: Définition non communiquée.
Namibie: Définition non communiquée.
Niger: Définition non communiquée.
Nigéria: Définition non communiquée.
Rwanda: Définition non communiquée.
Sénégal: Agglomérations de 10 000 habitants et plus.
Afrique du Sud: Zones avec quelque autorité locale.
Soudan: Localités dont le caractère est principalement administrat et/ou commercial ou localités ayant une population de 5 000 habitants et plus.
Swaziland: Localités déclarées urbaines.
Tunisie: Population vivant dans les communes.
Ouganda: Définition non communiquée.
République Unie de Tanzanie: 16 villes érigées en communes.
Zambie: Localités de 5 000 habitants et plus dont l'activité économique prédominante n'est pas de type agricole.

AMERIQUE DU NORD

Bahamas: Définition non communiquée.
Belize: Définition non communiquée.
Canada: Agglomérations de 1 000 habitants ou plus, ayant une densité de population de 400 ou plus habitants au kilomètre carrée.
Costa Rica: Chefs-lieux des cantons.
Cuba:Population vivant dans des agglomérations de 2 000 habitants ou plus.
République dominicaine:Chefs-lieux de municipios et districts municipaux, dont certains comprennent des zones suburbaines ayant des caractéristiques rurales.
El Salvador: Chef-lieux de municipios.
Groenland: Localités de 200 ou plus habitants.

Guatemala: Municipio du département de Guatemala et centres officiellement reconnues d'autres départments et municipalités.

Haïti: Chefs-lieux de communes.

Honduras: Localités de 2 000 ou plus ayant des caractéristiques essentiellement urbaines.

Jamaïque: Définition non communiquée.

Mexique: Localités de 2 500 et plus.

Nicaragua: Chefs-lieux de municipios et localités de 1 000 habitants ou plus avec rues et éclairage électrique.

Panama:Localités de 1 500 habitants et plus ayant des caractéristiques essentiellement urbaines. A partir de 1970, localités de 1 500 habitants et plus présentant des caractéristiques urbaines, telles que: rues, éclairage électrique, systèmes d'approvisionnement en eau et systèmes d'égouts.

Porto Rico: Localités de 2 500 habitants et plus et couronne urbaine á forte densité de population des zones urbainizées.

Etats Unis: Localités de 2 500 habitants et plus et zones urbanisées.

AMERIQUE DU SUD

Argentine: Centres de peuplement de 2 000 habitants et plus.

Bolivie: Localités de 2 000 habitants et plus.

Brésil: Zones urbaines et suburbaines des chefs lieux des municipios et des distritos.

Chili: Centres de peuplement ayant des caractéristiques nettement urbaines dues á la présence de certains services publics et municipaux.

Colombie: Définition non communiquée.

Equateur: Capitales des provinces et chefs-lieux de canton.

Iles Falkland (Malvinas): Ville de Stanley.

Paraguay: Grandes villes, villes et chefs-lieux des départements et des districts.

Pérou: Centres de peuplement de 100 logements ou plus qui sont occupés.

Suriname: Ville de Paramaribo.

Uruguay: Villes.

Venezuela: Centres de 1 000 habitants et plus.

ASIE

Arménie:Grandes villes et localités de type urbain, officiellement désignées comme telles, généralement sur la base du nombre d'habitants et de la prédominance des travailleurs agricoles ou non agricoles avec leur famille.

Azerbaïdjan: Grandes villes et localités de type urbain, officiellement désignées comme telles, généralement sur la base du nombre d'habitants et de la prédominance des travailleurs agricoles ou non agricoles avec leur famille.

Bahreïn: Communes ou villages de 2 500 et plus.

Brunei Darussalam: Définition non communiquée.

Cambodge: Villes.

Chine: Définition non communiquée.

Chypre: Zones municipaux, zones banlieues et quelques villes.

Géorgie: Grandes villes et localités de type urbain, officiellement désignées comme telles, généralement sur la base du nombre d'habitants et de la prédominance des travailleurs agricoles ou non agricoles avec leur famille.

Inde: Villes (localités dotées d'une charte municipale, d'un comité de zone municipal, d'un comité de zone déclarée urbaine ou d'un comité de zone de cantonnement); également toutes les localités qui ont une population de 5 000 habitants au moins, une densité de population d'au moins 1 000 habitants au mille carré ou 390 au kilomètre carré, des caractéristiques urbaines prononcées et où les trois quarts au moins des adultes du sexe masculin ont une occupation agricole.

Indonésie: Localités présentant des caractéristiques urbaines.

Iran (Rép. islamique): Tous les chefs-lieux de Shahrestan, quelle qu'en soit la dimension, et toutes les agglomérations avec centres municipaux.

Israël: Tous les peuplements de plus de 2 000 habitants á l'exception de ce où le tiers au moins des chefs de ménage faisant partie de la population civile active vivent de l'agriculture.

Japon: Villes (shi), comptant 50 000 habitants ou plus, où 60 p. 100 au moins des habitations sont situées dans les principales zones bâties, et dont 60 p. 100 au moins de population (dépendants compris) vit d'emplois s'e exerçant dans les industries manufacturières, le commerce et autres branches d'activités essentiellement urbaines. D'autre part, tout shi possédant les équipements et présentant les caractères définis comme urbains par l'administration préfectorale est considéré comme zone urbaine.

Kazakhstan: Grandes villes et localités de type urbain, officiellement désignées comme telles, généralement sur la base du nombre d'habitants et de la prédominance des travailleurs agricoles ou non agricoles avec leur famille.

Corée, rép. populaire dém. de: Définition non communiquée.

Corée, République de: Population vivant dans les villes irrespectueux de la dimension de la population.

Kirghizistan: Grandes villes et localités de type urbain, officiellement désignées comme telles, généralement sur la base du nombre d'habitants et de la prédominance des travailleurs agricoles ou non agricoles avec leur famille.

Malaisie: Zones déclarées telles et comptant au moins 10 000 habitants.

Maldives: Malé, la capitale.

Mongolie: Capitale et chefs-lieux de district.

Népal: Définition non communiquée.

Pakistan: Localités dotées d'une charte municipale, d'un comité municipale au d'un cantonnement.

Philippines: Définition non communiquée.

République arabe syrienne: Villes, centres de district (Mohafaza) et centres de sous district (Mantika), et communes de 20 000 habitants et plus.

Tadjikistan: Grandes villes et localités de type urbain, officiellement désignées comme telles, généralement sur la base du nombre d'habitants et de la prédominance des travailleurs agricoles ou non agricoles avec leur famille.

Thaïlande: Zones municipales.

Turquie: Population des localités contenues á l'intérieur des limites municipales des chefs-lieux des provinces et des districts.

Turkménistan: Grandes villes et localités de type urbain, officiellement désignées comme telles, généralement sur la base du nombre d'habitants et de la prédominance des travailleurs agricoles ou non agricoles avec leur famille.

Ouzbékistan: Grandes villes et localités de type urbain, officiellement désignées comme telles, généralement sur la base du nombre d'habitants et de la prédominance des travailleurs agricoles ou non agricoles avec leur famille.

Vietnam: Grandes villes, villes et districts de 2 000 habitants et plus.

Yémen: Définition non communiquée.

EUROPE

Albanie: Villes et autres centres industriels de plus de 400 habitants.

Autriche: Communes de plus de 5 000 habitants.

Bélarus: Grandes villes et localités de type urbain, officiellement désignées comme telles,généralement sur la base du nombre d'habitants et de la prédominance des travailleurs agricoles ou non agricoles avec leur famille.

Bulgarie: Villes, c'est-á-dire localités reconnues comme urbaines.

Croatie: Définition non communiquée.

Rép. Tchèque: Localités de 2 000 habitants et plus.

Estonie: Grandes villes et localités de type urbain, officiellement désignées comme telles, généralement sur la base du nombre d'habitants et de la prédominance des travailleurs agricoles
ou non agricoles avec leur famille.

Espagne: Localités de 2 000 habitants et plus.

Finlande: Communes urbaines. 1970: Localités.

France: Communes comprenant une agglomération de plus de 2 000 habitants vivant dans des habitations contiguës ou qui ne sont pas distantes les unes des autres de plus de 200 mètres et communes où la majeure partie de la population vit dans une agglomération multicommunale de cette nature.

Grèce: Municipalités et communes de 10 000 habitants et plus pour l'agglomération. Y compris également 18 agglomérations urbaines, selon la définition qui en a été donnée lors du recensement de 1991, a savoir: le Grand Athénes, Thessaloniki, Patra, Iraklio, Volos, Chania, Irannina, Chalkida, Agrinio, Kalamata, Katerini, Kerkyra, Salamina, Chios, Egio, Rethymno, Ermoupolis et Sparti.

Hongrie: Budapest et toutes les autres localités reconnues officiellement comme urbaines.

Islande: Localités de 200 habitants et plus.

Irlande: Villes de toutes dimensions, y compris leur banlieux, comptant 1 500 habitants ou plus.

Lettonie: Grandes villes et localités de type urbain, officiellement désignées comme telles, généralement sur la base du nombre d'habitants et de la prédominance des travailleurs agricoles ou non agricoles avec leur famille.

Lituanie: Grandes villes et localités de type urbain, officiellement désignées comme telles, généralement sur la base du nombre d'habitants et de la prédominance des travailleurs agricoles ou non agricoles avec leur famille.

Norvège: Localités de 2 000 habitants et plus.

Pays Bas: Régions urbaines: municipalités de 2 000 habitants et plus. Régions semi-urbaines: municipalités de moins de 2 000 habitants, mais où 20 p. 100 au maximum de la population active du sexe masculin pratiquent l'agriculture, et certaines municipalités de caractère résidentiel dont les habitants travaillent ailleurs.

Pologne: Villes et peuplements de type urbain, par exemple groupements de travailleurs ou de pêcheurs et stations climatiques.

Portugal: Agglomérations de 10 000 habitants et plus.

République de Moldova: Grandes villes et localités de type urbain, officiellement désignées comme telles, généralement sur la base du nombre d'habitants et de la prédominance des travailleurs agricoles ou non agricoles avec leur famille.

Roumanie: Grandes villes, municipalités et autres villes.

Russie, Fédération de: Grandes villes et localités de type urbain, officiellement désignées comme telles, généralement sur la base du nombre d'habitants et de la prédominance des travailleurs agricoles ou non agricoles avec leur famille.

Saint Marin: Définition non communiquée.

Slovaquie: 138 villages de 5 000 habitants et plus.
Slovénie: Définition non communiquée.
Suède: Définition non communiquée.
Suisse: Communes de 10 000 habitants et plus, et leurs banlieues.
L'ex. Rép. Yougoslave de Macédoine: Définition non communiquée.
Ukraine: Grandes villes et localités de type urbain, officiellement désignées comme telles, généralement sur la base du nombre d'habitants et de la prédominance des travailleurs agricoles ou non agricoles avec leur famille.
Yougoslavie: Définition non communiquée.

OCEANIE

Samoa américaines: Localités de 2 500 et plus et zones urbanisées.
Guam: Localités de 2 500 habitants et plus et zones urbanisées.
Nouvelle-Calédonie: Nouméa et communes de Païta, Dumbéa et Mont Dore.
Nouvelle-Zélande: Grandes villes, boroughs, chefs-lieux , municipalités et chefs-lieux des comtés de 1 000 habitants et plus.
Vanuatu: Centre Luganville et Vila urbaine.

_____

NOTES

[1] *Social and Demographic Statistics: Classifications of Size and Type of Locality and Urban/Rural Areas.* E/CN.3/551, United Nations, New York, 1980.
[2] *Annuaire démographique, Supplément historique, 1948-1997, cédérom, Publication des Narions Unies, numéro de vente E/F.99.XIII.12, Nations Unies, New York, 2000.*

6. Urban and total population by sex: 1992 - 2001
Population urbaine et population totale selon le sexe: 1992 - 2001

(See notes at end of table. — Voir notes à la fin du tableau.)

Continent, country or area and date / Continent, pays ou zone et date	Code[1]	Both sexes - Les deux sexes			Male - Masculin			Female - Féminin		
		Total	Urban - Urbaine		Total	Urban - Urbaine		Total	Urban - Urbaine	
			Number Nombre	Percent P.100		Number Nombre	Percent P.100		Number Nombre	Percent P.100
AFRICA — AFRIQUE										
Benin - Bénin										
15 II 1992	CDFC	4 915 555	1 756 197	35.7	2 390 336	857 191	35.9	2 525 219	899 006	35.6
1 VII 1993	ESDF	5 074 561	1 832 946	36.1	2 467 604	891 792	36.1	2 606 957	941 154	36.1
1 VII 1994	ESDF	5 241 843	1 917 100	36.6	2 548 310	932 172	36.6	2 693 533	984 928	36.6
1 VII 1995	ESDF	5 412 160	2 003 213	37.0	2 633 479	974 914	37.0	2 778 681	1 028 299	37.0
1 VII 1996	ESDF	5 594 499	2 098 699	37.5	2 722 854	1 019 980	37.5	2 871 645	1 078 719	37.6
1 VII 1997	ESDF	5 638 987	2 177 515	38.6	...	...	...	...	...	...
1 VII 1998	ESDF	5 816 488	2 278 190	39.2	...	...	...	...	...	...
1 VII 1999	ESDF	5 990 396	2 383 244	39.8	...	...	...	...	...	...
1 VII 2000	ESDF	6 169 084	2 492 967	40.4	3 013 705	1 220 905	40.5	3 155 379	1 272 062	40.3
Botswana[2]										
1 VII 1992	ESDF	1 358 639	650 000	47.8	650 088	...	...	708 551	...	...
1 VII 1994	ESDF	1 424 636	672 614	47.2	684 751	...	...	739 885	...	...
1 VII 1995	ESDF	1 458 828	696 282	47.7	701 603	...	...	757 225	...	...
1 VII 1996	ESDF	1 495 993	720 783	48.2	720 207	...	...	775 786	...	...
Burkina Faso										
1 VII 1992	ESDF	9 433 428	1 345 084	14.3	...	...	...	...	...	...
1 VII 1993	ESDF	9 682 470	1 405 478	14.5	...	...	...	...	...	...
1 VII 1994	ESDF	9 888 789	1 469 006	14.9	4 582 412	732 887	16.0	5 306 377	736 119	13.9
1 VII 1995	ESDF	10 200 453	1 534 524	15.0	4 985 642	...	...	5 214 811	...	...
Burundi										
1 VII 1993	ESDF	5 769 144	402 856	7.0	2 805 797	214 398	7.6	2 963 347	188 458	6.4
1 VII 1994	ESDF	5 875 413	420 826	7.2	2 857 267	221 304	7.7	3 018 146	199 522	6.6
1 VII 1995	ESDF	5 981 682	437 417	7.3	2 908 737	227 568	7.8	3 072 945	209 849	6.8
1 VII 1996	ESDF	6 087 951	454 661	7.5	2 960 208	233 221	7.9	3 127 743	221 440	7.1
1 VII 1997	ESDF	6 194 220	473 284	7.6	3 011 678	240 554	8.0	3 182 542	232 730	7.3
1 VII 1998	ESDF	6 300 489	493 297	7.8	3 064 211	...	...	3 236 278	...	...
Cameroon - Cameroun										
1 VII 1997	ESDF	14 297 617	6 748 475	47.2	...	...	...	...	...	...
1 VII 1998	ESDF	14 439 000	6 960 000	48.2	...	...	...	...	...	...
Côte d'Ivoire										
1 VII 1993	ESDF	13 175 000	6 008 000	45.6	6 718 000	3 063 000	45.6	6 457 000	2 944 000	45.6
Egypt - Égypte										
1 VII 1992	ESDF	54 082 000	23 366 000	43.2	27 694 000	11 965 000	43.2	26 388 000	11 401 000	43.2
1 VII 1993	ESDF	55 200 568	24 127 060	43.7	28 285 012	12 362 808	43.7	26 915 556	11 764 252	43.7
1 VII 1994	ESDF	56 343 786	24 481 023	43.4	28 874 917	12 545 982	43.4	27 468 869	11 935 041	43.4
1 VII 1995	ESDF	57 509 998	24 840 066	43.2	29 428 956	12 711 132	43.2	28 081 042	12 128 934	43.2
1 VII 1996	ESDF	58 755 211	25 019 402	42.6	30 063 860	12 801 923	42.6	28 691 351	12 217 479	42.6
19 XI 1996	CDFC	59 312 914	25 286 335	42.6	30 351 390	12 957 775	42.7	28 961 524	12 328 560	42.6
1 VII 1997	ESDF	60 080 063	25 589 396	42.6	30 736 254	13 091 232	42.6	29 343 809	12 498 164	42.6
1 VII 1998	ESDF	61 340 882	26 123 481	42.6	31 379 023	13 363 507	42.6	29 961 859	12 759 974	42.6
1 VII 1999	ESDF	62 652 065	26 641 192	42.5	32 059 065	13 632 299	42.5	30 593 000	13 008 893	42.5
1 VII 2000	ESDF	63 976 000	27 204 000	42.5	32 695 000	...	...	31 281 000	...	...
Ethiopia - Éthiopie										
1 VII 1992	ESDF	51 570 500	7 378 000	14.3	...	...	...	...	...	...
1 VII 1993	ESDF	53 236 400	7 789 100	14.6	...	...	...	...	...	...
11 X 1994	CDFC	53 477 265	7 323 207	13.7	26 910 698	3 534 805	13.1	26 566 567	3 788 402	14.3
1 VII 1995	ESDF	54 649 154	7 586 700	13.9	27 498 620	3 662 625	13.3	27 150 534	3 924 075	14.5
1 VII 1996	ESDF	56 372 000	7 950 000	14.1	28 344 000	3 885 000	13.7	28 028 000	4 065 000	14.5
1 VII 1997	ESDF	58 117 000	8 315 000	14.3	29 202 000	4 094 000	14.0	28 915 000	4 221 000	14.6
1 VII 1998	ESDF	59 882 000	8 691 000	14.5	30 071 000	4 299 000	14.3	29 811 000	4 392 000	14.7
1 VII 1999	ESDF	61 672 000	9 074 000	14.7	30 956 000	4 504 000	14.5	30 716 000	4 570 000	14.9
1 VII 2000	ESDF	63 494 702	9 472 971	14.9	...	...	...	...	...	...
1 VII 2001 *	ESDF	65 374 320	9 883 138	15.1	32 815 082	4 938 725	15.1	32 559 238	4 944 413	15.2
Gabon										
31 VII 1993	CDFC	1 014 976	742 296	73.1	501 784	371 622	74.1	513 192	370 674	72.2
Ghana										
26 III 2000	CDFC	18 912 079	8 274 270	43.8	9 357 382	...	...	9 554 697	...	...

6. Urban and total population by sex: 1992 - 2001
Population urbaine et population totale selon le sexe: 1992 - 2001
(continued — suite)

(See notes at end of table. — Voir notes à la fin du tableau.)

Continent, country or area and date / Continent, pays ou zone et date	Code[1]	Both sexes - Les deux sexes			Male - Masculin			Female - Féminin		
		Total	Urban - Urbaine		Total	Urban - Urbaine		Total	Urban - Urbaine	
			Number Nombre	Percent P.100		Number Nombre	Percent P.100		Number Nombre	Perce P.1
AFRICA — AFRIQUE										
Lesotho[3]										
14 IV 1996	CDJC	1 959 669	312 444	15.9	964 346	...	...	995 723	...	
1 VII 2001*	SSDJ	2 157 537	288 895	13.4	1 065 484	131 861	12.4	1 092 053	157 034	14
Liberia - Libéria										
1 VII 1992	ESDF	2 580 236	1 118 486	43.3	...	...	...	...	...	
1 VII 1993	ESDF	2 640 062	1 156 282	43.8	...	...	...	...	...	
1 VII 1994	ESDF	2 699 888	1 194 077	44.2	...	...	...	...	...	
1 VII 1995	ESDF	2 759 714	1 231 872	44.6	...	...	...	...	...	
1 VII 1996	ESDF	2 819 540	1 269 668	45.0	...	...	...	...	...	
1 VII 1997	ESDF	2 879 366	1 307 463	45.4	...	...	...	...	...	
Malawi										
1 VII 1992	ESDF	8 823 355	1 452 200	16.5	...	...	...	...	...	
1 VII 1993	ESDF	9 134 976	1 576 500	17.3	...	...	...	...	...	
1 VII 1994	ESDF	9 461 403	1 711 200	18.1	...	...	...	...	...	
1 VII 1995	ESDF	9 787 831	1 845 900	18.9	...	...	...	...	...	
1 VII 1996	ESDF	10 114 257	1 980 700	19.6	...	...	...	...	...	
1 IX 1998	CDFC	9 933 868	1 435 436	14.4	4 867 563	742 839	15.3	5 066 305	692 597	13
Mauritius - Maurice										
1 VII 1992	ESDJ	1 084 441	474 128	43.7	...	...	...	...	...	
1 VII 1993	ESDJ	1 097 374	478 329	43.6	...	...	...	...	...	
1 VII 1994	ESDJ	1 112 846	483 602	43.5	...	...	...	...	...	
1 VII 1995	ESDJ	1 122 457	486 294	43.3	...	...	...	...	...	
1 VII 1996	ESDJ	1 133 996	489 793	43.2	...	...	...	...	...	
1 VII 1997	ESDJ	1 148 284	494 446	43.1	...	...	...	...	...	
1 VII 1998	ESDJ	1 160 421	498 138	42.9	...	...	...	...	...	
1 VII 1999	ESDJ	1 175 267	502 958	42.8	...	...	...	...	...	
1 VII 2000	ESDJ	1 186 873	506 357	42.7	588 212	249 678	42.4	598 661	256 679	42
1 VII 2001*	ESDJ	1 199 881	510 822	42.6	594 490	251 721	42.3	605 391	259 101	42
Morocco - Maroc										
1 VII 1992	ESDF	25 547 000	12 725 000	49.8	12 529 000	6 378 000	50.9	13 018 000	6 347 000	48
1 VII 1993	ESDF	26 069 000	13 149 000	50.4	12 792 000	6 616 000	51.7	13 277 000	6 533 000	49
1 VII 1994	ESDF	25 926 000	13 270 000	51.2						
2 IX 1994	CDFC	26 019 280	13 356 246	51.3	12 944 517	6 632 953	51.2	13 074 763	6 723 293	51
1 VII 1995	ESDF	26 386 000	13 684 000	51.9	...	...	...	...	...	
1 VII 1996	ESDF	26 848 000	14 100 000	52.5	13 357 000	...	...	13 491 000	...	
1 VII 1997	ESDF	27 310 000	14 524 000	53.2	13 588 000	7 173 000	52.8	13 722 000	7 351 000	53
1 VII 1998	ESDF	27 775 000	14 957 000	53.9	13 819 000	7 373 000	53.4	13 956 000	7 584 000	54.
1 VII 1999	ESDF	28 238 000	15 401 000	54.5	14 049 000	7 580 000	54.0	14 189 000	7 821 000	55.
1 VII 2000*	ESDF	28 705 000	15 849 000	55.2	14 281 000	7 787 000	54.5	14 424 000	8 062 000	55
1 VII 2001*	ESDF	29 170 000	16 307 000	55.9	14 512 000	8 000 000	55.1	14 658 000	8 307 000	56
Mozambique[4]										
1 VIII 1997	CDFC	16 099 246	4 601 132	28.6	7 714 306	2 274 116	29.5	8 384 940	2 327 016	27
Saint Helena ex. dep. - Sainte-Hélène sans dép.										
8 III 1998	CDFC	5 157	884	17.1	2 612	452	17.3	2 545	432	17.
Senegal - Sénégal										
1 VII 1992	ESDF	7 703 826	2 964 355	38.5	...	...	...	...	...	
1 VII 1993	ESDF	7 913 090	3 497 584	44.2	...	...	...	...	...	
1 VII 1994	ESDF	8 127 374	3 324 304	40.9	...	...	...	...	...	
1 VII 1995	ESDF	8 346 998	3 447 804	41.3	...	...	...	...	...	
1 VII 1996	ESDF	8 572 004	3 575 365	41.7	...	...	...	...	...	
1 VII 1997	ESDF	8 802 304	3 618 255	41.1	...	...	...	...	...	
1 VII 1998	ESDF	9 037 906	3 842 820	42.5	...	...	...	...	...	
1 VII 1999	ESDF	9 278 617	3 982 772	42.9	...	...	...	...	...	
South Africa - Afrique du Sud[5,6]										
1 VII 1996	ESDF	40 342 300	21 659 400	53.7	19 394 900	10 604 600	54.7	20 947 400	11 054 800	52.
10 X 1996	CDFC	40 583 573	21 781 807	53.7	19 520 887	10 667 927	54.6	21 062 686	11 113 880	52.

6. Urban and total population by sex: 1992 - 2001
Population urbaine et population totale selon le sexe: 1992 - 2001
(continued — suite)

See notes at end of table. — Voir notes à la fin du tableau.)

Continent, country or area and date / Continent, pays ou zone et date	Code[1]	Both sexes - Les deux sexes			Male - Masculin			Female - Féminin		
		Total	Urban - Urbaine		Total	Urban - Urbaine		Total	Urban - Urbaine	
			Number Nombre	Percent P.100		Number Nombre	Percent P.100		Number Nombre	Percent P.100
AFRICA — AFRIQUE										
South Africa - Afrique du Sud[5,6]										
1 VII 1997	ESDF	41 226 700	22 107 800	53.6	19 857 000	10 836 700	54.6	21 369 700	11 271 100	52.7
1 VII 1998	ESDF	42 130 500	22 565 300	53.6	20 330 100	11 073 800	54.5	21 800 400	11 491 500	52.7
1 VII 1999	ESDF	43 054 306	23 032 381	53.5	20 814 425	11 316 037	54.4	22 239 881	11 716 344	52.7
1 VII 2000	ESDF	43 685 699	23 125 194	52.9	21 016 530	11 273 108	53.6	22 669 169	11 852 086	52.3
Sudan - Soudan										
1 VII 1992	ESDF	27 323 000	7 057 000	25.8	...	...	...	...	...	...
Swaziland										
1 VII 1992	ESDF	832 784	197 250	23.7	...	...	...	...	...	...
1 VII 1993	ESDF	850 628	206 203	24.2	...	...	...	...	...	...
1 VII 1994	ESDF	879 081	217 309	24.7	410 924	108 790	26.5	468 157	108 519	23.2
1 VII 1995	ESDF	908 119	225 074	24.8	...	...	...	...	...	...
1 VII 1996	ESDF	937 747	237 368	25.3	438 334	118 562	27.0	499 413	118 806	23.8
11 V 1997	CDFC	929 718	214 428	23.1	440 154	106 256	24.1	489 564	108 172	22.1
Tunisia - Tunisie										
20 IV 1994	CDFC	8 785 711	5 361 927	61.0	4 439 289	2 717 168	61.2	4 346 422	2 644 759	60.8
Uganda - Ouganda										
1 VII 1995	ESDF	19 262 626	2 587 105	13.4	9 504 221	...	...	9 758 406	...	...
1 VII 1996	ESDF	19 847 689	2 764 579	13.9	9 802 558	...	...	10 045 131	...	...
1 VII 1997	ESDF	20 752 400	2 732 878	13.2	...	...	...	...	...	...
1 VII 1998	ESDF	21 467 200	2 878 135	13.4	...	...	...	...	...	...
1 VII 1999	ESDF	22 206 600	3 026 742	13.6	...	...	...	...	...	...
1 VII 2000	ESDF	22 971 500	3 178 692	13.8	...	...	...	...	...	...
Zambia - Zambie										
1 VII 1995	ESDF	9 112 045	3 499 309	38.4	...	...	...	...	...	...
1 VII 2000	ESDF	10 722 854	4 111 548	38.3	...	...	...	...	...	...
Zimbabwe										
18 VIII 1997	SSDF	11 789 274	3 826 580	32.5	5 647 090	1 906 476	33.8	6 142 184	1 920 104	31.3
AMERICA, NORTH - AMERIQUE DU NORD										
Belize										
1 VII 1992	ESDF	199 000	92 688	46.6	101 000	45 467	45.0	98 000	47 221	48.2
1 VII 1993	ESDF	205 000	97 430	47.5	104 000	47 951	46.1	101 000	49 479	49.0
1 VII 1994	ESDF	211 000	106 975	50.7	104 000	52 000	50.0	107 000	54 975	51.4
1 VII 1995	ESDF	216 500	109 880	50.8	107 500	54 255	50.5	109 000	55 625	51.0
1 VII 1996	ESDF	222 000	113 640	51.2	111 000	54 440	49.0	111 000	59 200	53.3
1 VII 1997	ESDF	230 000	115 975	50.4	114 500	55 350	48.3	115 500	60 625	52.5
1 VII 1998	ESDF	238 500	120 110	50.4	118 500	57 095	48.2	120 000	63 015	52.5
12 V 2000	CDFC	240 204	114 541	47.7	121 278	56 565	46.6	118 926	57 976	48.7
1 VII 2000	ESDF	249 800	121 455	48.6	126 080	59 985	47.6	123 720	61 470	49.7
Canada[7,8]										
14 V 1996	CDJC	28 846 760	22 461 210	77.9	14 170 030	10 902 295	76.9	14 676 735	11 558 910	78.8
Costa Rica										
26 VI 2000	CDJC	3 810 179	2 249 414	59.0	1 902 614	1 096 248	57.6	1 907 565	1 153 166	60.5
Cuba										
1 VII 1992	ESDF	10 831 070	8 049 004	74.3	5 447 421	3 973 761	72.9	5 383 649	4 075 243	75.7
1 VII 1993	ESDF	10 904 466	8 111 613	74.4	5 482 360	4 001 875	73.0	5 422 106	4 109 738	75.8
1 VII 1994	ESDF	10 950 100	8 145 869	74.4	5 502 852	4 010 950	72.9	5 447 248	4 134 919	75.9
1 VII 1997	ESDF	11 065 878	8 295 762	75.0	5 541 552	4 069 554	73.4	5 524 326	4 226 208	76.5
1 VII 1998	ESDF	11 116 514	8 359 529	75.2	5 563 304	4 098 448	73.7	5 553 210	4 261 081	76.7
1 VII 1999	ESDF	11 159 991	8 395 944	75.2	5 580 344	4 112 359	73.7	5 579 647	4 283 585	76.8
1 VII 2000	ESDF	11 198 600	8 426 270	75.2	5 596 057	4 124 048	73.7	5 602 543	4 302 222	76.8
Dominican Republic - République dominicaine										
1 VII 1993	ESDF	7 620 395	4 615 596	60.6	...	...	...	...	...	...

6. Urban and total population by sex: 1992 - 2001
Population urbaine et population totale selon le sexe: 1992 - 2001
(continued — suite)

(See notes at end of table. — Voir notes à la fin du tableau.)

Continent, country or area and date / Continent, pays ou zone et date	Code[1]	Both sexes - Les deux sexes			Male - Masculin			Female - Féminin		
		Total	Urban - Urbaine		Total	Urban - Urbaine		Total	Urban - Urbaine	
			Number Nombre	Percent P.100		Number Nombre	Percent P.100		Number Nombre	Percent P.100
AMERICA, NORTH — AMERIQUE DU NORD										
El Salvador										
27 IX 1992	CDFC	5 118 599	2 581 834	50.4	2 485 613	1 220 024	49.1	2 632 986	1 361 810	51.7
1 VII 1995	ESDF	5 668 605	3 216 533	56.7	2 776 269	1 542 163	55.5	2 892 336	1 674 370	57.9
1 VII 1996	ESDF	5 787 093	3 305 082	57.1	2 835 313	1 585 186	55.9	2 951 780	1 719 896	58.3
1 VII 1997	ESDF	5 908 460	3 394 950	57.5	2 896 114	1 629 017	56.2	3 012 346	1 765 933	58.6
1 VII 1998	ESDF	6 031 326	3 485 465	57.8	2 957 835	1 673 250	56.6	3 073 491	1 812 215	59.0
1 VII 1999	ESDF	6 154 311	3 575 956	58.1	3 019 645	1 717 489	56.9	3 134 666	1 858 467	59.3
1 VII 2000	ESDF	6 276 037	3 665 747	58.4	3 080 704	1 761 327	57.2	3 195 333	1 904 420	59.6
1 VII 2001*	ESDF	6 396 890	3 754 903	58.7	3 141 208	1 804 804	57.5	3 255 682	1 950 099	59.9
Greenland - Groenland										
1 VII 1992	ESDJ	55 385	44 443	80.2	...	...	...	...	...	...
1 VII 1993	ESDJ	55 117	44 289	80.4	29 549	23 577	79.8	25 719	20 896	81.2
1 VII 1994	ESDJ	55 576	44 902	80.8	29 665	23 767	80.1	25 911	21 135	81.6
1 VII 1995	ESDJ	55 798	45 228	81.1	29 762	23 930	80.4	26 036	21 298	81.8
1 VII 1996	ESDJ	55 917	45 330	81.1	29 828	23 993	80.4	26 089	21 337	81.8
1 VII 1997	ESDJ	56 323	45 420	80.6	29 871	24 042	80.5	26 452	21 377	80.8
1 VII 1998	ESDJ	56 076	45 489	81.1	29 904	24 092	80.6	26 172	21 397	81.8
1 VII 1999	ESDJ	56 087	45 523	81.2	29 941	24 189	80.8	26 146	21 334	81.6
1 VII 2000	ESDJ	56 124	45 714	81.5	29 989	24 257	80.9	26 135	21 457	82.1
Haiti - Haïti										
1 VII 1992	ESDJ	6 763 746	2 082 204	30.8	...	...	...	...	...	...
1 VII 1993	ESDJ	6 902 596	2 165 805	31.4	...	...	...	...	...	...
1 VII 1994	ESDJ	7 041 445	2 251 351	32.0	...	...	...	...	...	...
1 VII 1995	ESDJ	7 180 294	2 338 842	32.6	...	...	...	...	...	...
1 VII 1996	ESDJ	7 336 028	2 433 878	33.2	...	...	...	...	...	...
1 VII 1997	ESDJ	7 491 762	2 531 060	33.8	...	...	...	...	...	...
1 VII 1998	ESDJ	7 647 496	2 630 383	34.4	...	...	...	...	...	...
1 VII 1999	ESDJ	7 803 230	2 731 843	35.0	...	...	...	...	...	...
1 VII 2000	ESDJ	7 958 964	2 835 433	35.6	...	...	...	...	...	...
Honduras										
1 VII 1992	ESDF	5 079 200	2 119 200	41.7	...	...	...	...	...	...
1 VII 1993	ESDF	5 248 000	2 219 800	42.3	...	...	...	...	...	...
1 VII 1994	ESDF	5 422 300	2 324 800	42.9	...	...	...	...	...	...
1 VII 1995	ESDF	5 602 500	2 434 300	43.5	...	...	...	...	...	...
1 VII 1996	ESDF	5 788 600	2 548 500	44.0	...	...	...	...	...	...
1 VII 1997	ESDF	5 980 900	2 667 600	44.6	...	...	...	...	...	...
1 VII 1998	ESDF	6 179 700	2 791 900	45.2	...	...	...	...	...	...
1 VII 1999	ESDF	6 385 000	2 921 400	45.8	...	...	...	...	...	...
Jamaica - Jamaïque										
10 IX 2001	CDFC	2 607 633	1 355 334	52.0	1 283 547	...	...	1 324 085	...	...
Mexico - Mexique										
1 VII 1992	ESDJ	87 113 817	62 956 129	72.3	...	...	...	...	...	...
1 VII 1993	ESDJ	88 754 928	64 536 499	72.7	...	...	...	...	...	...
1 VII 1994	ESDJ	90 385 688	66 093 327	73.1	...	...	...	...	...	...
1 VII 1995	ESDJ	91 992 118	67 601 543	73.5	...	...	...	...	...	...
5 XI 1995	SSDJ	91 158 290	67 003 515	73.5	...	...	...	...	...	...
1 VII 1996	ESDJ	93 571 559	69 047 515	73.8	...	...	...	...	...	...
1 VII 1997	ESDJ	95 127 443	70 438 407	74.0	...	...	...	...	...	...
1 VII 1998	ESDJ	96 648 885	71 775 640	74.3	...	...	...	...	...	...
1 VII 1999	ESDJ	98 132 370	73 066 860	74.5	48 641 698	...	...	49 490 720	...	...
14 II 2000	CDJC	97 483 412	72 759 822	74.6	47 592 253	35 317 569	74.2	49 891 159	37 442 253	75.0
1 VII 2000	ESDJ	100 248 699	74 823 781	74.6	...	...	...	...	...	...
1 VII 2001*	ESDJ	101 754 160	76 181 526	74.9	...	...	...	...	...	...
Nicaragua										
1 VII 1992	ESDJ	4 054 374	2 225 843	54.9	...	...	...	...	...	...

6. Urban and total population by sex: 1992 - 2001
Population urbaine et population totale selon le sexe: 1992 - 2001
(continued — suite)

(See notes at end of table. — Voir notes à la fin du tableau.)

Continent, country or area and date / Continent, pays ou zone et date	Code[1]	Both sexes - Les deux sexes			Male - Masculin			Female - Féminin		
		Total	Urban - Urbaine		Total	Urban - Urbaine		Total	Urban - Urbaine	
			Number Nombre	Percent P.100		Number Nombre	Percent P.100		Number Nombre	Percent P.100
AMERICA, NORTH — AMERIQUE DU NORD										
Nicaragua										
1 VII 1993	ESDJ	4 174 860	2 307 382	55.3	...	...	...	...	...	...
1 VII 1994	ESDJ	4 298 925	2 391 801	55.6	...	...	...	...	...	...
25 IV 1995	CDJC	4 357 099	2 370 810	54.4	2 147 105	...	...	2 209 994	...	...
1 VII 1995	ESDJ	4 426 677	2 479 178	56.0	2 199 918	1 192 131	54.2	2 226 759	1 287 047	57.8
1 VII 1996	ESDJ	4 548 755	2 535 091	55.7	2 261 141	1 221 317	54.0	2 287 614	1 313 774	57.4
1 VII 1997	ESDJ	4 674 199	2 621 328	56.1	2 324 066	1 264 550	54.4	2 350 133	1 356 778	57.7
1 VII 1998	ESDJ	4 803 102	2 710 381	56.4	2 388 742	1 309 236	54.8	2 414 360	1 401 145	58.0
1 VII 1999	ESDJ	4 935 559	2 802 340	56.8	2 455 217	1 355 417	55.2	2 480 342	1 446 923	58.3
1 VII 2000	ESDJ	5 071 671	2 897 293	57.1	2 523 541	1 403 141	55.6	2 548 129	1 494 152	58.6
Panama										
1 VII 1992	ESDF	2 488 333	1 350 002	54.3	1 259 517	657 496	52.2	1 228 816	692 506	56.4
1 VII 1993	ESDF	2 535 012	1 381 542	54.5	1 282 633	673 074	52.5	1 252 379	708 468	56.6
1 VII 1994	ESDF	2 582 566	1 413 083	54.7	1 306 173	688 653	52.7	1 276 393	724 430	56.8
1 VII 1995	ESDF	2 631 013	1 444 622	54.9	1 330 145	704 231	52.9	1 300 868	740 391	56.9
1 VII 1996	ESDF	2 674 490	1 476 665	55.2	1 351 574	719 973	53.3	1 322 916	756 692	57.2
1 VII 1997	ESDF	2 718 686	1 508 703	55.5	1 373 349	735 709	53.6	1 345 337	772 994	57.5
1 VII 1998	ESDF	2 763 612	1 540 742	55.8	1 395 475	751 450	53.8	1 368 137	789 292	57.7
1 VII 1999	ESDF	2 809 280	1 572 780	56.0	1 417 957	767 186	54.1	1 391 323	805 594	57.9
1 VII 2000	ESDF	2 855 703	1 604 823	56.2	1 440 801	782 928	54.3	1 414 902	821 895	58.1
Puerto Rico - Porto Rico[9]										
1 IV 2000*	CDJC	3 808 610	3 594 948	94.4	1 833 577	1 723 589	94.0	1 975 033	1 871 359	94.8
Saint Lucia - Sainte-Lucie										
1 VII 1994	ESDF	142 689	42 193	29.6	69 327	20 500	29.6	73 362	21 693	29.6
1 VII 1995	ESDF	145 437	43 005	29.6	70 725	20 913	29.6	74 715	22 092	29.6
1 VII 1996	ESDF	147 062	43 486	29.6	71 760	21 219	29.6	75 302	22 267	29.6
1 VII 1997	ESDF	149 666	44 256	29.6	73 114	21 620	29.6	76 552	22 636	29.6
1 VII 1998	ESDF	151 952	44 932	29.6	74 320	21 976	29.6	77 632	22 956	29.6
Saint Vincent and the Grenadines - Saint Vincent-et-les Grenadines										
1 VII 1992	ESDF	108 965	47 590	43.7	54 322	...	...	54 539	...	...
1 VII 1993	ESDF	109 653	47 890	43.7	...	...	...	...	...	...
1 VII 1994	ESDF	109 534	47 839	43.7	...	...	...	...	...	...
1 VII 1995	ESDF	110 724	48 353	43.7	...	...	...	...	...	...
1 VII 1996	ESDF	111 105	48 522	43.7	...	...	...	...	...	...
1 VII 1997	ESDF	111 655	48 761	43.7	55 713	...	...	55 942	...	...
1 VII 1998	ESDF	111 380	48 652	43.7	55 602	...	...	55 778	...	...
United States - États-Unis[10]										
1 IV 2000*	CDJC	281 421 906	222 360 539	79.0	138 053 563	108 375 797	78.5	143 368 343	113 984 742	79.5
AMERICA, SOUTH — AMERIQUE DU SUD										
Argentina - Argentine										
1 VII 1992	ESDF	33 421 199	29 226 537	87.4	...	...	...	...	...	...
1 VII 1993	ESDF	33 869 405	29 723 071	87.8	...	...	...	...	...	...
1 VII 1994	ESDF	34 318 469	30 220 944	88.1	16 836 555	...	...	17 481 914	...	...
1 VII 1995	ESDF	34 768 458	30 715 258	88.3	17 055 814	14 889 186	87.3	17 712 643	15 826 072	89.3
1 VII 1996	ESDF	35 219 612	31 206 336	88.6	17 275 885	...	...	17 943 728	...	...
1 VII 1997	ESDF	35 671 894	31 697 444	88.9	17 496 945	...	...	18 174 949	...	...
1 VII 1998	ESDF	36 124 933	32 188 095	89.1	17 718 738	...	...	18 406 194	...	...

6. Urban and total population by sex: 1992 - 2001
Population urbaine et population totale selon le sexe: 1992 - 2001
(continued — suite)

(See notes at end of table. — Voir notes à la fin du tableau.)

Continent, country or area and date / Continent, pays ou zone et date	Code[1]	Both sexes - Les deux sexes			Male - Masculin			Female - Féminin		
		Total	Urban - Urbaine		Total	Urban - Urbaine		Total	Urban - Urbaine	
			Number Nombre	Percent P.100		Number Nombre	Percent P.100		Number Nombre	Percent P.100
AMERICA, SOUTH — AMERIQUE DU SUD										
Argentina - Argentine										
1 VII 1999	ESDF	36 578 358	32 677 810	89.3	...	...	...	...	...	..
Bolivia - Bolivie[5,8]										
3 VI 1992	CDFC	6 420 792	3 694 846	57.5	3 171 265	1 793 445	56.6	3 249 527	1 901 401	58.5
1 VII 1992	ESDF	6 897 096	3 900 771	56.6	...	...	...	...	...	..
1 VII 1993	ESDF	7 065 211	4 063 965	57.5	...	...	...	...	...	..
1 VII 1994	ESDF	7 237 424	4 232 386	58.5	3 582 711	...	...	3 654 713	...	..
1 VII 1995	ESDF	7 413 834	4 406 129	59.4	3 680 139	2 139 324	58.1	3 733 695	2 266 805	60.7
1 VII 1996	ESDF	7 588 392	4 576 132	60.3	3 768 522	2 222 809	59.0	3 819 870	2 353 323	61.6
1 VII 1997	ESDF	7 767 059	4 751 190	61.2	3 859 028	2 308 866	59.8	3 908 031	2 442 324	62.5
1 VII 1998	ESDF	7 949 933	4 931 398	62.0	3 951 706	2 397 547	60.7	3 998 227	2 533 851	63.4
1 VII 1999	ESDF	8 137 113	5 116 850	62.9	4 046 609	2 488 906	61.5	4 090 504	2 627 944	64.3
1 VII 2000	ESDF	8 328 700	5 307 638	63.7	4 143 790	2 582 994	62.3	4 184 910	2 724 644	65.1
5 IX 2001	CDFC	8 274 325	5 165 230	62.4	4 123 850	2 517 106	61.0	4 150 475	2 648 124	63.8
Brazil - Brésil[11]										
1 VIII 1996	CDJC	157 070 163	123 076 831	78.4	77 442 865	59 716 389	77.1	79 627 298	63 360 442	79.6
1 VIII 2000	CDJC	169 799 170	137 953 959	81.2	83 576 015	66 882 993	80.0	86 223 155	71 070 966	82.4
Chile - Chili										
22 IV 1992	CDFC	13 348 401	11 140 405	83.5	6 553 254	5 364 760	81.9	6 795 147	5 775 645	85.0
1 VII 1992	ESDF	13 544 964	11 335 101	83.7	6 695 425	5 505 686	82.2	6 849 539	5 829 415	85.1
1 VII 1993	ESDF	13 771 187	11 561 902	84.0	6 809 060	5 619 865	82.5	6 962 127	5 942 037	85.3
1 VII 1994	ESDF	13 994 355	11 785 639	84.2	6 921 150	5 732 505	82.8	7 073 205	6 053 134	85.6
1 VII 1995	ESDF	14 210 429	12 002 308	84.5	7 029 597	5 841 532	83.1	7 180 832	6 160 776	85.8
1 VII 1996	ESDF	14 418 864	12 213 883	84.7	7 134 144	5 948 050	83.4	7 284 720	6 265 833	86.0
1 VII 1997	ESDF	14 622 354	12 420 506	84.9	7 236 189	6 052 039	83.6	7 386 165	6 368 467	86.2
1 VII 1998	ESDF	14 821 714	12 623 059	85.2	7 336 118	6 153 975	83.9	7 485 596	6 469 084	86.4
1 VII 1999	ESDF	15 017 760	12 822 261	85.4	7 434 317	6 254 136	84.1	7 583 443	6 568 125	86.6
1 VII 2000	ESDF	15 211 308	13 018 924	85.6	7 531 173	6 352 945	84.4	7 680 135	6 665 979	86.8
Colombia - Colombie										
24 X 1993	CDFC	33 109 840	23 514 070	71.0	16 296 539	11 211 708	68.8	16 813 301	12 302 362	73.2
Ecuador - Équateur[5,12]										
1 VII 1992	ESDF	10 740 799	6 115 572	56.9	5 398 462	...	...	5 342 337	...	..
1 VII 1993	ESDF	10 980 972	6 336 923	57.7	...	...	...	...	...	..
1 VII 1994	ESDF	11 221 070	6 560 382	58.5	5 638 647	...	...	5 582 423	...	..
1 VII 1995	ESDF	11 460 117	6 784 855	59.2	5 758 141	...	...	5 701 976	...	..
1 VII 1996	ESDF	11 698 496	7 011 072	59.9	5 877 274	...	...	5 821 222	...	..
1 VII 1997	ESDF	11 936 858	7 239 763	60.7	5 996 368	...	...	5 940 490	...	..
1 VII 1998	ESDF	12 174 628	7 469 833	61.4	6 115 124	...	...	6 059 504	...	..
1 VII 1999	ESDF	12 411 232	7 700 185	62.0	6 233 241	...	...	6 177 992	...	..
1 VII 2000	ESDF	12 646 095	7 929 722	62.7	6 350 427	3 907 419	61.5	6 295 668	4 022 303	63.8
25 XI 2001	CDFC	12 156 608	7 431 355	61.1	6 018 353	3 625 962	60.2	6 138 255	3 805 393	62.0
Paraguay[13]										
26 VIII 1992	CDFC	4 152 588	2 089 688	50.3	2 058 905	1 007 400	48.9	2 066 683	1 082 288	52.4
Peru - Pérou[5,14]										
1 VII 1992	ESDF	22 453 867	16 010 043	71.3	11 299 736	7 993 254	70.7	11 154 131	8 016 789	71.9
11 VII 1993	CDFC	22 048 356	15 458 599	70.1	10 956 375	7 606 489	69.4	11 091 981	7 852 110	70.8
1 VII 1995	ESDF	23 531 701	16 758 691	71.2	11 688 601	8 255 135	70.6	11 843 100	8 503 556	71.8
1 VII 1996	ESDF	23 946 779	17 775 935	74.2	11 887 773	8 869 457	74.6	12 059 006	8 906 470	73.9
1 VII 1998	ESDF	24 800 768	17 838 479	71.9	12 303 755	8 771 638	71.3	12 497 013	9 066 841	72.6
Suriname										
1 VII 1992	ESDF	403 312	283 000	70.2	202 035	...	...	201 279	...	..
1 VII 1993	ESDF	403 821	284 000	70.3	202 486	...	...	201 342	...	..
1 VII 1994	ESDF	405 013	285 000	70.4	203 261	...	...	201 749	...	..
1 VII 1995	ESDF	408 866	287 000	70.2	205 386	...	...	203 480	...	..
1 VII 1996	ESDF	413 427	288 000	69.7	...	...	...	...	...	..

6. Urban and total population by sex: 1992 - 2001
Population urbaine et population totale selon le sexe: 1992 - 2001
(continued — suite)

(see notes at end of table. — Voir notes à la fin du tableau.)

Continent, country area and date / Continent, pays zone et date	Code[1]	Both sexes - Les deux sexes			Male - Masculin			Female - Féminin		
		Total	Urban - Urbaine		Total	Urban - Urbaine		Total	Urban - Urbaine	
			Number Nombre	Percent P.100		Number Nombre	Percent P.100		Number Nombre	Percent P.100
AMERICA, SOUTH — AMERIQUE DU SUD										
Suriname										
1 VII 1997	ESDF	418 921	290 000	69.2	...	...	...	...	...	...
Uruguay[5]										
1 VII 1992	ESDF	3 149 177	2 866 527	91.0	1 527 450	1 365 241	89.4	1 621 727	1 501 286	92.6
1 VII 1993	ESDF	3 171 931	2 894 518	91.3	1 538 301	1 378 857	89.6	1 633 630	1 515 661	92.8
1 VII 1994	ESDF	3 195 009	2 922 589	91.5	1 549 423	1 392 577	89.9	1 645 586	1 530 012	93.0
1 VII 1995	ESDF	3 218 187	2 950 474	91.7	1 560 610	1 406 328	90.1	1 657 577	1 544 146	93.2
22 V 1996	CDFC	3 163 763	2 872 077	90.8	1 532 288	1 366 092	89.2	1 631 475	1 505 985	92.3
1 VII 1996	ESDF	3 241 576	2 978 306	91.9	1 571 925	1 420 193	90.3	1 669 651	1 558 113	93.3
1 VII 1997	ESDF	3 265 326	3 006 269	92.1	1 583 505	1 434 223	90.6	1 681 821	1 572 046	93.5
1 VII 1998	ESDF	3 289 270	3 034 154	92.2	1 595 257	1 448 290	90.8	1 694 013	1 585 864	93.6
1 VII 1999	ESDF	3 313 238	3 061 753	92.4	1 607 085	1 462 266	91.0	1 706 153	1 599 487	93.7
1 VII 2000*	ESDF	3 337 058	3 088 859	92.6	1 618 893	1 476 025	91.2	1 718 165	1 612 834	93.9
1 VII 2001*	ESDF	3 360 845	3 115 459	92.7	1 630 739	1 489 553	91.3	1 730 106	1 625 906	94.0
Venezuela[5,14]										
1 VII 1992	ESDF	20 441 298	17 235 382	84.3	10 302 691	...	...	10 138 607	...	...
1 VII 1993	ESDF	20 909 727	17 709 445	84.7	10 536 389	...	...	10 373 338	...	...
1 VII 1994	ESDF	21 377 426	18 183 104	85.1	10 769 620	...	...	10 607 806	...	...
1 VII 1995	ESDF	21 844 496	18 656 451	85.4	11 002 507	9 277 236	84.3	10 841 989	9 379 215	86.5
1 VII 1996	ESDF	22 311 094	19 137 416	85.8	11 235 137	9 514 592	84.7	11 075 957	9 622 824	86.9
1 VII 1997	ESDF	22 777 151	19 617 876	86.1	11 467 427	9 751 665	85.0	11 309 724	9 866 211	87.2
1 VII 1998	ESDF	23 242 435	20 097 795	86.5	11 699 249	9 988 424	85.4	11 543 186	10 109 371	87.6
1 VII 1999	ESDF	23 706 711	20 576 930	86.8	11 930 471	10 224 734	85.7	11 776 240	10 352 196	87.9
1 VII 2000	ESDF	24 169 744	21 055 245	87.1	12 160 964	10 460 568	86.0	12 008 780	10 594 677	88.2
ASIA — ASIE										
Armenia - Arménie										
1 VII 1992	ESDF	3 685 600	2 525 700	68.5	1 785 800	1 204 200	67.4	1 899 800	1 321 500	69.6
1 VII 1993	ESDF	3 731 300	2 534 300	67.9	1 807 100	1 208 500	66.9	1 924 200	1 325 800	68.9
1 VII 1994	ESDF	3 746 800	2 533 000	67.6	1 814 100	1 207 400	66.6	1 932 700	1 325 600	68.6
1 VII 1995	ESDF	3 759 950	2 534 250	67.4	1 820 165	1 207 260	66.3	1 939 785	1 326 990	68.4
1 VII 1996	ESDF	3 773 567	2 534 024	67.2	1 827 556	1 207 639	66.1	1 946 011	1 326 385	68.2
1 VII 1997	ESDF	3 785 982	2 534 076	66.9	1 835 093	1 208 745	65.9	1 950 889	1 325 331	67.9
1 VII 1998	ESDF	3 794 735	2 535 702	66.8	1 841 448	1 210 849	65.8	1 953 287	1 324 853	67.8
1 VII 1999	ESDF	3 800 817	2 535 846	66.7	1 846 592	1 212 207	65.6	1 954 225	1 323 639	67.7
1 VII 2000	ESDF	3 802 882	2 534 023	66.6	1 848 756	1 212 033	65.6	1 954 126	1 321 990	67.7
Azerbaijan - Azerbaïdjan										
1 VII 1992	ESDF	7 382 100	3 906 500	52.9	...	...	...	...	...	...
1 VII 1993	ESDF	7 494 800	3 949 700	52.7	...	...	...	...	...	...
1 VII 1994	ESDF	7 596 600	3 988 300	52.5	3 728 600	1 969 100	52.8	3 868 000	2 021 700	52.3
1 VII 1995	ESDF	7 684 900	4 020 100	52.3	3 778 700	1 977 600	52.3	3 906 200	2 042 500	52.3
1 VII 1996	ESDF	7 763 000	4 046 200	52.1	3 824 000	1 988 900	52.0	3 939 000	2 057 300	52.2
1 VII 1997	ESDF	7 838 300	4 070 200	51.9	3 864 300	2 006 500	51.9	3 974 000	2 063 700	51.9
1 VII 1998	ESDF	7 913 000	4 072 600	51.5	3 882 100	1 993 500	51.4	4 030 900	2 079 100	51.6
27 I 1999*	CDJC	7 953 438	4 053 584	51.0	3 883 155	1 970 022	50.7	4 070 283	2 083 562	51.2
1 VII 1999	ESDF	7 982 800	4 074 600	51.0	3 899 600	1 981 300	50.8	4 083 200	2 093 300	51.3
1 VII 2000	ESDF	8 048 600	4 096 900	50.9	3 936 400	1 994 300	50.7	4 112 200	2 102 600	51.1
1 VII 2001*	ESDF	8 111 200	4 118 800	50.8	3 971 600	2 006 800	50.5	4 139 600	2 112 000	51.0
Bangladesh										
22 I 2001	CDFC	123 151 246	28 808 477	23.4	62 735 988	15 360 059	24.5	60 415 258	13 448 418	22.3
Cambodia - Cambodge[15,16,17]										
1 VII 1996	ESDF	*10 340 000*	*1 540 000*	*14.9*	*5 119 000*	*738 000*	*14.4*	*5 583 000*	*802 000*	*14.4*
3 III 1998	CDFC	11 437 656	1 795 575	15.7	5 511 408	878 186	15.9	5 926 248	917 389	15.5

6. Urban and total population by sex: 1992 - 2001
Population urbaine et population totale selon le sexe: 1992 - 2001
(continued — suite)

(See notes at end of table. — Voir notes à la fin du tableau.)

Continent, country or area and date / Continent, pays ou zone et date	Code[1]	Both sexes - Les deux sexes			Male - Masculin			Female - Féminin		
		Total	Urban - Urbaine		Total	Urban - Urbaine		Total	Urban - Urbaine	
			Number Nombre	Percent P.100		Number Nombre	Percent P.100		Number Nombre	Percent P.100
ASIA — ASIE										
China - Chine[18,19,20]										
1 VII 1992	ESDF	1171710000	323 720 000	27.6	...	...	...	...	...	...
1 VII 1993	ESDF	1185170000	333 510 000	28.1	...	...	...	...	...	...
1 VII 1994	ESDF	1198500000	343 010 000	28.6	...	...	...	...	...	...
1 VII 1995	ESDF	1211210000	351 740 000	29.0	...	...	...	...	...	...
1 VII 1996	ESDF	1223890000	359 500 000	29.4	...	...	...	...	...	...
1 VII 1997	ESDF	1236260000	369 890 000	29.9	...	...	...	...	...	...
1 VII 1998	ESDF	1248100000	379 420 000	30.4	...	...	...	...	...	...
1 VII 1999	ESDF	1259090000	388 920 000	30.9	...	...	...	...	...	...
1 XI 2000	CDJC	1242612226	458 770 983	36.9	640 275 969	235 264 707	36.7	602 336 257	223 506 276	37.1
Cyprus - Chypre[21,22,23,24]										
1 X 1992	CDJC	602 025	407 324	67.7	299 614	201 811	67.4	302 411	205 513	68.0
1 X 2001	CDJC	689 565	474 450	68.8	338 497	231 128	68.3	351 068	243 322	69.3
Georgia - Géorgie										
1 VII 1992	ESDF	5 454 900	3 059 300	56.1	...	...	...	...	...	...
1 VII 1993	ESDF	5 440 300	3 039 500	55.9	...	...	...	...	...	...
1 VII 1994	ESDF	5 425 600	3 022 600	55.7	...	...	...	...	...	...
1 VII 1995	ESDF	5 416 900	3 013 600	55.6	...	...	...	...	...	...
1 VII 1996	ESDF	5 419 800	3 013 400	55.6	...	...	...	...	...	...
1 VII 1997	ESDF	5 430 600	3 019 800	55.6	...	...	...	...	...	...
1 VII 1998	ESDF	5 441 100	3 028 500	55.7	...	...	...	...	...	...
1 VII 1999	ESDF	4 604 500	2 660 200	57.8	...	...	...	...	...	...
1 VII 2000	ESDF	5 023 052	2 617 800	52.1	2 401 344	1 368 716	57.0	2 621 708	1 534 457	58.5
India - Inde[17,25]										
1 VII 1992	ESDF	869 845 000	225 953 000	26.0	...	...	...	...	...	...
1 VII 1993	ESDF	887 603 000	232 354 000	26.2	...	...	...	...	...	...
1 VII 1994	ESDF	905 508 000	238 858 000	26.4	...	...	...	...	...	...
1 VII 1995	ESDF	923 541 000	245 471 000	26.6	...	...	...	...	...	...
1 VII 1996	ESDF	941 681 000	252 200 000	26.8	487 475 000	134 819 000	27.7	452 065 000	121 947 000	27.0
1 VII 1997	ESDF	959 908 000	259 052 000	27.0	495 212 000	138 345 000	27.9	460 008 000	125 610 000	27.3
1 VII 1998	ESDF	978 199 000	266 035 000	27.2	503 002 000	141 939 000	28.2	467 931 000	129 333 000	27.6
1 VII 1999	ESDF	996 531 000	273 157 000	27.4	510 813 000	145 592 000	28.5	475 798 000	133 103 000	28.0
1 VII 2000	ESDF	1014877000	280 428 000	27.6	518 604 000	149 295 000	28.8	483 538 000	136 906 000	28.3
1 III 2001	CDFC	1027015247	285 354 954	27.8	531 277 078	150 135 894	28.3	495 738 169	135 219 060	27.3
1 VII 2001 *	ESDF	1033213000	287 857 000	27.9	534 319 000	153 031 000	28.6	498 932 000	140 738 000	28.2
Indonesia - Indonésie[17,26]										
1 VII 1992	ESDF	184 491 550	60 036 300	32.5	...	...	...	...	...	...
1 VII 1993	ESDF	187 589 500	62 898 800	33.5	...	...	...	...	...	...
1 VII 1994	ESDF	190 676 050	65 856 300	34.5	...	...	...	...	...	...
31 X 1995	SSDF	194 754 808	69 937 110	35.9	96 929 931	34 722 443	35.8	97 824 877	35 214 667	36.0
1 VII 1996	ESDF	198 320 000	73 640 300	37.1	...	...	...	...	...	...
1 VII 1997	ESDF	201 353 100	76 914 000	38.2	...	...	...	...	...	...
1 VII 1998	ESDF	204 392 500	80 275 300	39.3	...	...	...	...	...	...
1 VII 1999	ESDF	207 439 900	83 718 400	40.4	...	...	...	...	...	...
30 VI 2000	CDFC	206 264 595	86 601 850	42.0	103 417 180	43 368 496	41.9	102 847 415	43 233 354	42.0
Iran (Islamic Republic of) - Iran (République islamique d')										
1 VII 1992	ESDJ	56 656 431	32 775 768	57.9	...	...	...	...	...	...
1 VII 1993	ESDJ	57 487 720	33 742 643	58.7	29 414 643	17 326 790	58.9	28 073 077	16 415 853	58.5
1 VII 1994	ESDJ	59 331 206	34 738 041	58.5	29 846 228	17 839 668	59.8	28 484 978	16 898 373	59.3
1 VII 1995	ESDJ	59 187 068	35 762 803	60.4	30 284 145	18 364 139	60.6	28 902 923	17 398 664	60.2
23 X 1996	CDJC	60 055 488	36 817 789	61.3	30 515 159	18 805 023	61.6	29 540 329	18 012 766	61.0
1 VII 1997	ESDJ	60 938 837	37 826 305	62.1	31 011 770	19 249 804	62.1	29 927 067	18 576 501	62.1
1 VII 1998	ESDJ	61 835 591	38 839 280	62.8	...	...	...	...	...	...

6. **Urban and total population by sex: 1992 - 2001**
Population urbaine et population totale selon le sexe: 1992 - 2001
(continued — suite)

ee notes at end of table. — Voir notes à la fin du tableau.)

ontinent, country r area and date ontinent, pays u zone et date	Code[1]	Both sexes - Les deux sexes			Male - Masculin			Female - Féminin		
		Total	Urban - Urbaine		Total	Urban - Urbaine		Total	Urban - Urbaine	
			Number Nombre	Percent P.100		Number Nombre	Percent P.100		Number Nombre	Percent P.100
SIA — ASIE										
Iran (Islamic Republic of) - Iran (République islamique d')										
1 VII 1999	ESDJ	62 745 540	39 856 570	63.5	...	...	...	...	...	...
1 VII 2000	ESDJ	63 663 942	40 873 494	64.2	...	...	...	...	...	...
Iraq[27]										
16 X 1997	CDFC	19 184 543	12 945 776	67.5	9 536 570	6 466 325	67.8	9 647 973	6 479 451	67.2
Israel - Israël[5,28]										
1 VII 1992	ESDJ	5 123 500	4 603 900	89.9	2 542 900	2 276 300	89.5	2 580 400	2 328 400	90.2
1 VII 1993	ESDJ	5 261 400	4 723 500	89.8	2 609 400	2 333 200	89.4	2 652 000	2 390 300	90.1
1 VII 1994	ESDJ	5 399 300	4 843 700	89.7	2 675 800	2 390 900	89.4	2 723 500	2 453 000	90.1
1 VII 1995	ESDJ	5 544 900	4 970 500	89.6	2 746 500	2 452 000	89.3	2 798 400	2 518 200	90.0
4 XI 1995	CDJC	5 548 523	5 044 735	90.9	2 738 175	2 476 836	90.5	2 810 348	2 567 899	91.4
1 VII 1996	ESDJ	5 685 100	5 166 000	90.9	...	...	...	...	...	...
1 VII 1997	ESDJ	5 829 000	5 294 100	90.8	2 875 400	2 599 900	90.4	2 953 500	2 694 300	91.2
1 VII 1998	ESDJ	5 970 700	5 418 400	90.7	...	...	...	...	...	...
1 VII 1999	ESDJ	6 125 300	5 554 200	90.7	3 021 743	...	...	3 103 533	...	...
1 VII 2000	ESDJ	6 289 200	5 696 100	90.6	3 102 400	2 797 800	90.2	3 186 800	2 898 300	90.9
1 VII 2001*	ESDJ	6 439 000	5 900 700	91.6	3 176 600	2 900 200	91.3	3 262 500	3 000 500	92.0
Japan - Japon[29]										
1 X 1995	CDFC	125 570 246	98 009 107	78.1	61 574 398	48 210 196	78.3	63 995 848	49 798 911	77.8
1 X 2000	CDFC	126 925 843	99 865 289	78.7	62 110 764	49 005 691	78.9	64 815 079	50 859 598	78.5
Jordan - Jordanie[30]										
31 XII 1992	ESDF	3 844 000	2 997 975	78.0	...	...	...	...	...	...
10 XII 1994	CDFC	4 139 458	3 238 757	78.2	2 160 725	1 687 530	78.1	1 978 733	1 551 227	78.4
31 XII 1995	ESDF	4 291 000	3 355 511	78.2	...	...	...	...	...	...
31 XII 1996	ESDF	4 444 000	3 477 800	78.3	...	...	...	...	...	...
31 XII 1998	ESDF	4 755 750	3 743 070	78.7	...	...	...	...	...	...
31 XII 1999	ESDF	4 900 000	3 856 300	78.7	...	...	...	...	...	...
31 XII 2000	ESDF	5 039 000	3 965 693	78.7	2 635 400	2 066 126	78.4	2 403 600	1 899 567	79.0
Kazakhstan										
1 VII 1992	ESDF	16 517 600	9 354 800	56.6	8 211 040	4 613 957	56.2	8 691 660	5 070 443	58.3
1 VII 1993	ESDF	16 479 200	9 232 100	56.0	8 210 471	4 560 033	55.5	8 681 585	5 013 370	57.7
1 VII 1994	ESDF	16 296 800	9 026 300	55.4	...	...	...	...	...	...
1 VII 1995	ESDF	16 066 100	8 862 900	55.2	8 036 278	4 391 237	54.6	8 503 251	4 841 676	56.9
1 VII 1996	ESDF	15 920 897	8 782 513	55.2	7 738 053	4 175 974	54.0	8 182 844	4 606 539	56.3
1 VII 1997	ESDF	15 751 310	8 686 526	55.1	7 655 806	4 128 719	53.9	8 095 504	4 557 807	56.3
1 VII 1998	ESDF	15 072 983	8 434 080	56.0	7 263 077	3 945 189	54.3	7 809 906	4 488 891	57.5
26 II 1999	CDJC	14 953 126	8 377 303	56.0	7 201 785	3 918 556	54.4	7 751 341	4 458 747	57.5
1 VII 1999	ESDF	14 926 945	8 345 487	55.9	7 190 822	3 899 728	54.2	7 736 123	4 445 759	57.5
Korea (Dem. People's Republic of) - Corée (Rép. populaire dém. de)										
31 XII 1993	CDFC	21 213 378	12 501 217	58.9	10 329 699	5 951 077	57.6	10 883 679	6 550 140	60.2
Korea (Republic of) - Corée (République de)[13,17,31,32,33]										
1 XI 1995	CDFC	44 608 726	35 036 473	78.5	22 389 324	17 621 308	78.7	22 219 402	17 415 165	78.4
1 XI 2000	CDFC	46 136 101	36 755 144	79.7	23 158 582	18 484 139	79.8	22 977 519	18 271 005	79.5
Kyrgyzstan - Kirghizistan										
1 VII 1992	ESDF	4 533 600	1 708 100	37.7	...	...	...	...	...	...
1 VII 1993	ESDF	4 559 100	1 693 200	37.1	...	...	...	...	...	...
1 VII 1994	ESDF	4 526 100	1 650 300	36.5	...	...	...	...	...	...
1 VII 1995	ESDF	4 554 700	1 640 000	36.0	...	...	...	...	...	...
1 VII 1996	ESDF	4 625 200	1 652 600	35.7	...	...	...	...	...	...

6. Urban and total population by sex: 1992 - 2001
Population urbaine et population totale selon le sexe: 1992 - 2001
(continued — suite)

(See notes at end of table. — Voir notes à la fin du tableau.)

Continent, country or area and date / Continent, pays ou zone et date	Code[1]	Both sexes - Les deux sexes			Male - Masculin			Female - Féminin		
		Total	Urban - Urbaine		Total	Urban - Urbaine		Total	Urban - Urbaine	
			Number Nombre	Percent P.100		Number Nombre	Percent P.100		Number Nombre	Percent P.100
ASIA — ASIE										
Kyrgyzstan - Kirghizistan										
1 VII 1997	ESDF	4 689 700	1 667 800	35.6	2 289 300	...	...	2 345 600	...	...
1 VII 1998	ESDF	4 760 100	1 683 900	35.4	...	...	...	...	...	...
24 III 1999	CDJC	4 822 938	1 678 623	34.8	2 380 465	802 256	33.7	2 442 473	876 367	35.9
1 VII 1999	ESDF	4 833 900	1 709 900	35.4	...	...	...	...	...	...
1 VII 2000	ESDF	4 895 200	1 724 300	35.2	...	...	...	...	...	...
1 VII 2001*	ESDF	4 935 400	1 742 000	35.3	...	...	...	...	...	...
Lao People's Democratic Republic - République démocratique populaire lao										
1 III 1995	CDFC	4 574 848	781 753	17.1	2 260 986	...	...	2 313 862	...	...
Malaysia - Malaisie[34,35]										
1 VII 1992	ESDF	19 043 075	9 903 409	52.0	9 678 488	...	...	9 364 587	...	...
1 VII 1993	ESDF	19 563 728	10 354 587	52.9	9 956 183	...	...	9 607 545	...	...
1 VII 1994	ESDF	20 111 565	10 825 360	53.8	10 251 030	...	...	9 860 535	...	...
1 VII 1995	ESDF	20 689 344	11 317 218	54.7	10 563 895	...	...	10 125 449	...	...
5 VII 2000	CDJC	23 274 690	14 426 871	62.0	11 853 432	7 318 396	61.7	11 421 258	7 108 475	62.2
Maldives										
25 III 1995	CDFC	244 814	62 519	25.5	124 622	33 506	26.9	120 192	29 013	24.1
Mongolia - Mongolie										
1 VII 1996	ESDF	2 266 900	1 126 400	49.7	1 125 800	559 400	49.7	1 141 100	567 000	49.7
1 VII 1997	ESDF	2 296 900	1 138 800	49.6	1 140 300	565 300	49.6	1 156 600	573 400	49.6
1 VII 1998	ESDF	2 327 900	1 154 400	49.6	1 155 700	573 100	49.6	1 172 200	581 300	49.6
1 VII 1999	ESDF	2 359 000	1 382 000	58.6	1 170 900	686 000	58.6	1 188 100	696 100	58.6
5 I 2000	CDFC	2 373 493	1 344 516	56.6	1 177 981	657 081	55.8	1 195 512	687 435	57.5
1 VII 2000	ESDF	2 390 500	1 400 600	58.6	1 185 200	694 500	58.6	1 205 300	706 100	58.6
Myanmar[36]										
1 VII 1994	ESDF	43 922 000	9 249 467	21.1	21 832 000	4 601 468	21.1	22 090 000	4 647 999	21.0
Nepal - Népal[37]										
1 VII 1996	ESDJ	20 831 644	2 207 967	10.6	10 393 913	1 138 641	11.0	10 437 731	1 069 326	10.2
Occupied Palestinian Territory - Territoire palestinien occupé[38,39]										
1 VII 1997	ESDF	2 783 084	1 987 886	71.4	1 404 481	...	...	1 378 603	...	...
1 VII 1998	ESDF	2 897 452	2 070 547	71.5	1 462 532	...	...	1 434 920	...	...
1 VII 1999	ESDF	3 019 704	2 157 773	71.5	1 524 649	...	...	1 495 055	...	...
1 VII 2000	ESDF	3 150 056	2 251 337	71.5	1 590 945	...	...	1 559 111	...	...
1 VII 2001*	ESDF	3 298 951	2 357 971	71.5	1 666 805	...	...	1 632 146	...	...
Pakistan[40]										
2 III 1998	CDFC	130 579 571	42 458 339	32.5	67 840 137	22 419 286	33.0	62 739 434	20 039 053	31.9
1 III 1998	ESDF	131 510 000	42 910 000	32.6	68 290 000	22 100 000	32.4	63 220 000	20 810 000	32.9
Sri Lanka[41]										
17 VII 2001	CDFC	16 864 544	2 467 171	14.6	8 343 964	1 246 983	14.9	8 520 580	1 220 188	14.3
Syrian Arab Republic - République arabe syrienne[42]										
1 VII 1992	ESDF	12 958 000	6 594 000	50.9	6 620 000	3 408 000	51.5	6 338 000	3 186 000	50.3
1 VII 1993	ESDF	13 393 000	6 815 000	50.9	6 842 000	3 547 000	51.8	6 551 000	3 268 000	49.9
1 VII 1994	ESDF	13 844 000	7 112 000	51.4	7 071 000	3 702 000	52.4	6 773 000	3 410 000	50.3
3 IX 1994	CDFC	13 782 315	6 864 525	49.8	7 048 906	3 540 051	50.2	6 733 409	3 324 474	49.4

6. Urban and total population by sex: 1992 - 2001
Population urbaine et population totale selon le sexe: 1992 - 2001
(continued — suite)

(See notes at end of table. — Voir notes à la fin du tableau.)

Continent, country or area and date / Continent, pays ou zone et date	Code[1]	Both sexes - Les deux sexes			Male - Masculin			Female - Féminin		
		Total	Urban - Urbaine		Total	Urban - Urbaine		Total	Urban - Urbaine	
			Number Nombre	Percent P.100		Number Nombre	Percent P.100		Number Nombre	Percent P.100
ASIA — ASIE										
Syrian Arab Republic - République arabe syrienne[42]										
1 VII 2001*	ESDF	16 720 000	8 376 000	50.1	8 552 000	...	...	8 168 000	...	...
Tajikistan - Tadjikistan										
1 VII 1992	ESDF	5 571 200	1 675 400	30.1	2 764 200	814 500	29.5	2 807 000	860 900	30.7
1 VII 1993	ESDF	5 637 700	1 643 300	29.1	2 799 200	801 400	28.6	2 838 500	841 900	29.7
1 VII 1994	ESDF	5 744 700	1 631 300	28.4	...	...	...	...	...	...
Thailand - Thaïlande[43]										
1 IV 2000*	CDJC	60 617 200	18 833 700	31.1	29 850 100	9 085 400	30.4	30 767 100	9 748 300	31.7
Turkey - Turquie										
1 VII 1992	ESDF	58 379 000	35 329 006	60.5	29 582 000	...	...	28 819 000	...	...
1 VII 1993	ESDF	59 478 000	36 316 259	61.1	30 121 000	...	...	29 370 000	...	...
1 VII 1994	ESDF	60 587 000	37 321 027	61.6	30 653 000	...	...	29 923 000	...	...
1 VII 1995	ESDF	61 706 000	38 343 473	62.1	...	...	...	...	...	...
1 VII 1996	ESDF	62 841 000	39 387 527	62.7	31 312 000	...	...	30 216 000	...	...
1 VII 1997	ESDF	63 989 000	40 451 548	63.2	32 332 000	...	...	31 657 000	...	...
1 VII 1998	ESDF	65 145 000	41 532 552	63.8	32 904 000	...	...	32 241 000	...	...
1 VII 1999	ESDF	66 304 000	42 627 450	64.3	33 481 000	...	...	32 823 000	...	...
1 VII 2000*	ESDF	67 469 000	43 738 238	64.8	33 401 000	...	...	34 068 000	...	...
1 VII 2001*	ESDF	68 610 000	44 861 438	65.4	34 636 000	...	...	33 974 000	...	...
Uzbekistan - Ouzbékistan										
1 VII 1992	ESDF	21 359 700	8 473 800	39.7	10 572 300	4 155 000	39.3	10 787 400	4 318 800	40.0
1 VII 1993	ESDF	21 852 500	8 559 300	39.2	10 824 400	4 199 900	38.8	11 028 100	4 359 400	39.5
1 VII 1994	ESDF	22 282 400	8 634 700	38.8	11 044 600	4 237 600	38.4	11 237 800	4 397 100	39.1
1 VII 1995	ESDF	22 689 700	8 711 900	38.4	11 255 900	4 278 100	38.0	11 433 800	4 433 800	38.8
1 VII 1996	ESDF	23 130 400	8 817 600	38.1	11 487 300	4 335 600	37.7	11 643 100	4 482 000	38.5
1 VII 1997	ESDF	23 560 400	8 931 400	37.9	11 710 400	4 394 700	37.5	11 850 000	4 536 700	38.3
1 VII 1998	ESDF	24 051 000	9 109 700	37.9	...	...	...	...	...	...
1 VII 1999	ESDF	23 953 922	9 037 904	37.7	11 913 994	4 450 641	37.4	12 039 928	4 587 263	38.1
1 VII 2000	ESDF	24 650 415	9 195 435	37.3	12 278 626	4 538 871	37.0	12 371 789	4 656 564	37.6
1 VII 2001*	ESDF	24 964 433	9 256 101	37.1	12 442 510	4 573 055	36.8	12 521 923	4 683 046	37.4
Viet Nam										
1 VII 1992	ESDF	69 405 200	13 285 000	19.1	33 813 900	...	...	35 591 300	...	...
1 VII 1993	ESDF	71 025 600	13 663 000	19.2	34 670 800	...	...	36 354 800	...	...
1 VII 1994	ESDF	72 509 500	14 139 200	19.5	35 386 400	...	...	37 123 100	...	...
1 VII 1995	ESDF	73 962 400	14 575 400	19.7	36 095 400	...	...	37 867 000	...	...
1 VII 1996	ESDF	75 355 200	15 231 500	20.2	36 773 300	...	...	38 581 900	...	...
1 IV 1999*	CDJC	76 324 753	17 916 983	23.5	37 519 754	...	...	38 804 999	...	...
Yemen - Yémen										
1 VII 1992	ESDF	11 952 010	2 858 200	23.9	...	...	...	...	...	...
1 VII 1993	ESDF	12 301 970	3 091 990	25.1	...	...	...	...	...	...
1 VII 1994	ESDF	14 859 000	3 487 000	23.5	7 411 000	...	...	7 448 000	...	...
16 XII 1994	CDFC	14 587 807	3 423 518	23.5	7 473 540	1 856 602	24.8	7 114 267	1 566 916	22.0
1 VII 1995	ESDF	15 369 000	3 699 000	24.1	7 668 000	...	...	7 701 000	...	...
1 VII 1996	ESDF	15 915 000	3 913 000	24.6	7 943 000	...	...	7 972 000	...	...
1 VII 1997	ESDF	16 484 000	4 130 000	25.1	8 229 000	...	...	8 255 000	...	...
1 VII 2000	ESDF	18 261 000	4 802 000	26.3	9 143 000	2 587 000	28.3	9 118 000	2 215 000	24.3
EUROPE										
Albania - Albanie										
1 IV 2001	CDFC	3 069 275	1 292 875	42.1	1 530 443	...	...	1 538 832	...	...

Population urbaine et population totale selon le sexe: 1992 - 2001
(continued — suite)

(See notes at end of table. — Voir notes à la fin du tableau.)

Continent, country or area and date / Continent, pays ou zone et date	Code[1]	Both sexes - Les deux sexes			Male - Masculin			Female - Féminin		
		Total	Urban - Urbaine		Total	Urban - Urbaine		Total	Urban - Urbaine	
			Number Nombre	Percent P.100		Number Nombre	Percent P.100		Number Nombre	Percent P.100
EUROPE										
Austria - Autriche										
15 V 2001	CDJC	8 065 465	5 379 498	66.7	3 907 244	2 572 088	65.8	4 158 221	2 807 410	67.8
Belarus - Bélarus										
1 VII 1992	ESDF	10 313 300	6 988 900	67.8	4 847 300	3 284 800	67.8	5 466 000	3 704 100	67.8
1 VII 1993	ESDF	10 356 500	7 049 700	68.1	4 867 600	3 313 400	68.1	5 488 900	3 736 300	68.1
1 VII 1994	ESDF	10 308 318	7 048 784	68.4	4 828 086	3 326 708	68.9	5 480 232	3 722 076	67.9
1 VII 1995	ESDF	10 280 805	7 066 181	68.7	4 799 416	3 319 964	69.2	5 481 389	3 746 217	68.3
1 VII 1996	ESDF	10 250 250	7 080 710	69.1	4 784 616	3 324 087	69.5	5 465 634	3 756 623	68.7
1 VII 1997	ESDF	10 219 982	7 106 247	69.5	4 769 223	3 332 777	69.9	5 450 759	3 773 470	69.2
1 VII 1998	ESDF	10 191 479	7 140 980	70.1	4 753 951	3 345 660	70.4	5 437 528	3 795 320	69.8
16 II 1999	CDJC	10 045 237	6 961 516	69.3	4 717 621	3 279 196	69.5	5 327 616	3 682 320	69.1
1 VII 1999	ESDF	10 035 210	6 971 628	69.5	4 711 689	3 282 317	69.7	5 323 521	3 689 311	69.3
Bulgaria - Bulgarie										
1 VII 1992	ESDF	8 540 164	5 737 817	67.2	4 199 343	2 811 073	66.9	4 340 929	2 926 277	67.4
1 VII 1993	ESDF	8 472 313	5 712 671	67.4	4 160 386	2 794 209	67.2	4 311 927	2 918 462	67.7
1 VII 1994	ESDF	8 443 591	5 718 212	67.7	4 140 802	2 792 807	67.4	4 302 789	2 925 405	68.0
1 VII 1995	ESDF	8 406 067	5 702 133	67.8	4 116 667	2 780 230	67.5	4 289 400	2 921 903	68.1
1 VII 1996	ESDF	8 362 826	5 661 482	67.7	...	...	...	...	...	...
1 VII 1997	ESDF	8 312 068	5 623 899	67.7	4 061 233	2 734 426	67.3	4 250 835	2 889 473	68.0
1 VII 1998	ESDF	8 256 786	5 603 501	67.9	4 029 518	...	...	4 227 268	...	...
1 VII 2000	ESDF	8 170 172	5 577 216	68.3	3 979 292	2 700 131	67.9	4 190 880	2 877 085	68.3
1 III 2001	CDFC	7 928 901	5 474 534	69.0	3 862 465	2 651 312	68.6	4 066 436	2 823 222	69.4
1 VII 2001*	ESDF	7 913 301	5 477 604	69.2	3 853 710	2 652 367	68.8	4 059 591	2 825 237	69.6
Czech Republic - République tchèque										
1 VII 1992	ESDJ	10 317 807	7 716 953	74.8	5 009 229	...	...	5 308 578	...	...
1 VII 1993	ESDJ	10 330 607	7 719 966	74.7	5 016 950	...	...	5 313 657	...	...
1 VII 1994	ESDJ	10 336 162	7 722 404	74.7	5 021 408	...	...	5 314 754	...	...
1 VII 1995	ESDJ	10 330 759	7 715 655	74.7	5 020 163	...	...	5 310 596	...	...
1 VII 1996	ESDJ	10 315 353	7 701 911	74.7	5 014 667	...	...	5 300 686	...	...
1 VII 1997	ESDJ	10 303 642	7 692 120	74.7	5 010 531	...	...	5 293 111	...	...
1 VII 1998	ESDJ	10 294 943	7 675 220	74.6	5 007 480	...	...	5 287 463	...	...
1 VII 1999	ESDJ	10 282 784	7 659 954	74.5	5 002 823	...	...	5 279 961	...	...
1 VII 2000	ESDJ	10 272 503	7 641 415	74.4	4 999 326	...	...	5 273 177	...	...
1 III 2001	CDJC	10 292 933	7 620 108	74.0	5 019 381	3 690 375	73.5	5 273 552	3 929 733	74.5
1 VII 2001*	ESDJ	10 224 192	7 559 732	73.9	4 978 951	3 655 116	73.4	5 245 241	3 904 616	74.4
Estonia - Estonie										
1 VII 1992	ESDF	1 544 374	1 095 199	70.9	722 225	506 025	70.1	822 149	589 174	71.1
1 VII 1993	ESDF	1 516 728	1 068 133	70.4	708 438	492 432	69.5	808 290	575 701	71.2
1 VII 1994	ESDF	1 499 255	1 051 449	70.1	699 749	483 939	69.2	799 506	567 510	71.0
1 VII 1995	ESDF	1 483 942	1 037 099	69.9	691 934	476 322	68.8	792 008	560 777	70.8
1 VII 1996	ESDF	1 469 216	1 022 676	69.6	684 346	468 434	68.4	784 870	554 241	70.6
1 VII 1997	ESDF	1 457 987	1 011 012	69.3	678 674	462 004	68.1	779 313	549 008	70.4
1 VII 1998	ESDF	1 449 712	1 003 118	69.2	674 656	457 641	67.8	775 056	545 478	70.4
1 VII 1999	ESDF	1 442 389	997 188	69.1	671 130	454 363	67.7	771 259	542 825	70.4
31 III 2000	CDJC	1 370 052	923 211	67.4	631 851	415 515	65.8	738 201	507 696	68.8
1 VII 2000	ESDF	1 369 279	922 594	67.4	631 515	415 232	65.8	737 764	507 362	68.8
Finland - Finlande										
1 VII 1992	ESDJ	5 041 992	3 127 364	62.0	...	...	...	...	...	...
1 VII 1993	ESDJ	5 066 447	3 243 196	64.0	...	...	...	...	...	...
1 VII 1994	ESDJ	5 088 333	3 266 117	64.2	2 475 923	1 560 508	63.0	2 612 410	1 705 609	65.3
1 VII 1995	ESDJ	5 107 790	3 291 480	64.4	2 486 675	1 573 544	63.3	2 621 115	1 717 936	65.5
1 VII 1996	ESDJ	5 124 573	3 323 247	64.8	2 496 148	1 589 993	63.7	2 628 425	1 733 254	65.9
1 VII 1997	ESDJ	5 139 835	3 040 950	59.2	2 504 847	1 451 773	58.0	2 634 988	1 589 177	60.3
1 VII 1998	ESDJ	5 153 498	3 089 077	59.9	2 512 587	1 476 277	58.8	2 640 911	1 612 800	61.1
1 VII 1999	ESDJ	5 165 474	3 112 147	60.2	2 519 551	1 488 063	59.1	2 645 923	1 624 084	61.4
31 XII 2000	CDJC	5 181 115	3 167 668	61.1	2 529 341	1 516 812	60.0	2 651 774	1 650 856	62.3
1 VII 2001*	ESDJ	5 188 008	3 179 283	61.3	2 533 469	1 523 008	60.1	2 654 539	1 656 275	62.4

6. Urban and total population by sex: 1992 - 2001
Population urbaine et population totale selon le sexe: 1992 - 2001
(continued — suite)

(See notes at end of table. — Voir notes à la fin du tableau.)

Continent, country or area and date / Continent, pays ou zone et date	Code[1]	Both sexes - Les deux sexes			Male - Masculin			Female - Féminin		
		Total	Urban - Urbaine		Total	Urban - Urbaine		Total	Urban - Urbaine	
			Number Nombre	Percent P.100		Number Nombre	Percent P.100		Number Nombre	Percent P.100

EUROPE

Hungary - Hongrie										
1 VII 1992	ESDF	10 323 708	6 831 138	66.2	4 951 970	3 123 691	63.1	5 371 738	3 454 117	64.3
1 VII 1993	ESDF	10 293 574	6 819 270	66.2	4 933 180	3 113 807	63.1	5 360 394	3 449 975	64.4
1 VII 1994	ESDF	10 261 322	6 749 527	65.8	4 913 327	3 085 533	62.8	5 347 996	3 435 370	64.2
1 VII 1995	ESDF	10 228 988	6 670 673	65.2	4 893 810	3 038 844	62.1	5 335 179	3 401 226	63.8
1 VII 1996	ESDF	10 193 371	6 636 078	65.1	4 873 597	3 037 842	62.3	5 319 774	3 405 105	64.0
1 VII 1997	ESDF	10 154 900	6 596 923	65.0	4 852 592	3 051 927	62.9	5 302 308	3 424 289	64.6
1 VII 1998	ESDF	10 113 574	6 553 654	64.8	4 829 734	3 028 148	62.7	5 283 840	3 403 554	64.4
1 VII 1999	ESDF	10 067 506	6 508 854	64.7	4 804 690	3 016 494	62.8	5 262 817	3 395 530	64.5
1 VII 2000	ESDF	10 024 222	6 461 456	64.5	4 781 701	3 038 795	63.6	5 242 522	3 422 662	65.3
1 II 2001	CDFC	10 198 315	6 572 880	64.5	4 850 650	3 091 857	63.7	5 347 665	3 481 023	65.1
1 VII 2001*	ESDF	10 187 576	6 644 628	65.2	4 843 996	3 121 972	64.5	5 343 580	3 522 656	65.9
Iceland - Islande										
1 VII 1992	ESDJ	261 103	237 984	91.1	130 945	...	...	130 158	...	...
1 VII 1993	ESDJ	263 783	240 824	91.3	132 308	120 006	90.7	131 475	120 818	91.9
1 VII 1994	ESDJ	265 851	243 085	91.4	133 332	121 133	90.9	132 519	121 952	92.0
1 VII 1995	ESDJ	267 380	245 027	91.6	134 038	122 044	91.1	133 342	122 983	92.2
1 VII 1996	ESDJ	268 927	246 983	91.8	134 779	123 025	91.3	134 148	123 958	92.4
1 VII 1997	ESDJ	271 095	249 293	92.0	135 779	124 196	91.5	135 136	125 097	92.6
1 VII 1998	ESDJ	273 794	252 356	92.2	137 092	125 634	91.6	136 702	126 722	92.7
1 VII 1999	ESDJ	277 184	255 910	92.3	138 783	...	...	138 401	...	...
1 VII 2000	ESDJ	281 154	259 661	92.4	140 718	129 258	91.9	140 436	130 403	92.9
1 VII 2001*	ESDJ	285 054	263 409	92.4	142 757	131 217	91.9	142 297	132 192	92.9
Ireland - Irlande										
28 IV 1996	CDFC	3 626 087	2 107 991	58.1	1 800 232	1 018 779	56.6	1 825 855	1 089 212	59.7
Italy - Italie										
1 VII 1997	ESDJ	57 522 971	17 459 276	30.4	...	...	...	...	...	...
1 VII 1998	ESDJ	57 587 985	17 419 059	30.2	27 959 131	...	...	29 628 854	...	...
1 VII 1999	ESDJ	57 646 255	17 348 485	30.1	27 985 491	...	...	29 660 764	...	...
1 VII 2000	ESDJ	57 761 956	17 329 002	30.0	...	...	...	...	...	...
Latvia - Lettonie										
1 VII 1992	ESDF	2 614 338	1 796 491	68.7	...	...	...	...	...	...
1 VII 1993	ESDF	2 563 290	1 760 812	68.7	...	...	...	...	...	...
1 VII 1994	ESDF	2 520 742	1 734 300	68.8	1 181 408	807 576	68.4	1 366 291	953 832	69.8
1 VII 1995	ESDF	2 485 056	1 705 665	68.6	1 165 252	794 513	68.2	1 350 350	941 802	69.7
1 VII 1996	ESDF	2 457 222	1 685 462	68.6	1 153 326	785 853	68.1	1 337 439	933 233	69.8
1 VII 1997	ESDF	2 432 851	1 668 743	68.6	1 121 142	757 156	67.5	1 311 709	911 587	69.5
1 VII 1998	ESDF	2 410 019	1 651 759	68.5	1 110 461	747 636	67.3	1 299 558	904 123	69.6
1 VII 1999	ESDF	2 390 482	1 632 603	68.3	1 101 163	736 958	66.9	1 289 319	895 645	69.5
31 III 2000	CDJC	2 377 383	1 618 144	68.1	1 094 964	729 745	66.6	1 282 419	888 399	69.3
1 VII 2000	ESDF	2 372 985	1 614 159	68.0	1 092 871	727 722	66.6	1 280 114	886 437	69.2
1 VII 2001*	ESDF	2 355 011	1 599 272	67.9	1 084 484	720 359	66.4	1 270 527	878 913	69.2
Lithuania - Lituanie										
1 VII 1992	ESDF	3 700 114	2 520 925	68.1	1 749 383	1 186 067	67.8	1 950 731	1 334 858	68.4
1 VII 1993	ESDF	3 682 613	2 498 415	67.8	1 739 689	1 174 005	67.5	1 942 924	1 324 410	68.2
1 VII 1994	ESDF	3 657 144	2 473 011	67.6	1 725 290	1 159 235	67.2	1 931 854	1 313 776	68.0
1 VII 1995	ESDF	3 629 102	2 446 057	67.4	1 709 387	1 143 067	66.9	1 919 715	1 302 990	67.9
1 VII 1996	ESDF	3 601 613	2 430 578	67.5	1 693 703	1 131 996	66.8	1 907 910	1 298 582	68.1
1 VII 1997	ESDF	3 575 138	2 414 008	67.5	1 678 748	1 120 554	66.7	1 896 390	1 293 454	68.2
1 VII 1998	ESDF	3 549 332	2 388 283	67.3	1 664 608	1 105 323	66.4	1 884 724	1 282 960	68.1
1 VII 1999	ESDF	3 524 238	2 367 146	67.2	1 650 931	1 092 628	66.2	1 873 307	1 274 518	68.0
1 VII 2000	ESDF	3 499 537	2 345 640	67.0	1 637 616	1 079 945	65.9	1 861 921	1 265 695	68.0
6 IV 2001	CDJC	3 483 972	2 332 098	66.9	1 629 148	1 071 986	65.8	1 854 824	1 260 112	67.9
1 VII 2001*	ESDF	3 481 292	2 330 213	66.9	1 627 704	1 070 916	65.8	1 853 588	1 259 297	67.9
Netherlands - Pays-Bas[2]										
1 VII 1992	ESDJ	15 184 138	7 729 963	50.9	7 507 827	3 784 604	50.4	7 676 311	3 945 359	51.4
1 VII 1993	ESDJ	15 290 348	9 257 818	60.5	...	...	...	...	...	...
1 VII 1994	ESDJ	15 382 830	9 316 457	60.6	7 606 682	4 563 873	60.0	7 776 149	4 752 580	61.1

6. Urban and total population by sex: 1992 - 2001
Population urbaine et population totale selon le sexe: 1992 - 2001
(continued — suite)

(See notes at end of table. — Voir notes à la fin du tableau.)

Continent, country or area and date / Continent, pays ou zone et date	Code[1]	Both sexes - Les deux sexes Total	Urban - Urbaine Number Nombre	Urban - Urbaine Percent P.100	Male - Masculin Total	Urban - Urbaine Number Nombre	Urban - Urbaine Percent P.100	Female - Féminin Total	Urban - Urbaine Number Nombre	Urban - Urbaine Percent P.100
EUROPE										
Netherlands - Pays-Bas[2]										
1 VII 1995	ESDJ	15 458 995	9 419 243	60.9	7 644 888	4 616 362	60.4	7 814 107	4 802 881	61.5
1 VII 1996	ESDJ	15 530 509	9 467 677	61.0	7 679 546	4 640 765	60.4	7 850 963	4 826 912	61.5
1 VII 1997	ESDJ	15 610 640	9 672 080	62.0	7 718 434	4 742 775	61.4	7 892 206	4 929 305	62.5
1 VII 1998	ESDJ	15 707 209	9 755 109	62.1	7 766 673	4 785 293	61.6	7 940 536	4 969 818	62.6
Poland - Pologne[44]										
1 VII 1992	ESDF	38 364 729	23 817 297	62.1	18 685 863	11 236 993	60.1	19 678 866	12 237 984	62.2
1 VII 1993	ESDF	38 459 031	23 747 649	61.7	18 726 070	11 293 109	60.3	19 732 961	12 299 224	62.3
1 VII 1994	ESDF	38 543 577	23 689 765	61.5	18 763 139	11 339 127	60.4	19 780 438	12 350 638	62.4
1 VII 1995	ESDF	38 587 596	23 873 641	61.9	18 779 284	11 423 370	60.8	19 808 312	12 450 271	62.9
1 VII 1996	ESDF	38 618 019	23 896 823	61.9	18 789 243	11 429 857	60.8	19 828 776	12 466 966	62.9
1 VII 1997	ESDF	38 649 914	23 927 869	61.9	18 800 457	11 439 693	60.8	19 849 457	12 488 176	62.9
1 VII 1998	ESDF	38 666 145	23 931 229	61.9	18 801 934	11 436 090	60.8	19 864 211	12 495 139	62.9
1 VII 1999	ESDF	38 653 625	23 908 265	61.9	18 788 696	11 417 385	60.8	19 864 929	12 490 880	62.9
1 VII 2000	ESDF	38 646 201	23 897 484	61.8	...	...	...	...	...	...
Republic of Moldova - République de Moldova[45]										
1 VII 1992	ESDJ	4 347 800	2 039 200	46.9	...	...	...	...	...	...
1 VII 1993	ESDJ	4 348 032	2 021 681	46.5	2 075 556	971 446	46.8	2 272 476	1 050 235	46.2
1 VII 1994	ESDJ	4 348 087	2 018 599	46.4	2 076 475	969 941	46.7	2 271 612	1 048 658	46.2
1 VII 1995	ESDJ	4 348 100	2 018 600	46.4	2 076 500	970 000	46.7	2 271 600	1 048 600	46.2
1 VII 1996	ESDJ	4 327 200	1 999 700	46.2	2 067 700	960 900	46.5	2 259 500	1 038 800	46.0
1 VII 1997	ESDJ	3 654 208	1 525 600	41.7	1 749 374	733 792	41.9	1 904 834	791 808	41.6
1 VII 1998	ESDJ	3 652 200	1 535 200	42.0	1 748 400	739 800	42.3	1 903 800	795 400	41.8
1 VII 1999	ESDJ	3 646 400	1 530 500	42.0	1 745 550	738 850	42.3	1 900 850	791 650	41.6
1 VII 2000	ESDJ	3 639 000	1 513 300	41.6	1 742 300	730 800	41.9	1 896 700	782 500	41.3
1 VII 2001*	ESDJ	3 631 462	1 485 810	40.9	1 739 081	717 661	41.3	1 892 381	768 149	40.6
Romania - Roumanie										
7 I 1992	CDFC	22 810 035	12 391 819	54.3	11 213 763	6 047 785	53.9	11 596 272	6 344 034	54.7
1 VII 1992	ESDJ	22 788 969	12 367 358	54.3	11 200 695	6 018 859	53.7	11 588 274	6 348 499	54.8
1 VII 1993	ESDJ	22 755 260	12 406 204	54.5	11 176 390	6 032 330	54.0	11 578 870	6 373 874	55.0
1 VII 1994	ESDJ	22 730 622	12 427 612	54.7	11 156 807	6 037 065	54.1	11 573 815	6 390 547	55.2
1 VII 1995	ESDJ	22 680 951	12 457 195	54.9	11 123 977	6 047 572	54.4	11 556 974	6 409 623	55.5
1 VII 1996	ESDJ	22 607 620	12 411 174	54.9	11 080 933	6 016 714	54.3	11 526 687	6 394 460	55.5
1 VII 1997	ESDJ	22 545 925	12 404 690	55.0	11 041 414	6 007 827	54.4	11 504 511	6 396 863	55.6
1 VII 1998	ESDJ	22 502 803	12 347 886	54.9	11 012 110	5 971 134	54.2	11 490 693	6 376 752	55.5
1 VII 1999	ESDJ	22 458 022	12 302 729	54.8	10 984 529	...	...	11 473 493	...	...
1 VII 2000*	ESDJ	22 435 205	12 244 598	54.6	10 968 854	5 907 848	53.9	11 466 351	6 336 750	55.3
1 VII 2001*	ESDJ	22 408 393	12 243 748	54.6	10 949 490	5 903 537	53.9	11 458 903	6 340 211	55.3
Russian Federation - Fédération de Russie										
1 VII 1992	ESDF	148 310 200	108 833 400	73.4	...	...	...	...	...	...
1 VII 1993	ESDF	148 145 900	108 234 100	73.1	...	...	...	...	...	...
1 VII 1994	ESDF	147 967 800	107 948 600	73.0	69 479 594	50 517 227	72.7	78 488 219	57 431 371	73.2
1 VII 1995	ESDF	147 773 657	107 779 133	72.9	69 387 481	50 405 185	72.6	78 386 176	57 373 948	73.2
1 VII 1999	ESDF	145 943 393	106 488 089	73.0	68 405 752	49 622 408	72.5	77 537 641	56 865 681	73.3
San Marino - Saint-Marin										
1 VII 1992	ESDF	23 837	21 558	90.4	11 876	10 726	90.3	11 961	10 832	90.6
1 VII 1993	ESDF	24 360	22 031	90.4	12 118	10 945	90.3	12 242	11 086	90.6
1 VII 1994	ESDF	24 889	22 505	90.4	12 382	11 194	90.4	12 507	11 311	90.4
1 VII 1995	ESDF	24 988	22 339	89.4	12 375	11 063	89.4	12 613	11 276	89.4
1 VII 1997	ESDF	25 823	23 085	89.4	12 757	11 404	89.4	13 066	11 681	89.4
1 VII 2000	ESDF	26 941	22 738	84.4	13 185	11 787	89.4	13 756	10 951	79.6

6. Urban and total population by sex: 1992 - 2001
Population urbaine et population totale selon le sexe: 1992 - 2001
(continued — suite)

(See notes at end of table. — Voir notes à la fin du tableau.)

Continent, country or area and date / Continent, pays ou zone et date	Code[1]	Both sexes - Les deux sexes			Male - Masculin			Female - Féminin		
		Total	Urban - Urbaine		Total	Urban - Urbaine		Total	Urban - Urbaine	
			Number Nombre	Percent P.100		Number Nombre	Percent P.100		Number Nombre	Percent P.100

EUROPE

Serbia and Montenegro - Serbie-et-Montene-gro[46]

1 VII 1992	ESDJ	10 448 118	5 356 280	51.3	5 181 931	2 614 582	50.5	5 266 087	2 741 698	52.1
1 VII 1993	ESDJ	10 481 954	5 378 336	51.3	5 197 455	2 625 096	50.5	5 284 499	2 753 240	52.1
1 VII 1994	ESDJ	10 515 582	5 400 221	51.4	5 214 043	2 635 731	50.6	5 301 539	2 764 490	52.1
1 VII 1995	ESDJ	10 546 983	5 420 604	51.4	5 229 817	2 646 039	50.6	5 317 166	2 774 565	52.2
1 VII 1996	ESDJ	10 577 208	5 440 835	51.4	5 245 109	2 656 349	50.6	5 332 099	2 784 486	52.2
1 VII 1997	ESDJ	10 600 067	5 456 379	51.5	5 256 354	2 664 248	50.7	5 343 713	2 792 131	52.3
1 VII 1998	ESDJ	10 616 886	5 468 037	51.5	5 264 001	2 669 658	50.7	5 352 885	2 798 379	52.3
1 VII 1999	ESDJ	10 629 358	5 477 426	51.5	5 269 974	2 674 193	50.7	5 359 384	2 803 233	52.3
1 VII 2000	ESDJ	10 634 620	5 480 138	51.5	5 272 097	2 675 270	50.7	5 362 523	2 804 868	52.3
1 VII 2001*	ESDJ	10 650 937	5 491 849	51.6	...	...	...	...	...	...

Slovakia - Slovaquie

1 VII 1992	ESDJ	5 306 539	3 036 860	57.2	2 587 606	1 471 055	56.9	2 718 933	1 565 805	57.6
1 VII 1993	ESDJ	5 324 632	3 038 834	57.1	2 594 672	1 471 403	56.7	2 729 960	1 567 431	57.4
1 VII 1994	ESDJ	5 347 413	3 045 894	57.0	2 604 937	1 472 177	56.5	2 742 476	1 573 717	57.4
1 VII 1995	ESDJ	5 363 638	3 057 117	57.0	2 612 212	1 476 546	56.5	2 751 426	1 580 571	57.4
1 VII 1996	ESDJ	5 373 810	3 072 014	57.2	2 616 356	...	...	2 757 454	...	...
1 VII 1997	ESDJ	5 383 214	3 068 195	57.0	2 620 329	...	...	2 762 904	...	...
1 VII 1998	ESDJ	5 390 657	3 066 324	56.9	2 622 990	1 479 217	56.4	2 767 667	1 587 107	57.3
1 VII 1999	ESDJ	5 395 324	3 063 235	56.8	2 624 080	...	...	2 771 244	...	...

Slovenia - Slovénie

1 VII 1992	ESDJ	1 995 832	1 011 151	50.7	968 257	...	...	1 027 575	...	...
1 VII 1993	ESDJ	1 990 623	1 002 422	50.4	965 175	478 022	49.5	1 025 448	524 400	51.1
1 VII 1994	ESDJ	1 988 850	997 916	50.2	964 113	475 551	49.3	1 024 737	522 365	51.0

Switzerland - Suisse

1 VII 1992	ESDJ	6 875 364	4 689 392	68.2	3 357 791	...	...	3 517 573	...	...
1 VII 1993	ESDJ	6 938 265	4 719 177	68.0	3 388 890	...	...	3 549 375	...	...
1 VII 1994	ESDJ	6 993 795	4 745 834	67.9	3 416 116	...	...	3 577 679	...	...
1 VII 1995	ESDJ	7 040 687	4 768 417	67.7	3 438 605	2 304 085	67.0	3 602 082	2 464 332	68.4
1 VII 1996	ESDJ	7 071 851	4 783 434	67.6	3 453 232	2 311 082	66.9	3 618 619	2 472 352	68.3
1 VII 1997	ESDJ	7 088 906	4 789 234	67.6	3 461 432	2 314 317	66.9	3 627 474	2 474 917	68.2
1 VII 1998	ESDJ	7 110 002	4 799 607	67.5	3 471 966	2 320 098	66.8	3 638 036	2 479 509	68.2
1 VII 1999	ESDJ	7 143 991	4 823 202	67.5	3 489 699	2 333 007	66.9	3 654 292	2 490 195	68.1
1 VII 2000	ESDJ	7 184 250	4 854 390	67.6	3 510 203	2 349 347	66.9	3 674 047	2 505 043	68.2
5 XII 2000	CDJC	7 204 055	4 871 989	67.6	3 519 698	2 357 890	67.0	3 684 357	2 514 099	68.2
1 VII 2001*	ESDJ	7 232 634	4 894 456	67.7	3 534 394	...	...	3 698 239	...	...

The Former Yugoslav Rep. of Macedonia - L'ex-République yougoslave de Macédoine

20 VI 1994	CDJC	1 945 932	1 163 598	59.8	974 255	...	...	971 677	...	...
1 VII 1997	ESDF	1 996 869	1 189 442	59.6	999 595	590 300	59.1	997 274	599 142	60.1

Ukraine

1 VII 1992	ESDF	52 056 600	35 296 900	67.8	...	...	...	...	...	...
1 VII 1993	ESDF	52 244 100	35 471 000	67.9	...	...	...	...	...	...
1 VII 1994	ESDF	52 114 400	35 400 700	67.9	...	...	...	...	...	...
1 VII 1995	ESDF	51 728 400	35 118 800	67.9	...	...	...	...	...	...
1 VII 1996	ESDF	51 334 100	34 832 500	67.9	...	...	...	...	...	...
1 VII 1997	ESDF	50 893 500	34 521 800	67.8	...	...	...	...	...	...
1 VII 1998	ESDF	50 499 900	34 271 600	67.9	...	...	...	...	...	...
1 VII 1999	ESDF	50 105 600	34 017 400	67.9	...	...	...	...	...	...
1 VII 2000	ESDF	49 710 800	33 796 500	68.0	...	...	...	...	...	...

6. Urban and total population by sex: 1992 - 2001
Population urbaine et population totale selon le sexe: 1992 - 2001
(continued — suite)

(See notes at end of table. — Voir notes à la fin du tableau.)

Continent, country or area and date / Continent, pays ou zone et date	Code[1]	Both sexes - Les deux sexes			Male - Masculin			Female - Féminin		
		Total	Urban - Urbaine		Total	Urban - Urbaine		Total	Urban - Urbaine	
			Number Nombre	Percent P.100		Number Nombre	Percent P.100		Number Nombre	Percent P.100
EUROPE										
Ukraine										
5 XII 2001	CDJC	48 457 102	32 574 371	67.2	22 441 344	15 056 675	67.1	26 015 758	17 517 696	67.3
OCEANIA — OCEANIE										
Cook Islands - Îles Cook[47]										
1 XII 1996	CDFC	19 103	11 225	58.8	9 842	5 730	58.2	9 261	5 495	59.3
Fiji - Fidji										
25 VIII 1996	CDFC	775 077	359 495	46.4	393 931	180 119	45.7	381 146	179 376	47.1
Guam[9]										
1 VII 1992	ESDJ	139 371	53 174	38.2	74 258	29 033	39.1	65 113	24 141	37.1
1 VII 1993	ESDJ	142 589	54 402	38.2	...	...	...	...	...	...
1 VII 1994	ESDJ	145 881	55 658	38.2	...	...	...	...	...	...
1 VII 1995	ESDJ	149 249	56 943	38.2	...	...	...	...	...	...
1 VII 1996	ESDJ	152 694	58 257	38.2	...	...	...	...	...	...
1 VII 1997	ESDJ	156 200	59 603	38.2	...	...	...	...	...	...
New Caledonia - Nouvelle-Calédonie										
1 VII 1996	ESDF	*197 389*	*118 823*	*60.2*	*101 030*	...	...	*96 394*		
New Zealand - Nouvelle-Zélande										
5 III 1996	CDJC	3 618 303	3 091 740	85.4	1 777 464	1 503 444	84.6	1 840 839	1 588 296	86.3
Palau - Palaos										
9 IX 1995	CDFC	17 225	12 299	71.4	9 213	...	...	8 012	...	...
15 IV 2000	CDFC	19 129	13 303	69.5	...	...	...	...	...	...
Tonga										
30 XI 1996	CDFC	97 784	22 400	22.9	49 615	...	...	48 169	...	...
Vanuatu										
16 XI 1999	CDJC	186 678	40 094	21.5	95 682	...	...	90 996	...	...

GENERAL NOTES - NOTES GENERALES

Percentages urban are the number of persons resident in areas defined as 'urban' per 100 Total Population. For definition of 'urban', see end of Technical Notes for this table. For method of evaluation and limitations of data, see Technical Notes for this table. — Les pourcentages urbains réprésentent le nombre de personnes définies comme vivant dans des 'régions urbaines'. Pour la définitions des 'régions urbaines', se reporter à la fin des Notes Techniques pour ce tableau. Pour la méthode d'evaluation et les insuffisances des données, voir Notes techniques pour ce tableau.

Italics: estimates which are less reliable. — *Italiques:* estimations moins sûres.

FOOTNOTES - NOTES

* Provisional. — Données provisoires.

[1] 'Code' indicates the source of data, as follows:
CDFC - Census, de facto, complete tabulation
CDFS - Census, de facto, sample tabulation
CDJC - Census, de jure, complete tabulation
CDJS - Census, de jure, sample tabulation
SSDF - Sample survey, de facto
SSDJ - Sample survey, de jure
ESDF - Estimates, de facto
ESDJ - Estimates, de jure
Le 'Code' indique la source des données, comme suit:
CDFC - Recensement, population de fait, tabulation complète

CDFS - Recensement, population de fait, tabulation par sondage
CDJC - Recensement, population de droit, tabulation complète
CDJS - Recensement, population de droit, tabulation par sondage
SSDF - Enquête par sondage, population de fait
SSDJ - Enquête par sondage, population de droit
ESDF - Données estimatées, population de fait
ESDJ - Données estimatées, population de droit

[2] Series not strictly comparable due to differences of definitions of "urban". - - Les séries ne sont pas strictement comparables en raison de différences existant dans la définition des "regions urbaines".

[3] Data for urban and rural areas are not adjusted for under-enumeration, estimated around 5% for the total country. - Les donneés pour les zones urbaines et rurales n'ont pas été adjustées pour tenir en compte de la sous-estimation de 5% approximativement.

[4] Census results have been adjusted for underenumeration, estimated at 5.1 per cent. - Les résultat du recensement ont été ajustées pour compenser les lacunes du dénombrement, estimées à 5,1 p. 100.

[5] Mid-year estimates have been adjusted for underenumeration, at latest census. - Les estimations au millieu de l'année tiennent compte d'une ajustement destiné à compenser les lacunes du dénombrement lors du dernier recensement.

[6] Census results have been adjusted for underenumeration, estimated at 6.8 per cent. - Les résultat du recensement ont été ajustées pour compenser les lacunes du dénombrement, estimées à 6,8 p. 100.

[7] Because of rounding, totals are not in all cases the sum of the parts. - Les chiffres étant arrondis, les totaux ne correspondent pas toujours rigoureusement à la somme des chiffres partiels.

[8] Census data have not been adjusted for underenumeration. - Les données de recensement ne tiennent pas compte de d'une ajustement destiné à compenser les lacunes du dénombrement.

[9] Including armed forces stationed in the area. - Y compris les militaires en

garnison sur le territoire.

[10] Excluding armed forces overseas and civilian citizens absent from country for an extended period of time. - Non compris les militaires à l'étranger, et les civils hors du pays pendant une période prolongée.

[11] Data include persons in remote areas, military personel outside the country, merchant seamen at sea, civilian seasonal workers outside the country, and other civilians outside the country, and exclude nomads, foreign military, civilian aliens temporarily in the country, transients on ships and Indian jungle population. - Y compris les personnes dans des régions éloignées, le personel militaire en dehors du pays, les marins marchands, les ouvriers saisonniers civils de couture en dehors du pays, et autres civils en dehors du pays, et non compris les nomades, les militaires étrangers, les étrangers civils temporairement dans le pays, les transiteurs sur des bateaux et les Indiens de la jungle.

[12] Excluding nomadic Indian tribes. - Non compris les tribus d'Indiens nomades.

[13] Census data exclude adjustment for underenumeration. - Les données de recensement n'ont pas été ajustées pour compenser les lacunes du dénombrement.

[14] Excluding Indian jungle population. - Non compris les Indiens de la jungle.

[15] Excluding foreign diplomatic personnel and their dependants. - Non compris le personnel diplomatique étranger et les membres de leur famille les accompagnant.

[16] For 1996, based on results of a sample survey. - Pour 1996, d'après les résultats d'une enquête par sondage.

[17] Unrevised data. - Les données n'ont pas été révisées.

[18] For statistical purposes, the data for China do not include those for the Hong Kong Special Administrative Region (Hong Kong SAR), Macao special Administrative Region (Macao SAR) and Taiwan province of China. - Pour la présentation des statistiques, les données pour Chine ne comprend pas les Région Administrative Spéciale de Hong Kong (Hong Kong RAS), le Région Administrative Spéciale de Macao (Macao RAS) et Taïwan province de Chine.

[19] For the civilian population of 31 provinces, municipalities and autonomous regions. - Pour la population civile seulement de 31 provinces, municipalités et régions autonomes.

[20] Estimated data on the basis of the annual National Sample Survey on Population Changes. - Les données ont été estimées sur la base de l'enquête annuelle National Sample Survey on Population changes.

[21] Data refer to government controlled areas. - Les données se raportent aux zones contrôlées par le Gouvernement.

[22] Estimates of the number of Turkish Cypriots from 1974 onwards are the result of population projections based on the age and sex structure of the Turkish Cypriot community as at Census 1960 and with assumptions of fertility and mortality similar to the rest of the Cyprus Population. With regard to the migration of Turkish Cypriots after 1974, migration assumptions are based on figures obtained from Turkish Cypriot sources. Settlers from Turkey are not included. - - Les estimations du nombre de Chypriotes turcs depuis 1974 résultent des projections de population préparées sur la base de la structure par sexe et age de la communauté chypriote turque au recensement de 1960, et avec des hypothèses de fécondité et de mortalité similaires à celles du reste de la population de Chypre. En ce qui concerne la migration des Chypriotes turcs après 1974, les hypothèses sont basées sur les données obtenues de sources chypriotes turques. Les occupants venus de Turquie ne sont pas inclus.

[23] Data for the period 1993-2000 have been revised on the basis of the Population Census of 2001. - Des données pour 1993 à 2000 ont été calculées sur la base du recensement de population de 2001.

[24] Data include all population irrespective of citizenship, who at the time of the census have resided in the country or intended to reside for a period of at least one year. It does not distinguish between those present or absent at the time of census. - Les chiffres comprennent toute la population, quelle que soit la nationalité, qui à l'époque de recensement avait résidé dans le pays, ou avait l'intention de résider, pendant une période de au moins un an. Il n'y a pas de distinction entre les personnes présentes ou absentes au moment du recensement.

[25] Including data for the Indian-held part of Jammu and Kashmir, the final status of which has not yet been determined. - Y compris les données pour la partie du Jammu et du Cachemire occupée par l'Inde dont le statut définitif n'a pas encore été déterminé.

[26] The figure includes an estimated population of 459,557 persons in urban and 1, 857,659 persons in rural areas that were not directly enumerated, and a population of 566,403 persons in urban and 1,717,578 persons in rural areas that declined the participation. Also included are 421,399 non permanent residents (the homeless, the crew of ships carrying national flag, boat/floating house people, remote located tribesmen and refugees.) - Y compris la population estimée a 459,557 personnes dans les zones urbaines et de 1,857,659 personnes dans les zones rurales qui n'ont pas été énumérées directement, aussi que 566,403 personnes qui non pas répondu dans les zones urbaines et de 1,717,578 personnes dans les zones rurales. Y compris 421,399 résidants non permanents (les sans abri, l'équipage des bateaux portant le drapeau national, les habitants des embarcations ou des maisons flottantes, les habitants des tribus isolées et les réfugies.)

[27] For the 1997 Population Census, data exclude population in three autonomous provinces in the north of the country. - Pour le recensement de 1997, la population des trois provinces autonomes dans le nord du pays est exclue.

[28] Including data for East Jerusalem and Israeli residents in certain other territories under occupation by Israeli military forces since June 1967. - Y compris les données pour Jérusalem-Est et les résidents israéliens dans certains autres territoires occupés depuis 1967 par les forces armées israéliennes.

[29] Excluding diplomatic personnel outside country and foreign military and civilian personnel and their dependants stationed in the area. - Non compris le personnel diplomatique hors du pays ni les militaires et agents civils étrangers en poste sur le territoire et les membres de leur famille les accompagnant.

[30] Excluding data for Jordanian territory under occupation since June 1967 by Israeli military forces. Excluding foreigners, including registered Palestinian refugees. - Non compris les données pour le territoire jordanien occupé depuis juin 1967 par les forces armées israéliennes. Non compris les étrangers, mais y compris les réfugiés de Palestine immatriculés.

[31] Excluding alien armed forces, civilian aliens employed by armed forces, foreign diplomatic personnel and their dependants and Korean diplomatic personnel and their dependants outside the country. - Non compris les militaires étrangers, les civils étrangers employés par les forces armées, le personnel diplomatique étranger et les membres de leur famille les accompagnant et le personnel diplomatique coréen hors du pays et les membres de leurs familles les accompagnant.

[32] Urban/Rural: Places with 50,000 or more inhabitants are usually considered urban in Korea. However, the census data are composed in the basis of the minor administrative divisions such as Dongs (mostly urban areas) and Eups or Myeons (rural areas) rather than urban or rural residences. In this report, urban refers to Dongs and rural refers ro Eups and Myeons. - Urbaine/rurale: les lieux avec 50,000 habitants ou plus sont habituellement considérés urbains en Corée. Cependant, les résultats du recensement ont été préparés sur la base des divisions administratives mineures comme les Dongs (principalement des zones urbaines), et les Eups ou Myeons (des zones rurales) plutôt que sur les résidences urbaines ou rurales. Dans ce rapport urbaine se rapporte aux Dongs et rural aux Eups et aux Myeons.

[33] Including diplomats and their families abroad, but excluding foreign diplomats, foreign military personal, and their families in the country. - Y compris le personnel diplomatique et les membres de leurs familles à l'étranger, mais sans tenir compte du personnel diplomatique et militaire étranger et des membres de leurs familles.

[34] Excluding Malaysian citizens and permanent residents who were away or intended to be away from the country for more than six months. Excluding Malaysian military, naval and diplomatic personnel and their families outside the country, and tourists, businessmen who intended to be in Malaysia for less than six months. - Non compris les citoyens malaisiens et les résidents permanents qui étaient ou qui ont prévu d'être hors du pays pour six mois ou plus. Non compris le personnel militaire Malaisien, le personnel naval ou diplomatique et leurs familles hors du pays, et les touristes et les hommes d'affaires qui avaient l'intention de rester en Malaisie moins de six mois.

[35] Data have been adjusted for underenumeration, at 2000 census. - Les données ont été ajustées pour compenser les lacunes du dénombrement recensement de 2000.

[36] Data for urban refer to 170 towns out of 254 towns. - Les données urbaines se rapportent à 170 des 254 villes.

[37] Data including estimated population from household listing from Village Development Committees and Wards which could not be enumerated at the time of census. - Les données incluent la population estimée par les listes des ménages des comités de développement des villages et des circonscriptions qui n'ont pas pu être énumérée au moment du recensement.

[38] Data for urban including population in refugee camps. - Les données pour la population urbaine comprennent la population dans les camps réfugiés.

[39] Total population does not include Palestinian population living in those parts of Jerusalem governorate which were annexed by Israel in 1967, amounting to 210,209 persons. Likewise, the results does not include the estimates of not enumerated population based on the findings of the post enumeration study, i.e 83,805 persons. - Les données relatives à la population totale ne comprennent pas la population palestinienne équivalent à 210 209 personnes habitant dans les territoires du gouvernorat de Jérusalem qui ont été annexés par Israël en 1967. Egalement, les données ne tiennent pas compte des estimations de la population calculée sur la base des résultats de l'enquête postcensitaire, équivalent à 83 805 personnes.

[40] Excluding data for the Pakistan-held part of Jammu and Kashmir, the final status of which has not yet been determined. - Non compris les données concernant la partie du Jammu et Cachemire occupée par le Pakistan dont le statut définitif n'a pas été déterminé.

[41] The Population and Housing Census 2001 did not cover the whole area of the country due to the security problems; the Census was completed in 18 districts only; in three districts it was not possible to conduct it; and in four districts it was partially conducted. - Le recensement de la population et de l'habitat en 2001 n'a pas couvert la totalité du pays pour des problèmes de sécurité; le recensement a été complété seulement en 18 districts; dans 3 districts ça n'a pas été possible de conduire le recensement et dans 4 districts il a été partiellement conduit.

[42] Including Palestinian refugees. - Y compris les réfugiés de Palestine.

[43] Data for urban refer to population in municipalities, numbering 1,131 at the time of the census; data for rural refer to the population in non-municipal areas. - - Les données pour la zone urbaine se rapportent a la population des municipalités, comptant 1,131 au moment du recensement; les données pour la zone rurale se rapportent a la population au dehors des municipalités.

[44] Excluding civilian aliens within country, but including civilian nationals temporarily outside country. - Non compris les civils étrangers dans le pays, mais y compris les civils nationaux temporairement hors du pays.

[45] Data do not include information for Transnistria and the municipality of Bender. - Les données ne tiennent pas compte de l'information sur la Transnistria et la municipalité de Bender.

[46] Beginning with 1998, estimates of Kosovo and Metohia computed on the basis of natural increases from year 1997. - A partir du 1998, les estimations pour le Kosovo et la Metohia ont été calculées sur la base des incréments naturelles depuis 1997.

[47] The resident population consisted of 14,990 (7,738 males and 7,252 females). - Population résidente de 14 990 (7 738 hommes et 7 252 femmes).

Table 7

Table 7 presents population by age, sex and urban/rural residence for the latest available year between 1992 and 2001.

Description of variables: Data in this table are either population censuses figures or estimates, some of which are based on sample surveys. Data refer to the de facto population unless otherwise noted.

The reference date of the census or estimate appears in the stub of the table. In general, the estimates refer to mid-year (1 July).

Age is defined as age at last birthday, that is, the difference between the date of birth and the reference date of the age distribution expressed in completed solar years. The age classification used in this table is the following: under 1 year, 1-4 years, 5-year groups through 95-99 years, and 100 years and over.

The urban/rural classification of population by age and sex is that provided by each country or area; it is presumed to be based on the national census definitions of urban population that have been set forth at the end of the technical notes to table 6.

Estimates of population by age and sex presented in this table have been limited to countries or areas for which estimates have been based on the results of a sample survey or have been constructed by the component method from the results of a population census or sample survey. Estimations derived from distributing estimated total population according to percentages in each age-sex group at the time of a census or sample survey, are not acceptable, and they have not been included in this table.

Reliability of data: Estimates which are believed to be less reliable are set in *italics* rather than in roman type. No attempt has been made to take account of age-reporting accuracy, the evaluation of which has been described in section 3.1.3 of the Technical Notes.

Limitations: Statistics on population by age and sex are subject to the same qualifications as have been set forth for population statistics in general and age distributions in particular, as discussed in sections 3 and 3.1.3, respectively, of the Technical Notes.

Comparability of population data classified by age and sex is limited by variations in the definition of total population, discussed in detail in section 3 of the Technical Notes, and by the accuracy of the original enumeration. Both of these factors are more important in relation to certain age groups than to others. For example, under-enumeration is known to be more prevalent among infants and young children than among older persons. Similarly, the exclusion from the total population of certain groups that tend to be of selected ages (such as the armed forces) can markedly affect the age structure and its comparability with that for other countries or areas. Consideration should be given to the implications of these basic limitations in using the data.

In addition to these general qualifications are the special problems of comparability that arise in relation to age statistics in particular. Age distributions of population are known to suffer from certain deficiencies that have their origin in irregularities in age reporting. Although some of the irregularities tend to be obscured or eliminated when data are tabulated in five-year age groups rather than by single years, precision still continues to be affected, though the degree of distortion is not always readily seen.

Another factor limiting comparability is the age classification employed by the various countries or areas. Age may be based on the year of birth rather than the age at last birthday, in other words, calculated using the day, month and year of birth. Distributions based only on the year of birth are footnoted when known.

The absence of frequencies in the unknown age group does not necessarily indicate completely accurate reporting and tabulation of the age item. The unknowns may have been eliminated by assigning ages to them before tabulation, or by proportionately distributing the unknown category across the age groups after tabulation.

As noted in connection with table 5, intercensal estimates of total population are usually revised to accord with the results of a census of population if inexplicable discontinuities appear to exist. Postcensal age-sex distributions, however, are less likely to be revised in this way.   When it is known that a total population estimate for a given year has been revised and the corresponding age distribution has not been, the age distribution is shown as provisional. Distributions of this type should be used with caution when studying trends over a period of years, though their utility for studying age structure for the specified year is probably unimpaired.

The comparability of data by urban/rural residence is affected by the national definitions of urban and rural used in tabulating these data. When known, the definitions of urban used in national population censuses are presented at the end of the technical notes for table 6. As discussed in detail in the technical notes for table 6, these definitions vary considerably from one country or area to another.

Coverage: Population by age and sex is shown for 174 countries or areas.

Data are presented by urban/rural residence for 79 countries or areas.

Earlier data: Population by age, sex and urban/rural residence has been shown in previous issues of the *Demographic Yearbook*. For more information on specific topics, and years for which data are reported, readers should consult the Index.

Tableau 7

Le tableau 7 présente des données sur la population selon l'âge, le sexe et la résidence (urbaine/rurale) pour la dernière année disponible entre 1992 et 2001.

Description des variables : Les données de ce tableau sont tirées de recensements de la population, ou bien sont des estimations fondées, dans certains cas, sur des enquêtes par sondage. Sauf indication contraire, elles se rapportent à la population de fait.

La date de référence du recensement ou de l'estimation figure dans la colonne de gauche du tableau. En général, les estimations se rapportent au milieu de l'année (1er juillet).

L'âge désigne l'âge au dernier anniversaire, c'est-à-dire, la différence entre la date de naissance et la date de référence de la répartition par âge exprimée en années solaires révolues. La classification par âge utilisée dans ce tableau est la suivante : moins d'un an, 1 à 4 ans, groupes quinquennaux jusqu'à 95 - 99 ans et 100 ans et plus.

La classification par zones urbaines et rurales de la population selon l'âge et le sexe est celle qui est fournie par chaque pays ou zone; cette classification est présumée fonder sur les définitions utilisées dans les recensements nationaux de la population urbaine, qui sont reproduites à la fin du des notes techniques du tableau 6.

Les estimations de la population selon l'âge et le sexe qui figurent dans ce tableau ne concernent que les pays ou zones pour lesquels les estimations se fondent sur les résultats d'une enquête par sondage ou ont été établies par la méthode des composantes à partir des résultats d'un recensement de la population ou d'une enquête par sondage. Les répartitions par âge et par sexe obtenues en appliquant à l'estimation de la population totale les pourcentages enregistrés pour les divers groupes d'âge pour chaque sexe lors d'un recensement ou d'une enquête par sondage ne sont pas acceptables et n'ont pas été reproduites dans ce tableau.

Fiabilité des données : Les estimations considérées comme moins sûres sont indiquées en italique plutôt qu'en caractères romains. On n'a pas tenu compte des inexactitudes dans les déclarations d'âge, dont la méthode d'évaluation est exposée à la section 3.1.3 des Notes techniques.

Insuffisance des données : Les statistiques de la population selon l'âge et le sexe appellent les mêmes réserves que celles qui ont été respectivement formulées aux sections 3 et 3.1.3 des Notes techniques à l'égard des statistiques de la population en général et des répartitions par âge en particulier.

La comparabilité des statistiques de la population selon l'âge et le sexe est limitée par le manque d'uniformité dans la définition de la population totale (voir explications à la section 3 des Notes techniques) et par les lacunes des dénombrements. L'influence de ces deux facteurs varie selon les groupes d'âge. Ainsi, le dénombrement des enfants de moins d'un an et des jeunes enfants comporte souvent plus de lacunes que celui des personnes plus âgées. De même, l'exclusion du chiffre de la population totale de certains groupes de personnes appartenant souvent à des groupes d'âge déterminés, par exemple les militaires, peut influer sensiblement sur la structure par âge et sur la comparabilité des données avec celles d'autres pays ou zones. Il conviendra de tenir compte de ces facteurs fondamentaux lorsqu'on utilisera les données du tableau.

Outre ces difficultés d'ordre général, la comparabilité pose des problèmes particuliers lorsqu'il s'agit des données par âge. On sait que les répartitions de la population selon l'âge présentent certaines imperfections dues à l'inexactitude des déclarations d'âge. Certaines de ces anomalies ont tendance à s'estomper ou à disparaître lorsqu'on classe les données par groupes d'âge quinquennaux et non par années d'âge, mais une certaine imprécision demeure, même s'il n'est pas toujours facile de voir à quel point il y a distorsion.

Le degré de comparabilité dépend également de la classification par âge employée dans les divers pays ou zones. L'âge retenu peut être défini par date exacte (jour, mois et année) de naissance ou par celle du dernier anniversaire. Lorsqu'elles étaient connues, les répartitions établies seulement d'après l'année de la naissance ont été signalées en note à la fin du tableau.

Si aucun nombre ne figure dans la colonne réservée aux âges inconnus, cela ne signifie pas nécessairement que les déclarations d'âge et l'exploitation des données par âge aient été tout à fait exactes. C'est souvent une indication que l'on a attribué un âge aux personnes d'âge inconnu avant la mise en tableau ou que celles-ci ont été réparties proportionnellement entre les différents groupes après cette opération.

Comme on l'a indiqué à propos du tableau 5, les estimations intercensitaires de la population totale sont d'ordinaire rectifiées d'après les résultats des recensements de population si l'on constate des discontinuités inexplicables. Les données postcensitaires concernant la répartition de la population par âge et par sexe ont toutefois moins de chance d'être rectifiées de cette manière. Lorsqu'on savait qu'une estimation de la population totale pour une année donnée avait été rectifiée mais non la répartition par âge correspondante, cette dernière a été indiquée comme ayant un caractère provisoire. Les répartitions de ce type doivent être utilisées avec prudence lorsqu'on étudie les tendances sur un certain nombre d'années, quoique leur utilité pour l'étude de la structure par âge de la population pour l'année visée reste probablement entière.

La comparabilité des données selon la résidence (urbaine/rurale) peut être limitée par les définitions nationales des termes "urbain" et 'rural' utilisées pour la mise en tableaux de ces données. Les définitions du terme "urbain" utilisées pour les recensements nationaux de population ont été présentées à la fin des notes techniques du tableau 6 lorsqu'elles étaient connues. Comme on l'a précisé en détail dans les notes techniques relatives au tableau 6, ces définitions varient très sensiblement d'un pays ou d'une zone à l'autre.

Portée : Des statistiques de la population selon l'âge et le sexe sont présentées pour 174 pays ou zones.

La répartition selon la résidence (urbaine/rurale) et indiquée pour 79 pays ou zones.

Données publiées antérieurement : Des statistiques de la population selon l'âge, le sexe et la résidence (urbaine/rurale) ont été présentées dans des éditions antérieures de l'Annuaire démographique. Pour plus de précisions concernant les années et les sujets spécifiques pour lesquelles des données ont été publiées, se reporter à l'Index.

7. Population by age, sex and urban/rural residence: latest available year, 1992 - 2001
Population selon l'âge, le sexe et la résidence, urbaine/rurale: dernière année disponible, 1992 - 2001

(See notes at end of table. — Voir notes à la fin du tableau.)

Continent, country or area, date and age (in years) / Continent, pays ou zone, date et âge (en années)	Code[1]	Total			Urban - Urbaine			Rural - Rurale		
		Both sexes Les deux sexes	Male Masculin	Female Féminin	Both sexes Les deux sexes	Male Masculin	Female Féminin	Both sexes Les deux sexes	Male Masculin	Female Féminin
AFRICA — AFRIQUE										
Algeria - Algérie										
25 VI 1998										
Total	CDJC	29 100 867	14 698 589	14 402 278	...	...	...	...	...	...
0 - 4	CDJC	3 179 775	1 627 670	1 552 105	...	...	...	...	...	...
5 - 9	CDJC	3 574 197	1 820 858	1 753 339	...	...	...	...	...	...
10 - 14	CDJC	3 768 685	1 918 833	1 849 852	...	...	...	...	...	...
15 - 19	CDJC	3 499 291	1 782 614	1 716 677	...	...	...	...	...	...
20 - 24	CDJC	2 914 836	1 472 255	1 442 581	...	...	...	...	...	...
25 - 29	CDJC	2 502 614	1 259 989	1 242 625	...	...	...	...	...	...
30 - 34	CDJC	2 100 793	1 056 110	1 044 683	...	...	...	...	...	...
35 - 39	CDJC	1 667 371	841 768	825 603	...	...	...	...	...	...
40 - 44	CDJC	1 378 269	691 275	686 994	...	...	...	...	...	...
45 - 49	CDJC	1 108 870	565 289	543 581	...	...	...	...	...	...
50 - 54	CDJC	762 659	371 843	390 816	...	...	...	...	...	...
55 - 59	CDJC	698 499	345 318	353 181	...	...	...	...	...	...
60 - 64	CDJC	622 159	301 247	320 912	...	...	...	...	...	...
65 - 69	CDJC	510 617	252 003	258 614	...	...	...	...	...	...
70 - 74	CDJC	332 161	163 292	168 869	...	...	...	...	...	...
75 - 79	CDJC	217 975	107 732	110 243	...	...	...	...	...	...
80+	CDJC	237 820	111 711	126 109	...	...	...	...	...	...
Unk. - Inc.	CDJC	24 276	8 782	15 494	...	...	...	...	...	...
Benin - Bénin										
1 VII 2000										
Total	ESDF	6 169 084	3 013 705	3 155 379	2 492 967	1 220 905	1 272 062	3 676 117	1 792 800	1 883 317
0 - 4	ESDF	1 079 554	546 027	533 527	391 001	198 018	192 983	688 553	348 009	340 544
5 - 9	ESDF	897 767	449 283	448 484	328 285	162 197	166 088	569 482	287 086	282 396
10 - 14	ESDF	921 385	468 494	452 891	376 846	183 278	193 568	544 539	285 216	259 323
15 - 19	ESDF	757 852	395 867	361 985	329 941	172 182	157 759	427 911	223 685	204 226
20 - 24	ESDF	467 089	244 385	222 704	216 960	116 395	100 565	250 129	127 990	122 139
25 - 29	ESDF	387 118	179 632	207 486	171 245	82 819	88 426	215 873	96 813	119 060
30 - 34	ESDF	358 469	149 219	209 250	158 087	70 831	87 256	200 382	78 388	121 994
35 - 39	ESDF	325 169	137 686	187 483	139 841	62 837	77 004	185 328	74 849	110 479
40 - 44	ESDF	250 196	111 603	138 593	105 048	48 266	56 782	145 148	63 337	81 811
45 - 49	ESDF	200 864	90 725	110 139	81 818	37 658	44 160	119 046	53 067	65 979
50 - 54	ESDF	142 649	65 883	76 766	56 162	26 190	29 972	86 487	39 693	46 794
55 - 59	ESDF	111 888	51 260	60 628	44 354	20 390	23 964	67 534	30 870	36 664
60 - 64	ESDF	80 852	36 939	43 913	29 782	13 309	16 473	51 070	23 630	27 440
65 - 69	ESDF	58 328	26 402	31 926	21 850	9 392	12 458	36 478	17 010	19 468
70 - 74	ESDF	53 485	23 293	30 192	18 055	7 097	10 958	35 430	16 196	19 234
75 - 79	ESDF	29 333	13 747	15 586	9 931	4 171	5 760	19 402	9 576	9 826
80+	ESDF	47 086	23 260	23 826	13 761	5 875	7 886	33 325	17 385	15 940
1 VII 2001										
Total	ESDF	6 416 692	3 136 516	3 280 176	...	...	...	...	...	...
0 - 4	ESDF	1 114 233	563 594	550 639	...	...	...	...	...	...
5 - 9	ESDF	951 330	478 101	473 229	...	...	...	...	...	...
10 - 14	ESDF	881 265	444 239	437 026	...	...	...	...	...	...
15 - 19	ESDF	843 647	436 260	407 387	...	...	...	...	...	...
20 - 24	ESDF	510 694	270 545	240 149	...	...	...	...	...	...
25 - 29	ESDF	402 937	193 993	208 944	...	...	...	...	...	...
30 - 34	ESDF	354 910	149 768	205 142	...	...	...	...	...	...
35 - 39	ESDF	341 616	142 268	199 348	...	...	...	...	...	...
40 - 44	ESDF	260 713	115 027	145 686	...	...	...	...	...	...
45 - 49	ESDF	213 734	95 557	118 177	...	...	...	...	...	...
50 - 54	ESDF	153 520	70 293	83 227	...	...	...	...	...	...
55 - 59	ESDF	113 215	51 839	61 376	...	...	...	...	...	...
60 - 64	ESDF	91 038	41 028	50 010	...	...	...	...	...	...
65 - 69	ESDF	52 485	24 029	28 456	...	...	...	...	...	...
70 - 74	ESDF	57 896	24 995	32 901	...	...	...	...	...	...
75 - 79	ESDF	26 853	12 181	14 672	...	...	...	...	...	...

7. Population by age, sex and urban/rural residence: latest available year, 1992 - 2001
Population selon l'âge, le sexe et la résidence, urbaine/rurale: dernière année disponible, 1992 - 2001
(continued — suite)

(See notes at end of table. — Voir notes à la fin du tableau.)

Continent, country or area, date and age (in years) / Continent, pays ou zone, date et âge (en années)	Code[1]	Total			Urban - Urbaine			Rural - Rurale		
		Both sexes Les deux sexes	Male Masculin	Female Féminin	Both sexes Les deux sexes	Male Masculin	Female Féminin	Both sexes Les deux sexes	Male Masculin	Female Féminin
AFRICA — AFRIQUE										
Benin - Bénin										
1 VII 2001										
80+	ESDF	46 606	22 799	23 807	...	...	...	...	...	...
Botswana										
1 VII 2000										
Total	ESDF	1 653 061	799 735	853 326	...	...	...	...	...	...
0 - 1	ESDF	52 176	26 246	25 930	...	...	...	...	...	...
1 - 4	ESDF	187 593	94 292	93 301	...	...	...	...	...	...
5 - 9	ESDF	209 344	104 990	104 354	...	...	...	...	...	...
10 - 14	ESDF	189 965	94 642	95 323	...	...	...	...	...	...
15 - 19	ESDF	192 289	95 189	97 100	...	...	...	...	...	...
20 - 24	ESDF	169 860	82 760	87 100	...	...	...	...	...	...
25 - 29	ESDF	141 834	67 616	74 218	...	...	...	...	...	...
30+	ESDF	510 000	234 000	276 000	...	...	...	...	...	...
Burkina Faso										
10 XII 1996										
Total	CDFC	10 312 609	4 970 882	5 341 727	...	...	...	...	...	...
0 - 1	CDFC	346 453	173 583	172 870	...	...	...	...	...	...
1 - 4	CDFC	1 421 971	715 961	706 010	...	...	...	...	...	...
5 - 9	CDFC	1 798 242	913 006	885 236	...	...	...	...	...	...
10 - 14	CDFC	1 375 393	706 641	668 752	...	...	...	...	...	...
15 - 19	CDFC	1 082 487	534 025	548 462	...	...	...	...	...	...
20 - 24	CDFC	767 462	340 162	427 300	...	...	...	...	...	...
25 - 29	CDFC	666 645	285 292	381 353	...	...	...	...	...	...
30 - 34	CDFC	572 745	250 049	322 696	...	...	...	...	...	...
35 - 39	CDFC	467 470	205 558	261 912	...	...	...	...	...	...
40 - 44	CDFC	390 677	173 362	217 315	...	...	...	...	...	...
45 - 49	CDFC	311 624	145 091	166 533	...	...	...	...	...	...
50 - 54	CDFC	279 315	127 031	152 284	...	...	...	...	...	...
55 - 59	CDFC	208 700	102 910	105 790	...	...	...	...	...	...
60 - 64	CDFC	196 248	93 494	102 754	...	...	...	...	...	...
65 - 69	CDFC	132 659	66 895	65 764	...	...	...	...	...	...
70 - 74	CDFC	114 931	54 300	60 631	...	...	...	...	...	...
75 - 79	CDFC	62 654	31 623	31 031	...	...	...	...	...	...
80 - 84	CDFC	36 026	15 405	20 621	...	...	...	...	...	...
85 - 89	CDFC	14 151	6 253	7 898	...	...	...	...	...	...
90 - 94	CDFC	9 503	3 742	5 761	...	...	...	...	...	...
95+	CDFC	15 888	5 839	10 049	...	...	...	...	...	...
Unk. - Inc.	CDFC	41 365	20 660	20 705	...	...	...	...	...	...
Burundi										
1 VII 1993										
Total	ESDF	5 769 143	2 805 796	2 963 347	403 680	214 472	189 208	5 365 463	2 591 324	2 774 139
0 - 1	ESDF	224 612	112 804	111 808	12 371	6 101	6 270	212 241	106 703	105 538
1 - 4	ESDF	883 430	440 499	442 931	65 343	36 193	29 150	818 087	404 306	413 781
5 - 9	ESDF	897 159	445 841	451 318	62 896	34 079	28 817	834 263	411 762	422 501
10 - 14	ESDF	700 683	345 674	355 009	49 090	26 423	22 667	651 593	319 251	332 342
15 - 19	ESDF	575 666	281 702	293 964	40 303	21 533	18 770	535 364	260 169	275 195
20 - 24	ESDF	483 813	234 003	249 810	33 837	17 887	15 950	449 976	216 116	233 860
25 - 29	ESDF	408 301	196 125	212 176	28 539	14 992	13 547	379 761	181 134	198 627
30 - 34	ESDF	346 274	166 103	180 171	24 201	12 697	11 504	322 073	153 406	168 667
35 - 39	ESDF	284 561	135 801	148 760	19 877	10 380	9 497	264 682	125 421	139 261
40 - 44	ESDF	218 512	103 534	114 978	15 255	7 914	7 341	203 257	95 620	107 637
45 - 49	ESDF	173 824	81 368	92 456	12 123	6 220	5 903	161 701	75 148	86 553
50 - 54	ESDF	134 642	61 447	73 195	9 370	4 697	4 673	125 272	56 750	68 522
55 - 59	ESDF	108 961	49 101	59 860	7 577	3 753	3 824	101 386	45 348	56 038
60 - 64	ESDF	90 204	40 123	50 081	6 265	3 067	3 198	83 939	37 056	46 883
65 - 69	ESDF	73 426	32 828	40 598	5 101	2 509	2 592	68 325	30 319	38 006
70 - 74	ESDF	58 378	26 374	32 004	4 059	2 016	2 043	54 319	24 358	29 961
75 - 79	ESDF	45 623	21 325	24 298	3 181	1 630	1 551	42 442	19 694	22 748
80+	ESDF	61 074	31 144	29 930	4 292	2 381	1 911	56 782	28 763	28 019

130

7. Population by age, sex and urban/rural residence: latest available year, 1992 - 2001
Population selon l'âge, le sexe et la résidence, urbaine/rurale: dernière année disponible, 1992 - 2001
(continued — suite)

(See notes at end of table. — Voir notes à la fin du tableau.)

Continent, country or area, date and age (in years) / Continent, pays ou zone, date et âge (en années)	Code[1]	Total			Urban - Urbaine			Rural - Rurale		
		Both sexes Les deux sexes	Male Masculin	Female Féminin	Both sexes Les deux sexes	Male Masculin	Female Féminin	Both sexes Les deux sexes	Male Masculin	Female Féminin
AFRICA — AFRIQUE										
Chad - Tchad[2]										
1 VII 1992										
Total	ESDF	5 961 000	2 870 000	3 091 000	1 901 000	980 000	921 000	4 070 000	1 900 000	2 170 000
0 - 4	ESDF	975 000	486 000	489 000	277 000	139 000	138 000	708 000	357 000	351 000
5 - 9	ESDF	809 000	400 000	409 000	222 000	111 000	111 000	587 000	289 000	298 000
10 - 14	ESDF	686 000	339 000	347 000	200 000	102 000	98 000	486 000	237 000	249 000
15 - 19	ESDF	578 000	284 000	294 000	185 000	100 000	85 000	393 000	184 000	209 000
20 - 24	ESDF	532 000	258 000	274 000	182 000	101 000	81 000	350 000	157 000	193 000
25 - 29	ESDF	479 000	230 000	249 000	174 000	92 000	82 000	305 000	138 000	167 000
30 - 34	ESDF	409 000	195 000	214 000	152 000	79 000	73 000	257 000	116 000	141 000
35 - 39	ESDF	344 000	163 000	181 000	129 000	68 000	61 000	215 000	95 000	120 000
40 - 44	ESDF	288 000	136 000	152 000	106 000	53 000	53 000	182 000	83 000	99 000
45 - 49	ESDF	238 000	111 000	127 000	88 000	42 000	46 000	150 000	69 000	81 000
50 - 54	ESDF	192 000	87 000	105 000	70 000	34 000	36 000	122 000	53 000	69 000
55 - 59	ESDF	151 000	67 000	84 000	50 000	26 000	24 000	101 000	41 000	60 000
60+	ESDF	280 000	114 000	166 000	66 000	33 000	33 000	214 000	81 000	133 000
8 IV 1993[3]										
Total	CDJC	6 193 538	3 001 371	3 192 167	...	...	...	...	...	...
0 - 4	CDJC	1 125 473	565 539	559 934	...	...	...	...	...	...
5 - 9	CDJC	1 062 740	534 245	528 495	...	...	...	...	...	...
10 - 14	CDJC	777 185	400 917	376 268	...	...	...	...	...	...
15 - 19	CDJC	611 145	292 416	318 729	...	...	...	...	...	...
20 - 24	CDJC	453 417	204 657	248 760	...	...	...	...	...	...
25 - 29	CDJC	454 232	197 509	256 723	...	...	...	...	...	...
30 - 34	CDJC	354 363	163 792	190 571	...	...	...	...	...	...
35 - 39	CDJC	295 276	137 388	157 888	...	...	...	...	...	...
40 - 44	CDJC	257 420	117 788	139 632	...	...	...	...	...	...
45 - 49	CDJC	173 788	83 414	90 374	...	...	...	...	...	...
50 - 54	CDJC	176 935	81 489	95 446	...	...	...	...	...	...
55 - 59	CDJC	91 049	45 345	45 704	...	...	...	...	...	...
60 - 64	CDJC	127 259	60 027	67 232	...	...	...	...	...	...
65 - 69	CDJC	55 406	28 465	26 941	...	...	...	...	...	...
70 - 74	CDJC	74 940	36 932	38 008	...	...	...	...	...	...
75+	CDJC	78 654	41 237	37 417	...	...	...	...	...	...
Unk. - Inc.	CDJC	24 256	10 211	14 045	...	...	...	...	...	...
Egypt - Égypte										
19 XI 1996										
Total	CDFC	59 312 914	30 351 390	28 961 524	25 286 335	12 957 775	12 328 560	34 026 579	17 393 615	16 632 964
0 - 1	CDFC	560 622	288 082	272 540	238 653	122 073	116 580	321 969	166 009	155 960
1 - 4	CDFC	6 294 620	3 223 694	3 070 926	2 257 688	1 152 819	1 104 869	4 036 932	2 070 875	1 966 057
5 - 9	CDFC	7 626 252	3 939 121	3 687 131	2 852 218	1 464 520	1 387 698	4 774 034	2 474 601	2 299 433
10 - 14	CDFC	7 864 002	4 076 601	3 787 401	3 116 208	1 602 009	1 514 199	4 747 794	2 474 592	2 273 202
15 - 19	CDFC	6 901 611	3 602 857	3 298 754	2 930 311	1 510 230	1 420 081	3 971 300	2 092 627	1 878 673
20 - 24	CDFC	5 075 136	2 642 620	2 432 516	2 273 551	1 167 895	1 105 656	2 801 585	1 474 725	1 326 860
25 - 29	CDFC	4 370 522	2 105 063	2 265 459	1 916 234	933 765	982 469	2 454 288	1 171 298	1 282 990
30 - 34	CDFC	3 979 720	1 993 212	1 986 508	1 847 108	917 762	929 346	2 132 612	1 075 450	1 057 162
35 - 39	CDFC	3 860 105	1 914 367	1 945 738	1 776 094	879 215	896 879	2 084 011	1 035 152	1 048 859
40 - 44	CDFC	3 173 226	1 616 449	1 556 777	1 573 960	810 931	763 029	1 599 266	805 518	793 748
45 - 49	CDFC	2 696 169	1 408 498	1 287 671	1 296 912	687 877	609 035	1 399 257	720 621	678 636
50 - 54	CDFC	2 022 136	994 936	1 027 200	984 817	503 584	481 233	1 037 319	491 352	545 967
55 - 59	CDFC	1 476 673	776 537	700 136	686 141	372 516	313 625	790 532	404 021	386 511
60 - 64	CDFC	1 398 994	706 189	692 805	665 441	349 766	315 675	733 553	356 423	377 130
65 - 69	CDFC	930 576	507 085	423 491	404 645	232 503	172 142	525 931	274 582	251 349
70 - 74	CDFC	617 669	315 767	301 902	269 065	144 153	124 912	348 604	171 614	176 990
75+	CDFC	464 858	240 302	224 556	197 282	106 154	91 128	267 576	134 148	133 428
Unk. - Inc.	CDFC	23	10	13	7	3	4	16	7	9
1 VII 2000										
Total	ESDF	63 976 000	32 695 000	31 281 000	...	...	...	...	...	...
0 - 4	ESDF	7 394 000	3 783 000	3 611 000	...	...	...	...	...	...
5 - 9	ESDF	8 225 000	4 245 000	3 980 000	...	...	...	...	...	...

7. Population by age, sex and urban/rural residence: latest available year, 1992 - 2001
Population selon l'âge, le sexe et la résidence, urbaine/rurale: dernière année disponible, 1992 - 2001
(continued — suite)

(See notes at end of table. — Voir notes à la fin du tableau.)

Continent, country or area, date and age (in years) / Continent, pays ou zone, date et âge (en années)	Code[1]	Total			Urban - Urbaine			Rural - Rurale		
		Both sexes Les deux sexes	Male Masculin	Female Féminin	Both sexes Les deux sexes	Male Masculin	Female Féminin	Both sexes Les deux sexes	Male Masculin	Female Féminin
AFRICA — AFRIQUE										
Egypt - Égypte										
1 VII 2000										
10 - 14	ESDF	8 481 000	4 392 000	4 089 000	...	...	...	...	...	...
15 - 19	ESDF	7 445 000	3 882 000	3 563 000	...	...	...	...	...	...
20 - 24	ESDF	5 474 000	2 848 000	2 626 000	...	...	...	...	...	...
25 - 29	ESDF	4 714 000	2 266 000	2 448 000	...	...	...	...	...	...
30 - 34	ESDF	4 293 000	2 149 000	2 144 000	...	...	...	...	...	...
35 - 39	ESDF	4 164 000	2 064 000	2 100 000	...	...	...	...	...	...
40 - 44	ESDF	3 422 000	1 740 000	1 682 000	...	...	...	...	...	...
45 - 49	ESDF	2 909 000	1 516 000	1 393 000	...	...	...	...	...	...
50 - 54	ESDF	2 180 000	1 071 000	1 109 000	...	...	...	...	...	...
55 - 59	ESDF	1 593 000	835 000	758 000	...	...	...	...	...	...
60 - 64	ESDF	1 510 000	761 000	749 000	...	...	...	...	...	...
65 - 69	ESDF	1 003 000	546 000	457 000	...	...	...	...	...	...
70 - 74	ESDF	667 000	339 000	328 000	...	...	...	...	...	...
75+	ESDF	502 000	258 000	244 000	...	...	...	...	...	...
Ethiopia - Éthiopie										
1 VII 2001										
Total	ESDF	65 374 320	32 815 082	32 559 238	9 883 138	4 938 725	4 944 413	55 491 183	27 876 358	27 614 825
0 - 1	ESDF	2 606 442	1 316 319	1 290 123	276 267	147 795	128 472	2 330 176	1 168 525	1 161 651
1 - 4	ESDF	8 848 741	4 474 555	4 374 188	950 931	505 018	445 914	7 897 811	3 969 537	3 928 274
5 - 9	ESDF	8 996 168	4 561 463	4 434 705	1 085 739	557 741	527 998	7 910 428	4 003 720	3 906 708
10 - 14	ESDF	8 044 523	4 088 160	3 956 362	1 170 364	577 913	592 449	6 874 159	3 510 245	3 363 914
15 - 19	ESDF	7 221 370	3 671 616	3 549 755	1 223 381	591 467	631 914	5 997 989	3 080 148	2 917 842
20 - 24	ESDF	6 196 477	3 135 247	3 061 232	1 142 577	557 252	585 325	5 053 900	2 577 993	2 475 906
25 - 29	ESDF	5 043 379	2 505 588	2 537 791	959 959	471 661	488 299	4 083 419	2 033 927	2 049 493
30 - 34	ESDF	4 114 649	2 010 972	2 103 675	770 685	385 222	385 463	3 343 964	1 625 750	1 718 214
35 - 39	ESDF	3 289 852	1 578 799	1 711 054	595 281	300 315	294 966	2 694 572	1 278 483	1 416 089
40 - 44	ESDF	2 664 272	1 268 119	1 396 155	444 088	221 342	222 746	2 220 184	1 046 776	1 173 409
45 - 49	ESDF	2 188 270	1 064 969	1 123 301	348 085	178 781	169 304	1 840 185	886 188	953 997
50 - 54	ESDF	1 776 932	880 753	896 177	271 235	138 210	133 023	1 505 696	742 541	763 155
55 - 59	ESDF	1 390 250	702 299	687 952	205 332	102 132	103 200	1 184 919	600 166	584 753
60 - 64	ESDF	1 070 263	548 489	521 775	157 703	75 699	82 006	912 560	472 789	439 770
65 - 69	ESDF	795 595	411 183	384 414	118 258	54 975	63 284	677 338	356 207	321 131
70 - 74	ESDF	545 059	284 722	260 338	78 441	35 759	42 681	466 619	248 962	217 656
75 - 79	ESDF	324 329	171 787	152 542	46 055	20 867	25 186	278 277	150 918	127 358
80+	ESDF	257 747	140 050	117 698	38 759	16 570	22 190	218 988	123 480	95 508
Gabon										
31 VII 1993										
Total	CDFC	1 014 976	501 784	513 192	...	...	...	...	...	...
0 - 1	CDFC	35 791	17 875	17 916	...	...	...	...	...	...
1 - 4	CDFC	118 221	59 101	59 120	...	...	...	...	...	...
5 - 9	CDFC	140 487	70 051	70 436	...	...	...	...	...	...
10 - 14	CDFC	121 690	60 123	61 567	...	...	...	...	...	...
15 - 19	CDFC	100 800	48 841	51 959	...	...	...	...	...	...
20 - 24	CDFC	91 511	43 527	47 984	...	...	...	...	...	...
25 - 29	CDFC	81 750	40 475	41 275	...	...	...	...	...	...
30 - 34	CDFC	69 446	36 149	33 297	...	...	...	...	...	...
35 - 39	CDFC	52 254	28 364	23 890	...	...	...	...	...	...
40 - 44	CDFC	39 611	22 144	17 467	...	...	...	...	...	...
45 - 49	CDFC	32 206	16 706	15 500	...	...	...	...	...	...
50 - 54	CDFC	29 714	13 976	15 738	...	...	...	...	...	...
55 - 59	CDFC	29 442	13 384	16 058	...	...	...	...	...	...
60 - 64	CDFC	24 581	10 744	13 837	...	...	...	...	...	...
65 - 69	CDFC	18 091	7 882	10 209	...	...	...	...	...	...
70 - 74	CDFC	13 923	6 048	7 875	...	...	...	...	...	...
75 - 79	CDFC	8 081	3 637	4 444	...	...	...	...	...	...
80 - 84	CDFC	4 317	1 699	2 618	...	...	...	...	...	...
85 - 89	CDFC	1 813	633	1 180	...	...	...	...	...	...
90+	CDFC	1 247	425	822	...	...	...	...	...	...

7. Population by age, sex and urban/rural residence: latest available year, 1992 - 2001
Population selon l'âge, le sexe et la résidence, urbaine/rurale: dernière année disponible, 1992 - 2001
(continued — suite)

(See notes at end of table. — Voir notes à la fin du tableau.)

Continent, country or area, date and age (in years) Continent, pays ou zone, date et âge (en années)	Code[1]	Total			Urban - Urbaine			Rural - Rurale		
		Both sexes Les deux sexes	Male Masculin	Female Féminin	Both sexes Les deux sexes	Måle Masculin	Female Féminin	Both sexes Les deux sexes	Male Masculin	Female Féminin
AFRICA — AFRIQUE										
Gambia - Gambie										
15 IV 1993										
Total	CDFC	1 038 145	519 950	518 195	385 400	198 926	186 474	652 745	321 024	331 721
0 - 1	CDFC	29 047	14 817	14 230	10 476	5 326	5 150	18 571	9 491	9 080
1 - 4	CDFC	139 170	69 882	69 288	44 667	22 298	22 369	94 503	47 584	46 919
5 - 9	CDFC	163 791	81 904	81 887	49 744	24 132	25 612	114 047	57 772	56 275
10 - 14	CDFC	122 653	61 472	61 181	42 335	19 916	22 419	80 318	41 556	38 762
15 - 19	CDFC	108 525	52 499	56 026	45 171	21 305	23 866	63 354	31 194	32 160
20 - 24	CDFC	91 368	44 742	46 626	43 209	22 716	20 493	48 159	22 026	26 133
25 - 29	CDFC	88 049	40 923	47 126	38 409	20 306	18 103	49 640	20 617	29 023
30 - 34	CDFC	65 266	30 510	34 756	27 235	14 738	12 497	38 031	15 772	22 259
35 - 39	CDFC	49 453	24 924	24 529	20 588	11 713	8 875	28 865	13 211	15 654
40 - 44	CDFC	41 696	21 142	20 554	15 419	9 033	6 386	26 277	12 109	14 168
45 - 49	CDFC	29 042	16 593	12 449	11 067	6 898	4 169	17 975	9 695	8 280
50 - 54	CDFC	26 197	14 320	11 877	8 558	5 069	3 489	17 639	9 251	8 388
55 - 59	CDFC	14 826	9 041	5 785	5 162	3 152	2 010	9 664	5 889	3 775
60 - 64	CDFC	18 165	9 754	8 411	5 218	2 793	2 425	12 947	6 961	5 986
65 - 69	CDFC	9 223	5 251	3 972	3 031	1 618	1 413	6 192	3 633	2 559
70 - 74	CDFC	9 678	4 981	4 697	2 577	1 234	1 343	7 101	3 747	3 354
75 - 79	CDFC	4 529	2 474	2 055	1 320	656	664	3 209	1 818	1 391
80 - 84	CDFC	4 959	2 334	2 625	1 241	521	720	3 718	1 813	1 905
85 - 89	CDFC	1 692	855	837	443	192	251	1 249	663	586
90 - 94	CDFC	1 351	628	723	292	96	196	1 059	532	527
95+	CDFC	2 062	964	1 098	521	211	310	1 541	753	788
Unk. - Inc.	CDFC	17 403	9 940	7 463	8 717	5 003	3 714	8 686	4 937	3 749
Ghana										
26 III 2000										
Total	CDFC	18 912 079	9 357 382	9 554 697	...	...	...	...	...	...
0 - 1	CDFC	525 258	262 041	263 217	...	...	...	...	...	...
1 - 4	CDFC	2 244 163	1 117 729	1 126 434	...	...	...	...	...	...
5 - 9	CDFC	2 775 206	1 390 652	1 384 554	...	...	...	...	...	...
10 - 14	CDFC	2 262 216	1 151 131	1 111 085	...	...	...	...	...	...
15 - 19	CDFC	1 883 753	961 162	922 591	...	...	...	...	...	...
20 - 24	CDFC	1 600 820	763 051	837 769	...	...	...	...	...	...
25 - 29	CDFC	1 487 299	695 494	791 805	...	...	...	...	...	...
30 - 34	CDFC	1 206 809	566 439	640 370	...	...	...	...	...	...
35 - 39	CDFC	1 029 765	490 864	538 901	...	...	...	...	...	...
40 - 44	CDFC	886 931	443 284	443 647	...	...	...	...	...	...
45 - 49	CDFC	720 357	377 315	343 042	...	...	...	...	...	...
50 - 54	CDFC	568 369	279 950	288 419	...	...	...	...	...	...
55 - 59	CDFC	355 842	182 843	172 999	...	...	...	...	...	...
60 - 64	CDFC	366 351	177 347	189 004	...	...	...	...	...	...
65 - 69	CDFC	258 709	129 090	129 619	...	...	...	...	...	...
70 - 74	CDFC	225 158	106 513	118 645	...	...	...	...	...	...
75 - 79	CDFC	144 830	74 268	70 562	...	...	...	...	...	...
80 - 84	CDFC	140 847	66 941	73 906	...	...	...	...	...	...
85+	CDFC	229 396	121 268	108 128	...	...	...	...	...	...
Lesotho										
1 VII 2000										
Total	ESDF	2 144 146	1 059 014	1 085 132	...	...	...	...	...	...
0 - 1	ESDF	57 807	29 129	28 678	...	...	...	...	...	...
1 - 4	ESDF	236 417	120 151	116 266	...	...	...	...	...	...
5 - 9	ESDF	295 381	150 422	144 959	...	...	...	...	...	...
10 - 14	ESDF	279 827	141 855	137 972	...	...	...	...	...	...
15 - 19	ESDF	253 222	127 365	125 857	...	...	...	...	...	...
20 - 24	ESDF	220 504	107 951	112 553	...	...	...	...	...	...
25 - 29	ESDF	165 883	79 392	86 491	...	...	...	...	...	...
30 - 34	ESDF	124 767	60 343	64 424	...	...	...	...	...	...
35 - 39	ESDF	109 501	52 432	57 069	...	...	...	...	...	...
40 - 44	ESDF	92 099	44 207	47 892	...	...	...	...	...	...

7. Population by age, sex and urban/rural residence: latest available year, 1992 - 2001
Population selon l'âge, le sexe et la résidence, urbaine/rurale: dernière année disponible, 1992 - 2001
(continued — suite)

(See notes at end of table. — Voir notes à la fin du tableau.)

Continent, country or area, date and age (in years) / Continent, pays ou zone, date et âge (en années)	Code[1]	Total			Urban - Urbaine			Rural - Rurale		
		Both sexes Les deux sexes	Male Masculin	Female Féminin	Both sexes Les deux sexes	Male Masculin	Female Féminin	Both sexes Les deux sexes	Male Masculin	Female Féminin
AFRICA — AFRIQUE										
Lesotho										
1 VII 2000										
45 - 49	ESDF	76 631	37 536	39 095	...	...	...	...	...	...
50 - 54	ESDF	62 407	31 357	31 050	...	...	...	...	...	...
55 - 59	ESDF	49 589	24 111	25 478	...	...	...	...	...	...
60 - 64	ESDF	41 571	19 779	21 792	...	...	...	...	...	...
65 - 69	ESDF	38 206	16 650	21 556	...	...	...	...	...	...
70 - 74	ESDF	18 951	8 186	10 765	...	...	...	...	...	...
75+	ESDF	21 383	8 148	13 235	...	...	...	...	...	...
Malawi										
1 IX 1998										
Total	CDFC	9 933 868	4 867 563	5 066 305	1 435 436	742 839	692 597	8 498 432	4 124 724	4 373 708
0 - 1	CDFC	368 325	182 508	185 817	49 018	24 549	24 469	319 307	157 959	161 348
1 - 4	CDFC	1 292 065	641 117	650 948	166 030	83 011	83 019	1 126 035	558 106	567 929
5 - 9	CDFC	1 440 370	714 830	725 540	183 924	90 095	93 829	1 256 446	624 735	631 711
10 - 14	CDFC	1 232 500	616 445	616 055	180 430	84 521	95 909	1 052 070	531 924	520 146
15 - 19	CDFC	1 087 936	527 865	560 071	179 240	88 044	91 196	908 696	439 821	468 875
20 - 24	CDFC	979 060	435 138	543 922	185 677	89 626	96 051	793 383	345 512	447 871
25 - 29	CDFC	792 465	393 913	398 552	152 217	85 808	66 409	640 248	308 105	332 143
30 - 34	CDFC	601 241	303 080	298 161	105 241	60 855	44 386	496 000	242 225	253 775
35 - 39	CDFC	484 827	239 043	245 784	75 067	42 734	32 333	409 760	196 309	213 451
40 - 44	CDFC	360 709	180 167	180 542	50 294	30 145	20 149	310 415	150 022	160 393
45 - 49	CDFC	332 756	166 258	166 498	38 650	23 268	15 382	294 106	142 990	151 116
50 - 54	CDFC	238 846	120 193	118 653	24 745	15 195	9 550	214 101	104 998	109 103
55 - 59	CDFC	175 226	89 909	85 317	14 921	9 171	5 750	160 305	80 738	79 567
60 - 64	CDFC	153 084	72 251	80 833	10 405	5 973	4 432	142 679	66 278	76 401
65 - 69	CDFC	139 320	65 655	73 665	7 818	4 226	3 592	131 502	61 429	70 073
70 - 74	CDFC	98 049	45 310	52 739	4 936	2 407	2 529	93 113	42 903	50 210
75 - 79	CDFC	65 485	32 151	33 334	2 936	1 489	1 447	62 549	30 662	31 887
80 - 84	CDFC	45 632	20 495	25 137	1 968	873	1 095	43 664	19 622	24 042
85 - 89	CDFC	25 214	11 540	13 674	1 042	463	579	24 172	11 077	13 095
90 - 94	CDFC	11 167	5 180	5 987	521	227	294	10 646	4 953	5 693
95+	CDFC	9 591	4 515	5 076	356	159	197	9 235	4 356	4 879
Mauritania - Mauritanie										
24 IV 1993										
Total	ESDF	2 147 778	1 066 298	1 081 480	...	...	...	...	...	...
0 - 4	ESDF	390 397	196 530	193 867	...	...	...	...	...	...
5 - 9	ESDF	287 946	146 131	141 815	...	...	...	...	...	...
10 - 14	ESDF	294 024	152 069	141 955	...	...	...	...	...	...
15 - 19	ESDF	215 166	112 582	102 584	...	...	...	...	...	...
20 - 24	ESDF	185 066	90 442	94 624	...	...	...	...	...	...
25 - 29	ESDF	156 811	72 641	84 170	...	...	...	...	...	...
30 - 34	ESDF	140 238	64 843	75 395	...	...	...	...	...	...
35 - 39	ESDF	112 705	54 208	58 497	...	...	...	...	...	...
40 - 44	ESDF	85 646	42 337	43 309	...	...	...	...	...	...
45 - 49	ESDF	68 958	32 675	36 283	...	...	...	...	...	...
50 - 54	ESDF	51 822	25 394	26 428	...	...	...	...	...	...
55 - 59	ESDF	56 191	26 848	29 343	...	...	...	...	...	...
60 - 64	ESDF	27 591	14 406	13 185	...	...	...	...	...	...
65 - 69	ESDF	33 265	16 093	17 172	...	...	...	...	...	...
70 - 74	ESDF	16 779	8 307	8 472	...	...	...	...	...	...
75+	ESDF	25 173	10 792	14 381	...	...	...	...	...	...
Mauritius - Maurice										
2 VII 2000										
Total	CDJC	1 178 848	583 756	595 092	...	...	...	...	...	...
0 - 1	CDJC	18 915	9 574	9 341	...	...	...	...	...	...
1 - 4	CDJC	75 388	38 066	37 322	...	...	...	...	...	...
5 - 9	CDJC	105 189	53 037	52 152	...	...	...	...	...	...
10 - 14	CDJC	97 740	49 428	48 312	...	...	...	...	...	...

7. Population by age, sex and urban/rural residence: latest available year, 1992 - 2001
Population selon l'âge, le sexe et la résidence, urbaine/rurale: dernière année disponible, 1992 - 2001
(continued — suite)

(See notes at end of table. — Voir notes à la fin du tableau.)

Continent, country or area, date and age (in years) Continent, pays ou zone, date et âge (en années)	Code[1]	Total			Urban - Urbaine			Rural - Rurale		
		Both sexes Les deux sexes	Male Masculin	Female Féminin	Both sexes Les deux sexes	Male Masculin	Female Féminin	Both sexes Les deux sexes	Male Masculin	Female Féminin
AFRICA — AFRIQUE										
Mauritius - Maurice 2 VII 2000										
15 - 19	CDJC	102 088	51 671	50 417	...	...	...	...	...	...
20 - 24	CDJC	110 892	55 108	55 784	...	...	...	...	...	...
25 - 29	CDJC	93 797	46 749	47 048	...	...	...	...	...	...
30 - 34	CDJC	99 515	49 964	49 551	...	...	...	...	...	...
35 - 39	CDJC	101 946	51 621	50 325	...	...	...	...	...	...
40 - 44	CDJC	90 406	45 798	44 608	...	...	...	...	...	...
45 - 49	CDJC	77 931	39 133	38 798	...	...	...	...	...	...
50 - 54	CDJC	56 939	27 790	29 149	...	...	...	...	...	...
55 - 59	CDJC	40 491	19 228	21 263	...	...	...	...	...	...
60 - 64	CDJC	33 097	15 301	17 796	...	...	...	...	...	...
65 - 69	CDJC	25 768	11 758	14 010	...	...	...	...	...	...
70 - 74	CDJC	21 694	9 491	12 203	...	...	...	...	...	...
75 - 79	CDJC	14 910	6 047	8 863	...	...	...	...	...	...
80 - 84	CDJC	7 132	2 584	4 548	...	...	...	...	...	...
85 - 89	CDJC	3 498	1 049	2 449	...	...	...	...	...	...
90 - 94	CDJC	1 104	272	832	...	...	...	...	...	...
95+	CDJC	289	42	247	...	...	...	...	...	...
Unk. - Inc.	CDJC	119	45	74	...	...	...	...	...	...
Morocco - Maroc 1 VII 2001										
Total	ESDF	29 170 000	14 512 000	14 658 000	16 307 000	8 000 000	8 307 000	12 863 000	6 512 000	6 351 000
0 - 4	ESDF	2 990 000	1 526 000	1 464 000	1 483 000	758 000	725 000	1 507 000	768 000	739 000
5 - 9	ESDF	3 009 000	1 531 000	1 478 000	1 450 000	734 000	716 000	1 559 000	797 000	762 000
10 - 14	ESDF	3 218 000	1 640 000	1 578 000	1 568 000	776 000	792 000	1 650 000	864 000	786 000
15 - 19	ESDF	3 233 000	1 637 000	1 596 000	1 659 000	812 000	847 000	1 574 000	825 000	749 000
20 - 24	ESDF	2 971 000	1 481 000	1 490 000	1 632 000	790 000	842 000	1 339 000	691 000	648 000
25 - 29	ESDF	2 643 000	1 304 000	1 339 000	1 585 000	771 000	814 000	1 058 000	533 000	525 000
30 - 34	ESDF	2 194 000	1 062 000	1 132 000	1 427 000	682 000	745 000	767 000	380 000	387 000
35 - 39	ESDF	1 951 000	922 000	1 029 000	1 287 000	601 000	686 000	664 000	321 000	343 000
40 - 44	ESDF	1 699 000	841 000	858 000	1 104 000	547 000	557 000	595 000	294 000	301 000
45 - 49	ESDF	1 382 000	708 000	674 000	884 000	464 000	420 000	498 000	244 000	254 000
50 - 54	ESDF	952 000	474 000	478 000	597 000	311 000	286 000	355 000	163 000	192 000
55 - 59	ESDF	776 000	353 000	423 000	447 000	203 000	244 000	329 000	150 000	179 000
60 - 64	ESDF	668 000	314 000	354 000	378 000	174 000	204 000	290 000	140 000	150 000
65 - 69	ESDF	603 000	289 000	314 000	338 000	160 000	178 000	265 000	129 000	136 000
70 - 74	ESDF	420 000	205 000	215 000	234 000	110 000	124 000	186 000	95 000	91 000
75+	ESDF	461 000	225 000	236 000	234 000	107 000	127 000	227 000	118 000	109 000
Mozambique 1 VIII 1997										
Total	CDJC	15 278 334	7 320 948	7 957 386	4 454 859	2 201 292	2 253 567	10 823 475	5 119 656	5 703 819
0 - 1	CDJC	535 237	263 539	271 698	138 601	68 743	69 858	396 636	194 796	201 840
1 - 4	CDJC	2 206 319	1 089 667	1 116 652	558 601	277 008	281 593	1 647 718	812 659	835 059
5 - 9	CDJC	2 225 996	1 112 321	1 113 675	617 241	304 392	312 849	1 608 755	807 929	800 826
10 - 14	CDJC	1 825 665	947 236	878 429	600 911	301 921	298 990	1 224 754	645 315	579 439
15 - 19	CDJC	1 628 405	774 327	854 078	564 519	287 073	277 446	1 063 886	487 254	576 632
20 - 24	CDJC	1 464 727	637 113	827 614	461 071	217 269	243 802	1 003 656	419 844	583 812
25 - 29	CDJC	1 163 574	509 109	654 465	345 841	161 031	184 810	817 733	348 078	469 655
30 - 34	CDJC	887 710	410 148	477 562	284 119	137 905	146 214	603 591	272 243	331 348
35 - 39	CDJC	802 208	373 813	428 395	246 954	126 347	120 607	555 254	247 466	307 788
40 - 44	CDJC	573 193	270 046	303 147	173 329	90 578	82 751	399 864	179 468	220 396
45 - 49	CDJC	539 168	257 070	282 098	139 708	72 415	67 293	399 460	184 655	214 805
50 - 54	CDJC	390 962	178 902	212 060	95 508	48 098	47 410	295 454	130 804	164 650
55 - 59	CDJC	336 356	162 122	174 234	76 557	39 078	37 479	259 799	123 044	136 755
60 - 64	CDJC	239 431	114 335	125 096	57 172	27 663	29 509	182 259	86 672	95 587
65 - 69	CDJC	209 713	100 425	109 288	44 486	20 277	24 209	165 227	80 148	85 079
70 - 74	CDJC	98 014	47 407	50 607	21 390	9 542	11 848	76 624	37 865	38 759
75 - 79	CDJC	84 387	41 529	42 858	16 670	7 113	9 557	67 717	34 416	33 301
80 - 84	CDJC	32 631	15 305	17 326	6 162	2 542	3 620	26 469	12 763	13 706

7. Population by age, sex and urban/rural residence: latest available year, 1992 - 2001
Population selon l'âge, le sexe et la résidence, urbaine/rurale: dernière année disponible, 1992 - 2001
(continued — suite)

(See notes at end of table. — Voir notes à la fin du tableau.)

Continent, country or area, date and age (in years) / Continent, pays ou zone, date et âge (en annèes)	Code[1]	Total			Urban - Urbaine			Rural - Rurale		
		Both sexes Les deux sexes	Male Masculin	Female Féminin	Both sexes Les deux sexes	Male Masculin	Female Féminin	Both sexes Les deux sexes	Male Masculin	Female Féminin
AFRICA — AFRIQUE										
Mozambique										
1 VIII 1997										
85 - 89	CDJC	20 033	9 041	10 992	3 795	1 361	2 434	16 238	7 680	8 558
90 - 94	CDJC	7 179	3 537	3 642	1 114	430	684	6 065	3 107	2 958
95+	CDJC	7 426	3 956	3 470	1 110	506	604	6 316	3 450	2 866
1 VII 1998										
Total	ESDF	16 916 638	7 979 434	8 937 204	...	...	...	...	...	...
0 - 4	ESDF	3 068 070	1 494 852	1 573 218	...	...	...	...	...	...
5 - 9	ESDF	2 489 769	1 210 553	1 279 216	...	...	...	...	...	...
10 - 14	ESDF	2 145 744	1 039 085	1 106 659	...	...	...	...	...	...
15 - 19	ESDF	1 850 528	892 524	958 004	...	...	...	...	...	...
20 - 24	ESDF	1 495 883	706 574	789 309	...	...	...	...	...	...
25 - 29	ESDF	1 221 662	552 198	669 464	...	...	...	...	...	...
30 - 34	ESDF	961 492	412 024	549 468	...	...	...	...	...	...
35 - 39	ESDF	837 438	377 905	459 533	...	...	...	...	...	...
40 - 44	ESDF	719 643	336 269	383 374	...	...	...	...	...	...
45 - 49	ESDF	592 511	276 602	315 909	...	...	...	...	...	...
50 - 54	ESDF	474 269	218 567	255 702	...	...	...	...	...	...
55 - 59	ESDF	371 049	167 565	203 484	...	...	...	...	...	...
60 - 64	ESDF	276 146	122 743	153 403	...	...	...	...	...	...
65 - 69	ESDF	191 055	82 596	108 459	...	...	...	...	...	...
70 - 74	ESDF	117 727	48 663	69 064	...	...	...	...	...	...
75 - 79	ESDF	63 243	25 181	38 062	...	...	...	...	...	...
80+	ESDF	40 409	15 533	24 876	...	...	...	...	...	...
Namibia - Namibie										
1 VII 2000										
Total	ESDF	1 816 600	886 900	929 600	...	...	...	...	...	...
0 - 1	ESDF	61 500	30 900	30 600	...	...	...	...	...	...
1 - 4	ESDF	221 700	110 300	111 400	...	...	...	...	...	...
5 - 9	ESDF	271 600	135 600	137 000	...	...	...	...	...	...
10 - 14	ESDF	201 300	99 900	101 400	...	...	...	...	...	...
15 - 19	ESDF	186 300	92 500	93 800	...	...	...	...	...	...
20 - 24	ESDF	171 600	84 700	86 900	...	...	...	...	...	...
25 - 29	ESDF	155 800	76 000	79 800	...	...	...	...	...	...
30 - 34	ESDF	121 700	58 600	63 200	...	...	...	...	...	...
35 - 39	ESDF	102 100	48 000	54 000	...	...	...	...	...	...
40 - 44	ESDF	78 300	36 700	41 700	...	...	...	...	...	...
45 - 49	ESDF	60 300	28 900	31 400	...	...	...	...	...	...
50 - 54	ESDF	48 800	23 600	25 300	...	...	...	...	...	...
55 - 59	ESDF	38 100	18 300	19 900	...	...	...	...	...	...
60 - 64	ESDF	30 900	14 700	16 300	...	...	...	...	...	...
65 - 69	ESDF	21 500	10 100	11 500	...	...	...	...	...	...
70 - 74	ESDF	19 400	7 900	11 500	...	...	...	...	...	...
75 - 79	ESDF	12 900	5 300	7 800	...	...	...	...	...	...
80 - 84	ESDF	8 500	3 400	4 900	...	...	...	...	...	...
85+	ESDF	3 700	1 500	2 200	...	...	...	...	...	...
Nigeria - Nigéria[4]										
1 VII 2000										
Total	ESDF	115 224 312	57 750 754	57 473 558	...	...	...	...	...	...
0 - 4	ESDF	20 294 315	10 329 530	9 964 785	...	...	...	...	...	...
5 - 9	ESDF	16 626 314	8 475 111	8 151 203	...	...	...	...	...	...
10 - 14	ESDF	14 049 846	7 040 493	7 009 353	...	...	...	...	...	...
15 - 19	ESDF	11 614 242	5 860 447	5 753 795	...	...	...	...	...	...
20 - 24	ESDF	10 607 152	5 337 280	5 269 872	...	...	...	...	...	...
25 - 29	ESDF	8 949 326	4 425 396	4 523 930	...	...	...	...	...	...
30 - 34	ESDF	7 163 277	3 354 804	3 808 473	...	...	...	...	...	...
35 - 39	ESDF	6 009 160	2 804 124	3 205 036	...	...	...	...	...	...
40 - 44	ESDF	5 162 668	2 499 916	2 662 752	...	...	...	...	...	...
45 - 49	ESDF	4 212 419	2 088 777	2 123 642	...	...	...	...	...	...
50 - 54	ESDF	3 164 357	1 636 220	1 528 137	...	...	...	...	...	...

7. Population by age, sex and urban/rural residence: latest available year, 1992 - 2001
Population selon l'âge, le sexe et la résidence, urbaine/rurale: dernière année disponible, 1992 - 2001
(continued — suite)

(See notes at end of table. — Voir notes à la fin du tableau.)

Continent, country or area, date and age (in years) / Continent, pays ou zone, date et âge (en annèes)	Code[1]	Total			Urban - Urbaine			Rural - Rurale		
		Both sexes Les deux sexes	Male Masculin	Female Féminin	Both sexes Les deux sexes	Male Masculin	Female Féminin	Both sexes Les deux sexes	Male Masculin	Female Féminin
AFRICA — AFRIQUE										
Nigeria - Nigéria[4]										
1 VII 2000										
55 - 59	ESDF	2 413 817	1 275 577	1 138 240	...	...	...	...	...	...
60 - 64	ESDF	1 715 811	921 096	794 715	...	...	...	...	...	...
65 - 69	ESDF	1 258 407	675 255	583 152	...	...	...	...	...	...
70 - 74	ESDF	928 888	480 324	448 564	...	...	...	...	...	...
75 - 79	ESDF	578 124	297 076	281 048	...	...	...	...	...	...
80+	ESDF	476 189	249 328	226 861	...	...	...	...	...	...
Réunion										
1 I 1993										
Total	ESDJ	631 500	311 200	320 300	...	...	...	...	...	...
0 - 1	ESDJ	14 200	7 200	7 000	...	...	...	...	...	...
1 - 4	ESDJ	54 000	27 400	26 600	...	...	...	...	...	...
5 - 9	ESDJ	63 900	32 400	31 500	...	...	...	...	...	...
10 - 14	ESDJ	61 100	30 800	30 300	...	...	...	...	...	...
15 - 19	ESDJ	59 700	30 100	29 600	...	...	...	...	...	...
20 - 24	ESDJ	56 500	27 800	28 700	...	...	...	...	...	...
25 - 29	ESDJ	59 800	29 500	30 300	...	...	...	...	...	...
30 - 34	ESDJ	52 400	26 000	26 400	...	...	...	...	...	...
35 - 39	ESDJ	45 400	22 500	22 900	...	...	...	...	...	...
40 - 44	ESDJ	36 500	18 400	18 100	...	...	...	...	...	...
45 - 49	ESDJ	28 700	14 500	14 200	...	...	...	...	...	...
50 - 54	ESDJ	24 800	12 200	12 600	...	...	...	...	...	...
55 - 59	ESDJ	21 600	10 400	11 200	...	...	...	...	...	...
60 - 64	ESDJ	16 500	7 700	8 800	...	...	...	...	...	...
65 - 69	ESDJ	14 000	6 200	7 800	...	...	...	...	...	...
70 - 74	ESDJ	9 800	4 000	5 800	...	...	...	...	...	...
75 - 79	ESDJ	6 400	2 300	4 100	...	...	...	...	...	...
80+	ESDJ	6 200	1 800	4 400	...	...	...	...	...	...
Saint Helena ex. dep. - Sainte-Hélène sans dép.										
8 III 1998										
Total	CDJC	4 913	2 481	2 432	...	...	...	...	...	...
0 - 1	CDJC	60	33	27	...	...	...	...	...	...
1 - 4	CDJC	252	139	113	...	...	...	...	...	...
5 - 9	CDJC	369	197	172	...	...	...	...	...	...
10 - 14	CDJC	368	199	169	...	...	...	...	...	...
15 - 19	CDJC	452	217	235	...	...	...	...	...	...
20 - 24	CDJC	300	154	146	...	...	...	...	...	...
25 - 29	CDJC	370	185	185	...	...	...	...	...	...
30 - 34	CDJC	329	150	179	...	...	...	...	...	...
35 - 39	CDJC	391	181	210	...	...	...	...	...	...
40 - 44	CDJC	336	181	155	...	...	...	...	...	...
45 - 49	CDJC	340	173	167	...	...	...	...	...	...
50 - 54	CDJC	346	200	146	...	...	...	...	...	...
55 - 59	CDJC	230	124	106	...	...	...	...	...	...
60 - 64	CDJC	202	127	75	...	...	...	...	...	...
65 - 69	CDJC	190	86	104	...	...	...	...	...	...
70 - 74	CDJC	143	51	92	...	...	...	...	...	...
75 - 79	CDJC	111	41	70	...	...	...	...	...	...
80 - 84	CDJC	69	25	44	...	...	...	...	...	...
85 - 89	CDJC	26	7	19	...	...	...	...	...	...
90 - 94	CDJC	18	7	11	...	...	...	...	...	...
95+	CDJC	1	...	1	...	...	...	...	...	...
Unk. - Inc.	CDJC	10	4	6	...	...	...	...	...	...

7. Population by age, sex and urban/rural residence: latest available year, 1992 - 2001
Population selon l'âge, le sexe et la résidence, urbaine/rurale: dernière année disponible, 1992 - 2001
(continued — suite)

(See notes at end of table. — Voir notes à la fin du tableau.)

Continent, country or area, date and age (in years) / Continent, pays ou zone, date et âge (en annèes)	Code[1]	Total			Urban - Urbaine			Rural - Rurale		
		Both sexes Les deux sexes	Male Masculin	Female Féminin	Both sexes Les deux sexes	Male Masculin	Female Féminin	Both sexes Les deux sexes	Male Masculin	Female Féminin
AFRICA — AFRIQUE										
Saint Helena: Tristan da Cunha - Sainte-Hélène: Tristan da Cunha 1 VII 1996										
Total	ESDF	286	137	149	...	...	...	...	...	...
0 - 1	ESDF	1	1	...	...	...	...	...	...	...
1 - 4	ESDF	10	7	3	...	...	...	...	...	...
5 - 9	ESDF	14	9	5	...	...	...	...	...	...
10 - 14	ESDF	17	9	8	...	...	...	...	...	...
15 - 19	ESDF	13	8	5	...	...	...	...	...	...
20 - 24	ESDF	17	3	14	...	...	...	...	...	...
25 - 29	ESDF	35	17	18	...	...	...	...	...	...
30 - 34	ESDF	12	6	6	...	...	...	...	...	...
35 - 39	ESDF	19	10	9	...	...	...	...	...	...
40 - 44	ESDF	14	4	10	...	...	...	...	...	...
45 - 49	ESDF	24	14	10	...	...	...	...	...	...
50 - 54	ESDF	18	8	10	...	...	...	...	...	...
55 - 59	ESDF	22	6	16	...	...	...	...	...	...
60 - 64	ESDF	18	11	7	...	...	...	...	...	...
65 - 69	ESDF	12	5	7	...	...	...	...	...	...
70 - 74	ESDF	22	12	10	...	...	...	...	...	...
75 - 79	ESDF	10	5	5	...	...	...	...	...	...
80 - 84	ESDF	6	1	5	...	...	...	...	...	...
85 - 89	ESDF	1	1	...	...	...	...	...	...	...
90+	ESDF	1	...	1	...	...	...	...	...	...
Senegal - Sénégal 1 VII 1993										
Total	ESDJ	8 008 295	3 870 069	4 138 226	...	...	...	...	...	...
0 - 1	ESDJ	158 346	81 960	76 386	...	...	...	...	...	...
1 - 4	ESDJ	1 116 159	556 043	560 116	...	...	...	...	...	...
5 - 9	ESDJ	1 342 168	670 227	671 941	...	...	...	...	...	...
10 - 14	ESDJ	1 099 528	574 629	524 899	...	...	...	...	...	...
15 - 19	ESDJ	824 493	393 919	430 574	...	...	...	...	...	...
20 - 24	ESDJ	610 468	281 949	328 519	...	...	...	...	...	...
25 - 29	ESDJ	576 744	242 187	334 557	...	...	...	...	...	...
30 - 34	ESDJ	433 378	190 408	242 970	...	...	...	...	...	...
35 - 39	ESDJ	396 327	170 159	226 168	...	...	...	...	...	...
40 - 44	ESDJ	306 082	142 284	163 798	...	...	...	...	...	...
45 - 49	ESDJ	246 571	114 446	132 125	...	...	...	...	...	...
50 - 54	ESDJ	220 409	103 562	116 847	...	...	...	...	...	...
55 - 59	ESDJ	177 999	91 448	86 551	...	...	...	...	...	...
60 - 64	ESDJ	163 174	79 033	84 141	...	...	...	...	...	...
65 - 69	ESDJ	117 619	64 394	53 225	...	...	...	...	...	...
70 - 74	ESDJ	101 259	50 314	50 945	...	...	...	...	...	...
75 - 79	ESDJ	49 604	30 016	19 588	...	...	...	...	...	...
80 - 84	ESDJ	33 105	17 181	15 924	...	...	...	...	...	...
85 - 89	ESDJ	16 281	7 758	8 523	...	...	...	...	...	...
90+	ESDJ	18 581	8 152	10 429	...	...	...	...	...	...
Seychelles 1 VII 1998										
Total	ESDF	78 846	39 359	39 487	...	...	...	...	...	...
0 - 4	ESDF	7 515	3 899	3 616	...	...	...	...	...	...
5 - 9	ESDF	7 262	3 688	3 574	...	...	...	...	...	...
10 - 14	ESDF	7 043	3 554	3 489	...	...	...	...	...	...
15 - 19	ESDF	7 206	3 664	3 542	...	...	...	...	...	...
20 - 24	ESDF	6 831	3 452	3 379	...	...	...	...	...	...
25 - 29	ESDF	7 067	3 536	3 531	...	...	...	...	...	...
30 - 34	ESDF	7 362	3 640	3 722	...	...	...	...	...	...
35 - 39	ESDF	6 705	3 477	3 228	...	...	...	...	...	...

7. Population by age, sex and urban/rural residence: latest available year, 1992 - 2001
Population selon l'âge, le sexe et la résidence, urbaine/rurale: dernière année disponible, 1992 - 2001
(continued — suite)

(See notes at end of table. — Voir notes à la fin du tableau.)

Continent, country or area, date and age (in years) / Continent, pays ou zone, date et âge (en annèes)	Code[1]	Total			Urban - Urbaine			Rural - Rurale		
		Both sexes Les deux sexes	Male Masculin	Female Féminin	Both sexes Les deux sexes	Male Masculin	Female Féminin	Both sexes Les deux sexes	Male Masculin	Female Féminin
AFRICA — AFRIQUE										
Seychelles										
1 VII 1998										
40 - 44	ESDF	5 155	2 793	2 362	...	...	...	...	...	...
45 - 49	ESDF	3 376	1 788	1 588	...	...	...	...	...	...
50 - 54	ESDF	2 587	1 358	1 229	...	...	...	...	...	...
55 - 59	ESDF	2 746	1 339	1 407	...	...	...	...	...	...
60 - 64	ESDF	2 217	949	1 268	...	...	...	...	...	...
65 - 69	ESDF	1 954	827	1 127	...	...	...	...	...	...
70 - 74	ESDF	1 555	655	900	...	...	...	...	...	...
75 - 79	ESDF	1 113	432	681	...	...	...	...	...	...
80+	ESDF	1 152	308	844	...	...	...	...	...	...
South Africa - Afrique du Sud[5]										
10 X 1996										
Total	CDFC	40 583 573	19 520 887	21 062 686	21 781 807	10 667 927	11 113 880	18 801 766	8 852 960	9 948 806
0 - 1	CDFC	856 238	426 858	429 380	407 569	204 037	203 532	448 669	222 821	225 848
1 - 4	CDFC	3 587 383	1 789 905	1 797 478	1 608 627	801 912	806 715	1 978 756	987 993	990 763
5 - 9	CDFC	4 668 721	2 333 562	2 335 159	2 038 226	1 016 905	1 021 321	2 630 495	1 316 657	1 313 838
10 - 14	CDFC	4 654 098	2 308 758	2 345 340	2 061 009	1 016 787	1 044 222	2 593 089	1 291 971	1 301 118
15 - 19	CDFC	4 180 717	2 050 214	2 130 503	1 995 798	978 031	1 017 767	2 184 919	1 072 183	1 112 736
20 - 24	CDFC	3 982 354	1 917 919	2 064 435	2 271 339	1 120 919	1 150 420	1 711 015	797 000	914 015
25 - 29	CDFC	3 455 728	1 663 064	1 792 664	2 186 820	1 088 452	1 098 368	1 268 908	574 612	694 296
30 - 34	CDFC	3 074 202	1 463 499	1 610 703	1 970 405	972 890	997 515	1 103 797	490 609	613 188
35 - 39	CDFC	2 653 756	1 284 957	1 368 799	1 709 987	847 993	861 994	943 769	436 964	506 805
40 - 44	CDFC	2 138 626	1 030 597	1 108 029	1 360 825	676 387	684 438	777 801	354 210	423 591
45 - 49	CDFC	1 677 526	813 816	863 710	1 050 144	525 516	524 628	627 382	288 300	339 082
50 - 54	CDFC	1 268 895	600 476	668 419	775 141	383 915	391 226	493 754	216 561	277 193
55 - 59	CDFC	1 069 936	483 678	586 258	621 620	294 100	327 520	448 316	189 578	258 738
60 - 64	CDFC	890 537	352 053	538 484	482 701	208 117	274 584	407 836	143 936	263 900
65 - 69	CDFC	758 886	304 013	454 873	374 423	160 695	213 728	384 463	143 318	241 145
70 - 74	CDFC	482 162	195 119	287 043	254 856	105 173	149 683	227 306	89 946	137 360
75 - 79	CDFC	377 427	141 844	235 583	184 420	70 699	113 721	193 007	71 145	121 862
80 - 84	CDFC	178 903	62 072	116 831	96 886	32 757	64 129	82 017	29 315	52 702
85+	CDFC	137 284	43 230	94 054	69 901	21 596	48 305	67 383	21 634	45 749
Unk. - Inc.	CDFC	490 194	255 253	234 941	261 110	141 046	120 064	229 084	114 207	114 877
Sudan - Soudan										
15 IV 1993										
Total	CDFC	24 941 000	12 519 000	12 422 000	...	...	...	...	...	...
0 - 4	CDFC	4 305 000	2 173 000	2 132 000	...	...	...	...	...	...
5 - 9	CDFC	3 786 000	1 911 000	1 875 000	...	...	...	...	...	...
10 - 14	CDFC	2 627 000	1 285 000	1 341 000	...	...	...	...	...	...
15 - 19	CDFC	2 445 000	1 247 000	1 199 000	...	...	...	...	...	...
20 - 24	CDFC	2 255 000	1 158 000	1 098 000	...	...	...	...	...	...
25 - 29	CDFC	2 026 000	1 028 000	997 000	...	...	...	...	...	...
30 - 34	CDFC	1 624 000	802 000	822 000	...	...	...	...	...	...
35 - 39	CDFC	1 359 000	658 000	700 000	...	...	...	...	...	...
40 - 44	CDFC	1 109 000	526 000	582 000	...	...	...	...	...	...
45 - 49	CDFC	947 000	453 000	494 000	...	...	...	...	...	...
50 - 54	CDFC	766 000	377 000	388 000	...	...	...	...	...	...
55 - 59	CDFC	603 000	308 000	295 000	...	...	...	...	...	...
60 - 64	CDFC	433 000	229 000	205 000	...	...	...	...	...	...
65 - 69	CDFC	298 000	161 000	136 000	...	...	...	...	...	...
70 - 74	CDFC	195 000	109 000	85 000	...	...	...	...	...	...
75+	CDFC	163 000	94 000	73 000	...	...	...	...	...	...
Swaziland										
11 V 1997										
Total	CDFC	929 718	440 154	489 564	214 428	106 256	108 172	715 290	333 898	381 392
0 - 1	CDFC	24 405	12 049	12 356	5 123	2 519	2 604	19 282	9 530	9 752
1 - 4	CDFC	111 992	55 480	56 512	19 744	9 701	10 043	92 248	45 779	46 469
5 - 9	CDFC	139 245	68 976	70 269	22 232	10 663	11 569	117 013	58 313	58 700

7. Population by age, sex and urban/rural residence: latest available year, 1992 - 2001
Population selon l'âge, le sexe et la résidence, urbaine/rurale: dernière année disponible, 1992 - 2001
(continued — suite)

(See notes at end of table. — Voir notes à la fin du tableau.)

Continent, country or area, date and age (in years) / Continent, pays ou zone, date et âge (en années)	Code[1]	Total			Urban - Urbaine			Rural - Rurale		
		Both sexes Les deux sexes	Male Masculin	Female Féminin	Both sexes Les deux sexes	Male Masculin	Female Féminin	Both sexes Les deux sexes	Male Masculin	Female Féminin
AFRICA — AFRIQUE										
Swaziland										
11 V 1997										
10 - 14	CDFC	137 487	68 200	69 287	22 036	9 908	12 128	115 451	58 292	57 159
15 - 19	CDFC	112 356	54 775	57 581	24 504	10 716	13 788	87 852	44 059	43 793
20 - 24	CDFC	85 094	38 807	46 287	27 184	12 804	14 380	57 910	26 003	31 907
25 - 29	CDFC	68 043	30 147	37 896	24 731	12 610	12 121	43 312	17 537	25 775
30 - 34	CDFC	52 156	21 988	30 168	18 103	9 257	8 846	34 053	12 731	21 322
35 - 39	CDFC	45 802	19 645	26 157	15 043	7 841	7 202	30 759	11 804	18 955
40 - 44	CDFC	35 505	16 165	19 340	11 090	6 128	4 962	24 415	10 037	14 378
45 - 49	CDFC	30 371	14 461	15 910	8 627	5 068	3 559	21 744	9 393	12 351
50 - 54	CDFC	23 316	10 799	12 517	5 756	3 413	2 343	17 560	7 386	10 174
55 - 59	CDFC	17 920	8 758	9 162	3 759	2 275	1 484	14 161	6 483	7 678
60 - 64	CDFC	13 866	6 325	7 541	2 349	1 298	1 051	11 517	5 027	6 490
65 - 69	CDFC	10 152	4 645	5 507	1 340	710	630	8 812	3 935	4 877
70 - 74	CDFC	7 301	2 924	4 377	766	343	423	6 535	2 581	3 954
75 - 79	CDFC	5 269	2 175	3 094	527	256	271	4 742	1 919	2 823
80 - 84	CDFC	3 085	1 161	1 924	266	110	156	2 819	1 051	1 768
85 - 89	CDFC	1 765	707	1 058	145	64	81	1 620	643	977
90 - 94	CDFC	731	264	467	61	25	36	670	239	431
95+	CDFC	959	371	588	63	34	29	896	337	559
Unk. - Inc.	CDFC	2 898	1 332	1 566	979	513	466	1 919	819	1 100
Tunisia - Tunisie										
20 IV 1994										
Total	CDFC	8 785 711	4 439 289	4 346 422	5 361 927	2 717 168	2 644 759	3 423 784	1 722 121	1 701 663
0 - 1	CDFC	177 191	91 223	85 968	104 855	53 856	50 999	72 336	37 367	34 969
1 - 4	CDFC	791 125	405 657	385 468	447 380	229 089	218 291	343 745	176 568	167 177
5 - 9	CDFC	1 055 358	538 919	516 439	608 233	309 289	298 944	447 125	229 630	217 495
10 - 14	CDFC	1 034 646	530 178	504 468	605 460	307 625	297 835	429 186	222 553	206 633
15 - 19	CDFC	939 066	478 618	460 448	546 290	280 017	266 273	392 776	198 601	194 175
20 - 24	CDFC	818 718	412 463	406 255	497 919	254 409	243 510	320 799	158 054	162 745
25 - 29	CDFC	743 903	363 603	380 300	479 111	237 120	241 991	264 792	126 483	138 309
30 - 34	CDFC	656 615	326 172	330 443	443 690	223 004	220 686	212 925	103 168	109 757
35 - 39	CDFC	560 347	282 297	278 050	376 253	192 213	184 040	184 094	90 084	94 010
40 - 44	CDFC	437 893	219 789	218 104	291 220	150 579	140 641	146 673	69 210	77 463
45 - 49	CDFC	307 149	149 840	157 309	203 611	101 390	102 221	103 538	48 450	55 088
50 - 54	CDFC	270 357	133 005	137 352	169 597	84 240	85 357	100 760	48 765	51 995
55 - 59	CDFC	266 740	133 154	133 586	161 533	80 938	80 595	105 207	52 216	52 991
60 - 64	CDFC	251 363	127 279	124 084	150 315	75 525	74 790	101 048	51 754	49 294
65 - 69	CDFC	173 855	91 042	82 813	102 677	52 738	49 939	71 178	38 304	32 874
70 - 74	CDFC	137 177	69 561	67 616	79 962	38 819	41 143	57 215	30 742	26 473
75 - 79	CDFC	77 202	42 546	34 656	44 044	22 951	21 093	33 158	19 595	13 563
80 - 84	CDFC	58 593	30 245	28 348	33 199	15 977	17 222	25 394	14 268	11 126
85 - 89	CDFC	16 595	8 623	7 972	9 501	4 649	4 852	7 094	3 974	3 120
90 - 94	CDFC	9 663	4 194	5 469	5 746	2 255	3 491	3 917	1 939	1 978
95 - 99	CDFC	974	410	564	572	214	358	402	196	206
100+	CDFC	1 181	471	710	759	271	488	422	200	222
1 VII 1998										
Total	ESDF	*9 333 300*	*4 709 000*	*4 624 300*	...	...	...	...	...	...
0 - 4	ESDF	*978 500*	*500 700*	*477 800*	...	...	...	...	...	...
5 - 9	ESDF	*1 015 200*	*519 500*	*495 700*	...	...	...	...	...	...
10 - 14	ESDF	*1 058 900*	*541 400*	*517 500*	...	...	...	...	...	...
15 - 19	ESDF	*1 006 100*	*514 400*	*491 700*	...	...	...	...	...	...
20 - 24	ESDF	*898 500*	*455 600*	*443 000*	...	...	...	...	...	...
25 - 29	ESDF	*795 900*	*395 900*	*399 900*	...	...	...	...	...	...
30 - 34	ESDF	*714 800*	*351 200*	*363 600*	...	...	...	...	...	...
35 - 39	ESDF	*621 900*	*310 300*	*311 600*	...	...	...	...	...	...
40 - 44	ESDF	*512 500*	*257 400*	*255 100*	...	...	...	...	...	...
45 - 49	ESDF	*384 400*	*190 800*	*193 700*	...	...	...	...	...	...
50 - 54	ESDF	*291 800*	*142 200*	*149 600*	...	...	...	...	...	...
55 - 59	ESDF	*266 800*	*131 200*	*135 600*	...	...	...	...	...	...

7. **Population by age, sex and urban/rural residence: latest available year, 1992 - 2001**
Population selon l'âge, le sexe et la résidence, urbaine/rurale: dernière année disponible, 1992 - 2001
(continued — suite)

(See notes at end of table. — Voir notes à la fin du tableau.)

Continent, country or area, date and age (in years) / Continent, pays ou zone, date et âge (en années)	Code[1]	Total Both sexes Les deux sexes	Total Male Masculin	Total Female Féminin	Urban - Urbaine Both sexes Les deux sexes	Urban - Urbaine Male Masculin	Urban - Urbaine Female Féminin	Rural - Rurale Both sexes Les deux sexes	Rural - Rurale Male Masculin	Rural - Rurale Female Féminin
AFRICA — AFRIQUE										
Tunisia - Tunisie										
1 VII 1998										
60 - 64	ESDF	255 000	127 100	127 900	...	...	...	...	...	...
65 - 69	ESDF	208 200	105 500	102 700	...	...	...	...	...	...
70 - 74	ESDF	145 800	74 200	71 600	...	...	...	...	...	...
75 - 79	ESDF	94 700	48 500	46 200	...	...	...	...	...	...
80+	ESDF	84 100	43 000	41 000	...	...	...	...	...	...
Zambia - Zambie										
1 VII 1999										
Total	ESDF	10 406 681	5 198 440	5 208 241	...	...	...	...	...	...
0 - 1	ESDF	417 566	213 497	204 069	...	...	...	...	...	...
1 - 4	ESDF	1 616 964	831 505	785 459	...	...	...	...	...	...
5 - 9	ESDF	1 582 006	808 721	773 285	...	...	...	...	...	...
10 - 14	ESDF	1 058 901	525 113	533 788	...	...	...	...	...	...
15 - 19	ESDF	1 128 324	557 197	571 127	...	...	...	...	...	...
20 - 24	ESDF	1 046 144	518 297	527 847	...	...	...	...	...	...
25 - 29	ESDF	920 351	443 564	476 787	...	...	...	...	...	...
30 - 34	ESDF	652 208	307 240	344 968	...	...	...	...	...	...
35 - 39	ESDF	497 805	242 178	255 627	...	...	...	...	...	...
40 - 44	ESDF	390 682	196 760	193 922	...	...	...	...	...	...
45 - 49	ESDF	267 882	134 865	133 017	...	...	...	...	...	...
50 - 54	ESDF	236 880	115 634	121 246	...	...	...	...	...	...
55 - 59	ESDF	186 827	93 600	93 227	...	...	...	...	...	...
60 - 64	ESDF	159 960	78 755	81 205	...	...	...	...	...	...
65 - 69	ESDF	106 136	57 086	49 050	...	...	...	...	...	...
70 - 74	ESDF	74 555	38 623	35 932	...	...	...	...	...	...
75 - 79	ESDF	34 298	19 972	14 326	...	...	...	...	...	...
80+	ESDF	29 192	15 833	13 359	...	...	...	...	...	...
Zimbabwe										
18 VIII 1997										
Total	CDFC	11 789 274	5 647 090	6 142 184	3 826 580	1 906 476	1 920 104	7 962 694	3 740 614	4 222 080
0 - 1	CDFC	328 913	161 914	166 999	104 258	50 698	53 560	224 655	111 216	113 439
1 - 4	CDFC	1 281 912	638 067	643 846	379 808	189 440	190 368	902 105	448 628	453 478
5 - 9	CDFC	1 646 115	797 775	848 341	417 356	197 224	220 132	1 228 760	600 552	628 209
10 - 14	CDFC	1 803 558	882 644	920 911	453 547	213 501	240 046	1 350 010	669 145	680 866
15 - 19	CDFC	1 484 654	730 379	754 274	463 901	204 411	259 491	1 020 754	525 969	494 786
20 - 24	CDFC	1 147 871	521 360	626 511	492 556	229 928	262 628	655 314	291 432	363 883
25 - 29	CDFC	888 600	427 729	460 872	415 758	223 500	192 258	472 843	204 232	268 611
30 - 34	CDFC	624 978	287 946	337 032	280 744	139 782	140 962	344 235	148 165	196 071
35 - 39	CDFC	583 724	254 357	329 366	241 206	124 241	116 966	342 519	130 119	212 399
40 - 44	CDFC	442 692	203 372	239 319	176 245	99 272	76 973	266 445	104 100	162 346
45 - 49	CDFC	366 842	179 562	187 280	131 674	80 556	51 118	235 167	99 008	136 159
50 - 54	CDFC	306 227	130 448	175 779	88 621	48 258	40 363	217 606	82 190	135 415
55 - 59	CDFC	248 868	121 506	127 362	64 434	38 289	26 144	184 435	83 217	101 218
60 - 64	CDFC	195 169	98 104	97 066	47 494	29 051	18 442	147 675	69 052	78 623
65 - 69	CDFC	179 884	93 671	86 213	32 095	19 553	12 542	147 788	74 117	73 670
70 - 74	CDFC	99 500	46 063	53 437	18 242	9 667	8 575	81 256	36 395	44 862
75 - 79	CDFC	82 941	41 039	41 901	9 342	5 616	3 725	73 599	35 423	38 176
80 - 84	CDFC	36 224	14 650	21 571	5 644	2 343	3 300	30 577	12 307	18 271
85 - 89	CDFC	21 287	9 362	11 925	1 573	746	825	19 716	8 616	11 100
90 - 94	CDFC	6 974	2 681	4 295	272	...	272	6 702	2 681	4 023
95+	CDFC	12 342	4 456	7 884	1 810	399	1 412	10 531	4 057	6 474
1 VII 1999										
Total	ESDF	13 079 127	6 382 092	6 697 035	...	...	...	...	...	...
0 - 4	ESDF	2 310 243	1 139 151	1 171 092	...	...	...	...	...	...
5 - 9	ESDF	1 852 604	914 810	937 794	...	...	...	...	...	...
10 - 14	ESDF	1 546 743	769 315	777 428	...	...	...	...	...	...
15 - 19	ESDF	1 534 532	762 581	771 951	...	...	...	...	...	...
20 - 24	ESDF	1 314 285	651 638	662 647	...	...	...	...	...	...
25 - 29	ESDF	1 078 229	516 508	561 721	...	...	...	...	...	...

7. Population by age, sex and urban/rural residence: latest available year, 1992 - 2001
Population selon l'âge, le sexe et la résidence, urbaine/rurale: dernière année disponible, 1992 - 2001
(continued — suite)

(See notes at end of table. — Voir notes à la fin du tableau.)

Continent, country or area, date and age (in years) / Continent, pays ou zone, date et âge (en années)	Code[1]	Total			Urban - Urbaine			Rural - Rurale		
		Both sexes Les deux sexes	Male Masculin	Female Féminin	Both sexes Les deux sexes	Male Masculin	Female Féminin	Both sexes Les deux sexes	Male Masculin	Female Féminin
AFRICA — AFRIQUE										
Zimbabwe										
1 VII 1999										
30 - 34	ESDF	790 666	370 892	419 774	...	...	...	...	...	...
35 - 39	ESDF	621 821	288 864	332 957	...	...	...	...	...	...
40 - 44	ESDF	521 774	241 733	280 041	...	...	...	...	...	...
45 - 49	ESDF	393 469	185 239	208 230	...	...	...	...	...	...
50 - 54	ESDF	290 602	142 943	147 659	...	...	...	...	...	...
55 - 59	ESDF	264 199	125 792	138 407	...	...	...	...	...	...
60 - 64	ESDF	190 673	92 081	98 592	...	...	...	...	...	...
65 - 69	ESDF	146 583	75 988	70 595	...	...	...	...	...	...
70 - 74	ESDF	95 959	47 899	48 060	...	...	...	...	...	...
75+	ESDF	126 745	56 658	70 087	...	...	...	...	...	...
AMERICA, NORTH — AMERIQUE DU NORD										
Anguilla[6]										
9 V 2001										
Total	CDFC	11 430	5 628	5 802	...	...	...	...	...	...
0 - 1	CDFC	252	131	121	...	...	...	...	...	...
1 - 4	CDFC	821	394	427	...	...	...	...	...	...
5 - 9	CDFC	993	502	491	...	...	...	...	...	...
10 - 14	CDFC	1 136	563	573	...	...	...	...	...	...
15 - 19	CDFC	966	477	489	...	...	...	...	...	...
20 - 24	CDFC	788	375	413	...	...	...	...	...	...
25 - 29	CDFC	873	440	433	...	...	...	...	...	...
30 - 34	CDFC	999	494	505	...	...	...	...	...	...
35 - 39	CDFC	1 040	507	533	...	...	...	...	...	...
40 - 44	CDFC	881	429	452	...	...	...	...	...	...
45 - 49	CDFC	714	364	350	...	...	...	...	...	...
50 - 54	CDFC	468	236	232	...	...	...	...	...	...
55 - 59	CDFC	323	166	157	...	...	...	...	...	...
60 - 64	CDFC	304	144	160	...	...	...	...	...	...
65 - 69	CDFC	288	159	129	...	...	...	...	...	...
70 - 74	CDFC	211	82	129	...	...	...	...	...	...
75+	CDFC	373	165	208	...	...	...	...	...	...
Antigua and Barbuda - Antigua-et-Barbuda										
1 VII 1996										
Total	ESDF	68 612	33 080	35 532	...	...	...	...	...	...
0 - 4	ESDF	6 259	3 193	3 066	...	...	...	...	...	...
5 - 9	ESDF	6 656	3 328	3 328	...	...	...	...	...	...
10 - 14	ESDF	6 625	3 283	3 342	...	...	...	...	...	...
15 - 19	ESDF	6 284	3 163	3 120	...	...	...	...	...	...
20 - 24	ESDF	5 687	2 842	2 845	...	...	...	...	...	...
25 - 29	ESDF	6 158	3 014	3 143	...	...	...	...	...	...
30 - 34	ESDF	5 959	2 823	3 136	...	...	...	...	...	...
35 - 39	ESDF	5 370	2 533	2 837	...	...	...	...	...	...
40 - 44	ESDF	4 246	1 980	2 266	...	...	...	...	...	...
45 - 49	ESDF	3 476	1 628	1 848	...	...	...	...	...	...
50 - 54	ESDF	2 630	1 259	1 372	...	...	...	...	...	...
55 - 59	ESDF	1 981	961	1 020	...	...	...	...	...	...
60 - 64	ESDF	1 758	804	953	...	...	...	...	...	...
65 - 69	ESDF	1 679	724	955	...	...	...	...	...	...
70 - 74	ESDF	1 511	652	859	...	...	...	...	...	...
75 - 79	ESDF	1 123	463	660	...	...	...	...	...	...
80+	ESDF	1 212	430	782	...	...	...	...	...	...
Aruba										
31 XII 1997										
Total	ESDJ	91 363	45 349	46 014	...	...	...	...	...	...

7. Population by age, sex and urban/rural residence: latest available year, 1992 - 2001
Population selon l'âge, le sexe et la résidence, urbaine/rurale: dernière année disponible, 1992 - 2001
(continued — suite)

(See notes at end of table. — Voir notes à la fin du tableau.)

Continent, country or area, date and age (in years) / Continent, pays ou zone, date et âge (en années)	Code[1]	Total			Urban - Urbaine			Rural - Rurale		
		Both sexes Les deux sexes	Male Masculin	Female Féminin	Both sexes Les deux sexes	Male Masculin	Female Féminin	Both sexes Les deux sexes	Male Masculin	Female Féminin
AMERICA, NORTH — AMERIQUE DU NORD										
Aruba										
31 XII 1997										
0 - 4	ESDJ	7 249	3 758	3 491	...	...	...	...	...	...
5 - 9	ESDJ	7 005	3 594	3 411	...	...	...	...	...	...
10 - 14	ESDJ	6 573	3 373	3 200	...	...	...	...	...	...
15 - 19	ESDJ	5 783	2 980	2 803	...	...	...	...	...	...
20 - 24	ESDJ	6 128	3 123	3 005	...	...	...	...	...	...
25 - 29	ESDJ	7 798	3 939	3 858	...	...	...	...	...	...
30 - 34	ESDJ	8 874	4 464	4 409	...	...	...	...	...	...
35 - 39	ESDJ	8 882	4 445	4 437	...	...	...	...	...	...
40 - 44	ESDJ	7 957	3 928	4 029	...	...	...	...	...	...
45 - 49	ESDJ	6 548	3 214	3 334	...	...	...	...	...	...
50 - 54	ESDJ	5 130	2 479	2 651	...	...	...	...	...	...
55 - 59	ESDJ	4 084	1 937	2 147	...	...	...	...	...	...
60 - 64	ESDJ	3 144	1 462	1 682	...	...	...	...	...	...
65 - 69	ESDJ	2 265	1 039	1 225	...	...	...	...	...	...
70 - 74	ESDJ	1 573	698	875	...	...	...	...	...	...
75 - 79	ESDJ	1 020	419	601	...	...	...	...	...	...
80 - 84	ESDJ	664	253	411	...	...	...	...	...	...
85 - 89	ESDJ	386	135	250	...	...	...	...	...	...
90 - 94	ESDJ	186	62	124	...	...	...	...	...	...
95+	ESDJ	115	46	69	...	...	...	...	...	...
Bahamas										
1 V 2000										
Total	CDFC	303 611	147 715	155 896	...	...	...	...	...	...
0 - 1	CDFC	5 908	2 929	2 979	...	...	...	...	...	...
1 - 4	CDFC	23 212	11 737	11 475	...	...	...	...	...	...
5 - 9	CDFC	31 648	16 014	15 634	...	...	...	...	...	...
10 - 14	CDFC	28 561	14 149	14 412	...	...	...	...	...	...
15 - 19	CDFC	26 439	13 355	13 084	...	...	...	...	...	...
20 - 24	CDFC	24 772	12 140	12 632	...	...	...	...	...	...
25 - 29	CDFC	26 904	13 110	13 794	...	...	...	...	...	...
30 - 34	CDFC	26 117	12 601	13 516	...	...	...	...	...	...
35 - 39	CDFC	25 887	12 438	13 449	...	...	...	...	...	...
40 - 44	CDFC	21 014	9 971	11 043	...	...	...	...	...	...
45 - 49	CDFC	15 827	7 617	8 210	...	...	...	...	...	...
50 - 54	CDFC	11 978	5 749	6 229	...	...	...	...	...	...
55 - 59	CDFC	10 142	4 768	5 374	...	...	...	...	...	...
60 - 64	CDFC	8 011	3 750	4 261	...	...	...	...	...	...
65 - 69	CDFC	5 806	2 651	3 155	...	...	...	...	...	...
70 - 74	CDFC	4 072	1 689	2 383	...	...	...	...	...	...
75 - 79	CDFC	2 615	1 039	1 576	...	...	...	...	...	...
80 - 84	CDFC	1 919	714	1 205	...	...	...	...	...	...
85 - 89	CDFC	914	293	621	...	...	...	...	...	...
90+	CDFC	451	137	314	...	...	...	...	...	...
Unk. - Inc.	CDFC	1 414	864	550	...	...	...	...	...	...
Belize										
1 VII 1998										
Total	ESDF	238 500	118 500	120 000	...	...	...	...	...	...
0 - 4	ESDF	35 955	18 310	17 645	...	...	...	...	...	...
5 - 9	ESDF	33 205	16 840	16 365	...	...	...	...	...	...
10 - 14	ESDF	29 050	14 890	14 160	...	...	...	...	...	...
15 - 19	ESDF	28 235	14 095	14 140	...	...	...	...	...	...
20 - 24	ESDF	19 185	9 385	9 800	...	...	...	...	...	...
25 - 29	ESDF	15 810	7 185	8 625	...	...	...	...	...	...
30 - 34	ESDF	15 260	7 065	8 195	...	...	...	...	...	...
35 - 39	ESDF	14 120	6 715	7 405	...	...	...	...	...	...
40 - 44	ESDF	10 500	5 205	5 295	...	...	...	...	...	...

7. Population by age, sex and urban/rural residence: latest available year, 1992 - 2001
Population selon l'âge, le sexe et la résidence, urbaine/rurale: dernière année disponible, 1992 - 2001
(continued — suite)

(See notes at end of table. — Voir notes à la fin du tableau.)

Continent, country or area, date and age (in years) / Continent, pays ou zone, date et âge (en annèes)	Code[1]	Total			Urban - Urbaine			Rural - Rurale		
		Both sexes Les deux sexes	Male Masculin	Female Féminin	Both sexes Les deux sexes	Male Masculin	Female Féminin	Both sexes Les deux sexes	Male Masculin	Female Féminin
AMERICA, NORTH — AMERIQUE DU NORD										
Belize										
1 VII 1998										
45 - 49	ESDF	*8 350*	*4 275*	*4 075*	...	...	...	...	...	...
50 - 54	ESDF	*6 940*	*3 575*	*3 365*	...	...	...	...	...	...
55 - 59	ESDF	*5 725*	*2 950*	*2 775*	...	...	...	...	...	...
60 - 64	ESDF	*4 975*	*2 475*	*2 500*	...	...	...	...	...	...
65 - 69	ESDF	*3 985*	*1 910*	*2 075*	...	...	...	...	...	...
70 - 74	ESDF	*2 900*	*1 695*	*1 205*	...	...	...	...	...	...
75 - 79	ESDF	*1 805*	*825*	*980*	...	...	...	...	...	...
80 - 84	ESDF	*1 255*	*600*	*655*	...	...	...	...	...	...
85+	ESDF	*1 245*	*505*	*740*	...	...	...	...	...	...
Bermuda - Bermudes[7]										
1 VII 1997										
Total	ESDJ	60 331	29 210	31 122	...	...	...	...	...	...
0 - 4	ESDJ	4 020	1 979	2 042	...	...	...	...	...	...
5 - 9	ESDJ	4 041	2 012	2 028	...	...	...	...	...	...
10 - 14	ESDJ	3 822	1 935	1 887	...	...	...	...	...	...
15 - 19	ESDJ	3 387	1 689	1 699	...	...	...	...	...	...
20 - 24	ESDJ	4 077	2 063	2 015	...	...	...	...	...	...
25 - 29	ESDJ	5 502	2 802	2 700	...	...	...	...	...	...
30 - 34	ESDJ	5 938	2 952	2 986	...	...	...	...	...	...
35 - 39	ESDJ	5 600	2 766	2 834	...	...	...	...	...	...
40 - 44	ESDJ	4 866	2 316	2 549	...	...	...	...	...	...
45 - 49	ESDJ	4 140	2 009	2 131	...	...	...	...	...	...
50 - 54	ESDJ	3 333	1 597	1 736	...	...	...	...	...	...
55 - 59	ESDJ	2 821	1 335	1 487	...	...	...	...	...	...
60 - 64	ESDJ	2 629	1 250	1 378	...	...	...	...	...	...
65 - 69	ESDJ	2 154	967	1 188	...	...	...	...	...	...
70 - 74	ESDJ	1 691	702	989	...	...	...	...	...	...
75 - 79	ESDJ	1 109	426	684	...	...	...	...	...	...
80+	ESDJ	1 199	409	790	...	...	...	...	...	...
Canada[2]										
15 V 2001										
Total	CDJC	30 007 090	14 706 850	15 300 240	...	...	...	...	...	...
0 - 1	CDJC	317 455	162 700	154 750	...	...	...	...	...	...
1 - 4	CDJC	1 378 825	705 415	673 455	...	...	...	...	...	...
5 - 9	CDJC	1 976 135	1 011 470	964 670	...	...	...	...	...	...
10 - 14	CDJC	2 053 125	1 051 445	1 001 645	...	...	...	...	...	...
15 - 19	CDJC	2 053 325	1 052 150	1 001 180	...	...	...	...	...	...
20 - 24	CDJC	1 955 815	982 280	973 525	...	...	...	...	...	...
25 - 29	CDJC	1 898 185	935 510	962 685	...	...	...	...	...	...
30 - 34	CDJC	2 096 750	1 031 255	1 065 475	...	...	...	...	...	...
35 - 39	CDJC	2 522 850	1 245 005	1 277 860	...	...	...	...	...	...
40 - 44	CDJC	2 578 765	1 271 725	1 307 045	...	...	...	...	...	...
45 - 49	CDJC	2 333 530	1 151 155	1 182 380	...	...	...	...	...	...
50 - 54	CDJC	2 085 770	1 033 360	1 052 395	...	...	...	...	...	...
55 - 59	CDJC	1 594 235	789 205	805 030	...	...	...	...	...	...
60 - 64	CDJC	1 273 780	621 565	652 205	...	...	...	...	...	...
65 - 69	CDJC	1 133 625	543 820	589 800	...	...	...	...	...	...
70 - 74	CDJC	1 009 215	461 780	547 425	...	...	...	...	...	...
75 - 79	CDJC	813 670	338 820	474 845	...	...	...	...	...	...
80 - 84	CDJC	516 140	192 645	323 490	...	...	...	...	...	...
85 - 89	CDJC	281 795	91 440	190 355	...	...	...	...	...	...
90 - 94	CDJC	105 095	28 020	77 075	...	...	...	...	...	...
95 - 99	CDJC	25 225	5 380	19 845	...	...	...	...	...	...
100+	CDJC	3 795	740	3 055	...	...	...	...	...	...

7. Population by age, sex and urban/rural residence: latest available year, 1992 - 2001
Population selon l'âge, le sexe et la résidence, urbaine/rurale: dernière année disponible, 1992 - 2001
(continued — suite)

(See notes at end of table. — Voir notes à la fin du tableau.)

Continent, country or area, date and age (in years) / Continent, pays ou zone, date et âge (en années)	Code[1]	Total			Urban - Urbaine			Rural - Rurale		
		Both sexes Les deux sexes	Male Masculin	Female Féminin	Both sexes Les deux sexes	Male Masculin	Female Féminin	Both sexes Les deux sexes	Male Masculin	Female Féminin
AMERICA, NORTH — AMERIQUE DU NORD										
Costa Rica										
1 VII 1998										
Total	ESDJ	3 340 909	1 662 735	1 678 174	1 440 272	693 376	746 896	1 900 637	969 359	931 278
0 - 4	ESDJ	330 080	171 391	158 689	123 359	61 585	61 774	206 721	109 806	96 915
5 - 9	ESDJ	367 842	185 671	182 171	138 355	72 631	65 724	229 487	113 040	116 447
10 - 14	ESDJ	376 707	192 290	184 417	142 370	70 194	72 176	234 337	122 096	112 241
15 - 19	ESDJ	338 969	175 655	163 314	143 411	71 428	71 983	195 558	104 227	91 331
20 - 24	ESDJ	281 060	140 235	140 825	133 999	67 538	66 461	147 061	72 697	74 364
25 - 29	ESDJ	254 773	128 366	126 407	111 689	56 116	55 573	143 084	72 250	70 834
30 - 39	ESDJ	495 595	237 298	258 297	208 495	100 113	108 382	287 100	137 185	149 915
40 - 49	ESDJ	367 004	179 883	187 121	172 826	77 748	95 078	194 178	102 135	92 043
50 - 59	ESDJ	233 207	112 649	120 558	114 478	51 086	63 392	118 729	61 563	57 166
60 - 69	ESDJ	157 077	73 739	83 338	80 933	35 025	45 908	76 144	38 714	37 430
70+	ESDJ	132 966	63 457	69 509	67 095	28 850	38 245	65 871	34 607	31 264
Unk. - Inc.	ESDJ	5 629	2 101	3 528	3 262	1 062	2 200	2 367	1 039	1 328
26 VI 2000										
Total	CDJC	3 810 179	1 902 614	1 907 565	...	...	...	...	...	...
0 - 4	CDJC	376 584	192 287	184 297	...	...	...	...	...	...
5 - 9	CDJC	411 204	210 443	200 761	...	...	...	...	...	...
10 - 14	CDJC	429 019	219 467	209 552	...	...	...	...	...	...
15 - 19	CDJC	392 063	198 561	193 502	...	...	...	...	...	...
20 - 24	CDJC	342 728	171 679	171 049	...	...	...	...	...	...
25 - 29	CDJC	295 752	146 407	149 345	...	...	...	...	...	...
30 - 34	CDJC	296 738	146 377	150 361	...	...	...	...	...	...
35 - 39	CDJC	288 790	141 138	147 652	...	...	...	...	...	...
40 - 44	CDJC	241 262	118 853	122 409	...	...	...	...	...	...
45 - 49	CDJC	183 629	90 323	93 306	...	...	...	...	...	...
50 - 54	CDJC	146 024	71 727	74 297	...	...	...	...	...	...
55 - 59	CDJC	104 912	51 519	53 393	...	...	...	...	...	...
60 - 64	CDJC	88 142	43 089	45 053	...	...	...	...	...	...
65 - 69	CDJC	71 650	34 555	37 095	...	...	...	...	...	...
70 - 74	CDJC	57 641	27 765	29 876	...	...	...	...	...	...
75+	CDJC	84 041	38 424	45 617	...	...	...	...	...	...
Cuba										
1 VII 2000										
Total	ESDF	11 198 600	5 596 057	5 602 543	8 426 270	4 124 048	4 302 222	2 772 330	1 472 009	1 300 321
0 - 1	ESDF	146 483	75 608	70 875	106 254	54 826	51 428	40 229	20 782	19 447
1 - 4	ESDF	591 828	305 264	286 564	431 608	222 629	208 979	160 220	82 635	77 585
5 - 9	ESDF	786 471	404 878	381 593	572 393	294 190	278 203	214 078	110 688	103 390
10 - 14	ESDF	875 687	449 891	425 796	645 522	330 213	315 309	230 165	119 678	110 487
15 - 19	ESDF	750 005	382 025	367 980	552 436	279 450	272 986	197 569	102 575	94 994
20 - 24	ESDF	743 256	377 416	365 840	537 228	269 514	267 714	206 028	107 902	98 126
25 - 29	ESDF	1 037 088	521 620	515 468	755 893	374 015	381 878	281 195	147 605	133 590
30 - 34	ESDF	1 100 253	549 798	550 455	816 433	398 931	417 502	283 820	150 867	132 953
35 - 39	ESDF	1 038 271	514 601	523 670	804 045	390 074	413 971	234 226	124 527	109 699
40 - 44	ESDF	697 595	343 794	353 801	535 532	257 552	277 980	162 063	86 242	75 821
45 - 49	ESDF	691 144	340 795	350 349	536 245	257 949	278 296	154 899	82 846	72 053
50 - 54	ESDF	627 782	306 518	321 264	491 285	234 650	256 635	136 497	71 868	64 629
55 - 59	ESDF	540 310	266 888	273 422	422 112	203 137	218 975	118 198	63 751	54 447
60 - 64	ESDF	456 719	225 248	231 471	354 509	168 804	185 705	102 210	56 444	45 766
65 - 74	ESDF	633 747	309 967	323 780	489 475	227 721	261 754	144 272	82 246	62 026
75 - 84	ESDF	357 509	167 545	189 964	278 949	122 097	156 852	78 560	45 448	33 112
85+	ESDF	124 452	54 201	70 251	96 351	38 296	58 055	28 101	15 905	12 196
Dominica - Dominique										
31 XII 1998										
Total	ESDF	75 971	38 665	37 306	...	...	...	...	...	...
0 - 4	ESDF	8 085	4 115	3 970	...	...	...	...	...	...

7. Population by age, sex and urban/rural residence: latest available year, 1992 - 2001
Population selon l'âge, le sexe et la résidence, urbaine/rurale: dernière année disponible, 1992 - 2001
(continued — suite)

(See notes at end of table. — Voir notes à la fin du tableau.)

Continent, country or area, date and age (in years) / Continent, pays ou zone, date et âge (en années)	Code[1]	Total			Urban - Urbaine			Rural - Rurale		
		Both sexes Les deux sexes	Male Masculin	Female Féminin	Both sexes Les deux sexes	Male Masculin	Female Féminin	Both sexes Les deux sexes	Male Masculin	Female Féminin
AMERICA, NORTH — AMERIQUE DU NORD										
Dominica - Dominique										
31 XII 1998										
5 - 9	ESDF	8 721	4 413	4 308	...	...	...	...	...	...
10 - 14	ESDF	8 549	4 307	4 242	...	...	...	...	...	...
15 - 19	ESDF	7 945	4 124	3 821	...	...	...	...	...	...
20 - 24	ESDF	7 263	3 682	3 581	...	...	...	...	...	...
25 - 29	ESDF	6 158	3 296	2 862	...	...	...	...	...	...
30 - 34	ESDF	5 285	2 861	2 424	...	...	...	...	...	...
35 - 39	ESDF	4 131	2 233	1 898	...	...	...	...	...	...
40 - 44	ESDF	3 146	1 639	1 507	...	...	...	...	...	...
45 - 49	ESDF	2 658	1 374	1 284	...	...	...	...	...	...
50 - 54	ESDF	2 242	1 094	1 148	...	...	...	...	...	...
55 - 59	ESDF	2 153	1 011	1 142	...	...	...	...	...	...
60 - 64	ESDF	2 331	1 063	1 268	...	...	...	...	...	...
65 - 69	ESDF	2 154	1 052	1 102	...	...	...	...	...	...
70 - 74	ESDF	1 837	867	970	...	...	...	...	...	...
75 - 79	ESDF	1 417	678	739	...	...	...	...	...	...
80 - 84	ESDF	916	466	450	...	...	...	...	...	...
85+	ESDF	653	252	401	...	...	...	...	...	...
Unk. - Inc.	ESDF	327	138	189	...	...	...	...	...	...
Dominican Republic - République dominicaine										
1 VII 1995										
Total	ESDF	7 915 321	4 023 015	3 892 306	4 881 102	2 411 347	2 469 755	3 034 219	1 611 668	1 422 551
0 - 4	ESDF	996 573	507 476	489 097	588 141	298 800	289 341	408 432	208 676	199 756
5 - 9	ESDF	967 749	492 012	475 737	584 911	295 943	288 968	382 838	196 069	186 769
10 - 14	ESDF	904 707	459 734	444 973	537 560	270 978	266 582	367 148	188 757	178 391
15 - 19	ESDF	801 256	407 795	393 461	455 435	225 757	229 678	345 821	182 038	163 783
20 - 24	ESDF	748 440	381 701	366 739	449 740	223 909	225 831	298 700	157 792	140 908
25 - 29	ESDF	711 809	363 168	348 641	450 014	221 671	228 343	261 795	141 497	120 298
30 - 34	ESDF	631 345	321 798	309 547	414 605	203 401	211 204	216 740	118 397	98 343
35 - 39	ESDF	511 345	260 956	250 389	334 141	162 580	171 561	177 204	98 376	78 828
40 - 44	ESDF	400 507	205 055	195 452	258 532	125 072	133 460	141 975	79 983	61 992
45 - 49	ESDF	319 318	163 488	155 830	205 582	99 004	106 578	113 736	64 484	49 252
50 - 54	ESDF	249 286	127 076	122 210	166 209	80 001	86 208	83 077	47 075	36 002
55 - 59	ESDF	204 709	103 490	101 219	138 491	66 113	72 378	66 218	37 377	28 841
60 - 64	ESDF	163 452	81 041	82 411	109 207	50 777	58 430	54 245	30 264	23 981
65 - 69	ESDF	133 491	66 557	66 934	87 565	41 569	45 996	45 926	24 988	20 938
70 - 74	ESDF	79 588	38 926	40 662	45 173	20 948	24 225	34 414	17 977	16 437
75+	ESDF	91 746	42 742	49 004	55 796	24 824	30 972	35 950	17 918	18 032
El Salvador										
1 VII 2000										
Total	ESDF	6 276 037	3 080 704	3 195 333	3 665 747	1 761 327	1 904 420	2 610 290	1 319 377	1 290 913
0 - 1	ESDF	162 796	83 228	79 568	81 714	41 818	39 896	81 082	41 410	39 672
1 - 4	ESDF	634 364	323 642	310 722	347 269	176 918	170 351	287 095	146 724	140 371
5 - 9	ESDF	750 980	382 228	368 752	420 528	213 104	207 424	330 452	169 124	161 328
10 - 14	ESDF	685 981	348 284	337 697	359 569	180 791	178 778	326 412	167 493	158 919
15 - 19	ESDF	657 838	333 172	324 666	353 627	175 761	177 866	304 211	157 411	146 800
20 - 24	ESDF	675 749	339 998	335 751	382 307	186 592	195 715	293 442	153 406	140 036
25 - 29	ESDF	568 713	280 518	288 195	345 147	165 088	180 059	223 566	115 430	108 136
30 - 34	ESDF	439 544	207 031	232 513	283 100	130 033	153 067	156 444	76 998	79 446
35 - 39	ESDF	335 969	153 285	182 684	225 871	101 931	123 940	110 098	51 354	58 744
40 - 44	ESDF	292 475	134 591	157 884	191 221	86 574	104 647	101 254	48 017	53 237
45 - 49	ESDF	244 556	114 945	129 611	155 378	71 761	83 617	89 178	43 184	45 994
50 - 54	ESDF	210 268	99 860	110 408	130 442	60 868	69 574	79 826	38 992	40 834
55 - 59	ESDF	165 099	78 434	86 665	100 899	46 636	54 263	64 200	31 798	32 402

7. Population by age, sex and urban/rural residence: latest available year, 1992 - 2001
Population selon l'âge, le sexe et la résidence, urbaine/rurale: dernière année disponible, 1992 - 2001
(continued — suite)

(See notes at end of table. — Voir notes à la fin du tableau.)

Continent, country or area, date and age (in years) / Continent, pays ou zone, date et âge (en annèes)	Code[1]	Total			Urban - Urbaine			Rural - Rurale		
		Both sexes Les deux sexes	Male Masculin	Female Féminin	Both sexes Les deux sexes	Male Masculin	Female Féminin	Both sexes Les deux sexes	Male Masculin	Female Féminin
AMERICA, NORTH — AMERIQUE DU NORD										
El Salvador										
1 VII 2000										
60 - 64	ESDF	139 257	65 373	73 884	84 728	38 290	46 438	54 529	27 083	27 446
65 - 69	ESDF	117 414	54 043	63 371	71 968	31 621	40 347	45 446	22 422	23 024
70 - 74	ESDF	88 776	39 587	49 189	55 730	23 881	31 849	33 046	15 706	17 340
75 - 79	ESDF	45 080	18 998	26 082	29 330	11 955	17 375	36 577	16 413	20 164
80+	ESDF	47 043	17 359	29 684	37 861	13 904	23 957	9 182	3 455	5 727
Greenland - Groenland										
1 VII 2000										
Total	ESDJ	56 184	30 029	26 210	45 821	24 310	21 511	10 364	5 697	4 667
0 - 1	ESDJ	843	421	422	654	325	329	190	96	94
1 - 4	ESDJ	3 966	2 022	1 944	3 097	1 603	1 497	869	420	450
5 - 9	ESDJ	5 339	2 713	2 627	4 203	2 156	2 047	1 137	558	580
10 - 14	ESDJ	5 007	2 518	2 491	4 023	2 024	1 999	984	494	492
15 - 19	ESDJ	3 982	2 064	1 921	3 313	1 684	1 629	670	380	292
20 - 24	ESDJ	3 387	1 748	1 641	2 804	1 421	1 383	584	327	258
25 - 29	ESDJ	3 432	1 854	1 579	2 745	1 485	1 263	688	370	319
30 - 34	ESDJ	5 669	3 034	2 635	4 671	2 465	2 207	1 000	570	430
35 - 39	ESDJ	5 933	3 180	2 754	4 936	2 610	2 326	998	570	429
40 - 44	ESDJ	4 775	2 723	2 052	3 975	2 238	1 737	801	488	315
45 - 49	ESDJ	3 704	2 114	1 590	3 088	1 746	1 343	617	368	249
50 - 54	ESDJ	2 949	1 796	1 154	2 465	1 483	983	485	315	172
55 - 59	ESDJ	2 667	1 573	1 094	2 202	1 285	918	466	291	177
60 - 64	ESDJ	1 715	964	752	1 360	759	601	355	205	152
65 - 69	ESDJ	1 291	651	641	1 041	530	512	251	123	129
70 - 74	ESDJ	878	398	481	711	318	396	168	83	85
75 - 79	ESDJ	392	165	227	316	127	190	77	40	37
80 - 84	ESDJ	190	65	126	160	55	106	31	13	20
85 - 89	ESDJ	70	18	54	59	16	46	11	4	9
90 - 94	ESDJ	20	5	16	18	4	15	3	1	2
95+	ESDJ	3	3	...	2	2	...	1	1	...
Grenada - Grenade										
1 VII 2000										
Total	ESDF	101 308	50 200	51 108	...	...	...	...	...	...
0 - 4	ESDF	10 412	5 292	5 120	...	...	...	...	...	...
5 - 9	ESDF	11 547	5 798	5 749	...	...	...	...	...	...
10 - 14	ESDF	13 546	6 837	6 709	...	...	...	...	...	...
15 - 19	ESDF	11 911	6 077	5 834	...	...	...	...	...	...
20 - 24	ESDF	9 267	4 686	4 581	...	...	...	...	...	...
25 - 29	ESDF	7 290	3 883	3 407	...	...	...	...	...	...
30 - 34	ESDF	5 977	2 999	2 978	...	...	...	...	...	...
35 - 39	ESDF	6 537	3 294	3 243	...	...	...	...	...	...
40 - 44	ESDF	5 364	2 628	2 736	...	...	...	...	...	...
45 - 49	ESDF	3 780	1 955	1 825	...	...	...	...	...	...
50 - 54	ESDF	2 904	1 371	1 533	...	...	...	...	...	...
55 - 59	ESDF	2 472	1 160	1 312	...	...	...	...	...	...
60 - 64	ESDF	2 383	1 078	1 305	...	...	...	...	...	...
65 - 69	ESDF	2 356	1 010	1 346	...	...	...	...	...	...
70+	ESDF	5 562	2 132	3 430	...	...	...	...	...	...
Guadeloupe[8]										
1 I 1992										
Total	ESDJ	368 796	178 422	190 374	...	...	...	...	...	...
0 - 4	ESDJ	33 171	16 639	16 532	...	...	...	...	...	...
5 - 9	ESDJ	32 611	16 379	16 232	...	...	...	...	...	...
10 - 14	ESDJ	31 476	15 894	15 582	...	...	...	...	...	...
15 - 19	ESDJ	38 154	19 494	18 660	...	...	...	...	...	...
20 - 24	ESDJ	31 712	15 307	16 405	...	...	...	...	...	...

7. Population by age, sex and urban/rural residence: latest available year, 1992 - 2001
Population selon l'âge, le sexe et la résidence, urbaine/rurale: dernière année disponible, 1992 - 2001
(continued — suite)

(See notes at end of table. — Voir notes à la fin du tableau.)

Continent, country or area, date and age (in years) / Continent, pays ou zone, date et âge (en annèes)	Code[1]	Total			Urban - Urbaine			Rural - Rurale		
		Both sexes Les deux sexes	Male Masculin	Female Féminin	Both sexes Les deux sexes	Male Masculin	Female Féminin	Both sexes Les deux sexes	Male Masculin	Female Féminin
AMERICA, NORTH — AMERIQUE DU NORD										
Guadeloupe[8]										
1 I 1992										
25 - 29	ESDJ	32 906	16 051	16 855	...	...	...	...	...	...
30 - 34	ESDJ	29 320	14 452	14 868	...	...	...	...	...	...
35 - 39	ESDJ	25 375	11 881	13 494	...	...	...	...	...	...
40 - 44	ESDJ	22 614	10 690	11 924	...	...	...	...	...	...
45 - 49	ESDJ	18 055	8 721	9 334	...	...	...	...	...	...
50 - 54	ESDJ	14 841	7 098	7 743	...	...	...	...	...	...
55 - 59	ESDJ	14 042	6 584	7 458	...	...	...	...	...	...
60 - 64	ESDJ	12 032	5 526	6 506	...	...	...	...	...	...
65 - 69	ESDJ	11 044	5 022	6 022	...	...	...	...	...	...
70 - 74	ESDJ	8 553	3 874	4 679	...	...	...	...	...	...
75 - 79	ESDJ	5 947	2 420	3 527	...	...	...	...	...	...
80 - 84	ESDJ	3 883	1 487	2 396	...	...	...	...	...	...
85 - 89	ESDJ	1 966	655	1 311	...	...	...	...	...	...
90+	ESDJ	1 094	248	846	...	...	...	...	...	...
Guatemala										
1 VII 2001										
Total	ESDF	11 678 411	5 888 426	5 789 985	...	...	...	...	...	...
0 - 1	ESDF	387 025	197 549	189 476	...	...	...	...	...	...
1 - 4	ESDF	1 484 040	757 626	726 414	...	...	...	...	...	...
5 - 9	ESDF	1 689 604	862 809	826 795	...	...	...	...	...	...
10 - 14	ESDF	1 495 114	763 539	731 575	...	...	...	...	...	...
15 - 19	ESDF	1 320 329	673 506	646 823	...	...	...	...	...	...
20 - 24	ESDF	1 110 418	562 982	547 436	...	...	...	...	...	...
25 - 29	ESDF	894 268	449 807	444 461	...	...	...	...	...	...
30 - 34	ESDF	708 522	351 762	356 760	...	...	...	...	...	...
35 - 39	ESDF	571 673	281 068	290 605	...	...	...	...	...	...
40 - 44	ESDF	462 850	226 817	236 033	...	...	...	...	...	...
45 - 49	ESDF	386 977	190 123	196 854	...	...	...	...	...	...
50 - 54	ESDF	306 124	150 654	155 470	...	...	...	...	...	...
55 - 59	ESDF	244 215	121 084	123 131	...	...	...	...	...	...
60 - 64	ESDF	201 985	100 065	101 920	...	...	...	...	...	...
65 - 69	ESDF	166 701	81 453	85 248	...	...	...	...	...	...
70 - 74	ESDF	122 040	58 725	63 315	...	...	...	...	...	...
75 - 79	ESDF	74 787	35 391	39 396	...	...	...	...	...	...
80+	ESDF	51 739	23 466	28 273	...	...	...	...	...	...
Haiti - Haïti										
1 VII 1999										
Total	ESDJ	7 803 232	3 834 240	3 968 992	2 731 843	1 234 809	1 497 034	5 071 389	2 599 431	2 471 958
0 - 1	ESDJ	242 106	122 835	119 271	68 885	36 499	32 386	173 221	86 336	86 885
1 - 4	ESDJ	913 669	462 018	451 651	252 773	130 783	121 990	660 896	331 235	329 661
5 - 9	ESDJ	1 034 513	521 302	513 211	321 389	154 420	166 969	713 124	366 882	346 242
10 - 14	ESDJ	925 920	466 007	459 913	363 812	161 340	202 472	562 108	304 667	257 441
15 - 19	ESDJ	810 881	407 544	403 337	375 052	156 361	218 691	435 829	251 183	184 646
20 - 24	ESDJ	696 906	347 026	349 880	337 696	153 000	184 696	359 210	194 026	165 184
25 - 29	ESDJ	612 995	301 403	311 592	272 739	124 048	148 691	340 256	177 355	162 901
30 - 34	ESDJ	526 616	255 640	270 976	198 846	88 085	110 761	327 770	167 555	160 215
35 - 39	ESDJ	452 327	216 102	236 225	135 215	57 299	77 916	317 112	158 803	158 309
40 - 44	ESDJ	370 430	173 392	197 038	106 911	42 010	64 901	263 519	131 382	132 137
45 - 49	ESDJ	306 075	141 518	164 557	71 946	29 912	42 034	234 129	111 606	122 523
50 - 54	ESDJ	247 324	114 254	133 070	70 080	31 126	38 954	177 244	83 128	94 116
55 - 59	ESDJ	201 858	93 663	108 195	51 060	22 494	28 566	150 798	71 169	79 629
60 - 64	ESDJ	161 143	74 625	86 518	40 580	18 949	21 631	120 563	55 676	64 887
65 - 69	ESDJ	122 392	56 450	65 942	28 310	12 719	15 591	94 082	43 731	50 351
70 - 74	ESDJ	84 796	38 744	46 052	18 717	7 726	10 991	66 079	31 018	35 061
75 - 79	ESDJ	52 884	23 831	29 053	11 309	5 008	6 301	41 575	18 823	22 752
80+	ESDJ	40 397	17 886	22 511	6 523	3 030	3 493	33 874	14 856	19 018

7. Population by age, sex and urban/rural residence: latest available year, 1992 - 2001
Population selon l'âge, le sexe et la résidence, urbaine/rurale: dernière année disponible, 1992 - 2001
(continued — suite)

(See notes at end of table. — Voir notes à la fin du tableau.)

Continent, country or area, date and age (in years) / Continent, pays ou zone, date et âge (en années)	Code[1]	Total			Urban - Urbaine			Rural - Rurale		
		Both sexes Les deux sexes	Male Masculin	Female Féminin	Both sexes Les deux sexes	Male Masculin	Female Féminin	Both sexes Les deux sexes	Male Masculin	Female Féminin

AMERICA, NORTH — AMERIQUE DU NORD

Jamaica - Jamaïque
1 VII 1999

Total	ESDF	2 590 400	...	...	...	...	...	...	...	...
0 - 1	ESDF	56 428	...	...	...	...	...	...	...	...
1 - 4	ESDF	231 253	...	...	...	...	...	...	...	...
5 - 9	ESDF	266 869	...	...	...	...	...	...	...	...
10 - 14	ESDF	253 969	...	...	...	...	...	...	...	...
15 - 19	ESDF	247 768	...	...	...	...	...	...	...	...
20 - 24	ESDF	229 838	...	...	...	...	...	...	...	...
25 - 29	ESDF	229 441	...	...	...	...	...	...	...	...
30 - 34	ESDF	212 731	...	...	...	...	...	...	...	...
35 - 39	ESDF	190 099	...	...	...	...	...	...	...	...
40 - 44	ESDF	148 391	...	...	...	...	...	...	...	...
45 - 49	ESDF	109 839	...	...	...	...	...	...	...	...
50 - 54	ESDF	90 839	...	...	...	...	...	...	...	...
55 - 59	ESDF	74 092	...	...	...	...	...	...	...	...
60 - 64	ESDF	64 508	...	...	...	...	...	...	...	...
65 - 69	ESDF	58 754	...	...	...	...	...	...	...	...
70 - 74	ESDF	47 655	...	...	...	...	...	...	...	...
75+	ESDF	77 926	...	...	...	...	...	...	...	...

Martinique[8]
1 I 1992

Total	ESDJ	370 756	178 697	192 059	...	...	...	...	...	...
0 - 4	ESDJ	31 450	15 775	15 675	...	...	...	...	...	...
5 - 9	ESDJ	29 990	15 105	14 885	...	...	...	...	...	...
10 - 14	ESDJ	28 351	14 459	13 892	...	...	...	...	...	...
15 - 19	ESDJ	32 600	16 655	15 945	...	...	...	...	...	...
20 - 24	ESDJ	33 178	16 325	16 853	...	...	...	...	...	...
25 - 29	ESDJ	34 662	16 777	17 885	...	...	...	...	...	...
30 - 34	ESDJ	31 730	15 582	16 148	...	...	...	...	...	...
35 - 39	ESDJ	25 855	12 163	13 692	...	...	...	...	...	...
40 - 44	ESDJ	21 953	10 228	11 725	...	...	...	...	...	...
45 - 49	ESDJ	18 275	8 664	9 611	...	...	...	...	...	...
50 - 54	ESDJ	16 163	7 510	8 653	...	...	...	...	...	...
55 - 59	ESDJ	15 760	7 451	8 309	...	...	...	...	...	...
60 - 64	ESDJ	14 147	6 634	7 513	...	...	...	...	...	...
65 - 69	ESDJ	12 251	5 575	6 676	...	...	...	...	...	...
70 - 74	ESDJ	9 243	4 093	5 150	...	...	...	...	...	...
75 - 79	ESDJ	6 973	2 906	4 067	...	...	...	...	...	...
80 - 84	ESDJ	4 534	1 680	2 854	...	...	...	...	...	...
85 - 89	ESDJ	2 375	800	1 575	...	...	...	...	...	...
90+	ESDJ	1 266	315	951	...	...	...	...	...	...

Mexico - Mexique
14 II 2000

Total	CDJC	97 483 412	47 592 253	49 891 159	72 759 822	35 317 569	37 442 253	24 723 590	12 274 684	12 448 906
0 - 1	CDJC	2 061 431	1 049 375	1 012 056	1 483 607	755 457	728 150	577 824	293 918	283 906
1 - 4	CDJC	8 573 726	4 351 931	4 221 795	6 105 143	3 102 158	3 002 985	2 468 583	1 249 773	1 218 810
5 - 9	CDJC	11 215 323	5 677 711	5 537 612	7 865 897	3 984 541	3 881 356	3 349 426	1 693 170	1 656 256
10 - 14	CDJC	10 736 493	5 435 737	5 300 756	7 487 732	3 782 974	3 704 758	3 248 761	1 652 763	1 595 998
15 - 19	CDJC	9 992 135	4 909 648	5 082 487	7 389 092	3 623 560	3 765 532	2 603 043	1 286 088	1 316 955
20 - 24	CDJC	9 071 134	4 303 600	4 767 534	7 019 039	3 337 619	3 681 420	2 052 095	965 981	1 086 114
25 - 29	CDJC	8 157 743	3 861 482	4 296 261	6 454 014	3 053 121	3 400 893	1 703 729	808 361	895 368
30 - 34	CDJC	7 136 523	3 383 356	3 753 167	5 666 844	2 677 805	2 989 039	1 469 679	705 551	764 128
35 - 39	CDJC	6 352 538	3 023 328	3 329 210	5 025 577	2 381 668	2 643 909	1 326 961	641 660	685 301
40 - 44	CDJC	5 194 833	2 494 771	2 700 062	4 115 978	1 964 652	2 151 326	1 078 855	530 119	548 736
45 - 49	CDJC	4 072 091	1 957 177	2 114 914	3 155 008	1 504 805	1 650 203	917 083	452 372	464 711
50 - 54	CDJC	3 357 953	1 624 033	1 733 920	2 572 644	1 229 440	1 343 204	785 309	394 593	390 716
55 - 59	CDJC	2 559 231	1 234 072	1 325 159	1 893 913	898 926	994 987	665 318	335 146	330 172

7. Population by age, sex and urban/rural residence: latest available year, 1992 - 2001
Population selon l'âge, le sexe et la résidence, urbaine/rurale: dernière année disponible, 1992 - 2001
(continued — suite)

(See notes at end of table. — Voir notes à la fin du tableau.)

Continent, country or area, date and age (in years) Continent, pays ou zone, date et âge (en annèes)	Code[1]	Total			Urban - Urbaine			Rural - Rurale		
		Both sexes Les deux sexes	Male Masculin	Female Féminin	Both sexes Les deux sexes	Male Masculin	Female Féminin	Both sexes Les deux sexes	Male Masculin	Female Féminin
AMERICA, NORTH — AMERIQUE DU NORD										
Mexico - Mexique										
14 II 2000										
60 - 64	CDJC	2 198 146	1 045 404	1 152 742	1 592 246	735 836	856 410	605 900	309 568	296 332
65 - 69	CDJC	1 660 785	779 666	881 119	1 195 245	543 243	652 002	465 540	236 423	229 117
70 - 74	CDJC	1 245 674	589 106	656 568	889 049	402 401	486 648	356 625	186 705	169 920
75 - 79	CDJC	865 270	411 197	454 073	615 380	279 475	335 905	249 890	131 722	118 168
80 - 84	CDJC	483 876	217 330	266 546	340 470	144 998	195 472	143 406	72 332	71 074
85 - 89	CDJC	290 051	125 041	165 010	205 307	83 091	122 216	84 744	41 950	42 794
90 - 94	CDJC	122 006	50 843	71 163	84 105	32 603	51 502	37 901	18 240	19 661
95 - 99	CDJC	62 892	25 741	37 151	41 381	15 751	25 630	21 511	9 990	11 521
100+	CDJC	19 757	8 029	11 728	11 635	4 566	7 069	8 122	3 463	4 659
Unk. - Inc.	CDJC	2 053 801	1 033 675	1 020 126	1 550 516	778 879	771 637	503 285	254 796	248 489
Netherlands Antilles - Antilles néerlandaises										
29 I 2001										
Total	CDJC	175 653	82 521	93 132	...	...	...	...	...	...
0 - 1	CDJC	2 587	1 352	1 235	...	...	...	...	...	...
1 - 4	CDJC	10 336	5 235	5 101	...	...	...	...	...	...
5 - 9	CDJC	15 020	7 545	7 475	...	...	...	...	...	...
10 - 14	CDJC	14 573	7 349	7 224	...	...	...	...	...	...
15 - 19	CDJC	12 765	6 317	6 448	...	...	...	...	...	...
20 - 24	CDJC	8 431	4 147	4 284	...	...	...	...	...	...
25 - 29	CDJC	10 722	4 929	5 793	...	...	...	...	...	...
30 - 34	CDJC	13 421	6 135	7 286	...	...	...	...	...	...
35 - 39	CDJC	15 935	7 212	8 723	...	...	...	...	...	...
40 - 44	CDJC	15 358	6 985	8 373	...	...	...	...	...	...
45 - 49	CDJC	13 331	5 981	7 350	...	...	...	...	...	...
50 - 54	CDJC	11 359	5 325	6 034	...	...	...	...	...	...
55 - 59	CDJC	8 653	3 969	4 684	...	...	...	...	...	...
60 - 64	CDJC	6 937	3 171	3 766	...	...	...	...	...	...
65 - 69	CDJC	5 583	2 591	2 992	...	...	...	...	...	...
70 - 74	CDJC	4 078	1 792	2 286	...	...	...	...	...	...
75 - 79	CDJC	3 003	1 261	1 742	...	...	...	...	...	...
80 - 84	CDJC	2 010	759	1 251	...	...	...	...	...	...
85 - 89	CDJC	932	293	639	...	...	...	...	...	...
90 - 94	CDJC	473	141	332	...	...	...	...	...	...
95+	CDJC	146	32	114	...	...	...	...	...	...
Nicaragua										
1 VII 2000										
Total	ESDJ	5 071 670	2 523 542	2 548 128	2 897 293	1 403 141	1 494 152	2 174 377	1 120 400	1 053 977
0 - 4	ESDJ	801 055	408 066	392 989	415 325	212 904	202 421	385 730	195 162	190 568
5 - 9	ESDJ	730 885	371 680	359 205	393 844	200 271	193 573	337 041	171 409	165 632
10 - 14	ESDJ	629 819	319 734	310 085	350 185	175 868	174 317	279 634	143 866	135 768
15 - 19	ESDJ	602 356	304 085	298 271	340 251	167 250	173 001	262 105	136 835	125 270
20 - 24	ESDJ	482 531	240 909	241 622	277 409	132 917	144 492	205 122	107 992	97 130
25 - 29	ESDJ	398 727	196 347	202 380	242 869	115 174	127 695	155 858	81 173	74 685
30 - 34	ESDJ	322 729	157 017	165 711	206 092	96 966	109 126	116 636	60 051	56 585
35 - 39	ESDJ	264 515	127 961	136 553	166 298	77 637	88 661	98 216	50 324	47 892
40 - 44	ESDJ	215 410	103 959	111 451	133 403	62 101	71 302	82 007	41 858	40 149
45 - 49	ESDJ	173 111	83 521	89 590	103 070	47 405	55 665	70 041	36 116	33 925
50 - 54	ESDJ	124 207	59 916	64 290	73 390	32 989	40 401	50 816	26 927	23 889
55 - 59	ESDJ	94 762	45 306	49 456	56 034	24 690	31 344	38 728	20 616	18 112
60 - 64	ESDJ	77 002	36 388	40 614	45 973	19 943	26 030	31 029	16 445	14 584
65 - 69	ESDJ	59 388	27 292	32 097	35 718	14 971	20 747	23 671	12 321	11 350
70 - 74	ESDJ	44 784	19 903	24 882	26 895	10 666	16 229	17 890	9 237	8 653
75 - 79	ESDJ	29 641	13 017	16 624	17 911	6 949	10 962	11 730	6 068	5 662
80+	ESDJ	20 749	8 440	12 309	12 626	4 440	8 186	8 123	4 000	4 123

7. Population by age, sex and urban/rural residence: latest available year, 1992 - 2001
Population selon l'âge, le sexe et la résidence, urbaine/rurale: dernière année disponible, 1992 - 2001
(continued — suite)

(See notes at end of table. — Voir notes à la fin du tableau.)

Continent, country or area, date and age (in years) / Continent, pays ou zone, date et âge (en annèes)	Code[1]	Total			Urban - Urbaine			Rural - Rurale		
		Both sexes Les deux sexes	Male Masculin	Female Féminin	Both sexes Les deux sexes	Male Masculin	Female Féminin	Both sexes Les deux sexes	Male Masculin	Female Féminin
AMERICA, NORTH — AMERIQUE DU NORD										
Panama										
1 VII 2000										
Total	ESDF	2 855 703	1 440 801	1 414 902	1 604 823	782 928	821 895	1 250 880	657 873	593 007
0 - 1	ESDF	59 949	30 595	29 354	30 248	15 460	14 788	29 701	15 135	14 566
1 - 4	ESDF	241 433	123 553	117 880	121 253	62 069	59 184	120 180	61 484	58 696
5 - 9	ESDF	300 852	153 986	146 866	150 849	77 061	73 786	150 003	76 925	73 079
10 - 14	ESDF	291 489	148 579	142 911	148 812	75 471	73 342	142 678	73 109	69 569
15 - 19	ESDF	271 684	137 805	133 878	146 537	73 631	72 906	125 147	64 174	60 974
20 - 24	ESDF	254 772	129 237	125 536	146 169	72 295	73 875	108 605	56 944	51 661
25 - 29	ESDF	250 152	125 922	124 230	150 336	71 923	78 413	99 816	53 999	45 817
30 - 34	ESDF	230 835	115 884	114 951	141 488	67 582	73 906	89 347	48 302	41 045
35 - 39	ESDF	203 446	101 421	102 025	126 268	59 890	66 378	77 178	41 531	35 647
40 - 44	ESDF	170 180	84 702	85 478	105 158	50 101	55 057	65 022	34 601	30 421
45 - 49	ESDF	140 684	70 369	70 315	86 739	41 477	45 262	53 945	28 892	25 053
50 - 54	ESDF	115 342	58 278	57 064	69 710	33 225	36 485	45 632	25 053	20 579
55 - 59	ESDF	93 684	47 379	46 305	53 771	25 760	28 011	39 913	21 619	18 294
60 - 64	ESDF	73 087	36 664	36 423	40 256	18 795	21 461	32 831	17 869	14 962
65 - 69	ESDF	55 236	27 712	27 524	30 061	13 914	16 147	25 175	13 798	11 377
70 - 74	ESDF	43 900	21 495	22 405	24 076	10 692	13 384	19 824	10 803	9 021
75 - 79	ESDF	30 250	14 158	16 092	17 010	7 216	9 794	13 240	6 942	6 298
80+	ESDF	28 727	13 063	15 664	16 083	6 367	9 716	12 644	6 696	5 948
Puerto Rico - Porto Rico[9]										
1 VII 2000										
Total	ESDJ	3 817 633	1 837 619	1 980 014	...	...	...	...	...	...
0 - 1	ESDJ	57 239	29 276	27 963	...	...	...	...	...	...
1 - 4	ESDJ	238 043	121 974	116 069	...	...	...	...	...	...
5 - 9	ESDJ	304 922	156 148	148 774	...	...	...	...	...	...
10 - 14	ESDJ	305 036	155 603	149 433	...	...	...	...	...	...
15 - 19	ESDJ	313 153	159 181	153 972	...	...	...	...	...	...
20 - 24	ESDJ	301 587	149 672	151 915	...	...	...	...	...	...
25 - 29	ESDJ	271 597	133 153	138 444	...	...	...	...	...	...
30 - 34	ESDJ	263 101	126 372	136 729	...	...	...	...	...	...
35 - 39	ESDJ	265 648	124 816	140 832	...	...	...	...	...	...
40 - 44	ESDJ	251 518	116 588	134 930	...	...	...	...	...	...
45 - 49	ESDJ	234 237	108 205	126 032	...	...	...	...	...	...
50 - 54	ESDJ	231 992	107 006	124 986	...	...	...	...	...	...
55 - 59	ESDJ	190 322	87 771	102 551	...	...	...	...	...	...
60 - 64	ESDJ	161 633	74 767	86 866	...	...	...	...	...	...
65 - 69	ESDJ	134 905	61 236	73 669	...	...	...	...	...	...
70 - 74	ESDJ	107 248	47 668	59 580	...	...	...	...	...	...
75 - 79	ESDJ	83 521	36 129	47 392	...	...	...	...	...	...
80 - 84	ESDJ	53 764	22 822	30 942	...	...	...	...	...	...
85+	ESDJ	48 167	19 232	28 935	...	...	...	...	...	...
Saint Kitts-Nevis - Saint-Kitts-et-Nevis										
1 VII 2000										
Total	ESDF	40 410	20 400	20 010	...	...	...	...	...	...
0 - 4	ESDF	4 250	2 130	2 120	...	...	...	...	...	...
5 - 9	ESDF	4 100	2 140	1 960	...	...	...	...	...	...
10 - 14	ESDF	4 040	2 120	1 920	...	...	...	...	...	...
15 - 19	ESDF	3 870	2 000	1 870	...	...	...	...	...	...
20 - 24	ESDF	3 620	1 880	1 740	...	...	...	...	...	...
25 - 29	ESDF	3 240	1 640	1 600	...	...	...	...	...	...
30 - 34	ESDF	3 100	1 550	1 550	...	...	...	...	...	...
35 - 39	ESDF	2 910	1 430	1 480	...	...	...	...	...	...
40 - 44	ESDF	2 520	1 270	1 250	...	...	...	...	...	...
45 - 49	ESDF	1 880	900	980	...	...	...	...	...	...

7. Population by age, sex and urban/rural residence: latest available year, 1992 - 2001
Population selon l'âge, le sexe et la résidence, urbaine/rurale: dernière année disponible, 1992 - 2001
(continued — suite)

(See notes at end of table. — Voir notes à la fin du tableau.)

Continent, country or area, date and age (in years) / Continent, pays ou zone, date et âge (en annèes)	Code[1]	Total			Urban - Urbaine			Rural - Rurale		
		Both sexes Les deux sexes	Male Masculin	Female Féminin	Both sexes Les deux sexes	Male Masculin	Female Féminin	Both sexes Les deux sexes	Male Masculin	Female Féminin
AMERICA, NORTH — AMERIQUE DU NORD										
Saint Kitts-Nevis - Saint-Kitts-et-Nevis										
1 VII 2000										
50 - 54	ESDF	1 390	710	680	...	...	...	...	...	...
55 - 59	ESDF	1 100	560	540	...	...	...	...	...	...
60 - 64	ESDF	820	400	420	...	...	...	...	...	...
65 - 69	ESDF	840	410	430	...	...	...	...	...	...
70 - 74	ESDF	810	380	430	...	...	...	...	...	...
75 - 79	ESDF	700	330	370	...	...	...	...	...	...
80 - 84	ESDF	470	240	230	...	...	...	...	...	...
85+	ESDF	750	310	440	...	...	...	...	...	...
Saint Lucia - Sainte-Lucie										
22 V 2001										
Total	CDFC	158 147	77 264	80 883	...	...	...	...	...	...
0 - 1	CDFC	1 073	499	574	...	...	...	...	...	...
1 - 4	CDFC	13 608	6 719	6 889	...	...	...	...	...	...
5 - 9	CDFC	17 375	8 690	8 685	...	...	...	...	...	...
10 - 14	CDFC	17 310	8 606	8 704	...	...	...	...	...	...
15 - 19	CDFC	16 836	8 421	8 415	...	...	...	...	...	...
20 - 24	CDFC	13 706	6 826	6 880	...	...	...	...	...	...
25 - 29	CDFC	12 789	6 358	6 431	...	...	...	...	...	...
30 - 34	CDFC	12 212	5 867	6 345	...	...	...	...	...	...
35 - 39	CDFC	11 133	5 390	5 743	...	...	...	...	...	...
40 - 44	CDFC	9 144	4 451	4 693	...	...	...	...	...	...
45 - 49	CDFC	7 038	3 477	3 561	...	...	...	...	...	...
50 - 54	CDFC	5 451	2 645	2 806	...	...	...	...	...	...
55 - 59	CDFC	4 500	2 143	2 357	...	...	...	...	...	...
60 - 64	CDFC	3 935	1 814	2 121	...	...	...	...	...	...
65 - 69	CDFC	3 652	1 688	1 964	...	...	...	...	...	...
70 - 74	CDFC	2 766	1 278	1 488	...	...	...	...	...	...
75 - 79	CDFC	2 292	1 060	1 232	...	...	...	...	...	...
80 - 84	CDFC	1 711	684	1 027	...	...	...	...	...	...
85 - 89	CDFC	1 097	459	638	...	...	...	...	...	...
90 - 94	CDFC	349	133	216	...	...	...	...	...	...
95+	CDFC	170	56	114	...	...	...	...	...	...
Saint Vincent and the Grenadines - Saint Vincent-et-les Grenadines										
1 VII 2000										
Total	ESDF	111 821	55 797	56 024	...	...	...	...	...	...
0 - 1	ESDF	2 149	1 104	1 045	...	...	...	...	...	...
1 - 4	ESDF	10 539	5 371	5 168	...	...	...	...	...	...
5 - 9	ESDF	14 496	7 252	7 244	...	...	...	...	...	...
10 - 14	ESDF	14 402	7 307	7 095	...	...	...	...	...	...
15 - 19	ESDF	12 828	6 451	6 377	...	...	...	...	...	...
20 - 24	ESDF	10 224	5 244	4 980	...	...	...	...	...	...
25 - 29	ESDF	9 936	5 066	4 870	...	...	...	...	...	...
30 - 34	ESDF	8 063	4 164	3 899	...	...	...	...	...	...
35 - 39	ESDF	5 721	2 853	2 868	...	...	...	...	...	...
40 - 44	ESDF	4 254	2 182	2 072	...	...	...	...	...	...
45 - 49	ESDF	3 363	1 662	1 701	...	...	...	...	...	...
50 - 54	ESDF	3 115	1 516	1 599	...	...	...	...	...	...
55 - 59	ESDF	2 748	1 300	1 448	...	...	...	...	...	...
60 - 64	ESDF	2 702	1 283	1 419	...	...	...	...	...	...
65 - 69	ESDF	2 524	1 068	1 456	...	...	...	...	...	...
70 - 74	ESDF	1 948	862	1 086	...	...	...	...	...	...

7. Population by age, sex and urban/rural residence: latest available year, 1992 - 2001
Population selon l'âge, le sexe et la résidence, urbaine/rurale: dernière année disponible, 1992 - 2001
(continued — suite)

(See notes at end of table. — Voir notes à la fin du tableau.)

Continent, country or area, date and age (in years) / Continent, pays ou zone, date et âge (en années)	Code[1]	Total			Urban - Urbaine			Rural - Rurale		
		Both sexes Les deux sexes	Male Masculin	Female Féminin	Both sexes Les deux sexes	Male Masculin	Female Féminin	Both sexes Les deux sexes	Male Masculin	Female Féminin
AMERICA, NORTH — AMERIQUE DU NORD										
Saint Vincent and the Grenadines - Saint Vincent-et-les Grenadines										
1 VII 2000										
75 - 79	ESDF	1 360	584	776	...	...	...	...	...	...
80 - 84	ESDF	827	316	511	...	...	...	...	...	...
85+	ESDF	622	212	410	...	...	...	...	...	...
Trinidad and Tobago - Trinité-et-Tobago										
1 VII 1997										
Total	ESDF	1 274 799	636 340	638 459	...	...	...	...	...	...
0 - 1	ESDF	15 980	7 952	8 028	...	...	...	...	...	...
1 - 4	ESDF	76 520	38 818	37 702	...	...	...	...	...	...
5 - 9	ESDF	118 002	60 461	57 541	...	...	...	...	...	...
10 - 14	ESDF	133 509	67 766	65 743	...	...	...	...	...	...
15 - 19	ESDF	125 488	64 788	60 700	...	...	...	...	...	...
20 - 24	ESDF	113 206	57 922	55 284	...	...	...	...	...	...
25 - 29	ESDF	104 999	53 530	51 469	...	...	...	...	...	...
30 - 34	ESDF	103 806	51 190	52 616	...	...	...	...	...	...
35 - 39	ESDF	101 070	49 871	51 199	...	...	...	...	...	...
40 - 44	ESDF	89 922	45 331	44 591	...	...	...	...	...	...
45 - 49	ESDF	73 655	36 002	37 653	...	...	...	...	...	...
50 - 54	ESDF	58 076	28 693	29 383	...	...	...	...	...	...
55 - 59	ESDF	44 179	20 927	23 252	...	...	...	...	...	...
60 - 64	ESDF	34 112	16 462	17 650	...	...	...	...	...	...
65 - 69	ESDF	27 875	13 198	14 677	...	...	...	...	...	...
70 - 74	ESDF	22 245	9 516	12 729	...	...	...	...	...	...
75 - 79	ESDF	17 300	7 325	9 975	...	...	...	...	...	...
80+	ESDF	14 855	6 588	8 267	...	...	...	...	...	...
United States - États-Unis[10]										
1 VII 2000										
Total	ESDJ	275 306 000	134 554 000	140 752 000	...	...	...	...	...	...
0 - 4	ESDJ	18 865 000	9 639 000	9 227 000	...	...	...	...	...	...
5 - 9	ESDJ	19 781 000	10 122 000	9 659 000	...	...	...	...	...	...
10 - 14	ESDJ	19 908 000	10 196 000	9 712 000	...	...	...	...	...	...
15 - 19	ESDJ	19 897 000	10 227 000	9 670 000	...	...	...	...	...	...
20 - 24	ESDJ	18 518 000	9 433 000	9 085 000	...	...	...	...	...	...
25 - 29	ESDJ	17 861 000	8 876 000	8 984 000	...	...	...	...	...	...
30 - 34	ESDJ	19 580 000	9 682 000	9 898 000	...	...	...	...	...	...
35 - 39	ESDJ	22 276 000	11 071 000	11 205 000	...	...	...	...	...	...
40 - 44	ESDJ	22 618 000	11 218 000	11 400 000	...	...	...	...	...	...
45 - 49	ESDJ	19 901 000	9 776 000	10 125 000	...	...	...	...	...	...
50 - 54	ESDJ	17 265 000	8 398 000	8 867 000	...	...	...	...	...	...
55 - 59	ESDJ	13 324 000	6 397 000	6 927 000	...	...	...	...	...	...
60 - 64	ESDJ	10 677 000	5 046 000	5 631 000	...	...	...	...	...	...
65 - 69	ESDJ	9 436 000	4 334 000	5 102 000	...	...	...	...	...	...
70 - 74	ESDJ	8 753 000	3 876 000	4 877 000	...	...	...	...	...	...
75 - 79	ESDJ	7 422 000	3 103 000	4 319 000	...	...	...	...	...	...
80 - 84	ESDJ	4 913 000	1 866 000	3 047 000	...	...	...	...	...	...
85 - 89	ESDJ	2 705 000	883 000	1 821 000	...	...	...	...	...	...
90 - 94	ESDJ	1 179 000	319 000	861 000	...	...	...	...	...	...
95 - 99	ESDJ	364 000	81 000	283 000	...	...	...	...	...	...
100+	ESDJ	65 000	12 000	53 000	...	...	...	...	...	...

7. Population by age, sex and urban/rural residence: latest available year, 1992 - 2001
Population selon l'âge, le sexe et la résidence, urbaine/rurale: dernière année disponible, 1992 - 2001
(continued — suite)

(See notes at end of table. — Voir notes à la fin du tableau.)

Continent, country or area, date and age (in years) Continent, pays ou zone, date et âge (en années)	Code[1]	Total			Urban - Urbaine			Rural - Rurale		
		Both sexes Les deux sexes	Male Masculin	Female Féminin	Both sexes Les deux sexes	Male Masculin	Female Féminin	Both sexes Les deux sexes	Male Masculin	Female Féminin
AMERICA, NORTH — AMERIQUE DU NORD										
United States Virgin Islands - Îles Vierges américaines[11]										
1 IV 2000										
Total	CDJC	108 612	51 864	56 748	...	...	...	...	...	...
0 - 4	CDJC	8 553	...	...	...	...	...	...	...	...
5 - 9	CDJC	10 176	...	...	...	...	...	...	...	...
10 - 14	CDJC	9 676	...	...	...	...	...	...	...	...
15 - 19	CDJC	8 688	...	...	...	...	...	...	...	...
20 - 24	CDJC	5 916	...	...	...	...	...	...	...	...
25 - 34	CDJC	13 705	...	...	...	...	...	...	...	...
35 - 44	CDJC	15 746	...	...	...	...	...	...	...	...
45 - 54	CDJC	15 521	...	...	...	...	...	...	...	...
55 - 59	CDJC	6 757	...	...	...	...	...	...	...	...
60 - 64	CDJC	4 757	...	...	...	...	...	...	...	...
65 - 74	CDJC	5 845	...	...	...	...	...	...	...	...
75 - 84	CDJC	2 505	...	...	...	...	...	...	...	...
85+	CDJC	767	...	...	...	...	...	...	...	...
AMERICA, SOUTH — AMERIQUE DU SUD										
Argentina - Argentine[2]										
1 VII 1995										
Total	ESDF	34 768 457	16 976 701	17 609 936	30 556 905	14 820 662	15 736 243	4 029 732	2 156 039	1 873 693
0 - 4	ESDF	3 423 256	1 693 242	1 637 451	2 854 157	1 451 866	1 402 291	476 536	241 376	235 160
5 - 9	ESDF	3 339 853	1 692 161	1 638 391	2 860 036	1 452 476	1 407 560	470 516	239 685	230 831
10 - 14	ESDF	3 284 542	1 662 448	1 612 543	2 838 921	1 436 025	1 402 896	436 070	226 423	209 647
15 - 19	ESDF	3 349 962	1 683 418	1 646 642	2 943 654	1 473 952	1 469 702	386 406	209 466	176 940
20 - 24	ESDF	2 815 425	1 407 920	1 383 976	2 479 244	1 235 279	1 243 965	312 652	172 641	140 011
25 - 29	ESDF	2 470 850	1 234 773	1 220 298	2 182 440	1 085 594	1 096 846	272 631	149 179	123 452
30 - 34	ESDF	2 330 870	1 157 905	1 163 366	2 070 997	1 021 148	1 049 849	250 274	136 757	113 517
35 - 39	ESDF	2 198 005	1 072 637	1 118 988	1 960 731	946 918	1 013 813	230 894	125 719	105 175
40 - 44	ESDF	2 076 119	1 016 579	1 054 840	1 853 152	896 513	956 639	218 267	120 066	98 201
45 - 49	ESDF	1 851 125	923 726	943 144	1 669 726	813 793	855 933	197 144	109 933	87 211
50 - 54	ESDF	1 612 720	786 132	824 657	1 438 415	688 315	750 100	172 374	97 817	74 557
55 - 59	ESDF	1 431 429	683 301	746 669	1 280 730	598 896	681 834	149 240	84 405	64 835
60 - 64	ESDF	1 313 614	610 232	702 282	1 178 113	534 302	643 811	134 401	75 930	58 471
65 - 69	ESDF	1 173 708	527 186	645 792	1 055 243	462 065	593 178	117 735	65 121	52 614
70 - 74	ESDF	921 042	391 559	529 012	829 576	343 192	486 384	90 995	48 367	42 628
75 - 79	ESDF	637 312	249 995	386 978	574 790	219 340	355 450	62 183	30 655	31 528
80+	ESDF	538 624	183 487	354 907	486 980	160 988	325 992	51 414	22 499	28 915
1 VII 2000										
Total	ESDF	37 032 000	18 163 300	18 868 700	...	...	...	...	...	...
0 - 4	ESDF	3 498 600	1 778 300	1 720 300	...	...	...	...	...	...
5 - 9	ESDF	3 421 800	1 738 300	1 683 500	...	...	...	...	...	...
10 - 14	ESDF	3 344 600	1 697 800	1 646 800	...	...	...	...	...	...
15 - 19	ESDF	3 297 000	1 671 400	1 625 600	...	...	...	...	...	...
20 - 24	ESDF	3 361 100	1 695 900	1 665 200	...	...	...	...	...	...
25 - 29	ESDF	2 817 300	1 417 400	1 399 900	...	...	...	...	...	...
30 - 34	ESDF	2 465 400	1 237 100	1 228 300	...	...	...	...	...	...
35 - 39	ESDF	2 319 100	1 154 200	1 164 900	...	...	...	...	...	...
40 - 44	ESDF	2 178 100	1 062 700	1 115 400	...	...	...	...	...	...
45 - 49	ESDF	2 043 100	996 900	1 046 200	...	...	...	...	...	...
50 - 54	ESDF	1 802 800	873 700	929 100	...	...	...	...	...	...
55 - 59	ESDF	1 546 100	741 500	804 600	...	...	...	...	...	...
60 - 64	ESDF	1 343 900	625 100	718 800	...	...	...	...	...	...

7. Population by age, sex and urban/rural residence: latest available year, 1992 - 2001
Population selon l'âge, le sexe et la résidence, urbaine/rurale: dernière année disponible, 1992 - 2001
(continued — suite)

(See notes at end of table. — Voir notes à la fin du tableau.)

Continent, country or area, date and age (in years) Continent, pays ou zone, date et âge (en annèes)	Code[1]	Total			Urban - Urbaine			Rural - Rurale		
		Both sexes Les deux sexes	Male Masculin	Female Féminin	Both sexes Les deux sexes	Male Masculin	Female Féminin	Both sexes Les deux sexes	Male Masculin	Female Féminin
AMERICA, SOUTH — AMERIQUE DU SUD										
Argentina - Argentine[2]										
1 VII 2000										
65 - 69	ESDF	1 197 600	535 400	662 200	...	...	...	...	...	...
70 - 74	ESDF	1 019 500	433 700	585 800	...	...	...	...	...	...
75 - 79	ESDF	737 200	290 900	446 300	...	...	...	...	...	...
80+	ESDF	638 800	213 000	425 800	...	...	...	...	...	...
Bolivia - Bolivie										
5 IX 2001										
Total	CDFC	8 274 325	4 123 850	4 150 475	5 165 230	2 517 106	2 648 124	3 109 095	1 606 744	1 502 351
0 - 9	CDFC	2 170 998	1 115 775	1 055 223	1 259 066	646 912	612 154	911 932	468 863	443 069
10 - 19	CDFC	1 899 973	962 123	937 850	1 221 503	602 995	618 508	678 470	359 128	319 342
20 - 29	CDFC	1 391 959	680 985	710 974	977 334	466 107	511 227	414 625	214 878	199 747
30 - 39	CDFC	992 121	482 454	509 667	659 816	309 209	350 607	332 305	173 245	159 060
40 - 49	CDFC	750 600	370 905	379 695	474 487	226 920	247 567	276 113	143 985	132 128
50 - 59	CDFC	489 310	243 269	246 041	281 057	135 671	145 386	208 253	107 598	100 655
60 - 69	CDFC	309 873	148 018	161 855	157 647	71 880	85 767	152 226	76 138	76 088
70 - 79	CDFC	195 678	88 986	106 692	97 984	42 787	55 197	97 694	46 199	51 495
80 - 89	CDFC	59 651	25 484	34 167	30 453	12 422	18 031	29 198	13 062	16 136
90+	CDFC	14 162	5 851	8 311	5 883	2 203	3 680	8 279	3 648	4 631
Brazil - Brésil[12]										
1 VIII 2000										
Total	CDJC	169 799 170	83 576 015	86 223 155	137 953 959	66 882 993	71 070 966	31 845 211	16 693 022	15 152 189
0 - 1	CDJC	3 213 310	1 635 916	1 577 394	2 518 464	1 282 941	1 235 523	694 846	352 975	341 871
1 - 4	CDJC	13 162 418	6 691 010	6 471 408	10 242 356	5 207 423	5 034 933	2 920 062	1 483 587	1 436 475
5 - 9	CDJC	16 542 327	8 402 353	8 139 974	12 821 519	6 500 814	6 320 705	3 720 808	1 901 539	1 819 269
10 - 14	CDJC	17 348 067	8 777 639	8 570 428	13 530 190	6 803 898	6 726 292	3 817 877	1 973 741	1 844 136
15 - 19	CDJC	17 939 815	9 019 130	8 920 685	14 403 539	7 132 822	7 270 717	3 536 276	1 886 308	1 649 968
20 - 24	CDJC	16 141 515	8 048 218	8 093 297	13 352 132	6 549 365	6 802 767	2 789 383	1 498 853	1 290 530
25 - 29	CDJC	13 849 665	6 814 328	7 035 337	11 570 969	5 606 425	5 964 544	2 278 696	1 207 903	1 070 793
30 - 34	CDJC	13 028 944	6 363 983	6 664 961	10 918 396	5 248 443	5 669 953	2 110 548	1 115 540	995 008
35 - 39	CDJC	12 261 529	5 955 875	6 305 654	10 326 271	4 929 130	5 397 141	1 935 258	1 026 745	908 513
40 - 44	CDJC	10 546 694	5 116 439	5 430 255	8 913 019	4 249 804	4 663 215	1 633 675	866 635	767 040
45 - 49	CDJC	8 721 541	4 216 418	4 505 123	7 309 621	3 472 375	3 837 246	1 411 920	744 043	667 877
50 - 54	CDJC	7 062 601	3 415 678	3 646 923	5 833 659	2 764 708	3 068 951	1 228 942	650 970	577 972
55 - 59	CDJC	5 444 715	2 585 244	2 859 471	4 387 995	2 032 135	2 355 860	1 056 720	553 109	503 611
60 - 64	CDJC	4 600 929	2 153 209	2 447 720	3 712 213	1 676 323	2 035 890	888 716	476 886	411 830
65 - 69	CDJC	3 581 106	1 639 325	1 941 781	2 916 899	1 284 812	1 632 087	664 207	354 513	309 694
70 - 74	CDJC	2 742 302	1 229 329	1 512 973	2 249 617	966 115	1 283 502	492 685	263 214	229 471
75 - 79	CDJC	1 779 587	780 571	999 016	1 456 665	610 767	845 898	322 922	169 804	153 118
80 - 84	CDJC	1 036 034	428 501	607 533	841 798	331 002	510 796	194 236	97 499	96 737
85 - 89	CDJC	534 871	208 088	326 783	436 121	160 379	275 742	98 750	47 709	51 041
90 - 94	CDJC	180 426	65 117	115 309	147 784	50 531	97 253	32 642	14 586	18 056
95 - 99	CDJC	56 198	19 221	36 977	45 682	14 899	30 783	10 516	4 322	6 194
100+	CDJC	24 576	10 423	14 153	19 050	7 882	11 168	5 526	2 541	2 985
1 VII 2001										
Total	ESDF	172 385 826	84 953 370	87 432 456	...	...	...	...	...	...
0 - 1	ESDF	3 321 908	1 695 047	1 626 861	...	...	...	...	...	...
1 - 4	ESDF	12 970 704	6 610 813	6 359 891	...	...	...	...	...	...
5 - 9	ESDF	16 108 258	8 207 298	7 900 960	...	...	...	...	...	...
10 - 14	ESDF	16 658 052	8 474 638	8 183 414	...	...	...	...	...	...
15 - 19	ESDF	17 302 346	8 760 444	8 541 902	...	...	...	...	...	...
20 - 24	ESDF	16 992 351	8 493 070	8 499 281	...	...	...	...	...	...
25 - 29	ESDF	14 911 837	7 347 459	7 564 378	...	...	...	...	...	...
30 - 34	ESDF	13 627 689	6 664 294	6 963 395	...	...	...	...	...	...
35 - 39	ESDF	13 087 533	6 364 773	6 722 760	...	...	...	...	...	...
40 - 44	ESDF	11 275 605	5 459 067	5 816 538	...	...	...	...	...	...
45 - 49	ESDF	9 417 878	4 551 079	4 866 799	...	...	...	...	...	...

7. Population by age, sex and urban/rural residence: latest available year, 1992 - 2001
Population selon l'âge, le sexe et la résidence, urbaine/rurale: dernière année disponible, 1992 - 2001
(continued — suite)

(See notes at end of table. — Voir notes à la fin du tableau.)

Continent, country or area, date and age (in years) / Continent, pays ou zone, date et âge (en années)	Code[1]	Total			Urban - Urbaine			Rural - Rurale		
		Both sexes Les deux sexes	Male Masculin	Female Féminin	Both sexes Les deux sexes	Male Masculin	Female Féminin	Both sexes Les deux sexes	Male Masculin	Female Féminin
AMERICA, SOUTH — AMERIQUE DU SUD										
Brazil - Brésil[12]										
1 VII 2001										
50 - 54	ESDF	7 536 842	3 632 576	3 904 266	...	...	...	...	...	...
55 - 59	ESDF	5 712 650	2 727 518	2 985 132	...	...	...	...	...	...
60 - 64	ESDF	4 673 555	2 188 770	2 484 785	...	...	...	...	...	...
65 - 69	ESDF	3 482 520	1 584 984	1 897 536	...	...	...	...	...	...
70 - 74	ESDF	2 598 972	1 134 174	1 464 798	...	...	...	...	...	...
75 - 79	ESDF	1 560 749	640 605	920 144	...	...	...	...	...	...
80+	ESDF	1 146 377	416 761	729 616	...	...	...	...	...	...
Chile - Chili										
1 VII 2000										
Total	ESDF	15 211 308	7 531 173	7 680 135	13 018 924	6 352 945	6 665 979	2 192 384	1 178 228	1 014 156
0 - 4	ESDF	1 440 866	733 592	707 274	1 224 658	622 989	601 669	216 208	110 603	105 605
5 - 9	ESDF	1 461 182	743 576	717 606	1 248 393	633 532	614 861	212 789	110 044	102 745
10 - 14	ESDF	1 426 153	725 469	700 684	1 224 991	618 425	606 566	201 162	107 044	94 118
15 - 19	ESDF	1 279 053	649 887	629 166	1 103 859	554 218	549 641	175 194	95 669	79 525
20 - 24	ESDF	1 197 174	606 134	591 040	1 024 934	511 652	513 282	172 240	94 482	77 758
25 - 29	ESDF	1 209 954	609 474	600 480	1 043 437	516 015	527 422	166 517	93 459	73 058
30 - 34	ESDF	1 219 036	611 703	607 333	1 048 092	519 414	528 678	170 944	92 289	78 655
35 - 39	ESDF	1 209 347	603 456	605 891	1 046 014	515 637	530 377	163 333	87 819	75 514
40 - 44	ESDF	1 050 666	521 975	528 691	904 669	441 723	462 946	145 997	80 252	65 745
45 - 49	ESDF	859 652	424 342	435 310	738 454	357 927	380 527	121 198	66 415	54 783
50 - 54	ESDF	711 475	347 131	364 344	607 922	290 083	317 839	103 553	57 048	46 505
55 - 59	ESDF	596 467	285 846	310 621	509 276	237 913	271 363	87 191	47 933	39 258
60 - 64	ESDF	459 896	215 333	244 563	380 966	172 137	208 829	78 930	43 196	35 734
65 - 69	ESDF	385 756	173 297	212 459	326 324	141 236	185 088	59 432	32 061	27 371
70 - 74	ESDF	302 413	129 810	172 603	251 398	102 803	148 595	51 015	27 007	24 008
75 - 79	ESDF	203 438	81 273	122 165	169 162	63 652	105 510	34 276	17 621	16 655
80+	ESDF	198 780	68 875	129 905	166 375	53 589	112 786	32 405	15 286	17 119
Colombia - Colombie										
24 X 1993										
Total	CDFC	33 109 840	16 296 539	16 813 301	23 514 070	11 211 708	12 302 362	9 595 770	5 084 831	4 510 939
0 - 1	CDFC	655 167	335 257	319 910	428 832	218 599	210 233	226 335	116 658	109 677
1 - 4	CDFC	3 099 703	1 579 134	1 520 569	2 060 730	1 045 612	1 015 118	1 038 973	533 522	505 451
5 - 9	CDFC	3 816 670	1 943 375	1 873 295	2 533 072	1 280 393	1 252 679	1 283 598	662 982	620 616
10 - 14	CDFC	3 840 632	1 947 256	1 893 376	2 598 400	1 289 824	1 308 576	1 242 232	657 432	584 800
15 - 19	CDFC	3 301 436	1 614 187	1 687 249	2 316 196	1 077 176	1 239 020	985 240	537 011	448 229
20 - 24	CDFC	3 156 530	1 508 254	1 648 276	2 302 417	1 053 570	1 248 847	854 113	454 684	399 429
25 - 29	CDFC	2 977 533	1 420 298	1 557 235	2 242 535	1 032 450	1 210 085	734 998	387 848	347 150
30 - 34	CDFC	2 693 270	1 303 844	1 389 426	2 061 372	967 247	1 094 125	631 898	336 597	295 301
35 - 39	CDFC	2 219 750	1 060 353	1 159 397	1 666 555	769 837	896 718	553 195	290 516	262 679
40 - 44	CDFC	1 735 926	864 685	871 241	1 293 477	623 693	669 784	442 449	240 992	201 457
45 - 49	CDFC	1 323 815	650 119	673 696	959 787	456 546	503 241	364 028	193 573	170 455
50 - 54	CDFC	1 139 501	559 518	579 983	810 259	381 569	428 690	329 242	177 949	151 293
55 - 59	CDFC	855 265	413 838	441 427	614 592	284 877	329 715	240 673	128 961	111 712
60 - 64	CDFC	798 234	388 860	409 374	560 005	257 531	302 474	238 229	131 329	106 900
65 - 69	CDFC	539 716	260 405	279 311	385 937	176 277	209 660	153 779	84 128	69 651
70 - 74	CDFC	417 485	201 401	216 084	292 756	131 927	160 829	124 729	69 474	55 255
75 - 79	CDFC	260 423	123 908	136 515	187 273	83 108	104 165	73 150	40 800	32 350
80 - 84	CDFC	161 961	73 107	88 854	115 289	48 381	66 908	46 672	24 726	21 946
85 - 89	CDFC	72 282	30 793	41 489	53 497	21 345	32 152	18 785	9 448	9 337
90+	CDFC	44 541	17 947	26 594	31 089	11 746	19 343	13 452	6 201	7 251
1 VII 2001										
Total	ESDF	43 070 704	21 282 227	21 788 477	...	...	...	...	...	...
0 - 1	ESDF	984 025	504 869	479 157	...	...	...	...	...	...
1 - 4	ESDF	3 800 557	1 937 134	1 863 423	...	...	...	...	...	...
5 - 9	ESDF	4 740 463	2 416 547	2 323 916	...	...	...	...	...	...
10 - 14	ESDF	4 437 450	2 258 914	2 178 536	...	...	...	...	...	...

7. Population by age, sex and urban/rural residence: latest available year, 1992 - 2001
Population selon l'âge, le sexe et la résidence, urbaine/rurale: dernière année disponible, 1992 - 2001
(continued — suite)

(See notes at end of table. — Voir notes à la fin du tableau.)

Continent, country or area, date and age (in years) / Continent, pays ou zone, date et âge (en annèes)	Code[1]	Total			Urban - Urbaine			Rural - Rurale		
		Both sexes Les deux sexes	Male Masculin	Female Féminin	Both sexes Les deux sexes	Male Masculin	Female Féminin	Both sexes Les deux sexes	Male Masculin	Female Féminin
AMERICA, SOUTH — AMERIQUE DU SUD										
Colombia - Colombie										
1 VII 2001										
15 - 19	ESDF	4 172 571	2 117 485	2 055 086	...	...	...	...	...	...
20 - 24	ESDF	3 968 778	1 997 333	1 971 445	...	...	...	...	...	...
25 - 29	ESDF	3 569 416	1 769 645	1 799 771	...	...	...	...	...	...
30 - 34	ESDF	3 490 371	1 707 191	1 783 180	...	...	...	...	...	...
35 - 39	ESDF	3 164 551	1 534 352	1 630 199	...	...	...	...	...	...
40 - 44	ESDF	2 641 518	1 267 405	1 374 113	...	...	...	...	...	...
45 - 49	ESDF	2 186 046	1 039 265	1 146 781	...	...	...	...	...	...
50 - 54	ESDF	1 691 528	803 277	888 251	...	...	...	...	...	...
55 - 59	ESDF	1 236 111	589 886	646 225	...	...	...	...	...	...
60 - 64	ESDF	937 510	440 313	497 197	...	...	...	...	...	...
65 - 69	ESDF	731 260	334 521	396 739	...	...	...	...	...	...
70 - 74	ESDF	551 286	245 849	305 437	...	...	...	...	...	...
75 - 79	ESDF	389 200	169 322	219 878	...	...	...	...	...	...
80+	ESDF	378 063	148 919	229 144	...	...	...	...	...	...
Ecuador - Équateur[13]										
25 XI 2001										
Total	CDFC	12 156 608	6 018 353	6 138 255	7 431 355	3 625 962	3 805 393	4 725 253	2 392 391	2 332 862
0 - 1	CDFC	237 209	120 000	117 209	132 634	67 302	65 332	104 575	52 698	51 877
1 - 4	CDFC	1 099 651	558 576	541 075	612 787	311 551	301 236	486 864	247 025	239 839
5 - 9	CDFC	1 362 121	689 123	672 998	771 344	389 609	381 735	590 777	299 514	291 263
10 - 14	CDFC	1 341 039	679 271	661 768	767 207	384 630	382 577	573 832	294 641	279 191
15 - 19	CDFC	1 240 531	617 087	623 444	754 865	368 673	386 192	485 666	248 414	237 252
20 - 24	CDFC	1 168 637	571 018	597 619	751 887	362 536	389 351	416 750	208 482	208 268
25 - 29	CDFC	947 395	457 309	490 086	619 497	295 689	323 808	327 898	161 620	166 278
30 - 34	CDFC	863 071	423 372	439 699	570 009	274 727	295 282	293 062	148 645	144 417
35 - 39	CDFC	774 543	374 505	400 038	513 318	243 762	269 556	261 225	130 743	130 482
40 - 44	CDFC	673 871	332 177	341 694	446 548	217 269	229 279	227 323	114 908	112 415
45 - 49	CDFC	538 983	264 970	274 013	349 836	169 592	180 244	189 147	95 378	93 769
50 - 54	CDFC	462 855	230 263	232 592	289 840	141 453	148 387	173 015	88 810	84 205
55 - 59	CDFC	339 411	168 060	171 351	205 081	99 313	105 768	134 330	68 747	65 583
60 - 64	CDFC	293 667	143 933	149 734	169 775	80 579	89 196	123 892	63 354	60 538
65 - 69	CDFC	244 031	117 495	126 536	141 921	65 770	76 151	102 110	51 725	50 385
70 - 74	CDFC	194 686	95 101	99 585	112 608	52 841	59 767	82 078	42 260	39 818
75 - 79	CDFC	142 949	69 055	73 894	82 944	38 340	44 604	60 005	30 715	29 290
80 - 84	CDFC	97 462	45 092	52 370	57 223	25 332	31 891	40 239	19 760	20 479
85 - 89	CDFC	63 167	28 985	34 182	38 910	17 333	21 577	24 257	11 652	12 605
90 - 94	CDFC	39 386	18 351	21 035	24 906	11 477	13 429	14 480	6 874	7 606
95+	CDFC	31 943	14 610	17 333	18 215	8 184	10 031	13 728	6 426	7 302
Falkland Islands (Malvinas) - Îles Falkland (Malvinas)										
8 IV 2001										
Total	CDFC	2 913	1 598	1 315	...	...	...	...	...	...
0 - 4	CDFC	137	70	67	...	...	...	...	...	...
5 - 9	CDFC	146	71	75	...	...	...	...	...	...
10 - 14	CDFC	155	87	68	...	...	...	...	...	...
15 - 19	CDFC	149	69	80	...	...	...	...	...	...
20 - 24	CDFC	223	111	112	...	...	...	...	...	...
25 - 29	CDFC	271	143	128	...	...	...	...	...	...
30 - 34	CDFC	292	173	119	...	...	...	...	...	...
35 - 39	CDFC	277	159	118	...	...	...	...	...	...
40 - 44	CDFC	250	124	126	...	...	...	...	...	...
45 - 49	CDFC	241	152	89	...	...	...	...	...	...
50 - 54	CDFC	233	139	94	...	...	...	...	...	...
55 - 59	CDFC	188	117	71	...	...	...	...	...	...

7. Population by age, sex and urban/rural residence: latest available year, 1992 - 2001
Population selon l'âge, le sexe et la résidence, urbaine/rurale: dernière année disponible, 1992 - 2001
(continued — suite)

(See notes at end of table. — Voir notes à la fin du tableau.)

Continent, country or area, date and age (in years) / Continent, pays ou zone, date et âge (en annèes)	Code[1]	Total			Urban - Urbaine			Rural - Rurale		
		Both sexes Les deux sexes	Male Masculin	Female Féminin	Both sexes Les deux sexes	Male Masculin	Female Féminin	Both sexes Les deux sexes	Male Masculin	Female Féminin
AMERICA, SOUTH — AMERIQUE DU SUD										
Falkland Islands (Malvinas) - Îles Falkland (Malvinas)										
8 IV 2001										
60 - 64	CDFC	110	68	42	...	...	...	...	...	...
65 - 69	CDFC	90	50	40	...	...	...	...	...	...
70 - 74	CDFC	64	26	38	...	...	...	...	...	...
75 - 79	CDFC	29	15	14	...	...	...	...	...	...
80+	CDFC	58	24	34	...	...	...	...	...	...
French Guiana - Guyane Française										
8 III 1999										
Total	CDJC	156 790	78 963	77 827	...	...	...	...	...	...
0 - 1	CDJC	671	357	314	...	...	...	...	...	...
1 - 4	CDJC	16 739	8 537	8 202	...	...	...	...	...	...
5 - 9	CDJC	19 330	9 818	9 512	...	...	...	...	...	...
10 - 14	CDJC	16 533	8 410	8 123	...	...	...	...	...	...
15 - 19	CDJC	14 587	7 315	7 272	...	...	...	...	...	...
20 - 24	CDJC	10 862	5 667	5 195	...	...	...	...	...	...
25 - 29	CDJC	12 467	5 754	6 713	...	...	...	...	...	...
30 - 34	CDJC	13 130	6 384	6 746	...	...	...	...	...	...
35 - 39	CDJC	12 709	6 280	6 429	...	...	...	...	...	...
40 - 44	CDJC	10 736	5 433	5 303	...	...	...	...	...	...
45 - 49	CDJC	8 729	4 583	4 146	...	...	...	...	...	...
50 - 54	CDJC	6 557	3 517	3 040	...	...	...	...	...	...
55 - 59	CDJC	4 344	2 346	1 998	...	...	...	...	...	...
60 - 64	CDJC	2 971	1 529	1 442	...	...	...	...	...	...
65 - 69	CDJC	2 188	1 148	1 040	...	...	...	...	...	...
70 - 74	CDJC	1 597	783	814	...	...	...	...	...	...
75 - 79	CDJC	1 266	561	705	...	...	...	...	...	...
80 - 84	CDJC	726	301	425	...	...	...	...	...	...
85 - 89	CDJC	423	154	269	...	...	...	...	...	...
90 - 94	CDJC	152	53	99	...	...	...	...	...	...
95 - 99	CDJC	68	31	37	...	...	...	...	...	...
100+	CDJC	5	2	3	...	...	...	...	...	...
Paraguay										
26 VIII 1992										
Total	CDFC	4 152 588	2 085 905	2 066 683	2 089 688	1 007 400	1 082 288	2 062 900	1 078 505	984 395
0 - 1	CDFC	118 192	60 024	58 168	54 555	27 665	26 890	63 637	32 359	31 278
1 - 4	CDFC	491 014	250 071	240 943	216 256	109 958	106 298	274 758	140 113	134 645
5 - 9	CDFC	594 283	302 325	291 958	262 086	131 958	130 128	332 197	170 367	161 830
10 - 14	CDFC	521 614	265 289	256 325	242 292	119 058	123 234	279 322	146 231	133 091
15 - 19	CDFC	393 220	196 052	197 168	207 202	96 993	110 209	186 018	99 059	86 959
20 - 24	CDFC	347 259	171 483	175 776	191 354	88 600	102 754	155 905	82 883	73 022
25 - 29	CDFC	310 953	154 005	156 948	172 849	81 176	91 673	138 104	72 829	65 275
30 - 34	CDFC	286 081	144 986	141 095	159 198	77 005	82 193	126 883	67 981	58 902
35 - 39	CDFC	240 051	121 493	118 558	132 610	64 666	67 944	107 441	56 827	50 614
40 - 44	CDFC	190 182	98 338	91 844	102 913	50 941	51 972	87 269	47 397	39 872
45 - 49	CDFC	152 250	76 655	75 595	81 277	39 647	41 630	70 973	37 008	33 965
50 - 54	CDFC	131 107	66 260	64 847	68 228	32 593	35 635	62 879	33 667	29 212
55 - 59	CDFC	93 226	46 195	47 031	48 192	22 528	25 664	45 034	23 667	21 367
60 - 64	CDFC	93 260	45 959	47 301	48 431	21 949	26 482	44 829	24 010	20 819
65 - 69	CDFC	67 077	32 017	35 060	35 682	15 667	20 015	31 395	16 350	15 045
70 - 74	CDFC	50 510	23 457	27 053	26 428	10 979	15 449	24 082	12 478	11 604
75 - 79	CDFC	35 248	16 234	19 014	19 303	8 202	11 101	15 945	8 032	7 913
80 - 84	CDFC	21 591	9 238	12 353	12 155	4 830	7 325	9 436	4 408	5 028
85 - 89	CDFC	10 486	4 130	6 356	5 878	2 100	3 778	4 608	2 030	2 578
90+	CDFC	4 984	1 694	3 290	2 799	885	1 914	2 185	809	1 376

7. Population by age, sex and urban/rural residence: latest available year, 1992 - 2001
Population selon l'âge, le sexe et la résidence, urbaine/rurale: dernière année disponible, 1992 - 2001
(continued — suite)

(See notes at end of table. — Voir notes à la fin du tableau.)

Continent, country or area, date and age (in years) — Continent, pays ou zone, date et âge (en années)	Code[1]	Total			Urban - Urbaine			Rural - Rurale		
		Both sexes Les deux sexes	Male Masculin	Female Féminin	Both sexes Les deux sexes	Male Masculin	Female Féminin	Both sexes Les deux sexes	Male Masculin	Female Féminin
AMERICA, SOUTH — AMERIQUE DU SUD										
Paraguay										
1 VII 1994										
Total	ESDF	4 699 855	2 368 072	2 331 783	...	...	...	...	...	...
0 - 4	ESDF	715 014	364 150	350 864	...	...	...	...	...	...
5 - 9	ESDF	654 658	332 801	321 857	...	...	...	...	...	...
10 - 14	ESDF	586 281	297 813	288 468	...	...	...	...	...	...
15 - 19	ESDF	470 439	238 954	231 485	...	...	...	...	...	...
20 - 24	ESDF	411 468	208 846	202 622	...	...	...	...	...	...
25 - 29	ESDF	372 517	189 181	183 336	...	...	...	...	...	...
30 - 34	ESDF	329 185	166 900	162 285	...	...	...	...	...	...
35 - 39	ESDF	284 549	144 628	139 921	...	...	...	...	...	...
40 - 44	ESDF	246 627	126 630	119 997	...	...	...	...	...	...
45 - 49	ESDF	151 622	77 050	74 572	...	...	...	...	...	...
50 - 54	ESDF	128 128	64 973	63 155	...	...	...	...	...	...
55 - 59	ESDF	105 906	51 990	53 916	...	...	...	...	...	...
60 - 64	ESDF	76 980	34 849	42 131	...	...	...	...	...	...
65 - 69	ESDF	63 014	27 121	35 893	...	...	...	...	...	...
70 - 74	ESDF	45 379	19 310	26 069	...	...	...	...	...	...
75 - 79	ESDF	31 578	12 945	18 633	...	...	...	...	...	...
80+	ESDF	26 510	9 931	16 579	...	...	...	...	...	...
Peru - Pérou[14,15]										
1 VII 1998										
Total	ESDF	24 800 768	12 303 755	12 497 013	17 838 479	8 771 638	9 066 841	6 962 289	3 532 117	3 430 172
0 - 4	ESDF	2 900 190	1 476 026	1 424 164	1 855 712	945 850	909 862	1 044 478	530 176	514 302
5 - 9	ESDF	2 851 273	1 447 069	1 404 204	1 870 911	957 601	913 310	980 362	489 468	490 894
10 - 14	ESDF	2 781 819	1 409 773	1 372 046	1 904 255	966 710	937 545	877 564	443 063	434 501
15 - 19	ESDF	2 654 997	1 341 124	1 313 873	1 929 521	957 468	972 053	725 476	383 656	341 820
20 - 24	ESDF	2 446 999	1 225 205	1 221 794	1 865 335	917 815	947 520	581 664	307 390	274 274
25 - 29	ESDF	2 120 187	1 044 092	1 076 095	1 624 964	786 633	838 331	495 223	257 459	237 764
30 - 34	ESDF	1 830 822	888 261	942 561	1 411 958	673 764	738 194	418 864	214 497	204 367
35 - 39	ESDF	1 555 372	750 728	804 644	1 204 983	573 829	631 154	350 389	176 899	173 490
40 - 44	ESDF	1 289 468	624 829	664 639	999 183	480 094	519 089	290 285	144 735	145 550
45 - 49	ESDF	1 065 036	520 173	544 863	809 869	394 768	415 101	255 167	125 405	129 762
50 - 54	ESDF	858 806	420 725	438 081	634 806	311 616	323 190	224 000	109 109	114 891
55 - 59	ESDF	708 473	345 545	362 928	510 973	248 325	262 648	197 500	97 220	100 280
60 - 64	ESDF	588 760	284 358	304 402	415 491	198 352	217 139	173 269	86 006	87 263
65 - 69	ESDF	455 376	216 257	239 119	317 789	148 462	169 327	137 587	67 795	69 792
70 - 74	ESDF	319 388	147 990	171 398	222 130	100 692	121 438	97 258	47 298	49 960
75 - 79	ESDF	205 437	91 784	113 653	143 212	62 333	80 879	62 225	29 451	32 774
80+	ESDF	168 365	69 816	98 549	117 387	47 326	70 061	50 978	22 490	28 488
Suriname										
1 VII 2000										
Total	ESDF	435 797	218 677	217 120	...	...	...	...	...	...
0 - 4	ESDF	52 793	28 129	24 664	...	...	...	...	...	...
5 - 9	ESDF	44 683	23 928	20 755	...	...	...	...	...	...
10 - 14	ESDF	46 670	23 655	23 015	...	...	...	...	...	...
15 - 19	ESDF	46 248	22 544	23 704	...	...	...	...	...	...
20 - 24	ESDF	36 554	18 061	18 493	...	...	...	...	...	...
25 - 29	ESDF	33 413	16 508	16 905	...	...	...	...	...	...
30 - 34	ESDF	34 407	17 179	17 228	...	...	...	...	...	...
35 - 39	ESDF	32 015	16 568	15 447	...	...	...	...	...	...
40 - 44	ESDF	25 168	12 717	12 451	...	...	...	...	...	...
45 - 49	ESDF	19 825	9 247	10 578	...	...	...	...	...	...
50 - 54	ESDF	14 717	7 195	7 522	...	...	...	...	...	...
55 - 59	ESDF	12 436	5 511	6 925	...	...	...	...	...	...
60 - 64	ESDF	11 833	5 597	6 236	...	...	...	...	...	...
65 - 69	ESDF	10 669	5 056	5 613	...	...	...	...	...	...
70 - 74	ESDF	6 856	3 512	3 344	...	...	...	...	...	...

7. **Population by age, sex and urban/rural residence: latest available year, 1992 - 2001**
Population selon l'âge, le sexe et la résidence, urbaine/rurale: dernière année disponible, 1992 - 2001
(continued — suite)

(See notes at end of table. — Voir notes à la fin du tableau.)

Continent, country or area, date and age (in years) Continent, pays ou zone, date et âge (en années)	Code[1]	Total			Urban - Urbaine			Rural - Rurale		
		Both sexes Les deux sexes	Male Masculin	Female Féminin	Both sexes Les deux sexes	Male Masculin	Female Féminin	Both sexes Les deux sexes	Male Masculin	Female Féminin
AMERICA, SOUTH — AMERIQUE DU SUD										
Suriname										
1 VII 2000										
75 - 79	ESDF	4 165	1 843	2 322	...	...	...	...	...	...
80+	ESDF	3 345	1 427	1 918	...	...	...	...	...	...
Uruguay[15]										
1 VII 1999										
Total	ESDF	3 313 239	1 607 086	1 706 153	3 061 753	1 462 266	1 599 487	251 486	144 820	106 666
0 - 1	ESDF	56 956	29 095	27 861	52 963	27 056	25 907	3 993	2 039	1 954
1 - 4	ESDF	226 007	115 402	110 605	210 400	107 404	102 996	15 607	7 998	7 609
5 - 9	ESDF	276 500	141 239	135 261	257 983	131 787	126 196	18 517	9 452	9 065
10 - 14	ESDF	263 801	134 681	129 120	247 283	126 411	120 872	16 518	8 270	8 248
15 - 19	ESDF	257 829	131 364	126 465	241 024	122 444	118 580	16 805	8 920	7 885
20 - 24	ESDF	271 052	137 674	133 378	252 456	127 267	125 189	18 596	10 407	8 189
25 - 29	ESDF	247 250	125 054	122 196	229 771	114 406	115 365	17 479	10 648	6 831
30 - 34	ESDF	220 167	108 945	111 222	202 243	97 529	104 714	17 924	11 416	6 508
35 - 39	ESDF	218 260	106 409	111 851	201 856	96 634	105 222	16 404	9 775	6 629
40 - 44	ESDF	204 154	98 972	105 182	188 080	89 678	98 402	16 074	9 294	6 780
45 - 49	ESDF	182 137	88 501	93 636	166 094	79 074	87 020	16 043	9 427	6 616
50 - 54	ESDF	167 953	80 210	87 743	152 457	70 693	81 764	15 496	9 517	5 979
55 - 59	ESDF	153 608	72 387	81 221	139 810	63 743	76 067	13 798	8 644	5 154
60 - 64	ESDF	143 348	65 280	78 068	129 800	56 911	72 889	13 548	8 369	5 179
65 - 69	ESDF	137 944	61 510	76 434	125 241	53 486	71 755	12 703	8 024	4 679
70 - 74	ESDF	116 782	48 926	67 856	106 718	42 798	63 920	10 064	6 128	3 936
75 - 79	ESDF	83 309	32 483	50 826	76 788	28 698	48 090	6 521	3 785	2 736
80 - 84	ESDF	50 131	17 370	32 761	46 642	15 530	31 112	3 489	1 840	1 649
85+	ESDF	36 051	11 584	24 467	34 144	10 717	23 427	1 907	867	1 040
1 VII 2000										
Total	ESDF	3 322 141	1 609 199	1 712 942	...	...	...	...	...	...
0 - 1	ESDF	53 272	27 097	26 175	...	...	...	...	...	...
1 - 4	ESDF	223 611	113 764	109 847	...	...	...	...	...	...
5 - 9	ESDF	275 757	140 838	134 919	...	...	...	...	...	...
10 - 14	ESDF	270 998	137 785	133 213	...	...	...	...	...	...
15 - 19	ESDF	268 367	136 320	132 047	...	...	...	...	...	...
20 - 24	ESDF	252 458	127 174	125 284	...	...	...	...	...	...
25 - 29	ESDF	234 190	116 913	117 277	...	...	...	...	...	...
30 - 34	ESDF	226 990	112 334	114 656	...	...	...	...	...	...
35 - 39	ESDF	221 452	108 460	112 992	...	...	...	...	...	...
40 - 44	ESDF	205 578	100 259	105 319	...	...	...	...	...	...
45 - 49	ESDF	187 016	90 841	96 175	...	...	...	...	...	...
50 - 54	ESDF	170 437	82 045	88 392	...	...	...	...	...	...
55 - 59	ESDF	152 548	72 515	80 033	...	...	...	...	...	...
60 - 64	ESDF	142 474	65 916	76 558	...	...	...	...	...	...
65 - 69	ESDF	134 895	60 173	74 722	...	...	...	...	...	...
70 - 74	ESDF	118 796	50 345	68 451	...	...	...	...	...	...
75 - 79	ESDF	84 643	33 635	51 008	...	...	...	...	...	...
80 - 84	ESDF	53 923	19 262	34 661	...	...	...	...	...	...
85 - 89	ESDF	29 259	9 192	20 067	...	...	...	...	...	...
90 - 94	ESDF	11 600	3 350	8 250	...	...	...	...	...	...
95+	ESDF	3 877	981	2 896	...	...	...	...	...	...
Venezuela[14]										
1 VII 1998										
Total	ESDF	23 242 435	11 699 249	11 543 186	20 097 795	9 988 424	10 109 371	3 144 640	1 710 825	1 433 815
0 - 4	ESDF	2 784 819	1 422 439	1 362 380	2 337 635	1 187 902	1 149 733	447 184	234 537	212 647
5 - 9	ESDF	2 733 236	1 395 141	1 338 095	2 310 403	1 171 369	1 139 034	422 833	223 772	199 061
10 - 14	ESDF	2 604 204	1 327 839	1 276 365	2 211 369	1 114 612	1 096 757	392 835	213 227	179 608
15 - 19	ESDF	2 385 499	1 213 909	1 171 590	2 054 541	1 026 836	1 027 705	330 958	187 073	143 885
20 - 24	ESDF	2 125 428	1 078 510	1 046 918	1 851 454	925 854	925 600	273 974	152 656	121 318
25 - 29	ESDF	1 882 713	951 600	931 113	1 644 717	819 904	824 813	237 996	131 696	106 300

7. Population by age, sex and urban/rural residence: latest available year, 1992 - 2001
Population selon l'âge, le sexe et la résidence, urbaine/rurale: dernière année disponible, 1992 - 2001
(continued — suite)

(See notes at end of table. — Voir notes à la fin du tableau.)

Continent, country or area, date and age (in years) / Continent, pays ou zone, date et âge (en années)	Code[1]	Total			Urban - Urbaine			Rural - Rurale		
		Both sexes Les deux sexes	Male Masculin	Female Féminin	Both sexes Les deux sexes	Male Masculin	Female Féminin	Both sexes Les deux sexes	Male Masculin	Female Féminin
AMERICA, SOUTH — AMERIQUE DU SUD										
Venezuela[14]										
1 VII 1998										
30 - 34	ESDF	1 783 275	897 333	885 942	1 582 498	787 063	795 435	200 777	110 270	90 507
35 - 44	ESDF	1 569 757	786 995	782 762	1 401 415	696 175	705 240	168 342	90 820	77 522
45 - 49	ESDF	1 099 658	550 105	549 553	989 289	489 901	499 388	110 369	60 204	50 165
50 - 54	ESDF	856 609	426 942	429 667	755 213	371 229	383 984	101 396	55 713	45 683
55 - 59	ESDF	631 474	310 100	321 374	545 596	262 781	282 815	85 878	47 319	38 559
60 - 64	ESDF	485 775	234 536	251 239	408 104	191 857	216 247	77 671	42 679	34 992
65 - 69	ESDF	392 733	186 379	206 354	338 907	156 628	182 279	53 826	29 751	24 075
70 - 74	ESDF	288 337	132 603	155 734	245 705	108 200	137 505	42 632	24 403	18 229
75 - 79	ESDF	181 084	79 183	101 901	151 996	62 928	89 068	29 088	16 255	12 833
80+	ESDF	135 888	54 297	81 591	103 086	37 391	65 695	32 802	16 906	15 896
Unk. - Inc.	ESDF	1 301 946	651 338	650 608	1 165 867	577 794	588 073	136 079	73 544	62 535
1 VII 2000										
Total	ESDF	24 169 744	12 160 964	12 008 780	...	...	...	...	...	...
0 - 4	ESDF	2 797 567	1 429 119	1 368 448	...	...	...	...	...	...
5 - 9	ESDF	2 751 023	1 404 448	1 346 575	...	...	...	...	...	...
10 - 14	ESDF	2 678 361	1 366 152	1 312 209	...	...	...	...	...	...
15 - 19	ESDF	2 460 374	1 252 234	1 208 140	...	...	...	...	...	...
20 - 24	ESDF	2 249 613	1 141 582	1 108 031	...	...	...	...	...	...
25 - 29	ESDF	1 932 177	977 045	955 132	...	...	...	...	...	...
30 - 34	ESDF	1 826 960	919 710	907 250	...	...	...	...	...	...
35 - 39	ESDF	1 676 569	840 642	835 927	...	...	...	...	...	...
40 - 44	ESDF	1 378 725	689 104	689 621	...	...	...	...	...	...
45 - 49	ESDF	1 180 062	588 949	591 113	...	...	...	...	...	...
50 - 54	ESDF	946 008	471 554	474 454	...	...	...	...	...	...
55 - 59	ESDF	698 720	343 749	354 971	...	...	...	...	...	...
60 - 64	ESDF	518 199	249 901	268 298	...	...	...	...	...	...
65 - 69	ESDF	411 489	194 794	216 695	...	...	...	...	...	...
70 - 74	ESDF	315 146	145 085	170 061	...	...	...	...	...	...
75 - 79	ESDF	198 478	87 048	111 430	...	...	...	...	...	...
80+	ESDF	150 273	59 848	90 425	...	...	...	...	...	...
ASIA — ASIE										
Armenia - Arménie										
1 VII 2000										
Total	ESDF	3 802 883	1 848 756	1 954 127	2 534 024	1 212 033	1 321 991	1 268 859	636 723	632 136
0 - 1	ESDF	34 891	18 906	15 985	21 590	11 614	9 976	13 301	7 292	6 009
1 - 4	ESDF	169 569	90 611	78 958	104 205	55 097	49 108	65 364	35 514	29 850
5 - 9	ESDF	312 705	161 455	151 250	188 935	97 424	91 511	123 770	64 031	59 739
10 - 14	ESDF	379 750	194 643	185 107	241 824	123 850	117 974	137 926	70 793	67 133
15 - 19	ESDF	369 535	188 966	180 569	247 129	126 344	120 785	122 406	62 622	59 784
20 - 24	ESDF	321 344	164 463	156 881	222 694	113 608	109 086	98 650	50 855	47 795
25 - 29	ESDF	286 588	145 710	140 878	191 905	97 913	93 992	94 683	47 797	46 886
30 - 34	ESDF	276 202	136 057	140 145	176 690	83 992	92 698	99 512	52 065	47 447
35 - 39	ESDF	316 118	149 145	166 973	205 547	92 740	112 807	110 571	56 405	54 166
40 - 44	ESDF	317 256	148 299	168 957	221 801	98 689	123 112	95 455	49 610	45 845
45 - 49	ESDF	235 188	108 547	126 641	172 439	76 613	95 826	62 749	31 934	30 815
50 - 54	ESDF	157 083	71 439	85 644	118 721	53 337	65 384	38 362	18 102	20 260
55 - 59	ESDF	107 984	48 437	59 547	78 600	35 358	43 242	29 384	13 079	16 305
60 - 64	ESDF	172 088	77 132	94 956	116 202	51 505	64 697	55 886	25 627	30 259
65 - 69	ESDF	128 212	57 050	71 162	80 146	34 801	45 345	48 066	22 249	25 817
70 - 74	ESDF	119 367	51 915	67 452	75 990	33 282	42 708	43 377	18 633	24 744
75 - 79	ESDF	51 263	18 907	32 356	35 135	13 333	21 802	16 128	5 574	10 554
80 - 84	ESDF	23 824	7 828	15 996	17 343	5 862	11 481	6 481	1 966	4 515
85+	ESDF	23 916	9 246	14 670	17 128	6 671	10 457	6 788	2 575	4 213

7. Population by age, sex and urban/rural residence: latest available year, 1992 - 2001
Population selon l'âge, le sexe et la résidence, urbaine/rurale: dernière année disponible, 1992 - 2001
(continued — suite)

(See notes at end of table. — Voir notes à la fin du tableau.)

Continent, country or area, date and age (in years) / Continent, pays ou zone, date et âge (en années)	Code[1]	Total			Urban - Urbaine			Rural - Rurale		
		Both sexes Les deux sexes	Male Masculin	Female Féminin	Both sexes Les deux sexes	Male Masculin	Female Féminin	Both sexes Les deux sexes	Male Masculin	Female Féminin
ASIA — ASIE										
Azerbaijan - Azerbaïdjan										
1 VII 2001										
Total	ESDF	8 111 200	3 971 600	4 139 600	4 118 800	2 006 800	2 112 000	3 992 400	1 964 800	2 027 600
0 - 1	ESDF	113 700	61 100	52 600	49 600	26 900	22 700	64 100	34 200	29 900
1 - 4	ESDF	593 200	314 800	278 400	256 400	137 500	118 900	336 800	177 300	159 500
5 - 9	ESDF	843 400	435 700	407 700	391 000	203 300	187 700	452 400	232 400	220 000
10 - 14	ESDF	931 800	477 400	454 400	465 900	239 200	226 700	465 900	238 200	227 700
15 - 19	ESDF	831 800	424 200	407 600	425 500	217 100	208 400	406 300	207 100	199 200
20 - 24	ESDF	693 900	342 100	351 800	356 100	175 300	180 800	337 800	166 800	171 000
25 - 29	ESDF	614 900	292 400	322 500	301 400	138 400	163 000	313 500	154 000	159 500
30 - 34	ESDF	658 100	310 700	347 400	324 300	148 600	175 700	333 800	162 100	171 700
35 - 39	ESDF	693 700	328 800	364 900	364 100	169 600	194 500	329 600	159 200	170 400
40 - 44	ESDF	637 600	309 300	328 300	355 500	172 700	182 800	282 100	136 600	145 500
45 - 49	ESDF	415 400	201 400	214 000	244 700	119 100	125 600	170 700	82 300	88 400
50 - 54	ESDF	281 000	135 800	145 200	170 700	83 400	87 300	110 300	52 400	57 900
55 - 59	ESDF	151 000	70 500	80 500	89 600	42 100	47 500	61 400	28 400	33 000
60 - 64	ESDF	269 400	122 000	147 400	138 500	63 600	74 900	130 900	58 400	72 500
65 - 69	ESDF	217 400	98 500	118 900	102 000	45 600	56 400	115 400	52 900	62 500
70 - 74	ESDF	150 900	66 300	84 600	72 500	31 000	41 500	78 400	35 300	43 100
75 - 79	ESDF	68 600	25 900	42 700	35 200	12 800	22 400	33 400	13 100	20 300
80 - 84	ESDF	30 500	8 800	21 700	14 200	4 400	9 800	16 300	4 400	11 900
85 - 89	ESDF	15 100	4 100	11 000	6 700	1 900	4 800	8 400	2 200	6 200
90 - 94	ESDF	7 800	1 800	6 000	2 800	800	2 000	5 000	1 000	4 000
95 - 99	ESDF	3 500	700	2 800	1 200	300	900	2 300	400	1 900
100+	ESDF	2 200	400	1 800	500	100	400	1 700	300	1 400
Unk. - Inc.	ESDF	69 400	41 800	27 600	69 400	41 800	27 600	...	...	...
Bahrain - Bahreïn										
1 VII 2001										
Total	ESDF	654 619	375 674	278 945	...	...	...	...	...	...
0 - 4	ESDF	59 727	30 599	29 128	...	...	...	...	...	...
5 - 9	ESDF	62 092	31 411	30 681	...	...	...	...	...	...
10 - 14	ESDF	59 155	30 504	28 651	...	...	...	...	...	...
15 - 19	ESDF	51 596	26 668	24 928	...	...	...	...	...	...
20 - 24	ESDF	59 047	32 379	26 668	...	...	...	...	...	...
25 - 29	ESDF	69 131	42 731	26 400	...	...	...	...	...	...
30 - 34	ESDF	72 017	44 425	27 592	...	...	...	...	...	...
35 - 39	ESDF	65 954	39 946	26 008	...	...	...	...	...	...
40 - 44	ESDF	56 704	36 174	20 530	...	...	...	...	...	...
45 - 49	ESDF	39 014	25 878	13 136	...	...	...	...	...	...
50 - 54	ESDF	21 738	14 452	7 286	...	...	...	...	...	...
55 - 59	ESDF	12 319	7 188	5 131	...	...	...	...	...	...
60 - 64	ESDF	9 539	4 945	4 594	...	...	...	...	...	...
65 - 69	ESDF	6 448	3 157	3 291	...	...	...	...	...	...
70 - 74	ESDF	4 962	2 530	2 432	...	...	...	...	...	...
75 - 79	ESDF	2 711	1 403	1 308	...	...	...	...	...	...
80 - 84	ESDF	1 504	812	692	...	...	...	...	...	...
85 - 89	ESDF	605	302	303	...	...	...	...	...	...
90+	ESDF	356	170	186	...	...	...	...	...	...
Bhutan - Bhoutan										
31 XII 2001										
Total	ESDF	698 949	352 935	346 014	...	...	...	...	...	...
0 - 4	ESDF	107 990	54 115	53 875	...	...	...	...	...	...
5 - 9	ESDF	101 236	50 268	50 968	...	...	...	...	...	...
10 - 14	ESDF	84 687	42 889	41 798	...	...	...	...	...	...
15 - 19	ESDF	62 845	31 877	30 968	...	...	...	...	...	...
20 - 24	ESDF	55 493	27 570	27 923	...	...	...	...	...	...
25 - 29	ESDF	47 633	23 827	23 806	...	...	...	...	...	...
30 - 34	ESDF	42 745	21 569	21 176	...	...	...	...	...	...

7. Population by age, sex and urban/rural residence: latest available year, 1992 - 2001
Population selon l'âge, le sexe et la résidence, urbaine/rurale: dernière année disponible, 1992 - 2001
(continued — suite)

(See notes at end of table. — Voir notes à la fin du tableau.)

Continent, country or area, date and age (in years) / Continent, pays ou zone, date et âge (en annèes)	Code[1]	Total			Urban - Urbaine			Rural - Rurale		
		Both sexes Les deux sexes	Male Masculin	Female Féminin	Both sexes Les deux sexes	Male Masculin	Female Féminin	Both sexes Les deux sexes	Male Masculin	Female Féminin
ASIA — ASIE										
Bhutan - Bhoutan										
31 XII 2001										
35 - 39	ESDF	39 156	20 229	18 927	...	...	...	...	...	...
40 - 44	ESDF	33 001	17 015	15 986	...	...	...	...	...	...
45 - 49	ESDF	26 534	13 766	12 768	...	...	...	...	...	...
50 - 54	ESDF	25 170	12 955	12 215	...	...	...	...	...	...
55 - 59	ESDF	22 270	11 509	10 761	...	...	...	...	...	...
60 - 64	ESDF	20 451	10 555	9 896	...	...	...	...	...	...
65 - 69	ESDF	12 335	6 072	6 263	...	...	...	...	...	...
70 - 74	ESDF	8 388	4 201	4 187	...	...	...	...	...	...
75+	ESDF	9 015	4 518	4 497	...	...	...	...	...	...
Brunei Darussalam - Brunéi Darussalam										
1 VII 1992										
Total	ESDF	267 800	141 300	126 500	...	...	...	...	...	...
0 - 4	ESDF	34 800	18 000	16 800	...	...	...	...	...	...
5 - 9	ESDF	30 700	15 800	14 900	...	...	...	...	...	...
10 - 14	ESDF	26 800	13 800	13 000	...	...	...	...	...	...
15 - 19	ESDF	23 000	11 800	11 200	...	...	...	...	...	...
20 - 24	ESDF	25 200	12 900	12 300	...	...	...	...	...	...
25 - 29	ESDF	27 600	14 500	13 100	...	...	...	...	...	...
30 - 34	ESDF	27 700	14 900	12 800	...	...	...	...	...	...
35 - 39	ESDF	22 600	12 600	10 000	...	...	...	...	...	...
40 - 44	ESDF	15 900	9 100	6 800	...	...	...	...	...	...
45 - 49	ESDF	9 300	5 300	4 000	...	...	...	...	...	...
50 - 54	ESDF	7 500	4 000	3 500	...	...	...	...	...	...
55 - 59	ESDF	5 300	2 700	2 600	...	...	...	...	...	...
60 - 64	ESDF	4 000	2 100	1 900	...	...	...	...	...	...
65 - 69	ESDF	2 700	1 400	1 300	...	...	...	...	...	...
70 - 74	ESDF	2 000	1 100	900	...	...	...	...	...	...
75 - 79	ESDF	1 200	600	600	...	...	...	...	...	...
80 - 84	ESDF	900	400	500	...	...	...	...	...	...
85+	ESDF	600	300	300	...	...	...	...	...	...
Cambodia - Cambodge[16]										
3 III 1998										
Total	CDFC	11 437 656	5 511 408	5 926 248	1 795 575	878 186	917 389	9 642 081	4 633 222	5 008 859
0 - 1	CDFC	231 609	118 075	113 534	32 869	16 851	16 018	198 740	101 224	97 516
1 - 4	CDFC	1 235 183	629 217	605 966	160 680	82 377	78 303	1 074 503	546 840	527 663
5 - 9	CDFC	1 772 820	903 976	868 844	239 934	122 652	117 282	1 532 886	781 324	751 562
10 - 14	CDFC	1 658 196	851 139	807 057	246 998	126 217	120 781	1 411 198	724 922	686 276
15 - 19	CDFC	1 344 258	664 184	680 074	233 677	113 229	120 448	1 110 581	550 955	559 626
20 - 24	CDFC	745 687	354 100	391 587	128 884	63 561	65 323	616 803	290 539	326 264
25 - 29	CDFC	888 540	426 968	461 572	157 736	79 241	78 495	730 804	347 727	383 077
30 - 34	CDFC	782 682	370 090	412 592	137 139	69 093	68 046	645 543	300 997	344 546
35 - 39	CDFC	695 868	325 331	370 537	123 310	61 255	62 055	572 558	264 076	308 482
40 - 44	CDFC	497 067	199 722	297 345	92 433	40 499	51 934	404 634	159 223	245 411
45 - 49	CDFC	415 931	175 052	240 879	72 681	32 868	39 813	343 250	142 184	201 066
50 - 54	CDFC	312 463	132 413	180 050	50 505	22 227	28 278	261 958	110 186	151 772
55 - 59	CDFC	256 930	110 189	146 741	37 186	16 284	20 902	219 744	93 905	125 839
60 - 64	CDFC	204 994	86 602	118 392	28 433	11 627	16 806	176 561	74 975	101 586
65 - 69	CDFC	166 928	70 660	96 268	21 891	8 614	13 277	145 037	62 046	82 991
70 - 74	CDFC	112 213	46 769	65 444	14 851	5 535	9 316	97 362	41 234	56 128
75 - 79	CDFC	67 528	27 838	39 690	9 135	3 337	5 798	58 393	24 501	33 892
80 - 84	CDFC	30 652	12 159	18 493	4 288	1 515	2 773	26 364	10 644	15 720
85 - 89	CDFC	13 368	5 029	8 339	1 874	592	1 282	11 494	4 437	7 057
90 - 94	CDFC	2 867	1 026	1 841	453	157	296	2 414	869	1 545
95+	CDFC	1 872	869	1 003	618	455	163	1 254	414	840

7. Population by age, sex and urban/rural residence: latest available year, 1992 - 2001
Population selon l'âge, le sexe et la résidence, urbaine/rurale: dernière année disponible, 1992 - 2001
(continued — suite)

(See notes at end of table. — Voir notes à la fin du tableau.)

Continent, country or area, date and age (in years) / Continent, pays ou zone, date et âge (en années)	Code[1]	Total			Urban - Urbaine			Rural - Rurale		
		Both sexes Les deux sexes	Male Masculin	Female Féminin	Both sexes Les deux sexes	Male Masculin	Female Féminin	Both sexes Les deux sexes	Male Masculin	Female Féminin
ASIA — ASIE										
Cambodia - Cambodge[16]										
1 VII 2001										
Total	ESDF	13 310 858	6 457 461	6 853 358	...	...	...	...	...	...
0 - 1	ESDF	432 372	220 633	211 740	...	...	...	...	...	...
1 - 4	ESDF	1 602 406	814 171	788 228	...	...	...	...	...	...
5 - 9	ESDF	1 855 761	941 159	914 605	...	...	...	...	...	...
10 - 14	ESDF	1 779 246	909 977	869 272	...	...	...	...	...	...
15 - 19	ESDF	1 621 602	825 261	796 342	...	...	...	...	...	...
20 - 24	ESDF	1 169 447	569 576	599 872	...	...	...	...	...	...
25 - 29	ESDF	745 132	352 695	392 438	...	...	...	...	...	...
30 - 34	ESDF	894 227	427 957	466 271	...	...	...	...	...	...
35 - 39	ESDF	762 794	359 780	403 016	...	...	...	...	...	...
40 - 44	ESDF	643 364	290 642	352 722	...	...	...	...	...	...
45 - 49	ESDF	462 912	183 251	279 661	...	...	...	...	...	...
50 - 54	ESDF	383 052	161 890	221 158	...	...	...	...	...	...
55 - 59	ESDF	285 309	120 354	164 954	...	...	...	...	...	...
60 - 64	ESDF	230 857	97 852	133 003	...	...	...	...	...	...
65 - 69	ESDF	176 866	73 537	103 324	...	...	...	...	...	...
70 - 74	ESDF	133 468	55 861	77 600	...	...	...	...	...	...
75+	ESDF	132 060	52 885	79 174	...	...	...	...	...	...
China - Chine[17]										
1 XI 2000										
Total	CDJC	1242612226	640 275 969	602 336 257	458 770 983	235 264 707	223 506 276	783 841 243	405 011 262	378 829 981
0 - 1	CDJC	13 793 799	7 460 206	6 333 593	4 449 020	2 376 585	2 072 435	9 344 779	5 083 621	4 261 158
1 - 4	CDJC	55 184 575	30 188 488	24 996 087	17 669 697	9 525 854	8 143 843	37 514 878	20 662 634	16 852 244
5 - 9	CDJC	90 152 587	48 303 208	41 849 379	26 588 363	14 180 433	12 407 930	63 564 224	34 122 775	29 441 449
10 - 14	CDJC	125 396 633	65 344 739	60 051 894	35 802 884	18 701 307	17 101 577	89 593 749	46 643 432	42 950 317
15 - 19	CDJC	103 031 165	52 878 170	50 152 995	42 231 585	21 086 911	21 144 674	60 799 580	31 791 259	29 008 321
20 - 24	CDJC	94 573 174	47 937 766	46 635 408	41 021 887	20 651 361	20 370 526	53 551 287	27 286 405	26 264 882
25 - 29	CDJC	117 602 265	60 230 758	57 371 507	48 788 516	24 820 721	23 967 795	68 813 749	35 410 037	33 403 712
30 - 34	CDJC	127 314 298	65 360 456	61 953 842	49 723 640	25 760 568	23 963 072	77 590 658	39 599 888	37 990 770
35 - 39	CDJC	109 147 295	56 141 391	53 005 904	44 518 164	23 269 889	21 248 275	64 629 131	32 871 502	31 757 629
40 - 44	CDJC	81 242 945	42 243 187	38 999 758	33 518 610	17 499 183	16 019 427	47 724 335	24 744 004	22 980 331
45 - 49	CDJC	85 521 045	43 939 603	41 581 442	31 708 706	16 245 324	15 463 382	53 812 339	27 694 279	26 118 060
50 - 54	CDJC	63 304 200	32 804 125	30 500 075	22 335 748	11 462 314	10 873 434	40 968 452	21 341 811	19 626 641
55 - 59	CDJC	46 370 375	24 061 506	22 308 869	16 004 389	8 077 159	7 927 230	30 365 986	15 984 347	14 381 639
60 - 64	CDJC	41 703 848	21 674 478	20 029 370	14 944 552	7 519 377	7 425 175	26 759 296	14 155 101	12 604 195
65 - 69	CDJC	34 780 460	17 549 348	17 231 112	12 174 470	6 128 605	6 045 865	22 605 990	11 420 743	11 185 247
70 - 74	CDJC	25 574 149	12 436 154	13 137 995	8 479 487	4 216 193	4 263 294	17 094 662	8 219 961	8 874 701
75 - 79	CDJC	15 928 330	7 175 811	8 752 519	5 000 134	2 291 543	2 708 591	10 928 196	4 884 268	6 043 928
80 - 84	CDJC	7 989 158	3 203 868	4 785 290	2 472 016	1 004 359	1 467 657	5 517 142	2 199 509	3 317 633
85 - 89	CDJC	3 030 698	1 056 941	1 973 757	994 079	347 550	646 529	2 036 619	709 391	1 327 228
90 - 94	CDJC	783 594	229 758	553 836	276 586	80 189	196 397	507 008	149 569	357 439
95 - 99	CDJC	169 756	51 373	118 383	62 255	17 827	44 428	107 501	33 546	73 955
100+	CDJC	17 877	4 635	13 242	6 195	1 455	4 740	11 682	3 180	8 502
China: Hong Kong SAR - Chine: Hong-Kong RAS										
1 VII 2001										
Total	ESDJ	6 724 900	3 287 000	3 437 900	...	...	...	...	...	...
0 - 1	ESDJ	50 000	26 200	23 800	...	...	...	...	...	...
1 - 4	ESDJ	226 300	117 700	108 600	...	...	...	...	...	...
5 - 9	ESDJ	397 700	206 000	191 700	...	...	...	...	...	...
10 - 14	ESDJ	430 100	221 400	208 700	...	...	...	...	...	...
15 - 19	ESDJ	446 000	229 500	216 500	...	...	...	...	...	...
20 - 24	ESDJ	466 700	225 100	241 600	...	...	...	...	...	...
25 - 29	ESDJ	524 800	240 700	284 100	...	...	...	...	...	...
30 - 34	ESDJ	583 900	256 300	327 600	...	...	...	...	...	...

7. **Population by age, sex and urban/rural residence: latest available year, 1992 - 2001**
Population selon l'âge, le sexe et la résidence, urbaine/rurale: dernière année disponible, 1992 - 2001
(continued — suite)

(See notes at end of table. — Voir notes à la fin du tableau.)

Continent, country or area, date and age (in years) / Continent, pays ou zone, date et âge (en années)	Code[1]	Total			Urban - Urbaine			Rural - Rurale		
		Both sexes Les deux sexes	Male Masculin	Female Féminin	Both sexes Les deux sexes	Male Masculin	Female Féminin	Both sexes Les deux sexes	Male Masculin	Female Féminin
ASIA — ASIE										
China: Hong Kong SAR - Chine: Hong-Kong RAS										
1 VII 2001										
35 - 39	ESDJ	684 600	312 900	371 700	...	...	...	...	...	...
40 - 44	ESDJ	679 800	335 700	344 100	...	...	...	...	...	...
45 - 49	ESDJ	540 000	270 400	269 600	...	...	...	...	...	...
50 - 54	ESDJ	437 800	227 000	210 800	...	...	...	...	...	...
55 - 59	ESDJ	252 800	136 000	116 800	...	...	...	...	...	...
60 - 64	ESDJ	250 800	133 800	117 000	...	...	...	...	...	...
65 - 69	ESDJ	250 300	128 300	122 000	...	...	...	...	...	...
70 - 74	ESDJ	210 400	102 500	107 900	...	...	...	...	...	...
75 - 79	ESDJ	144 100	63 700	80 400	...	...	...	...	...	...
80 - 84	ESDJ	86 200	34 200	52 000	...	...	...	...	...	...
85+	ESDJ	62 600	19 600	43 000	...	...	...	...	...	...
China: Macao SAR - Chine: Macao RAS										
23 VIII 2001										
Total	CDJC	435 235	208 865	226 370	...	...	...	...	...	...
0 - 1	CDJC	3 252	1 692	1 560	...	...	...	...	...	...
1 - 4	CDJC	17 444	9 086	8 358	...	...	...	...	...	...
5 - 9	CDJC	32 278	16 785	15 493	...	...	...	...	...	...
10 - 14	CDJC	41 247	21 261	19 986	...	...	...	...	...	...
15 - 19	CDJC	35 972	17 938	18 034	...	...	...	...	...	...
20 - 24	CDJC	28 974	12 242	16 732	...	...	...	...	...	...
25 - 29	CDJC	31 804	13 758	18 046	...	...	...	...	...	...
30 - 34	CDJC	34 943	14 447	20 496	...	...	...	...	...	...
35 - 39	CDJC	45 256	19 952	25 304	...	...	...	...	...	...
40 - 44	CDJC	46 214	23 082	23 132	...	...	...	...	...	...
45 - 49	CDJC	37 357	19 448	17 909	...	...	...	...	...	...
50 - 54	CDJC	25 167	13 579	11 588	...	...	...	...	...	...
55 - 59	CDJC	13 728	7 324	6 404	...	...	...	...	...	...
60 - 64	CDJC	9 911	5 106	4 805	...	...	...	...	...	...
65 - 69	CDJC	9 882	4 512	5 370	...	...	...	...	...	...
70 - 74	CDJC	8 978	3 836	5 142	...	...	...	...	...	...
75 - 79	CDJC	6 336	2 479	3 857	...	...	...	...	...	...
80 - 84	CDJC	3 844	1 465	2 379	...	...	...	...	...	...
85+	CDJC	2 648	873	1 775	...	...	...	...	...	...
Cyprus - Chypre[18]										
1 X 1992[19]										
Total	CDJC	602 025	299 614	302 411	407 324	201 811	205 513	194 701	97 803	96 898
0 - 1	CDJC	10 551	5 395	5 156	6 967	3 515	3 452	3 584	1 880	1 704
1 - 4	CDJC	40 015	20 695	19 320	26 768	13 783	12 985	13 247	6 912	6 335
5 - 9	CDJC	51 923	26 806	25 117	34 529	17 837	16 692	17 394	8 969	8 425
10 - 14	CDJC	49 290	25 382	23 908	32 793	16 896	15 897	16 497	8 486	8 011
15 - 19	CDJC	42 222	21 568	20 654	28 619	14 570	14 049	13 603	6 998	6 605
20 - 24	CDJC	43 359	21 899	21 460	30 299	15 071	15 228	13 060	6 828	6 232
25 - 29	CDJC	45 913	23 024	22 889	32 030	15 820	16 210	13 883	7 204	6 679
30 - 34	CDJC	49 081	24 615	24 466	34 580	17 034	17 546	14 501	7 581	6 920
35 - 39	CDJC	44 208	22 324	21 884	30 944	15 314	15 630	13 264	7 010	6 254
40 - 44	CDJC	41 224	20 522	20 702	29 337	14 455	14 882	11 887	6 067	5 820
45 - 49	CDJC	37 145	18 604	18 541	26 789	13 385	13 404	10 356	5 219	5 137
50 - 54	CDJC	29 731	14 599	15 132	20 666	10 298	10 368	9 065	4 301	4 764
55 - 59	CDJC	26 421	12 721	13 700	17 740	8 763	8 977	8 681	3 958	4 723
60 - 64	CDJC	23 803	10 859	12 944	15 254	7 067	8 187	8 549	3 792	4 757
65 - 69	CDJC	21 187	9 862	11 325	13 085	6 085	7 000	8 102	3 777	4 325
70 - 74	CDJC	16 682	7 751	8 931	9 993	4 611	5 382	6 689	3 140	3 549
75 - 79	CDJC	13 311	5 984	7 327	7 600	3 310	4 290	5 711	2 674	3 037
80 - 84	CDJC	9 438	4 075	5 363	5 338	2 241	3 097	4 100	1 834	2 266

7. Population by age, sex and urban/rural residence: latest available year, 1992 - 2001
Population selon l'âge, le sexe et la résidence, urbaine/rurale: dernière année disponible, 1992 - 2001
(continued — suite)

(See notes at end of table. — Voir notes à la fin du tableau.)

Continent, country or area, date and age (in years) / Continent, pays ou zone, date et âge (en années)	Code[1]	Total			Urban - Urbaine			Rural - Rurale		
		Both sexes Les deux sexes	Male Masculin	Female Féminin	Both sexes Les deux sexes	Male Masculin	Female Féminin	Both sexes Les deux sexes	Male Masculin	Female Féminin
ASIA — ASIE										
Cyprus - Chypre[18]										
1 X 1992[19]										
85 - 89	CDJC	3 859	1 671	2 188	2 234	918	1 316	1 625	753	872
90 - 94	CDJC	1 293	537	756	749	298	451	544	239	305
95 - 99	CDJC	228	74	154	120	33	87	108	41	67
100+	CDJC	49	19	30	28	10	18	21	9	12
Unk. - Inc.	CDJC	1 092	628	464	862	497	365	230	131	99
31 XII 2000										
Total	ESDJ	759 100	379 000	380 100	...	...	...	...	...	...
0 - 1	ESDJ	9 500	5 000	4 500	...	...	...	...	...	...
1 - 4	ESDJ	41 000	21 000	20 000	...	...	...	...	...	...
5 - 9	ESDJ	60 500	31 300	29 200	...	...	...	...	...	...
10 - 14	ESDJ	61 200	31 600	29 600	...	...	...	...	...	...
15 - 19	ESDJ	61 700	32 000	29 700	...	...	...	...	...	...
20 - 24	ESDJ	55 300	28 400	26 900	...	...	...	...	...	...
25 - 29	ESDJ	50 400	25 400	25 000	...	...	...	...	...	...
30 - 34	ESDJ	52 900	26 600	26 300	...	...	...	...	...	...
35 - 39	ESDJ	56 800	28 700	28 100	...	...	...	...	...	...
40 - 44	ESDJ	56 000	28 400	27 600	...	...	...	...	...	...
45 - 49	ESDJ	50 200	25 200	25 000	...	...	...	...	...	...
50 - 54	ESDJ	46 200	23 100	23 100	...	...	...	...	...	...
55 - 59	ESDJ	39 400	19 400	20 000	...	...	...	...	...	...
60 - 64	ESDJ	31 200	14 900	16 300	...	...	...	...	...	...
65 - 69	ESDJ	27 500	12 600	14 900	...	...	...	...	...	...
70 - 74	ESDJ	23 200	10 200	13 000	...	...	...	...	...	...
75 - 79	ESDJ	17 400	7 600	9 800	...	...	...	...	...	...
80+	ESDJ	18 700	7 600	11 100	...	...	...	...	...	...
Georgia - Géorgie										
1 VII 2000										
Total	ESDF	4 945 553	2 364 247	2 581 306	2 860 786	1 348 715	1 512 071	2 084 767	1 015 532	1 069 235
0 - 1	ESDF	42 247	22 938	19 309	26 206	14 152	12 054	16 041	8 786	7 255
1 - 4	ESDF	197 055	104 267	92 788	119 229	63 120	56 109	77 826	41 147	36 679
5 - 9	ESDF	361 619	185 741	175 878	208 452	107 038	101 414	153 167	78 703	74 464
10 - 14	ESDF	409 671	209 366	200 305	229 154	116 874	112 280	180 517	92 492	88 025
15 - 19	ESDF	388 789	198 066	190 723	222 064	113 224	108 840	166 725	84 842	81 883
20 - 24	ESDF	376 407	191 927	184 480	213 454	108 613	104 841	162 953	83 314	79 639
25 - 29	ESDF	350 129	181 759	168 370	213 415	110 488	102 927	136 714	71 271	65 443
30 - 34	ESDF	363 659	175 712	187 947	214 156	100 573	113 583	149 503	75 139	74 364
35 - 39	ESDF	403 179	191 543	211 636	241 215	109 394	131 821	161 964	82 149	79 815
40 - 44	ESDF	353 366	168 218	185 148	216 428	98 958	117 470	136 938	69 260	67 678
45 - 49	ESDF	305 841	143 921	161 920	193 528	88 504	105 024	112 313	55 417	56 896
50 - 54	ESDF	216 111	100 444	115 667	137 119	62 640	74 479	78 992	37 804	41 188
55 - 59	ESDF	225 223	99 437	125 786	130 629	56 530	74 099	94 594	42 907	51 687
60 - 64	ESDF	280 405	126 438	153 967	155 346	68 463	86 883	125 059	57 975	67 084
65 - 69	ESDF	242 085	102 877	139 208	123 373	51 091	72 282	118 712	51 786	66 926
70 - 74	ESDF	218 503	85 840	132 663	111 805	41 553	70 252	106 698	44 287	62 411
75 - 79	ESDF	113 417	34 835	78 582	56 587	16 900	39 687	56 830	17 935	38 895
80 - 84	ESDF	59 039	24 600	34 439	29 156	12 606	16 550	29 883	11 994	17 889
85 - 89	ESDF	27 302	11 583	15 719	13 332	5 601	7 731	13 970	5 982	7 988
90 - 94	ESDF	8 410	3 605	4 805	4 432	1 819	2 613	3 978	1 786	2 192
95 - 99	ESDF	2 730	1 020	1 710	1 510	527	983	1 220	493	727
100+	ESDF	366	110	256	196	47	149	170	63	107
India - Inde[20]										
1 VII 2001										
Total	ESDF	1017544000	526 356 000	491 187 000	...	...	...	...	...	...
0 - 4	ESDF	109 047 000	55 987 000	53 060 000	...	...	...	...	...	...
5 - 9	ESDF	116 737 000	59 531 000	57 206 000	...	...	...	...	...	...
10 - 14	ESDF	123 531 000	63 879 000	59 653 000	...	...	...	...	...	...
15 - 19	ESDF	109 619 000	57 958 000	51 661 000	...	...	...	...	...	...

7. Population by age, sex and urban/rural residence: latest available year, 1992 - 2001
Population selon l'âge, le sexe et la résidence, urbaine/rurale: dernière année disponible, 1992 - 2001
(continued — suite)

(See notes at end of table. — Voir notes à la fin du tableau.)

Continent, country or area, date and age (in years) / Continent, pays ou zone, date et âge (en années)	Code[1]	Total			Urban - Urbaine			Rural - Rurale		
		Both sexes Les deux sexes	Male Masculin	Female Féminin	Both sexes Les deux sexes	Male Masculin	Female Féminin	Both sexes Les deux sexes	Male Masculin	Female Féminin
ASIA — ASIE										
India - Inde[20]										
1 VII 2001										
20 - 24	ESDF	90 680 000	47 966 000	42 714 000	...	...	...	...	...	...
25 - 29	ESDF	81 887 000	41 598 000	40 289 000	...	...	...	...	...	...
30 - 34	ESDF	75 555 000	37 661 000	37 894 000	...	...	...	...	...	...
35 - 39	ESDF	65 743 000	33 527 000	32 215 000	...	...	...	...	...	...
40 - 44	ESDF	56 436 000	29 644 000	26 792 000	...	...	...	...	...	...
45 - 49	ESDF	46 993 000	24 945 000	22 047 000	...	...	...	...	...	...
50 - 54	ESDF	39 099 000	20 715 000	18 384 000	...	...	...	...	...	...
55 - 59	ESDF	31 287 000	16 558 000	14 729 000	...	...	...	...	...	...
60 - 64	ESDF	24 184 000	12 513 000	11 671 000	...	...	...	...	...	...
65 - 69	ESDF	19 438 000	9 871 000	9 567 000	...	...	...	...	...	...
70 - 74	ESDF	13 120 000	6 647 000	6 473 000	...	...	...	...	...	...
75 - 79	ESDF	8 352 000	4 317 000	4 035 000	...	...	...	...	...	...
80+	ESDF	5 837 000	3 040 000	2 798 000	...	...	...	...	...	...
Indonesia - Indonésie[21]										
30 VI 2000										
Total	CDFC	201 241 999	100 934 962	100 307 037	85 380 627	42 759 571	42 621 056	115 861 372	58 175 391	57 685 981
0 - 1	CDFC	3 492 259	1 799 525	1 692 734	1 529 180	790 207	738 973	1 963 079	1 009 318	953 761
1 - 4	CDFC	16 810 117	8 496 176	8 313 941	6 642 545	3 361 599	3 280 946	10 167 572	5 134 577	5 032 995
5 - 9	CDFC	20 494 091	10 433 865	10 060 226	7 962 806	4 034 352	3 928 454	12 531 285	6 399 513	6 131 772
10 - 14	CDFC	20 453 732	10 460 908	9 992 824	7 951 997	4 017 276	3 934 721	12 501 735	6 443 632	6 058 103
15 - 19	CDFC	21 149 517	10 649 348	10 500 169	9 501 797	4 656 022	4 845 775	11 647 720	5 993 326	5 654 394
20 - 24	CDFC	19 258 101	9 237 464	10 020 637	9 394 813	4 528 914	4 865 899	9 863 288	4 708 550	5 154 738
25 - 29	CDFC	18 640 937	9 130 504	9 510 433	8 720 487	4 321 110	4 399 377	9 920 450	4 809 394	5 111 056
30 - 34	CDFC	16 399 720	8 204 302	8 195 418	7 499 021	3 795 282	3 703 739	8 900 699	4 409 020	4 491 679
35 - 39	CDFC	14 904 226	7 432 840	7 471 386	6 430 999	3 230 371	3 200 628	8 473 227	4 202 469	4 270 758
40 - 44	CDFC	12 467 848	6 433 438	6 034 410	5 322 075	2 767 298	2 554 777	7 145 773	3 666 140	3 479 633
45 - 49	CDFC	9 656 005	5 087 252	4 568 753	4 015 532	2 137 790	1 877 742	5 640 473	2 949 462	2 691 011
50 - 54	CDFC	7 384 968	3 791 185	3 593 783	2 905 386	1 500 733	1 404 653	4 479 582	2 290 452	2 189 130
55 - 59	CDFC	5 678 664	2 883 226	2 795 438	2 235 074	1 145 432	1 089 642	3 443 590	1 737 794	1 705 796
60 - 64	CDFC	5 321 019	2 597 076	2 723 943	1 951 238	949 193	1 002 045	3 369 781	1 647 883	1 721 898
65 - 69	CDFC	3 564 926	1 666 191	1 898 735	1 310 805	600 348	710 457	2 254 121	1 065 843	1 188 278
70 - 74	CDFC	2 837 037	1 368 190	1 468 847	1 016 304	479 243	537 061	1 820 733	888 947	931 786
75+	CDFC	2 716 985	1 257 526	1 459 459	986 136	442 204	543 932	1 730 849	815 322	915 527
Unk. - Inc.	CDFC	11 847	5 946	5 901	4 432	2 197	2 235	7 415	3 749	3 666
Iran (Islamic Republic of) - Iran (République islamique d')										
23 X 1996										
Total	CDJC	60 055 488	30 515 159	29 540 329	36 817 789	18 805 023	18 012 766	23 026 293	11 604 972	11 421 321
0 - 1	CDJC	1 020 936	524 927	496 009	577 065	296 189	280 876	438 331	225 870	212 461
1 - 4	CDJC	5 142 088	2 639 181	2 502 907	2 849 490	1 460 895	1 388 595	2 265 600	1 164 225	1 101 375
5 - 9	CDJC	8 481 845	4 324 165	4 157 680	4 878 478	2 482 469	2 396 009	3 568 961	1 824 356	1 744 605
10 - 14	CDJC	9 080 676	4 622 473	4 458 203	5 519 239	2 815 729	2 703 510	3 532 506	1 792 962	1 739 544
15 - 19	CDJC	7 115 547	3 579 875	3 535 672	4 312 401	2 192 258	2 120 143	2 776 791	1 375 316	1 401 475
20 - 24	CDJC	5 221 982	2 566 453	2 655 529	3 154 588	1 552 571	1 602 017	2 049 270	1 005 536	1 043 734
25 - 29	CDJC	4 709 154	2 365 834	2 343 320	3 058 756	1 542 685	1 516 071	1 636 320	816 297	820 023
30 - 34	CDJC	3 980 066	2 012 720	1 967 346	2 709 279	1 379 337	1 329 942	1 260 670	628 651	632 019
35 - 39	CDJC	3 571 779	1 817 609	1 754 170	2 433 263	1 253 499	1 179 764	1 128 946	559 452	569 494
40 - 44	CDJC	2 812 086	1 431 062	1 381 024	1 907 112	999 736	907 376	896 847	427 395	469 452
45 - 49	CDJC	2 013 040	990 158	1 022 882	1 326 036	679 081	646 955	680 701	308 103	372 598
50 - 54	CDJC	1 529 078	768 621	760 457	978 343	508 898	469 445	545 616	257 191	288 425
55 - 59	CDJC	1 366 728	717 251	649 477	830 201	443 453	386 748	532 070	271 309	260 761
60 - 64	CDJC	1 382 946	753 502	629 444	783 511	426 040	357 471	593 925	324 115	269 810
65 - 69	CDJC	1 076 373	577 189	499 184	601 575	313 942	287 633	470 975	260 734	210 241
70 - 74	CDJC	846 509	463 018	383 491	479 380	253 061	226 319	364 876	208 499	156 377

7. Population by age, sex and urban/rural residence: latest available year, 1992 - 2001
Population selon l'âge, le sexe et la résidence, urbaine/rurale: dernière année disponible, 1992 - 2001
(continued — suite)

(See notes at end of table. — Voir notes à la fin du tableau.)

Continent, country or area, date and age (in years) / Continent, pays ou zone, date et âge (en années)	Code[1]	Total			Urban - Urbaine			Rural - Rurale		
		Both sexes Les deux sexes	Male Masculin	Female Féminin	Both sexes Les deux sexes	Male Masculin	Female Féminin	Both sexes Les deux sexes	Male Masculin	Female Féminin
ASIA — ASIE										
Iran (Islamic Republic of) - Iran (République islamique d')										
23 X 1996										
75 - 79	CDJC	364 118	192 898	171 220	213 209	108 117	105 092	150 168	84 342	65 826
80 - 84	CDJC	146 470	74 081	72 389	86 330	41 073	45 257	59 770	32 783	26 987
85 - 89	CDJC	76 476	35 182	41 294	43 625	18 287	25 338	32 657	16 781	15 876
90 - 94	CDJC	44 780	19 977	24 803	25 563	10 855	14 708	19 067	9 050	10 017
95+	CDJC	40 455	20 103	20 352	21 018	10 022	10 996	19 224	9 963	9 261
Unk. - Inc.	CDJC	32 356	18 880	13 476	29 327	16 826	12 501	3 002	2 042	960
Iraq										
1 VII 2001										
Total	ESDF	24 813 365	12 424 655	12 388 710	16 786 216	8 435 417	8 350 799	8 027 149	3 989 238	4 037 911
0 - 4	ESDF	4 204 992	2 152 617	2 052 375	2 662 981	1 363 117	1 299 864	1 542 011	789 500	752 511
5 - 9	ESDF	3 530 274	1 792 771	1 737 503	2 271 485	1 152 236	1 119 249	1 258 789	640 535	618 254
10 - 14	ESDF	3 143 756	1 597 209	1 546 547	2 062 610	1 047 953	1 014 657	1 081 146	549 256	531 890
15 - 19	ESDF	2 704 919	1 372 868	1 332 051	1 814 193	921 904	892 289	890 726	450 964	439 762
20 - 24	ESDF	2 316 564	1 169 700	1 146 864	1 581 702	800 938	780 764	734 862	368 762	366 100
25 - 29	ESDF	1 952 402	977 701	974 701	1 359 271	684 350	674 921	593 131	293 351	299 780
30 - 34	ESDF	1 614 198	800 214	813 984	1 143 674	571 922	571 752	470 524	228 292	242 232
35 - 39	ESDF	1 279 987	623 408	656 579	927 093	458 110	468 983	352 894	165 298	187 596
40 - 44	ESDF	1 032 328	499 170	533 158	756 211	372 260	383 951	276 117	126 910	149 207
45 - 49	ESDF	807 388	388 977	418 411	595 650	293 047	302 603	211 738	95 930	115 808
50 - 54	ESDF	638 860	308 112	330 748	472 597	232 751	239 846	166 263	75 361	90 902
55 - 59	ESDF	491 447	239 599	251 848	362 238	179 763	182 475	129 209	59 836	69 373
60 - 64	ESDF	373 297	179 995	193 302	274 281	134 244	140 037	99 016	45 751	53 265
65 - 69	ESDF	267 876	125 726	142 150	195 763	92 766	102 997	72 113	32 960	39 153
70 - 74	ESDF	190 384	86 113	104 271	135 525	61 375	74 150	54 859	24 738	30 121
75 - 79	ESDF	125 816	53 516	72 300	84 924	35 403	49 521	40 892	18 113	22 779
80+	ESDF	138 877	56 959	81 918	86 018	33 278	52 740	52 859	23 681	29 178
Israel - Israël[22]										
1 VII 2000										
Total	ESDJ	6 289 200	3 102 400	3 186 800	5 696 100	2 797 800	2 898 300	593 100	304 700	288 500
0 - 1	ESDJ	133 900	68 800	65 100	...	...	...	...	...	...
0 - 4	ESDJ	...	...	...	575 400	295 600	279 800	70 500	36 100	34 400
1 - 4	ESDJ	512 000	262 900	249 100	...	...	...	...	...	...
5 - 9	ESDJ	590 200	302 600	287 500	524 600	268 900	255 700	65 500	33 700	31 800
10 - 14	ESDJ	562 200	287 800	274 200	500 600	255 700	244 900	61 500	32 200	29 300
15 - 19	ESDJ	546 300	280 300	266 100	485 000	247 100	237 900	61 300	33 200	28 100
20 - 24	ESDJ	536 300	272 100	264 200	486 800	245 900	240 900	49 400	26 100	23 300
25 - 29	ESDJ	498 500	251 700	246 900	456 300	230 100	226 200	42 300	21 700	20 600
30 - 34	ESDJ	416 300	207 500	208 800	376 800	187 500	189 300	39 600	19 900	19 700
35 - 39	ESDJ	382 500	188 000	194 400	344 000	168 600	175 400	38 500	19 400	19 100
40 - 44	ESDJ	375 100	182 100	193 100	339 100	163 600	175 500	36 000	18 400	17 600
45 - 49	ESDJ	370 900	179 600	191 200	337 400	162 300	175 100	33 500	17 300	16 200
50 - 54	ESDJ	332 300	160 400	172 000	305 800	146 600	159 200	26 500	13 700	12 800
55 - 59	ESDJ	206 500	99 200	107 300	...	...	...	...	...	...
55 - 64	ESDJ	...	...	...	386 700	180 900	205 800	30 800	15 900	14 900
60 - 64	ESDJ	210 900	97 500	113 400	...	...	...	...	...	...
65 - 69	ESDJ	180 100	81 100	99 100	...	...	...	...	...	...
65 - 74	ESDJ	...	...	...	324 700	142 000	182 700	20 200	9 400	10 800
70 - 74	ESDJ	164 900	70 200	94 700	...	...	...	...	...	...
75+	ESDJ	...	...	...	252 900	103 000	149 900	17 500	7 500	10 000
75 - 79	ESDJ	135 100	56 300	79 100	...	...	...	...	...	...
80 - 84	ESDJ	70 000	29 100	40 800	...	...	...	...	...	...
85 - 89	ESDJ	46 800	18 100	28 700	...	...	...	...	...	...
90+	ESDJ	18 600	7 300	11 300	...	...	...	...	...	...

7. Population by age, sex and urban/rural residence: latest available year, 1992 - 2001
Population selon l'âge, le sexe et la résidence, urbaine/rurale: dernière année disponible, 1992 - 2001
(continued — suite)

(See notes at end of table. — Voir notes à la fin du tableau.)

Continent, country or area, date and age (in years) / Continent, pays ou zone, date et âge (en années)	Code[1]	Total			Urban - Urbaine			Rural - Rurale		
		Both sexes Les deux sexes	Male Masculin	Female Féminin	Both sexes Les deux sexes	Male Masculin	Female Féminin	Both sexes Les deux sexes	Male Masculin	Female Féminin
ASIA — ASIE										
Japan - Japon[23]										
1 X 2000										
Total	CDFC	126 925 843	62 110 764	64 815 079	99 865 289	49 005 691	50 859 598	27 060 554	13 105 073	13 955 481
0 - 1	CDFC	1 171 652	600 466	571 186	946 482	485 130	461 352	225 170	115 336	109 834
1 - 4	CDFC	4 732 446	2 422 055	2 310 391	3 771 724	1 930 430	1 841 294	960 722	491 625	469 097
5 - 9	CDFC	6 021 789	3 083 431	2 938 358	4 686 566	2 399 688	2 286 878	1 335 223	683 743	651 480
10 - 14	CDFC	6 546 612	3 353 150	3 193 462	5 000 556	2 560 796	2 439 760	1 546 056	792 354	753 702
15 - 19	CDFC	7 488 165	3 833 984	3 654 181	5 878 320	3 010 056	2 868 264	1 609 845	823 928	785 917
20 - 24	CDFC	8 421 460	4 307 242	4 114 218	6 989 577	3 582 379	3 407 198	1 431 883	724 863	707 020
25 - 29	CDFC	9 790 309	4 965 277	4 825 032	8 149 612	4 131 227	4 018 385	1 640 697	834 050	806 647
30 - 34	CDFC	8 776 610	4 436 818	4 339 792	7 301 831	3 699 586	3 602 245	1 474 779	737 232	737 547
35 - 39	CDFC	8 114 865	4 096 286	4 018 579	6 578 179	3 330 783	3 247 396	1 536 686	765 503	771 183
40 - 44	CDFC	7 800 219	3 924 171	3 876 048	6 099 826	3 068 796	3 031 030	1 700 393	855 375	845 018
45 - 49	CDFC	8 916 008	4 467 772	4 448 236	6 895 939	3 440 338	3 455 601	2 020 069	1 027 434	992 635
50 - 54	CDFC	10 441 990	5 210 038	5 231 952	8 237 639	4 085 392	4 152 247	2 204 351	1 124 646	1 079 705
55 - 59	CDFC	8 734 172	4 290 239	4 443 933	6 965 529	3 418 751	3 546 778	1 768 643	871 488	897 155
60 - 64	CDFC	7 735 833	3 749 528	3 986 305	6 039 491	2 935 344	3 104 147	1 696 342	814 184	882 158
65 - 69	CDFC	7 105 939	3 357 281	3 748 658	5 374 653	2 546 769	2 827 884	1 731 286	810 512	920 774
70 - 74	CDFC	5 900 576	2 670 270	3 230 306	4 304 854	1 951 802	2 353 052	1 595 722	718 468	877 254
75 - 79	CDFC	4 150 600	1 625 822	2 524 778	2 979 368	1 169 120	1 810 248	1 171 232	456 702	714 530
80 - 84	CDFC	2 614 689	915 268	1 699 421	1 864 830	652 632	1 212 198	749 859	262 636	487 223
85 - 89	CDFC	1 532 323	477 083	1 055 240	1 089 747	341 275	748 472	442 576	135 808	306 768
90 - 94	CDFC	570 281	149 295	420 986	401 755	105 381	296 374	168 526	43 914	124 612
95 - 99	CDFC	118 488	25 070	93 418	82 972	17 454	65 518	35 516	7 616	27 900
100+	CDFC	12 256	2 027	10 229	8 403	1 355	7 048	3 853	672	3 181
Unk. - Inc.	CDFC	228 561	148 191	80 370	217 436	141 207	76 229	11 125	6 984	4 141
1 X 2001										
Total	ESDF	127 291 000	62 244 000	65 047 000	...	...	...	...	...	...
0 - 1	ESDF	1 177 000	605 000	572 000	...	...	...	...	...	...
1 - 4	ESDF	4 724 000	2 419 000	2 304 000	...	...	...	...	...	...
5 - 9	ESDF	6 001 000	3 074 000	2 925 000	...	...	...	...	...	...
10 - 14	ESDF	6 382 000	3 271 000	3 111 000	...	...	...	...	...	...
15 - 19	ESDF	7 350 000	3 767 000	3 584 000	...	...	...	...	...	...
20 - 24	ESDF	8 202 000	4 197 000	4 004 000	...	...	...	...	...	...
25 - 29	ESDF	9 704 000	4 923 000	4 780 000	...	...	...	...	...	...
30 - 34	ESDF	9 327 000	4 717 000	4 611 000	...	...	...	...	...	...
35 - 39	ESDF	8 012 000	4 043 000	3 966 000	...	...	...	...	...	...
40 - 44	ESDF	7 757 000	3 906 000	3 850 000	...	...	...	...	...	...
45 - 49	ESDF	8 526 000	4 275 000	4 251 000	...	...	...	...	...	...
50 - 54	ESDF	11 017 000	5 498 000	5 520 000	...	...	...	...	...	...
55 - 59	ESDF	8 327 000	4 092 000	4 236 000	...	...	...	...	...	...
60 - 64	ESDF	7 919 000	3 840 000	4 079 000	...	...	...	...	...	...
65 - 69	ESDF	7 277 000	3 445 000	3 833 000	...	...	...	...	...	...
70 - 74	ESDF	6 059 000	2 755 000	3 306 000	...	...	...	...	...	...
75 - 79	ESDF	4 431 000	1 783 000	2 647 000	...	...	...	...	...	...
80 - 84	ESDF	2 720 000	944 000	1 778 000	...	...	...	...	...	...
85 - 89	ESDF	1 606 000	499 000	1 107 000	...	...	...	...	...	...
90+	ESDF	774 000	192 000	582 000	...	...	...	...	...	...
Jordan - Jordanie[24]										
10 XII 1994										
Total	CDFC	4 139 458	2 160 725	1 978 733	3 238 757	1 687 530	1 551 227	900 701	473 195	427 506
0 - 1	CDFC	123 963	63 377	60 586	95 860	49 143	46 717	28 103	14 234	13 869
1 - 4	CDFC	492 953	252 930	240 023	377 855	193 790	184 065	115 098	59 140	55 958
5 - 9	CDFC	566 406	289 767	276 639	432 615	220 987	211 628	133 791	68 780	65 011
10 - 14	CDFC	529 059	271 179	257 880	406 464	207 860	198 604	122 595	63 319	59 276
15 - 19	CDFC	483 548	251 160	232 388	374 507	194 129	180 378	109 041	57 031	52 010
20 - 24	CDFC	453 423	243 622	209 801	357 900	191 806	166 094	95 523	51 816	43 707
25 - 29	CDFC	378 952	209 365	169 587	302 167	166 150	136 017	76 785	43 215	33 570
30 - 34	CDFC	272 376	145 584	126 792	221 111	117 967	103 144	51 265	27 617	23 648

7. Population by age, sex and urban/rural residence: latest available year, 1992 - 2001
Population selon l'âge, le sexe et la résidence, urbaine/rurale: dernière année disponible, 1992 - 2001
(continued — suite)

(See notes at end of table. — Voir notes à la fin du tableau.)

Continent, country or area, date and age (in years) / Continent, pays ou zone, date et âge (en années)	Code[1]	Total			Urban - Urbaine			Rural - Rurale		
		Both sexes Les deux sexes	Male Masculin	Female Féminin	Both sexes Les deux sexes	Male Masculin	Female Féminin	Both sexes Les deux sexes	Male Masculin	Female Féminin
ASIA — ASIE										
Jordan - Jordanie[24]										
10 XII 1994										
35 - 39	CDFC	188 510	98 364	90 146	152 152	79 303	72 849	36 358	19 061	17 297
40 - 44	CDFC	141 140	73 128	68 012	111 873	57 507	54 366	29 267	15 621	13 646
45 - 49	CDFC	127 400	63 161	64 239	103 397	51 162	52 235	24 003	11 999	12 004
50 - 54	CDFC	114 318	61 149	53 169	92 506	49 729	42 777	21 812	11 420	10 392
55 - 59	CDFC	91 621	48 299	43 322	73 611	38 940	34 671	18 010	9 359	8 651
60 - 64	CDFC	68 005	35 251	32 754	53 549	27 704	25 845	14 456	7 547	6 909
65 - 69	CDFC	42 232	22 799	19 433	33 797	18 037	15 760	8 435	4 762	3 673
70 - 74	CDFC	29 618	13 621	15 997	22 472	10 222	12 250	7 146	3 399	3 747
75 - 79	CDFC	14 497	7 507	6 990	11 050	5 615	5 435	3 447	1 892	1 555
80+	CDFC	17 786	8 328	9 458	13 145	5 835	7 310	4 641	2 493	2 148
Unk. - Inc.	CDFC	3 651	2 134	1 517	2 726	1 644	1 082	925	490	435
31 XII 2000										
Total	ESDF	5 039 000	2 635 400	2 403 600	...	...	...	...	...	...
0 - 1	ESDF	151 875	78 140	73 735	...	...	...	...	...	...
1 - 4	ESDF	573 740	293 450	280 290	...	...	...	...	...	...
5 - 9	ESDF	665 150	339 965	325 185	...	...	...	...	...	...
10 - 14	ESDF	604 680	310 975	293 705	...	...	...	...	...	...
15 - 19	ESDF	549 250	279 350	269 900	...	...	...	...	...	...
20 - 24	ESDF	508 940	266 175	242 765	...	...	...	...	...	...
25 - 29	ESDF	483 745	268 810	214 935	...	...	...	...	...	...
30 - 34	ESDF	403 120	224 010	179 110	...	...	...	...	...	...
35 - 39	ESDF	277 145	150 220	126 925	...	...	...	...	...	...
40 - 44	ESDF	211 640	110 690	100 950	...	...	...	...	...	...
45 - 49	ESDF	151 170	79 060	72 110	...	...	...	...	...	...
50 - 54	ESDF	120 935	63 250	57 685	...	...	...	...	...	...
55 - 59	ESDF	110 860	57 980	52 880	...	...	...	...	...	...
60 - 64	ESDF	90 700	47 440	43 260	...	...	...	...	...	...
65+	ESDF	136 050	65 885	70 165	...	...	...	...	...	...
Kazakhstan										
1 VII 1999										
Total	ESDF	14 926 945	7 190 822	7 736 123	8 345 487	3 899 728	4 445 759	6 581 458	3 291 094	3 290 364
0 - 1	ESDF	211 476	109 032	102 444	106 072	54 673	51 399	105 404	54 359	51 045
1 - 4	ESDF	942 069	480 483	461 586	450 352	228 274	222 078	491 717	252 209	239 508
5 - 9	ESDF	1 473 993	749 028	724 965	714 638	359 526	355 112	759 355	389 502	369 853
10 - 14	ESDF	1 604 524	806 408	798 116	807 352	402 630	404 722	797 172	403 778	393 394
15 - 19	ESDF	1 410 883	705 773	705 110	708 647	347 233	361 414	702 236	358 540	343 696
20 - 24	ESDF	1 297 244	643 622	653 622	713 214	335 201	378 013	584 030	308 421	275 609
25 - 29	ESDF	1 159 446	599 070	560 376	733 915	355 654	378 261	425 531	243 416	182 115
30 - 34	ESDF	1 062 048	532 510	529 538	643 431	313 951	329 480	418 617	218 559	200 058
35 - 39	ESDF	1 188 588	582 510	606 078	708 424	339 024	369 400	480 164	243 486	236 678
40 - 44	ESDF	1 050 684	507 944	542 740	642 428	303 479	338 949	408 256	204 465	203 791
45 - 49	ESDF	862 641	407 386	455 255	537 783	249 038	288 745	324 858	158 348	166 510
50 - 54	ESDF	569 824	264 005	305 819	356 757	161 784	194 973	213 067	102 221	110 846
55 - 59	ESDF	506 020	225 000	281 020	290 289	124 351	165 938	215 731	100 649	115 082
60 - 64	ESDF	583 940	252 751	331 189	341 540	141 312	200 228	242 400	111 439	130 961
65 - 69	ESDF	345 932	137 790	208 142	205 076	77 009	128 067	140 856	60 781	80 075
70 - 74	ESDF	336 102	112 166	223 936	203 819	65 078	138 741	132 283	47 088	85 195
75 - 79	ESDF	159 885	41 880	118 005	94 818	23 730	71 088	65 067	18 150	46 917
80 - 84	ESDF	84 296	19 271	65 025	48 436	10 711	37 725	35 860	8 560	27 300
85 - 89	ESDF	52 338	9 969	42 369	27 087	5 190	21 897	25 251	4 779	20 472
90 - 94	ESDF	19 680	3 219	16 461	8 815	1 404	7 411	10 865	1 815	9 050
95 - 99	ESDF	4 803	880	3 923	2 174	409	1 765	2 629	471	2 158
100+	ESDF	529	125	404	420	67	353	109	58	51

7. Population by age, sex and urban/rural residence: latest available year, 1992 - 2001
Population selon l'âge, le sexe et la résidence, urbaine/rurale: dernière année disponible, 1992 - 2001
(continued — suite)

(See notes at end of table. — Voir notes à la fin du tableau.)

Continent, country or area, date and age (in years) / Continent, pays ou zone, date et âge (en annèes)	Code[1]	Total			Urban - Urbaine			Rural - Rurale		
		Both sexes Les deux sexes	Male Masculin	Female Féminin	Both sexes Les deux sexes	Male Masculin	Female Féminin	Both sexes Les deux sexes	Male Masculin	Female Féminin
ASIA — ASIE										
Korea (Dem. People's Republic of) - Corée (Rép. populaire dém. de)										
31 XII 1993										
Total	CDJC	20 522 351	9 677 663	10 844 688	12 501 217	5 951 077	6 550 140	8 021 134	3 726 586	4 294 548
0 - 1	CDJC	416 088	213 149	202 939	228 730	117 280	111 450	187 358	95 869	91 489
1 - 4	CDJC	1 672 420	858 805	813 615	955 496	490 788	464 708	716 924	368 017	348 907
5 - 9	CDJC	1 866 583	957 583	909 000	1 102 774	565 845	536 929	763 809	391 738	372 071
10 - 14	CDJC	1 767 112	904 764	862 348	1 081 711	554 589	527 122	685 401	350 175	335 226
15 - 19	CDJC	1 528 298	708 790	819 508	957 833	450 199	507 634	570 465	258 591	311 874
20 - 24	CDJC	1 862 989	765 479	1 097 510	1 158 144	493 090	665 054	704 845	272 389	432 456
25 - 29	CDJC	2 019 525	987 095	1 032 430	1 256 838	630 044	626 794	762 687	357 051	405 636
30 - 34	CDJC	1 607 929	791 117	816 812	1 002 111	498 143	503 968	605 818	292 974	312 844
35 - 39	CDJC	1 386 454	682 990	703 464	901 104	440 315	460 789	485 350	242 675	242 675
40 - 44	CDJC	990 787	482 309	508 478	638 616	306 319	332 297	352 171	175 990	176 181
45 - 49	CDJC	1 243 077	603 230	639 847	786 240	377 375	408 865	456 837	225 855	230 982
50 - 54	CDJC	1 208 802	582 990	625 812	754 557	361 150	393 407	454 245	221 840	232 405
55 - 59	CDJC	1 063 657	487 276	576 381	635 339	290 490	344 849	428 318	196 786	231 532
60 - 64	CDJC	748 594	301 764	446 830	437 753	187 062	250 691	310 841	114 702	196 139
65 - 69	CDJC	506 061	174 925	331 136	275 918	101 045	174 873	230 143	73 880	156 263
70 - 74	CDJC	339 533	102 975	236 558	177 353	53 214	124 139	162 180	49 761	112 419
75 - 79	CDJC	187 260	49 324	137 936	95 721	23 326	72 395	91 539	25 998	65 541
80 - 84	CDJC	81 332	19 005	62 327	41 691	8 893	32 798	39 641	10 112	29 529
85 - 89	CDJC	20 835	3 565	17 270	10 559	1 671	8 888	10 276	1 894	8 382
90 - 94	CDJC	4 100	485	3 615	2 145	217	1 928	1 955	268	1 687
95+	CDJC	818	40	778	530	20	510	288	20	268
Unk. - Inc.	CDJC	97	3	94	54	2	52	43	1	42
Korea (Republic of) - Corée (République de)[25]										
1 XI 1995										
Total	CDJC	44 553 710	22 357 352	22 196 358	34 991 964	17 595 723	17 396 241	9 561 746	4 761 629	4 800 117
0 - 1	CDJC	655 707	349 050	306 657	547 347	291 276	256 071	108 360	57 774	50 586
1 - 4	CDJC	2 771 702	1 472 300	1 299 402	2 287 750	1 215 282	1 072 468	483 952	257 018	226 934
5 - 9	CDJC	3 096 115	1 626 922	1 469 193	2 514 837	1 325 013	1 189 824	581 278	301 909	279 369
10 - 14	CDJC	3 711 980	1 913 801	1 798 179	2 956 665	1 533 376	1 423 289	755 315	380 425	374 890
15 - 19	CDJC	3 863 491	1 987 044	1 876 447	3 083 565	1 589 448	1 494 117	779 926	397 596	382 330
20 - 24	CDJC	4 304 378	2 237 940	2 066 438	3 509 790	1 758 084	1 751 706	794 588	479 856	314 732
25 - 29	CDJC	4 137 913	2 078 417	2 059 496	3 473 377	1 725 122	1 748 255	664 536	353 295	311 241
30 - 34	CDJC	4 230 239	2 146 351	2 083 888	3 517 693	1 774 770	1 742 923	712 546	371 581	340 965
35 - 39	CDJC	4 133 864	2 103 016	2 030 848	3 428 662	1 731 271	1 697 391	705 202	371 745	333 457
40 - 44	CDJC	3 071 101	1 579 850	1 491 251	2 519 966	1 295 738	1 224 228	551 135	284 112	267 023
45 - 49	CDJC	2 464 295	1 261 509	1 202 786	1 951 493	1 004 316	947 177	512 802	257 193	255 609
50 - 54	CDJC	2 063 768	1 028 887	1 034 881	1 516 333	774 968	741 365	547 435	253 919	293 516
55 - 59	CDJC	1 913 461	923 625	989 836	1 264 170	626 873	637 297	649 291	296 752	352 539
60 - 64	CDJC	1 495 082	673 719	821 363	905 622	413 690	491 932	589 460	260 029	329 431
65 - 69	CDJC	1 043 979	420 873	623 106	612 437	242 461	369 976	431 542	178 412	253 130
70 - 74	CDJC	762 544	293 696	468 848	437 794	159 518	278 276	324 750	134 178	190 572
75 - 79	CDJC	455 673	160 498	295 175	255 966	83 390	172 576	199 707	77 108	122 599
80 - 84	CDJC	246 191	71 267	174 924	137 645	36 561	101 084	108 546	34 706	73 840
85+	CDJC	131 818	28 370	103 448	70 675	14 468	56 207	61 143	13 902	47 241
Unk. - Inc.	CDJC	409	217	192	177	98	79	232	119	113
1 VII 2001										
Total	ESDF	*47 342 828*	*23 835 309*	*23 507 519*	...	...	...	...	...	...
0 - 1	ESDF	*602 111*	*314 833*	*287 278*	...	...	...	...	...	...
1 - 4	ESDF	*2 558 890*	*1 344 123*	*1 214 767*	...	...	...	...	...	...
5 - 9	ESDF	*3 535 918*	*1 884 073*	*1 651 845*	...	...	...	...	...	...
10 - 14	ESDF	*3 163 082*	*1 675 429*	*1 487 653*	...	...	...	...	...	...

7. Population by age, sex and urban/rural residence: latest available year, 1992 - 2001
Population selon l'âge, le sexe et la résidence, urbaine/rurale: dernière année disponible, 1992 - 2001
(continued — suite)

(See notes at end of table. — Voir notes à la fin du tableau.)

Continent, country or area, date and age (in years) / Continent, pays ou zone, date et âge (en annèes)	Code[1]	Total			Urban - Urbaine			Rural - Rurale		
		Both sexes Les deux sexes	Male Masculin	Female Féminin	Both sexes Les deux sexes	Male Masculin	Female Féminin	Both sexes Les deux sexes	Male Masculin	Female Féminin
ASIA — ASIE										
Korea (Republic of) - Corée (République de)[25]										
1 VII 2001										
15 - 19	ESDF	3 622 701	1 880 835	1 741 866	...	...	...	...	...	...
20 - 24	ESDF	3 931 424	2 024 541	1 906 883	...	...	...	...	...	...
25 - 29	ESDF	4 215 329	2 172 995	2 042 334	...	...	...	...	...	...
30 - 34	ESDF	4 316 019	2 202 687	2 113 332	...	...	...	...	...	...
35 - 39	ESDF	4 224 047	2 160 796	2 063 251	...	...	...	...	...	...
40 - 44	ESDF	4 145 438	2 106 885	2 038 553	...	...	...	...	...	...
45 - 49	ESDF	3 160 749	1 597 510	1 563 239	...	...	...	...	...	...
50 - 54	ESDF	2 422 687	1 222 647	1 200 040	...	...	...	...	...	...
55 - 59	ESDF	2 006 055	989 183	1 016 872	...	...	...	...	...	...
60 - 64	ESDF	1 859 165	875 062	984 103	...	...	...	...	...	...
65 - 69	ESDF	1 465 332	640 071	825 261	...	...	...	...	...	...
70 - 74	ESDF	966 910	373 486	593 424	...	...	...	...	...	...
75 - 79	ESDF	631 802	224 802	407 000	...	...	...	...	...	...
80 - 84	ESDF	329 847	102 313	227 534	...	...	...	...	...	...
85 - 89	ESDF	138 845	34 538	104 307	...	...	...	...	...	...
90 - 94	ESDF	38 881	7 499	31 382	...	...	...	...	...	...
95+	ESDF	7 596	1 001	6 595	...	...	...	...	...	...
Kuwait - Koweït										
1 VII 1998										
Total	ESDF	2 027 103	1 226 774	800 329	...	...	...	...	...	...
0 - 1	ESDF	38 759	19 737	19 022	...	...	...	...	...	...
1 - 4	ESDF	162 578	82 913	79 665	...	...	...	...	...	...
5 - 9	ESDF	178 527	91 301	87 226	...	...	...	...	...	...
10 - 14	ESDF	162 295	82 540	79 755	...	...	...	...	...	...
15 - 19	ESDF	135 096	69 853	65 243	...	...	...	...	...	...
20 - 24	ESDF	154 165	81 411	72 754	...	...	...	...	...	...
25 - 29	ESDF	245 307	156 663	88 644	...	...	...	...	...	...
30 - 34	ESDF	273 922	186 112	87 810	...	...	...	...	...	...
35 - 39	ESDF	228 935	152 744	76 191	...	...	...	...	...	...
40 - 44	ESDF	173 732	119 508	54 224	...	...	...	...	...	...
45 - 49	ESDF	110 552	77 575	32 977	...	...	...	...	...	...
50 - 54	ESDF	66 987	46 236	20 751	...	...	...	...	...	...
55 - 59	ESDF	41 362	27 964	13 398	...	...	...	...	...	...
60 - 64	ESDF	25 882	16 652	9 230	...	...	...	...	...	...
65 - 69	ESDF	13 541	7 701	5 840	...	...	...	...	...	...
70 - 74	ESDF	7 631	4 004	3 627	...	...	...	...	...	...
75 - 79	ESDF	4 060	1 998	2 062	...	...	...	...	...	...
80 - 84	ESDF	2 111	1 073	1 038	...	...	...	...	...	...
85+	ESDF	1 661	789	872	...	...	...	...	...	...
Kyrgyzstan - Kirghizistan										
1 I 2001										
Total	ESDF	4 907 594	2 423 983	2 483 611	1 706 709	815 457	891 252	3 200 885	1 608 526	1 592 359
0 - 1	ESDF	95 064	48 578	46 486	27 474	14 086	13 388	67 590	34 492	33 098
1 - 4	ESDF	412 439	210 381	202 058	110 094	56 189	53 905	302 345	154 192	148 153
5 - 9	ESDF	585 995	296 861	289 134	163 230	82 352	80 878	422 765	214 509	208 256
10 - 14	ESDF	594 835	300 834	294 001	171 763	85 815	85 948	423 072	215 019	208 053
15 - 19	ESDF	522 588	262 782	259 806	166 047	80 462	85 585	356 541	182 320	174 221
20 - 24	ESDF	447 630	226 191	221 439	188 768	92 128	96 640	258 862	134 063	124 799
25 - 29	ESDF	397 523	200 160	197 363	153 886	74 403	79 483	243 637	125 757	117 880
30 - 34	ESDF	357 711	179 819	177 892	141 293	68 852	72 441	216 418	110 967	105 451
35 - 39	ESDF	341 584	168 896	172 688	131 552	63 220	68 332	210 032	105 676	104 356
40 - 44	ESDF	303 948	148 964	154 984	118 684	56 247	62 437	185 264	92 717	92 547
45 - 49	ESDF	218 371	105 716	112 655	87 431	40 985	46 446	130 940	64 731	66 209
50 - 54	ESDF	157 332	74 859	82 473	67 236	30 839	36 397	90 096	44 020	46 076

7. Population by age, sex and urban/rural residence: latest available year, 1992 - 2001
Population selon l'âge, le sexe et la résidence, urbaine/rurale: dernière année disponible, 1992 - 2001
(continued — suite)

(See notes at end of table. — Voir notes à la fin du tableau.)

Continent, country or area, date and age (in years) / Continent, pays ou zone, date et âge (en annèes)	Code[1]	Total			Urban - Urbaine			Rural - Rurale		
		Both sexes Les deux sexes	Male Masculin	Female Féminin	Both sexes Les deux sexes	Male Masculin	Female Féminin	Both sexes Les deux sexes	Male Masculin	Female Féminin
ASIA — ASIE										
Kyrgyzstan - Kirghizistan										
1 I 2001										
55 - 59	ESDF	76 973	36 706	40 267	30 626	13 796	16 830	46 347	22 910	23 437
60 - 64	ESDF	127 753	57 856	69 897	50 542	21 685	28 857	77 211	36 171	41 040
65 - 69	ESDF	95 017	41 816	53 201	33 766	13 729	20 037	61 251	28 087	33 164
70 - 74	ESDF	89 693	37 299	52 394	32 857	11 874	20 983	56 836	25 425	31 411
75 - 79	ESDF	46 887	16 461	30 426	18 082	5 333	12 749	28 805	11 128	17 677
80 - 84	ESDF	20 187	5 842	14 345	7 911	2 186	5 725	12 276	3 656	8 620
85 - 89	ESDF	9 848	2 595	7 253	3 871	909	2 962	5 977	1 686	4 291
90 - 94	ESDF	3 994	973	3 021	1 193	295	898	2 801	678	2 123
95 - 99	ESDF	1 475	300	1 175	303	62	241	1 172	238	934
100+	ESDF	747	94	653	100	10	90	647	84	563
Lao People's Democratic Republic - République démocratique populaire lao										
1 VII 2000										
Total	ESDF	5 218 300	2 579 000	2 639 300	...	...	...	...	...	...
0 - 4	ESDF	685 000	345 600	340 500	...	...	...	...	...	...
5 - 9	ESDF	807 100	407 400	398 500	...	...	...	...	...	...
10 - 14	ESDF	784 100	389 400	393 300	...	...	...	...	...	...
15 - 19	ESDF	550 600	276 000	274 500	...	...	...	...	...	...
20 - 24	ESDF	371 100	175 400	198 000	...	...	...	...	...	...
25 - 29	ESDF	357 800	165 100	192 700	...	...	...	...	...	...
30 - 34	ESDF	308 000	144 400	163 600	...	...	...	...	...	...
35 - 39	ESDF	326 900	159 900	166 300	...	...	...	...	...	...
40 - 44	ESDF	251 600	131 500	118 800	...	...	...	...	...	...
45 - 49	ESDF	205 100	110 900	95 000	...	...	...	...	...	...
50 - 54	ESDF	164 000	72 200	92 400	...	...	...	...	...	...
55 - 59	ESDF	124 700	61 900	63 300	...	...	...	...	...	...
60 - 64	ESDF	98 200	51 600	47 500	...	...	...	...	...	...
65 - 69	ESDF	73 500	36 100	37 000	...	...	...	...	...	...
70 - 74	ESDF	51 000	25 800	23 800	...	...	...	...	...	...
75+	ESDF	60 000	25 800	34 300	...	...	...	...	...	...
Malaysia - Malaisie										
5 VII 2000										
Total	CDJC	23 274 690	11 853 432	11 421 258	14 426 871	7 318 396	7 108 475	8 847 819	4 535 036	4 312 783
0 - 4	CDJC	2 612 744	1 347 633	1 265 111	1 574 757	812 456	762 301	1 037 987	535 177	502 810
5 - 9	CDJC	2 646 527	1 364 984	1 281 543	1 534 452	792 519	741 933	1 112 075	572 465	539 610
10 - 14	CDJC	2 491 777	1 276 348	1 215 429	1 383 003	709 140	673 863	1 108 774	567 208	541 566
15 - 19	CDJC	2 367 021	1 195 803	1 171 218	1 408 673	707 968	700 705	958 348	487 835	470 513
20 - 24	CDJC	2 087 173	1 050 916	1 036 257	1 436 911	708 607	728 304	650 262	342 309	307 953
25 - 29	CDJC	1 921 052	972 668	948 384	1 315 940	653 627	662 313	605 112	319 041	286 071
30 - 34	CDJC	1 800 196	915 814	884 382	1 207 148	606 473	600 675	593 048	309 341	283 707
35 - 39	CDJC	1 705 044	866 212	838 832	1 141 371	577 947	563 424	563 673	288 265	275 408
40 - 44	CDJC	1 487 498	764 706	722 792	976 771	504 183	472 588	510 727	260 523	250 204
45 - 49	CDJC	1 168 527	604 844	563 683	743 757	389 417	354 340	424 770	215 427	209 343
50 - 54	CDJC	918 868	480 261	438 607	562 704	298 115	264 589	356 164	182 146	174 018
55 - 59	CDJC	616 598	320 119	296 479	356 078	186 312	169 766	260 520	133 807	126 713
60 - 64	CDJC	551 027	274 216	276 811	306 351	153 941	152 410	244 676	120 275	124 401
65 - 69	CDJC	346 725	164 943	181 782	189 063	89 783	99 280	157 662	75 160	82 502
70 - 74	CDJC	264 119	125 883	138 236	138 716	64 354	74 362	125 403	61 529	63 874
75+	CDJC	289 794	128 082	161 712	151 176	63 554	87 622	138 618	64 528	74 090
Maldives										
25 III 1995										
Total	CDFC	244 814	124 622	120 192	62 519	33 506	29 013	182 295	91 116	91 179
0 - 1	CDFC	7 044	3 593	3 451	1 149	592	557	5 895	3 001	2 894

7. Population by age, sex and urban/rural residence: latest available year, 1992 - 2001
Population selon l'âge, le sexe et la résidence, urbaine/rurale: dernière année disponible, 1992 - 2001
(continued — suite)

(See notes at end of table. — Voir notes à la fin du tableau.)

Continent, country or area, date and age (in years) / Continent, pays ou zone, date et âge (en annèes)	Code[1]	Total			Urban - Urbaine			Rural - Rurale		
		Both sexes Les deux sexes	Male Masculin	Female Féminin	Both sexes Les deux sexes	Male Masculin	Female Féminin	Both sexes Les deux sexes	Male Masculin	Female Féminin
ASIA — ASIE										
Maldives										
25 III 1995										
1 - 4	CDFC	29 928	15 520	14 408	4 978	2 603	2 375	24 950	12 917	12 033
5 - 9	CDFC	40 759	20 840	19 919	7 203	3 671	3 532	33 556	17 169	16 387
10 - 14	CDFC	35 870	18 286	17 584	8 441	4 256	4 185	27 429	14 030	13 399
15 - 19	CDFC	24 905	12 343	12 562	9 745	5 328	4 417	15 160	7 015	8 145
20 - 24	CDFC	21 021	9 944	11 077	7 339	4 075	3 264	13 682	5 869	7 813
25 - 29	CDFC	18 191	8 802	9 389	5 854	3 229	2 625	12 337	5 573	6 764
30 - 34	CDFC	15 364	7 579	7 785	4 656	2 526	2 130	10 708	5 053	5 655
35 - 39	CDFC	12 632	6 315	6 317	3 572	1 911	1 661	9 060	4 404	4 656
40 - 44	CDFC	6 922	3 625	3 297	2 061	1 216	845	4 861	2 409	2 452
45 - 49	CDFC	6 584	3 369	3 215	1 892	1 021	871	4 692	2 348	2 344
50 - 54	CDFC	6 247	3 205	3 042	1 643	885	758	4 604	2 320	2 284
55 - 59	CDFC	5 962	3 240	2 722	1 341	725	616	4 621	2 515	2 106
60 - 64	CDFC	5 294	3 010	2 284	1 061	563	498	4 233	2 447	1 786
65 - 69	CDFC	3 201	1 897	1 304	606	335	271	2 595	1 562	1 033
70 - 74	CDFC	2 101	1 279	822	387	222	165	1 714	1 057	657
75 - 79	CDFC	968	617	351	186	99	87	782	518	264
80 - 84	CDFC	695	394	301	102	44	58	593	350	243
85 - 89	CDFC	326	220	106	47	24	23	279	196	83
90 - 94	CDFC	163	86	77	27	12	15	136	74	62
95+	CDFC	94	67	27	17	9	8	77	58	19
Unk. - Inc.	CDFC	543	391	152	212	160	52	331	231	100
31 III 2000										
Total	CDFC	270 101	137 200	132 901	...	...	...	...	...	...
0 - 1	CDFC	5 515	2 780	2 735	...	...	...	...	...	...
1 - 4	CDFC	25 397	12 919	12 478	...	...	...	...	...	...
5 - 9	CDFC	37 927	19 336	18 591	...	...	...	...	...	...
10 - 14	CDFC	41 089	20 897	20 192	...	...	...	...	...	...
15 - 19	CDFC	33 266	16 590	16 676	...	...	...	...	...	...
20 - 24	CDFC	23 514	11 620	11 894	...	...	...	...	...	...
25 - 29	CDFC	20 090	9 805	10 285	...	...	...	...	...	...
30 - 34	CDFC	18 161	8 890	9 271	...	...	...	...	...	...
35 - 39	CDFC	15 699	7 828	7 871	...	...	...	...	...	...
40 - 44	CDFC	12 402	6 272	6 130	...	...	...	...	...	...
45 - 49	CDFC	7 461	3 977	3 484	...	...	...	...	...	...
50 - 54	CDFC	5 967	3 051	2 916	...	...	...	...	...	...
55 - 59	CDFC	5 996	3 131	2 865	...	...	...	...	...	...
60 - 64	CDFC	6 312	3 370	2 942	...	...	...	...	...	...
65 - 69	CDFC	4 611	2 650	1 961	...	...	...	...	...	...
70 - 74	CDFC	2 873	1 737	1 136	...	...	...	...	...	...
75 - 79	CDFC	1 410	859	551	...	...	...	...	...	...
80 - 84	CDFC	679	407	272	...	...	...	...	...	...
85 - 89	CDFC	284	162	122	...	...	...	...	...	...
90 - 94	CDFC	96	59	37	...	...	...	...	...	...
95+	CDFC	76	45	31	...	...	...	...	...	...
Unk. - Inc.	CDFC	1 276	815	461	...	...	...	...	...	...
Mongolia - Mongolie										
5 I 2000										
Total	CDFC	2 373 493	1 177 981	1 195 512	1 344 516	657 081	687 435	1 028 977	520 900	508 077
0 - 1	CDFC	49 804	25 356	24 448	23 778	12 119	11 659	26 026	13 237	12 789
1 - 4	CDFC	196 219	99 126	97 093	91 687	46 096	45 591	104 532	53 030	51 502
5 - 9	CDFC	285 664	144 315	141 349	150 401	75 700	74 701	135 263	68 615	66 648
10 - 14	CDFC	317 434	159 294	158 140	179 974	89 670	90 304	137 460	69 624	67 836
15 - 19	CDFC	263 358	133 327	130 031	154 244	75 040	79 204	109 114	58 287	50 827
20 - 24	CDFC	235 751	118 023	117 728	135 694	66 010	69 684	100 057	52 013	48 044
25 - 29	CDFC	216 652	107 962	108 690	125 644	61 274	64 370	91 008	46 688	44 320
30 - 34	CDFC	187 872	92 473	95 399	113 537	54 332	59 205	74 335	38 141	36 194
35 - 39	CDFC	172 606	84 846	87 760	108 347	52 275	56 072	64 259	32 571	31 688

7. Population by age, sex and urban/rural residence: latest available year, 1992 - 2001
Population selon l'âge, le sexe et la résidence, urbaine/rurale: dernière année disponible, 1992 - 2001
(continued — suite)

(See notes at end of table. — Voir notes à la fin du tableau.)

Continent, country or area, date and age (in years) / Continent, pays ou zone, date et âge (en années)	Code[1]	Total			Urban - Urbaine			Rural - Rurale		
		Both sexes Les deux sexes	Male Masculin	Female Féminin	Both sexes Les deux sexes	Male Masculin	Female Féminin	Both sexes Les deux sexes	Male Masculin	Female Féminin
ASIA — ASIE										
Mongolia - Mongolie										
5 I 2000										
40 - 44	CDFC	127 220	62 619	64 601	79 563	38 840	40 723	47 657	23 779	23 878
45 - 49	CDFC	82 888	40 562	42 326	50 873	25 089	25 784	32 015	15 473	16 542
50 - 54	CDFC	57 835	27 707	30 128	35 016	17 094	17 922	22 819	10 613	12 206
55 - 59	CDFC	55 895	27 379	28 516	30 397	15 011	15 386	25 498	12 368	13 130
60 - 64	CDFC	42 292	20 778	21 514	21 889	10 658	11 231	20 403	10 120	10 283
65 - 69	CDFC	35 415	15 982	19 433	18 480	8 145	10 335	16 935	7 837	9 098
70 - 74	CDFC	20 239	8 766	11 473	10 946	4 579	6 367	9 293	4 187	5 106
75 - 79	CDFC	14 843	5 832	9 011	7 963	3 197	4 766	6 880	2 635	4 245
80 - 84	CDFC	7 036	2 329	4 707	3 777	1 281	2 496	3 259	1 048	2 211
85 - 89	CDFC	3 376	991	2 385	1 746	519	1 227	1 630	472	1 158
90 - 94	CDFC	869	257	612	441	125	316	428	132	296
95 - 99	CDFC	196	53	143	104	24	80	92	29	63
100+	CDFC	29	4	25	15	3	12	14	1	13
1 I 2001										
Total	ESDF	*2 407 488*	*1 192 415*	*1 215 073*	...	...	...	...	...	...
0 - 1	ESDF	*42 354*	*21 422*	*20 932*	...	...	...	...	...	...
1 - 4	ESDF	*188 339*	*95 160*	*93 179*	...	...	...	...	...	...
5 - 9	ESDF	*267 992*	*135 329*	*132 663*	...	...	...	...	...	...
10 - 14	ESDF	*314 824*	*157 923*	*156 901*	...	...	...	...	...	...
15 - 19	ESDF	*276 626*	*138 551*	*138 075*	...	...	...	...	...	...
20 - 24	ESDF	*249 447*	*122 680*	*126 767*	...	...	...	...	...	...
25 - 29	ESDF	*219 824*	*108 963*	*110 861*	...	...	...	...	...	...
30 - 34	ESDF	*190 603*	*93 735*	*96 868*	...	...	...	...	...	...
35 - 39	ESDF	*172 606*	*85 266*	*87 340*	...	...	...	...	...	...
40 - 44	ESDF	*139 384*	*68 554*	*70 830*	...	...	...	...	...	...
45 - 49	ESDF	*90 233*	*44 648*	*45 585*	...	...	...	...	...	...
50 - 54	ESDF	*66 975*	*32 675*	*34 300*	...	...	...	...	...	...
55 - 59	ESDF	*57 203*	*28 099*	*29 104*	...	...	...	...	...	...
60 - 64	ESDF	*46 237*	*22 418*	*23 819*	...	...	...	...	...	...
65 - 69	ESDF	*35 173*	*16 382*	*18 791*	...	...	...	...	...	...
70 - 74	ESDF	*21 783*	*9 688*	*12 095*	...	...	...	...	...	...
75 - 79	ESDF	*15 268*	*6 473*	*8 795*	...	...	...	...	...	...
80 - 84	ESDF	*7 633*	*2 806*	*4 827*	...	...	...	...	...	...
85 - 89	ESDF	*3 685*	*1 222*	*2 463*	...	...	...	...	...	...
90 - 94	ESDF	*1 053*	*348*	*705*	...	...	...	...	...	...
95 - 99	ESDF	*204*	*65*	*139*	...	...	...	...	...	...
100+	ESDF	*42*	*8*	*34*	...	...	...	...	...	...
Myanmar										
1 VII 1997										
Total	ESDF	*46 402 000*	*23 039 000*	*23 363 000*	...	...	...	...	...	...
0 - 4	ESDF	*5 786 000*	*2 879 000*	*2 907 000*	...	...	...	...	...	...
5 - 9	ESDF	*4 959 000*	*2 558 000*	*2 401 000*	...	...	...	...	...	...
10 - 14	ESDF	*4 708 000*	*2 440 000*	*2 268 000*	...	...	...	...	...	...
15 - 19	ESDF	*4 593 000*	*2 343 000*	*2 250 000*	...	...	...	...	...	...
20 - 24	ESDF	*4 299 000*	*2 165 000*	*2 134 000*	...	...	...	...	...	...
25 - 29	ESDF	*3 952 000*	*1 961 000*	*1 991 000*	...	...	...	...	...	...
30 - 34	ESDF	*3 555 000*	*1 745 000*	*1 810 000*	...	...	...	...	...	...
35 - 39	ESDF	*3 060 000*	*1 496 000*	*1 564 000*	...	...	...	...	...	...
40 - 44	ESDF	*2 594 000*	*1 263 000*	*1 331 000*	...	...	...	...	...	...
45 - 49	ESDF	*2 131 000*	*1 035 000*	*1 096 000*	...	...	...	...	...	...
50 - 54	ESDF	*1 747 000*	*842 000*	*905 000*	...	...	...	...	...	...
55 - 59	ESDF	*1 466 000*	*695 000*	*771 000*	...	...	...	...	...	...
60 - 64	ESDF	*1 202 000*	*561 000*	*641 000*	...	...	...	...	...	...
65+	ESDF	*2 350 000*	*1 056 000*	*1 294 000*	...	...	...	...	...	...
Nepal - Népal										
1 VII 1996										
Total	ESDJ	*20 831 644*	*10 393 913*	*10 437 731*	*2 207 967*	*1 138 641*	*1 069 326*	*18 623 677*	*9 255 272*	*9 368 405*

7. Population by age, sex and urban/rural residence: latest available year, 1992 - 2001
Population selon l'âge, le sexe et la résidence, urbaine/rurale: dernière année disponible, 1992 - 2001
(continued — suite)

(See notes at end of table. — Voir notes à la fin du tableau.)

Continent, country or area, date and age (in years) / Continent, pays ou zone, date et âge (en années)	Code[1]	Total			Urban - Urbaine			Rural - Rurale		
		Both sexes Les deux sexes	Male Masculin	Female Féminin	Both sexes Les deux sexes	Male Masculin	Female Féminin	Both sexes Les deux sexes	Male Masculin	Female Féminin
ASIA — ASIE										
Nepal - Népal										
1 VII 1996										
0 - 4	ESDJ	3 235 783	1 658 100	1 577 683	283 174	139 204	143 970	2 952 609	1 518 896	1 433 713
5 - 9	ESDJ	2 838 712	1 447 733	1 390 979	280 407	151 796	128 611	2 558 305	1 295 937	1 262 368
10 - 14	ESDJ	2 521 943	1 275 549	1 246 394	241 904	124 110	117 794	2 280 040	1 151 439	1 128 601
15 - 19	ESDJ	2 149 812	1 041 495	1 108 317	233 403	110 195	123 208	1 916 408	931 300	985 108
20 - 24	ESDJ	1 839 716	882 635	957 081	237 790	118 604	119 186	1 601 926	764 031	837 895
25 - 29	ESDJ	1 565 942	766 431	799 511	222 983	122 864	100 119	1 342 960	643 568	699 392
30 - 34	ESDJ	1 310 586	648 320	662 266	170 140	93 500	76 640	1 140 446	554 820	585 626
35 - 39	ESDJ	1 139 089	570 183	568 906	133 684	73 273	60 411	1 005 405	496 910	508 495
40 - 44	ESDJ	983 519	494 106	489 413	105 506	56 085	49 421	878 013	438 021	439 992
45 - 49	ESDJ	839 008	423 529	415 479	81 831	44 633	37 198	757 176	378 896	378 280
50 - 54	ESDJ	698 161	351 396	346 765	62 770	32 371	30 399	635 391	319 025	316 366
55 - 59	ESDJ	566 009	283 271	282 738	49 332	24 253	25 079	516 677	259 019	257 658
60 - 64	ESDJ	438 536	216 857	221 679	38 025	17 312	20 713	400 511	199 545	200 966
65 - 69	ESDJ	318 278	154 732	163 546	28 023	13 376	14 647	290 255	141 356	148 899
70 - 74	ESDJ	208 529	98 933	109 596	19 466	8 853	10 613	189 062	90 079	98 983
75 - 79	ESDJ	115 654	53 285	62 369	12 217	4 965	7 252	103 437	48 320	55 117
80+	ESDJ	62 367	27 358	35 009	7 312	3 247	4 065	55 056	24 110	30 946
22 VI 2001										
Total	CDJC	22 736 934	11 359 378	11 377 556	...	...	...	...	...	...
0 - 1	CDJC	494 813	252 519	242 294	...	...	...	...	...	...
1 - 4	CDJC	2 260 400	1 143 196	1 117 204	...	...	...	...	...	...
5 - 9	CDJC	3 211 442	1 633 087	1 578 355	...	...	...	...	...	...
10 - 14	CDJC	2 981 932	1 533 806	1 448 126	...	...	...	...	...	...
15 - 19	CDJC	2 389 002	1 185 826	1 203 176	...	...	...	...	...	...
20 - 24	CDJC	2 016 768	946 742	1 070 026	...	...	...	...	...	...
25 - 29	CDJC	1 725 478	821 014	904 464	...	...	...	...	...	...
30 - 34	CDJC	1 489 503	726 040	763 463	...	...	...	...	...	...
35 - 39	CDJC	1 310 653	651 351	659 302	...	...	...	...	...	...
40 - 44	CDJC	1 088 044	539 993	548 051	...	...	...	...	...	...
45 - 49	CDJC	923 373	469 695	453 678	...	...	...	...	...	...
50 - 54	CDJC	766 054	392 659	373 395	...	...	...	...	...	...
55 - 59	CDJC	602 093	318 610	283 483	...	...	...	...	...	...
60 - 64	CDJC	520 908	262 255	258 653	...	...	...	...	...	...
65 - 69	CDJC	387 223	196 053	191 170	...	...	...	...	...	...
70 - 74	CDJC	273 789	141 678	132 111	...	...	...	...	...	...
75 - 79	CDJC	165 764	82 335	83 429	...	...	...	...	...	...
80 - 84	CDJC	84 255	41 192	43 063	...	...	...	...	...	...
85 - 89	CDJC	27 947	13 630	14 317	...	...	...	...	...	...
90 - 94	CDJC	11 421	5 082	6 339	...	...	...	...	...	...
95 - 99	CDJC	6 072	2 615	3 457	...	...	...	...	...	...
Occupied Palestinian Territory - Territoire palestinien occupé										
1 VII 2001										
Total	ESDF	3 298 951	1 666 805	1 632 146	...	...	...	...	...	...
0 - 1	ESDF	128 140	65 188	62 952	...	...	...	...	...	...
1 - 4	ESDF	475 455	241 853	233 602	...	...	...	...	...	...
5 - 9	ESDF	511 081	259 730	251 351	...	...	...	...	...	...
10 - 14	ESDF	424 637	215 996	208 641	...	...	...	...	...	...
15 - 19	ESDF	343 574	176 042	167 532	...	...	...	...	...	...
20 - 24	ESDF	289 729	147 917	141 812	...	...	...	...	...	...
25 - 29	ESDF	245 225	124 626	120 599	...	...	...	...	...	...
30 - 34	ESDF	205 318	104 841	100 477	...	...	...	...	...	...
35 - 39	ESDF	170 462	88 237	82 225	...	...	...	...	...	...
40 - 44	ESDF	132 417	68 330	64 087	...	...	...	...	...	...
45 - 49	ESDF	91 979	46 766	45 213	...	...	...	...	...	...
50 - 54	ESDF	71 298	34 947	36 351	...	...	...	...	...	...

7. Population by age, sex and urban/rural residence: latest available year, 1992 - 2001
Population selon l'âge, le sexe et la résidence, urbaine/rurale: dernière année disponible, 1992 - 2001
(continued — suite)

(See notes at end of table. — Voir notes à la fin du tableau.)

Continent, country or area, date and age (in years) / Continent, pays ou zone, date et âge (en années)	Code[1]	Total			Urban - Urbaine			Rural - Rurale		
		Both sexes Les deux sexes	Male Masculin	Female Féminin	Both sexes Les deux sexes	Male Masculin	Female Féminin	Both sexes Les deux sexes	Male Masculin	Female Féminin
ASIA — ASIE										
Occupied Palestinian Territory - Territoire palestinien occupé										
1 VII 2001										
55 - 59	ESDF	55 474	25 109	30 365	...	...	...	...	...	...
60 - 64	ESDF	46 407	20 271	26 136	...	...	...	...	...	...
65 - 69	ESDF	41 152	17 820	23 332	...	...	...	...	...	...
70 - 74	ESDF	30 410	13 050	17 360	...	...	...	...	...	...
75 - 79	ESDF	19 366	8 333	11 033	...	...	...	...	...	...
80+	ESDF	16 827	7 749	9 078	...	...	...	...	...	...
Oman										
1 VII 2000										
Total	ESDF	2 401 256	1 401 589	999 667	...	...	...	...	...	...
0 - 4	ESDF	278 495	141 993	136 502	...	...	...	...	...	...
5 - 9	ESDF	287 685	146 348	141 337	...	...	...	...	...	...
10 - 14	ESDF	274 048	139 490	134 558	...	...	...	...	...	...
15 - 19	ESDF	245 717	125 772	119 945	...	...	...	...	...	...
20 - 24	ESDF	249 244	138 545	110 699	...	...	...	...	...	...
25 - 29	ESDF	256 961	168 923	88 038	...	...	...	...	...	...
30 - 34	ESDF	217 901	153 718	64 183	...	...	...	...	...	...
35 - 39	ESDF	183 236	131 348	51 888	...	...	...	...	...	...
40 - 44	ESDF	131 676	91 727	39 949	...	...	...	...	...	...
45 - 49	ESDF	86 000	56 444	29 556	...	...	...	...	...	...
50 - 54	ESDF	58 778	36 083	22 695	...	...	...	...	...	...
55 - 59	ESDF	41 620	23 454	18 166	...	...	...	...	...	...
60 - 64	ESDF	31 756	17 258	14 498	...	...	...	...	...	...
65 - 69	ESDF	22 713	12 168	10 545	...	...	...	...	...	...
70 - 74	ESDF	15 691	8 389	7 302	...	...	...	...	...	...
75+	ESDF	19 123	9 317	9 806	...	...	...	...	...	...
Unk. - Inc.	ESDF	612	612	...	...	...	...	...	...	...
Pakistan[26,27]										
2 III 1998										
Total	CDFC	127 441 708	66 204 793	61 236 915	42 375 208	22 374 052	20 001 156	85 066 500	43 830 741	41 235 759
0 - 4	CDFC	18 611 101	9 488 106	9 122 995	5 369 807	2 699 426	2 670 381	13 241 294	6 788 680	6 452 614
5 - 9	CDFC	19 944 265	10 376 230	9 568 035	5 860 782	2 975 132	2 885 650	14 083 483	7 401 098	6 682 385
10 - 14	CDFC	16 487 551	8 681 970	7 805 581	5 434 781	2 777 214	2 657 567	11 052 770	5 904 756	5 148 014
15 - 19	CDFC	13 193 775	6 780 579	6 413 196	4 720 114	2 404 205	2 315 909	8 473 661	4 376 374	4 097 287
20 - 24	CDFC	11 491 380	5 766 195	5 725 185	4 182 102	2 211 952	1 970 150	7 309 278	3 554 243	3 755 035
25 - 29	CDFC	9 565 376	4 964 363	4 601 013	3 579 238	2 022 092	1 557 146	5 986 138	2 942 271	3 043 867
30 - 34	CDFC	8 103 504	4 330 684	3 772 820	3 122 406	1 796 023	1 326 383	4 981 098	2 534 661	2 446 437
35 - 39	CDFC	6 144 394	3 278 330	2 866 064	2 373 755	1 336 906	1 036 849	3 770 639	1 941 424	1 829 215
40 - 44	CDFC	5 640 767	2 847 692	2 793 075	2 057 973	1 100 661	957 312	3 582 794	1 747 031	1 835 763
45 - 49	CDFC	4 494 396	2 294 132	2 200 264	1 528 816	815 066	713 750	2 965 580	1 479 066	1 486 514
50 - 54	CDFC	4 080 253	2 151 291	1 928 962	1 325 717	705 053	620 664	2 754 536	1 446 238	1 308 298
55 - 59	CDFC	2 698 411	1 448 731	1 249 680	861 236	471 026	390 210	1 837 175	977 705	859 470
60 - 64	CDFC	2 618 383	1 406 681	1 211 702	780 898	418 241	362 657	1 837 485	988 440	849 045
65 - 69	CDFC	1 509 437	828 153	681 284	447 364	243 412	203 952	1 062 073	584 741	477 332
70 - 74	CDFC	1 353 974	744 456	609 518	360 539	196 885	163 654	993 435	547 571	445 864
75+	CDFC	1 504 741	817 200	687 541	369 680	200 758	168 922	1 135 061	616 442	518 619
Philippines										
1 IX 1995										
Total	CDJC	68 616 536	34 584 170	34 032 366	...	...	...	...	...	...
0 - 1	CDJC	1 878 319	970 072	908 247	...	...	...	...	...	...
1 - 4	CDJC	7 483 799	3 857 196	3 626 603	...	...	...	...	...	...
5 - 9	CDJC	8 893 430	4 566 569	4 326 861	...	...	...	...	...	...
10 - 14	CDJC	8 040 658	4 081 676	3 958 982	...	...	...	...	...	...
15 - 19	CDJC	7 465 451	3 726 799	3 738 652	...	...	...	...	...	...
20 - 24	CDJC	6 270 557	3 119 589	3 150 968	...	...	...	...	...	...
25 - 29	CDJC	5 752 631	2 879 753	2 872 878	...	...	...	...	...	...

7. Population by age, sex and urban/rural residence: latest available year, 1992 - 2001
Population selon l'âge, le sexe et la résidence, urbaine/rurale: dernière année disponible, 1992 - 2001
(continued — suite)

(See notes at end of table. — Voir notes à la fin du tableau.)

Continent, country or area, date and age (in years) / Continent, pays ou zone, date et âge (en annèes)	Code[1]	Total			Urban - Urbaine			Rural - Rurale		
		Both sexes Les deux sexes	Male Masculin	Female Féminin	Both sexes Les deux sexes	Male Masculin	Female Féminin	Both sexes Les deux sexes	Male Masculin	Female Féminin
ASIA — ASIE										
Philippines										
1 IX 1995										
30 - 34	CDJC	4 861 116	2 454 570	2 406 546	...	...	...	...	...	...
35 - 39	CDJC	4 318 168	2 195 627	2 122 541	...	...	...	...	...	...
40 - 44	CDJC	3 402 813	1 729 637	1 673 176	...	...	...	...	...	...
45 - 49	CDJC	2 734 379	1 384 973	1 349 406	...	...	...	...	...	...
50 - 54	CDJC	2 063 363	1 032 912	1 030 451	...	...	...	...	...	...
55 - 59	CDJC	1 715 069	844 164	870 905	...	...	...	...	...	...
60 - 64	CDJC	1 322 088	641 970	680 118	...	...	...	...	...	...
65 - 69	CDJC	955 878	448 557	507 321	...	...	...	...	...	...
70 - 74	CDJC	654 459	299 990	354 469	...	...	...	...	...	...
75 - 79	CDJC	410 024	184 175	225 849	...	...	...	...	...	...
80 - 84	CDJC	252 035	107 048	144 987	...	...	...	...	...	...
85 - 89	CDJC	95 865	39 625	56 240	...	...	...	...	...	...
90 - 94	CDJC	37 294	15 469	21 825	...	...	...	...	...	...
95 - 99	CDJC	7 592	3 221	4 371	...	...	...	...	...	...
100+	CDJC	1 548	578	970	...	...	...	...	...	...
Saudi Arabia - Arabie saoudite										
27 IX 1992										
Total	CDFC	16 948 388	9 479 973	7 468 415	...	...	...	...	...	...
0 - 1	CDFC	513 850	262 345	251 505	...	...	...	...	...	...
1 - 4	CDFC	2 040 375	1 037 484	1 002 891	...	...	...	...	...	...
5 - 9	CDFC	2 469 655	1 243 974	1 225 681	...	...	...	...	...	...
10 - 14	CDFC	2 052 250	1 043 533	1 008 717	...	...	...	...	...	...
15 - 19	CDFC	1 495 805	740 526	755 279	...	...	...	...	...	...
20 - 24	CDFC	1 403 072	784 713	618 359	...	...	...	...	...	...
25 - 29	CDFC	1 639 795	1 028 036	611 759	...	...	...	...	...	...
30 - 34	CDFC	1 507 079	960 572	546 507	...	...	...	...	...	...
35 - 39	CDFC	1 191 004	764 240	426 764	...	...	...	...	...	...
40 - 44	CDFC	759 834	500 822	259 012	...	...	...	...	...	...
45 - 49	CDFC	523 529	325 684	197 845	...	...	...	...	...	...
50 - 54	CDFC	407 061	236 052	171 009	...	...	...	...	...	...
55 - 59	CDFC	260 278	157 287	102 991	...	...	...	...	...	...
60 - 64	CDFC	250 626	148 295	102 331	...	...	...	...	...	...
65 - 69	CDFC	132 067	78 998	53 069	...	...	...	...	...	...
70 - 74	CDFC	127 407	70 296	57 111	...	...	...	...	...	...
75 - 79	CDFC	60 490	35 070	25 420	...	...	...	...	...	...
80+	CDFC	114 211	62 046	52 165	...	...	...	...	...	...
Singapore - Singapour[28]										
30 VI 2000										
Total	CDJC	3 263 200	1 630 300	1 632 900	...	...	...	...	...	...
0 - 4	CDJC	213 300	110 300	102 900	...	...	...	...	...	...
5 - 9	CDJC	252 100	129 900	122 100	...	...	...	...	...	...
10 - 14	CDJC	235 400	121 700	113 700	...	...	...	...	...	...
15 - 19	CDJC	211 300	109 100	102 300	...	...	...	...	...	...
20 - 24	CDJC	212 600	106 500	106 100	...	...	...	...	...	...
25 - 29	CDJC	267 600	129 500	138 100	...	...	...	...	...	...
30 - 34	CDJC	290 900	142 200	148 700	...	...	...	...	...	...
35 - 39	CDJC	323 100	162 300	160 700	...	...	...	...	...	...
40 - 44	CDJC	313 000	158 000	155 100	...	...	...	...	...	...
45 - 49	CDJC	262 600	132 700	129 900	...	...	...	...	...	...
50 - 54	CDJC	207 100	104 100	103 000	...	...	...	...	...	...
55 - 59	CDJC	125 500	62 200	63 300	...	...	...	...	...	...
60 - 64	CDJC	111 100	54 400	56 700	...	...	...	...	...	...
65 - 69	CDJC	89 200	42 700	46 400	...	...	...	...	...	...
70 - 74	CDJC	68 000	31 900	36 100	...	...	...	...	...	...
75 - 79	CDJC	40 100	17 900	22 200	...	...	...	...	...	...

7. **Population by age, sex and urban/rural residence: latest available year, 1992 - 2001**
Population selon l'âge, le sexe et la résidence, urbaine/rurale: dernière année disponible, 1992 - 2001
(continued — suite)

(See notes at end of table. — Voir notes à la fin du tableau.)

Continent, country or area, date and age (in years) / Continent, pays ou zone, date et âge (en annèes)	Code[1]	Total			Urban - Urbaine			Rural - Rurale		
		Both sexes Les deux sexes	Male Masculin	Female Féminin	Both sexes Les deux sexes	Male Masculin	Female Féminin	Both sexes Les deux sexes	Male Masculin	Female Féminin
ASIA — ASIE										
Singapore - Singapour[28]										
30 VI 2000										
80+	CDJC	40 400	14 900	25 500	...	...	...	...	...	...
Sri Lanka										
1 VII 1998										
Total	ESDF	18 774 000	9 570 000	9 204 000	...	...	...	...	...	...
0 - 4	ESDF	2 345 000	1 194 000	1 151 000	...	...	...	...	...	...
5 - 9	ESDF	2 128 000	1 082 000	1 046 000	...	...	...	...	...	...
10 - 14	ESDF	2 136 000	1 090 000	1 046 000	...	...	...	...	...	...
15 - 19	ESDF	2 028 000	1 028 000	1 000 000	...	...	...	...	...	...
20 - 24	ESDF	1 931 000	969 000	962 000	...	...	...	...	...	...
25 - 29	ESDF	1 612 000	807 000	805 000	...	...	...	...	...	...
30 - 34	ESDF	1 424 000	721 000	703 000	...	...	...	...	...	...
35 - 39	ESDF	1 060 000	533 000	527 000	...	...	...	...	...	...
40 - 44	ESDF	883 000	455 000	428 000	...	...	...	...	...	...
45 - 49	ESDF	770 000	390 000	380 000	...	...	...	...	...	...
50 - 54	ESDF	682 000	360 000	322 000	...	...	...	...	...	...
55 - 59	ESDF	534 000	281 000	253 000	...	...	...	...	...	...
60 - 64	ESDF	431 000	232 000	199 000	...	...	...	...	...	...
65 - 69	ESDF	318 000	168 000	150 000	...	...	...	...	...	...
70+	ESDF	492 000	260 000	232 000	...	...	...	...	...	...
Syrian Arab Republic - République arabe syrienne[29]										
1 VII 2001										
Total	ESDF	16 720 000	8 552 000	8 168 000	8 376 000	4 319 000	4 057 000	8 344 000	4 233 000	4 111 000
0 - 1	ESDF	401 000	205 000	196 000	147 000	74 000	73 000	254 000	131 000	123 000
1 - 4	ESDF	1 705 000	880 000	825 000	791 000	410 000	381 000	914 000	470 000	444 000
5 - 9	ESDF	2 274 000	1 166 000	1 108 000	1 013 000	518 000	495 000	1 261 000	648 000	613 000
10 - 14	ESDF	2 382 000	1 213 000	1 169 000	1 093 000	553 000	540 000	1 289 000	660 000	629 000
15 - 19	ESDF	2 241 000	1 142 000	1 099 000	1 115 000	583 000	532 000	1 126 000	559 000	567 000
20 - 24	ESDF	1 572 000	792 000	780 000	834 000	436 000	398 000	738 000	356 000	382 000
25 - 29	ESDF	1 228 000	608 000	620 000	640 000	324 000	316 000	588 000	284 000	304 000
30 - 34	ESDF	1 006 000	500 000	506 000	552 000	276 000	276 000	454 000	224 000	230 000
35 - 39	ESDF	868 000	419 000	449 000	472 000	229 000	243 000	396 000	190 000	206 000
40 - 44	ESDF	731 000	360 000	371 000	406 000	199 000	207 000	325 000	161 000	164 000
45 - 49	ESDF	593 000	312 000	281 000	335 000	173 000	162 000	258 000	139 000	119 000
50 - 54	ESDF	540 000	279 000	261 000	306 000	160 000	146 000	234 000	119 000	115 000
55 - 59	ESDF	344 000	180 000	164 000	201 000	108 000	93 000	143 000	72 000	71 000
60 - 64	ESDF	318 000	175 000	143 000	180 000	99 000	81 000	138 000	76 000	62 000
65+	ESDF	517 000	321 000	196 000	291 000	177 000	114 000	226 000	144 000	82 000
Tajikistan - Tadjikistan										
1 VII 1993										
Total	ESDF	5 621 727	2 799 853	2 821 874	1 630 259	802 998	827 261	3 991 468	1 996 855	1 994 613
0 - 1	ESDF	184 774	94 831	89 943	40 106	20 635	19 471	144 668	74 196	70 472
1 - 4	ESDF	766 931	391 834	375 097	178 075	91 008	87 067	588 856	300 826	288 030
5 - 9	ESDF	850 331	430 324	420 007	216 453	109 526	106 927	633 878	320 798	313 080
10 - 14	ESDF	662 636	334 838	327 798	173 587	87 552	86 035	489 049	247 286	241 763
15 - 19	ESDF	556 944	280 895	276 049	154 090	78 932	75 158	402 854	201 963	200 891
20 - 24	ESDF	508 529	253 281	255 248	159 737	87 175	72 562	348 792	166 106	182 686
25 - 29	ESDF	442 462	214 034	228 428	128 423	62 552	65 871	314 039	151 482	162 557
30 - 34	ESDF	407 674	201 357	206 317	126 932	60 776	66 156	280 742	140 581	140 161
35 - 39	ESDF	288 358	142 831	145 527	101 141	48 758	52 383	187 217	94 073	93 144
40 - 44	ESDF	207 948	102 260	105 688	79 581	37 810	41 771	128 367	64 450	63 917
45 - 49	ESDF	117 936	61 378	56 558	45 662	22 419	23 243	72 274	38 959	33 315
50 - 54	ESDF	144 526	75 203	69 323	54 095	26 162	27 933	90 431	49 041	41 390
55 - 59	ESDF	141 142	69 598	71 544	51 033	23 940	27 093	90 109	45 658	44 451

7. Population by age, sex and urban/rural residence: latest available year, 1992 - 2001
Population selon l'âge, le sexe et la résidence, urbaine/rurale: dernière année disponible, 1992 - 2001
(continued — suite)

(See notes at end of table. — Voir notes à la fin du tableau.)

Continent, country or area, date and age (in years) / Continent, pays ou zone, date et âge (en années)	Code[1]	Total			Urban - Urbaine			Rural - Rurale		
		Both sexes Les deux sexes	Male Masculin	Female Féminin	Both sexes Les deux sexes	Male Masculin	Female Féminin	Both sexes Les deux sexes	Male Masculin	Female Féminin
ASIA — ASIE										
Tajikistan - Tadjikistan										
1 VII 1993										
60 - 64	ESDF	124 190	59 376	64 814	42 695	18 867	23 828	81 495	40 509	40 986
65 - 69	ESDF	91 521	41 320	50 201	33 770	13 001	20 769	57 751	28 319	29 432
70 - 74	ESDF	52 809	19 600	33 209	18 809	6 118	12 691	34 000	13 482	20 518
75 - 79	ESDF	31 647	11 305	20 342	12 670	3 774	8 896	18 977	7 531	11 446
80 - 84	ESDF	22 997	8 403	14 594	8 345	2 529	5 816	14 652	5 874	8 778
85 - 89	ESDF	11 267	4 426	6 841	3 458	992	2 466	7 809	3 434	4 375
90 - 94	ESDF	6 068	2 300	3 768	1 316	378	938	4 752	1 922	2 830
95 - 99	ESDF	711	327	384	198	74	124	513	253	260
100+	ESDF	326	132	194	83	20	63	243	112	131
Thailand - Thaïlande										
1 IV 2000										
Total	CDJC	60 617 200	29 850 200	30 767 100	18 833 700	9 085 500	9 748 200	41 783 500	20 764 700	21 018 800
0 - 4	CDJC	4 387 100	2 266 700	2 120 300	1 145 800	588 700	557 100	3 241 300	1 678 000	1 563 300
5 - 9	CDJC	5 030 900	2 610 800	2 420 100	1 295 500	674 200	621 300	3 735 400	1 936 600	1 798 800
10 - 14	CDJC	5 203 500	2 621 100	2 582 300	1 377 900	693 100	684 800	3 825 600	1 928 100	1 897 500
15 - 19	CDJC	5 341 300	2 709 300	2 632 000	1 640 100	822 000	818 100	3 701 200	1 887 300	1 813 800
20 - 24	CDJC	4 931 600	2 463 300	2 468 300	1 804 100	870 600	933 500	3 127 600	1 592 700	1 534 900
25 - 29	CDJC	5 248 500	2 536 400	2 712 100	1 868 900	891 100	977 800	3 379 600	1 645 300	1 734 300
30 - 34	CDJC	5 448 700	2 604 900	2 843 800	1 814 600	851 200	963 400	3 634 200	1 753 800	1 880 400
35 - 39	CDJC	5 386 900	2 615 600	2 771 300	1 742 200	814 100	928 100	3 644 700	1 801 500	1 843 300
40 - 44	CDJC	4 849 700	2 385 900	2 463 900	1 606 100	772 000	834 100	3 243 600	1 613 900	1 629 800
45 - 49	CDJC	3 876 700	1 915 600	1 961 100	1 254 200	606 000	648 200	2 622 500	1 309 700	1 312 800
50 - 54	CDJC	2 914 700	1 416 700	1 498 000	916 700	438 900	477 800	1 998 100	977 800	1 020 300
55 - 59	CDJC	2 284 500	1 094 900	1 189 600	672 300	309 800	362 500	1 612 200	785 100	827 200
60 - 64	CDJC	1 998 200	946 100	1 052 100	593 900	277 800	316 100	1 404 300	668 300	736 000
65 - 69	CDJC	1 526 000	704 900	821 100	437 000	195 100	241 900	1 089 100	509 900	579 200
70 - 74	CDJC	1 043 400	475 700	567 700	312 000	136 500	175 500	731 400	339 100	392 200
75 - 79	CDJC	594 900	263 700	331 200	174 400	75 800	98 600	420 500	187 900	232 700
80 - 84	CDJC	323 800	131 500	192 300	101 900	41 500	60 400	221 900	90 000	131 900
85+	CDJC	226 800	87 000	139 700	76 400	27 100	49 300	150 300	59 900	90 400
1 VII 2001										
Total	ESDJ	62 968 056	31 330 878	31 637 177	...	...	...	...	...	...
0 - 1	ESDJ	997 630	508 463	489 166	...	...	...	...	...	...
1 - 4	ESDJ	3 960 770	2 019 088	1 941 682	...	...	...	...	...	...
5 - 9	ESDJ	4 841 092	2 484 331	2 356 760	...	...	...	...	...	...
10 - 14	ESDJ	4 799 809	2 456 446	2 343 363	...	...	...	...	...	...
15 - 19	ESDJ	5 023 327	2 559 814	2 463 511	...	...	...	...	...	...
20 - 24	ESDJ	5 607 809	2 842 478	2 765 330	...	...	...	...	...	...
25 - 29	ESDJ	5 802 849	2 919 377	2 883 471	...	...	...	...	...	...
30 - 34	ESDJ	5 987 991	2 980 906	3 007 084	...	...	...	...	...	...
35 - 39	ESDJ	5 723 494	2 831 784	2 891 709	...	...	...	...	...	...
40 - 44	ESDJ	4 922 426	2 427 052	2 495 374	...	...	...	...	...	...
45 - 49	ESDJ	3 995 042	1 952 028	2 043 015	...	...	...	...	...	...
50 - 54	ESDJ	3 031 402	1 476 610	1 554 792	...	...	...	...	...	...
55 - 59	ESDJ	2 257 375	1 098 567	1 158 810	...	...	...	...	...	...
60 - 64	ESDJ	1 934 305	928 302	1 006 003	...	...	...	...	...	...
65 - 69	ESDJ	1 583 007	743 168	839 839	...	...	...	...	...	...
70+	ESDJ	2 499 725	1 102 462	1 397 263	...	...	...	...	...	...
Turkey - Turquie										
1 VII 2001										
Total	ESDF	68 610 000	34 636 000	33 974 000	...	...	...	...	...	...
0 - 1	ESDF	1 478 000	755 000	723 000	...	...	...	...	...	...
1 - 4	ESDF	5 691 000	2 900 000	2 790 000	...	...	...	...	...	...
5 - 9	ESDF	6 612 000	3 360 000	3 251 000	...	...	...	...	...	...
10 - 14	ESDF	6 600 000	3 375 000	3 225 000	...	...	...	...	...	...
15 - 19	ESDF	6 766 000	3 454 000	3 312 000	...	...	...	...	...	...

7. Population by age, sex and urban/rural residence: latest available year, 1992 - 2001
Population selon l'âge, le sexe et la résidence, urbaine/rurale: dernière année disponible, 1992 - 2001
(continued — suite)

(See notes at end of table. — Voir notes à la fin du tableau.)

Continent, country or area, date and age (in years) / Continent, pays ou zone, date et âge (en années)	Code[1]	Total			Urban - Urbaine			Rural - Rurale		
		Both sexes Les deux sexes	Male Masculin	Female Féminin	Both sexes Les deux sexes	Male Masculin	Female Féminin	Both sexes Les deux sexes	Male Masculin	Female Féminin
ASIA — ASIE										
Turkey - Turquie										
1 VII 2001										
20 - 24	ESDF	6 705 000	3 410 000	3 294 000	...	...	...	...	...	...
25 - 29	ESDF	6 108 000	3 111 000	2 997 000	...	...	...	...	...	...
30 - 34	ESDF	5 315 000	2 698 000	2 617 000	...	...	...	...	...	...
35 - 39	ESDF	5 027 000	2 564 000	2 463 000	...	...	...	...	...	...
40 - 44	ESDF	4 312 000	2 210 000	2 102 000	...	...	...	...	...	...
45 - 49	ESDF	3 551 000	1 810 000	1 741 000	...	...	...	...	...	...
50 - 54	ESDF	2 807 000	1 413 000	1 395 000	...	...	...	...	...	...
55 - 59	ESDF	2 136 000	1 043 000	1 093 000	...	...	...	...	...	...
60 - 64	ESDF	1 760 000	819 000	942 000	...	...	...	...	...	...
65 - 69	ESDF	1 594 000	752 000	843 000	...	...	...	...	...	...
70 - 74	ESDF	1 182 000	544 000	638 000	...	...	...	...	...	...
75+	ESDF	966 000	418 000	548 000	...	...	...	...	...	...
Turkmenistan - Turkménistan										
10 I 1995										
Total	CDFC	4 483 251	2 225 331	2 257 920	...	...	...	...	...	...
0 - 4	CDFC	674 693	344 429	330 264	...	...	...	...	...	...
5 - 9	CDFC	619 381	315 453	303 928	...	...	...	...	...	...
10 - 14	CDFC	516 995	263 071	253 924	...	...	...	...	...	...
15 - 19	CDFC	455 727	231 593	224 134	...	...	...	...	...	...
20 - 24	CDFC	414 632	204 256	210 376	...	...	...	...	...	...
25 - 29	CDFC	366 538	181 317	185 221	...	...	...	...	...	...
30 - 34	CDFC	351 856	173 927	177 929	...	...	...	...	...	...
35 - 39	CDFC	281 039	138 462	142 577	...	...	...	...	...	...
40 - 44	CDFC	204 313	99 575	104 738	...	...	...	...	...	...
45 - 49	CDFC	126 864	62 244	64 620	...	...	...	...	...	...
50 - 54	CDFC	97 136	48 330	48 806	...	...	...	...	...	...
55 - 59	CDFC	114 232	54 283	59 949	...	...	...	...	...	...
60 - 64	CDFC	91 473	43 379	48 094	...	...	...	...	...	...
65 - 69	CDFC	73 263	32 176	41 087	...	...	...	...	...	...
70 - 74	CDFC	43 818	15 709	28 109	...	...	...	...	...	...
75 - 79	CDFC	22 707	7 301	15 406	...	...	...	...	...	...
80 - 84	CDFC	15 942	5 060	10 882	...	...	...	...	...	...
85 - 89	CDFC	5 813	1 782	4 031	...	...	...	...	...	...
90 - 94	CDFC	2 611	737	1 874	...	...	...	...	...	...
95 - 99	CDFC	639	179	460	...	...	...	...	...	...
100+	CDFC	722	274	448	...	...	...	...	...	...
Unk. - Inc.	CDFC	2 857	1 794	1 063	...	...	...	...	...	...
Uzbekistan - Ouzbékistan										
1 VII 2001										
Total	ESDF	24 964 433	12 442 510	12 521 923	9 256 101	4 573 055	4 683 046	15 708 332	7 869 455	7 838 877
0 - 1	ESDF	513 043	263 408	249 635	158 893	81 393	77 500	354 150	182 015	172 135
1 - 4	ESDF	2 219 863	1 138 212	1 081 651	693 448	355 999	337 449	1 526 415	782 213	744 202
5 - 9	ESDF	3 237 989	1 653 776	1 584 213	1 015 989	519 360	496 629	2 222 000	1 134 416	1 087 584
10 - 14	ESDF	3 203 022	1 627 673	1 575 349	1 049 577	533 870	515 707	2 153 445	1 093 803	1 059 642
15 - 19	ESDF	2 821 926	1 422 296	1 399 630	984 385	497 725	486 660	1 837 541	924 571	912 970
20 - 24	ESDF	2 296 834	1 157 998	1 138 836	841 326	425 348	415 978	1 455 508	732 650	722 858
25 - 29	ESDF	2 030 200	1 023 174	1 007 026	788 176	397 184	390 992	1 242 024	625 990	616 034
30 - 34	ESDF	1 749 557	861 368	888 189	726 099	372 846	353 253	1 023 458	488 522	534 936
35 - 39	ESDF	1 672 397	816 665	855 732	660 932	323 492	337 440	1 011 465	493 173	518 292
40 - 44	ESDF	1 479 057	728 780	750 277	612 755	297 460	315 295	866 302	431 320	434 982
45 - 49	ESDF	1 034 628	506 734	527 894	464 375	223 425	240 950	570 253	283 309	286 944
50 - 54	ESDF	696 648	337 634	359 014	340 008	161 069	178 939	356 640	176 565	180 075
55 - 59	ESDF	394 997	197 700	197 297	185 073	88 314	96 759	209 924	109 386	100 538
60 - 64	ESDF	553 697	265 428	288 269	254 409	115 715	138 694	299 288	149 713	149 575
65 - 69	ESDF	399 550	185 653	213 897	171 869	75 277	96 592	227 681	110 376	117 305

7. Population by age, sex and urban/rural residence: latest available year, 1992 - 2001
Population selon l'âge, le sexe et la résidence, urbaine/rurale: dernière année disponible, 1992 - 2001
(continued — suite)

(See notes at end of table. — Voir notes à la fin du tableau.)

Continent, country or area, date and age (in years) / Continent, pays ou zone, date et âge (en annèes)	Code[1]	Total			Urban - Urbaine			Rural - Rurale		
		Both sexes Les deux sexes	Male Masculin	Female Féminin	Both sexes Les deux sexes	Male Masculin	Female Féminin	Both sexes Les deux sexes	Male Masculin	Female Féminin
ASIA — ASIE										
Uzbekistan - Ouzbékistan										
1 VII 2001										
70 - 74	ESDF	325 230	143 466	181 764	146 702	57 100	89 602	178 528	86 366	92 162
75 - 79	ESDF	185 449	67 568	117 881	87 515	27 439	60 076	97 934	40 129	57 805
80 - 84	ESDF	78 794	23 459	55 335	39 138	10 729	28 409	39 656	12 730	26 926
85 - 89	ESDF	41 343	10 761	30 582	20 793	4 904	15 889	20 550	5 857	14 693
90 - 94	ESDF	19 195	6 220	12 975	9 150	2 774	6 376	10 045	3 446	6 599
95 - 99	ESDF	10 114	4 171	5 943	4 954	1 461	3 493	5 160	2 710	2 450
100+	ESDF	900	366	534	535	171	364	365	195	170
Viet Nam										
31 XII 1992										
Total	ESDF	69 175 080	33 312 978	35 862 102	13 485 405	6 510 756	6 974 649	55 689 675	26 802 222	28 887 453
0 - 1	ESDF	2 001 535	1 020 783	980 752	380 372	198 134	182 238	1 621 163	822 649	798 514
1 - 4	ESDF	7 434 032	3 905 228	3 528 804	1 476 562	796 303	680 259	5 957 470	3 108 925	2 848 545
5 - 9	ESDF	9 417 737	4 845 729	4 572 008	1 850 121	946 795	903 326	7 567 616	3 898 934	3 668 682
10 - 14	ESDF	8 506 356	4 412 810	4 093 546	1 619 359	831 098	788 261	6 886 997	3 581 712	3 305 285
15 - 19	ESDF	7 549 286	3 725 455	3 823 831	1 437 113	700 936	736 177	6 112 173	3 024 519	3 087 654
20 - 24	ESDF	6 360 986	2 902 592	3 458 394	1 233 318	545 113	688 205	5 127 668	2 357 479	2 770 189
25 - 29	ESDF	5 385 675	2 286 311	3 099 364	1 132 681	552 042	580 639	4 252 994	1 734 269	2 518 725
30 - 34	ESDF	5 134 977	2 427 883	2 707 094	978 248	455 218	523 030	4 156 729	1 972 665	2 184 064
35 - 39	ESDF	3 627 005	1 689 916	1 937 089	690 239	315 472	374 767	2 936 766	1 374 444	1 562 322
40 - 44	ESDF	2 452 443	1 145 069	1 307 374	466 578	212 297	254 281	1 985 865	932 772	1 053 093
45 - 49	ESDF	2 180 257	991 028	1 189 229	414 748	183 127	231 621	1 765 509	807 901	957 608
50 - 54	ESDF	1 944 942	862 243	1 082 699	410 614	180 576	230 038	1 534 328	681 667	852 661
55 - 59	ESDF	1 912 388	827 661	1 084 727	392 739	181 080	211 659	1 519 649	646 581	873 068
60 - 64	ESDF	1 776 884	821 777	955 107	340 055	152 727	187 328	1 436 829	669 050	767 779
65 - 69	ESDF	1 401 409	611 955	789 454	266 498	112 991	153 507	1 134 911	498 964	635 947
70 - 74	ESDF	916 907	385 883	531 024	174 183	70 182	104 001	742 724	315 701	427 023
75 - 79	ESDF	647 829	257 607	390 222	122 944	45 891	77 053	524 885	211 716	313 169
80 - 84	ESDF	333 454	123 517	209 937	63 082	20 499	42 583	270 372	103 018	167 354
85+	ESDF	190 978	69 531	121 447	35 951	10 275	25 676	155 027	59 256	95 771
Yemen - Yémen										
16 XII 1994										
Total	CDFC	14 587 807	7 473 540	7 114 267	3 423 518	1 856 602	1 566 916	11 164 289	5 616 938	5 547 351
0 - 1	CDFC	474 719	245 925	228 794	98 756	50 872	47 884	375 963	195 053	180 910
1 - 4	CDFC	1 920 253	969 884	950 369	372 120	189 919	182 201	1 548 133	779 965	768 168
5 - 9	CDFC	2 735 850	1 404 417	1 331 433	535 411	272 246	263 165	2 200 439	1 132 171	1 068 268
10 - 14	CDFC	2 202 884	1 186 231	1 016 653	492 788	260 979	231 809	1 710 096	925 252	784 844
15 - 19	CDFC	1 486 755	785 127	701 628	401 317	220 977	180 340	1 085 438	564 150	521 288
20 - 24	CDFC	990 006	514 157	475 849	316 136	185 604	130 532	673 870	328 553	345 317
25 - 29	CDFC	914 142	433 650	480 492	257 640	142 812	114 828	656 502	290 838	365 664
30 - 34	CDFC	780 524	370 666	409 858	219 905	123 317	96 588	560 619	247 349	313 270
35 - 39	CDFC	739 189	357 761	381 428	192 980	108 179	84 801	546 209	249 582	296 627
40 - 44	CDFC	534 930	267 057	267 873	134 608	77 669	56 939	400 322	189 388	210 934
45 - 49	CDFC	414 427	212 507	201 920	107 327	62 215	45 112	307 100	150 292	156 808
50 - 54	CDFC	383 799	193 636	190 163	88 698	49 044	39 654	295 101	144 592	150 509
55 - 59	CDFC	207 589	109 372	98 217	50 432	28 990	21 442	157 157	80 382	76 775
60 - 64	CDFC	284 731	149 934	134 797	57 530	31 440	26 090	227 201	118 494	108 707
65 - 69	CDFC	134 878	72 661	62 217	28 131	15 841	12 290	106 747	56 820	49 927
70 - 74	CDFC	171 999	89 830	82 169	30 560	15 868	14 692	141 439	73 962	67 477
75 - 79	CDFC	63 288	34 421	28 867	12 541	6 990	5 551	50 747	27 431	23 316
80 - 84	CDFC	80 755	40 421	40 334	13 648	6 582	7 066	67 107	33 839	33 268
85+	CDFC	66 040	35 095	30 945	12 457	6 596	5 861	53 583	28 499	25 084
Unk. - Inc.	CDFC	1 049	788	261	533	462	71	516	326	190
1 VII 1997										
Total	ESDF	16 484 000	8 227 000	8 257 000	...	...	...	...	...	...
0 - 1	ESDF	712 000	363 000	349 000	...	...	...	...	...	...
1 - 4	ESDF	2 446 000	1 247 000	1 199 000	...	...	...	...	...	...

7. Population by age, sex and urban/rural residence: latest available year, 1992 - 2001
Population selon l'âge, le sexe et la résidence, urbaine/rurale: dernière année disponible, 1992 - 2001
(continued — suite)

(See notes at end of table. — Voir notes à la fin du tableau.)

Continent, country or area, date and age (in years) / Continent, pays ou zone, date et âge (en années)	Code[1]	Total			Urban - Urbaine			Rural - Rurale		
		Both sexes Les deux sexes	Male Masculin	Female Féminin	Both sexes Les deux sexes	Male Masculin	Female Féminin	Both sexes Les deux sexes	Male Masculin	Female Féminin
ASIA — ASIE										
Yemen - Yémen										
1 VII 1997										
5 - 9	ESDF	2 384 000	1 213 000	1 171 000	...	...	...	...	...	...
10 - 14	ESDF	2 203 000	1 129 000	1 074 000	...	...	...	...	...	...
15 - 19	ESDF	2 024 000	1 047 000	977 000	...	...	...	...	...	...
20 - 24	ESDF	1 426 000	717 000	709 000	...	...	...	...	...	...
25 - 29	ESDF	957 000	456 000	501 000	...	...	...	...	...	...
30 - 34	ESDF	878 000	405 000	473 000	...	...	...	...	...	...
35 - 39	ESDF	821 000	377 000	444 000	...	...	...	...	...	...
40 - 44	ESDF	645 000	302 000	343 000	...	...	...	...	...	...
45 - 49	ESDF	495 000	240 000	255 000	...	...	...	...	...	...
50 - 54	ESDF	385 000	188 000	197 000	...	...	...	...	...	...
55 - 59	ESDF	297 000	146 000	151 000	...	...	...	...	...	...
60 - 64	ESDF	238 000	113 000	125 000	...	...	...	...	...	...
65 - 69	ESDF	198 000	99 000	99 000	...	...	...	...	...	...
70 - 74	ESDF	149 000	74 000	75 000	...	...	...	...	...	...
75+	ESDF	226 000	111 000	115 000	...	...	...	...	...	...
EUROPE										
Andorra - Andorre										
31 XII 1994										
Total	ESDF	64 311	34 083	30 228	...	...	...	...	...	...
0 - 4	ESDF	3 314	1 725	1 589	...	...	...	...	...	...
5 - 9	ESDF	3 243	1 697	1 546	...	...	...	...	...	...
10 - 14	ESDF	3 513	1 795	1 718	...	...	...	...	...	...
15 - 19	ESDF	3 943	2 074	1 869	...	...	...	...	...	...
20 - 24	ESDF	5 312	2 726	2 586	...	...	...	...	...	...
25 - 29	ESDF	7 000	3 608	3 392	...	...	...	...	...	...
30 - 34	ESDF	7 131	3 822	3 309	...	...	...	...	...	...
35 - 39	ESDF	6 160	3 394	2 766	...	...	...	...	...	...
40 - 44	ESDF	5 058	2 840	2 218	...	...	...	...	...	...
45 - 49	ESDF	4 296	2 389	1 907	...	...	...	...	...	...
50 - 54	ESDF	3 441	1 845	1 596	...	...	...	...	...	...
55 - 59	ESDF	2 659	1 417	1 242	...	...	...	...	...	...
60 - 64	ESDF	2 589	1 375	1 214	...	...	...	...	...	...
65 - 69	ESDF	2 267	1 181	1 086	...	...	...	...	...	...
70 - 74	ESDF	1 816	911	905	...	...	...	...	...	...
75 - 79	ESDF	1 095	565	530	...	...	...	...	...	...
80 - 84	ESDF	815	423	392	...	...	...	...	...	...
85+	ESDF	659	296	363	...	...	...	...	...	...
Austria - Autriche										
1 VII 2001										
Total	ESDJ	8 130 328	3 953 689	4 176 639	...	...	...	...	...	...
0 - 4	ESDJ	405 816	207 666	198 151	...	...	...	...	...	...
5 - 9	ESDJ	467 493	239 465	228 028	...	...	...	...	...	...
10 - 14	ESDJ	470 380	241 436	228 944	...	...	...	...	...	...
15 - 19	ESDJ	482 814	246 789	236 025	...	...	...	...	...	...
20 - 24	ESDJ	477 512	242 430	235 082	...	...	...	...	...	...
25 - 29	ESDJ	547 414	272 695	274 720	...	...	...	...	...	...
30 - 34	ESDJ	688 020	348 425	339 595	...	...	...	...	...	...
35 - 39	ESDJ	719 857	368 178	351 679	...	...	...	...	...	...
40 - 44	ESDJ	636 263	324 800	311 463	...	...	...	...	...	...
45 - 49	ESDJ	534 462	269 277	265 185	...	...	...	...	...	...
50 - 54	ESDJ	515 183	258 592	256 592	...	...	...	...	...	...
55 - 59	ESDJ	460 235	226 284	233 952	...	...	...	...	...	...
60 - 64	ESDJ	460 975	222 945	238 030	...	...	...	...	...	...
65 - 69	ESDJ	336 646	155 082	181 564	...	...	...	...	...	...
70 - 74	ESDJ	330 287	142 315	187 973	...	...	...	...	...	...

7. Population by age, sex and urban/rural residence: latest available year, 1992 - 2001
Population selon l'âge, le sexe et la résidence, urbaine/rurale: dernière année disponible, 1992 - 2001
(continued — suite)

(See notes at end of table. — Voir notes à la fin du tableau.)

Continent, country or area, date and age (in years) / Continent, pays ou zone, date et âge (en annèes)	Code[1]	Total			Urban - Urbaine			Rural - Rurale		
		Both sexes Les deux sexes	Male Masculin	Female Féminin	Both sexes Les deux sexes	Male Masculin	Female Féminin	Both sexes Les deux sexes	Male Masculin	Female Féminin
EUROPE										
Austria - Autriche										
1 VII 2001										
75 - 79	ESDJ	293 211	100 409	192 802	...	...	...	...	...	...
80 - 84	ESDJ	158 771	48 911	109 860	...	...	...	...	...	...
85+	ESDJ	144 993	37 993	107 000	...	...	...	...	...	...
Belarus - Bélarus										
1 I 2000										
Total	ESDF	10 019 480	4 703 212	5 316 268	6 985 363	3 287 017	3 698 346	3 034 117	1 416 195	1 617 922
0 - 1	ESDF	92 149	47 450	44 699	66 093	33 975	32 118	26 056	13 475	12 581
1 - 4	ESDF	372 413	191 609	180 804	256 418	132 152	124 266	115 995	59 457	56 538
5 - 9	ESDF	618 128	317 019	301 109	431 228	221 492	209 736	186 900	95 527	91 373
10 - 14	ESDF	814 878	416 701	398 177	584 645	299 000	285 645	230 233	117 701	112 532
15 - 19	ESDF	808 294	413 476	394 818	633 471	320 815	312 656	174 823	92 661	82 162
20 - 24	ESDF	719 670	366 025	353 645	564 196	284 647	279 549	155 474	81 378	74 096
25 - 29	ESDF	694 571	346 998	347 573	524 206	257 332	266 874	170 365	89 666	80 699
30 - 34	ESDF	690 345	342 870	347 475	509 435	245 807	263 628	180 910	97 063	83 847
35 - 39	ESDF	820 911	405 999	414 912	615 185	292 917	322 268	205 726	113 082	92 644
40 - 44	ESDF	825 230	402 509	422 721	622 986	291 953	331 033	202 244	110 556	91 688
45 - 49	ESDF	690 189	330 521	359 668	526 124	243 026	283 098	164 065	87 495	76 570
50 - 54	ESDF	535 490	251 826	283 664	399 033	183 992	215 041	136 457	67 834	68 623
55 - 59	ESDF	432 273	192 521	239 752	278 875	125 173	153 702	153 398	67 348	86 050
60 - 64	ESDF	572 720	238 988	333 732	338 370	142 345	196 025	234 350	96 643	137 707
65 - 69	ESDF	475 227	184 904	290 323	230 518	88 716	141 802	244 709	96 188	148 521
70 - 74	ESDF	424 930	145 812	279 118	206 532	72 916	133 616	218 398	72 896	145 502
75 - 79	ESDF	242 158	65 791	176 367	112 640	30 589	82 051	129 518	35 202	94 316
80+	ESDF	189 904	42 193	147 711	85 408	20 170	65 238	104 496	22 023	82 473
Belgium - Belgique										
1 VII 2001										
Total	ESDJ	10 286 570	5 030 154	5 256 416	...	...	...	...	...	...
0 - 4	ESDJ	576 522	294 355	282 167	...	...	...	...	...	...
5 - 9	ESDJ	606 496	310 040	296 456	...	...	...	...	...	...
10 - 14	ESDJ	622 150	318 551	303 599	...	...	...	...	...	...
15 - 19	ESDJ	605 416	309 290	296 126	...	...	...	...	...	...
20 - 24	ESDJ	639 016	322 484	316 533	...	...	...	...	...	...
25 - 29	ESDJ	670 599	338 963	331 636	...	...	...	...	...	...
30 - 34	ESDJ	746 501	378 524	367 977	...	...	...	...	...	...
35 - 39	ESDJ	810 810	411 048	399 762	...	...	...	...	...	...
40 - 44	ESDJ	788 991	398 444	390 548	...	...	...	...	...	...
45 - 49	ESDJ	729 676	367 753	361 923	...	...	...	...	...	...
50 - 54	ESDJ	690 564	347 583	342 981	...	...	...	...	...	...
55 - 59	ESDJ	552 150	274 449	277 701	...	...	...	...	...	...
60 - 64	ESDJ	509 618	246 897	262 721	...	...	...	...	...	...
65 - 69	ESDJ	504 903	235 899	269 004	...	...	...	...	...	...
70 - 74	ESDJ	465 273	204 203	261 070	...	...	...	...	...	...
75 - 79	ESDJ	382 573	153 256	229 317	...	...	...	...	...	...
80 - 84	ESDJ	203 575	71 455	132 120	...	...	...	...	...	...
85+	ESDJ	181 741	46 965	134 777	...	...	...	...	...	...
Bulgaria - Bulgarie										
1 VII 2001										
Total	ESDF	7 913 301	3 853 710	4 059 591	5 477 604	2 652 367	2 825 237	2 435 697	1 201 343	1 234 354
0 - 1	ESDF	66 613	34 223	32 390	46 878	24 102	22 776	19 735	10 121	9 614
1 - 4	ESDF	254 762	130 936	123 826	176 758	90 781	85 977	78 004	40 155	37 849
5 - 9	ESDF	378 215	193 961	184 254	259 551	132 920	126 631	118 664	61 041	57 623
10 - 14	ESDF	502 298	257 462	244 836	360 752	184 230	176 522	141 546	73 232	68 314
15 - 19	ESDF	536 439	275 517	260 922	408 132	208 212	199 920	128 307	67 305	61 002
20 - 24	ESDF	573 093	294 132	278 961	436 144	220 505	215 639	136 949	73 627	63 322
25 - 29	ESDF	573 614	292 578	281 036	433 829	218 720	215 109	139 785	73 858	65 927
30 - 34	ESDF	545 853	277 133	268 720	405 938	202 107	203 831	139 915	75 026	64 889
35 - 39	ESDF	522 219	262 769	259 450	387 522	190 261	197 261	134 697	72 508	62 189

7. Population by age, sex and urban/rural residence: latest available year, 1992 - 2001
Population selon l'âge, le sexe et la résidence, urbaine/rurale: dernière année disponible, 1992 - 2001
(continued — suite)

(See notes at end of table. — Voir notes à la fin du tableau.)

Continent, country or area, date and age (in years) / Continent, pays ou zone, date et âge (en annèes)	Code[1]	Total			Urban - Urbaine			Rural - Rurale		
		Both sexes Les deux sexes	Male Masculin	Female Féminin	Both sexes Les deux sexes	Male Masculin	Female Féminin	Both sexes Les deux sexes	Male Masculin	Female Féminin
EUROPE										
Bulgaria - Bulgarie										
1 VII 2001										
40 - 44	ESDF	548 877	273 898	274 979	410 885	199 821	211 064	137 992	74 077	63 915
45 - 49	ESDF	564 354	277 929	286 425	421 046	203 084	217 962	143 308	74 845	68 463
50 - 54	ESDF	587 494	285 029	302 465	424 072	203 130	220 942	163 422	81 899	81 523
55 - 59	ESDF	490 385	232 716	257 669	322 515	153 739	168 776	167 870	78 977	88 893
60 - 64	ESDF	437 459	201 979	235 480	260 018	119 975	140 043	177 441	82 004	95 437
65 - 69	ESDF	456 243	204 824	251 419	253 543	111 056	142 487	202 700	93 768	108 932
70 - 74	ESDF	384 387	165 781	218 606	212 559	90 259	122 300	171 828	75 522	96 306
75 - 79	ESDF	293 805	118 683	175 122	155 597	61 938	93 659	138 208	56 745	81 463
80 - 84	ESDF	122 994	47 556	75 438	63 776	24 240	39 536	59 218	23 316	35 902
85 - 89	ESDF	56 497	20 638	35 859	28 867	10 211	18 656	27 630	10 427	17 203
90 - 94	ESDF	15 543	5 321	10 222	8 126	2 734	5 392	7 417	2 587	4 830
95 - 99	ESDF	1 970	593	1 377	1 001	311	690	969	282	687
100+	ESDF	187	52	135	95	31	64	92	21	71
Channel Islands: Guernsey - Îles Anglo-Normandes: Guernesey										
31 III 1996										
Total	CDFC	58 681	28 244	30 437	...	...	...	...	...	...
0 - 1	CDFC	599	300	299	...	...	...	...	...	...
1 - 4	CDFC	2 781	1 436	1 345	...	...	...	...	...	...
5 - 9	CDFC	3 624	1 813	1 811	...	...	...	...	...	...
10 - 14	CDFC	3 339	1 727	1 612	...	...	...	...	...	...
15 - 19	CDFC	3 351	1 682	1 669	...	...	...	...	...	...
20 - 24	CDFC	4 075	1 935	2 140	...	...	...	...	...	...
25 - 29	CDFC	4 659	2 202	2 457	...	...	...	...	...	...
30 - 34	CDFC	4 691	2 301	2 390	...	...	...	...	...	...
35 - 39	CDFC	4 342	2 125	2 217	...	...	...	...	...	...
40 - 44	CDFC	4 044	2 057	1 987	...	...	...	...	...	...
45 - 49	CDFC	4 610	2 282	2 328	...	...	...	...	...	...
50 - 54	CDFC	3 309	1 669	1 640	...	...	...	...	...	...
55 - 59	CDFC	3 250	1 642	1 608	...	...	...	...	...	...
60 - 64	CDFC	2 798	1 360	1 438	...	...	...	...	...	...
65 - 69	CDFC	2 621	1 210	1 411	...	...	...	...	...	...
70 - 74	CDFC	2 329	1 031	1 298	...	...	...	...	...	...
75 - 79	CDFC	1 810	727	1 083	...	...	...	...	...	...
80 - 84	CDFC	1 349	468	881	...	...	...	...	...	...
85 - 89	CDFC	709	194	515	...	...	...	...	...	...
90 - 94	CDFC	316	74	242	...	...	...	...	...	...
95 - 99	CDFC	66	9	57	...	...	...	...	...	...
100+	CDFC	9	...	9	...	...	...	...	...	...
Channel Islands: Jersey - Îles Anglo-Normandes: Jersey										
10 III 1996										
Total	CDFC	85 150	41 394	43 756	...	...	...	...	...	...
0 - 1	CDFC	951	505	446	...	...	...	...	...	...
1 - 4	CDFC	3 942	2 037	1 905	...	...	...	...	...	...
5 - 9	CDFC	4 868	2 486	2 382	...	...	...	...	...	...
10 - 14	CDFC	4 356	2 231	2 125	...	...	...	...	...	...
15 - 19	CDFC	4 278	2 134	2 144	...	...	...	...	...	...
20 - 24	CDFC	5 637	2 706	2 931	...	...	...	...	...	...
25 - 29	CDFC	7 821	3 806	4 015	...	...	...	...	...	...
30 - 34	CDFC	8 074	3 961	4 113	...	...	...	...	...	...
35 - 39	CDFC	7 109	3 527	3 582	...	...	...	...	...	...
40 - 44	CDFC	6 269	3 103	3 166	...	...	...	...	...	...

7. Population by age, sex and urban/rural residence: latest available year, 1992 - 2001
Population selon l'âge, le sexe et la résidence, urbaine/rurale: dernière année disponible, 1992 - 2001
(continued — suite)

(See notes at end of table. — Voir notes à la fin du tableau.)

Continent, country or area, date and age (in years) / Continent, pays ou zone, date et âge (en années)	Code[1]	Total			Urban - Urbaine			Rural - Rurale		
		Both sexes Les deux sexes	Male Masculin	Female Féminin	Both sexes Les deux sexes	Male Masculin	Female Féminin	Both sexes Les deux sexes	Male Masculin	Female Féminin
EUROPE										
Channel Islands: Jersey - Îles Anglo-Normandes: Jersey										
10 III 1996										
45 - 49	CDFC	6 374	3 195	3 179	...	...	...	...	...	...
50 - 54	CDFC	4 876	2 419	2 457	...	...	...	...	...	...
55 - 59	CDFC	4 654	2 377	2 277	...	...	...	...	...	...
60 - 64	CDFC	3 981	2 003	1 978	...	...	...	...	...	...
65 - 69	CDFC	3 441	1 635	1 806	...	...	...	...	...	...
70 - 74	CDFC	2 994	1 360	1 634	...	...	...	...	...	...
75 - 79	CDFC	2 209	850	1 359	...	...	...	...	...	...
80 - 84	CDFC	1 833	654	1 179	...	...	...	...	...	...
85 - 89	CDFC	1 026	301	725	...	...	...	...	...	...
90 - 94	CDFC	378	85	293	...	...	...	...	...	...
95 - 99	CDFC	73	17	56	...	...	...	...	...	...
100+	CDFC	6	2	4	...	...	...	...	...	...
Croatia - Croatie										
1 I 2001										
Total	ESDJ	4 437 460	2 135 900	2 301 560	...	...	...	...	...	...
0 - 1	ESDJ	42 942	22 097	20 845	...	...	...	...	...	...
1 - 4	ESDJ	194 580	99 621	94 959	...	...	...	...	...	...
5 - 9	ESDJ	248 528	127 274	121 254	...	...	...	...	...	...
10 - 14	ESDJ	268 584	137 175	131 409	...	...	...	...	...	...
15 - 19	ESDJ	298 606	152 676	145 930	...	...	...	...	...	...
20 - 24	ESDJ	305 631	155 739	149 892	...	...	...	...	...	...
25 - 29	ESDJ	294 497	148 666	145 831	...	...	...	...	...	...
30 - 34	ESDJ	295 431	147 920	147 511	...	...	...	...	...	...
35 - 39	ESDJ	317 273	158 506	158 767	...	...	...	...	...	...
40 - 44	ESDJ	333 403	166 499	166 904	...	...	...	...	...	...
45 - 49	ESDJ	333 576	168 290	165 286	...	...	...	...	...	...
50 - 54	ESDJ	299 773	148 224	151 549	...	...	...	...	...	...
55 - 59	ESDJ	229 775	108 673	121 102	...	...	...	...	...	...
60 - 64	ESDJ	262 016	120 667	141 349	...	...	...	...	...	...
65 - 69	ESDJ	252 947	110 459	142 488	...	...	...	...	...	...
70 - 74	ESDJ	203 885	81 884	122 001	...	...	...	...	...	...
75 - 79	ESDJ	137 201	44 149	93 052	...	...	...	...	...	...
80 - 84	ESDJ	56 954	17 040	39 914	...	...	...	...	...	...
85 - 89	ESDJ	30 833	8 682	22 151	...	...	...	...	...	...
90 - 94	ESDJ	10 265	2 571	7 694	...	...	...	...	...	...
95 - 99	ESDJ	1 371	302	1 069	...	...	...	...	...	...
100+	ESDJ	84	21	63	...	...	...	...	...	...
Unk. - Inc.	ESDJ	19 305	8 765	10 540	...	...	...	...	...	...
Czech Republic - République tchèque										
31 XII 2000										
Total	ESDJ	10 266 546	4 996 731	5 269 815	7 630 951	3 689 243	3 941 708	2 635 595	1 307 488	1 328 107
0 - 1	ESDJ	90 622	46 884	43 738	66 578	34 473	32 105	24 044	12 411	11 633
1 - 4	ESDJ	359 496	184 532	174 964	262 147	134 077	128 070	97 349	50 455	46 894
5 - 9	ESDJ	571 430	293 457	277 973	420 491	215 862	204 629	150 939	77 595	73 344
10 - 14	ESDJ	642 886	328 994	313 892	477 299	243 827	233 472	165 587	85 167	80 420
15 - 19	ESDJ	682 333	348 835	333 498	503 523	257 204	246 319	178 810	91 631	87 179
20 - 24	ESDJ	852 548	435 295	417 253	631 242	321 307	309 935	221 306	113 988	107 318
25 - 29	ESDJ	867 051	442 176	424 875	648 311	326 976	321 335	218 740	115 200	103 540
30 - 34	ESDJ	690 760	352 733	338 027	521 109	263 150	257 959	169 651	89 583	80 068
35 - 39	ESDJ	690 042	351 500	338 542	521 110	262 973	258 137	168 932	88 527	80 405
40 - 44	ESDJ	681 116	343 740	337 376	508 441	253 211	255 230	172 675	90 529	82 146
45 - 49	ESDJ	793 726	395 591	398 135	595 416	293 241	302 175	198 310	102 350	95 960
50 - 54	ESDJ	813 556	400 825	412 731	609 596	295 403	314 193	203 960	105 422	98 538

7. Population by age, sex and urban/rural residence: latest available year, 1992 - 2001
Population selon l'âge, le sexe et la résidence, urbaine/rurale: dernière année disponible, 1992 - 2001
(continued — suite)

(See notes at end of table. — Voir notes à la fin du tableau.)

Continent, country or area, date and age (in years) / Continent, pays ou zone, date et âge (en années)	Code[1]	Total			Urban - Urbaine			Rural - Rurale		
		Both sexes Les deux sexes	Male Masculin	Female Féminin	Both sexes Les deux sexes	Male Masculin	Female Féminin	Both sexes Les deux sexes	Male Masculin	Female Féminin
EUROPE										
Czech Republic - République tchèque										
31 XII 2000										
55 - 59	ESDJ	635 761	305 457	330 304	482 794	229 574	253 220	152 967	75 883	77 084
60 - 64	ESDJ	472 216	218 856	253 360	349 997	161 559	188 438	122 219	57 297	64 922
65 - 69	ESDJ	438 862	192 510	246 352	320 986	140 123	180 863	117 876	52 387	65 489
70 - 74	ESDJ	408 243	164 661	243 582	297 147	119 824	177 323	111 096	44 837	66 259
75 - 79	ESDJ	326 131	115 946	210 185	237 693	84 415	153 278	88 438	31 531	56 907
80 - 84	ESDJ	130 579	42 126	88 453	94 466	30 131	64 335	36 113	11 995	24 118
85 - 89	ESDJ	85 294	24 210	61 084	60 587	16 770	43 817	24 707	7 440	17 267
90 - 94	ESDJ	27 537	6 880	20 657	18 475	4 316	14 159	9 062	2 564	6 498
95 - 99	ESDJ	5 403	1 333	4 070	3 076	720	2 356	2 327	613	1 714
100+	ESDJ	954	190	764	467	107	360	487	83	404
1 VII 2001										
Total	ESDJ	10 268 136	5 001 120	5 267 017	...	...	...	...	...	...
0 - 4	ESDJ	449 644	231 178	218 466	...	...	...	...	...	...
5 - 9	ESDJ	553 508	284 274	269 234	...	...	...	...	...	...
10 - 14	ESDJ	644 951	330 301	314 651	...	...	...	...	...	...
15 - 19	ESDJ	680 052	347 823	332 229	...	...	...	...	...	...
20 - 24	ESDJ	835 616	426 642	408 974	...	...	...	...	...	...
25 - 29	ESDJ	882 459	450 374	432 085	...	...	...	...	...	...
30 - 34	ESDJ	697 469	356 378	341 091	...	...	...	...	...	...
35 - 39	ESDJ	694 419	353 937	340 483	...	...	...	...	...	...
40 - 44	ESDJ	669 438	338 376	331 062	...	...	...	...	...	...
45 - 49	ESDJ	786 609	392 654	393 955	...	...	...	...	...	...
50 - 54	ESDJ	811 650	400 306	411 344	...	...	...	...	...	...
55 - 59	ESDJ	658 486	316 874	341 613	...	...	...	...	...	...
60 - 64	ESDJ	482 182	223 954	258 228	...	...	...	...	...	...
65 - 69	ESDJ	432 106	190 108	241 999	...	...	...	...	...	...
70 - 74	ESDJ	407 563	165 081	242 482	...	...	...	...	...	...
75 - 79	ESDJ	325 483	116 089	209 395	...	...	...	...	...	...
80 - 84	ESDJ	143 124	46 138	96 986	...	...	...	...	...	...
85+	ESDJ	113 381	30 638	82 744	...	...	...	...	...	...
Denmark - Danemark[30]										
1 VII 2001										
Total	ESDJ	5 358 783	2 649 233	2 709 551	...	...	...	...	...	...
0 - 4	ESDJ	336 474	172 453	164 021	...	...	...	...	...	...
5 - 9	ESDJ	349 643	179 401	170 242	...	...	...	...	...	...
10 - 14	ESDJ	313 662	161 118	152 544	...	...	...	...	...	...
15 - 19	ESDJ	280 761	143 284	137 477	...	...	...	...	...	...
20 - 24	ESDJ	321 164	162 414	158 750	...	...	...	...	...	...
25 - 29	ESDJ	381 036	192 262	188 774	...	...	...	...	...	...
30 - 34	ESDJ	396 618	202 318	194 300	...	...	...	...	...	...
35 - 39	ESDJ	419 558	214 265	205 293	...	...	...	...	...	...
40 - 44	ESDJ	377 204	191 681	185 524	...	...	...	...	...	...
45 - 49	ESDJ	367 450	185 871	181 580	...	...	...	...	...	...
50 - 54	ESDJ	383 616	193 303	190 314	...	...	...	...	...	...
55 - 59	ESDJ	367 917	185 146	182 771	...	...	...	...	...	...
60 - 64	ESDJ	270 408	133 183	137 226	...	...	...	...	...	...
65 - 69	ESDJ	221 911	105 584	116 328	...	...	...	...	...	...
70 - 74	ESDJ	192 264	87 401	104 864	...	...	...	...	...	...
75 - 79	ESDJ	163 983	68 162	95 822	...	...	...	...	...	...
80 - 84	ESDJ	116 390	42 953	73 438	...	...	...	...	...	...
85+	ESDJ	98 728	28 440	70 288	...	...	...	...	...	...
Estonia - Estonie										
1 VII 2000										
Total	ESDF	1 369 279	631 515	737 764	922 594	415 232	507 362	446 685	216 283	230 402
0 - 1	ESDF	12 513	6 469	6 044	8 251	4 285	3 966	4 262	2 184	2 078

7. Population by age, sex and urban/rural residence: latest available year, 1992 - 2001
Population selon l'âge, le sexe et la résidence, urbaine/rurale: dernière année disponible, 1992 - 2001
(continued — suite)

(See notes at end of table. — Voir notes à la fin du tableau.)

Continent, country or area, date and age (in years) / Continent, pays ou zone, date et âge (en années)	Code[1]	Total			Urban - Urbaine			Rural - Rurale		
		Both sexes Les deux sexes	Male Masculin	Female Féminin	Both sexes Les deux sexes	Male Masculin	Female Féminin	Both sexes Les deux sexes	Male Masculin	Female Féminin
EUROPE										
Estonia - Estonie										
1 VII 2000										
1 - 4	ESDF	48 954	25 199	23 755	31 030	15 905	15 125	17 924	9 294	8 630
5 - 9	ESDF	78 115	40 027	38 088	47 457	24 257	23 200	30 658	15 770	14 888
10 - 14	ESDF	106 823	54 825	51 998	67 867	34 847	33 020	38 956	19 978	18 978
15 - 19	ESDF	104 062	53 030	51 032	70 183	35 195	34 988	33 879	17 835	16 044
20 - 24	ESDF	95 020	48 370	46 650	70 661	34 608	36 053	24 359	13 762	10 597
25 - 29	ESDF	94 290	47 234	47 056	67 740	33 221	34 519	26 550	14 013	12 537
30 - 34	ESDF	89 676	43 981	45 695	61 055	29 369	31 686	28 621	14 612	14 009
35 - 39	ESDF	95 972	46 484	49 488	64 752	30 337	34 415	31 220	16 147	15 073
40 - 44	ESDF	99 366	47 375	51 991	68 087	31 147	36 940	31 279	16 228	15 051
45 - 49	ESDF	95 297	44 468	50 829	66 380	29 628	36 752	28 917	14 840	14 077
50 - 54	ESDF	86 431	39 304	47 127	59 404	25 907	33 497	27 027	13 397	13 630
55 - 59	ESDF	73 569	32 497	41 072	47 887	20 079	27 808	25 682	12 418	13 264
60 - 64	ESDF	82 300	34 436	47 864	55 940	22 541	33 399	26 360	11 895	14 465
65 - 69	ESDF	69 419	27 244	42 175	45 951	17 442	28 509	23 468	9 802	13 666
70 - 74	ESDF	61 183	21 270	39 913	41 744	14 358	27 386	19 439	6 912	12 527
75 - 79	ESDF	39 739	10 685	29 054	25 742	6 766	18 976	13 997	3 919	10 078
80 - 84	ESDF	18 455	4 624	13 831	11 554	2 931	8 623	6 901	1 693	5 208
85 - 89	ESDF	12 591	2 769	9 822	7 547	1 640	5 907	5 044	1 129	3 915
90 - 94	ESDF	4 202	767	3 435	2 454	416	2 038	1 748	351	1 397
95 - 99	ESDF	697	116	581	418	71	347	279	45	234
100+	ESDF	66	6	60	39	3	36	27	3	24
Unk. - Inc.	ESDF	539	335	204	451	279	172	88	56	32
1 I 2001										
Total	ESDF	1 366 723	630 385	736 338	...	...	...	...	...	...
0 - 4	ESDF	61 517	31 764	29 753	...	...	...	...	...	...
5 - 9	ESDF	74 552	38 158	36 394	...	...	...	...	...	...
10 - 14	ESDF	106 287	54 620	51 667	...	...	...	...	...	...
15 - 19	ESDF	104 726	53 360	51 366	...	...	...	...	...	...
20 - 24	ESDF	95 448	48 593	46 855	...	...	...	...	...	...
25 - 29	ESDF	93 957	47 163	46 794	...	...	...	...	...	...
30 - 34	ESDF	90 265	44 327	45 938	...	...	...	...	...	...
35 - 39	ESDF	94 480	45 786	48 694	...	...	...	...	...	...
40 - 44	ESDF	99 232	47 295	51 937	...	...	...	...	...	...
45 - 49	ESDF	95 900	44 733	51 167	...	...	...	...	...	...
50 - 54	ESDF	88 466	40 209	48 257	...	...	...	...	...	...
55 - 59	ESDF	71 493	31 587	39 906	...	...	...	...	...	...
60 - 64	ESDF	82 297	34 394	47 903	...	...	...	...	...	...
65 - 69	ESDF	68 746	26 980	41 766	...	...	...	...	...	...
70 - 74	ESDF	61 911	21 828	40 083	...	...	...	...	...	...
75 - 79	ESDF	41 009	11 014	29 995	...	...	...	...	...	...
80 - 84	ESDF	18 426	4 582	13 844	...	...	...	...	...	...
85+	ESDF	17 472	3 657	13 815	...	...	...	...	...	...
Unk. - Inc.	ESDF	539	335	204	...	...	...	...	...	...
Finland - Finlande										
31 XII 2000										
Total	CDJC	5 181 115	2 529 341	2 651 774	3 167 668	1 516 812	1 650 856	2 013 447	1 012 529	1 000 918
0 - 1	CDJC	56 550	29 124	27 426	36 051	18 551	17 500	20 499	10 573	9 926
1 - 4	CDJC	234 725	119 727	114 998	144 628	73 577	71 051	90 097	46 150	43 947
5 - 9	CDJC	326 424	166 231	160 193	192 415	97 653	94 762	134 009	68 578	65 431
10 - 14	CDJC	318 634	162 947	155 687	180 374	91 943	88 431	138 260	71 004	67 256
15 - 19	CDJC	331 778	169 617	162 161	193 281	96 323	96 958	138 497	73 294	65 203
20 - 24	CDJC	327 230	167 084	160 146	234 805	115 297	119 508	92 425	51 787	40 638
25 - 29	CDJC	306 202	156 842	149 360	220 633	112 147	108 486	85 569	44 695	40 874
30 - 34	CDJC	346 890	176 839	170 051	232 819	118 043	114 776	114 071	58 796	55 275
35 - 39	CDJC	378 646	192 915	185 731	238 927	120 395	118 532	139 719	72 520	67 199
40 - 44	CDJC	382 265	193 976	188 289	230 988	114 880	116 108	151 277	79 096	72 181
45 - 49	CDJC	399 427	201 745	197 682	239 170	116 581	122 589	160 257	85 164	75 093

188

7. Population by age, sex and urban/rural residence: latest available year, 1992 - 2001
Population selon l'âge, le sexe et la résidence, urbaine/rurale: dernière année disponible, 1992 - 2001
(continued — suite)

(See notes at end of table. — Voir notes à la fin du tableau.)

Continent, country or area, date and age (in years) Continent, pays ou zone, date et âge (en années)	Code[1]	Total			Urban - Urbaine			Rural - Rurale		
		Both sexes Les deux sexes	Male Masculin	Female Féminin	Both sexes Les deux sexes	Male Masculin	Female Féminin	Both sexes Les deux sexes	Male Masculin	Female Féminin
EUROPE										
Finland - Finlande										
31 XII 2000										
50 - 54	CDJC	428 147	215 979	212 168	259 794	126 361	133 433	168 353	89 618	78 735
55 - 59	CDJC	310 083	154 028	156 055	188 611	90 754	97 857	121 472	63 274	58 198
60 - 64	CDJC	256 916	123 117	133 799	147 915	68 345	79 570	109 001	54 772	54 229
65 - 69	CDJC	225 524	103 778	121 746	125 981	55 352	70 629	99 543	48 426	51 117
70 - 74	CDJC	211 265	88 852	122 413	115 373	45 851	69 522	95 892	43 001	52 891
75 - 79	CDJC	163 283	58 256	105 027	88 620	29 935	58 685	74 663	28 321	46 342
80 - 84	CDJC	98 731	29 459	69 272	54 096	15 335	38 761	44 635	14 124	30 511
85 - 89	CDJC	55 758	14 095	41 663	30 571	7 147	23 424	25 187	6 948	18 239
90 - 94	CDJC	19 179	4 121	15 058	10 668	2 032	8 636	8 511	2 089	6 422
95 - 99	CDJC	3 190	571	2 619	1 814	290	1 524	1 376	281	1 095
100+	CDJC	268	38	230	134	20	114	134	18	116
1 VII 2001										
Total	ESDJ	5 188 008	2 533 469	2 654 539	...	...	...	...	...	...
0 - 4	ESDJ	289 034	147 648	141 386	...	...	...	...	...	...
5 - 9	ESDJ	324 101	165 169	158 932	...	...	...	...	...	...
10 - 14	ESDJ	320 826	163 953	156 873	...	...	...	...	...	...
15 - 19	ESDJ	330 499	169 009	161 491	...	...	...	...	...	...
20 - 24	ESDJ	326 415	166 667	159 748	...	...	...	...	...	...
25 - 29	ESDJ	309 196	158 539	150 657	...	...	...	...	...	...
30 - 34	ESDJ	340 981	173 759	167 222	...	...	...	...	...	...
35 - 39	ESDJ	377 592	192 373	185 219	...	...	...	...	...	...
40 - 44	ESDJ	380 178	192 848	187 330	...	...	...	...	...	...
45 - 49	ESDJ	398 992	201 429	197 563	...	...	...	...	...	...
50 - 54	ESDJ	424 544	214 216	210 328	...	...	...	...	...	...
55 - 59	ESDJ	317 874	158 054	159 820	...	...	...	...	...	...
60 - 64	ESDJ	265 495	127 505	137 990	...	...	...	...	...	...
65 - 69	ESDJ	225 374	103 853	121 521	...	...	...	...	...	...
70 - 74	ESDJ	211 870	89 625	122 245	...	...	...	...	...	...
75 - 79	ESDJ	164 819	59 571	105 248	...	...	...	...	...	...
80 - 84	ESDJ	101 195	30 322	70 874	...	...	...	...	...	...
85+	ESDJ	79 028	18 934	60 094	...	...	...	...	...	...
France[31]										
1 I 2001										
Total	ESDJ	59 039 713	28 677 636	30 362 077	...	...	...	...	...	...
0 - 1	ESDJ	768 571	394 048	374 523	...	...	...	...	...	...
1 - 4	ESDJ	2 887 638	1 478 959	1 408 679	...	...	...	...	...	...
5 - 9	ESDJ	3 607 494	1 846 977	1 760 517	...	...	...	...	...	...
10 - 14	ESDJ	3 837 589	1 962 654	1 874 935	...	...	...	...	...	...
15 - 19	ESDJ	3 903 836	1 993 782	1 910 054	...	...	...	...	...	...
20 - 24	ESDJ	3 757 032	1 897 801	1 859 231	...	...	...	...	...	...
25 - 29	ESDJ	4 083 848	2 045 442	2 038 406	...	...	...	...	...	...
30 - 34	ESDJ	4 225 041	2 104 052	2 120 989	...	...	...	...	...	...
35 - 39	ESDJ	4 349 402	2 155 790	2 193 612	...	...	...	...	...	...
40 - 44	ESDJ	4 248 310	2 095 907	2 152 403	...	...	...	...	...	...
45 - 49	ESDJ	4 175 461	2 063 148	2 112 313	...	...	...	...	...	...
50 - 54	ESDJ	4 194 399	2 090 468	2 103 931	...	...	...	...	...	...
55 - 59	ESDJ	2 821 303	1 400 926	1 420 377	...	...	...	...	...	...
60 - 64	ESDJ	2 661 723	1 283 052	1 378 671	...	...	...	...	...	...
65 - 69	ESDJ	2 679 893	1 234 100	1 445 793	...	...	...	...	...	...
70 - 74	ESDJ	2 467 162	1 071 537	1 395 625	...	...	...	...	...	...
75 - 79	ESDJ	2 093 089	836 758	1 256 331	...	...	...	...	...	...
80 - 84	ESDJ	1 057 191	386 444	670 747	...	...	...	...	...	...
85 - 89	ESDJ	776 129	233 525	542 604	...	...	...	...	...	...
90 - 94	ESDJ	350 657	84 491	266 166	...	...	...	...	...	...
95 - 99	ESDJ	84 089	16 221	67 868	...	...	...	...	...	...
100+	ESDJ	9 856	1 554	8 302	...	...	...	...	...	...

7. **Population by age, sex and urban/rural residence: latest available year, 1992 - 2001**
Population selon l'âge, le sexe et la résidence, urbaine/rurale: dernière année disponible, 1992 - 2001
(continued — suite)

(See notes at end of table. — Voir notes à la fin du tableau.)

Continent, country or area, date and age (in years) / Continent, pays ou zone, date et âge (en années)	Code[1]	Total			Urban - Urbaine			Rural - Rurale		
		Both sexes Les deux sexes	Male Masculin	Female Féminin	Both sexes Les deux sexes	Male Masculin	Female Féminin	Both sexes Les deux sexes	Male Masculin	Female Féminin
EUROPE										
Germany - Allemagne										
1 VII 2001										
Total	ESDJ	82 349 925	40 215 606	42 134 319	...	...	...	...	...	...
0 - 4	ESDJ	3 918 414	2 011 427	1 906 987	...	...	...	...	...	...
5 - 9	ESDJ	4 045 252	2 075 174	1 970 078	...	...	...	...	...	...
10 - 14	ESDJ	4 734 378	2 430 415	2 303 963	...	...	...	...	...	...
15 - 19	ESDJ	4 626 530	2 373 194	2 253 336	...	...	...	...	...	...
20 - 24	ESDJ	4 699 187	2 390 391	2 308 797	...	...	...	...	...	...
25 - 29	ESDJ	4 840 453	2 472 720	2 367 734	...	...	...	...	...	...
30 - 34	ESDJ	6 561 489	3 376 296	3 185 193	...	...	...	...	...	...
35 - 39	ESDJ	7 241 945	3 731 192	3 510 753	...	...	...	...	...	...
40 - 44	ESDJ	6 496 132	3 321 945	3 174 188	...	...	...	...	...	...
45 - 49	ESDJ	5 748 750	2 901 110	2 847 640	...	...	...	...	...	...
50 - 54	ESDJ	5 109 639	2 569 701	2 539 939	...	...	...	...	...	...
55 - 59	ESDJ	4 686 005	2 338 699	2 347 306	...	...	...	...	...	...
60 - 64	ESDJ	5 761 886	2 824 687	2 937 199	...	...	...	...	...	...
65 - 69	ESDJ	4 267 501	2 016 900	2 250 601	...	...	...	...	...	...
70 - 74	ESDJ	3 603 931	1 567 615	2 036 316	...	...	...	...	...	...
75 - 79	ESDJ	2 842 706	969 079	1 873 627	...	...	...	...	...	...
80 - 84	ESDJ	1 589 337	467 756	1 121 581	...	...	...	...	...	...
85+	ESDJ	1 576 394	377 310	1 199 085	...	...	...	...	...	...
Greece - Grèce[32]										
1 VII 1998										
Total	ESDF	10 516 366	5 183 147	5 333 219	...	...	...	...	...	...
0 - 1	ESDF	100 841	51 955	48 886	...	...	...	...	...	...
1 - 4	ESDF	405 370	208 990	196 380	...	...	...	...	...	...
5 - 9	ESDF	529 098	272 273	256 825	...	...	...	...	...	...
10 - 14	ESDF	604 465	310 569	293 896	...	...	...	...	...	...
15 - 19	ESDF	728 568	374 505	354 063	...	...	...	...	...	...
20 - 24	ESDF	784 483	399 369	385 114	...	...	...	...	...	...
25 - 29	ESDF	808 127	409 297	398 830	...	...	...	...	...	...
30 - 34	ESDF	795 833	398 588	397 245	...	...	...	...	...	...
35 - 39	ESDF	750 348	373 325	377 023	...	...	...	...	...	...
40 - 44	ESDF	716 783	357 777	359 006	...	...	...	...	...	...
45 - 49	ESDF	676 343	339 070	337 273	...	...	...	...	...	...
50 - 54	ESDF	638 436	316 425	322 011	...	...	...	...	...	...
55 - 59	ESDF	588 076	286 255	301 821	...	...	...	...	...	...
60 - 64	ESDF	630 119	301 195	328 924	...	...	...	...	...	...
65 - 69	ESDF	596 049	280 767	315 282	...	...	...	...	...	...
70 - 74	ESDF	482 754	217 301	265 453	...	...	...	...	...	...
75 - 79	ESDF	311 600	133 387	178 213	...	...	...	...	...	...
80 - 84	ESDF	192 538	78 670	113 868	...	...	...	...	...	...
85 - 89	ESDF	120 451	48 844	71 607	...	...	...	...	...	...
90 - 94	ESDF	41 144	17 938	23 206	...	...	...	...	...	...
95 - 99	ESDF	12 579	5 486	7 093	...	...	...	...	...	...
100+	ESDF	2 361	1 161	1 200	...	...	...	...	...	...
Hungary - Hongrie										
1 VII 2001										
Total	ESDF	10 187 576	4 843 996	5 343 580	6 644 628	3 121 972	3 522 656	3 542 948	1 722 024	1 820 924
0 - 1	ESDF	95 958	49 191	46 767	59 649	30 566	29 082	36 309	18 624	17 684
1 - 4	ESDF	387 012	198 406	188 605	235 144	120 276	114 868	151 868	78 130	73 738
5 - 9	ESDF	571 574	292 634	278 940	347 258	177 732	169 526	224 316	114 902	109 414
10 - 14	ESDF	621 512	317 686	303 825	386 180	196 876	189 304	235 332	120 811	114 521
15 - 19	ESDF	661 768	337 332	324 436	443 616	223 360	220 256	218 153	113 972	104 180
20 - 24	ESDF	796 748	408 116	388 632	540 701	273 746	266 954	256 048	134 370	121 678
25 - 29	ESDF	802 172	408 497	393 676	545 854	275 167	270 686	256 319	133 330	122 989
30 - 34	ESDF	708 394	359 097	349 298	469 415	236 196	233 219	238 980	122 901	116 078
35 - 39	ESDF	611 276	305 759	305 516	390 138	191 483	198 654	221 138	114 276	106 862

7. **Population by age, sex and urban/rural residence: latest available year, 1992 - 2001**
Population selon l'âge, le sexe et la résidence, urbaine/rurale: dernière année disponible, 1992 - 2001
(continued — suite)

(See notes at end of table. — Voir notes à la fin du tableau.)

Continent, country or area, date and age (in years) Continent, pays ou zone, date et âge (en années)	Code[1]	Total			Urban - Urbaine			Rural - Rurale		
		Both sexes Les deux sexes	Male Masculin	Female Féminin	Both sexes Les deux sexes	Male Masculin	Female Féminin	Both sexes Les deux sexes	Male Masculin	Female Féminin
EUROPE										
Hungary - Hongrie										
1 VII 2001										
40 - 44	ESDF	692 456	340 352	352 104	439 022	209 258	229 764	253 434	131 094	122 340
45 - 49	ESDF	830 283	402 465	427 818	552 034	259 058	292 976	278 248	143 406	134 842
50 - 54	ESDF	713 712	339 644	374 068	479 139	222 283	256 856	234 573	117 360	117 212
55 - 59	ESDF	609 360	279 862	329 498	412 962	188 077	224 885	196 398	91 785	104 612
60 - 64	ESDF	536 902	230 931	305 972	347 545	149 186	198 360	189 358	81 746	107 612
65 - 69	ESDF	488 179	200 689	287 490	309 392	127 322	182 071	178 786	73 368	105 419
70 - 74	ESDF	435 032	167 968	267 064	277 420	107 887	169 534	157 612	60 080	97 531
75 - 79	ESDF	338 389	118 004	220 385	216 381	74 870	141 512	122 008	43 134	78 874
80 - 84	ESDF	164 284	52 622	111 662	108 666	34 763	73 904	55 617	17 858	37 758
85 - 89	ESDF	85 586	24 788	60 797	58 660	17 107	41 554	26 925	7 682	19 244
90+	ESDF	36 978	9 952	27 026	25 451	6 759	18 692	11 528	3 194	8 334
Iceland - Islande										
1 VII 2001										
Total	ESDJ	284 968	142 660	142 308	...	...	...	...	...	...
0 - 4	ESDJ	21 351	10 849	10 502	...	...	...	...	...	...
5 - 9	ESDJ	22 476	11 497	10 979	...	...	...	...	...	...
10 - 14	ESDJ	22 227	11 444	10 783	...	...	...	...	...	...
15 - 19	ESDJ	20 940	10 588	10 353	...	...	...	...	...	...
20 - 24	ESDJ	21 858	11 021	10 838	...	...	...	...	...	...
25 - 29	ESDJ	21 468	10 897	10 571	...	...	...	...	...	...
30 - 34	ESDJ	20 063	10 148	9 915	...	...	...	...	...	...
35 - 39	ESDJ	21 628	10 815	10 813	...	...	...	...	...	...
40 - 44	ESDJ	21 249	10 773	10 476	...	...	...	...	...	...
45 - 49	ESDJ	19 078	9 708	9 371	...	...	...	...	...	...
50 - 54	ESDJ	16 613	8 515	8 098	...	...	...	...	...	...
55 - 59	ESDJ	13 175	6 677	6 498	...	...	...	...	...	...
60 - 64	ESDJ	9 785	4 847	4 938	...	...	...	...	...	...
65 - 69	ESDJ	9 458	4 554	4 904	...	...	...	...	...	...
70 - 74	ESDJ	8 877	4 199	4 679	...	...	...	...	...	...
75 - 79	ESDJ	6 791	3 043	3 748	...	...	...	...	...	...
80 - 84	ESDJ	4 444	1 858	2 587	...	...	...	...	...	...
85+	ESDJ	3 491	1 231	2 261	...	...	...	...	...	...
Ireland - Irlande										
28 IV 1996										
Total	CDFC	3 626 087	1 800 232	1 825 855	2 107 991	1 018 779	1 089 212	1 518 096	781 453	736 643
0 - 1	CDFC	48 854	25 231	23 623	29 896	15 513	14 383	18 958	9 718	9 240
1 - 4	CDFC	201 540	103 509	98 031	118 528	61 039	57 489	83 012	42 470	40 542
5 - 9	CDFC	282 943	145 335	137 608	157 226	80 627	76 599	125 717	64 708	61 009
10 - 14	CDFC	326 087	167 377	158 710	175 127	89 533	85 594	150 960	77 844	73 116
15 - 19	CDFC	339 536	173 950	165 586	194 941	98 329	96 612	144 595	75 621	68 974
20 - 24	CDFC	293 354	149 143	144 211	197 224	95 289	101 935	96 130	53 854	42 276
25 - 29	CDFC	259 045	129 363	129 682	173 299	83 739	89 560	85 746	45 624	40 122
30 - 34	CDFC	260 929	127 735	133 194	165 281	79 336	85 945	95 648	48 399	47 249
35 - 39	CDFC	255 676	126 140	129 536	149 768	72 677	77 091	105 908	53 463	52 445
40 - 44	CDFC	240 441	120 064	120 377	135 108	65 555	69 553	105 333	54 509	50 824
45 - 49	CDFC	225 400	113 816	111 584	125 882	61 577	64 305	99 518	52 239	47 279
50 - 54	CDFC	186 647	94 818	91 829	105 304	51 683	53 621	81 343	43 135	38 208
55 - 59	CDFC	153 807	77 809	75 998	88 442	43 004	45 438	65 365	34 805	30 560
60 - 64	CDFC	137 946	68 690	69 256	77 165	36 701	40 464	60 781	31 989	28 792
65 - 69	CDFC	126 809	60 256	66 553	68 099	30 401	37 698	58 710	29 855	28 855
70 - 74	CDFC	112 542	50 124	62 418	58 341	24 103	34 238	54 201	26 021	28 180
75 - 79	CDFC	84 097	35 228	48 869	41 905	15 784	26 121	42 192	19 444	22 748
80 - 84	CDFC	55 771	21 074	34 697	27 877	9 143	18 734	27 894	11 931	15 963
85 - 89	CDFC	25 052	8 063	16 989	13 219	3 545	9 674	11 833	4 518	7 315
90 - 94	CDFC	7 833	2 083	5 750	4 408	1 004	3 404	3 425	1 079	2 346
95 - 99	CDFC	1 501	356	1 145	808	169	639	693	187	506
100+	CDFC	277	68	209	143	28	115	134	40	94

7. Population by age, sex and urban/rural residence: latest available year, 1992 - 2001
Population selon l'âge, le sexe et la résidence, urbaine/rurale: dernière année disponible, 1992 - 2001
(continued — suite)

(See notes at end of table. — Voir notes à la fin du tableau.)

Continent, country or area, date and age (in years) / Continent, pays ou zone, date et âge (en années)	Code[1]	Total			Urban - Urbaine			Rural - Rurale		
		Both sexes Les deux sexes	Male Masculin	Female Féminin	Both sexes Les deux sexes	Male Masculin	Female Féminin	Both sexes Les deux sexes	Male Masculin	Female Féminin
EUROPE										
Ireland - Irlande										
1 VII 2001										
Total	ESDF	3 854 311	1 914 492	1 939 820	...	...	...	...	...	...
0 - 4	ESDF	272 860	140 438	132 423	...	...	...	...	...	...
5 - 9	ESDF	261 814	134 586	127 228	...	...	...	...	...	...
10 - 14	ESDF	287 568	146 677	140 891	...	...	...	...	...	...
15 - 19	ESDF	324 115	166 418	157 697	...	...	...	...	...	...
20 - 24	ESDF	338 033	169 806	168 227	...	...	...	...	...	...
25 - 29	ESDF	319 158	161 058	158 101	...	...	...	...	...	...
30 - 34	ESDF	278 796	139 724	139 072	...	...	...	...	...	...
35 - 39	ESDF	272 203	134 058	138 145	...	...	...	...	...	...
40 - 44	ESDF	260 977	129 343	131 635	...	...	...	...	...	...
45 - 49	ESDF	244 446	122 274	122 172	...	...	...	...	...	...
50 - 54	ESDF	226 400	113 847	112 554	...	...	...	...	...	...
55 - 59	ESDF	187 258	94 616	92 642	...	...	...	...	...	...
60 - 64	ESDF	150 039	74 909	75 130	...	...	...	...	...	...
65 - 69	ESDF	129 887	63 279	66 608	...	...	...	...	...	...
70 - 74	ESDF	110 884	50 894	59 991	...	...	...	...	...	...
75 - 79	ESDF	88 919	37 078	51 841	...	...	...	...	...	...
80 - 84	ESDF	57 283	21 729	35 554	...	...	...	...	...	...
85+	ESDF	43 678	13 763	29 915	...	...	...	...	...	...
Isle of Man - Îles de Man										
14 IV 1996										
Total	CDJC	71 714	34 797	36 917	...	...	...	...	...	...
0 - 1	CDJC	766	412	354	...	...	...	...	...	...
1 - 4	CDJC	3 380	1 719	1 661	...	...	...	...	...	...
5 - 9	CDJC	4 278	2 180	2 098	...	...	...	...	...	...
10 - 14	CDJC	4 200	2 132	2 068	...	...	...	...	...	...
15 - 19	CDJC	4 179	2 171	2 008	...	...	...	...	...	...
20 - 24	CDJC	4 515	2 251	2 264	...	...	...	...	...	...
25 - 29	CDJC	4 898	2 452	2 446	...	...	...	...	...	...
30 - 34	CDJC	5 252	2 654	2 598	...	...	...	...	...	...
35 - 39	CDJC	4 945	2 417	2 528	...	...	...	...	...	...
40 - 44	CDJC	4 612	2 313	2 299	...	...	...	...	...	...
45 - 49	CDJC	5 461	2 745	2 716	...	...	...	...	...	...
50 - 54	CDJC	4 532	2 259	2 273	...	...	...	...	...	...
55 - 59	CDJC	4 015	2 023	1 992	...	...	...	...	...	...
60 - 64	CDJC	3 516	1 728	1 788	...	...	...	...	...	...
65 - 69	CDJC	3 409	1 539	1 870	...	...	...	...	...	...
70 - 74	CDJC	3 377	1 480	1 897	...	...	...	...	...	...
75 - 79	CDJC	2 612	1 040	1 572	...	...	...	...	...	...
80 - 84	CDJC	2 093	786	1 307	...	...	...	...	...	...
85 - 89	CDJC	1 189	379	810	...	...	...	...	...	...
90 - 94	CDJC	411	101	310	...	...	...	...	...	...
95 - 99	CDJC	65	16	49	...	...	...	...	...	...
100+	CDJC	9	...	9	...	...	...	...	...	...
Italy - Italie										
1 I 2001										
Total	ESDJ	57 844 017	28 094 857	29 749 160	...	...	...	...	...	...
0 - 1	ESDJ	542 368	279 471	262 897	...	...	...	...	...	...
0 - 4	ESDJ	2 140 683	1 101 174	1 039 509	...	...	...	...	...	...
5 - 9	ESDJ	2 769 342	1 423 960	1 345 382	...	...	...	...	...	...
10 - 14	ESDJ	2 851 511	1 465 981	1 385 530	...	...	...	...	...	...
15 - 19	ESDJ	3 045 511	1 561 200	1 484 311	...	...	...	...	...	...
20 - 24	ESDJ	3 556 119	1 814 088	1 742 031	...	...	...	...	...	...
25 - 29	ESDJ	4 399 252	2 228 786	2 170 466	...	...	...	...	...	...
30 - 34	ESDJ	4 704 263	2 382 026	2 322 237	...	...	...	...	...	...
35 - 39	ESDJ	4 678 953	2 362 595	2 316 358	...	...	...	...	...	...

7. Population by age, sex and urban/rural residence: latest available year, 1992 - 2001
Population selon l'âge, le sexe et la résidence, urbaine/rurale: dernière année disponible, 1992 - 2001
(continued — suite)

(See notes at end of table. — Voir notes à la fin du tableau.)

Continent, country or area, date and age (in years) Continent, pays ou zone, date et âge (en années)	Code[1]	Total			Urban - Urbaine			Rural - Rurale		
		Both sexes Les deux sexes	Male Masculin	Female Féminin	Both sexes Les deux sexes	Male Masculin	Female Féminin	Both sexes Les deux sexes	Male Masculin	Female Féminin
EUROPE										
Italy - Italie										
1 I 2001										
40 - 44	ESDJ	4 100 240	2 057 653	2 042 587	...	...	...	...	...	...
45 - 49	ESDJ	3 766 985	1 876 731	1 890 254	...	...	...	...	...	...
50 - 54	ESDJ	3 976 685	1 967 589	2 009 096	...	...	...	...	...	...
55 - 59	ESDJ	3 274 229	1 597 722	1 676 507	...	...	...	...	...	...
60 - 64	ESDJ	3 481 941	1 664 824	1 817 117	...	...	...	...	...	...
65 - 69	ESDJ	3 107 325	1 434 161	1 673 164	...	...	...	...	...	...
70 - 74	ESDJ	2 796 956	1 216 241	1 580 715	...	...	...	...	...	...
75 - 79	ESDJ	2 262 700	890 414	1 372 286	...	...	...	...	...	...
80 - 84	ESDJ	1 136 061	402 355	733 706	...	...	...	...	...	...
85 - 89	ESDJ	868 459	271 288	597 171	...	...	...	...	...	...
90 - 94	ESDJ	315 174	81 933	233 241	...	...	...	...	...	...
95 - 99	ESDJ	61 100	12 965	48 135	...	...	...	...	...	...
100+	ESDJ	8 160	1 700	6 460	...	...	...	...	...	...
Latvia - Lettonie										
1 VII 2001										
Total	ESDF	2 355 011	1 084 484	1 270 527	1 599 272	720 359	878 913	755 739	364 125	391 614
0 - 1	ESDF	19 934	10 159	9 775	12 568	6 416	6 152	7 366	3 743	3 623
1 - 4	ESDF	74 960	38 464	36 496	46 381	23 854	22 527	28 579	14 610	13 969
5 - 9	ESDF	125 311	64 080	61 231	76 145	38 842	37 303	49 166	25 238	23 928
10 - 14	ESDF	179 913	91 863	88 050	113 139	57 709	55 430	66 774	34 154	32 620
15 - 19	ESDF	182 346	92 961	89 385	121 088	61 155	59 933	61 258	31 806	29 452
20 - 24	ESDF	161 401	82 073	79 328	110 565	55 369	55 196	50 836	26 704	24 132
25 - 29	ESDF	162 580	82 230	80 350	112 158	55 525	56 633	50 422	26 705	23 717
30 - 34	ESDF	160 262	79 440	80 822	109 643	52 983	56 660	50 619	26 457	24 162
35 - 39	ESDF	167 540	82 128	85 412	114 409	54 144	60 265	53 131	27 984	25 147
40 - 44	ESDF	177 674	85 722	91 952	123 993	57 450	66 543	53 681	28 272	25 409
45 - 49	ESDF	157 187	73 711	83 476	112 811	50 697	62 114	44 376	23 014	21 362
50 - 54	ESDF	145 751	66 517	79 234	106 229	46 488	59 741	39 522	20 029	19 493
55 - 59	ESDF	129 664	56 764	72 900	89 468	37 844	51 624	40 196	18 920	21 276
60 - 64	ESDF	148 409	62 017	86 392	104 499	42 516	61 983	43 910	19 501	24 409
65 - 69	ESDF	118 828	45 877	72 951	80 663	30 620	50 043	38 165	15 257	22 908
70 - 74	ESDF	107 794	37 735	70 059	75 193	26 396	48 797	32 601	11 339	21 262
75 - 79	ESDF	73 160	18 245	54 915	50 264	12 689	37 575	22 896	5 556	17 340
80 - 84	ESDF	33 162	8 292	24 870	21 837	5 638	16 199	11 325	2 654	8 671
85 - 89	ESDF	19 962	4 337	15 625	12 559	2 869	9 690	7 403	1 468	5 935
90 - 94	ESDF	7 612	1 589	6 023	4 688	988	3 700	2 924	601	2 323
95 - 99	ESDF	1 417	261	1 156	883	156	727	534	105	429
100+	ESDF	144	19	125	89	11	78	55	8	47
Liechtenstein										
1 VII 2001										
Total	ESDF	33 104	16 195	16 909	...	...	...	...	...	...
0 - 1	ESDF	195	110	85	...	...	...	...	...	...
1 - 4	ESDF	1 617	789	828	...	...	...	...	...	...
5 - 9	ESDF	2 036	1 013	1 023	...	...	...	...	...	...
10 - 14	ESDF	2 088	1 098	990	...	...	...	...	...	...
15 - 19	ESDF	2 017	1 005	1 012	...	...	...	...	...	...
20 - 24	ESDF	2 095	1 065	1 030	...	...	...	...	...	...
25 - 29	ESDF	2 342	1 127	1 215	...	...	...	...	...	...
30 - 34	ESDF	2 855	1 417	1 438	...	...	...	...	...	...
35 - 39	ESDF	2 928	1 431	1 497	...	...	...	...	...	...
40 - 44	ESDF	2 829	1 384	1 445	...	...	...	...	...	...
45 - 49	ESDF	2 558	1 263	1 295	...	...	...	...	...	...
50 - 54	ESDF	2 381	1 243	1 138	...	...	...	...	...	...
55 - 59	ESDF	2 073	1 062	1 011	...	...	...	...	...	...
60 - 64	ESDF	1 498	744	754	...	...	...	...	...	...
65 - 69	ESDF	1 065	486	579	...	...	...	...	...	...
70 - 74	ESDF	855	378	477	...	...	...	...	...	...

7. Population by age, sex and urban/rural residence: latest available year, 1992 - 2001
Population selon l'âge, le sexe et la résidence, urbaine/rurale: dernière année disponible, 1992 - 2001
(continued — suite)

(See notes at end of table. — Voir notes à la fin du tableau.)

Continent, country or area, date and age (in years) Continent, pays ou zone, date et âge (en années)	Code[1]	Total			Urban - Urbaine			Rural - Rurale		
		Both sexes Les deux sexes	Male Masculin	Female Féminin	Both sexes Les deux sexes	Male Masculin	Female Féminin	Both sexes Les deux sexes	Male Masculin	Female Féminin
EUROPE										
Liechtenstein										
1 VII 2001										
75 - 79	ESDF	789	274	515	...	...	...	...	...	...
80 - 84	ESDF	496	191	305	...	...	...	...	...	...
85 - 89	ESDF	279	93	186	...	...	...	...	...	...
90 - 94	ESDF	89	15	74	...	...	...	...	...	...
95 - 99	ESDF	18	7	11	...	...	...	...	...	...
100+	ESDF	1	...	1	...	...	...	...	...	...
Lithuania - Lituanie										
1 VII 2001										
Total	ESDF	3 481 292	1 627 704	1 853 588	2 330 213	1 070 916	1 259 297	1 151 079	556 788	594 291
0 - 1	ESDF	32 311	16 609	15 702	20 460	10 518	9 942	11 851	6 091	5 760
1 - 4	ESDF	144 552	74 510	70 042	93 299	48 121	45 178	51 253	26 389	24 864
5 - 9	ESDF	225 158	115 144	110 014	143 787	73 538	70 249	81 371	41 606	39 765
10 - 14	ESDF	271 066	138 516	132 550	174 451	88 835	85 616	96 615	49 681	46 934
15 - 19	ESDF	267 820	136 538	131 282	181 392	91 177	90 215	86 428	45 361	41 067
20 - 24	ESDF	235 058	119 120	115 938	170 150	83 266	86 884	64 908	35 854	29 054
25 - 29	ESDF	238 934	119 109	119 825	172 118	83 754	88 364	66 816	35 355	31 461
30 - 34	ESDF	255 277	126 013	129 264	178 802	86 210	92 592	76 475	39 803	36 672
35 - 39	ESDF	269 465	132 721	136 744	189 116	89 917	99 199	80 349	42 804	37 545
40 - 44	ESDF	268 839	129 145	139 694	189 620	87 319	102 301	79 219	41 826	37 393
45 - 49	ESDF	219 505	103 898	115 607	155 956	70 617	85 339	63 549	33 281	30 268
50 - 54	ESDF	196 848	89 979	106 869	137 180	60 018	77 162	59 668	29 961	29 707
55 - 59	ESDF	183 140	80 498	102 642	121 310	51 810	69 500	61 830	28 688	33 142
60 - 64	ESDF	183 422	76 957	106 465	117 194	48 053	69 141	66 228	28 904	37 324
65 - 69	ESDF	167 065	65 888	101 177	100 068	39 045	61 023	66 997	26 843	40 154
70 - 74	ESDF	143 499	51 824	91 675	85 021	30 942	54 079	58 478	20 882	37 596
75 - 79	ESDF	97 734	28 831	68 903	55 567	15 989	39 578	42 167	12 842	29 325
80 - 84	ESDF	43 872	12 311	31 561	24 000	6 540	17 460	19 872	5 771	14 101
85 - 89	ESDF	24 469	6 091	18 378	13 502	3 248	10 254	10 967	2 843	8 124
90 - 94	ESDF	10 382	3 086	7 296	5 721	1 539	4 182	4 661	1 547	3 114
95 - 99	ESDF	2 087	635	1 452	1 076	293	783	1 011	342	669
100+	ESDF	464	107	357	214	46	168	250	61	189
Unk. - Inc.	ESDF	325	174	151	209	121	88	116	53	63
Luxembourg										
1 VII 2001										
Total	ESDJ	441 795	217 680	224 115	...	...	...	...	...	...
0 - 4	ESDJ	27 869	14 312	13 557	...	...	...	...	...	...
5 - 9	ESDJ	28 624	14 669	13 955	...	...	...	...	...	...
10 - 14	ESDJ	26 753	13 674	13 079	...	...	...	...	...	...
15 - 19	ESDJ	24 827	12 704	12 123	...	...	...	...	...	...
20 - 24	ESDJ	25 916	13 059	12 858	...	...	...	...	...	...
25 - 29	ESDJ	30 799	15 362	15 438	...	...	...	...	...	...
30 - 34	ESDJ	37 598	18 818	18 780	...	...	...	...	...	...
35 - 39	ESDJ	39 195	19 944	19 251	...	...	...	...	...	...
40 - 44	ESDJ	35 803	18 226	17 578	...	...	...	...	...	...
45 - 49	ESDJ	31 475	15 982	15 493	...	...	...	...	...	...
50 - 54	ESDJ	27 807	14 404	13 403	...	...	...	...	...	...
55 - 59	ESDJ	22 888	11 667	11 221	...	...	...	...	...	...
60 - 64	ESDJ	20 491	9 946	10 545	...	...	...	...	...	...
65 - 69	ESDJ	18 445	8 669	9 777	...	...	...	...	...	...
70 - 74	ESDJ	17 725	7 940	9 786	...	...	...	...	...	...
75 - 79	ESDJ	12 217	4 385	7 833	...	...	...	...	...	...
80 - 84	ESDJ	7 129	2 286	4 843	...	...	...	...	...	...
85+	ESDJ	6 237	1 638	4 600	...	...	...	...	...	...
Malta - Malte[33]										
1 VII 2001										
Total	ESDJ	393 028	194 526	198 502	...	...	...	...	...	...
0 - 4	ESDJ	22 499	11 519	10 981	...	...	...	...	...	...

7. Population by age, sex and urban/rural residence: latest available year, 1992 - 2001
Population selon l'âge, le sexe et la résidence, urbaine/rurale: dernière année disponible, 1992 - 2001
(continued — suite)

(See notes at end of table. — Voir notes à la fin du tableau.)

Continent, country or area, date and age (in years) / Continent, pays ou zone, date et âge (en années)	Code[1]	Total			Urban - Urbaine			Rural - Rurale		
		Both sexes Les deux sexes	Male Masculin	Female Féminin	Both sexes Les deux sexes	Male Masculin	Female Féminin	Both sexes Les deux sexes	Male Masculin	Female Féminin
EUROPE										
Malta - Malte[33]										
1 VII 2001										
5 - 9	ESDJ	25 804	13 333	12 471	...	...	...	...	...	...
10 - 14	ESDJ	28 330	14 527	13 804	...	...	...	...	...	...
15 - 19	ESDJ	29 061	14 993	14 068	...	...	...	...	...	...
20 - 24	ESDJ	29 795	15 325	14 471	...	...	...	...	...	...
25 - 29	ESDJ	27 842	14 248	13 594	...	...	...	...	...	...
30 - 34	ESDJ	23 939	12 201	11 738	...	...	...	...	...	...
35 - 39	ESDJ	26 608	13 450	13 158	...	...	...	...	...	...
40 - 44	ESDJ	29 995	15 037	14 958	...	...	...	...	...	...
45 - 49	ESDJ	28 734	14 490	14 244	...	...	...	...	...	...
50 - 54	ESDJ	30 467	15 181	15 287	...	...	...	...	...	...
55 - 59	ESDJ	23 233	11 309	11 925	...	...	...	...	...	...
60 - 64	ESDJ	17 745	8 327	9 419	...	...	...	...	...	...
65 - 69	ESDJ	16 189	7 220	8 969	...	...	...	...	...	...
70 - 74	ESDJ	12 890	5 472	7 418	...	...	...	...	...	...
75 - 79	ESDJ	10 051	4 182	5 869	...	...	...	...	...	...
80 - 84	ESDJ	5 908	2 409	3 499	...	...	...	...	...	...
85+	ESDJ	3 944	1 309	2 635	...	...	...	...	...	...
Monaco										
1 VII 2000										
Total	CDJC	32 017	15 544	16 473	...	...	...	...	...	...
0 - 14	CDJC	4 237	2 206	2 031	...	...	...	...	...	...
15 - 24	CDJC	2 634	1 367	1 267	...	...	...	...	...	...
25 - 44	CDJC	8 698	4 370	4 328	...	...	...	...	...	...
45 - 64	CDJC	9 250	4 552	4 698	...	...	...	...	...	...
65+	CDJC	7 181	3 042	4 139	...	...	...	...	...	...
Unk. - Inc.	CDJC	17	7	10	...	...	...	...	...	...
Netherlands - Pays-Bas										
1 I 2001										
Total	ESDJ	15 987 075	7 909 855	8 077 220	10 329 289	5 075 331	5 253 958	5 657 786	2 834 524	2 823 262
0 - 1	ESDJ	207 097	105 856	101 241	133 671	68 349	65 322	73 426	37 507	35 919
1 - 4	ESDJ	793 988	406 535	387 453	501 344	256 426	244 918	292 644	150 109	142 535
5 - 9	ESDJ	995 828	509 250	486 578	617 734	315 692	302 042	378 094	193 558	184 536
10 - 14	ESDJ	980 625	501 302	479 323	605 246	308 946	296 300	375 379	192 356	183 023
15 - 19	ESDJ	930 515	476 586	453 929	589 667	299 658	290 009	340 848	176 928	163 920
20 - 24	ESDJ	962 691	486 741	475 950	674 486	332 507	341 979	288 205	154 234	133 971
25 - 29	ESDJ	1 118 821	564 302	554 519	791 485	397 134	394 351	327 336	167 168	160 168
30 - 34	ESDJ	1 317 579	671 663	645 916	889 386	455 177	434 209	428 193	216 486	211 707
35 - 39	ESDJ	1 328 013	677 179	650 834	866 714	442 881	423 833	461 299	234 298	227 001
40 - 44	ESDJ	1 235 328	625 769	609 559	792 450	400 606	391 844	442 878	225 163	217 715
45 - 49	ESDJ	1 142 667	578 271	564 396	724 942	364 533	360 409	417 725	213 738	203 987
50 - 54	ESDJ	1 181 742	600 629	581 113	741 141	375 277	365 864	440 601	225 352	215 249
55 - 59	ESDJ	875 129	443 775	431 354	532 285	267 874	264 411	342 844	175 901	166 943
60 - 64	ESDJ	742 551	368 632	373 919	458 473	224 934	233 539	284 078	143 698	140 380
65 - 69	ESDJ	643 835	306 379	337 456	401 469	187 728	213 741	242 366	118 651	123 715
70 - 74	ESDJ	558 536	248 156	310 380	359 665	157 088	202 577	198 871	91 068	107 803
75 - 79	ESDJ	455 493	180 771	274 722	301 710	117 611	184 099	153 783	63 160	90 623
80 - 84	ESDJ	288 303	98 886	189 417	193 155	64 804	128 351	95 148	34 082	61 066
85 - 89	ESDJ	158 004	44 311	113 693	106 714	28 765	77 949	51 290	15 546	35 744
90 - 94	ESDJ	57 530	12 515	45 015	38 921	7 939	30 982	18 609	4 576	14 033
95 - 99	ESDJ	11 712	2 174	9 538	7 889	1 300	6 589	3 823	874	2 949
100+	ESDJ	1 088	173	915	742	102	640	346	71	275
Norway - Norvège[34]										
1 VII 2001										
Total	ESDJ	4 513 751	2 236 618	2 277 134	...	...	...	...	...	...
0 - 4	ESDJ	298 658	153 166	145 492	...	...	...	...	...	...
5 - 9	ESDJ	308 119	158 468	149 651	...	...	...	...	...	...

7. Population by age, sex and urban/rural residence: latest available year, 1992 - 2001
Population selon l'âge, le sexe et la résidence, urbaine/rurale: dernière année disponible, 1992 - 2001
(continued — suite)

(See notes at end of table. — Voir notes à la fin du tableau.)

Continent, country or area, date and age (in years) / Continent, pays ou zone, date et âge (en années)	Code[1]	Total			Urban - Urbaine			Rural - Rurale		
		Both sexes Les deux sexes	Male Masculin	Female Féminin	Both sexes Les deux sexes	Male Masculin	Female Féminin	Both sexes Les deux sexes	Male Masculin	Female Féminin
EUROPE										
Norway - Norvège[34]										
1 VII 2001										
10 - 14	ESDJ	297 590	152 525	145 065	...	...	...	...	...	...
15 - 19	ESDJ	267 082	137 079	130 003	...	...	...	...	...	...
20 - 24	ESDJ	273 970	139 176	134 794	...	...	...	...	...	...
25 - 29	ESDJ	320 890	162 549	158 341	...	...	...	...	...	...
30 - 34	ESDJ	351 681	179 218	172 463	...	...	...	...	...	...
35 - 39	ESDJ	336 389	172 394	163 995	...	...	...	...	...	...
40 - 44	ESDJ	319 516	162 884	156 633	...	...	...	...	...	...
45 - 49	ESDJ	308 162	156 659	151 504	...	...	...	...	...	...
50 - 54	ESDJ	304 491	155 657	148 834	...	...	...	...	...	...
55 - 59	ESDJ	259 926	131 492	128 435	...	...	...	...	...	...
60 - 64	ESDJ	189 957	93 467	96 490	...	...	...	...	...	...
65 - 69	ESDJ	163 989	78 035	85 954	...	...	...	...	...	...
70 - 74	ESDJ	161 924	73 664	88 261	...	...	...	...	...	...
75 - 79	ESDJ	152 231	63 676	88 555	...	...	...	...	...	...
80 - 84	ESDJ	112 998	41 475	71 524	...	...	...	...	...	...
85+	ESDJ	86 182	25 039	61 144	...	...	...	...	...	...
Poland - Pologne[35]										
1 VII 1999										
Total	ESDF	38 653 625	18 788 696	19 864 929	23 908 265	11 417 385	12 490 880	14 745 360	7 371 311	7 374 049
0 - 1	ESDF	387 325	199 592	187 733	209 988	108 287	101 701	177 337	91 305	86 032
1 - 4	ESDF	1 691 030	868 884	822 146	918 097	472 039	446 058	772 933	396 845	376 088
5 - 9	ESDF	2 575 178	1 320 209	1 254 969	1 418 313	727 875	690 438	1 156 865	592 334	564 531
10 - 14	ESDF	3 057 596	1 564 305	1 493 291	1 795 759	918 726	877 033	1 261 837	645 579	616 258
15 - 19	ESDF	3 354 769	1 710 552	1 644 217	2 101 899	1 066 209	1 035 690	1 252 870	644 343	608 527
20 - 24	ESDF	3 140 940	1 598 940	1 542 000	1 995 021	1 001 458	993 563	1 145 919	597 482	548 437
25 - 29	ESDF	2 707 897	1 378 608	1 329 289	1 655 689	828 730	826 959	1 052 208	549 878	502 330
30 - 34	ESDF	2 430 207	1 236 424	1 193 783	1 468 385	723 489	744 896	961 822	512 935	448 887
35 - 39	ESDF	2 730 412	1 375 580	1 354 832	1 697 824	823 238	874 586	1 032 588	552 342	480 246
40 - 44	ESDF	3 233 372	1 615 737	1 617 635	2 141 900	1 028 239	1 113 661	1 091 472	587 498	503 974
45 - 49	ESDF	3 053 669	1 504 186	1 549 483	2 087 422	993 412	1 094 010	966 247	510 774	455 473
50 - 54	ESDF	2 291 423	1 107 929	1 183 494	1 565 775	741 882	823 893	725 648	366 047	359 601
55 - 59	ESDF	1 645 830	769 709	876 121	1 081 904	498 567	583 337	563 926	271 142	292 784
60 - 64	ESDF	1 733 364	778 568	954 796	1 089 723	480 729	608 994	643 641	297 839	345 802
65 - 69	ESDF	1 642 836	704 538	938 298	991 759	421 016	570 743	651 077	283 522	367 555
70 - 74	ESDF	1 346 060	519 579	826 481	779 395	297 863	481 532	566 665	221 716	344 949
75 - 79	ESDF	894 985	314 834	580 151	499 492	171 310	328 182	395 493	143 524	251 969
80 - 84	ESDF	385 259	122 127	263 132	209 779	62 572	147 207	175 480	59 555	115 925
85+	ESDF	351 473	98 395	253 078	200 141	51 744	148 397	151 332	46 651	104 681
1 VII 2001										
Total	ESDF	38 638 332	18 766 876	19 871 456	...	...	...	...	...	...
0 - 4	ESDF	1 949 075	1 002 625	946 450	...	...	...	...	...	...
5 - 9	ESDF	2 369 813	1 214 601	1 155 212	...	...	...	...	...	...
10 - 14	ESDF	2 827 276	1 449 777	1 377 499	...	...	...	...	...	...
15 - 19	ESDF	3 339 571	1 702 562	1 637 009	...	...	...	...	...	...
20 - 24	ESDF	3 213 911	1 634 590	1 579 321	...	...	...	...	...	...
25 - 29	ESDF	2 904 762	1 476 629	1 428 133	...	...	...	...	...	...
30 - 34	ESDF	2 462 707	1 255 626	1 207 082	...	...	...	...	...	...
35 - 39	ESDF	2 539 886	1 281 474	1 258 412	...	...	...	...	...	...
40 - 44	ESDF	3 072 329	1 536 402	1 535 927	...	...	...	...	...	...
45 - 49	ESDF	3 145 209	1 551 430	1 593 779	...	...	...	...	...	...
50 - 54	ESDF	2 690 874	1 304 805	1 386 069	...	...	...	...	...	...
55 - 59	ESDF	1 654 442	775 773	878 669	...	...	...	...	...	...
60 - 64	ESDF	1 679 399	755 200	924 199	...	...	...	...	...	...
65 - 69	ESDF	1 601 185	685 536	915 649	...	...	...	...	...	...
70 - 74	ESDF	1 398 276	553 352	844 925	...	...	...	...	...	...
75 - 79	ESDF	993 478	343 260	650 219	...	...	...	...	...	...
80 - 84	ESDF	451 354	146 644	304 711	...	...	...	...	...	...

7. Population by age, sex and urban/rural residence: latest available year, 1992 - 2001
Population selon l'âge, le sexe et la résidence, urbaine/rurale: dernière année disponible, 1992 - 2001
(continued — suite)

(See notes at end of table. — Voir notes à la fin du tableau.)

Continent, country or area, date and age (in years) / Continent, pays ou zone, date et âge (en annèes)	Code[1]	Total			Urban - Urbaine			Rural - Rurale		
		Both sexes Les deux sexes	Male Masculin	Female Féminin	Both sexes Les deux sexes	Male Masculin	Female Féminin	Both sexes Les deux sexes	Male Masculin	Female Féminin
EUROPE										
Poland - Pologne[35]										
1 VII 2001										
85+	ESDF	344 790	96 594	248 196	...	...	...	...	...	...
Portugal										
1 VII 2001										
Total	ESDF	10 299 218	4 972 470	5 326 749	...	...	...	...	...	...
0 - 4	ESDF	561 037	288 862	272 176	...	...	...	...	...	...
5 - 9	ESDF	529 841	270 489	259 352	...	...	...	...	...	...
10 - 14	ESDF	554 943	283 380	271 563	...	...	...	...	...	...
15 - 19	ESDF	673 654	344 094	329 560	...	...	...	...	...	...
20 - 24	ESDF	789 944	399 328	390 616	...	...	...	...	...	...
25 - 29	ESDF	822 919	412 846	410 074	...	...	...	...	...	...
30 - 34	ESDF	739 989	368 958	371 031	...	...	...	...	...	...
35 - 39	ESDF	747 041	365 460	381 581	...	...	...	...	...	...
40 - 44	ESDF	736 905	360 281	376 624	...	...	...	...	...	...
45 - 49	ESDF	681 455	331 343	350 113	...	...	...	...	...	...
50 - 54	ESDF	652 168	314 775	337 393	...	...	...	...	...	...
55 - 59	ESDF	573 658	269 790	303 868	...	...	...	...	...	...
60 - 64	ESDF	541 317	251 624	289 694	...	...	...	...	...	...
65 - 69	ESDF	528 611	238 257	290 354	...	...	...	...	...	...
70 - 74	ESDF	463 078	201 631	261 447	...	...	...	...	...	...
75 - 79	ESDF	347 464	142 852	204 612	...	...	...	...	...	...
80 - 84	ESDF	204 539	77 906	126 633	...	...	...	...	...	...
85+	ESDF	150 660	50 596	100 064	...	...	...	...	...	...
Republic of Moldova - République de Moldova[36]										
1 VII 2001										
Total	ESDJ	3 631 462	1 739 081	1 892 381	1 485 810	717 661	768 149	2 145 652	1 021 420	1 124 232
0 - 1	ESDJ	36 154	18 683	17 471	12 375	6 382	5 993	23 779	12 301	11 478
1 - 4	ESDJ	163 486	83 879	79 607	54 940	28 388	26 552	108 546	55 491	53 055
5 - 9	ESDJ	265 849	136 032	129 817	91 997	47 343	44 654	173 852	88 689	85 163
10 - 14	ESDJ	342 528	174 380	168 148	131 643	67 171	64 472	210 885	107 209	103 676
15 - 19	ESDJ	358 256	181 313	176 943	138 195	70 555	67 640	220 061	110 758	109 303
20 - 24	ESDJ	311 125	157 511	153 614	125 492	64 527	60 965	185 633	92 984	92 649
25 - 29	ESDJ	278 536	138 764	139 772	121 619	59 132	62 487	156 917	79 632	77 285
30 - 34	ESDJ	220 424	109 446	110 978	115 277	60 084	55 193	105 147	49 362	55 785
35 - 39	ESDJ	252 947	120 779	132 168	116 372	55 069	61 303	136 575	65 710	70 865
40 - 44	ESDJ	296 336	141 422	154 914	136 071	63 406	72 665	160 265	78 016	82 249
45 - 49	ESDJ	261 855	124 040	137 815	120 880	56 391	64 489	140 975	67 649	73 326
50 - 54	ESDJ	215 274	100 018	115 256	99 291	47 140	52 151	115 983	52 878	63 105
55 - 59	ESDJ	129 171	56 522	72 649	52 066	24 466	27 600	77 105	32 056	45 049
60 - 64	ESDJ	153 192	65 592	87 600	59 320	26 526	32 794	93 872	39 066	54 806
65 - 69	ESDJ	128 222	52 901	75 321	41 206	17 517	23 689	87 016	35 384	51 632
70 - 74	ESDJ	106 178	40 904	65 274	33 558	12 769	20 789	72 620	28 135	44 485
75 - 79	ESDJ	67 967	22 867	45 100	21 517	6 808	14 709	46 450	16 059	30 391
80 - 84	ESDJ	28 835	9 912	18 923	8 542	2 635	5 907	20 293	7 277	13 016
85+	ESDJ	15 127	4 116	11 011	5 449	1 352	4 097	9 678	2 764	6 914
Romania - Roumanie										
1 VII 2001										
Total	ESDJ	22 408 393	10 949 490	11 458 903	12 243 748	5 903 537	6 340 211	10 164 645	5 045 953	5 118 692
0 - 1	ESDJ	223 424	114 720	108 704	104 532	53 717	50 815	118 892	61 003	57 889
1 - 4	ESDJ	912 082	468 135	443 947	416 818	214 339	202 479	495 264	253 796	241 468
5 - 9	ESDJ	1 198 739	614 934	583 805	556 507	286 058	270 449	642 232	328 876	313 356
10 - 14	ESDJ	1 651 378	841 537	809 841	914 538	465 618	448 920	736 840	375 919	360 921
15 - 19	ESDJ	1 623 469	827 601	795 868	963 409	489 291	474 118	660 060	338 310	321 750
20 - 24	ESDJ	1 924 862	981 654	943 208	1 122 480	564 277	558 203	802 382	417 377	385 005
25 - 29	ESDJ	1 854 851	949 210	905 641	1 015 159	499 491	515 668	839 692	449 719	389 973
30 - 34	ESDJ	1 945 710	982 655	963 055	1 167 832	553 462	614 370	777 878	429 193	348 685

7. **Population by age, sex and urban/rural residence: latest available year, 1992 - 2001**
Population selon l'âge, le sexe et la résidence, urbaine/rurale: dernière année disponible, 1992 - 2001
(continued — suite)

(See notes at end of table. — Voir notes à la fin du tableau.)

Continent, country or area, date and age (in years) Continent, pays ou zone, date et âge (en années)	Code[1]	Total			Urban - Urbaine			Rural - Rurale		
		Both sexes Les deux sexes	Male Masculin	Female Féminin	Both sexes Les deux sexes	Male Masculin	Female Féminin	Both sexes Les deux sexes	Male Masculin	Female Féminin
EUROPE										
Romania - Roumanie										
1 VII 2001										
35 - 39	ESDJ	1 237 934	624 153	613 781	780 955	369 681	411 274	456 979	254 472	202 507
40 - 44	ESDJ	1 530 486	761 761	768 725	1 012 632	481 220	531 412	517 854	280 541	237 313
45 - 49	ESDJ	1 613 704	793 361	820 343	1 064 132	519 338	544 794	549 572	274 023	275 549
50 - 54	ESDJ	1 396 413	677 776	718 637	821 606	405 755	415 851	574 807	272 021	302 786
55 - 59	ESDJ	1 063 257	503 230	560 027	538 301	257 753	280 548	524 956	245 477	279 479
60 - 64	ESDJ	1 177 981	536 973	641 008	537 530	246 474	291 056	640 451	290 499	349 952
65 - 69	ESDJ	1 099 482	488 436	611 046	456 364	200 336	256 028	643 118	288 100	355 018
70 - 74	ESDJ	904 691	386 886	517 805	360 827	151 313	209 514	543 864	235 573	308 291
75 - 79	ESDJ	626 576	247 252	379 324	237 328	88 769	148 559	389 248	158 483	230 765
80 - 84	ESDJ	245 859	86 422	159 437	95 965	31 477	64 488	149 894	54 945	94 949
85+	ESDJ	177 495	62 794	114 701	76 833	25 168	51 665	100 662	37 626	63 036
Russian Federation - Fédération de Russie										
1 VII 1999										
Total	ESDF	145 943 393	68 405 752	77 537 641	106 488 089	49 622 408	56 865 681	39 455 304	18 783 344	20 671 960
0 - 1	ESDF	1 247 988	641 652	606 336	857 488	441 150	416 338	390 500	200 502	189 998
1 - 4	ESDF	5 273 255	2 703 604	2 569 651	3 601 015	1 848 352	1 752 663	1 672 240	855 252	816 988
5 - 9	ESDF	8 624 225	4 423 897	4 200 328	5 853 019	3 003 247	2 849 772	2 771 206	1 420 650	1 350 556
10 - 14	ESDF	12 073 276	6 152 074	5 921 202	8 414 270	4 291 221	4 123 049	3 659 006	1 860 853	1 798 153
15 - 19	ESDF	11 640 353	5 903 004	5 737 349	8 427 541	4 235 850	4 191 691	3 212 812	1 667 154	1 545 658
20 - 24	ESDF	10 694 954	5 403 032	5 291 922	8 002 226	3 994 587	4 007 639	2 692 728	1 408 445	1 284 283
25 - 29	ESDF	10 132 910	5 223 463	4 909 447	7 823 180	4 033 537	3 789 643	2 309 730	1 189 926	1 119 804
30 - 34	ESDF	9 601 516	4 839 812	4 761 704	7 139 919	3 594 303	3 545 616	2 461 597	1 245 509	1 216 088
35 - 39	ESDF	12 142 415	6 036 862	6 105 553	8 979 325	4 386 590	4 592 735	3 163 090	1 650 272	1 512 818
40 - 44	ESDF	12 503 481	6 112 856	6 390 625	9 386 098	4 492 980	4 893 118	3 117 383	1 619 876	1 497 507
45 - 49	ESDF	11 209 888	5 366 036	5 843 852	8 637 306	4 051 810	4 585 496	2 572 582	1 314 226	1 258 356
50 - 54	ESDF	7 681 472	3 578 859	4 102 613	6 070 884	2 786 751	3 284 133	1 610 588	792 108	818 480
55 - 59	ESDF	6 440 897	2 807 088	3 633 809	4 772 163	2 063 501	2 708 662	1 668 734	743 587	925 147
60 - 64	ESDF	8 409 982	3 506 323	4 903 659	6 059 829	2 487 725	3 572 104	2 350 153	1 018 598	1 331 555
65 - 69	ESDF	6 341 925	2 423 364	3 918 561	4 335 136	1 620 168	2 714 968	2 006 789	803 196	1 203 593
70 - 74	ESDF	6 028 319	1 968 872	4 059 447	4 152 137	1 369 386	2 782 751	1 876 182	599 486	1 276 696
75 - 79	ESDF	2 941 515	713 392	2 228 123	2 034 447	501 317	1 533 130	907 068	212 075	694 993
80 - 84	ESDF	1 589 627	340 138	1 249 489	1 074 249	242 399	831 850	515 378	97 739	417 639
85 - 89	ESDF	1 000 845	192 218	808 627	642 772	132 578	510 194	358 073	59 640	298 433
90 - 94	ESDF	284 809	50 479	234 330	176 436	32 916	143 520	108 373	17 563	90 810
95 - 99	ESDF	66 543	14 515	52 028	40 569	9 526	31 043	25 974	4 989	20 985
100+	ESDF	13 198	4 212	8 986	8 080	2 514	5 566	5 118	1 698	3 420
1 I 2001										
Total	ESDF	143 954 391	67 287 019	76 667 372	...	...	...	...	...	...
0 - 1	ESDF	1 309 841	673 515	636 326	...	...	...	...	...	...
0 - 4	ESDF	4 996 000	2 566 260	2 429 740	...	...	...	...	...	...
5 - 9	ESDF	7 123 120	3 652 229	3 470 891	...	...	...	...	...	...
10 - 14	ESDF	10 825 129	5 532 869	5 292 260	...	...	...	...	...	...
15 - 19	ESDF	12 208 011	6 199 698	6 008 313	...	...	...	...	...	...
20 - 24	ESDF	10 901 116	5 494 678	5 406 438	...	...	...	...	...	...
25 - 29	ESDF	10 422 406	5 259 573	5 162 833	...	...	...	...	...	...
30 - 34	ESDF	9 534 224	4 879 484	4 654 740	...	...	...	...	...	...
35 - 39	ESDF	10 587 806	5 256 996	5 330 810	...	...	...	...	...	...
40 - 44	ESDF	12 594 636	6 146 961	6 447 675	...	...	...	...	...	...
45 - 49	ESDF	11 625 074	5 538 814	6 086 260	...	...	...	...	...	...
50 - 54	ESDF	9 832 545	4 553 051	5 279 494	...	...	...	...	...	...
55 - 59	ESDF	4 840 576	2 134 498	2 706 078	...	...	...	...	...	...
60 - 64	ESDF	8 624 902	3 525 417	5 099 485	...	...	...	...	...	...
65 - 69	ESDF	5 973 442	2 284 876	3 688 566	...	...	...	...	...	...
70 - 74	ESDF	5 966 463	2 033 884	3 932 579	...	...	...	...	...	...
75 - 79	ESDF	3 758 139	960 722	2 797 417	...	...	...	...	...	...
80 - 84	ESDF	1 533 539	338 265	1 195 274	...	...	...	...	...	...

7. Population by age, sex and urban/rural residence: latest available year, 1992 - 2001
Population selon l'âge, le sexe et la résidence, urbaine/rurale: dernière année disponible, 1992 - 2001
(continued — suite)

(See notes at end of table. — Voir notes à la fin du tableau.)

Continent, country or area, date and age (in years) / Continent, pays ou zone, date et âge (en annèes)	Code[1]	Total			Urban - Urbaine			Rural - Rurale		
		Both sexes Les deux sexes	Male Masculin	Female Féminin	Both sexes Les deux sexes	Male Masculin	Female Féminin	Both sexes Les deux sexes	Male Masculin	Female Féminin
EUROPE										
Russian Federation - Fédération de Russie										
1 I 2001										
85 - 89	ESDF	884 600	168 050	716 550	...	...	...	...	...	...
90 - 94	ESDF	299 404	59 221	240 183	...	...	...	...	...	...
95 - 99	ESDF	83 799	19 285	64 514	...	...	...	...	...	...
100+	ESDF	29 619	8 673	20 946	...	...	...	...	...	...
San Marino - Saint-Marin										
31 XII 2000										
Total	ESDF	26 941	13 185	13 756	...	...	...	...	...	...
0 - 1	ESDF	285	149	136	...	...	...	...	...	...
1 - 4	ESDF	1 187	627	560	...	...	...	...	...	...
5 - 9	ESDF	1 316	686	630	...	...	...	...	...	...
10 - 14	ESDF	1 230	635	595	...	...	...	...	...	...
15 - 19	ESDF	1 346	709	637	...	...	...	...	...	...
20 - 24	ESDF	1 601	803	798	...	...	...	...	...	...
25 - 29	ESDF	1 932	962	970	...	...	...	...	...	...
30 - 34	ESDF	2 422	1 154	1 268	...	...	...	...	...	...
35 - 39	ESDF	2 530	1 235	1 295	...	...	...	...	...	...
40 - 44	ESDF	2 109	1 063	1 046	...	...	...	...	...	...
45 - 49	ESDF	1 822	906	916	...	...	...	...	...	...
50 - 54	ESDF	1 848	913	935	...	...	...	...	...	...
55 - 59	ESDF	1 527	747	780	...	...	...	...	...	...
60 - 64	ESDF	1 443	717	726	...	...	...	...	...	...
65 - 69	ESDF	1 311	625	686	...	...	...	...	...	...
70 - 74	ESDF	1 085	501	584	...	...	...	...	...	...
75 - 79	ESDF	940	396	544	...	...	...	...	...	...
80 - 84	ESDF	537	211	326	...	...	...	...	...	...
85 - 89	ESDF	337	112	225	...	...	...	...	...	...
90 - 94	ESDF	107	29	78	...	...	...	...	...	...
95 - 99	ESDF	24	5	19	...	...	...	...	...	...
100+	ESDF	2	...	2	...	...	...	...	...	...
Serbia and Montenegro - Serbie-et-Monteneg-ro[37]										
1 VII 2000										
Total	ESDJ	10 633 508	5 271 588	5 361 920	5 482 862	2 676 715	2 806 147	5 150 646	2 594 873	2 555 773
0 - 1	ESDJ	124 833	64 923	59 910	65 403	33 965	31 438	59 430	30 958	28 472
1 - 4	ESDJ	521 569	270 305	251 264	270 429	140 097	130 332	251 140	130 208	120 932
5 - 9	ESDJ	698 840	361 765	337 075	360 042	185 150	174 892	338 798	176 615	162 183
10 - 14	ESDJ	772 963	396 370	376 593	374 454	190 369	184 085	398 509	206 001	192 508
15 - 19	ESDJ	792 267	405 080	387 187	401 854	203 968	197 886	390 413	201 112	189 301
20 - 24	ESDJ	805 115	411 765	393 350	409 656	207 424	202 232	395 459	204 341	191 118
25 - 29	ESDJ	774 329	394 880	379 449	386 468	193 832	192 636	387 861	201 048	186 813
30 - 34	ESDJ	734 554	373 161	361 393	369 752	180 931	188 821	364 802	192 230	172 572
35 - 39	ESDJ	716 009	361 759	354 250	380 637	183 347	197 290	335 372	178 412	156 960
40 - 44	ESDJ	732 707	368 944	363 763	406 042	195 635	210 407	326 665	173 309	153 356
45 - 49	ESDJ	781 354	392 557	388 797	446 557	215 265	231 292	334 797	177 292	157 505
50 - 54	ESDJ	663 329	328 278	335 051	384 676	183 940	200 736	278 653	144 338	134 315
55 - 59	ESDJ	497 729	241 182	256 547	270 006	128 641	141 365	227 723	112 541	115 182
60 - 64	ESDJ	558 705	263 403	295 302	294 935	138 591	156 344	263 770	124 812	138 958
65 - 69	ESDJ	541 997	248 176	293 821	263 183	121 354	141 829	278 814	126 822	151 992
70 - 74	ESDJ	445 900	194 017	251 883	200 298	87 149	113 149	245 602	106 868	138 734
75 - 79	ESDJ	282 116	114 811	167 305	123 548	52 195	71 353	158 568	62 616	95 952
80 - 84	ESDJ	103 019	40 326	62 693	39 501	17 023	22 478	63 518	23 303	40 215
85 - 89	ESDJ	58 616	26 299	32 317	24 532	11 474	13 058	34 084	14 825	19 259
90 - 94	ESDJ	20 981	10 131	10 850	7 973	4 553	3 420	13 008	5 578	7 430

7. Population by age, sex and urban/rural residence: latest available year, 1992 - 2001
Population selon l'âge, le sexe et la résidence, urbaine/rurale: dernière année disponible, 1992 - 2001
(continued — suite)

(See notes at end of table. — Voir notes à la fin du tableau.)

Continent, country or area, date and age (in years) / Continent, pays ou zone, date et âge (en années)	Code[1]	Total			Urban - Urbaine			Rural - Rurale		
		Both sexes Les deux sexes	Male Masculin	Female Féminin	Both sexes Les deux sexes	Male Masculin	Female Féminin	Both sexes Les deux sexes	Male Masculin	Female Féminin
EUROPE										
Serbia and Montenegro - Serbie-et-Monteneg-ro[37]										
1 VII 2000										
95 - 99	ESDJ	5 758	2 991	2 767	2 548	1 557	991	3 210	1 434	1 776
100+	ESDJ	818	465	353	368	255	113	450	210	240
Slovakia - Slovaquie										
1 VII 2001										
Total	ESDJ	5 391 001	2 619 288	2 771 713	...	...	...	...	...	...
0 - 1	ESDJ	23 757	11 766	11 985	...	...	...	...	...	...
1 - 4	ESDJ	281 636	144 406	137 230	...	...	...	...	...	...
5 - 9	ESDJ	344 274	176 171	168 103	...	...	...	...	...	...
10 - 14	ESDJ	400 050	204 326	195 724	...	...	...	...	...	...
15 - 19	ESDJ	441 911	225 697	216 214	...	...	...	...	...	...
20 - 24	ESDJ	469 706	239 400	230 307	...	...	...	...	...	...
25 - 29	ESDJ	434 413	220 497	213 917	...	...	...	...	...	...
30 - 34	ESDJ	363 293	183 806	179 487	...	...	...	...	...	...
35 - 39	ESDJ	384 836	193 744	191 093	...	...	...	...	...	...
40 - 44	ESDJ	403 893	202 997	200 897	...	...	...	...	...	...
45 - 49	ESDJ	413 086	204 429	208 657	...	...	...	...	...	...
50 - 54	ESDJ	341 086	165 119	175 967	...	...	...	...	...	...
55 - 59	ESDJ	254 996	117 144	137 852	...	...	...	...	...	...
60 - 64	ESDJ	218 645	96 149	122 496	...	...	...	...	...	...
65 - 69	ESDJ	199 681	83 503	116 179	...	...	...	...	...	...
70 - 74	ESDJ	175 869	68 244	107 625	...	...	...	...	...	...
75 - 79	ESDJ	136 590	48 556	88 034	...	...	...	...	...	...
80 - 84	ESDJ	56 091	18 964	37 128	...	...	...	...	...	...
85+	ESDJ	47 188	14 370	32 818	...	...	...	...	...	...
Slovenia - Slovénie										
1 VII 1994										
Total	ESDJ	1 988 850	964 113	1 024 737	997 916	475 551	522 365	990 934	488 562	502 372
0 - 1	ESDJ	19 466	9 965	9 501	8 919	4 561	4 358	10 547	5 404	5 143
1 - 4	ESDJ	84 824	43 560	41 264	40 025	20 631	19 394	44 799	22 929	21 870
5 - 9	ESDJ	126 259	64 622	61 637	62 686	32 057	30 629	63 573	32 565	31 008
10 - 14	ESDJ	143 077	73 368	69 709	72 117	36 869	35 248	70 960	36 499	34 461
15 - 19	ESDJ	150 443	77 203	73 240	74 594	38 194	36 400	75 849	39 009	36 840
20 - 24	ESDJ	141 774	72 151	69 623	67 878	34 154	33 724	73 896	37 997	35 899
25 - 29	ESDJ	150 162	74 501	75 661	74 217	35 380	38 837	75 945	39 121	36 824
30 - 34	ESDJ	153 228	76 673	76 555	79 738	38 212	41 526	73 490	38 461	35 029
35 - 39	ESDJ	159 755	80 980	78 775	85 018	41 357	43 661	74 737	39 623	35 114
40 - 44	ESDJ	160 954	82 711	78 243	86 108	42 867	43 241	74 846	39 844	35 002
45 - 49	ESDJ	122 858	62 532	60 326	65 369	31 995	33 374	57 489	30 537	26 952
50 - 54	ESDJ	120 990	60 326	60 664	62 438	30 037	32 401	58 552	30 289	28 263
55 - 59	ESDJ	110 516	53 644	56 872	55 402	26 734	28 668	55 114	26 910	28 204
60 - 64	ESDJ	107 888	48 901	58 987	52 495	23 397	29 098	55 393	25 504	29 889
65 - 69	ESDJ	88 952	35 178	53 774	42 991	16 883	26 108	45 961	18 295	27 666
70 - 74	ESDJ	66 671	22 855	43 816	31 712	11 191	20 521	34 959	11 664	23 295
75 - 79	ESDJ	30 035	10 058	19 977	14 001	4 754	9 247	16 034	5 304	10 730
80 - 84	ESDJ	32 852	10 224	22 628	14 292	4 419	9 873	18 560	5 805	12 755
85 - 89	ESDJ	13 983	3 740	10 243	6 032	1 485	4 547	7 951	2 255	5 696
90 - 94	ESDJ	3 646	834	2 812	1 629	335	1 294	2 017	499	1 518
95 - 99	ESDJ	463	80	383	240	38	202	246	46	200
100+	ESDJ	54	7	47	15	1	14	16	2	14
1 VII 2001										
Total	ESDJ	1 992 060	973 872	1 018 188	...	...	...	...	...	...
0 - 4	ESDJ	90 723	46 780	43 943	...	...	...	...	...	...
5 - 9	ESDJ	99 389	51 047	48 342	...	...	...	...	...	...
10 - 14	ESDJ	119 952	61 471	58 481	...	...	...	...	...	...

7. Population by age, sex and urban/rural residence: latest available year, 1992 - 2001
Population selon l'âge, le sexe et la résidence, urbaine/rurale: dernière année disponible, 1992 - 2001
(continued — suite)

(See notes at end of table. — Voir notes à la fin du tableau.)

Continent, country or area, date and age (in years) / Continent, pays ou zone, date et âge (en années)	Code[1]	Total			Urban - Urbaine			Rural - Rurale		
		Both sexes Les deux sexes	Male Masculin	Female Féminin	Both sexes Les deux sexes	Male Masculin	Female Féminin	Both sexes Les deux sexes	Male Masculin	Female Féminin
EUROPE										
Slovenia - Slovénie										
1 VII 2001										
15 - 19	ESDJ	134 730	68 913	65 817	...	...	...	...	...	...
20 - 24	ESDJ	151 354	78 270	73 084	...	...	...	...	...	...
25 - 29	ESDJ	147 551	76 000	71 551	...	...	...	...	...	...
30 - 34	ESDJ	145 824	73 931	71 893	...	...	...	...	...	...
35 - 39	ESDJ	156 207	79 058	77 150	...	...	...	...	...	...
40 - 44	ESDJ	155 484	79 356	76 128	...	...	...	...	...	...
45 - 49	ESDJ	159 960	82 969	76 991	...	...	...	...	...	...
50 - 54	ESDJ	136 754	69 863	66 891	...	...	...	...	...	...
55 - 59	ESDJ	105 563	51 715	53 848	...	...	...	...	...	...
60 - 64	ESDJ	103 595	49 230	54 365	...	...	...	...	...	...
65 - 69	ESDJ	96 030	41 939	54 091	...	...	...	...	...	...
70 - 74	ESDJ	82 159	32 161	49 998	...	...	...	...	...	...
75 - 79	ESDJ	58 249	18 017	40 232	...	...	...	...	...	...
80 - 84	ESDJ	25 992	7 449	18 543	...	...	...	...	...	...
85+	ESDJ	22 548	5 707	16 842	...	...	...	...	...	...
Spain - Espagne										
1 VII 2001										
Total	ESDJ	40 265 502	19 709 429	20 556 073	...	...	...	...	...	...
0 - 4	ESDJ	1 902 858	979 921	922 937	...	...	...	...	...	...
5 - 9	ESDJ	1 927 628	994 121	933 507	...	...	...	...	...	...
10 - 14	ESDJ	2 056 138	1 056 798	999 340	...	...	...	...	...	...
15 - 19	ESDJ	2 454 000	1 258 136	1 195 865	...	...	...	...	...	...
20 - 24	ESDJ	3 109 192	1 588 556	1 520 636	...	...	...	...	...	...
25 - 29	ESDJ	3 449 474	1 759 656	1 689 818	...	...	...	...	...	...
30 - 34	ESDJ	3 375 823	1 718 359	1 657 465	...	...	...	...	...	...
35 - 39	ESDJ	3 217 265	1 621 882	1 595 383	...	...	...	...	...	...
40 - 44	ESDJ	2 921 760	1 459 858	1 461 903	...	...	...	...	...	...
45 - 49	ESDJ	2 552 551	1 269 686	1 282 865	...	...	...	...	...	...
50 - 54	ESDJ	2 404 106	1 185 309	1 218 797	...	...	...	...	...	...
55 - 59	ESDJ	2 173 917	1 059 892	1 114 026	...	...	...	...	...	...
60 - 64	ESDJ	1 874 949	892 133	982 816	...	...	...	...	...	...
65 - 69	ESDJ	2 042 372	945 204	1 097 168	...	...	...	...	...	...
70 - 74	ESDJ	1 824 273	808 936	1 015 337	...	...	...	...	...	...
75 - 79	ESDJ	1 422 655	585 838	836 818	...	...	...	...	...	...
80 - 84	ESDJ	884 919	321 079	563 840	...	...	...	...	...	...
85+	ESDJ	671 626	204 068	467 558	...	...	...	...	...	...
Sweden - Suède										
1 VII 2001										
Total	ESDJ	8 895 960	4 400 599	4 495 361	...	...	...	...	...	...
0 - 4	ESDJ	456 809	234 563	222 246	...	...	...	...	...	...
5 - 9	ESDJ	571 656	292 850	278 806	...	...	...	...	...	...
10 - 14	ESDJ	597 072	306 523	290 549	...	...	...	...	...	...
15 - 19	ESDJ	513 821	264 295	249 526	...	...	...	...	...	...
20 - 24	ESDJ	516 178	262 811	253 367	...	...	...	...	...	...
25 - 29	ESDJ	586 539	298 382	288 157	...	...	...	...	...	...
30 - 34	ESDJ	623 457	318 069	305 388	...	...	...	...	...	...
35 - 39	ESDJ	641 582	328 926	312 657	...	...	...	...	...	...
40 - 44	ESDJ	583 889	297 248	286 641	...	...	...	...	...	...
45 - 49	ESDJ	584 590	296 212	288 378	...	...	...	...	...	...
50 - 54	ESDJ	632 828	319 212	313 616	...	...	...	...	...	...
55 - 59	ESDJ	607 289	307 546	299 744	...	...	...	...	...	...
60 - 64	ESDJ	448 777	222 994	225 783	...	...	...	...	...	...
65 - 69	ESDJ	379 269	181 526	197 743	...	...	...	...	...	...
70 - 74	ESDJ	360 252	163 925	196 327	...	...	...	...	...	...
75 - 79	ESDJ	333 568	143 424	190 145	...	...	...	...	...	...
80 - 84	ESDJ	252 038	98 475	153 563	...	...	...	...	...	...
85+	ESDJ	206 349	63 621	142 728	...	...	...	...	...	...

7. Population by age, sex and urban/rural residence: latest available year, 1992 - 2001
Population selon l'âge, le sexe et la résidence, urbaine/rurale: dernière année disponible, 1992 - 2001
(continued — suite)

(See notes at end of table. — Voir notes à la fin du tableau.)

Continent, country or area, date and age (in years) / Continent, pays ou zone, date et âge (en annèes)	Code[1]	Total			Urban - Urbaine			Rural - Rurale		
		Both sexes Les deux sexes	Male Masculin	Female Féminin	Both sexes Les deux sexes	Male Masculin	Female Féminin	Both sexes Les deux sexes	Male Masculin	Female Féminin

EUROPE

Switzerland - Suisse
1 VII 2001

Total	ESDJ	7 232 633	3 534 394	3 698 239	...	...	...	...	...	...
0 - 4	ESDJ	394 366	202 602	191 764	...	...	...	...	...	...
5 - 9	ESDJ	420 191	216 211	203 980	...	...	...	...	...	...
10 - 14	ESDJ	430 871	221 866	209 006	...	...	...	...	...	...
15 - 19	ESDJ	419 181	215 463	203 718	...	...	...	...	...	...
20 - 24	ESDJ	420 015	211 809	208 206	...	...	...	...	...	...
25 - 29	ESDJ	467 026	230 756	236 270	...	...	...	...	...	...
30 - 34	ESDJ	568 828	280 926	287 903	...	...	...	...	...	...
35 - 39	ESDJ	623 992	314 476	309 516	...	...	...	...	...	...
40 - 44	ESDJ	565 686	286 295	279 391	...	...	...	...	...	...
45 - 49	ESDJ	506 569	254 527	252 043	...	...	...	...	...	...
50 - 54	ESDJ	491 750	246 648	245 102	...	...	...	...	...	...
55 - 59	ESDJ	451 127	225 413	225 715	...	...	...	...	...	...
60 - 64	ESDJ	356 372	172 486	183 886	...	...	...	...	...	...
65 - 69	ESDJ	316 122	146 782	169 340	...	...	...	...	...	...
70 - 74	ESDJ	275 261	119 364	155 897	...	...	...	...	...	...
75 - 79	ESDJ	229 628	91 791	137 837	...	...	...	...	...	...
80 - 84	ESDJ	154 081	56 414	97 668	...	...	...	...	...	...
85+	ESDJ	141 571	40 570	101 002	...	...	...	...	...	...

The Former Yugoslav Rep. of Macedonia - L'ex-République yougoslave de Macédoine
20 VI 1994

Total	CDJC	1 935 034	968 931	966 103	1 156 297	574 461	581 836	778 737	394 470	384 267
0 - 1	CDJC	28 626	14 688	13 938	15 006	7 678	7 328	13 620	7 010	6 610
1 - 4	CDJC	122 661	63 281	59 380	65 521	33 772	31 749	57 140	29 509	27 631
5 - 9	CDJC	162 672	83 649	79 023	91 559	47 127	44 432	71 113	36 522	34 591
10 - 14	CDJC	166 993	85 716	81 277	97 231	49 572	47 659	69 762	36 144	33 618
15 - 19	CDJC	161 947	82 731	79 216	93 395	47 311	46 084	68 552	35 420	33 132
20 - 24	CDJC	152 720	77 984	74 736	87 496	44 132	43 364	65 224	33 852	31 372
25 - 29	CDJC	150 545	76 309	74 236	87 079	42 986	44 093	63 466	33 323	30 143
30 - 34	CDJC	147 733	74 873	72 860	89 325	44 130	45 195	58 408	30 743	27 665
35 - 39	CDJC	145 144	74 150	70 994	94 448	47 380	47 068	50 696	26 770	23 926
40 - 44	CDJC	136 590	68 684	67 906	94 134	47 158	46 976	42 456	21 526	20 930
45 - 49	CDJC	109 351	53 715	55 636	74 941	36 941	38 000	34 410	16 774	17 636
50 - 54	CDJC	99 300	48 653	50 647	64 263	31 747	32 516	35 037	16 906	18 131
55 - 59	CDJC	95 419	46 243	49 176	59 768	29 374	30 394	35 651	16 869	18 782
60 - 64	CDJC	88 511	42 203	46 308	52 236	24 720	27 516	36 275	17 483	18 792
65 - 69	CDJC	67 323	31 107	36 216	38 531	17 705	20 826	28 792	13 402	15 390
70 - 74	CDJC	50 502	22 826	27 676	27 771	12 443	15 328	22 731	10 383	12 348
75 - 79	CDJC	20 709	9 552	11 157	10 415	4 565	5 850	10 294	4 987	5 307
80 - 84	CDJC	17 372	8 030	9 342	8 587	3 792	4 795	8 785	4 238	4 547
85 - 89	CDJC	5 708	2 616	3 092	2 854	1 252	1 602	2 854	1 364	1 490
90 - 94	CDJC	1 651	671	980	844	343	501	807	328	479
95 - 99	CDJC	279	114	165	150	58	92	129	56	73
100+	CDJC	112	38	74	52	19	33	60	19	41
Unk. - Inc.	CDJC	3 166	1 098	2 068	691	256	435	2 475	842	1 633

1 I 2001

Total	ESDJ	2 031 112	1 016 237	1 014 875	...	...	...	...	...	...
0 - 1	ESDJ	25 861	13 457	12 404	...	...	...	...	...	...
1 - 4	ESDJ	107 864	55 950	51 914	...	...	...	...	...	...
5 - 9	ESDJ	153 009	79 040	73 969	...	...	...	...	...	...
10 - 14	ESDJ	160 991	83 090	77 901	...	...	...	...	...	...
15 - 19	ESDJ	167 147	85 641	81 506	...	...	...	...	...	...

7. Population by age, sex and urban/rural residence: latest available year, 1992 - 2001
Population selon l'âge, le sexe et la résidence, urbaine/rurale: dernière année disponible, 1992 - 2001
(continued — suite)

(See notes at end of table. — Voir notes à la fin du tableau.)

Continent, country or area, date and age (in years) / Continent, pays ou zone, date et âge (en années)	Code[1]	Total			Urban - Urbaine			Rural - Rurale		
		Both sexes Les deux sexes	Male Masculin	Female Féminin	Both sexes Les deux sexes	Male Masculin	Female Féminin	Both sexes Les deux sexes	Male Masculin	Female Féminin
EUROPE										
The Former Yugoslav Rep. of Macedonia - L'ex-République yougoslave de Macédoine										
1 I 2001										
20 - 24	ESDJ	164 671	84 166	80 505	...	...	...	...	...	...
25 - 29	ESDJ	157 090	80 106	76 984	...	...	...	...	...	...
30 - 34	ESDJ	150 815	76 656	74 159	...	...	...	...	...	...
35 - 39	ESDJ	148 956	75 320	73 636	...	...	...	...	...	...
40 - 44	ESDJ	116 740	59 417	57 323	...	...	...	...	...	...
45 - 49	ESDJ	138 761	70 027	68 734	...	...	...	...	...	...
50 - 54	ESDJ	117 700	57 408	60 292	...	...	...	...	...	...
55 - 59	ESDJ	93 752	45 260	48 492	...	...	...	...	...	...
60 - 64	ESDJ	89 931	42 803	47 128	...	...	...	...	...	...
65 - 69	ESDJ	82 391	38 278	44 113	...	...	...	...	...	...
70 - 74	ESDJ	60 082	26 833	33 249	...	...	...	...	...	...
75 - 79	ESDJ	38 092	16 275	21 817	...	...	...	...	...	...
80 - 84	ESDJ	14 840	6 331	8 509	...	...	...	...	...	...
85 - 89	ESDJ	6 861	2 918	3 943	...	...	...	...	...	...
90 - 94	ESDJ	2 097	845	1 252	...	...	...	...	...	...
95+	ESDJ	827	304	523	...	...	...	...	...	...
Ukraine										
1 I 2000										
Total	ESDF	49 456 088	22 978 364	26 477 724	33 505 862	15 617 268	17 888 594	15 950 226	7 361 096	8 589 130
0 - 1	ESDF	384 980	198 354	186 626	236 787	122 275	114 512	148 193	76 079	72 114
1 - 4	ESDF	1 788 699	919 015	869 684	1 111 882	571 821	540 061	676 817	347 194	329 623
5 - 9	ESDF	2 916 281	1 494 369	1 421 912	1 883 784	967 011	916 773	1 032 497	527 358	505 139
10 - 14	ESDF	3 735 293	1 902 893	1 832 400	2 512 646	1 280 784	1 231 862	1 222 647	622 109	600 538
15 - 19	ESDF	3 765 026	1 911 977	1 853 049	2 658 519	1 339 952	1 318 567	1 106 507	572 025	534 482
20 - 24	ESDF	3 591 292	1 819 369	1 771 923	2 558 515	1 283 993	1 274 522	1 032 777	535 376	497 401
25 - 29	ESDF	3 572 343	1 824 781	1 747 562	2 547 820	1 295 618	1 252 202	1 024 523	529 163	495 360
30 - 34	ESDF	3 237 966	1 613 622	1 624 344	2 251 564	1 099 648	1 151 916	986 402	513 974	472 428
35 - 39	ESDF	3 764 789	1 841 151	1 923 638	2 702 737	1 294 593	1 408 144	1 062 052	546 558	515 494
40 - 44	ESDF	3 778 496	1 815 712	1 962 784	2 757 518	1 297 091	1 460 427	1 020 978	518 621	502 357
45 - 49	ESDF	3 510 913	1 651 749	1 859 164	2 601 842	1 203 492	1 398 350	909 071	448 257	460 814
50 - 54	ESDF	2 751 783	1 255 818	1 495 965	2 023 520	918 093	1 105 427	728 263	337 725	390 538
55 - 59	ESDF	2 504 490	1 088 853	1 415 637	1 628 499	713 950	914 549	875 991	374 903	501 088
60 - 64	ESDF	3 324 060	1 400 640	1 923 420	2 151 452	909 188	1 242 264	1 172 608	491 452	681 156
65 - 69	ESDF	2 105 700	833 941	1 271 759	1 221 364	490 866	730 498	884 336	343 075	541 261
70 - 74	ESDF	2 288 411	786 754	1 501 657	1 348 209	479 513	868 696	940 202	307 241	632 961
75 - 79	ESDF	1 326 381	361 585	964 796	717 931	201 080	516 851	608 450	160 505	447 945
80 - 84	ESDF	580 522	141 516	439 006	322 726	85 139	237 587	257 796	56 377	201 419
85 - 89	ESDF	387 150	86 878	300 272	198 310	48 289	150 021	188 840	38 589	150 251
90 - 94	ESDF	117 445	23 065	94 380	57 130	11 590	45 540	60 315	11 475	48 840
95 - 99	ESDF	22 689	5 518	17 171	12 130	2 765	9 365	10 559	2 753	7 806
100+	ESDF	1 379	804	575	977	517	460	402	287	115
1 I 2001										
Total	ESDF	49 036 519	22 775 737	26 260 782	...	...	...	...	...	...
0 - 1	ESDF	381 239	197 071	184 168	...	...	...	...	...	...
1 - 4	ESDF	1 687 309	867 322	819 987	...	...	...	...	...	...
5 - 9	ESDF	2 743 948	1 406 999	1 336 949	...	...	...	...	...	...
10 - 14	ESDF	3 617 476	1 846 278	1 771 198	...	...	...	...	...	...
15 - 19	ESDF	3 787 495	1 921 596	1 865 899	...	...	...	...	...	...
20 - 24	ESDF	3 593 205	1 823 294	1 769 911	...	...	...	...	...	...
25 - 29	ESDF	3 610 466	1 840 033	1 770 433	...	...	...	...	...	...
30 - 34	ESDF	3 245 562	1 622 179	1 623 383	...	...	...	...	...	...
35 - 39	ESDF	3 591 935	1 756 452	1 835 483	...	...	...	...	...	...

7. Population by age, sex and urban/rural residence: latest available year, 1992 - 2001
Population selon l'âge, le sexe et la résidence, urbaine/rurale: dernière année disponible, 1992 - 2001
(continued — suite)

(See notes at end of table. — Voir notes à la fin du tableau.)

Continent, country or area, date and age (in years) / Continent, pays ou zone, date et âge (en annèes)	Code[1]	Total Both sexes Les deux sexes	Total Male Masculin	Total Female Féminin	Urban Both sexes	Urban Male	Urban Female	Rural Both sexes	Rural Male	Rural Female
EUROPE										
Ukraine										
1 I 2001										
40 - 44	ESDF	3 846 074	1 849 684	1 996 390	...	...	...	...	...	...
45 - 49	ESDF	3 491 859	1 641 602	1 850 257	...	...	...	...	...	...
50 - 54	ESDF	3 061 899	1 398 143	1 663 756	...	...	...	...	...	...
55 - 59	ESDF	2 173 474	942 392	1 231 082	...	...	...	...	...	...
60 - 64	ESDF	3 357 166	1 398 561	1 958 605	...	...	...	...	...	...
65 - 69	ESDF	2 047 769	821 034	1 226 735	...	...	...	...	...	...
70 - 74	ESDF	2 276 909	793 749	1 483 160	...	...	...	...	...	...
75 - 79	ESDF	1 430 314	393 268	1 037 046	...	...	...	...	...	...
80 - 84	ESDF	589 808	145 003	444 805	...	...	...	...	...	...
85 - 89	ESDF	372 258	78 363	293 895	...	...	...	...	...	...
90 - 94	ESDF	100 867	25 010	75 857	...	...	...	...	...	...
95 - 99	ESDF	25 971	6 572	19 399	...	...	...	...	...	...
100+	ESDF	3 516	1 132	2 384	...	...	...	...	...	...
United Kingdom - Royaume-Uni										
1 VII 1999										
Total	ESDF	59 500 915	29 298 873	30 202 042	...	...	...	...	...	...
0 - 4	ESDF	3 624 572	1 858 000	1 766 572	...	...	...	...	...	...
5 - 9	ESDF	3 906 613	2 001 191	1 905 422	...	...	...	...	...	...
10 - 14	ESDF	3 855 988	1 978 480	1 877 508	...	...	...	...	...	...
15 - 19	ESDF	3 682 658	1 890 892	1 791 766	...	...	...	...	...	...
20 - 24	ESDF	3 516 500	1 803 294	1 713 206	...	...	...	...	...	...
25 - 29	ESDF	4 261 094	2 189 108	2 071 986	...	...	...	...	...	...
30 - 34	ESDF	4 803 199	2 453 378	2 349 821	...	...	...	...	...	...
35 - 39	ESDF	4 707 589	2 395 827	2 311 762	...	...	...	...	...	...
40 - 44	ESDF	4 038 253	2 029 357	2 008 896	...	...	...	...	...	...
45 - 49	ESDF	3 794 836	1 897 407	1 897 429	...	...	...	...	...	...
50 - 54	ESDF	3 999 336	1 992 852	2 006 484	...	...	...	...	...	...
55 - 59	ESDF	3 156 477	1 563 394	1 593 083	...	...	...	...	...	...
60 - 64	ESDF	2 860 674	1 400 454	1 460 220	...	...	...	...	...	...
65 - 69	ESDF	2 595 637	1 233 008	1 362 629	...	...	...	...	...	...
70 - 74	ESDF	2 333 352	1 050 881	1 282 471	...	...	...	...	...	...
75 - 79	ESDF	2 055 261	841 054	1 214 207	...	...	...	...	...	...
80 - 84	ESDF	1 166 572	414 014	752 558	...	...	...	...	...	...
85+	ESDF	1 142 304	306 282	836 022	...	...	...	...	...	...
OCEANIA — OCEANIE										
American Samoa - Samoas américaines[11]										
1 IV 2000										
Total	CDJC	57 291	29 264	28 027	...	...	...	...	...	...
0 - 4	CDJC	7 820	...	...	...	...	...	...	...	...
5 - 9	CDJC	7 788	...	...	...	...	...	...	...	...
10 - 14	CDJC	6 604	...	...	...	...	...	...	...	...
15 - 19	CDJC	5 223	...	...	...	...	...	...	...	...
20 - 24	CDJC	4 476	...	...	...	...	...	...	...	...
25 - 34	CDJC	8 707	...	...	...	...	...	...	...	...
35 - 44	CDJC	7 361	...	...	...	...	...	...	...	...
45 - 54	CDJC	4 733	...	...	...	...	...	...	...	...
55 - 59	CDJC	1 474	...	...	...	...	...	...	...	...
60 - 64	CDJC	1 204	...	...	...	...	...	...	...	...
65 - 74	CDJC	1 345	...	...	...	...	...	...	...	...
75 - 84	CDJC	465	...	...	...	...	...	...	...	...
85+	CDJC	91	...	...	...	...	...	...	...	...

204

7. Population by age, sex and urban/rural residence: latest available year, 1992 - 2001
Population selon l'âge, le sexe et la résidence, urbaine/rurale: dernière année disponible, 1992 - 2001
(continued — suite)

(See notes at end of table. — Voir notes à la fin du tableau.)

Continent, country or area, date and age (in years) / Continent, pays ou zone, date et âge (en années)	Code[1]	Total			Urban - Urbaine			Rural - Rurale		
		Both sexes Les deux sexes	Male Masculin	Female Féminin	Both sexes Les deux sexes	Male Masculin	Female Féminin	Both sexes Les deux sexes	Male Masculin	Female Féminin
OCEANIA — OCEANIE										
Australia - Australie										
1 VII 2001										
Total	ESDJ	19 386 663	9 655 422	9 731 241	...	...	...	...	...	...
0 - 1	ESDJ	247 936	127 190	120 746	...	...	...	...	...	...
1 - 4	ESDJ	1 009 535	517 663	491 872	...	...	...	...	...	...
5 - 9	ESDJ	1 328 290	681 781	646 509	...	...	...	...	...	...
10 - 14	ESDJ	1 337 457	685 397	652 060	...	...	...	...	...	...
15 - 19	ESDJ	1 362 106	697 641	664 465	...	...	...	...	...	...
20 - 24	ESDJ	1 382 408	706 106	676 302	...	...	...	...	...	...
25 - 29	ESDJ	1 453 387	733 221	720 166	...	...	...	...	...	...
30 - 34	ESDJ	1 461 251	730 244	731 007	...	...	...	...	...	...
35 - 39	ESDJ	1 478 222	738 014	740 208	...	...	...	...	...	...
40 - 44	ESDJ	1 474 085	736 361	737 724	...	...	...	...	...	...
45 - 49	ESDJ	1 360 860	679 714	681 146	...	...	...	...	...	...
50 - 54	ESDJ	1 286 335	650 508	635 827	...	...	...	...	...	...
55 - 59	ESDJ	998 401	507 117	491 284	...	...	...	...	...	...
60 - 64	ESDJ	804 278	404 506	399 772	...	...	...	...	...	...
65 - 69	ESDJ	673 063	329 739	343 324	...	...	...	...	...	...
70 - 74	ESDJ	628 418	297 158	331 260	...	...	...	...	...	...
75 - 79	ESDJ	513 860	223 507	290 353	...	...	...	...	...	...
80 - 84	ESDJ	324 113	127 346	196 767	...	...	...	...	...	...
85 - 89	ESDJ	177 639	59 234	118 405	...	...	...	...	...	...
90 - 94	ESDJ	65 701	18 246	47 455	...	...	...	...	...	...
95 - 99	ESDJ	15 340	3 534	11 806	...	...	...	...	...	...
100+	ESDJ	3 978	1 195	2 783	...	...	...	...	...	...
Cook Islands - Îles Cook										
1 XII 1996										
Total	CDFC	18 034	9 297	8 737	...	...	...	...	...	...
0 - 1	CDFC	508	280	228	...	...	...	...	...	...
1 - 4	CDFC	1 887	971	916	...	...	...	...	...	...
5 - 9	CDFC	2 193	1 151	1 042	...	...	...	...	...	...
10 - 14	CDFC	1 879	971	908	...	...	...	...	...	...
15 - 19	CDFC	1 628	861	767	...	...	...	...	...	...
20 - 24	CDFC	1 563	786	777	...	...	...	...	...	...
25 - 29	CDFC	1 455	727	728	...	...	...	...	...	...
30 - 34	CDFC	1 333	706	627	...	...	...	...	...	...
35 - 39	CDFC	1 075	545	530	...	...	...	...	...	...
40 - 44	CDFC	817	393	424	...	...	...	...	...	...
45 - 49	CDFC	769	409	360	...	...	...	...	...	...
50 - 54	CDFC	713	356	357	...	...	...	...	...	...
55 - 59	CDFC	703	359	344	...	...	...	...	...	...
60 - 64	CDFC	565	299	266	...	...	...	...	...	...
65 - 69	CDFC	389	209	180	...	...	...	...	...	...
70 - 74	CDFC	268	145	123	...	...	...	...	...	...
75 - 79	CDFC	157	75	82	...	...	...	...	...	...
80 - 84	CDFC	91	42	49	...	...	...	...	...	...
85 - 89	CDFC	38	12	26	...	...	...	...	...	...
90+	CDFC	3	...	3	...	...	...	...	...	...
Fiji - Fidji										
25 VIII 1996										
Total	CDFC	775 077	393 931	381 146	359 495	180 119	179 376	415 582	213 812	201 770
0 - 1	CDFC	18 239	9 282	8 957	8 136	4 213	3 923	10 103	5 069	5 034
1 - 4	CDFC	75 975	39 281	36 694	32 702	16 877	15 825	43 273	22 404	20 869
5 - 9	CDFC	87 095	44 937	42 158	35 977	18 271	17 706	51 118	26 666	24 452
10 - 14	CDFC	92 855	47 709	45 146	40 497	20 644	19 853	52 358	27 065	25 293
15 - 19	CDFC	83 682	42 829	40 853	41 404	20 748	20 656	42 278	22 081	20 197
20 - 24	CDFC	66 955	34 444	32 511	35 678	17 936	17 742	31 277	16 508	14 769
25 - 29	CDFC	61 660	31 283	30 377	30 706	15 554	15 152	30 954	15 729	15 225

7. **Population by age, sex and urban/rural residence: latest available year, 1992 - 2001**
Population selon l'âge, le sexe et la résidence, urbaine/rurale: dernière année disponible, 1992 - 2001
(continued — suite)

(See notes at end of table. — Voir notes à la fin du tableau.)

Continent, country or area, date and age (in years) / Continent, pays ou zone, date et âge (en annèes)	Code[1]	Total			Urban - Urbaine			Rural - Rurale		
		Both sexes Les deux sexes	Male Masculin	Female Féminin	Both sexes Les deux sexes	Male Masculin	Female Féminin	Both sexes Les deux sexes	Male Masculin	Female Féminin
OCEANIA — OCEANIE										
Fiji - Fidji										
25 VIII 1996										
30 - 34	CDFC	60 841	30 727	30 114	28 905	14 318	14 587	31 936	16 409	15 527
35 - 39	CDFC	55 779	28 525	27 254	26 975	13 523	13 452	28 804	15 002	13 802
40 - 44	CDFC	44 180	22 341	21 839	21 863	10 765	11 098	22 317	11 576	10 741
45 - 49	CDFC	37 081	18 482	18 599	18 007	8 913	9 094	19 074	9 569	9 505
50 - 54	CDFC	28 683	14 286	14 397	13 300	6 567	6 733	15 383	7 719	7 664
55 - 59	CDFC	22 245	10 857	11 388	9 562	4 560	5 002	12 683	6 297	6 386
60 - 64	CDFC	15 459	7 605	7 854	6 389	3 039	3 350	9 070	4 566	4 504
65 - 69	CDFC	10 761	5 138	5 623	4 191	1 941	2 250	6 570	3 197	3 373
70 - 74	CDFC	6 357	3 054	3 303	2 473	1 129	1 344	3 884	1 925	1 959
75 - 79	CDFC	4 152	1 881	2 271	1 558	654	904	2 594	1 227	1 367
80 - 84	CDFC	1 938	843	1 095	782	339	443	1 156	504	652
85 - 89	CDFC	772	290	482	266	97	169	506	193	313
90 - 94	CDFC	265	100	165	82	23	59	183	77	106
95+	CDFC	103	37	66	42	8	34	61	29	32
French Polynesia - Polynésie française										
1 I 1999										
Total	ESDF	227 525	117 738	109 787	...	...	...	...	...	...
0 - 1	ESDF	4 268	2 177	2 091	...	...	...	...	...	...
1 - 4	ESDF	18 470	9 604	8 866	...	...	...	...	...	...
5 - 9	ESDF	25 518	13 178	12 340	...	...	...	...	...	...
10 - 14	ESDF	25 533	13 055	12 478	...	...	...	...	...	...
15 - 19	ESDF	22 126	11 290	10 836	...	...	...	...	...	...
20 - 24	ESDF	19 077	9 884	9 193	...	...	...	...	...	...
25 - 29	ESDF	19 574	10 141	9 433	...	...	...	...	...	...
30 - 34	ESDF	19 667	10 179	9 488	...	...	...	...	...	...
35 - 39	ESDF	17 032	8 941	8 091	...	...	...	...	...	...
40 - 44	ESDF	14 421	7 640	6 781	...	...	...	...	...	...
45 - 49	ESDF	11 037	5 830	5 207	...	...	...	...	...	...
50 - 54	ESDF	9 001	4 790	4 211	...	...	...	...	...	...
55 - 59	ESDF	7 202	3 845	3 357	...	...	...	...	...	...
60 - 64	ESDF	5 518	2 899	2 619	...	...	...	...	...	...
65 - 69	ESDF	3 998	2 042	1 956	...	...	...	...	...	...
70 - 74	ESDF	2 600	1 244	1 356	...	...	...	...	...	...
75 - 79	ESDF	1 365	585	780	...	...	...	...	...	...
80+	ESDF	1 118	414	704	...	...	...	...	...	...
Guam[11]										
1 IV 2000										
Total	CDJC	154 805	79 181	75 624	...	...	...	...	...	...
0 - 4	CDJC	16 785	...	...	...	...	...	...	...	...
5 - 9	CDJC	16 090	...	...	...	...	...	...	...	...
10 - 14	CDJC	14 281	...	...	...	...	...	...	...	...
15 - 19	CDJC	12 379	...	...	...	...	...	...	...	...
20 - 24	CDJC	11 989	...	...	...	...	...	...	...	...
25 - 34	CDJC	25 850	...	...	...	...	...	...	...	...
35 - 44	CDJC	23 141	...	...	...	...	...	...	...	...
45 - 54	CDJC	16 548	...	...	...	...	...	...	...	...
55 - 59	CDJC	4 993	...	...	...	...	...	...	...	...
60 - 64	CDJC	4 534	...	...	...	...	...	...	...	...
65 - 74	CDJC	5 860	...	...	...	...	...	...	...	...
75 - 84	CDJC	2 000	...	...	...	...	...	...	...	...
85+	CDJC	355	...	...	...	...	...	...	...	...
Marshall Islands - Îles Marshall										
1 VII 2001										
Total	ESDF	54 584	27 960	26 624	...	...	...	...	...	...
0 - 4	ESDF	9 016	4 684	4 332	...	...	...	...	...	...

7. Population by age, sex and urban/rural residence: latest available year, 1992 - 2001
Population selon l'âge, le sexe et la résidence, urbaine/rurale: dernière année disponible, 1992 - 2001
(continued — suite)

(See notes at end of table. — Voir notes à la fin du tableau.)

Continent, country or area, date and age (in years) / Continent, pays ou zone, date et âge (en années)	Code[1]	Total			Urban - Urbaine			Rural - Rurale		
		Both sexes Les deux sexes	Male Masculin	Female Féminin	Both sexes Les deux sexes	Male Masculin	Female Féminin	Both sexes Les deux sexes	Male Masculin	Female Féminin
OCEANIA — OCEANIE										
Marshall Islands - Îles Marshall										
1 VII 2001										
5 - 9	ESDF	6 653	3 391	3 262	...	...	...	...	...	...
10 - 14	ESDF	7 272	3 745	3 527	...	...	...	...	...	...
15 - 19	ESDF	6 998	3 576	3 422	...	...	...	...	...	...
20 - 24	ESDF	5 190	2 594	2 596	...	...	...	...	...	...
25 - 29	ESDF	3 982	1 991	1 991	...	...	...	...	...	...
30 - 34	ESDF	3 407	1 736	1 671	...	...	...	...	...	...
35 - 39	ESDF	2 996	1 538	1 458	...	...	...	...	...	...
40 - 44	ESDF	2 558	1 276	1 282	...	...	...	...	...	...
45 - 49	ESDF	2 174	1 155	1 019	...	...	...	...	...	...
50 - 54	ESDF	1 618	883	735	...	...	...	...	...	...
55 - 59	ESDF	957	514	443	...	...	...	...	...	...
60 - 64	ESDF	623	318	305	...	...	...	...	...	...
65 - 69	ESDF	478	236	242	...	...	...	...	...	...
70 - 74	ESDF	289	159	130	...	...	...	...	...	...
75+	ESDF	373	164	209	...	...	...	...	...	...
Micronesia, Federated States of - Micronésie, États Fédérés de La										
18 IX 1994										
Total	CDJC	105 506	53 923	51 583	...	...	...	...	...	...
0 - 4	CDJC	15 854	8 211	7 643	...	...	...	...	...	...
5 - 9	CDJC	15 330	8 051	7 279	...	...	...	...	...	...
10 - 14	CDJC	14 749	7 534	7 215	...	...	...	...	...	...
15 - 19	CDJC	12 251	6 431	5 820	...	...	...	...	...	...
20 - 24	CDJC	8 828	4 321	4 507	...	...	...	...	...	...
25 - 29	CDJC	7 063	3 496	3 567	...	...	...	...	...	...
30 - 34	CDJC	6 598	3 311	3 287	...	...	...	...	...	...
35 - 39	CDJC	6 079	3 077	3 002	...	...	...	...	...	...
40 - 44	CDJC	5 071	2 661	2 410	...	...	...	...	...	...
45 - 49	CDJC	3 579	1 930	1 649	...	...	...	...	...	...
50 - 54	CDJC	2 219	1 101	1 118	...	...	...	...	...	...
55 - 59	CDJC	2 105	1 033	1 072	...	...	...	...	...	...
60 - 64	CDJC	1 985	1 018	967	...	...	...	...	...	...
65 - 69	CDJC	1 395	668	727	...	...	...	...	...	...
70 - 74	CDJC	1 229	567	662	...	...	...	...	...	...
75 - 79	CDJC	581	274	307	...	...	...	...	...	...
80 - 84	CDJC	354	150	204	...	...	...	...	...	...
85+	CDJC	236	89	147	...	...	...	...	...	...
New Caledonia - Nouvelle-Calédonie										
16 IV 1996										
Total	CDFC	196 836	100 762	96 074	...	...	...	...	...	...
0 - 9	CDFC	41 383	21 463	19 920	...	...	...	...	...	...
10 - 19	CDFC	36 398	18 526	17 872	...	...	...	...	...	...
20 - 29	CDFC	36 027	18 335	17 692	...	...	...	...	...	...
30 - 39	CDFC	30 266	15 315	14 951	...	...	...	...	...	...
40 - 49	CDFC	22 393	11 752	10 641	...	...	...	...	...	...
50 - 59	CDFC	15 589	8 220	7 369	...	...	...	...	...	...
60 - 69	CDFC	9 022	4 592	4 430	...	...	...	...	...	...
70 - 79	CDFC	4 146	1 913	2 233	...	...	...	...	...	...
80 - 89	CDFC	1 443	593	850	...	...	...	...	...	...
90+	CDFC	169	53	116	...	...	...	...	...	...

7. Population by age, sex and urban/rural residence: latest available year, 1992 - 2001
Population selon l'âge, le sexe et la résidence, urbaine/rurale: dernière année disponible, 1992 - 2001
(continued — suite)

(See notes at end of table. — Voir notes à la fin du tableau.)

Continent, country or area, date and age (in years) / Continent, pays ou zone, date et âge (en années)	Code[1]	Total			Urban - Urbaine			Rural - Rurale		
		Both sexes Les deux sexes	Male Masculin	Female Féminin	Both sexes Les deux sexes	Male Masculin	Female Féminin	Both sexes Les deux sexes	Male Masculin	Female Féminin
OCEANIA — OCEANIE										
New Zealand - Nouvelle-Zélande										
5 III 1996										
Total	CDJC	3 618 303	1 777 461	1 840 842	3 090 408	1 502 502	1 587 906	526 563	274 020	252 543
0 - 1	CDJC	54 747	28 293	26 454	46 440	24 021	22 422	8 301	4 272	4 032
1 - 4	CDJC	224 856	115 821	109 032	188 793	97 101	91 692	36 042	18 705	17 334
5 - 9	CDJC	288 294	147 723	140 571	238 686	122 124	116 559	49 566	25 560	23 997
10 - 14	CDJC	264 186	135 663	128 523	218 820	112 236	106 590	45 324	23 403	21 918
15 - 19	CDJC	262 980	133 575	129 405	228 459	114 618	113 835	34 419	18 885	15 537
20 - 24	CDJC	271 761	134 835	136 926	244 119	119 538	124 584	27 498	15 180	12 321
25 - 29	CDJC	273 303	132 453	140 850	240 270	115 875	124 386	32 931	16 491	16 437
30 - 34	CDJC	293 484	142 452	151 032	250 455	121 329	129 123	42 882	21 033	21 855
35 - 39	CDJC	285 216	139 293	145 923	238 338	115 833	122 502	46 737	23 352	23 385
40 - 44	CDJC	255 039	125 439	129 600	212 982	103 296	109 689	41 910	22 047	19 857
45 - 49	CDJC	241 191	120 249	120 942	201 657	99 564	102 093	39 396	20 592	18 807
50 - 54	CDJC	186 717	93 351	93 366	155 691	77 049	78 636	30 930	16 230	14 700
55 - 59	CDJC	158 601	78 783	79 818	132 129	64 716	67 407	26 400	14 004	12 393
60 - 64	CDJC	135 264	67 419	67 845	114 234	55 845	58 383	20 994	11 538	9 453
65 - 69	CDJC	132 972	65 184	67 788	115 509	55 380	60 129	17 430	9 783	7 644
70 - 74	CDJC	113 664	51 762	61 902	101 553	45 249	56 301	12 087	6 495	5 592
75 - 79	CDJC	82 287	33 561	48 726	74 937	29 880	45 060	7 332	3 675	3 663
80 - 84	CDJC	55 281	20 412	34 869	51 240	18 540	32 700	4 041	1 869	2 169
85 - 89	CDJC	27 024	8 385	18 642	25 302	7 698	17 613	1 716	687	1 035
90 - 94	CDJC	9 225	2 382	6 840	8 712	2 205	6 504	513	177	336
95 - 99	CDJC	1 950	393	1 557	1 842	366	1 479	105	27	78
100+	CDJC	261	33	225	252	33	216	6	3	6
1 VII 2000										
Total	ESDJ	3 830 800	1 886 900	1 943 900	...	...	...	...	...	...
0 - 1	ESDJ	57 140	29 490	27 650	...	...	...	...	...	...
1 - 4	ESDJ	228 370	117 340	111 040	...	...	...	...	...	...
5 - 9	ESDJ	301 850	155 590	146 250	...	...	...	...	...	...
10 - 14	ESDJ	289 150	148 240	140 910	...	...	...	...	...	...
15 - 19	ESDJ	272 880	140 530	132 340	...	...	...	...	...	...
20 - 24	ESDJ	256 220	130 230	126 000	...	...	...	...	...	...
25 - 29	ESDJ	264 990	128 570	136 410	...	...	...	...	...	...
30 - 34	ESDJ	285 500	136 920	148 580	...	...	...	...	...	...
35 - 39	ESDJ	307 450	149 430	158 010	...	...	...	...	...	...
40 - 44	ESDJ	288 430	141 760	146 660	...	...	...	...	...	...
45 - 49	ESDJ	256 780	127 310	129 480	...	...	...	...	...	...
50 - 54	ESDJ	237 180	118 750	118 430	...	...	...	...	...	...
55 - 59	ESDJ	183 790	91 600	92 210	...	...	...	...	...	...
60 - 64	ESDJ	149 990	73 930	76 060	...	...	...	...	...	...
65 - 69	ESDJ	129 410	63 490	65 920	...	...	...	...	...	...
70 - 74	ESDJ	119 280	56 600	62 670	...	...	...	...	...	...
75 - 79	ESDJ	94 860	40 480	54 390	...	...	...	...	...	...
80 - 84	ESDJ	59 970	22 240	37 720	...	...	...	...	...	...
85 - 89	ESDJ	33 300	10 840	22 470	...	...	...	...	...	...
90+	ESDJ	14 260	3 550	10 710	...	...	...	...	...	...
Niue - Nioué										
17 VIII 1997										
Total	CDFC	2 088	1 053	1 035	...	...	...	...	...	...
0 - 4	CDFC	210	107	103	...	...	...	...	...	...
5 - 9	CDFC	229	124	105	...	...	...	...	...	...
10 - 14	CDFC	243	115	128	...	...	...	...	...	...
15 - 19	CDFC	195	105	90	...	...	...	...	...	...
20 - 24	CDFC	116	62	54	...	...	...	...	...	...
25 - 29	CDFC	126	66	60	...	...	...	...	...	...
30 - 34	CDFC	145	76	69	...	...	...	...	...	...
35 - 39	CDFC	122	68	54	...	...	...	...	...	...

7. Population by age, sex and urban/rural residence: latest available year, 1992 - 2001
Population selon l'âge, le sexe et la résidence, urbaine/rurale: dernière année disponible, 1992 - 2001
(continued — suite)

(See notes at end of table. — Voir notes à la fin du tableau.)

Continent, country or area, date and age (in years) / Continent, pays ou zone, date et âge (en annèes)	Code[1]	Total			Urban - Urbaine			Rural - Rurale		
		Both sexes Les deux sexes	Male Masculin	Female Féminin	Both sexes Les deux sexes	Male Masculin	Female Féminin	Both sexes Les deux sexes	Male Masculin	Female Féminin
OCEANIA — OCEANIE										
Niue - Nioué										
17 VIII 1997										
40 - 44	CDFC	125	64	61	...	...	...	...	...	...
45 - 49	CDFC	94	40	54	...	...	...	...	...	...
50 - 54	CDFC	100	53	47	...	...	...	...	...	...
55 - 59	CDFC	109	52	57	...	...	...	...	...	...
60 - 64	CDFC	101	48	53	...	...	...	...	...	...
65 - 69	CDFC	51	23	28	...	...	...	...	...	...
70 - 74	CDFC	44	24	20	...	...	...	...	...	...
75+	CDFC	78	26	52	...	...	...	...	...	...
Northern Mariana Islands - Îles Mariannes septentrionales										
1 IV 2000										
Total	CDFC	69 221	31 984	37 237	...	...	...	...	...	...
0 - 4	CDFC	5 792	...	...	...	...	...	...	...	...
5 - 9	CDFC	5 420	...	...	...	...	...	...	...	...
10 - 14	CDFC	4 377	...	...	...	...	...	...	...	...
15 - 19	CDFC	3 943	...	...	...	...	...	...	...	...
20 - 24	CDFC	7 566	...	...	...	...	...	...	...	...
25 - 34	CDFC	20 181	...	...	...	...	...	...	...	...
35 - 44	CDFC	12 651	...	...	...	...	...	...	...	...
45 - 54	CDFC	6 208	...	...	...	...	...	...	...	...
55 - 59	CDFC	1 199	...	...	...	...	...	...	...	...
60 - 64	CDFC	837	...	...	...	...	...	...	...	...
65 - 74	CDFC	748	...	...	...	...	...	...	...	...
75 - 84	CDFC	233	...	...	...	...	...	...	...	...
85+	CDFC	66	...	...	...	...	...	...	...	...
Palau - Palaos										
9 IX 1995										
Total	CDFC	17 225	9 213	8 012	...	...	...	...	...	...
0 - 4	CDFC	1 762	916	846	...	...	...	...	...	...
5 - 9	CDFC	1 551	797	754	...	...	...	...	...	...
10 - 14	CDFC	1 527	798	729	...	...	...	...	...	...
15 - 19	CDFC	1 282	684	598	...	...	...	...	...	...
20 - 24	CDFC	1 427	723	704	...	...	...	...	...	...
25 - 29	CDFC	1 741	929	812	...	...	...	...	...	...
30 - 34	CDFC	1 717	1 005	712	...	...	...	...	...	...
35 - 39	CDFC	1 583	927	656	...	...	...	...	...	...
40 - 44	CDFC	1 261	727	534	...	...	...	...	...	...
45 - 49	CDFC	943	553	390	...	...	...	...	...	...
50 - 54	CDFC	603	329	274	...	...	...	...	...	...
55 - 59	CDFC	488	249	239	...	...	...	...	...	...
60 - 64	CDFC	361	174	187	...	...	...	...	...	...
65 - 69	CDFC	328	145	183	...	...	...	...	...	...
70 - 74	CDFC	278	122	156	...	...	...	...	...	...
75+	CDFC	373	135	238	...	...	...	...	...	...
15 IV 2000										
Total	CDFC	19 129	...	...	...	...	...	...	...	...
0 - 4	CDFC	1 308	...	...	...	...	...	...	...	...
5 - 9	CDFC	1 700	...	...	...	...	...	...	...	...
10 - 14	CDFC	1 555	...	...	...	...	...	...	...	...
15 - 19	CDFC	1 382	...	...	...	...	...	...	...	...
20 - 24	CDFC	1 342	...	...	...	...	...	...	...	...
25 - 29	CDFC	1 910	...	...	...	...	...	...	...	...
30 - 34	CDFC	2 169	...	...	...	...	...	...	...	...
35 - 39	CDFC	1 891	...	...	...	...	...	...	...	...
40 - 44	CDFC	1 651	...	...	...	...	...	...	...	...

7. Population by age, sex and urban/rural residence: latest available year, 1992 - 2001
Population selon l'âge, le sexe et la résidence, urbaine/rurale: dernière année disponible, 1992 - 2001
(continued — suite)

(See notes at end of table. — Voir notes à la fin du tableau.)

Continent, country or area, date and age (in years) Continent, pays ou zone, date et âge (en annèes)	Code[1]	Total			Urban - Urbaine			Rural - Rurale		
		Both sexes Les deux sexes	Male Masculin	Female Féminin	Both sexes Les deux sexes	Male Masculin	Female Féminin	Both sexes Les deux sexes	Male Masculin	Female Féminin
OCEANIA — OCEANIE										
Palau - Palaos										
15 IV 2000										
45 - 49	CDFC	1 272	...	...	...	...	...	...	...	...
50 - 54	CDFC	886	...	...	...	...	...	...	...	...
55 - 59	CDFC	563	...	...	...	...	...	...	...	...
60 - 64	CDFC	463	...	...	...	...	...	...	...	...
65 - 69	CDFC	318	...	...	...	...	...	...	...	...
70 - 74	CDFC	274	...	...	...	...	...	...	...	...
75+	CDFC	445	...	...	...	...	...	...	...	...
Pitcairn										
31 XII 1993										
Total	ESDF	53	25	28	...	...	...	...	...	...
0 - 1	ESDF	1	1	...	...	...	...	...	...	...
1 - 4	ESDF	2	1	1	...	...	...	...	...	...
5 - 9	ESDF	6	3	3	...	...	...	...	...	...
10 - 14	ESDF	5	1	4	...	...	...	...	...	...
15 - 19	ESDF	4	3	1	...	...	...	...	...	...
20 - 24	ESDF	2	2	...	...	...	...	...	...	...
25 - 29	ESDF	...	...	...	...	...	...	...	...	...
30 - 34	ESDF	5	1	4	...	...	...	...	...	...
35 - 39	ESDF	8	6	2	...	...	...	...	...	...
40 - 44	ESDF	3	1	2	...	...	...	...	...	...
45 - 49	ESDF	1	...	1	...	...	...	...	...	...
50 - 54	ESDF	3	...	3	...	...	...	...	...	...
55 - 59	ESDF	2	1	1	...	...	...	...	...	...
60 - 64	ESDF	3	2	1	...	...	...	...	...	...
65 - 69	ESDF	4	1	3	...	...	...	...	...	...
70 - 74	ESDF	2	1	1	...	...	...	...	...	...
75 - 79	ESDF	1	1	...	...	...	...	...	...	...
80 - 84	ESDF	...	...	...	...	...	...	...	...	...
85+	ESDF	1	...	1	...	...	...	...	...	...
Tonga										
1 VII 1999										
Total	ESDF	*99 821*	*50 731*	*49 088*	...	...	...	...	...	...
0 - 4	ESDF	*13 365*	*6 835*	*6 529*	...	...	...	...	...	...
5 - 9	ESDF	*12 407*	*6 565*	*5 842*	...	...	...	...	...	...
10 - 14	ESDF	*12 129*	*6 415*	*5 714*	...	...	...	...	...	...
15 - 19	ESDF	*11 685*	*6 020*	*5 665*	...	...	...	...	...	...
20 - 24	ESDF	*9 056*	*4 630*	*4 426*	...	...	...	...	...	...
25 - 29	ESDF	*7 217*	*3 664*	*3 553*	...	...	...	...	...	...
30 - 34	ESDF	*6 373*	*3 263*	*3 111*	...	...	...	...	...	...
35 - 39	ESDF	*5 042*	*2 495*	*2 547*	...	...	...	...	...	...
40 - 44	ESDF	*4 312*	*2 037*	*2 275*	...	...	...	...	...	...
45 - 49	ESDF	*3 763*	*1 755*	*2 008*	...	...	...	...	...	...
50 - 54	ESDF	*3 287*	*1 518*	*1 769*	...	...	...	...	...	...
55 - 59	ESDF	*3 076*	*1 491*	*1 585*	...	...	...	...	...	...
60 - 64	ESDF	*2 677*	*1 360*	*1 318*	...	...	...	...	...	...
65 - 69	ESDF	*2 132*	*1 082*	*1 050*	...	...	...	...	...	...
70 - 74	ESDF	*1 507*	*763*	*744*	...	...	...	...	...	...
75+	ESDF	*1 792*	*837*	*954*	...	...	...	...	...	...

GENERAL NOTES - NOTES GENERALES

Unless otherwise specified, age is defined as age at last birthday (completed years). For definition of urban, see Technical notes for table 6. For method of evaluation and limitation of data, see Technical Notes for this table. — Sauf indication contraire, l'âge dernier anniversaire (années révolues). Pour la définitions de "zones urbaines", voir les Notes techniques relatives au tableau 6. Pour le méthode d'évaluation et les insuffissances des données, voire Notes techniques, pour ce tableau.

Italics: estimates which are less reliable. — *Italiques:* estimations moins sûres.

FOOTNOTES - NOTES

[1] 'Code' indicates the source of data, as follows:
CDFC - Census, de facto, complete tabulation
CDFS - Census, de facto, sample tabulation
CDJC - Census, de jure, complete tabulation

CDJS - Census, de jure, sample tabulation
SSDF - Sample survey, de facto
SSDJ - Sample survey, de jure
ESDF - Estimates, de facto
ESDJ - Estimates, de jure
Le 'Code' indique la source des données, comme suit:
CDFC - Recensement, population de fait, tabulation complète
CDFS - Recensement, population de fait, tabulation par sondage
CDJC - Recensement, population de droit, tabulation complète
CDJS - Recensement, population de droit, tabulation par sondage
SSDF - Enquête par sondage, population de fait
SSDJ - Enquête par sondage, population de droit
ESDF - Estimations, population de fait
ESDJ - Estimations, population de droit

[2] Because of rounding, totals are not in all cases the sum of the parts. - Les chiffres étant arrondis, les totaux ne correspondent pas toujours rigoureusement à la somme des chiffres partiels.

[3] For 1993, data have not been adjusted for underenumeration, estimated at 1.4 per cent.- Pour 1993, les données n'ont pas été ajustées pour compenser les lacunes du dénombrement, estimées à 1,4 p. 100.

[4] Data refer to national projections. — Les données se referent aux projections nationales.

[5] Data have been adjusted for underenumeration estimated at 6.8 per cent.- Les données ont été ajustées pour compenser les lacunes du dénombrement estimées à 6,8 p. 100.

[6] Total population excludes persons who were not contacted at the time of the census.- La population non comprend pas les personnes qui n'ont pas été contactées à l'heure du recensement.

[7] Excluding institutional population.- Non compris la population dans les institutions.

[8] Age classification based on year of birth rather than on completed years of age. - La classification par âge est fondée sur l'année de naissance et non sur l'âge en années révolues.

[9] Including armed forces stationed in the area. - Y compris les militaires en garnison sur le territoire.

[10] De jure population, but excluding civilian citizens absent from country for an extended period of time. - Population de droit, mais non compris les civils hors du pays pendant une période prolongée.

[11] Including armed forces stationed in the area.- Y compris les militaires en garnison sur le territoire.

[12] Data include persons in remote areas, military personel outside the country, merchant seamen at sea, civilian seasonal workers outside the country, and other civilians outside the country, and exclude nomads, foreign military, civilian aliens temporarily in the country, transients on ships and Indian jungle population.- Y compris les personnes dans des régions éloignées, le personel militaire en dehors du pays, les marins marchands, les ouvriers saisonniers civils de couture en dehors du pays, et autres civils en dehors du pays, et non compris les nomades, les militaires étrangers, les étrangers civils temporairement dans le pays, les transiteurs sur des bateaux et les Indiens de la jungle.

[13] Excluding nomadic Indian tribes. - Non compris les tribus d'Indiens nomades.

[14] Excluding Indian jungle population. - Non compris les Indiens de la jungle.

[15] Mid-year estimates have been adjusted for underenumeration, at latest census.- Les estimations au millieu de l''année tiennent compte d''une ajustement destiné à compenser les lacunes du dénombrement lors du dernier recensement.

[16] For 2001, figures for male and female do not add up to the total, since only the figures for the total were adjusted for underenumeration.- Pour 2001, les données pour la population masculine et la population féminine ne s'ajoutent pas au total, parce-que elles n'ont pas été ajustées pour compenser les lacunes du dénombrement.

[17] For statistical purposes, the data for China do not include those for the Hong Kong Special Administrative Region (Hong Kong SAR), Macao special Administrative Region (Macao SAR) and Taiwan province of China. - Pour la présentation des statistiques, les données pour Chine ne comprend pas la Région Administrative Spéciale de Hong Kong (Hong Kong RAS), la Région Administrative Spéciale de Macao (Macao RAS) et Taïwan province de Chine.

[18] For 2000, including estimates of Turkish Cypriots in the occupied area. - - Pour 2000, y compris des évaluations des Chypriotes turcs dans le secteur occupé.

[19] Data refer to government controlled areas.- Les données se raportent aux zones contrôlées par le Gouvernement.

[20] Including data for the Indian-held part of Jammu and Kashmir, the final status of which has not yet been determined. - Y compris les données pour la partie du Jammu et du Cachemire occupée par l'Inde dont le statut définitif n'a pas encore été déterminé.

[21] Data refer to only enumerated population with permanent residence.- Les données se rapportent à la population énumérée avec la résidence permanente.

[22] Including data for East Jerusalem and Israeli residents in certain other territories under occupation by Israeli military forces since June 1967. - Y compris les données pour Jérusalem-Est et les résidents israéliens dans certains autres territoires occupés depuis 1967 par les forces armées israéliennes.

[23] Excluding diplomatic personnel outside country and foreign military and civilian personnel and their dependants stationed in the area. - Non compris le personnel diplomatique hors du pays ni les militaires et agents civils étrangers en poste sur le territoire et les membres de leur famille les accompagnant.

[24] Excluding data for Jordanian territory under occupation since June 1967 by Israeli military forces. Excluding foreigners, including registered Palestinian refugees. - Non compris les données pour le territoire jordanien occupé depuis juin 1967 par les forces armées israéliennes. Non compris les étrangers, mais y compris les réfugiés de Palestine enregistrés.

[25] Excluding alien armed forces, civilian aliens employed by armed forces, foreign diplomatic personnel and their dependants and Korean diplomatic personnel and their dependants outside the country. - Non compris les militaires étrangers, les civils étrangers employés par les forces armées, le personnel diplomatique étranger et les membres de leur famille les accompagnant et le personnel diplomatique coréen hors du pays et les membres de leurs familles les accompagnant.

[26] Excluding data for the Pakistan-held part of Jammu and Kashmir, the final status of which has not yet been determined. - Non compris les données concernant la partie du Jammu et Cachemire occupée par le Pakistan dont le statut définitif n'a pas été déterminé.

[27] Excluding the Federal Administrative tribal areas.- Non compris les zones tribales administrées par le gouvernement fédéral.

[28] Excluding transients afloat and non-locally domiciled military and civilian services personnel and their dependants. - Non compris les personnes de passage à bord de navires ni les militaires et agents civils non-résidents et les membres de leur famille les accompagnant.

[29] Including Palestinian refugees. - Y compris les réfugiés de Palestine.

[30] Excluding Faeroe Islands and Greenland. - Non compris les îles Féroé et Gröenland.

[31] Excluding Overseas Departments, namely French Guiana, Guadeloupe, Martinique and Reunion, shown separately. De jure population but excluding diplomatic personnel outside country and including members of alien armed forces not living in military camps and foreign diplomatic personnel not living in embassies or consulates. - Non compris les départements d'outre-mer, c'est-à-dire la Guyane française, la Guadeloupe, la Martinique et la Réunion, qui font l'objet de rubriques distinctes. Population de droit, non compris le personnel diplomatique hors du pays et y compris les militaires étrangers ne vivant pas dans des camps militaires et le personnel diplomatique étranger ne vivant pas dans les ambassades ou les consulats.

[32] Mid-year population excludes armed forces stationed outside the country, but includes alien armed forces stationed in the area. - Les estimations au millieu de l'année non comprises les militaires en garnison hors du pays, mais y compris les militaires étrangers en garnison sur le territoire.

[33] Maltese population only. - Population Maltaise seulement.

[34] Including residents temporarily outside the country. - Y compris les résidents se trouvant temporairement hors du pays.

[35] For 1999, excluding civilian aliens within country, but including civilian nationals temporarily outside country.- Pour 1999, non compris les civils étrangers dans le pays, mais y compris les civils nationaux temporairement hors du pays.

[36] Data do not include information for Transnistria and the municipality of Bender.- Les données ne tiennent compte d''information sur la Transnistria et la municipalité de Bender.

[37] Beginning with 1998, estimates of Kosovo and Metohia computed on the basis of natural increases from year 1997.- A partir du 1998, les estimations pour le Kosovo et la Metohia ont été calculées sur la base des incréments naturelles depuis 1997.

Table 8

Table 8 presents population of capital cities and cities of 100,000 or more inhabitants for the latest available year.

Description of variables: Since the way in which cities are delimited differs from one country or area to another, the table not only presents data for the so-called city proper, but also for the urban agglomeration, if available.

City proper is defined as a locality with legally fixed boundaries and an administratively recognized urban status, usually characterized by some form of local government.

Urban agglomeration has been defined as comprising the city or town proper and also the suburban fringe or densely settled territory lying outside of, but adjacent to, the city boundaries.

For some countries or areas, however, the data relate to entire administrative divisions known, for example, as shi or municipalities (municipios) which are composed of a populated centre and adjoining territory, some of which may contain other, often separate urban localities or may be distinctively rural in character. For this group of countries or areas the type of civil division is given in a footnote.

The surface area of the city or urban agglomeration is shown at the end of the table, when available.

City names are presented in the original language of the country or area in which the cities are located. In cases where the original names are not in the Roman alphabet, they have been Romanized. Cities are listed in English alphabetical order.

Capital cities are shown in the table regardless of their population size. The names of the capital cities are printed in capital letters. The designation of any specific city as a capital city is as was reported by the country or area.

The table also covers cities with, or whose urban agglomeration is of a population of 100,000 and more; that is, while the urban agglomeration should have a population of 100,000 or more to be included in the table, the city proper may be of a smaller population size.

The reference date of each population figure appears in the stub of the table. Estimates based on results of sample surveys and city censuses as well as those derived from other sources are noted in the "code" column.

Reliability of data: Specific information is generally not available on the reliability of the estimates of the population of cities or urban agglomerations presented in this table.

In the absence of such quality assessment, data from population censuses, sample surveys and city censuses are considered to be reliable and, therefore, set in roman type. Other estimates are considered to be reliable if they are based on a complete census (or a sample survey), and have been adjusted by a continuous population register or adjusted on the basis of the calculated balance of births, deaths, and migration.

Limitations: Statistics on the population of capital cities and cities of 100,000 or more inhabitants are subject to the same qualifications as have been set forth for population statistics in general as discussed in section 3 of the Technical Notes.

International comparability of data on city population is limited to a great extent by variations in national concepts and definitions. Although an effort is made to reduce the sources of non-comparability somewhat by presenting the data for both city proper and urban agglomeration, many serious problems of comparability remain.

Data presented in the "city proper" column for some countries represent an urban administrative area legally distinguished from surrounding rural territory, while for other countries these data represent a commune or an equally small administrative unit. In still other countries, the administrative units may be relatively extensive and thereby include considerable territories beyond the urban centre itself.

City data are also especially affected by whether the data refer to de facto or de jure population, as well as variations among countries in how each of these concepts is applied. With reference to the total population, the difference between the de facto and de jure population is discussed at length in section 3.1.1 of the Technical Notes.

Data on city populations based on intercensal estimates present additional problems: comparability is impaired by the different methods used in making the estimates and by the loss of precision in applying to selected segments of the population, methods best suited for the whole population. For example, it is far more difficult to apply the component method of estimating population growth to cities than it is to the entire country.

Births and deaths occurring in the cities do not all originate in the population present in or resident of that area. Therefore, the use of natural increase to estimate the probable size of the city population is a potential source of error. Internal migration is another component of population change that cannot be measured with accuracy in many areas. Because of these factors, estimates in this table may be less valuable in general and in particular limited for purposes of international comparison.

City data, even when set in roman type, are often not as reliable as estimates for the total population of the country or area. Furthermore, because the sources of these data include censuses (national or city), surveys and estimates, the years to which they refer vary widely. In addition, because city boundaries may alter over time, comparisons covering different years should be carried out with caution.

Coverage: Cities are shown for 228 countries or areas.

Earlier data: Population of capital cities and cities with a population of 100,000 or more have been shown in previous issues of the *Demographic Yearbook*. For more information on specific topics and years for which data are reported, readers should consult the Index.

Tableau 8

Le tableau 8 présente des données sur la population des capitales et des villes de 100 000 habitants et plus pour la dernière année disponible.

Description des variables : Etant donné que les villes ne sont pas délimitées de la même manière dans tous les pays ou zones, on s'est efforcé de donner, dans ce tableau, des chiffres correspondant non seulement aux villes proprement dites, mais aussi, le cas échéant, aux agglomérations urbaines.

On entend par villes proprement dites les localités qui ont des limites juridiquement définies et sont administrativement considérées comme villes, ce qui se caractérise généralement par l'existence d'une autorité locale.

L'agglomération urbaine comprend, par définition, la ville proprement dite ainsi que la proche banlieue, c'est-à-dire la zone fortement peuplée qui est extérieure, mais contiguë aux limites de la ville.

En outre, dans certains pays ou zones, les données se rapportent à des divisions administratives entières, connues par exemple sous le nom de shi ou de municipios, qui comportent une agglomération et le territoire avoisinant, lequel peut englober d'autres agglomérations urbaines tout à fait distinctes ou être de caractère essentiellement rural. Pour ce groupe de pays ou zones, le type de division administrative est indiqué en note.

On trouvera à la fin du tableau la superficie de la ville ou agglomération urbaine chaque fois que possible.

Les noms des villes sont indiqués dans la langue du pays ou zone où ces villes sont situées. Les noms de villes qui ne sont pas à l'origine libellés en caractères latins ont été romanisés. Les villes sont énumérées dans l'ordre alphabétique anglais.

Les capitales figurent dans le tableau quel que soit le chiffre de leur population et leur nom a été imprimé en lettres majuscules. Ne sont indiquées comme capitales que les villes ainsi désignées par le pays ou zone intéressé.

En ce qui concerne les autres villes, le tableau indique celles dont la population est égale ou supérieure à 100 000 habitants. Ce chiffre limite s'applique à l'agglomération urbaine et non à la ville proprement dite, dont la population peut être moindre.

La date de référence du chiffre correspondant à chaque population figure dans la colonne de gauche du tableau. Lorsqu'on savait que les estimations étaient fondées sur les résultats d'enquêtes par sondage ou de recensements municipaux ou étaient tirées d'autres sources, on l'a indiqué en note.

Fiabilité des données : On ne possède généralement pas de renseignements précis sur la fiabilité des estimations de la population des villes ou agglomérations urbaines présentées dans ce tableau.

Les données provenant de recensements de la population, d'enquêtes par sondage ou de recensements municipaux sont jugées sûres et figurent par conséquent en caractères romains. D'autres estimations sont considérées comme sûres si sont fondées sur un recensement complet (ou une enquête par sondage) et ont été ajustées en fonction des données fournies par un registre de population permanent ou en fonction de la balance, établie par le calcul des naissances, des décès et des migrations.

Insuffisance des données : Les statistiques portant sur la population des capitales et des villes de 100 000 habitants et plus appellent toutes les réserves qui ont été faites à la section 3 des Notes techniques à propos des statistiques de la population en général.

La comparabilité internationale des données portant sur la population des villes est compromise dans une large mesure par la diversité des définitions nationales. Bien que l'on se soit efforcé de réduire les facteurs de non-comparabilité en présentant à la fois dans le tableau les données relatives aux villes proprement dites et celles concernant les agglomérations urbaines, de nombreux et graves problèmes de comparabilité n'en subsistent pas moins.

Pour certain pays, les données figurant dans la colonne intitulée "ville proprement dite" correspondent à une zone administrative urbaine juridiquement distincte du territoire rural environnant, tandis que pour d'autres pays ces données correspondent à une commune ou petite unité administrative analogue. Pour d'autres encore, les unités administratives en cause peuvent être relativement étendues et comporter par conséquent un vaste territoire au-delà du centre urbain lui-même.

L'emploi de données se rapportant tantôt à la population de fait, tantôt à la population de droit, ainsi que les différences de traitement de ces deux concepts d'un pays à l'autre influent particulièrement sur les statistiques urbaines. En ce qui concerne la population totale, la différence entre population de fait et population de droit est expliquée en détail à la section 3.1.1 des Notes techniques.

Les statistiques des populations urbaines qui sont fondées sur des estimations intercensitaires posent encore plus de problèmes que les données de recensement. Leur comparabilité est compromise par la diversité des méthodes employées pour établir les estimations et par le manque possible de précision dans l'application de telle ou telle méthode.

La méthode des composantes, par exemple, est beaucoup plus difficile à appliquer en vue de l'estimation de l'accroissement de la population lorsqu'il s'agit de villes que lorsqu'il s'agit de pays entiers.

Les naissances et décès qui surviennent dans les villes ne correspondent pas tous à la population présente ou résidente. En conséquence, des erreurs peuvent se produire si l'on établit pour les villes des estimations fondées sur l'accroissement naturel de la population. Les migrations intérieures constituent un second élément d'estimation que, dans bien des régions, on ne peut pas toujours mesurer avec exactitude. Pour ces raisons, les estimations présentées dans ce table risquent dans l'ensemble d'être peu fiables et leur valeur est particulièrement limitée du point de vue des comparaisons internationales.

Même lorsqu'elles figurent en caractères romains, il arrive souvent que les statistiques urbaines ne soient pas aussi sûres que les estimations concernant la population totale du pays ou zone en cause. De surcroît, comme ces statistiques proviennent aussi bien de recensements (nationaux ou municipaux) que d'enquêtes ou d'estimations, les années auxquelles elles se rapportent sont extrêmement variables. Enfin, comme les limites urbaines varient parfois d'une époque à une autre, il y a lieu d'être prudent lorsque l'on compare des données se rapportant à des années différentes.

Portée : Ce tableau fournit des données sur la population des villes de 228 pays ou zones.

Données publiées antérieurement : Des statistiques de la population des capitales et des villes de 100 000 habitants ou plus ont été présentées dans des éditions antérieures de l'Annuaire démographique. Pour plus de précisions concernant les sujets spécifiques et les années pour lesquelles des données ont été publiées, se reporter à l'Index.

8. Population of capital cities and cities of 100 000 and more inhabitants: latest available year
Population des capitales et des villes de 100 000 habitants et plus: dernière année disponible

(See notes at end of table. — Voir notes à la fin du tableau.)

Continent, country or area, date and city Continent, pays ou zone, date et ville	Code[1]	City proper — Ville proprement dite Population				Urban agglomeration — Agglomération urbaine Population			
		Both sexes Les deux sexes	Male Masculin	Female Féminin	Surface area Superficie (km²)	Both sexes Les deux sexes	Male Masculin	Female Féminin	Surface area Superficie (km²)
AFRICA — AFRIQUE									
Algeria — Algérie									
1998									
Annaba	CDJC	348 554	...	...	...	...	...	...	...
Batna	CDJC	242 514	...	...	...	...	...	...	...
Béchar	CDJC	131 010	...	...	...	...	...	...	...
Bejaïa	CDJC	147 076	...	...	...	...	...	...	...
Beskra	CDJC	170 956	...	...	...	...	...	...	...
Bordj Bou Arreridj	CDJC	128 535	...	...	...	...	...	...	...
Ech Cheliff (El Asnam)	CDJC	179 768	...	...	...	...	...	...	...
El Boulaïda (Blida)	CDJC	226 512	...	...	...	...	...	...	...
EL DJAZAIR (ALGER, ALGIERS)	CDJC	1 519 570	...	...	...	...	...	...	...
El Djelfa	CDJC	154 265	...	...	...	...	...	...	...
El Eulma	CDJC	105 130	...	...	...	...	...	...	...
El Wad	CDJC	104 801	...	...	...	...	...	...	...
Ghardaïa	CDJC	110 724	...	...	...	...	...	...	...
Ghilizane	CDJC	104 285	...	...	...	...	...	...	...
Guelma	CDJC	108 734	...	...	...	...	...	...	...
Jijel	CDJC	106 003	...	...	...	...	...	...	...
Khenchla	CDJC	106 082	...	...	...	...	...	...	...
Lemdiyya (Medea)	CDJC	123 535	...	...	...	...	...	...	...
Mestghanem (Mostaganem)	CDJC	124 399	...	...	...	...	...	...	...
Qacentina (Constantine)	CDJC	462 187	...	...	...	...	...	...	...
Saïda	CDJC	110 865	...	...	...	...	...	...	...
Sidi-bel-Abbès	CDJC	180 260	...	...	...	...	...	...	...
Skikda	CDJC	152 335	...	...	...	...	...	...	...
Souq Ahras	CDJC	115 882	...	...	...	...	...	...	...
Stif (Sétif)	CDJC	211 859	...	...	...	...	...	...	...
Tbessa	CDJC	153 246	...	...	...	...	...	...	...
Tihert	CDJC	145 332	...	...	...	...	...	...	...
Tilimsen (Tlemcen)	CDJC	155 162	...	...	...	...	...	...	...
Touggourt	CDJC	113 625	...	...	...	...	...	...	...
Wahran (Oran)	CDJC	692 516	...	...	...	...	...	...	...
Wargla	CDJC	129 402	...	...	...	...	...	...	...
Angola									
1993									
Huambo	ESDF	...	...	...	...	*400 000*	...	...	...
LUANDA	ESDF	...	...	...	...	*1 822 407*	*855 676*	*936 731*	...
Benin — Bénin									
2000									
Cotonou	ESDF	*650 660*	*318 752*	*331 908*	79	...	...	...	...
Parakou	ESDF	*144 627*	*73 603*	*71 024*	441	...	...	...	...
PORTO-NOVO	ESDF	*232 756*	*113 737*	*119 019*	50	...	...	...	...
Botswana									
2001									
Francistown	CDFC	83 023	...	...	79	113 315	...	...	...
GABORONE	CDFC	186 007	...	...	169	282 150	...	...	...
Burkina Faso									
1996									
Bobo Dioulasso	CDFC	309 771	157 021	152 750	...	...	...	...	...
OUAGADOUGOU	CDFC	709 736	364 674	345 062	...	750 398	384 807	365 591	...
Burundi									
1990									
BUJUMBURA	CDFC	235 440	129 195	106 245	...	...	...	...	...
Cameroon — Cameroun									
1998									
Bafoussam	ESDF	*205 620*	...	...	...	...	...	...	...
Bamenda	ESDF	*252 083*	...	...	...	...	...	...	...
Bertoua	ESDF	*129 067*	...	...	...	...	...	...	...
Douala	ESDF	*1 382 900*	...	...	...	...	...	...	...
Edéa	ESDF	*101 200*	...	...	...	...	...	...	...

8. Population of capital cities and cities of 100 000 and more inhabitants: latest available year
Population des capitales et des villes de 100 000 habitants et plus: dernière année disponible (continued — suite)

(See notes at end of table. — Voir notes à la fin du tableau.)

Continent, country or area, date and city / Continent, pays ou zone, date et ville	Code[1]	City proper — Ville proprement dite Population				Urban agglomeration — Agglomération urbaine Population			
		Both sexes Les deux sexes	Male Masculin	Female Féminin	Surface area Superficie (km²)	Both sexes Les deux sexes	Male Masculin	Female Féminin	Surface area Superficie (km²)
AFRICA — AFRIQUE									
Cameroon — Cameroun									
1998									
Garoua	ESDF	293 081	...	...	...	...	...	...	...
Kousséri	ESDF	233 280	...	...	...	...	...	...	...
Kumba	ESDF	110 860	...	...	...	...	...	...	...
Loum	ESDF	115 781	...	...	...	...	...	...	...
Maroua	ESDF	225 469	...	...	...	...	...	...	...
Ngaoundéré	ESDF	156 804	...	...	...	...	...	...	...
Nkongsamba	ESDF	104 908	...	...	...	...	...	...	...
YAOUNDE	ESDF	1 293 000	...	...	...	...	...	...	...
Cape Verde — Cap-Vert									
1990									
PRAIA	CDFC	61 644	...	...	...	...	...	...	...
Central African Republic — République centrafricaine									
1988									
BANGUI	CDFC	451 690	...	...	...	...	...	...	...
Chad — Tchad									
1993									
N'DJAMENA	CDFC	530 965	...	...	...	...	...	...	...
Comoros — Comores									
1991									
MORONI	CDFC	30 365	...	...	...	...	...	...	...
Congo									
1984									
BRAZZAVILLE	CDFC	596 200	...	...	...	...	...	...	...
Pointe-Noire	CDFC	298 014	...	...	...	...	...	...	...
Côte d'Ivoire									
1988									
Abidjan	CDFC	1 929 079	...	...	...	...	...	...	...
Bouake	CDFC	329 850	...	...	...	362 192	...	...	...
Daloa	CDFC	121 842	...	...	...	127 923	...	...	...
Korhogo	CDFC	109 445	...	...	...	112 888	...	...	...
YAMOUSSOUKRO	CDFC	106 786	...	...	...	126 191	...	...	...
Democratic Republic of the Congo — République démocratique du Congo									
1984									
Boma	ESDF	197 617	...	...	...	...	...	...	...
Bukavu	ESDF	167 950	...	...	...	...	...	...	...
Kananga	ESDF	298 693	...	...	...	...	...	...	...
Kikwit	ESDF	149 296	...	...	...	...	...	...	...
KINSHASA	ESDF	2 664 309	...	...	...	...	...	...	...
Kisangani	ESDF	317 581	...	...	...	...	...	...	...
Kolwezi	ESDF	416 122	...	...	...	...	...	...	...
Likasi (Jadotville)	ESDF	213 862	...	...	...	...	...	...	...
Lubumbashi	ESDF	564 830	...	...	...	...	...	...	...
Matadi	ESDF	138 798	...	...	...	...	...	...	...
Mbandaka	ESDF	137 291	...	...	...	...	...	...	...
Mbuji-Mayi	ESDF	486 235	...	...	...	...	...	...	...
Djibouti									
1970									
DJIBOUTI	ESDF	62 000	...	...	...	...	...	...	...
Egypt — Égypte									
1996									
Alexandria	CDFC	3 339 076	1 707 477	1 631 599	...	...	...	...	...
Al Orizah	CDFC	100 482	53 081	47 401	...	...	...	...	...
Assyût	CDFC	343 662	182 151	161 511	...	...	...	...	...
Aswan	CDFC	219 541	111 640	107 901	...	...	...	...	...
Banha	CDFC	135 892	69 154	66 738	...	...	...	...	...
Beni-Suef	CDFC	171 734	87 105	84 629	...	...	...	...	...
CAIRO	CDFC	6 800 992	3 486 260	3 314 732	...	...	...	...	...

8. Population of capital cities and cities of 100 000 and more inhabitants: latest available year
Population des capitales et des villes de 100 000 habitants et plus: dernière année disponible (continued — suite)

(See notes at end of table. — Voir notes à la fin du tableau.)

Continent, country or area, date and city / Continent, pays ou zone, date et ville	Code[1]	City proper — Ville proprement dite Population				Urban agglomeration — Agglomération urbaine Population			
		Both sexes Les deux sexes	Male Masculin	Female Féminin	Surface area Superficie (km²)	Both sexes Les deux sexes	Male Masculin	Female Féminin	Surface area Superficie (km²)
AFRICA — AFRIQUE									
Egypt — Égypte									
1996									
Damanhûr	CDFC	209 423	107 965	101 458	...	...	...	...	...
El-Mahalla El-Kubra	CDFC	394 924	199 100	195 824	...	...	...	...	...
Faiyûm	CDFC	260 830	134 462	126 368	...	...	...	...	...
Giza	CDFC	2 221 817	1 139 665	1 082 152	...	...	...	...	...
Imbaba	CDFC	523 265	266 793	256 472	...	...	...	...	...
Ismailia	CDFC	255 134	129 004	126 130	...	...	...	...	...
Kafr-El-Dwar	CDFC	101 056	51 491	49 565	...	...	...	...	...
Kena	CDFC	155 382	79 038	76 344	...	...	...	...	...
Luxer	CDFC	153 758	79 753	74 005	...	...	...	...	...
Mansûra	CDFC	369 409	187 622	181 787	...	...	...	...	...
Menia	CDFC	201 440	103 428	98 012	...	...	...	...	...
Port Said	CDFC	472 335	242 502	229 833	...	...	...	...	...
Shebin-El-Kom	CDFC	156 794	79 868	76 926	...	...	...	...	...
Shubra-El-Khema	CDFC	870 776	449 271	421 505	...	...	...	...	...
Sohag	CDFC	170 417	85 918	84 499	...	...	...	...	...
Suez	CDFC	417 527	214 133	203 394	...	...	...	...	...
Tanta	CDFC	372 893	188 594	184 299	...	...	...	...	...
Zagazig	CDFC	267 469	136 094	131 375	...	...	...	...	...
Equatorial Guinea — Guinée équatoriale									
1983									
MALABO	CDFC	30 418	...	...	...	...	...	...	...
Eritrea — Érythrée									
1990									
ASMARA	ESDF	358 100	...	...	...	...	...	...	...
Ethiopia — Ethiopie									
2001									
ADDIS ABABA	ESDF	2 570 000	1 237 000	1 333 000	...	...	...	...	...
Bahir Dar	ESDF	134 062	69 588	64 474	28	...	...	...	...
Debre Zeit	ESDF	103 569	51 147	52 422	...	...	...	...	...
Dessie	ESDF	135 529	69 436	66 093	15	...	...	...	...
Dire Dawa	ESDF	227 494	114 125	113 369	18	...	...	...	...
Gondar	ESDF	156 087	78 670	77 417	40	...	...	...	...
Harar	ESDF	101 000	51 000	50 000	...	...	...	...	...
Jimma	ESDF	125 569	64 009	61 560	...	...	...	...	...
Mekele	ESDF	134 996	68 572	66 424	24	...	...	...	...
Nazareth	ESDF	180 537	90 403	90 134	...	...	...	...	...
Gabon									
1993									
LIBREVILLE	CDFC	362 386	184 192	178 194	...	418 616	212 383	206 233	...
Gambia — Gambie									
1993									
BANJUL[2]	CDFC	42 326	22 268	20 058	12	...	...	...	...
Ghana									
1984									
ACCRA[3]	CDFC	867 459	...	...	...	1 160 112	...	...	...
Kumasi	CDFC	376 246	...	...	...	489 586	...	...	...
Sekondi-Takoradi[4]	CDFC	93 400	...	...	...	178 257	...	...	...
Tamale	CDFC	135 952	...	...	...	167 778	...	...	...
Tema	CDFC	100 052	...	...	...	...	...	...	...
Guinea — Guinée									
1996									
CONAKRY	CDFC	1 091 500	...	...	...	...	...	...	...
Kankan	CDFC	...	...	...	...	261 341	...	...	...
Kindia	CDFC	...	...	...	...	287 607	...	...	...
Labé	CDFC	...	...	...	...	249 515	...	...	...
Nzérékoré	CDFC	...	...	...	...	282 772	...	...	...

8. Population of capital cities and cities of 100 000 and more inhabitants: latest available year
Population des capitales et des villes de 100 000 habitants et plus: dernière année disponible (continued — suite)

(See notes at end of table. — Voir notes à la fin du tableau.)

Continent, country or area, date and city / Continent, pays ou zone, date et ville	Code[1]	City proper — Ville proprement dite Population				Urban agglomeration — Agglomération urbaine Population			
		Both sexes Les deux sexes	Male Masculin	Female Féminin	Surface area Superficie (km²)	Both sexes Les deux sexes	Male Masculin	Female Féminin	Surface area Superficie (km²)
AFRICA — AFRIQUE									
Guinea-Bissau — Guinée-Bissau									
1991									
BISSAU	CDFC	197 600	...	...	...	...	...	...	...
Kenya									
1999									
Eldoret	CDFC	167 016	...	...	...	...	...	...	...
Kisumu	CDFC	322 734	...	...	...	...	...	...	...
Machakos	CDFC	144 109	...	...	...	...	...	...	...
Meru	CDFC	126 427	...	...	...	...	...	...	...
Mombasa	CDFC	665 018	...	...	...	...	...	...	...
NAIROBI	CDFC	2 143 254	...	...	...	...	...	...	...
Nakuru	CDFC	219 366	...	...	...	...	...	...	...
Lesotho									
1986									
MASERU	CDFC	109 382	...	...	...	...	...	...	...
Liberia — Libéria									
1984									
MONROVIA	CDFC	421 053	...	...	...	...	...	...	...
Libyan Arab Jamahiriya — Jamahiriya arabe libyenne									
1990									
Al Khums	ESDJ	*200 000*	...	...	...	...	...	...	...
BENGHAZI[5]	ESDJ	*800 000*	...	...	...	...	...	...	...
Misurata	ESDJ	*360 000*	...	...	...	...	...	...	...
Sebha	ESDJ	*150 000*	...	...	...	...	...	...	...
TRIPOLI[5]	ESDJ	*1 500 000*	...	...	...	...	...	...	...
Zuwarah	ESDJ	*280 000*	...	...	...	...	...	...	...
Madagascar									
1993									
ANTANANARIVO[6]	CDJC	710 236	346 073	364 163	72	...	...	...	...
Antsirabe	CDJC	126 062	62 288	63 774	112	...	...	...	...
Fianarantsoa	CDJC	109 260	52 757	56 504	85	...	...	...	...
Mahajanga	CDJC	106 780	52 711	54 068	14	...	...	...	...
Toamasina	CDJC	137 782	66 844	70 938	20	...	...	...	...
Malawi									
1998									
Blantyre-Limbe	CDFC	502 053	...	...	220	...	...	...	...
LILONGWE	CDFC	440 471	...	...	328	...	...	...	...
Mali									
1996									
BAMAKO	ESDJ	*809 552*	*388 775*	*420 777*	252	...	...	...	...
1998									
BAMAKO	CDJC	1 016 167	520 688	495 479	252	...	...	...	...
Mauritania — Mauritanie									
2000									
NOUAKCHOTT	CDFC	558 195	...	...	...	...	...	...	...
Mauritius — Maurice									
2000									
Beau Bassin - Rose Hill	ESDJ	102 770	51 258	51 512	20	...	...	...	...
PORT LOUIS	ESDJ	148 761	74 511	74 250	46	...	...	...	...
Vacoas - Phoenix	ESDJ	101 000	50 382	50 618	54	...	...	...	...
Morocco — Maroc									
1994									
Agadir	CDFC	155 244	...	...	...	...	...	...	...
Béni-Mellal	CDFC	140 212	...	...	...	...	...	...	...
Casablanca (Dar-el-Beida)	CDFC	2 765 931	...	...	...	...	...	...	...
El-Jadida	CDFC	119 083	...	...	...	...	...	...	...
Fès	CDFC	506 585	...	...	...	...	...	...	...
Kénitra	CDFC	292 627	...	...	...	...	...	...	...
Khouribga	CDFC	152 090	...	...	...	...	...	...	...
Ksar-el-Kebir	CDFC	107 065	...	...	...	...	...	...	...

(See notes at end of table. — Voir notes à la fin du tableau.)

Continent, country or area, date and city / Continent, pays ou zone, date et ville	Code[1]	City proper — Ville proprement dite Population				Urban agglomeration — Agglomération urbaine Population			
		Both sexes Les deux sexes	Male Masculin	Female Féminin	Surface area Superficie (km²)	Both sexes Les deux sexes	Male Masculin	Female Féminin	Surface area Superficie (km²)
AFRICA — AFRIQUE									
Morocco — Maroc									
1994									
Marrakech	CDFC	656 325	...	...	...	...	...	...	...
Meknès	CDFC	443 214	...	...	...	...	...	...	...
Mohammedia	CDFC	170 063	...	...	...	...	...	...	...
Nador	CDFC	112 450	...	...	...	...	...	...	...
Oujda	CDFC	351 878	...	...	...	...	...	...	...
RABAT[7]	CDFC	1 359 209	...	...	...	...	...	...	...
Safi	CDFC	262 276	...	...	...	...	...	...	...
Tanger	CDFC	497 147	...	...	...	...	...	...	...
Tétouan	CDFC	277 516	...	...	...	...	...	...	...
Mozambique									
1997									
Beira	CDFC	397 368	...	...	...	...	...	...	...
Chimoio	CDFC	171 056	...	...	...	...	...	...	...
MAPUTO	CDFC	966 837	...	...	...	1 391 499	...	...	...
Matola	CDFC	424 662	...	...	...	...	...	...	...
Mocuba	CDFC	124 650	...	...	...	...	...	...	...
Nacala	CDFC	158 248	...	...	...	...	...	...	...
Nampula	CDFC	303 346	...	...	...	...	...	...	...
Quelimane	CDFC	150 116	...	...	...	...	...	...	...
Tete	CDFC	101 984	...	...	...	...	...	...	...
Namibia — Namibie									
1991									
WINDHOEK	CDFC	147 056	...	...	...	...	...	...	...
Niger[8]									
1988									
Maradi	CDJC	110 739	54 355	56 384	...	...	...	...	...
NIAMEY	CDJC	397 437	203 172	194 265	...	...	...	...	...
Zinder	CDJC	120 160	60 936	59 224	...	...	...	...	...
Nigeria — Nigéria									
1991									
Aba	CDFC	500 183	...	...	...	...	...	...	...
Abeokuta	CDFC	352 735	...	...	...	...	...	...	...
ABUJA	CDFC	107 069	...	...	...	378 671	...	...	...
Ado-Ekiti	CDFC	156 122	...	...	...	...	...	...	...
Akure	CDFC	239 124	...	...	...	...	...	...	...
Awka	CDFC	104 682	...	...	...	...	...	...	...
Bauchi	CDFC	206 537	...	...	...	...	...	...	...
Benin City	CDFC	762 719	...	...	...	...	...	...	...
Bida	CDFC	111 245	...	...	...	...	...	...	...
Calabar	CDFC	310 839	...	...	...	...	...	...	...
Damaturu	CDFC	141 897	...	...	...	...	...	...	...
Ede	CDFC	142 363	...	...	...	...	...	...	...
Effon-Alaiye	CDFC	158 977	...	...	...	...	...	...	...
Enugu	CDFC	407 756	...	...	...	...	...	...	...
Gboko	CDFC	101 281	...	...	...	...	...	...	...
Gombe	CDFC	163 604	...	...	...	...	...	...	...
Gusau	CDFC	132 393	...	...	...	...	...	...	...
Ibadan	CDFC	1 835 300	...	...	...	...	...	...	...
Ife	CDFC	186 856	...	...	...	...	...	...	...
Ijebu-Ode	CDFC	124 313	...	...	...	...	...	...	...
Ikare	CDFC	103 843	...	...	...	...	...	...	...
Ikire	CDFC	111 435	...	...	...	...	...	...	...
Ikorodu	CDFC	184 674	...	...	...	...	...	...	...
Ikot Ekpene	CDFC	119 402	...	...	...	...	...	...	...
Ilawe-Ekiti	CDFC	104 049	...	...	...	...	...	...	...
Ilesha	CDFC	139 445	...	...	...	...	...	...	...
Ilorin	CDFC	532 089	...	...	...	...	...	...	...
Ise	CDFC	108 136	...	...	...	...	...	...	...
Iseyin	CDFC	170 936	...	...	...	...	...	...	...

(See notes at end of table. — Voir notes à la fin du tableau.)

Continent, country or area, date and city / Continent, pays ou zone, date et ville	Code[1]	City proper — Ville proprement dite Population				Urban agglomeration — Agglomération urbaine Population			
		Both sexes Les deux sexes	Male Masculin	Female Féminin	Surface area Superficie (km²)	Both sexes Les deux sexes	Male Masculin	Female Féminin	Surface area Superficie (km²)
AFRICA — AFRIQUE									
Nigeria — Nigéria									
1991									
Iwo	CDFC	125 645	...	...	...	...	...	...	...
Jimeta	CDFC	141 724	...	...	...	...	...	...	...
Jos	CDFC	510 300	...	...	...	...	...	...	...
Kaduna	CDFC	993 642	...	...	...	...	...	...	...
Kano	CDFC	2 166 554	...	...	...	...	...	...	...
Katsina	CDFC	259 315	...	...	...	...	...	...	...
Lagos	CDFC	5 195 247	...	...	...	...	...	...	...
Maiduguri	CDFC	618 278	...	...	...	...	...	...	...
Makurdi	CDFC	151 515	...	...	...	...	...	...	...
Minna	CDFC	189 191	...	...	...	...	...	...	...
Mubi	CDFC	128 900	...	...	...	...	...	...	...
Nnewi	CDFC	121 065	...	...	...	...	...	...	...
Ogbomosho	CDFC	433 030	...	...	...	...	...	...	...
Okene	CDFC	312 775	...	...	...	...	...	...	...
Okpogho	CDFC	105 127	...	...	...	...	...	...	...
Ondo	CDFC	146 051	...	...	...	...	...	...	...
Onitsha	CDFC	350 280	...	...	...	...	...	...	...
Oshogbo	CDFC	250 951	...	...	...	...	...	...	...
Owerri	CDFC	119 711	...	...	...	...	...	...	...
Owo	CDFC	157 181	...	...	...	...	...	...	...
Oyo	CDFC	369 894	...	...	...	...	...	...	...
Port Harcourt	CDFC	703 421	...	...	...	...	...	...	...
Sagamu	CDFC	127 513	...	...	...	...	...	...	...
Sango Otta	CDFC	103 332	...	...	...	...	...	...	...
Sapele	CDFC	109 576	...	...	...	...	...	...	...
Sokoto	CDFC	329 639	...	...	...	...	...	...	...
Suleja	CDFC	105 075	...	...	...	...	...	...	...
Ugep	CDFC	134 773	...	...	...	...	...	...	...
Umuahia	CDFC	147 167	...	...	...	...	...	...	...
Warri	CDFC	363 382	...	...	...	...	...	...	...
Zaria	CDFC	612 257	...	...	...	...	...	...	...
Réunion									
1999									
SAINT-DENIS[9]	CDFC	131 557	...	...	143	158 139	...	...	...
Saint-Pierre	CDFC	68 915	...	...	...	129 238	...	...	...
Rwanda									
1991									
KIGALI	CDJC	233 640	125 550	108 090	...	...	...	...	...
St. Helena ex. dep. — Sainte-Hélène sans dép.									
1998									
JAMESTOWN	CDFC	1 768	904	864	40	...	...	...	...
Sao Tome and Principe — Sao Tomé-et-Principe									
1991									
SAO TOME	CDJC	43 400	...	...	...	...	...	...	...
Senegal — Sénégal									
1999									
DAKAR	ESDF	879 703	...	...	500	1 976 533	...	...	...
Kaolack	ESDF	227 915	...	...	...	...	...	...	...
Mbour	ESDF	135 619	...	...	...	...	...	...	...
Pikine-Guediaway[10]	ESDF	1 096 830	...	...	...	...	...	...	...
Saint Louis	ESDF	147 961	...	...	...	...	...	...	...
Thiès	ESDF	256 113	...	...	...	...	...	...	...
Ziguinchor	ESDF	199 871	...	...	...	...	...	...	...
Seychelles									
1997									
VICTORIA	CDFC	...	...	...	...	24 701	...	...	...

(See notes at end of table. — Voir notes à la fin du tableau.)

Continent, country or area, date and city / Continent, pays ou zone, date et ville	Code[1]	City proper — Ville proprement dite Population				Urban agglomeration — Agglomération urbaine Population			
		Both sexes Les deux sexes	Male Masculin	Female Féminin	Surface area Superficie (km²)	Both sexes Les deux sexes	Male Masculin	Female Féminin	Surface area Superficie (km²)
AFRICA — AFRIQUE									
Sierra Leone									
1985									
FREETOWN	CDFC	469 776	...	...	...	...	...	...	...
Somalia — Somalie									
1972									
MOGADISHU	ESDF	*230 000*	...	...	...	...	...	...	...
South Africa — Afrique du Sud									
1996									
Alexandra	CDFC	171 284	...	...	...	...	...	...	...
Benoni	CDFC	366 343	...	...	...	...	...	...	...
Bloemfontein	CDFC	350 504	...	...	...	...	...	...	...
Boksburg	CDFC	263 179	...	...	...	...	...	...	...
Botshabelo	CDFC	177 971	...	...	...	...	...	...	...
CAPE TOWN[11]	CDFC	987 007	...	...	...	...	...	...	...
Durban	CDFC	669 242	...	...	...	...	...	...	...
Germiston	CDFC	164 252	...	...	...	...	...	...	...
Johannesburg	CDFC	752 349	...	...	...	...	...	...	...
Kathlehong	CDFC	344 803	...	...	...	...	...	...	...
Kempton Park	CDFC	344 426	...	...	...	...	...	...	...
Khayelitsa	CDFC	314 239	...	...	...	...	...	...	...
Kimberley	CDFC	206 070	...	...	...	...	...	...	...
Mangaung	CDFC	176 525	...	...	...	...	...	...	...
Pietermaritzburg	CDFC	405 385	...	...	...	...	...	...	...
Port Elizabeth	CDFC	775 255	...	...	...	...	...	...	...
PRETORIA[11]	CDFC	692 348	340 363	351 985	...	...	...	...	...
Roodepoort	CDFC	279 340	...	...	...	...	...	...	...
Soweto	CDFC	904 165	...	...	...	...	...	...	...
Springs	CDFC	163 304	...	...	...	...	...	...	...
Tembisa	CDFC	237 676	...	...	...	...	...	...	...
Umlazi	CDFC	339 715	...	...	...	...	...	...	...
Vereeniging	CDFC	379 638	...	...	...	...	...	...	...
Sudan — Soudan									
1993									
Al-Fasher	CDFC	141 884	...	...	...	...	...	...	...
Al-Gadarif	CDFC	191 164	...	...	...	...	...	...	...
Al-Gezira	CDFC	211 362	...	...	...	...	...	...	...
Al-Obeid	CDFC	229 425	...	...	...	...	...	...	...
Juba	CDFC	114 980	...	...	...	...	...	...	...
Kassala	CDFC	234 622	...	...	...	...	...	...	...
KHARTOUM	CDFC	947 483	...	...	...	2 919 773	...	...	...
Khartoum North	CDFC	700 887	...	...	...	...	...	...	...
Kosti	CDFC	173 599	...	...	...	...	...	...	...
Nyala	CDFC	227 183	...	...	...	...	...	...	...
Omdurman	CDFC	1 271 403	...	...	...	...	...	...	...
Port Sudan	CDFC	308 195	...	...	...	...	...	...	...
Swaziland									
1986									
MBABANE	CDFC	38 290	...	...	...	...	...	...	...
Togo									
1990									
LOME	ESDF	*450 000*	...	...	...	...	...	...	...
Tunisia — Tunisie									
1998									
Bizerte	ESDF	*105 520*	...	...	...	...	...	...	...
Gabes	ESDF	*104 950*	...	...	...	...	...	...	...
Kairouan	ESDF	*110 280*	...	...	...	...	...	...	...
Sfax	ESDF	*248 800*	...	...	...	...	...	...	...
TUNIS	ESDF	*702 330*	...	...	...	...	...	...	...
Uganda — Ouganda									
1991									
KAMPALA	CDFC	774 241	377 225	397 016	...	...	...	...	...

8. Population of capital cities and cities of 100 000 and more inhabitants: latest available year
Population des capitales et des villes de 100 000 habitants et plus: dernière année disponible (continued — suite)

(See notes at end of table. — Voir notes à la fin du tableau.)

Continent, country or area, date and city / Continent, pays ou zone, date et ville	Code[1]	City proper — Ville proprement dite Population				Urban agglomeration — Agglomération urbaine Population			
		Both sexes Les deux sexes	Male Masculin	Female Féminin	Surface area Superficie (km²)	Both sexes Les deux sexes	Male Masculin	Female Féminin	Surface area Superficie (km²)
AFRICA — AFRIQUE									
Uganda — Ouganda									
2002									
Gulu	CDFC	113 144	...	...	...	...	...	...	...
KAMPALA	CDFC	1 208 544	588 433	620 111	...	...	...	...	...
United Republic of Tanzania — République Unie de Tanzanie									
1988									
Arusha	CDFC	134 708	69 875	64 833	...	...	...	...	...
Dar es Salaam	CDFC	1 360 850	715 925	644 925	...	...	...	...	...
DODOMA	CDFC	203 833	101 437	102 396	...	...	...	...	...
Mbeya	CDFC	152 844	74 259	78 585	...	...	...	...	...
Morogoro	CDFC	117 760	59 144	58 616	...	...	...	...	...
Mwanza	CDFC	223 013	113 779	109 234	...	...	...	...	...
Shinyanga	CDFC	100 724	50 117	50 607	...	...	...	...	...
Tanga	CDFC	187 455	96 259	91 196	...	...	...	...	...
Zanzibar	CDFC	157 634	77 787	79 847	...	...	...	...	...
Western Sahara — Sahara occidental									
1974									
EL AAIUN	CDFC	20 010	...	...	...	...	...	...	...
Zambia — Zambie									
1999									
Chingola	ESDF	*211 755*	*108 236*	*103 519*	...	...	...	...	...
Kabwe	ESDF	*233 197*	*120 476*	*112 721*	...	...	...	...	...
Kitwe	ESDF	*467 084*	*244 865*	*222 219*	...	...	...	...	...
Luanshya	ESDF	*186 372*	*98 614*	*87 758*	...	...	...	...	...
LUSAKA	ESDF	*1 269 848*	*638 918*	*630 930*	...	...	...	...	...
Mufulira	ESDF	*204 104*	*107 080*	*97 024*	...	...	...	...	...
Ndola	ESDF	*441 624*	*231 511*	*210 113*	...	...	...	...	...
Zimbabwe									
1992									
Bulawayo	CDFC	621 742	309 864	311 878	479	...	...	...	...
Chitungwiza	CDFC	274 912	137 890	137 022	...	...	...	...	...
Gweru	CDFC	128 037	64 472	63 565	...	...	...	...	...
HARARE	CDFC	1 189 103	623 345	565 758	872	...	...	...	...
Mutare	CDFC	131 367	68 413	62 954	...	...	...	...	...
AMERICA, NORTH — AMERIQUE DU NORD									
Anguilla									
2001									
THE VALLEY	CDJC	1 169	...	...	...	...	...	...	...
Antigua and Barbuda — Antigua-et-Barbuda									
1991									
ST. JOHN	CDFC	22 342	...	...	...	...	...	...	...
Aruba									
1991									
ORANJESTAD	CDFC	20 045	9 441	10 604	...	...	...	...	...
Bahamas									
2000									
NASSAU	CDFC	...	...	...	...	210 832	...	...	...
Barbados — Barbade									
1980									
BRIDGETOWN	CDFC	7 466	...	...	...	...	...	...	...
Belize									
2000									
BELMOPAN	ESDF	*8 305*	*4 050*	*4 255*	...	...	...	...	...
Bermuda — Bermudes[12]									
1991									
HAMILTON	CDJC	1 100	...	...	...	...	...	...	...

(See notes at end of table. — Voir notes à la fin du tableau.)

Continent, country or area, date and city / Continent, pays ou zone, date et ville	Code[1]	City proper — Ville proprement dite Population				Urban agglomeration — Agglomération urbaine Population			
		Both sexes Les deux sexes	Male Masculin	Female Féminin	Surface area Superficie (km²)	Both sexes Les deux sexes	Male Masculin	Female Féminin	Surface area Superficie (km²)
AMERICA, NORTH — AMERIQUE DU NORD									
British Virgin Islands — Iles Vierges britanniques									
1992									
ROAD TOWN	ESDF	*3 500*	...	...	...	...	...	...	...
Canada[13]									
1996									
Abbotsford	CDJC	105 403	52 190	53 210	344	136 480	67 990	68 490	610
Barrie	CDJC	79 191	38 445	40 745	77	118 695	58 170	60 525	897
Brampton	CDJC	268 251	133 355	134 895	265	...	...	...	...
Brantford	CDJC	84 764	40 775	43 985	71	100 238	48 415	51 825	324
Burlington	CDJC	136 976	66 510	70 460	177	...	...	...	...
Burnaby	CDJC	179 209	88 000	91 205	88	...	...	...	...
Calgary	CDJC	768 082	382 065	386 015	717	845 493	424 359	421 134	5 083
Cambridge	CDJC	101 429	49 815	51 615	116	...	...	...	...
Cape Breton	CDJC	114 733	54 900	59 830	2 460	117 849	56 450	61 400	2 473
Chicoutimi-Jonquière	CDJC	119 564	58 325	61 235	366	162 949	80 900	82 049	1 723
Coquitlam	CDJC	101 820	50 495	51 325	123	...	...	...	...
East York	CDJC	107 822	50 330	57 490	21	...	...	...	...
Edmonton	CDJC	616 306	302 760	313 545	670	885 123	441 328	443 795	9 537
Etobicoke	CDJC	328 718	158 490	170 225	124	...	...	...	...
Gatineau	CDJC	100 702	49 465	51 235	141	...	...	...	...
Gloucester	CDJC	104 022	51 015	53 005	294	...	...	...	...
Guelph	CDJC	95 821	46 785	49 040	87	105 420	51 720	53 700	391
Halifax	CDJC	113 910	53 195	60 715	79	341 463	166 590	174 873	2 503
Hamilton	CDJC	322 352	156 085	166 265	123	642 729	315 374	327 355	1 359
Kelowna	CDJC	89 442	42 985	46 455	213	136 541	66 435	70 105	3 007
Kingston	CDJC	99 703	47 735	51 965	239	143 416	70 605	72 815	1 629
Kitchener	CDJC	178 420	87 560	90 860	135	395 208	195 741	199 467	824
Laval	CDJC	330 393	161 500	168 895	245	...	...	...	...
London	CDJC	325 646	156 740	168 910	438	410 407	200 084	210 323	2 105
Longueuil	CDJC	127 977	61 645	66 330	43	...	...	...	...
Markham	CDJC	173 383	85 145	88 240	212	...	...	...	...
Mississauga	CDJC	544 382	268 205	276 180	274	...	...	...	...
Moncton	CDJC	67 982	32 445	35 540	746	113 491	55 060	58 430	2 153
Montréal	CDJC	1 016 376	489 035	527 340	177	3 393 739	1 657 540	1 736 199	4 024
Nepean	CDJC	115 100	56 445	58 660	217	...	...	...	...
North York	CDJC	589 653	280 980	308 675	177	...	...	...	...
Oakville	CDJC	128 405	63 120	65 285	138	...	...	...	...
Oshawa	CDJC	134 364	65 835	68 530	143	277 073	137 669	139 404	894
OTTAWA	CDJC	323 340	154 800	168 540	110	1 037 853	511 024	526 829	5 686
Peterborough	CDJC	69 535	32 445	37 090	54	100 193	47 755	52 440	1 164
Québec	CDJC	167 264	78 735	88 530	89	683 741	332 345	351 396	3 150
Regina	CDJC	180 400	87 115	93 290	114	199 527	97 507	102 020	3 422
Richmond	CDJC	148 867	72 340	76 525	124	...	...	...	...
Richmond Hill	CDJC	101 725	49 840	51 880	99	...	...	...	...
Saanich	CDJC	101 388	48 635	52 755	103	...	...	...	...
St. Catharines	CDJC	130 926	62 730	68 195	94	382 813	186 934	195 879	1 400
St. John's	CDJC	101 936	48 240	53 695	432	177 054	86 104	90 950	324
Saint John	CDJC	72 494	34 040	38 455	323	128 029	62 433	65 596	3 509
Saskatoon	CDJC	193 647	93 435	100 215	137	225 963	110 526	115 437	5 322
Scarborough	CDJC	558 960	269 110	289 850	188	...	...	...	...
Sherbrooke	CDJC	76 786	35 810	40 975	58	150 098	72 855	77 243	980
Sudbury	CDJC	92 059	44 125	47 935	263	165 009	81 500	83 509	2 612
Surrey	CDJC	304 477	151 810	152 665	302	...	...	...	...
Thunder Bay	CDJC	113 662	55 580	58 080	323	129 089	63 935	65 154	2 295
Toronto	CDJC	653 734	319 490	334 245	97	4 403 092	2 161 726	2 241 366	5 868
Trois-Rivières	CDJC	48 419	22 640	25 780	78	142 234	69 047	73 187	872
Vancouver	CDJC	514 008	252 990	261 020	113	1 912 120	948 827	963 293	2 821
Vaughan	CDJC	132 549	65 920	66 625	275	...	...	...	...

8. Population of capital cities and cities of 100 000 and more inhabitants: latest available year
Population des capitales et des villes de 100 000 habitants et plus: dernière année disponible (continued — suite)

(See notes at end of table. — Voir notes à la fin du tableau.)

Continent, country or area, date and city / Continent, pays ou zone, date et ville	Code[1]	City proper — Ville proprement dite Population				Urban agglomeration — Agglomération urbaine Population			
		Both sexes Les deux sexes	Male Masculin	Female Féminin	Surface area Superficie (km²)	Both sexes Les deux sexes	Male Masculin	Female Féminin	Surface area Superficie (km²)
AMERICA, NORTH — AMERIQUE DU NORD									
Canada[13]									
1996									
Victoria	CDJC	73 504	33 770	39 730	19	316 828	152 701	164 127	633
Windsor	CDJC	197 694	95 635	102 060	120	287 486	141 375	146 111	862
Winnipeg	CDJC	618 477	298 390	320 085	464	679 174	332 173	347 001	4 078
York	CDJC	146 534	69 290	77 250	23	...	...	...	...
2002									
Calgary	ESDJ	...	...	...	...	993 182	498 990	494 192	5 083
Chicoutimi-Jonquière	ESDJ	...	...	...	...	156 942	77 702	79 240	1 723
Edmonton	ESDJ	...	...	...	...	967 166	483 891	483 275	9 537
Halifax	ESDJ	...	...	...	...	363 211	177 158	186 053	2 503
Hamilton	ESDJ	...	...	...	...	686 882	337 132	349 750	1 359
Kitchener	ESDJ	...	...	...	...	437 952	218 072	219 880	824
London	ESDJ	...	...	...	...	427 296	208 700	218 596	2 105
Montréal	ESDJ	...	...	...	...	3 548 775	1 738 355	1 810 420	4 024
Oshawa	ESDJ	...	...	...	...	310 027	153 673	156 354	894
OTTAWA	ESDJ	...	...	...	...	1 128 914	557 231	571 683	5 686
Québec	ESDJ	...	...	...	...	697 753	339 467	358 286	3 150
Regina	ESDJ	...	...	...	...	197 027	95 823	101 204	3 422
St. John's	ESDJ	...	...	...	...	177 235	85 789	91 446	790
Saint John	ESDJ	...	...	...	...	126 958	61 545	65 413	3 509
Saskatoon	ESDJ	...	...	...	...	231 834	113 616	118 218	5 322
Sherbrooke	ESDJ	...	...	...	...	156 519	76 414	80 105	980
Sudbury	ESDJ	...	...	...	...	155 947	76 639	79 308	2 612
Thunder Bay	ESDJ	...	...	...	...	125 109	61 862	63 247	2 295
Toronto	ESDJ	...	...	...	...	5 029 855	2 478 517	2 551 338	5 868
Trois-Rivières	ESDJ	...	...	...	...	141 360	68 657	72 703	872
Vancouver	ESDJ	...	...	...	...	2 122 684	1 049 597	1 073 087	2 821
Victoria	ESDJ	...	...	...	...	318 864	153 857	165 007	633
Windsor	ESDJ	...	...	...	...	319 873	159 019	160 854	862
Winnipeg	ESDJ	...	...	...	...	685 507	336 204	349 303	4 078
Cayman Islands — Iles Caïmanes									
1989									
GEORGE TOWN	CDFC	12 921	...	...	...	...	...	...	...
1999									
GEORGE TOWN	CDFC	20 626	...	...	...	...	...	...	...
Costa Rica									
2000									
Alajuela	CDJC	222 853	111 649	111 204	388	...	...	...	...
Cartago	CDJC	132 057	65 418	66 639	288	...	...	...	...
Heredia	CDJC	103 894	50 241	53 653	...	...	...	...	...
Puntarenas	CDJC	102 504	52 248	50 256	1 842	...	...	...	...
SAN JOSE[14]	CDJC	309 672	149 647	160 025	45	1 345 750	656 205	689 545	4 966
Cuba									
2000									
Bayamo	ESDF	143 700	...	...	...	...	...	...	...
Camagüey	ESDF	308 288	...	...	...	...	...	...	...
Ciego de Avila	ESDF	103 350	...	...	...	...	...	...	...
Cienfuegos	ESDF	138 965	...	...	...	...	...	...	...
Guantánamo	ESDF	209 269	...	...	...	...	...	...	...
Holguín	ESDF	262 100	...	...	...	...	...	...	...
LA HABANA	ESDF	2 186 632	...	...	727	...	...	...	...
Las Tunas	ESDF	139 051	...	...	...	...	...	...	...
Matanzas	ESDF	125 466	...	...	...	...	...	...	...
Pinar del Río	ESDF	148 300	...	...	...	...	...	...	...
Sancti Spíritus	ESDF	105 568	...	...	...	...	...	...	...
Santa Clara	ESDF	210 568	...	...	...	...	...	...	...
Santiago de Cuba	ESDF	443 064	...	...	...	...	...	...	...

8. Population of capital cities and cities of 100 000 and more inhabitants: latest available year
Population des capitales et des villes de 100 000 habitants et plus: dernière année disponible (continued — suite)

(See notes at end of table. — Voir notes à la fin du tableau.)

Continent, country or area, date and city / Continent, pays ou zone, date et ville	Code[1]	City proper — Ville proprement dite Population				Urban agglomeration — Agglomération urbaine Population			
		Both sexes Les deux sexes	Male Masculin	Female Féminin	Surface area Superficie (km²)	Both sexes Les deux sexes	Male Masculin	Female Féminin	Surface area Superficie (km²)
AMERICA, NORTH — AMERIQUE DU NORD									
Dominica — Dominique									
1991									
ROSEAU	CDFC	16 243	...	...	...	...	...	...	...
Dominican Republic — République dominicaine									
2001									
San Pedro de Macoris	ESDF	266 629	...	...	...	...	...	...	...
Santiago de los Caballeros	ESDF	836 614	...	...	...	...	...	...	...
SANTO DOMINGO	ESDF	2 677 056	...	...	...	...	...	...	...
El Salvador[15]									
2000									
Ahuachapan	ESDF	107 533	...	...	245	...	...	...	...
Apopa	ESDF	171 833	...	...	52	...	...	...	...
Ciudad Delgado	ESDF	153 350	...	...	33	...	...	...	...
Ilopango	ESDF	132 231	...	...	35	...	...	...	...
Mejicanos	ESDF	189 392	...	...	22	...	...	...	...
Nueva San Salvador	ESDF	158 206	...	...	112	...	...	...	...
SAN SALVADOR	ESDF	479 605	...	...	72	1 959 036	...	...	543
San Miguel	ESDF	239 037	...	...	594	...	...	...	...
Santa Ana	ESDF	248 964	...	...	400	...	...	...	...
Soyapango	ESDF	285 286	...	...	30	...	...	...	...
Greenland — Groenland									
2000									
NUUK (GODTHAB)	ESDJ	13 552	7 265	6 287	...	...	...	...	...
Grenada — Grenade									
1981									
ST. GEORGE'S	CDFC	4 788	...	...	...	...	...	...	...
Guadeloupe									
1999									
BASSE-TERRE	CDJC	...	...	...	...	44 864	...	...	...
Pointe-à-Pitre	CDJC	...	...	...	...	171 773	...	...	...
Guatemala									
2001									
GUATEMALA	ESDF	1 022 001	491 891	530 110	228	...	...	...	...
Escuintla	ESDF	114 626	57 893	56 733	332	...	...	...	...
Mixco	ESDF	452 134	221 928	230 206	99	...	...	...	...
Quetzaltenango	ESDF	152 223	76 272	75 951	120	...	...	...	...
Villa Nueva	ESDF	390 329	192 238	198 091	114	...	...	...	...
Haiti — Haïti									
1999									
Cap-Haitien	ESDJ	113 555	50 064	63 491	10	...	...	...	...
Carrefour	ESDJ	336 222	146 838	189 384	23	...	...	...	...
Delmas	ESDJ	284 079	124 774	159 305	26	...	...	...	...
PORT-AU-PRINCE	ESDJ	990 558	436 170	554 388	21	...	...	...	...
Honduras									
2001									
Choloma	CDJC	126 402	59 834	66 568	...	...	...	...	...
La Ceiba	CDJC	126 721	60 313	66 408	...	...	...	...	...
San Pedro Sula	CDJC	483 384	230 662	252 722	...	...	...	...	...
TEGUCIGALPA	CDJC	819 867	385 110	434 757	...	...	...	...	...
Jamaica — Jamaïque									
1991									
KINGSTON	CDFC	103 962	...	...	22	538 144	250 369	287 775	...
Martinique									
1999									
FORT-DE-FRANCE	CDJC	94 049	...	...	...	134 727	...	...	...
Mexico — Mexique									
2000									
Acapulco (de Juárez)	CDJC	620 656	297 398	323 258	...	...	...	...	...

8. Population of capital cities and cities of 100 000 and more inhabitants: latest available year
Population des capitales et des villes de 100 000 habitants et plus: dernière année disponible (continued — suite)

(See notes at end of table. — Voir notes à la fin du tableau.)

Continent, country or area, date and city / Continent, pays ou zone, date et ville	Code[1]	City proper — Ville proprement dite Population				Urban agglomeration — Agglomération urbaine Population			
		Both sexes Les deux sexes	Male Masculin	Female Féminin	Surface area Superficie (km²)	Both sexes Les deux sexes	Male Masculin	Female Féminin	Surface area Superficie (km²)
AMERICA, NORTH — AMERIQUE DU NORD									
Mexico — Mexique									
2000									
Aguascalientes	CDJC	594 092	286 074	308 018	...	...	...	...	...
Alvaro Obregon	CDJC	686 807	327 321	359 486	...	...	...	...	...
Azcapotzalco	CDJC	441 008	210 101	230 907	...	...	...	...	...
Benito Juárez	CDJC	360 478	160 409	200 069	...	...	...	...	...
Buenavista	CDJC	193 707	95 741	97 966	...	...	...	...	...
Campeche	CDJC	190 813	91 742	99 071	...	...	...	...	...
Cancun	CDJC	397 191	203 471	193 720	...	...	...	...	...
Celaya	CDJC	277 750	132 820	144 930	...	...	...	...	...
Chalco de Diaz Covarrubias	CDJC	125 027	61 946	63 081	...	...	...	...	...
Chetumal	CDJC	121 602	59 500	62 102	...	...	...	...	...
Chihuahua	CDJC	657 876	318 929	338 947	...	...	...	...	...
Chilpacingo (de los Bravo)	CDJC	142 746	67 790	74 956	...	...	...	...	...
Chimalhuacan	CDJC	482 530	239 285	243 245	...	...	...	...	...
Ciudad Acuña	CDJC	108 159	55 310	52 849	...	...	...	...	...
Ciudad Apodaca	CDJC	270 369	135 776	134 593	...	...	...	...	...
Ciudad Del Carmen	CDJC	126 024	62 398	63 626	...	...	...	...	...
Ciudad General Escobedo	CDJC	230 556	116 254	114 302	...	...	...	...	...
Ciudad Juárez	CDJC	1 187 275	596 584	590 691	...	...	...	...	...
Ciudad López Mateos	CDJC	467 544	228 449	239 095	...	...	...	...	...
Ciudad Madero	CDJC	182 325	86 944	95 381	...	...	...	...	...
Ciudad Obregón	CDJC	250 790	122 250	128 540	...	...	...	...	...
Ciudad Santa Catarina	CDJC	225 976	112 850	113 126	...	...	...	...	...
Ciudad Valles	CDJC	105 721	50 211	55 510	...	...	...	...	...
Ciudad Victoria	CDJC	249 029	120 978	128 051	...	...	...	...	...
Coatzacoalcos	CDJC	225 973	108 270	117 703	...	...	...	...	...
Colimas	CDJC	119 639	57 899	61 740	...	...	...	...	...
Córdoba	CDJC	133 807	62 024	71 783	...	...	...	...	...
Coyoacan	CDJC	640 423	300 429	339 994	...	...	...	...	...
Cuajimalpa de Morelos	CDJC	132 605	62 683	69 922	...	...	...	...	...
Cuauhtemoc	CDJC	516 255	241 750	274 505	...	...	...	...	...
Cuautitlan Izcalli	CDJC	433 830	211 991	221 839	...	...	...	...	...
Cuautla	CDJC	136 932	65 114	71 818	...	...	...	...	...
Cuernavaca	CDJC	327 162	155 030	172 132	...	...	...	...	...
Culiacán Rosales	CDJC	540 823	262 372	278 451	...	...	...	...	...
Durango (Victoria de Durango)	CDJC	427 135	205 006	222 129	...	...	...	...	...
Ecatepec (de Morelos)	CDJC	1 621 827	797 461	824 366	...	...	...	...	...
Ensenada	CDJC	223 492	110 534	112 958	...	...	...	...	...
Gómez Palacio	CDJC	210 113	102 576	107 537	...	...	...	...	...
Guadalajara	CDJC	1 646 183	788 174	858 009	...	...	...	...	...
Guadalupe	CDJC	669 842	332 809	337 033	...	...	...	...	...
Gustavo A. Madero	CDJC	1 235 542	595 133	640 409	...	...	...	...	...
Hermosillo	CDJC	545 928	269 701	276 227	...	...	...	...	...
Iguala (de la Independencia)	CDJC	104 759	49 675	55 084	...	...	...	...	...
Irapuato	CDJC	319 148	153 229	165 919	...	...	...	...	...
Ixtapaluca	CDJC	235 827	115 981	119 846	...	...	...	...	...
Iztacalco	CDJC	553 780	264 453	289 327	...	...	...	...	...
Iztapalapa	CDJC	1 773 343	864 239	909 104	...	...	...	...	...
La Magdalena Contreras	CDJC	221 645	106 264	115 381	...	...	...	...	...
La Paz	CDJC	162 954	80 946	82 008	...	...	...	...	...
León (de los Aldama)	CDJC	1 020 818	497 863	522 955	...	...	...	...	...
Los Mochis	CDJC	200 906	96 933	103 973	...	...	...	...	...
Los Reyes Acaquilpan	CDJC	211 298	104 025	107 273	...	...	...	...	...
Matamoros	CDJC	376 279	184 173	192 106	...	...	...	...	...
Mazatlán	CDJC	327 989	159 941	168 048	...	...	...	...	...
Mérida	CDJC	662 530	317 826	344 704	...	...	...	...	...
Metepec	CDJC	158 695	76 336	82 359	...	...	...	...	...
Mexicali	CDJC	549 873	274 649	275 224	...	...	...	...	...

8. Population of capital cities and cities of 100 000 and more inhabitants: latest available year
Population des capitales et des villes de 100 000 habitants et plus: dernière année disponible (continued — suite)

(See notes at end of table. — Voir notes à la fin du tableau.)

Continent, country or area, date and city Continent, pays ou zone, date et ville	Code[1]	City proper — Ville proprement dite Population				Urban agglomeration — Agglomération urbaine Population			
		Both sexes Les deux sexes	Male Masculin	Female Féminin	Surface area Superficie (km²)	Both sexes Les deux sexes	Male Masculin	Female Féminin	Surface area Superficie (km²)
AMERICA, NORTH — AMERIQUE DU NORD									
Mexico — Mexique									
2000									
MEXICO, CIUDAD DE	CDJC	8 605 239	4 110 485	4 494 754	...	...	...	...	...
Miguel Hidalgo	CDJC	352 640	160 132	192 508	...	...	...	...	...
Minatitlán	CDJC	109 193	51 517	57 676	...	...	...	...	...
Monclova	CDJC	192 554	95 214	97 340	...	...	...	...	...
Monterrey	CDJC	1 110 909	547 567	563 342	...	...	...	...	...
Morelia	CDJC	549 996	261 973	288 023	...	...	...	...	...
Naucalpan de Juárez	CDJC	835 053	404 275	430 778	...	...	...	...	...
Naucalpan de Juárez (Huixquilucan)	CDJC	107 951	49 736	58 215	...	...	...	...	...
Netzahualcóyotl	CDJC	1 225 083	594 809	630 274	...	...	...	...	...
Nogales	CDJC	156 854	79 540	77 314	...	...	...	...	...
Nuevo Laredo	CDJC	308 828	153 920	154 908	...	...	...	...	...
Oaxaca de Juárez	CDJC	251 846	117 309	134 537	...	...	...	...	...
Orizaba	CDJC	118 552	55 183	63 369	...	...	...	...	...
Pachuca (de Soto)	CDJC	231 602	110 197	121 405	...	...	...	...	...
Piedras Negras	CDJC	126 386	62 399	63 987	...	...	...	...	...
Poza Rica de Hidalgo	CDJC	151 441	70 397	81 044	...	...	...	...	...
Puebla de Zaragoza	CDJC	1 271 673	607 507	664 166	...	...	...	...	...
Puerto Vallarta	CDJC	151 432	75 845	75 587	...	...	...	...	...
Querétaro	CDJC	536 463	258 418	278 045	...	...	...	...	...
Reynosa	CDJC	403 718	199 414	204 304	...	...	...	...	...
Salamanca	CDJC	137 000	66 062	70 938	...	...	...	...	...
Saltillo	CDJC	562 587	278 785	283 802	...	...	...	...	...
San Cristobal de las Casas	CDJC	112 442	53 938	58 504	...	...	...	...	...
San Francisco Coacalco	CDJC	252 291	122 775	129 516	...	...	...	...	...
San Luis Potosí	CDJC	629 208	299 686	329 522	...	...	...	...	...
San Luis Rio Colorado	CDJC	126 645	63 323	63 322	...	...	...	...	...
San Nicolas de los Garza	CDJC	496 878	246 483	250 395	...	...	...	...	...
San Pablo de las Salinas	CDJC	146 560	71 628	74 932	...	...	...	...	...
San Pedro Garza Garcia	CDJC	125 945	58 363	67 582	...	...	...	...	...
Soledad de Graciano Sanchez	CDJC	169 574	81 932	87 642	...	...	...	...	...
Tampico	CDJC	295 442	141 046	154 396	...	...	...	...	...
Tapachula (de Cordova y Ordoñez)	CDJC	179 839	85 062	94 777	...	...	...	...	...
Tehuacán	CDJC	204 598	97 612	106 986	...	...	...	...	...
Tepic	CDJC	265 817	127 632	138 185	...	...	...	...	...
Texcoco de Mora	CDJC	101 711	50 447	51 264	...	...	...	...	...
Tijuana	CDJC	1 148 681	579 014	569 667	...	...	...	...	...
Tlahuac	CDJC	257 092	124 846	132 246	...	...	...	...	...
Tlalnepantla	CDJC	714 735	346 784	367 951	...	...	...	...	...
Tlalpan	CDJC	534 905	256 927	277 978	...	...	...	...	...
Tlaquepaque	CDJC	458 674	226 614	232 060	...	...	...	...	...
Toluca (de Lerdo)	CDJC	435 125	207 566	227 559	...	...	...	...	...
Tonala	CDJC	315 278	156 300	158 978	...	...	...	...	...
Torreón	CDJC	502 964	244 067	258 897	...	...	...	...	...
Tuxtla Gutiérrez	CDJC	424 579	203 912	220 667	...	...	...	...	...
Uruapan	CDJC	225 816	108 433	117 383	...	...	...	...	...
Venustiano Carranza	CDJC	462 806	219 200	243 606	...	...	...	...	...
Veracruz	CDJC	411 582	193 271	218 311	...	...	...	...	...
Veracruz (Boca del Rio)	CDJC	123 891	57 856	66 035	...	...	...	...	...
Villa Nicolas Romero	CDJC	216 192	106 837	109 355	...	...	...	...	...
Villahermosa	CDJC	330 846	157 818	173 028	...	...	...	...	...
Xalapa-Enriquez	CDJC	373 076	172 799	200 277	...	...	...	...	...
Xico	CDJC	322 784	160 613	162 171	...	...	...	...	...
Xochimilco	CDJC	364 647	179 268	185 379	...	...	...	...	...
Zacatecas	CDJC	113 947	54 285	59 662	...	...	...	...	...
Zamora de Hidalgo	CDJC	122 881	58 951	63 930	...	...	...	...	...

8. Population of capital cities and cities of 100 000 and more inhabitants: latest available year
Population des capitales et des villes de 100 000 habitants et plus: dernière année disponible (continued — suite)

(See notes at end of table. — Voir notes à la fin du tableau.)

Continent, country or area, date and city / Continent, pays ou zone, date et ville	Code[1]	City proper — Ville proprement dite Population				Urban agglomeration — Agglomération urbaine Population			
		Both sexes Les deux sexes	Male Masculin	Female Féminin	Surface area Superficie (km²)	Both sexes Les deux sexes	Male Masculin	Female Féminin	Surface area Superficie (km²)
AMERICA, NORTH — AMERIQUE DU NORD									
Mexico — Mexique									
2000									
Zapopan	CDJC	910 690	442 244	468 446	...	...	...	...	...
Montserrat									
1980									
PLYMOUTH	CDFC	1 478	...	...	...	...	...	...	...
Netherlands Antilles — Antilles néerlandaises									
1992									
WILLEMSTAD	CDJC	2 345	...	...	...	...	...	...	...
Nicaragua									
2000									
Chinandega	ESDF	...	...	...	...	247 336	121 653	125 683	...
Granada	ESDF	...	...	...	...	115 315	56 191	59 124	...
Leon	ESDF	...	...	...	...	216 695	104 524	112 171	...
MANAGUA	ESDF	...	...	...	...	1 147 730	555 720	592 010	...
Masaya	ESDF	...	...	...	...	170 683	83 729	86 954	...
Panama									
2000									
PANAMA[16]	ESDF	484 261	230 747	253 514	107	...	...	...	...
San Miguelito	ESDF	331 692	161 901	169 791	50	...	...	...	...
Puerto Rico — Porto Rico[17]									
2000									
Arecibo	CDJC	100 131	48 545	51 586	326	...	...	...	...
Bayamón	CDJC	224 044	107 504	116 540	115	...	...	...	...
Caguas	CDJC	140 502	66 396	74 106	152	...	...	...	...
Carolina	CDJC	186 076	86 680	99 396	117	...	...	...	...
Guaynabo	CDJC	100 053	47 857	52 196	70	...	...	...	...
Ponce[18]	CDJC	186 475	89 941	96 534	297	...	...	...	...
SAN JUAN[19]	CDJC	434 374	199 785	234 589	124	...	...	...	...
Saint Kitts-Nevis — Saint-Kitts-et-Nevis									
1980									
BASSETERRE	CDFC	14 161	...	...	...	...	...	...	...
Saint Lucia — Sainte-Lucie									
1998									
CASTRIES	ESDF	2 301	...	...	...	...	...	...	...
Saint Pierre and Miquelon — Saint Pierre-et-Miquelon									
1999									
SAINT-PIERRE	CDFC	5 618	...	...	...	...	...	...	...
Saint Vincent and the Grenadines — Saint Vincent-et-les Grenadines									
1991									
KINGSTOWN	CDFC	15 466	...	...	...	...	...	...	...
Trinidad and Tobago — Trinité-et-Tobago									
1996									
PORT-OF-SPAIN	ESDF	43 396	20 739	22 657	12	...	...	...	...
Turks and Caicos Islands — Iles Turques et Caïques									
1990									
GRAND TURK	CDFC	3 691	...	...	...	...	...	...	...
United States — Etats-Unis[20]									
2000									
Abilene (TX)	CDJC	115 930	...	...	272	126 555	...	...	2 372
Akron (OH)[21]	CDJC	217 074	...	...	161	...	...	...	...
Albuquerque (NM)	CDJC	448 607	...	...	468	712 738	...	...	15 394
Alexandria (VA)[22]	CDJC	128 283	...	...	39	...	...	...	...

8. Population of capital cities and cities of 100 000 and more inhabitants: latest available year
Population des capitales et des villes de 100 000 habitants et plus: dernière année disponible (continued — suite)

(See notes at end of table. — Voir notes à la fin du tableau.)

Continent, country or area, date and city / Continent, pays ou zone, date et ville	Code[1]	City proper — Ville proprement dite Population				Urban agglomeration — Agglomération urbaine Population			
		Both sexes Les deux sexes	Male Masculin	Female Féminin	Surface area Superficie (km²)	Both sexes Les deux sexes	Male Masculin	Female Féminin	Surface area Superficie (km²)
AMERICA, NORTH — AMERIQUE DU NORD									
United States — Etats-Unis[20]									
2000									
Allentown (PA)[23]	CDJC	106 632	...	...	46	637 958	...	...	2 857
Amarillo (TX)	CDJC	173 627	...	...	2 337	217 858	...	...	4 724
Anaheim (CA)[24]	CDJC	328 014	...	...	12	...	...	...	...
Anchorage (AK)	CDJC	260 283	...	...	4 396	260 283	...	...	4 397
Ann Arbor (MI)[25]	CDJC	114 024	...	...	70	...	...	...	...
Arlington (TX)[26]	CDJC	332 969	...	...	248	...	...	...	...
Arlington (VA)[22]	CDJC	189 453	...	...	67	...	...	...	...
Arvada (CO)	CDJC	102 153	...	...	85	...	...	...	...
Athens (GA)	CDJC	100 266	...	...	305	153 444	...	...	1 531
Atlanta (GA)	CDJC	416 474	...	...	341	4 112 198	...	...	15 867
Augusta (GA)	CDJC	195 182	...	...	783	477 441	...	...	6 343
Aurora (CO)[27]	CDJC	276 393	...	...	369	...	...	...	...
Aurora (IL)[28]	CDJC	142 990	...	...	100	...	...	...	...
Austin (TX)	CDJC	656 562	...	...	651	1 249 763	...	...	10 945
Bakersfield (CA)	CDJC	247 057	...	...	293	661 645	...	...	21 087
Baltimore (MD)[22]	CDJC	651 154	...	...	209	...	...	...	...
Baton Rouge (LA)	CDJC	227 818	...	...	199	602 894	...	...	4 109
Beaumont (TX)[29]	CDJC	113 866	...	...	220	385 090	...	...	5 580
Bellevue (WA)	CDJC	109 569	...	...	80	...	...	...	...
Berkeley (CA)[30]	CDJC	102 743	...	...	27	...	...	...	...
Birmingham (AL)	CDJC	242 820	...	...	388	921 106	...	...	8 255
Boise City (ID)	CDJC	185 787	...	...	165	432 345	...	...	4 260
Boston (MA)[31]	CDJC	589 141	...	...	125	5 819 100	...	...	14 569
Bridgeport (CT)[32]	CDJC	139 529	...	...	41	...	...	...	...
Brownsville (TX)[33]	CDJC	139 722	...	...	208	335 227	...	...	2 345
Buffalo (NY)[34]	CDJC	292 648	...	...	105	1 170 111	...	...	4 060
Burbank (CA)	CDJC	100 316	...	...	45	...	...	...	...
Cambridge (MA)	CDJC	101 355	...	...	17	...	...	...	...
Cape Coral (FL)	CDJC	102 286	...	...	272	440 888	...	...	2 081
Carrollton (TX)	CDJC	109 576	...	...	95	...	...	...	...
Cedar Rapids (IA)	CDJC	120 758	...	...	164	191 701	...	...	1 858
Chandler (AZ)	CDJC	176 581	...	...	150	...	...	...	...
Charlotte (NC)[35]	CDJC	540 828	...	...	628	1 499 293	...	...	8 751
Chattanooga (TN)	CDJC	155 554	...	...	350	465 161	...	...	4 726
Chesapeake (VA)[36]	CDJC	199 184	...	...	883	...	...	...	...
Chicago (IL)[37]	CDJC	2 896 016	...	...	588	9 157 540	...	...	17 950
Chula Vista (CA)[38]	CDJC	173 556	...	...	127	...	...	...	...
Cincinnati (OH)[39]	CDJC	331 285	...	...	202	1 979 202	...	...	9 867
Clarksville (TN)[40]	CDJC	103 455	...	...	246	207 033	...	...	3 265
Clearwater (FL)[41]	CDJC	108 787	...	...	66	...	...	...	...
Cleveland (OH)[42]	CDJC	478 403	...	...	201	2 945 831	...	...	9 357
Colorado Springs (CO)	CDJC	360 890	...	...	481	516 929	...	...	5 508
Columbia (SC)	CDJC	116 278	...	...	324	536 691	...	...	3 775
Columbus (GA)	CDJC	185 781	...	...	560	274 624	...	...	4 066
Columbus (OH)	CDJC	711 470	...	...	545	1 540 157	...	...	8 138
Concord (CA)[30]	CDJC	121 780	...	...	78	...	...	...	...
Coral Springs (FL)	CDJC	117 549	...	...	62	...	...	...	...
Corona (CA)	CDJC	124 966	...	...	91	...	...	...	...
Corpus Christi (TX)	CDJC	277 454	...	...	401	380 783	...	...	3 957
Costa Mesa (CA)	CDJC	108 724	...	...	41	...	...	...	...
Dallas (TX)[43]	CDJC	1 188 580	...	...	887	5 221 801	...	...	23 581
Daly City (CA)	CDJC	103 621	...	...	20	...	...	...	...
Dayton (OH)[44]	CDJC	166 179	...	...	145	950 558	...	...	4 361
Denver (CO)[45]	CDJC	554 636	...	...	397	2 581 506	...	...	22 005
Des Moines (IA)	CDJC	198 682	...	...	196	456 022	...	...	4 475
Detroit (MI)[46]	CDJC	951 270	...	...	359	5 456 428	...	...	17 006
Downey (CA)	CDJC	107 323	...	...	32	...	...	...	...

8. Population of capital cities and cities of 100 000 and more inhabitants: latest available year
Population des capitales et des villes de 100 000 habitants et plus: dernière année disponible (continued — suite)

(See notes at end of table. — Voir notes à la fin du tableau.)

Continent, country or area, date and city — Continent, pays ou zone, date et ville	Code[1]	City proper — Ville proprement dite Population				Urban agglomeration — Agglomération urbaine Population			
		Both sexes Les deux sexes	Male Masculin	Female Féminin	Surface area Superficie (km²)	Both sexes Les deux sexes	Male Masculin	Female Féminin	Surface area Superficie (km²)
AMERICA, NORTH — AMERIQUE DU NORD									
United States — Etats-Unis[20]									
2000									
Durham (NC)[47]	CDJC	187 035	...	...	245	...	...	...	...
El Monte (CA)[24]	CDJC	115 965	...	...	25	...	...	...	...
El Paso (TX)	CDJC	563 662	...	...	645	679 622	...	...	2 624
Elizabeth (NJ)[32]	CDJC	120 568	...	...	32	...	...	...	...
Erie (PA)	CDJC	103 717	...	...	57	280 843	...	...	2 077
Escondido (CA)[38]	CDJC	133 559	...	...	94	...	...	...	...
Eugene (OR)[48]	CDJC	137 893	...	...	105	322 959	...	...	11 795
Evansville (IN)	CDJC	121 582	...	...	105	296 195	...	...	3 800
Fayetteville (NC)	CDJC	121 015	...	...	152	302 963	...	...	1 692
Flint (MI)[25]	CDJC	124 943	...	...	87	...	...	...	...
Fontana (CA)[24]	CDJC	128 929	...	...	94	...	...	...	...
Fort Collins (CO)[49]	CDJC	118 652	...	...	121	251 494	...	...	6 738
Fort Lauderdale (FL)[50]	CDJC	152 397	...	...	82	...	...	...	...
Fort Wayne (IN)	CDJC	205 727	...	...	205	502 141	...	...	6 340
Fort Worth (TX)[26]	CDJC	534 694	...	...	758	...	...	...	...
Fremont (CA)[30]	CDJC	203 413	...	...	199	...	...	...	...
Fresno (CA)	CDJC	427 652	...	...	270	922 516	...	...	20 983
Fullerton (CA)[24]	CDJC	126 003	...	...	58	...	...	...	...
Garden Grove (CA)[24]	CDJC	165 196	...	...	47	...	...	...	...
Garland (TX)[26]	CDJC	215 768	...	...	148	...	...	...	...
Gary (IN)[28]	CDJC	102 746	...	...	130	...	...	...	...
Gilbert (AZ)	CDJC	109 697	...	...	111	...	...	...	...
Glendale (AZ)[51]	CDJC	218 812	...	...	144	...	...	...	...
Glendale (CA)[24]	CDJC	194 973	...	...	79	...	...	...	...
Grand Prairie (TX)[26]	CDJC	127 427	...	...	185	...	...	...	...
Grand Rapids (MI)	CDJC	197 800	...	...	116	1 088 514	...	...	7 145
Green Bay (WI)	CDJC	102 313	...	...	114	226 778	...	...	1 369
Greensboro (NC)[52]	CDJC	223 891	...	...	271	1 251 509	...	...	10 057
Hampton (VA)[36]	CDJC	146 437	...	...	134	...	...	...	...
Hartford (CT)[53]	CDJC	121 578	...	...	45	1 183 110	...	...	4 344
Hayward (CA)[30]	CDJC	140 030	...	...	115	...	...	...	...
Henderson (NV)	CDJC	175 381	...	...	206	...	...	...	...
Hialeah (FL)[50]	CDJC	226 419	...	...	50	...	...	...	...
Hollywood (FL)[50]	CDJC	139 357	...	...	71	...	...	...	...
Honolulu (HI)	CDJC	371 657	...	...	222	876 156	...	...	1 555
Houston (TX)[54]	CDJC	1 953 631	...	...	1 501	4 669 571	...	...	19 960
Huntington Beach (CA)[24]	CDJC	189 594	...	...	68	...	...	...	...
Huntsville (AL)	CDJC	158 216	...	...	451	342 376	...	...	3 556
Independence (MO)[55]	CDJC	113 288	...	...	203	...	...	...	...
Indianapolis (IN)	CDJC	781 870	...	...	936	1 607 486	...	...	9 125
Inglewood (CA)[24]	CDJC	112 580	...	...	24	...	...	...	...
Irvine (CA)	CDJC	143 072	...	...	120	...	...	...	...
Irving (TX)[26]	CDJC	191 615	...	...	174	...	...	...	...
Jackson (MS)	CDJC	184 256	...	...	272	440 801	...	...	6 120
Jacksonville (FL)	CDJC	735 617	...	...	1 962	1 100 491	...	...	6 826
Jersey City (NJ)[32]	CDJC	240 055	...	...	39	...	...	...	...
Joliet (IL)	CDJC	106 221	...	...	99	...	...	...	...
Kansas City (KS)[55]	CDJC	146 866	...	...	322	...	...	...	...
Kansas City (MO)	CDJC	441 545	...	...	812	1 776 062	...	...	14 003
Knoxville (TN)	CDJC	173 890	...	...	240	687 249	...	...	6 343
Lafayette (LA)	CDJC	110 257	...	...	123	385 647	...	...	6 718
Lakewood (CO)[27]	CDJC	144 126	...	...	105	...	...	...	...
Lancaster (CA)	CDJC	118 718	...	...	244	...	...	...	...
Lansing (MI)[56]	CDJC	119 128	...	...	91	447 728	...	...	4 422
Laredo (TX)	CDJC	176 576	...	...	203	193 117	...	...	8 695
Las Vegas (NV)	CDJC	478 434	...	...	294	1 563 282	...	...	101 969
Lexington-Fayette (KY)	CDJC	260 512	...	...	737	479 198	...	...	4 973

(See notes at end of table. — Voir notes à la fin du tableau.)

Continent, country or area, date and city / Continent, pays ou zone, date et ville	Code[1]	City proper — Ville proprement dite Population				Urban agglomeration — Agglomération urbaine Population			
		Both sexes Les deux sexes	Male Masculin	Female Féminin	Surface area Superficie (km²)	Both sexes Les deux sexes	Male Masculin	Female Féminin	Surface area Superficie (km²)
AMERICA, NORTH — AMERIQUE DU NORD									
United States — Etats-Unis[20]									
2000									
Lincoln (NE)	CDJC	225 581	...	...	193	250 291	...	...	2 173
Little Rock (AR)[57]	CDJC	183 133	...	...	301	583 845	...	...	7 533
Livonia (MI)[25]	CDJC	100 545	...	...	93	...	...	...	...
Long Beach (CA)[24]	CDJC	461 522	...	...	131	...	...	...	...
Los Angeles (CA)[58]	CDJC	3 694 820	...	...	1 215	16 373 645	...	...	87 972
Louisville (KY)	CDJC	256 231	...	...	161	1 025 598	...	...	5 367
Lowell (MA)	CDJC	105 167	...	...	36	...	...	...	...
Lubbock (TX)	CDJC	199 564	...	...	297	242 628	...	...	2 330
Madison (WI)	CDJC	208 054	...	...	178	426 526	...	...	3 114
Manchester (NH)	CDJC	107 006	...	...	86	...	...	...	...
McAllen (TX)	CDJC	106 414	...	...	119	569 463	...	...	4 064
Memphis (TN)	CDJC	650 100	...	...	723	1 135 614	...	...	7 790
Mesa (AZ)[51]	CDJC	396 375	...	...	324	...	...	...	...
Mesquite (TX)[26]	CDJC	124 523	...	...	112	...	...	...	...
Miami (FL)[59]	CDJC	362 470	...	...	92	3 876 380	...	...	8 168
Milwaukee (WI)[60]	CDJC	596 974	...	...	249	1 689 572	...	...	4 644
Minneapolis (MN)[61]	CDJC	382 618	...	...	142	2 968 806	...	...	15 707
Mobile (AL)	CDJC	198 915	...	...	305	540 258	...	...	7 329
Modesto (CA)	CDJC	188 856	...	...	93	446 997	...	...	3 871
Montgomery (AL)	CDJC	201 568	...	...	402	333 055	...	...	5 199
Moreno Valley (CA)[24]	CDJC	142 381	...	...	133	...	...	...	...
Naperville (IL)	CDJC	128 358	...	...	92	...	...	...	...
Nashville-Davidson (TN)	CDJC	545 524	...	...	1 226	1 231 311	...	...	10 549
New Haven (CT)[32]	CDJC	123 626	...	...	49	...	...	...	...
New Orleans (LA)	CDJC	484 674	...	...	468	1 337 726	...	...	8 805
New York (NY)[62]	CDJC	8 008 278	...	...	786	21 199 865	...	...	27 082
Newark (NJ)[32]	CDJC	273 546	...	...	62	...	...	...	...
Newport News (VA)[36]	CDJC	180 150	...	...	177	...	...	...	...
Norfolk (VA)[63]	CDJC	234 403	...	...	139	1 569 541	...	...	6 083
North Las Vegas (NV)	CDJC	115 488	...	...	203	...	...	...	...
Norwalk (CA)	CDJC	103 298	...	...	25	...	...	...	...
Oakland (CA)[30]	CDJC	399 484	...	...	145	...	...	...	...
Oceanside (CA)[38]	CDJC	161 029	...	...	105	...	...	...	...
Oklahoma City (OK)	CDJC	506 132	...	...	1 572	1 083 346	...	...	11 001
Omaha (NE)	CDJC	390 007	...	...	300	716 998	...	...	6 412
Ontario (CA)[24]	CDJC	158 007	...	...	129	...	...	...	...
Orange (CA)[24]	CDJC	128 821	...	...	61	...	...	...	...
Orlando (FL)	CDJC	185 951	...	...	242	1 644 561	...	...	9 042
Overland Park (KS)[55]	CDJC	149 080	...	...	147	...	...	...	...
Oxnard (CA)[24]	CDJC	170 358	...	...	66	...	...	...	...
Palmdale (CA)[24]	CDJC	116 670	...	...	272	...	...	...	...
Pasadena (CA)[24]	CDJC	133 936	...	...	60	...	...	...	...
Pasadena (TX)[64]	CDJC	141 674	...	...	114	...	...	...	...
Paterson (NJ)[32]	CDJC	149 222	...	...	22	...	...	...	...
Pembroke Pines (FL)	CDJC	137 427	...	...	86	...	...	...	...
Peoria (AZ)	CDJC	108 364	...	...	358	...	...	...	...
Peoria (IL)	CDJC	112 936	...	...	115	347 387	...	...	4 653
Philadelphia (PA)[65]	CDJC	1 517 550	...	...	350	6 188 463	...	...	15 375
Phoenix (AZ)[66]	CDJC	1 321 045	...	...	1 230	3 251 876	...	...	37 747
Pittsburgh (PA)	CDJC	334 563	...	...	144	2 358 695	...	...	11 976
Plano (TX)[26]	CDJC	222 030	...	...	185	...	...	...	...
Pomona (CA)[24]	CDJC	149 473	...	...	59	...	...	...	...
Portland (OR)[67]	CDJC	529 121	...	...	348	2 265 223	...	...	18 010
Portsmouth (VA)[36]	CDJC	100 565	...	...	86	...	...	...	...
Providence (RI)[68]	CDJC	173 618	...	...	48	1 188 613	...	...	2 956
Provo (UT)[69]	CDJC	105 166	...	...	103	368 536	...	...	5 176
Pueblo (CO)	CDJC	102 121	...	...	117	141 472	...	...	6 187

8. Population of capital cities and cities of 100 000 and more inhabitants: latest available year
Population des capitales et des villes de 100 000 habitants et plus: dernière année disponible (continued — suite)

(See notes at end of table. — Voir notes à la fin du tableau.)

Continent, country or area, date and city Continent, pays ou zone, date et ville	Code[1]	City proper — Ville proprement dite Population				Urban agglomeration — Agglomération urbaine Population			
		Both sexes Les deux sexes	Male Masculin	Female Féminin	Surface area Superficie (km²)	Both sexes Les deux sexes	Male Masculin	Female Féminin	Surface area Superficie (km²)
AMERICA, NORTH — AMERIQUE DU NORD									
United States — Etats-Unis[20]									
2000									
Raleigh (NC)[70]	CDJC	276 093	...	...	297	1 187 941	...	...	9 042
Rancho Cucamonga (CA)[24]	CDJC	127 743	...	...	97	...	...	...	...
Reno (NV)	CDJC	180 480	...	...	179	339 486	...	...	16 427
Richmond (VA)[71]	CDJC	197 790	...	...	156	996 512	...	...	7 627
Riverside (CA)[24]	CDJC	255 166	...	...	202	...	...	...	...
Rochester (NY)	CDJC	219 773	...	...	93	1 098 201	...	...	8 873
Rockford (IL)	CDJC	150 115	...	...	145	371 236	...	...	4 025
Sacramento (CA)[72]	CDJC	407 018	...	...	252	1 796 857	...	...	13 194
St. Louis (MO)	CDJC	348 189	...	...	160	2 603 607	...	...	16 558
St. Paul (MN)[73]	CDJC	287 151	...	...	137	...	...	...	...
St. Petersburg (FL)[41]	CDJC	248 232	...	...	154	...	...	...	...
Salem (OR)[74]	CDJC	136 924	...	...	118	...	...	...	...
Salinas (CA)[75]	CDJC	151 060	...	...	49	401 762	...	...	8 604
Salt Lake City (UT)[76]	CDJC	181 743	...	...	283	1 333 914	...	...	4 189
San Antonio (TX)	CDJC	1 144 646	...	...	1 056	1 592 383	...	...	8 616
San Bernardino (CA)[24]	CDJC	185 401	...	...	152	...	...	...	...
San Buenaventura (CA)	CDJC	100 916	...	...	55	...	...	...	...
San Diego (CA)	CDJC	1 223 400	...	...	840	2 813 833	...	...	10 890
San Francisco (CA)[77]	CDJC	776 733	...	...	121	7 039 362	...	...	19 084
San Jose (CA)[30]	CDJC	894 943	...	...	453	...	...	...	...
Santa Ana (CA)[24]	CDJC	337 977	...	...	70	...	...	...	...
Santa Clara (CA)	CDJC	102 361	...	...	48	...	...	...	...
Santa Clarita (CA)[24]	CDJC	151 088	...	...	124	...	...	...	...
Santa Rosa (CA)[30]	CDJC	147 595	...	...	104	...	...	...	...
Savannah (GA)	CDJC	131 510	...	...	194	293 000	...	...	3 527
Scottsdale (AZ)[51]	CDJC	202 705	...	...	477	...	...	...	...
Seattle (WA)[78]	CDJC	563 374	...	...	217	3 554 760	...	...	18 709
Shreveport (LA)	CDJC	200 145	...	...	267	392 302	...	...	6 020
Simi Valley (CA)[24]	CDJC	111 351	...	...	102	...	...	...	...
Sioux Falls (SD)	CDJC	123 975	...	...	146	172 412	...	...	3 593
South Bend (IN)[79]	CDJC	107 789	...	...	100	265 559	...	...	1 185
Spokane (WA)	CDJC	195 629	...	...	150	417 939	...	...	4 568
Springfield (IL)	CDJC	111 454	...	...	140	201 437	...	...	3 063
Springfield (MA)	CDJC	152 082	...	...	83	591 932	...	...	1 905
Springfield (MO)	CDJC	151 580	...	...	190	325 721	...	...	4 744
Stamford (CT)[32]	CDJC	117 083	...	...	98	...	...	...	...
Sterling Heights (MI)[25]	CDJC	124 471	...	...	95	...	...	...	...
Stockton (CA)	CDJC	243 771	...	...	142	563 598	...	...	3 624
Sunnyvale (CA)[30]	CDJC	131 760	...	...	57	...	...	...	...
Syracuse (NY)	CDJC	147 306	...	...	65	732 117	...	...	7 984
Tacoma (WA)[80]	CDJC	193 556	...	...	130	...	...	...	...
Tallahassee (FL)	CDJC	150 624	...	...	248	284 539	...	...	3 064
Tampa (FL)[81]	CDJC	303 447	...	...	290	2 395 997	...	...	6 616
Tempe (AZ)[51]	CDJC	158 625	...	...	104	...	...	...	...
Thousand Oaks (CA)[24]	CDJC	117 005	...	...	142	...	...	...	...
Toledo (OH)	CDJC	313 619	...	...	209	618 203	...	...	3 534
Topeka (KS)	CDJC	122 377	...	...	145	169 871	...	...	1 424
Torrance (CA)[24]	CDJC	137 946	...	...	53	...	...	...	...
Tucson (AZ)	CDJC	486 699	...	...	504	843 746	...	...	23 794
Tulsa (OK)	CDJC	393 049	...	...	473	803 235	...	...	12 989
Vallejo (CA)[30]	CDJC	116 760	...	...	78	...	...	...	...
Vancouver (WA)	CDJC	143 560	...	...	111	...	...	...	...
Virginia Beach (VA)[36]	CDJC	425 257	...	...	643	...	...	...	...
Waco (TX)	CDJC	113 726	...	...	218	213 517	...	...	2 699
Warren (MI)[25]	CDJC	138 247	...	...	89	...	...	...	...
WASHINGTON (DC)[82]	CDJC	572 059	...	...	...	7 608 070	...	...	6 758
Waterbury (CT)[32]	CDJC	107 271	...	...	74	...	...	...	...

8. Population of capital cities and cities of 100 000 and more inhabitants: latest available year
Population des capitales et des villes de 100 000 habitants et plus: dernière année disponible (continued — suite)

(See notes at end of table. — Voir notes à la fin du tableau.)

Continent, country or area, date and city Continent, pays ou zone, date et ville	Code[1]	City proper — Ville proprement dite Population				Urban agglomeration — Agglomération urbaine Population			
		Both sexes Les deux sexes	Male Masculin	Female Féminin	Surface area Superficie (km²)	Both sexes Les deux sexes	Male Masculin	Female Féminin	Surface area Superficie (km²)
AMERICA, NORTH — AMERIQUE DU NORD									
United States — Etats-Unis[20]									
2000									
West Covina (CA)[24]	CDJC	105 080	...	...	42	...	...	...	...
West Valley City (UT)	CDJC	108 896	...	...	92	...	...	...	...
Westminster (CO)	CDJC	100 940	...	...	82	...	...	...	...
Wichita (KS)	CDJC	344 284	...	...	352	545 220	...	...	7 687
Wichita Falls (TX)	CDJC	104 197	...	...	183	140 518	...	...	3 982
Winston-Salem (NC)[83]	CDJC	185 776	...	...	282	...	...	...	...
Worcester (MA)[84]	CDJC	172 648	...	...	97	...	...	...	...
Yonkers (NY)[32]	CDJC	196 086	...	...	47	...	...	...	...
United States Virgin Islands — Iles Vierges américaines[17]									
1990									
CHARLOTTE AMALIE	CDFC	12 331	...	...	...	20 589	...	...	...
2000									
CHARLOTTE AMALIE	CDFC	11 004	...	...	...	18 914	...	...	...
AMERICA, SOUTH — AMERIQUE DU SUD									
Argentina — Argentine									
1991									
Avellaneda	CDFC	344 024	...	...	...	...	...	...	...
Bahía Blanca	CDFC	260 096	...	...	...	...	...	...	...
BUENOS AIRES	CDFC	2 965 403	...	...	...	11 298 030	...	...	...
Catamarca	CDFC	109 882	...	...	...	132 626	...	...	...
Comodoro Rivadavia	CDFC	124 104	...	...	...	...	...	...	...
Concordia	CDFC	116 485	...	...	...	...	...	...	...
Córdoba	CDFC	1 157 507	...	...	...	1 208 554	...	...	...
Corrientes	CDFC	258 103	...	...	...	...	...	...	...
Formosa	CDFC	147 636	...	...	...	...	...	...	...
General San Martín	CDFC	406 809	...	...	...	...	...	...	...
La Matanza	CDFC	1 120 088	...	...	...	...	...	...	...
Lanus	CDFC	468 561	...	...	...	...	...	...	...
La Plata	CDFC	521 936	...	...	...	642 979	...	...	...
Lomas de Zamora	CDFC	574 330	...	...	...	...	...	...	...
Mar del Plata	CDFC	512 880	...	...	...	...	...	...	...
Mendoza	CDFC	121 620	...	...	...	773 113	...	...	...
Morón	CDFC	643 553	...	...	...	...	...	...	...
Neuquén	CDFC	167 296	...	...	...	183 579	...	...	...
Paraná	CDFC	207 041	...	...	...	211 936	...	...	...
Posadas	CDFC	201 273	...	...	...	210 755	...	...	...
Quilmes	CDFC	511 234	...	...	...	...	...	...	...
Resistencia	CDFC	229 212	...	...	...	292 287	...	...	...
Río Cuarto	CDFC	134 355	...	...	...	138 853	...	...	...
Rosario	CDFC	907 718	...	...	...	1 118 905	...	...	...
Salta	CDFC	367 550	...	...	...	370 904	...	...	...
San Fernando	CDFC	141 063	...	...	...	...	...	...	...
San Isidro	CDFC	299 023	...	...	...	...	...	...	...
San Juan	CDFC	119 423	...	...	...	352 691	...	...	...
San Miguel de Tucumán	CDFC	470 809	...	...	...	622 324	...	...	...
San Nicolás	CDFC	119 302	...	...	...	...	...	...	...
San Salvador de Jujuy	CDFC	178 748	...	...	...	180 102	...	...	...
Santa Fé	CDFC	353 063	...	...	...	406 388	...	...	...
Santiago del Estero	CDFC	189 947	...	...	...	263 471	...	...	...
Vicente López	CDFC	289 505	...	...	...	...	...	...	...
Bolivia — Bolivie									
2000									
Cochabamba	ESDF	607 129	290 640	316 489	...	...	...	...	...

8. Population of capital cities and cities of 100 000 and more inhabitants: latest available year
Population des capitales et des villes de 100 000 habitants et plus: dernière année disponible (continued — suite)

(See notes at end of table. — Voir notes à la fin du tableau.)

Continent, country or area, date and city / Continent, pays ou zone, date et ville	Code[1]	City proper — Ville proprement dite Population				Urban agglomeration — Agglomération urbaine Population			
		Both sexes Les deux sexes	Male Masculin	Female Féminin	Surface area Superficie (km²)	Both sexes Les deux sexes	Male Masculin	Female Féminin	Surface area Superficie (km²)
AMERICA, SOUTH — AMERIQUE DU SUD									
Bolivia — Bolivie									
2000									
El Alto	ESDF	*568 919*	*284 495*	*284 424*	...	...	...	...	...
LA PAZ[85]	ESDF	*1 000 899*	*478 964*	*521 935*	...	...	...	...	...
Oruro	ESDF	*232 311*	*114 207*	*118 104*	...	...	...	...	...
Potosí	ESDF	*147 351*	*71 878*	*75 473*	...	...	...	...	...
Santa Cruz	ESDF	*1 016 137*	*499 045*	*517 092*	...	...	...	...	...
SUCRE[85]	ESDF	*192 238*	*91 750*	*100 488*	...	...	...	...	...
Tarija	ESDF	*135 679*	*66 489*	*69 193*	...	...	...	...	...
2001									
Cochabamba	CDFC	778 422	374 428	403 994	...	...	...	...	...
El Alto	CDFC	694 749	340 497	354 252	...	...	...	...	...
LA PAZ[85]	CDFC	1 487 248	718 617	768 631	...	...	...	...	...
Oruro	CDFC	202 010	97 164	104 846	...	...	...	...	...
Potosí	CDFC	133 268	63 662	69 606	...	...	...	...	...
Santa Cruz	CDFC	1 114 095	545 303	568 792	...	...	...	...	...
SUCRE[85]	CDFC	194 888	92 142	102 746	...	...	...	...	...
Tarija	CDFC	135 651	65 027	70 624	...	...	...	...	...
Brazil — Brésil[15]									
2000									
Abaeteluba	CDJC	...	...	...	...	119 152	60 595	58 557	1 090
Aguas Lindas de Goiás	CDJC	...	...	...	...	105 746	53 164	52 582	...
Alagoinhas	CDJC	...	...	...	...	130 095	62 068	68 027	761
Alvorada	CDJC	...	...	...	...	183 968	90 422	93 546	...
Americana	CDJC	...	...	...	...	182 593	90 335	92 258	...
Ananindeua	CDJC	...	...	...	...	393 569	190 307	203 262	485
Anápolis	CDJC	...	...	...	...	288 085	140 485	147 600	...
Angra dos Reis	CDJC	...	...	...	...	119 247	60 089	59 158	...
Aparecida de Goiania	CDJC	...	...	...	...	336 392	166 916	169 476	...
Apucarana	CDJC	...	...	...	...	107 827	52 825	55 002	556
Aracaju	CDJC	...	...	...	...	461 534	215 887	245 647	151
Araçatuba	CDJC	...	...	...	...	169 254	81 984	87 270	2 668
Araguaina	CDJC	...	...	...	...	113 143	55 224	57 919	...
Araguario	CDJC	...	...	...	...	101 974	50 766	51 208	...
Arapiraca	CDJC	...	...	...	...	186 466	89 183	97 283	...
Araraquara	CDJC	...	...	...	...	182 471	88 742	93 729	...
Araras	CDJC	...	...	...	...	104 196	52 079	52 117	...
Atibaia	CDJC	...	...	...	...	111 300	55 335	55 965	...
Bagé	CDJC	...	...	...	...	118 767	57 042	61 725	7 185
Barbacena	CDJC	...	...	...	...	114 126	54 697	59 429	...
Barueri	CDJC	...	...	...	...	208 281	102 884	105 397	...
Barra Mansa	CDJC	...	...	...	...	170 753	83 072	87 681	830
Barreiras	CDJC	...	...	...	...	131 849	66 177	65 672	...
Barretos	CDJC	...	...	...	...	103 913	50 667	53 246	...
Bauru	CDJC	...	...	...	...	316 064	154 435	161 629	702
Belém	CDJC	...	...	...	...	1 280 614	608 253	672 361	736
Belford Roxo	CDJC	...	...	...	...	434 474	211 285	223 189	...
Belo Horizonte	CDJC	...	...	...	...	2 238 526	1 057 263	1 181 263	335
Betim	CDJC	...	...	...	...	306 675	152 880	153 795	376
Blumenou	CDJC	...	...	...	...	261 808	128 298	133 510	509
Boa Vista	CDJC	...	...	...	...	200 568	100 334	100 234	...
Botucatu	CDJC	...	...	...	...	108 306	52 876	55 430	...
Bragança Paulista	CDJC	...	...	...	...	125 031	61 902	63 129	770
BRASILIA	CDJC	...	...	...	...	2 051 146	981 356	1 069 790	5 794
Cabo de Santo Agostinho	CDJC	...	...	...	...	152 977	75 246	77 731	...
Cabo Frio	CDJC	...	...	...	...	126 828	63 033	63 795	...
Cachoeirinha	CDJC	...	...	...	...	107 564	52 491	55 073	...
Cachoeiro de Itapemirim	CDJC	...	...	...	...	174 879	85 705	89 174	892
Camacari	CDJC	...	...	...	...	161 727	80 962	80 765	718

8. Population of capital cities and cities of 100 000 and more inhabitants: latest available year
Population des capitales et des villes de 100 000 habitants et plus: dernière année disponible (continued — suite)

(See notes at end of table. — Voir notes à la fin du tableau.)

Continent, country or area, date and city / Continent, pays ou zone, date et ville	Code[1]	City proper — Ville proprement dite Population				Urban agglomeration — Agglomération urbaine Population			
		Both sexes Les deux sexes	Male Masculin	Female Féminin	Surface area Superficie (km²)	Both sexes Les deux sexes	Male Masculin	Female Féminin	Surface area Superficie (km²)
AMERICA, SOUTH — AMERIQUE DU SUD									
Brazil — Brésil[15]									
2000									
Camaragibe	CDJC	...	...	...	...	128 702	62 579	66 123	...
Campina Grande	CDJC	...	...	...	...	355 331	168 236	187 095	970
Campinas	CDJC	...	...	...	...	969 396	472 175	497 221	781
Campo Grande	CDJC	...	...	...	...	663 621	322 703	340 918	8 091
Campos dos Goytacazes	CDJC	...	...	...	...	406 989	196 711	210 278	4 536
Canoas	CDJC	...	...	...	...	306 093	148 860	157 233	...
Carapicuíba	CDJC	...	...	...	...	344 596	168 851	175 745	...
Cariacica	CDJC	...	...	...	...	324 285	159 433	164 852	279
Caruaru	CDJC	...	...	...	...	253 634	120 296	133 338	936
Cascavel	CDJC	...	...	...	...	245 369	119 634	125 735	2 074
Castanhal	CDJC	...	...	...	...	134 496	65 902	68 594	1 003
Catanduva	CDJC	...	...	...	...	105 847	51 869	53 978	...
Caucaia	CDJC	...	...	...	...	250 479	123 299	127 180	1 293
Caxias	CDJC	...	...	...	...	139 756	67 914	71 842	6 724
Caxias do Sul	CDJC	...	...	...	...	360 419	176 959	183 460	1 601
Chapecó	CDJC	...	...	...	...	146 967	72 600	74 367	...
Codo	CDJC	...	...	...	...	111 146	54 407	56 739	4 923
Colatina	CDJC	...	...	...	...	112 711	55 275	57 436	2 094
Colombo	CDJC	...	...	...	...	183 329	91 236	92 093	...
Conselheiro Lafaiete	CDJC	...	...	...	...	102 836	49 816	53 020	...
Contagem	CDJC	...	...	...	...	538 017	263 390	274 627	167
Cotia	CDJC	...	...	...	...	148 987	73 646	75 341	...
Crato	CDJC	...	...	...	...	104 646	49 570	55 076	...
Criciúma	CDJC	...	...	...	...	170 420	83 971	86 449	...
Cubatao	CDJC	...	...	...	...	108 309	54 524	53 785	...
Cuiabá	CDJC	...	...	...	...	483 346	235 568	247 778	3 922
Curitiba	CDJC	...	...	...	...	1 587 315	760 848	826 467	427
Diadema	CDJC	...	...	...	...	357 064	175 108	181 956	...
Divinópolis	CDJC	...	...	...	...	183 962	89 978	93 984	716
Dourados	CDJC	...	...	...	...	164 949	81 015	83 934	4 082
Duque de Caxias	CDJC	...	...	...	...	775 456	375 732	399 724	463
Embu	CDJC	...	...	...	...	207 663	102 190	105 473	...
Feira de Santana	CDJC	...	...	...	...	480 949	229 656	251 293	1 344
Ferraz de Vasconcelos	CDJC	...	...	...	...	142 377	70 199	72 178	...
Florianópolis	CDJC	...	...	...	...	342 315	165 694	176 621	440
Fortaleza	CDJC	...	...	...	...	2 141 402	1 002 236	1 139 166	336
Foz do Iguaçu	CDJC	...	...	...	...	258 543	127 739	130 804	596
Franca	CDJC	...	...	...	...	287 737	142 159	145 578	...
Francisco Morato	CDJC	...	...	...	...	133 738	66 702	67 036	...
Franco da Rocha	CDJC	...	...	...	...	108 122	55 975	52 147	...
Garanhuns	CDJC	...	...	...	...	117 749	55 654	62 095	456
Goiânia	CDJC	...	...	...	...	1 093 007	521 055	571 952	788
Governador Valadares	CDJC	...	...	...	...	247 131	118 267	128 864	2 447
Gravatai	CDJC	...	...	...	...	232 629	114 837	117 792	...
Guaratinguetá	CDJC	...	...	...	...	104 219	50 895	53 324	...
Guarapuava	CDJC	...	...	...	...	155 161	76 205	78 956	5 365
Guarujá	CDJC	...	...	...	...	264 812	130 875	133 937	...
Guarulhos	CDJC	...	...	...	...	1 072 717	527 487	545 230	...
Hortolandia	CDJC	...	...	...	...	152 523	76 291	76 232	...
Ibirité	CDJC	...	...	...	...	133 044	66 190	66 854	...
Ilhéus	CDJC	...	...	...	...	222 127	110 445	111 682	1 712
Imperatriz	CDJC	...	...	...	...	230 566	110 947	119 619	6 014
Indaiatuba	CDJC	...	...	...	...	147 050	73 436	73 614	...
Ipatinga	CDJC	...	...	...	...	212 496	104 089	108 407	231
Itaboraí	CDJC	...	...	...	...	187 479	92 689	94 790	569
Itabuna	CDJC	...	...	...	...	196 675	94 385	102 290	...
Itajaí	CDJC	...	...	...	...	147 494	72 353	75 141	...

8. Population of capital cities and cities of 100 000 and more inhabitants: latest available year
Population des capitales et des villes de 100 000 habitants et plus: dernière année disponible (continued — suite)

(See notes at end of table. — Voir notes à la fin du tableau.)

Continent, country or area, date and city / Continent, pays ou zone, date et ville	Code[1]	City proper — Ville proprement dite Population				Urban agglomeration — Agglomération urbaine Population			
		Both sexes Les deux sexes	Male Masculin	Female Féminin	Surface area Superficie (km²)	Both sexes Les deux sexes	Male Masculin	Female Féminin	Surface area Superficie (km²)
AMERICA, SOUTH — AMERIQUE DU SUD									
Brazil — Brésil[15]									
2000									
Itapetininga	CDJC	...	...	...	...	125 559	62 882	62 677	2 035
Itapecerica da Serra	CDJC	...	...	...	...	129 685	64 101	65 584	...
Itapevi	CDJC	...	...	...	...	162 433	80 401	82 032	...
Itaquaquecetuba	CDJC	...	...	...	...	272 942	136 213	136 729	...
Itu	CDJC	...	...	...	...	135 366	67 465	67 901	640
Jaboatao dos Guarapes	CDJC	...	...	...	...	581 556	277 955	303 601	...
Jacareí	CDJC	...	...	...	...	191 291	94 634	96 657	...
Jaraguá do Sul	CDJC	...	...	...	...	108 489	54 694	53 795	...
Jaú	CDJC	...	...	...	...	112 104	55 399	56 705	...
Jequié	CDJC	...	...	...	...	147 202	71 899	75 303	3 113
Ji-Paraná	CDJC	...	...	...	...	106 800	53 251	53 549	...
Joao Pessoa	CDJC	...	...	...	...	597 934	279 476	318 458	...
Joinville	CDJC	...	...	...	...	426 604	213 535	213 069	1 080
Juazeiro	CDJC	...	...	...	...	174 567	86 339	88 228	5 615
Juàzeiro do Norte	CDJC	...	...	...	...	212 133	100 140	111 993	...
Juiz de Fora	CDJC	...	...	...	...	456 796	217 411	239 385	1 424
Jundiaí	CDJC	...	...	...	...	323 397	158 591	164 806	432
Lages	CDJC	...	...	...	...	157 682	76 620	81 062	5 287
Lauro de Freitas	CDJC	...	...	...	...	113 543	55 529	58 014	...
Limeira	CDJC	...	...	...	...	249 046	123 609	125 437	...
Linhares	CDJC	...	...	...	...	112 617	56 027	56 590	4 388
Londrina	CDJC	...	...	...	...	447 065	215 816	231 249	2 129
Luziânia	CDJC	...	...	...	...	141 082	70 789	70 293	4 653
Macae	CDJC	...	...	...	...	132 461	65 523	66 938	...
Macapá	CDJC	...	...	...	...	283 308	139 344	143 964	...
Maceió	CDJC	...	...	...	...	797 759	376 572	421 187	517
Magé	CDJC	...	...	...	...	205 830	101 317	104 513	744
Manaus	CDJC	...	...	...	...	1 405 835	685 444	720 391	11 349
Maraba	CDJC	...	...	...	...	168 020	84 709	83 311	14 320
Maracanau	CDJC	...	...	...	...	179 732	88 406	91 326	...
Marília	CDJC	...	...	...	...	197 342	96 502	100 840	1 194
Maringá	CDJC	...	...	...	...	288 653	138 514	150 139	490
Mauá	CDJC	...	...	...	...	363 392	178 837	184 555	...
Moji das Cruzes	CDJC	...	...	...	...	330 241	162 636	167 605	749
Moji-Guaçu	CDJC	...	...	...	...	124 228	62 410	61 818	960
Montes Claros	CDJC	...	...	...	...	306 947	148 459	158 488	4 135
Mossoró	CDJC	...	...	...	...	213 841	102 823	111 018	2 108
Natal	CDJC	...	...	...	...	712 317	334 355	377 962	...
Nilópolis	CDJC	...	...	...	...	153 712	72 563	81 149	...
Niterói	CDJC	...	...	...	...	459 451	213 984	245 467	131
Nossa Senhora do Socorro	CDJC	...	...	...	...	131 679	64 517	67 162	...
Nova Friburgo	CDJC	...	...	...	...	173 418	84 281	89 137	930
Nova Iguaçu	CDJC	...	...	...	...	920 599	445 609	474 990	795
Nôvo Hamburgo	CDJC	...	...	...	...	236 193	115 432	120 761	...
Olinda	CDJC	...	...	...	...	367 902	172 251	195 651	...
Osasco	CDJC	...	...	...	...	652 593	317 575	335 018	...
Palhoça	CDJC	...	...	...	...	102 742	51 432	51 310	...
Palmas	CDJC	...	...	...	...	137 355	68 735	68 620	...
Paranaguá	CDJC	...	...	...	...	127 339	63 439	63 900	1 015
Parnaíba	CDJC	...	...	...	...	132 282	62 813	69 469	1 053
Parnamirim	CDJC	...	...	...	...	124 690	60 533	64 157	...
Passo Fundo	CDJC	...	...	...	...	168 458	80 766	87 692	1 596
Patos de Minas	CDJC	...	...	...	...	123 881	61 213	62 668	3 336
Paulista	CDJC	...	...	...	...	262 237	125 009	137 228	...
Pelotas	CDJC	...	...	...	...	323 158	153 342	169 816	1 924
Petrolina	CDJC	...	...	...	...	218 538	106 611	111 927	6 116
Petrópolis	CDJC	...	...	...	...	286 537	138 114	148 423	771

(See notes at end of table. — Voir notes à la fin du tableau.)

Continent, country or area, date and city Continent, pays ou zone, date et ville	Code[1]	City proper — Ville proprement dite Population				Urban agglomeration — Agglomération urbaine Population			
		Both sexes Les deux sexes	Male Masculin	Female Féminin	Surface area Superficie (km²)	Both sexes Les deux sexes	Male Masculin	Female Féminin	Surface area Superficie (km²)
AMERICA, SOUTH — AMERIQUE DU SUD									
Brazil — Brésil[15]									
2000									
Pindamonhangaba	CDJC	...	...	...	...	126 026	62 877	63 149	719
Pinhais	CDJC	...	...	...	...	102 985	50 822	52 163	...
Piracicaba	CDJC	...	...	...	...	329 158	162 433	166 725	1 426
Poços de Caldas	CDJC	...	...	...	...	135 627	66 190	69 437	533
Ponta Grossa	CDJC	...	...	...	...	273 616	133 197	140 419	2 212
Porto Alegre	CDJC	...	...	...	...	1 360 590	635 820	724 770	...
Porto Velho	CDJC	...	...	...	...	334 661	166 737	167 924	...
Pouso Alegre	CDJC	...	...	...	...	106 776	52 715	54 061	...
Praia Grande	CDJC	...	...	...	...	193 582	94 521	99 061	...
Presidente Prudente	CDJC	...	...	...	...	189 186	91 797	97 389	554
Queimados	CDJC	...	...	...	...	121 993	59 504	62 489	...
Recife	CDJC	...	...	...	...	1 422 905	661 690	761 215	...
Resende	CDJC	...	...	...	...	104 549	51 170	53 379	...
Ribeirao das Neves	CDJC	...	...	...	...	246 846	123 531	123 315	...
Ribeirao Prêto	CDJC	...	...	...	...	504 923	243 032	261 891	...
Ribeirao Pires	CDJC	...	...	...	...	104 508	51 634	52 874	...
Rio Branco	CDJC	...	...	...	...	253 059	123 248	129 811	...
Rio Claro	CDJC	...	...	...	...	168 218	82 232	85 986	503
Rio de Janeiro	CDJC	...	...	...	...	5 857 904	2 748 143	3 109 761	1 256
Rio Grande	CDJC	...	...	...	...	186 544	90 413	96 131	2 825
Rio Verde	CDJC	...	...	...	...	116 552	58 500	58 052	9 136
Rondonópolis	CDJC	...	...	...	...	150 227	75 287	74 940	4 594
Sabára	CDJC	...	...	...	...	115 352	56 239	59 113	...
Salvador	CDJC	...	...	...	...	2 443 107	1 150 252	1 292 855	313
Santa Bárbara D'Oeste	CDJC	...	...	...	...	170 078	84 943	85 135	...
Santa Cruz do Sul	CDJC	...	...	...	...	107 632	52 105	55 527	...
Santa Luzia (Minas Gerais)	CDJC	...	...	...	...	184 903	90 740	94 163	...
Santa Maria	CDJC	...	...	...	...	243 611	115 983	127 628	3 279
Santa Rita	CDJC	...	...	...	...	115 844	56 406	59 438	...
Santarém	CDJC	...	...	...	...	262 538	130 402	132 136	...
Santo André	CDJC	...	...	...	...	649 331	313 815	335 516	...
Santos	CDJC	...	...	...	...	417 983	193 222	224 761	725
Sao Bernardo do Campo	CDJC	...	...	...	...	703 177	342 107	361 070	319
Sao Caetano do Sul	CDJC	...	...	...	...	140 159	65 517	74 642	...
Sao Carlo	CDJC	...	...	...	...	192 998	95 585	97 413	1 120
Sao Gonçalo	CDJC	...	...	...	...	891 119	429 404	461 715	...
Sao Joao de Meriti	CDJC	...	...	...	...	449 476	216 014	233 462	...
Sao José	CDJC	...	...	...	...	173 559	84 591	88 968	...
Sao José de Ribamar	CDJC	...	...	...	...	107 384	52 591	54 793	...
Sao José do Rio Prêto	CDJC	...	...	...	...	358 523	173 476	185 047	586
Sao José dos Campos	CDJC	...	...	...	...	539 313	266 469	272 844	1 186
Sao José dos Pinhais	CDJC	...	...	...	...	204 316	102 412	101 904	923
Sao Leopoldo	CDJC	...	...	...	...	193 547	94 684	98 863	...
Sao Luís	CDJC	...	...	...	...	870 028	406 400	463 628	822
Sao Paulo	CDJC	...	...	...	...	10 434 252	4 972 678	5 461 574	1 493
Sao Vicente	CDJC	...	...	...	...	303 551	147 207	156 344	...
Sapucaia do Sul	CDJC	...	...	...	...	122 751	60 297	62 454	...
Serra	CDJC	...	...	...	...	321 181	158 458	162 723	549
Sete Lagoas	CDJC	...	...	...	...	184 871	89 925	94 946	...
Sobral	CDJC	...	...	...	...	155 276	75 275	80 001	1 646
Sorocaba	CDJC	...	...	...	...	493 468	242 787	250 681	...
Sumaré	CDJC	...	...	...	...	196 723	98 717	98 006	208
Susano	CDJC	...	...	...	...	228 690	113 251	115 439	...
Taboao da Serra	CDJC	...	...	...	...	197 644	95 357	102 287	...
Taubaté	CDJC	...	...	...	...	244 165	120 309	123 856	...
Teixeira de Freitas	CDJC	...	...	...	...	107 486	53 189	54 297	...
Teófilo Otoni	CDJC	...	...	...	...	129 424	62 177	67 247	...

8. Population of capital cities and cities of 100 000 and more inhabitants: latest available year
Population des capitales et des villes de 100 000 habitants et plus: dernière année disponible (continued — suite)

(See notes at end of table. — Voir notes à la fin du tableau.)

Continent, country or area, date and city / Continent, pays ou zone, date et ville	Code[1]	City proper — Ville proprement dite Population				Urban agglomeration — Agglomération urbaine Population			
		Both sexes Les deux sexes	Male Masculin	Female Féminin	Surface area Superficie (km²)	Both sexes Les deux sexes	Male Masculin	Female Féminin	Surface area Superficie (km²)
AMERICA, SOUTH — AMERIQUE DU SUD									
Brazil — Brésil[15]									
2000									
Teresina	CDJC	...	...	...	...	715 360	335 251	380 109	1 356
Teresópolis	CDJC	...	...	...	...	138 081	67 111	70 970	768
Timon	CDJC	...	...	...	...	129 692	63 042	66 650	1 702
Uberaba	CDJC	...	...	...	...	252 051	122 353	129 698	4 524
Uberlândia	CDJC	...	...	...	...	501 214	245 701	255 513	4 040
Uruguaiana	CDJC	...	...	...	...	126 936	62 755	64 181	6 763
Varginha	CDJC	...	...	...	...	108 998	53 765	55 233	...
Varzea Grande	CDJC	...	...	...	...	215 298	107 641	107 657	900
Viamao	CDJC	...	...	...	...	227 429	111 567	115 862	...
Vila Velha	CDJC	...	...	...	...	345 965	165 970	179 995	...
Vitória	CDJC	...	...	...	...	292 304	137 938	154 366	...
Vitória da Conquista	CDJC	...	...	...	...	262 494	127 636	134 858	3 743
Vitória de Santo Antao	CDJC	...	...	...	...	117 609	56 978	60 631	344
Volta Redonda	CDJC	...	...	...	...	242 063	116 740	125 323	...
2001									
Abaeteluba	ESDJ	...	...	...	...	121 415	...	...	1 090
Aguas Lindas de Goiás	ESDJ	...	...	...	...	116 122	...	...	...
Alagoinhas	ESDJ	...	...	...	...	131 179	...	...	761
Alvorada	ESDJ	...	...	...	...	188 756	...	...	...
Americana	ESDJ	...	...	...	...	185 552	...	...	...
Ananindeua	ESDJ	...	...	...	...	410 234	...	...	485
Anápolis	ESDJ	...	...	...	...	288 814	...	...	...
Angra dos Reis	ESDJ	...	...	...	...	123 307	...	...	...
Aparecida de Goiania	ESDJ	...	...	...	...	355 171	...	...	...
Apucarana	ESDJ	...	...	...	...	109 386	...	...	556
Aracaju	ESDJ	...	...	...	...	468 297	...	...	151
Araçatuba	ESDJ	...	...	...	...	171 289	...	...	2 668
Araguaina	ESDJ	...	...	...	...	115 901	...	...	...
Araguario	ESDJ	...	...	...	...	103 243	...	...	...
Arapiraca	ESDJ	...	...	...	...	188 988	...	...	...
Araraquara	ESDJ	...	...	...	...	185 064	...	...	...
Araras	ESDJ	...	...	...	...	106 261	...	...	...
Atibaia	ESDJ	...	...	...	...	114 090	...	...	...
Bagé	ESDJ	...	...	...	...	116 084	...	...	7 185
Barbacena	ESDJ	...	...	...	...	115 856	...	...	...
Barueri	ESDJ	...	...	...	...	217 510	...	...	...
Barra Mansa	ESDJ	...	...	...	...	171 470	...	...	830
Barreiras	ESDJ	...	...	...	...	116 874	...	...	...
Barretos	ESDJ	...	...	...	...	104 913	...	...	...
Bauru	ESDJ	...	...	...	...	322 554	...	...	702
Belém	ESDJ	...	...	...	...	1 304 314	...	...	736
Belford Roxo	ESDJ	...	...	...	...	442 012	...	...	...
Belo Horizonte	ESDJ	...	...	...	...	2 258 857	...	...	335
Betim	ESDJ	...	...	...	...	323 188	...	...	376
Blumenou	ESDJ	...	...	...	...	267 580	...	...	509
Boa Vista	ESDJ	...	...	...	...	208 514	...	...	...
Botucatu	ESDJ	...	...	...	...	110 242	...	...	...
Bragança Paulista	ESDJ	...	...	...	...	127 959	...	...	770
BRASILIA	ESDJ	...	...	...	...	2 097 447	...	...	5 794
Cabo de Santo Agostinho	ESDJ	...	...	...	...	156 004	...	...	...
Cabo Frio	ESDJ	...	...	...	...	133 341	...	...	...
Cachoeirinha	ESDJ	...	...	...	...	109 839	...	...	...
Cachoeiro de Itapemirim	ESDJ	...	...	...	...	178 013	...	...	892
Camacari	ESDJ	...	...	...	...	166 985	...	...	718
Camaragibe	ESDJ	...	...	...	...	132 215	...	...	...
Campina Grande	ESDJ	...	...	...	...	358 526	...	...	970
Campinas	ESDJ	...	...	...	...	982 977	...	...	781

8. Population of capital cities and cities of 100 000 and more inhabitants: latest available year
Population des capitales et des villes de 100 000 habitants et plus: dernière année disponible (continued — suite)

(See notes at end of table. — Voir notes à la fin du tableau.)

Continent, country or area, date and city / Continent, pays ou zone, date et ville	Code[1]	City proper — Ville proprement dite Population				Urban agglomeration — Agglomération urbaine Population			
		Both sexes Les deux sexes	Male Masculin	Female Féminin	Surface area Superficie (km²)	Both sexes Les deux sexes	Male Masculin	Female Féminin	Surface area Superficie (km²)
AMERICA, SOUTH — AMERIQUE DU SUD									
Brazil — Brésil[15]									
2001									
Campo Grande	ESDJ	...	...	...	...	679 281	...	...	8 091
Campos dos Goytacazes	ESDJ	...	...	...	...	410 220	...	...	4 536
Canoas	ESDJ	...	...	...	...	310 187	...	...	...
Carapicuíba	ESDJ	...	...	...	...	351 041	...	...	...
Cariacica	ESDJ	...	...	...	...	329 918	...	...	279
Caruaru	ESDJ	...	...	...	...	258 176	...	...	936
Cascavel	ESDJ	...	...	...	...	251 460	...	...	2 074
Castanhal	ESDJ	...	...	...	...	138 417	...	...	1 003
Catanduva	ESDJ	...	...	...	...	107 612	...	...	...
Caucaia	ESDJ	...	...	...	...	260 700	...	...	1 293
Caxias	ESDJ	...	...	...	...	140 450	...	...	6 724
Caxias do Sul	ESDJ	...	...	...	...	368 776	...	...	1 601
Chapecó	ESDJ	...	...	...	...	15 153	...	...	...
Codo	ESDJ	...	...	...	...	111 587	...	...	4 923
Colatina	ESDJ	...	...	...	...	104 702	...	...	2 094
Colombo	ESDJ	...	...	...	...	191 381	...	...	...
Conselheiro Lafaiete	ESDJ	...	...	...	...	104 338	...	...	...
Contagem	ESDJ	...	...	...	...	548 637	...	...	167
Cotia	ESDJ	...	...	...	...	153 070	...	...	...
Crato	ESDJ	...	...	...	...	106 078	...	...	...
Criciúma	ESDJ	...	...	...	...	173 269	...	...	...
Cubatao	ESDJ	...	...	...	...	109 963	...	...	...
Cuiabá	ESDJ	...	...	...	...	492 894	...	...	3 922
Curitiba	ESDJ	...	...	...	...	1 620 219	...	...	427
Diadema	ESDJ	...	...	...	...	362 663	...	...	...
Divinópolis	ESDJ	...	...	...	...	187 730	...	...	716
Dourados	ESDJ	...	...	...	...	168 197	...	...	4 082
Duque de Caxias	ESDJ	...	...	...	...	783 517	...	...	463
Embu	ESDJ	...	...	...	...	213 017	...	...	...
Feira de Santana	ESDJ	...	...	...	...	490 307	...	...	1 344
Ferraz de Vasconcelos	ESDJ	...	...	...	...	147 966	...	...	...
Florianópolis	ESDJ	...	...	...	...	352 401	...	...	440
Fortaleza	ESDJ	...	...	...	...	2 183 612	...	...	336
Foz do Iguaçu	ESDJ	...	...	...	...	266 771	...	...	596
Franca	ESDJ	...	...	...	...	294 067	...	...	...
Francisco Morato	ESDJ	...	...	...	...	139 309	...	...	...
Franco da Rocha	ESDJ	...	...	...	...	110 755	...	...	...
Garanhuns	ESDJ	...	...	...	...	119 336	...	...	456
Goiânia	ESDJ	...	...	...	...	1 111 622	...	...	788
Governador Valadares	ESDJ	...	...	...	...	248 960	...	...	2 447
Gravatai	ESDJ	...	...	...	...	238 759	...	...	...
Guaratinguetá	ESDJ	...	...	...	...	105 459	...	...	...
Guarapuava	ESDJ	...	...	...	...	157 283	...	...	5 365
Guarujá	ESDJ	...	...	...	...	271 902	...	...	...
Guarulhos	ESDJ	...	...	...	...	1 106 064	...	...	...
Hortolandia	ESDJ	...	...	...	...	159 749	...	...	...
Ibirité	ESDJ	...	...	...	...	139 703	...	...	...
Ilhéus	ESDJ	...	...	...	...	221 654	...	...	1 712
Imperatriz	ESDJ	...	...	...	...	230 768	...	...	6 014
Indaiatuba	ESDJ	...	...	...	...	152 462	...	...	...
Ipatinga	ESDJ	...	...	...	...	216 429	...	...	231
Itaboraí	ESDJ	...	...	...	...	192 649	...	...	569
Itabuna	ESDJ	...	...	...	...	197 829	...	...	...
Itajaí	ESDJ	...	...	...	...	150 804	...	...	...
Itapetininga	ESDJ	...	...	...	...	128 306	...	...	2 035
Itapecerica da Serra	ESDJ	...	...	...	...	134 499	...	...	...
Itapevi	ESDJ	...	...	...	...	169 106	...	...	...

8. Population of capital cities and cities of 100 000 and more inhabitants: latest available year
Population des capitales et des villes de 100 000 habitants et plus: dernière année disponible (continued — suite)

(See notes at end of table. — Voir notes à la fin du tableau.)

Continent, country or area, date and city / Continent, pays ou zone, date et ville	Code[1]	City proper — Ville proprement dite Population				Urban agglomeration — Agglomération urbaine Population			
		Both sexes Les deux sexes	Male Masculin	Female Féminin	Surface area Superficie (km²)	Both sexes Les deux sexes	Male Masculin	Female Féminin	Surface area Superficie (km²)
AMERICA, SOUTH — AMERIQUE DU SUD									
Brazil — Brésil[15]									
2001									
Itaquaquecetuba	ESDJ	...	...	...	...	285 610	...	...	...
Itu	ESDJ	...	...	...	...	138 741	...	...	640
Jaboatao dos Guarapes	ESDJ	...	...	...	...	592 297	...	...	...
Jacareí	ESDJ	...	...	...	...	194 733	...	...	...
Jaraguá do Sul	ESDJ	...	...	...	...	112 245	...	...	...
Jaú	ESDJ	...	...	...	...	113 952	...	...	...
Jequié	ESDJ	...	...	...	...	147 403	...	...	3 113
Ji-Paraná	ESDJ	...	...	...	...	107 869	...	...	...
Joao Pessoa	ESDJ	...	...	...	...	607 441	...	...	...
Joinville	ESDJ	...	...	...	...	446 064	...	...	1 080
Juazeiro	ESDJ	...	...	...	...	179 667	...	...	5 615
Juàzeiro do Norte	ESDJ	...	...	...	...	216 560	...	...	...
Juiz de Fora	ESDJ	...	...	...	...	465 080	...	...	1 424
Jundiaí	ESDJ	...	...	...	...	326 915	...	...	432
Lages	ESDJ	...	...	...	...	158 681	...	...	5 287
Lauro de Freitas	ESDJ	...	...	...	...	118 678	...	...	...
Limeira	ESDJ	...	...	...	...	253 649	...	...	...
Linhares	ESDJ	...	...	...	...	114 332	...	...	4 388
Londrina	ESDJ	...	...	...	...	454 871	...	...	2 129
Luziânia	ESDJ	...	...	...	...	148 453	...	...	4 653
Macae	ESDJ	...	...	...	...	136 145	...	...	...
Macapá	ESDJ	...	...	...	...	295 898	...	...	...
Maceió	ESDJ	...	...	...	...	817 444	...	...	517
Magé	ESDJ	...	...	...	...	210 861	...	...	744
Manaus	ESDJ	...	...	...	...	1 451 958	...	...	11 349
Maraba	ESDJ	...	...	...	...	173 301	...	...	14 320
Maracanau	ESDJ	...	...	...	...	174 741	...	...	...
Marília	ESDJ	...	...	...	...	201 574	...	...	1 194
Maringá	ESDJ	...	...	...	...	294 380	...	...	490
Mauá	ESDJ	...	...	...	...	371 475	...	...	...
Mesquita	ESDJ	...	...	...	...	168 041	...	...	...
Moji das Cruzes	ESDJ	...	...	...	...	336 618	...	...	749
Moji-Guaçu	ESDJ	...	...	...	...	127 001	...	...	960
Montes Claros	ESDJ	...	...	...	...	313 688	...	...	4 135
Mossoró	ESDJ	...	...	...	...	215 610	...	...	2 108
Natal	ESDJ	...	...	...	...	722 144	...	...	...
Nilópolis	ESDJ	...	...	...	...	153 017	...	...	...
Niterói	ESDJ	...	...	...	...	461 204	...	...	131
Nossa Senhora do Socorro	ESDJ	...	...	...	...	138 662	...	...	...
Nova Friburgo	ESDJ	...	...	...	...	174 087	...	...	930
Nova Iguaçu	ESDJ	...	...	...	...	764 879	...	...	795
Nôvo Hamburgo	ESDJ	...	...	...	...	239 790	...	...	...
Olinda	ESDJ	...	...	...	...	372 014	...	...	...
Osasco	ESDJ	...	...	...	...	661 155	...	...	...
Palhoça	ESDJ	...	...	...	...	106 875	...	...	...
Palmas	ESDJ	...	...	...	...	150 884	...	...	...
Paranaguá	ESDJ	...	...	...	...	130 548	...	...	1 015
Parnaíba	ESDJ	...	...	...	...	134 122	...	...	1 053
Parnamirim	ESDJ	...	...	...	...	132 237	...	...	...
Passo Fundo	ESDJ	...	...	...	...	171 734	...	...	1 596
Patos de Minas	ESDJ	...	...	...	...	126 257	...	...	3 336
Paulista	ESDJ	...	...	...	...	268 282	...	...	...
Pelotas	ESDJ	...	...	...	...	324 752	...	...	1 924
Petrolina	ESDJ	...	...	...	...	225 199	...	...	6 116
Petrópolis	ESDJ	...	...	...	...	290 139	...	...	771
Pindamonhangaba	ESDJ	...	...	...	...	128 627	...	...	719
Pinhais	ESDJ	...	...	...	...	106 314	...	...	...

8. Population of capital cities and cities of 100 000 and more inhabitants: latest available year
Population des capitales et des villes de 100 000 habitants et plus: dernière année disponible (continued — suite)

(See notes at end of table. — Voir notes à la fin du tableau.)

Continent, country or area, date and city / Continent, pays ou zone, date et ville	Code[1]	City proper — Ville proprement dite Population				Urban agglomeration — Agglomération urbaine Population			
		Both sexes Les deux sexes	Male Masculin	Female Féminin	Surface area Superficie (km²)	Both sexes Les deux sexes	Male Masculin	Female Féminin	Surface area Superficie (km²)
AMERICA, SOUTH — AMERIQUE DU SUD									
Brazil — Brésil[15]									
2001									
Piracicaba	ESDJ	...	...	...	...	334 402	...	...	1 426
Poços de Caldas	ESDJ	...	...	...	...	138 691	...	...	533
Ponta Grossa	ESDJ	...	...	...	...	278 660	...	...	2 212
Porto Alegre	ESDJ	...	...	...	...	1 373 313	...	...	...
Porto Seguro	ESDJ	...	...	...	...	103 155	...	...	...
Porto Velho	ESDJ	...	...	...	...	342 264	...	...	...
Pouso Alegre	ESDJ	...	...	...	...	109 660	...	...	...
Praia Grande	ESDJ	...	...	...	...	200 199	...	...	...
Presidente Prudente	ESDJ	...	...	...	...	192 004	...	...	554
Queimados	ESDJ	...	...	...	...	124 495	...	...	...
Recife	ESDJ	...	...	...	...	1 437 190	...	...	...
Resende	ESDJ	...	...	...	...	106 995	...	...	...
Ribeirao das Neves	ESDJ	...	...	...	...	259 203	...	...	...
Ribeirao Prêto	ESDJ	...	...	...	...	514 160	...	...	...
Ribeirao Pires	ESDJ	...	...	...	...	106 700	...	...	...
Rio Branco	ESDJ	...	...	...	...	261 430	...	...	...
Rio Claro	ESDJ	...	...	...	...	171 750	...	...	503
Rio de Janeiro	ESDJ	...	...	...	...	5 897 485	...	...	1 256
Rio Grande	ESDJ	...	...	...	...	188 215	...	...	2 825
Rio Verde	ESDJ	...	...	...	...	119 829	...	...	9 136
Rondonópolis	ESDJ	...	...	...	...	153 281	...	...	4 594
Sabára	ESDJ	...	...	...	...	118 429	...	...	...
Salvador	ESDJ	...	...	...	...	2 485 702	...	...	313
Santa Bárbara D'Oeste	ESDJ	...	...	...	...	172 739	...	...	...
Santa Cruz do Sul	ESDJ	...	...	...	...	109 606	...	...	...
Santa Luzia (Minas Gerais)	ESDJ	...	...	...	...	190 479	...	...	...
Santa Maria	ESDJ	...	...	...	...	247 766	...	...	3 279
Santa Rita	ESDJ	...	...	...	...	118 207	...	...	...
Santarém	ESDJ	...	...	...	...	264 992	...	...	...
Santo André	ESDJ	...	...	...	...	652 305	...	...	...
Santos	ESDJ	...	...	...	...	417 817	...	...	725
Sao Bernardo do Campo	ESDJ	...	...	...	...	717 790	...	...	319
Sao Caetano do Sul	ESDJ	...	...	...	...	138 993	...	...	...
Sao Carlo	ESDJ	...	...	...	...	197 184	...	...	1 120
Sao Gonçalo	ESDJ	...	...	...	...	903 333	...	...	...
Sao Joao de Meriti	ESDJ	...	...	...	...	452 109	...	...	...
Sao José	ESDJ	...	...	...	...	177 775	...	...	...
Sao José de Ribamar	ESDJ	...	...	...	...	111 884	...	...	...
Sao José do Rio Prêto	ESDJ	...	...	...	...	367 247	...	...	586
Sao José dos Campos	ESDJ	...	...	...	...	550 762	...	...	1 186
Sao José dos Pinhais	ESDJ	...	...	...	...	213 625	...	...	923
Sao Leopoldo	ESDJ	...	...	...	...	196 531	...	...	...
Sao Luís	ESDJ	...	...	...	...	889 129	...	...	822
Sao Paulo	ESDJ	...	...	...	...	10 499 133	...	...	1 493
Sao Vicente	ESDJ	...	...	...	...	306 860	...	...	...
Sapucaia do Sul	ESDJ	...	...	...	...	124 862	...	...	...
Serra	ESDJ	...	...	...	...	334 840	...	...	549
Sete Lagoas	ESDJ	...	...	...	...	189 686	...	...	...
Sobral	ESDJ	...	...	...	...	158 513	...	...	1 646
Sorocaba	ESDJ	...	...	...	...	508 848	...	...	...
Sumaré	ESDJ	...	...	...	...	202 813	...	...	208
Susano	ESDJ	...	...	...	...	236 985	...	...	...
Taboao da Serra	ESDJ	...	...	...	...	202 049	...	...	...
Taubaté	ESDJ	...	...	...	...	248 667	...	...	...
Teixeira de Freitas	ESDJ	...	...	...	...	109 908	...	...	...
Teófilo Otoni	ESDJ	...	...	...	...	128 741	...	...	...
Teresina	ESDJ	...	...	...	...	728 881	...	...	1 356

8. Population of capital cities and cities of 100 000 and more inhabitants: latest available year
Population des capitales et des villes de 100 000 habitants et plus: dernière année disponible (continued — suite)

(See notes at end of table. — Voir notes à la fin du tableau.)

Continent, country or area, date and city / Continent, pays ou zone, date et ville	Code[1]	City proper — Ville proprement dite Population				Urban agglomeration — Agglomération urbaine Population			
		Both sexes Les deux sexes	Male Masculin	Female Féminin	Surface area Superficie (km²)	Both sexes Les deux sexes	Male Masculin	Female Féminin	Surface area Superficie (km²)
AMERICA, SOUTH — AMERIQUE DU SUD									
Brazil — Brésil[15]									
2001									
Teresópolis	ESDJ	...	...	...	...	*140 144*	...	...	*768*
Timon	ESDJ	...	...	...	...	*131 821*	...	...	*1 702*
Uberaba	ESDJ	...	...	...	...	*256 539*	...	...	*4 524*
Uberlândia	ESDJ	...	...	...	...	*516 870*	...	...	*4 040*
Uruguaiana	ESDJ	...	...	...	...	*128 186*	...	...	*6 763*
Varginha	ESDJ	...	...	...	...	*111 480*	...	...	...
Varzea Grande	ESDJ	...	...	...	...	*221 825*	...	...	*900*
Viamao	ESDJ	...	...	...	...	*232 755*	...	...	...
Vila Velha	ESDJ	...	...	...	...	*355 739*	...	...	...
Vitória	ESDJ	...	...	...	...	*296 012*	...	...	...
Vitória da Conquista	ESDJ	...	...	...	...	*267 189*	...	...	*3 743*
Vitória de Santo Antao	ESDJ	...	...	...	...	*118 894*	...	...	*344*
Volta Redonda	ESDJ	...	...	...	...	*244 715*	...	...	...
Chile — Chili									
2000									
Antofagasta	ESDF	251 868	124 419	127 449	...	...	...	...	...
Arica	ESDF	185 622	92 114	93 508	...	...	...	...	...
Calama	ESDF	128 073	64 732	63 341	...	...	...	...	...
Chillán	ESDF	171 207	81 327	89 880	...	...	...	...	...
Concepción	ESDF	379 860	185 399	194 461	...	...	...	...	...
Copiapó	ESDF	122 441	62 086	60 355	...	...	...	...	...
Coquimbo	ESDF	135 622	66 025	69 597	...	...	...	...	...
Iquique	ESDF	169 997	86 726	83 271	...	...	...	...	...
La Serena	ESDF	130 426	63 009	67 417	...	...	...	...	...
Los Angeles	ESDF	116 739	56 780	59 959	...	...	...	...	...
Osorno	ESDF	131 666	63 373	68 293	...	...	...	...	...
Puente Alto	ESDF	425 056	208 546	216 510	...	...	...	...	...
Puerto Montt	ESDF	138 138	67 700	70 438	...	...	...	...	...
Punta Arenas	ESDF	124 246	63 922	60 324	...	...	...	...	...
Quilpué	ESDF	120 597	56 770	63 827	...	...	...	...	...
Rancagua	ESDF	213 735	103 691	110 044	...	...	...	...	...
San Bernardo	ESDF	246 491	123 225	123 266	...	...	...	...	...
SANTIAGO[86]	ESDF	4 788 543	2 301 070	2 487 473	...	...	...	...	...
Talca	ESDF	182 445	87 010	95 435	...	...	...	...	...
Talcahuano	ESDF	280 941	137 927	143 014	...	...	...	...	...
Temuco	ESDF	273 223	130 336	142 887	...	...	...	...	...
Valdivia	ESDF	125 999	61 350	64 649	...	...	...	...	...
Valparaíso	ESDF	285 262	139 545	145 717	...	...	...	...	...
Viña del Mar	ESDF	342 715	163 694	179 021	...	...	...	...	...
Colombia — Colombie									
2001									
Armenia	ESDF	*300 026*	...	...	115	...	...	...	...
Barrancabermeja	ESDF	*199 937*	...	...	1 274	...	...	...	...
Barranquilla	ESDF	*1 278 521*	...	...	166	...	...	...	...
Bello	ESDF	*360 054*	...	...	151	...	...	...	...
Bucaramanga	ESDF	*539 805*	...	...	154	...	...	...	...
Buenaventura	ESDF	*268 723*	...	...	6 785	...	...	...	...
Buga	ESDF	*127 745*	...	...	873	...	...	...	...
Cali	ESDF	*2 212 430*	...	...	552	...	...	...	...
Cartagena	ESDF	*927 117*	...	...	570	...	...	...	...
Cartago	ESDF	*133 938*	...	...	260	...	...	...	...
Cucuta	ESDF	*662 599*	...	...	1 098	...	...	...	...
Dos Quebradas	ESDF	*178 334*	...	...	80	...	...	...	...
Duitama	ESDF	*114 732*	...	...	229	...	...	...	...
Envigado	ESDF	*155 569*	...	...	51	...	...	...	...
Florencia	ESDF	*134 438*	...	...	2 292	...	...	...	...
Floridablanca	ESDF	*238 602*	...	...	101	...	...	...	...

8. Population of capital cities and cities of 100 000 and more inhabitants: latest available year
Population des capitales et des villes de 100 000 habitants et plus: dernière année disponible (continued — suite)

(See notes at end of table. — Voir notes à la fin du tableau.)

Continent, country or area, date and city Continent, pays ou zone, date et ville	Code[1]	City proper — Ville proprement dite Population				Urban agglomeration — Agglomération urbaine Population			
		Both sexes Les deux sexes	Male Masculin	Female Féminin	Surface area Superficie (km²)	Both sexes Les deux sexes	Male Masculin	Female Féminin	Surface area Superficie (km²)
AMERICA, SOUTH — AMERIQUE DU SUD									
Colombia — Colombie									
2001									
Girardot	ESDF	121 354	...	...	130	...	...	...	...
Ibagué	ESDF	430 400	...	...	1 439	...	...	...	...
Itagüi	ESDF	251 627	...	...	17	...	...	...	...
Maicao	ESDF	123 437	...	...	2 229	...	...	...	...
Manizales	ESDF	368 867	...	...	477	...	...	...	...
Medellín	ESDF	2 003 780	...	...	387	...	...	...	...
Monteria	ESDF	330 144	...	...	3 043	...	...	...	...
Neiva	ESDF	339 768	...	...	1 468	...	...	...	...
Palmira	ESDF	279 554	...	...	1 044	...	...	...	...
Pasto	ESDF	396 007	...	...	1 181	...	...	...	...
Popayan	ESDF	227 200	...	...	464	...	...	...	...
Pereira	ESDF	478 001	...	...	702	...	...	...	...
SANTA FE DE BOGOTA	ESDF	6 573 291	...	...	1 605	...	...	...	...
Santa Marta	ESDF	398 368	...	...	2 369	...	...	...	...
Sincelejo	ESDF	241 706	...	...	292	...	...	...	...
Soacha	ESDF	290 574	...	...	187	...	...	...	...
Sogamoso	ESDF	150 981	...	...	214	...	...	...	...
Soledad	ESDF	312 254	...	...	67	...	...	...	...
Tulua	ESDF	182 526	...	...	818	...	...	...	...
Tunja	ESDF	121 525	...	...	118	...	...	...	...
Valledupar	ESDF	331 547	...	...	4 225	...	...	...	...
Villavicencio	ESDF	331 417	...	...	1 328	...	...	...	...
Ecuador — Equateur									
2000									
Ambato	ESDF	174 261	...	...	27	...	...	...	...
Cuenca	ESDF	278 035	...	...	47	...	...	...	...
Esmeraldas	ESDF	125 914	...	...	8	...	...	...	...
Guayaquil	ESDF	2 117 553	...	...	193	...	...	...	...
Ibarra	ESDF	136 558	...	...	39	...	...	...	...
Loja	ESDF	127 200	...	...	21	...	...	...	...
Machala	ESDF	216 901	...	...	23	...	...	...	...
Manta	ESDF	168 642	...	...	38	...	...	...	...
Milagro	ESDF	126 433	...	...	17	...	...	...	...
Portoviejo	ESDF	180 641	...	...	38	...	...	...	...
Quevedo	ESDF	133 996	...	...	20	...	...	...	...
QUITO	ESDF	1 615 809	...	...	170	...	...	...	...
Riobamba	ESDF	126 101	...	...	24	...	...	...	...
Santo Domingo de los Colorados	ESDF	211 732	...	...	43	...	...	...	...
Falkland Islands (Malvinas) — Iles Falkland (Malvinas)									
2001									
STANLEY	CDFC	1 989	1 009	980	...	...	...	...	...
French Guiana — Guyane Française									
1999									
CAYENNE[9]	CDFC	50 395	24 496	25 899	24	...	...	...	...
Guyana									
1976									
GEORGETOWN	ESDF	72 049	...	...	...	187 056	...	...	...
Paraguay									
2002									
ASUNCION[87]	CDFC	513 399	...	...	117	1 620 483	...	...	...
Capiatá	CDFC	154 469	...	...	...	...	...	...	...
Ciudad del Este	CDFC	223 350	...	...	57	333 535	...	...	...
Fernando de la Mora	CDFC	114 332	...	...	...	...	...	...	...
Lambaré	CDFC	119 984	...	...	...	...	...	...	...
Luque	CDFC	170 433	...	...	...	...	...	...	...

(See notes at end of table. — Voir notes à la fin du tableau.)

Continent, country or area, date and city / Continent, pays ou zone, date et ville	Code[1]	City proper — Ville proprement dite Population				Urban agglomeration — Agglomération urbaine Population			
		Both sexes Les deux sexes	Male Masculin	Female Féminin	Surface area Superficie (km²)	Both sexes Les deux sexes	Male Masculin	Female Féminin	Surface area Superficie (km²)
AMERICA, SOUTH — AMERIQUE DU SUD									
Paraguay									
2002									
San Lorenzo	CDFC	202 745	...	...	91	...	...	...	...
Peru — Pérou									
1993									
Arequipa	CDFC	619 156	...	...	...	642 478	...	...	...
Ayacucho	CDFC	105 918	...	...	...	110 745	...	...	...
Cajamarca	CDFC	92 447	...	...	...	101 627	...	...	...
Chiclayo	CDFC	411 536	...	...	...	566 027	...	...	...
Chimbote	CDFC	268 979	...	...	...	309 435	...	...	...
Cuzco	CDFC	255 568	...	...	...	257 543	...	...	...
Huancayo	CDFC	258 209	...	...	...	342 843	...	...	...
Huánuco	CDFC	118 814	...	...	...	125 686	...	...	...
Ica	CDFC	122 667	...	...	...	161 406	...	...	...
Iquitos	CDFC	274 759	...	...	...	287 429	...	...	...
Juliaca	CDFC	142 576	...	...	...	145 724	...	...	...
LIMA[88]	CDFC	5 681 941	...	...	...	6 321 173	...	...	...
Piura	CDFC	277 964	...	...	...	...	...	...	...
Pucallpa	CDFC	172 286	...	...	...	180 664	...	...	...
Sullana	CDFC	147 361	...	...	...	206 706	...	...	...
Tacna	CDFC	174 336	...	...	...	177 058	...	...	...
Trujillo	CDFC	509 312	...	...	...	588 638	...	...	...
1998									
LIMA[88]	ESDF	7 200 936	3 539 354	3 661 582	...	...	...	...	...
Suriname									
1995									
PARAMARIBO	ESDF	216 000	...	...	183	265 000	...	...	626
Uruguay									
1996									
MONTEVIDEO	CDFC	1 303 182	605 658	697 524	530	...	...	...	...
Venezuela									
1998									
Acarigua-Araure	ESDF	227 684	...	...	1 065	...	...	...	...
Barcelona	ESDF	301 595	...	...	463	...	...	...	...
Barcelona-Puerto La Cruz	ESDF	484 149	...	...	707	...	...	...	...
Barinas	ESDF	221 558	...	...	848	...	...	...	...
Barquisimeto	ESDF	810 809	...	...	2 645	...	...	...	...
Cabimas	ESDF	213 290	...	...	175	...	...	...	...
CARACAS[89]	ESDF	1 975 294	...	...	433	...	...	...	...
Carúpano	ESDF	116 107	...	...	203	...	...	...	...
Catia la Mar	ESDF	117 013	...	...	76	...	...	...	...
Ciudad Bolívar	ESDF	278 525	...	...	5 851	...	...	...	...
Ciudad Guayana	ESDF	641 998	...	...	1 612	...	...	...	...
Coro	ESDF	167 048	...	...	438	...	...	...	...
Cumaná	ESDF	265 621	...	...	405	...	...	...	...
Guarenas	ESDF	169 202	...	...	180	...	...	...	...
Los Teques	ESDF	176 292	...	...	98	...	...	...	...
Maracaibo	ESDF	1 706 547	...	...	604	...	...	...	...
Maracay	ESDF	458 761	...	...	169	...	...	...	...
Maturín	ESDF	262 167	...	...	...	...	...	...	...
Mérida	ESDF	272 437	...	...	482	...	...	...	...
Puerto Cabello	ESDF	176 347	...	...	309	...	...	...	...
Punto Fijo	ESDF	118 126	...	...	31	...	...	...	...
San Cristóbal	ESDF	272 374	...	...	248	...	...	...	...
San Fernando de Apure	ESDF	121 949	...	...	...	...	...	...	...
Turmero	ESDF	203 434	...	...	208	...	...	...	...
Valencia	ESDF	1 263 888	...	...	1 212	...	...	...	...
Valera	ESDF	121 090	...	...	55	...	...	...	...

8. Population of capital cities and cities of 100 000 and more inhabitants: latest available year
Population des capitales et des villes de 100 000 habitants et plus: dernière année disponible (continued — suite)

(See notes at end of table. — Voir notes à la fin du tableau.)

Continent, country or area, date and city Continent, pays ou zone, date et ville	Code[1]	City proper — Ville proprement dite Population				Urban agglomeration — Agglomération urbaine Population			
		Both sexes Les deux sexes	Male Masculin	Female Féminin	Surface area Superficie (km²)	Both sexes Les deux sexes	Male Masculin	Female Féminin	Surface area Superficie (km²)
ASIA — ASIE									
Afghanistan									
1988									
Herat	ESDF	*177 300*	...	...	...	...	...	...	...
KABUL	ESDF	*1 424 400*	...	...	...	...	...	...	...
Kandahar (Quandahar)	ESDF	*225 500*	...	...	...	...	...	...	...
Mazar-i-Sharif	ESDF	*130 600*	...	...	...	...	...	...	...
Armenia — Arménie									
1999									
Kirovakan (Vanadzoz)	ESDF	172 600	82 850	89 750	27	...	...	...	...
Leninakan (Gyumzi)	ESDF	211 650	101 590	110 060	50	...	...	...	...
YEREVAN	ESDF	1 248 461	601 642	646 819	210	...	...	...	...
Azerbaijan — Azerbaïdjan									
1999									
BAKU	CDJC	1 788 854	869 689	919 165	2 130	...	...	...	...
Ganja	CDJC	299 342	143 478	155 864	110	...	...	...	...
Sumgayit	CDJC	283 184	138 739	144 445	80	...	...	...	...
2000									
BAKU	ESDF	1 802 000	877 500	924 500	2 130	...	...	...	...
Ganja	ESDF	300 700	144 300	156 400	110	...	...	...	...
Sumgayit	ESDF	286 000	140 300	145 700	80	...	...	...	...
2001									
BAKU	ESDF	1 817 900	886 000	931 900	2 130	...	...	...	...
Ganja	ESDF	301 400	144 700	156 700	110	...	...	...	...
Sumgayit	ESDF	288 400	141 700	146 700	80	...	...	...	...
Bahrain — Bahreïn									
1992									
MANAMA	ESDF	*140 401*	...	...	26	...	...	...	...
Bangladesh									
1991									
Barisal	CDFC	...	...	...	...	163 481	...	...	...
Chittagong	CDFC	...	...	...	...	1 363 998	...	...	...
Comilla	CDFC	...	...	...	...	143 282	...	...	...
DHAKA	CDFC	...	...	...	...	3 397 187	...	...	...
Dinajpur	CDFC	...	...	...	...	126 189	...	...	...
Jamalpur	CDFC	...	...	...	...	101 242	...	...	...
Jessore	CDFC	...	...	...	...	160 198	...	...	...
Khulna	CDFC	...	...	...	...	545 849	...	...	...
Mymensingh	CDFC	...	...	...	...	185 517	...	...	...
Narayanganj	CDFC	...	...	...	...	268 952	...	...	...
Nawabganj	CDFC	...	...	...	...	121 205	...	...	...
Pabna	CDFC	...	...	...	...	104 479	...	...	...
Rajshahi	CDFC	...	...	...	...	299 671	...	...	...
Rangpur	CDFC	...	...	...	...	203 931	...	...	...
Saidpur	CDFC	...	...	...	...	102 030	...	...	...
Tangail	CDFC	...	...	...	...	104 387	...	...	...
Tongi	CDFC	...	...	...	...	154 175	...	...	...
Bhutan — Bhoutan									
1977									
THIMPHU	ESDF	*8 922*	...	...	...	...	...	...	...
Brunei Darussalam — Brunéi Darussalam									
1981									
BANDAR SERI BEGAWAN	CDFC	49 902	...	...	...	...	...	...	...
Cambodia — Cambodge									
2002									
Bat Dambang	ESDF	*171 382*	*82 785*	*88 597*	...	...	...	...	...
PHNOM PENH	ESDF	*703 963*	*339 763*	*364 200*	...	*1 234 444*	...	...	...
Seam Reab	ESDF	*140 966*	*69 052*	*71 914*	...	...	...	...	...

8. Population of capital cities and cities of 100 000 and more inhabitants: latest available year
Population des capitales et des villes de 100 000 habitants et plus: dernière année disponible (continued — suite)

(See notes at end of table. — Voir notes à la fin du tableau.)

Continent, country or area, date and city — Continent, pays ou zone, date et ville	Code[1]	City proper — Ville proprement dite Population				Urban agglomeration — Agglomération urbaine Population			
		Both sexes Les deux sexes	Male Masculin	Female Féminin	Surface area Superficie (km²)	Both sexes Les deux sexes	Male Masculin	Female Féminin	Surface area Superficie (km²)
ASIA — ASIE									
China — Chine									
1999									
Chiayi	ESDF	264 286	133 270	131 016	...	...	...	...	...
Hsinchu	ESDF	359 087	183 682	175 405	...	...	...	...	...
Kaohsiung[90]	ESDF	1 468 586	744 243	724 343	...	...	...	...	...
Keelung	ESDF	383 272	196 952	186 320	...	...	...	...	...
Taichung	ESDF	930 175	461 069	469 106	...	...	...	...	...
Tainan	ESDF	725 445	366 061	359 384	...	...	...	...	...
Taipei[90]	ESDF	2 640 322	1 310 368	1 329 954	...	...	...	...	...
2000									
Acheng	CDJC	638 894	327 774	311 120	...	...	...	...	...
Akesu	CDJC	561 822	295 811	266 011	...	...	...	...	...
Aletai	CDJC	178 510	91 207	87 303	...	...	...	...	...
Anda	CDJC	473 091	243 349	229 742	...	...	...	...	...
An'guo	CDJC	378 830	189 944	188 886	...	...	...	...	...
Ankang	CDJC	843 426	443 270	400 156	...	...	...	...	...
Anlu	CDJC	611 990	314 089	297 901	...	...	...	...	...
Anning	CDJC	295 173	161 481	133 692	...	...	...	...	...
Anqing	CDJC	582 751	293 884	288 867	...	...	...	...	...
Anqiu	CDJC	1 096 782	554 403	542 379	...	...	...	...	...
Anshan	CDJC	1 556 285	787 838	768 447	...	...	...	...	...
Anshun	CDJC	767 307	395 894	371 413	...	...	...	...	...
Anyang	CDJC	768 992	390 120	378 872	...	...	...	...	...
Atushi	CDJC	200 345	101 867	98 478	...	...	...	...	...
Baicheng	CDJC	484 979	244 453	240 526	...	...	...	...	...
Baise	CDJC	340 483	177 310	163 173	...	...	...	...	...
Baishan	CDJC	335 400	172 109	163 291	...	...	...	...	...
Baiyin	CDJC	460 982	243 672	217 310	...	...	...	...	...
Baoding	CDJC	902 496	455 625	446 871	...	...	...	...	...
Baoji	CDJC	600 377	308 493	291 884	...	...	...	...	...
Baoshan	CDJC	846 865	430 076	416 789	...	...	...	...	...
Baotou	CDJC	1 671 181	862 495	808 686	...	...	...	...	...
Bazhong	CDJC	1 185 862	616 323	569 539	...	...	...	...	...
Bazhou	CDJC	557 901	285 321	272 580	...	...	...	...	...
Beian	CDJC	442 474	226 743	215 731	...	...	...	...	...
Beihai	CDJC	558 635	290 544	268 091	...	...	...	...	...
BEIJING (PEKING)	CDJC	11 509 595	6 020 903	5 488 692	...	...	...	...	...
Beiliu	CDJC	1 049 035	557 967	491 068	...	...	...	...	...
Beining	CDJC	527 217	270 153	257 064	...	...	...	...	...
Beipiao	CDJC	573 836	291 584	282 252	...	...	...	...	...
Bengbu	CDJC	809 399	413 444	395 955	...	...	...	...	...
Benxi	CDJC	980 069	495 102	484 967	...	...	...	...	...
Bijie	CDJC	1 128 230	589 537	538 693	...	...	...	...	...
Binzhou	CDJC	600 883	299 952	300 931	...	...	...	...	...
Bole	CDJC	224 869	116 506	108 363	...	...	...	...	...
Botou	CDJC	550 888	280 209	270 679	...	...	...	...	...
Bozhou	CDJC	1 351 939	697 126	654 813	...	...	...	...	...
Cangzhou	CDJC	443 561	223 648	219 913	...	...	...	...	...
Cenxi	CDJC	731 623	384 212	347 411	...	...	...	...	...
Changchun	CDJC	3 225 557	1 647 216	1 578 341	...	...	...	...	...
Changde	CDJC	1 346 739	686 467	660 272	...	...	...	...	...
Changge	CDJC	646 306	332 022	314 284	...	...	...	...	...
Changji	CDJC	387 169	202 275	184 894	...	...	...	...	...
Changle	CDJC	689 815	358 963	330 852	...	...	...	...	...
Changning	CDJC	795 223	428 332	366 891	...	...	...	...	...
Changsha	CDJC	2 122 873	1 099 304	1 023 569	...	...	...	...	...
Changshu	CDJC	1 239 637	598 034	641 603	...	...	...	...	...
Changyi	CDJC	683 182	340 763	342 419	...	...	...	...	...
Changzhi	CDJC	648 981	332 246	316 735	...	...	...	...	...
Changzhou	CDJC	1 081 845	552 850	528 995	...	...	...	...	...

(See notes at end of table. — Voir notes à la fin du tableau.)

Continent, country or area, date and city / Continent, pays ou zone, date et ville	Code[1]	City proper — Ville proprement dite Population				Urban agglomeration — Agglomération urbaine Population			
		Both sexes Les deux sexes	Male Masculin	Female Féminin	Surface area Superficie (km²)	Both sexes Les deux sexes	Male Masculin	Female Féminin	Surface area Superficie (km²)

ASIA — ASIE

China — Chine
2000

Chaohu	CDJC	778 864	396 961	381 903	...	...	...	...	...
Chaoyang (Guangdong)	CDJC	2 470 812	1 256 428	1 214 384	...	...	...	...	...
Chaoyang (Liaoning)	CDJC	475 038	238 128	236 910	...	...	...	...	...
Chaozhou	CDJC	363 582	181 260	182 322	...	...	...	...	...
Chengde	CDJC	437 251	221 221	216 030	...	...	...	...	...
Chengdu	CDJC	4 333 541	2 258 996	2 074 545	...	...	...	...	...
Chenghai	CDJC	860 003	428 157	431 846	...	...	...	...	...
Chenzhou	CDJC	655 014	340 799	314 215	...	...	...	...	...
Chibi	CDJC	510 926	267 233	243 693	...	...	...	...	...
Chifeng	CDJC	1 153 723	589 450	564 273	...	...	...	...	...
Chishui	CDJC	251 780	130 227	121 553	...	...	...	...	...
Chizhou	CDJC	555 489	280 395	275 094	...	...	...	...	...
Chongqing	CDJC	9 691 901	5 013 398	4 678 503	...	...	...	...	...
Chongzhou	CDJC	650 698	330 345	320 353	...	...	...	...	...
Chuxiong	CDJC	503 682	261 315	242 367	...	...	...	...	...
Chuzhou	CDJC	493 735	251 117	242 618	...	...	...	...	...
Cixi	CDJC	1 214 537	615 279	599 258	...	...	...	...	...
Conghua	CDJC	517 552	264 150	253 402	...	...	...	...	...
Daan	CDJC	430 512	219 682	210 830	...	...	...	...	...
Dafeng	CDJC	756 766	383 391	373 375	...	...	...	...	...
Dali	CDJC	521 169	262 564	258 605	...	...	...	...	...
Dalian	CDJC	3 245 191	1 641 485	1 603 706	...	...	...	...	...
Dandong	CDJC	780 414	389 277	391 137	...	...	...	...	...
Dangyang	CDJC	495 946	253 125	242 821	...	...	...	...	...
Danjiangkou	CDJC	501 126	262 922	238 204	...	...	...	...	...
Danyang	CDJC	877 232	442 296	434 936	...	...	...	...	...
Danzhou	CDJC	835 465	442 636	392 829	...	...	...	...	...
Daqing	CDJC	1 380 051	704 765	675 286	...	...	...	...	...
Dashiqiao	CDJC	714 670	370 713	343 957	...	...	...	...	...
Datong	CDJC	1 526 744	785 754	740 990	...	...	...	...	...
Daye	CDJC	873 859	460 417	413 442	...	...	...	...	...
Dazhou	CDJC	384 525	192 819	191 706	...	...	...	...	...
Dehui	CDJC	878 349	448 146	430 203	...	...	...	...	...
Dengfeng	CDJC	609 085	321 081	288 004	...	...	...	...	...
Dengta	CDJC	502 149	259 895	242 254	...	...	...	...	...
Dengzhou	CDJC	1 290 656	677 791	612 865	...	...	...	...	...
Dexing	CDJC	297 784	155 178	142 606	...	...	...	...	...
Deyang	CDJC	628 876	324 823	304 053	...	...	...	...	...
Dezhou	CDJC	552 445	277 994	274 451	...	...	...	...	...
Dingzhou	CDJC	1 107 903	559 214	548 689	...	...	...	...	...
Dongfang	CDJC	358 318	188 840	169 478	...	...	...	...	...
Donggang	CDJC	640 340	324 344	315 996	...	...	...	...	...
Dongguan	CDJC	6 445 777	3 035 742	3 410 035	...	...	...	...	...
Dongsheng	CDJC	252 566	129 512	123 054	...	...	...	...	...
Dongtai	CDJC	1 164 653	583 122	581 531	...	...	...	...	...
Dongxing	CDJC	108 131	58 939	49 192	...	...	...	...	...
Dongyang	CDJC	753 094	375 565	377 529	...	...	...	...	...
Dongying	CDJC	788 844	407 241	381 603	...	...	...	...	...
Dujiangyan	CDJC	621 980	314 845	307 135	...	...	...	...	...
Dunhua	CDJC	480 834	247 966	232 868	...	...	...	...	...
Dunhuang	CDJC	187 578	96 679	90 899	...	...	...	...	...
Duyun	CDJC	463 426	241 421	222 005	...	...	...	...	...
Enping	CDJC	464 898	240 765	224 133	...	...	...	...	...
Enshi	CDJC	755 725	397 284	358 441	...	...	...	...	...
Emeishan	CDJC	423 070	217 201	205 869	...	...	...	...	...
Ezhou	CDJC	1 023 285	533 940	489 345	...	...	...	...	...
Fangchenggang	CDJC	422 514	233 979	188 535	...	...	...	...	...
Feicheng	CDJC	948 602	476 032	472 570	...	...	...	...	...

(See notes at end of table. — Voir notes à la fin du tableau.)

Continent, country or area, date and city / Continent, pays ou zone, date et ville	Code[1]	City proper — Ville proprement dite Population				Urban agglomeration — Agglomération urbaine Population			
		Both sexes Les deux sexes	Male Masculin	Female Féminin	Surface area Superficie (km²)	Both sexes Les deux sexes	Male Masculin	Female Féminin	Surface area Superficie (km²)
ASIA — ASIE									
China — Chine									
2000									
Fengcheng (Jiangxi)	CDJC	1 216 412	644 029	572 383	...	...	...	...	...
Fengcheng (Liaoning)	CDJC	560 384	288 402	271 982	...	...	...	...	...
Fenghua	CDJC	471 558	239 252	232 306	...	...	...	...	...
Fengnan	CDJC	550 872	285 442	265 430	...	...	...	...	...
Fengzhen	CDJC	264 204	137 562	126 642	...	...	...	...	...
Fenyang	CDJC	387 046	199 129	187 917	...	...	...	...	...
Foshan	CDJC	768 656	398 973	369 683	...	...	...	...	...
Fuan	CDJC	554 057	296 379	257 678	...	...	...	...	...
Fuding	CDJC	521 070	276 419	244 651	...	...	...	...	...
Fujin	CDJC	420 579	215 650	204 929	...	...	...	...	...
Fukang	CDJC	152 965	80 372	72 593	...	...	...	...	...
Fuqing	CDJC	1 174 540	597 890	576 650	...	...	...	...	...
Fuquan	CDJC	292 720	155 972	136 748	...	...	...	...	...
Fushun	CDJC	1 434 447	722 549	711 898	...	...	...	...	...
Fuxin	CDJC	627 855	311 912	315 943	...	...	...	...	...
Fuyang (Anhui)	CDJC	628 633	324 172	304 461	...	...	...	...	...
Fuyang (Zhejiang)	CDJC	1 719 057	878 560	840 497	...	...	...	...	...
Fuzhou (Fujian)	CDJC	2 124 435	1 086 638	1 037 797	...	...	...	...	...
Fuzhou (Jiangxi)	CDJC	1 007 391	533 936	473 455	...	...	...	...	...
Gaizhou	CDJC	883 811	455 641	428 170	...	...	...	...	...
Ganzhou	CDJC	494 600	254 272	240 328	...	...	...	...	...
Gaoan	CDJC	788 329	416 678	371 651	...	...	...	...	...
Gaobeidian	CDJC	538 582	268 027	270 555	...	...	...	...	...
Gaocheng	CDJC	758 269	380 317	377 952	...	...	...	...	...
Gaomi	CDJC	842 403	420 956	421 447	...	...	...	...	...
Gaoming	CDJC	301 041	159 746	141 295	...	...	...	...	...
Gaoping	CDJC	471 671	236 439	235 232	...	...	...	...	...
Gaoyao	CDJC	625 125	314 474	310 651	...	...	...	...	...
Gaoyou	CDJC	797 752	392 863	404 889	...	...	...	...	...
Gaozhou	CDJC	1 219 132	639 497	579 635	...	...	...	...	...
Geermu	CDJC	135 897	73 572	62 325	...	...	...	...	...
Gejiu	CDJC	453 311	243 377	209 934	...	...	...	...	...
Genhe	CDJC	157 337	80 485	76 852	...	...	...	...	...
Gongyi	CDJC	777 202	395 784	381 418	...	...	...	...	...
Gongzhuling	CDJC	1 041 735	532 134	509 601	...	...	...	...	...
Guang'an	CDJC	1 093 103	561 454	531 649	...	...	...	...	...
Guanghan	CDJC	577 298	289 596	287 702	...	...	...	...	...
Guangshui	CDJC	885 936	458 607	427 329	...	...	...	...	...
Guangyuan	CDJC	905 057	467 422	437 635	...	...	...	...	...
Guangzhou	CDJC	8 524 826	4 445 052	4 079 774	...	...	...	...	...
Guigang	CDJC	1 413 128	731 298	681 830	...	...	...	...	...
Guilin	CDJC	804 571	414 004	390 567	...	...	...	...	...
Guiping	CDJC	1 359 035	716 617	642 418	...	...	...	...	...
Guixi	CDJC	535 517	282 662	252 855	...	...	...	...	...
Guiyang	CDJC	2 985 105	1 568 544	1 416 561	...	...	...	...	...
Gujiao	CDJC	205 702	110 105	95 597	...	...	...	...	...
Haerbin	CDJC	3 481 504	1 759 609	1 721 895	...	...	...	...	...
Haicheng	CDJC	1 181 130	606 805	574 325	...	...	...	...	...
Haikou	CDJC	830 192	431 774	398 418	...	...	...	...	...
Hailaer	CDJC	262 184	132 849	129 335	...	...	...	...	...
Hailin	CDJC	435 677	222 525	213 152	...	...	...	...	...
Hailun	CDJC	720 008	368 751	351 257	...	...	...	...	...
Haimen	CDJC	942 952	431 066	511 886	...	...	...	...	...
Haining	CDJC	666 080	331 349	334 731	...	...	...	...	...
Haiyang	CDJC	654 594	329 202	325 392	...	...	...	...	...
Hami	CDJC	388 714	201 005	187 709	...	...	...	...	...
Hancheng	CDJC	387 041	201 881	185 160	...	...	...	...	...
Hanchuan	CDJC	1 057 396	552 093	505 303	...	...	...	...	...

(See notes at end of table. — Voir notes à la fin du tableau.)

Continent, country or area, date and city	Code[1]	City proper — Ville proprement dite Population				Urban agglomeration — Agglomération urbaine Population			
Continent, pays ou zone, date et ville		Both sexes Les deux sexes	Male Masculin	Female Féminin	Surface area Superficie (km²)	Both sexes Les deux sexes	Male Masculin	Female Féminin	Surface area Superficie (km²)
ASIA — ASIE									
China — Chine									
2000									
Handan	CDJC	1 329 734	693 882	635 852	...	...	...	...	...
Hangzhou	CDJC	2 451 319	1 301 103	1 150 216	...	...	...	...	...
Hanzhong	CDJC	503 871	258 142	245 729	...	...	...	...	...
Hebi	CDJC	495 336	260 212	235 124	...	...	...	...	...
Hechi	CDJC	318 348	167 526	150 822	...	...	...	...	...
Hechuan	CDJC	1 420 520	732 503	688 017	...	...	...	...	...
Hefei	CDJC	1 659 075	879 749	779 326	...	...	...	...	...
Hegang	CDJC	694 640	354 262	340 378	...	...	...	...	...
Heihe	CDJC	192 764	97 488	95 276	...	...	...	...	...
Hejian	CDJC	757 581	383 621	373 960	...	...	...	...	...
Hejin	CDJC	368 572	195 677	172 895	...	...	...	...	...
Helong	CDJC	215 266	110 051	105 215	...	...	...	...	...
Hengshui	CDJC	422 761	212 417	210 344	...	...	...	...	...
Hengyang	CDJC	879 051	450 222	428 829	...	...	...	...	...
Heshan (Guangdong)	CDJC	405 779	202 461	203 318	...	...	...	...	...
Heshan (Guangxi)	CDJC	131 249	69 205	62 044	...	...	...	...	...
Hetian	CDJC	186 127	94 034	92 093	...	...	...	...	...
Heyuan	CDJC	227 773	115 330	112 443	...	...	...	...	...
Heze	CDJC	1 280 031	656 790	623 241	...	...	...	...	...
Hezhou	CDJC	850 023	446 208	403 815	...	...	...	...	...
Honghu	CDJC	877 775	459 997	417 778	...	...	...	...	...
Hongjiang	CDJC	485 061	250 434	234 627	...	...	...	...	...
Houma	CDJC	225 123	113 997	111 126	...	...	...	...	...
Huadian	CDJC	444 415	228 624	215 791	...	...	...	...	...
Huaian	CDJC	1 200 679	619 541	581 138	...	...	...	...	...
Huaibei	CDJC	741 195	382 444	358 751	...	...	...	...	...
Huaihua	CDJC	346 522	178 221	168 301	...	...	...	...	...
Huainan	CDJC	1 357 228	701 205	656 023	...	...	...	...	...
Huaiyin	CDJC	555 052	282 186	272 866	...	...	...	...	...
Huanggang	CDJC	373 568	194 607	178 961	...	...	...	...	...
Huanghua	CDJC	483 273	251 128	232 145	...	...	...	...	...
Huangshan	CDJC	406 200	208 004	198 196	...	...	...	...	...
Huangshi (Hubei)	CDJC	653 722	334 712	319 010	...	...	...	...	...
Huayin	CDJC	242 488	125 006	117 482	...	...	...	...	...
Huaying	CDJC	352 257	183 962	168 295	...	...	...	...	...
Huazhou	CDJC	1 007 796	529 550	478 246	...	...	...	...	...
Huhehaote	CDJC	1 406 955	724 328	682 627	...	...	...	...	...
Huixian	CDJC	776 326	394 763	381 563	...	...	...	...	...
Huiyang	CDJC	862 822	429 006	433 816	...	...	...	...	...
Huizhou	CDJC	591 686	292 216	299 470	...	...	...	...	...
Hulin	CDJC	311 509	160 842	150 667	...	...	...	...	...
Huludao	CDJC	900 936	456 211	444 725	...	...	...	...	...
Hunchun	CDJC	211 091	108 873	102 218	...	...	...	...	...
Huozhou	CDJC	274 955	142 316	132 639	...	...	...	...	...
Huzhou	CDJC	1 145 414	573 421	571 993	...	...	...	...	...
Jiamusi	CDJC	859 944	433 369	426 575	...	...	...	...	...
Jian (Jiangxi)	CDJC	473 113	244 476	228 637	...	...	...	...	...
Jian (Jilin)	CDJC	239 849	124 475	115 374	...	...	...	...	...
Jiande	CDJC	473 062	242 606	230 456	...	...	...	...	...
Jiangdu	CDJC	1 053 023	512 151	540 872	...	...	...	...	...
Jiangjin	CDJC	1 322 890	686 106	636 784	...	...	...	...	...
Jiangmen	CDJC	536 317	271 693	264 624	...	...	...	...	...
Jiangshan	CDJC	473 222	241 301	231 921	...	...	...	...	...
Jiangyan	CDJC	861 321	419 333	441 988	...	...	...	...	...
Jiangyin	CDJC	1 315 472	665 719	649 753	...	...	...	...	...
Jiangyou	CDJC	849 761	436 112	413 649	...	...	...	...	...
Jian'ou	CDJC	478 651	249 624	229 027	...	...	...	...	...
Jianyang (Sichuan)	CDJC	1 412 523	728 353	684 170	...	...	...	...	...

(See notes at end of table. — Voir notes à la fin du tableau.)

Continent, country or area, date and city / Continent, pays ou zone, date et ville	Code[1]	City proper — Ville proprement dite Population				Urban agglomeration — Agglomération urbaine Population			
		Both sexes Les deux sexes	Male Masculin	Female Féminin	Surface area Superficie (km²)	Both sexes Les deux sexes	Male Masculin	Female Féminin	Surface area Superficie (km²)
ASIA — ASIE									
China — Chine									
2000									
Jianyang (Fujian)	CDJC	317 848	167 066	150 782	...	...	...	...	...
Jiaohe	CDJC	474 109	243 510	230 599	...	...	...	...	...
Jiaonan	CDJC	827 771	419 331	408 440	...	...	...	...	...
Jiaozhou	CDJC	783 478	388 207	395 271	...	...	...	...	...
Jiaozuo	CDJC	747 299	384 395	362 904	...	...	...	...	...
Jiaxing	CDJC	881 923	445 646	436 277	...	...	...	...	...
Jiayuguan	CDJC	159 541	85 959	73 582	...	...	...	...	...
Jieshou	CDJC	640 878	327 384	313 494	...	...	...	...	...
Jiexiu	CDJC	372 993	190 675	182 318	...	...	...	...	...
Jieyang	CDJC	633 570	324 831	308 739	...	...	...	...	...
Jilin	CDJC	1 953 134	984 762	968 372	...	...	...	...	...
Jimo	CDJC	1 111 202	553 261	557 941	...	...	...	...	...
Ji'nan	CDJC	2 999 934	1 539 067	1 460 867	...	...	...	...	...
Jinchang	CDJC	204 902	106 725	98 177	...	...	...	...	...
Jincheng	CDJC	304 221	157 663	146 558	...	...	...	...	...
Jingdezhen	CDJC	444 720	228 747	215 973	...	...	...	...	...
Jinggangshan	CDJC	145 769	74 722	71 047	...	...	...	...	...
Jinghong	CDJC	443 672	229 846	213 826	...	...	...	...	...
Jingjiang	CDJC	639 665	316 885	322 780	...	...	...	...	...
Jingmen	CDJC	583 373	300 284	283 089	...	...	...	...	...
Jingzhou	CDJC	1 177 150	598 951	578 199	...	...	...	...	...
Jinhua	CDJC	424 859	216 773	208 086	...	...	...	...	...
Jining (Shandong)	CDJC	1 050 522	530 322	520 200	...	...	...	...	...
Jining (Inner Mongolia)	CDJC	272 448	136 913	135 535	...	...	...	...	...
Jinjiang	CDJC	1 479 259	772 066	707 193	...	...	...	...	...
Jinshi	CDJC	243 242	126 619	116 623	...	...	...	...	...
Jintan	CDJC	533 350	256 798	276 552	...	...	...	...	...
Jinzhong	CDJC	534 357	274 957	259 400	...	...	...	...	...
Jinzhou (Liaoning)	CDJC	861 991	430 777	431 214	...	...	...	...	...
Jinzhou (Hebei)	CDJC	520 942	265 012	255 930	...	...	...	...	...
Jishou	CDJC	294 297	151 422	142 875	...	...	...	...	...
Jiujiang	CDJC	551 329	280 126	271 203	...	...	...	...	...
Jiuquan	CDJC	346 258	177 943	168 315	...	...	...	...	...
Jiutai	CDJC	799 729	411 067	388 662	...	...	...	...	...
Jixi	CDJC	910 782	467 547	443 235	...	...	...	...	...
Jiyuan	CDJC	626 478	323 554	302 924	...	...	...	...	...
Jizhou	CDJC	373 825	187 005	186 820	...	...	...	...	...
Jurong	CDJC	594 316	302 713	291 603	...	...	...	...	...
Kaifeng	CDJC	796 171	398 133	398 038	...	...	...	...	...
Kaili	CDJC	433 236	230 692	202 544	...	...	...	...	...
Kaiping	CDJC	668 692	326 560	342 132	...	...	...	...	...
Kaiyuan (Liaoning)	CDJC	529 736	271 422	258 314	...	...	...	...	...
Kaiyuan (Yunnan)	CDJC	292 039	152 771	139 268	...	...	...	...	...
Kashi (Xinjiang)	CDJC	340 640	172 136	168 504	...	...	...	...	...
Kelamayi	CDJC	270 232	143 500	126 732	...	...	...	...	...
Kuerle	CDJC	381 943	199 344	182 599	...	...	...	...	...
Kuitun	CDJC	285 299	148 740	136 559	...	...	...	...	...
Kunming	CDJC	3 035 406	1 615 096	1 420 310	...	...	...	...	...
Kunshan	CDJC	750 074	377 433	372 641	...	...	...	...	...
Laiwu	CDJC	1 233 525	626 549	606 976	...	...	...	...	...
Laixi	CDJC	728 796	366 400	362 396	...	...	...	...	...
Laiyang	CDJC	897 681	453 293	444 388	...	...	...	...	...
Laizhou	CDJC	889 361	450 192	439 169	...	...	...	...	...
Langfang	CDJC	715 388	363 094	352 294	...	...	...	...	...
Langzhong	CDJC	787 809	400 390	387 419	...	...	...	...	...
Lanxi	CDJC	607 196	314 090	293 106	...	...	...	...	...
Lanzhou	CDJC	2 087 759	1 092 661	995 098	...	...	...	...	...
Laohekou	CDJC	509 468	257 204	252 264	...	...	...	...	...

(See notes at end of table. — Voir notes à la fin du tableau.)

Continent, country or area, date and city / Continent, pays ou zone, date et ville	Code[1]	City proper — Ville proprement dite Population				Urban agglomeration — Agglomération urbaine Population			
		Both sexes Les deux sexes	Male Masculin	Female Féminin	Surface area Superficie (km²)	Both sexes Les deux sexes	Male Masculin	Female Féminin	Surface area Superficie (km²)
ASIA — ASIE									
China — Chine									
2000									
Lasa	CDJC	223 001	117 004	105 997	...	...	...	...	...
Lechang	CDJC	423 444	223 788	199 656	...	...	...	...	...
Leiyang	CDJC	1 180 235	631 431	548 804	...	...	...	...	...
Leizhou	CDJC	1 268 298	674 213	594 085	...	...	...	...	...
Leling	CDJC	615 833	313 642	302 191	...	...	...	...	...
Lengshuijiang	CDJC	339 701	175 071	164 630	...	...	...	...	...
Leping	CDJC	729 639	381 937	347 702	...	...	...	...	...
Leqing	CDJC	1 162 765	605 494	557 271	...	...	...	...	...
Leshan	CDJC	1 120 158	567 028	553 130	...	...	...	...	...
Lianjiang	CDJC	1 205 764	642 214	563 550	...	...	...	...	...
Lianyuan	CDJC	996 893	521 941	474 952	...	...	...	...	...
Lianyungang	CDJC	687 242	354 350	332 892	...	...	...	...	...
Lianzhou	CDJC	409 360	212 292	197 068	...	...	...	...	...
Liaocheng	CDJC	950 319	474 976	475 343	...	...	...	...	...
Liaoyang	CDJC	728 492	365 833	362 659	...	...	...	...	...
Liaoyuan	CDJC	462 233	234 701	227 532	...	...	...	...	...
Lichuan	CDJC	786 984	417 988	368 996	...	...	...	...	...
Liling	CDJC	934 396	484 127	450 269	...	...	...	...	...
Lin'an	CDJC	514 238	261 852	252 386	...	...	...	...	...
Linfen	CDJC	724 403	367 377	357 026	...	...	...	...	...
Lingbao	CDJC	722 890	377 872	345 018	...	...	...	...	...
Linghai	CDJC	647 310	332 906	314 404	...	...	...	...	...
Lingwu	CDJC	249 890	128 364	121 526	...	...	...	...	...
Lingyuan	CDJC	620 121	324 554	295 567	...	...	...	...	...
Linhai	CDJC	948 618	479 625	468 993	...	...	...	...	...
Linhe	CDJC	510 965	260 835	250 130	...	...	...	...	...
Linjiang	CDJC	184 901	94 904	89 997	...	...	...	...	...
Linqing	CDJC	694 247	348 411	345 836	...	...	...	...	...
Linxia	CDJC	202 498	104 017	98 481	...	...	...	...	...
Linxiang	CDJC	448 452	235 723	212 729	...	...	...	...	...
Linyi	CDJC	1 938 510	988 940	949 570	...	...	...	...	...
Linzhou	CDJC	982 254	501 659	480 595	...	...	...	...	...
Lishi	CDJC	235 678	121 253	114 425	...	...	...	...	...
Lishui	CDJC	348 241	178 908	169 333	...	...	...	...	...
Liuan	CDJC	1 559 037	807 902	751 135	...	...	...	...	...
Liupanshui	CDJC	995 055	523 692	471 363	...	...	...	...	...
Liuyang	CDJC	1 307 572	680 610	626 962	...	...	...	...	...
Liuzhou	CDJC	1 220 392	634 909	585 483	...	...	...	...	...
Liyang	CDJC	740 871	375 694	365 177	...	...	...	...	...
Longhai	CDJC	816 318	415 936	400 382	...	...	...	...	...
Longjing	CDJC	261 551	132 150	129 401	...	...	...	...	...
Longkou	CDJC	671 335	337 507	333 828	...	...	...	...	...
Longquan	CDJC	250 398	131 534	118 864	...	...	...	...	...
Longyan	CDJC	543 731	298 481	245 250	...	...	...	...	...
Loudi	CDJC	398 577	205 172	193 405	...	...	...	...	...
Lucheng	CDJC	213 944	111 293	102 651	...	...	...	...	...
Lufeng	CDJC	1 164 767	600 959	563 808	...	...	...	...	...
Luoding	CDJC	866 190	449 131	417 059	...	...	...	...	...
Luohe	CDJC	304 105	150 273	153 832	...	...	...	...	...
Luoyang	CDJC	1 491 680	759 425	732 255	...	...	...	...	...
Luquan	CDJC	397 449	202 340	195 109	...	...	...	...	...
Luxi (Yunnan)	CDJC	337 406	172 038	165 368	...	...	...	...	...
Luzhou	CDJC	1 252 884	636 652	616 232	...	...	...	...	...
Maanshan	CDJC	567 576	292 994	274 582	...	...	...	...	...
Macheng	CDJC	1 129 047	595 391	533 656	...	...	...	...	...
Manzhouli	CDJC	181 112	92 853	88 259	...	...	...	...	...
Maoming	CDJC	644 301	335 713	308 588	...	...	...	...	...
Meihekou	CDJC	617 674	317 226	300 448	...	...	...	...	...

(See notes at end of table. — Voir notes à la fin du tableau.)

Continent, country or area, date and city / Continent, pays ou zone, date et ville	Code[1]	City proper — Ville proprement dite Population				Urban agglomeration — Agglomération urbaine Population			
		Both sexes Les deux sexes	Male Masculin	Female Féminin	Surface area Superficie (km²)	Both sexes Les deux sexes	Male Masculin	Female Féminin	Surface area Superficie (km²)
ASIA — ASIE									
China — Chine									
2000									
Meishan	CDJC	799 309	402 889	396 420	...	...	...	...	...
Meixian	CDJC	313 821	160 925	152 896	...	...	...	...	...
Meizhou	CDJC	354 302	178 658	175 644	...	...	...	...	...
Mianyang	CDJC	1 162 962	604 414	558 548	...	...	...	...	...
Mianzhu	CDJC	515 830	263 098	252 732	...	...	...	...	...
Miluo	CDJC	658 867	342 113	316 754	...	...	...	...	...
Mingguang	CDJC	569 585	290 126	279 459	...	...	...	...	...
Miquan	CDJC	180 952	95 368	85 584	...	...	...	...	...
Mishan	CDJC	438 277	224 565	213 712	...	...	...	...	...
Mudanjiang	CDJC	1 014 206	512 000	502 206	...	...	...	...	...
Muling	CDJC	310 096	158 623	151 473	...	...	...	...	...
Nan'an	CDJC	1 385 276	700 218	685 058	...	...	...	...	...
Nanchang	CDJC	1 844 253	952 504	891 749	...	...	...	...	...
Nanchong	CDJC	1 771 920	922 452	849 468	...	...	...	...	...
Nanchuan	CDJC	631 853	326 307	305 546	...	...	...	...	...
Nan'gong	CDJC	467 356	234 978	232 378	...	...	...	...	...
Nanhai	CDJC	2 133 741	1 111 731	1 022 010	...	...	...	...	...
Nanjing	CDJC	3 624 234	1 935 931	1 688 303	...	...	...	...	...
Nankang	CDJC	694 987	338 836	356 151	...	...	...	...	...
Nanning	CDJC	1 766 701	924 916	841 785	...	...	...	...	...
Nanping	CDJC	488 818	257 352	231 466	...	...	...	...	...
Nantong	CDJC	771 386	386 206	385 180	...	...	...	...	...
Nanxiong	CDJC	372 844	185 330	187 514	...	...	...	...	...
Nanyang	CDJC	1 584 715	814 822	769 893	...	...	...	...	...
Nehe	CDJC	672 295	343 873	328 422	...	...	...	...	...
Neijiang	CDJC	1 391 931	709 053	682 878	...	...	...	...	...
Ning'an	CDJC	437 328	223 201	214 127	...	...	...	...	...
Ningbo	CDJC	1 567 499	804 850	762 649	...	...	...	...	...
Ningde	CDJC	400 293	213 131	187 162	...	...	...	...	...
Ningguo	CDJC	381 842	199 915	181 927	...	...	...	...	...
Panjin	CDJC	602 541	309 377	293 164	...	...	...	...	...
Panshi	CDJC	530 470	273 219	257 251	...	...	...	...	...
Panzhihua	CDJC	690 739	363 585	327 154	...	...	...	...	...
Penglai	CDJC	500 408	252 726	247 682	...	...	...	...	...
Pengzhou	CDJC	770 749	389 697	381 052	...	...	...	...	...
Pingdingshan	CDJC	900 903	470 362	430 541	...	...	...	...	...
Pingdu	CDJC	1 321 975	670 685	651 290	...	...	...	...	...
Pinghu	CDJC	507 899	249 848	258 051	...	...	...	...	...
Pingliang	CDJC	454 996	236 426	218 570	...	...	...	...	...
Pingxiang (Jiangxi)	CDJC	783 445	402 198	381 247	...	...	...	...	...
Pingxiang (Guangxi)	CDJC	107 046	57 445	49 601	...	...	...	...	...
Pizhou	CDJC	1 539 922	791 332	748 590	...	...	...	...	...
Pulandian	CDJC	757 844	385 636	372 208	...	...	...	...	...
Puning	CDJC	1 856 402	954 242	902 160	...	...	...	...	...
Putian	CDJC	443 926	216 578	227 348	...	...	...	...	...
Puyang	CDJC	448 290	229 387	218 903	...	...	...	...	...
Qian'an	CDJC	632 704	323 330	309 374	...	...	...	...	...
Qianjiang	CDJC	992 438	506 290	486 148	...	...	...	...	...
Qidong	CDJC	1 057 073	495 819	561 254	...	...	...	...	...
Qingdao	CDJC	2 720 972	1 359 527	1 361 445	...	...	...	...	...
Qingtongxia	CDJC	248 640	129 121	119 519	...	...	...	...	...
Qingyuan	CDJC	506 680	258 819	247 861	...	...	...	...	...
Qingzhen	CDJC	471 305	248 079	223 226	...	...	...	...	...
Qingzhou	CDJC	894 468	450 090	444 378	...	...	...	...	...
Qinhuangdao	CDJC	817 487	411 355	406 132	...	...	...	...	...
Qinyang	CDJC	446 404	224 725	221 679	...	...	...	...	...
Qinzhou	CDJC	1 035 504	578 428	457 076	...	...	...	...	...
Qionghai	CDJC	449 845	236 560	213 285	...	...	...	...	...

(See notes at end of table. — Voir notes à la fin du tableau.)

Continent, country or area, date and city / Continent, pays ou zone, date et ville	Code[1]	City proper — Ville proprement dite Population				Urban agglomeration — Agglomération urbaine Population			
		Both sexes Les deux sexes	Male Masculin	Female Féminin	Surface area Superficie (km²)	Both sexes Les deux sexes	Male Masculin	Female Féminin	Surface area Superficie (km²)
ASIA — ASIE									
China — Chine									
2000									
Qionglai	CDJC	631 577	321 382	310 195	...	...	...	...	...
Qiongshan	CDJC	678 149	355 557	322 592	...	...	...	...	...
Qiqihaer	CDJC	1 540 089	776 191	763 898	...	...	...	...	...
Qitaihe	CDJC	486 704	254 500	232 204	...	...	...	...	...
Qixia	CDJC	651 357	331 148	320 209	...	...	...	...	...
Quanzhou	CDJC	1 192 286	616 826	575 460	...	...	...	...	...
Qufu	CDJC	625 313	317 685	307 628	...	...	...	...	...
Qujing	CDJC	648 956	333 756	315 200	...	...	...	...	...
Quzhou	CDJC	286 271	148 054	138 217	...	...	...	...	...
Renhuai	CDJC	520 759	270 091	250 668	...	...	...	...	...
Renqiu	CDJC	768 900	390 649	378 251	...	...	...	...	...
Rizhao	CDJC	1 148 190	576 050	572 140	...	...	...	...	...
Rongcheng	CDJC	732 147	368 156	363 991	...	...	...	...	...
Rugao	CDJC	1 362 533	659 720	702 813	...	...	...	...	...
Ruian	CDJC	1 207 788	627 593	580 195	...	...	...	...	...
Ruichang	CDJC	398 844	209 755	189 089	...	...	...	...	...
Ruijin	CDJC	535 499	280 328	255 171	...	...	...	...	...
Ruili	CDJC	155 210	80 532	74 678	...	...	...	...	...
Rushan	CDJC	580 326	291 047	289 279	...	...	...	...	...
Ruzhou	CDJC	923 245	474 090	449 155	...	...	...	...	...
Sanhe	CDJC	456 882	229 788	227 094	...	...	...	...	...
Sanmenxia	CDJC	288 746	149 846	138 900	...	...	...	...	...
Sanming	CDJC	337 105	178 031	159 074	...	...	...	...	...
Sanshui	CDJC	440 119	230 835	209 284	...	...	...	...	...
Sanya	CDJC	482 296	254 293	228 003	...	...	...	...	...
Shahe	CDJC	474 260	243 171	231 089	...	...	...	...	...
Shanghai	CDJC	14 348 535	7 414 274	6 934 261	...	...	...	...	...
Shangqiu	CDJC	1 428 983	729 319	699 664	...	...	...	...	...
Shangrao	CDJC	327 703	164 698	163 005	...	...	...	...	...
Shangyu	CDJC	722 523	354 917	367 606	...	...	...	...	...
Shangzhi	CDJC	582 764	298 966	283 798	...	...	...	...	...
Shangzhou	CDJC	530 883	279 160	251 723	...	...	...	...	...
Shantou	CDJC	1 270 112	636 189	633 923	...	...	...	...	...
Shanwei	CDJC	409 677	211 746	197 931	...	...	...	...	...
Shaoguan	CDJC	535 979	282 515	253 464	...	...	...	...	...
Shaowu	CDJC	288 401	151 117	137 284	...	...	...	...	...
Shaoxing	CDJC	633 118	310 860	322 258	...	...	...	...	...
Shaoyang	CDJC	607 868	309 563	298 305	...	...	...	...	...
Shengzhou	CDJC	671 221	345 614	325 607	...	...	...	...	...
Shenyang	CDJC	5 303 053	2 700 380	2 602 673	...	...	...	...	...
Shenzhen	CDJC	7 008 831	3 454 392	3 554 439	...	...	...	...	...
Shenzhou	CDJC	568 558	289 086	279 472	...	...	...	...	...
Shifang	CDJC	432 579	218 447	214 132	...	...	...	...	...
Shihezi	CDJC	590 115	305 253	284 862	...	...	...	...	...
Shijiazhuang	CDJC	1 969 975	1 005 476	964 499	...	...	...	...	...
Shishi	CDJC	498 786	264 700	234 086	...	...	...	...	...
Shishou	CDJC	602 649	310 486	292 163	...	...	...	...	...
Shiyan	CDJC	589 824	309 552	280 272	...	...	...	...	...
Shizuishan	CDJC	314 296	163 261	151 035	...	...	...	...	...
Shouguang	CDJC	1 081 991	548 020	533 971	...	...	...	...	...
Shuangcheng	CDJC	749 182	382 673	366 509	...	...	...	...	...
Shuangliao	CDJC	404 499	206 071	198 428	...	...	...	...	...
Shuangyashan	CDJC	487 294	248 542	238 752	...	...	...	...	...
Shulan	CDJC	660 065	340 293	319 772	...	...	...	...	...
Shunde	CDJC	1 694 152	893 580	800 572	...	...	...	...	...
Shuozhou	CDJC	563 896	290 621	273 275	...	...	...	...	...
Sihui	CDJC	409 804	209 936	199 868	...	...	...	...	...
Simao	CDJC	230 834	120 071	110 763	...	...	...	...	...

8. Population of capital cities and cities of 100 000 and more inhabitants: latest available year
Population des capitales et des villes de 100 000 habitants et plus: dernière année disponible (continued — suite)

(See notes at end of table. — Voir notes à la fin du tableau.)

Continent, country or area, date and city Continent, pays ou zone, date et ville	Code[1]	City proper — Ville proprement dite Population				Urban agglomeration — Agglomération urbaine Population			
		Both sexes Les deux sexes	Male Masculin	Female Féminin	Surface area Superficie (km²)	Both sexes Les deux sexes	Male Masculin	Female Féminin	Surface area Superficie (km²)
ASIA — ASIE									
China — Chine									
2000									
Siping	CDJC	492 841	247 416	245 425	...	...	...	...	...
Songyuan	CDJC	538 469	273 101	265 368	...	...	...	...	...
Songzi	CDJC	859 941	437 980	421 961	...	...	...	...	...
Suihua	CDJC	800 207	405 382	394 825	...	...	...	...	...
Suining	CDJC	1 355 388	696 590	658 798	...	...	...	...	...
Suizhou	CDJC	1 598 752	818 936	779 816	...	...	...	...	...
Suqian	CDJC	244 651	124 719	119 932	...	...	...	...	...
Suzhou (Anhui)	CDJC	1 601 181	819 067	782 114	...	...	...	...	...
Suzhou (Jiangsu)	CDJC	1 344 709	686 919	657 790	...	...	...	...	...
Tacheng	CDJC	149 210	76 056	73 154	...	...	...	...	...
Taian	CDJC	1 538 211	775 346	762 865	...	...	...	...	...
Taicang	CDJC	515 063	250 788	264 275	...	...	...	...	...
Taishan	CDJC	948 716	478 773	469 943	...	...	...	...	...
Taixing	CDJC	1 235 454	618 158	617 296	...	...	...	...	...
Taiyuan	CDJC	2 558 382	1 321 216	1 237 166	...	...	...	...	...
Taizhou (Zhejiang)	CDJC	1 491 963	766 497	725 466	...	...	...	...	...
Taizhou (Jiangsu)	CDJC	607 660	303 078	304 582	...	...	...	...	...
Tangshan	CDJC	1 711 311	863 091	848 220	...	...	...	...	...
Taonan	CDJC	441 096	224 878	216 218	...	...	...	...	...
Tengzhou	CDJC	1 548 817	811 999	736 818	...	...	...	...	...
Tianchang	CDJC	590 745	297 550	293 195	...	...	...	...	...
Tianjin	CDJC	7 499 181	3 825 069	3 674 112	...	...	...	...	...
Tianmen	CDJC	1 613 739	849 283	764 456	...	...	...	...	...
Tianshui	CDJC	1 146 986	594 508	552 478	...	...	...	...	...
Tiefa	CDJC	239 636	121 471	118 165	...	...	...	...	...
Tieli	CDJC	354 601	181 024	173 577	...	...	...	...	...
Tieling	CDJC	433 799	217 795	216 004	...	...	...	...	...
Tongcheng	CDJC	660 772	321 098	339 674	...	...	...	...	...
Tongchuan	CDJC	404 257	211 294	192 963	...	...	...	...	...
Tonghua	CDJC	460 148	231 960	228 188	...	...	...	...	...
Tongjiang	CDJC	164 595	85 426	79 169	...	...	...	...	...
Tongliao	CDJC	793 913	400 930	392 983	...	...	...	...	...
Tongling	CDJC	362 477	188 130	174 347	...	...	...	...	...
Tongren	CDJC	308 583	163 632	144 951	...	...	...	...	...
Tongshi	CDJC	100 836	53 146	47 690	...	...	...	...	...
Tongxiang	CDJC	713 399	360 567	352 832	...	...	...	...	...
Tongzhou	CDJC	1 371 498	652 777	718 721	...	...	...	...	...
Tulufan	CDJC	251 652	129 183	122 469	...	...	...	...	...
Tumen	CDJC	132 368	67 067	65 301	...	...	...	...	...
Urumqi	CDJC	1 753 298	911 328	841 970	...	...	...	...	...
Wafangdian	CDJC	956 063	489 377	466 686	...	...	...	...	...
Wanning	CDJC	513 604	272 751	240 853	...	...	...	...	...
Wanyuan	CDJC	536 685	278 918	257 767	...	...	...	...	...
Weifang	CDJC	1 380 300	696 720	683 580	...	...	...	...	...
Weihai	CDJC	609 219	307 867	301 352	...	...	...	...	...
Weihui	CDJC	464 371	233 151	231 220	...	...	...	...	...
Weinan	CDJC	888 866	451 028	437 838	...	...	...	...	...
Wenchang	CDJC	509 271	260 432	248 839	...	...	...	...	...
Wendeng	CDJC	675 061	335 330	339 731	...	...	...	...	...
Wenling	CDJC	1 162 783	604 031	558 752	...	...	...	...	...
Wenzhou	CDJC	1 915 548	1 028 001	887 547	...	...	...	...	...
Wuan	CDJC	720 196	373 108	347 088	...	...	...	...	...
Wuchang	CDJC	888 782	454 587	434 195	...	...	...	...	...
Wuchuan	CDJC	822 482	429 336	393 146	...	...	...	...	...
Wudalianchi	CDJC	338 689	176 002	162 687	...	...	...	...	...
Wugang (Hunan)	CDJC	694 847	363 904	330 943	...	...	...	...	...
Wugang (Henan)	CDJC	313 089	164 347	148 742	...	...	...	...	...
Wuhai	CDJC	427 553	223 947	203 606	...	...	...	...	...

8. Population of capital cities and cities of 100 000 and more inhabitants: latest available year
Population des capitales et des villes de 100 000 habitants et plus: dernière année disponible (continued — suite)

(See notes at end of table. — Voir notes à la fin du tableau.)

Continent, country or area, date and city / Continent, pays ou zone, date et ville	Code[1]	City proper — Ville proprement dite Population				Urban agglomeration — Agglomération urbaine Population			
		Both sexes Les deux sexes	Male Masculin	Female Féminin	Surface area Superficie (km²)	Both sexes Les deux sexes	Male Masculin	Female Féminin	Surface area Superficie (km²)
ASIA — ASIE									
China — Chine									
2000									
Wuhan	CDJC	8 312 700	4 306 729	4 005 971		...	...	...	...
Wuhu	CDJC	697 197	359 560	337 637		...	...	...	...
Wujiang	CDJC	857 104	426 423	430 681		...	...	...	...
Wujin	CDJC	1 420 204	719 200	701 004		...	...	...	...
Wulanhaote	CDJC	269 162	135 406	133 756		...	...	...	...
Wusu	CDJC	190 359	100 288	90 071		...	...	...	...
Wuwei	CDJC	946 506	488 872	457 634		...	...	...	...
Wuxi	CDJC	1 425 766	732 231	693 535		...	...	...	...
Wuxian	CDJC	1 128 429	557 717	570 712		...	...	...	...
Wuxue	CDJC	719 426	381 959	337 467		...	...	...	...
Wuyishan	CDJC	212 156	112 006	100 150		...	...	...	...
Wuzhong	CDJC	355 442	181 909	173 533		...	...	...	...
Wuzhou	CDJC	381 043	193 424	187 619		...	...	...	...
Xiamen	CDJC	2 053 070	1 061 697	991 373		...	...	...	...
Xi'an	CDJC	4 481 508	2 320 642	2 160 866		...	...	...	...
Xiangcheng	CDJC	1 052 468	546 760	505 708		...	...	...	...
Xiangfan	CDJC	871 388	443 899	427 489		...	...	...	...
Xiangtan	CDJC	707 783	363 619	344 164		...	...	...	...
Xiangxiang	CDJC	807 718	413 489	394 229		...	...	...	...
Xianning	CDJC	567 598	295 836	271 762		...	...	...	...
Xiantao	CDJC	1 474 078	774 487	699 591		...	...	...	...
Xianyang	CDJC	953 860	493 153	460 707		...	...	...	...
Xiaogan	CDJC	883 123	454 917	428 206		...	...	...	...
Xiaoshan	CDJC	1 233 348	613 229	620 119		...	...	...	...
Xiaoyi	CDJC	414 154	215 941	198 213		...	...	...	...
Xichang	CDJC	615 212	318 658	296 554		...	...	...	...
Xifeng	CDJC	317 669	163 228	154 441		...	...	...	...
Xilin'haote	CDJC	173 796	89 527	84 269		...	...	...	...
Xingcheng	CDJC	524 527	269 567	254 960		...	...	...	...
Xinghua	CDJC	1 441 659	745 856	695 803		...	...	...	...
Xingning	CDJC	871 507	436 749	434 758		...	...	...	...
Xingping	CDJC	551 523	284 879	266 644		...	...	...	...
Xingtai	CDJC	536 282	272 661	263 621		...	...	...	...
Xingyang	CDJC	619 840	316 049	303 791		...	...	...	...
Xingyi	CDJC	719 605	375 079	344 526		...	...	...	...
Xinhui	CDJC	932 425	467 557	464 868		...	...	...	...
Xi'ning	CDJC	854 466	440 359	414 107		...	...	...	...
Xinji	CDJC	623 219	314 536	308 683		...	...	...	...
Xinle	CDJC	439 644	220 811	218 833		...	...	...	...
Xinmi	CDJC	779 014	406 291	372 723		...	...	...	...
Xinmin	CDJC	653 719	333 683	320 036		...	...	...	...
Xintai	CDJC	1 344 395	687 569	656 826		...	...	...	...
Xinxiang	CDJC	775 941	394 224	381 717		...	...	...	...
Xinyang	CDJC	1 255 750	644 031	611 719		...	...	...	...
Xinyi (Guangdong)	CDJC	907 978	464 088	443 890		...	...	...	...
Xinyi (Jiangsu)	CDJC	962 656	491 509	471 147		...	...	...	...
Xinyu	CDJC	778 391	408 940	369 451		...	...	...	...
Xinzheng	CDJC	609 173	315 462	293 711		...	...	...	...
Xinzhou	CDJC	496 608	251 708	244 900		...	...	...	...
Xishan	CDJC	1 181 073	599 540	581 533		...	...	...	...
Xuancheng	CDJC	822 707	428 470	394 237		...	...	...	...
Xuanwei	CDJC	1 292 825	691 846	600 979		...	...	...	...
Xuchang	CDJC	373 387	188 476	184 911		...	...	...	...
Xuzhou	CDJC	1 679 626	866 686	812 940		...	...	...	...
Yaan	CDJC	334 475	171 237	163 238		...	...	...	...
Yakeshi	CDJC	405 806	207 451	198 355		...	...	...	...
Yan'an	CDJC	403 868	209 240	194 628		...	...	...	...
Yancheng	CDJC	683 663	347 576	336 087		...	...	...	...

(See notes at end of table. — Voir notes à la fin du tableau.)

Continent, country or area, date and city Continent, pays ou zone, date et ville	Code[1]	City proper — Ville proprement dite Population				Urban agglomeration — Agglomération urbaine Population			
		Both sexes Les deux sexes	Male Masculin	Female Féminin	Surface area Superficie (km²)	Both sexes Les deux sexes	Male Masculin	Female Féminin	Surface area Superficie (km²)
ASIA — ASIE									
China — Chine									
2000									
Yangchun	CDJC	840 581	440 930	399 651	...	...	...	...	...
Yangjiang	CDJC	538 069	276 769	261 300	...	...	...	...	...
Yangquan	CDJC	655 317	346 209	309 108	...	...	...	...	...
Yangzhong	CDJC	301 672	150 538	151 134	...	...	...	...	...
Yangzhou	CDJC	711 993	362 425	349 568	...	...	...	...	...
Yanji	CDJC	432 339	223 342	208 997	...	...	...	...	...
Yanshi	CDJC	816 026	414 890	401 136	...	...	...	...	...
Yantai	CDJC	1 724 404	871 452	852 952	...	...	...	...	...
Yibin	CDJC	809 099	419 397	389 702	...	...	...	...	...
Yichang	CDJC	712 738	371 510	341 228	...	...	...	...	...
Yicheng	CDJC	522 835	266 340	256 495	...	...	...	...	...
Yichun (Jiangxi)	CDJC	920 357	480 945	439 412	...	...	...	...	...
Yichun (Heilongjiang)	CDJC	814 016	413 071	400 945	...	...	...	...	...
Yidu	CDJC	385 779	196 716	189 063	...	...	...	...	...
Yima	CDJC	136 543	73 411	63 132	...	...	...	...	...
Yinchuan	CDJC	807 487	415 203	392 284	...	...	...	...	...
Yingcheng	CDJC	650 485	340 907	309 578	...	...	...	...	...
Yingde	CDJC	810 446	421 964	388 482	...	...	...	...	...
Yingkou	CDJC	698 059	353 751	344 308	...	...	...	...	...
Yingtan	CDJC	178 406	92 050	86 356	...	...	...	...	...
Yi'ning	CDJC	357 519	179 862	177 657	...	...	...	...	...
Yiwu	CDJC	912 670	461 103	451 567	...	...	...	...	...
Yixing	CDJC	1 164 275	592 095	572 180	...	...	...	...	...
Yiyang	CDJC	1 228 881	629 842	599 039	...	...	...	...	...
Yizheng	CDJC	610 356	311 144	299 212	...	...	...	...	...
Yizhou	CDJC	549 434	288 084	261 350	...	...	...	...	...
Yong'an	CDJC	334 852	180 109	154 743	...	...	...	...	...
Yongcheng	CDJC	1 264 607	654 047	610 560	...	...	...	...	...
Yongchuan	CDJC	984 730	507 848	476 882	...	...	...	...	...
Yongkang	CDJC	557 067	290 946	266 121	...	...	...	...	...
Yongji	CDJC	421 244	214 446	206 798	...	...	...	...	...
Yongzhou	CDJC	976 539	508 021	468 518	...	...	...	...	...
Yuanjiang	CDJC	700 236	363 730	336 506	...	...	...	...	...
Yuanping	CDJC	471 853	244 751	227 102	...	...	...	...	...
Yucheng	CDJC	494 301	248 103	246 198	...	...	...	...	...
Yueyang	CDJC	912 993	471 170	441 823	...	...	...	...	...
Yuhang	CDJC	817 715	419 877	397 838	...	...	...	...	...
Yulin (Shaanxi)	CDJC	451 337	232 951	218 386	...	...	...	...	...
Yulin (Guangxi)	CDJC	918 229	491 729	426 500	...	...	...	...	...
Yumen	CDJC	188 931	99 832	89 099	...	...	...	...	...
Yuncheng	CDJC	604 381	304 489	299 892	...	...	...	...	...
Yunfu	CDJC	261 636	136 789	124 847	...	...	...	...	...
Yunzhou	CDJC	598 387	303 581	294 806	...	...	...	...	...
Yushu	CDJC	1 155 670	592 213	563 457	...	...	...	...	...
Yuxi	CDJC	409 044	206 139	202 905	...	...	...	...	...
Yuyao	CDJC	852 719	429 835	422 884	...	...	...	...	...
Yuzhou	CDJC	1 122 669	587 728	534 941	...	...	...	...	...
Zaoyang	CDJC	1 054 374	538 588	515 786	...	...	...	...	...
Zaozhuang	CDJC	1 996 798	1 025 190	971 608	...	...	...	...	...
Zengcheng	CDJC	899 644	466 540	433 104	...	...	...	...	...
Zhalantun	CDJC	409 051	211 922	197 129	...	...	...	...	...
Zhangjiagang	CDJC	957 223	466 771	490 452	...	...	...	...	...
Zhangjiajie	CDJC	453 723	234 454	219 269	...	...	...	...	...
Zhangjiakou	CDJC	903 348	455 048	448 300	...	...	...	...	...
Zhangping	CDJC	264 757	140 779	123 978	...	...	...	...	...
Zhangqiu	CDJC	977 324	485 925	491 399	...	...	...	...	...
Zhangshu	CDJC	527 823	273 691	254 132	...	...	...	...	...
Zhangye	CDJC	486 688	248 469	238 219	...	...	...	...	...

8. Population of capital cities and cities of 100 000 and more inhabitants: latest available year
Population des capitales et des villes de 100 000 habitants et plus: dernière année disponible (continued — suite)

(See notes at end of table. — Voir notes à la fin du tableau.)

Continent, country or area, date and city Continent, pays ou zone, date et ville	Code[1]	City proper — Ville proprement dite Population				Urban agglomeration — Agglomération urbaine Population			
		Both sexes Les deux sexes	Male Masculin	Female Féminin	Surface area Superficie (km²)	Both sexes Les deux sexes	Male Masculin	Female Féminin	Surface area Superficie (km²)
ASIA — ASIE									
China — Chine									
2000									
Zhangzhou	CDJC	567 884	291 597	276 287	...	...	...	...	...
Zhanjiang	CDJC	1 350 665	707 187	643 478	...	...	...	...	...
Zhaodong	CDJC	832 657	424 694	407 963	...	...	...	...	...
Zhaoqing	CDJC	507 834	254 086	253 748	...	...	...	...	...
Zhaotong	CDJC	727 959	377 931	350 028	...	...	...	...	...
Zhaoyuan	CDJC	593 705	297 504	296 201	...	...	...	...	...
Zhengzhou	CDJC	2 589 387	1 347 037	1 242 350	...	...	...	...	...
Zhenjiang	CDJC	695 663	364 429	331 234	...	...	...	...	...
Zhijiang	CDJC	508 835	257 013	251 822	...	...	...	...	...
Zhongshan	CDJC	2 363 322	1 175 587	1 187 735	...	...	...	...	...
Zhongxiang	CDJC	1 021 998	516 758	505 240	...	...	...	...	...
Zhoukou	CDJC	323 738	162 443	161 295	...	...	...	...	...
Zhoushan	CDJC	715 685	362 426	353 259	...	...	...	...	...
Zhuanghe	CDJC	835 062	422 677	412 385	...	...	...	...	...
Zhucheng	CDJC	1 053 695	531 390	522 305	...	...	...	...	...
Zhuhai	CDJC	833 908	414 067	419 841	...	...	...	...	...
Zhuji	CDJC	1 070 675	535 820	534 855	...	...	...	...	...
Zhumadian	CDJC	338 036	170 485	167 551	...	...	...	...	...
Zhuozhou	CDJC	546 754	275 834	270 920	...	...	...	...	...
Zhuzhou	CDJC	879 996	454 057	425 939	...	...	...	...	...
Zibo	CDJC	2 817 479	1 429 838	1 387 641	...	...	...	...	...
Zigong	CDJC	1 051 384	532 479	518 905	...	...	...	...	...
Zixing	CDJC	351 581	181 632	169 949	...	...	...	...	...
Ziyang	CDJC	1 016 034	527 326	488 708	...	...	...	...	...
Zoucheng	CDJC	1 101 003	571 761	529 242	...	...	...	...	...
Zunhua	CDJC	683 662	348 121	335 541	...	...	...	...	...
Zunyi	CDJC	691 694	358 839	332 855	...	...	...	...	...
China - Hong-Kong SAR — Chine - Hong-Kong RAS									
2001									
HONG KONG	CDJC	6 708 389	3 285 344	3 423 045	1 099	...	...	...	...
China - Macao SAR — Chine - Macao RAS									
2001									
MACAO	CDJC	435 235	208 865	226 370	26	...	...	...	...
2002									
MACAO	ESDJ	439 162	210 642	228 520	26	...	...	...	...
Cyprus — Chypre									
2000									
LEFKOSIA[91]	ESDJ	...	...	...	...	197 800	...	...	...
Lemesos[92]	ESDJ	...	...	...	...	157 600	...	...	...
2001									
LEFKOSIA[91]	CDJC	47 832	22 978	24 854	...	200 686	97 157	103 529	...
Lemesos[92]	CDJC	94 250	45 474	48 776	...	156 939	76 314	80 625	...
Georgia — Géorgie									
1990									
Batumi	ESDF	137 000	...	...	...	...	...	...	...
Kutaisi	ESDF	236 000	...	...	...	...	...	...	...
Rustavi	ESDF	160 000	...	...	...	...	...	...	...
Sukhumi	ESDF	122 000	...	...	...	...	...	...	...
TBILISI	ESDF	1 268 000	...	...	...	...	...	...	...
India — Inde[93]									
2001									
Abohar	CDFC	124 303	66 434	57 869	23	...	...	...	...
Achalpur	CDFC	107 304	55 678	51 626	...	...	...	...	...
Adilabad	CDFC	108 233	55 023	53 210	...	128 196	64 883	63 313	...
Adityapur	CDFC	119 221	63 855	55 366	...	...	...	...	...
Adoni	CDFC	155 969	78 908	77 061	30	161 125	81 577	79 548	...

(See notes at end of table. — Voir notes à la fin du tableau.)

Continent, country or area, date and city / Continent, pays ou zone, date et ville	Code[1]	City proper — Ville proprement dite Population				Urban agglomeration — Agglomération urbaine Population			
		Both sexes Les deux sexes	Male Masculin	Female Féminin	Surface area Superficie (km²)	Both sexes Les deux sexes	Male Masculin	Female Féminin	Surface area Superficie (km²)
ASIA — ASIE									
India — Inde[93]									
2001									
Agartala	CDFC	189 327	94 398	94 929	16	...	...	...	...
Agra	CDFC	1 259 979	674 902	585 077	121	1 321 410	708 622	612 788	141
Ahmedabad	CDFC	3 515 361	1 863 886	1 651 475	...	4 519 278	2 397 728	2 121 550	...
Ahmednagar	CDFC	307 455	159 409	148 046	18	347 396	184 604	162 792	30
Aizawl	CDFC	229 714	116 983	112 731	110	...	...	...	...
Ajmer	CDFC	485 197	253 854	231 343	242	490 138	256 379	233 759	...
Akola	CDFC	399 978	206 433	193 545	23	...	...	...	...
Alandur	CDFC	146 154	74 784	71 370	...	...	...	...	...
Alappuzha	CDFC	177 079	85 708	91 371	70	282 727	137 232	145 495	84
Aligarh	CDFC	667 732	357 152	310 580	34	...	...	...	...
Alipurduar	CDFC	...	...	...	...	114 069	58 527	55 542	26
Allahabad	CDFC	990 298	549 754	440 544	...	1 049 579	581 876	467 703	...
Alwal	CDFC	106 424	56 562	49 862	...	...	...	...	...
Alwar	CDFC	260 245	139 141	121 104	...	265 850	143 238	122 612	58
Ambala	CDFC	139 222	73 956	65 266	17	168 003	92 610	75 393	38
Ambala Sadar	CDFC	106 378	55 461	50 917	...	...	...	...	...
Ambarnath	CDFC	203 795	107 378	96 417	...	...	...	...	...
Ambattur	CDFC	302 492	156 237	146 255	...	...	...	...	...
Amravati	CDFC	549 370	283 789	265 581	122	...	...	...	...
Amritsar	CDFC	975 695	524 127	451 568	...	1 011 327	543 638	467 689	...
Amroha	CDFC	164 890	86 836	78 054	6	...	...	...	...
Anand	CDFC	130 462	68 032	62 430	...	218 064	115 183	102 881	...
Anantapur	CDFC	220 951	112 273	108 678	...	243 359	123 976	119 383	...
Anklesvar	CDFC	...	...	...	...	112 648	60 265	52 383	...
Arcot	CDFC	...	...	...	...	126 975	62 938	64 037	19
Arrah	CDFC	203 395	109 876	93 519	31	...	...	...	...
Asansol	CDFC	486 304	256 551	229 753	25	1 090 171	576 813	513 358	223
Ashoknagar Kalyangarh	CDFC	111 475	56 340	55 135	...	...	...	...	...
Aurangabad	CDFC	872 667	458 869	413 798	139	891 841	468 815	423 026	148
Avadi	CDFC	230 913	119 187	111 726	...	...	...	...	...
Azamgarh	CDFC	104 943	51 284	53 659	...	...	...	...	...
Bahadurgarh	CDFC	119 839	65 835	54 004	...	131 924	72 851	59 073	...
Baharampur	CDFC	160 168	81 795	78 373	17	170 343	87 038	83 305	19
Bahraich	CDFC	168 376	89 532	78 844	13	...	...	...	...
Baidyabati	CDFC	108 231	56 429	51 802	...	...	...	...	...
Baleshwar	CDFC	106 032	55 637	50 395	...	156 274	82 034	74 240	42
Ballia	CDFC	102 226	55 123	47 103	...	...	...	...	...
Bally	CDFC	261 575	149 810	111 765	12	...	...	...	...
Balurghat	CDFC	135 516	68 822	66 694	...	143 095	72 687	70 408	8
Banda	CDFC	134 822	72 663	62 159	...	139 387	75 172	64 215	...
Bangalore	CDFC	4 292 223	2 240 956	2 051 267	...	5 686 844	2 983 926	2 702 918	446
Bangaon	CDFC	102 115	52 489	49 626	...	...	...	...	...
Bankura	CDFC	128 811	66 333	62 478	19	...	...	...	...
Bansberia	CDFC	104 453	55 403	49 050	...	...	...	...	...
Baranagar	CDFC	250 615	132 701	117 914	7	...	...	...	...
Barasat	CDFC	231 515	118 367	113 148	...	...	...	...	...
Barddhaman	CDFC	285 871	148 824	137 047	23	...	...	...	...
Bareilly	CDFC	699 839	368 022	331 817	107	729 800	386 418	343 382	124
Baripada	CDFC	...	...	...	...	100 593	53 610	46 983	...
Barrackpur	CDFC	144 331	76 268	68 063	14	...	...	...	...
Barshi	CDFC	104 786	53 894	50 892	...	...	...	...	...
Basirhat	CDFC	113 120	57 876	55 244	22	...	...	...	...
Basti	CDFC	106 985	56 813	50 172	...	...	...	...	...
Batala	CDFC	126 646	67 026	59 620	...	147 753	78 342	69 411	...
Bathinda	CDFC	217 389	117 359	100 030	97	...	...	...	...
Beawar	CDFC	123 701	64 394	59 307	...	125 923	65 569	60 354	18
Begusarai	CDFC	...	...	...	...	107 203	57 349	49 854	...
Belgaum	CDFC	399 600	204 846	194 754	142	506 235	261 862	244 373	155

(See notes at end of table. — Voir notes à la fin du tableau.)

Continent, country or area, date and city / Continent, pays ou zone, date et ville	Code[1]	City proper — Ville proprement dite Population				Urban agglomeration — Agglomération urbaine Population			
		Both sexes Les deux sexes	Male Masculin	Female Féminin	Surface area Superficie (km²)	Both sexes Les deux sexes	Male Masculin	Female Féminin	Surface area Superficie (km²)
ASIA — ASIE									
India — Inde[93]									
2001									
Bellary	CDFC	317 000	163 082	153 918	66	...	...	...	...
Bettiah	CDFC	116 692	61 803	54 889	...	...	...	...	...
Bhadravati	CDFC	160 392	81 260	79 132	...	...	...	...	...
Bhadreswar	CDFC	105 944	57 991	47 953	...	...	...	...	...
Bhagalpur	CDFC	340 349	182 704	157 645	30	349 709	187 627	162 082	31
Bhalswa Jahangir Pur	CDFC	151 427	83 289	68 138	...	...	...	...	...
Bharatpur	CDFC	204 456	109 809	94 647	41	205 104	110 148	94 956	51
Bharuch	CDFC	148 391	76 568	71 823	...	176 531	91 273	85 258	...
Bhatpara	CDFC	441 956	243 065	198 891	16	...	...	...	...
Bhavani	CDFC	...	...	...	...	104 285	52 804	51 481	...
Bhavnagar	CDFC	510 958	267 019	243 939	...	517 578	270 458	247 120	...
Bheemavaram	CDFC	137 327	69 487	67 840	26	141 975	71 938	70 037	...
Bhilai Nagar	CDFC	553 837	289 853	263 984	89	...	...	...	...
Bhilwara	CDFC	280 185	148 642	131 543	118	...	...	...	...
Bhind	CDFC	153 768	83 009	70 759	17	...	...	...	...
Bhiwandi	CDFC	598 703	367 858	230 845	26	621 390	382 493	238 897	28
Bhiwani	CDFC	169 424	91 726	77 698	28	...	...	...	...
Bhopal	CDFC	1 433 875	755 685	678 190	285	1 454 830	766 602	688 228	...
Bhubaneswar	CDFC	647 302	360 476	286 826	125	657 477	365 848	291 629	...
Bhusawal	CDFC	172 366	89 187	83 179	13	187 524	97 192	90 332	25
Bid	CDFC	138 091	71 790	66 301	8	...	...	...	...
Bidar	CDFC	172 298	89 715	82 583	...	173 678	90 449	83 229	47
Bidhan Nagar	CDFC	167 848	85 215	82 633	...	...	...	...	...
Bihar	CDFC	231 972	121 813	110 159	24	...	...	...	...
Bijapur	CDFC	245 946	126 554	119 392	...	253 307	130 237	123 070	75
Bikaner	CDFC	529 007	282 450	246 557	166	...	...	...	...
Bilaspur	CDFC	265 178	137 273	127 905	36	330 291	170 898	159 393	46
Birnagar	CDFC	...	...	...	...	115 104	59 179	55 925	...
Bokaro Steel City	CDFC	394 173	213 044	181 129	163	497 855	268 668	229 187	183
Bommanahalli	CDFC	201 220	108 040	93 180	...	...	...	...	...
Botad	CDFC	100 059	52 668	47 391	...	...	...	...	...
Brahmapur	CDFC	289 724	150 089	139 635	80	...	...	...	...
Budaun	CDFC	148 138	78 294	69 844	4	...	...	...	...
Bulandshahr	CDFC	176 256	93 066	83 190	12	...	...	...	...
Burhanpur	CDFC	194 360	100 031	94 329	13	...	...	...	...
Byatarayanapura	CDFC	180 931	94 683	86 248	...	...	...	...	...
Chakdaha	CDFC	...	...	...	...	101 278	51 321	49 957	...
Champdani	CDFC	103 232	57 874	45 358	...	...	...	...	...
Chandan Nagar	CDFC	162 166	84 222	77 944	10	...	...	...	...
Chandausi	CDFC	103 757	55 167	48 590	...	...	...	...	...
Chandigarh	CDFC	808 796	451 387	357 409	70	...	...	...	...
Chandrapur	CDFC	297 612	148 499	149 113	56	...	...	...	...
Chapra	CDFC	178 835	96 077	82 758	17	...	...	...	...
Chennai (Madras)	CDFC	4 216 268	2 161 605	2 054 663	174	6 424 624	3 294 328	3 130 296	612
Cherthala	CDFC	...	...	...	...	141 512	68 740	72 772	93
Chhatarpur	CDFC	...	...	...	...	109 021	58 393	50 628	...
Chhindwara	CDFC	122 309	63 583	58 726	...	153 635	79 889	73 746	...
Chikmagalur	CDFC	101 022	51 611	49 411	...	...	...	...	...
Chirala	CDFC	...	...	...	...	166 877	83 262	83 615	48
Chirkunda	CDFC	...	...	...	...	106 200	56 528	49 672	...
Chitradurga	CDFC	122 594	62 811	59 783	...	125 060	64 075	60 985	16
Chittoor	CDFC	152 966	77 044	75 922	33	...	...	...	...
Churu	CDFC	...	...	...	...	101 853	53 099	48 754	...
Coimbatore	CDFC	923 085	476 056	447 029	106	1 446 034	743 161	702 873	317
Coonoor	CDFC	...	...	...	...	101 234	51 089	50 145	...
Cuddalore	CDFC	158 569	80 113	78 456	28	...	...	...	...
Cuddapah	CDFC	125 725	63 165	62 560	42	260 899	132 297	128 602	78
Cuttack	CDFC	535 139	286 192	248 947	122	587 637	314 435	273 202	153

(See notes at end of table. — Voir notes à la fin du tableau.)

Continent, country or area, date and city / Continent, pays ou zone, date et ville	Code[1]	City proper — Ville proprement dite Population				Urban agglomeration — Agglomération urbaine Population			
		Both sexes Les deux sexes	Male Masculin	Female Féminin	Surface area Superficie (km²)	Both sexes Les deux sexes	Male Masculin	Female Féminin	Surface area Superficie (km²)
ASIA — ASIE									
India — Inde[93]									
2001									
Dallo Pura	CDFC	132 628	71 349	61 279	...	...	...	...	...
Damoh	CDFC	112 160	58 898	53 262	...	127 939	67 244	60 695	36
Darbhanga	CDFC	266 834	142 042	124 792	19	...	...	...	...
Darjiling	CDFC	107 530	53 325	54 205	...	109 163	54 131	55 032	...
Dasarahalli	CDFC	263 636	143 225	120 411	...	...	...	...	...
Davangere	CDFC	363 780	187 603	176 177	...	...	...	...	...
Dehradun	CDFC	447 808	236 852	210 956	37	527 859	279 653	248 206	86
Dehri	CDFC	119 007	63 552	55 455	...	...	...	...	...
Delhi[94]	CDFC	9 817 439	5 378 658	4 438 781	431	12 791 458	7 021 896	5 769 562	624
Delhi Cantonment	CDFC	124 452	75 700	48 752	...	...	...	...	...
Deoghar	CDFC	...	...	...	...	112 501	61 405	51 096	...
Deoli	CDFC	119 432	66 575	52 857	...	...	...	...	...
Deoria	CDFC	104 222	54 737	49 485	...	...	...	...	...
Dewas	CDFC	230 658	120 610	110 048	100	...	...	...	...
Dhanbad	CDFC	198 963	108 400	90 563	23	1 064 357	578 602	485 755	201
Dharmavaram	CDFC	103 400	52 799	50 601	...	...	...	...	...
Dhule	CDFC	341 473	177 631	163 842	46	...	...	...	...
Dibrugarh	CDFC	122 523	65 736	56 787	15	137 879	74 239	63 640	16
Dimapur	CDFC	107 382	61 595	45 787	...	...	...	...	...
Dinapur Nizamat	CDFC	130 339	69 024	61 315	...	...	...	...	...
Dindigul	CDFC	196 619	98 969	97 650	14	...	...	...	...
Dohad	CDFC	...	...	...	...	112 087	57 765	54 322	...
Dumdum	CDFC	101 319	52 868	48 451	...	...	...	...	...
Durg	CDFC	231 182	118 896	112 286	51	...	...	...	...
Durgapur	CDFC	492 996	263 426	229 570	154	...	...	...	...
Durg-Bhilai Nagar	CDFC	...	...	...	...	923 559	480 432	443 127	183
Eluru	CDFC	189 772	92 405	97 367	15	215 343	104 987	110 356	...
English Bazar	CDFC	161 448	82 932	78 516	...	224 392	115 454	108 938	19
Erode	CDFC	151 184	76 726	74 458	8	391 169	199 306	191 863	132
Etah	CDFC	107 098	56 960	50 138	...	...	...	...	...
Etawah	CDFC	211 460	112 833	98 627	9	...	...	...	...
Faizabad	CDFC	144 924	76 078	68 846	33	208 164	114 252	93 912	63
Faridabad	CDFC	1 054 981	580 548	474 433	178	...	...	...	...
Farrukhabad-cum-Fategarh	CDFC	227 876	120 783	107 093	17	242 558	129 608	112 950	21
Fatehpur	CDFC	151 757	79 836	71 921	57	...	...	...	...
Firozabad	CDFC	278 801	147 980	130 821	9	432 213	230 477	201 736	12
Gadag-Betgeri	CDFC	154 849	78 672	76 177	35	...	...	...	...
Gajuwaka	CDFC	258 944	133 461	125 483	...	...	...	...	...
Gandhinagar	CDFC	195 891	103 814	92 077	57	...	...	...	...
Ganganagar	CDFC	210 788	115 412	95 376	21	222 833	121 877	100 956	...
Gangawati	CDFC	...	...	...	...	101 397	51 253	50 144	...
Gaya	CDFC	383 197	203 252	179 945	29	394 185	209 926	184 259	32
Ghatlodiya	CDFC	106 259	56 040	50 219	...	...	...	...	...
Ghaziabad	CDFC	968 521	521 408	447 113	64	...	...	...	...
Ghazipur	CDFC	...	...	...	...	103 283	54 321	48 962	...
Giridih	CDFC	...	...	...	...	105 212	55 154	50 058	...
Godhra	CDFC	121 852	63 143	58 709	...	131 144	67 933	63 211	...
Gonda	CDFC	122 164	67 400	54 764	...	...	...	...	...
Gondiya	CDFC	120 878	61 435	59 443	18	...	...	...	...
Gorakhpur	CDFC	624 570	330 450	294 120	137	...	...	...	...
Gudivada	CDFC	112 245	55 439	56 806	13	...	...	...	...
Gudiyatham	CDFC	...	...	...	...	100 021	49 822	50 199	...
Gulbarga	CDFC	427 929	222 623	205 306	...	435 631	226 848	208 783	43
Guna	CDFC	137 132	72 462	64 670	46	...	...	...	...
Guntakul	CDFC	117 403	59 364	58 039	52	...	...	...	...
Guntur	CDFC	514 707	257 939	256 768	30	...	...	...	...
Gurgaon	CDFC	173 542	92 985	80 557	15	229 243	123 370	105 873	24
Guruvayur	CDFC	...	...	...	...	138 676	64 550	74 126	50

261

8. Population of capital cities and cities of 100 000 and more inhabitants: latest available year
Population des capitales et des villes de 100 000 habitants et plus: dernière année disponible (continued — suite)

(See notes at end of table. — Voir notes à la fin du tableau.)

Continent, country or area, date and city / Continent, pays ou zone, date et ville	Code[1]	City proper — Ville proprement dite Population				Urban agglomeration — Agglomération urbaine Population			
		Both sexes Les deux sexes	Male Masculin	Female Féminin	Surface area Superficie (km²)	Both sexes Les deux sexes	Male Masculin	Female Féminin	Surface area Superficie (km²)
ASIA — ASIE									
India — Inde[93]									
2001									
Guwahati	CDFC	808 021	441 347	366 674	217	814 575	445 649	368 926	...
Gwalior	CDFC	826 919	442 484	384 435	290	865 800	465 388	400 412	303
Habra	CDFC	127 695	65 263	62 432	18	239 170	121 603	117 567	37
Hajipur	CDFC	119 276	63 762	55 514	...	...	...	...	...
Haldia	CDFC	170 695	89 886	80 809	69	...	...	...	...
Haldwani-cum-Kathgodam	CDFC	129 140	68 826	60 314	11	159 020	84 611	74 409	...
Halisahar	CDFC	124 479	67 124	57 355	...	...	...	...	...
Hanumangarh	CDFC	129 654	69 583	60 071	...	...	...	...	...
Haora (Howrah)	CDFC	1 008 704	547 969	460 735	52	...	...	...	...
Hapur	CDFC	211 987	112 962	99 025	14	...	...	...	...
Hardoi	CDFC	112 474	59 877	52 597	...	...	...	...	...
Hardwar	CDFC	175 010	94 650	80 360	15	220 433	119 159	101 274	42
Hassan	CDFC	117 386	60 225	57 161	...	133 317	68 337	64 980	27
Hathras	CDFC	123 243	65 908	57 335	8	126 352	67 568	58 784	...
Hazaribag	CDFC	127 243	67 905	59 338	...	135 446	72 296	63 150	...
Hindupur	CDFC	125 056	64 159	60 897	38	...	...	...	...
Hisar	CDFC	256 810	140 240	116 570	45	263 070	143 816	119 254	49
Hoshiarpur	CDFC	148 243	78 946	69 297	28	...	...	...	...
Hospet	CDFC	163 284	83 430	79 854	28	...	...	...	...
Hubli-Dharwad	CDFC	786 018	403 270	382 748	191	...	...	...	...
Hugli-Chinsurah	CDFC	170 201	86 728	83 473	17	...	...	...	...
Hyderabad	CDFC	3 449 878	1 773 899	1 675 979	...	5 533 640	2 854 938	2 678 702	...
Ichalakaranji	CDFC	257 572	135 988	121 584	30	285 795	150 934	134 861	38
Imphal	CDFC	217 275	107 593	109 682	33	245 967	121 588	124 379	37
Indore	CDFC	1 597 441	839 843	757 598	...	1 639 044	861 758	777 286	165
Itarsi	CDFC	...	...	...	...	109 288	57 118	52 170	...
Jabalpur	CDFC	951 469	496 829	454 640	154	1 117 200	588 556	528 644	224
Jagadhri	CDFC	101 300	55 910	45 390	...	...	...	...	...
Jagdalpur	CDFC	...	...	...	...	103 216	53 048	50 168	...
Jaipur	CDFC	2 324 319	1 239 711	1 084 608	200	...	...	...	...
Jalandhar	CDFC	701 223	376 925	324 298	80	709 255	381 116	328 139	...
Jalgaon	CDFC	368 579	193 464	175 115	62	...	...	...	...
Jalna	CDFC	235 529	121 728	113 801	82	...	...	...	...
Jalpaiguri	CDFC	100 212	50 570	49 642	...	...	...	...	...
Jammu	CDFC	378 431	206 061	172 370	...	607 642	330 769	276 873	...
Jamnagar	CDFC	447 734	235 093	212 641	...	558 462	292 954	265 508	...
Jamshedpur	CDFC	570 349	300 081	270 268	60	1 101 804	580 336	521 468	160
Jamuria	CDFC	129 456	68 741	60 715	...	...	...	...	...
Jaunpur	CDFC	159 996	84 179	75 817	25	...	...	...	...
Jetpur Navagadh	CDFC	104 311	54 772	49 539	...	...	...	...	...
Jhansi	CDFC	383 248	203 003	180 245	48	463 281	246 495	216 786	83
Jhunjhunun	CDFC	100 476	52 814	47 662	...	...	...	...	...
Jind	CDFC	136 089	73 557	62 532	...	...	...	...	...
Jodhpur	CDFC	846 408	450 816	395 592	79	856 034	455 860	400 174	...
Jorhat	CDFC	...	...	...	60	135 091	71 837	63 254	69
Junagadh	CDFC	168 686	86 935	81 751	...	252 138	130 318	121 820	...
Kaithal	CDFC	117 226	63 090	54 136	...	...	...	...	...
Kakinada	CDFC	289 920	143 905	146 015	39	368 672	183 619	185 053	58
Kalol	CDFC	100 021	53 098	46 923	...	112 025	59 532	52 493	...
Kalyan	CDFC	1 193 266	633 395	559 871	225	...	...	...	...
Kamarhati	CDFC	314 334	168 633	145 701	11	...	...	...	...
Kamptee	CDFC	...	...	...	...	137 056	71 633	65 423	36
Kancheepuram	CDFC	152 984	77 058	75 926	12	188 349	94 942	93 407	40
Kanchrapara	CDFC	126 118	65 197	60 921	13	...	...	...	...
Kanhangad	CDFC	...	...	...	...	129 364	61 954	67 410	84
Kannur	CDFC	...	...	...	...	498 175	237 101	261 074	145
Kanpur	CDFC	2 532 138	1 354 581	1 177 557	267	2 690 486	1 440 140	1 250 346	299
Kapra	CDFC	159 176	82 914	76 262	...	...	...	...	...

(See notes at end of table. — Voir notes à la fin du tableau.)

Continent, country or area, date and city / Continent, pays ou zone, date et ville	Code[1]	City proper — Ville proprement dite Population				Urban agglomeration — Agglomération urbaine Population			
		Both sexes Les deux sexes	Male Masculin	Female Féminin	Surface area Superficie (km²)	Both sexes Les deux sexes	Male Masculin	Female Féminin	Surface area Superficie (km²)
ASIA — ASIE									
India — Inde[93]									
2001									
Karaikkudi	CDFC	...	...	...	...	125 185	62 230	62 955	79
Karawal Nagar	CDFC	148 549	80 364	68 185	...	...	...	...	...
Karimnagar	CDFC	203 819	104 514	99 305	24	215 782	110 479	105 303	...
Karnal	CDFC	210 476	112 263	98 213	22	222 017	118 428	103 589	24
Karur	CDFC	...	...	...	...	153 123	77 130	75 993	19
Katihar	CDFC	175 169	93 567	81 602	25	190 862	102 126	88 736	...
Khammam	CDFC	158 022	80 072	77 950	...	196 763	100 255	96 508	26
Khandwa	CDFC	171 976	88 859	83 117	36	...	...	...	...
Khanna	CDFC	103 059	55 290	47 769	...	...	...	...	...
Kharagpur	CDFC	207 984	107 506	100 478	91	296 323	152 700	143 623	125
Khardaha	CDFC	116 252	61 254	54 998	...	...	...	...	...
Khargone	CDFC	...	...	...	...	103 980	54 236	49 744	...
Kirari Suleman Nagar	CDFC	153 874	84 908	68 966	...	...	...	...	...
Kishangarh	CDFC	116 156	61 025	55 131	...	...	...	...	...
Koch Bihar	CDFC	...	...	...	...	102 922	52 186	50 736	...
Kochi	CDFC	596 473	295 351	301 122	109	1 355 406	670 462	684 944	373
Kolar	CDFC	113 299	57 773	55 526	...	...	...	...	...
Kolhapur	CDFC	485 183	251 958	233 225	67	497 554	258 400	239 154	67
Kolkata (Calcutta)[95]	CDFC	4 580 544	2 506 029	2 074 515	185	13 216 546	7 072 114	6 144 432	897
Kollam	CDFC	361 441	177 586	183 855	41	379 975	186 842	193 133	68
Korba	CDFC	315 695	165 028	150 667	35	...	...	...	...
Kota	CDFC	695 899	369 897	326 002	221	704 731	374 570	330 161	...
Kothagudem	CDFC	...	...	...	...	105 265	52 377	52 888	35
Kottayam	CDFC	...	...	...	...	172 867	84 915	87 952	64
Kozhikode	CDFC	436 527	211 785	224 742	96	880 168	428 984	451 184	233
Krishnanagar	CDFC	139 070	70 512	68 558	16	148 645	75 381	73 264	...
Krishnarajapura	CDFC	187 453	98 107	89 346	...	...	...	...	...
Kukatpalle	CDFC	290 591	152 159	138 432	...	...	...	...	...
Kulti	CDFC	290 057	152 947	137 110	...	...	...	...	...
Kumbakonam	CDFC	140 021	69 607	70 414	13	160 827	80 012	80 815	15
Kurnool	CDFC	267 739	135 859	131 880	15	320 619	163 071	157 548	46
L.B. Nagar	CDFC	261 987	135 636	126 351	...	...	...	...	...
Lakhimpur	CDFC	120 566	64 804	55 762	...	...	...	...	...
Lalitpur	CDFC	111 810	58 901	52 909	...	...	...	...	...
Latur	CDFC	299 828	156 477	143 351	21	...	...	...	...
Loni	CDFC	120 659	64 976	55 683	...	...	...	...	...
Lucknow	CDFC	2 207 340	1 165 932	1 041 408	310	2 266 933	1 199 273	1 067 660	338
Ludhiana	CDFC	1 395 053	789 868	605 185	135	...	...	...	...
Machilipatnam	CDFC	183 370	91 400	91 970	27	...	...	...	...
Madanapalle	CDFC	...	...	...	...	107 262	54 507	52 755	...
Madhyamgram	CDFC	155 503	79 716	75 787	...	...	...	...	...
Madurai	CDFC	922 913	466 909	456 004	47	1 194 665	604 728	589 937	115
Mahadevapura	CDFC	135 597	72 803	62 794	...	...	...	...	...
Mahbubnagar	CDFC	130 849	67 019	63 830	14	139 483	71 508	67 975	...
Mahesana	CDFC	...	...	...	...	141 367	74 928	66 439	...
Maheshtala	CDFC	389 214	204 734	184 480	...	...	...	...	...
Mainpuri	CDFC	...	...	...	...	102 007	54 043	47 964	...
Malappuram	CDFC	...	...	...	...	170 364	83 669	86 695	111
Malegaon	CDFC	409 190	208 744	200 446	13	...	...	...	...
Malerkotla	CDFC	106 802	56 872	49 930	...	...	...	...	...
Malkajgiri	CDFC	175 000	90 000	85 000	...	...	...	...	...
Mancherial	CDFC	...	...	...	...	118 047	60 371	57 676	...
Mandsaur	CDFC	116 483	60 269	56 214	...	117 532	60 860	56 672	...
Mandya	CDFC	131 211	66 630	64 581	17	...	...	...	...
Mangalore	CDFC	398 745	200 234	198 511	75	538 560	269 176	269 384	155
Mango	CDFC	166 091	87 322	78 769	...	...	...	...	...
Mathura	CDFC	298 827	159 249	139 578	9	319 235	171 516	147 719	22
Maunath Bhanjan	CDFC	210 071	108 696	101 375	9	...	...	...	...

8. Population of capital cities and cities of 100 000 and more inhabitants: latest available year
Population des capitales et des villes de 100 000 habitants et plus: dernière année disponible (continued — suite)

(See notes at end of table. — Voir notes à la fin du tableau.)

Continent, country or area, date and city / Continent, pays ou zone, date et ville	Code[1]	City proper — Ville proprement dite Population				Urban agglomeration — Agglomération urbaine Population			
		Both sexes Les deux sexes	Male Masculin	Female Féminin	Surface area Superficie (km²)	Both sexes Les deux sexes	Male Masculin	Female Féminin	Surface area Superficie (km²)
ASIA — ASIE									
India — Inde[93]									
2001									
Medinipur	CDFC	153 349	78 365	74 984	15	...	...	...	...
Meerut	CDFC	1 074 229	571 074	503 155	142	1 167 399	624 904	542 495	178
Mira-Bhayandar	CDFC	520 301	286 458	233 843	...	...	...	...	...
Mirzapur-cum-Vindhyachal	CDFC	205 264	109 872	95 392	39	...	...	...	...
Modinagar	CDFC	112 918	60 260	52 658	10	139 642	74 570	65 072	17
Moga	CDFC	124 624	66 843	57 781	...	134 242	71 996	62 246	...
Moradabad	CDFC	641 240	340 217	301 023	34	...	...	...	...
Morena	CDFC	150 890	82 281	68 609	96	...	...	...	...
Mormugoa	CDFC	...	...	...	...	104 689	55 927	48 762	...
Motihari	CDFC	101 506	54 629	46 877	...	109 250	59 517	49 733	...
Mughalsarai	CDFC	...	...	...	...	116 246	61 572	54 674	...
Mumbai (Bombay)	CDFC	11 914 398	6 577 902	5 336 496	466	16 368 084	8 979 172	7 388 912	1 041
Munger	CDFC	187 311	100 374	86 937	18	...	...	...	...
Murwara (Katni)	CDFC	186 738	97 666	89 072	107	...	...	...	...
Muzaffarnagar	CDFC	316 452	166 998	149 454	...	331 403	174 877	156 526	12
Muzaffarpur	CDFC	305 465	163 907	141 558	26	...	...	...	...
Mysore	CDFC	742 261	377 132	365 129	103	785 800	399 904	385 896	129
Nabadwip	CDFC	115 036	58 268	56 768	...	125 346	63 544	61 802	...
Nadiad	CDFC	192 799	100 452	92 347	...	196 679	102 469	94 210	...
Nagaon	CDFC	107 471	56 888	50 583	...	123 054	64 976	58 078	...
Nagercoil	CDFC	208 149	103 075	105 074	24	...	...	...	...
Nagpur	CDFC	2 051 320	1 058 692	992 628	217	2 122 965	1 097 723	1 025 242	229
Naihati	CDFC	215 432	113 706	101 726	4	...	...	...	...
Nala Sopara	CDFC	184 664	99 629	85 035	...	...	...	...	...
Nalgonda	CDFC	110 651	56 495	54 156	...	111 745	57 042	54 703	...
Nanded	CDFC	430 598	224 766	205 832	21	...	...	...	...
Nandyal	CDFC	151 771	76 914	74 857	15	156 216	79 145	77 071	...
Nangloi Jat	CDFC	150 371	82 358	68 013	...	...	...	...	...
Nashik	CDFC	1 076 967	579 638	497 329	259	1 152 048	619 962	532 086	322
Navghar-Manikpur	CDFC	116 700	61 806	54 894	...	...	...	...	...
Navi Mumbai (New Bombay)	CDFC	703 947	395 891	308 056	...	...	...	...	...
Navsari	CDFC	134 009	69 766	64 243	...	229 323	122 335	106 988	...
Neemuch	CDFC	107 496	56 509	50 987	...	112 691	59 250	53 441	...
Nellore	CDFC	378 947	191 283	187 664	48	404 922	204 269	200 653	...
NEW DELHI[96,97]	CDFC	294 783	161 596	133 187	...	...	...	...	...
Neyveli	CDFC	128 133	65 632	62 501	97	138 387	70 920	67 467	116
Nizamabad	CDFC	286 956	145 457	141 499	37	...	...	...	...
Noida	CDFC	293 908	162 306	131 602	90	...	...	...	...
North Barrackpur	CDFC	123 523	63 827	59 696	...	...	...	...	...
North Dumdum	CDFC	220 032	112 868	107 164	...	...	...	...	...
Ongole	CDFC	149 589	76 134	73 455	8	152 945	77 862	75 083	20
Orai	CDFC	139 444	74 974	64 470	...	...	...	...	...
Ozhukarai	CDFC	217 623	110 038	107 585	...	...	...	...	...
Palakkad	CDFC	130 736	64 293	66 443	30	197 281	96 790	100 491	59
Palanpur	CDFC	110 383	58 019	52 364	...	122 279	64 343	57 936	...
Pali	CDFC	187 571	99 258	88 313	84	...	...	...	...
Pallavaram	CDFC	143 984	73 152	70 832	...	...	...	...	...
Palwal	CDFC	100 528	53 577	46 951	...	...	...	...	...
Panchkula Urban Estate	CDFC	140 992	75 925	65 067	...	...	...	...	...
Panihati	CDFC	348 379	180 068	168 311	19	...	...	...	...
Panipat	CDFC	261 665	143 565	118 100	21	353 983	194 697	159 286	...
Panvel	CDFC	104 031	54 967	49 064	...	...	...	...	...
Parbhani	CDFC	259 170	133 892	125 278	58	...	...	...	...
Patan	CDFC	112 038	59 031	53 007	...	113 568	59 889	53 679	...
Pathankot	CDFC	159 559	87 505	72 054	...	168 275	91 998	76 277	...
Patiala	CDFC	302 870	162 465	140 405	...	323 309	173 412	149 897	...
Patna	CDFC	1 376 950	749 868	627 082	107	1 707 429	925 857	781 572	129
Phagwara	CDFC	...	...	...	...	102 111	55 224	46 887	...

8. Population of capital cities and cities of 100 000 and more inhabitants: latest available year
Population des capitales et des villes de 100 000 habitants et plus: dernière année disponible (continued — suite)

(See notes at end of table. — Voir notes à la fin du tableau.)

Continent, country or area, date and city — Continent, pays ou zone, date et ville	Code[1]	City proper — Ville proprement dite Population				Urban agglomeration — Agglomération urbaine Population			
		Both sexes Les deux sexes	Male Masculin	Female Féminin	Surface area Superficie (km²)	Both sexes Les deux sexes	Male Masculin	Female Féminin	Surface area Superficie (km²)
ASIA — ASIE									
India — Inde[93]									
2001									
Phusro	CDFC	...	...	...	...	174 367	93 656	80 711	84
Pilibhit	CDFC	124 082	65 824	58 258	10	...	...	...	...
Pimpri Chinchwad	CDFC	1 006 417	543 436	462 981		...	...	...	...
Pollachi	CDFC	...	...	...	...	127 993	64 417	63 576	43
Pondicherry	CDFC	220 749	109 386	111 363	20	505 715	253 336	252 379	67
Porbandar	CDFC	133 083	68 261	64 822	...	197 414	101 882	95 532	...
Port Blair	CDFC	100 186	55 507	44 679	...	...	...	...	...
Proddatur	CDFC	164 932	82 826	82 106	7	...	...	...	...
Pudukkottai	CDFC	108 947	54 537	54 410	...	...	...	...	...
Pune	CDFC	2 540 069	1 325 694	1 214 375	146	3 755 525	1 980 941	1 774 584	423
Puri	CDFC	157 610	82 229	75 381	17	...	...	...	...
Purnia	CDFC	171 235	92 573	78 662	45	196 757	106 051	90 706	60
Puruliya	CDFC	113 766	59 171	54 595	...	...	...	...	...
Quthbullapur	CDFC	225 816	118 463	107 353	...	...	...	...	...
Rae Bareli	CDFC	169 285	88 961	80 324	50	...	...	...	...
Raichur	CDFC	205 634	105 714	99 920	...	...	...	...	...
Raiganj	CDFC	165 222	87 489	77 733	11	175 064	92 742	82 322	15
Raigarh	CDFC	110 987	57 465	53 522	...	115 740	59 916	55 824	...
Raipur	CDFC	605 131	314 369	290 762	...	699 264	364 034	335 230	64
Rajahmundry	CDFC	313 347	158 027	155 320	52	408 341	205 655	202 686	64
Rajapalayam	CDFC	121 982	61 080	60 902	11	...	...	...	...
Rajarhat Gopalpur	CDFC	271 781	140 179	131 602	...	...	...	...	...
Rajkot	CDFC	966 642	506 915	459 727	...	1 002 160	525 797	476 363	...
Rajnandgaon	CDFC	143 727	72 964	70 763	93	...	...	...	...
Rajpur Sonarpur	CDFC	336 390	173 591	162 799	...	...	...	...	...
Ramagundam	CDFC	235 540	120 307	115 233	28	236 623	120 871	115 752	...
Rampur	CDFC	281 549	146 621	134 928	20	...	...	...	...
Ranaghat	CDFC	...	...	...	...	145 172	73 804	71 368	25
Ranchi	CDFC	846 454	450 514	395 940	177	862 850	459 251	403 599	182
Raniganj	CDFC	122 891	65 360	57 531	...	...	...	...	...
Ratlam	CDFC	221 267	113 982	107 285	39	233 480	120 473	113 007	41
Raurkela	CDFC	224 601	121 028	103 573	133	484 292	258 466	225 826	157
Rewa	CDFC	183 232	98 476	84 756	55	...	...	...	...
Rewari	CDFC	100 946	54 111	46 835	...	...	...	...	...
Rishra	CDFC	113 259	62 602	50 657	...	...	...	...	...
Robertson Pet	CDFC	141 294	70 568	70 726	...	156 961	78 574	78 387	...
Rohtak	CDFC	286 773	154 153	132 620	28	294 537	158 299	136 238	...
Roorkee	CDFC	...	...	...	...	114 811	63 861	50 950	...
S.A.S. Nagar (Mohali)	CDFC	123 284	65 570	57 714	...	...	...	...	...
Sagar	CDFC	232 321	122 491	109 830	36	309 164	163 018	146 146	52
Saharanpur	CDFC	452 925	239 456	213 469	25	...	...	...	...
Saharasa	CDFC	124 015	67 010	57 005	...	...	...	...	...
Salem	CDFC	693 236	352 770	340 466	20	748 513	381 042	367 471	93
Sambalpur	CDFC	154 164	79 914	74 250	50	226 966	117 954	109 012	90
Sambhal	CDFC	182 930	97 264	85 666	16	...	...	...	...
Sangli-Miraj-Kupwad	CDFC	436 639	224 195	212 444	...	447 632	229 852	217 780	...
Santipur	CDFC	138 195	70 084	68 111	25	...	...	...	...
Sasaram	CDFC	131 042	69 665	61 377	...	...	...	...	...
Satara	CDFC	108 043	55 935	52 108	...	...	...	...	...
Satna	CDFC	225 468	120 203	105 265	...	229 323	122 335	106 988	...
Sawai Madhopur	CDFC	...	...	...	...	101 994	53 942	48 052	...
Secunderabad	CDFC	204 182	103 274	100 908	...	...	...	...	...
Serampore	CDFC	197 955	105 613	92 342	6	...	...	...	...
Serilingampalle	CDFC	150 525	75 462	75 063	...	...	...	...	...
Shahjahanpur	CDFC	297 932	162 796	135 136	13	323 166	176 910	146 256	23
Shillong	CDFC	132 876	66 129	66 747	10	267 881	134 416	133 465	25
Shimla	CDFC	142 161	80 772	61 389	32	144 578	82 424	62 154	35
Shimoga	CDFC	274 105	140 107	133 998	...	...	...	...	...

(See notes at end of table. — Voir notes à la fin du tableau.)

Continent, country or area, date and city Continent, pays ou zone, date et ville	Code[1]	City proper — Ville proprement dite Population				Urban agglomeration — Agglomération urbaine Population			
		Both sexes Les deux sexes	Male Masculin	Female Féminin	Surface area Superficie (km²)	Both sexes Les deux sexes	Male Masculin	Female Féminin	Surface area Superficie (km²)
ASIA — ASIE									
India — Inde[93]									
2001									
Shivapuri	CDFC	146 859	78 395	68 464	81	...	...	...	...
Sikar	CDFC	184 904	96 327	88 577	23	185 506	96 646	88 860	...
Silchar	CDFC	142 393	72 727	69 666	16	184 285	94 321	89 964	...
Siliguri	CDFC	470 275	249 942	220 333	16	...	...	...	...
Singrauli	CDFC	185 580	100 342	85 238	...	...	...	...	...
Sirsa	CDFC	160 129	85 802	74 327	19	...	...	...	...
Sitapur	CDFC	151 827	79 682	72 145	26	...	...	...	...
Sivakasi	CDFC	...	...	...	...	121 312	60 923	60 389	13
Siwan	CDFC	108 172	57 223	50 949	...	...	...	...	...
Solapur	CDFC	873 037	444 885	428 152	...	...	...	...	...
Sonipat	CDFC	216 213	117 654	98 559	28	225 151	122 488	102 663	...
South Dum Dum	CDFC	392 150	200 182	191 968	11	...	...	...	...
Srikakulam	CDFC	109 666	54 788	54 878	...	117 066	58 613	58 453	...
Srinagar	CDFC	894 940	481 750	413 190	...	971 357	523 017	448 340	...
Sultan Pur Majra	CDFC	163 716	88 313	75 403	...	...	...	...	...
Sultanpur	CDFC	100 085	53 163	46 922	...	...	...	...	...
Surat	CDFC	2 433 787	1 372 307	1 061 480	...	2 811 466	1 597 093	1 214 373	...
Surendranagar Dudhrej	CDFC	156 417	81 430	74 987	...	...	...	...	...
Tadepalligudem	CDFC	102 303	50 476	51 827	...	...	...	...	...
Tambaram	CDFC	137 609	70 181	67 428	...	...	...	...	...
Tenali	CDFC	149 839	74 868	74 971	15	...	...	...	...
Thane	CDFC	1 261 517	674 660	586 857	144	...	...	...	...
Thanesar	CDFC	120 072	65 786	54 286	...	122 704	67 239	55 465	...
Thanjavur	CDFC	215 725	106 950	108 775	15	...	...	...	...
Thiruvananthapuram	CDFC	744 739	365 899	378 840	142	889 191	437 009	452 182	178
Thoothukkudi (Tuticorin)	CDFC	216 058	107 781	108 277	13	242 860	121 205	121 655	140
Thrissur	CDFC	317 474	154 188	163 286	...	330 067	160 386	169 681	88
Tinsukia	CDFC	...	...	...	...	108 102	59 515	48 587	...
Tiruchchirappalli	CDFC	746 062	373 541	372 521	23	847 131	424 541	422 590	166
Tirunelveli	CDFC	411 298	203 173	208 125	15	431 603	213 399	218 204	87
Tirupati	CDFC	227 657	117 786	109 871	16	302 678	154 845	147 833	20
Tiruppur	CDFC	346 551	180 629	165 922	44	542 787	282 872	259 915	91
Tiruvannamalai	CDFC	130 301	66 026	64 275	14	...	...	...	...
Tiruvottiyur	CDFC	211 768	108 938	102 830	...	...	...	...	...
Titagarh	CDFC	124 198	70 608	53 590	3	...	...	...	...
Tonk	CDFC	135 663	70 135	65 528	...	...	...	...	...
Tumkur	CDFC	248 592	129 215	119 377	...	...	...	...	...
Udaipur	CDFC	389 317	205 319	183 998	64	...	...	...	...
Udupi	CDFC	113 039	55 933	57 106	...	127 060	62 644	64 416	73
Ujjain	CDFC	429 933	223 745	206 188	...	430 669	224 223	206 446	92
Ulhasnagar	CDFC	472 943	251 610	221 333	22	...	...	...	...
Uluberia	CDFC	202 095	105 735	96 360	...	...	...	...	...
Unnao	CDFC	144 917	76 474	68 443	16	...	...	...	...
Uppal Kalan	CDFC	118 259	61 299	56 960	...	...	...	...	...
Uttarpara Kotrung	CDFC	150 204	78 661	71 543	...	...	...	...	...
Vadakara	CDFC	...	...	...	...	123 965	59 743	64 222	39
Vadodara	CDFC	1 306 035	684 130	621 905	...	1 492 398	783 237	709 161	...
Valsad	CDFC	...	...	...	...	145 650	75 322	70 328	...
Vaniyambadi	CDFC	...	...	...	...	103 841	51 668	52 173	...
Varanasi	CDFC	1 100 748	584 514	516 234	83	1 211 749	644 922	566 827	105
Vasai	CDFC	...	...	...	...	174 382	91 121	83 261	...
Vejalpur	CDFC	113 304	58 828	54 476	...	...	...	...	...
Vellore	CDFC	177 413	88 048	89 365	12	388 211	193 779	194 432	62
Veraval	CDFC	141 207	72 074	69 133	...	157 869	80 813	77 056	...
Vidisha	CDFC	125 457	66 579	58 878	...	...	...	...	...
Vijayawada	CDFC	825 436	436 366	389 070	...	1 011 152	531 084	480 068	105
Virar	CDFC	118 945	63 762	55 183	...	...	...	...	...
Visakhapatnam	CDFC	969 608	489 038	480 570	78	1 329 472	674 080	655 392	318

8. Population of capital cities and cities of 100 000 and more inhabitants: latest available year
Population des capitales et des villes de 100 000 habitants et plus: dernière année disponible (continued — suite)

(See notes at end of table. — Voir notes à la fin du tableau.)

Continent, country or area, date and city / Continent, pays ou zone, date et ville	Code[1]	City proper — Ville proprement dite Population				Urban agglomeration — Agglomération urbaine Population			
		Both sexes Les deux sexes	Male Masculin	Female Féminin	Surface area Superficie (km²)	Both sexes Les deux sexes	Male Masculin	Female Féminin	Surface area Superficie (km²)
ASIA — ASIE									
India — Inde[93]									
2001									
Vizianagarm	CDFC	174 324	86 111	88 213	21	195 462	96 771	98 691	30
Wadhwan	CDFC	...	...	...	...	219 828	114 217	105 611	...
Warangal	CDFC	528 570	267 820	260 750	57	577 190	292 709	284 481	67
Wardha	CDFC	111 070	57 447	53 623	8	...	...	...	...
Yamunanagar	CDFC	189 587	101 888	87 699	16	306 640	166 324	140 316	42
Yavatmal	CDFC	122 906	62 838	60 068	10	141 970	72 883	69 087	13
Indonesia — Indonésie									
2000									
Ambon	CDFC	205 664	103 399	102 265	...	...	...	...	...
Balikpapan	CDFC	409 862	212 264	197 598	...	...	...	...	...
Banda Aceh	CDFC	215 542	110 298	105 244	...	...	...	...	...
Bandar Lampung	CDFC	743 127	374 517	368 610	...	...	...	...	...
Bandjarmasin	CDFC	530 908	263 987	266 921	...	...	...	...	...
Bandung	CDFC	2 138 066	1 074 862	1 063 204	...	...	...	...	...
Batam	CDFC	439 971	211 516	228 455	...	...	...	...	...
Bengkulu	CDFC	281 605	141 481	140 124	...	...	...	...	...
Binjai	CDFC	224 516	112 796	111 720	...	...	...	...	...
Bitung	CDFC	147 671	75 774	71 897	...	...	...	...	...
Blitar	CDFC	119 426	58 646	60 780	...	...	...	...	...
Bogor	CDFC	751 211	378 648	372 563	...	...	...	...	...
Cirebon	CDFC	272 597	135 602	136 995	...	...	...	...	...
Denpasar	CDFC	533 252	271 067	262 185	...	...	...	...	...
Gorontalo	CDFC	135 087	65 717	69 370	...	...	...	...	...
JAKARTA	CDFC	8 389 443	4 245 606	4 143 837	...	...	...	...	...
Jambi	CDFC	417 568	211 810	205 758	...	...	...	...	...
Jayapura	CDFC	166 201	89 196	77 005	...	...	...	...	...
Kediri	CDFC	244 705	121 813	122 892	...	...	...	...	...
Madiun	CDFC	164 048	78 503	85 545	...	...	...	...	...
Magelang	CDFC	117 715	57 626	60 089	...	...	...	...	...
Makasar (Ujung Pandang)	CDFC	1 101 933	543 169	558 764	...	...	...	...	...
Malang	CDFC	757 383	375 348	382 035	...	...	...	...	...
Manado	CDFC	382 451	192 164	190 287	...	...	...	...	...
Mataram	CDFC	317 374	156 606	160 768	...	...	...	...	...
Medan	CDFC	1 911 997	950 180	961 817	...	...	...	...	...
Mojokerto	CDFC	109 073	53 174	55 899	...	...	...	...	...
Padang	CDFC	716 283	352 871	363 412	...	...	...	...	...
Pakalongan	CDFC	262 678	130 364	132 314	...	...	...	...	...
Pakanbaru	CDFC	587 842	298 945	288 897	...	...	...	...	...
Palangkaraya	CDFC	160 572	81 843	78 729	...	...	...	...	...
Palembang	CDFC	1 458 664	722 818	735 846	...	...	...	...	...
Pangkal Pinang	CDFC	125 835	63 385	62 450	...	...	...	...	...
Pare Pare	CDFC	108 452	53 194	55 258	...	...	...	...	...
Pasuruan	CDFC	168 629	83 237	85 392	...	...	...	...	...
Pematang Siantar	CDFC	242 756	120 045	122 711	...	...	...	...	...
Pontianak	CDFC	473 360	238 249	235 111	...	...	...	...	...
Probolinggo	CDFC	191 674	94 300	97 374	...	...	...	...	...
Salatiga	CDFC	151 527	74 442	77 085	...	...	...	...	...
Samarinda	CDFC	523 119	266 857	256 262	...	...	...	...	...
Semarang	CDFC	1 427 207	700 940	726 267	...	...	...	...	...
Sukabumi	CDFC	252 688	126 753	125 935	...	...	...	...	...
Surabaya	CDFC	2 610 477	1 296 859	1 313 618	...	...	...	...	...
Surakarta	CDFC	491 272	238 458	252 814	...	...	...	...	...
Tangerang	CDFC	1 326 015	660 897	665 118	...	...	...	...	...
Tanjung Balai	CDFC	132 503	66 476	66 027	...	...	...	...	...
Tebing Tinggi	CDFC	125 211	61 990	63 221	...	...	...	...	...
Tegal	CDFC	237 250	118 125	119 125	...	...	...	...	...
Yogyakarta	CDFC	397 431	194 488	202 943	...	...	...	...	...

8. Population of capital cities and cities of 100 000 and more inhabitants: latest available year
Population des capitales et des villes de 100 000 habitants et plus: dernière année disponible (continued — suite)

(See notes at end of table. — Voir notes à la fin du tableau.)

Continent, country or area, date and city / Continent, pays ou zone, date et ville	Code[1]	City proper — Ville proprement dite Population				Urban agglomeration — Agglomération urbaine Population			
		Both sexes Les deux sexes	Male Masculin	Female Féminin	Surface area Superficie (km²)	Both sexes Les deux sexes	Male Masculin	Female Féminin	Surface area Superficie (km²)
ASIA — ASIE									
Iran (Islamic Republic of) — Iran (République islamique d')									
1996									
Abadan	CDJC	206 073	104 252	101 821	...	...	...	...	...
Ahwaz	CDJC	804 980	410 328	394 652	...	...	...	...	...
Amol	CDJC	159 092	79 562	79 530	...	...	...	...	...
Andimeshk	CDJC	106 923	54 142	52 781	...	...	...	...	...
Arak	CDJC	380 755	193 112	187 643	...	...	...	...	...
Ardabil	CDJC	340 386	174 586	165 800	...	...	...	...	...
Babol	CDJC	158 346	79 703	78 643	...	...	...	...	...
Bandar-e-Abbas	CDJC	273 578	143 166	130 412	...	...	...	...	...
Birjand	CDJC	127 608	67 838	59 770	...	...	...	...	...
Bojnurd	CDJC	134 835	69 026	65 809	...	...	...	...	...
Borujerd	CDJC	217 804	109 196	108 608	...	...	...	...	...
Bukand	CDJC	120 020	61 001	59 019	...	...	...	...	...
Bushehr	CDJC	143 641	76 626	67 015	...	...	...	...	...
Dezful	CDJC	202 639	106 660	95 979	...	...	...	...	...
Esfahan	CDJC	1 266 072	651 270	614 802	...	...	...	...	...
Gonbad-e-Kavus	CDJC	111 253	55 601	55 652	...	...	...	...	...
Gorgan	CDJC	188 710	95 395	93 315	...	...	...	...	...
Hamadan	CDJC	401 281	205 007	196 274	...	...	...	...	...
Ilam	CDJC	126 346	64 551	61 795	...	...	...	...	...
Islam Shahr (Qasemabad)	CDJC	265 450	135 110	130 340	...	...	...	...	...
Karaj	CDJC	940 968	482 486	458 482	...	...	...	...	...
Kashan	CDJC	201 372	103 203	98 169	...	...	...	...	...
Kerman	CDJC	384 991	201 674	183 317	...	...	...	...	...
Kermanshah	CDJC	692 986	356 449	336 537	...	...	...	...	...
Khomeini shahr	CDJC	165 888	86 175	79 713	...	...	...	...	...
Khoramabad	CDJC	272 815	139 020	133 795	...	...	...	...	...
Khoramshahr	CDJC	105 636	53 541	52 095	...	...	...	...	...
Kord-Shahr	CDJC	100 477	50 995	49 482	...	...	...	...	...
Khoy	CDJC	148 944	75 429	73 515	...	...	...	...	...
Mahabad	CDJC	107 799	56 287	51 512	...	...	...	...	...
Malayer	CDJC	144 373	72 531	71 842	...	...	...	...	...
Marvadsht	CDJC	103 579	52 578	51 001	...	...	...	...	...
Maraqeh	CDJC	132 318	66 625	65 693	...	...	...	...	...
Mashhad	CDJC	1 887 405	957 345	930 060	...	...	...	...	...
Masjed Soleyman	CDJC	116 882	59 498	57 384	...	...	...	...	...
Najafabad	CDJC	178 498	90 601	87 897	...	...	...	...	...
Neyshabur	CDJC	158 847	79 568	79 279	...	...	...	...	...
Orumiyeh	CDJC	435 200	222 871	212 329	...	...	...	...	...
Qaem shahr	CDJC	143 286	71 491	71 795	...	...	...	...	...
Qazvin	CDJC	291 117	149 910	141 207	...	...	...	...	...
Qarchak	CDJC	142 690	73 326	69 364	...	...	...	...	...
Qods	CDJC	138 278	70 803	67 475	...	...	...	...	...
Qom	CDJC	777 677	397 638	380 039	...	...	...	...	...
Rasht	CDJC	417 748	209 495	208 253	...	...	...	...	...
Sabzewar	CDJC	170 738	86 789	83 949	...	...	...	...	...
Sanandaj	CDJC	277 808	144 326	133 482	...	...	...	...	...
Saqez	CDJC	115 394	58 652	56 742	...	...	...	...	...
Sari	CDJC	195 882	98 805	97 077	...	...	...	...	...
Shahrud	CDJC	104 765	54 586	50 179	...	...	...	...	...
Shiraz	CDJC	1 053 025	541 307	511 718	...	...	...	...	...
Sirjan	CDJC	135 024	69 347	65 677	...	...	...	...	...
Tabriz	CDJC	1 191 043	609 813	581 230	...	...	...	...	...
TEHRAN	CDJC	6 758 845	3 468 946	3 289 899	...	...	...	...	...
Varamin	CDJC	107 233	54 492	52 741	...	...	...	...	...
Yazd	CDJC	326 776	168 834	157 942	...	...	...	...	...
Zabol	CDJC	100 887	51 074	49 813	...	...	...	...	...
Zahedan	CDJC	419 518	215 836	203 682	...	...	...	...	...

8. Population of capital cities and cities of 100 000 and more inhabitants: latest available year
Population des capitales et des villes de 100 000 habitants et plus: dernière année disponible (continued — suite)

(See notes at end of table. — Voir notes à la fin du tableau.)

Continent, country or area, date and city / Continent, pays ou zone, date et ville	Code[1]	City proper — Ville proprement dite Population				Urban agglomeration — Agglomération urbaine Population			
		Both sexes Les deux sexes	Male Masculin	Female Féminin	Surface area Superficie (km²)	Both sexes Les deux sexes	Male Masculin	Female Féminin	Surface area Superficie (km²)
ASIA — ASIE									
Iran (Islamic Republic of) — Iran (République islamique d')									
1996									
Zanjan	CDJC	286 295	146 150	140 145	...	...	...	...	...
Iraq									
1987									
Adhamiyah	CDFC	464 151	...	...	...	...	...	...	...
Amara	CDFC	208 797	...	...	...	...	...	...	...
BAGHDAD[98]	CDFC	3 841 268	...	...	...	...	...	...	...
Basra	CDFC	406 296	...	...	...	...	...	...	...
Diwaniya	CDFC	196 519	...	...	...	...	...	...	...
Erbil	CDFC	485 968	...	...	...	...	...	...	...
Hilla	CDFC	268 834	...	...	...	...	...	...	...
Kadhimain	CDFC	521 444	...	...	...	...	...	...	...
Karradah Sharqiyah	CDFC	235 554	...	...	...	...	...	...	...
Kerbala	CDFC	296 705	...	...	...	...	...	...	...
Kirkuk	CDFC	418 624	...	...	...	...	...	...	...
Kut	CDFC	183 183	...	...	...	...	...	...	...
Majnoon	CDFC	244 545	...	...	...	...	...	...	...
Mosul	CDFC	664 221	...	...	...	...	...	...	...
Najaf	CDFC	309 010	...	...	...	...	...	...	...
Nasariya	CDFC	265 937	...	...	...	...	...	...	...
Ramadi	CDFC	192 556	...	...	...	...	...	...	...
Sulamaniya	CDFC	364 096	...	...	...	...	...	...	...
Israel — Israël									
2000									
Ashdod	ESDJ	170 000	83 100	86 900	44	...	...	...	...
Bat Yam	ESDJ	137 100	65 400	71 700	8	...	...	...	...
Be'er Sheva	ESDJ	170 900	83 000	87 900	55	...	...	...	...
Bene Beraq	ESDJ	135 800	67 700	68 100	8	...	...	...	...
Haifa	ESDJ	269 400	129 300	140 100	60	...	...	...	...
Holon	ESDJ	165 000	79 600	85 400	19	...	...	...	...
JERUSALEM[99,100]	ESDJ	651 900	323 600	328 300	126	...	...	...	...
Netanya	ESDJ	160 100	77 100	83 000	29	...	...	...	...
Petah Tiqwa	ESDJ	165 700	80 200	85 500	37	...	...	...	...
Ramat Gan	ESDJ	127 300	59 900	67 400	14	...	...	...	...
Rishon Leziyyon	ESDJ	199 800	97 300	102 500	51	...	...	...	...
Tel Aviv-Yafo	ESDJ	352 600	167 500	185 100	52	2 705 600	1 313 800	1 391 800	...
Japan — Japon[101,102,103]									
2001									
Abiko	ESDF	129 043	64 197	64 846	43	...	...	...	...
Ageo	ESDF	213 988	107 317	106 671	46	...	...	...	...
Aizuwakamatsu	ESDF	117 945	56 414	61 531	315	...	...	...	...
Akashi	ESDF	293 091	143 420	149 671	49	...	...	...	...
Akishima	ESDF	106 637	53 834	52 803	17	...	...	...	...
Akita	ESDF	317 999	151 908	166 091	460	...	...	...	...
Amagasaki	ESDF	464 497	227 423	237 074	50	...	...	...	...
Anjo	ESDF	160 411	81 461	78 950	86	...	...	...	...
Aomori	ESDF	297 508	140 474	157 034	692	...	...	...	...
Asaka	ESDF	121 057	63 332	57 725	18	...	...	...	...
Ashikaga	ESDF	162 834	79 751	83 083	178	...	...	...	...
Atsugi	ESDF	219 343	114 472	104 871	94	...	...	...	...
Beppu	ESDF	126 779	57 054	69 725	125	...	...	...	...
Chiba	ESDF	893 782	450 532	443 250	272	...	...	...	...
Chigasaki	ESDF	222 122	109 908	112 214	36	...	...	...	...
Chofu	ESDF	206 310	104 606	101 704	22	...	...	...	...
Daito	ESDF	129 042	64 715	64 327	18	...	...	...	...
Ebina	ESDF	118 800	60 690	58 110	26	...	...	...	...
Fuchyu	ESDF	230 295	120 418	109 877	29	...	...	...	...
Fuji	ESDF	235 514	116 962	118 552	214	...	...	...	...

8. Population of capital cities and cities of 100 000 and more inhabitants: latest available year
Population des capitales et des villes de 100 000 habitants et plus: dernière année disponible (continued — suite)

(See notes at end of table. — Voir notes à la fin du tableau.)

Continent, country or area, date and city Continent, pays ou zone, date et ville	Code[1]	City proper — Ville proprement dite Population				Urban agglomeration — Agglomération urbaine Population			
		Both sexes Les deux sexes	Male Masculin	Female Féminin	Surface area Superficie (km²)	Both sexes Les deux sexes	Male Masculin	Female Féminin	Surface area Superficie (km²)
ASIA — ASIE									
Japan — Japon[101,102,103]									
2001									
Fujieda	ESDF	128 739	62 925	65 814	141	...	...	...	...
Fujimi	ESDF	103 428	51 979	51 449	20	...	...	...	...
Fujinomiya	ESDF	120 712	59 400	61 312	315	...	...	...	...
Fujisawa	ESDF	382 008	192 251	189 757	70	...	...	...	...
Fukaya	ESDF	103 820	51 925	51 895	69	...	...	...	...
Fukui	ESDF	251 970	122 882	129 088	341	...	...	...	...
Fukuoka	ESDF	1 350 981	651 380	699 601	339	...	...	...	...
Fukushima	ESDF	291 277	140 927	150 350	746	...	...	...	...
Fukuyama	ESDF	379 620	184 203	195 417	364	...	...	...	...
Funabashi	ESDF	552 441	281 664	270 777	86	...	...	...	...
Gifu	ESDF	403 379	191 285	212 094	195	...	...	...	...
Habikino	ESDF	119 856	57 490	62 366	26	...	...	...	...
Hachinohe	ESDF	241 988	116 877	125 111	214	...	...	...	...
Hachioji	ESDF	539 630	275 315	264 315	186	...	...	...	...
Hadano	ESDF	168 244	87 146	81 098	104	...	...	...	...
Hamamatsu	ESDF	585 303	291 629	293 674	257	...	...	...	...
Handa	ESDF	111 485	55 275	56 210	47	...	...	...	...
Higashihiroshima	ESDF	124 525	63 812	60 713	288	...	...	...	...
Higashikurume	ESDF	113 837	56 540	57 297	13	...	...	...	...
Higashimurayama	ESDF	142 713	70 939	71 774	17	...	...	...	...
Higashiosaka	ESDF	514 728	253 752	260 976	62	...	...	...	...
Hikone	ESDF	108 271	53 450	54 821	98	...	...	...	...
Himeji	ESDF	478 843	230 717	248 126	276	...	...	...	...
Hino	ESDF	168 777	87 317	81 460	28	...	...	...	...
Hirakata	ESDF	402 970	195 369	207 601	65	...	...	...	...
Hiratsuka	ESDF	255 173	129 522	125 651	68	...	...	...	...
Hirosaki	ESDF	176 592	81 219	95 373	274	...	...	...	...
Hiroshima	ESDF	1 129 432	548 711	580 721	741	...	...	...	...
Hitachi	ESDF	192 542	96 525	96 017	153	...	...	...	...
Hitachinaka	ESDF	152 026	76 723	75 303	99	...	...	...	...
Hofu	ESDF	118 487	56 957	61 530	189	...	...	...	...
Ibaraki	ESDF	261 085	129 116	131 969	77	...	...	...	...
Ichihara	ESDF	278 812	143 419	135 393	368	...	...	...	...
Ichikawa	ESDF	453 106	234 738	218 368	57	...	...	...	...
Ichinomiya	ESDF	275 352	134 792	140 560	82	...	...	...	...
Iida	ESDF	107 422	51 272	56 150	325	...	...	...	...
Ikeda	ESDF	101 370	49 770	51 600	22	...	...	...	...
Ikoma	ESDF	113 225	54 171	59 054	53	...	...	...	...
Imabari	ESDF	117 586	54 341	63 245	75	...	...	...	...
Inazawa	ESDF	100 090	49 902	50 188	48	...	...	...	...
Iruma	ESDF	148 799	74 101	74 698	45	...	...	...	...
Isesaki	ESDF	127 412	63 481	63 931	65	...	...	...	...
Ishinomaki	ESDF	119 335	57 759	61 576	137	...	...	...	...
Itami	ESDF	191 351	94 690	96 661	25	...	...	...	...
Iwakuni	ESDF	105 285	50 207	55 078	221	...	...	...	...
Iwatsuki	ESDF	109 238	54 877	54 361	49	...	...	...	...
Izumi (Osaka)	ESDF	173 651	84 643	89 008	85	...	...	...	...
Joetsu	ESDF	134 849	65 728	69 121	249	...	...	...	...
Kadoma	ESDF	134 898	67 249	67 649	12	...	...	...	...
Kagoshima	ESDF	552 200	257 911	294 289	290	...	...	...	...
Kakamigahara	ESDF	132 295	64 840	67 455	80	...	...	...	...
Kakogawa	ESDF	266 224	130 401	135 823	139	...	...	...	...
Kamagaya	ESDF	102 841	51 316	51 525	21	...	...	...	...
Kamakura	ESDF	167 718	80 585	87 133	40	...	...	...	...
Kanazawa	ESDF	456 392	222 550	233 842	468	...	...	...	...
Kariya	ESDF	133 163	69 436	63 727	50	...	...	...	...
Kashihara	ESDF	125 202	60 238	64 964	40	...	...	...	...
Kashiwa	ESDF	328 966	164 655	164 311	73	...	...	...	...

8. Population of capital cities and cities of 100 000 and more inhabitants: latest available year
Population des capitales et des villes de 100 000 habitants et plus: dernière année disponible (continued — suite)

(See notes at end of table. — Voir notes à la fin du tableau.)

Continent, country or area, date and city / Continent, pays ou zone, date et ville	Code[1]	City proper — Ville proprement dite Population				Urban agglomeration — Agglomération urbaine Population			
		Both sexes Les deux sexes	Male Masculin	Female Féminin	Surface area Superficie (km²)	Both sexes Les deux sexes	Male Masculin	Female Féminin	Surface area Superficie (km²)

ASIA — ASIE

Japan — Japon[101,102,103]
2001

Kasuga	ESDF	105 767	52 052	53 715	14	...	...	...	...
Kasugai	ESDF	289 198	144 788	144 410	93	...	...	...	...
Kasukabe	ESDF	204 276	101 886	102 390	38	...	...	...	...
Kawachinagano	ESDF	120 282	57 387	62 895	110	...	...	...	...
Kawagoe	ESDF	331 150	167 711	163 439	109	...	...	...	...
Kawaguchi	ESDF	464 775	237 534	227 241	56	...	...	...	...
Kawanishi	ESDF	154 353	73 773	80 580	53	...	...	...	...
Kawasaki	ESDF	1 263 827	656 654	607 173	143	...	...	...	...
Kiryu	ESDF	114 583	55 342	59 241	137	...	...	...	...
Kisarazu	ESDF	122 649	61 341	61 308	139	...	...	...	...
Kishiwada	ESDF	200 929	97 244	103 685	72	...	...	...	...
Kitakyushu[104]	ESDF	1 008 942	476 905	532 037	484	...	...	...	...
Kobe	ESDF	1 500 991	716 353	784 638	550	...	...	...	...
Kochi	ESDF	331 999	155 234	176 765	145	...	...	...	...
Kodaira	ESDF	180 435	90 307	90 128	20	...	...	...	...
Kofu	ESDF	196 247	96 809	99 438	172	...	...	...	...
Koganei	ESDF	112 158	57 049	55 109	11	...	...	...	...
Kokubunji	ESDF	113 012	57 276	55 736	11	...	...	...	...
Komaki	ESDF	144 117	73 200	70 917	63	...	...	...	...
Komatsu	ESDF	108 587	52 597	55 990	371	...	...	...	...
Koriyama	ESDF	335 554	166 236	169 318	757	...	...	...	...
Koshigaya	ESDF	309 709	155 577	154 132	60	...	...	...	...
Kumagaya	ESDF	156 552	78 845	77 707	85	...	...	...	...
Kumamoto	ESDF	664 703	315 564	349 139	267	...	...	...	...
Kurashiki	ESDF	431 482	208 125	223 357	299	...	...	...	...
Kure	ESDF	202 406	97 737	104 669	146	...	...	...	...
Kurume	ESDF	236 842	112 486	124 356	125	...	...	...	...
Kusatsu	ESDF	116 855	60 589	56 266	48	...	...	...	...
Kuwana	ESDF	108 763	53 353	55 410	57	...	...	...	...
Kyoto	ESDF	1 467 252	703 259	763 993	610	...	...	...	...
Machida	ESDF	383 565	190 748	192 817	72	...	...	...	...
Maebashi	ESDF	284 027	138 716	145 311	147	...	...	...	...
Matsubara	ESDF	132 387	64 679	67 708	17	...	...	...	...
Matsudo	ESDF	466 562	235 277	231 285	61	...	...	...	...
Matsue	ESDF	152 719	74 023	78 696	221	...	...	...	...
Matsumoto	ESDF	209 556	103 882	105 674	266	...	...	...	...
Matsusaka	ESDF	124 238	59 874	64 364	210	...	...	...	...
Matsuyama	ESDF	474 531	223 881	250 650	289	...	...	...	...
Minoh	ESDF	124 599	60 338	64 261	48	...	...	...	...
Misato	ESDF	130 680	66 635	64 045	30	...	...	...	...
Mishima	ESDF	111 071	54 378	56 693	62	...	...	...	...
Mitaka	ESDF	172 750	86 897	85 853	17	...	...	...	...
Mito	ESDF	246 728	120 218	126 510	176	...	...	...	...
Miyakonojo	ESDF	131 856	62 189	69 667	306	...	...	...	...
Miyazaki	ESDF	306 136	143 727	162 409	287	...	...	...	...
Moriguchi	ESDF	151 187	74 114	77 073	13	...	...	...	...
Morioka	ESDF	288 614	138 281	150 333	489	...	...	...	...
Musashino	ESDF	135 701	66 024	69 677	11	...	...	...	...
Nagano	ESDF	360 824	175 824	185 000	404	...	...	...	...
Nagaoka	ESDF	193 826	95 254	98 572	262	...	...	...	...
Nagareyama	ESDF	150 805	74 769	76 036	35	...	...	...	...
Nagasaki	ESDF	421 341	195 191	226 150	241	...	...	...	...
Nagoya	ESDF	2 175 404	1 082 026	1 093 378	326	...	...	...	...
Naha	ESDF	302 556	145 601	156 955	39	...	...	...	...
Nara	ESDF	365 550	173 213	192 337	212	...	...	...	...
Narashino	ESDF	154 774	78 704	76 070	21	...	...	...	...
Neyagawa	ESDF	249 495	123 015	126 480	25	...	...	...	...
Niigata	ESDF	528 311	256 509	271 802	206	...	...	...	...

8. Population of capital cities and cities of 100 000 and more inhabitants: latest available year
Population des capitales et des villes de 100 000 habitants et plus: dernière année disponible (continued — suite)

(See notes at end of table. — Voir notes à la fin du tableau.)

Continent, country or area, date and city / Continent, pays ou zone, date et ville	Code[1]	City proper — Ville proprement dite Population				Urban agglomeration — Agglomération urbaine Population			
		Both sexes Les deux sexes	Male Masculin	Female Féminin	Surface area Superficie (km²)	Both sexes Les deux sexes	Male Masculin	Female Féminin	Surface area Superficie (km²)
ASIA — ASIE									
Japan — Japon[101,102,103]									
2001									
Niihama	ESDF	125 380	59 950	65 430	161	...	...	...	...
Niiza	ESDF	149 596	75 600	73 996	23	...	...	...	...
Nishio	ESDF	101 186	50 814	50 372	76	...	...	...	...
Nishinomiya	ESDF	444 458	212 265	232 193	99	...	...	...	...
Nishitokyo	ESDF	181 875	90 785	91 090	16	...	...	...	...
Nobeoka	ESDF	124 421	58 360	66 061	284	...	...	...	...
Noda	ESDF	120 184	60 217	59 967	74	...	...	...	...
Numazu	ESDF	207 268	102 595	104 673	152	...	...	...	...
Ogaki	ESDF	150 509	73 087	77 422	80	...	...	...	...
Oita	ESDF	438 499	211 591	226 908	361	...	...	...	...
Okayama	ESDF	628 262	302 710	325 552	513	...	...	...	...
Okazaki	ESDF	339 156	169 522	169 634	227	...	...	...	...
Okinawa	ESDF	121 013	58 342	62 671	49	...	...	...	...
Omuta	ESDF	137 688	62 733	74 955	82	...	...	...	...
Osaka	ESDF	2 606 611	1 275 495	1 331 116	221	...	...	...	...
Ota	ESDF	149 237	75 342	73 895	98	...	...	...	...
Otsu	ESDF	290 310	141 173	149 137	302	...	...	...	...
Oume	ESDF	141 589	71 251	70 338	103	...	...	...	...
Oyama	ESDF	156 119	78 596	77 523	172	...	...	...	...
Saga	ESDF	167 566	79 485	88 081	104	...	...	...	...
Sagamihara	ESDF	609 795	310 042	299 753	90	...	...	...	...
Sakai	ESDF	792 865	384 328	408 537	137	...	...	...	...
Sakata	ESDF	101 453	48 804	52 649	176	...	...	...	...
Sakura	ESDF	171 330	84 236	87 094	104	...	...	...	...
Sanda	ESDF	112 500	54 863	57 637	210	...	...	...	...
Sasebo	ESDF	240 737	113 179	127 558	248	...	...	...	...
Sayama	ESDF	161 009	81 585	79 424	49	...	...	...	...
Sendai	ESDF	1 012 546	497 232	515 314	784	...	...	...	...
Seto	ESDF	132 046	65 306	66 740	112	...	...	...	...
Shimizu	ESDF	236 055	115 485	120 570	228	...	...	...	...
Shimonoseki	ESDF	251 208	117 849	133 359	224	...	...	...	...
Shizuoka	ESDF	468 757	228 399	240 358	1 146	...	...	...	...
Soka	ESDF	226 820	116 540	110 280	27	...	...	...	...
Suita	ESDF	349 739	172 341	177 398	36	...	...	...	...
Suzuka	ESDF	188 143	93 613	94 530	195	...	...	...	...
Tachikawa	ESDF	165 653	82 976	82 677	24	...	...	...	...
Tajimi	ESDF	104 137	50 500	53 637	78	...	...	...	...
Takamatsu	ESDF	333 434	161 608	171 826	194	...	...	...	...
Takaoka	ESDF	171 579	82 134	89 445	151	...	...	...	...
Takarazuka	ESDF	215 195	101 530	113 665	102	...	...	...	...
Takasaki	ESDF	240 420	118 377	122 043	111	...	...	...	...
Takatsuki	ESDF	355 564	173 669	181 895	105	...	...	...	...
Tama	ESDF	145 213	73 324	71 889	21	...	...	...	...
Toda	ESDF	108 914	57 218	51 696	18	...	...	...	...
Tokai	ESDF	100 556	52 341	48 215	43	...	...	...	...
Tokorozawa	ESDF	331 789	166 525	165 264	72	...	...	...	...
Tokushima	ESDF	267 404	127 022	140 382	191	...	...	...	...
Tokuyama	ESDF	104 079	50 385	53 694	340	...	...	...	...
TOKYO[105]	ESDF	8 197 738	4 074 045	4 123 693	621	...	...	...	...
Tondabayashi	ESDF	126 383	60 527	65 856	40	...	...	...	...
Tottori	ESDF	150 867	73 723	77 144	237	...	...	...	...
Toyama	ESDF	325 705	157 869	167 836	209	...	...	...	...
Toyota	ESDF	353 360	186 469	166 891	290	...	...	...	...
Toyohashi	ESDF	366 927	182 187	184 740	261	...	...	...	...
Toyokawa	ESDF	117 732	58 430	59 302	65	...	...	...	...
Toyonaka	ESDF	390 603	189 647	200 956	36	...	...	...	...
Tsu	ESDF	163 463	79 355	84 108	102	...	...	...	...
Tsuchiura	ESDF	135 135	67 231	67 904	82	...	...	...	...

8. Population of capital cities and cities of 100 000 and more inhabitants: latest available year
Population des capitales et des villes de 100 000 habitants et plus: dernière année disponible (continued — suite)

(See notes at end of table. — Voir notes à la fin du tableau.)

Continent, country or area, date and city / Continent, pays ou zone, date et ville	Code[1]	City proper — Ville proprement dite Population				Urban agglomeration — Agglomération urbaine Population			
		Both sexes Les deux sexes	Male Masculin	Female Féminin	Surface area Superficie (km²)	Both sexes Les deux sexes	Male Masculin	Female Féminin	Surface area Superficie (km²)
ASIA — ASIE									
Japan — Japon[101,102,103]									
2001									
Tsukuba	ESDF	167 338	86 854	80 484	260	...	...	...	...
Tsuruoka	ESDF	100 494	48 087	52 407	234	...	...	...	...
Ube	ESDF	174 099	83 469	90 630	210	...	...	...	...
Ueda	ESDF	125 846	62 020	63 826	177	...	...	...	...
Uji	ESDF	188 419	92 146	96 273	68	...	...	...	...
Urasoe	ESDF	103 090	50 612	52 478	19	...	...	...	...
Urayasu	ESDF	137 265	70 986	66 279	17	...	...	...	...
Utsunomiya	ESDF	444 135	222 152	221 983	312	...	...	...	...
Wakayama	ESDF	385 414	182 472	202 942	209	...	...	...	...
Yachiyo	ESDF	171 232	85 075	86 157	51	...	...	...	...
Yaizu	ESDF	118 864	57 826	61 038	46	...	...	...	...
Yamagata	ESDF	255 313	123 164	132 149	381	...	...	...	...
Yamaguchi	ESDF	141 207	67 453	73 754	357	...	...	...	...
Yamato	ESDF	214 707	109 309	105 398	27	...	...	...	...
Yao	ESDF	274 488	133 748	140 740	42	...	...	...	...
Yatsushiro	ESDF	105 789	49 499	56 290	147	...	...	...	...
Yokkaichi	ESDF	292 361	143 976	148 385	197	...	...	...	...
Yokohama	ESDF	3 454 375	1 748 356	1 706 019	437	...	...	...	...
Yokosuka	ESDF	430 284	216 873	213 411	101	...	...	...	...
Yonago	ESDF	139 089	66 172	72 917	106	...	...	...	...
Zama	ESDF	125 784	64 622	61 162	18	...	...	...	...
Jordan — Jordanie									
1999									
AMMAN	ESDF	*1 117 605*	...	...	...	...	...	...	...
Irbid	ESDF	*240 188*	...	...	...	...	...	...	...
Russiefa	ESDF	*212 086*	...	...	...	...	...	...	...
Zarqa	ESDF	*416 279*	...	...	...	...	...	...	...
2000									
AMMAN	ESDF	*1 147 447*	...	...	...	...	...	...	...
Irbid	ESDF	*247 275*	...	...	...	...	...	...	...
Russiefa	ESDF	*218 211*	...	...	...	...	...	...	...
Zarqa	ESDF	*428 623*	...	...	...	...	...	...	...
Kazakhstan									
1999									
Aktau	CDJC	143 396	69 805	73 591	...	...	...	...	...
Aktobe	CDJC	253 088	117 568	135 520	...	...	...	...	...
Almaty	CDJC	1 129 356	511 917	617 439	...	...	...	...	...
ASTANA	CDJC	312 965	145 442	167 523	...	319 324	148 607	170 717	252
Atirau	CDJC	142 497	66 989	75 508	...	...	...	...	...
Ekibastuz	CDJC	127 197	60 079	67 118	...	...	...	...	...
Karaganda	CDJC	436 864	201 246	235 618	...	...	...	...	...
Koktshetau	CDJC	123 389	56 364	67 025	...	...	...	...	...
Kustanai	CDJC	221 429	101 706	119 723	...	...	...	...	...
Kyzylorda	CDJC	157 364	75 011	82 353	...	...	...	...	...
Pavlodar	CDJC	300 503	138 811	161 692	...	...	...	...	...
Petropavlovsk (Severo-Kazakhstanskaya oblast)	CDJC	203 523	92 536	110 987	...	...	...	...	...
Rudni	CDJC	109 515	50 721	58 794	...	...	...	...	...
Semipalatinsk	CDJC	269 574	122 916	146 658	...	...	...	...	...
Shimkent	CDJC	360 078	167 628	192 450	...	...	...	...	...
Taraz	CDJC	330 125	153 394	176 731	...	...	...	...	...
Temirtau	CDJC	170 481	78 990	91 491	...	...	...	...	...
Uralsk	CDJC	195 459	88 723	106 736	...	...	...	...	...
Ust-Kamenogorsk	CDJC	310 950	142 151	168 799	...	...	...	...	...
2000									
Aktau	ESDF	142 600	...	...	...	157 900	...	...	706
Aktobe	ESDF	249 200	...	...	...	277 800	...	...	...
Almaty	ESDF	1 135 400	...	...	...	1 135 400	...	...	230

8. Population of capital cities and cities of 100 000 and more inhabitants: latest available year
Population des capitales et des villes de 100 000 habitants et plus: dernière année disponible (continued — suite)

(See notes at end of table. — Voir notes à la fin du tableau.)

Continent, country or area, date and city Continent, pays ou zone, date et ville	Code[1]	City proper — Ville proprement dite Population				Urban agglomeration — Agglomération urbaine Population			
		Both sexes Les deux sexes	Male Masculin	Female Féminin	Surface area Superficie (km²)	Both sexes Les deux sexes	Male Masculin	Female Féminin	Surface area Superficie (km²)
ASIA — ASIE									
Kazakhstan									
2000									
ASTANA	ESDF	322 400	...	...	...	322 400	...	...	252
Atirau	ESDF	142 700	...	...	...	194 600	...	...	
Karaganda	ESDF	434 300	...	...	...	434 600	...	...	600
Koktshetau	ESDF	123 500	...	...	...	134 100	...	...	230
Kustanai	ESDF	216 700	...	...	...	216 700	...	...	...
Kyzylorda	ESDF	158 300	...	...	...	194 900	...	...	88
Pavlodar	ESDF	295 400	...	...	...	312 600	...	...	
Petropavlovsk (Severo-Kazakhstanskaya oblast)	ESDF	201 500	...	...	...	202 400	...	...	155
Shimkent	ESDF	359 600	...	...	...	419 400	...	...	78
Taldykorgan	ESDF	97 200	...	...	...	117 100	...	...	59
Taraz	ESDF	329 200	...	...	...	329 200	...	...	
Uralsk	ESDF	190 900	...	...	...	217 300	...	...	232
Ust-Kamenogorsk	ESDF	307 900	...	...	...	317 400	...	...	23
Korea (Dem. People's Republic of) — Corée (Rép. populaire dém. de)									
1993									
Chongjin	CDFC	582 480	...	...	...	...	...	...	...
Haeju	CDFC	229 172	...	...	...	...	...	...	...
Hamhung	CDFC	709 730	...	...	...	...	...	...	...
Hyesan	CDFC	178 020	...	...	...	...	...	...	...
Kaesong	CDFC	334 433	...	...	...	...	...	...	...
Kanggye	CDFC	223 410	...	...	...	...	...	...	...
Nampho	CDFC	731 448	...	...	...	...	...	...	...
Phyongsong	CDFC	272 934	...	...	...	...	...	...	...
PYONGYANG	CDFC	2 741 260	...	...	...	...	...	...	...
Sariwon	CDFC	254 146	...	...	...	...	...	...	...
Sinuiji	CDFC	326 011	...	...	...	...	...	...	...
Wonsan	CDFC	300 148	...	...	...	...	...	...	...
Korea (Republic of) — Corée (République de)									
1995									
Andong	CDJC	188 443	93 435	95 008	1 518	...	...	...	...
Ansan	CDJC	510 314	266 181	244 133	144	...	...	...	...
Anyang	CDJC	591 106	295 296	295 810	58	...	...	...	...
Bucheon (Puchon)	CDJC	779 412	393 280	386 132	53	...	...	...	...
Busan (Pusan)	CDJC	3 814 325	1 900 519	1 913 806	748	...	...	...	...
Changwon	CDJC	481 694	248 276	233 418	293	...	...	...	...
Cheonan	CDJC	330 259	168 016	162 243	637	...	...	...	...
Cheongju	CDJC	531 376	264 612	266 764	153	...	...	...	...
Chuncheon	CDJC	234 528	117 524	117 004	1 117	...	...	...	...
Chungju	CDJC	205 206	104 218	100 988	984	...	...	...	...
Daegu (Taegu)	CDJC	2 449 420	1 233 712	1 215 708	885	...	...	...	...
Daejeon (Taejon)	CDJC	1 272 121	643 078	629 043	539	...	...	...	...
Gangneung (Kangnung)	CDJC	220 403	110 719	109 684	1 039	...	...	...	...
Gimhae (Kimhae)	CDJC	256 370	128 682	127 688	463	...	...	...	...
Gumi (Kumi)	CDJC	311 431	157 820	153 611	127	...	...	...	...
Gunpo (Kunpo)	CDJC	235 233	118 763	116 470	36	...	...	...	...
Gunsan (Kunsan)	CDJC	266 569	134 797	131 772	388	...	...	...	...
Guri (Kuri)	CDJC	142 173	71 617	70 556	33	...	...	...	...
Gwangju (Kwangchu)	CDJC	1 257 636	627 127	630 509	501	...	...	...	...
Gwangmyeong (Kwangmyong)	CDJC	350 914	174 892	176 022	38	...	...	...	...
Gyeongju (Kyongju)	CDJC	273 968	136 887	137 081	1 324	...	...	...	...
Hanam	CDJC	115 812	58 998	56 814	93	...	...	...	...
Iksan (Iri)	CDJC	322 685	160 986	161 699	507	...	...	...	...
Incheon	CDJC	2 308 188	1 166 160	1 142 028	955	...	...	...	...
Jecheon (Chechon)	CDJC	137 070	69 113	67 957	882	...	...	...	...
Jeju (Cheju)	CDJC	258 511	127 710	130 801	255	...	...	...	...

8. Population of capital cities and cities of 100 000 and more inhabitants: latest available year
Population des capitales et des villes de 100 000 habitants et plus: dernière année disponible (continued — suite)

(See notes at end of table. — Voir notes à la fin du tableau.)

Continent, country or area, date and city Continent, pays ou zone, date et ville	Code[1]	City proper — Ville proprement dite Population				Urban agglomeration — Agglomération urbaine Population			
		Both sexes Les deux sexes	Male Masculin	Female Féminin	Surface area Superficie (km²)	Both sexes Les deux sexes	Male Masculin	Female Féminin	Surface area Superficie (km²)
ASIA — ASIE									
Korea (Republic of) — Corée (République de)									
1995									
Jeongeup	CDJC	139 111	67 854	71 257	692	...	...	...	...
Jeonju (Chonchu)	CDJC	563 153	280 042	283 111	206	...	...	...	...
Jinju (Chinju)	CDJC	329 886	162 923	166 963	712	...	...	...	...
Masan	CDJC	441 242	219 804	221 438	329	...	...	...	...
Mokpo	CDJC	247 452	124 122	123 330	46	...	...	...	...
Pohang	CDJC	508 899	259 364	249 535	1 126	...	...	...	...
Seongnam	CDJC	869 094	437 481	431 613	141	...	...	...	...
SEOUL	CDJC	10 231 217	5 138 935	5 092 282	605	...	...	...	...
Siheung	CDJC	133 443	68 309	65 134	123	...	...	...	...
Suncheon	CDJC	249 263	125 061	124 202	907	...	...	...	...
Suwon (Puwan)	CDJC	755 550	379 960	375 590	121	...	...	...	...
Uijeongbu (Eujeongbu)	CDJC	276 111	138 118	137 993	81	...	...	...	...
Ulsan	CDJC	967 429	500 724	466 705	1 055	...	...	...	...
Wonju	CDJC	237 460	119 881	117 579	865	...	...	...	...
Yeosu	CDJC	183 596	92 229	91 367	45	...	...	...	...
2000									
Andong	CDFC	182 098	89 823	92 275	1 518	...	...	...	...
Asan	CDFC	180 763	90 812	89 951	...	...	...	...	...
Boryeong	CDFC	109 535	55 390	54 145	...	...	...	...	...
Bucheon (Puchon)	CDFC	761 389	384 935	376 454	53	...	...	...	...
Busan (Pusan)	CDFC	3 662 884	1 827 062	1 835 822	748	...	...	...	...
Changwon	CDFC	517 410	265 941	251 469	293	...	...	...	...
Cheonan	CDFC	417 835	212 874	204 961	637	...	...	...	...
Cheongju	CDFC	586 700	292 144	294 556	153	...	...	...	...
Chuncheon	CDFC	252 547	125 605	126 942	1 117	...	...	...	...
Chungju	CDFC	217 927	110 540	107 387	984	...	...	...	...
Daegu (Taegu)	CDFC	2 480 578	1 247 562	1 233 016	885	...	...	...	...
Daejeon (Taejon)	CDFC	1 368 207	690 600	677 607	539	...	...	...	...
Gangneung (Kangnung)	CDFC	228 232	113 826	114 406	1 039	...	...	...	...
Geoje	CDFC	168 022	87 169	80 853	...	...	...	...	...
Gimcheon	CDFC	147 855	73 629	74 226	...	...	...	...	...
Gimhae (Kimhae)	CDFC	331 979	167 255	164 724	463	...	...	...	...
Gimje	CDFC	102 589	50 067	52 522	...	...	...	...	...
Gongju	CDFC	130 376	64 537	65 839	...	...	...	...	...
Goyang	CDFC	763 971	381 072	382 899	...	...	...	...	...
Gumi (Kumi)	CDFC	341 550	173 253	168 297	127	...	...	...	...
Gunpo (Kunpo)	CDFC	263 760	133 013	130 747	36	...	...	...	...
Gunsan (Kunsan)	CDFC	272 715	138 537	134 178	388	...	...	...	...
Gwangju (Kwangchu)	CDFC	1 352 797	674 228	678 569	501	...	...	...	...
Gwangmyeong (Kwangmyong)	CDFC	334 089	167 115	166 974	38	...	...	...	...
Gwangyang	CDFC	132 639	67 629	65 010	...	...	...	...	...
Gyeongju (Kyongju)	CDFC	275 842	136 891	138 951	1 324	...	...	...	...
Gyeongsan	CDFC	228 206	114 162	114 044	...	...	...	...	...
Icheon	CDFC	179 719	88 460	91 259	...	...	...	...	...
Iksan (Iri)	CDFC	323 687	161 231	162 456	507	...	...	...	...
Incheon	CDFC	2 475 139	1 250 383	1 224 756	955	...	...	...	...
Jecheon (Chechon)	CDFC	143 710	72 855	70 855	882	...	...	...	...
Jeju (Cheju)	CDFC	279 996	138 932	141 064	255	...	...	...	...
Jeongeup	CDFC	129 152	62 902	66 250	...	...	...	...	...
Jeonju (Chonchu)	CDFC	616 468	306 661	309 807	206	...	...	...	...
Jinhae (Chinhae)	CDFC	127 578	64 317	63 261	...	...	...	...	...
Jinju (Chinju)	CDFC	339 791	168 576	171 215	712	...	...	...	...
Masan	CDFC	434 371	218 050	216 321	329	...	...	...	...
Miryang	CDFC	115 962	56 855	59 107	...	...	...	...	...
Mokpo	CDFC	250 480	125 922	124 558	46	...	...	...	...
Nonsan	CDFC	137 452	68 799	68 653	...	...	...	...	...
Pohang	CDFC	515 714	264 319	251 395	1 126	...	...	...	...

8. Population of capital cities and cities of 100 000 and more inhabitants: latest available year
Population des capitales et des villes de 100 000 habitants et plus: dernière année disponible (continued — suite)

(See notes at end of table. — Voir notes à la fin du tableau.)

Continent, country or area, date and city Continent, pays ou zone, date et ville	Code[1]	City proper — Ville proprement dite Population				Urban agglomeration — Agglomération urbaine Population			
		Both sexes Les deux sexes	Male Masculin	Female Féminin	Surface area Superficie (km²)	Both sexes Les deux sexes	Male Masculin	Female Féminin	Surface area Superficie (km²)
ASIA — ASIE									
Korea (Republic of) — Corée (République de)									
2000									
Sacheon	CDFC	111 078	55 285	55 793	...	...	...	...	...
Sangju	CDFC	116 493	57 152	59 341	...	...	...	...	...
Seongnam	CDFC	914 590	461 011	453 579	141	...	...	...	...
Seosan	CDFC	143 154	73 100	70 054	...	...	...	...	...
SEOUL	CDFC	9 895 217	4 966 993	4 928 224	605	...	...	...	...
Suncheon	CDFC	265 930	133 064	132 866	907	...	...	...	...
Suwon (Puwan)	CDFC	946 704	476 639	470 065	121	...	...	...	...
Tongyeong	CDFC	123 842	62 017	61 825	...	...	...	...	...
Uijeongbu (Eujeongbu)	CDFC	355 380	177 657	177 723	81	...	...	...	...
Ulsan	CDFC	1 014 428	522 062	492 366	1 055	...	...	...	...
Wonju	CDFC	268 352	134 901	133 451	865	...	...	...	...
Yangsan	CDFC	191 975	96 551	95 424	...	...	...	...	...
Yeongcheon	CDFC	111 392	55 176	56 216	...	...	...	...	...
Yeongju	CDFC	126 507	63 556	62 951	...	...	...	...	...
Yeosu	CDFC	303 233	152 836	150 397	45	...	...	...	...
Kuwait — Koweït									
1995									
Jaleeb Al-Shuykh	CDFC	102 169	78 748	23 421	...	...	...	...	...
KUWAIT CITY	CDFC	28 747	23 601	5 146	...	...	...	...	...
Salmiya	CDFC	129 775	77 672	52 103	...	...	...	...	...
Kyrgyzstan — Kirghizistan									
2001									
BISHKEK	ESDF	780 800	374 400	406 400	127	...	...	...	...
Osh	ESDF	218 100	104 300	113 800	24	...	...	...	...
Lao People's Democratic Republic — République démocratique populaire lao									
1985									
VIENTIANE	CDFC	160 000	...	...	...	377 400	...	...	...
1995									
VIENTIANE	CDFC	...	...	...	...	528 100	...	...	...
Lebanon — Liban									
1970									
BEIRUT	SSDF	474 870	239 130	235 740	...	938 940	...	...	...
Tripoli	SSDF	127 611	...	...	...	...	...	...	...
Malaysia: Peninsular Malaysia — Malaysie: Malaisie Péninsulaire									
1991									
Alor Setar	CDFC	124 412	...	...	...	164 444	...	...	...
George Town	CDFC	219 603	...	...	...	...	...	...	...
Ipoh	CDFC	382 853	...	...	...	468 841	...	...	...
Johore Bharu	CDFC	328 436	...	...	...	441 703	...	...	...
Klang	CDFC	243 355	...	...	...	368 379	...	...	...
Kota Bahru	CDFC	219 582	...	...	...	234 581	...	...	...
KUALA LUMPUR	CDFC	1 145 342	...	...	...	...	...	...	...
Kuala Terengganu	CDFC	228 119	...	...	...	...	...	...	...
Kuantan	CDFC	199 484	...	...	...	202 445	...	...	...
Petaling Jaya	CDFC	254 350	...	...	...	350 995	...	...	...
Seleyang Baru	CDFC	124 228	...	...	...	134 197	...	...	...
Seremban	CDFC	182 869	...	...	...	193 237	...	...	...
Shah Alam	CDFC	102 019	...	...	...	117 027	...	...	...
Sungai Petani	CDFC	114 763	...	...	...	116 977	...	...	...
Taiping	CDFC	183 261	...	...	...	200 324	...	...	...
Malaysia: Sabah — Malaisie: Sabah									
1991									
KOTA KINABALU	CDFC	76 120	...	...	...	160 184	...	...	...
Sandakan	CDFC	125 841	...	...	...	156 675	...	...	...

8. Population of capital cities and cities of 100 000 and more inhabitants: latest available year
Population des capitales et des villes de 100 000 habitants et plus: dernière année disponible (continued — suite)

(See notes at end of table. — Voir notes à la fin du tableau.)

Continent, country or area, date and city / Continent, pays ou zone, date et ville	Code[1]	City proper — Ville proprement dite Population				Urban agglomeration — Agglomération urbaine Population			
		Both sexes Les deux sexes	Male Masculin	Female Féminin	Surface area Superficie (km²)	Both sexes Les deux sexes	Male Masculin	Female Féminin	Surface area Superficie (km²)
ASIA — ASIE									
Malaysia: Sarawak — Malaisie: Sarawak									
1991									
KUCHING	CDFC	148 059	...	...	...	277 905	...	...	...
Sibu	CDFC	126 381	...	...	...	133 479	...	...	...
Maldives									
2000									
MALE	CDFC	74 069	38 559	35 510	...	...	...	...	...
Mongolia — Mongolie									
2000									
ULAANBAATAR	CDFC	760 077	369 146	390 931	...	...	...	...	...
2001									
ULAANBAATAR	ESDF	*773 267*	*378 901*	*394 366*	...	...	...	...	...
Myanmar									
1983									
Bassein	CDFC	144 096	...	...	...	...	...	...	...
Mandalay	CDFC	532 949	...	...	...	...	...	...	...
Monywa	CDFC	106 843	...	...	...	...	...	...	...
Moulmein	CDFC	219 961	...	...	...	...	...	...	...
Pegu	CDFC	150 528	...	...	...	...	...	...	...
Sittwe	CDFC	107 621	...	...	...	...	...	...	...
Taunggyi	CDFC	108 231	...	...	...	...	...	...	...
YANGON	CDFC	2 513 023	...	...	...	...	...	...	...
Nepal — Népal									
1991									
Biratnagar	CDJC	129 388	...	...	...	...	...	...	...
KATHMANDU	CDJC	421 258	...	...	...	...	...	...	...
Lalitpur	CDJC	115 865	...	...	...	...	...	...	...
Occupied Palestinian Territory — Territoire palestinien occupé									
1997									
Gaza	CDFC	291 596	148 517	143 079	38	...	...	...	...
Hebron	CDFC	119 401	62 005	57 396	49	...	...	...	...
Nablus	CDFC	100 231	50 990	49 241	26	...	...	...	...
2001									
Gaza	ESDF	343 904	175 241	168 663	38	...	...	...	...
Hebron	ESDF	140 055	72 753	67 302	49	...	...	...	...
Khan Yunis	ESDF	105 095	53 603	51 492	...	...	...	...	...
Nablus	ESDF	115 872	59 016	56 856	26	...	...	...	...
Oman									
1993									
MUSCAT	CDFC	40 856	...	...	...	...	...	...	...
Salalah	CDFC	131 802	...	...	...	...	...	...	...
Pakistan[106]									
1998									
Abbotabad	CDFC	106 101	61 698	44 403	...	...	...	...	...
Bahawalnagar	CDFC	111 313	57 779	53 534	...	...	...	...	...
Bahawalpur	CDFC	408 395	222 228	186 167	...	...	...	...	...
Burewala	CDFC	152 097	78 726	73 371	...	...	...	...	...
Chiniot	CDFC	172 522	90 474	82 048	...	...	...	...	...
Chishtian	CDFC	102 287	52 427	49 860	...	...	...	...	...
Dadu	CDFC	102 550	53 508	49 042	...	...	...	...	...
Daska	CDFC	102 883	52 359	50 524	...	...	...	...	...
Dera Ghazi Khan	CDFC	190 542	98 738	91 804	...	...	...	...	...
Faisalabad (Lyallpur)	CDFC	2 008 861	1 053 085	955 776	...	...	...	...	...
Gojra	CDFC	117 872	60 598	57 294	...	...	...	...	...
Gujranwala	CDFC	1 132 509	588 512	543 997	...	...	...	...	...
Gujrat	CDFC	251 792	128 524	123 268	...	...	...	...	...
Hafizabad	CDFC	133 678	69 231	64 447	...	...	...	...	...
Hyderabad	CDFC	1 166 894	612 283	554 611	...	...	...	...	...

8. Population of capital cities and cities of 100 000 and more inhabitants: latest available year
Population des capitales et des villes de 100 000 habitants et plus: dernière année disponible (continued — suite)

(See notes at end of table. — Voir notes à la fin du tableau.)

Continent, country or area, date and city / Continent, pays ou zone, date et ville	Code[1]	City proper — Ville proprement dite Population				Urban agglomeration — Agglomération urbaine Population			
		Both sexes Les deux sexes	Male Masculin	Female Féminin	Surface area Superficie (km²)	Both sexes Les deux sexes	Male Masculin	Female Féminin	Surface area Superficie (km²)
ASIA — ASIE									
Pakistan[106]									
1998									
ISLAMABAD	CDFC	529 180	290 717	238 463	...	...	...	...	...
Jacobabad	CDFC	138 780	71 854	66 926	...	...	...	...	...
Jaranwala	CDFC	106 785	55 819	51 166	...	...	...	...	...
Jhang	CDFC	293 366	153 123	140 243	...	...	...	...	...
Jhelum	CDFC	147 392	79 169	68 223	...	...	...	...	...
Kamoke	CDFC	152 288	78 848	73 440	...	...	...	...	...
Karachi	CDFC	9 339 023	5 029 900	4 309 123	...	...	...	...	...
Kasur	CDFC	245 321	129 553	115 768	...	...	...	...	...
Khairpur	CDFC	105 637	55 358	50 279	...	...	...	...	...
Khanewal	CDFC	133 986	69 145	64 841	...	...	...	...	...
Khanpur	CDFC	120 382	62 371	58 011	...	...	...	...	...
Kohat	CDFC	126 627	71 505	55 122	...	...	...	...	...
Lahore	CDFC	5 143 495	2 707 220	2 436 275	...	...	...	...	...
Larkana	CDFC	270 283	140 622	129 661	...	...	...	...	...
Mangora	CDFC	173 868	91 742	82 126	...	...	...	...	...
Mardan	CDFC	245 926	129 247	116 679	...	...	...	...	...
Mirpur Khas	CDFC	189 671	97 940	91 731	...	...	...	...	...
Multan	CDFC	1 197 384	637 911	559 473	...	...	...	...	...
Muridke	CDFC	111 951	58 210	53 741	...	...	...	...	...
Muzaffargharh	CDFC	123 404	66 556	56 848	...	...	...	...	...
Nawabshah	CDFC	189 244	98 116	91 128	...	...	...	...	...
Okara	CDFC	201 815	104 245	97 570	...	...	...	...	...
Pakpattan	CDFC	109 033	56 676	52 357	...	...	...	...	...
Peshawar	CDFC	982 816	521 901	460 915	...	...	...	...	...
Quetta	CDFC	565 137	307 759	257 378	...	...	...	...	...
Rahimyar Khan	CDFC	233 537	121 446	112 091	...	...	...	...	...
Rawalpindi	CDFC	1 409 768	750 530	659 238	...	...	...	...	...
Sadiqabad	CDFC	144 391	75 217	69 174	...	...	...	...	...
Sahiwal	CDFC	208 778	108 992	99 786	...	...	...	...	...
Sargodha	CDFC	458 440	239 837	218 603	...	...	...	...	...
Shakkarpur	CDFC	134 883	69 713	65 170	...	...	...	...	...
Sheikhu Pura	CDFC	280 263	146 739	133 524	...	...	...	...	...
Sialkote	CDFC	421 502	227 398	194 104	...	...	...	...	...
Sukkur	CDFC	335 551	175 679	159 872	...	...	...	...	...
Tandoadam	CDFC	104 907	54 670	50 237	...	...	...	...	...
Wah Cantonment	CDFC	198 891	104 230	94 661	...	...	...	...	...
Philippines									
1994									
MANILA	ESDJ	...	...	...	...	8 594 150	...	...	...
1995									
Angeles	CDJC	234 011	116 877	117 134	60	...	...	...	...
Bacolod	CDJC	402 345	196 601	205 744	156	...	...	...	...
Bago	CDJC	132 338	67 916	64 422	362	...	...	...	...
Baguio	CDJC	226 883	111 185	115 698	49	...	...	...	...
Batangas	CDJC	211 879	105 855	106 024	283	...	...	...	...
Butuan	CDJC	247 074	124 811	122 263	345	...	...	...	...
Cabanatuan	CDJC	201 033	100 195	100 838	283	...	...	...	...
Cadiz	CDJC	125 943	64 080	61 863	210	...	...	...	...
Cagayan de Oro	CDJC	428 314	211 796	216 518	373	...	...	...	...
Calbayog	CDJC	129 216	66 275	62 941	903	...	...	...	...
Caloocan	CDJC	1 023 159	...	...	56	...	...	...	...
Cebu	CDJC	662 299	324 964	337 335	281	...	...	...	...
Cotabato	CDJC	146 779	71 624	75 155	144	...	...	...	...
Dagupan	CDJC	126 214	62 728	63 486	37	...	...	...	...
Davao	CDJC	1 006 840	502 782	504 058	1 211	...	...	...	...
General Santos	CDJC	327 173	165 792	161 381	402	...	...	...	...
Iligan	CDJC	273 004	136 172	136 832	673	...	...	...	...
Iloilo	CDJC	334 539	161 988	172 551	56	...	...	...	...

278

8. Population of capital cities and cities of 100 000 and more inhabitants: latest available year
Population des capitales et des villes de 100 000 habitants et plus: dernière année disponible (continued — suite)

(See notes at end of table. — Voir notes à la fin du tableau.)

Continent, country or area, date and city Continent, pays ou zone, date et ville	Code[1]	City proper — Ville proprement dite Population				Urban agglomeration — Agglomération urbaine Population			
		Both sexes Les deux sexes	Male Masculin	Female Féminin	Surface area Superficie (km²)	Both sexes Les deux sexes	Male Masculin	Female Féminin	Surface area Superficie (km²)
ASIA — ASIE									
Philippines									
1995									
Lapu-Lapu	CDJC	173 744	85 899	87 845	58	...	...	...	...
Legasp	CDJC	141 657	70 134	71 523	154	...	...	...	...
Lipa	CDJC	177 894	89 819	88 075	209	...	...	...	...
Lucena City	CDJC	177 750	88 897	88 853	80	...	...	...	...
Makati	CDJC	484 176	...	...	...	...	...	...	...
Mandaue	CDJC	194 745	96 440	98 305	12	...	...	...	...
Mandaluyong	CDJC	286 870	...	...	...	...	...	...	...
MANILA	CDJC	1 654 671	...	...	614	...	...	...	...
Marawi	CDJC	114 389	56 236	58 153	23	...	...	...	...
Muntinlupa	CDJC	399 846	...	...	47	...	...	...	...
Naga	CDJC	126 972	62 051	64 921	85	...	...	...	...
Olongapo	CDJC	179 754	88 472	91 282	103	...	...	...	...
Ormoc	CDJC	144 003	73 298	70 705	491	...	...	...	...
Ozamis	CDJC	101 944	50 707	51 237	343	...	...	...	...
Pagadian	CDJC	125 182	62 266	62 916	332	...	...	...	...
Pasay	CDJC	408 610	...	...	14	...	...	...	...
Pasig	CDJC	471 075	...	...	...	...	...	...	...
Puerto Princesa	CDJC	129 577	66 991	62 586	2	...	...	...	...
Quezon City	CDJC	1 989 419	...	...	166	...	...	...	...
Roxas	CDJC	118 715	58 859	59 856	95	...	...	...	...
San Carlos (Negros Occidental)	CDJC	101 429	51 303	50 126	384	...	...	...	...
San Carlos (Pangasinan)	CDJC	134 039	67 274	66 765	169	...	...	...	...
San Pablo	CDJC	183 757	90 960	92 797	198	...	...	...	...
Silay	CDJC	122 748	61 583	61 165	167	...	...	...	...
Surigao	CDJC	104 909	52 045	52 864	225	...	...	...	...
Tacloban	CDJC	167 310	82 250	85 060	101	...	...	...	...
Toledo	CDJC	121 469	61 937	59 532	200	...	...	...	...
Zamboanga	CDJC	511 139	256 319	254 820	464	...	...	...	...
Qatar									
1997									
Al-Rayyan	CDJC	169 774	110 588	59 186	893	...	...	...	...
DOHA	CDJC	264 009	171 791	92 218	159	...	...	...	...
Saudi Arabia — Arabie saoudite									
1992									
Abha	CDFC	112 148	62 676	49 472	...	...	...	...	...
Ad-Dammam	CDFC	482 117	297 284	184 833	...	...	...	...	...
Al-Hufuf	CDFC	225 840	121 231	104 609	...	...	...	...	...
Al-Kharj	CDFC	148 687	83 339	65 348	...	...	...	...	...
Al-Khubar	CDFC	142 981	92 632	50 349	...	...	...	...	...
Al-Madinah	CDFC	609 318	333 229	276 089	...	...	...	...	...
Al-Mubarraz	CDFC	219 097	116 469	102 628	...	...	...	...	...
Ar'ar	CDFC	105 752	57 563	48 189	...	...	...	...	...
Ath-Thuqbah	CDFC	126 014	77 513	48 501	...	...	...	...	...
At-Ta'if	CDFC	408 129	217 879	190 250	...	...	...	...	...
Buraydah	CDFC	240 091	133 957	106 134	...	...	...	...	...
Hafar al-Batin	CDFC	138 401	73 863	64 538	...	...	...	...	...
Ha'il	CDFC	175 518	95 915	79 603	...	...	...	...	...
Jiddah	CDFC	2 021 095	1 196 740	824 355	...	...	...	...	...
Khamis Mushayt	CDFC	217 990	121 245	96 745	...	...	...	...	...
Makkah	CDFC	952 429	514 298	438 131	...	...	...	...	...
RIYADH	CDFC	2 723 222	1 594 407	1 128 819	...	...	...	...	...
Tabuk	CDFC	286 384	162 789	123 595	...	...	...	...	...
Singapore — Singapour									
1999									
SINGAPORE	ESDF	3 894 000	...	...	...	...	...	...	...

8. Population of capital cities and cities of 100 000 and more inhabitants: latest available year
Population des capitales et des villes de 100 000 habitants et plus: dernière année disponible (continued — suite)

(See notes at end of table. — Voir notes à la fin du tableau.)

Continent, country or area, date and city / Continent, pays ou zone, date et ville	Code[1]	City proper — Ville proprement dite Population				Urban agglomeration — Agglomération urbaine Population			
		Both sexes Les deux sexes	Male Masculin	Female Féminin	Surface area Superficie (km²)	Both sexes Les deux sexes	Male Masculin	Female Féminin	Surface area Superficie (km²)
ASIA — ASIE									
Sri Lanka									
1990									
COLOMBO	ESDF	615 000	...	...	...	...	...	...	...
Dehiwala-Mount Lavinia	ESDF	196 000	...	...	...	...	...	...	...
Jaffna	ESDF	129 000	...	...	...	...	...	...	...
Kandy	ESDF	104 000	...	...	...	...	...	...	...
Moratuwa	ESDF	170 000	...	...	...	...	...	...	...
Syrian Arab Republic — République arabe syrienne									
1994									
Aleppo	CDFC	1 582 930	824 302	758 628	...	1 813 355	943 079	870 276	...
Al-Hasakeh	CDFC	119 798	62 090	57 708	...	143 844	64 861	78 983	...
Al-Kamishli	CDFC	144 286	73 994	70 292	...	188 825	96 744	92 081	...
Al-Rakka	CDFC	165 195	84 823	80 372	...	201 114	103 233	97 881	...
DAMASCUS	CDFC	1 394 322	720 338	673 984	...	...	...	...	...
Deir El-Zor	CDFC	140 459	73 528	66 931	...	201 306	104 867	96 439	...
Hama	CDFC	264 348	136 769	127 579	...	343 279	176 795	166 484	...
Homs	CDFC	540 133	277 576	262 557	...	659 282	338 970	320 312	...
Lattakia	CDFC	311 784	160 027	151 757	...	357 562	183 465	174 097	...
Tajikistan — Tadjikistan									
1993									
DUSHANBE	ESDJ	528 600	...	...	...	...	...	...	...
Thailand — Thaïlande									
2000									
BANGKOK	CDJC	...	...	...	...	6 320 174	3 010 913	3 309 261	1 569
Buri Ram	CDJC	...	...	...	...	204 716	99 403	105 313	10 323
Chachoengsao	CDJC	...	...	...	...	131 600	62 984	68 616	5 351
Chaiyaphum	CDJC	...	...	...	...	176 838	86 930	89 908	12 778
Chanthaburi	CDJC	...	...	...	...	474 221	233 314	240 907	6 338
Chiang Mai	CDJC	...	...	...	...	387 537	186 130	201 407	20 107
Chiang Rai	CDJC	...	...	...	...	196 249	96 635	99 614	11 678
Chon Buri	CDJC	...	...	...	...	555 285	272 028	283 257	4 363
Kalasin	CDJC	...	...	...	...	187 426	92 314	95 112	6 947
Kanchanaburi	CDJC	...	...	...	...	171 834	85 421	86 413	19 483
Khon Kaen	CDJC	...	...	...	...	375 058	184 150	190 908	10 886
Lampang	CDJC	...	...	...	...	223 624	108 825	114 799	12 534
Loei	CDJC	...	...	...	...	101 162	50 882	50 280	11 425
Lop Buri	CDJC	...	...	...	...	119 183	58 599	60 584	6 200
Maha Sarakham	CDJC	...	...	...	...	114 236	54 733	59 503	5 292
Nakhon Pathom	CDJC	...	...	...	...	218 441	105 031	113 410	2 168
Nakhon Ratchasima	CDJC	...	...	...	...	535 459	258 038	277 421	20 494
Nakhon Sawan	CDJC	...	...	...	...	229 647	109 731	119 916	9 598
Nakhon Si Thammarat	CDJC	...	...	...	...	259 190	125 225	133 965	9 943
Narathiwat	CDJC	...	...	...	...	162 031	79 686	82 345	4 475
Nong Bua Lam Phu	CDJC	...	...	...	...	110 026	54 472	55 554	3 859
Nong Khai	CDJC	...	...	...	...	182 530	90 205	92 325	7 332
Nonthaburi	CDJC	...	...	...	...	538 235	259 444	278 791	622
Pathum Thani	CDJC	...	...	...	...	310 484	151 496	158 988	1 526
Pattani	CDJC	...	...	...	...	115 640	56 537	59 103	1 940
Phayao	CDJC	...	...	...	...	110 612	54 113	56 499	6 335
Phetchabun	CDJC	...	...	...	...	158 840	76 453	82 387	12 668
Phetchaburi	CDJC	...	...	...	...	155 707	74 561	81 146	6 225
Phichit	CDJC	...	...	...	...	117 217	55 769	61 448	4 531
Phitsanulok	CDJC	...	...	...	...	154 643	73 577	81 066	10 816
Phra Nakhon Si Ayutthaya	CDJC	...	...	...	...	238 233	113 170	125 063	2 557
Phrae	CDJC	...	...	...	...	106 537	51 863	54 674	6 539
Phuket	CDJC	...	...	...	...	100 224	48 240	51 984	543
Prachuap Khiri Khan	CDJC	...	...	...	...	162 630	78 532	84 098	6 368
Ratchaburi	CDJC	...	...	...	...	241 572	116 294	125 278	5 197
Rayong	CDJC	...	...	...	...	205 140	101 725	103 415	3 552

8. Population of capital cities and cities of 100 000 and more inhabitants: latest available year
Population des capitales et des villes de 100 000 habitants et plus: dernière année disponible (continued — suite)

(See notes at end of table. — Voir notes à la fin du tableau.)

Continent, country or area, date and city / Continent, pays ou zone, date et ville	Code[1]	City proper — Ville proprement dite Population				Urban agglomeration — Agglomération urbaine Population			
		Both sexes Les deux sexes	Male Masculin	Female Féminin	Surface area Superficie (km²)	Both sexes Les deux sexes	Male Masculin	Female Féminin	Surface area Superficie (km²)
ASIA — ASIE									
Thailand — Thaïlande									
2000									
Roi Et	CDJC	...	...	...	...	151 518	74 903	76 615	8 299
Sakon Nakhon	CDJC	...	...	...	...	145 609	71 829	73 780	9 606
Samut Prakan	CDJC	...	...	...	...	640 311	309 397	330 914	1 004
Samut Sakhon	CDJC	...	...	...	...	191 973	91 504	100 469	872
Saraburi	CDJC	...	...	...	...	223 313	111 836	111 477	3 577
Si Sa Ket	CDJC	...	...	...	...	148 293	73 051	75 242	8 840
Songkhla	CDJC	...	...	...	...	404 105	191 918	212 187	7 394
Sukhothai	CDJC	...	...	...	...	115 698	55 022	60 676	6 596
Suphan Buri	CDJC	...	...	...	...	147 902	69 768	78 134	5 358
Surat Thani	CDJC	...	...	...	...	268 075	131 124	136 951	12 892
Surin	CDJC	...	...	...	...	103 864	49 736	54 128	8 124
Tak	CDJC	...	...	...	...	116 714	57 048	59 666	16 407
Trang	CDJC	...	...	...	...	118 649	56 619	62 030	4 918
Ubon Ratchathani	CDJC	...	...	...	...	266 448	129 877	136 571	15 745
Udon Thani	CDJC	...	...	...	...	396 016	195 485	200 531	11 730
Yala	CDJC	...	...	...	...	114 621	55 825	58 796	4 521
2002									
BANGKOK	ESDJ	...	...	...	...	7 917 000	3 777 000	4 140 000	1 569
Buri Ram	ESDJ	...	...	...	...	209 422	103 236	106 186	10 323
Chachoengsao	ESDJ	...	...	...	...	136 757	66 900	69 857	5 351
Chaiyaphum	ESDJ	...	...	...	...	183 160	91 174	91 986	12 778
Chanthaburi	ESDJ	...	...	...	...	151 738	75 128	76 610	6 338
Chiang Mai	ESDJ	...	...	...	...	390 445	194 072	196 373	20 107
Chiang Rai	ESDJ	...	...	...	...	197 793	99 969	97 824	11 678
Chon Buri	ESDJ	...	...	...	...	556 545	275 351	281 194	4 363
Kalasin	ESDJ	...	...	...	...	191 744	96 148	95 596	6 947
Kanchanaburi	ESDJ	...	...	...	...	164 353	80 691	83 662	19 483
Khon Kaen	ESDJ	...	...	...	...	398 533	197 778	200 755	10 886
Lampang	ESDJ	...	...	...	...	226 503	112 418	114 085	12 534
Loei	ESDJ	...	...	...	...	101 540	51 723	49 817	11 425
Lop Buri	ESDJ	...	...	...	...	122 123	60 891	61 232	6 200
Lumphun	ESDJ	...	...	...	...	106 226	53 335	52 891	4 506
Maha Sarakham	ESDJ	...	...	...	...	120 926	58 649	62 277	5 292
Nakhon Pathom	ESDJ	...	...	...	...	243 813	117 596	126 217	2 168
Nakhon Ratchasima	ESDJ	...	...	...	...	566 104	276 925	289 179	20 494
Nakhon Sawan	ESDJ	...	...	...	...	236 163	113 951	122 212	9 598
Nakhon Si Thammarat	ESDJ	...	...	...	...	287 761	139 923	147 838	9 943
Narathiwat	ESDJ	...	...	...	...	166 081	83 082	82 999	4 475
Nong Bua Lam Phu	ESDJ	...	...	...	...	111 176	55 872	55 304	3 859
Nong Khai	ESDJ	...	...	...	...	185 556	93 325	92 231	7 332
Nonthaburi	ESDJ	...	...	...	...	564 835	273 604	291 231	622
Pathum Thani	ESDJ	...	...	...	...	280 365	136 072	144 293	1 526
Pattani	ESDJ	...	...	...	...	123 675	61 406	62 269	1 940
Phayao	ESDJ	...	...	...	...	111 195	56 311	54 884	6 335
Phetchabun	ESDJ	...	...	...	...	152 980	74 615	78 365	12 668
Phetchaburi	ESDJ	...	...	...	...	163 340	79 317	84 023	6 225
Phichit	ESDJ	...	...	...	...	120 795	57 339	63 456	4 531
Phitsanulok	ESDJ	...	...	...	...	158 628	76 015	82 613	10 816
Phra Nakhon Si Ayutthaya	ESDJ	...	...	...	...	243 518	116 101	127 417	2 557
Phrae	ESDJ	...	...	...	...	113 542	56 168	57 374	6 539
Prachuap Khiri Khan	ESDJ	...	...	...	...	163 070	79 845	83 225	6 368
Ratchaburi	ESDJ	...	...	...	...	250 650	120 854	129 796	5 197
Rayong	ESDJ	...	...	...	...	212 129	106 858	105 271	3 552
Roi Et	ESDJ	...	...	...	...	154 162	77 163	76 999	8 299
Sakon Nakhon	ESDJ	...	...	...	...	146 795	72 790	74 005	9 606
Samut Prakan	ESDJ	...	...	...	...	680 363	332 881	347 482	1 004
Samut Sakhon	ESDJ	...	...	...	...	190 595	91 375	99 220	872
Saraburi	ESDJ	...	...	...	...	209 274	104 501	104 773	3 577

8. Population of capital cities and cities of 100 000 and more inhabitants: latest available year
Population des capitales et des villes de 100 000 habitants et plus: dernière année disponible (continued — suite)

(See notes at end of table. — Voir notes à la fin du tableau.)

Continent, country or area, date and city Continent, pays ou zone, date et ville	Code[1]	City proper — Ville proprement dite Population				Urban agglomeration — Agglomération urbaine Population			
		Both sexes Les deux sexes	Male Masculin	Female Féminin	Surface area Superficie (km²)	Both sexes Les deux sexes	Male Masculin	Female Féminin	Surface area Superficie (km²)
ASIA — ASIE									
Thailand — Thaïlande									
2002									
Si Sa Ket	ESDJ	...	...	...	...	151 251	74 862	76 389	8 840
Songkhla	ESDJ	...	...	...	...	437 747	213 072	224 675	7 394
Sukhothai	ESDJ	...	...	...	...	116 026	55 681	60 345	6 596
Suphan Buri	ESDJ	...	...	...	...	154 249	73 024	81 225	5 358
Surat Thani	ESDJ	...	...	...	...	281 161	137 869	143 292	12 892
Surin	ESDJ	...	...	...	...	106 835	51 563	55 272	8 124
Trang	ESDJ	...	...	...	...	127 194	61 557	65 637	4 918
Ubon Ratchathani	ESDJ	...	...	...	...	274 120	135 579	138 541	15 745
Udon Thani	ESDJ	...	...	...	...	403 467	202 154	201 313	11 730
Yala	ESDJ	...	...	...	...	117 076	58 502	58 574	4 521
Timor-Leste									
1960									
DILI	CDFC	52 158	...	...	...	...	...	...	...
Turkey — Turquie[107]									
1997									
Adana[108]	CDFC	1 041 509	...	...	1 952	...	...	...	...
Adiyaman	CDFC	212 475	...	...	...	...	...	...	...
Afyon	CDFC	113 510	...	...	...	...	...	...	...
Aksaray	CDFC	101 187	...	...	...	...	...	...	...
Alanya[109]	CDFC	117 311	...	...	...	...	...	...	...
ANKARA[110]	CDFC	2 984 099	...	...	1 814	...	...	...	...
Antalya	CDFC	512 086	...	...	1 953	...	...	...	...
Aydin	CDFC	133 757	...	...	...	...	...	...	...
Balikesir	CDFC	189 987	...	...	1 446	...	...	...	...
Batman	CDFC	212 726	...	...	615	...	...	...	...
Bismil[109]	CDFC	101 409	...	...	...	...	...	...	...
Bursa[111]	CDFC	1 066 559	...	...	1 174	...	...	...	...
Corlu[109]	CDFC	123 266	...	...	...	...	...	...	...
Corum	CDFC	147 112	...	...	...	...	...	...	...
Denizli	CDFC	233 651	...	...	784	...	...	...	...
Diyarbakir	CDFC	511 640	...	...	2 330	...	...	...	...
Edirne	CDFC	115 083	...	...	...	...	...	...	...
Elazig	CDFC	250 534	...	...	2 275	...	...	...	...
Erzincan	CDFC	102 304	...	...	...	...	...	...	...
Erzurum	CDFC	298 735	...	...	1 280	...	...	...	...
Esenyurt[109]	CDFC	103 830	...	...	...	...	...	...	...
Eskisehir	CDFC	454 536	...	...	2 535	...	...	...	...
Gaziantep[112]	CDFC	712 800	...	...	2 105	...	...	...	...
Gebze[109]	CDFC	235 211	...	...	...	...	...	...	...
Hatay	CDFC	139 046	...	...	689	...	...	...	...
Içel	CDFC	501 398	...	...	1 772	...	...	...	...
Iskenderun[109]	CDFC	161 728	...	...	759	...	...	...	...
Isparta	CDFC	134 271	...	...	558	...	...	...	...
Istanbul[113]	CDFC	8 260 438	...	...	1 991	...	...	...	...
Izmir[114]	CDFC	2 081 556	...	...	763	...	...	...	...
Kahramanmaras	CDFC	303 594	...	...	2 913	...	...	...	...
Karabuk	CDFC	103 806	...	...	...	...	...	...	...
Karaman	CDFC	104 154	...	...	...	...	...	...	...
Kayseri[115]	CDFC	498 233	...	...	721	...	...	...	...
Kirikkale	CDFC	203 496	...	...	195	...	...	...	...
Kiziltepe[109]	CDFC	112 015	...	...	...	...	...	...	...
Kocaeli	CDFC	198 200	...	...	1 197	...	...	...	...
Konya[116]	CDFC	623 333	...	...	5 983	...	...	...	...
Kütahya	CDFC	162 319	...	...	2 572	...	...	...	...
Malatya	CDFC	400 248	...	...	968	...	...	...	...
Manisa	CDFC	201 340	...	...	2 125	...	...	...	...
Ordu	CDFC	117 699	...	...	...	...	...	...	...
Osmaniye	CDFC	160 854	...	...	974	...	...	...	...

8. Population of capital cities and cities of 100 000 and more inhabitants: latest available year
Population des capitales et des villes de 100 000 habitants et plus: dernière année disponible (continued — suite)

(See notes at end of table. — Voir notes à la fin du tableau.)

Continent, country or area, date and city / Continent, pays ou zone, date et ville	Code[1]	City proper — Ville proprement dite Population				Urban agglomeration — Agglomération urbaine Population			
		Both sexes Les deux sexes	Male Masculin	Female Féminin	Surface area Superficie (km²)	Both sexes Les deux sexes	Male Masculin	Female Féminin	Surface area Superficie (km²)
ASIA — ASIE									
Turkey — Turquie[107]									
1997									
Sakarya	CDFC	183 265	...	...	646	...	...	...	...
Samsun	CDFC	338 387	...	...	716	...	...	...	...
Sanliurfa	CDFC	410 762	...	...	3 791	...	...	...	...
Siirt	CDFC	107 067	...	...	273	...	...	...	...
Sivas	CDFC	232 352	...	...	2 857	...	...	...	...
Sultanbeyli[109]	CDFC	144 932	...	...		...	...	...	...
Tarsus[109]	CDFC	190 184	...	...	144	...	...	...	...
Tekirdag	CDFC	100 557	...	...	...	...	...	...	...
Trabzon	CDFC	182 552	...	...	168	...	...	...	...
Usak	CDFC	124 356	...	...		...	...	...	...
Van	CDFC	226 965	...	...	2 048	...	...	...	...
Viransehir[109]	CDFC	106 363	...	...	...	...	...	...	...
Zonguldak	CDFC	106 176	...	...	637	...	...	...	...
2000									
Adana[108]	CDFC	1 088 157	...	...	1 952	...	...	...	...
Adiyaman	CDFC	270 409	...	...	...	...	...	...	...
Afyon	CDFC	120 189	...	...	...	...	...	...	...
Aksaray	CDFC	104 723	...	...	...	...	...	...	...
Alanya[109]	CDFC	154 249	...	...	...	...	...	...	...
ANKARA[110]	CDFC	3 136 527	...	...	1 814	...	...	...	...
Antalya	CDFC	561 104	...	...	1 953	...	...	...	...
Aydin	CDFC	144 284	...	...	...	...	...	...	...
Balikesir	CDFC	197 435	...	...	1 446	...	...	...	...
Batman	CDFC	240 162	...	...	615	...	...	...	...
Bismil[109]	CDFC	139 081	...	...	...	...	...	...	...
Bursa[111]	CDFC	1 163 441	...	...	1 174	...	...	...	...
Corlu[109]	CDFC	146 077	...	...	...	...	...	...	...
Corum	CDFC	157 678	...	...	...	...	...	...	...
Denizli	CDFC	253 402	...	...	784	...	...	...	...
Derince[109]	CDFC	112 332	...	...	...	...	...	...	...
Diyarbakir	CDFC	560 038	...	...	2 330	...	...	...	...
Edirne	CDFC	119 292	...	...	...	...	...	...	...
Elazig	CDFC	265 228	...	...	2 275	...	...	...	...
Elbistan[109]	CDFC	100 306	...	...	...	...	...	...	...
Erzincan	CDFC	104 202	...	...	...	...	...	...	...
Erzurum	CDFC	317 068	...	...	1 280	...	...	...	...
Eskisehir	CDFC	468 016	...	...	2 535	...	...	...	...
Gaziantep[112]	CDFC	755 091	...	...	2 105	...	...	...	...
Gebze[109]	CDFC	268 686	...	...	...	...	...	...	...
Hatay	CDFC	145 051	...	...	689	...	...	...	...
Içel	CDFC	529 665	...	...	1 772	...	...	...	...
Iskenderun[109]	CDFC	164 365	...	...	759	...	...	...	...
Isparta	CDFC	142 273	...	...	558	...	...	...	...
Istanbul[113]	CDFC	8 892 927	...	...	1 991	...	...	...	...
Izmir[114]	CDFC	2 209 767	...	...	763	...	...	...	...
Kahramanmaras	CDFC	332 781	...	...	2 913	...	...	...	...
Karabuk	CDFC	101 730	...	...	...	...	...	...	...
Karaman	CDFC	114 785	...	...	...	...	...	...	...
Kayseri[115]	CDFC	523 936	...	...	721	...	...	...	...
Kirikkale	CDFC	208 574	...	...	195	...	...	...	...
Kiziltepe[109]	CDFC	136 692	...	...	...	...	...	...	...
Kocaeli	CDFC	199 187	...	...	1 197	...	...	...	...
Konya[116]	CDFC	667 159	...	...	5 983	...	...	...	...
Kütahya	CDFC	174 600	...	...	2 572	...	...	...	...
Malatya	CDFC	453 574	...	...	968	...	...	...	...
Manavgat[109]	CDFC	101 453	...	...	...	...	...	...	...
Manisa	CDFC	218 665	...	...	2 125	...	...	...	...
Ordu	CDFC	122 912	...	...	...	...	...	...	...

8. Population of capital cities and cities of 100 000 and more inhabitants: latest available year
Population des capitales et des villes de 100 000 habitants et plus: dernière année disponible (continued — suite)

(See notes at end of table. — Voir notes à la fin du tableau.)

Continent, country or area, date and city / Continent, pays ou zone, date et ville	Code[1]	City proper — Ville proprement dite Population				Urban agglomeration — Agglomération urbaine Population			
		Both sexes Les deux sexes	Male Masculin	Female Féminin	Surface area Superficie (km²)	Both sexes Les deux sexes	Male Masculin	Female Féminin	Surface area Superficie (km²)
ASIA — ASIE									
Turkey — Turquie[107]									
2000									
Osmaniye	CDFC	176 438	...	...	974	...	...	...	...
Sakarya	CDFC	323 175	...	...	646	...	...	...	...
Samsun	CDFC	351 342	...	...	716	...	...	...	...
Sanliurfa	CDFC	467 287	...	...	3 791	...	...	...	...
Siirt	CDFC	123 261	...	...	273	...	...	...	...
Silifke[109]	CDFC	102 053	...	...	...	...	...	...	...
Sultanbeyli[109]	CDFC	175 009	...	...	...	...	...	...	...
Tarsus[109]	CDFC	189 738	...	...	144	...	...	...	...
Tekirdag	CDFC	107 718	...	...	...	...	...	...	...
Tokat	CDFC	105 015	...	...	...	...	...	...	...
Trabzon	CDFC	192 261	...	...	168	...	...	...	...
Usak	CDFC	131 877	...	...	...	...	...	...	...
Van	CDFC	256 557	...	...	2 048	...	...	...	...
Viransehir[109]	CDFC	131 073	...	...	...	...	...	...	...
Zonguldak	CDFC	101 216	...	...	637	...	...	...	...
Turkmenistan — Turkménistan									
1990									
ASHKHABAD	ESDF	407 000	...	...	...	...	...	...	...
Chardzhou	ESDF	164 000	...	...	...	...	...	...	...
Tashauz	ESDF	114 000	...	...	...	...	...	...	...
United Arab Emirates — Emirats Arabes Unis									
1995									
ABU DHABI	CDFC	398 695	269 834	128 861	...	...	...	...	...
Ajman	CDFC	114 395	68 389	46 006	...	...	...	...	...
Al-Ayn	CDFC	225 970	144 693	81 277	...	...	...	...	...
Al-Sharjah	CDFC	320 095	204 729	115 366	...	...	...	...	...
Dubai	CDFC	669 181	463 479	205 702	...	...	...	...	...
2002									
ABU DHABI	ESDF	527 000	359 000	168 000	...	...	...	...	...
Ajman	ESDF	205 000	122 000	83 000	...	...	...	...	...
Al-Ayn	ESDF	328 000	215 000	113 000	...	...	...	...	...
Al-Sharjah	ESDF	488 000	317 000	171 000	...	...	...	...	...
Dubai	ESDF	1 089 000	759 000	330 000	...	...	...	...	...
Uzbekistan — Ouzbékistan									
2000									
Almalyk	ESDF	114 000	56 600	57 400	...	...	...	...	...
Andizhan	ESDF	336 500	166 100	170 400	...	...	...	...	...
Angren	ESDF	129 100	64 000	65 100	...	...	...	...	...
Bukhara	ESDF	238 800	120 200	118 600	...	...	...	...	...
Chirchik	ESDF	142 700	70 600	72 100	...	...	...	...	...
Banjzak	ESDF	129 800	67 600	62 200	...	...	...	...	...
Fergana	ESDF	184 800	90 600	94 200	...	...	...	...	...
Karshi	ESDF	202 400	103 000	99 400	...	...	...	...	...
Kokand	ESDF	198 000	96 700	101 300	...	...	...	...	...
Margilan	ESDF	156 800	76 600	80 200	...	...	...	...	...
Namangan	ESDF	388 300	194 700	193 600	...	...	...	...	...
Navoi	ESDF	141 100	71 800	69 300	...	...	...	...	...
Nukus	ESDF	208 600	102 600	106 000	...	...	...	...	...
Samarkand	ESDF	361 100	178 800	182 300	...	...	...	...	...
TASHKENT	ESDF	2 133 300	1 038 800	1 094 500	...	...	...	...	...
Termez	ESDF	114 400	57 100	57 300	...	...	...	...	...
Urgentch	ESDF	139 000	68 100	70 900	...	...	...	...	...
Viet Nam									
1992									
Buonmathuot	ESDF	282 095	...	...	...	...	...	...	...
Campha	ESDF	209 086	...	...	...	...	...	...	...
Cantho	ESDF	215 587	...	...	...	...	...	...	...

8. Population of capital cities and cities of 100 000 and more inhabitants: latest available year
Population des capitales et des villes de 100 000 habitants et plus: dernière année disponible (continued — suite)

(See notes at end of table. — Voir notes à la fin du tableau.)

Continent, country or area, date and city Continent, pays ou zone, date et ville	Code[1]	City proper — Ville proprement dite Population				Urban agglomeration — Agglomération urbaine Population			
		Both sexes Les deux sexes	Male Masculin	Female Féminin	Surface area Superficie (km²)	Both sexes Les deux sexes	Male Masculin	Female Féminin	Surface area Superficie (km²)
ASIA — ASIE									
Viet Nam									
1992									
Dalat	ESDF	106 409	...	...	...	...	...	...	...
Da Nang	ESDF	382 674	...	...	...	...	...	...	...
Haiphong	ESDF	783 133	...	...	22	...	...	...	...
HANOI	ESDF	1 073 760	...	...	46	...	...	...	...
Ho Chi Minh[117]	ESDF	3 015 743	...	...	140	...	...	...	...
Hon Gai	ESDF	127 484	...	...	...	...	...	...	...
Hué	ESDF	219 149	...	...	...	...	...	...	...
Longxuyen	ESDF	132 681	...	...	...	...	...	...	...
Mytho	ESDF	108 404	...	...	...	...	...	...	...
Namdinh	ESDF	171 699	...	...	...	...	...	...	...
Nhatrang	ESDF	221 331	...	...	...	...	...	...	...
Qui Nhon	ESDF	163 385	...	...	...	...	...	...	...
Rach Gia	ESDF	141 132	...	...	...	...	...	...	...
Thai Nguyen	ESDF	127 643	...	...	...	...	...	...	...
Vinh	ESDF	112 455	...	...	...	...	...	...	...
Vungtau	ESDF	145 145	...	...	...	...	...	...	...
Yemen — Yémen									
1994									
Adan	CDFC	398 294	...	...	...	...	...	...	...
Al-Hudaydah (Hodeidah)	CDFC	298 452	...	...	...	...	...	...	...
Al-Mukalla	CDFC	122 359	...	...	...	...	...	...	...
Ibb	CDFC	103 312	...	...	...	...	...	...	...
SANA'A	CDFC	954 448	...	...	...	...	...	...	...
Ta'izz	CDFC	317 571	...	...	...	...	...	...	...
EUROPE									
Albania — Albanie									
1990									
TIRANA	ESDF	244 153	...	...	...	...	...	...	...
Andorra — Andorre									
1990									
ANDORRA LA VELLA	ESDF	...	...	...	...	20 437	...	...	...
1999									
ANDORRA LA VELLA	ESDF	18 526	...	...	...	21 189	...	...	...
2002									
ANDORRA LA VELLA	ESDF	18 142	...	...	...	20 724	...	...	...
Austria — Autriche									
2001									
Bregenz	CDJC	...	...	...	...	180 987	88 830	92 157	150
Graz	CDJC	226 892	106 609	120 283	128	287 903	136 415	151 488	349
Innsbruck	CDJC	113 826	53 434	60 392	105	183 661	87 315	96 346	110
Klagenfurt	CDJC	90 257	41 482	48 775	120	100 513	46 440	54 073	187
Linz	CDJC	186 266	88 332	97 934	96	273 722	131 310	142 412	249
Salzburg	CDJC	144 817	67 464	77 353	66	212 666	100 360	112 306	259
WIEN	CDJC	1 562 482	738 168	824 314	415	1 838 225	870 893	967 332	1 161
Belarus — Bélarus									
2000									
Baranovichi	ESDF	168 300	79 100	89 200	55	...	...	...	...
Bobruisk	ESDF	221 200	104 100	117 100	77	...	...	...	...
Borisov	ESDF	151 100	71 500	79 600	47	...	...	...	...
Brest	ESDF	288 900	134 300	154 600	74	...	...	...	...
Gomel	ESDF	...	...	...	...	487 400	223 200	264 200	117
Grodno	ESDF	304 100	142 000	162 100	93	...	...	...	...
Lida	ESDF	100 500	47 400	53 100	38	...	...	...	...
MINSK	ESDF	...	...	...	...	1 688 100	790 800	897 300	256
Mogilev	ESDF	358 400	167 500	190 900	99	...	...	...	...
Mozir	ESDF	110 200	53 400	56 800	36	...	...	...	...

8. Population of capital cities and cities of 100 000 and more inhabitants: latest available year
Population des capitales et des villes de 100 000 habitants et plus: dernière année disponible (continued — suite)

(See notes at end of table. — Voir notes à la fin du tableau.)

Continent, country or area, date and city / Continent, pays ou zone, date et ville	Code[1]	City proper — Ville proprement dite Population				Urban agglomeration — Agglomération urbaine Population			
		Both sexes Les deux sexes	Male Masculin	Female Féminin	Surface area Superficie (km²)	Both sexes Les deux sexes	Male Masculin	Female Féminin	Surface area Superficie (km²)
EUROPE									
Belarus — Bélarus									
2000									
Novopolotsk	ESDF	106 600	51 200	55 400	48	...	...	...	...
Orsha	ESDF	...	...	...	...	136 400	65 700	70 700	36
Pinsk	ESDF	131 000	61 900	69 100	42	...	...	...	...
Soligorsk	ESDF	101 400	48 100	53 300	8	...	...	...	...
Vitebsk	ESDF	...	...	...	...	348 700	158 000	190 700	89
Belgium — Belgique[118]									
2000									
Antwerpen (Anvers)	ESDJ	445 570	216 319	229 251	205	...	...	...	...
Brugge	ESDJ	116 559	56 436	60 123	138	...	...	...	...
BRUXELLES (BRUSSEL)	ESDJ	964 405	461 065	503 340	161	...	...	...	...
Charleroi	ESDJ	200 233	96 214	104 019	102	...	...	...	...
Gent (Gand)	ESDJ	224 685	109 142	115 543	156	...	...	...	...
Liège (Luik)	ESDJ	184 550	89 176	95 374	69	...	...	...	...
Namur	ESDJ	105 248	50 251	54 997	176	...	...	...	...
Bosnia and Herzegovina — Bosnie-Herzégovine									
1991									
Banja Luka	ESDJ	195 994	...	...	1 239	...	...	...	...
Doboj	ESDJ	102 624	...	...	697	...	...	...	...
Mostar	ESDJ	127 034	...	...	1 227	...	...	...	...
Prijedor	ESDJ	112 635	...	...	834	...	...	...	...
SARAJEVO	ESDJ	529 021	...	...	2 095	...	...	...	...
Tuzla	ESDJ	131 866	...	...	303	...	...	...	...
Zenica	ESDJ	145 837	...	...	505	...	...	...	...
Bulgaria — Bulgarie									
2000									
Bourgas	ESDF	194 526	94 520	100 006	...	196 974	95 723	101 251	481
Plévène	ESDF	119 849	58 281	61 568	...	124 762	60 736	64 026	817
Plovdiv	ESDF	...	...	...	...	345 525	164 384	181 141	74
Roussé	ESDF	...	...	...	...	165 972	79 910	86 062	437
Slivène	ESDF	104 848	50 824	54 024	...	107 199	51 988	55 211	1 354
SOFIA	ESDF	1 137 668	539 334	598 334	...	1 164 066	552 454	611 612	1 311
Stara Zagora	ESDF	...	...	...	...	148 356	72 323	76 033	1 005
Varna	ESDF	...	...	...	...	294 458	143 645	150 813	210
2001									
Bourgas	ESDF	192 773	93 648	99 125	...	194 886	94 689	100 197	481
Plévène	ESDF	122 201	59 504	62 697	...	126 992	61 881	65 111	817
Plovdiv	ESDF	...	...	...	...	339 442	162 331	177 111	74
Roussé	ESDF	...	...	...	...	161 738	78 163	83 575	437
Slivène	ESDF	100 422	48 588	51 834	...	102 625	49 701	52 924	1 354
SOFIA	ESDF	1 095 765	518 016	577 749	...	1 120 411	530 021	590 390	1 311
Stara Zagora	ESDF	...	...	...	...	143 903	70 485	73 418	1 005
Varna	ESDF	...	...	...	...	313 480	152 230	161 250	210
Channel Islands: Guernsey — Iles Anglo-Normandes: Guernesey									
1996									
ST. PETER PORT	CDFC	16 194	...	...	...	...	...	...	...
2001									
ST. PETER PORT	CDJC	16 488	...	...	...	...	...	...	...
Channel Islands — Iles Anglo-Normandes: Jersey									
2001									
ST. HELIER	CDJC	28 310	13 669	14 641	9	...	...	...	...
Croatia — Croatie									
2000									
Rijeka	ESDJ	143 000	...	...	...	...	...	...	...
Split	ESDJ	174 000	...	...	...	...	...	...	...
ZAGREB	ESDJ	682 000	...	...	1 405	...	...	...	...

8. Population of capital cities and cities of 100 000 and more inhabitants: latest available year
Population des capitales et des villes de 100 000 habitants et plus: dernière année disponible (continued — suite)

(See notes at end of table. — Voir notes à la fin du tableau.)

Continent, country or area, date and city / Continent, pays ou zone, date et ville	Code[1]	City proper — Ville proprement dite Population				Urban agglomeration — Agglomération urbaine Population			
		Both sexes Les deux sexes	Male Masculin	Female Féminin	Surface area Superficie (km²)	Both sexes Les deux sexes	Male Masculin	Female Féminin	Surface area Superficie (km²)
EUROPE									
Croatia — Croatie									
2001									
Rijeka	ESDJ	143 800	68 382	75 418	...	...	...	...	...
Split	ESDJ	175 140	83 720	91 420	...	...	...	...	...
ZAGREB	ESDJ	691 724	321 507	370 217	1 405	...	...	...	...
Czech Republic — République tchéque									
2000									
Brno	ESDJ	383 569	181 736	201 833	230	...	...	...	...
Olomouc	ESDJ	103 015	48 778	54 237	103	...	...	...	...
Ostrava	ESDJ	321 263	155 423	165 840	214	...	...	...	...
Plzen	ESDJ	167 534	80 620	86 914	125	...	...	...	...
PRAHA	ESDJ	1 186 855	561 960	624 895	496	...	...	...	...
2001									
Brno	CDJC	379 185	179 998	199 187	230	...	...	...	...
Olomouc	CDJC	103 293	48 961	54 332	103	...	...	...	...
Ostrava	CDJC	319 293	154 483	164 810	214	...	...	...	...
Plzen	CDJC	166 274	80 117	86 157	125	...	...	...	...
PRAHA	CDJC	1 178 576	560 030	618 546	496	...	...	...	...
Denmark — Danemark									
2001									
Ålborg	ESDJ	161 661	79 829	81 832	560	...	...	...	...
Århus	ESDJ	286 668	140 451	146 217	469	...	...	...	...
KOBENHAVN	ESDJ	499 148	244 025	255 123	123	...	...	...	...
Odense	ESDJ	183 691	89 341	94 350	364	...	...	...	...
Estonia — Estonie									
2000									
TALLINN	ESDF	400 398	180 277	220 121	158	...	...	...	...
Tartu	ESDF	101 257	45 002	56 255	39	...	...	...	...
2001									
TALLINN	ESDF	399 850	180 077	219 773	158	...	...	...	...
Tartu	ESDF	101 240	45 009	56 231	39	...	...	...	...
Faeroe Islands — Iles Féroé									
1992									
THORSHAVN	ESDJ	14 671	...	...	63	16 218	...	...	79
Finland — Finlande									
2000									
Espoo	CDJC	213 271	104 104	109 167	312	...	...	...	...
HELSINKI	CDJC	555 474	257 399	298 075	185	955 748	452 712	503 036	743
Oulu	CDJC	120 753	58 590	62 163	328	...	...	...	...
Tampere	CDJC	195 468	92 847	102 621	523	...	...	...	...
Turku	CDJC	172 561	80 473	92 088	243	...	...	...	...
Vantaa	CDJC	178 471	87 121	91 350	241	...	...	...	...
France[119,120]									
1990									
Aix-en-Provence	CDJC	123 778	...	...	...	...	...	...	...
Amiens	CDJC	131 880	...	...	...	156 140	...	...	...
Angers	CDJC	141 354	...	...	...	208 222	...	...	...
Besançon	CDJC	113 835	...	...	...	122 633	...	...	...
Bordeaux	CDJC	210 467	...	...	...	696 819	...	...	...
Boulogne-Billancourt[121]	CDJC	101 569	...	...	...	...	...	...	...
Brest	CDJC	147 888	...	...	...	201 442	...	...	...
Caen	CDJC	112 872	...	...	...	191 505	...	...	...
Clermont-Ferrand	CDJC	136 180	...	...	...	254 451	...	...	...
Dijon	CDJC	146 723	...	...	...	230 469	...	...	...
Grenoble	CDJC	150 815	...	...	...	404 837	...	...	...
Le Havre	CDJC	195 932	...	...	...	253 675	...	...	...
Le Mans	CDJC	145 439	...	...	...	189 032	...	...	...
Lille[122]	CDJC	172 149	...	...	...	959 433	...	...	...
Limoges	CDJC	133 469	...	...	...	170 072	...	...	...

(See notes at end of table. — Voir notes à la fin du tableau.)

Continent, country or area, date and city Continent, pays ou zone, date et ville	Code[1]	City proper — Ville proprement dite Population				Urban agglomeration — Agglomération urbaine Population			
		Both sexes Les deux sexes	Male Masculin	Female Féminin	Surface area Superficie (km²)	Both sexes Les deux sexes	Male Masculin	Female Féminin	Surface area Superficie (km²)
EUROPE									
France[119],[120]									
1990									
Lyon[123]	CDJC	415 479	...	...	...	1 262 342	...	...	...
Marseille	CDJC	800 309	...	...	...	1 230 871	...	...	...
Metz	CDJC	119 598	...	...	...	193 160	...	...	...
Montpellier	CDJC	208 103	...	...	...	248 429	...	...	...
Mulhouse	CDJC	108 358	...	...	...	223 878	...	...	...
Nantes	CDJC	244 514	...	...	...	495 229	...	...	...
Nice	CDJC	342 903	...	...	...	517 291	...	...	...
Nîmes	CDJC	128 549	...	...	...	138 610	...	...	...
Orléans	CDJC	105 099	...	...	...	243 137	...	...	...
PARIS[124]	CDJC	2 152 329	1 000 712	1 151 617	...	9 319 367	4 503 580	4 815 787	...
Perpignan	CDJC	105 869	...	...	...	157 755	...	...	...
Reims	CDJC	180 611	...	...	...	206 446	...	...	...
Rennes	CDJC	197 497	...	...	...	244 998	...	...	...
Rouen	CDJC	102 722	...	...	...	380 220	...	...	...
Saint-Étienne	CDJC	199 528	...	...	...	313 467	...	...	...
Strasbourg[122]	CDJC	252 274	...	...	...	388 466	...	...	...
Toulon	CDJC	167 788	...	...	...	437 825	...	...	...
Toulouse	CDJC	358 598	...	...	...	650 311	...	...	...
Tours	CDJC	129 506	...	...	...	282 193	...	...	...
Villeurbanne	CDJC	116 851	...	...	...	262 342	...	...	...
Germany — Allemagne									
1999									
Aachen	ESDJ	243 825	121 671	122 154	161	...	...	...	...
Augsburg	ESDJ	254 867	121 846	133 021	147	...	...	...	...
Bergisch Gladbach	ESDJ	106 150	50 723	55 427	83	...	...	...	...
BERLIN	ESDJ	3 386 667	1 644 575	1 742 092	891	...	...	...	...
Bielefeld	ESDJ	321 125	152 701	168 424	258	...	...	...	...
Bochum	ESDJ	392 830	190 433	202 397	145	...	...	...	...
Bonn	ESDJ	301 048	143 416	157 632	141	...	...	...	...
Bottrop	ESDJ	121 097	58 490	62 607	101	...	...	...	...
Braunschweig	ESDJ	246 322	119 350	126 972	192	...	...	...	...
Bremen	ESDJ	540 330	259 439	280 891	327	...	...	...	...
Bremerhaven	ESDJ	122 735	59 991	62 744	78	...	...	...	...
Chemnitz	ESDJ	263 222	125 123	138 099	176	...	...	...	...
Cottbus	ESDJ	110 894	53 712	57 182	150	...	...	...	...
Darmstadt	ESDJ	137 776	67 680	70 096	122	...	...	...	...
Dortmund	ESDJ	590 213	286 880	303 333	280	...	...	...	...
Dresden	ESDJ	476 668	229 565	247 103	237	...	...	...	...
Duisburg	ESDJ	519 793	252 735	267 058	233	...	...	...	...
Düsseldorf	ESDJ	568 855	268 630	300 225	217	...	...	...	...
Erfurt	ESDJ	201 267	96 937	104 330	269	...	...	...	...
Erlangen	ESDJ	100 750	48 939	51 811	77	...	...	...	...
Essen	ESDJ	599 515	286 350	313 165	210	...	...	...	...
Frankfurt am Main	ESDJ	643 821	314 431	329 390	248	...	...	...	...
Freiburg im Breisgau	ESDJ	202 455	96 025	106 430	153	...	...	...	...
Fürth	ESDJ	109 771	52 773	56 998	63	...	...	...	...
Gelsenkirchen	ESDJ	281 979	135 781	146 198	105	...	...	...	...
Gera	ESDJ	114 718	55 211	59 507	152	...	...	...	...
Göttingen	ESDJ	124 775	60 334	64 441	117	...	...	...	...
Hagen	ESDJ	205 201	98 338	106 863	160	...	...	...	...
Halle	ESDJ	254 360	121 314	133 046	135	...	...	...	...
Hamburg	ESDJ	1 704 735	824 686	880 049	755	...	...	...	...
Hamm	ESDJ	181 804	89 307	92 497	226	...	...	...	...
Hannover	ESDJ	514 718	245 017	269 701	204	...	...	...	...
Heidelberg	ESDJ	139 672	65 694	73 978	109	...	...	...	...
Heilbronn	ESDJ	119 526	58 400	61 126	100	...	...	...	...
Herne	ESDJ	175 661	85 577	90 084	51	...	...	...	...
Hildesheim	ESDJ	104 013	48 910	55 103	93	...	...	...	...

(See notes at end of table. — Voir notes à la fin du tableau.)

Continent, country or area, date and city / Continent, pays ou zone, date et ville	Code[1]	City proper — Ville proprement dite Population				Urban agglomeration — Agglomération urbaine Population			
		Both sexes Les deux sexes	Male Masculin	Female Féminin	Surface area Superficie (km²)	Both sexes Les deux sexes	Male Masculin	Female Féminin	Surface area Superficie (km²)
EUROPE									
Germany — Allemagne									
1999									
Ingolstadt	ESDJ	114 826	56 417	58 409	133	...	...	...	...
Kaiserslautern	ESDJ	100 025	49 247	50 778	140	...	...	...	...
Karlsruhe	ESDJ	277 204	134 775	142 429	173	...	...	...	...
Kassel	ESDJ	196 211	93 058	103 153	107	...	...	...	...
Kiel	ESDJ	233 795	113 274	120 521	117	...	...	...	...
Koblenz	ESDJ	108 003	51 340	56 663	105	...	...	...	...
Köln	ESDJ	962 507	466 543	495 964	405	...	...	...	...
Krefeld	ESDJ	241 769	117 087	124 682	138	...	...	...	...
Leipzig	ESDJ	489 532	235 789	253 743	176	...	...	...	...
Leverkusen	ESDJ	160 841	78 116	82 725	79	...	...	...	...
Lübeck	ESDJ	213 326	101 024	112 302	214	...	...	...	...
Lüdwigshafen am Rhein	ESDJ	163 771	81 257	82 514	78	...	...	...	...
Magdeburg	ESDJ	235 073	112 839	122 234	193	...	...	...	...
Mainz	ESDJ	183 134	89 093	94 041	98	...	...	...	...
Mannheim	ESDJ	307 730	151 145	156 585	145	...	...	...	...
Moers	ESDJ	106 837	51 824	55 013	68	...	...	...	...
Mönchengladbach	ESDJ	263 697	126 721	136 976	170	...	...	...	...
Mülheim an der Ruhr	ESDJ	173 895	82 677	91 218	91	...	...	...	...
München	ESDJ	1 194 560	571 363	623 197	311	...	...	...	...
Münster (Westf.)	ESDJ	264 670	123 825	140 845	303	...	...	...	...
Neuss	ESDJ	149 702	72 522	77 180	99	...	...	...	...
Nürnberg	ESDJ	486 628	233 415	253 213	186	...	...	...	...
Oberhausen	ESDJ	222 349	107 562	114 787	77	...	...	...	...
Offenbach am Main	ESDJ	116 627	57 539	59 088	45	...	...	...	...
Oldenburg	ESDJ	154 125	73 572	80 553	103	...	...	...	...
Osnabrück	ESDJ	164 539	77 981	86 558	120	...	...	...	...
Paderborn	ESDJ	137 647	67 010	70 637	179	...	...	...	...
Pforzheim	ESDJ	117 227	55 738	61 489	98	...	...	...	...
Potsdam	ESDJ	128 983	62 651	66 332	109	...	...	...	...
Recklinghausen	ESDJ	125 022	60 456	64 566	66	...	...	...	...
Regensburg	ESDJ	125 236	59 600	65 636	81	...	...	...	...
Remscheid	ESDJ	120 125	57 923	62 202	75	...	...	...	...
Reutlingen	ESDJ	110 343	53 564	56 779	87	...	...	...	...
Rostock	ESDJ	203 279	99 627	103 652	181	...	...	...	...
Saarbrücken	ESDJ	183 836	87 875	95 961	167	...	...	...	...
Salzgitter	ESDJ	112 934	54 808	58 126	224	...	...	...	...
Schwerin	ESDJ	102 878	49 428	53 450	130	...	...	...	...
Siegen	ESDJ	109 225	53 585	55 640	115	...	...	...	...
Solingen	ESDJ	165 583	79 712	85 871	89	...	...	...	...
Stuttgart	ESDJ	582 443	284 977	297 466	207	...	...	...	...
Ulm	ESDJ	116 103	56 511	59 592	119	...	...	...	...
Wiesbaden	ESDJ	268 716	129 032	139 684	204	...	...	...	...
Witten	ESDJ	103 384	49 545	53 839	72	...	...	...	...
Wolfsburg	ESDJ	121 954	59 761	62 193	204	...	...	...	...
Wuppertal	ESDJ	368 993	176 350	192 643	168	...	...	...	...
Würzburg	ESDJ	127 350	58 801	68 549	88	...	...	...	...
Zwickau	ESDJ	104 146	49 513	54 633	73	...	...	...	...
Gibraltar									
1991									
GIBRALTAR	CDFC	28 074	...	...	...	...	...	...	...
Greece — Grèce[125]									
1991									
ATHINAI	CDFC	772 072	...	...	39	3 072 922	...	...	457
Calithèa[126]	CDFC	114 233	...	...	5	...	...	...	...
Iraclion	CDFC	116 178	...	...	52	132 117	...	...	78
Larissa[126]	CDFC	113 090	...	...	88	...	...	...	...
Patrai	CDFC	153 344	...	...	57	170 452	...	...	104
Pésterion[126]	CDFC	137 288	...	...	10	...	...	...	...

(See notes at end of table. — Voir notes à la fin du tableau.)

Continent, country or area, date and city / Continent, pays ou zone, date et ville	Code[1]	City proper — Ville proprement dite Population				Urban agglomeration — Agglomération urbaine Population			
		Both sexes Les deux sexes	Male Masculin	Female Féminin	Surface area Superficie (km²)	Both sexes Les deux sexes	Male Masculin	Female Féminin	Surface area Superficie (km²)
EUROPE									
Greece — Grèce[125]									
1991									
Piraiévs[126]	CDFC	182 671	...	...	11	...	...	...	...
Salonika	CDFC	...	...	...	...	749 048	...	...	131
Volos	CDFC	116 031	...	...	18	383 967	...	...	98
Holy See — Saint-Siège[127]									
1988									
VATICAN CITY	ESDF	766	...	...	...	...	...	...	...
Hungary — Hongrie									
2000									
BUDAPEST	ESDF	1 797 222	816 805	980 417	525	...	...	...	...
Debrecen	ESDF	202 636	95 345	107 291	462	...	...	...	...
Győr	ESDF	126 714	59 332	67 382	175	...	...	...	...
Kecskemét	ESDF	105 551	49 653	55 898	321	...	...	...	...
Miskolc	ESDF	171 263	79 095	92 168	237	...	...	...	...
Nyiregyhaza	ESDF	112 234	53 408	58 826	274	...	...	...	...
Pécs	ESDF	156 617	72 459	84 158	163	...	...	...	...
Szeged	ESDF	156 993	72 680	84 313	281	...	...	...	...
Székesfehérvar	ESDF	104 893	49 437	55 456	171	...	...	...	...
2001									
BUDAPEST	ESDF	1 749 389	799 279	950 110	525	...	...	...	...
Debrecen	ESDF	207 094	96 567	110 528	462	...	...	...	...
Győr	ESDF	129 610	61 404	68 206	175	...	...	...	...
Kecskemét	ESDF	107 441	50 084	57 356	321	...	...	...	...
Miskolc	ESDF	183 988	85 778	98 209	237	...	...	...	...
Nyiregyhaza	ESDF	117 239	54 706	62 532	274	...	...	...	...
Pécs	ESDF	160 540	74 343	86 197	163	...	...	...	...
Szeged	ESDF	164 684	76 082	88 602	281	...	...	...	...
Székesfehérvar	ESDF	104 444	49 605	54 840	171	...	...	...	...
Iceland — Islande									
2000									
REYKJAVIK	ESDJ	110 903	54 420	56 483	100	173 710	85 609	88 101	...
Ireland — Irlande									
1996									
Cork	CDFC	127 187	61 254	65 933	40	179 954	87 304	92 650	...
DUBLIN	CDFC	481 854	228 401	253 453	118	952 692	456 350	496 342	922
Isle of Man — Ile de Man									
1996									
DOUGLAS	CDJC	23 487	...	...	...	...	...	...	...
2001									
DOUGLAS	CDJC	25 347	12 460	12 887	...	...	...	...	...
Italy — Italie									
2001									
Ancona	CDJC	100 402	48 049	52 353	124	...	...	...	...
Bari	CDJC	312 452	150 311	162 141	116	...	...	...	...
Bergamo	CDJC	110 691	51 445	59 246	40	...	...	...	...
Bologna	CDJC	369 955	171 722	198 233	141	...	...	...	...
Brescia	CDJC	187 865	90 011	97 854	91	...	...	...	...
Cagliari	CDJC	158 351	73 952	84 399	86	...	...	...	...
Catania	CDJC	306 464	144 419	162 045	181	...	...	...	...
Ferrara	CDJC	130 461	60 975	69 486	404	...	...	...	...
Firenze	CDJC	352 227	164 356	187 871	102	...	...	...	...
Foggia	CDJC	146 072	71 029	75 043	508	...	...	...	...
Forli	CDJC	108 363	51 873	56 490	228	...	...	...	...
Genova	CDJC	603 560	282 002	321 558	244	...	...	...	...
Latina	CDJC	108 711	52 086	56 625	278	...	...	...	...
Livorno	CDJC	148 143	70 290	77 853	104	...	...	...	...
Messina	CDJC	236 621	112 995	123 626	211	...	...	...	...
Milano	CDJC	1 182 693	550 270	632 423	182	...	...	...	...
Modena	CDJC	175 442	83 953	91 489	183	...	...	...	...

8. Population of capital cities and cities of 100 000 and more inhabitants: latest available year
Population des capitales et des villes de 100 000 habitants et plus: dernière année disponible (continued — suite)

(See notes at end of table. — Voir notes à la fin du tableau.)

Continent, country or area, date and city Continent, pays ou zone, date et ville	Code[1]	City proper — Ville proprement dite Population				Urban agglomeration — Agglomération urbaine Population			
		Both sexes Les deux sexes	Male Masculin	Female Féminin	Surface area Superficie (km²)	Both sexes Les deux sexes	Male Masculin	Female Féminin	Surface area Superficie (km²)

EUROPE

Italy — Italie
2001

Monza	CDJC	117 068	56 046	61 022	33	...	...	...	...
Napoli	CDJC	993 386	475 342	518 044	117	...	...	...	...
Novara	CDJC	101 921	48 280	53 641	103	...	...	...	...
Padova	CDJC	203 350	95 498	107 852	93	...	...	...	...
Palermo	CDJC	652 640	311 648	340 992	159	...	...	...	...
Parma	CDJC	156 172	73 799	82 373	261	...	...	...	...
Perugia	CDJC	148 575	70 622	77 953	450	...	...	...	...
Pescara	CDJC	115 197	54 469	60 728	34	...	...	...	...
Prato	CDJC	170 388	82 662	87 726	98	...	...	...	...
Ravenna	CDJC	138 204	67 075	71 129	653	...	...	...	...
Reggio di Calabria	CDJC	179 384	86 607	92 777	236	...	...	...	...
Reggio nell'Emilia	CDJC	141 383	68 047	73 336	232	...	...	...	...
Rimini	CDJC	128 301	61 699	66 602	135	...	...	...	...
ROMA	CDJC	2 459 776	1 155 247	1 304 529	1 285	...	...	...	...
Salerno	CDJC	144 078	69 044	75 034	59	...	...	...	...
Sassari	CDJC	112 959	53 958	59 001	546	...	...	...	...
Siracusa	CDJC	121 000	58 958	62 042	204	...	...	...	...
Taranto	CDJC	201 349	96 114	105 235	218	...	...	...	...
Terni	CDJC	103 964	49 276	54 688	212	...	...	...	...
Torino	CDJC	857 433	406 001	451 432	130	...	...	...	...
Trento	CDJC	104 844	50 136	54 708	158	...	...	...	...
Trieste	CDJC	209 520	97 325	112 195	85	...	...	...	...
Venezia	CDJC	266 181	125 846	140 335	413	...	...	...	...
Verona	CDJC	243 474	114 918	128 556	207	...	...	...	...
Vicenza	CDJC	106 069	50 174	55 895	81	...	...	...	...

Latvia — Lettonie
2000

Daugavpils	ESDF	114 642	51 782	62 860	72	...	...	...	...
RIGA	ESDF	762 825	340 561	422 264	307	...	...	...	...

2001

Daugavpils	ESDF	113 945	51 457	62 488	72	...	...	...	...
RIGA	ESDF	751 892	335 621	416 271	307	...	...	...	...

Liechtenstein
2001

VADUZ	ESDF	4 911	2 313	2 598	17	...	...	...	...

Lithuania — Lituanie
2000

Kaunas	ESDF	412 639	...	...	157	...	...	...	...
Klaipeda	ESDF	202 451	...	...	98	...	...	...	...
Panevezhis	ESDF	133 695	...	...	50	...	...	...	...
Shauliai	ESDF	146 563	...	...	81	...	...	...	...
VILNIUS	ESDF	577 969	...	...	394	...	...	...	...

2001

Kaunas	ESDF	378 141	170 714	207 427	157	...	...	...	...
Klaipeda	ESDF	192 859	89 464	103 395	98	...	...	...	...
Panevezhis	ESDF	119 612	54 487	65 125	50	...	...	...	...
Shauliai	ESDF	133 780	61 152	72 628	81	...	...	...	...
VILNIUS	ESDF	542 202	247 040	295 162	394	...	...	...	...

Luxembourg
1996

LUXEMBOURG-VILLE	ESDJ	77 400	...	...	51	...	...	...	...

Malta — Malte[128]
1999

VALLETTA	ESDF	7 073	3 382	3 691	...	...	...	...	...

2000

VALLETTA	ESDF	7 212	3 430	3 780	...	...	...	...	...

(See notes at end of table. — Voir notes à la fin du tableau.)

Continent, country or area, date and city / Continent, pays ou zone, date et ville	Code[1]	City proper — Ville proprement dite Population				Urban agglomeration — Agglomération urbaine Population			
		Both sexes Les deux sexes	Male Masculin	Female Féminin	Surface area Superficie (km²)	Both sexes Les deux sexes	Male Masculin	Female Féminin	Surface area Superficie (km²)
EUROPE									
Monaco									
1999									
MONACO	ESDJ	33 268	...	...	...	...	...	...	...
Netherlands — Pays-Bas[129,130]									
2000									
Almere	ESDJ	158 902	79 270	79 632	132	...	...	...	...
Amersfoort	ESDJ	129 720	63 343	66 377	63	158 758	77 636	81 122	122
AMSTERDAM	ESDJ	735 526	362 669	372 857	165	1 009 247	496 093	513 154	366
Apeldoorn	ESDJ	154 859	76 045	78 814	340	...	...	...	...
Arnhem	ESDJ	140 736	69 320	71 416	99	142 265	70 068	72 197	127
Breda	ESDJ	163 427	79 541	83 886	127	...	...	...	...
Dordrecht	ESDJ	120 222	59 140	61 082	81	242 291	119 075	123 216	153
Ede	ESDJ	103 708	51 001	52 707	318	...	...	...	...
Eindhoven	ESDJ	204 776	102 806	101 970	87	...	...	...	...
Emmen	ESDJ	108 367	53 660	54 707	341	...	...	...	...
Enschede	ESDJ	151 346	76 947	74 399	141	...	...	...	...
Geleen-Sittard	ESDJ	97 953	48 314	49 639	80	141 593	70 059	71 534	122
Groningen	ESDJ	175 569	86 656	88 913	80	194 213	95 412	98 801	126
Haarlem	ESDJ	147 831	71 714	76 117	29	190 826	91 903	98 923	77
Haarlemmermeer	ESDJ	118 553	59 289	59 264	180	...	...	...	...
Heerlen-Kerkrade	ESDJ	95 004	46 654	48 350	45	216 187	106 291	109 896	109
Leiden	ESDJ	117 170	57 256	59 914	22	252 708	123 637	129 071	88
Maastricht	ESDJ	122 005	58 638	63 367	57	...	...	...	...
Nijmegen	ESDJ	154 616	74 512	80 104	54	...	...	...	...
Rotterdam	ESDJ	598 660	293 952	304 708	209	1 005 394	493 646	511 748	356
s-Gravenhage	ESDJ	457 726	223 661	234 065	83	622 404	302 267	320 137	191
s-Hertogenbosch	ESDJ	131 697	64 882	66 815	85	...	...	...	...
Tilburg	ESDJ	197 358	97 463	99 895	117	219 875	108 690	111 185	159
Utrecht	ESDJ	260 625	125 701	134 924	96	395 300	192 151	203 149	169
Zaanstad	ESDJ	137 669	67 808	69 861	75	...	...	...	...
Zoetermeer	ESDJ	110 500	54 150	56 350	36	...	...	...	...
Zwolle	ESDJ	109 000	52 989	56 011	113	...	...	...	...
2001									
Almere	ESDJ	150 398	74 886	75 512	132	...	...	...	...
Amersfoort	ESDJ	128 035	62 439	65 596	63	156 868	76 644	80 224	122
AMSTERDAM	ESDJ	734 594	361 662	372 932	165	1 006 449	494 249	512 200	365
Apeldoorn	ESDJ	153 683	75 374	78 309	340	...	...	...	...
Arnhem	ESDJ	139 329	68 456	70 873	99	140 835	69 189	71 646	127
Breda	ESDJ	162 308	78 992	83 316	127	...	...	...	...
Dordrecht	ESDJ	120 021	59 042	60 979	81	241 733	118 780	122 953	153
Ede	ESDJ	102 405	50 300	52 105	318	...	...	...	...
Eindhoven	ESDJ	203 397	101 828	101 569	87	304 972	152 472	152 500	181
Emmen	ESDJ	107 422	53 187	54 235	341	...	...	...	...
Enschede	ESDJ	150 449	76 473	73 976	141	...	...	...	...
Geleen-Sittard	ESDJ	...	...	...	...	141 556	70 065	71 491	122
Groningen	ESDJ	174 250	85 801	88 449	80	192 948	94 591	98 357	126
Haarlem	ESDJ	148 377	71 767	76 610	29	191 211	91 915	99 296	77
Haarlemmermeer	ESDJ	113 553	56 741	56 812	180	...	...	...	...
Heerlen-Kerkrade	ESDJ	...	...	...	...	217 379	106 800	110 579	109
Leiden	ESDJ	117 022	57 067	59 955	22	251 669	123 006	128 663	87
Maastricht	ESDJ	122 163	58 724	63 439	57	...	...	...	...
Nijmegen	ESDJ	153 705	73 886	79 819	54	...	...	...	...
Rotterdam	ESDJ	595 255	291 647	303 608	209	996 604	488 859	507 745	356
s-Gravenhage	ESDJ	442 356	215 627	226 729	68	615 417	298 376	317 041	187
s-Hertogenbosch	ESDJ	130 477	64 250	66 227	85	155 946	76 864	79 082	119
Tilburg	ESDJ	195 819	96 710	99 109	117	218 208	107 866	110 342	161
Utrecht	ESDJ	256 420	123 471	132 949	96	389 993	189 441	200 552	169
Zaanstad	ESDJ	136 115	67 102	69 013	75	...	...	...	...
Zoetermeer	ESDJ	110 129	54 001	56 128	36	...	...	...	...
Zwolle	ESDJ	107 373	52 157	55 216	113	107 373	52 157	55 216	113

8. Population of capital cities and cities of 100 000 and more inhabitants: latest available year
Population des capitales et des villes de 100 000 habitants et plus: dernière année disponible (continued — suite)

(See notes at end of table. — Voir notes à la fin du tableau.)

Continent, country or area, date and city Continent, pays ou zone, date et ville	Code[1]	City proper — Ville proprement dite Population				Urban agglomeration — Agglomération urbaine Population			
		Both sexes Les deux sexes	Male Masculin	Female Féminin	Surface area Superficie (km²)	Both sexes Les deux sexes	Male Masculin	Female Féminin	Surface area Superficie (km²)
EUROPE									
Norway — Norvège									
2000									
Bergen	ESDJ	230 222	112 908	117 314	445	...	...	...	...
OSLO	ESDJ	508 097	245 859	262 237	427	...	...	...	...
Stavanger	ESDJ	108 833	53 543	55 289	66	...	...	...	...
Trondheim	ESDJ	149 513	73 252	76 260	321	...	...	...	...
Poland — Pologne									
2000									
Bialystok	ESDF	285 507	...	...	90	...	...	...	...
Bielsko-Biala	ESDF	179 314	...	...	125	...	...	...	...
Bydgoszcz	ESDF	384 537	...	...	174	...	...	...	...
Bytom	ESDF	201 942	...	...	69	...	...	...	...
Chorzów	ESDF	120 450	...	...	34	...	...	...	...
Czestochowa	ESDF	255 549	...	...	160	...	...	...	...
Dabrowa Górnicza	ESDF	130 250	...	...	188	...	...	...	...
Elblag	ESDF	130 160	...	...	80	...	...	...	...
Gdansk	ESDF	456 574	...	...	262	...	...	...	...
Gdynia	ESDF	255 416	...	...	136	...	...	...	...
Gliwice	ESDF	209 356	...	...	134	...	...	...	...
Grudziadz	ESDF	102 344	...	...	59	...	...	...	...
Gorzów Wielkopolski	ESDF	126 285	...	...	77	...	...	...	...
Jastrzebie-Zdrój	ESDF	101 387	...	...	85	...	...	...	...
Kalisz	ESDF	108 097	...	...	55	...	...	...	...
Katowice	ESDF	340 539	...	...	164	...	...	...	...
Kielce	ESDF	210 956	...	...	109	...	...	...	...
Koszalin	ESDF	111 618	...	...	83	...	...	...	...
Kraków	ESDF	741 510	...	...	327	...	...	...	...
Legnica	ESDF	109 124	...	...	56	...	...	...	...
Lódz	ESDF	793 217	...	...	295	...	...	...	...
Lublin	ESDF	355 803	...	...	148	...	...	...	...
Olsztyn	ESDF	174 271	...	...	88	...	...	...	...
Opole	ESDF	128 927	...	...	96	...	...	...	...
Plock	ESDF	130 830	...	...	88	...	...	...	...
Poznan	ESDF	574 896	...	...	261	...	...	...	...
Radom	ESDF	231 341	...	...	112	...	...	...	...
Ruda Slaska	ESDF	154 228	...	...	78	...	...	...	...
Rybnik	ESDF	143 883	...	...	135	...	...	...	...
Rzeszów	ESDF	162 501	...	...	54	...	...	...	...
Slupsk	ESDF	102 244	...	...	43	...	...	...	...
Sosnowiec	ESDF	241 102	...	...	91	...	...	...	...
Szczecin	ESDF	416 485	...	...	301	...	...	...	...
Tarnów	ESDF	121 828	...	...	72	...	...	...	...
Torun	ESDF	204 322	...	...	116	...	...	...	...
Tychy	ESDF	130 832	...	...	82	...	...	...	...
Walbrzych	ESDF	134 720	...	...	85	...	...	...	...
WARSZAWA	ESDF	1 610 470	...	...	494	...	...	...	...
Wloclawek	ESDF	123 349	...	...	85	...	...	...	...
Wroclaw	ESDF	638 571	...	...	293	...	...	...	...
Zabrze	ESDF	197 910	...	...	80	...	...	...	...
Zielona Góra	ESDF	118 987	...	...	58	...	...	...	...
Portugal									
2001									
Almada	CDFC	101 501	47 970	53 531	15	...	...	...	...
Amadora	CDFC	175 872	84 394	91 478	24	...	...	...	...
Braga	CDFC	117 272	55 810	61 462	32	...	...	...	...
Coimbra	CDFC	101 069	46 487	54 582	59	...	...	...	...
Funchal	CDFC	103 932	48 483	55 449	34	...	...	...	...
LISBOA[131]	CDFC	564 657	257 987	306 670	85	2 682 687	1 286 194	1 396 493	3 213
Porto[132]	CDFC	263 131	119 715	143 416	42	1 260 680	603 985	656 695	814
Vila Nova de Gaia	CDFC	178 255	85 527	92 728	56	...	...	...	...

8. Population of capital cities and cities of 100 000 and more inhabitants: latest available year
Population des capitales et des villes de 100 000 habitants et plus: dernière année disponible (continued — suite)

(See notes at end of table. — Voir notes à la fin du tableau.)

Continent, country or area, date and city / Continent, pays ou zone, date et ville	Code[1]	City proper — Ville proprement dite Population				Urban agglomeration — Agglomération urbaine Population			
		Both sexes Les deux sexes	Male Masculin	Female Féminin	Surface area Superficie (km²)	Both sexes Les deux sexes	Male Masculin	Female Féminin	Surface area Superficie (km²)
EUROPE									
Republic of Moldova — République de Moldova									
2001									
Beltsy	ESDF	144 371	71 171	73 200	41	...	...	...	...
KISHINEV	ESDF	654 927	316 591	338 336	121	...	...	...	...
Romania — Roumanie									
2001									
Arad	ESDJ	183 352	86 415	96 937	267	...	...	...	...
Bacau	ESDJ	206 765	100 376	106 389	43	...	...	...	...
Baia Mare	ESDJ	149 989	72 790	77 199	234	...	...	...	...
Botosani	ESDJ	126 628	61 541	65 087	41	...	...	...	...
Braila	ESDJ	230 687	110 662	120 025	33	...	...	...	...
Brasov	ESDJ	307 046	148 577	158 469	267	...	...	...	...
BUCURESTI	ESDJ	1 996 814	934 530	1 062 284	238	...	...	...	...
Buzau	ESDJ	145 335	70 263	75 072	81	...	...	...	...
Cluj-Napoca	ESDJ	331 992	158 557	173 435	180	...	...	...	...
Constanta	ESDJ	336 309	161 429	174 880	125	...	...	...	...
Craiova	ESDJ	311 326	150 490	160 836	81	...	...	...	...
Drobeta Turnu-Severin	ESDJ	116 342	57 294	59 048	55	...	...	...	...
Galati	ESDJ	325 057	159 760	165 297	246	...	...	...	...
Iasi	ESDJ	348 705	167 115	181 590	94	...	...	...	...
Oradea	ESDJ	221 487	105 708	115 779	111	...	...	...	...
Piatra Neamt	ESDJ	123 966	59 803	64 163	78	...	...	...	...
Pitesti	ESDJ	186 238	90 375	95 863	41	...	...	...	...
Ploiesti	ESDJ	248 399	118 142	130 257	58	...	...	...	...
Rimnicu Vilcea	ESDJ	120 363	58 515	61 848	90	...	...	...	...
Satu-Mare	ESDJ	129 523	61 742	67 781	150	...	...	...	...
Sibiu	ESDJ	167 377	78 860	88 517	122	...	...	...	...
Suceava	ESDJ	117 214	57 080	60 134	52	...	...	...	...
Timisoara	ESDJ	328 263	154 847	173 416	129	...	...	...	...
Tirgu-Mures	ESDJ	163 267	77 846	85 421	49	...	...	...	...
Russian Federation — Fédération de Russie									
1999									
Abakan	ESDF	168 047	77 027	91 020	...	...	...	...	...
Achinsk	ESDF	121 419	57 161	64 258	...	122 800	...	...	...
Almetievsk	ESDF	141 764	68 085	73 679	...	151 850	...	...	...
Angarsk	ESDF	265 410	130 419	134 991	...	270 750	...	...	...
Arkhangelsk	ESDF	364 985	169 342	195 643	...	372 200	...	...	...
Armavir	ESDF	163 832	75 976	87 856	...	180 700	...	...	...
Arzamas	ESDF	110 465	51 174	59 291	...	...	...	...	...
Astrakhan	ESDF	482 402	224 336	258 066	...	...	...	...	...
Balakovo	ESDF	208 030	97 808	110 222	...	208 650	...	...	...
Balashikha	ESDF	132 559	59 927	72 632	...	...	...	...	...
Barnaul	ESDF	579 900	268 946	310 954	...	647 600	...	...	...
Belgorod	ESDF	338 308	156 067	182 241	...	...	...	...	...
Berezniki	ESDF	182 900	92 307	90 593	...	185 150	...	...	...
Biisk	ESDF	224 493	103 772	120 721	...	236 250	...	...	...
Blagoveshchensk (Amurskaya oblast)	ESDF	220 102	106 277	113 825	...	223 500	...	...	...
Bratsk	ESDF	279 664	134 389	145 275	...	...	...	...	...
Bryansk	ESDF	455 158	213 605	241 553	...	477 450	...	...	...
Cheboksary	ESDF	459 156	216 659	242 497	...	471 650	...	...	...
Chelyabinsk	ESDF	1 084 208	501 602	582 606	...	1 111 100	...	...	...
Cherepovets	ESDF	323 545	153 635	169 910	...	...	...	...	...
Cherkessk	ESDF	121 032	56 199	64 833	...	...	...	...	...
Chita	ESDF	308 863	146 756	162 107	...	309 300	...	...	...
Dimitrovgrad	ESDF	136 605	65 234	71 371	...	...	...	...	...
Dzerzhinsk (Novgorodskaya oblast)	ESDF	278 246	129 783	148 463	...	289 100	...	...	...

8. Population of capital cities and cities of 100 000 and more inhabitants: latest available year
Population des capitales et des villes de 100 000 habitants et plus: dernière année disponible (continued — suite)

(See notes at end of table. — Voir notes à la fin du tableau.)

Continent, country or area, date and city / Continent, pays ou zone, date et ville	Code[1]	City proper — Ville proprement dite Population				Urban agglomeration — Agglomération urbaine Population			
		Both sexes Les deux sexes	Male Masculin	Female Féminin	Surface area Superficie (km²)	Both sexes Les deux sexes	Male Masculin	Female Féminin	Surface area Superficie (km²)
EUROPE									
Russian Federation — Fédération de Russie									
1999									
Ekaterinoburg	ESDF	1 267 393	578 680	688 713	...	1 313 750	...	...	...
Elektrostal	ESDF	147 159	67 416	79 743	...	...	...	...	...
Elets	ESDF	118 987	55 033	63 954	...	...	...	...	...
Elista	ESDF	102 189	47 480	54 709	...	106 150	...	...	...
Engels	ESDF	189 826	88 715	101 111	...	224 800	...	...	...
Glazov	ESDF	106 473	49 720	56 753	...	...	...	...	...
Ioshkap-Ola	ESDF	249 550	114 431	135 119	...	278 500	...	...	...
Irkutsk	ESDF	591 047	264 536	326 511	...	...	...	...	...
Ivanovo	ESDF	458 531	206 380	252 151	...	...	...	...	...
Izhevsk	ESDF	653 691	302 203	351 488	...	...	...	...	...
Kaliningrad (Kaliningradskaya oblast)	ESDF	425 089	204 456	220 633	...	...	...	...	...
Kaluga	ESDF	339 703	155 720	183 983	...	357 100	...	...	...
Kamensk-Uralsky	ESDF	190 352	88 328	102 024	...	192 000	...	...	...
Kamyshin	ESDF	125 901	58 968	66 933	...	...	...	...	...
Kansk	ESDF	108 063	51 654	56 409	...	...	...	...	...
Kazan	ESDF	1 091 656	499 838	591 818	...	1 092 150	...	...	...
Kemerovo	ESDF	492 240	222 475	269 765	...	532 200	...	...	...
Khabarovsk	ESDF	608 853	296 436	312 417	...	...	...	...	...
Khimki	ESDF	134 962	60 229	74 733	...	136 300	...	...	...
Kirov (Azerbaidzhanskaya SSR)	ESDF	465 628	213 653	251 975	...	508 150	...	...	...
Kiselevsk	ESDF	110 005	51 798	58 207	...	115 900	...	...	...
Kislovodsk	ESDF	112 481	51 301	61 180	...	117 100	...	...	...
Kolomna	ESDF	150 905	69 344	81 561	...	...	...	...	...
Komsomolsk-na-Amure	ESDF	294 268	140 015	154 253	...	...	...	...	...
Korolev	ESDF	133 789	60 577	73 212	...	161 600	...	...	...
Kostroma	ESDF	287 818	132 062	155 756	...	...	...	...	...
Kovrov	ESDF	161 298	73 154	88 144	...	...	...	...	...
Krasnodar	ESDF	639 917	298 694	341 223	...	757 150	...	...	...
Krasnoyarsk	ESDF	876 418	394 992	481 426	...	...	...	...	...
Kurgan	ESDF	364 211	168 153	196 058	...	...	...	...	...
Kursk	ESDF	440 208	200 923	239 285	...	...	...	...	...
Leninsk-Kuznetsky	ESDF	114 079	54 109	59 970	...	153 800	...	...	...
Lipetsk	ESDF	518 926	243 479	275 447	...	...	...	...	...
Lyubertsy	ESDF	164 210	73 397	90 813	...	...	...	...	...
Maikop	ESDF	166 860	75 470	91 390	...	178 550	...	...	...
Magadan	ESDF	121 330	59 226	62 104	...	130 450	...	...	...
Magnitogorsk	ESDF	426 866	199 646	227 220	...	427 300	...	...	...
Makhachkala	ESDF	330 942	163 560	167 382	...	378 650	...	...	...
Mezhdurechensk	ESDF	104 551	50 729	53 822	...	...	...	...	...
Miass	ESDF	165 811	77 932	87 879	...	179 400	...	...	...
Michurinsk	ESDF	118 610	53 026	65 584	...	...	...	...	...
MOSKVA	ESDF	8 297 056	3 724 694	4 572 362	...	8 537 700	...	...	...
Murmansk	ESDF	378 552	187 960	190 592	...	...	...	...	...
Murom	ESDF	140 993	65 615	75 378	...	...	...	...	...
Mytishchi	ESDF	156 631	69 397	87 234	...	...	...	...	...
Naberezhnye Tchelny	ESDF	521 282	250 577	270 705	...	524 400	...	...	...
Nakhodka	ESDF	158 559	80 172	78 387	...	188 150	...	...	...
Naltchik	ESDF	230 131	108 218	121 913	...	250 600	...	...	...
Neftekamsk	ESDF	117 352	55 296	62 056	...	124 650	...	...	...
Nevinnomyssk	ESDF	132 111	62 335	69 776	...	...	...	...	...
Nizhnekamsk	ESDF	224 426	105 993	118 433	...	...	...	...	...
Nizhenvartovsk	ESDF	238 071	118 840	119 231	...	...	...	...	...
Nizhny Tagil	ESDF	392 942	184 439	208 503	...	...	...	...	...
Nizhny Novgorod	ESDF	1 357 555	619 859	737 696	...	1 366 100	...	...	...
Noginsk	ESDF	117 446	52 784	64 662	...	...	...	...	...

8. Population of capital cities and cities of 100 000 and more inhabitants: latest available year
Population des capitales et des villes de 100 000 habitants et plus: dernière année disponible (continued — suite)

(See notes at end of table. — Voir notes à la fin du tableau.)

Continent, country or area, date and city / Continent, pays ou zone, date et ville	Code[1]	City proper — Ville proprement dite Population				Urban agglomeration — Agglomération urbaine Population			
		Both sexes Les deux sexes	Male Masculin	Female Féminin	Surface area Superficie (km²)	Both sexes Les deux sexes	Male Masculin	Female Féminin	Surface area Superficie (km²)
EUROPE									
Russian Federation — Fédération de Russie									
1999									
Norilsk	ESDF	148 797	75 009	73 788	...	244 450	...	...	...
Novocheboksarsk	ESDF	124 628	58 624	66 004	...	124 900	...	...	...
Novocherkassk	ESDF	184 306	92 582	91 724	...	198 950	...	...	...
Novokuybishevsk	ESDF	115 758	51 706	64 052	...	117 900	...	...	...
Novokuznetsk	ESDF	564 353	262 313	302 040	...	579 250	...	...	...
Novomoskovsk (Tulskaya oblast)	ESDF	138 220	61 797	76 423	...	...	...	...	...
Novorossiysk	ESDF	204 652	97 198	107 454	...	248 850	...	...	...
Novoshakhtinsk	ESDF	101 566	48 083	53 483	...	118 450	...	...	...
Novosibirsk	ESDF	1 400 328	636 563	763 765	...	...	...	...	...
Novotroitsk	ESDF	109 681	53 577	56 104	...	117 400	...	...	...
Obninsk	ESDF	108 029	52 965	55 064	...	...	...	...	...
Odintsovo	ESDF	128 227	58 345	69 882	...	...	...	...	...
Oktyabrsky	ESDF	111 423	53 153	58 270	...	...	...	...	...
Omsk	ESDF	1 153 314	536 759	616 555	...	1 177 000	...	...	...
Orekhovo-Zuevo	ESDF	125 399	55 394	70 005	...	...	...	...	...
Orel	ESDF	341 854	155 373	186 481	...	...	...	...	...
Orenburg	ESDF	522 643	238 134	284 509	...	541 500	...	...	...
Orsk	ESDF	274 849	130 618	144 231	...	280 000	...	...	...
Penza	ESDF	528 140	243 904	284 236	...	528 500	...	...	...
Perm	ESDF	1 014 360	472 602	541 758	...	1 024 250	...	...	...
Pervouralsk	ESDF	135 588	64 826	70 762	...	163 850	...	...	...
Petropavlovsk-Kamchatsky	ESDF	198 424	102 034	96 390	...	209 650	...	...	...
Petrozavodsk	ESDF	282 401	130 133	152 268	...	282 650	...	...	...
Podolsk	ESDF	193 735	86 646	107 089	...	...	...	...	...
Prokopyevsk	ESDF	236 174	111 692	124 482	...	236 350	...	...	...
Pskov	ESDF	201 846	91 042	110 804	...	...	...	...	...
Pyatigorsk	ESDF	128 257	56 836	71 421	...	184 600	...	...	...
Rostov-na-Donu	ESDF	1 003 482	461 383	542 099	...	...	...	...	...
Rubtsovsk	ESDF	163 252	77 811	85 441	...	...	...	...	...
Ryazan	ESDF	528 116	241 727	286 389	...	531 200	...	...	...
Rybinsk	ESDF	241 450	111 568	129 882	...	...	...	...	...
Salavat	ESDF	157 847	74 820	83 027	...	...	...	...	...
Samara (Samarskaya oblast)	ESDF	1 164 859	522 584	642 275	...	1 183 350	...	...	...
Saransk	ESDF	316 086	143 809	172 277	...	344 700	...	...	...
Sarapyul	ESDF	105 623	48 418	57 205	...	106 350	...	...	...
Saratov	ESDF	875 256	404 967	470 289	...	...	...	...	...
Sergiev Posad	ESDF	111 256	49 010	62 246	...	...	...	...	...
Serpukhov	ESDF	133 685	62 466	71 219	...	...	...	...	...
Severodvinsk	ESDF	235 799	120 852	114 947	...	238 250	...	...	...
Seversk	ESDF	119 146	56 316	62 830	...	...	...	...	...
Shakhty	ESDF	221 538	101 638	119 900	...	250 900	...	...	...
Shchelkovo	ESDF	104 847	46 819	58 028	...	...	...	...	...
Smolensk	ESDF	351 498	161 833	189 665	...	...	...	...	...
Sochi	ESDF	334 009	153 852	180 157	...	395 800	...	...	...
Solikamsk	ESDF	106 164	52 534	53 630	...	...	...	...	...
St. Petersburg	ESDF	4 678 102	2 110 381	2 567 721	...	...	...	...	...
Starsy Oskol	ESDF	212 182	100 715	111 467	...	...	...	...	...
Stavropol	ESDF	342 642	157 317	185 325	...	342 700	...	...	...
Sterlitamak	ESDF	264 729	125 804	138 925	...	...	...	...	...
Surgut	ESDF	277 781	138 507	139 274	...	...	...	...	...
Syktivkar	ESDF	229 879	108 010	121 869	...	246 800	...	...	...
Syzran	ESDF	186 367	83 947	102 420	...	...	...	...	...
Taganrog	ESDF	284 850	131 569	153 281	...	...	...	...	...
Tambov	ESDF	312 453	141 980	170 473	...	...	...	...	...
Tolyatti	ESDF	720 430	350 308	370 122	...	734 300	...	...	...
Tomsk	ESDF	481 462	231 737	249 725	...	...	...	...	...

8. Population of capital cities and cities of 100 000 and more inhabitants: latest available year
Population des capitales et des villes de 100 000 habitants et plus: dernière année disponible (continued — suite)

(See notes at end of table. — Voir notes à la fin du tableau.)

Continent, country or area, date and city / Continent, pays ou zone, date et ville	Code[1]	City proper — Ville proprement dite Population				Urban agglomeration — Agglomération urbaine Population			
		Both sexes Les deux sexes	Male Masculin	Female Féminin	Surface area Superficie (km²)	Both sexes Les deux sexes	Male Masculin	Female Féminin	Surface area Superficie (km²)
EUROPE									
Russian Federation — Fédération de Russie									
1999									
Tula	ESDF	506 147	230 960	275 187	...	554 650	...	...	...
Tver	ESDF	450 795	208 622	242 173	...	455 150	...	...	...
Tyumen	ESDF	502 214	235 033	267 181	...	556 200	...	...	...
Ufa	ESDF	1 087 788	510 451	577 337	...	1 093 700	...	...	...
Uhta	ESDF	101 192	48 564	52 628	...	129 200	...	...	...
Ulan-Ude	ESDF	370 175	174 278	195 897	...	394 400	...	...	...
Ulyanovsk	ESDF	668 030	314 674	353 356	...	690 300	...	...	...
Usolie Sibirskoye	ESDF	103 831	51 374	52 457	...	...	...	...	...
Ussuriisk	ESDF	157 095	74 155	82 940	...	...	...	...	...
Ust-Ulimsk	ESDF	106 502	52 501	54 001	...	...	...	...	...
Uzno-Sakhalinsk	ESDF	176 515	83 990	92 525	...	184 500	...	...	...
Velikie Luky	ESDF	116 275	53 704	62 571	...	...	...	...	...
Velikiy Novgorod	ESDF	229 461	108 308	121 153	...	238 000	...	...	...
Vladikavkaz (Osetinskaya ASSR)	ESDF	308 810	142 412	166 398	...	322 500	...	...	...
Vladimir	ESDF	335 083	157 803	177 280	...	356 850	...	...	...
Vladivostok	ESDF	606 895	291 561	315 334	...	636 600	...	...	...
Volgodonsk	ESDF	179 712	88 832	90 880	...	187 000	...	...	...
Volgograd	ESDF	992 341	459 366	532 975	...	1 024 900	...	...	...
Vologda	ESDF	300 449	137 301	163 148	...	309 750	...	...	...
Volzhsky	ESDF	285 920	134 010	151 910	...	294 850	...	...	...
Voronezh	ESDF	903 224	416 952	486 272	...	978 100	...	...	...
Votkinsk	ESDF	102 102	47 727	54 375	...	...	...	...	...
Yakutsk	ESDF	196 417	93 210	103 207	...	228 350	...	...	...
Yaroslave	ESDF	614 095	278 692	335 403	...	...	...	...	...
Zelenodolsk	ESDF	101 300	45 749	55 551	...	...	...	...	...
Zelenograd	ESDF	207 501	97 718	109 783	...	...	...	...	...
Zlatoust	ESDF	197 928	91 663	106 265	...	200 350	...	...	...
San Marino — Saint-Marin									
2000									
SAN MARINO	ESDF	2 822	1 341	1 481	7	4 508	2 174	2 334	...
Serbia and Montenegro — Serbie-et-Montenegro									
2000									
BEOGRAD	ESDJ	1 583 985	764 082	819 903	3 224	...	...	...	...
Cacak	ESDJ	115 000	56 201	58 799	636	...	...	...	...
Djakovica	ESDJ	131 634	67 547	64 087	588	...	...	...	...
Gnjilane	ESDJ	118 026	60 599	57 427	515	...	...	...	...
Kosovska Mitrovica	ESDJ	114 406	58 664	55 742	336	...	...	...	...
Kragujevac	ESDJ	180 311	88 186	92 125	835	...	...	...	...
Kraljevo	ESDJ	124 652	61 406	63 246	1 529	...	...	...	...
Krusevac	ESDJ	136 635	66 619	70 016	854	...	...	...	...
Leskovac	ESDJ	161 217	80 367	80 850	1 024	...	...	...	...
Nis	ESDJ	248 818	122 473	126 345	597	...	...	...	...
Novi Sad	ESDJ	266 067	127 446	138 621	699	...	...	...	...
Pancevo	ESDJ	122 797	59 999	62 798	755	...	...	...	...
Pec	ESDJ	141 121	72 518	68 603	603	...	...	...	...
Podgorica	ESDJ	166 476	82 803	83 673	1 441	...	...	...	...
Pristina	ESDJ	241 565	122 990	118 575	572	...	...	...	...
Prizren	ESDJ	204 629	104 677	99 952	765	...	...	...	...
Sabac	ESDJ	122 021	59 788	62 233	795	...	...	...	...
Smederevo	ESDJ	116 728	57 816	58 912	481	...	...	...	...
Subotica	ESDJ	143 068	68 762	74 306	1 007	...	...	...	...
Urosevac	ESDJ	127 250	65 651	61 599	345	...	...	...	...
Zrenjanin	ESDJ	130 846	63 411	67 435	1 326	...	...	...	...

8. Population of capital cities and cities of 100 000 and more inhabitants: latest available year
Population des capitales et des villes de 100 000 habitants et plus: dernière année disponible (continued — suite)

(See notes at end of table. — Voir notes à la fin du tableau.)

Continent, country or area, date and city Continent, pays ou zone, date et ville	Code[1]	City proper — Ville proprement dite Population				Urban agglomeration — Agglomération urbaine Population			
		Both sexes Les deux sexes	Male Masculin	Female Féminin	Surface area Superficie (km²)	Both sexes Les deux sexes	Male Masculin	Female Féminin	Surface area Superficie (km²)
EUROPE									
Slovakia — Slovaquie									
2001									
BRATISLAVA	CDJC	428 672	200 541	228 131	368	...	...	...	...
Kosice	CDJC	236 093	112 915	123 178	244	...	...	...	...
Slovenia — Slovénie									
2000									
LJUBLJANA	ESDJ	256 595	119 311	137 284	275	...	...	...	...
2001									
LJUBLJANA	ESDJ	251 070	116 484	134 586	275	...	...	...	...
Spain — Espagne									
1999									
Alcalá de Henares	ESDJ	164 463	81 942	82 521	878	...	...	...	...
Alcorcón	ESDJ	142 048	70 208	71 840	337	...	...	...	...
Algeciras	ESDJ	103 106	50 684	52 422	851	...	...	...	...
Badalona	ESDJ	209 635	103 531	106 104	210	...	...	...	...
Cartagena	ESDJ	177 709	87 825	89 884	5 583	...	...	...	...
Elche	ESDJ	193 174	95 470	97 704	3 261	...	...	...	...
Fuenlabrada	ESDJ	171 173	86 315	84 858	387	...	...	...	...
Getafe	ESDJ	145 371	72 184	73 187	784	...	...	...	...
Gijón	ESDJ	267 980	127 095	140 885	1 816	...	...	...	...
Hospitalet de Llobregat	ESDJ	247 986	121 347	126 639	125	...	...	...	...
Jérez de la Frontera	ESDJ	182 660	89 164	93 496	14 118	...	...	...	...
Leganés	ESDJ	173 163	86 270	86 893	431	...	...	...	...
Mataró	ESDJ	104 095	51 054	53 041	223	...	...	...	...
Móstoles	ESDJ	195 351	96 829	98 522	454	...	...	...	...
Sabadell	ESDJ	184 859	89 881	94 978	376	...	...	...	...
San Cristóbal de La Laguna	ESDJ	127 945	62 703	65 242	1 021	...	...	...	...
Santa Coloma de Gramanet	ESDJ	120 802	60 100	60 702	71	...	...	...	...
Terrassa	ESDJ	168 695	82 369	86 326	702	...	...	...	...
Vigo	ESDJ	283 670	134 490	149 180	1 091	...	...	...	...
2000									
Albacete	ESDJ	149 410	72 875	76 535	12 431	...	...	...	...
Alicante	ESDJ	271 864	129 942	141 922	2 008	...	...	...	...
Almería	ESDJ	171 273	82 896	88 377	2 962	...	...	...	...
Badajoz	ESDJ	126 868	61 327	65 541	15 302	...	...	...	...
Barcelona	ESDJ	1 404 571	651 259	753 312	991	...	...	...	...
Bilbao	ESDJ	344 218	162 148	182 070	413	...	...	...	...
Burgos	ESDJ	161 918	78 043	83 875	1 084	...	...	...	...
Cádiz	ESDJ	138 152	66 407	71 745	112	...	...	...	...
Castellón de la Plana	ESDJ	136 795	66 475	70 320	1 075	...	...	...	...
Córdoba	ESDJ	308 652	148 359	160 293	12 533	...	...	...	...
Donostia - San Sebastián	ESDJ	177 851	83 494	94 357	615	...	...	...	...
Granada	ESDJ	240 089	111 821	128 268	882	...	...	...	...
Huelva	ESDJ	139 050	67 288	71 762	1 513	...	...‥	...	...
Jaén	ESDJ	106 301	51 239	55 062	4 243	...	...	...	...
La Coruña	ESDJ	239 423	111 474	127 949	376	...	...	...	...
Las Palmas de Gran Canaria	ESDJ	353 004	173 168	179 836	1 005	...	...	...	...
León	ESDJ	142 491	66 142	76 349	392	...	...	...	...
Lleida	ESDJ	110 427	53 646	56 781	2 120	...	...	...	...
Logroño	ESDJ	123 485	58 977	64 508	796	...	...	...	...
MADRID	ESDJ	2 781 857	1 293 753	1 488 104	6 058	...	...	...	...
Málaga	ESDJ	539 425	258 143	281 282	3 930	...	...	...	...
Murcia	ESDJ	353 986	171 867	182 119	8 865	...	...	...	...
Ourense	ESDJ	107 682	50 443	57 239	845	...	...	...	...
Oviedo	ESDJ	197 942	91 719	106 223	1 866	...	...	...	...
Palma de Mallorca	ESDJ	299 937	144 410	155 527	2 008	...	...	...	...
Pamplona	ESDJ	159 534	75 328	84 206	238	...	...	...	...
Salamanca	ESDJ	156 849	73 295	83 554	386	...	...	...	...
Santa Cruz de Tenerife	ESDJ	202 452	97 038	105 414	1 506	...	...	...	...
Santander	ESDJ	180 212	84 237	95 975	348	...	...	...	...

8. Population of capital cities and cities of 100 000 and more inhabitants: latest available year
Population des capitales et des villes de 100 000 habitants et plus: dernière année disponible (continued — suite)

(See notes at end of table. — Voir notes à la fin du tableau.)

Continent, country or area, date and city — Continent, pays ou zone, date et ville	Code[1]	City proper — Ville proprement dite Population				Urban agglomeration — Agglomération urbaine Population			
		Both sexes Les deux sexes	Male Masculin	Female Féminin	Surface area Superficie (km²)	Both sexes Les deux sexes	Male Masculin	Female Féminin	Surface area Superficie (km²)
EUROPE									
Spain — Espagne									
2000									
Sevilla	ESDJ	694 536	331 314	363 222	1 413	...	...	...	...
Tarragona	ESDJ	110 931	53 738	57 193	624	...	...	...	...
Valencia	ESDJ	726 678	344 682	381 996	1 346	...	...	...	...
Valladolid	ESDJ	314 136	150 895	163 241	1 975	...	...	...	...
Vitoria-Gasteiz	ESDJ	216 760	106 155	110 605	2 768	...	...	...	...
Zaragoza	ESDJ	600 449	287 904	312 545	10 631	...	...	...	...
Sweden — Suède									
1999									
Göteborg	ESDJ	462 470	226 323	236 147	449	788 970	389 432	399 538	...
Helsingborg	ESDJ	116 870	56 377	60 493	346	...	...	...	...
Jönköping	ESDJ	116 344	56 809	59 535	1 485	...	...	...	...
Linköping	ESDJ	132 500	66 412	66 088	1 431	...	...	...	...
Malmö	ESDJ	257 574	123 610	133 964	154	518 506	252 814	265 692	...
Norrköping	ESDJ	122 212	60 089	62 123	1 491	...	...	...	...
Orebro	ESDJ	123 503	59 759	63 744	1 371	...	...	...	...
STOCKHOLM	ESDJ	743 703	356 604	387 099	187	1 643 366	800 874	842 492	...
Umeå	ESDJ	103 970	51 325	52 645	2 316	...	...	...	...
Uppsala	ESDJ	188 478	91 600	96 878	2 465	...	...	...	...
Västerås	ESDJ	125 433	62 033	63 400	956	...	...	...	...
Switzerland — Suisse									
2000									
Bâle	CDJC	166 009	78 371	87 638	24	...	...	...	...
BERNE	CDJC	122 484	56 697	65 787	52	...	...	...	...
Genève	CDJC	174 999	82 009	92 990	16	...	...	...	...
Lausanne	CDJC	114 889	53 479	61 410	41	...	...	...	...
Zürich	CDJC	337 900	161 221	176 679	88	...	...	...	...
2001									
Bâle	ESDJ	165 356	78 073	87 283	24	401 610	192 661	208 949	271
BERNE	ESDJ	122 427	56 721	65 706	52	320 058	152 617	167 441	410
Genève	ESDJ	175 403	82 201	93 202	16	467 040	223 324	243 716	436
Lausanne	ESDJ	115 208	53 701	61 507	41	290 881	139 072	151 809	275
Zürich	ESDJ	339 234	162 164	177 070	88	960 310	468 595	491 715	847
The Former Yougoslav Rep. of Macedonia — L'ex-République yougoslave de Macédoine									
1994									
SKOPLJE	CDJC	429 964	212 466	217 498		...	...	...	...
Ukraine									
2000									
Alchevsk	ESDF	118 750	54 607	64 143		...	...	...	...
Belaya Tserkov (Bila Crkva)	ESDF	212 979	101 266	111 713		...	...	...	...
Berdyansk	ESDF	129 016	59 035	69 981		...	...	...	...
Cherkassy	ESDF	307 753	141 735	166 018		...	...	...	...
Chernigov	ESDF	309 511	144 196	165 315		...	...	...	...
Chernovtsy	ESDF	260 239	121 484	138 755		...	...	...	...
Dneprodzerzhinsk	ESDF	268 312	124 545	143 767		...	...	...	...
Dnepropetrovsk	ESDF	1 098 623	507 409	591 214		...	...	...	...
Donetsk (Donestskaya oblast)	ESDF	1 042 405	480 621	561 784		...	...	...	...
Enakievo (Yenakievo)	ESDF	104 136	47 772	56 364		...	...	...	...
Evpatoriya	ESDF	105 014	47 573	57 441		...	...	...	...
Gorlovka	ESDF	298 648	137 539	161 109		...	...	...	...
Ivano-Frankovsk	ESDF	234 406	113 863	120 543		...	...	...	...
Kamenetz-Podolsky	ESDF	109 696	52 869	56 827		...	...	...	...
Kertch	ESDF	164 799	78 225	86 574		...	...	...	...
Kharkov	ESDF	1 484 449	677 575	806 874		...	...	...	...
Kherson	ESDF	351 449	161 184	190 265		...	...	...	...
Khmelnitsky (Hmilnyk)	ESDF	259 351	121 922	137 429		...	...	...	...
KIEV	ESDF	2 595 012	1 220 120	1 374 892		...	...	...	...

(See notes at end of table. — Voir notes à la fin du tableau.)

Continent, country or area, date and city / Continent, pays ou zone, date et ville	Code[1]	City proper — Ville proprement dite Population				Urban agglomeration — Agglomération urbaine Population			
		Both sexes Les deux sexes	Male Masculin	Female Féminin	Surface area Superficie (km²)	Both sexes Les deux sexes	Male Masculin	Female Féminin	Surface area Superficie (km²)
EUROPE									
Ukraine									
2000									
Kirovograd	ESDF	264 236	121 904	142 332	...	...	...	...	...
Krasny Lutch	ESDF	101 525	47 108	54 417	...	...	...	...	...
Kramatorsk	ESDF	185 210	83 607	101 603	...	...	...	...	...
Krementchug	ESDF	238 416	109 645	128 771	...	...	...	...	...
Kryvy Rig	ESDF	698 408	322 315	376 093	...	...	...	...	...
Lysychansk	ESDF	116 349	53 350	62 999	...	...	...	...	...
Lugansk	ESDF	464 432	211 023	253 409	...	...	...	...	...
Lutsk	ESDF	215 093	100 672	114 421	...	...	...	...	...
Lvov	ESDF	784 149	378 084	406 065	...	...	...	...	...
Makeyevka	ESDF	381 933	175 889	206 044	...	...	...	...	...
Mariupol	ESDF	486 473	223 646	262 827	...	...	...	...	...
Melitopol	ESDF	168 793	77 977	90 816	...	...	...	...	...
Mykolaiv (Nikolaevskaya oblast)	ESDF	505 849	231 636	274 213	...	...	...	...	...
Nikopol	ESDF	148 347	68 088	80 259	...	...	...	...	...
Odessa	ESDF	993 091	469 132	523 959	...	...	...	...	...
Pavlograd	ESDF	126 362	59 458	66 904	...	...	...	...	...
Poltava	ESDF	310 865	143 040	167 825	...	...	...	...	...
Rovno	ESDF	244 454	115 725	128 729	...	...	...	...	...
Sevastopol	ESDF	348 313	164 373	183 940	...	...	...	...	...
Severodonetsk	ESDF	126 739	58 649	68 090	...	...	...	...	...
Simferopol	ESDF	336 796	151 986	184 810	...	...	...	...	...
Slavyansk	ESDF	123 883	56 374	67 509	...	...	...	...	...
Stakhanov	ESDF	100 850	45 859	54 991	...	...	...	...	...
Sumy	ESDF	293 073	136 622	156 451	...	...	...	...	...
Ternopol	ESDF	233 349	112 731	120 618	...	...	...	...	...
Uzhgorod	ESDF	125 482	58 843	66 639	...	...	...	...	...
Vinnutsya	ESDF	384 899	183 776	201 123	...	...	...	...	...
Zaporozhye	ESDF	842 446	387 336	455 110	...	...	...	...	...
Zhitomir	ESDF	297 000	141 563	155 437	...	...	...	...	...
United Kingdom — Royaume-Uni[133]									
1996									
Aberdeen	ESDF	217 260	106 198	111 062	186	...	...	...	...
Aberdeenshire	ESDF	227 430	113 042	114 388	6 318	...	...	...	...
Amber Valley	ESDF	115 224	57 285	57 939	265	...	...	...	...
Angus	ESDF	110 780	54 044	56 736	2 181	...	...	...	...
Arun	ESDF	137 978	65 564	72 414	221	...	...	...	...
Ashfield	ESDF	108 558	53 753	54 805	110	...	...	...	...
Aylesbury Vale	ESDF	154 927	77 051	77 876	903	...	...	...	...
Barking & Dagenham[134]	ESDF	153 715	75 092	78 623	34	...	...	...	...
Barnet[134]	ESDF	319 353	155 895	163 458	89	...	...	...	...
Barnsley	ESDF	227 213	111 642	115 571	328	...	...	...	...
Basildon	ESDF	163 280	80 407	82 873	110	...	...	...	...
Basingstoke & Deane	ESDF	147 914	73 469	74 445	634	...	...	...	...
Bassetlaw	ESDF	106 303	52 748	53 555	637	...	...	...	...
Bath & North East Somerset	ESDF	164 725	80 342	84 383	351	...	...	...	...
Bedford	ESDF	137 451	68 477	68 974	477	...	...	...	...
Belfast[135]	ESDF	297 300	...	...	110	...	...	...	...
Bexley[134]	ESDF	219 311	107 360	111 951	61	...	...	...	...
Birmingham	ESDF	1 020 589	504 342	516 247	265	...	...	...	...
Blackburn	ESDF	139 491	68 701	70 790	137	...	...	...	...
Blackpool	ESDF	152 459	73 875	78 584	35	...	...	...	...
Bolton	ESDF	265 449	130 861	134 588	140	...	...	...	...
Bournemouth	ESDF	160 749	76 297	84 452	46	...	...	...	...
Bracknell Forest	ESDF	110 092	55 725	54 367	109	...	...	...	...
Bradford	ESDF	483 422	238 407	245 015	366	...	...	...	...
Braintree	ESDF	126 236	62 500	63 736	612	...	...	...	...
Breckland	ESDF	113 654	55 573	58 081	1 305	...	...	...	...

8. Population of capital cities and cities of 100 000 and more inhabitants: latest available year
Population des capitales et des villes de 100 000 habitants et plus: dernière année disponible (continued — suite)

(See notes at end of table. — Voir notes à la fin du tableau.)

Continent, country or area, date and city / Continent, pays ou zone, date et ville	Code[1]	City proper — Ville proprement dite Population				Urban agglomeration — Agglomération urbaine Population			
		Both sexes Les deux sexes	Male Masculin	Female Féminin	Surface area Superficie (km²)	Both sexes Les deux sexes	Male Masculin	Female Féminin	Surface area Superficie (km²)
EUROPE									
United Kingdom — Royaume-Uni[133]									
1996									
Brent[134]	ESDF	247 525	123 645	123 880	44	...	...	...	...
Bridgend	ESDF	130 080	63 056	67 024	246	...	...	...	...
Brighton	ESDF	156 124	76 842	79 282	58	...	...	...	...
Bristol	ESDF	399 633	198 167	201 466	110	...	...	...	...
Broadland	ESDF	113 896	55 984	57 912	552	...	...	...	...
Bromley[134]	ESDF	295 584	143 424	152 160	152	...	...	...	...
Broxtowe	ESDF	111 429	55 215	56 214	81	...	...	...	...
Bury	ESDF	181 873	90 104	91 769	99	...	...	...	...
Caerphilly	ESDF	169 125	83 049	86 076	278	...	...	...	...
Calderdale	ESDF	192 844	94 093	98 751	363	...	...	...	...
Cambridge	ESDF	116 701	58 498	58 203	41	...	...	...	...
Camden[134]	ESDF	189 119	92 370	96 749	22	...	...	...	...
Canterbury	ESDF	136 481	66 429	70 052	309	...	...	...	...
Cardiff[136]	ESDF	315 040	154 656	160 384	140	...	...	...	...
Carlisle	ESDF	103 102	50 308	52 794	1 040	...	...	...	...
Carmarthenshire	ESDF	169 108	82 270	86 838	2 395	...	...	...	...
Charnwood	ESDF	155 724	77 740	77 984	279	...	...	...	...
Chelmsford	ESDF	156 601	77 147	79 454	342	...	...	...	...
Cheltenham	ESDF	106 692	52 428	54 264	47	...	...	...	...
Cherwell	ESDF	132 687	65 387	67 300	589	...	...	...	...
Chester	ESDF	119 221	58 314	60 907	448	...	...	...	...
Chesterfield	ESDF	100 673	49 514	51 159	66	...	...	...	...
Chichester	ESDF	104 112	47 863	56 249	786	...	...	...	...
Colchester	ESDF	154 176	76 091	78 085	334	...	...	...	...
Conwy	ESDF	110 596	52 510	58 086	1 130	...	...	...	...
Coventry	ESDF	306 503	151 502	155 001	97	...	...	...	...
Crewe & Nantwich	ESDF	113 670	56 612	57 058	430	...	...	...	...
Croydon[134]	ESDF	333 787	163 998	169 789	87	...	...	...	...
Dacorum	ESDF	134 733	66 410	68 323	212	...	...	...	...
Darlington	ESDF	101 257	49 307	51 950	197	...	...	...	...
Derby	ESDF	233 708	115 901	117 807	78	...	...	...	...
Derry	ESDF	104 400	...	...	380	...	...	...	...
Doncaster	ESDF	291 804	143 806	147 998	581	...	...	...	...
Dover	ESDF	107 398	52 359	55 039	315	...	...	...	...
Dudley	ESDF	312 194	154 918	157 276	98	...	...	...	...
Dumfries & Galloway	ESDF	147 600	71 703	75 897	6 439	...	...	...	...
Dundee	ESDF	150 250	71 740	78 510	65	...	...	...	...
Ealing[134]	ESDF	297 033	148 140	148 893	55	...	...	...	...
East Ayrshire	ESDF	122 350	59 110	63 240	1 252	...	...	...	...
East Devon	ESDF	123 105	57 740	65 365	814	...	...	...	...
East Dunbartonshire	ESDF	110 750	54 125	56 625	172	...	...	...	...
East Hampshire	ESDF	110 761	53 872	56 889	515	...	...	...	...
East Hertfordshire	ESDF	123 553	61 771	61 782	477	...	...	...	...
East Lindsey	ESDF	123 058	59 401	63 657	1 760	...	...	...	...
East Riding of Yorkshire	ESDF	308 689	150 842	157 847	2 415	...	...	...	...
East Staffordshire	ESDF	100 421	49 951	50 470	390	...	...	...	...
Eastleigh	ESDF	111 732	55 310	56 422	80	...	...	...	...
Edinburgh[137]	ESDF	448 850	216 730	232 120	262	...	...	...	...
Elmbridge	ESDF	124 539	60 298	64 241	97	...	...	...	...
Enfield[134]	ESDF	262 613	129 236	133 377	81	...	...	...	...
Epping Forest	ESDF	119 512	58 424	61 088	340	...	...	...	...
Erewash	ESDF	106 818	53 033	53 785	109	...	...	...	...
Exeter	ESDF	107 729	53 152	54 577	47	...	...	...	...
Falkirk	ESDF	143 040	69 469	73 571	299	...	...	...	...
Fareham	ESDF	103 748	50 413	53 335	74	...	...	...	...
Fife	ESDF	349 300	169 204	180 096	1 323	...	...	...	...
Flintshire	ESDF	144 918	71 443	73 475	438	...	...	...	...
Gateshead	ESDF	200 968	98 242	102 726	143	...	...	...	...

8. Population of capital cities and cities of 100 000 and more inhabitants: latest available year
Population des capitales et des villes de 100 000 habitants et plus: dernière année disponible (continued — suite)

(See notes at end of table. — Voir notes à la fin du tableau.)

Continent, country or area, date and city Continent, pays ou zone, date et ville	Code[1]	City proper — Ville proprement dite Population				Urban agglomeration — Agglomération urbaine Population			
		Both sexes Les deux sexes	Male Masculin	Female Féminin	Surface area Superficie (km²)	Both sexes Les deux sexes	Male Masculin	Female Féminin	Surface area Superficie (km²)
EUROPE									
United Kingdom — Royaume-Uni[133]									
1996									
Gedling	ESDF	112 194	54 985	57 209	120	...	...	...	...
Glasgow	ESDF	616 430	294 237	322 193	175	...	...	...	...
Gloucester	ESDF	106 834	53 328	53 506	41	...	...	...	...
Greenwich[134]	ESDF	212 073	103 156	108 917	48	...	...	...	...
Guildford	ESDF	124 567	61 520	63 047	271	...	...	...	...
Gwynedd	ESDF	117 775	57 195	60 580	2 548	...	...	...	...
Hackney[134]	ESDF	193 843	95 559	98 284	20	...	...	...	...
Halton	ESDF	123 038	60 479	62 559	74	...	...	...	...
Hammersmith & Fulham[134]	ESDF	156 718	74 635	82 083	16	...	...	...	...
Haringey[134]	ESDF	216 111	107 188	108 923	30	...	...	...	...
Harrogate	ESDF	147 635	70 360	77 275	1 333	...	...	...	...
Harrow[134]	ESDF	210 670	103 517	107 153	51	...	...	...	...
Havant & Waterloo	ESDF	117 341	56 816	60 525	55	...	...	...	...
Havering[134]	ESDF	230 909	113 300	117 609	118	...	...	...	...
Highland	ESDF	208 700	102 383	106 317	25 784	...	...	...	...
Hillingdon[134]	ESDF	247 718	122 684	125 034	110	...	...	...	...
Horsham	ESDF	118 569	58 198	60 371	530	...	...	...	...
Hounslow[134]	ESDF	205 798	102 875	102 923	58	...	...	...	...
Huntingdonshire	ESDF	152 742	75 372	77 370	923	...	...	...	...
Ipswich	ESDF	113 642	55 641	58 001	39	...	...	...	...
Isle of Wight	ESDF	125 466	60 464	65 002	380	...	...	...	...
Islington[134]	ESDF	175 990	85 525	90 465	15	...	...	...	...
Kensington & Chelsea[134]	ESDF	159 039	77 469	81 570	12	...	...	...	...
Kings Lynn & West Norfolk	ESDF	131 214	64 551	66 663	1 429	...	...	...	...
Kingston-upon-Hull	ESDF	266 775	132 393	134 382	71	...	...	...	...
Kingston-upon-Thames[134]	ESDF	141 837	69 980	71 857	38	...	...	...	...
Kirklees	ESDF	388 807	191 176	197 631	410	...	...	...	...
Knowsley	ESDF	154 053	74 838	79 215	97	...	...	...	...
Lambeth[134]	ESDF	264 727	129 763	134 964	27	...	...	...	...
Lancaster	ESDF	136 948	66 569	70 379	576	...	...	...	...
Leeds	ESDF	726 939	359 351	367 588	562	...	...	...	...
Leicester	ESDF	294 830	146 359	148 471	73	...	...	...	...
Lewisham[134]	ESDF	241 495	116 451	125 044	35	...	...	...	...
Lisburn	ESDF	108 400	...	...	447	...	...	...	...
Liverpool	ESDF	467 995	228 398	239 597	113	...	...	...	...
LONDON[138]	ESDF	7 074 265	3 474 931	3 599 334	1 578	...	...	...	...
Luton	ESDF	181 468	91 012	90 456	43	...	...	...	...
Macclesfield	ESDF	152 604	74 565	78 039	525	...	...	...	...
Maidstone	ESDF	140 664	69 243	71 421	393	...	...	...	...
Manchester	ESDF	430 818	212 530	218 288	116	...	...	...	...
Mansfield	ESDF	101 355	50 288	51 067	77	...	...	...	...
Merton[134]	ESDF	182 291	89 704	92 587	38	...	...	...	...
Mid Bedfordshire	ESDF	118 945	58 957	59 988	503	...	...	...	...
Mid Sussex	ESDF	125 329	61 787	63 542	333	...	...	...	...
Middlesborough	ESDF	146 778	71 871	74 907	54	...	...	...	...
Milton Keynes	ESDF	197 131	98 274	98 857	309	...	...	...	...
Neath Port Talbot	ESDF	139 459	68 064	71 395	442	...	...	...	...
Newark & Sherwood	ESDF	104 464	51 558	52 906	651	...	...	...	...
Newbury	ESDF	143 727	71 390	72 337	704	...	...	...	...
Newcastle-under-Lyme	ESDF	122 314	60 137	62 177	211	...	...	...	...
Newcastle-upon-Tyne	ESDF	282 338	138 883	143 455	112	...	...	...	...
Newham[134]	ESDF	228 857	114 740	114 117	36	...	...	...	...
New Forest	ESDF	169 513	82 041	87 472	753	...	...	...	...
Newport	ESDF	136 789	66 839	69 950	190	...	...	...	...
North Ayrshire	ESDF	139 520	67 163	72 357	884	...	...	...	...
North East Lincolnshire	ESDF	158 503	77 615	80 888	192	...	...	...	...
North Hertfordshire	ESDF	114 941	56 925	58 016	375	...	...	...	...
North Lanarkshire	ESDF	325 940	158 347	167 593	474	...	...	...	...

8. Population of capital cities and cities of 100 000 and more inhabitants: latest available year
Population des capitales et des villes de 100 000 habitants et plus: dernière année disponible (continued — suite)

(See notes at end of table. — Voir notes à la fin du tableau.)

Continent, country or area, date and city Continent, pays ou zone, date et ville	Code[1]	City proper — Ville proprement dite Population				Urban agglomeration — Agglomération urbaine Population			
		Both sexes Les deux sexes	Male Masculin	Female Féminin	Surface area Superficie (km²)	Both sexes Les deux sexes	Male Masculin	Female Féminin	Surface area Superficie (km²)
EUROPE									
United Kingdom — Royaume-Uni[133]									
1996									
North Lincolnshire	ESDF	152 767	75 457	77 310	838	...	...	...	...
North Somerset	ESDF	185 340	90 218	95 122	375	...	...	...	...
North Tyneside	ESDF	193 619	92 875	100 744	84	...	...	...	...
North Wiltshire	ESDF	121 747	60 947	60 800	768	...	...	...	...
Northampton	ESDF	192 382	94 840	97 542	81	...	...	...	...
Norwich	ESDF	126 221	61 878	64 343	39	...	...	...	...
Nottingham	ESDF	283 969	140 237	143 732	75	...	...	...	...
Nuneaton & Bedworth	ESDF	118 340	59 060	59 280	79	...	...	...	...
Oldham	ESDF	220 172	107 764	112 408	141	...	...	...	...
Oxford	ESDF	137 343	69 220	68 123	46	...	...	...	...
Pembrokeshire	ESDF	113 597	55 413	58 184	1 590	...	...	...	...
Perth & Kinross	ESDF	132 570	63 937	68 633	5 311	...	...	...	...
Peterborough	ESDF	158 674	79 264	79 410	333	...	...	...	...
Plymouth	ESDF	255 826	125 854	129 972	80	...	...	...	...
Poole	ESDF	139 226	67 391	71 835	65	...	...	...	...
Portsmouth	ESDF	190 370	97 010	93 360	40	...	...	...	...
Powys	ESDF	124 418	61 771	62 647	5 196	...	...	...	...
Preston	ESDF	134 818	67 195	67 623	142	...	...	...	...
Reading	ESDF	142 851	72 310	70 541	40	...	...	...	...
Redbridge[134]	ESDF	230 578	113 277	117 301	56	...	...	...	...
Redcar & Cleveland	ESDF	139 785	68 465	71 320	245	...	...	...	...
Reigate & Banstead	ESDF	119 307	58 576	60 731	129	...	...	...	...
Renfrewshire	ESDF	178 550	86 208	92 342	261	...	...	...	...
Rhondda, Cynon, Taff	ESDF	240 117	118 610	121 507	424	...	...	...	...
Richmond-upon-Thames[134]	ESDF	179 877	87 176	92 701	55	...	...	...	...
Rochdale	ESDF	207 563	101 884	105 679	160	...	...	...	...
Rochester-upon-Medway	ESDF	144 478	71 379	73 099	160	...	...	...	...
Rotherham	ESDF	255 342	126 360	128 982	283	...	...	...	...
Rushcliffe	ESDF	103 500	51 092	52 408	409	...	...	...	...
St. Albans	ESDF	130 267	64 373	65 894	161	...	...	...	...
St. Helens	ESDF	179 483	88 293	91 190	133	...	...	...	...
Salford	ESDF	229 179	113 589	115 590	97	...	...	...	...
Salisbury	ESDF	112 534	54 503	58 031	1 004	...	...	...	...
Sandwell	ESDF	292 196	143 434	148 762	86	...	...	...	...
Scarborough	ESDF	108 258	51 709	56 549	817	...	...	...	...
Scottish Borders	ESDF	106 100	51 101	54 999	4 734	...	...	...	...
Sedgemoor	ESDF	101 866	50 178	51 688	564	...	...	...	...
Sefton	ESDF	289 739	138 360	151 379	153	...	...	...	...
Sevenoaks	ESDF	110 476	53 984	56 492	368	...	...	...	...
Sheffield	ESDF	530 375	263 775	266 600	367	...	...	...	...
Slough	ESDF	110 462	54 664	55 798	27	...	...	...	...
Solihull	ESDF	203 922	99 688	104 234	179	...	...	...	...
South Ayrshire	ESDF	114 630	54 802	59 828	1 202	...	...	...	...
South Bedfordshire	ESDF	110 949	55 159	55 790	213	...	...	...	...
South Cambridgeshire	ESDF	128 422	63 498	64 924	902	...	...	...	...
South Gloucestershire	ESDF	235 129	117 579	117 550	497	...	...	...	...
South Lakeland	ESDF	100 889	48 658	52 231	1 554	...	...	...	...
South Lanarkshire	ESDF	307 450	148 701	158 749	1 771	...	...	...	...
South Kesteven	ESDF	119 951	58 374	61 577	943	...	...	...	...
South Norfolk	ESDF	105 778	52 113	53 665	908	...	...	...	...
South Oxfordshire	ESDF	124 637	61 467	63 170	679	...	...	...	...
South Ribble	ESDF	103 020	50 250	52 770	113	...	...	...	...
South Somerset	ESDF	150 710	73 645	77 065	959	...	...	...	...
South Staffordshire	ESDF	103 284	51 022	52 262	408	...	...	...	...
South Tyneside	ESDF	156 078	75 999	80 079	64	...	...	...	...
Southampton	ESDF	214 859	108 325	106 534	50	...	...	...	...
Southend-on-Sea	ESDF	172 266	82 911	89 355	42	...	...	...	...
Southwark[134]	ESDF	229 871	113 282	116 589	29	...	...	...	...

(See notes at end of table. — Voir notes à la fin du tableau.)

Continent, country or area, date and city / Continent, pays ou zone, date et ville	Code[1]	City proper — Ville proprement dite Population				Urban agglomeration — Agglomération urbaine Population			
		Both sexes Les deux sexes	Male Masculin	Female Féminin	Surface area Superficie (km²)	Both sexes Les deux sexes	Male Masculin	Female Féminin	Surface area Superficie (km²)
EUROPE									
United Kingdom — Royaume-Uni[133]									
1996									
Stafford	ESDF	124 531	61 660	62 871	599	...	...	...	...
Stockport	ESDF	291 080	141 315	149 765	126	...	...	...	...
Stockton-on-Tees	ESDF	179 009	88 068	90 941	204	...	...	...	...
Stoke-on-Trent	ESDF	254 438	126 133	128 305	93	...	...	...	...
Stratford-on-Avon	ESDF	111 211	54 170	57 041	977	...	...	...	...
Stroud	ESDF	108 022	53 091	54 931	461	...	...	...	...
Suffolk Coastal	ESDF	118 681	58 278	60 403	892	...	...	...	...
Sunderland	ESDF	294 261	143 574	150 687	138	...	...	...	...
Sutton[134]	ESDF	175 527	85 353	90 174	43	...	...	...	...
Swale	ESDF	117 562	58 744	58 818	373	...	...	...	...
Swansea	ESDF	230 180	112 876	117 304	378	...	...	...	...
Tameside	ESDF	220 722	109 005	111 717	103	...	...	...	...
Teignbridge	ESDF	116 743	56 289	60 454	674	...	...	...	...
Tendring	ESDF	132 265	62 860	69 405	337	...	...	...	...
Test Valley	ESDF	107 182	53 019	54 163	637	...	...	...	...
Thamesdown	ESDF	174 598	87 176	87 422	230	...	...	...	...
Thanet	ESDF	125 543	59 567	65 976	103	...	...	...	...
The Wrekin	ESDF	144 154	71 507	72 647	290	...	...	...	...
Thurrock	ESDF	132 283	65 807	66 476	164	...	...	...	...
Tonbridge & Malling	ESDF	104 991	52 141	52 850	240	...	...	...	...
Torbay	ESDF	123 413	57 936	65 477	63	...	...	...	...
Tower Hamlets[134]	ESDF	176 635	88 852	87 783	20	...	...	...	...
Trafford	ESDF	218 893	107 360	111 533	106	...	...	...	...
Tunbridge Wells	ESDF	102 616	49 544	53 072	332	...	...	...	...
Vale of Glamorgan	ESDF	119 358	58 142	61 216	335	...	...	...	...
Vale of White Horse	ESDF	112 545	56 987	55 558	579	...	...	...	...
Vale Royal	ESDF	115 233	56 748	58 485	380	...	...	...	...
Wakefield	ESDF	317 342	157 184	160 158	333	...	...	...	...
Walsall	ESDF	262 593	130 111	132 482	106	...	...	...	...
Waltham Forest[134]	ESDF	220 249	108 187	112 062	40	...	...	...	...
Wandsworth[134]	ESDF	266 169	129 106	137 063	35	...	...	...	...
Warrington	ESDF	189 012	93 732	95 280	176	...	...	...	...
Warwick	ESDF	122 506	60 228	62 278	282	...	...	...	...
Waveney	ESDF	107 731	52 025	55 706	370	...	...	...	...
Waverley	ESDF	114 133	55 348	58 785	345	...	...	...	...
Wealden	ESDF	138 030	65 888	72 142	836	...	...	...	...
West Lancashire	ESDF	109 763	54 031	55 732	338	...	...	...	...
West Lothian	ESDF	150 770	74 178	76 592	425	...	...	...	...
West Wiltshire	ESDF	108 889	53 732	55 157	517	...	...	...	...
Westminster[134]	ESDF	204 063	101 174	102 889	22	...	...	...	...
Wigan	ESDF	309 786	153 353	156 433	199	...	...	...	...
Winchester	ESDF	106 007	51 653	54 354	661	...	...	...	...
Windsor & Maidenhead	ESDF	141 548	70 387	71 161	198	...	...	...	...
Wirral	ESDF	329 179	157 640	171 539	159	...	...	...	...
Wokingham	ESDF	142 361	71 935	70 426	179	...	...	...	...
Wolverhampton	ESDF	244 453	120 455	123 998	69	...	...	...	...
Wrexham Maelor	ESDF	123 308	59 817	63 491	498	...	...	...	...
Wychavon	ESDF	108 009	52 849	55 160	664	...	...	...	...
Wycombe	ESDF	164 045	81 812	82 233	325	...	...	...	...
Wyre	ESDF	104 348	49 847	54 501	284	...	...	...	...
York	ESDF	175 095	85 359	89 736	271	...	...	...	...
OCEANIA — OCEANIE									
American Samoa — Samoa américaines[17]									
2000									
PAGO PAGO	CDFC	4 278	...	...	...	...	...	...	...

8. Population of capital cities and cities of 100 000 and more inhabitants: latest available year
Population des capitales et des villes de 100 000 habitants et plus: dernière année disponible (continued — suite)

(See notes at end of table. — Voir notes à la fin du tableau.)

Continent, country or area, date and city Continent, pays ou zone, date et ville	Code[1]	City proper — Ville proprement dite Population				Urban agglomeration — Agglomération urbaine Population			
		Both sexes Les deux sexes	Male Masculin	Female Féminin	Surface area Superficie (km²)	Both sexes Les deux sexes	Male Masculin	Female Féminin	Surface area Superficie (km²)
OCEANIA — OCEANIE									
Australia — Australie[139]									
2000									
Adelaide	ESDJ	...	...	...	...	1 095 924	537 147	558 777	1 826
Brisbane	ESDJ	...	...	...	...	1 627 076	804 837	822 239	4 703
Cairns	ESDJ	115 647	59 043	56 604	489	...	...	...	...
CANBERRA	ESDJ	310 675	154 712	155 963	808	350 275	174 648	175 627	2 789
Geelong	ESDJ	157 961	77 755	80 206	388	...	...	...	...
Gold Coast	ESDJ	404 385	199 273	205 112	1 235	...	...	...	...
Greater Wollongong	ESDJ	264 335	131 737	132 598	1 089	...	...	...	...
Hobart	ESDJ	...	...	...	...	194 197	94 448	99 749	1 358
Melbourne	ESDJ	...	...	...	...	3 466 707	1 710 831	1 755 876	7 694
Newcastle	ESDJ	483 219	239 330	243 889	4 042	...	...	...	...
Perth	ESDJ	...	...	...	...	1 380 982	687 099	693 883	5 386
Sunshine Coast	ESDJ	178 038	87 185	90 853	459	...	...	...	...
Sydney	ESDJ	...	...	...	...	4 084 971	2 030 159	2 054 812	12 144
Townsville	ESDJ	130 015	66 165	63 850	456	...	...	...	...
Cook Islands — Iles Cook									
2001									
RAROTONGA	CDFC	12 188	...	...	...	...	...	...	...
Fiji — Fidji									
1986									
SUVA	CDFC	69 665	34 660	35 005	...	141 273	70 408	70 865	...
1996									
SUVA	CDFC	77 366	38 518	38 848	...	167 975	83 910	84 065	...
French Polynesia — Polynésie francaise									
1996									
PAPEETE	CDFC	25 553	...	...	...	113 412	...	...	...
2002									
PAPEETE	CDFC	26 181	...	...	...	124 864	...	...	...
Guam[17]									
1990									
AGANA	CDJC	1 139	...	...	3	40 877	...	...	...
Kiribati									
2000									
TARAWA	CDFC	...	...	...	...	36 717	...	...	...
Marshall Islands — Iles Marshall									
1980									
MAJURO	CDFC	11 791	...	...	...	...	...	...	...
1988									
MAJURO	CDFC	19 664	...	...	...	...	...	...	...
1999									
MAJURO	CDFC	23 676	12 075	11 601	...	...	...	...	...
Micronesia, Federated States of — Micronésie, États fédérés de									
1989									
PALIKIR	CDJC	5 399	...	...	...	...	...	...	...
1994									
PALIKIR	CDJC	5 773	...	...	...	...	...	...	...
2000									
PALIKIR	CDJC	6 227	...	...	...	...	...	...	...
Nauru									
1983									
YAREN	CDFC	559	...	...	...	...	...	...	...
1992									
YAREN	CDFC	672	...	...	...	...	...	...	...
New Caledonia — Nouvelle-Calédonie									
1996									
NOUMEA	CDFC	76 293	38 443	37 850	46	118 823	60 327	58 496	1 643

8. Population of capital cities and cities of 100 000 and more inhabitants: latest available year
Population des capitales et des villes de 100 000 habitants et plus: dernière année disponible (continued — suite)

(See notes at end of table. — Voir notes à la fin du tableau.)

Continent, country or area, date and city Continent, pays ou zone, date et ville	Code[1]	City proper — Ville proprement dite Population				Urban agglomeration — Agglomération urbaine Population			
		Both sexes Les deux sexes	Male Masculin	Female Féminin	Surface area Superficie (km²)	Both sexes Les deux sexes	Male Masculin	Female Féminin	Surface area Superficie (km²)
OCEANIA — OCEANIE									
New Zealand — Nouvelle-Zélande									
2000									
Auckland	ESDJ	386 100	...	...	75	1 105 700	...	...	...
Christchurch	ESDJ	324 800	...	...	106	342 000	...	...	...
Dunedin	ESDJ	119 200	...	...	...	111 700	...	...	...
Hamilton	ESDJ	118 100	...	...	...	170 900	...	...	...
Manukau[140]	ESDJ	286 800	...	...	566	...	...	...	...
Napier-Hastings	ESDJ	...	...	...	...	114 500	...	...	...
Northshore	ESDJ	189 700	...	...	...	...	...	...	...
Waitakere	ESDJ	174 100	...	...	376	...	...	...	...
WELLINGTON	ESDJ	167 400	...	...	263	346 500	...	...	...
Niue — Nioué									
1981									
ALOFI	CDFC	986	...	...	...	...	...	...	...
1991									
ALOFI	CDFC	682	...	...	...	...	...	...	...
2001									
ALOFI	CDFC	615	...	...	...	...	...	...	...
Northern Mariana Islands — Iles Mariannes du Nord									
1980									
GARAPAN	CDFC	2 063	...	...	...	...	...	...	...
1990									
GARAPAN	CDFC	3 904	...	...	...	...	...	...	...
2000									
GARAPAN	CDFC	3 588	...	...	...	...	...	...	...
Palau — Palaos									
1990									
KOROR	CDFC	9 018	...	...	...	...	...	...	...
2000									
KOROR	CDFC	10 600	...	...	...	...	...	...	...
Papua New Guinea — Papouasie-Nouvelle-Guinée									
1990									
PORT MORESBY	CDFC	195 570	...	...	...	...	...	...	...
2000									
PORT MORESBY	CDFC	254 158	138 974	115 184	...	...	...	...	...
Pitcairn									
1993									
ADAMSTOWN	CDFC	53	...	...	5	...	...	...	...
Samoa									
1981									
APIA	CDFC	33 170	...	...	...	...	...	...	...
1991									
APIA	CDFC	34 126	...	...	...	...	...	...	...
2001									
APIA	CDFC	38 836	...	...	...	...	...	...	...
Solomon Islands — Iles Salomon									
1999									
HONIARA	CDFC	49 107	...	...	...	...	...	...	...
Tonga									
2000									
NUKU'ALOFA	ESDF	21 538	10 625	10 913	...	30 336	15 115	15 221	...
Tuvalu									
1985									
FUNAFUTI	CDFC	2 810	...	...	...	...	...	...	...
1991									
FUNAFUTI	CDFC	3 839	...	...	...	...	...	...	...

8. Population of capital cities and cities of 100 000 and more inhabitants: latest available year
Population des capitales et des villes de 100 000 habitants et plus: dernière année disponible (continued — suite)

(See notes at end of table. — Voir notes à la fin du tableau.)

Continent, country or area, date and city / Continent, pays ou zone, date et ville	Code[1]	City proper — Ville proprement dite Population				Urban agglomeration — Agglomération urbaine Population			
		Both sexes Les deux sexes	Male Masculin	Female Féminin	Surface area Superficie (km²)	Both sexes Les deux sexes	Male Masculin	Female Féminin	Surface area Superficie (km²)
OCEANIA — OCEANIE									
Vanuatu									
1999									
PORT VILA	CDFC	29 356	...	...	...	...	...	...	...
Wallis and Futuna Islands — Iles Wallis et Futuna									
1990									
META-UTU	CDFC	1 222	...	...	...	...	...	...	...
1996									
META-UTU	CDFC	1 137	...	...	...	...	...	...	...

GENERAL NOTES - NOTES GENERALES

The capital city of each country is shown in capital letters. Figures in italics are estimates of questionable reliability. For definition of city proper and urban agglomeration, method of evaluation and limitations of data see Technical Notes for this table. — Le nom de la capitale de chaque pays est imprimé en majuscules. Les chiffres en italiques sont des estimations de qualité douteuse. Pour la définition de la ville proprement dite et de l'agglomération urbaine, et pour les méthodes d'évaluation et les insuffisances des données voir Notes techniques pour ce tableau.

FOOTNOTES - NOTES

[1] 'Code' indicates the source of data, as follows:
CDFC - Census, de facto, complete tabulation
CDFS - Census, de facto, sample tabulation
CDJC - Census, de jure, complete tabulation
CDJS - Census, de jure, sample tabulation
SSDF - Sample survey, de facto
SSDJ - Sample survey, de jure
ESDF - Estimates, de facto
ESDJ - Estimates, de jure
Le 'Code' indique la source des données, comme suit:
CDFC - Recensement, population de fait, tabulation complète
CDFS - Recensement, population de fait, tabulation par sondage
CDJC - Recensement, population de droit, tabulation complète
CDJS - Recensement, population de droit, tabulation par sondage
SSDF - Enquête par sondage, population de fait
SSDJ - Enquête par sondage, population de droit
ESDF - Données estimatées, population de fait
ESDJ - Données estimatées, population de droit
[2] Data for urban agglomeration includes Kombo St. Mary. — Les données relatives à l'agglomération urbaine se rapportent à Kombo St. Mary.
[3] Data for urban agglomeration refer to 'Accra-Tema Metropolitan area'. — Les données relatives à l'agglomération urbaine se rapportent à la 'zone métropolitaine d'Accra-Tema'.
[4] Data for urban agglomeration refer to the Sekondi-Takoradi Municipal Council. Including Sekondi (population 31 916) and Takoradi (population 61 484). — Les données concernant l'agglomération urbaine se rapportent au Conseil municipal de Sekondi-Takoradi. Y compris Sekondi (31 916 personnes) et Takoradi (61 484 personnes).
[5] Dual capitals. — Le pays a deux capitales.
[6] For the urban commune of Antananarivo. — Pour la commune urbaine de Antananarivo.
[7] Including Salé and Temara. — Y compris Salé et Temara.
[8] Data for cities proper refer to communes. — Les données pour les villes se réfèrent aux communes.
[9] For communes which may contain rural areas as well as urban centre. — Commune(s) pouvant comprendre un centre urbain et une zone rurale.

[10] Included in urban agglomeration of Dakar. — Comprise dans l'agglomération urbaine de Dakar.
[11] Pretoria is the administrative capital, Cape Town the legislative capital. — Pretoria est la capitale administrative, Le Cap la capitale législative.
[12] Excluding persons residing in institutions. — Non compris les personnes dans les institutions.
[13] Due to random rounding technique figures for males and females do not add up to the total. — La somme des données pour hommes et femmes ne correspond pas au total grâce a la technique de l'arrondissement aléatoire.
[14] Data for urban agglomeration refer to 'metropolitan area', comprising central of San José (including San José city) cantones Curridabat, Escazu, Montes de Oca, Tibas and parts of cantones of Alajuelita, Desamparados, Goicoechea and Moravia. — Les données pour l'agglomération urbaine se rapportent à la 'zone métropolitaine' comprenant le canton central de San José (et la ville de San José), les cantons de Curridabat, Escazu, Montes de Oca et Tibas et certaines parties des cantons de Alajuelita, Desamparados, Goicoechea et Moravia.
[15] For municipalities which may contain an urban centre as well as a rural area. — Pour municipios qui peuvent comprendre un centre urbain et aussi une zone rurale.
[16] Including municipalities of Bella Vista, Betania, Calidonia, Curundu, El Chorillo, Juan Diaz, Parque Lefevre, Pedregal, Pueblo Nuevo, Rio Abajo, San Felipe, San Francisco and Santa Ana. — Y compris les corregimientos de Bella Vista, Betania, Calidonia, Curundu, El Chorillo, Juan Diaz, Parque Lefevre, Pedregal, Pueblo Nuevo, Rio Abajo, San Felipe, San Francisco et Santa Ana.
[17] Including armed forces stationed in the area. — Y compris les militaires en garnison sur le territoire.
[18] Data for urban agglomeration refer to 'standard metropolitan area' comprised of municipality of Ponce, which includes Ponce proper. — Les données relatives à l'agglomération urbaine se rapportent à la 'zone métropolitaine officielle' qui comprend la municipalité de Ponce, comprenant Ponce proprement dite.
[19] Data for urban agglomeration refer to 'metropolitan statistical area', comprising municipalities of San Juan, Caguas, Carolina, Catano, Guaynabo, Rio Piedras and Trujillo Alto. — Les données concernant l'agglomération urbaine se rapportent à la 'zone métropolitaine statistique' qui comprend les municipios de San Juan, Caguas, Carolina, Catano, Guaynabo, Rio Piedras et Trujillo Alto.
[20] Excluding armed forces overseas and civilian citizens absent from country for extended period of time. — Non compris les militaires à l'étranger et les civils hors du pays pendant une période prolongée.
[21] Included in urban agglomeration of Cleveland. — Comprise dans l'agglomération urbaine de Cleveland.
[22] Included in urban agglomeration of Washington, D.C. — Comprise dans l'agglomération urbaine de Washington, D.C.
[23] Data for urban agglomeration refer to Allentown-Bethlehem-Easton, Pennsylvania-New Jersey 'metropolitan statistical area'. — Les données pour l'agglomération urbaine se rapportent à la 'zone métropolitaine statistique' d'Allentown-Bethlehem-Easton (Pennsylvania-New Jersey).
[24] Included in urban agglomeration of Los Angeles. — Comprise dans l'agglomération urbaine de Los Angeles.

25 Included in urban agglomeration of Detroit. — Comprise dans
l'agglomération urbaine de Detroit.
26 Included in urban agglomeration of Dallas. — Comprise dans
l'agglomération urbaine de Dallas.
27 Included in urban agglomeration of Denver. — Comprise dans
l'agglomération urbaine de Denver.
28 Included in urban agglomeration of Chicago. — Comprise dans
l'agglomération urbaine de Chicago.
29 Data for urban agglomeration refer to Beaumont-Port Arthur, Texas
'metropolitan statistical area'. — Les données pour l'agglomération urbaine
se rapportent à la 'zone métropolitaine statistique' de Beaumont-Port Arthur
(Texas).
30 Included in urban agglomeration of San Francisco. — Comprise dans
l'agglomération urbaine de San Francisco.
31 Data for urban agglomeration refer to Boston-Worcester-Lawrence
'consolidated metropolitan statistical area', comprising 'metropolitan
statistical area' of Boston, Brockton, Fitchburg-Leominster, Lawrence, Lowell,
Manchester, Nashua, New Bedford, Portsmouth-Gloucester and Worcester.
— Les données pour l'agglomération urbaine se rapportent à la 'zone
métropolitaine statistique unifiée' de Boston-Worcester-Lawrence,
comprenant la 'zone métropolitaine statistique' de Boston, de Brockton, de
Fitchburg-Leominster, de Lawrence, de Lowwell, Manchester, Nashua, New
Bedford, Portsmouth-Rochester et Worcester.
32 Included in urban agglomeration of New York. — Comprise dans
l'agglomération urbaine de New York.
33 Data for urban agglomeration refer to Brownsville-Harlingen-San Benito,
Texas 'metropolitan statistical area'. — Les données pour l'agglomération
urbaine se rapportent à la 'zone métropolitaine statistique' de
Brownsville-Harlingen-San Benito (Texas).
34 Data for urban agglomeration refer to Buffalo-Niagara Falls
'consolidated metropolitan statistical area', comprising 'metropolitan
statistical area' of Buffalo and Niagara Falls. — Les données pour
l'agglomération urbaine se rapportent à la 'zone métropolitaine statistique
unifiée' de Buffalo-Niagara Falls, comprenant la 'zone métropolitaine
statistique' de Buffalo et Niagara Falls.
35 Data for urban agglomeration refer to Charlotte-Gastonia-Rock Hill
'metropolitan statistical area'. — Les données pour l'agglomération urbaine
se rapportent à la 'zone métropolitaine statistique' de
Charlotte-Gastonia-Rock Hill.
36 Included in urban agglomeration of Norfolk. — Comprise dans
l'agglomération urbaine de Norfolk.
37 Data for urban agglomeration refer to Chicago-Gary-Kenosha
'consolidated metropolitan statistical area', comprising 'metropolitan
statistical area' of Chicago, Gary, Kankakee and Kenosha. — Les données
pour l'agglomération urbaine se rapportent à la 'zone métropolitaine
statistique unifiée' de Chicago-Gary-Kenosha, comprenant la 'zone
métropolitaine statistique' de Chicago, de Gary, de Kankakee et de Kenosha.
38 Included in urban agglomeration of San Diego. — Comprise dans
l'agglomération urbaine de San Diego.
39 Data for urban agglomeration refer to Cincinnati-Hamilton 'consolidated
metropolitan statistical area', comprising 'metropolitan statistical area' of
Cincinnati and Hamilton-Middletown. — Les données pour l'agglomération
urbaine se rapportent à la 'zone métropolitaine statistique unifiée' de
Cincinnati comprenant la 'zone métropolitaine statistique' de Cincinnati et de
Hamilton-Middletown.
40 Data for urban agglomeration refer to Clarksville-Hopkinsville
'metropolitan statistical area'. — Les données pour l'agglomération urbaine
se rapportent à la 'zone métropolitaine statistique' de Clarksville-Hopkinsville.
41 Included in urban agglomeration of Tampa. — Comprise dans
l'agglomération urbaine de Tampa.
42 Data for urban agglomeration refer to Cleveland-Akron 'consolidated
metropolitan statistical area', comprising 'metropolitan statistical area' of
Akron and Cleveland-Lorain-Elyria. — Les données pour l'agglomération
urbaine se rapportent à la 'zone métropolitaine statistique unifiée' de
Cleveland-Akron comprenant la 'zone métropolitaine statistique' de Akron et
de Cleveland-Lorain-Elyria.
43 Data for urban agglomeration refer to Dallas-Fort Worth 'consolidated
metropolitan statistical area', comprising 'metropolitan statistical area' of
Dallas and Fort Worth-Arlington. — Les données pour l'agglomération
urbaine se rapportent à la 'zone métropolitaine statistique unifiée' de
Dallas-Fort Worth, comprenant la 'zone métropolitaine statistique' de Dallas
et de Fort Worth-Arlington.
44 Data for urban agglomeration refer to Dayton-Springfield 'metropolitan
statistical area'. — Les données pour l'agglomération urbaine se rapportent à
la 'zone métropolitaine statistique' de Dayton-Springfield.
45 Data for urban agglomeration refer to Denver-Boulder-Greeley
'consolidated metropolitan statistical area', comprising 'metropolitan
statistical area' of Boulder-Longmont, Denver and Greeley. — Les données
pour l'agglomération urbaine se rapportent à la 'zone métropolitaine
statistique unifiée' de Denver-Boulder-Greeley, comprenant la 'zone
métropolitaine statistique' de Boulder-Longmont, de Denver et de Greeley.
46 Data for urban agglomeration refer to Detroit-Ann Arbor-Flint

'consolidated metropolitan statistical area', comprising 'metropolitan
statistical area' of Detroit, Ann Arbor and Flint. — Les données pour
l'agglomération urbaine se rapportent à la 'zone métropolitaine statistique
unifiée' de Detroit-Ann Arbor- Flint comprenant la 'zone métropolitaine
statistique' de Detroit, de Ann Arbor et de Flint.
47 Included in urban agglomeration of Raleigh. — Comprise dans
l'agglomération urbaine de Raleigh.
48 Data for urban agglomeration refer to Eugene-Springfield 'metropolitan
statistical area'. — Les données pour l'agglomération urbaine se rapportent à
la 'zone métropolitaine statistique' d'Eugene-Springfield.
49 Data for urban agglomeration refer to Fort Collins-Loveland
'metropolitan statistical area'. — Les données pour l'agglomération urbaine
se rapportent à la 'zone métropolitaine statistique' de Fort Collins-Loveland.
50 Included in urban agglomeration of Miami. — Comprise dans
l'agglomération urbaine de Miami.
51 Included in urban agglomeration of Phoenix. — Comprise dans
l'agglomération urbaine de Phoenix.
52 Data for urban agglomeration refer to Greensboro-Winston-Salem-High
Point, North Carolina 'metropolitan statistical area'. — Les données pour
l'agglomération urbaine se rapportent à la 'zone métropolitaine statistique' de
Greensboro-Winston-Salem-High Point (Caroline du Nord).
53 Data for urban agglomeration refer to Hartford 'consolidated
metropolitan statistical area', comprising 'metropolitan statistical area' of
Hartford. — Les données pour l'agglomération urbaine se rapportent à la
'zone métropolitaine statistique unifiée' de Hartford, comprenant la 'zone
métropolitaine statistique' de Hartford.
54 Data for urban agglomeration refer to Houston-Galveston-Brazoria
'consolidated metropolitan statistical area', comprising 'metropolitan
statistical area' of Houston, Galveston-Texas City and Brazoria. — Les
données pour l'agglomération urbaine se rapportent à la 'zone métropolitaine
statistique unifiée' de Houston-Galveston-Brazoria, comprenant la 'zone
métropolitaine statistique' de Houston, de Galveston-Texas City et de
Brazoria.
55 Included in urban agglomeration of Kansas City, Mo. — Comprise dans
l'agglomération urbaine de Kansas City (Mo.).
56 Data for urban agglomeration refer to Lansing-East Lansing
'metropolitan statistical area'. — Les données pour l'agglomération urbaine
se rapportent à la 'zone métropolitaine statistique' de Lansing-East Lansing.
57 Data for urban agglomeration refer to Little Rock-North Little Rock
'metropolitan statistical area'. — Les données pour l'agglomération urbaine
se rapportent à la 'zone métropolitaine statistique' de Little Rock-North Little
Rock (Arkansas).
58 Data for urban agglomeration refer to Los Angeles-Riverside-Orange
County 'consolidated metropolitan statistical area' of Los Angeles-Long
Beach, Orange County, Ventura and Riverside-San Bernardino. — Les
données pour l'agglomération urbaine se rapportent à la 'zone métropolitaine
statistique unifiée' de Los Angeles-Riverside-Orange County comprenant la
'zone métropolitaine statistique' de Los Angeles-Long Beach, de Orange
County, de Ventura et de Riverside-San Bernardino.
59 Data for urban agglomeration refer to Miami-Fort Lauderdale
'consolidated metropolitan statistical area', comprising 'metropolitan
statistical area' of Miami and Fort Lauderdale. — Les données pour
l'agglomération urbaine se rapportent à la 'zone métropolitaine statistique
unifiée' de Miami-Fort Lauderdale, comprenant la 'zone métropolitaine
statistique' de Miami et de Fort Lauderdale.
60 Data for urban agglomeration refer to Milwaukee-Racine 'consolidated
metropolitan statistical area', comprising 'metropolitan statistical area' of
Milwaukee-Waukesha and Racine. — Les données pour l'agglomération
urbaine se rapportent à la 'zone métropolitaine statistique unifiée' de
Milwaukee-Racine, comprenant la 'zone métropolitaine statistique' de
Milwaukee-Waukesha et de Racine.
61 Data for urban agglomeration refer to Minneapolis-St. Paul, Minnesota
'metropolitan statistical area'. — Les données pour l'agglomération urbaine
se rapportent à la 'zone métropolitaine statistique' de Minneapolis-St. Paul
(Minnesota).
62 Data for urban agglomeration refer to New York-Northern New
Jersey-Long Island 'consolidated metropolitan statistical area', comprising
'metropolitan statistical area' of New York, Bergen-Passaic, Bridgeport,
Danbury, Jersey City, Dutchess County, New Haven-Meriden,
Middlesex-Somerset-Hunterdon, Monmouth-Ocean, Newburgh,
Nassau-Suffolk, Newark, Stamford-Norwalk, Trenton and Waterbury. — Les
données pour l'agglomération urbaine se rapportent à la 'zone métropolitaine
statistique unifiée' de New York-New Jersey-Long Island, comprenant la
'zone métropolitaine statistique' de New York, de Bergen-Passaic, de
Bridgeport, de Danbury, de Jersey City, de Dutchess County, de New
Haven-Meriden, Dutchess County, de New Haven-Meriden, de
Middlesex-Somerset-Hunterdon, de Monmouth-Ocean, de Nassau-Suffolk,
de Trenton, de Newark, de Waterbury, de Newburgh et de
Stamford-Norwalk.
63 Data for urban agglomeration refer to Norfolk-Virginia Beach-Newport
News 'metropolitan statistical area'. — Les données pour l'agglomération

urbaine se rapportent à la 'zone métropolitaine statistique' de Norfolk-Virginia Beach-Newport News.

[64] Included in urban agglomeration of Houston. — Comprise dans l'agglomération urbaine de Houston.

[65] Data for urban agglomeration refer to Philadephia-Wilmington-Atlantic City 'consolidated metropolitan statistical area', comprising 'metropolitan statistical area' of Philadelphia, Atlantic-Cape May, Wilmington-Newark and Vineland-Milville-Bridgeton. — Les données pour l'agglomération urbaine se rapportent à la 'zone métropolitaine statistique unifiée' de Philadelphie-Wilmington-Trenton, comprenant la 'zone métropolitaine statistique' de Philadelphie, de Wilmington, Del.-N.J.-Md., Atlantic-Cape May, de Wilmington-Newark et de Vineland-Milville-Bridgeton.

[66] Data for urban agglomeration refer to Phoenix-Mesa 'metropolitan statistical area'. — Les données pour l'agglomération urbaine se rapportent à la 'zone métropolitaine statistique' de Phoenix-Mesa.

[67] Data for urban agglomeration refer to Portland-Salem 'consolidated metropolitan statistical area', comprising 'standard metropolitan statistical area' of Portland-Vancouver and Salem. — Les données pour l'agglomération urbaine se rapportent à la 'zone métropolitaine statistique unifiée' de Portland-Salem, comprenant la 'zone métropolitaine statistique' de Portland-Vancouver et de Salem.

[68] Data for urban agglomeration refer to Providence-Fall River-Warwick 'consolidated metropolitan statistical area', comprising 'metropolitan statistical area' of Fall River Warwick and Providence. — Les données pour l'agglomération urbaine se rapportent à la 'zone métropolitaine statistique unifiée' de Providence-Fall River-Warwick, comprenant la 'zone métropolitaine statistique' de Fall River de Warwick et de Providence.

[69] Data for urban agglomeration refer to Provo-Orem, Utah 'metropolitan statistical area'. — Les données pour l'agglomération urbaine se rapportent à la 'zone métropolitaine statistique' de Provo-Orem (Utah).

[70] Data for urban agglomeration refer to Raleigh-Durham-Chapel Hill 'metropolitan statistical area'. — Les données pour l'agglomération urbaine se rapportent à la 'zone métropolitaine statistique' de Raleigh-Durham-Chapel Hill.

[71] Data for urban agglomeration refer to Richmond-Petersburg 'metropolitan statistical area'. — Les données pour l'agglomération urbaine se rapportent à la 'zone métropolitaine statistique' de Richmond-Petersburg.

[72] Data for urban agglomeration refer to Sacramento-Yolo 'consolidated metropolitan statistical area', comprising 'metropolitan statistical area' of Sacramento and Yolo. — Les données pour l'agglomération urbaine se rapportent à la 'zone métropolitaine statistique unifiée' de Sacramento-Yolo, comprenant la 'zone métropolitaine statistique' de Sacramento et Yolo.

[73] Included in urban agglomeration of Minneapolis. — Comprise dans l'agglomération urbaine de Minneapolis.

[74] Included in urban agglomeration of Portland. — Comprise dans l'agglomération urbaine de Portland.

[75] Data for urban agglomeration refer to Salinas, California 'metropolitan statistical area'. — Les données pour l'agglomération urbaine se rapportent à la 'zone métropolitaine statistique' de Salinas (Californie).

[76] Data for urban agglomeration refer to Salt Lake City-Ogden 'metropolitan statistical area'. — Les données pour l'agglomération urbaine se rapportent à la 'zone métropolitaine statistique' de Salt Lake City-Ogden.

[77] Data for urban agglomeration refer to San Francisco-Oakland-San Jose 'consolidated metropolitan statistical area', comprising 'metropolitan statistical area' of Oakland, San Francisco, San Jose, Santa Cruz-Watsonville, Santa Rosa and Vallejo-Fairfield-Napa. — Les données pour l'agglomération urbaine se rapportent à la 'zone métropolitaine statistique unifiée' de San Francisco-Oakland-San José, comprenant la 'zone métropolitaine statistique' de Oakland, de San Francisco, de San José, de Santa Cruz-Watsonville de Santa Rosa et de Vallejo-Fairfield-Napa.

[78] Data for urban agglomeration refer to Seattle-Tacoma-Bremerton 'consolidated metropolitan statistical area', comprising 'metropolitan statistical area' of Bremerton, Olympia, Seattle-Bellevue-Everett and Tacoma. — Les données pour l'agglomération urbaine se rapportent à la 'zone métropolitaine statistique unifiée' de Seattle-Tacoma-Bremerton comprenant la 'zone métropolitaine statistique' de Bremerton, de Olympia, de Seattle-Bellevue-Everett, et de Tacoma.

[79] Data for urban agglomeration refer to South Bend-Mishawaka 'metropolitan statistical area'. — Les données pour l'agglomération urbaine se rapportent à la 'zone métropolitaine statistique' de South Bend-Mishawaka.

[80] Included in urban agglomeration of Seattle. — Comprise dans l'agglomération urbaine de Seattle.

[81] Data for urban agglomeration refer to Tampa-St. Petersburg-Clearwater, Florida 'metropolitan statistical area'. — Les données pour l'agglomération urbaine se rapportent à la 'zone métropolitaine statistique' de Tampa-St. Petersburg-Clearwater (Florida).

[82] Data for urban agglomeration refer to Washington-Baltimore 'consolidated metropolitan statistical area'. — Les données pour l'agglomération urbaine se rapportent à la 'zone métropolitaine statistique unifiée' de Washington-Baltimore.

[83] Included in urban agglomeration of Greensboro. — Comprise dans

l'agglomération urbaine de Greensboro.

[84] Included in urban agglomeration of Boston. — Comprise dans l'agglomération urbaine de Boston.

[85] La Paz is the actual capital and the seat of the Government but Sucre is the legal capital and the seat of the judiciary. — La Paz est la capitale effective et le siège du gouvernement, mais Sucre est la capitale constitutionnelle et le siège du pouvoir judiciaire.

[86] 'Metropolitan area' Gran Santiago. — 'Zone métropolitaine' Grand Santiago.

[87] Data for urban agglomeration refer to 'metropolitan area', comprising Asuncion proper and localities of Trinidad, Zeballos Cué, Campo Grande and Lamboré. — Les données pour l'agglomération urbaine se rapportent à la 'zone métropolitaine' comprenant la ville d'Asuncion proprement dite et les localités de Trinidad, Zeballos Cué, Campo Grande et Lamboré.

[88] Data for urban agglomeration refer to 'metropolitan area' Gran Lima. — Les données pour l'agglomération urbaine se rapportent à la 'zone métropolitaine' Grand Lima.

[89] Data for urban agglomeration refer to 'metropolitan area', comprising Caracas proper (the urban parishes of Department of Libertador) and a part of district of Sucre in State of Miranda. — Les données pour l'agglomération urbaine se rapportent à la 'zone métropolitaine', comprenant la ville de Caracas proprement dite (paroisses urbaines du département du Libertador) et une partie du district de Sucre dans l'Etat de Miranda.

[90] For municipalities which may contain rural area as well as urban centre. — Pour les municipalités qui peuvent comprendre un centre urbaine et une zone rurale.

[91] Lefkosia urban agglomeration is composed of Lefkosia municipality, Agios Dometios, Egkomi, Strovolos, Aglangia, Lakatameia, Anthoupoli, Latsia and Geri. — L'agglomération urbaine de Lefkosia se comprend de la municipalité de Lefkosia et Agios Dometios, Egkomi, Strovolos, Aglangia, Lakatameia, Anthoupoli, Latsia et Geri.

[92] Lemesos urban agglomeration is composed of Lemesos municipality, Mesa Geitonia, Agios Athanasios, Germasogeia, Pano Polemidia, Ypsonas, Kato Polemidia, and parts of Mouttagiaka, Agios Tychon, Parekklisia, Monagrouli, Moni, Pyrgos and Tserkezoi. — L'agglomération urbaine de Lemesos se comprend de la municipalité de Lemesos et Mesa Geitonia, Agios Athanasios, Germasogeia, Pano Polemidia, Ypsonas, Kato Polemidia, et certaines parties des Mouttagiaka, Agios Tychon, Parekklisia, Monagrouli, Moni, Pyrgos et Tserkezoi.

[93] Including data for the India-held part of Jammu and Kashmir, the final status of which has not yet been determined. Excluding cities for Assam state. — Y compris les données concernant la partie de Jammu-et-Cachemire occupée par l'Inde, dont le statut définitif n'a pas encore été déterminé. Non compris les villes de l'état d'Assam.

[94] Data for urban agglomeration includes New Delhi. — Les données pour l'agglomération urbaine y compris New Delhi.

[95] Data for urban agglomeration include Bally, Baranagar, Barrackpur, Bhatpara, Calcutta Municipal Corporation, Chandan Nagar, Garden Reach, Houghly-Chinsura, Howrah, Jadarpur, Kamarhati, Naihati, Panihati, Serampore, South Dum Dum, South Suburban, and Titagarh. — Les données pour l'agglomération urbaine y compris Bally, Baranagar, Barrackpur, Bhatpara, Calcutta Municipal Corporation, Chandan Nagar, Garden Reach, Houghly Chinsura, Howrah, Jadarpur, Kamarhati, Naihati, Panihati, Serampore, South Dum Dum, South Suburban et Titagarh.

[96] Included in urban agglomeration of Delhi. — Comprise dans l'agglomération urbaine de Delhi.

[97] Data refer to the New Delhi Municipal Council. — Les données se rapportent au New Delhi Municipal Council.

[98] Including Karkh, Rassaiah, Adhamiya and Kadhimain Qadha Centres and Maamoon, Mansour and Karradah-Sharqiyah Nahlyas. — Y compris les cazas de Karkh, Adhamiya et Kadhimain ainsi que les nahiyas de Maamoon, Mansour et Karradah-Sharqiyah.

[99] Designation and data provided by Israel. The position of the United Nations on the question of Jerusalem is contained in General Assembly resolution 181 (II) and subsequent resolutions of the General Assembly and the Security Council concerning this question. — Appelation de données fournies par Israel. La position des Nations Unies concernant la question de Jérusalem est décrite dans la resolution 181 (II) de l'Assemblée générale et résolutions ultérieures de l'Assemblée générale et du Conseil de sécurité sur cette question.

[100] Including East Jerusalem. — Y compris Jérusalem-Est.

[101] Excluding diplomatic personnel outside country and foreign military and civilian personnel and their dependants stationed in the area. — Non compris le personnel diplomatique hors du territoire, les militaires et agents civils étrangers en poste sur le territoire et les membres de leur famille les accompagnant.

[102] Except for Tokyo, all data refer to shi, a minor division which may include some scattered or rural population as well as an urban centre. — Sauf pour Tokyo, toutes les données se rapportent à des shi, petites divisions administratives qui peuvent comprendre des peuplements dispersés ou ruraux en plus d'un centre urbain.

[103] Data excluding Hokkaido region. — Non compris la region de Hokkaido.

[104] Including Kokura, Moji, Tobata, Wakamatsu and Yahata (Yawata). — Y compris Kokura, Moji, Tobata, Wakamatsu et Yahata (Yawata).

[105] Data for city proper refer to 23 wards (ku) of the old city. The urban agglomeration figures refer to Tokyo-to (Tokyo Prefecture), comprising the 23 wards plus 14 urban counties (shi), 18 towns (machi) and 8 villages (mura). The 'Tokyo Metropolitan Area' comprises the 23 wards of Tokyo-to plus 21 cities, 20 towns and 2 villages. The 'Keihin Metropolitan Area' (Tokyo-Yokohama Metropolitan Area) plus 9 cities (one of which is Yokohama City) and two towns, with a total population of 20 485 542 on 1 October 1965. — Les données concernant la ville proprement dite se rapportent aux 23 circonscriptions de la vieille ville. Les chiffres pour l'agglomération urbaine se rapportent à Tokyo-to (préfecture de Tokyo), comprenant les 23 circonscriptions plus 14 cantons urbains (Shi), 18 villes (machi) et 8 villages (mura). La 'zone métropolitaine de Tokyo' comprend les 23 circonscriptions de Tokyo-to plus 21 municipalités, 20 villes et 2 villages. La 'zone métropolitaine de Keihin' (zone métropolitaine de Tokyo-Yokohama) comprend la zone métropolitaine de Tokyo, plus 9 municipalités, dont l'une est Yokohama et 2 villes, elle comptait 20 485 542 habitants au 1er octobre 1965.

[106] Excluding data for the Pakistan-held part of Jammu and Kashmir, the final status of which has not yet been determined, and for Junagardh, Manavadar, Gilgit and Baltistan. — Non compris les données pour la partie de Jammu-Cachemire occupée par le Pakistan dont le status definitif n'a pas encore été déterminé, et le Junagardh, le Manavadar, le Gilgit et le Baltistan.

[107] City defined as a main municipality, a province centre or a district centre. A main municipality consists of city portions of more than one district, each of which having its own municipality. — La ville est définie comme une municipalité principale, la capitale de la province ou le centre d'un district. Une municipalité principale se comprennent des parts d'une ville qui sont fais des plusieurs districts, et chacun a son municipalité.

[108] Covers population of Seyhan and Yuregir districts within Adana municipal boundaries. — Y compris la population des districts de Seyhan et Yuregir de la municipalité d'Adana.

[109] District centre. — Le centre du district.

[110] Covers population of Altindag, Cankaya, Etimesgut, Golbasi, Kecioren, Mamak, Sincan and Yenimahalle districts within Ankara municipal boundaries. — Y compris la population des districts de Altindag, Cankaya, Etimesgut, Golbasi, Kecioren, Mamak, Sincan et Yenimahalle de la municipalité d'Ankara.

[111] Covers population of Nilufer, Osmangazi and Yildirim districts within Bursa municipal boundaries. — Y compris la population des districts de Nilufer, Osmangazi et Yildirim de la municipalité d'Bursa.

[112] Covers population of Sahinbey and Sehitkamil districts within Gaziantep municipal boundaries. — Y compris la population des districts de Sahinbey et Sehitkamil de la municipalité d'Gaziantep.

[113] Covers population of Adalar, Avcilar, Bagcilar, Bahcelievler, Bakirkoy, Bayrampasa, Besiktas, Beykoz, Beyoglu, Eminonu, Esenler, Eyup, Fatih, Gaziosmanpasa, Gungoren, Kadikoy, Kagithane, Kartal, Kucukcekmece, Maltepe, Pendik, Sariyer, Sisli, Tuzla, Umraniye, Uskudar and Zeytinburnu districts within Istanbul municipal boundaries. — Y compris la population des districts de Adalar, Avcilar, Bagcilar, Bahcelievler, Bakirkoy, Bayrampasa, Besiktas, Beykoz, Beyoglu, Eminonu, Esenler, Eyup, Fatih, Gaziosmanpasa, Gungoren, Kadikoy, Kagithane, Kartal, Kucukcekmece, Maltepe, Pendik, Sariyer, Sisli, Tuzla, Umraniye, Uskudar et Zeytinburnu de la municipalité d'Istanbul.

[114] Covers population of Balcova, Bornova, Buca, Cigli, Gaziemir, Guzelbahce, Karsiyaka, Konak, and Narlidere districts within Izmir municipal boundaries. — Y compris la population des districts de Balcova, Bornova, Buca, Cigli, Gaziemir, Guzelbahce, Karsiyaka, Konak et Narlidere de la municipalité d'Izmir.

[115] Covers population of Kocasinan and Melikgazi districts within Kayseri municipal boundaries . — Y compris la population des districts de Kocasinan et Melikgazi de la municipalité d'Kayseri.

[116] Covers population of Karatay, Meram and Selcuklu districts within Konya municipal boundaries. — Y compris la population des districts de Karatay, Meram et Selcuklu de la municipalité d'Konya.

[117] Including Cholon. — Y compris Cholon.

[118] Data for cities proper refer to communes which may contain an urban centre and a rural area. — Les données concernant les villes proprement dites se rapportent à des communes qui peuvent comprendre un centre urbain et une zone rurale.

[119] Data for cities proper refer to communes which are centres for urban agglomeration. — Les données concernant les villes proprement dites se rapportent à des communes qui sont des centres d'agglomérations urbaines.

[120] De jure population, but excluding diplomatic personnel outside the country and including foreign diplomatic personnel not living in embassies or consulates. — Population de droit, mais non compris le personnel diplomatique hors du pays et y compris le personnel diplomatique étranger qui ne vit pas dans les ambassades ou les consulats.

[121] Included in urban agglomeration of Paris. — Comprise dans l'agglomération urbaine de Paris.

[122] Data refer to French territory of this international agglomeration. — Les données se rapportent aux habitants de cette agglomération internationale qui vivent en territoire francais.

[123] Including Villeurbanne. — Y compris Villeurbanne.

[124] Data for urban agglomeration refer to the extended agglomeration, comprising the city of Paris, 73 communes in Department of Essonne, 36 communes in Department of Hauts-de-Seine, 13 communes in the Department of Seine-et-Marne, 40 communes in Department of Seine-Saint-Denis, 47 communes in Department of Val-de-Marne, 58 communes in Department of Val-d'Oise and 42 communes in the Department of Yvelines. — Les données pour l'agglomération urbaine se rapportent à l'agglomération étendue, qui comprend la ville de Paris, 73 communes dans le département de l'Essonne, 36 communes dans le département des Hauts-de-Seine, 13 communes dans le département de la Seine-et-Marne, 40 communes dans le département de la Seine-Saint-Denis , 47 communes dans le département du Val-de-Marne, 58 communes dans le département du Val-d'Oise et 42 communes dans le département des Yvelines.

[125] Including armed forces stationed outside the country but excluding alien armed forces stationed in the area. — Y compris les militaires en garnison hors du pays, mais non compris les militaires étrangers en garnison sur le territoire.

[126] Included in urban agglomeration of Athens. — Comprise dans l'agglomération urbaine d'Athènes.

[127] Data refer to the Vatican City State. — Les données se rapportent aux Etat du Saint-Siège.

[128] Including civilian nationals temporarily outside the country. — Y compris les civils nationaux temporairement hors du pays.

[129] Data for cities proper refer to administrative units (municipalities). — Les données concernant les villes proprement dites se rapportent à des unités administratives (municipalités).

[130] Data for urban agglomeration refer to 'metropolitan agglomeration' defined as an urban area with more than 100,000 inhabitants, more than 50,000 jobs and more than 150,000 potential regional users of facilities. The metropolitan agglomerations were demarcated on the basis of digital land use maps for 1996. — Les données pour les agglomérations urbaines se réfèrent aux 'agglomérations métropolitaines' définies comme zones urbaines avec plus de 100,000 habitants, plus de 50,000 emplois et plus de 150,000 utilisateurs potentiels des facilitées régionales. Les agglomérations métropolitaines ont été définies sur la base des cartes digitales du territoire de 1996.

[131] 'Lisbon Metropolitan Area' includes the whole area of each of the municipalities of Alcochete, Almada, Amadora, Azambuja, Barreiro, Cascais, Lisboa, Loures, Mafra, Moita, Montijo, Oeiras, Odivelas, Palmela Sesimbra, Setúbal, Seixal, Sintra and Vila Franca de Xira. — La zone métropolitaine de Lisbon se comprennent de municipalités entières de Alcochete, Almada, Amadora, Azambuja, Barreiro, Cascais, Lisboa, Al Loures, Mafra, Moita, Montijo, Oeiras, Odivelas, Palmela Sesimbra, Setúbal, Seixal, Sintra et Vila Franca de Xira.

[132] 'Porto Metropilitan Area' includes the whole area of each of the municipalities of Espinho, Gondomar, Maia, Matosinhos, Porto, Póvoa de Varzim, Valongo, Vila do Conde e Vila Nova de Gaia. — La zone métropolitaine de Porto se comprennent de municipalités entières de Espinho, Gondomar, Maia, Matosinhos, Porto, Póvoa de Varzim, Valongo, Vila do Conde e Vila Nova de Gaia.

[133] For county districts, unitary authorities and London boroughs. — Pour les districts de province, autorités d'unité et cartiers de Londres.

[134] Greater London Borough included in figure for 'Greater London' conurbation. — Le chiffre relatif à l'ensemble urbain du 'Grand Londres' comprend le Greater London Borough.

[135] Capital of Northern Ireland. — Capitale de l'Irlande du Nord.

[136] Capital of Wales for certain purposes. — Considérée à certains égards comme la capitale du pays de Galles.

[137] Capital of Scotland. — Capitale de l'Ecosse.

[138] 'Greater London' conurbation as reconstituted in 1965 and comprising 32 new Greater London Boroughs. — Ensemble urbain du 'Grand Londres', tel qu'il a été reconstitué en 1965, comprenant 32 nouveaux Greater London Boroughs.

[139] Data for urban agglomeration refer to metropolitan areas defined for census purposes and normally comprising city proper (municipality) and contiguous urban areas. — Les données relatives aux agglomérations urbaines se rapportent à la zone métropolitaine définie aux fins du recensement qui comprend généralement la ville proprement dite (municipalité) et la zone urbaine contigue.

[140] Included in urban agglomeration of Auckland. — Comprise dans l'agglomération urbaine d'Auckland.

Table 9

Table 9 presents live births and live-birth rates by urban/rural residence for as many years as possible between 1997 and 2001.

Description of variables: Live birth is defined as the complete expulsion or extraction from its mother of a product of conception, irrespective of the duration of pregnancy, which after such separation, breathes or shows any other evidence of life such as beating of the heart, pulsation of the umbilical cord, or definite movements of voluntary muscles, whether or not the umbilical cord has been cut or the placenta is attached; each product of such a birth is considered live-born[1].

Statistics on the number of live births are obtained from civil registers unless otherwise noted. For those countries or areas where civil registration statistics on live births are considered reliable (estimated completeness of 90 per cent or more) the birth rates shown have been calculated on the basis of registered live births. However, for countries or areas where civil registration of live births is non-existent or considered unreliable (estimated completeness of less than 90 per cent or of unknown completeness), estimated rates provided by national statistical authorities are presented and are identified by the code "|" in the first column.

The urban/rural classification of birth may refer to the residence of mother or the place of delivery, as the national practices vary and is provided by each country or area; it is presumed to be based on the national census definitions of urban population that have been set forth at the end of the technical notes for table 6.

Rate computation: Crude live-birth rates are the annual number of live births per 1 000 mid-year population.

Rates by urban/rural residence are the annual number of live births, in the appropriate urban or rural category, per 1 000 corresponding mid-year population. Rates are calculated only for data considered complete, that is, coded with a "C". These rates have been calculated by the Statistics Division of the United Nations Department for Economic and Social Affairs.

Rates presented in this table are limited to those countries or areas having a minimum number of 30 live births in a given year.

In addition, some rates have been obtained from sample surveys, using different methods[2]; to distinguish them from civil registration data, estimated rates are identified by a footnote.

Reliability of data: Each country or area has been asked to indicate the estimated completeness of the live births recorded in its civil register. These national assessments are indicated by the quality codes (C) and (U) that appear in the first column of this table.

C indicates that the data are estimated to be virtually complete, that is, representing at least 90 per cent of the live births occurring each year, while U indicates that data are estimated to be incomplete, that is, representing less than 90 per cent of the live births occurring each year. A third code (...) indicates that no information was provided regarding completeness.

Data from civil registers which are reported as incomplete or of unknown completeness (coded U or ...) are considered unreliable. They appear in italics in this table. Rates are not calculated for these data, since they are not considered completely reliable.

These quality codes apply only to data from civil registers. If data from other sources are presented, the symbol (|) is shown instead of the quality code. For more information about the quality of vital statistics data in general, and the information available on the basis of the completeness estimates in particular, see section 4.2 of the Technical Notes.

Limitations. Statistics on live births are subject to the same qualifications as have been set forth for vital statistics in general and birth statistics in particular as discussed in section 4 of the Technical Notes.

The reliability of data, an indication of which is described above, is an important factor in considering the limitations. In addition, some live births are tabulated by date of registration and not by date of occurrence; these have been indicated by a plus sign "+". Whenever the lag between the date of occurrence and date of registration is prolonged and, therefore, a large proportion of the live-birth registrations are delayed, birth statistics for any given year may be seriously affected.

Another factor which limits international comparability is the practice of some countries or areas not to include in live-birth statistics infants who were born alive but died before the registration of the birth or within the first 24 hours of life, thus underestimating the total number of life births. Statistics of this type are footnoted.

In addition, it should be noted that rates are affected also by the quality and limitations of the population estimates that are used in their computation. The problems of under-enumeration or over-enumeration and, to some extent, the differences in definition of total population have been discussed in section 3 of the Technical Notes dealing with population data in general, and specific information pertaining to individual countries or areas is given in the footnotes to table 3.

The rates estimated from the results of sample surveys are subject to possibilities of considerable error as a result of omissions in reporting of births, or as a result of erroneous reporting of births, which occurred outside the reference period. However, rates estimated from sample surveys do have an outstanding advantage, and that is the availability of a built-in and strictly corresponding population base.

It should be emphasized that crude birth rates - like crude death, marriage and divorce rates - may be seriously affected by the age-sex structure of the populations to which they relate. Nevertheless, they do provide a simple measure of the level of and changes in natality.

The comparability of data by urban/rural residence is affected by the national definition of urban and rural used in tabulating these data. It is assumed, in the absence of specific information to the contrary, that the definitions of urban and rural used in connection with the national population census were also used in the compilation of the vital statistics for each country or area. However, the possibility cannot be excluded that, for a given country or area, the same definitions of urban and rural are not used for both the vital statistics data and the population census data. When known, the definitions of urban used in national population census are presented at the end of the technical notes to table 6. As discussed in detail in the technical notes to table 6, these definitions vary considerably from one area or country to another. Urban/rural differentials in vital rates may also be affected by whether the vital events have been tabulated in terms of place of occurrence or place of usual residence. This problem is discussed in more detail in section 4.1.4.1 of the Technical notes.

Coverage: Live births are shown for 157 countries or areas. Data are presented by urban/rural residence for 59 countries or areas.

Earlier data: Live births have been shown in each issue of the *Demographic Yearbook*. Data included in this table update the series covering a period of years as follows:

Issue	Years Covered
Special Edition on Natality, CD, 1999	
- Numbers	1980 - 1999
- Rates	1985 - 1999
Historical Supplement, CD, 1997	1948 – 1997
1992	1983 – 1992
1986	1967 – 1986
1981	1962 – 1981
Historical Supplement, 1979	1948 - 1977

For further information on years covered prior to 1948, readers should consult the Index.

NOTES

[1] *Principles and Recommendations for a Vital Statistics System Revision 2*, Sales No. E. 01.XVII.10, United Nations, New York, 2001.
[2] *Manual X: Indirect Techniques for Demographic Estimation*, United Nations publication, Sale No. E.83.XIII.2, United Nations, New York, 1983.

Tableau 9

Le tableau 9 présente des données sur les naissances vivantes et les taux bruts de natalité selon la résidence (urbaine/rurale) pour le plus grand nombre d'années possible entre 1997 et 2001.

Description des variables: La naissance vivante est l'expulsion ou l'extraction complète du corps de la mère, indépendamment de la durée de gestation, d'un produit de la conception qui, après cette séparation, respire ou manifeste tout autre signe de vie, tel que battement de cœur, pulsation du cordon ombilical ou contraction effective d'un muscle soumis à l'action de la volonté, que le cordon ombilical ait été coupé ou non et que le placenta soit ou non demeuré attaché; tout produit d'une telle naissance est considéré comme "enfant né vivant"[1].

Sauf indication contraire, les statistiques du nombre de naissances vivantes sont établies sur la base des registres de l'état civil. Pour les pays ou zones où les statistiques obtenues de l'enregistrement des naissances vivantes par les services de l'état civil sont jugées sûres (complétude estimée à 90 p. 100 ou plus), les taux de natalité indiqués ont été calculés par la Division de la statistiques de l'ONU d'après les naissances vivantes enregistrées. En revanche, pour les pays, ou zones où l'enregistrement des naissances vivantes par les services de l'état civil n'existe pas ou est de qualité douteuse (complétude estimée à moins de 90 p. 100 ou degré de complétude inconnu), on a présenté, autant que possible, des taux estimatifs nationaux signalés avec un code '|'.

La classification des naissances selon la résidence (urbaine/rurale) peut se rapporter au lieu de résidence de la mère ou au lieu d'occurrence et elle a été fournie par chaque pays ou zone; il faut en conclure qu'elle repose sur les définitions de la population urbaine utilisées pour les recensements de la population nationaux telles qu'elles sont reproduites à la fin des notes techniques du tableau 6.

Calcul des taux: Les taux bruts de natalité représentent le nombre annuel de naissances vivantes pour 1 000 habitants ou milieu de l'année.

Les taux selon la résidence (urbaine/rurale) représentent le nombre annuel de naissances vivantes, classées selon la catégorie urbaine ou rurale appropriée pour 1 000 habitants au milieu de l'année. Les taux ont été calculés seulement pour les données considérées complète, ayant un code 'C'. Ces taux ont été calculés par la Division de Statistique du Département des Affaires Economiques et Sociales des Nations Unies.

Les taux présentés dans ce tableau se rapportent seulement aux pays ou zones où l'on a enregistré un nombre minimal de 30 naissances vivantes au cours d'une année donnée.

Dans certains cas, les données ont été obtenues de sources différentes de l'état civil, en utilisant un nombre de techniques indirectes d'estimation démographique[2]. Pour les distinguer des données qui proviennent des registres de l'état civil, ces taux estimatifs ont été identifiés par une note au bas du tableau.

Fiabilité des données: Il a été demandé à chaque pays ou zone d'indiquer le degré estimatif de complétude des données sur les naissances vivantes figurant dans ses registres d'état civil. Ces évaluations nationales sont désignées par les codes de qualité (C) et (U) qui apparaissent dans la première colonne du tableau.

La lettre (C) indique que les données sont jugées à peu près complète, c'est-à-dire qu'elles représentent au moins 90 p. 100 des naissances vivantes survenues chaque année; la lettre (U) indique que les données sont jugées incomplètes, c'est-à-dire qu'elles représentent moins de 90 p. 100 des, naissances vivantes survenues chaque année. Un troisième code (...) indique qu'aucun renseignement n'a été fourni quant à la complétude des données.

Les données provenant des registres de l'état civil qui sont déclarés incomplets ou dont le degré de complétude n'est pas connu (et qui sont affectées de la lettre (U) ou du code (...) sont jugées douteuses. Elles apparaissent en italique dans le présent tableau. Les taux pour ces données ne sont pas calculés.

Ces codes de qualité ne s'appliquent qu'aux données tirées des registres de l'état civil.   Si l'on présente des données autres que celles de l'état civil, le signe (|) est utilisé à la place du code de qualité. Pour plus de précisions sur la qualité des données reposant sur les statistiques de l'état civil en général, voir la section 4.2 des Notes techniques, qui fournit aussi des renseignements sur les estimations de complétude.

Insuffisance des données: Les statistiques des naissances vivantes appellent toutes les réserves qui ont été faites à propos des statistiques de l'état civil en général et des statistiques des naissances en particulier (voir explications données à la section 4 des Notes techniques).

La fiabilité des données, au sujet de laquelle des indications ont été fournies plus haut, est un facteur important. Il faut également tenir compte du fait que, dans certains cas, les données relatives aux naissances vivantes sont exploitées selon la date de l'enregistrement et non la date de l'événement; ces cas ont été identifiés par le signe ' +'. Là où le décalage entre l'événement et son enregistrement est grand, c'est-à-dire là où une forte proportion des naissances vivantes fait l'objet d'un enregistrement tardif, les statistiques des naissances vivantes pour une année donnée peuvent être sérieusement faussées.

Un autre facteur qui nuit à la comparabilité internationale est la pratique de certains pays ou zones qui consiste à ne pas inclure dans les statistiques des naissances vivantes les enfants nés vivants mais décédés avant l'enregistrement de leur naissance ou dans les 24 heures qui ont suivi la naissance, pratique qui conduit à sous-estimer le nombre total de naissances vivantes. Quant tel était le cas, on l'a signalé en note au bas du tableau.

Les taux estimatifs fondés sur les résultats d'enquêtes par sondage comportent des possibilités d'erreurs considérables dues soit à des omissions dans les déclarations, soit au fait que l'on a déclaré à tort des naissances survenues en réalité hors de la période considérée. Toutefois, les taux estimatifs fondés sur les résultats d'enquêtes par sondage présentent un gros avantage: le chiffre de population utilisé comme base est, par définition, rigoureusement correspondant.

Il faut souligner que les taux bruts de natalité, de même que les taux bruts de mortalité, de nuptialité et de divortialité, peuvent varier très sensiblement selon la structure par âge et par sexe de la population à laquelle ils se rapportent. Ils offrent néanmoins un moyen simple de mesurer le niveau et l'évolution de la natalité.

La comparabilité des données selon la résidence (urbaine/rurale) peut être limitée par les définitions nationales des termes "urbain" et "rural" utilisées pour la mise en tableaux de ces données. En l'absence d'indications contraires, on a supposé que les définitions des termes "urbain" et "rural" pour le recensement national de la population avaient été utilisées aussi pour l'établissement des statistiques de l'état civil pour chaque pays ou zone. Toutefois, on ne peut exclure la possibilité que, pour un pays ou zone donnée, les mêmes définitions des termes "urbain" et "rural" n'aient pas été utilisées dans les deux cas. Les définitions du terme "urbain" pour les recensements nationaux de population ont été présentées à la fin des notes Techniques du tableau 6 lorsqu'elles étaient connues. Comme on l'a précisé en détail dans les notes techniques relatives au tableau 6, ces définitions varient très sensiblement d'un pays ou d'une zone à l'autre. La différence entre ces taux pour les zones urbaines et rurales pourra aussi être faussée selon que les faits d'état civil auront été classés d'après le lieu de l'événement ou le lieu de résidence habituelle. Ce problème est examiné plus en détail à la section 4.1.4.1 des Notes techniques.

Portée: Le tableau 9 présente des statistiques des naissances vivantes pour 157 pays ou zones. Les répartitions selon la résidence (urbaine/rurale) intéressent 59 pays ou zones.

Données publiées antérieurement : Des données sur les naissances vivantes ont été présentées dans chaque édition de l'Annuaire démographique. Les données présentées dans ce tableau mettent à jour les périodes d'années suivantes :

Editions	Années considérées
Edition spéciale sur les Statistiques de la natalité (CD), 1999	
- Nombre	1980 - 1999
- Taux	1985 - 1999
Supplément rétrospectif (CD), 1997	1948 – 1997
1992	1983 – 1992
1986	1967 – 1986
1981	1962 – 1981
Supplément rétrospectif, 1979	1948 - 1977

Pour plus d'information concernant les années antérieures à 1948, vous êtes priés de consulter l'Index.

NOTES

[1] *Principes et recommandations pour un système de statistique de l'état civil, deuxième révision, Numéro de vente: F.01.XVII.10, Nations Unies, New York, 2003.*
[2] *Manuel X, techniques indirectes d'estimation démographique, Numéro de vents F.83.XIII.2, Nations Unies, New York, 1984.*

9. Live births and crude birth rates, by urban/rural residence: 1997 - 2001
Naissances vivantes et taux bruts de natalité selon la résidence, urbaine/rurale: 1997 - 2001

(See notes at end of table. — Voir notes à la fin du tableau.)

Continent, country or area and urban/rural residence / Continent, pays ou zone et résidence urbaine/rurale	Code[a]	Number - Nombre					Rate - Taux				
		1997	1998	1999	2000	2001	1997	1998	1999	2000	2001
AFRICA — AFRIQUE											
Algeria - Algérie[1,2]	C										
Total		628 342	620 322	593 643	588 628	618 380	21.6	21.0	19.8	19.4	20.1
Benin - Bénin[3]	I										
Total		255 620	260 610	265 980	272 640	263 726	45.3	44.8	44.4	44.2	41.1
Botswana[3]	I										
Total		49 546	50 606	53 407	...	53 735	32.3	32.2	33.2	...	32.0
Burundi[3]	I										
Total		284 528	290 982	...	...	...	45.9	46.2	...	...	...
Cape Verde - Cap-Vert	C										
Total		...	*15 460	...	...	...	...	*37.1	...	...	...
Chad - Tchad	U										
Total		...	...	...	...	397 896	...	...	...	...	...
Côte d'Ivoire[3]	I										
Total		...	614 667	...	655 904		...	40.0	...	40.0	...
Egypt - Égypte											
Total	C	1 654 695	1 687 252	1 693 025	...		27.5	27.5	27.0	...	...
Urban-Urbaine	C	721 905	685 233	657 902	...		28.2	26.2	24.7	...	...
Rural-Rurale	C	932 790	1 002 019	1 035 123	...		27.0	28.5	28.7	...	...
Ethiopia - Éthiopie											
Total	...	...	...	2 186 023			...	...	...	...	...
Urban-Urbaine	...	...	...	171 698			...	...	...	...	...
Rural-Rurale	...	...	...	2 014 325			...	...	...	...	...
Libyan Arab Jamahiriya - Jamahiriya arabe libyenne											
Total	C	...	...	...	98 752	99 187	...	...	...	19.3	18.7
Malawi[3,4]	I										
Total!		...	496 524	531 160	543 654	555 558	...	50.0	...	...	49.9
Mali	U										
Total		...	...	...	...	525 685	...	...	...	...	...
Mauritius - Maurice											
Total	+C	20 012	19 434	20 311	20 205	19 696	17.4	16.7	17.3	17.0	16.4
Urban-Urbaine	+C	8 106	7 886	8 140	7 994	7 768	16.4	15.8	16.2	15.8	15.2
Rural-Rurale	+C	11 906	11 548	12 171	12 211	11 928	18.2	17.4	18.1	17.9	17.3
Morocco - Maroc[5]											
Total	C	552 141	540 907	529 383	...		20.2	19.5	18.7	...	...
Urban-Urbaine	C	258 464	256 491	256 501	...		17.8	17.1	16.7	...	...
Rural-Rurale	C	292 669	283 667	272 069	...		22.9	22.1	21.2	...	...
Mozambique[3]	I										
Total		...	...	...	...	753 252	...	...	...	...	42.7
Réunion[1]	C										
Total		13 712	13 538	14 153	14 842	14 541	20.0	19.4	19.9	20.6	19.8
Saint Helena ex. dep. - Sainte-Hélène sans dép.	C										
Total		64	59	52	56	36	...	11.4	...	...	...
Seychelles	+C										
Total		1 475	1 412	1 460	1 512	1 440	19.1	17.9	18.2	18.6	17.7
South Africa - Afrique du Sud	U										
Total		1 046 095	1 216 337	1 363 800	1 407 833		...	...	...	...	...
Swaziland[6]											
Total	I	31 087	...	...	...	...	33.4	...	...	...	...
Urban-Urbaine	I	6 915	...	...	...	...	32.2	...	...	...	...
Rural-Rurale	I	24 172	...	...	...	...	33.8	...	...	...	...
Tunisia - Tunisie	C										
Total		173 757	166 718	160 169	...	*163 300	18.9	17.9	16.9	...	*16.9
AMERICA, NORTH — AMERIQUE DU NORD											
Anguilla	+C										
Total		169	155	176	193	*183	16.3	14.5	16.1	17.1	*15.8

9. Live births and crude birth rates, by urban/rural residence: 1997 - 2001
Naissances vivantes et taux bruts de natalité selon la résidence, urbaine/rurale: 1997 - 2001
(continued — suite)

(See notes at end of table. — Voir notes à la fin du tableau.)

Continent, country or area and urban/rural residence — Continent, pays ou zone et résidence urbaine/rurale	Code[a]	Number - Nombre					Rate - Taux				
		1997	1998	1999	2000	2001	1997	1998	1999	2000	2001
AMERICA, NORTH — AMERIQUE DU NORD											
Antigua and Barbuda - Antigua-et-Barbuda											
Total	+C	1 448	1 366	1 329	1 528	...	...	...	...	...	...
Aruba											
Total	+U	*1 457*	*1 315*	*1 225*	*1 294*	*1 266*	...	...	...	...	...
Bahamas											
Total	U	...	...	*6 367*			...	...	...	...	...
Barbados - Barbade											
Total	+U	...	...	...	*3 762*		...	...	...	...	...
Belize											
Total	U	*7 348*	*5 986*	*6 218*	*7 313*	*7 082*	...	...	...	...	...
Bermuda - Bermudes											
Total	C	849	825	...	*838	831	14.1	...	...	...	13.4
British Virgin Islands - Îles Vierges britanniques											
Total	+C	...	...	...	*318		...	...	...	...	*15.4
Canada[7]											
Total	C	348 598	342 418	337 249	327 882	333 744	11.7	11.4	11.1	10.7	10.8
Cayman Islands - Îles Caïmanes											
Total	C	572	545	604	619	*622	15.9	14.5	15.5	15.4	*15.0
Costa Rica											
Total	C	78 018	76 982	78 526	78 178	76 401	22.5	21.8	21.9	19.9	19.2
Urban-Urbaine	C	33 528	...	35 326	34 958	...	...	...	...	...	...
Rural-Rurale	C	44 490	...	43 200	43 219	...	...	...	...	...	...
Cuba											
Total	C	152 681	151 080	150 785	143 528	*138 718	13.8	13.6	13.5	12.8	*12.4
Urban-Urbaine	C	107 838	109 024	109 028	104 521	...	13.0	13.0	13.0	12.4	...
Rural-Rurale	C	44 843	42 056	41 757	39 007	...	16.2	15.3	15.1	14.1	...
Dominica - Dominique											
Total	+C	1 340	1 230	1 291	1 199	...	17.7	16.2	...	16.8	...
Dominican Republic - République dominicaine											
Total	+U	*164 556*	*179 372*	*193 418*	*189 332*		...	...	...	...	...
El Salvador											
Total	C	164 143	158 350	153 636	150 176	*138 354	27.8	26.3	25.0	23.9	*21.6
Urban-Urbaine	C	93 335	102 332	100 458	92 959	*83 478	27.5	29.4	28.1	25.4	*22.2
Rural-Rurale	C	70 808	56 018	53 178	57 217	*54 876	28.2	22.0	20.6	21.9	*20.8
Greenland - Groenland											
Total	C	1 100	986	947	...	...	19.5	17.6	16.9	...	...
Urban-Urbaine	C	839	770	734	...	...	18.5	16.9	16.1	...	...
Rural-Rurale	C	261	216	213	...	...	24.6	20.4	20.2	...	...
Grenada - Grenade											
Total	+C	2 191	1 938	1 791	1 883	*1 899	22.0	19.4	17.8	18.6	*18.8
Guatemala											
Total	C	387 862	489 829	360 759	*426 346	*403 532	36.9	45.4	32.5	*37.4	*34.5
Urban-Urbaine	C	155 660	207 773	140 491	...	...	...	...	...	...	...
Rural-Rurale	C	232 202	282 056	220 268	...	...	...	...	...	...	...
Jamaica - Jamaïque											
Total	+C	59 385	56 937	56 911	*54 035	*55 270	23.3	22.1	22.0	*20.7	*21.1
Mexico - Mexique[5]											
Total	+U	*2 698 425*	*2 668 428*	*2 769 089*	*2 798 339*	*2 767 610*	...	...	...	...	...
Urban-Urbaine	+U	*1 753 593*	*1 776 675*	*1 804 415*	*1 806 199*	*1 749 126*	...	...	...	...	...
Rural-Rurale	+U	*808 915*	*767 725*	*786 089*	*762 200*	*748 772*	...	...	...	...	...
Netherlands Antilles - Antilles néerlandaises											
Total	C	3 558	3 111	2 803	...	...	17.1	15.0	13.7	...	...
Nicaragua											
Total	+U	*113 498*	*111 154*	*91 670*	*92 859*	...	...	...	...	...	...
Urban-Urbaine	+U	*89 059*	*84 869*	*78 240*	*60 962*	...	...	...	...	...	...

9. Live births and crude birth rates, by urban/rural residence: 1997 - 2001
Naissances vivantes et taux bruts de natalité selon la résidence, urbaine/rurale: 1997 - 2001
(continued — suite)

(See notes at end of table. — Voir notes à la fin du tableau.)

Continent, country or area and urban/rural residence — Continent, pays ou zone et résidence urbaine/rurale	Code[a]	Number - Nombre					Rate - Taux				
		1997	1998	1999	2000	2001	1997	1998	1999	2000	2001
AMERICA, NORTH — AMERIQUE DU NORD											
Nicaragua											
Rural-Rurale	+U	24 439	26 285	13 430	31 897	...	...	...	...	...	...
Panama											
Total	C	68 009	62 351	64 248	64 839	63 900	25.0	22.6	22.9	22.7	22.1
Urban-Urbaine	C	35 804	31 751	32 724	32 510	...	23.7	20.6	20.8	20.3	...
Rural-Rurale	C	32 205	30 600	31 524	32 329	...	26.6	25.0	25.5	25.8	...
Puerto Rico - Porto Rico[5]											
Total	C	64 214	60 518	59 684	59 460	55 982	17.3	16.1	15.8	15.6	14.6
Urban-Urbaine	C	32 473	30 575	30 561	30 464	29 323	...	...	...	...	...
Rural-Rurale	C	31 728	29 931	29 096	28 967	26 635	...	...	...	...	...
Saint Kitts and Nevis - Saint-Kitts-et-Nevis											
Total	+C	875	865	864	838	*803	21.5	21.6	20.3	20.7	*17.4
Saint Lucia - Sainte-Lucie[8]											
Total	C	3 303	2 950	2 997	2 840	*2 919	22.1	19.4	19.5	18.2	*18.5
Urban-Urbaine	C	1 018	846	...	...	...	23.0	18.8	...	...	...
Rural-Rurale	C	2 426	2 014	...	...	...	23.0	18.8	...	...	...
Saint Vincent and the Grenadines - Saint Vincent-et-les Grenadines[8]											
Total	+C	2 311	2 112	2 149	2 171	*1 967	20.7	19.0	19.3	19.4	*18.0
Trinidad and Tobago - Trinité-et-Tobago											
Total	C	18 452	...	...	...	...	14.5	...	...	...	...
United States - États-Unis											
Total	C	3 880 894	3 941 553	3 959 417	4 058 814	4 025 933	14.5	14.6	14.5	14.7	14.1
AMERICA, SOUTH — AMERIQUE DU SUD											
Argentina - Argentine											
Total	C	692 357	683 301	686 748	701 878	683 495	19.4	18.9	18.8	19.0	18.2
Bolivia - Bolivie											
Total	U	...	...	...	264 941	...	...	...	...	...	...
Brazil - Brésil[9,8]											
Total	U	...	2 459 275	2 657 613	2 611 422	2 509 354	...	...	...	...	...
Chile - Chili											
Total	C	259 959	257 105	250 674	...	...	17.8	17.3	16.7	...	...
Urban-Urbaine	C	225 816	224 097	218 607	...	...	18.2	17.8	17.0	...	...
Rural-Rurale	C	34 143	33 008	32 067	...	...	15.5	15.0	14.6	...	...
Colombia - Colombie[10]											
Total	+U	990 057	718 880	746 194	734 081	...	...	...	...	...	...
Urban-Urbaine	+U	...	680 093	707 014	700 583	...	...	...	...	...	...
Rural-Rurale	+U	...	29 788	33 169	31 008	...	...	...	...	...	...
Ecuador - Équateur[11]											
Total	U	169 869	199 079	*218 108	*202 257	...	...	...	...	...	...
Urban-Urbaine	U	124 571	142 383	...	...	...	...	...	...	...	...
Rural-Rurale	U	45 298	56 696	...	...	...	...	...	...	...	...
Falkland Islands (Malvinas) - Îles Falkland (Malvinas)											
Total	+C	29	28	33	27	...	...	...	...	...	...
French Guiana - Guyane française[1]											
Total	C	4 453	4 696	4 907	...	...	...	...	31.0	...	...
Peru - Pérou[9,12]											
Total	C	652 467	648 075	642 874	636 064	630 947	26.8	26.1	25.5	24.8	23.9
Suriname											
Total	C	10 794	10 221	10 144	9 804	...	25.8	24.1	23.6	22.5	...
Urban-Urbaine	C	6 987	6 848	6 875	6 018	...	24.1	...	...	...	...
Rural-Rurale	C	3 807	3 373	3 269	3 786	...	29.5	...	...	...	...

9. Live births and crude birth rates, by urban/rural residence: 1997 - 2001
Naissances vivantes et taux bruts de natalité selon la résidence, urbaine/rurale: 1997 - 2001
(continued — suite)

(See notes at end of table. — Voir notes à la fin du tableau.)

Continent, country or area and urban/rural residence / Continent, pays ou zone et résidence urbaine/rurale	Code[a]	Number - Nombre					Rate - Taux				
		1997	1998	1999	2000	2001	1997	1998	1999	2000	2001
AMERICA, SOUTH — AMERIQUE DU SUD											
Uruguay											
Total	+C	58 032	54 127	54 004	52 770	...	17.8	16.5	16.3	15.8	...
Venezuela[9]											
Total	C	516 636	501 808	527 888	544 416	529 552	22.7	21.6	22.3	22.5	21.5
ASIA — ASIE											
Armenia - Arménie[13]											
Total	C	43 929	39 366	36 502	34 276	32 065	11.6	10.4	9.6	9.0	8.4
Urban-Urbaine	C	26 904	24 535	22 458	21 390	...	10.6	9.7	8.9	8.4	...
Rural-Rurale	C	17 025	14 831	14 044	12 886	...	13.6	11.8	11.1	10.2	...
Azerbaijan - Azerbaïdjan[13]											
Total	+C	132 052	123 996	117 539	116 994	110 356	16.8	15.7	14.7	14.5	13.6
Urban-Urbaine	+C	57 031	53 217	50 083	49 631	49 676	14.0	13.1	12.3	12.1	12.1
Rural-Rurale	+C	75 021	70 779	67 456	67 363	60 680	19.9	18.4	17.3	17.0	15.2
Bahrain - Bahreïn											
Total	U	13 382	13 381	14 280	13 947	13 468	...	...	...	...	...
Bangladesh											
Total	U	3 057 000	...	...	...	...	...	...	...	...	...
Brunei Darussalam - Brunéi Darussalam											
Total	+C	7 459	7 411	7 408	7 481	...	23.7	22.9	22.4	22.1	...
China - Chine[14]											
Total	I	20380000	19910000	19090000	...	...	16.5	16.0	15.2	...	...
China: Hong Kong SAR - Chine: Hong Kong RAS											
Total	C	59 250	52 977	51 281	54 134	48 219	9.1	8.1	7.8	8.1	7.2
China: Macao SAR - Chine: Macao RAS											
Total	C	5 031	4 434	4 148	3 849	3 241	12.1	10.5	9.7	8.9	7.5
Cyprus - Chypre[15,5]											
Total	C	9 275	8 879	8 505	8 447	8 167	12.2	11.6	11.0	10.8	10.4
Urban-Urbaine	C	6 100	5 906	5 640	5 732	...	...	...	...	...	...
Rural-Rurale	C	3 036	2 839	2 789	2 648	...	...	...	...	...	...
Georgia - Géorgie[13]											
Total	C	52 000	46 800	40 778	40 392	40 416	9.6	8.6	8.9	8.0	8.2
Urban-Urbaine	C	30 800	28 000	25 862	25 520	25 078	10.2	9.2	9.7	9.7	...
Rural-Rurale	C	21 200	18 800	14 916	14 872	15 338	8.8	7.8	7.7	7.8	...
Iran (Islamic Republic of) - Iran (République islamique d')											
Total	C	1 179 260	1 185 639	1 177 557	...	...	19.4	19.2	18.8	...	...
Urban-Urbaine	C	711 629	738 225	744 839	...	...	18.8	19.0	18.7	...	...
Rural-Rurale	C	467 631	447 414	432 718	...	...	20.2	19.5	18.9	...	...
Iraq[16]											
Total	U	520 787	519 216	532 916	471 886	...	...	...	...	...	...
Israel - Israël[17]											
Total	C	124 478	130 080	131 936	136 390	136 638	21.4	21.8	21.5	21.7	21.2
Urban-Urbaine	C	111 547	116 527	...	121 700	124 640	21.1	21.5	...	21.4	21.1
Rural-Rurale	C	12 931	13 553	...	14 690	11 998	24.2	24.5	...	24.8	22.3
Japan - Japon[18,5]											
Total	C	1 191 665	1 203 147	1 177 669	1 190 547	1 170 662	9.5	9.5	9.3	9.4	9.2
Urban-Urbaine	C	958 324	970 682	951 533	962 392	947 755	...	...	...	...	...
Rural-Rurale	C	233 035	232 176	225 894	227 945	222 709	...	...	...	...	...
Jordan - Jordanie[19]											
Total	+C	130 633	133 714	135 266	126 016	...	28.4	28.1	27.6	25.0	...
Kazakhstan[13]											
Total	C	232 356	222 380	211 815	*217 379	*220 748	14.8	14.8	14.2	*14.6	*14.9
Urban-Urbaine	C	112 458	112 002	106 541	...	...	12.9	13.3	12.8	...	...
Rural-Rurale	C	119 898	110 378	105 274	...	...	17.0	16.6	16.0	...	...

9. Live births and crude birth rates, by urban/rural residence: 1997 - 2001
Naissances vivantes et taux bruts de natalité selon la résidence, urbaine/rurale: 1997 - 2001
(continued — suite)

(See notes at end of table. — Voir notes à la fin du tableau.)

Continent, country or area and urban/rural residence / Continent, pays ou zone et résidence urbaine/rurale	Code[a]	Number - Nombre					Rate - Taux				
		1997	1998	1999	2000	2001	1997	1998	1999	2000	2001
ASIA — ASIE											
Korea (Republic of) - Corée (République de)[20]											
Total	C	675 227	640 126	616 322	636 780	557 228	14.7	13.8	13.2	13.5	11.8
Urban-Urbaine	C	554 676	523 452	500 744	519 767	453 431	...	...	...	...	...
Rural-Rurale	C	120 551	116 674	115 578	117 013	103 797	...	...	...	...	...
Kuwait - Koweït											
Total	C	42 815	41 424	41 135	41 843	*41 342	21.6	20.4	19.5	19.1	*18.2
Kyrgyzstan - Kirghizistan[13]											
Total	C	102 050	104 183	104 068	96 770	98 138	21.8	21.9	21.5	19.8	19.9
Urban-Urbaine	C	25 919	28 494	28 328	28 193	28 491	15.5	16.9	16.6	16.4	16.4
Rural-Rurale	C	76 131	75 689	75 740	68 577	69 647	25.2	24.6	24.2	21.6	21.8
Lebanon - Liban[16]											
Total	U	85 018	84 250	85 516	85 760	...	...	...	...	...	...
Malaysia - Malaisie											
Total	C	540 486	524 696	554 200	569 500	...	24.9	23.7	24.4	24.5	...
Maldives											
Total	C	6 184	5 687	5 226	5 314	4 882	23.9	21.3	18.8	19.6	17.7
Urban-Urbaine	C	1 562	1 467	1 489	1 567	1 636	...	...	...	...	...
Rural-Rurale	C	4 622	4 220	3 737	3 747	3 246	...	...	...	...	...
Mongolia - Mongolie											
Total	C	49 488	49 256	49 461	48 721	49 685	21.5	21.2	21.0	20.4	20.5
Urban-Urbaine	C	21 858	22 393	24 219	23 828	24 691	19.2	19.4	17.5	17.0	...
Rural-Rurale	C	27 630	26 863	25 242	24 893	24 994	23.9	22.9	25.8	25.1	...
Occupied Palestinian Territory - Territoire palestinien occupé											
Total	U	97 473	99 587	96 486	97 529	93 596	...	...	...	...	...
Oman[16]											
Total	...	45 482	45 303	44 067	...	...	...	...	...	...	...
Pakistan[21,22]											
Total	I	4 143 507	...	...	...	...	32.3	...	...	...	...
Urban-Urbaine	I	1 198 286	...	...	...	...	...	...	...	...	...
Rural-Rurale	I	2 945 221	...	...	...	...	...	...	...	...	...
Philippines											
Total	C	1 653 236	1 632 859	1 613 335	1 766 440	...	23.1	22.3	21.6	23.1	...
Qatar											
Total	C	10 447	10 781	10 846	*11 250	12 118	20.0	19.8	...	...	20.3
Saudi Arabia - Arabie saoudite											
Total	...	...	...	509 352	578 772		...	...	...	...	...
Singapore - Singapour											
Total	C	47 333	43 664	43 336	46 997	41 451	12.5	11.1	11.0	11.7	10.0
Sri Lanka											
Total	+C	332 626	329 148	329 121	...	...	17.9	17.5	17.3	...	...
Syrian Arab Republic - République arabe syrienne[1,23]											
Total	C	496 140	505 008	503 473	505 484	524 212	32.9	32.4	31.3	31.0	31.4
Tajikistan - Tadjikistan[13]											
Total	C	...	...	*110 300	...	...	...	...	*17.7	...	...
Thailand - Thaïlande											
Total	+U	897 604	897 495	772 604	773 009	790 425	...	...	...	...	...
Urban-Urbaine	+U	...	...	116 268	119 794	...	...	...	...	...	...
Rural-Rurale	+U	...	...	656 336	653 215	...	...	...	...	...	...
Turkey - Turquie[24,8]											
Total	I	1 477 000	1 488 000	1 498 000	1 508 000	1 507 000	23.1	22.8	22.6	22.4	22.0
Turkmenistan - Turkménistan[13]											
Total	C	...	*98 461	...	...	...	...	*20.3	...	...	...
Uzbekistan - Ouzbékistan[13]											
Total	C	602 694	...	553 745	527 580	512 950	25.6	...	23.1	21.4	20.5

319

9. Live births and crude birth rates, by urban/rural residence: 1997 - 2001
Naissances vivantes et taux bruts de natalité selon la résidence, urbaine/rurale: 1997 - 2001
(continued — suite)

(See notes at end of table. — Voir notes à la fin du tableau.)

Continent, country or area and urban/rural residence / Continent, pays ou zone et résidence urbaine/rurale	Code[a]	Number - Nombre					Rate - Taux				
		1997	1998	1999	2000	2001	1997	1998	1999	2000	2001
ASIA — ASIE											
Uzbekistan - Ouzbékistan[13]											
Urban-Urbaine	C	187 104	...	173 209	163 834	159 492	20.9	...	19.2	17.8	17.2
Rural-Rurale	C	415 590	...	380 536	363 746	353 458	28.4	...	25.5	23.5	22.5
EUROPE											
Albania - Albanie											
Total	C	61 739	60 139	...	...	...	16.5	15.9	...	...	...
Andorra - Andorre											
Total	C	730	781	833	747	777	11.1	11.8	12.6	11.3	11.6
Austria - Autriche											
Total	C	84 045	81 233	78 138	78 268	75 458	10.4	10.1	9.7	9.7	9.3
Belarus - Bélarus[13]											
Total	C	89 586	92 645	92 975	...	...	8.8	9.1	9.3	...	...
Urban-Urbaine	C	61 462	64 856	66 380	...	...	8.6	9.1	9.5	...	...
Rural-Rurale	C	28 124	27 789	26 595	...	...	9.0	9.1	8.7	...	...
Belgium - Belgique[25]											
Total	C	115 864	114 276	113 469	114 883	*114 014	11.4	11.2	11.1	11.2	*11.1
Bosnia and Herzegovina - Bosnie-Herzégovine											
Total	C	48 397	45 007	...	...	...	12.9	12.3	...	...	...
Bulgaria - Bulgarie											
Total	C	64 125	65 360	72 291	73 679	68 180	7.7	7.9	8.8	9.0	8.6
Urban-Urbaine	C	45 746	...	...	52 789	48 567	8.1	...	...	9.5	8.9
Rural-Rurale	C	18 379	...	...	20 890	19 613	6.8	...	...	8.1	8.1
Channel Islands: Guernsey - Îles Anglo-Normandes: Guernesey											
Total	C	672	669	672	644	...	11.4	11.3	11.2	10.7	...
Croatia - Croatie											
Total	C	55 501	47 068	45 179	43 746	40 993	12.1	10.5	9.9	10.0	9.2
Urban-Urbaine	C	33 025	26 819	...	24 768	22 938	...	...	...	...	...
Rural-Rurale	C	22 476	20 249	...	18 978	18 055	...	...	...	...	...
Czech Republic - République tchèque											
Total	C	90 657	90 535	89 471	90 910	90 715	8.8	8.8	8.7	8.8	8.9
Urban-Urbaine	C	66 508	66 622	65 460	66 868	67 081	8.6	8.7	8.5	8.8	8.9
Rural-Rurale	C	24 149	23 913	24 011	24 042	23 634	9.2	9.1	9.2	9.1	8.9
Denmark - Danemark[26]											
Total	C	67 636	66 170	66 232	67 081	65 450	12.8	12.5	12.4	12.6	12.2
Estonia - Estonie[13,5]											
Total	C	12 626	12 170	12 545	13 089	*12 629	8.7	8.4	8.7	9.6	*9.3
Finland - Finlande[27]											
Total	C	59 329	57 108	57 574	56 742	56 189	11.5	11.1	11.1	11.0	10.8
Urban-Urbaine	C	37 430	36 103	36 621	...	36 191	12.3	11.7	11.8	...	11.4
Rural-Rurale	C	21 899	21 005	20 953	...	19 998	10.4	10.2	10.2	...	10.0
France[28,29]											
Total	C	726 768	738 080	744 791	774 782	774 600	12.4	12.6	12.7	13.2	13.1
Urban-Urbaine	C	562 475	567 675	570 503	589 608	...	...	...	...	...	...
Rural-Rurale	C	162 948	168 952	172 966	183 787	...	...	...	...	...	...
Germany - Allemagne											
Total	C	812 173	797 541	770 744	766 999	*743 500	9.9	9.7	9.4	9.3	*9.0
Gibraltar[30]											
Total	C	427	411	381	408	399	15.7	15.2	14.0	15.1	14.1
Greece - Grèce											
Total	C	102 038	100 894	116 038	117 140	102 282	9.7	9.6	11.0	11.7	10.2
Urban-Urbaine	C	69 898	69 490	...	...	...	...	...	...	...	...
Rural-Rurale	C	32 140	31 404	...	...	...	...	...	...	...	...
Hungary - Hongrie[5]											
Total	C	100 350	97 301	94 645	97 597	97 047	9.9	9.6	9.4	9.7	9.5
Urban-Urbaine	C	59 290	58 358	57 113	59 029	59 119	9.0	8.9	8.8	9.1	8.9

9. Live births and crude birth rates, by urban/rural residence: 1997 - 2001
Naissances vivantes et taux bruts de natalité selon la résidence, urbaine/rurale: 1997 - 2001
(continued — suite)

(See notes at end of table. — Voir notes à la fin du tableau.)

Continent, country or area and urban/rural residence / Continent, pays ou zone et résidence urbaine/rurale	Code[a]	Number - Nombre					Rate - Taux				
		1997	1998	1999	2000	2001	1997	1998	1999	2000	2001
EUROPE											
Hungary - Hongrie[5]											
Rural-Rurale	C	40 496	38 341	36 836	37 781	37 019	11.4	10.8	10.4	10.6	10.4
Iceland - Islande											
Total	C	4 151	4 178	4 100	4 315	4 091	15.3	15.3	14.8	15.3	14.4
Urban-Urbaine	C	3 900	3 904	...	3 993	3 849	15.6	15.5	...	15.4	14.6
Rural-Rurale	C	251	274	...	322	242	11.6	12.8	...	15.0	11.2
Ireland - Irlande[31]											
Total	+C	52 775	53 551	53 354	54 239	57 882	14.4	14.5	14.2	14.3	15.0
Urban-Urbaine	+C	28 657	28 857	30 827	...	...	...	...	...	...	...
Rural-Rurale	+C	24 118	24 694	22 527	...	...	...	...	...	...	...
Isle of Man - Îles de Man											
Total	+C	...	...	894	*830	...	...	...	...	*11.1	...
Italy - Italie											
Total	C	534 461	515 439	523 463	543 039	535 282	9.3	9.0	9.1	9.4	9.2
Latvia - Lettonie[13]											
Total	C	18 830	18 410	19 396	20 248	19 664	7.7	7.6	8.1	8.5	8.3
Urban-Urbaine	C	11 698	11 328	12 072	12 737	12 531	7.0	6.9	7.4	7.9	7.8
Rural-Rurale	C	7 132	7 082	7 324	7 511	7 133	9.3	9.3	9.7	9.9	9.4
Liechtenstein											
Total	C	435	...	...	...	...	13.9	...	...	...	...
Lithuania - Lituanie[13]											
Total	C	37 812	37 019	36 415	34 149	31 546	10.6	10.4	10.3	9.8	9.1
Urban-Urbaine	C	23 732	23 066	...	21 008	19 672	9.8	9.7	...	9.0	8.4
Rural-Rurale	C	14 080	13 953	...	13 141	11 874	12.1	12.0	...	11.4	10.3
Luxembourg											
Total	C	5 503	5 386	5 582	5 723	5 459	13.1	12.6	12.9	13.1	12.4
Malta - Malte[32,33]											
Total	C	4 835	4 488	4 308	4 255	3 859	12.6	11.6	11.1	10.9	9.8
Monaco											
Total	C	713	681	...	760	...	22.3	...	...	22.8	...
Netherlands - Pays-Bas[34]											
Total	C	192 443	199 408	200 445	206 619	202 603	12.3	12.7	12.7	13.0	12.6
Urban-Urbaine	C	118 751	123 487	...	132 318	132 295	12.3	12.7	...	...	...
Rural-Rurale	C	73 692	75 921	...	74 301	70 308	12.4	12.8	...	...	...
Norway - Norvège[35]											
Total	C	59 801	58 352	59 298	59 234	56 696	13.6	13.2	13.3	13.2	12.6
Poland - Pologne											
Total	C	412 635	395 619	382 002	378 700	368 205	10.7	10.2	9.9	9.8	9.5
Urban-Urbaine	C	221 078	214 074	208 173	...	...	9.2	8.9	8.7	...	...
Rural-Rurale	C	191 557	181 545	173 829	...	...	13.0	12.3	11.8	...	...
Portugal											
Total	C	113 047	113 510	116 002	118 551	112 774	11.4	11.4	11.6	11.8	10.9
Republic of Moldova - République de Moldova[13]											
Total	C	49 804	41 332	38 501	36 939	36 448	13.6	11.3	10.6	10.2	10.0
Urban-Urbaine	C	...	14 221	13 238	12 722	12 542	...	9.3	8.6	8.4	8.4
Rural-Rurale	C	...	27 111	25 263	24 217	23 906	...	12.8	11.9	11.4	11.1
Romania - Roumanie											
Total	C	236 891	237 297	234 600	234 521	220 368	10.5	10.5	10.4	10.5	9.8
Urban-Urbaine	C	110 009	110 186	...	108 254	102 432	8.9	8.9	...	8.8	8.4
Rural-Rurale	C	126 882	127 111	...	126 267	117 936	12.5	12.5	...	12.4	11.6
Russian Federation - Fédération de Russie[13]											
Total	C	1 259 943	1 283 292	1 214 689	1 266 800	1 311 604	8.6	8.8	8.3	8.7	9.1
Urban-Urbaine	C	...	...	842 640	...	...	...	...	7.9	...	...
Rural-Rurale	C	...	...	372 049	...	...	...	...	9.4	...	...
San Marino - Saint-Marin											
Total	+C	287	285	303	290	...	11.1	10.9	11.5	10.8	...
Urban-Urbaine	+C	256	...	...	259	...	11.1	...	...	11.4	...
Rural-Rurale	+C	31	...	...	31	...	11.3	...	...	7.4	...

9. Live births and crude birth rates, by urban/rural residence: 1997 - 2001
Naissances vivantes et taux bruts de natalité selon la résidence, urbaine/rurale: 1997 - 2001
(continued — suite)

(See notes at end of table. — Voir notes à la fin du tableau.)

Continent, country or area and urban/rural residence / Continent, pays ou zone et résidence urbaine/rurale	Code[a]	Number - Nombre					Rate - Taux				
		1997	1998	1999	2000	2001	1997	1998	1999	2000	2001
EUROPE											
Serbia and Montenegro - Serbie-et-Montenegro											
Total	C	131 394	128 461	123 970	125 868	131 449	12.4	12.1	11.7	11.8	12.3
Urban-Urbaine	C	67 773	66 885	64 489	66 409	...	12.4	12.2	11.8	12.1	...
Rural-Rurale	C	63 621	61 576	59 481	59 459	...	12.4	12.0	11.5	11.5	...
Slovakia - Slovaquie											
Total	C	59 310	57 582	56 223	55 103	51 136	11.0	10.7	10.4	10.2	9.5
Urban-Urbaine	C	...	29 725	28 693	...	26 106	...	9.7	9.4	...	...
Rural-Rurale	C	...	27 857	27 530	...	25 030	...	12.0	11.8	...	...
Slovenia - Slovénie											
Total	C	18 165	17 856	17 533	18 180	17 477	9.1	9.0	8.8	9.1	8.8
Urban-Urbaine	C	...	...	8 017	8 306	8 039	...	...	...	...	...
Rural-Rurale	C	...	...	9 516	9 874	9 438	...	...	...	...	...
Spain - Espagne											
Total	C	369 035	365 193	380 130	*386 450	*407 135	9.4	9.3	9.6	*9.7	*10.1
Sweden - Suède											
Total	C	90 383	89 028	88 173	90 441	91 466	10.2	10.1	10.0	10.2	10.3
Switzerland - Suisse											
Total	C	80 584	78 949	78 408	78 458	73 509	11.4	11.1	11.0	10.9	10.2
Urban-Urbaine	C	52 589	51 684	51 771	52 393	49 292	11.0	10.8	10.7	10.8	10.1
Rural-Rurale	C	27 995	27 265	26 637	26 065	24 217	12.2	11.8	11.5	11.2	10.4
The Former Yugoslav Rep. of Macedonia - L'ex-République yougoslave de Macédoine											
Total	C	29 478	...	27 309	29 308	27 010	14.8	...	13.5	...	13.3
Urban-Urbaine	C	15 411	...	14 375	15 579	14 761	13.0	...	...	...	...
Rural-Rurale	C	14 067	...	12 934	13 729	12 249	17.4	...	...	...	...
Ukraine[13]											
Total	C	442 581	419 238	...	385 126	376 478	8.7	8.3	...	7.7	7.7
Urban-Urbaine	C	274 961	258 724	...	...	237 228	8.0	7.5	...	...	...
Rural-Rurale	C	167 620	160 514	...	...	139 250	10.2	9.9	...	...	...
United Kingdom - Royaume-Uni[36]											
Total	C	726 622	716 888	699 976	679 029	668 777	12.3	12.1	11.8	11.4	11.2
OCEANIA — OCEANIE											
American Samoa - Samoas américaines											
Total	C	1 634	1 688	1 736	1 730	...	29.7	30.3	30.6	30.0	...
Australia - Australie											
Total	+C	251 842	249 616	248 870	249 636	*245 759	13.6	13.3	13.1	13.0	*12.7
Cook Islands - Îles Cook											
Total	+C	413	386	346	...	...	22.6	22.2	21.1	...	...
Fiji - Fidji											
Total	+C	...	17 944	16 916	...	...	...	22.5	21.0	...	...
French Polynesia - Polynésie française											
Total	C	4 702	4 562	4 580	4 900	...	21.1	20.2	20.1	21.2	...
Guam[37]											
Total	C	4 318	4 322	4 037	3 790	...	27.6	29.0	26.6	24.5	...
Marshall Islands - Îles Marshall[38]											
Total	+U	1 607	1 651	1 478	...	*1 511	...	...	...	...	...
Micronesia, Federated States of - Micronésie, États fédérés de											
Total	U	2 575	...	...	...	...	...	...	...	...	...

9. Live births and crude birth rates, by urban/rural residence: 1997 - 2001
Naissances vivantes et taux bruts de natalité selon la résidence, urbaine/rurale: 1997 - 2001
(continued — suite)

(See notes at end of table. — Voir notes à la fin du tableau.)

Continent, country or area and urban/rural residence / Continent, pays ou zone et résidence urbaine/rurale	Code[a]	Number - Nombre					Rate - Taux				
		1997	1998	1999	2000	2001	1997	1998	1999	2000	2001
OCEANIA — OCEANIE											
New Caledonia - Nouvelle-Calédonie											
Total	C	4 490	4 352	4 316	...	...	22.4	21.3	20.8	...	...
New Zealand - Nouvelle-Zélande[5]											
Total	+C	57 734	55 349	57 053	56 605	...	15.4	14.6	15.0	14.8	...
Urban-Urbaine	+C	50 218	48 337	49 536	49 374	...	...	...	...	...	...
Rural-Rurale	+C	7 516	6 717	7 293	7 126	...	...	...	...	...	...
Northern Mariana Islands - Îles Mariannes septentrionales											
Total	U	*1 536*	*1 421*	*1 448*	...	...	...	...	...	...	...
Palau - Palaos											
Total	C	330	280	250	...	...	18.3	15.1	13.2	...	...
Tonga											
Total	+C	2 700	2 737	2 599	2 471	...	27.4	27.6	26.0	24.6	...

GENERAL NOTES - NOTES GENERALES

For certain countries, there is a discrepancy between the total number of live births shown in this table and those shown in subsequent tables for the same year. Usually this discrepancy arises because the total number of births occurring in a given year is revised, although the remaining tabulations are not. Rates are the number of live births per 1 000 mid-year population. For definitions of 'urban', see end of Technical Notes for table 6. For method of evaluation and limitations of data, see Technical Notes for this table. — Pour quelques pays il y a une discordance entre le nombre total des naissances vivantes présenté dans ce tableau et ceux présentés pour la mème année dans d'autres tableaux. Habituellement ces différences apparaîssent lorsque le nombre total des naissances pour une certaine année a été révisé; alors que les autres tabulations ne l'ont pas été. Les taux représentent le nombre de naissances vivantes pour 1 000 personnes au milieu de l'année. Pour les définitions des 'régions urbaines', se reporter à la fin des Notes techniques du tableau 6. Pour la méthode d'évaluation et les limitations des données, voir Notes techniques pour ce tableau.

Italics: data from civil registers which are incomplete or of unknown completeness. — Italiques: données incomplètes ou dont le degré de complétude n'est pas connu provenant des registres de l'état civil.

FOOTNOTES - NOTES

  * Provisional. — Données provisoires.
  [a] 'Code' indicates the source of data, as follows:
C - Civil registration, estimated over 90% complete
U - Civil registration, estimated less than 90% complete
I - Other source, estimated reliable
+ - Data tabulated by date of registration rather than occurence.
... - Information not available

Le 'Code' indique la source des données, comme suit:
C - Registres de l'état civil considérés complèts à 90 p. 100 au moins.
U - Registres de l'état civil qui ne sont pas considérés complèts à 90 p. 100 au moins.
I - Autre source, considérée pas douteuses.
+ - Données exploitées selon la date de l'enregistrement et non la date de l'événement.
... - Information pas disponible.

  [1] Excluding live-born infants dying before registration of birth. - Non compris les enfants nés vivants décédés avant l'enregistrement de leur naissance.
  [2] For Algerian population only. - Pour la population algérienne seulement.
  [3] Data refer to national projections. - Les données se referent aux projections nationales.
  [4] Data on births refer to the 1998 Population and Housing Census, adjusted for under-enumeration. - Les données sur les naissances referent au Recensement de la population et de l'habitat, ajustés pour compenser les lacunes de dénombrement.
  [5] Figures for urban and rural areas do not add up to the total, since they do not include the category 'Unknown residence'. - La somme des donées pour la residence urbaine et rurale n'est pas égale au total parce qu'elle n'inclue pas la catégorie 'Residence inconnue'.
  [6] Data for 1997 refer to last twelve months preceding population and housing census of 1997. - Les données pour 1997 se réfèrent au douze mois précédant le recensement de population et de l'habitat de 1997.
  [7] Including Canadian residents temporarily in the United States, but excluding United States residents temporarily in Canada. - Y compris les résidents canadiens se trouvant temporairement aux Etats-Unis, mais ne comprenant pas les résidents des Etats-Unis se trouvant temporairement au Canada.
  [8] Data as reported by national statistical authorities; they may differ from data presented in other tables. - Les données comme ils ont été déclarés par l'institut national de la statistique; ils peuvent etre different de ceux presentés dans autre tableaux.
  [9] Excluding Indian jungle population. - Non compris les Indiens de la jungle.
  [10] Data on live births and deaths are based on a civil registration system put in place in January 1998. - Les données sur les naissances et les décès sont basées sur un système d'enregistrement des faits d'état civil mis en place en janvier 1998.
  [11] Excluding nomadic Indian tribes. - Non compris les tribus d'Indiens nomades.
  [12] Including an upward adjustment for under-registration. - Y compris un ajustement pour sous-enregistrement.
  [13] Excluding infants born alive with less than 28 weeks gestation, less than 1 000 grams in weight and 35 centimeters in length, who die within seven days of birth. - Non compris les enfants nés vivants avant 28 semaines de gestation, pesant moins de 1 000 grammes, mesurant moins de 35 centimètres et décédés dans les sept jours qui ont suivi leur naissance.
  [14] For statistical purposes, the data for China do not include those for the Hong Kong Special Administrative Region (Hong Kong SAR), Macao special Administrative Region (Macao SAR) and Taiwan province of China. - Pour la présentation des statistiques, les données pour Chine ne comprend pas la Région Administrative Spéciale de Hong Kong (Hong Kong RAS), la Région Administrative Spéciale de Macao (Macao RAS) et Taïwan province de Chine.

15 Data refer to government controlled areas. - Les données se raportent aux zones contrôlées par le Gouvernement.

16 Published by the United Nations Economic and Social Commission for Western Asia. - Publié par la Commission économique et sociale des Nations Unies pour l'Asie occidentale.

17 Including data for East Jerusalem and Israeli residents in certain other territories under occupation by Israeli military forces since June 1967. - Y compris les données pour Jérusalem-Est et les résidents israéliens dans certains autres territoires occupés depuis 1967 par les forces armées israéliennes.

18 For Japanese nationals in Japan only. - Pour les nationaux japonais au Japon seulement.

19 Excluding data for Jordanian territory under occupation since June 1967 by Israeli military forces. Excluding foreigners, including registered Palestinian refugees. - Non compris les données pour le territoire jordanien occupé depuis juin 1967 par les forces armées israéliennes. Non compris les étrangers, mais y compris les réfugiés de Palestine enregistrés.

20 Excluding alien armed forces, civilian aliens employed by armed forces, and foreign diplomatic personnel and their dependants. - Non compris les militaires étrangers, les civils étrangers employés par les forces armées ni le personnel diplomatique étranger et les membres de leur famille les accompagnant.

21 Based on the results of the Population Growth Survey. - D'après les résultats de la 'Population Growth Survey.'

22 Excluding data for the Pakistan-held part of Jammu and Kashmir, the final status of which has not yet been determined. - Non compris les données concernant la partie du Jammu et Cachemire occupée par le Pakistan dont le statut définitif n'a pas été déterminé.

23 Excluding nomad population and Palestinian refugees. - Non compris la population nomade et les réfugiés de Palestine.

24 Based on the results of the Population Demographic Survey. - D'après les résultats de la Population Demographic Survey.

25 Including armed forces stationed outside the country, but excluding alien armed forces stationed in the area. - Y compris les militaires nationaux hors du pays, mais non compris les militaires étrangers en garnison sur le territoire.

26 Excluding Faeroe Islands and Greenland. - Non compris les îles Féroé et Gröenland.

27 Including nationals temporarily outside the country. - Y compris les nationaux se trouvant temporairement hors du pays.

28 Including armed forces stationed outside the country. - Y compris les militaires nationaux hors du pays.

29 Data for urban and rural areas exclude births of nationals outside the country.- Les chiffres pour la residence urbaine et rurale ne comprennent pas les naissances de nationaux hors du pays.

30 Excluding armed forces. - Non compris les militaires en garnison.

31 Events registered within one year of occurrence. - Evénements enregistrés dans l'année qui suit l'événement.

32 Computed on population including civilian nationals temporarily outside the country. - Les taux sont calculés sur la base d'un chiffre de population qui comprend les civils nationaux temporairement hors du pays.

33 Live births to Maltese parents only. - Naissances vivantes aux parents maltais seulement.

34 Including residents outside the country if listed in a Netherlands population register. - Y compris les résidents hors du pays, s'ils sont inscrits sur un registre de population néerlandais.

35 Including residents temporarily outside the country. - Y compris les résidents se trouvant temporairement hors du pays.

36 Data revised to exclude births in Northern Ireland to non-residents of Northern Ireland. - Données révisées non compris des naissances en Irlande du Nord aux non-résidents de l'Irlande du Nord.

37 Including United States military personnel, their dependants and contract employees. - Y compris les militaires des Etats-Unis, les membres de leur famille les accompagnant et les agents contractuels des Etats-Unis.

38 There is still a significant underregistration of births in the Republic of Marshall Islands.- Il y encore un sous-enregistrement considérable des naissances vivantes dans la République des Iles Marshall.

Table 10

Table 10 presents live births by age of mother, sex of the child and urban/rural residence for the latest available year in the period 1992-2001.

Description of variables: Age is defined as age at last birthday, that is, the difference between the date of birth and the date of the occurrence of the event, expressed in completed solar years. The age classification used in this table is the following: under 15 years, 5-year age groups through 45-49 years, and 50 years and over.

Reliability of data: Data from civil registers of live births which are reported as incomplete (less than 90 per cent completeness) or of unknown completeness are considered unreliable and are set in *italics* rather than in roman type. Table 9 and the technical notes for that table provide more detailed information on the completeness of live-birth registration. For more information about the quality of vital statistics data in general, see section 4.2 of the Technical Notes.

Limitations: Statistics on live births by age of mother are subject to the same qualifications as have been set forth for vital statistics in general and birth statistics in particular as discussed in section 4 of the Technical Notes.

The reliability of the data described above, is an important factor in considering the limitations. In addition, some live births are tabulated by date of registration and not by date of occurrence; these have been indicated by a plus sign "+". Whenever the lag between the date of occurrence and date of registration is prolonged and, therefore, a large proportion of the live-birth registrations are delayed, birth statistics for any given year may be seriously affected.

Another factor which limits international comparability is the practice of some countries or areas of not including in live-birth statistics infants who were born alive but died before the registration of the birth or within the first 24 hours of life, thus underestimating the total number of live births. Statistics of this type are footnoted.

Because these statistics are classified according to age, they are subject to the limitations with respect to accuracy of age reporting similar to those already discussed in connection with section 3.1.3 of the Technical Notes. The factors influencing the accuracy of reporting may be somewhat dissimilar in vital statistics (because of the differences in the method of taking a census and registering a birth) but, in general, the same errors can be observed.

The absence of frequencies in the unknown age group does not necessarily indicate completely accurate reporting and tabulation of the age item. It is often an indication that the unknowns have been eliminated by assigning ages to them before tabulation, or by proportionate distribution after tabulation.

On the other hand, large frequencies in the unknown age category may indicate that a large proportion of the births are born outside of wedlock, the records for which tend to be incomplete in so far as characteristics of the parents are concerned.

Another limitation of age reporting may result from calculating age of mother at birth of child (or at time of registration) from year of birth rather than from day, month and year of birth. Information on this factor is given in footnotes when known.

When birth statistics are tabulated by date of registration rather than by date of occurrence, the age of the mother will almost always refer to the date of registration rather than to the date of birth of the child. Hence, in those countries or areas where registration of births is delayed, possibly for years, statistics on births by age of mother should be used with caution.

In few countries, data by age refer to confinements (deliveries) rather than to live births causing under-enumeration in the event of a multiple birth. This practice leads to lack of strict comparability, both among countries or areas relying on this practice and between data shown in this table and table 9.

The comparability of data by urban/rural residence is affected by the national definitions of urban and rural used in tabulating these data. It is assumed, in the absence of specific information to the contrary, that the definitions of urban and rural used in connection with the national population census were also used in the compilation of the vital statistics for each country or area. However, the possibility cannot be excluded that, for a given country or area, the same definitions of urban and rural are not used for both the vital statistics data and the population census data. When known, the definitions of urban used in national population censuses are presented at the end of table 6. As discussed in detail in the technical notes for table 6, these definitions vary considerably from one country or area to another.

Coverage: Live births by age of mother are shown for 130 countries or areas. Data are presented by urban/rural residence for 52 countries or areas.

Earlier data: Live births by age of mother have been shown for the latest available year in each issue of the Yearbook. Data included in this table update the series covering period of years as follows:

Issue	Years Covered
Special Edition on Natality, CD, 1999	1990 – 1998
Historical Supplement CD, 1997	1948 – 1997
1992	1983 – 1992
1986	1977 – 1988
1981	1972 – 1980
Historical Supplement, 1979	1948 - 1977

For further information on years covered prior to 1948, readers should consult the Index.

Tableau 10

Le tableau 10 présente des données sur les naissances vivantes selon l'âge de la mère, le sexe de l'enfant et la résidence (urbaine/rurale) pour la dernière année disponible.

Description des variables : L'âge désigne l'âge au dernier anniversaire, c'est-à-dire la différence entre la date de naissance et la date de l'événement exprimée en années solaires révolues. La classification par âge utilisée dans ce tableau comprend les catégories suivantes : moins de 15 ans, groupes quinquennaux jusqu'à 45 - 49 ans, 50 ans et plus, et âge inconnu.

Fiabilité des données : Les données sur les naissances vivantes provenant des registres de l'état civil qui sont déclarés incomplets (degré de complétude inférieur à 90 p. 100) ou dont le degré de complétude n'est pas connu sont jugées douteuses et apparaissent en italique et non en caractères romains. Le tableau 9 et les notes techniques se rapportant à ce tableau présentent des renseignements plus détaillés sur le degré de complétude de l'enregistrement des naissances vivantes. Pour plus de précisions sur la qualité des statistiques de l'état civil en général, voir la section 4.2 des notes techniques.

Insuffisance des données : Les statistiques des naissances vivantes selon l'âge de la mère appellent toutes les réserves qui ont été faites à propos des statistiques de l'état civil en général et des statistiques de naissances en particulier (voir explications à la section 4 des Notes techniques).

La fiabilité des données, au sujet de laquelle des indications ont été fournies plus haut, est un facteur important. Il faut également tenir compte du fait que, dans certains cas, les données relatives aux naissances vivantes exploitées selon la date de l'enregistrement et non la date de l'événement; ces cas ont été identifiés par le signe "+". Là où le décalage entre l'événement et son enregistrement est grand, c'est-à-dire quand une forte proportion des naissances vivantes fait l'objet d'un enregistrement tardif, les statistiques des naissances vivantes pour une année donnée peuvent être sérieusement faussées.

Un autre facteur qui nuit à la comparabilité internationale est la pratique de certains pays ou zones qui consiste à ne pas inclure dans les statistiques des naissances vivantes les enfants nés vivants mais décédés avant l'enregistrement de leur naissance ou dans les 24 heures qui ont suivi la naissance, pratique qui conduit à sous-estimer le nombre total de naissances vivantes. Quand tel était le cas, on l'a signalé en note au bas du tableau.

Etant donné que ces statistiques sont classées selon l'âge, elles appellent les mêmes réserves concernant l'exactitude des déclarations d'âge que celles dont il a déjà été fait mention dans la section 3.1.3 des Notes techniques. Dans le cas des statistiques de l'état civil, les facteurs qui interviennent à cet égard sont parfois différents, étant donné que le recensement de la population et l'enregistrement des naissances se font par des méthodes différentes, mais, d'une manière générale, les erreurs observées seront les mêmes.

Si aucun nombre ne figure dans la colonne réservée aux âges inconnus, cela ne signifie pas nécessairement que les déclarations d'âge et l'exploitation des données par âge été tout à fait exactes. C'est souvent une indication que l'on a attribué un âge aux personnes d'âge inconnu avant l'exploitation des données ou que celles-ci ont été réparties proportionnellement entre les différents groupes après cette opération.

D'autre part, lorsque le nombre des personnes d'âge inconnu est important, cela peut signifier que la proportion de naissances de mère pas mariée est élevée, étant donné qu'en pareil cas l'acte de naissance ne contient pas toutes les caractéristiques concernant les parents.

Les déclarations par âge peuvent comporter des distorsions, du fait que l'âge de la mère au moment de la naissance d'un enfant (ou de la déclaration de naissance) est donné par année de naissance et non par date exacte (jour, mois et année).

Il convient de noter que, lorsque les statistiques de la natalité sont établies selon la date de l'enregistrement et non celle de l'événement, l'âge de la mère représente presque toujours son âge à la date de l'enregistrement et non à la date de la naissance de l'enfant. Ainsi, dans les pays ou zones où l'enregistrement des naissances est tardif le retard atteignant souvent plusieurs années, il faut utiliser avec prudence les statistiques de naissances selon l'âge de la mère.

Dans quelques pays, la classification par âges se réfère aux accouchements, et non aux naissances vivantes, ce qui conduit à un sous-dénombrement en cas de naissances gémellaires. Cette pratique est une cause d'incomparabilité, à la fois entre pays ou zones de ce tableau et les données du tableau 9.

La comparabilité des données selon la résidence (urbaine/rurale) peut être limitée par les définitions nationales des termes "urbain" et "rural" utilisés pour la mise en tableaux de ces données. En l'absence d'indications contraires, on a supposé que les définitions des termes urbain et rural pour le recensement national de la population aient été utilisées aussi pour l'établissement des statistiques de l'état civil pour chaque pays ou zone. Toutefois, on ne peut exclure la possibilité que, pour un pays ou zone donnée, les mêmes définitions des termes urbain" et rural n'aient pas été utilisées dans les deux cas. Les définitions du terme "urbain" pour les recensements nationaux de population ont été présentées à la fin du tableau 6 lorsqu'elles étaient connues. Comme on l'a précisé en détail dans les Notes techniques relatives au tableau 6, ces définitions varient très sensiblement d'un pays ou d'une zone à l'autre.

Portée : Le tableau 10 présente des données sur les naissances vivantes classées selon l'âge de la mère pour 130 pays ou zones. Des répartitions selon le sexe de l'enfant sont présentées pour 81 pays ou zones. Les répartitions selon la résidence (urbaine/rurale) intéressent 52 pays ou zones.

Données publiées antérieurement: Des statistiques des naissances vivantes selon l'âge de la mère ont été présentées pour la dernière année disponible dans chaque édition de l'Annuaire démographique. Les données présentées dans ce tableau mettent à jour les périodes d'années suivantes :

Editions	Années considérées
Edition spéciale, Statistiques de la natalité (CD), 1999	1990 – 1998
Supplément rétrospectif (CD), 1997	1948 – 1997
1992	1983 – 1992
1986	1977 – 1988
1981	1972 – 1980
Supplément rétrospectif, 1979	1948 – 1977

Pour plus de précision sur les années antérieur à 1948, on se reportera à l'index.

10. Live births by age of mother, sex of the child and urban/rural residence: latest available year
Naissances vivantes selon l'âge de la mère , le sexe de l'enfant et la résidence, urbaine/rurale: dernière année disponible

(See notes at end of table.— Voir notes à la fin du tableau.)

Continent, country or area, year and age (in years) / Continent, pays ou zone, année et âge (en années)	Codeª	Total			Urban - Urbaine			Rural - Rurale		
		Both sexes - Les deux sexes	Male - Masculin	Female - Féminin	Both sexes - Les deux sexes	Male - Masculin	Female - Féminin	Both sexes - Les deux sexes	Male - Masculin	Female - Féminin
AFRICA — AFRIQUE										
Benin - Bénin										
1992										
Total	I	179 264	90 631	88 633	55 094	27 920	27 174	124 170	62 711	61 459
0 - 14	I	6 361	3 236	3 125	1 977	1 015	962	4 384	2 221	2 163
15 - 19	I	54 858	27 748	27 110	12 491	6 302	6 189	42 367	21 446	20 921
20 - 24	I	65 930	33 296	32 634	20 593	10 448	10 145	45 337	22 848	22 489
25 - 29	I	30 735	15 528	15 207	12 044	6 079	5 965	18 691	9 449	9 242
30 - 34	I	13 700	6 931	6 769	4 974	2 520	2 454	8 726	4 411	4 315
35 - 39	I	4 891	2 439	2 452	2 200	1 122	1 078	2 691	1 317	1 374
40 - 44	I	2 371	1 222	1 149	607	326	281	1 764	896	868
45 - 49	I	57	35	22	-	-	-	57	35	22
50+	I	361	196	165	208	108	100	153	88	65
Egypt - Égypte										
1999										
Total	C	1 693 025	870 195	822 830	657 902	338 638	319 264	1 035 123	531 557	503 566
0 - 19	C	58 512	29 955	28 557	20 778	10 785	9 993	37 734	19 170	18 564
20 - 24	C	449 584	231 642	217 942	169 931	87 629	82 302	279 653	144 013	135 640
25 - 29	C	491 555	252 991	238 564	187 184	96 644	90 540	304 371	156 347	148 024
30 - 34	C	309 972	159 186	150 786	124 244	63 653	60 591	185 728	95 533	90 195
35 - 39	C	163 663	83 988	79 675	61 243	31 423	29 820	102 420	52 565	49 855
40 - 44	C	38 298	19 828	18 470	13 614	7 005	6 609	24 684	12 823	11 861
45+	C	8 219	4 201	4 018	2 341	1 193	1 148	5 878	3 008	2 870
Unk.- Inc.	C	173 222	88 404	84 818	78 567	40 306	38 261	94 655	48 098	46 557
Libyan Arab Jamahiriya - Jamahiriya arabe libyenne										
2000										
Total	C	98 752	50 751	48 001	...	...	...	...	...	...
0 - 19	C	4 743	2 494	2 249	...	...	...	...	...	...
20 - 24	C	14 368	7 315	7 053	...	...	...	...	...	...
25 - 29	C	27 733	14 249	13 484	...	...	...	...	...	...
30 - 34	C	28 008	14 313	13 695	...	...	...	...	...	...
35 - 39	C	16 581	8 521	8 060	...	...	...	...	...	...
40 - 44	C	6 227	3 270	2 957	...	...	...	...	...	...
45+	C	928	507	421	...	...	...	...	...	...
Unk.- Inc.	C	164	82	82	...	...	...	...	...	...
Mauritius - Maurice										
2000										
Total	+C	20 237	10 368	9 869	...	...	...	...	...	...
0 - 14	+C	36	21	15	...	...	...	...	...	...
15 - 19	+C	1 924	979	945	...	...	...	...	...	...
20 - 24	+C	6 764	3 520	3 244	...	...	...	...	...	...
25 - 29	+C	5 654	2 848	2 806	...	...	...	...	...	...
30 - 34	+C	3 714	1 882	1 832	...	...	...	...	...	...
35 - 39	+C	1 715	887	828	...	...	...	...	...	...
40 - 44	+C	360	199	161	...	...	...	...	...	...
45 - 49	+C	23	10	13	...	...	...	...	...	...
50+	+C	1	1	-	...	...	...	...	...	...
Unk.- Inc.	+C	46	21	25	...	...	...	...	...	...
Morocco - Maroc										
1999										
Total	C	529 383	270 719	258 664	256 501	131 296	125 205	272 069	138 979	133 090
0 - 14	C	494	274	220	188	104	84	303	167	136
15 - 19	C	48 067	24 686	23 381	18 485	9 474	9 011	29 529	15 182	14 347
20 - 24	C	125 963	64 787	61 176	55 702	28 748	26 954	70 091	35 952	34 139
25 - 29	C	134 263	68 787	65 476	67 453	34 607	32 846	66 585	34 060	32 525
30 - 34	C	116 005	59 164	56 841	62 250	31 782	30 468	53 558	27 260	26 298
35 - 39	C	74 432	37 762	36 670	39 356	19 988	19 368	34 957	17 710	17 247
40 - 44	C	24 443	12 351	12 092	11 339	5 732	5 607	13 071	6 606	6 465

10. Live births by age of mother, sex of the child and urban/rural residence: latest available year
Naissances vivantes selon l'âge de la mère , le sexe de l'enfant et la résidence, urbaine/rurale: dernière année disponible (continued — suite)

(See notes at end of table.— Voir notes à la fin du tableau.)

Continent, country or area, year and age (in years) / Continent, pays ou zone, année et âge (en années)	Code[a]	Total			Urban - Urbaine			Rural - Rurale		
		Both sexes - Les deux sexes	Male - Masculin	Female - Féminin	Both sexes - Les deux sexes	Male - Masculin	Female - Féminin	Both sexes - Les deux sexes	Male - Masculin	Female - Féminin
AFRICA — AFRIQUE										
Morocco - Maroc										
1999										
45 - 49	C	4 555	2 327	2 228	1 431	712	719	3 118	1 612	1 506
50+	C	1 138	566	572	286	141	145	851	425	426
Unk.- Inc.	C	23	15	8	11	8	3	6	5	1
Réunion										
1998										
Total	C	13 538	-	-	...	...	...	...	...	...
0 - 14	C	12	-	-	...	...	...	...	...	...
15 - 19	C	1 114	-	-	...	...	...	...	...	...
20 - 24	C	2 955	-	-	...	...	...	...	...	...
25 - 29	C	3 910	-	-	...	...	...	...	...	...
30 - 34	C	3 433	-	-	...	...	...	...	...	...
35 - 39	C	1 671	-	-	...	...	...	...	...	...
40 - 44	C	427	-	-	...	...	...	...	...	...
45 - 49	C	16	-	-	...	...	...	...	...	...
Saint Helena ex. dep. - Sainte - Hélène sans dép.										
2000										
Total	C	56	32	24	...	...	...	...	...	...
15 - 19	C	7	3	4	...	...	...	...	...	...
20 - 24	C	16	10	6	...	...	...	...	...	...
25 - 29	C	12	5	7	...	...	...	...	...	...
30 - 34	C	13	9	4	...	...	...	...	...	...
35 - 39	C	7	4	3	...	...	...	...	...	...
40 - 44	C	1	1	-	...	...	...	...	...	...
Seychelles										
1993										
Total	+C	1 689	860	829	...	...	...	...	...	...
0 - 14	+C	3	2	1	...	...	...	...	...	...
15 - 19	+C	271	157	114	...	...	...	...	...	...
20 - 24	+C	522	254	268	...	...	...	...	...	...
25 - 29	+C	473	246	227	...	...	...	...	...	...
30 - 34	+C	275	137	138	...	...	...	...	...	...
35 - 39	+C	126	56	70	...	...	...	...	...	...
40 - 44	+C	16	7	9	...	...	...	...	...	...
45+	+C	3	1	2	...	...	...	...	...	...
South Africa - Afrique du Sud										
1999										
Total	U	*1 363 800*	-	-	...	...	...	...	...	...
15 - 19	U	*195 560*	-	-	...	...	...	...	...	...
20 - 24	U	*362 872*	-	-	...	...	...	...	...	...
25 - 29	U	*339 586*	-	-	...	...	...	...	...	...
30 - 34	U	*246 119*	-	-	...	...	...	...	...	...
35 - 39	U	*140 344*	-	-	...	...	...	...	...	...
40 - 44	U	*52 428*	-	-	...	...	...	...	...	...
45 - 49	U	*13 437*	-	-	...	...	...	...	...	...
50+	U	*4 439*	-	-	...	...	...	...	...	...
Unk.- Inc.	U	*9 015*	-	-	...	...	...	...	...	...
Swaziland[1]										
1997										
Total	I	31 087	-	-	6 915	-	-	24 172	-	-
15 - 19	I	4 192	-	-	897	-	-	3 295	-	-
20 - 24	I	8 927	-	-	2 107	-	-	6 820	-	-
25 - 29	I	7 537	-	-	1 895	-	-	5 642	-	-
30 - 34	I	4 893	-	-	1 021	-	-	3 872	-	-
35 - 39	I	3 413	-	-	664	-	-	2 749	-	-
40 - 44	I	1 247	-	-	194	-	-	1 053	-	-

10. Live births by age of mother, sex of the child and urban/rural residence: latest available year
Naissances vivantes selon l'âge de la mère , le sexe de l'enfant et la résidence, urbaine/rurale: dernière année disponible (continued — suite)

(See notes at end of table.— Voir notes à la fin du tableau.)

Continent, country or area, year and age (in years) / Continent, pays ou zone, année et âge (en années)	Code[a]	Total			Urban - Urbaine			Rural - Rurale		
		Both sexes - Les deux sexes	Male - Masculin	Female - Féminin	Both sexes - Les deux sexes	Male - Masculin	Female - Féminin	Both sexes - Les deux sexes	Male - Masculin	Female - Féminin
AFRICA — AFRIQUE										
Swaziland[1]										
1997										
45 - 49	I	564	-	-	78	-	-	486	-	-
50+	I	230	-	-	32	-	-	198	-	-
Unk.- Inc.	I	84	-	-	27	-	-	57	-	-
Tunisia - Tunisie										
1998										
Total	C	166 718	-	-	...	...	...	...	...	...
15 - 19	C	3 650	-	-	...	...	...	...	...	...
20 - 24	C	28 802	-	-	...	...	...	...	...	...
25 - 29	C	44 260	-	-	...	...	...	...	...	...
30 - 34	C	39 518	-	-	...	...	...	...	...	...
35 - 39	C	19 869	-	-	...	...	...	...	...	...
40 - 44	C	5 327	-	-	...	...	...	...	...	...
45+	C	650	-	-	...	...	...	...	...	...
Unk.- Inc.	C	2 446	-	-	...	...	...	...	...	...
Zimbabwe[2]										
1992										
Total	I	359 286	181 007	178 279	107 597	54 099	53 498	251 689	126 908	124 781
0 - 14	I	400	196	204	69	35	34	331	161	170
15 - 19	I	51 532	25 946	25 586	12 885	6 536	6 349	38 647	19 410	19 237
20 - 24	I	113 965	57 541	56 424	39 078	19 741	19 337	74 887	37 800	37 087
25 - 29	I	77 393	38 894	38 499	26 902	13 395	13 507	50 491	25 499	24 992
30 - 34	I	58 693	29 648	29 045	16 898	8 559	8 339	41 795	21 089	20 706
35 - 39	I	37 559	18 926	18 633	8 746	4 334	4 412	28 813	14 592	14 221
40 - 44	I	15 224	7 568	7 656	2 520	1 240	1 280	12 704	6 328	6 376
45+	I	4 520	2 288	2 232	499	259	240	4 021	2 029	1 992
AMERICA, NORTH — AMERIQUE DU NORD										
Anguilla										
1999										
Total	+C	176	-	-	...	...	...	...	...	...
0 - 14	+C	1	-	-	...	...	...	...	...	...
15 - 19	+C	28	-	-	...	...	...	...	...	...
20 - 24	+C	42	-	-	...	...	...	...	...	...
25 - 29	+C	43	-	-	...	...	...	...	...	...
30 - 34	+C	35	-	-	...	...	...	...	...	...
35 - 39	+C	22	-	-	...	...	...	...	...	...
40+	+C	4	-	-	...	...	...	...	...	...
Unk.- Inc.	+C	1	-	-	...	...	...	...	...	...
Antigua and Barbuda - Antigua - et - Barbuda										
1995										
Total	+C	1 347	-	-	...	...	...	...	...	...
0 - 14	+C	4	-	-	...	...	...	...	...	...
15 - 19	+C	209	-	-	...	...	...	...	...	...
20 - 24	+C	377	-	-	...	...	...	...	...	...
25 - 29	+C	350	-	-	...	...	...	...	...	...
30 - 34	+C	246	-	-	...	...	...	...	...	...
35 - 39	+C	128	-	-	...	...	...	...	...	...
40 - 44	+C	23	-	-	...	...	...	...	...	...
45+	+C	2	-	-	...	...	...	...	...	...
Unk.- Inc.	+C	8	-	-	...	...	...	...	...	...
Aruba										
1996										
Total	+U	1 452	-	-	...	...	...	...	...	...
0 - 14	+U	6	-	-	...	...	...	...	...	...

10. Live births by age of mother, sex of the child and urban/rural residence: latest available year
Naissances vivantes selon l'âge de la mère , le sexe de l'enfant et la résidence, urbaine/rurale: dernière année disponible (continued — suite)

(See notes at end of table.— Voir notes à la fin du tableau.)

Continent, country or area, year and age (in years) Continent, pays ou zone, année et âge (en années)	Code[a]	Total			Urban - Urbaine			Rural - Rurale		
		Both sexes - Les deux sexes	Male - Masculin	Female - Féminin	Both sexes - Les deux sexes	Male - Masculin	Female - Féminin	Both sexes - Les deux sexes	Male - Masculin	Female - Féminin
AMERICA, NORTH — AMERIQUE DU NORD										
Aruba										
1996										
15 - 19	+U	122	-	-	...	...	...	...	...	...
20 - 24	+U	320	-	-	...	...	...	...	...	...
25 - 29	+U	409	-	-	...	...	...	...	...	...
30 - 34	+U	384	-	-	...	...	...	...	...	...
35 - 39	+U	185	-	-	...	...	...	...	...	...
40+	+U	26	-	-	...	...	...	...	...	...
Bahamas										
1996										
Total	U	5 873	3 027	2 846	...	...	...	...	...	...
0 - 14	U	10	4	6	...	...	...	...	...	...
15 - 19	U	803	424	379	...	...	...	...	...	...
20 - 24	U	1 561	829	732	...	...	...	...	...	...
25 - 29	U	1 525	748	777	...	...	...	...	...	...
30 - 34	U	1 238	640	598	...	...	...	...	...	...
35 - 39	U	601	316	285	...	...	...	...	...	...
40 - 44	U	106	58	48	...	...	...	...	...	...
45 - 49	U	6	3	3	...	...	...	...	...	...
50+	U	23	5	18	...	...	...	...	...	...
Belize										
1998										
Total	U	5 986	3 047	2 939	...	...	...	...	...	...
0 - 14	U	24	14	10	...	...	...	...	...	...
15 - 19	U	1 081	530	551	...	...	...	...	...	...
20 - 24	U	1 783	916	867	...	...	...	...	...	...
25 - 29	U	1 454	749	705	...	...	...	...	...	...
30 - 34	U	893	472	421	...	...	...	...	...	...
35 - 39	U	465	234	231	...	...	...	...	...	...
40 - 44	U	108	53	55	...	...	...	...	...	...
45+	U	18	8	10	...	...	...	...	...	...
Unk.- Inc.	U	160	71	89	...	...	...	...	...	...
Bermuda - Bermudes										
1998										
Total	C	825	416	409	...	...	...	...	...	...
0 - 14	C	-	-	-	...	...	...	...	...	...
15 - 19	C	66	34	32	...	...	...	...	...	...
20 - 24	C	142	63	79	...	...	...	...	...	...
25 - 29	C	187	102	85	...	...	...	...	...	...
30 - 34	C	265	139	126	...	...	...	...	...	...
35 - 39	C	141	68	73	...	...	...	...	...	...
40+	C	24	10	14	...	...	...	...	...	...
Canada[3]										
2000										
Total	C	327 882	168 387	159 495	...	...	...	...	...	...
0 - 14	C	153	87	66	...	...	...	...	...	...
15 - 19	C	17 350	8 777	8 573	...	...	...	...	...	...
20 - 24	C	59 523	30 623	28 900	...	...	...	...	...	...
25 - 29	C	101 072	52 139	48 933	...	...	...	...	...	...
30 - 34	C	96 353	49 514	46 839	...	...	...	...	...	...
35 - 39	C	45 393	23 113	22 280	...	...	...	...	...	...
40 - 44	C	7 643	3 928	3 715	...	...	...	...	...	...
45 - 49	C	278	148	130	...	...	...	...	...	...
50+	C	3	2	1	...	...	...	...	...	...
Unk.- Inc.	C	114	56	58	...	...	...	...	...	...

10. Live births by age of mother, sex of the child and urban/rural residence: latest available year
Naissances vivantes selon l'âge de la mère , le sexe de l'enfant et la résidence, urbaine/rurale: dernière année disponible (continued — suite)

(See notes at end of table.— Voir notes à la fin du tableau.)

Continent, country or area, year and age (in years) / Continent, pays ou zone, année et âge (en années)	Code[a]	Total			Urban - Urbaine			Rural - Rurale		
		Both sexes - Les deux sexes	Male - Masculin	Female - Féminin	Both sexes - Les deux sexes	Male - Masculin	Female - Féminin	Both sexes - Les deux sexes	Male - Masculin	Female - Féminin
AMERICA, NORTH — AMERIQUE DU NORD										
Cayman Islands - Îles Caïmanes										
1994										
Total	+C	531	246	285	...	...	...	...	...	...
0 - 14	+C	2	1	1	...	...	...	...	...	...
15 - 19	+C	62	31	31	...	...	...	...	...	...
20 - 24	+C	136	69	67	...	...	...	...	...	...
25 - 29	+C	139	55	84	...	...	...	...	...	...
30 - 34	+C	142	64	78	...	...	...	...	...	...
35 - 39	+C	37	20	17	...	...	...	...	...	...
40+	+C	13	6	7	...	...	...	...	...	...
Costa Rica										
1999										
Total	C	78 526	-	-	...	...	...	...	...	...
0 - 14	C	597	-	-	...	...	...	...	...	...
15 - 19	C	15 444	-	-	...	...	...	...	...	...
20 - 24	C	22 540	-	-	...	...	...	...	...	...
25 - 29	C	18 322	-	-	...	...	...	...	...	...
30 - 34	C	12 872	-	-	...	...	...	...	...	...
35 - 39	C	6 568	-	-	...	...	...	...	...	...
40 - 44	C	1 669	-	-	...	...	...	...	...	...
45+	C	106	-	-	...	...	...	...	...	...
Unk.- Inc.	C	408	-	-	...	...	...	...	...	...
Cuba										
2000										
Total	C	143 528	74 610	68 918	104 521	54 415	50 106	39 007	20 195	18 812
0 - 14	C	510	285	225	301	166	135	209	119	90
15 - 19	C	18 235	9 556	8 679	11 352	5 976	5 376	6 883	3 580	3 303
20 - 24	C	35 317	18 449	16 868	24 907	13 035	11 872	10 410	5 414	4 996
25 - 29	C	45 965	23 902	22 063	34 159	17 766	16 393	11 806	6 136	5 670
30 - 34	C	30 253	15 561	14 692	23 367	12 082	11 285	6 886	3 479	3 407
35 - 39	C	11 750	6 068	5 682	9 310	4 808	4 502	2 440	1 260	1 180
40 - 44	C	1 343	706	637	1 004	516	488	339	190	149
45 - 49	C	63	33	30	42	23	19	21	10	11
50+	C	24	11	13	16	7	9	8	4	4
Unk.- Inc.	C	68	39	29	63	36	27	5	3	2
Dominican Republic - République dominicaine										
1999										
Total	+U	193 418	99 127	94 291	...	...	...	...	...	...
0 - 14	+U	1 665	909	756	...	...	...	...	...	...
15 - 19	+U	23 353	11 880	11 473	...	...	...	...	...	...
20 - 24	+U	53 145	27 213	25 932	...	...	...	...	...	...
25 - 29	+U	51 520	26 568	24 952	...	...	...	...	...	...
30 - 34	+U	32 644	16 649	15 995	...	...	...	...	...	...
35 - 39	+U	15 335	7 867	7 468	...	...	...	...	...	...
40 - 44	+U	6 015	3 124	2 891	...	...	...	...	...	...
45 - 49	+U	2 624	1 388	1 236	...	...	...	...	...	...
50+	+U	2 558	1 238	1 320	...	...	...	...	...	...
Unk.- Inc.	+U	4 559	2 291	2 268	...	...	...	...	...	...
El Salvador										
2000										
Total	C	150 176	77 398	72 778	92 959	47 804	45 155	57 217	29 594	27 623
0 - 14	C	1 399	741	658	770	399	371	629	342	287
15 - 19	C	30 610	15 970	14 640	18 028	9 444	8 584	12 582	6 526	6 056
20 - 24	C	48 853	25 158	23 695	31 134	16 021	15 113	17 719	9 137	8 582
25 - 29	C	35 030	18 068	16 962	22 677	11 630	11 047	12 353	6 438	5 915

10. Live births by age of mother, sex of the child and urban/rural residence: latest available year
Naissances vivantes selon l'âge de la mère , le sexe de l'enfant et la résidence, urbaine/rurale: dernière année disponible (continued — suite)

(See notes at end of table.— Voir notes à la fin du tableau.)

Continent, country or area, year and age (in years) / Continent, pays ou zone, année et âge (en années)	Code[a]	Total			Urban - Urbaine			Rural - Rurale		
		Both sexes - Les deux sexes	Male - Masculin	Female - Féminin	Both sexes - Les deux sexes	Male - Masculin	Female - Féminin	Both sexes - Les deux sexes	Male - Masculin	Female - Féminin
AMERICA, NORTH — AMERIQUE DU NORD										
El Salvador 2000										
30 - 34	C	20 068	10 287	9 781	12 854	6 590	6 264	7 214	3 697	3 517
35 - 39	C	10 388	5 242	5 146	5 767	2 841	2 926	4 621	2 401	2 220
40 - 44	C	3 416	1 731	1 685	1 548	783	765	1 868	948	920
45 - 49	C	360	173	187	154	80	74	206	93	113
50+	C	48	26	22	23	14	9	25	12	13
Unk.- Inc.	C	4	2	2	4	2	2	...	...	...
Greenland - Groenland 1999										
Total	C	947	472	475	734	365	369	213	107	106
0 - 14	C	6	2	4	6	2	4	-	-	-
15 - 19	C	77	37	40	58	28	30	19	9	10
20 - 24	C	246	115	131	185	84	101	61	31	30
25 - 29	C	197	111	86	140	81	59	57	30	27
30 - 34	C	257	127	130	209	104	105	48	23	25
35 - 39	C	130	66	64	108	55	53	22	11	11
40 - 44	C	31	13	18	25	10	15	6	3	3
45 - 49	C	2	-	2	2	-	2	-	-	-
50+	C	1	1	-	1	1	-	-	-	-
Grenada - Grenade 2000										
Total	+C	1 883	-	-	...	...	...	...	...	...
0 - 14	+C	9	-	-	...	...	...	...	...	...
15 - 19	+C	310	-	-	...	...	...	...	...	...
20 - 24	+C	490	-	-	...	...	...	...	...	...
25 - 29	+C	452	-	-	...	...	...	...	...	...
30 - 34	+C	339	-	-	...	...	...	...	...	...
35 - 39	+C	208	-	-	...	...	...	...	...	...
40 - 44	+C	73	-	-	...	...	...	...	...	...
45+	+C	2	-	-	...	...	...	...	...	...
Guatemala 1999										
Total	C	360 759	183 621	177 138	140 491	-	-	220 268	-	-
0 - 14	C	1 776	892	884	677	-	-	1 099	-	-
15 - 19	C	65 999	33 808	32 191	25 674	-	-	40 325	-	-
20 - 24	C	108 223	54 947	53 276	44 487	-	-	63 736	-	-
25 - 29	C	79 683	40 608	39 075	32 492	-	-	47 191	-	-
30 - 34	C	53 921	27 473	26 448	20 520	-	-	33 401	-	-
35 - 39	C	34 730	17 623	17 107	11 694	-	-	23 036	-	-
40 - 44	C	13 305	6 722	6 583	3 955	-	-	9 350	-	-
45 - 49	C	1 981	973	1 008	502	-	-	1 479	-	-
50+	C	557	288	269	119	-	-	438	-	-
Unk.- Inc.	C	584	287	297	371	-	-	213	-	-
Jamaica - Jamaïque 1996										
Total	+C	54 164	-	-	...	...	...	...	...	...
0 - 14	+C	400	-	-	...	...	...	...	...	...
15 - 19	+C	10 760	-	-	...	...	...	...	...	...
20 - 24	+C	15 881	-	-	...	...	...	...	...	...
25 - 29	+C	12 949	-	-	...	...	...	...	...	...
30 - 34	+C	8 824	-	-	...	...	...	...	...	...
35 - 39	+C	4 277	-	-	...	...	...	...	...	...
40 - 44	+C	974	-	-	...	...	...	...	...	...
45+	+C	99	-	-	...	...	...	...	...	...

10. Live births by age of mother, sex of the child and urban/rural residence: latest available year
Naissances vivantes selon l'âge de la mère , le sexe de l'enfant et la résidence, urbaine/rurale: dernière année disponible (continued — suite)

(See notes at end of table.— Voir notes à la fin du tableau.)

Continent, country or area, year and age (in years) — Continent, pays ou zone, année et âge (en années)	Code[a]	Total			Urban - Urbaine			Rural - Rurale		
		Both sexes - Les deux sexes	Male - Masculin	Female - Féminin	Both sexes - Les deux sexes	Male - Masculin	Female - Féminin	Both sexes - Les deux sexes	Male - Masculin	Female - Féminin
AMERICA, NORTH — AMERIQUE DU NORD										
Martinique[4,5]										
1992										
Total	C	6 305	3 190	3 115	...	...	...	...	...	...
0 - 14	C	15	8	7	...	...	...	...	...	...
15 - 19	C	430	221	209	...	...	...	...	...	...
20 - 24	C	1 486	746	740	...	...	...	...	...	...
25 - 29	C	2 029	1 022	1 007	...	...	...	...	...	...
30 - 34	C	1 495	769	726	...	...	...	...	...	...
35 - 39	C	675	339	336	...	...	...	...	...	...
40 - 44	C	143	70	73	...	...	...	...	...	...
45+	C	8	5	3	...	...	...	...	...	...
Unk.- Inc.	C	24	10	14	...	...	...	...	...	...
Mexico - Mexique[6]										
2000										
Total	+U	2 798 339	1 398 877	1 398 703	...	...	...	...	...	...
0 - 14	+U	12 175	5 977	6 196	...	...	...	...	...	...
15 - 19	+U	433 600	220 214	213 360	...	...	...	...	...	...
20 - 24	+U	797 421	404 579	392 773	...	...	...	...	...	...
25 - 29	+U	686 367	347 862	338 444	...	...	...	...	...	...
30 - 34	+U	418 706	211 519	207 157	...	...	...	...	...	...
35 - 39	+U	196 536	98 672	97 850	...	...	...	...	...	...
40 - 44	+U	56 696	28 373	28 318	...	...	...	...	...	...
45 - 49	+U	8 552	4 259	4 293	...	...	...	...	...	...
50+	+U	2 988	1 385	1 603	...	...	...	...	...	...
Unk.- Inc.	+U	185 298	76 037	108 709	...	...	...	...	...	...
Nicaragua										
2000										
Total	+U	92 859	-	-	...	...	...	...	...	...
0 - 14	+U	857	-	-	...	...	...	...	...	...
15 - 19	+U	28 472	-	-	...	...	...	...	...	...
20 - 24	+U	29 223	-	-	...	...	...	...	...	...
25 - 29	+U	17 693	-	-	...	...	...	...	...	...
30 - 34	+U	9 671	-	-	...	...	...	...	...	...
35 - 39	+U	5 323	-	-	...	...	...	...	...	...
40 - 44	+U	1 391	-	-	...	...	...	...	...	...
45 - 49	+U	182	-	-	...	...	...	...	...	...
50+	+U	22	-	-	...	...	...	...	...	...
Unk.- Inc.	+U	25	-	-	...	...	...	...	...	...
Panama										
1999										
Total	C	64 248	33 077	31 171	32 724	16 894	15 830	31 524	16 183	15 341
0 - 14	C	537	290	247	205	114	91	332	176	156
15 - 19	C	12 126	6 288	5 838	5 594	2 893	2 701	6 532	3 395	3 137
20 - 24	C	18 281	9 435	8 846	9 344	4 846	4 498	8 937	4 589	4 348
25 - 29	C	15 488	7 964	7 524	8 369	4 321	4 048	7 119	3 643	3 476
30 - 34	C	10 451	5 314	5 137	5 822	2 989	2 833	4 629	2 325	2 304
35 - 39	C	4 925	2 581	2 344	2 553	1 309	1 244	2 372	1 272	1 100
40 - 44	C	1 076	528	548	448	226	222	628	302	326
45 - 49	C	95	46	49	14	9	5	81	37	44
50+	C	23	9	14	1	-	1	22	9	13
Unk.- Inc.	C	1 246	622	624	374	187	187	872	435	437
2000										
Total	C	64 839	-	-	...	...	...	...	...	...
0 - 14	C	513	-	-	...	...	...	...	...	...
15 - 19	C	12 089	-	-	...	...	...	...	...	...
20 - 24	C	18 343	-	-	...	...	...	...	...	...
25 - 29	C	15 649	-	-	...	...	...	...	...	...
30 - 34	C	10 709	-	-	...	...	...	...	...	...

10. Live births by age of mother, sex of the child and urban/rural residence: latest available year
Naissances vivantes selon l'âge de la mère , le sexe de l'enfant et la résidence, urbaine/rurale: dernière année disponible (continued — suite)

(See notes at end of table.— Voir notes à la fin du tableau.)

Continent, country or area, year and age (in years) / Continent, pays ou zone, année et âge (en années)	Code[a]	Total			Urban - Urbaine			Rural - Rurale		
		Both sexes - Les deux sexes	Male - Masculin	Female - Féminin	Both sexes - Les deux sexes	Male - Masculin	Female - Féminin	Both sexes - Les deux sexes	Male - Masculin	Female - Féminin
AMERICA, NORTH — AMERIQUE DU NORD										
Panama										
2000										
35 - 39	C	5 092	-	-	...	...	...	...	...	...
40 - 44	C	1 194	-	-	...	...	...	...	...	...
45 - 49	C	105	-	-	...	...	...	...	...	...
50+	C	18	-	-	...	...	...	...	...	...
Unk.- Inc.	C	1 127	-	-	...	...	...	...	...	...
Puerto Rico - Porto Rico[7]										
2000										
Total	C	59 460	30 593	28 867	30 464	15 589	14 875	28 967	14 991	13 976
0 - 14	C	272	155	117	115	62	53	156	93	63
15 - 19	C	11 118	5 735	5 383	4 972	2 552	2 420	6 140	3 181	2 959
20 - 24	C	19 423	10 005	9 418	9 360	4 804	4 556	10 057	5 197	4 860
25 - 29	C	15 152	7 806	7 346	8 167	4 169	3 998	6 983	3 637	3 346
30 - 34	C	8 902	4 515	4 387	5 123	2 586	2 537	3 779	1 929	1 850
35 - 39	C	3 762	1 974	1 788	2 243	1 176	1 067	1 518	797	721
40 - 44	C	748	362	386	437	218	219	311	144	167
45 - 49	C	29	14	15	18	7	11	10	7	3
Unk.- Inc.	C	54	27	27	29	15	14	13	6	7
Saint Kitts and Nevis - Saint - Kitts - et - Nevis										
1996										
Total	+C	833	-	-	...	...	...	...	...	...
10 - 14	+C	5	-	-	...	...	...	...	...	...
15 - 19	+C	153	-	-	...	...	...	...	...	...
20 - 24	+C	230	-	-	...	...	...	...	...	...
25 - 29	+C	195	-	-	...	...	...	...	...	...
30 - 34	+C	140	-	-	...	...	...	...	...	...
35 - 39	+C	90	-	-	...	...	...	...	...	...
40 - 44	+C	18	-	-	...	...	...	...	...	...
45+	+C	2	-	-	...	...	...	...	...	...
Saint Lucia - Sainte - Lucie[8]										
2000										
Total	C	2 843	-	-	...	...	...	...	...	...
0 - 14	C	7	-	-	...	...	...	...	...	...
15 - 19	C	466	-	-	...	...	...	...	...	...
20 - 24	C	780	-	-	...	...	...	...	...	...
25 - 29	C	667	-	-	...	...	...	...	...	...
30 - 34	C	557	-	-	...	...	...	...	...	...
35 - 39	C	280	-	-	...	...	...	...	...	...
40 - 44	C	82	-	-	...	...	...	...	...	...
45+	C	4	-	-	...	...	...	...	...	...
Saint Vincent and the Grenadines - Saint Vincent-et-les Grenadines[8]										
2000										
Total	+C	2 149	1 104	1 045	...	...	...	...	...	...
0 - 14	+C	10	3	7	...	...	...	...	...	...
15 - 19	+C	454	232	222	...	...	...	...	...	...
20 - 24	+C	638	340	298	...	...	...	...	...	...
25 - 29	+C	486	244	242	...	...	...	...	...	...
30 - 34	+C	311	157	154	...	...	...	...	...	...
35 - 39	+C	208	107	101	...	...	...	...	...	...
40 - 44	+C	34	15	19	...	...	...	...	...	...

10. Live births by age of mother, sex of the child and urban/rural residence: latest available year
Naissances vivantes selon l'âge de la mère , le sexe de l'enfant et la résidence, urbaine/rurale: dernière année disponible (continued — suite)

(See notes at end of table.— Voir notes à la fin du tableau.)

Continent, country or area, year and age (in years) / Continent, pays ou zone, année et âge (en années)	Code[a]	Total			Urban - Urbaine			Rural - Rurale		
		Both sexes - Les deux sexes	Male - Masculin	Female - Féminin	Both sexes - Les deux sexes	Male - Masculin	Female - Féminin	Both sexes - Les deux sexes	Male - Masculin	Female - Féminin
AMERICA, NORTH — AMERIQUE DU NORD										
Saint Vincent and the Grenadines - Saint Vincent-et-les Grenadines[8]										
2000										
45 - 49	+C	1	1	-	...	...	...	...	...	...
Unk.- Inc.	+C	7	5	2	...	...	...	...	...	...
Trinidad and Tobago - Trinité-et-Tobago										
1997										
Total	C	18 452	9 343	9 109	...	...	...	...	...	...
0 - 14	C	37	20	17	...	...	...	...	...	...
15 - 19	C	2 588	1 323	1 265	...	...	...	...	...	...
20 - 24	C	5 353	2 721	2 632	...	...	...	...	...	...
25 - 29	C	4 519	2 297	2 222	...	...	...	...	...	...
30 - 34	C	3 678	1 877	1 801	...	...	...	...	...	...
35 - 39	C	1 804	879	925	...	...	...	...	...	...
40 - 44	C	417	198	219	...	...	...	...	...	...
45+	C	24	11	13	...	...	...	...	...	...
Unk.- Inc.	C	32	17	15	...	...	...	...	...	...
United States - États-Unis										
2001										
Total	C	4 025 933	-	-	...	...	...	...	...	...
0 - 14	C	7 781	-	-	...	...	...	...	...	...
15 - 19	C	445 944	-	-	...	...	...	...	...	...
20 - 24	C	1 021 627	-	-	...	...	...	...	...	...
25 - 29	C	1 058 265	-	-	...	...	...	...	...	...
30 - 34	C	942 697	-	-	...	...	...	...	...	...
35 - 39	C	451 723	-	-	...	...	...	...	...	...
40 - 44	C	92 813	-	-	...	...	...	...	...	...
45 - 49	C	4 844	-	-	...	...	...	...	...	...
50 - 54	C	239	-	-	...	...	...	...	...	...
United States Virgin Islands - Îles Vierges américaines										
1993										
Total	C	2 529	1 290	1 239	...	...	...	...	...	...
0 - 14	C	18	7	11	...	...	...	...	...	...
15 - 19	C	404	201	203	...	...	...	...	...	...
20 - 24	C	733	377	356	...	...	...	...	...	...
25 - 29	C	612	319	293	...	...	...	...	...	...
30 - 34	C	462	232	230	...	...	...	...	...	...
35 - 39	C	227	123	104	...	...	...	...	...	...
40+	C	42	17	25	...	...	...	...	...	...
Unk.- Inc.	C	31	14	17	...	...	...	...	...	...
AMERICA, SOUTH — AMERIQUE DU SUD										
Argentina - Argentine										
2000										
Total	C	701 878	-	-	...	...	...	...	...	...
0 - 14	C	3 208	-	-	...	...	...	...	...	...
15 - 19	C	103 129	-	-	...	...	...	...	...	...
20 - 24	C	192 871	-	-	...	...	...	...	...	...
25 - 29	C	176 768	-	-	...	...	...	...	...	...
30 - 34	C	129 374	-	-	...	...	...	...	...	...

10. Live births by age of mother, sex of the child and urban/rural residence: latest available year
Naissances vivantes selon l'âge de la mère , le sexe de l'enfant et la résidence, urbaine/rurale: dernière année disponible (continued — suite)

(See notes at end of table.— Voir notes à la fin du tableau.)

Continent, country or area, year and age (in years) / Continent, pays ou zone, année et âge (en années)	Code[a]	Total			Urban - Urbaine			Rural - Rurale		
		Both sexes - Les deux sexes	Male - Masculin	Female - Féminin	Both sexes - Les deux sexes	Male - Masculin	Female - Féminin	Both sexes - Les deux sexes	Male - Masculin	Female - Féminin
AMERICA, SOUTH — AMERIQUE DU SUD										
Argentina - Argentine										
2000										
35 - 39	C	69 733	-	-	...	...	...	...	...	...
40 - 44	C	19 767	-	-	...	...	...	...	...	...
45 - 49	C	1 575	-	-	...	...	...	...	...	...
50+	C	163	-	-	...	...	...	...	...	...
Unk.- Inc.	C	5 290	-	-	...	...	...	...	...	...
Brazil - Brésil[9,8]										
1998										
Total	U	2 461 486	1 254 111	1 207 375	...	...	...	...	...	...
0 - 14	U	16 113	8 148	7 965	...	...	...	...	...	...
15 - 19	U	499 478	254 952	244 526	...	...	...	...	...	...
20 - 24	U	745 623	380 397	365 226	...	...	...	...	...	...
25 - 29	U	589 329	300 363	288 966	...	...	...	...	...	...
30 - 34	U	370 787	188 692	182 095	...	...	...	...	...	...
35 - 39	U	165 575	83 966	81 609	...	...	...	...	...	...
40 - 44	U	43 555	21 865	21 690	...	...	...	...	...	...
45 - 49	U	4 432	2 200	2 232	...	...	...	...	...	...
50+	U	415	204	211	...	...	...	...	...	...
Unk.- Inc.	U	26 179	13 324	12 855	...	...	...	...	...	...
Chile - Chili										
1999										
Total	C	250 674	128 256	122 418	...	...	...	...	...	...
0 - 14	C	1 052	559	493	...	...	...	...	...	...
15 - 19	C	39 387	20 158	19 229	...	...	...	...	...	...
20 - 24	C	59 293	30 405	28 888	...	...	...	...	...	...
25 - 29	C	64 135	32 959	31 176	...	...	...	...	...	...
30 - 34	C	51 086	25 980	25 106	...	...	...	...	...	...
35 - 39	C	28 720	14 613	14 107	...	...	...	...	...	...
40 - 44	C	6 700	3 427	3 273	...	...	...	...	...	...
45 - 49	C	298	152	146	...	...	...	...	...	...
50+	C	3	3	-	...	...	...	...	...	...
Colombia - Colombie										
2000										
Total	U	734 081	377 341	356 740	700 583	360 499	340 084	31 008	15 576	15 432
0 - 14	U	5 684	2 921	2 763	5 392	2 773	2 619	276	140	136
15 - 19	U	156 613	80 422	76 191	149 194	76 688	72 506	7 064	3 560	3 504
20 - 24	U	213 728	110 370	103 358	204 538	105 792	98 746	8 766	4 370	4 396
25 - 29	U	162 217	83 273	78 944	155 823	80 065	75 758	6 122	3 063	3 059
30 - 34	U	114 068	58 609	55 459	109 760	56 422	53 338	4 107	2 086	2 021
35 - 39	U	59 325	30 253	29 072	56 753	28 948	27 805	2 457	1 245	1 212
40 - 44	U	14 736	7 574	7 162	13 819	7 107	6 712	866	441	425
45 - 49	U	1 220	634	586	1 085	570	515	129	61	68
50+	U	184	101	83	162	92	70	20	9	11
Unk.- Inc.	U	6 306	3 184	3 122	4 057	2 042	2 015	1 201	601	600
Ecuador - Équateur[10]										
1998										
Total	U	199 079	101 862	97 217	142 383	73 064	69 319	56 696	28 798	27 898
0 - 14	U	703	348	355	515	261	254	188	87	101
15 - 19	U	35 007	17 835	17 172	25 024	12 781	12 243	9 983	5 054	4 929
20 - 24	U	60 739	31 190	29 549	43 856	22 647	21 209	16 883	8 543	8 340
25 - 29	U	46 481	23 862	22 619	34 129	17 597	16 532	12 352	6 265	6 087
30 - 34	U	30 639	15 659	14 980	22 385	11 400	10 985	8 254	4 259	3 995
35 - 39	U	16 895	8 591	8 304	11 262	5 722	5 540	5 633	2 869	2 764
40 - 44	U	5 834	2 983	2 851	3 370	1 720	1 650	2 464	1 263	1 201
45 - 49	U	888	430	458	466	229	237	422	201	221
50+	U	130	64	66	66	37	29	64	27	37
Unk.- Inc.	U	1 763	900	863	1 310	670	640	453	230	223

10. Live births by age of mother, sex of the child and urban/rural residence: latest available year
Naissances vivantes selon l'âge de la mère , le sexe de l'enfant et la résidence, urbaine/rurale: dernière année disponible (continued — suite)

(See notes at end of table.— Voir notes à la fin du tableau.)

Continent, country or area, year and age (in years) / Continent, pays ou zone, année et âge (en années)	Code[a]	Total			Urban - Urbaine			Rural - Rurale		
		Both sexes - Les deux sexes	Male - Masculin	Female - Féminin	Both sexes - Les deux sexes	Male - Masculin	Female - Féminin	Both sexes - Les deux sexes	Male - Masculin	Female - Féminin
AMERICA, SOUTH — AMERIQUE DU SUD										
Falkland Islands (Malvinas) - Îles Falkland (Malvinas)										
1992										
Total	+C	27	16	11	22	14	8	5	2	3
0 - 14	+C	-	-	-	-	-	-	-	-	-
15 - 19	+C	4	3	1	4	3	1	-	-	-
20 - 24	+C	5	1	4	2	1	1	3	-	3
25 - 29	+C	10	7	3	8	5	3	2	2	-
30 - 34	+C	7	5	2	7	5	2	-	-	-
35+	+C	1	-	1	1	-	1	-	-	-
French Guiana - Guyane française[4]										
1999										
Total	C	4 907	2 445	2 462	...	...	...	...	...	...
0 - 14	C	41	20	21	...	...	...	...	...	...
15 - 19	C	706	343	363	...	...	...	...	...	...
20 - 24	C	1 058	538	520	...	...	...	...	...	...
25 - 29	C	1 309	656	653	...	...	...	...	...	...
30 - 34	C	1 025	485	540	...	...	...	...	...	...
35 - 39	C	607	323	284	...	...	...	...	...	...
40 - 44	C	149	71	78	...	...	...	...	...	...
45+	C	12	9	3	...	...	...	...	...	...
Suriname										
2000										
Total	C	9 804	-	-	6 018	-	-	3 786	-	-
0 - 14	C	52	-	-	31	-	-	21	-	-
15 - 19	C	1 495	-	-	904	-	-	591	-	-
20 - 24	C	2 652	-	-	1 720	-	-	932	-	-
25 - 29	C	2 395	-	-	1 606	-	-	789	-	-
30 - 34	C	1 717	-	-	1 108	-	-	609	-	-
35 - 39	C	830	-	-	536	-	-	294	-	-
40 - 44	C	190	-	-	108	-	-	82	-	-
45+	C	18	-	-	1	-	-	17	-	-
Unk.- Inc.	C	455	-	-	4	-	-	451	-	-
Uruguay[6]										
2000										
Total	+C	52 770	27 119	25 641	...	...	...	...	...	...
0 - 14	+C	206	91	116	...	...	...	...	...	...
15 - 19	+C	8 268	4 293	3 974	...	...	...	...	...	...
20 - 24	+C	13 173	6 729	6 442	...	...	...	...	...	...
25 - 29	+C	12 404	6 460	5 943	...	...	...	...	...	...
30 - 34	+C	11 342	5 792	5 547	...	...	...	...	...	...
35 - 39	+C	5 373	2 765	2 606	...	...	...	...	...	...
40 - 44	+C	1 340	669	670	...	...	...	...	...	...
45+	+C	71	34	37	...	...	...	...	...	...
Unk.- Inc.	+C	593	286	306	...	...	...	...	...	...
Venezuela[9]										
2000										
Total	C	544 416	290 687	253 729	...	...	...	...	...	...
0 - 14	C	5 583	3 049	2 534	...	...	...	...	...	...
15 - 19	C	110 933	59 152	51 781	...	...	...	...	...	...
20 - 24	C	162 060	86 830	75 230	...	...	...	...	...	...
25 - 29	C	123 758	65 862	57 896	...	...	...	...	...	...
30 - 34	C	81 700	43 665	38 035	...	...	...	...	...	...
35 - 39	C	41 508	22 122	19 386	...	...	...	...	...	...
40 - 44	C	11 497	6 101	5 396	...	...	...	...	...	...
45 - 49	C	1 583	863	720	...	...	...	...	...	...

10. Live births by age of mother, sex of the child and urban/rural residence: latest available year
Naissances vivantes selon l'âge de la mère , le sexe de l'enfant et la résidence, urbaine/rurale: dernière année disponible (continued — suite)

(See notes at end of table.— Voir notes à la fin du tableau.)

Continent, country or area, year and age (in years) / Continent, pays ou zone, année et âge (en années)	Code[a]	Total			Urban - Urbaine			Rural - Rurale		
		Both sexes - Les deux sexes	Male - Masculin	Female - Féminin	Both sexes - Les deux sexes	Male - Masculin	Female - Féminin	Both sexes - Les deux sexes	Male - Masculin	Female - Féminin
AMERICA, SOUTH — AMERIQUE DU SUD										
Venezuela[9]										
2000										
50+	C	374	190	184	...	...	...	...	...	...
Unk.- Inc.	C	5 420	2 853	2 567	...	...	...	...	...	...
ASIA — ASIE										
Armenia - Arménie[11]										
2000										
Total	C	34 276	-	-	21 390	-	-	12 886	-	-
15 - 19	C	4 937	-	-	2 673	-	-	2 264	-	-
20 - 24	C	16 183	-	-	10 067	-	-	6 116	-	-
25 - 29	C	7 562	-	-	5 029	-	-	2 533	-	-
30 - 34	C	3 292	-	-	2 100	-	-	1 192	-	-
35 - 39	C	1 765	-	-	1 154	-	-	611	-	-
40 - 44	C	501	-	-	343	-	-	158	-	-
45 - 49	C	21	-	-	13	-	-	8	-	-
50+	C	15	-	-	11	-	-	4	-	-
Azerbaijan - Azerbaïdjan[11]										
2001										
Total	+C	110 356	59 495	50 861	49 676	26 989	22 687	60 680	32 506	28 174
15 - 19	+C	10 741	5 522	5 219	4 083	2 108	1 975	6 658	3 414	3 244
20 - 24	+C	43 306	22 871	20 435	19 340	10 255	9 085	23 966	12 616	11 350
25 - 29	+C	30 243	16 529	13 714	14 308	7 899	6 409	15 935	8 630	7 305
30 - 34	+C	16 810	9 365	7 445	7 663	4 302	3 361	9 147	5 063	4 084
35 - 39	+C	7 331	4 172	3 159	3 431	1 977	1 454	3 900	2 195	1 705
40 - 44	+C	1 795	968	827	795	414	381	1 000	554	446
45 - 49	+C	107	57	50	50	30	20	-	27	30
50+	+C	23	11	12	6	4	2	17	-	10
Bahrain - Bahreïn										
1999										
Total	U	14 280	-	-	...	...	...	...	...	...
0 - 14	U	2	-	-	...	...	...	...	...	...
15 - 19	U	345	-	-	...	...	...	...	...	...
20 - 24	U	2 804	-	-	...	...	...	...	...	...
25 - 29	U	4 122	-	-	...	...	...	...	...	...
30 - 34	U	3 769	-	-	...	...	...	...	...	...
35 - 39	U	2 382	-	-	...	...	...	...	...	...
40 - 44	U	723	-	-	...	...	...	...	...	...
45 - 49	U	97	-	-	...	...	...	...	...	...
50+	U	13	-	-	...	...	...	...	...	...
Unk.- Inc.	U	23	-	-	...	...	...	...	...	...
Brunei Darussalam - Brunéi Darussalam										
2000										
Total	+C	7 481	3 852	3 629	...	...	...	...	...	...
0 - 14	+C	4	3	1	...	...	...	...	...	...
15 - 19	+C	442	241	201	...	...	...	...	...	...
20 - 24	+C	1 507	793	714	...	...	...	...	...	...
25 - 29	+C	2 276	1 169	1 107	...	...	...	...	...	...
30 - 34	+C	1 901	964	937	...	...	...	...	...	...
35 - 39	+C	1 041	508	533	...	...	...	...	...	...
40 - 44	+C	294	168	126	...	...	...	...	...	...
45 - 49	+C	13	6	7	...	...	...	...	...	...
Unk.- Inc.	+C	3	-	3	...	...	...	...	...	...

10. Live births by age of mother, sex of the child and urban/rural residence: latest available year
Naissances vivantes selon l'âge de la mère , le sexe de l'enfant et la résidence, urbaine/rurale: dernière année disponible (continued — suite)

(See notes at end of table.— Voir notes à la fin du tableau.)

Continent, country or area, year and age (in years) / Continent, pays ou zone, année et âge (en années)	Code[a]	Total			Urban - Urbaine			Rural - Rurale		
		Both sexes - Les deux sexes	Male - Masculin	Female - Féminin	Both sexes - Les deux sexes	Male - Masculin	Female - Féminin	Both sexes - Les deux sexes	Male - Masculin	Female - Féminin
ASIA — ASIE										
China: Hong Kong SAR - Chine: Hong Kong RAS[6]										
2000										
Total	C	54 134	28 273	25 848	...	...	...	...	...	...
0 - 14	C	12	8	4	...	...	...	...	...	...
15 - 19	C	969	509	460	...	...	...	...	...	...
20 - 24	C	6 572	3 473	3 099	...	...	...	...	...	...
25 - 29	C	16 103	8 348	7 755	...	...	...	...	...	...
30 - 34	C	18 941	9 907	9 034	...	...	...	...	...	...
35 - 39	C	10 018	5 241	4 776	...	...	...	...	...	...
40 - 44	C	1 388	726	662	...	...	...	...	...	...
45 - 49	C	57	32	25	...	...	...	...	...	...
50+	C	1	1	-	...	...	...	...	...	...
Unk.- Inc.	C	73	28	33	...	...	...	...	...	...
China: Macao SAR - Chine: Macao RAS										
2000										
Total	C	3 849	2 031	1 818	...	...	...	...	...	...
0 - 14	C	1	1	-	...	...	...	...	...	...
15 - 19	C	92	49	43	...	...	...	...	...	...
20 - 24	C	451	248	203	...	...	...	...	...	...
25 - 29	C	1 326	703	623	...	...	...	...	...	...
30 - 34	C	1 243	652	591	...	...	...	...	...	...
35 - 39	C	628	320	308	...	...	...	...	...	...
40 - 44	C	106	57	49	...	...	...	...	...	...
45 - 49	C	2	1	1	...	...	...	...	...	...
Cyprus - Chypre[7,12]										
2001										
Total	C	8 167	-	-	...	...	...	...	...	...
15 - 19	C	189	-	-	...	...	...	...	...	...
20 - 24	C	1 531	-	-	...	...	...	...	...	...
25 - 29	C	2 603	-	-	...	...	...	...	...	...
30 - 34	C	1 836	-	-	...	...	...	...	...	...
35 - 39	C	819	-	-	...	...	...	...	...	...
40 - 44	C	144	-	-	...	...	...	...	...	...
45 - 49	C	6	-	-	...	...	...	...	...	...
50+	C	5	-	-	...	...	...	...	...	...
Georgia - Géorgie[11]										
2001										
Total	C	40 416	21 906	18 510	25 078	13 427	11 651	15 338	8 479	6 859
0 - 14	C	86	45	41	53	31	22	33	14	19
15 - 19	C	4 814	2 557	2 257	2 769	1 440	1 329	2 045	1 117	928
20 - 24	C	15 733	8 392	7 341	9 193	4 883	4 310	6 540	3 509	3 031
25 - 29	C	9 640	5 334	4 306	6 397	3 501	2 896	3 243	1 833	1 410
30 - 34	C	5 992	3 291	2 701	3 896	2 098	1 798	2 096	1 193	903
35 - 39	C	3 058	1 686	1 372	2 046	1 097	949	1 012	589	423
40 - 44	C	809	449	360	535	287	248	274	162	112
45 - 49	C	146	80	66	89	42	47	57	38	19
50+	C	38	17	21	26	11	15	12	6	6
Unk.- Inc.	C	100	55	45	74	37	37	26	18	8
Iran (Islamic Republic of) - Iran (République islamique d')										
1994										
Total	U	*1 304 255*	-	-	*657 275*	-	-	*646 980*	-	-
0 - 14	U	*2 059*	-	-	*1 647*	-	-	*412*	-	-
15 - 19	U	*150 317*	-	-	*70 834*	-	-	*79 483*	-	-
20 - 24	U	*411 003*	-	-	*216 621*	-	-	*194 382*	-	-

10. Live births by age of mother, sex of the child and urban/rural residence: latest available year
Naissances vivantes selon l'âge de la mère , le sexe de l'enfant et la résidence, urbaine/rurale: dernière année disponible (continued — suite)

(See notes at end of table.— Voir notes à la fin du tableau.)

Continent, country or area, year and age (in years) / Continent, pays ou zone, année et âge (en années)	Code[a]	Total			Urban - Urbaine			Rural - Rurale		
		Both sexes - Les deux sexes	Male - Masculin	Female - Féminin	Both sexes - Les deux sexes	Male - Masculin	Female - Féminin	Both sexes - Les deux sexes	Male - Masculin	Female - Féminin
ASIA — ASIE										
Iran (Islamic Republic of) - Iran (République islamique d')										
1994										
25 - 29	U	338 933	-	-	177 085	-	-	161 848	-	-
30 - 34	U	212 503	-	-	102 545	-	-	109 958	-	-
35 - 39	U	126 843	-	-	66 304	-	-	60 539	-	-
40 - 44	U	45 713	-	-	17 297	-	-	28 416	-	-
45 - 49	U	12 355	-	-	2 883	-	-	9 472	-	-
50+	U	4 529	-	-	2 059	-	-	2 470	-	-
Iraq[13]										
2000										
Total	U	471 886	-	-	...	...	...	...	...	...
15 - 19	U	21 367	-	-	...	...	...	...	...	...
20 - 24	U	115 973	-	-	...	...	...	...	...	...
25 - 29	U	149 287	-	-	...	...	...	...	...	...
30 - 34	U	110 981	-	-	...	...	...	...	...	...
35 - 39	U	52 196	-	-	...	...	...	...	...	...
40 - 44	U	16 717	-	-	...	...	...	...	...	...
45+	U	5 365	-	-	...	...	...	...	...	...
Israel - Israël[14]										
2000										
Total	C	136 390	70 173	66 217	121 700	62 659	59 041	14 690	7 514	7 176
0 - 14	C	6	3	3	6	3	3	...	...	...
15 - 19	C	4 538	2 334	2 204	4 138	2 132	2 006	400	202	198
20 - 24	C	30 883	16 048	14 835	28 068	14 621	13 447	2 815	1 427	1 388
25 - 29	C	45 956	23 498	22 458	41 073	20 992	20 081	4 883	2 506	2 377
30 - 34	C	33 695	17 322	16 373	29 704	15 244	14 460	3 991	2 078	1 913
35 - 39	C	16 576	8 551	8 025	14 496	7 519	6 977	2 080	1 032	1 048
40 - 44	C	3 998	2 010	1 988	3 535	1 777	1 758	463	233	230
45 - 49	C	299	165	134	279	152	127	20	13	7
50+	C	28	14	14	27	13	14	1	1	-
Unk.- Inc.	C	411	228	183	374	206	168	37	22	15
Japan - Japon[7,15]										
2000										
Total	C	1 190 547	612 148	578 399	...	...	...	...	...	...
0 - 14	C	43	22	21	...	...	...	...	...	...
15 - 19	C	19 729	10 330	9 399	...	...	...	...	...	...
20 - 24	C	161 361	82 870	78 491	...	...	...	...	...	...
25 - 29	C	470 833	242 106	228 727	...	...	...	...	...	...
30 - 34	C	396 901	203 949	192 952	...	...	...	...	...	...
35 - 39	C	126 409	65 090	61 319	...	...	...	...	...	...
40 - 44	C	14 848	7 561	7 287	...	...	...	...	...	...
45 - 49	C	396	210	186	...	...	...	...	...	...
50+	C	6	1	5	...	...	...	...	...	...
Unk.- Inc.	C	21	9	12	...	...	...	...	...	...
Kazakhstan[11]										
1999										
Total	C	211 815	-	-	106 541	-	-	105 274	-	-
0 - 14	C	38	-	-	21	-	-	17	-	-
15 - 19	C	22 334	-	-	11 329	-	-	11 005	-	-
20 - 24	C	80 991	-	-	40 087	-	-	40 904	-	-
25 - 29	C	56 876	-	-	29 008	-	-	27 868	-	-
30 - 34	C	32 276	-	-	16 490	-	-	15 786	-	-
35 - 39	C	15 542	-	-	7 748	-	-	7 794	-	-
40 - 44	C	3 120	-	-	1 444	-	-	1 676	-	-
45 - 49	C	205	-	-	79	-	-	126	-	-
50+	C	31	-	-	4	-	-	27	-	-
Unk.- Inc.	C	402	-	-	331	-	-	71	-	-

(See notes at end of table.— Voir notes à la fin du tableau.)

Continent, country or area, year and age (in years) / Continent, pays ou zone, année et âge (en années)	Code[a]	Total			Urban - Urbaine			Rural - Rurale		
		Both sexes - Les deux sexes	Male - Masculin	Female - Féminin	Both sexes - Les deux sexes	Male - Masculin	Female - Féminin	Both sexes - Les deux sexes	Male - Masculin	Female - Féminin
ASIA — ASIE										
Korea (Dem. People's Republic of) - Corée (Rép. populaire dém. de)										
1993										
Total	U	420 576	215 444	205 132	230 111	117 944	112 167	190 465	97 500	92 965
0 - 24	U	54 774	27 978	26 796	27 672	14 130	13 542	27 102	13 848	13 254
25 - 29	U	268 774	137 297	131 477	149 546	76 348	73 198	119 228	60 949	58 279
30 - 34	U	82 021	42 255	39 766	45 049	23 258	21 791	36 972	18 997	17 975
35 - 39	U	12 617	6 557	6 060	6 683	3 538	3 145	5 934	3 019	2 915
40 - 44	U	1 679	917	762	811	456	355	868	461	407
45+	U	711	440	271	350	214	136	361	226	135
Korea (Republic of) - Corée (République de)[16]										
2000										
Total	C	636 780	333 797	302 983	...	...	...	...	...	...
0 - 14	C	9	3	6	...	...	...	...	...	...
15 - 19	C	4 603	2 403	2 200	...	...	...	...	...	...
20 - 24	C	74 440	38 457	35 983	...	...	...	...	...	...
25 - 29	C	329 113	170 947	158 166	...	...	...	...	...	...
30 - 34	C	183 930	97 689	86 241	...	...	...	...	...	...
35 - 39	C	37 203	20 300	16 903	...	...	...	...	...	...
40 - 44	C	5 071	2 707	2 364	...	...	...	...	...	...
45 - 49	C	292	146	146	...	...	...	...	...	...
50+	C	50	34	16	...	...	...	...	...	...
Unk.- Inc.	C	2 069	1 111	958	...	...	...	...	...	...
Kuwait - Koweït										
2000										
Total	C	41 843	21 332	20 511	...	...	...	...	...	...
15 - 19	C	1 271	655	616	...	...	...	...	...	...
20 - 24	C	8 918	4 543	4 375	...	...	...	...	...	...
25 - 29	C	13 227	6 795	6 432	...	...	...	...	...	...
30 - 34	C	10 156	5 214	4 942	...	...	...	...	...	...
35 - 39	C	5 674	2 853	2 821	...	...	...	...	...	...
40 - 44	C	1 613	794	819	...	...	...	...	...	...
45+	C	213	116	97	...	...	...	...	...	...
Unk.- Inc.	C	771	362	409	...	...	...	...	...	...
Kyrgyzstan - Kirghizistan[11]										
2000										
Total	C	96 770	49 566	47 204	28 193	14 497	13 696	68 577	35 069	33 508
0 - 14	C	11	5	6	4	2	2	7	3	4
15 - 19	C	8 716	4 504	4 212	2 223	1 147	1 076	6 493	3 357	3 136
20 - 24	C	35 918	18 380	17 538	9 738	4 974	4 764	26 180	13 406	12 774
25 - 29	C	26 102	13 245	12 857	8 027	4 144	3 883	18 075	9 101	8 974
30 - 34	C	15 526	8 051	7 475	4 918	2 534	2 384	10 608	5 517	5 091
35 - 39	C	7 977	4 071	3 906	2 457	1 272	1 185	5 520	2 799	2 721
40 - 44	C	2 005	1 045	960	594	300	294	1 411	745	666
45 - 49	C	261	132	129	73	39	34	188	93	95
50+	C	70	39	31	21	11	10	49	28	21
Unk.- Inc.	C	184	94	90	138	74	64	46	20	26
Malaysia: Peninsular Malaysia - Malaisie: Malaisie Péninsulaire[4]										
1998										
Total	C	457 642	236 683	220 959	...	...	...	...	...	...
0 - 14	C	174	100	74	...	...	...	...	...	...
15 - 19	C	14 194	7 390	6 804	...	...	...	...	...	...

10. Live births by age of mother, sex of the child and urban/rural residence: latest available year
Naissances vivantes selon l'âge de la mère , le sexe de l'enfant et la résidence, urbaine/rurale: dernière année disponible (continued — suite)

(See notes at end of table.— Voir notes à la fin du tableau.)

Continent, country or area, year and age (in years) Continent, pays ou zone, année et âge (en années)	Code[a]	Total			Urban - Urbaine			Rural - Rurale		
		Both sexes - Les deux sexes	Male - Masculin	Female - Féminin	Both sexes - Les deux sexes	Male - Masculin	Female - Féminin	Both sexes - Les deux sexes	Male - Masculin	Female - Féminin
ASIA — ASIE										
Malaysia: Peninsular Malaysia - Malaisie: Malaisie Péninsulaire[4]										
1998										
20 - 24	C	95 312	49 381	45 931	...	...	...	...	...	...
25 - 29	C	150 270	77 295	72 975	...	...	...	...	...	...
30 - 34	C	117 590	61 249	56 341	...	...	...	...	...	...
35 - 39	C	61 106	31 430	29 676	...	...	...	...	...	...
40 - 44	C	17 424	9 031	8 393	...	...	...	...	...	...
45 - 49	C	1 385	712	673	...	...	...	...	...	...
50+	C	46	26	20	...	...	...	...	...	...
Unk.- Inc.	C	141	69	72	...	...	...	...	...	...
Maldives										
1999										
Total	C	5 225	2 641	2 584	1 489	753	736	3 736	1 888	1 848
0 - 14	C	2	2	-	-	-	-	2	2	-
15 - 19	C	587	286	301	157	74	83	430	212	218
20 - 24	C	1 581	830	751	479	245	234	1 102	585	517
25 - 29	C	1 364	672	692	421	202	219	943	470	473
30 - 34	C	972	479	493	264	137	127	708	342	366
35 - 39	C	547	271	276	130	67	63	417	204	213
40 - 44	C	147	89	58	29	23	6	118	66	52
45 - 49	C	24	11	13	8	4	4	16	7	9
50+	C	1	1	-	1	1	-	-	-	-
Mongolia - Mongolie										
2000										
Total	C	48 721	24 832	23 889	23 828	-	-	24 893	-	-
0 - 14	C	18	8	10	6	-	-	12	-	-
15 - 19	C	3 648	1 862	1 786	1 616	-	-	2 032	-	-
20 - 24	C	17 418	8 800	8 618	8 517	-	-	8 901	-	-
25 - 29	C	14 813	7 607	7 206	7 314	-	-	7 499	-	-
30 - 34	C	8 231	4 162	4 069	4 239	-	-	3 992	-	-
35 - 39	C	3 487	1 816	1 671	1 637	-	-	1 850	-	-
40 - 44	C	921	478	443	421	-	-	500	-	-
45 - 49	C	138	73	65	56	-	-	82	-	-
50+	C	47	26	21	22	-	-	25	-	-
Oman[13]										
1999										
Total	...	44 067	-	-	...	...	...	...	...	...
15 - 19	...	4 096	-	-	...	...	...	...	...	...
20 - 24	...	13 224	-	-	...	...	...	...	...	...
25 - 29	...	11 504	-	-	...	...	...	...	...	...
30 - 34	...	7 759	-	-	...	...	...	...	...	...
35 - 39	...	5 563	-	-	...	...	...	...	...	...
40 - 44	...	1 739	-	-	...	...	...	...	...	...
45+	...	182	-	-	...	...	...	...	...	...
Pakistan[17,18]										
1997										
Total	I	4 143 506	2 149 035	1 994 471	1 198 287	627 177	571 110	2 945 220	1 521 858	1 423 362
15 - 19	I	332 071	171 847	160 224	82 658	43 309	39 349	249 413	128 538	120 875
20 - 24	I	1 226 263	649 834	576 429	339 841	185 462	154 379	886 422	464 372	422 050
25 - 29	I	1 168 672	612 292	556 380	376 770	198 244	178 526	791 901	414 047	377 854
30 - 34	I	736 912	369 551	367 361	222 775	108 885	113 890	514 137	260 666	253 471
35 - 39	I	450 566	231 371	219 195	123 740	66 522	57 218	326 827	164 849	161 978
40 - 44	I	162 938	79 703	83 235	40 370	19 237	21 133	122 569	60 467	62 102
45+	I	66 084	34 437	31 647	12 133	5 518	6 615	53 951	28 919	25 032
Philippines										
1998										
Total	C	1 632 859	853 304	779 555	...	...	...	...	...	...

10. Live births by age of mother, sex of the child and urban/rural residence: latest available year
Naissances vivantes selon l'âge de la mère , le sexe de l'enfant et la résidence, urbaine/rurale: dernière année disponible (continued — suite)

(See notes at end of table.— Voir notes à la fin du tableau.)

Continent, country or area, year and age (in years) / Continent, pays ou zone, année et âge (en années)	Code[a]	Total			Urban - Urbaine			Rural - Rurale		
		Both sexes - Les deux sexes	Male - Masculin	Female - Féminin	Both sexes - Les deux sexes	Male - Masculin	Female - Féminin	Both sexes - Les deux sexes	Male - Masculin	Female - Féminin
ASIA — ASIE										
Philippines										
1998										
0 - 14	C	721	364	357	...	...	...	...	...	...
15 - 19	C	114 519	59 848	54 671	...	...	...	...	...	...
20 - 24	C	452 083	236 565	215 518	...	...	...	...	...	...
25 - 29	C	473 598	247 658	225 940	...	...	...	...	...	...
30 - 34	C	326 807	171 318	155 489	...	...	...	...	...	...
35 - 39	C	189 249	98 338	90 911	...	...	...	...	...	...
40 - 44	C	64 254	33 258	30 996	...	...	...	...	...	...
45 - 49	C	7 971	4 093	3 878	...	...	...	...	...	...
50+	C	760	378	382	...	...	...	...	...	...
Unk.- Inc.	C	2 897	1 484	1 413	...	...	...	...	...	...
Qatar										
1999										
Total	C	10 846	-	-	...	...	...	...	...	...
15 - 19	C	390	-	-	...	...	...	...	...	...
20 - 24	C	2 170	-	-	...	...	...	...	...	...
25 - 29	C	3 296	-	-	...	...	...	...	...	...
30 - 34	C	2 733	-	-	...	...	...	...	...	...
35 - 39	C	1 568	-	-	...	...	...	...	...	...
40 - 44	C	464	-	-	...	...	...	...	...	...
45 - 49	C	58	-	-	...	...	...	...	...	...
50+	C	17	-	-	...	...	...	...	...	...
Unk.- Inc.	C	150	-	-	...	...	...	...	...	...
Singapore - Singapour[19]										
2000										
Total	+C	46 631	24 346	22 285	...	...	...	...	...	...
0 - 14	+C	12	8	4	...	...	...	...	...	...
15 - 19	+C	927	474	453	...	...	...	...	...	...
20 - 24	+C	4 596	2 397	2 199	...	...	...	...	...	...
25 - 29	+C	15 663	8 220	7 443	...	...	...	...	...	...
30 - 34	+C	16 890	8 760	8 130	...	...	...	...	...	...
35 - 39	+C	7 294	3 840	3 454	...	...	...	...	...	...
40 - 44	+C	1 209	625	584	...	...	...	...	...	...
45 - 49	+C	30	16	14	...	...	...	...	...	...
50+	+C	1	-	1	...	...	...	...	...	...
Unk.- Inc.	+C	9	6	3	...	...	...	...	...	...
Sri Lanka										
1996										
Total	+C	340 649	173 603	167 046	234 715	119 540	115 175	105 934	54 063	51 871
0 - 14	+C	139	73	66	109	59	50	30	14	16
15 - 19	+C	28 271	14 483	13 788	18 849	9 594	9 255	9 422	4 889	4 533
20 - 24	+C	83 244	42 548	40 696	54 727	27 881	26 846	28 517	14 667	13 850
25 - 29	+C	101 510	51 840	49 670	70 277	35 933	34 344	31 233	15 907	15 326
30 - 34	+C	76 096	38 601	37 495	55 159	27 969	27 190	20 937	10 632	10 305
35 - 39	+C	42 130	21 467	20 663	28 886	14 765	14 121	13 244	6 702	6 542
40 - 44	+C	8 378	4 168	4 210	6 143	3 076	3 067	2 235	1 092	1 143
45 - 49	+C	804	386	418	534	250	284	270	136	134
50+	+C	77	37	40	31	13	18	46	24	22
Tajikistan - Tadjikistan[11]										
1994										
Total	C	162 152	-	-	38 006	-	-	124 146	-	-
0 - 19	C	15 886	-	-	3 832	-	-	12 054	-	-
20 - 24	C	59 943	-	-	14 476	-	-	45 467	-	-
25 - 29	C	43 322	-	-	10 202	-	-	33 120	-	-
30 - 34	C	28 073	-	-	6 393	-	-	21 680	-	-
35 - 39	C	11 323	-	-	2 351	-	-	8 972	-	-

10. Live births by age of mother, sex of the child and urban/rural residence: latest available year
Naissances vivantes selon l'âge de la mère , le sexe de l'enfant et la résidence, urbaine/rurale: dernière année disponible (continued — suite)

(See notes at end of table.— Voir notes à la fin du tableau.)

Continent, country or area, year and age (in years) / Continent, pays ou zone, année et âge (en années)	Code[a]	Total			Urban - Urbaine			Rural - Rurale		
		Both sexes - Les deux sexes	Male - Masculin	Female - Féminin	Both sexes - Les deux sexes	Male - Masculin	Female - Féminin	Both sexes - Les deux sexes	Male - Masculin	Female - Féminin
ASIA — ASIE										
Tajikistan - Tadjikistan[11]										
1994										
40 - 44	C	2 936	-	-	494	-	-	2 442	-	-
45 - 49	C	282	-	-	45	-	-	237	-	-
50+	C	41	-	-	4	-	-	37	-	-
Unk.- Inc.	C	346	-	-	209	-	-	137	-	-
Thailand - Thaïlande										
2000										
Total	+U	773 009	397 523	375 486	...	...	...	...	...	...
0 - 14	+U	1 478	779	699	...	...	...	...	...	...
15 - 19	+U	86 675	44 787	41 888	...	...	...	...	...	...
20 - 24	+U	207 225	106 314	100 911	...	...	...	...	...	...
25 - 29	+U	218 767	112 516	106 251	...	...	...	...	...	...
30 - 34	+U	154 337	79 321	75 016	...	...	...	...	...	...
35 - 39	+U	68 568	35 298	33 270	...	...	...	...	...	...
40 - 44	+U	16 339	8 497	7 842	...	...	...	...	...	...
45 - 49	+U	1 850	932	918	...	...	...	...	...	...
50+	+U	421	212	209	...	...	...	...	...	...
Unk.- Inc.	+U	17 349	8 867	8 482	...	...	...	...	...	...
Turkey - Turquie[17,8]										
1997										
Total	I	1 377 000	-	-	...	...	...	...	...	...
0 - 14	I	-	-	-	...	...	...	...	...	...
15 - 19	I	165 000	-	-	...	...	...	...	...	...
20 - 24	I	531 000	-	-	...	...	...	...	...	...
25 - 29	I	387 000	-	-	...	...	...	...	...	...
30 - 34	I	182 000	-	-	...	...	...	...	...	...
35 - 39	I	79 000	-	-	...	...	...	...	...	...
40 - 44	I	28 000	-	-	...	...	...	...	...	...
45+	I	5 000	-	-	...	...	...	...	...	...
Uzbekistan - Ouzbékistan[11]										
2000										
Total	C	527 580	-	-	163 834	-	-	363 746	-	-
15 - 19	C	28 179	-	-	10 217	-	-	17 962	-	-
20 - 24	C	228 743	-	-	69 369	-	-	159 374	-	-
25 - 29	C	160 082	-	-	48 315	-	-	111 767	-	-
30 - 34	C	78 316	-	-	25 084	-	-	53 232	-	-
35 - 39	C	26 866	-	-	9 095	-	-	17 771	-	-
40 - 44	C	4 979	-	-	1 639	-	-	3 340	-	-
45 - 49	C	348	-	-	96	-	-	252	-	-
50+	C	67	-	-	19	-	-	48	-	-
EUROPE										
Austria - Autriche										
2001										
Total	C	75 458	-	-	...	...	...	...	...	...
15 - 19	C	3 245	-	-	...	...	...	...	...	...
20 - 24	C	14 181	-	-	...	...	...	...	...	...
25 - 29	C	25 009	-	-	...	...	...	...	...	...
30 - 34	C	22 379	-	-	...	...	...	...	...	...
35 - 39	C	8 972	-	-	...	...	...	...	...	...
40 - 44	C	1 591	-	-	...	...	...	...	...	...
45 - 49	C	67	-	-	...	...	...	...	...	...
50+	C	5	-	-	...	...	...	...	...	...

10. Live births by age of mother, sex of the child and urban/rural residence: latest available year
Naissances vivantes selon l'âge de la mère , le sexe de l'enfant et la résidence, urbaine/rurale: dernière année disponible (continued — suite)

(See notes at end of table.— Voir notes à la fin du tableau.)

Continent, country or area, year and age (in years) / Continent, pays ou zone, année et âge (en années)	Code[a]	Total			Urban - Urbaine			Rural - Rurale		
		Both sexes - Les deux sexes	Male - Masculin	Female - Féminin	Both sexes - Les deux sexes	Male - Masculin	Female - Féminin	Both sexes - Les deux sexes	Male - Masculin	Female - Féminin
EUROPE										
Belarus - Bélarus[11]										
1999										
Total	C	92 975	47 945	45 030	66 380	34 176	32 209	26 595	13 769	12 826
0 - 19	C	11 506	6 001	5 505	7 642	3 985	3 657	3 864	2 016	1 848
20 - 24	C	38 926	20 193	18 733	28 058	14 516	13 542	10 868	5 677	5 191
25 - 29	C	25 520	13 030	12 490	18 590	9 472	9 118	6 930	3 558	3 372
30 - 34	C	11 749	5 985	5 764	8 430	4 308	4 122	3 319	1 677	1 642
35 - 39	C	4 351	2 259	2 092	3 064	1 577	1 487	1 287	682	605
40 - 44	C	847	438	409	542	288	254	305	150	155
45 - 49	C	39	22	17	21	15	6	18	7	11
50+	C	2	-	-	2	-	2	-	-	-
Unk.- Inc.	C	35	17	18	31	15	16	4	2	2
Belgium - Belgique[20]										
1992										
Total	C	124 774	63 883	60 891	...	...	...	...	...	...
0 - 14	C	29	14	15	...	...	...	...	...	...
15 - 19	C	3 576	1 802	1 774	...	...	...	...	...	...
20 - 24	C	26 290	13 464	12 826	...	...	...	...	...	...
25 - 29	C	54 442	27 797	26 645	...	...	...	...	...	...
30 - 34	C	30 484	15 659	14 825	...	...	...	...	...	...
35 - 39	C	8 604	4 437	4 167	...	...	...	...	...	...
40 - 44	C	1 253	662	591	...	...	...	...	...	...
45 - 49	C	53	25	28	...	...	...	...	...	...
50+	C	6	5	1	...	...	...	...	...	...
Unk.- Inc.	C	37	18	19	...	...	...	...	...	...
Bosnia and Herzegovina - Bosnie - Herzégovine										
1998										
Total	C	45 007	-	-	...	...	...	...	...	...
0 - 14	C	2	-	-	...	...	...	...	...	...
15 - 19	C	3 191	-	-	...	...	...	...	...	...
20 - 24	C	14 515	-	-	...	...	...	...	...	...
25 - 29	C	12 937	-	-	...	...	...	...	...	...
30 - 34	C	7 971	-	-	...	...	...	...	...	...
35 - 39	C	3 577	-	-	...	...	...	...	...	...
40 - 44	C	756	-	-	...	...	...	...	...	...
45 - 49	C	53	-	-	...	...	...	...	...	...
50+	C	4	-	-	...	...	...	...	...	...
Unk.- Inc.	C	2 001	-	-	...	...	...	...	...	...
Bulgaria - Bulgarie										
2001										
Total	C	68 180	35 125	33 055	48 567	25 068	23 499	19 613	10 057	9 556
0 - 14	C	376	213	163	246	133	113	130	80	50
15 - 19	C	11 253	5 893	5 360	6 626	3 489	3 137	4 627	2 404	2 223
20 - 24	C	24 180	12 414	11 766	16 388	8 462	7 926	7 792	3 952	3 840
25 - 29	C	20 382	10 433	9 949	15 809	8 057	7 752	4 573	2 376	2 197
30 - 34	C	8 876	4 584	4 292	7 078	3 696	3 382	1 798	888	910
35 - 39	C	2 559	1 302	1 257	1 979	1 003	976	580	299	281
40 - 44	C	491	252	239	383	199	184	108	53	55
45 - 49	C	22	9	13	21	8	13	1	1	-
50+	C	1	1	-	...	...	...	1	1	-
Unk.- Inc.	C	40	24	16	37	21	16	3	3	-
Channel Islands: Guernsey - Îles Anglo - Normandes: Guernesey										
2000										
Total	C	644	336	308	...	...	...	...	...	...

10. Live births by age of mother, sex of the child and urban/rural residence: latest available year
Naissances vivantes selon l'âge de la mère , le sexe de l'enfant et la résidence, urbaine/rurale: dernière année disponible (continued — suite)

(See notes at end of table.— Voir notes à la fin du tableau.)

Continent, country or area, year and age (in years) / Continent, pays ou zone, année et âge (en années)	Code[a]	Total			Urban - Urbaine			Rural - Rurale		
		Both sexes - Les deux sexes	Male - Masculin	Female - Féminin	Both sexes - Les deux sexes	Male - Masculin	Female - Féminin	Both sexes - Les deux sexes	Male - Masculin	Female - Féminin
EUROPE										
Channel Islands: Guernsey - Îles Anglo - Normandes: Guernesey										
2000										
15 - 19	C	42	15	27	...	...	...	...	...	...
20 - 24	C	84	49	35	...	...	...	...	...	...
25 - 29	C	192	101	91	...	...	...	...	...	...
30 - 34	C	200	102	98	...	...	...	...	...	...
35 - 39	C	106	60	46	...	...	...	...	...	...
40 - 44	C	20	9	11	...	...	...	...	...	...
Channel Islands: Jersey - Îles Anglo - Normandes: Jersey										
1994										
Total	+C	1 142	589	553	...	...	...	...	...	...
0 - 14	+C	1	1	-	...	...	...	...	...	...
15 - 19	+C	31	17	14	...	...	...	...	...	...
20 - 24	+C	161	86	75	...	...	...	...	...	...
25 - 29	+C	390	201	189	...	...	...	...	...	...
30 - 34	+C	398	198	200	...	...	...	...	...	...
35 - 39	+C	140	77	63	...	...	...	...	...	...
40+	+C	21	9	12	...	...	...	...	...	...
Croatia - Croatie										
2001										
Total	C	40 993	21 019	19 974	22 938	11 777	11 161	18 055	9 242	8 813
0 - 14	C	8	6	2	4	2	2	4	4	-
15 - 19	C	2 246	1 152	1 094	895	466	429	1 351	686	665
20 - 24	C	10 788	5 412	5 376	5 067	2 556	2 511	5 721	2 856	2 865
25 - 29	C	14 206	7 305	6 901	8 250	4 197	4 053	5 956	3 108	2 848
30 - 34	C	9 108	4 762	4 346	5 826	3 056	2 770	3 282	1 706	1 576
35 - 39	C	3 806	1 981	1 825	2 382	1 257	1 125	1 424	724	700
40 - 44	C	712	350	362	427	209	218	285	141	144
45 - 49	C	35	13	22	21	8	13	...	...	...
50+	C	2	-	-	...	...	...	-	-	-
Unk.- Inc.	C	82	38	44	64	26	38	18	12	6
Czech Republic - République tchèque										
2001										
Total	C	90 715	46 616	44 099	67 081	34 518	32 563	23 634	12 098	11 536
0 - 14	C	17	10	7	15	8	7	2	2	-
15 - 19	C	3 810	1 918	1 892	2 819	1 413	1 406	991	505	486
20 - 24	C	24 985	12 953	12 032	17 197	8 917	8 280	7 788	4 036	3 752
25 - 29	C	39 512	20 204	19 308	29 420	15 070	14 350	10 092	5 134	4 958
30 - 34	C	16 356	8 396	7 960	12 894	6 620	6 274	3 462	1 776	1 686
35 - 39	C	5 183	2 701	2 482	4 085	2 149	1 936	1 098	552	546
40 - 44	C	822	419	403	632	334	298	190	85	105
45 - 49	C	29	14	15	18	6	12	11	8	3
50+	C	1	1	-	1	1	-	...	...	...
Denmark - Danemark[21]										
2001										
Total	C	65 450	-	-	...	...	...	...	...	...
15 - 19	C	1 044	-	-	...	...	...	...	...	...
20 - 24	C	8 149	-	-	...	...	...	...	...	...
25 - 29	C	23 974	-	-	...	...	...	...	...	...
30 - 34	C	21 946	-	-	...	...	...	...	...	...
35 - 39	C	9 037	-	-	...	...	...	...	...	...
40 - 44	C	1 257	-	-	...	...	...	...	...	...

10. Live births by age of mother, sex of the child and urban/rural residence: latest available year
Naissances vivantes selon l'âge de la mère , le sexe de l'enfant et la résidence, urbaine/rurale: dernière année disponible (continued — suite)

(See notes at end of table.— Voir notes à la fin du tableau.)

Continent, country or area, year and age (in years) / Continent, pays ou zone, année et âge (en années)	Code[a]	Total			Urban - Urbaine			Rural - Rurale		
		Both sexes - Les deux sexes	Male - Masculin	Female - Féminin	Both sexes - Les deux sexes	Male - Masculin	Female - Féminin	Both sexes - Les deux sexes	Male - Masculin	Female - Féminin
EUROPE										
Denmark - Danemark[21]										
2001										
45 - 49	C	39	-	-	...	...	...	...	...	...
50+	C	1	-	-	...	...	...	...	...	...
Estonia - Estonie[7,11]										
2000										
Total	C	13 086	6 834	6 252	8 684	4 581	4 103	4 402	2 253	2 149
0 - 14	C	4	3	1	2	2	-	2	1	1
15 - 19	C	1 306	703	603	796	423	373	510	280	230
20 - 24	C	4 041	2 130	1 911	2 708	1 471	1 237	1 333	659	674
25 - 29	C	4 016	2 001	2 015	2 732	1 362	1 370	1 284	639	645
30 - 34	C	2 475	1 338	1 137	1 641	894	747	834	444	390
35 - 39	C	984	522	462	662	352	310	322	170	152
40 - 44	C	250	132	118	134	72	62	116	60	56
45 - 49	C	9	4	5	8	4	4	1	-	1
Unk.- Inc.	C	1	1	-	1	1	-	...	...	...
2001										
Total	C	12 632	-	-	...	...	...	...	...	...
15 - 19	C	1 226	-	-	...	...	...	...	...	...
20 - 24	C	3 795	-	-	...	...	...	...	...	...
25 - 29	C	3 872	-	-	...	...	...	...	...	...
30 - 34	C	2 462	-	-	...	...	...	...	...	...
35 - 39	C	1 045	-	-	...	...	...	...	...	...
40 - 44	C	219	-	-	...	...	...	...	...	...
45 - 49	C	8	-	-	...	...	...	...	...	...
50+	C	-	-	-	...	...	...	...	...	...
Finland - Finlande[22]										
2001										
Total	C	56 189	28 701	27 488	36 191	18 569	17 622	19 998	10 132	9 866
0 - 14	C	6	3	3	3	1	2	3	2	1
15 - 19	C	1 714	894	820	1 109	593	516	605	301	304
20 - 24	C	9 542	4 860	4 682	6 137	3 126	3 011	3 405	1 734	1 671
25 - 29	C	17 191	8 734	8 457	11 147	5 686	5 461	6 044	3 048	2 996
30 - 34	C	17 038	8 707	8 331	10 999	5 687	5 312	6 039	3 020	3 019
35 - 39	C	8 793	4 538	4 255	5 656	2 892	2 764	3 137	1 646	1 491
40 - 44	C	1 808	913	895	1 087	562	525	721	351	370
45 - 49	C	94	51	43	51	22	29	43	29	14
50+	C	3	-	2	2	-	2	-	1	-
France[5,23]										
2000										
Total	C	773 395	396 638	376 757	589 608	302 146	287 462	183 787	94 492	89 295
0 - 14	C	49	22	27	41	18	23	8	4	4
15 - 19	C	15 646	7 995	7 651	13 267	6 707	6 560	2 379	1 288	1 091
20 - 24	C	103 451	53 181	50 270	83 572	42 960	40 612	19 879	10 221	9 658
25 - 29	C	273 133	140 100	133 033	204 106	104 653	99 453	69 027	35 447	33 580
30 - 34	C	247 171	126 914	120 257	184 175	94 477	89 698	62 996	32 437	30 559
35 - 39	C	109 626	56 084	53 542	84 690	43 250	41 440	24 936	12 834	12 102
40 - 44	C	23 273	11 812	11 461	18 880	9 634	9 246	4 393	2 178	2 215
45 - 49	C	1 006	513	493	841	432	409	165	81	84
50+	C	40	17	23	36	15	21	4	2	2
Unk.- Inc.	C	-	-	-	-	-	-	-	-	-
Germany - Allemagne										
2000										
Total	C	766 999	-	-	...	...	...	...	...	...
0 - 14	C	466	-	-	...	...	...	...	...	...
15 - 19	C	38 731	-	-	...	...	...	...	...	...
20 - 24	C	137 851	-	-	...	...	...	...	...	...
25 - 29	C	240 571	-	-	...	...	...	...	...	...

10. Live births by age of mother, sex of the child and urban/rural residence: latest available year
Naissances vivantes selon l'âge de la mère , le sexe de l'enfant et la résidence, urbaine/rurale: dernière année disponible (continued — suite)

(See notes at end of table.— Voir notes à la fin du tableau.)

Continent, country or area, year and age (in years) / Continent, pays ou zone, année et âge (en années)	Code[a]	Total			Urban - Urbaine			Rural - Rurale		
		Both sexes - Les deux sexes	Male - Masculin	Female - Féminin	Both sexes - Les deux sexes	Male - Masculin	Female - Féminin	Both sexes - Les deux sexes	Male - Masculin	Female - Féminin
EUROPE										
Germany - Allemagne										
2000										
30 - 34	C	247 389	-	-	...	...	...	...	...	...
35 - 39	C	90 368	-	-	...	...	...	...	...	...
40 - 44	C	11 315	-	-	...	...	...	...	...	...
45 - 49	C	285	-	-	...	...	...	...	...	...
50+	C	23	-	-	...	...	...	...	...	...
Gibraltar										
1997										
Total	C	427	-	-	...	...	...	...	...	...
0 - 14	C	-	-	-	...	...	...	...	...	...
15 - 19	C	18	-	-	...	...	...	...	...	...
20 - 24	C	93	-	-	...	...	...	...	...	...
25 - 29	C	143	-	-	...	...	...	...	...	...
30 - 34	C	117	-	-	...	...	...	...	...	...
35 - 39	C	51	-	-	...	...	...	...	...	...
40 - 44	C	4	-	-	...	...	...	...	...	...
45+	C	1	-	-	...	...	...	...	...	...
Greece - Grèce										
2001										
Total	C	102 282	-	-	...	...	...	...	...	...
0 - 14	C	148	-	-	...	...	...	...	...	...
15 - 19	C	3 650	-	-	...	...	...	...	...	...
20 - 24	C	17 859	-	-	...	...	...	...	...	...
25 - 29	C	34 421	-	-	...	...	...	...	...	...
30 - 34	C	31 656	-	-	...	...	...	...	...	...
35 - 39	C	12 123	-	-	...	...	...	...	...	...
40 - 44	C	2 169	-	-	...	...	...	...	...	...
45 - 49	C	186	-	-	...	...	...	...	...	...
50+	C	65	-	-	...	...	...	...	...	...
Hungary - Hongrie[7]										
2001										
Total	C	96 138	49 562	46 576	59 119	30 418	28 701	37 019	19 144	17 875
0 - 14	C	103	54	49	43	21	22	60	33	27
15 - 19	C	7 004	3 604	3 400	3 360	1 720	1 640	3 644	1 884	1 760
20 - 24	C	24 951	12 892	12 059	13 440	6 913	6 527	11 511	5 979	5 532
25 - 29	C	36 195	18 558	17 637	23 514	12 041	11 473	12 681	6 517	6 164
30 - 34	C	20 147	10 404	9 743	13 757	7 056	6 701	6 390	3 348	3 042
35 - 39	C	6 378	3 352	3 026	4 141	2 213	1 928	2 237	1 139	1 098
40 - 44	C	1 302	667	635	834	436	398	468	231	237
45 - 49	C	58	31	27	30	18	12	28	13	15
Iceland - Islande										
2000										
Total	C	4 315	2 192	2 123	3 993	2 021	1 972	322	171	151
15 - 19	C	241	130	111	223	119	104	18	11	7
20 - 24	C	936	489	447	883	461	422	53	28	25
25 - 29	C	1 351	684	667	1 276	646	630	75	38	37
30 - 34	C	1 129	548	581	1 028	496	532	101	52	49
35 - 39	C	545	288	257	480	248	232	65	40	25
40 - 44	C	109	52	57	100	50	50	9	2	7
45 - 49	C	4	1	3	3	1	2	1	-	1
2001										
Total	C	4 091	-	-	...	...	...	...	...	...
15 - 19	C	203	-	-	...	...	...	...	...	...
20 - 24	C	858	-	-	...	...	...	...	...	...
25 - 29	C	1 346	-	-	...	...	...	...	...	...
30 - 34	C	991	-	-	...	...	...	...	...	...
35 - 39	C	584	-	-	...	...	...	...	...	...
40 - 44	C	105	-	-	...	...	...	...	...	...

10. Live births by age of mother, sex of the child and urban/rural residence: latest available year
Naissances vivantes selon l'âge de la mère , le sexe de l'enfant et la résidence, urbaine/rurale: dernière année disponible (continued — suite)

(See notes at end of table.— Voir notes à la fin du tableau.)

Continent, country or area, year and age (in years) / Continent, pays ou zone, année et âge (en années)	Code[a]	Total			Urban - Urbaine			Rural - Rurale		
		Both sexes - Les deux sexes	Male - Masculin	Female - Féminin	Both sexes - Les deux sexes	Male - Masculin	Female - Féminin	Both sexes - Les deux sexes	Male - Masculin	Female - Féminin
EUROPE										
Iceland - Islande										
2001										
45 - 49	C	3	-	-	...	...	...	...	...	...
50+	C	-	-	-	...	...	...	...	...	...
Ireland - Irlande[24]										
2001										
Total	+C	57 882	-	-	...	...	...	...	...	...
15 - 19	+C	3 087	-	-	...	...	...	...	...	...
20 - 24	+C	8 335	-	-	...	...	...	...	...	...
25 - 29	+C	14 134	-	-	...	...	...	...	...	...
30 - 34	+C	19 305	-	-	...	...	...	...	...	...
35 - 39	+C	10 798	-	-	...	...	...	...	...	...
40 - 44	+C	1 839	-	-	...	...	...	...	...	...
45 - 49	+C	76	-	-	...	...	...	...	...	...
50+	+C	1	-	-	...	...	...	...	...	...
Italy - Italie										
2000										
Total	C	543 039	279 953	263 086	...	...	...	...	...	...
0 - 14	C	68	19	20	...	...	...	...	...	...
15 - 19	C	21 280	5 537	5 143	...	...	...	...	...	...
20 - 24	C	122 014	31 609	29 466	...	...	...	...	...	...
25 - 29	C	332 192	85 537	80 510	...	...	...	...	...	...
30 - 34	C	391 294	100 799	94 784	...	...	...	...	...	...
35 - 39	C	186 572	48 055	45 242	...	...	...	...	...	...
40 - 44	C	31 017	7 980	7 525	...	...	...	...	...	...
45 - 49	C	1 349	349	327	...	...	...	...	...	...
50+	C	273	68	69	...	...	...	...	...	...
Unk.- Inc.	C	21	-	-	...	...	...	...	...	...
Latvia - Lettonie[11]										
2001										
Total	C	19 664	9 987	9 677	12 531	6 357	6 174	7 133	3 630	3 503
0 - 14	C	4	3	1	2	2	-	2	1	1
15 - 19	C	1 531	808	723	850	428	422	681	380	301
20 - 24	C	5 969	3 005	2 964	3 534	1 786	1 748	2 435	1 219	1 216
25 - 29	C	6 138	3 120	3 018	4 092	2 081	2 011	2 046	1 039	1 007
30 - 34	C	3 807	1 930	1 877	2 597	1 318	1 279	1 210	612	598
35 - 39	C	1 722	869	853	1 145	586	559	577	283	294
40 - 44	C	463	235	228	292	145	147	171	90	81
45 - 49	C	24	15	9	14	9	5	10	6	4
50+	C	-	-	-	-	-	-	...	...	...
Unk.- Inc.	C	6	2	4	5	2	3	1	-	1
Liechtenstein										
1997										
Total	C	435	-	-	...	...	...	...	...	...
0 - 14	C	-	-	-	...	...	...	...	...	...
15 - 19	C	2	-	-	...	...	...	...	...	...
20 - 24	C	72	-	-	...	...	...	...	...	...
25 - 29	C	133	-	-	...	...	...	...	...	...
30 - 34	C	149	-	-	...	...	...	...	...	...
35 - 39	C	68	-	-	...	...	...	...	...	...
40 - 44	C	10	-	-	...	...	...	...	...	...
45+	C	1	-	-	...	...	...	...	...	...
Lithuania - Lituanie[11]										
2001										
Total	C	31 546	16 139	15 407	19 672	10 023	9 649	11 874	6 116	5 758
0 - 14	C	10	3	7	6	-	6	4	3	1
15 - 19	C	2 776	1 375	1 401	1 482	722	760	1 294	653	641
20 - 24	C	9 905	5 016	4 889	5 804	2 914	2 890	4 101	2 102	1 999
25 - 29	C	9 915	5 069	4 846	6 501	3 293	3 208	3 414	1 776	1 638

10. Live births by age of mother, sex of the child and urban/rural residence: latest available year
Naissances vivantes selon l'âge de la mère , le sexe de l'enfant et la résidence, urbaine/rurale: dernière année disponible (continued — suite)

(See notes at end of table.— Voir notes à la fin du tableau.)

Continent, country or area, year and age (in years) / Continent, pays ou zone, année et âge (en années)	Code[a]	Total			Urban - Urbaine			Rural - Rurale		
		Both sexes - Les deux sexes	Male - Masculin	Female - Féminin	Both sexes - Les deux sexes	Male - Masculin	Female - Féminin	Both sexes - Les deux sexes	Male - Masculin	Female - Féminin
EUROPE										
Lithuania - Lituanie[11]										
2001										
30 - 34	C	5 766	3 042	2 724	3 853	2 029	1 824	1 913	1 013	900
35 - 39	C	2 530	1 303	1 227	1 635	854	781	895	449	446
40 - 44	C	609	312	297	373	199	174	236	113	123
45 - 49	C	23	13	10	10	7	3	13	6	7
Unk.- Inc.	C	12	6	6	8	5	3	4	1	3
Luxembourg										
2001										
Total	C	4 241	-	-	...	...	...	...	...	...
15 - 19	C	52	-	-	...	...	...	...	...	...
20 - 24	C	492	-	-	...	...	...	...	...	...
25 - 29	C	1 388	-	-	...	...	...	...	...	...
30 - 34	C	1 564	-	-	...	...	...	...	...	...
35 - 39	C	647	-	-	...	...	...	...	...	...
40 - 44	C	96	-	-	...	...	...	...	...	...
45 - 49	C	2	-	-	...	...	...	...	...	...
50+	C	-			...	...	...	...	...	...
Malta - Malte[25]										
2001										
Total	C	3 859	-	-	...	...	...	...	...	...
15 - 19	C	240	-	-	...	...	...	...	...	...
20 - 24	C	767	-	-	...	...	...	...	...	...
25 - 29	C	1 509	-	-	...	...	...	...	...	...
30 - 34	C	902	-	-	...	...	...	...	...	...
35 - 39	C	340	-	-	...	...	...	...	...	...
40 - 44	C	97	-	-	...	...	...	...	...	...
45 - 49	C	4	-	-	...	...	...	...	...	...
Netherlands - Pays - Bas[26]										
2001										
Total	C	202 603	103 806	98 797	132 295	67 706	64 589	70 308	36 100	34 208
0 - 14	C	10	8	5	10	6	4	3	2	1
15 - 19	C	6 126	1 379	1 294	2 181	1 122	1 059	492	257	235
20 - 24	C	39 616	8 872	8 599	13 178	6 652	6 526	4 293	2 220	2 073
25 - 29	C	118 145	27 547	26 291	34 744	17 781	16 963	19 094	9 766	9 328
30 - 34	C	176 025	43 980	41 636	53 394	27 399	25 995	32 222	16 581	15 641
35 - 39	C	74 917	19 160	18 185	24 760	12 710	12 050	12 585	6 450	6 135
40 - 44	C	10 537	2 769	2 682	3 881	1 966	1 915	1 570	803	767
45 - 49	C	388	91	105	147	70	77	49	21	28
50+	C	1	-	-	...	...	...	...	...	...
Norway - Norvège[5]										
2001										
Total	C	56 696	29 041	27 655	...	...	...	...	...	...
0 - 14	C	6	4	2	...	...	...	...	...	...
15 - 19	C	1 435	752	683	...	...	...	...	...	...
20 - 24	C	8 449	4 394	4 055	...	...	...	...	...	...
25 - 29	C	19 571	9 994	9 577	...	...	...	...	...	...
30 - 34	C	18 610	9 536	9 074	...	...	...	...	...	...
35 - 39	C	7 486	3 786	3 700	...	...	...	...	...	...
40 - 44	C	1 091	548	543	...	...	...	...	...	...
45 - 49	C	48	27	21	...	...	...	...	...	...
Poland - Pologne										
2001										
Total	C	368 205	-	-	...	...	...	...	...	...
15 - 19	C	25 777	-	-	...	...	...	...	...	...
20 - 24	C	117 267	-	-	...	...	...	...	...	...
25 - 29	C	128 314	-	-	...	...	...	...	...	...
30 - 34	C	62 546	-	-	...	...	...	...	...	...

10. Live births by age of mother, sex of the child and urban/rural residence: latest available year
Naissances vivantes selon l'âge de la mère , le sexe de l'enfant et la résidence, urbaine/rurale: dernière année disponible (continued — suite)

(See notes at end of table.— Voir notes à la fin du tableau.)

Continent, country or area, year and age (in years) / Continent, pays ou zone, année et âge (en années)	Code[a]	Total			Urban - Urbaine			Rural - Rurale		
		Both sexes - Les deux sexes	Male - Masculin	Female - Féminin	Both sexes - Les deux sexes	Male - Masculin	Female - Féminin	Both sexes - Les deux sexes	Male - Masculin	Female - Féminin
EUROPE										
Poland - Pologne										
2001										
35 - 39	C	26 620	-	-	...	...	...	...	...	...
40 - 44	C	7 275	-	-	...	...	...	...	...	...
45 - 49	C	350	-	-	...	...	...	...	...	...
50+	C	1	-	-	...	...	...	...	...	...
Portugal										
2001										
Total	C	112 774	-	-	...	...	...	...	...	...
15 - 19	C	6 783	-	-	...	...	...	...	...	...
20 - 24	C	21 726	-	-	...	...	...	...	...	...
25 - 29	C	37 570	-	-	...	...	...	...	...	...
30 - 34	C	30 852	-	-	...	...	...	...	...	...
35 - 39	C	13 157	-	-	...	...	...	...	...	...
40 - 44	C	2 441	-	-	...	...	...	...	...	...
45 - 49	C	145	-	-	...	...	...	...	...	...
50+	C	4	-	-	...	...	...	...	...	...
Republic of Moldova - République de Moldova[11]										
2001										
Total	C	36 448	18 784	17 664	12 542	6 545	5 997	23 906	12 239	11 667
0 - 14	C	17	7	10	5	4	1	12	3	9
15 - 19	C	5 923	3 025	2 898	1 451	743	708	4 472	2 282	2 190
20 - 24	C	15 046	7 732	7 314	5 114	2 654	2 460	9 932	5 078	4 854
25 - 29	C	9 426	4 906	4 520	3 598	1 931	1 667	5 828	2 975	2 853
30 - 34	C	3 994	2 082	1 912	1 612	844	768	2 382	1 238	1 144
35 - 39	C	1 589	802	787	593	288	305	996	514	482
40 - 44	C	409	211	198	147	73	74	262	138	124
45 - 49	C	21	9	12	8	3	5	13	6	7
50+	C	3	1	2	1	1	-	2	-	2
Unk.- Inc.	C	20	9	11	13	4	9	7	5	2
Romania - Roumanie										
2001										
Total	C	220 368	113 599	106 769	102 432	52 753	49 679	117 936	60 846	57 090
0 - 14	C	627	319	308	232	118	114	395	201	194
15 - 19	C	28 503	14 604	13 899	9 329	4 706	4 623	19 174	9 898	9 276
20 - 24	C	77 518	40 024	37 494	32 306	16 765	15 541	45 212	23 259	21 953
25 - 29	C	66 793	34 598	32 195	34 305	17 697	16 608	32 488	16 901	15 587
30 - 34	C	36 063	18 493	17 570	20 766	10 677	10 089	15 297	7 816	7 481
35 - 39	C	8 395	4 274	4 121	4 358	2 210	2 148	4 037	2 064	1 973
40 - 44	C	2 327	1 220	1 107	1 081	553	528	1 246	667	579
45 - 49	C	139	65	74	54	26	28	85	39	46
50+	C	3	2	-	1	1	-	2	1	1
Russian Federation - Fédération de Russie[11]										
1999										
Total	C	1 214 689	-	-	842 640	-	-	372 049	-	-
0 - 14	C	2 884	-	-	1 602	-	-	1 282	-	-
15 - 19	C	164 881	-	-	103 737	-	-	61 144	-	-
20 - 24	C	488 888	-	-	342 101	-	-	146 787	-	-
25 - 29	C	317 816	-	-	228 500	-	-	89 316	-	-
30 - 34	C	154 625	-	-	108 749	-	-	45 876	-	-
35 - 39	C	68 187	-	-	46 375	-	-	21 812	-	-
40 - 44	C	14 167	-	-	8 989	-	-	5 178	-	-
45 - 49	C	672	-	-	425	-	-	247	-	-
50+	C	19	-	-	14	-	-	5	-	-
Unk.- Inc.	C	2 550	-	-	2 148	-	-	402	-	-

10. Live births by age of mother, sex of the child and urban/rural residence: latest available year
Naissances vivantes selon l'âge de la mère , le sexe de l'enfant et la résidence, urbaine/rurale: dernière année disponible (continued — suite)

(See notes at end of table.— Voir notes à la fin du tableau.)

Continent, country or area, year and age (in years) / Continent, pays ou zone, année et âge (en années)	Code[a]	Total			Urban - Urbaine			Rural - Rurale		
		Both sexes - Les deux sexes	Male - Masculin	Female - Féminin	Both sexes - Les deux sexes	Male - Masculin	Female - Féminin	Both sexes - Les deux sexes	Male - Masculin	Female - Féminin
EUROPE										
San Marino - Saint - Marin										
2000										
Total	+C	290	151	139	...	...	...	...	...	...
20 - 24	+C	18	13	5	...	...	...	...	...	...
25 - 29	+C	65	34	31	...	...	...	...	...	...
30 - 34	+C	142	74	68	...	...	...	...	...	...
35 - 39	+C	55	24	31	...	...	...	...	...	...
40 - 44	+C	9	6	3	...	...	...	...	...	...
45 - 49	+C	1	-	1	...	...	...	...	...	...
Serbia and Montenegro - Serbie-et-Montenegro										
2000										
Total	C	125 868	65 403	60 465	66 409	34 508	31 901	59 459	30 895	28 564
0 - 14	C	68	40	28	41	22	19	27	18	9
15 - 19	C	9 602	5 008	4 594	4 220	2 197	2 023	5 382	2 811	2 571
20 - 24	C	41 126	21 243	19 883	19 694	10 193	9 501	21 432	11 050	10 382
25 - 29	C	40 983	21 134	19 849	22 176	11 481	10 695	18 807	9 653	9 154
30 - 34	C	22 422	11 884	10 538	13 213	6 933	6 280	9 209	4 951	4 258
35 - 39	C	8 611	4 491	4 120	5 313	2 741	2 572	3 298	1 750	1 548
40 - 44	C	1 778	918	860	1 082	578	504	696	340	356
45 - 49	C	160	87	73	78	39	39	82	48	34
50+	C	31	13	18	13	6	7	18	7	11
Unk.- Inc.	C	1 087	585	502	579	318	261	508	267	241
Slovakia - Slovaquie										
2001										
Total	C	51 136	26 439	24 697	26 106	13 543	12 563	25 030	12 896	12 134
0 - 14	C	42	20	22	17	6	11	25	14	11
15 - 19	C	4 600	2 404	2 196	1 893	982	911	2 707	1 422	1 285
20 - 24	C	16 895	8 738	8 157	7 776	4 086	3 690	9 119	4 652	4 467
25 - 29	C	18 216	9 356	8 860	9 975	5 104	4 871	8 241	4 252	3 989
30 - 34	C	7 823	4 051	3 772	4 520	2 344	2 176	3 303	1 707	1 596
35 - 39	C	2 942	1 549	1 393	1 601	859	742	1 341	690	651
40 - 44	C	594	307	287	314	158	156	280	149	131
45 - 49	C	24	14	-	-	4	-	14	10	4
50+	C	-	-	-	-	-	-	-	-	-
Slovenia - Slovénie										
2001										
Total	C	17 477	9 064	8 413	8 039	4 172	3 867	9 438	4 892	4 546
0 - 14	C	1	-	1	...	...	...	1	-	1
15 - 19	C	441	242	199	186	101	85	255	141	114
20 - 24	C	3 761	1 946	1 815	1 445	754	691	2 316	1 192	1 124
25 - 29	C	7 028	3 611	3 417	3 127	1 594	1 533	3 901	2 017	1 884
30 - 34	C	4 505	2 373	2 132	2 370	1 262	1 108	2 135	1 111	1 024
35 - 39	C	1 514	773	741	782	389	393	732	384	348
40 - 44	C	220	114	106	126	69	57	94	45	49
45 - 49	C	7	5	-	3	3	-	4	2	2
Spain - Espagne										
1998										
Total	C	365 193	188 997	176 196	...	...	...	...	...	...
0 - 14	C	97	58	39	...	...	...	...	...	...
15 - 19	C	10 804	5 548	5 256	...	...	...	...	...	...
20 - 24	C	38 473	20 097	18 376	...	...	...	...	...	...
25 - 29	C	110 492	57 257	53 235	...	...	...	...	...	...
30 - 34	C	142 219	73 558	68 661	...	...	...	...	...	...
35 - 39	C	55 084	28 401	26 683	...	...	...	...	...	...
40 - 44	C	7 721	3 934	3 787	...	...	...	...	...	...
45 - 49	C	294	139	155	...	...	...	...	...	...

10. Live births by age of mother, sex of the child and urban/rural residence: latest available year
Naissances vivantes selon l'âge de la mère , le sexe de l'enfant et la résidence, urbaine/rurale: dernière année disponible (continued — suite)

(See notes at end of table.— Voir notes à la fin du tableau.)

Continent, country or area, year and age (in years) Continent, pays ou zone, année et âge (en années)	Code[a]	Total			Urban - Urbaine			Rural - Rurale		
		Both sexes - Les deux sexes	Male - Masculin	Female - Féminin	Both sexes - Les deux sexes	Male - Masculin	Female - Féminin	Both sexes - Les deux sexes	Male - Masculin	Female - Féminin
EUROPE										
Spain - Espagne										
1998										
50+	C	9	5	4	...	...	...	...	...	...
Sweden - Suède										
2001										
Total	C	91 466	-	-	...	...	...	...	...	...
15 - 19	C	1 648	-	-	...	...	...	...	...	...
20 - 24	C	11 825	-	-	...	...	...	...	...	...
25 - 29	C	30 063	-	-	...	...	...	...	...	...
30 - 34	C	31 282	-	-	...	...	...	...	...	...
35 - 39	C	14 190	-	-	...	...	...	...	...	...
40 - 44	C	2 361	-	-	...	...	...	...	...	...
45 - 49	C	87	-	-	...	...	...	...	...	...
50+	C	2	-	-	...	...	...	...	...	...
Switzerland - Suisse										
2001										
Total	C	73 509	37 739	35 770	49 292	25 221	24 071	24 217	12 518	11 699
0 - 14	C	2	2	-	2	2	-	...	...	...
15 - 19	C	1 144	588	556	825	427	398	319	161	158
20 - 24	C	8 919	4 578	4 341	6 131	3 098	3 033	2 788	1 480	1 308
25 - 29	C	22 003	11 362	10 641	14 119	7 276	6 843	7 884	4 086	3 798
30 - 34	C	27 327	14 025	13 302	18 207	9 356	8 851	9 120	4 669	4 451
35 - 39	C	12 187	6 193	5 994	8 587	4 347	4 240	3 600	1 846	1 754
40 - 44	C	1 856	947	909	1 367	683	684	489	264	225
45 - 49	C	60	37	23	43	25	18	17	12	5
50+	C	11	-	4	11	-	4	...	...	...
The Former Yugoslav Rep. of Macedonia - L'ex - République yougoslave de Macédoine										
2001										
Total	C	27 010	13 977	13 033	14 761	7 572	7 189	12 249	6 405	5 844
0 - 14	C	39	17	22	28	11	17	11	6	5
15 - 19	C	2 163	1 117	1 046	1 091	557	534	1 072	560	512
20 - 24	C	9 228	4 823	4 405	4 675	2 441	2 234	4 553	2 382	2 171
25 - 29	C	9 474	4 919	4 555	5 334	2 732	2 602	4 140	2 187	1 953
30 - 34	C	4 492	2 286	2 206	2 678	1 351	1 327	1 814	935	879
35 - 39	C	1 363	685	678	803	402	401	560	283	277
40 - 44	C	219	113	106	129	64	65	90	49	41
45 - 49	C	15	8	7	11	7	4	4	1	3
50+	C	1	-	1	1	-	1	...	...	...
Unk.- Inc.	C	16	9	7	11	7	4	5	2	3
Ukraine[11]										
2001										
Total	C	376 478	-	-	237 228	-	-	139 250	-	-
0 - 14	C	149	-	-	69	-	-	80	-	-
15 - 19	C	54 859	-	-	29 509	-	-	25 350	-	-
20 - 24	C	156 246	-	-	98 007	-	-	58 239	-	-
25 - 29	C	99 608	-	-	65 776	-	-	33 832	-	-
30 - 34	C	44 502	-	-	30 090	-	-	14 412	-	-
35 - 39	C	16 019	-	-	10 413	-	-	5 606	-	-
40 - 44	C	3 683	-	-	2 181	-	-	1 502	-	-
45 - 49	C	165	-	-	90	-	-	75	-	-
50+	C	5	-	-	8	-	-	1	-	-
Unk.- Inc.	C	1 242	-	-	1 089	-	-	153	-	-

10. Live births by age of mother, sex of the child and urban/rural residence: latest available year
Naissances vivantes selon l'âge de la mère , le sexe de l'enfant et la résidence, urbaine/rurale: dernière année disponible (continued — suite)

(See notes at end of table.— Voir notes à la fin du tableau.)

Continent, country or area, year and age (in years) / Continent, pays ou zone, année et âge (en années)	Code[a]	Total			Urban - Urbaine			Rural - Rurale		
		Both sexes - Les deux sexes	Male - Masculin	Female - Féminin	Both sexes - Les deux sexes	Male - Masculin	Female - Féminin	Both sexes - Les deux sexes	Male - Masculin	Female - Féminin
EUROPE										
United Kingdom - Royaume - Uni										
2000										
Total	C	679 029	347 941	331 088	...	...	...	...	...	...
0 - 14	C	328	178	150	...	...	...	...	...	...
15 - 19	C	51 731	26 592	25 139	...	...	...	...	...	...
20 - 24	C	120 305	61 703	58 602	...	...	...	...	...	...
25 - 29	C	191 583	98 096	93 487	...	...	...	...	...	...
30 - 34	C	202 893	103 928	98 965	...	...	...	...	...	...
35 - 39	C	95 400	48 867	46 533	...	...	...	...	...	...
40 - 44	C	16 032	8 191	7 841	...	...	...	...	...	...
45 - 49	C	663	335	328	...	...	...	...	...	...
50+	C	45	29	16	...	...	...	...	...	...
Unk.- Inc.	C	49	22	27	...	...	...	...	...	...
2001										
Total	C	668 777	-	-	...	...	...	...	...	...
0 - 14	C	299	-	-	...	...	...	...	...	...
15 - 19	C	48 865	-	-	...	...	...	...	...	...
20 - 24	C	123 845	-	-	...	...	...	...	...	...
25 - 29	C	171 852	-	-	...	...	...	...	...	...
30 - 34	C	203 261	-	-	...	...	...	...	...	...
35 - 39	C	101 379	-	-	...	...	...	...	...	...
40 - 44	C	18 273	-	-	...	...	...	...	...	...
45 - 49	C	890	-	-	...	...	...	...	...	...
50+	C	78	-	-	...	...	...	...	...	...
Unk.- Inc.	C	35	-	-	...	...	...	...	...	...
OCEANIA — OCEANIE										
American Samoa - Samoas américaines										
1993										
Total	C	1 998	-	-	...	...	...	...	...	...
0 - 14	C	2	-	-	...	...	...	...	...	...
15 - 19	C	137	-	-	...	...	...	...	...	...
20 - 24	C	574	-	-	...	...	...	...	...	...
25 - 29	C	614	-	-	...	...	...	...	...	...
30 - 34	C	433	-	-	...	...	...	...	...	...
35 - 39	C	197	-	-	...	...	...	...	...	...
40+	C	41	-	-	...	...	...	...	...	...
Australia - Australie										
2000										
Total	+C	249 636	128 190	121 446	...	...	...	...	...	...
0 - 14	+C	79	50	29	...	...	...	...	...	...
15 - 19	+C	11 395	5 873	5 522	...	...	...	...	...	...
20 - 24	+C	37 604	19 530	18 074	...	...	...	...	...	...
25 - 29	+C	78 409	40 213	38 196	...	...	...	...	...	...
30 - 34	+C	78 663	40 217	38 446	...	...	...	...	...	...
35 - 39	+C	36 803	18 820	17 983	...	...	...	...	...	...
40 - 44	+C	6 342	3 308	3 034	...	...	...	...	...	...
45 - 49	+C	249	135	114	...	...	...	...	...	...
50+	+C	13	8	5	...	...	...	...	...	...
Unk.- Inc.	+C	79	36	43	...	...	...	...	...	...
Guam[7,27]										
1992										
Total	C	4 214	2 179	2 035	3 438	1 758	1 680	775	421	354
0 - 14	C	10	4	6	9	4	5	-	-	-
15 - 19	C	614	335	279	525	284	241	89	51	38
20 - 24	C	1 285	659	626	1 054	543	511	231	116	115

10. Live births by age of mother, sex of the child and urban/rural residence: latest available year
Naissances vivantes selon l'âge de la mère , le sexe de l'enfant et la résidence, urbaine/rurale: dernière année disponible (continued — suite)

(See notes at end of table.— Voir notes à la fin du tableau.)

Continent, country or area, year and age (in years) / Continent, pays ou zone, année et âge (en années)	Code[a]	Total			Urban - Urbaine			Rural - Rurale		
		Both sexes - Les deux sexes	Male - Masculin	Female - Féminin	Both sexes - Les deux sexes	Male - Masculin	Female - Féminin	Both sexes - Les deux sexes	Male - Masculin	Female - Féminin
OCEANIA — OCEANIE										
Guam[7,27]										
1992										
25 - 29	C	1 227	655	572	971	508	463	256	147	109
30 - 34	C	706	356	350	555	280	275	151	76	75
35 - 39	C	302	141	161	258	112	146	45	29	16
40 - 44	C	67	26	41	63	24	39	3	2	1
45+	C	3	3	-	3	3	-	-	-	-
Marshall Islands - Îles Marshall[28]										
1999										
Total	+U	1 478	-	-	...	...	...	...	...	...
0 - 14	+U	3	-	-	...	...	...	...	...	...
15 - 19	+U	279	-	-	...	...	...	...	...	...
20 - 24	+U	482	-	-	...	...	...	...	...	...
25 - 29	+U	373	-	-	...	...	...	...	...	...
30 - 34	+U	211	-	-	...	...	...	...	...	...
35 - 39	+U	108	-	-	...	...	...	...	...	...
40 - 44	+U	19	-	-	...	...	...	...	...	...
50+	+U	1	-	-	...	...	...	...	...	...
New Caledonia - Nouvelle - Calédonie										
1999										
Total	C	4 316	-	-	...	...	...	...	...	...
15 - 19	C	129	-	-	...	...	...	...	...	...
20 - 24	C	984	-	-	...	...	...	...	...	...
25 - 29	C	1 391	-	-	...	...	...	...	...	...
30 - 34	C	1 113	-	-	...	...	...	...	...	...
35 - 39	C	550	-	-	...	...	...	...	...	...
40 - 44	C	143	-	-	...	...	...	...	...	...
45 - 49	C	6	-	-	...	...	...	...	...	...
New Zealand - Nouvelle - Zélande[7]										
2000										
Total	+C	56 605	29 157	27 448	49 374	25 407	23 967	7 126	3 681	3 445
0 - 14	+C	31	18	13	26	14	12	4	3	1
15 - 19	+C	3 787	1 961	1 826	3 419	1 766	1 653	357	189	168
20 - 24	+C	9 881	5 081	4 794	8 844	4 554	4 290	1 012	520	492
25 - 29	+C	15 766	8 139	7 627	13 647	7 036	6 611	2 087	1 078	1 009
30 - 34	+C	17 163	8 879	8 284	14 882	7 682	7 200	2 256	1 178	1 078
35 - 39	+C	8 430	4 291	4 139	7 223	3 688	3 535	1 197	598	599
40 - 44	+C	1 497	759	738	1 289	646	643	207	113	94
45 - 49	+C	50	23	27	44	21	23	6	2	4
Palau - Palaos										
1999										
Total	C	250	-	-	...	...	...	...	...	...
15 - 19	C	20	-	-	...	...	...	...	...	...
20 - 24	C	40	-	-	...	...	...	...	...	...
25 - 29	C	70	-	-	...	...	...	...	...	...
30 - 34	C	77	-	-	...	...	...	...	...	...
35 - 39	C	33	-	-	...	...	...	...	...	...
40 - 44	C	10	-	-	...	...	...	...	...	...
Tonga										
2000										
Total	+C	2 471	-	-	...	...	...	...	...	...
0 - 14	+C	2	-	-	...	...	...	...	...	...
15 - 19	+C	101	-	-	...	...	...	...	...	...
20 - 24	+C	528	-	-	...	...	...	...	...	...
25 - 29	+C	695	-	-	...	...	...	...	...	...
30 - 34	+C	688	-	-	...	...	...	...	...	...

10. Live births by age of mother, sex of the child and urban/rural residence: latest available year
Naissances vivantes selon l'âge de la mère , le sexe de l'enfant et la résidence, urbaine/rurale: dernière année disponible (continued — suite)

(See notes at end of table.— Voir notes à la fin du tableau.)

Continent, country or area, year and age (in years) / Continent, pays ou zone, année et âge (en années)	Code[a]	Total			Urban - Urbaine			Rural - Rurale		
		Both sexes - Les deux sexes	Male - Masculin	Female - Féminin	Both sexes - Les deux sexes	Male - Masculin	Female - Féminin	Both sexes - Les deux sexes	Male - Masculin	Female - Féminin
OCEANIA — OCEANIE										
Tonga										
2000										
35 - 39	+C	314	-	-	...	...	...	...	...	...
40 - 44	+C	122	-	-	...	...	...	...	...	...
45 - 49	+C	14	-	-	...	...	...	...	...	...
Unk.- Inc.	+C	7	-	-	...	...	...	...	...	...

GENERAL NOTES - NOTES GENERALES

For definition of 'urban', see end of Technical Notes for table 6. For method of evaluation and limitations of data, see Technical Notes for this table. — Pour les définitions des 'régions urbaines', se reporter à la fin des Notes techniques du tableau 6. Pour la méthode d"evaluations et les limitations des données, voir Notes techniques, pour ce tableau.

Italics: data from civil registers which are incomplete or of unknown completeness. — *Italiques:* données incomplètes ou dont le degré d'exactitude n'est pas connu provenant des registres de l'état civil.

FOOTNOTES - NOTES

[a] 'Code' indicates the source of data, as follows:
C - Civil registration, estimated over 90% complete
U - Civil registration, estimated less than 90% complete
I - Other source, estimated reliable
+ - Data tabulated by date of registration rather than occurence.
... - Information not available

Le 'Code' indique la source des données, comme suit:
C - Registres de l'état civil considérés complèts à 90 p. 100 au moins.
U - Registres de l'état civil qui ne sont pas considérés complèts à 90 p. 100 au moins.
I - Autre source, considérée pas douteuses.
+ - Données exploitées selon la date de l'enregistrement et non la date de l'événement.
... - Information pas disponible.

[1] Data for 1997 refer to last twelve months preceding population and housing census of 1997. - Les données pour 1997 se réfèrent au douze mois précédant le recensement de population et de l'habitat de 1997.
[2] Based on the results of the population census. - D'après les résultats du recensement de la population.
[3] Including Canadian residents temporarily in the United States, but excluding United States residents temporarily in Canada. - Y compris les résidents canadiens se trouvant temporairement aux Etats-Unis, mais ne comprennant pas les résidents des Etats-Unis se trouvant temporairement au Canada.
[4] Excluding live-born infants dying before registration of birth. - Non compris les enfants nés vivants décédés avant l'enregistrement de leur naissance.
[5] Age classification based on age the mother reached during the year, not on the exact age of the mother at the moment of birth. - Le classement selon l'âge est basé sur l'âge que la mère a atteint dans l'année de référence et non sur l'âge exacte de la mère au moment de naissance de l'enfant.
[6] Including unknown sex. - Y compris le sexe inconnu.
[7] Figures for urban and rural areas do not add up to the total, since they do not include the category 'Unknown residence'. - La somme des

donées pour la residence urbaine et rurale n'est pas égale au total parce qu'elle n'inclue pas la catégorie 'Residence inconnue'.
[8] Data as reported by national statistical authorities; they may differ from data presented in other tables. - Les donées comme ils ont été déclarés par l'institut national de la statistique; ils peuvent etre different de ceux presentés dans autre tableaux.
[9] Excluding Indian jungle population. - Non compris les Indiens de la jungle.
[10] Excluding nomadic Indian tribes. - Non compris les tribus d'Indiens nomades.
[11] Excluding infants born alive with less than 28 weeks gestation, less than 1 000 grams in weight and 35 centimeters in length, who die within seven days of birth. - Non compris les enfants nés vivants avant 28 semaines de gestation, pesant moins de 1 000 grammes, mesurant moins de 35 centimètres et décédés dans les sept jours qui ont suivi leur naissance.
[12] Data refer to government controlled areas. - Les données se raportent aux zones contrôlées par le Gouvernement.
[13] Published by the United Nations Economic and Social Commission for Western Asia. - Publié par la Commission économique et sociale des Nations Unies pour l'Asie occidentale.
[14] Beginning 1970, including data for East Jerusalem and Israeli residents in certain other territories under occupation by Israeli military forces since 1967. - A partir de 1970, y compris les données pour Jérusalem-Est et les résidents israéliens dans certains autres territoires occupés depuis juin 1967 par les forces armées israéliennes.
[15] For Japanese nationals in Japan only. - Pour les nationaux japonais au Japon seulement.
[16] Excluding alien armed forces, civilian aliens employed by armed forces, and foreign diplomatic personnel and their dependants. - Non compris les militaires étrangers, les civils étrangers employés par les forces armées ni le personnel diplomatique étranger et les membres de leur famille les accompagnant.
[17] Based on the results of the Population Growth Survey. - D'après les résultats de la 'Population Growth Survey.'
[18] Excluding data for the Pakistan-held part of Jammu and Kashmir, the final status of which has not yet been determined. - Non compris les données concernant la partie du Jammu et Cachemire occupée par le Pakistan dont le statut définitif n'a pas été déterminé.
[19] Excluding transients afloat and military and civilian services personnel and their dependants abroad. - Non compris les personnes de passage à bord de navires ni les militaires et agents civils et les membres de leur famille les accompagnant à l'étranger.
[20] Including armed forces stationed outside the country, but excluding alien armed forces stationed in the area. - Y compris les militaires nationaux hors du pays, mais non compris les militaires étrangers en garnison sur le territoire.
[21] Excluding Faeroe Islands and Greenland. - Non compris les îles Féroé et Gröenland.
[22] Including nationals temporarily outside the country. - Y compris les nationaux se trouvant temporairement hors du pays.
[23] Including armed forces stationed outside the country. - Y compris les militaires nationaux hors du pays.
[24] Births registered within one year of occurrence. - Naissances

enregistrées dans l'année qui suit l'événement.

[25] Live births to Maltese parents only. - Naissances vivantes aux parents maltais seulement.

[26] Including residents outside the country if listed in a Netherlands population register. - Y compris les résidents hors du pays, s'ils sont inscrits sur un registre de population néerlandais.

[27] Including United States military personnel, their dependants and contract employees. - Y compris les militaires des Etats-Unis, les membres de leur famille les accompagnant et les agents contractuels des Etats-Unis.

[28] Excluding United States military personnel, their dependants and contract employees. - Non compris les militaires des Etats-Unis, les membres de leur famille les accompagnant et les agents contractuels des Etats-Unis.

Table 11

Table 11 presents live-birth rates by age of mother and urban/rural residence for the latest available year in the period 1992-2001.

Description of variables: Age is defined as age at last birthday preceding the live birth, that is, the difference between the date of birth and the date of the occurrence of the event, expressed in completed solar years. The age classification used in this table is the following: under 20 years, 5-year age groups through 40-44 years, and 45 years or over.

The urban/rural classification of births is that provided by each country or area; it is presumed to be based on the national census definitions of urban population set forth at the end of the technical notes for table 6.

Rate computation: Live-birth rates specific to age of mother are the annual number of births to women in each age group (as shown in table 10) per 1 000 female population in the same age group.

Birth rates by age of mother and urban/rural residence are the annual number of live births that occurred to a specific age-urban/rural group (as shown in table 10) per 1 000 females in the corresponding age-urban/rural group. These rates have been calculated by the Statistics Division of the United Nations.

Since relatively few births occur to women below 15 or above 50 years of age, birth rates for women under 20 years of age and for those 45 years of age or over are computed on the female population aged 15-19 and 45-49, respectively. Similarly, the rate for women of "All ages" is based on all live births irrespective of age of mother, and is computed on the female population aged 15-49 years. This rate for "All ages" is known as the general fertility rate.

Births to mothers of unknown age have been distributed proportionately across the age groups, by the Statistics Division of the United Nations, in accordance with the distribution of births by age of mother prior to the calculation of the rates.

The population used in computing the rates is estimated or enumerated distributions of females by age. First priority was given to an estimate for the mid-point of the same year (as shown in table 7), second priority to census returns of the year to which the births referred, and third priority to an estimate for some other point of time in the year.

Rates presented in this table have been limited to those for countries or areas having at least a total of 100 live births in a given year.

Reliability of data: Rates are not computed if the data on live births from civil registers are reported as incomplete (less than 90 per cent completeness) or of unknown completeness. Table 9 and the technical notes for that table provide more detailed information on the completeness of live-birth registration. For more information about the quality of vital statistics data in general, and the information available on the basis of the completeness of estimates in particular, see section 4.2 of the Technical Notes.

Limitations: Rates shown in this table are subject to the same limitations that affect the corresponding frequencies and are set forth in the technical notes for table 10. These include differences in the completeness of registration, the treatment of infants who were born alive but died before the registration of the birth or within the first 24 hours of life, the method used to determine age of mother and the quality of the reported information relating to age of mother. In addition, some rates are based on births tabulated by date of registration and not by date of occurrence; these have been indicated by a plus sign "+".

The effect of including delayed registration on the distribution of births by age of mother may be noted in the age-specific fertility rates for women at older ages. In some cases, high age-specific rates for women aged 45 years and over may reflect age of mother at registration of birth and not fertility at these older ages.

The comparability of data by urban/rural residence is affected by the national definitions of urban and rural used in tabulating these data. It is assumed, in the absence of specific information to the contrary, that the definitions of urban and rural used in connection with the national population census were also used in the compilation of the vital statistics for each country or area. However, it is possible that, for a given country or area, the definitions of urban and rural used for both the vital statistics data and the population census data are not the same. When known, the definitions of urban used in national population censuses are presented at the end of the technical notes for table 6. As discussed in detail in the technical notes for table 6, these definitions vary considerably from one country or area to another.

In addition to problems of comparability, vital rates classified by urban/rural residence are also subject to certain special types of bias. If, when calculating vital rates, different definitions of urban are used in connection with the vital events and the population data and if this results in a net difference between the numerator and denominator of the rate in the population at risk, then the vital rates would be biased. Urban/rural differentials in vital rates may also be affected by whether the vital events have been tabulated in terms of place of occurrence or place of usual residence. This problem is discussed in more detail in section 4.1.4.1 of the Technical Notes.

Coverage: Live-birth rates specific for age of mother are shown for 92 countries or areas. Rates are presented by urban/rural residence for 30 countries or areas.

Earlier data: Live-birth rates specific for age of mother have been shown for the latest available year in each issue of the Yearbook. Data included in this table update the series covering a period of years as follows:

Issue	Years Covered
Special Topic on Natality, CD, 1999	1990 – 1998
Historical Supplement CD, 1997	1948 – 1997
1992	1983 – 1992
1986	1977 – 1985
1981	1972 – 1980
Historical Supplement, 1979	1948 - 1977

Tableau 11

Le tableau 11 présente des taux des naissances vivantes selon l'âge de la mère et selon la résidence (urbaine/rurale) pour la dernière année disponible dans le période 1992-2001.

Description des variables : L'âge désigne l'âge au dernier anniversaire précédant la naissance, c'est-à-dire la différence entre la date de naissance et la date de l'événement, exprimée en années solaires révolues. La classification par âge utilisée dans le tableau 11 comprend les catégories suivantes: moins de 20 ans, groupes quinquennaux jusqu'à 40 à 44 ans, et 45 et plus.

La classification des naissances selon la résidence urbaine/rurale est celle qui a été fournie par chaque pays ou zone; il faut en conclure qu'elle repose sur les définitions de la population urbaine utilisées pour les recensements nationaux, telles qu'elles sont reproduites à la fin des notes technique du tableau 6.

Calcul des taux: Les taux des naissances vivantes selon l'âge de la mère représentent le nombre annuel de naissances dans chaque groupe d'âge (fréquences du tableau 10) pour 1 000 femmes des mêmes groupes d'âge.

Les taux de natalité selon l'âge de la mère et la résidence (urbaine/rurale) représentent le nombre annuel de naissances vivantes intervenues dans un groupe d'âge donné dans la population urbaine ou rurale (comme il est indiqué au tableau 10) pour 1 000 femmes du groupe d'âge correspondant dans la population urbaine ou rurale. Ces taux ont été calculés par la Division de statistique de l'ONU.

Etant donné que le nombre de naissances parmi les femmes de moins de 15 ans ou de plus de 50 ans est relativement peu élevé, les taux de natalité parmi les femmes âgées de moins de 20 ans et celles de 45 ans et plus ont été calculés sur la base des populations féminines âgées de 15 à 19 ans et de 45 à 49 ans, respectivement. De la même façon, le taux pour les femmes de "tous âges" est fondé sur la totalité des naissances vivantes, indépendamment de l'âge de la mère et ce chiffre est rapporté à l'effectif de la population féminine âgée de 15 à 49 ans. Ce taux "tous âges" est le taux global de fécondité.

Les naissances pour lesquelles l'âge de la mère était inconnu ont été réparties par la Division de statistique de l'ONU, avant le calcul des taux, suivant les proportions observées pour celles où l'âge de la mère était connu.

Les chiffres de population utilisés pour le calcul des taux proviennent de dénombrements ou de répartitions estimatives de la population féminine selon l'âge. On a utilisé de préférence les estimations de la population au milieu de l'année considérée selon les indications du tableau 7; à défaut, on s'est contenté des données censitaires se rapportant à l'année des naissances et, si ces données manquaient également, d'estimations établies pour une autre date de l'année.

Les taux présentés dans ce tableau ne concernent que les pays ou zones où l'on a enregistré un total d'au moins 100 naissances vivantes dans une année donnée.

Fiabilité des données : Les taux établis à partir de données sur les naissances vivantes provenant des registres de l'état civil qui sont déclarées incompletes (degré de complétude inférieur à 90 p. 100) ou dont le degré de complétude n'est pas connu sont jugés douteux et ils n'ont pas été calculés ou présentés dans ce tableau. Le tableau 9 et les Notes techniques se rapportant à ce tableau présentent des renseignements plus détaillés sur le degré de complétude de l'enregistrement des naissances vivantes. Pour plus de précisions sur la qualité des données reposant sur les statistiques de l'état civil en général, voir la section 4.2 des Notes techniques, qui fournit aussi des renseignements fondés sur les estimations de complétude.

Insuffisance des données : Les taux du tableau 11 appellent les mêmes réserves que les fréquences correspondantes; voir à ce sujet les explications données dans les notes techniques relatives au tableau 10. Leurs imperfections tiennent notamment au degré de complétude de l'enregistrement, au classement des enfants nés vivants décédés avant l'enregistrement de leur naissance ou dans les 24 heures qui ont suivi la naissance, à la méthode utilisée pour déterminer l'âge de la mère et à l'exactitude des renseignements fournis sur l'âge de la mère. En outre, dans certains cas, les données relatives aux naissances sont exploitées selon la date de l'enregistrement et non selon la date de l'événement; ces cas ont été identifiés par le signe "+".

On peut se rendre compte, d'après les taux relatifs aux groupes d'âge les plus avancés, des conséquences que peut avoir l'inclusion, dans les statistiques des naissances selon l'âge de la mère, des naissances enregistrées tardivement. Dans certains cas, il se peut que des taux élevés pour le groupe d'âge 45 ans et plus ne traduisent pas le niveau de la fécondité de ce groupe d'âge, mais l'âge de la mère au moment où la naissances a été enregistrée.

La comparabilité des données selon la résidence (urbaine/rurale) peut être limitée par les définitions nationales des termes "urbain" et "rural" utilisées pour la mise en tableaux de ces données. En l'absence d'indications contraires, on a supposé que les définitions des termes urbain et rural utilisés pour le recensement national de la population avaient été utilisées aussi pour l'établissement de statistiques de l'état civil pour chaque pays ou zone. Toutefois, on ne peut exclure la possibilité que, pour un pays ou zone donné, les mêmes définitions des termes "urbain" et "rural" n'aient pas été utilisées dans deux cas. Les définitions du terme "urbain" utilisées pour les recensements nationaux de population ont été présentées à la fin des Notes techniques du tableau 6 lorsqu'elles étaient connues. Comme on l'a précisé en détail dans les Notes techniques relatives au tableau 6, ces définitions varient très sensiblement d'un pays ou d'une zone à l'autre.

Outre ces problèmes de comparabilité, les taux démographiques classés selon la résidence (urbaine/rurale) sont également sujets à certains types particuliers d'erreurs. Si, lors du calcul de ces taux, des définitions différentes du terme "urbain" sont utilisées pour classer les faits d'état civil et les données relatives à la population et s'il en résulte une différence nette entre le numérateur et le dénominateur pour le taux de la population exposée au risque, les taux démographiques s'en trouveront faussés. La différence entre ces taux pour les zones urbaines et rurales pourra aussi être faussée selon que les faits d'état civil auront été classés d'après le lieu de l'événement ou le lieu de résidence habituelle. Ce problème est examiné plus en détail à la section 4.1.4.1 des Notes techniques.

Portée : Le tableau 11 présente des taux des naissances vivantes selon l'âge de la mère pour 92 pays ou zones. Les taux selon la résidence (urbaine/rurale) intéressent 30 pays ou zones.

Données publiées antérieurement : Des taux des naissances vivantes selon l'âge de la mère ont déjà été publiés pour la dernière année disponible dans chaque édition de l'Annuaire démographique. Les données présentées dans ce tableau mettent à jour les périodes d'années suivantes:

Editions	Années considérées
Edition spéciale, Statistiques de la natalité (CD), 1999	1990 – 1998
Supplément rétrospectif (CD), 1997	1948 – 1997
1992	1983 – 1992
1986	1977 – 1985
1981	1972 – 1980
Supplément rétrospectif, 1979	1948 - 1977

11. Live-birth rates by age of mother and urban/rural residence: latest available year
Naissances vivantes, taux selon l'âge de la mère et la résidence, urbaine/rurale: dernière année disponible

(See notes at end of table. — Voir notes à la fin du tableau.)

Continent, pays ou zone, année, et résidence urbaine/rurale	All ages Tous âges[1]	-20[2]	20-24	25-29	30-34	35-39	40-44	45+[3]
AFRICA — AFRIQUE								
Benin - Bénin								
1992								
Total	160.7	276.4	305.1	141.4	84.6	37.0	24.8	5.9
Urban - Urbaine	131.0	156.7	243.5	150.8	84.1	47.2	18.1	8.5
Rural - Rurale	178.7	362.1	344.6	135.9	84.9	31.5	28.4	4.5
Egypt - Égypte								
1999								
Total	108.4	18.5	192.8	226.3	162.8	87.7	25.7	6.7
Mauritius - Maurice+								
2000								
Total	60.7	38.7	122.1	122.1	77.5	34.5	8.1	♦0.6
Morocco - Maroc								
1999								
Total	68.6	30.8	88.6	105.2	109.5	74.3	32.1	9.2
Urban - Urbaine	56.1	22.6	70.2	87.4	90.4	61.3	23.6	4.7
Rural - Rurale	86.4	39.6	111.6	132.1	144.8	97.1	46.7	15.7
Swaziland[4]								
1997								
Total	133.2	73.0	193.4	199.4	162.6	130.8	64.7	50.0
Urban - Urbaine	106.6	65.3	147.1	157.0	115.9	92.6	39.2	31.0
Rural - Rurale	143.5	75.4	214.3	219.4	182.0	145.4	73.4	55.5
Tunisia - Tunisie								
1998								
Total	67.8	7.5	66.0	112.3	110.3	64.7	21.2	3.4
Zimbabwe[5]								
1992								
Total	146.6	82.1	217.9	205.6	179.9	144.7	80.3	31.5
Urban - Urbaine	123.2	63.6	181.5	172.4	139.9	100.7	46.7	13.6
Rural - Rurale	159.5	90.9	243.3	229.0	203.4	166.8	93.7	37.7
AMERICA, NORTH — AMERIQUE DU NORD								
Bermuda - Bermudes								
1997								
Total	50.2	33.0	75.4	67.4	88.7	57.5	6.6	...
Canada[6]								
1997								
Total	44.0	20.2	64.0	103.8	84.4	32.5	5.2	0.2
Cuba								
2000								
Total	47.4	51.0	96.6	89.2	55.0	22.4	3.8	0.2
Urban - Urbaine	45.2	42.7	93.1	89.5	56.0	22.5	3.6	0.2
Rural - Rurale	54.4	74.7	106.1	88.4	51.8	22.2	4.5	♦0.4
El Salvador								
2000								
Total	90.9	98.6	145.5	121.6	86.3	56.9	21.6	3.1
Urban - Urbaine	91.2	105.7	159.1	125.9	84.0	46.5	14.8	2.1
Rural - Rurale	90.5	90.0	126.5	114.2	90.8	78.7	35.1	5.0
Greenland - Groenland								
1999								
Total	66.9	44.3	160.3	106.9	87.7	50.0	16.3	♦2.0
Urban - Urbaine	62.3	41.0	145.3	94.5	85.7	49.4	♦15.6	♦2.4
Rural - Rurale	90.3	♦60.9	232.8	157.9	97.4	♦53.4	♦20.6	♦0.0
Grenada - Grenade								
2000								
Total	76.5	54.7	107.0	132.7	113.8	64.1	26.7	♦1.1
Guatemala								
1999								
Total	141.4	110.3	211.2	193.4	162.6	128.3	60.1	13.8

364

11. Live-birth rates by age of mother and urban/rural residence: latest available year
Naissances vivantes, taux selon l'âge de la mère et la résidence, urbaine/rurale: dernière année disponible (continued — suite)

(See notes at end of table. — Voir notes à la fin du tableau.)

Continent, country or area, year and urban/rural residence Continent, pays ou zone, année, et résidence urbaine/rurale	All ages Tous âges[1]	-20[2]	20-24	25-29	30-34	35-39	40-44	45+[3]
					Age of mother (in years) - Age de la mère (en années)			
AMERICA, NORTH — **AMERIQUE DU NORD**								
Jamaica - Jamaïque[+] 1995								
Total	91.2	98.6	141.1	125.8	96.9	57.6	17.9	1.3
Martinique[7,8] 1992								
Total	61.9	28.0	88.5	113.9	92.9	49.5	12.2	♦0.8
Panama 1999								
Total	86.6	97.4	148.3	128.8	95.0	51.0	13.3	1.8
Urban - Urbaine	71.7	81.1	127.1	109.7	81.7	40.3	8.5	♦0.3
Rural - Rurale	110.6	117.3	179.0	161.1	118.7	70.7	22.0	4.4
2000								
Total	85.7	95.8	148.7	128.2	94.8	50.8	14.2	1.8
Puerto Rico - Porto Rico 2000								
Total	60.5	74.0	128.0	109.5	65.2	26.7	5.5	♦0.2
Saint Kitts and Nevis - Saint-Kitts-et-Nevis[+] 1996								
Total	76.9	74.2	126.4	122.6	83.3	59.2	♦15.0	♦2.2
Saint Lucia - Sainte-Lucie 2000								
Total	66.0	57.5	99.5	93.9	86.5	50.0	18.5	♦1.2
Saint Vincent and the Grenadines - Saint Vincent-et-les Grenadines 2000								
Total	80.3	73.0	128.5	100.1	80.0	72.8	16.5	♦0.6
Trinidad and Tobago - Trinité-et-Tobago 1997								
Total	52.2	43.3	97.0	88.0	70.0	35.3	9.4	♦0.6
United States - États-Unis 2000								
Total	57.7	49.4	112.0	121.1	93.9	40.3	7.9	0.4
AMERICA, SOUTH — **AMERIQUE DU SUD**								
Argentina - Argentine 2000								
Total	75.9	65.9	116.7	127.2	106.1	60.3	17.9	1.7
Chile - Chili 1999								
Total	63.4	64.9	99.8	106.4	84.0	48.5	13.1	0.7
French Guiana - Guyane française[7] 1999								
Total	117.4	102.7	203.7	195.0	151.9	94.4	28.1	♦2.9
Suriname 2000								
Total	85.4	68.3	150.1	148.2	104.3	56.2	16.0	♦1.8
Uruguay[+] 2000								
Total	65.7	64.9	106.3	107.0	100.0	48.1	12.9	0.7
Venezuela[9] 2000								
Total	86.5	97.4	147.7	130.9	90.9	50.1	16.8	3.3

11. Live-birth rates by age of mother and urban/rural residence: latest available year
Naissances vivantes, taux selon l'âge de la mère et la résidence, urbaine/rurale: dernière année disponible (continued — suite)

(See notes at end of table. — Voir notes à la fin du tableau.)

Continent, country or area, year and urban/rural residence / Continent, pays ou zone,année, et résidence urbaine/rurale	All ages Tous âges[1]	Age of mother (in years) - Age de la mère (en années)						
		-20[2]	20-24	25-29	30-34	35-39	40-44	45+[3]
ASIA — ASIE								
Armenia - Arménie[10]								
2000								
Total	31.7	27.3	103.2	53.7	23.5	10.6	3.0	0.3
Urban - Urbaine	28.6	22.1	92.3	53.5	22.7	10.2	2.8	♦0.3
Rural - Rurale	38.7	37.9	128.0	54.0	25.1	11.3	3.4	♦0.4
Azerbaijan - Azerbaïdjan[10]								
2001								
Total	47.2	26.4	123.1	93.8	48.4	20.1	5.5	0.6
Urban - Urbaine	40.4	19.6	107.0	87.8	43.6	17.6	4.3	0.4
Rural - Rurale	54.9	33.4	140.2	99.9	53.3	22.9	6.9	♦0.2
Brunei Darussalam - Brunéi Darussalam+								
1992								
Total	103.8	41.0	142.3	175.2	135.7	83.9	27.5	♦5.3
China: Hong Kong SAR - Chine: Hong Kong RAS[11]								
2000								
Total	26.3	4.4	30.5	59.2	56.1	26.3	4.0	0.2
China: Macao SAR - Chine: Macao RAS								
2000								
Total	27.1	5.4	25.7	63.7	56.4	25.6	4.6	♦0.1
Cyprus - Chypre[12]								
1999								
Total	45.3	10.9	76.9	118.0	79.7	31.2	6.3	♦0.7
Georgia - Géorgie[10]								
2000								
Total	31.3	30.9	82.5	59.5	30.2	12.9	3.9	0.7
Urban - Urbaine	32.5	31.6	86.7	64.2	34.2	14.4	4.4	0.8
Rural - Rurale	29.4	30.0	77.0	52.1	24.1	10.5	3.1	0.6
Israel - Israël[13]								
2000								
Total	87.2	17.1	117.2	186.7	161.9	85.5	20.8	1.7
Urban - Urbaine	85.7	17.5	116.9	182.1	157.4	82.9	20.2	1.8
Rural - Rurale	101.6	14.3	121.1	237.6	203.1	109.2	26.4	♦1.3
Japan - Japon[14]								
2000								
Total	40.7	5.4	39.2	97.6	91.5	31.5	3.8	0.1
Kazakhstan[10]								
1999								
Total	52.3	31.8	124.1	101.7	61.1	25.7	5.8	0.5
Urban - Urbaine	43.6	31.5	106.4	76.9	50.2	21.0	4.3	0.3
Rural - Rurale	65.5	32.1	148.5	153.1	79.0	33.0	8.2	0.9
Korea (Republic of) - Corée (République de)[15]								
2000								
Total	47.5	2.5	39.9	156.2	89.0	18.0	2.6	0.2
Kuwait - Koweït								
1998								
Total	86.7	20.8	131.5	147.3	113.7	71.0	31.2	6.4
Kyrgyzstan - Kirghizistan[10]								
2000								
Total	76.2	34.7	165.4	134.6	88.5	45.8	13.7	3.1
Urban - Urbaine	56.2	25.0	108.2	102.9	70.1	35.8	10.1	2.1
Rural - Rurale	89.4	40.0	206.1	156.1	100.8	52.3	16.1	3.8
Maldives								
1996								
Total	119.8	54.4	190.9	176.5	137.7	114.2	40.0	♦6.8

11. Live-birth rates by age of mother and urban/rural residence: latest available year
Naissances vivantes, taux selon l'âge de la mère et la résidence, urbaine/rurale: dernière année disponible (continued — suite)

(See notes at end of table. — Voir notes à la fin du tableau.)

Continent, country or area, year and urban/rural residence Continent, pays ou zone,année, et résidence urbaine/rurale	All ages Tous âges[1]	-20[2]	20-24	25-29	30-34	35-39	40-44	45+[3]
			Age of mother (in years) - Age de la mère (en années)					

ASIA — ASIE

Mongolia - Mongolie
2000

	All ages	-20	20-24	25-29	30-34	35-39	40-44	45+
Total	75.4	28.2	148.0	136.3	86.3	39.7	14.3	4.4
Urban - Urbaine	60.3	20.5	122.2	113.6	71.6	29.2	10.3	3.0
Rural - Rurale	99.0	40.2	185.3	169.2	110.3	58.4	20.9	6.5

Pakistan[16,17]
1997

Total	152.8	52.3	231.0	273.2	211.2	142.9	68.4	30.7
Urban - Urbaine	131.5	38.1	189.7	258.0	189.8	116.6	52.6	17.6
Rural - Rurale	163.6	59.6	251.9	281.1	222.0	156.3	75.9	36.8

Singapore - Singapour[*,18]
2000

Total	49.6	9.2	43.3	113.4	113.6	45.4	7.8	0.2

Sri Lanka[+]
1996

Total	72.6	29.1	88.7	129.1	110.9	81.8	20.0	2.4

Tajikistan - Tadjikistan[10]
1993

Total	146.4	53.9	271.9	225.5	159.6	93.6	35.7	6.9
Urban - Urbaine	101.4	46.0	215.7	167.7	104.2	50.0	13.8	2.2
Rural - Rurale	166.8	56.9	294.3	248.9	185.7	118.1	50.0	10.2

Turkey - Turquie[16]
1997

Total	81.1	50.0	173.6	144.9	73.3	36.1	15.5	3.4

Uzbekistan - Ouzbékistan[10]
2000

Total	82.7	21.1	205.4	161.4	89.7	31.5	7.0	0.8
Urban - Urbaine	65.7	21.8	167.9	123.6	73.0	26.6	5.4	0.5
Rural - Rurale	93.6	20.7	227.5	185.9	100.6	34.7	8.2	1.1

EUROPE

Austria - Autriche
2001

Total	37.5	13.7	60.3	91.0	65.9	25.5	5.1	0.3

Belarus - Bélarus[10]
1999

Total	34.5	29.0	106.0	73.1	32.4	10.0	2.0	0.1
Urban - Urbaine	31.5	24.9	98.5	67.6	30.4	8.9	1.6	♦0.1
Rural - Rurale	45.4	43.2	131.7	93.8	39.1	13.8	3.5	♦0.2

Belgium - Belgique[19]
1992

Total	50.4	11.9	75.1	140.8	77.2	23.0	3.6	0.2

Bulgaria - Bulgarie
2001

Total	35.7	44.6	86.7	72.6	33.1	9.9	1.8	♦0.1
Urban - Urbaine	33.2	34.4	76.1	73.5	34.8	10.0	1.8	♦0.1
Rural - Rurale	43.6	78.0	123.1	69.4	27.7	9.3	1.7	0.0

Croatia - Croatie
2001

Total	38.0	15.5	72.1	97.6	61.9	24.0	4.3	0.2

Czech Republic - République tchèque
2001

Total	35.2	11.5	61.1	91.4	48.0	15.2	2.5	♦0.1

Denmark - Danemark[20]
2001

Total	52.3	7.6	51.3	127.0	112.9	44.0	6.8	0.2

11. Live-birth rates by age of mother and urban/rural residence: latest available year
Naissances vivantes, taux selon l'âge de la mère et la résidence, urbaine/rurale: dernière année disponible (continued — suite)

(See notes at end of table. — Voir notes à la fin du tableau.)

Continent, country or area, year and urban/rural residence / Continent, pays ou zone, année, et résidence urbaine/rurale	Age of mother (in years) - Age de la mère (en années)							
	All ages Tous âges[1]	-20[2]	20-24	25-29	30-34	35-39	40-44	45+[3]
EUROPE								
Estonia - Estonie[10]								
2000								
Total	38.2	25.7	86.6	85.4	54.2	19.9	4.8	♦0.2
Urban - Urbaine	35.4	22.8	75.1	79.2	51.8	19.2	3.6	♦0.2
Rural - Rurale	45.2	31.9	125.8	102.4	59.5	21.4	7.7	♦0.1
2001								
Total	36.9	23.9	81.0	82.7	53.6	21.5	4.2	♦0.2
Finland - Finlande[21]								
2001								
Total	46.5	10.7	59.7	114.1	101.9	47.5	9.7	0.5
France[8,22]								
2000								
Total	53.1	8.1	56.0	128.9	114.7	49.8	10.8	0.5
Germany - Allemagne								
1997								
Total	41.1	9.6	54.7	90.2	80.2	31.3	5.4	0.3
Greece - Grèce								
1998								
Total	38.7	11.8	53.2	89.6	71.9	26.4	4.9	0.5
Hungary - Hongrie								
2001								
Total	37.8	21.9	64.2	91.9	57.7	20.9	3.7	0.1
Urban - Urbaine	34.5	15.5	50.3	86.9	59.0	20.8	3.6	♦0.1
Rural - Rurale	44.7	35.6	94.6	103.1	55.0	20.9	3.8	♦0.2
Iceland - Islande								
2000								
Total	60.1	23.2	87.6	128.7	113.4	51.1	10.5	♦0.4
Urban - Urbaine	59.7	23.5	89.2	128.3	110.0	48.3	10.3	♦0.3
Rural - Rurale	65.7	♦20.3	67.8	137.6	166.7	88.4	♦12.6	♦1.6
2001								
Total	56.6	19.6	79.2	127.3	99.9	54.0	10.0	♦0.3
Ireland - Irlande[+,23]								
2001								
Total	57.0	19.6	49.5	89.4	138.8	78.2	14.0	0.6
Italy - Italie								
1999								
Total	38.2	6.9	33.8	76.5	81.6	39.1	7.3	1.0
Latvia - Lettonie[10]								
2001								
Total	33.3	17.2	75.3	76.4	47.1	20.2	5.0	♦0.3
Urban - Urbaine	30.0	14.2	64.1	72.3	45.9	19.0	4.4	♦0.2
Rural - Rurale	41.1	23.2	100.9	86.3	50.1	22.9	6.7	♦0.5
Liechtenstein								
1997								
Total	49.7	♦2.0	62.1	101.0	104.8	48.6	♦7.8	♦0.9
Lithuania - Lituanie[10]								
2001								
Total	35.5	21.2	85.5	82.8	44.6	18.5	4.4	♦0.2
Urban - Urbaine	30.5	16.5	66.8	73.6	41.6	16.5	3.6	♦0.1
Rural - Rurale	48.8	31.6	141.2	108.6	52.2	23.8	6.3	♦0.4
Luxembourg								
2001								
Total	38.0	4.3	38.3	89.9	83.3	33.6	5.5	♦0.1
Malta - Malte[24]								
2001								
Total	40.1	17.1	53.0	111.0	76.8	25.8	6.5	♦0.3
Netherlands - Pays-Bas[25]								
2001								
Total	51.2	13.5	83.2	213.1	272.5	115.1	17.3	0.7
Urban - Urbaine	50.2	7.6	38.5	88.1	123.0	58.4	9.9	0.4

11. Live-birth rates by age of mother and urban/rural residence: latest available year
Naissances vivantes, taux selon l'âge de la mère et la résidence, urbaine/rurale: dernière année disponible (continued — suite)

(See notes at end of table. — Voir notes à la fin du tableau.)

Continent, country or area, year and urban/rural residence / Continent, pays ou zone, année, et résidence urbaine/rurale	All ages Tous âges[1]	-20[2]	20-24	25-29	30-34	35-39	40-44	45+[3]
EUROPE								
Netherlands - Pays-Bas[25]								
2001								
Rural - Rurale	53.3	3.0	32.0	119.2	152.2	55.4	7.2	0.2
Norway - Norvège[8]								
2001								
Total	53.1	11.1	62.7	123.6	107.9	45.6	7.0	0.3
Poland - Pologne								
2001								
Total	36.0	15.7	74.3	89.8	51.8	21.2	4.7	0.2
Portugal								
2001								
Total	43.2	20.6	55.6	91.6	83.2	34.5	6.5	0.4
Republic of Moldova - République de Moldova[10]								
2001								
Total	36.2	33.6	98.0	67.5	36.0	12.0	2.6	♦0.2
Urban - Urbaine	28.2	21.5	84.0	57.6	29.2	9.7	2.0	♦0.1
Rural - Rurale	42.6	41.0	107.2	75.4	42.7	14.1	3.2	♦0.2
Romania - Roumanie								
2001								
Total	37.9	36.6	82.2	73.8	37.4	13.7	3.0	0.2
Urban - Urbaine	28.1	20.2	57.9	66.5	33.8	10.6	2.0	0.1
Rural - Rurale	54.6	60.8	117.4	83.3	43.9	19.9	5.3	0.3
Russian Federation - Fédération de Russie[10]								
1999								
Total	31.1	29.3	92.6	64.9	32.5	11.2	2.2	0.1
Urban - Urbaine	28.5	25.2	85.6	60.4	30.7	10.1	1.8	0.1
Rural - Rurale	39.4	40.4	114.4	79.8	37.8	14.4	3.5	0.2
San Marino - Saint-Marin+								
2000								
Total	41.8	...	♦22.6	67.0	112.0	42.5	♦8.6	♦1.1
Serbia and Montenegro - Serbie-et-Montenegro								
2000								
Total	47.9	25.2	105.5	108.9	62.6	24.5	4.9	0.5
Urban - Urbaine	46.7	21.7	98.2	116.1	70.6	27.2	5.2	0.4
Rural - Rurale	49.2	28.8	113.1	101.5	53.8	21.2	4.6	0.6
Slovakia - Slovaquie								
2001								
Total	35.5	21.5	73.4	85.2	43.6	15.4	3.0	♦0.1
Slovenia - Slovénie								
2001								
Total	34.1	6.7	51.5	98.2	62.7	19.6	2.9	♦0.1
Spain - Espagne								
1998								
Total	35.8	8.0	24.0	68.6	90.1	37.1	5.8	0.2
Sweden - Suède								
2001								
Total	46.1	6.6	46.7	104.3	102.4	45.4	8.2	0.3
Switzerland - Suisse								
2001								
Total	41.4	5.6	42.8	93.1	94.9	39.4	6.6	0.3
The Former Yugoslav Rep. of Macedonia - L'ex-République yougoslave de Macédoine								
2001								
Total	52.7	27.0	114.7	123.1	60.6	18.5	3.8	♦0.2

11. Live-birth rates by age of mother and urban/rural residence: latest available year
Naissances vivantes, taux selon l'âge de la mère et la résidence, urbaine/rurale: dernière année disponible (continued — suite)

(See notes at end of table. — Voir notes à la fin du tableau.)

Continent, country or area, year and urban/rural residence Continent, pays ou zone,année, et résidence urbaine/rurale	All ages Tous âges[1]	Age of mother (in years) - Age de la mère (en années)						
		-20[2]	20-24	25-29	30-34	35-39	40-44	45+[3]
EUROPE								
Ukraine[10]								
2001								
Total	29.6	29.6	88.6	56.4	27.5	8.8	1.9	0.1
United Kingdom - Royaume-Uni[26]								
1999								
Total	49.5	30.7	72.4	98.9	88.9	39.5	7.6	0.4
OCEANIA — OCEANIE								
Australia - Australie[+]								
2000								
Total	50.8	17.4	56.5	107.0	110.5	49.1	8.8	0.4
New Caledonia - Nouvelle-Calédonie								
1994								
Total	89.5	33.9	140.3	182.3	130.0	60.8	16.4	♦1.1
New Zealand - Nouvelle-Zélande								
2000								
Total	57.9	28.8	78.4	115.6	115.5	53.4	10.2	0.4
Tonga								
1999								
Total	110.2	28.3	128.3	220.2	201.6	128.2	49.3	♦3.2

GENERAL NOTES - NOTES GENERALES

Rates are the number of live births by age of mother per 1 000 corresponding female population. For definitions of 'urban', see end of Technical Notes for table 6. For method of evaluation and limitations of data, see Technical Notes for this table. — Les taux représentent les nombres vivantes selon l'âge de la mère pour 1 000 femmes du même groupe d'âge. Pour les définitions des 'régions urbaines', se reporter à la fin des Notes techniques du tableau 6. Pour la méthode d'évaluation et les insuffisances des données, voir Notes techniques pour ce tableau.

FOOTNOTES - NOTES

* Provisional. — Données provisoires.
♦ Rates based on 30 or fewer live births. — Taux basés sur 30 naissances vivantes ou moins.
+ Data tabulated by date of registration rather than occurrence. — Données exploitées selon la date de l'enregistrement et non la date de l'événement.

[1] Rates computed on female population aged 15-49. — Taux calculés sur la base de la population féminine de 15 à 49 ans.
[2] Rates computed on female population aged 15-19. — Taux calculés sur la base de la population féminine de 15 à 19 ans.
[3] Rates computed on female population aged 45-49. — Taux calculés sur la base de la population féminine de 45 à 49 ans.
[4] Data for 1997 refer to last twelve months preceding population and housing census of 1997. - Les données pour 1997 se réfèrent au douze mois précédant le recensement de population et de l'habitat de 1997.
[5] Based on the results of the population census. - D'après les résultats du recensement de la population.
[6] Including Canadian residents temporarily in the United States, but excluding United States residents temporarily in Canada. - Y compris les résidents canadiens se trouvant temporairement aux Etats-Unis, mais ne comprennent pas les résidents des Etats-Unis se trouvant temporairement au Canada.
[7] Excluding live-born infants who died before birth was registered. - - Non compris les enfants nés vivants décédés avant l'enregistrement de leur naissance.
[8] Age classification based on age the mother reached during the year, not on the exact age of the mother at the moment of birth. - Le classement selon l'âge est basé sur l'âge que la mère a atteint dans l'année de référence et non sur l'âge exacte de la mère au moment de naissance de l'enfant.
[9] Excluding Indian jungle population. - Non compris les Indiens de la jungle.
[10] Excluding infants born alive with less than 28 weeks gestation, less than 1 000 grams in weight and 35 centimeters in length, who die within seven days of birth. - Non compris les enfants nés vivants avant 28 semaines de gestation, pesant moins de 1 000 grammes, mesurant moins de 35 centimètres et décédés dans les sept jours qui ont suivi leur naissance.
[11] Including unknown sex. - Y compris le sexe inconnu.
[12] Data refer to government controlled areas. - Les données se raportent aux zones contrôlées par le Gouvernement.
[13] Beginning 1970, including data for East Jerusalem and Israeli residents in certain other territories under occupation by Israeli military forces since 1967. - A partir de 1970, y compris les données pour Jérusalem-Est et les résidents israéliens dans certains autres territoires occupés depuis juin 1967 par les forces armées israéliennes.
[14] For Japanese nationals in Japan only. - Pour les nationaux japonais au Japon seulement.
[15] Excluding alien armed forces, civilian aliens employed by armed forces, and foreign diplomatic personnel and their dependants. - Non compris les militaires étrangers, les civils étrangers employés par les forces armées ni le personnel diplomatique étranger et les membres de leur famille les accompagnant.
[16] Based on the results of the Population Growth Survey. - D'après les résultats de la 'Population Growth Survey.'
[17] Excluding data for the Pakistan-held part of Jammu and Kashmir,

the final status of which has not yet been determined. - Non compris les données concernant la partie du Jammu et Cachemire occupée par le Pakistan dont le statut définitif n'a pas été déterminé.

[18] Excluding transients afloat and non-locally domiciled military and civilian services personnel and their dependants. - Non compris les personnes de passage à bord de navires ni les militaires et agents civils non-résidents et les membres de leur famille les accompagnant.

[19] Including armed forces stationed outside the country, but excluding alien armed forces stationed in the area. - Y compris les militaires nationaux hors du pays, mais non compris les militaires étrangers en garnison sur le territoire.

[20] Excluding Faeroe Islands and Greenland. - Non compris les îles Féroé et Gröenland.

[21] Including nationals temporarily outside the country. - Y compris les nationaux se trouvant temporairement hors du pays.

[22] Including armed forces stationed outside the country. - Y compris les militaires nationaux hors du pays.

[23] Births registered within one year of occurrence. - Naissances enregistrées dans l'année qui suit l'événement.

[24] Live births to Maltese parents only. - Naissances vivantes aux parents maltais seulement.

[25] Including residents outside the country if listed in a Netherlands population register. - Y compris les résidents hors du pays, s'ils sont inscrits sur un registre de population néerlandais.

[26] Data revised to exclude births in Northern Ireland to non-residents of Northern Ireland. - Données révisées non compris des naissances en Irlande du Nord aux non-résidents de l'Irlande du Nord.

Table 12

Table 12 presents late foetal deaths and late foetal-death ratios by urban/rural residence for as many years as possible between 1997 and 2001.

Description of variables: Late foetal deaths are foetal deaths[i] of 28 or more completed weeks of gestation. Foetal deaths of unknown gestational age are included with those 28 or more weeks.

Statistics on the number of late foetal deaths are obtained from civil registers unless otherwise noted.

The urban/rural classification of late foetal deaths is as provided by each country or area; it is presumed to be based on the national census definitions of urban population that have been set forth at the end of the technical notes for table 6.

Ratio computation: Late foetal-death ratios are the annual number of late foetal deaths per 1 000 live births (as shown in table 9) in the same year. The live-birth base was adopted because it is assumed to be more comparable from one country or area to another than the combination of live births and foetal deaths.

Ratios by urban/rural residence are the annual number of late foetal deaths, in the appropriate urban or rural category, per 1 000 corresponding live births (as shown in table 9). These ratios have been calculated by the Statistics Division of the United Nations.

Ratios presented in this table have been limited to those for countries or areas having at least a total of 1 000 late foetal deaths in a given year.

Reliability of data: Each country or area has been asked to indicate the estimated completeness of the late foetal deaths recorded in its civil register. These national assessments are indicated by the quality codes, C and U that appear in the first column of this table.

C indicates that the data are estimated to be virtually complete, that is, representing at least 90 per cent of the late foetal deaths occurring each year, while U indicates that data are estimated to be incomplete, that is, representing less than 90 per cent of the late foetal deaths occurring each year. The code ... indicates that no information was provided regarding completeness.

Data from civil registers which are reported as incomplete or of unknown completeness (coded U or ...) are considered unreliable. They appear in italics in this table. Ratios are not computed for data so coded.

For more information about the quality of vital statistics data in general, see section 4.2 of the Technical Notes.

Limitations: Statistics on late foetal deaths are subject to the same qualifications as have been set forth for vital statistics in general and foetal-death statistics in particular as discussed in section 4 of the Technical Notes.

The reliability of the data is a very important factor. Of all vital statistics, the registration of foetal deaths is probably the most incomplete.

Variation in the definition of foetal deaths, and in particular late foetal deaths, also limits international comparability. The criterion of 28 or more completed weeks of gestation to distinguish late foetal deaths is not universally used; some countries or areas use different durations of gestation or other criteria such as size of the foetus. In addition, the difficulty of accurately determining gestational age further reduces comparability. However, to promote comparability, late foetal deaths shown in this table are restricted to those of at least 28 or more completed weeks of gestation. Wherever this is not possible a footnote is provided.

Another factor introducing variation in the definition of late foetal deaths is the practice by some countries or areas of including in late foetal-death statistics infants who were born alive but died before the registration of the birth or within the first 24 hours of life, thus overestimating the total number of late foetal deaths. Statistics of this type are footnoted.

In addition, late foetal-death ratios are subject to the limitations of the data on live births with which they have been calculated. These have been set forth in the technical notes for table 9.

Regarding the computation of the ratios, it must be pointed out that when late foetal deaths and live births are both under registered, the resulting ratios may be of quite reasonable magnitude. As a matter of fact, for the countries or areas where live-birth registration is poorest, the late foetal-death ratios may be the largest, effectively masking the completeness of the base data. For this reason, possible variations in birth-registration completeness as well as the reported completeness of late foetal deaths must always be borne in mind in evaluating late foetal-death ratios.

In addition to the indirect effect of live-birth under-registration, late foetal-death ratios may be seriously affected by date-of-registration tabulation of live births. When the annual number of live births registered and reported fluctuates over a wide range due to changes in legislation or to special needs for proof of birth on the part of large segments of the population, then the late foetal-death ratios will also fluctuate, but inversely. Because of these effects, data for countries or areas known to tabulate live births by date of registration should be used with caution.

Finally, it may be noted that the counting of live-born infants as late foetal deaths, because they died before the registration of the birth or within the first 24 hours of life, has the effect of inflating the late foetal-death ratios unduly by decreasing the birth denominator and increasing the foetal-death numerator. This factor should not be overlooked in using data from this table.

The comparability of data by urban/rural residence is affected by the national definitions of urban and rural used in tabulating these data. It is assumed, in the absence of specific information to the contrary, that the definitions of urban and rural used in connection with the national population census were also used in the compilation of the vital statistics for each country or area. However, the possibility cannot be excluded that, for a given country or area, the same definitions of urban and rural are not used for both the vital statistics data and the population census data. When known, the definitions of urban used in national population censuses are presented at the end of the technical notes for table 6. As discussed in detail in the technical notes for table 6, these definitions vary considerably from one country or area to another.

Urban/rural differentials in late foetal death ratios may also be affected by whether the late foetal deaths and live births have been tabulated in terms of place of occurrence or place of usual residence. This problem is discussed in more detail in section 4.1.4.1 of the Technical Notes.

Coverage: Late foetal deaths are shown for 78 countries or areas. Data are presented by urban/rural residence for 40 countries or areas.

Earlier data: Late foetal deaths and late foetal-death ratios have been shown in each issue of the Demographic Yearbook beginning with the 1951 issue. A special topic CD on natality published in 2001 presents the data for all available years from 1990 to 1998. For more information on specific topics, and years for which data are reported, readers should consult the Index.

NOTES

[i] For definition, see section 4.1.1.3 of the Technical Notes.

Tableau 12

Le tableau 12 présente des données sur les morts fœtales tardives et des rapports de mortinatalité selon la résidence (urbaine/rurale) pour le plus grand nombre d'années possible entre 1997 et 2001.

Description des variables : Par mort fœtale tardive, on entend décès d'un fœtus[1] survenu après 28 semaines complètes de gestation au moins. Les morts fœtales pour lesquelles la durée de la période de gestation n'est pas connue sont comprises dans cette catégorie.

Sauf indication contraire, les statistiques du nombre de morts fœtales tardives sont établies sur la base des registres de l'état civil.

La classification des morts fœtales tardives selon la résidence (urbaine/rurale) est celle qui a été fournie par chaque pays ou zone; il faut en conclure qu'elle repose sur les définitions de la population urbaine utilisées pour les recensements nationaux, telles qu'elles sont reproduites à la fin des Notes techniques du tableau 6.

Calcul des rapports : Les rapports de mortinatalité représentent le nombre annuel de morts fœtales tardives pour 1,000 naissances vivantes (telles qu'elles sont présentées au tableau 9) survenues pendant la même année. On a pris pour base de calcul les naissances vivantes parce qu'on pense qu'elle sont plus facilement comparables d'un pays ou d'une zone à l'autre que la combinaison des naissances vivantes et des morts fœtales.

Les rapports selon la résidence (urbaine/rurale) représentent le nombre annuel de morts fœtales tardives, classées selon la catégorie urbaine ou rurale appropriée pour 1 000 naissances vivantes (telles qu'elles sont présentées au tableau 9) survenues dans la population correspondante. Ces rapports ont été calculés par la Division de statistique de l'ONU.

Les rapports présentés dans le tableau 12 ne concernent que les pays ou zones où l'on a enregistré un total d'au moins 1 000 morts fœtales tardives dans une année donnée.

Fiabilité des données : Il a été demandé à chaque pays ou zone d'indiquer le degré estimatif de complétude des données sur les morts fœtales tardives figurant dans ses registres d'état civil. Ces évaluations nationales sont désignées par les codes de qualité "C", "U", et "..." qui apparaissent dans la première colonne du tableau.

La lettre "C" indique que les données sont jugées à peu près complètes, c'est-à-dire qu'elles représentent au moins 90 p. 100 des morts fœtales tardives survenues chaque année; la lettre "U" indique que les données sont jugées incomplètes, c'est-à-dire qu'elles représentent moins de 90 p.100 des morts fœtales tardives survenues chaque année. Le signe "..." indique qu'aucun renseignement n'a été fourni quant à la complétude des données.

Les données provenant des registres de l'état civil qui sont déclarées incomplètes ou dont le degré de complétude n'est pas connu (et qui sont affectées de la lettre "U" ou du signe "...") sont jugées douteuses. Elles apparaissent en italique dans le présent tableau ; les rapports, dans ces cas, n'ont pas été calculés.

Pour plus de précisions sur la qualité des données reposant sur les statistiques de l'état civil en général, voir la section 4.2 des notes techniques.

Insuffisance des données : Les statistiques des morts fœtales tardives appellent toutes les réserves qui ont été faites à propos des statistiques de l'état civil en général et des statistiques des morts fœtales en particulier (voir explication figurant à la section 4 des notes techniques).

La fiabilité des données est un facteur très important. Les statistiques des morts fœtales sont probablement les moins complètes de toutes les statistiques de l'état civil.

L'hétérogénéité des définitions de la mort fœtales et, en particulier, de la mort fœtale tardive nuit aussi à la comparabilité internationale des données. Le critère des 28 semaines complètes de gestation au moins n'est pas universellement utilisé; certains pays ou zones utilisent des critères différents pour la durée de la période de gestation ou d'autres critères tels que la taille du fœtus. Pour faciliter les comparaisons, les morts fœtales tardives considérées ici sont exclusivement celles qui sont survenues au terme de 28 semaines de gestation au moins. Les exceptions sont signalées en note.

Un autre facteur d'hétérogénéité dans la définition de la mort fœtale tardive est la pratique de certains pays ou zones qui consiste à inclure dans les statistiques des morts fœtales tardives les enfants nés vivants mais décédés avant l'enregistrement de leur naissance ou dans les 24 heures qui ont suivi la naissance, pratique qui conduit à surestimer le nombre total des morts fœtales tardives. Quand tel était le cas, on l'a signalé en note au bas du tableau.

Les rapports de mortinatalité appellent en outre toutes les réserves qui ont été formulées à propos des statistiques des naissances vivantes qui ont servi à leur calcul. Voir à ce sujet les Notes techniques relatives au tableau 9.

En ce qui concerne le calcul des rapports, il convient de noter que, si l'enregistrement est défectueux à la fois pour les morts fœtales tardives et pour les naissances vivantes, les rapports de mortinatalité peuvent être tout à fait raisonnables. En fait, c'est parfois pour les pays ou zones où l'enregistrement des naissances vivantes laisse le plus à désirer que les rapports de mortinatalité sont les plus élevés, ce qui masque l'incomplétude des données de base. Aussi, pour porter un jugement sur la qualité des rapports de mortinatalité, il ne faut jamais oublier que la complétude de l'enregistrement des naissances comme celle de l'enregistrement des morts fœtales tardives peut varier sensiblement.

En dehors des effets indirects des lacunes de l'enregistrement des naissances vivantes, il arrive que les rapports de mortinatalité soient sérieusement faussés lorsque l'exploitation des données relatives aux naissances se fait d'après la date de l'enregistrement. Si le nombre des naissances vivantes enregistrées vient à varier notablement d'une année à l'autre par suite de modifications de la législation ou parce que des groupes importants de la population ont besoin de posséder une attestation de naissance, les rapports de mortinatalité varient également, mais en sens contraire. Il convient donc d'utiliser avec prudence le données des pays ou zones où les statistiques sont établies d'après la date de l'enregistrement.

Enfin, on notera que l'inclusion parmi les morts fœtales tardives des décès d'enfants nés vivants qui sont décédés avant l'enregistrement de leur naissance ou dans les 24 heures qui ont suivi la naissance conduit à des rapports de mortinatalité exagérés parce que le dénominateur (nombre de naissances) se trouve alors diminué et le numérateur (morts fœtales) augmenté. Il importe de ne pas négliger ce facteur lorsqu'on utilise les données du présent tableau.

La comparabilité des données selon la résidence (urbaine/rurale)peut être limitée par les définitions nationales des termes "urbain" et "rural" utilisées pour la mise en tableaux de ces données. En l'absence d'indications contraires, on a supposé que les définitions des termes "urbain" et "rural" utilisées pour le recensement national de la population avaient été utilisées aussi pour l'établissement des statistiques de l'état civil pour chaque pays ou zone. Toutefois, on ne peut exclure la possibilité que, pour un pays ou zone donné, les mêmes définitions des termes "urbain" et "rural" n'aient pas été utilisées dans les deux cas. Les définitions du terme urbain utilisées pour les recensements nationaux de population ont été présentées à la fin des notes techniques du tableau 6 lorsqu'elles étaient connues. Comme on l'a précisé en détail dans les notes techniques relatives au tableau 6, ces définitions varient très sensiblement d'un pays ou d'une zone à l'autre.

La différence entre les rapports de mortinatalité pour les zones urbaines et rurales pourra aussi être faussée selon que les morts fœtales tardives et les naissances vivantes auront été classées d'après le lieu de l'événement ou le lieu de la résidence habituelle. Ce problème est examiné plus en détail à la section 4.1.4.1 des Notes techniques.

Portée: Ce tableau présente des données sur les morts fœtales tardives pour 78 pays ou zones. Les répartitions selon la résidence (urbaine/rurale)intéressent 40 pays ou zones.

Ce tableau présente également des données sur les rapports de mortinatalité pour 16 pays ou zones. Les rapports ventilés selon la résidence (urbaine/rurale) intéressent 12 pays ou zones.

Données publiées antérieurement : Des statistiques des morts fœtales tardives et des rapports de mortinatalité ont été publiées dans toutes les éditions de l'Annuaire démographique à partir de celle de 1951. Un CD-ROM sur la natalité publié en 2001 présente les données pour toutes les années disponibles de 1990 à 1998. Pour plus de précisions concernant les années et les sujets spécifiques pour lesquelles des données ont été publiées, se reporter à l'Index.

NOTES

[1] *Pour la définition, voir la section 4.1.1.3 des Notes techniques.*

12. Late foetal deaths and late foetal death ratios, by urban/rural residence; 1997 - 2001
Morts foetales tardives et rapports de mortinatalité, selon la résidence, urbaine/rurale: 1997 - 2001

(See notes at end of table. — Voir notes à la fin du tableau.)

Continent, country or area and urban/rural residence Continent, pays ou zone et résidence, urbaine/rurale	Code[1]	Number - Nombre					Ratio - Rapport				
		1997	1998	1999	2000	2001	1997	1998	1999	2000	2001
AFRICA — AFRIQUE											
Algeria - Algérie											
Total	+C	5 245	5 344	14 420	14 891	15 654	...	...	...	...	...
Egypt - Égypte[2]											
Total	+U	5 670	6 526	5 782	...	...	...	...	...	...	...
Urban - Urbaine	+U	4 753	5 361	4 630	...	...	...	...	...	...	...
Rural - Rurale	+U	917	1 165	1 152	...	...	...	...	...	...	...
Mauritius - Maurice											
Total	+C	257	227	226	266	244	...	...	...	...	...
Urban - Urbaine	+C	99	91	90	115	83	...	...	...	...	...
Rural - Rurale	+C	158	136	136	151	161	...	...	...	...	...
Tunisia - Tunisie											
Total	...	1 920	...	...	...	...	...	...	...	...	...
AMERICA, NORTH — **AMERIQUE DU NORD**											
Bermuda - Bermudes											
Total	C	3	...	...	...	...	...	...	...	...	...
Canada[3]											
Total	C	1 174	...	1 087	1 060	...	3.4	...	3.2	3.2	...
Costa Rica											
Total	C	...	...	...	528	510	...	...	...	...	...
Cuba											
Total	C	1 655	1 680	1 643	...	...	10.8	11.1	10.9	...	...
Urban - Urbaine	C	...	...	1 202	...	...	...	...	11.0	...	...
Rural - Rurale	C	...	...	441	...	...	...	...	10.6	...	...
El Salvador											
Total	C	823	664	621	766	706	...	...	...	...	...
Urban - Urbaine	C	673	538	491	557	611	...	...	...	...	...
Rural - Rurale	C	150	126	130	209	95	...	...	...	...	...
Greenland - Groenland											
Total	C	4	3	...	...	...	...	...	...	...	...
Urban - Urbaine	C	4	3	...	...	...	...	...	...	...	...
Rural - Rurale	C	-	-	...	...	...	...	...	...	...	...
Guatemala											
Total	C	6 176	6 531	6 253	...	...	15.9	13.3	17.3	...	...
Urban - Urbaine	C	3 836	4 091	4 124	...	...	24.6	19.7	29.4	...	...
Rural - Rurale	C	2 340	2 440	2 129	...	...	10.1	8.7	9.7	...	...
Mexico - Mexique[4]											
Total	...	17 435	17 700	16 916	16 487	15 432	...	...	...	...	...
Urban - Urbaine	...	12 468	12 735	...	12 347	...	...	...	...	...	...
Rural - Rurale	...	4 697	4 710	...	4 064	...	...	...	...	...	...
Panama[5]											
Total	U	411	343	428	...	394	...	...	...	...	...
Urban - Urbaine	U	207	184	217	...	...	...	...	...	...	...
Rural - Rurale	U	204	159	211	...	...	...	...	...	...	...
Puerto Rico - Porto Rico[4]											
Total	C	740	692	684	651	584	...	...	...	...	...
Urban - Urbaine	C	...	...	...	360	361	...	...	...	...	...
Rural - Rurale	C	...	...	...	290	220	...	...	...	...	...
Saint Lucia - Sainte-Lucie											
Total	...	53	39	46	49	...	...	...	...	...	...
Saint Vincent and the Grenadines - Saint Vincent-et-les Grenadines											
Total	+C	24	...	...	...	...	...	...	...	...	...
United States - États-Unis											
Total	C	13 116	14 043	12 968	...	12 859	3.4	3.6	3.3	...	3.2

12. Late foetal deaths and late foetal death ratios, by urban/rural residence; 1997 - 2001
Morts foetales tardives et rapports de mortinatalité, selon la résidence, urbaine/rurale: 1997 - 2001
(continued — suite)

(See notes at end of table. — Voir notes à la fin du tableau.)

Continent, country or area and urban/rural residence — Continent, pays ou zone et résidence, urbaine/rurale	Code[1]	Number - Nombre					Ratio - Rapport				
		1997	1998	1999	2000	2001	1997	1998	1999	2000	2001
AMERICA, SOUTH — AMERIQUE DU SUD											
Argentina - Argentine											
Total	C	4 869	5 039	4 296	...	5 314	...	...	...	...	7.8
Brazil - Brésil[6]											
Total	...	...	...	19 849	19 298	18 341	...	...	...	...	...
Chile - Chili											
Total	C	1 240	1 161	1 080	...	...	4.8	4.5	4.3	...	...
Urban - Urbaine	C	1 020	954	915	...	...	4.5	4.3	4.2	...	...
Rural - Rurale	C	220	207	165	...	...	6.4	6.3	5.1	...	...
Colombia - Colombie											
Total	...	4 343	5 489	4 490	4 540	...	...	...	...	...	...
Urban - Urbaine	...	...	...	4 008	4 031	...	...	...	...	...	...
Rural - Rurale	...	...	...	434	448	...	...	...	...	...	...
Ecuador - Équateur[7]											
Total	C	2 287	2 792	...	...	...	13.5	14.0	...	...	...
Urban - Urbaine	C	...	2 318	...	...	...	...	16.3	...	...	...
Rural - Rurale	C	...	474	...	...	...	...	8.4	...	...	...
Suriname											
Total	...	117	106	108	...	...	...	...	...	...	...
Uruguay											
Total	+C	426	441	535	436	...	...	...	...	...	...
Venezuela[6]											
Total	...	...	...	...	4 529	...	...	...	...	...	...
ASIA — ASIE											
Armenia - Arménie											
Total	C	316	283	292	289	269	...	...	...	...	...
Urban - Urbaine	C	266	239	234	215	...	...	...	...	...	...
Rural - Rurale	C	50	44	58	74	...	...	...	...	...	...
Azerbaijan - Azerbaïdjan											
Total	+C	576	561	425	418	425	...	...	...	...	...
China: Hong Kong SAR - Chine: Hong Kong RAS											
Total	...	243	226	228	301	221	...	...	...	...	...
China: Macao SAR - Chine: Macao RAS											
Total	C	22	13	10	12	8	...	...	...	...	...
Georgia - Géorgie											
Total	C	...	...	794	693	...	...	...	...	...	...
Urban - Urbaine	C	...	...	790	690	...	...	...	...	...	...
Rural - Rurale	C	...	...	4	3	...	...	...	...	...	...
Japan - Japon[8,4]											
Total	C	3 359	3 296	3 139	3 050	2 882	2.8	2.7	2.7	2.6	2.5
Urban - Urbaine	C	2 692	2 606	2 509	2 424	2 345	2.8	2.7	2.6	2.5	2.5
Rural - Rurale	C	663	675	625	624	534	2.8	2.9	2.8	2.7	2.4
Kazakhstan											
Total	C	2 109	2 015	1 897	...	...	9.1	9.1	9.0	...	...
Urban - Urbaine	C	1 404	1 294	1 191	...	...	12.5	11.6	11.2	...	...
Rural - Rurale	C	705	721	706	...	...	5.9	6.5	6.7	...	...
Kuwait - Koweït											
Total	C	...	299	255	269	...	...	...	...	...	...
Kyrgyzstan - Kirghizistan											
Total	C	619	654	660	608	617	...	...	...	...	...
Urban - Urbaine	C	...	...	...	361	335	...	...	...	...	...
Rural - Rurale	C	...	...	...	247	282	...	...	...	...	...
Malaysia - Malaisie[9]											
Total	...	2 378	2 042	...	...	...	...	...	...	...	...

12. Late foetal deaths and late foetal death ratios, by urban/rural residence; 1997 - 2001
Morts foetales tardives et rapports de mortinatalité, selon la résidence, urbaine/rurale: 1997 - 2001
(continued — suite)

(See notes at end of table. — Voir notes à la fin du tableau.)

Continent, country or area and urban/rural residence Continent, pays ou zone et résidence, urbaine/rurale	Code[1]	Number - Nombre					Ratio - Rapport				
		1997	1998	1999	2000	2001	1997	1998	1999	2000	2001
ASIA — ASIE											
Malaysia: Peninsular Malaysia - Malaisie: Malaisie Péninsulaire											
Total	...	2 168	1 910	...	...	...	...	...	...	...	...
Urban - Urbaine	...	1 161	981	...	...	...	...	...	...	...	...
Rural - Rurale	...	1 007	929	...	...	...	...	...	...	...	...
Philippines											
Total	...	4 761	3 082	4 721	5 127	...	...	...	...	...	...
Qatar											
Total	...	55	...	77	...	...	...	...	...	...	...
Singapore - Singapour											
Total	C	139	133	125	143	107	...	...	...	...	...
Uzbekistan - Ouzbékistan											
Total	C	4 188	...	3 600	3 062	2 902	6.9	...	6.5	5.8	5.7
Urban - Urbaine	C	1 622	...	1 441	1 148	1 138	8.7	...	8.3	7.0	7.1
Rural - Rurale	C	2 566	...	2 159	1 914	1 764	6.2	...	5.7	5.3	5.0
EUROPE											
Austria - Autriche											
Total	C	272	256	316	331	278	...	...	...	...	...
Belgium - Belgique[10,11]											
Total	C	492	513	556	554	583	...	...	...	...	...
Bulgaria - Bulgarie											
Total	C	484	...	540	555	500	...	...	...	...	...
Urban - Urbaine	C	324	...	...	365	246	...	...	...	...	...
Rural - Rurale	C	160	...	...	190	254	...	...	...	...	...
Channel Islands: Guernsey - Îles Anglo-Normandes: Guernesey											
Total	C	4	7	1	4	...	...	...	...	...	...
Croatia - Croatie											
Total	C	253	225	205	229	216	...	...	...	...	...
Urban - Urbaine	C	152	129	...	127	111	...	...	...	...	...
Rural - Rurale	C	101	96	...	102	105	...	...	...	...	...
Czech Republic - République tchèque											
Total	C	273	294	303	259	263	...	...	...	...	...
Urban - Urbaine	C	188	205	215	197	200	...	...	...	...	...
Rural - Rurale	C	85	89	88	62	63	...	...	...	...	...
Estonia - Estonie											
Total	C	108	...	82	67	69	...	...	...	...	...
Urban - Urbaine	C	...	...	...	41	...	...	...	...	...	...
Rural - Rurale	C	...	...	...	24	...	...	...	...	...	...
Finland - Finlande[12]											
Total	C	174	150	...	...	185	...	...	...	...	...
Urban - Urbaine	C	...	87	...	...	94	...	...	...	...	...
Rural - Rurale	C	...	63	...	...	91	...	...	...	...	...
France[2,13]											
Total	C	3 576	3 685	3 442	...	...	4.9	5.0	4.6	...	...
Urban - Urbaine	C	2 784	2 869	2 674	...	...	4.9	5.1	4.7	...	...
Rural - Rurale	C	760	788	719	...	...	4.7	4.7	4.2	...	...
Germany - Allemagne											
Total	C	3 510	...	3 118	...	3 084	4.3	...	4.0	...	4.1
Greece - Grèce[14]											
Total	C	538	517	550	...	588	...	...	...	...	...
Urban - Urbaine	C	442	398	...	...	...	...	...	...	...	...
Rural - Rurale	C	186	199	...	...	...	...	...	...	...	...
Hungary - Hongrie[4]											
Total	C	480	556	471	538	550	...	...	...	...	...
Urban - Urbaine	C	252	296	241	313	304	...	...	...	...	...

12. Late foetal deaths and late foetal death ratios, by urban/rural residence; 1997 - 2001
Morts foetales tardives et rapports de mortinatalité, selon la résidence, urbaine/rurale: 1997 - 2001
(continued — suite)

(See notes at end of table. — Voir notes à la fin du tableau.)

Continent, country or area and urban/rural residence Continent, pays ou zone et résidence, urbaine/rurale	Code[1]	Number - Nombre					Ratio - Rapport				
		1997	1998	1999	2000	2001	1997	1998	1999	2000	2001
EUROPE											
Hungary - Hongrie[4]											
Rural - Rurale	C	227	257	225	225	244	...	...	...	...	...
Iceland - Islande											
Total	C	13	9	19	15	10	...	...	...	...	...
Urban - Urbaine	C	13	7	...	13	9	...	...	...	...	...
Rural - Rurale	C	...	2	...	2	1	...	...	...	...	...
Ireland - Irlande											
Total	+C	368	...	311	...	...	...	...	...	...	...
Isle of Man - Îles de Man											
Total	+C	...	...	4	3	...	...	...	...	...	...
Italy - Italie											
Total	C	1 928	...	...	...	...	3.6	...	...	...	...
Latvia - Lettonie											
Total	C	169	179	165	158	138	...	...	...	...	...
Urban - Urbaine	C	106	115	93	99	88	...	...	...	...	...
Rural - Rurale	C	63	64	72	59	50	...	...	...	...	...
Lithuania - Lituanie											
Total	C	194	205	207	221	167	...	...	...	...	...
Urban - Urbaine	C	...	...	...	120	90	...	...	...	...	...
Rural - Rurale	C	...	...	...	101	77	...	...	...	...	...
Luxembourg											
Total	C	...	32	14	...	23	...	...	...	...	...
Netherlands - Pays-Bas[15]											
Total	C	985	970	944	...	...	...	...	...	...	...
Norway - Norvège											
Total	C	230	247	241	225	241	...	...	...	...	...
Poland - Pologne											
Total	C	2 013	1 983	1 882	...	1 574	4.9	5.0	4.9	...	4.3
Urban - Urbaine	C	1 007	990	983	...	...	4.6	4.6	4.7	...	...
Rural - Rurale	C	1 006	993	899	...	...	5.3	5.5	5.2	...	...
Portugal											
Total	C	506	...	...	...	390	...	...	...	...	...
Romania - Roumanie											
Total	C	1 483	1 514	1 459	1 393	1 282	6.3	6.4	6.2	5.9	5.8
Urban - Urbaine	C	689	714	...	612	567	6.3	6.5	...	5.7	5.5
Rural - Rurale	C	794	800	...	781	715	6.3	6.3	...	6.2	6.1
Russian Federation - Fédération de Russie											
Total	C	...	...	8 864	...	...	...	...	7.3	...	...
Urban - Urbaine	C	...	...	6 472	...	...	...	...	7.7	...	...
Rural - Rurale	C	...	...	2 392	...	...	...	...	6.4	...	...
San Marino - Saint-Marin											
Total	+C	3	...	1	2	...	...	...	...	...	...
Urban - Urbaine	+C	3	...	...	2	...	...	...	...	...	...
Rural - Rurale	+C	...	...	...	...	...	...	...	...	...	...
Serbia and Montenegro - Serbie-et-Monténégro											
Total	C	809	786	722	715	741	...	...	...	...	...
Slovakia - Slovaquie											
Total	C	...	281	259	...	207	...	...	...	...	...
Urban - Urbaine	C	...	141	117	...	100	...	...	...	...	...
Rural - Rurale	C	...	140	142	...	107	...	...	...	...	...
Slovenia - Slovénie											
Total	C	...	83	66	68	85	...	...	...	...	...
Urban - Urbaine	C	...	...	...	32	38	...	...	...	...	...
Rural - Rurale	C	...	...	...	36	46	...	...	...	...	...
Spain - Espagne											
Total	C	1 338	1 267	1 275	...	...	3.6	3.5	3.4	...	...
Sweden - Suède											
Total	C	337	303	321	342	349	...	...	...	...	...

12. Late foetal deaths and late foetal death ratios, by urban/rural residence; 1997 - 2001
Morts foetales tardives et rapports de mortinatalité, selon la résidence, urbaine/rurale: 1997 - 2001
(continued — suite)

(See notes at end of table. — Voir notes à la fin du tableau.)

Continent, country or area and urban/rural residence Continent, pays ou zone et résidence, urbaine/rurale	Code[1]	Number - Nombre					Ratio - Rapport				
		1997	1998	1999	2000	2001	1997	1998	1999	2000	2001
EUROPE											
Switzerland - Suisse											
Total	C	336	308	277	283	279	...	...	...	...	...
Urban - Urbaine	C	211	218	165	170	176	...	...	...	...	...
Rural - Rurale	C	125	90	112	113	103	...	...	...	...	...
The Former Yugoslav Rep. of Macedonia - L'ex-République yougoslave de Macédoine											
Total	C	299	...	...	266	284	...	...	...	...	...
Urban - Urbaine	C	171	...	...	150	182	...	...	...	...	...
Rural - Rurale	C	128	...	...	116	102	...	...	...	...	...
Ukraine											
Total	C	2 966	2 597	...	...	1 830	6.7	6.2	...	...	4.9
Urban - Urbaine	C	2 021	1 744	...	...	1 214	7.4	6.7	...	...	5.1
Rural - Rurale	C	945	853	...	...	616	5.6	5.3	...	...	4.4
United Kingdom - Royaume-Uni											
Total	C	3 889	3 890	3 723	3 594	...	5.4	5.4	5.3	5.3	...
OCEANIA — OCEANIE											
Australia - Australie											
Total	+C	982	858	799	802		...	...	...	...	...
New Caledonia - Nouvelle-Calédonie											
Total	+C	34	41	28			...	...	...	...	...
New Zealand - Nouvelle-Zélande											
Total	+C	171	...	172	168		...	...	...	...	...
Urban - Urbaine	+C	149	...	147	137		...	...	...	...	...
Rural - Rurale	+C	22	...	25	31		...	...	...	...	...

GENERAL NOTES - NOTES GENERALES

Late foetal deaths are deaths of foetuses of 28 or more completed weeks of gestation. Data include foetal deaths of unknown gestational age. Ratios are the number of late foetal deaths per 1 000 live births. Ratios are shown only for countries or areas having at least a total of 1 000 late foetal deaths in a given year. For definitions of 'urban', see end of Technical Notes for table 6. For method of evaluation and limitations of data, see Technical Notes for this table. — Les morts foetales tardives sont celles qui surviennent après 28 semaines complètes de gestation au moins. Les données comprennent les morts foetales survenues après une période de gestation de durée inconnue. Les rapports représentent le nombre de morts foetales tardives pour 1 000 naissances vivantes. Les rapports présentés ne se rapportent qu'aux pays ou zones ou l'on enregistré un total d'au moins 1 000 morts foetales tardives dans une année donnée. Pour les définitions des 'régions urbaines', se reporter à la fin des Notes techniques du tableau 6. Pour la méthode d'évaluation et les insuffisances des données, voir Notes techniques, pour ce tableau.

Italics: data from civil registers which are incomplete or of unknown completeness. — Italiques: données incomplètes ou dont le degré d'exactitude n'est pas connu, provenant des registres de l'état civil.

FOOTNOTES - NOTES

* Provisional. — Données provisoires.
+ Data tabulated by date of registration rather than occurence. — Données

exploitées selon la date de l'enregistrement et non la date de l'événement.

[1] 'Code' indicates the source of data, as follows:
C - Civil registration, estimated over 90% complete
U - Civil registration, estimated less than 90% complete
I - Other source, estimated reliable
+ - Data tabulated by date of registration rather than occurence.
... - Information not available

Le 'Code' indique la source des données, comme suit:
C - Registres de l'état civil considérés complèts à 90 p. 100 au moins.
U - Registres de l'état civil qui ne sont pas considérés complèts à 90 p. 100 au moins.
I - Autre source, considérée pas douteuses.
+ - Données exploitées selon la date de l'enregistrement et non la date de l'événement.
... - Information pas disponible.

[2] Foetal deaths after at least 180 days (6 calendar months or 26 weeks) of gestation. - Morts foetales survenues après 180 jours (6 mois civils ou 26 semaines) au moins de gestation.
[3] Including Canadian residents temporarily in the United States, but excluding United States residents temporarily in Canada. - Y compris les résidents canadiens se trouvant temporairement aux Etats-Unis, mais ne comprennent pas les résidents des Etats-Unis se trouvant temporairement au Canada.
[4] Data for urban and rural areas exclude foetal deaths of unknown residence. - Les données urbaines/rurales ne comprennent pas les morts foetales tardives dont on ignore la résidence.
[5] Excluding tribal Indian population. - Non compris les Indiens vivant en tribus.
[6] Excluding Indian jungle population. - Non compris les Indiens de la

jungle.

[7] Excluding nomadic Indian tribes. - Non compris les tribus d'Indiens nomades.

[8] For Japanese nationals in Japan only. - Pour les nationaux japonais au Japon seulement.

[9] Total was revised to include late registration. - Le total a été revisé avec les enregistrements tardives.

[10] Including armed forces stationed outside the country, but excluding alien armed forces stationed in the area. - Y compris les militaires nationaux hors du pays, mais non compris les militaires étrangers en garnison sur le territoire.

[11] Unrevised data. - Les données n'ont pas été révisées.

[12] Including nationals temporarily outside the country. - Y compris les nationaux se trouvant temporairement hors du pays.

[13] Ratios computed on live births in the population including national armed forces outside the country. - Rapports calculés sur la base des naissances vivantes qui comprennent les militaires nationaux hors du pays.

[14] For urban/rural, foetal deaths after at least 150 days (5 calendar months or 20 weeks) of gestation. - Pour les chiffres urbaine/rurale, morts foetales survenues après 150 jours (5 mois civils ou 26 semaines) ou moins de gestation.

[15] Including residents outside the country if listed in a Netherlands population register. - Y compris les résidents hors du pays, s'ils sont inscrits sur un registre de population néerlandais.

Table 13

Table 13 presents legally induced abortions for as many years as possible between 1993 and 2001.

Description of variables: Abortion is defined, with reference to the women, as any interruption of pregnancy before 28 weeks of gestation with a dead foetus.[i] There are two major categories of abortion: spontaneous and induced. Induced abortions are those initiated by deliberate action undertaken with the intention of terminating pregnancy; all other abortions are considered as spontaneous.

The induction of abortion is subject to governmental regulation in most, if not all, countries or areas. This regulation varies from complete prohibition in some countries or areas to abortion on request, with services provided by governmental health authorities, in others. More generally, governments have attempted to define the conditions under which pregnancy may lawfully be terminated and have established procedures for authorizing abortion in individual cases.

Legally induced abortions are further classified according to the legal grounds on which induced abortion may be performed. A code shown next to the country or area name indicates the grounds on which induced abortion is legal in that particular country or area, the meanings of which are shown below:

a) Continuation of pregnancy would involve risk to the life of the pregnant woman greater than if the pregnancy were terminated.

b) Continuation of pregnancy would involve greater risk of injury to the physical health of the pregnant woman than if the pregnancy were terminated.

c) Continuation of pregnancy would involve risk of injury to the mental health of the pregnant woman greater than if the pregnancy were terminated.

d) Continuation of pregnancy would involve risk of injury to mental or physical health of any existing children of the family greater than if the pregnancy were terminated.

e) There is a substantial risk that if the child were born it would suffer from such physical or mental abnormalities as to be seriously handicapped.

f) Other.

Reliability of data: Unlike data on live births and foetal deaths, which are generally collected through systems of vital registration, data on abortion are collected from a variety of sources. Because of this, the quality specification, showing the completeness of civil registers, which is presented for other tables, does not appear here.

Limitations: With regard to the collection of information on abortions, a variety of sources are used, but hospital records are the most common source of information. This obviously implies that most cases that have no contact with hospitals are missed. Data from other sources are probably also incomplete. The data in the present table are limited to legally induced abortions which by their nature, might be assumed to be more complete than data on all induced abortions.

Coverage: Legally induced abortions are shown for 52 countries or areas.

Earlier data: Legally induced abortions have been shown previously in all issues of the *Demographic Yearbook* since the 1971 issue.

NOTES

[i] *Manual of the International Statistical Classification of Diseases, Injuries and Causes of Death, 1965 Revision, volume. I*, World Health Organization, Geneva, 1967. p. 243.

Tableau 13

Ce tableau présente des données sur les avortements provoqués légalement pour le plus grand nombre d'années possible entre 1993 et 2001.

Descriptions des variables: Le terme avortement est défini, en ce qui concerne la femme, comme toute interruption d'une grossesse avant la 28ème semaine avec présence d'un fœtus mort.[1] L'avortement peut être spontané ou provoqué. L'avortement provoqué est celui qui résulte de manœuvres délibérées, entreprises dans le dessein d'interrompre la grossesse; toutes les autres avortements sont considérés comme spontanés.

L'interruption délibérée de la grossesse fait l'objet d'une réglementation officielle dans la plupart des pays ou zones, sinon dans tous. Cette réglementation va de l'interdiction totale à l'autorisation de l'avortement sur demande, pratiqué par des services de santé publique. Le plus souvent, les gouvernements se sont efforcés de définir les circonstances dans lesquelles la grossesse peut être interrompue licitement et de fixer une procédure d'autorisation.

Les interruptions légales de grossesse sont également classées selon le motif d'autorisation. Un code, affiché à côté du pays ou de la zone, signale les motifs d'autorisation de l'avortement. Le signifié de ces codes est le suivant:

a) La non-interruption de la grossesse comporterait, pour la vie de la femme enceinte, un risque plus grave que celui de l'avortement.

b) La non-interruption de la grossesse comporterait, pour la santé physique de la femme enceinte, un risque plus grave que celui de l'avortement.

c) La non-interruption de la grossesse comporterait, pour la santé mentale de la femme, un risque plus grave que celui de l'avortement.

d) La non-interruption de la grossesse comporterait, pour la santé mentale ou physique d'un enfant déjà né dans la famille, un risque plus grave que celui de l'avortement.

e) L'enfant né à terme courrait un risque substantiel de souffrir d'anomalies physiques ou mentales entraînant pour lui un grave handicap.

f) Autres motifs.

Fiabilité des données: A la différence des données sur les naissances vivantes et les morts fœtales, qui proviennent généralement des registres d'état civil, les données sur l'avortement sont tirées de sources diverses. Aussi ne trouve-t-on pas ici une évaluation de la qualité des données semblable à celle qui indique, pour les autres tableaux, le degré d'exhaustivité des données de l'état civil.

Insuffisances des données: En ce qui concerne les renseignements sur l'avortement, un grand nombre de sources sont utilisées[33], mais les relevés hospitaliers constituent la source la plus fréquente d'information. Il s'ensuit que la plupart des cas qui ne passent pas par les hôpitaux sont ignorés. Les données du tableau 13 se limitent aux avortements provoqués pour raisons légales dont on peut supposer, en raison de leur nature même, que les statistiques sont plus complètes que les données concernant l'ensemble des avortements provoqués.

Portée: Ce tableau présente des données sur les avortements provoqués pour raisons légales concernant 52 pays ou zones.

Données publiées antérieurement: Des statistiques des avortements provoqués pour raisons légales ont déjà été publiées dans toutes les éditions de l'Annuaire démographique depuis celle de 1971.

NOTES

[1] *Manual of the International Statistical Classification of Diseases, Injuries and Causes of Death, 1965 Revision, volume. I*, World Health Organization, Geneva, 1967. p. 243.

13. Legally induced abortions: 1993 - 2001
Avortements provoqués légalement: 1993 - 2001

(See notes at end of table. — Voir notes à la fin du tableau.)

Continent and country or area / Continent et pays ou zone	Number — Nombre								
	1993	1994	1995	1996	1997	1998	1999	2000	200[1]
AFRICA — AFRIQUE									
South Africa - Afrique du Sud[1]	...	...	...	...	...	28 978	...	...	
AMERICA, NORTH — AMERIQUE DU NORD									
Canada[a,b,c]	72 434	71 630	70 549	...	...	110 331	...	...	
Cuba	86 906	89 421	83 963	...	80 097	75 109	80 037	76 293	
Dominican Republic - République dominicaine	...	...	18 377	20 852	22 911	31 068	...	...	
Greenland - Groenland	977	1 000	879	862	865	913	816	...	
Mexico - Mexique	...	...	...	2 724	2 938	3 189	3 486	3 281	
Panama[2]	...	...	...	...	...	...	...	11	
ASIA — ASIE									
Armenia - Arménie	27 907	30 571	30 726	31 323	25 266	18 286	14 403	11 769	10 41
Azerbaijan - Azerbaïdjan	33 951	33 280	28 610	28 375	25 182	24 914	20 878	17 501	18 33
China: Hong Kong SAR - Chine: Hong-Kong RAS	26 057	26 049	25 363	25 041	23 939	22 086	20 891	21 375	20 23
Georgia - Géorgie	45 131	48 953	43 549	...	...	...	...	...	
Israel - Israël[3,4]	17 164	16 903	17 627	17 447	18 771	18 210	18 532	...	
Japan - Japon[5,a,b,c,d,e]	386 807	364 350	343 024	338 867	337 799	333 220	337 314	341 164	
Kazakhstan	206 877	260 200	224 100	193 462	156 222	148 799	137 808	...	
Kyrgyzstan - Kirghizistan	52 724	49 325	27 111	...	31 598	28 090	25 790	22 044	23 390
Mongolia - Mongolie	...	...	...	15 588	12 870	...	...	...	
Singapore - Singapour[a,b,c,d,e]	16 476	15 690	14 504	14 362	13 827	13 838	13 753	13 734	
Tajikistan - Tadjikistan	40 078	35 709	...	...	...	...	...	...	
Uzbekistan - Ouzbékistan	...	120 434	104 400	104 620	...	...	...	...	
EUROPE									
Belarus - Bélarus	212 729	207 658	193 280	174 098	152 660	145 339	135 824	...	
Belgium - Belgique	...	...	...	...	...	11 999	12 734	13 762	14 775
Bulgaria - Bulgarie	107 416	97 567	97 092	...	87 896	...	...	61 378	51 165
Channel Islands: Guernsey - Îles Anglo-Normandes: Guernesey	...	...	...	...	57	104	92	89	
Channel Islands: Jersey - Îles Anglo-Normandes: Jersey	296	...	...	...	...	...	...	...	
Croatia - Croatie	25 179	19 673	14 282	12 339	10 036	8 907	8 064	7 534	
Czech Republic - République tchèque[a,b,c,e]	70 634	54 836	49 531	48 086	45 022	42 959	39 382	34 623	32 513
Denmark - Danemark[6,a,b,c,d,e]	18 607	17 598	17 720	18 135	17 152	16 592	16 271	15 681	
Estonia - Estonie	23 284	19 784	17 671	16 887	16 615	...	14 503	12 743	
Finland - Finlande[a,b,c,e,f]	10 342	10 013	9 884	10 437	10 238	10 744	10 819	10 930	10 694
France[a,b,c,e]	157 886	152 963	146 433	...	163 985	...	...	...	
Germany - Allemagne	111 236	103 586	97 937	...	130 890	...	130 471	134 609	
Greece - Grèce[a,b,c,e,f]	12 289	12 608	...	12 542	...	...	...	...	
Hungary - Hongrie[a,b,c,d,e,f]	75 258	74 491	76 957	76 600	74 564	68 971	65 981	59 249	56 405
Iceland - Islande[a,b,c,e,f]	827	775	807	854	921	...	945	947	996
italy - Italie	145 229	135 956	134 137	138 925	140 166	138 354	138 708	...	
Latvia - Lettonie	31 348	26 795	25 933	24 227	21 768	19 964	18 031	17 240	15 647
Lithuania - Lituanie	38 864	30 326	31 278	27 832	22 680	21 022	18 846	16 259	13 677
Netherlands - Pays-Bas[a,b,c,e,f]	19 804	20 811	20 932	22 441	...	24 141	...	...	
Norway - Norvège[a,b,c,d,e,f]	14 909	...	13 672	...	...	14 028	14 251	14 635	13 867
Poland - Pologne[7,a,b,c,e,f]	1 208	874	559	491	3 171	312	151	138	123
Republic of Moldova - République de Moldavie	...	...	44 252	46 010	...	31 293	27 908	20 395	16 028
Romania - Roumanie	585 761	530 191	502 840	456 221	347 126	259 888	...	257 865	198 086
Russian Federation - Fédération de Russie	3 243 957	2 481 493	2 766 362	...	...	...	...	...	
Serbia and Montenegro - Serbie-et-Montenegro	119 254	98 942	96 854	83 577	64 099	58 739	...	...	
Slovakia - Slovaquie	38 852	34 883	35 879	...	...	21 109	19 949	...	18 026
Slovenia - Slovénie	12 154	11 324	10 791	10 218	...	9 116	8 707	8 429	7 799
Spain - Espagne	...	47 832	...	51 002	46 902	53 847	58 399	63 756	

(ee notes at end of table. — Voir notes à la fin du tableau.)

ontinent and country or area ontinent et pays ou zone	Number — Nombre								
	1993	1994	1995	1996	1997	1998	1999	2000	2001
JROPE									
Sweden - Suède	34 169	32 293	31 441	32 117	31 433	31 008	...	30 980	31 772
The Former Yugoslav Rep. of Macedonia - L'ex-République yougoslave de Macédoine	...	...	...	...	12 028	...	...	...	...
United Kingdom - Royaume-Uni[a,b,c,d,e,f] ...	173 686	169 964	167 297	189 473	191 855	199 887	195 394	197 366	197 913
CEANIA — OCEANIE									
New Caledonia - Nouvelle-Calédonie	...	...	...	...	1 528	1 466	...	...	...
New Zealand - Nouvelle-Zélande	11 893	12 835	13 652	14 805	15 208	15 029	15 501	...	...

ENERAL NOTES - NOTES GENERALES

or method of evaluation and limitations of data, see Technical Notes, for this ble. — Pour la méthode d'évaluation et les insuffisances des données, voir otes techniques, pour ce tableau.

OOTNOTES - NOTES

* Provisional. — Données provisoires.

a Continuation of pregnancy would involve risk to the life of the pregnant oman greater than if the pregnancy were terminated. — La prolongation de la rossesse exposerait la vie de la femme enceinte davantage que son interruption.

b Continuation of pregnancy would involve risk to the physical health of the regnant woman greater than if the pregnancy were terminated. — La rolongation de la grossesse couserait des complication pouvant affecter la santé hysique de la femme enceinte davantage que son interruption.

c Continuation of pregnancy would involve risk of injury to the mental health of e pregnant woman greater than if the pregnancy were terminated. — La rolongation de la grossesse couserait des complications affectant les facultés nentales de la femme enceinte davantage que son interruption.

d Continuation of pregnancy would involve risk of injury to the mental or hysical health of any existing children of the family greater than if the pregnancy vere terminated. — La prolongation de la grossesse couserait des complications affectant les facultés mentales ou physiques des enfants vivants de cettee famille, davantage que son interruption.

e There is a substaintial risk that if the child were born it would suffer from such physical or mental abnormalities as to be seriously handicapped. — Il y aurait des risques majeurs pour l'enfant de naître avec des anomalies physiques ou mentales qui l'handicaperaient gravement.

f Other. — Autres.

1 Data refer to both 1997 and 1998. - Les données se rapportent à 1997 et à 1998.

2 Data refer to abortions granted for medical reasons by the Comision Multidisciplinaria Nacional de Aborto Terapéutico. - Les données se référent aux avortements autorisés pour des raisons médicales par la Comision Multidisciplinaria Nacional de Aborto Terapéutico.

3 Including data for East Jerusalem and Israeli residents in certain other territories under occupation by Israeli military forces since June 1967. - Y compris les données pour Jérusalem-Est et les résidents israéliens dans certains autres territoires occupés depuis 1967 par les forces armées israéliennes.

4 Data refer to authorization to interrupt pregancy. - Les données se rapportent à l'autorisation d'interrompre le pregancy.

5 For Japanese nationals in Japan only. - Pour les nationaux japonais au Japon seulement.

6 Excluding Faeroe Islands and Greenland. - Non compris les îles Féroé et Gröenland.

7 Based on hospital and polyclinic records. - D'après les registres des hôpitaux et des polycliniques.

Table 14

Table 14 presents legally induced abortions by age and number of previous live births of women for the latest available year.

Description of variables: The technical notes for table 13 provide more detailed information on the classification of legally induced abortion.

Age is defined as age at last birthday, that is, the difference between the date of birth and the date of the occurrence of the event, expressed in complete solar years. The age classification used in this table is the following: under 15 years, 5-year age groups through 45-49 years and 50 years and over.

Except where otherwise indicated, eight categories are used in classifying the number of previous live births: 0 through 5, 6 or more live births, and, if required, number of live births unknown.

Reliability of data: Unlike data on live births and foetal deaths, which are generally collected through systems of vital registration, data on abortion are collected from a variety of sources. Because of this, the quality specification, showing the completeness of civil registers, which is presented for other tables, does not appear here.

Limitations: With regard to the collection of information on abortions, a variety of sources are used, but hospital records are the most common source of information. This obviously implies that most cases that have no contact with hospitals are missed. Data from other sources are probably also incomplete. The data in the present table are limited to legally induced abortions that, by their nature, might be assumed to be more complete than data on all induced abortions.

In addition, deficiencies in reporting of age and number of previous live births of the woman, differences in the method used for obtaining the age of the woman, and the proportion of abortions for which age or previous live births of the woman are unknown must all be taken into account in using these data.

Coverage: Legally induced abortions by age and number of previous live births of woman are shown for 39 countries or areas.

Earlier data: Legally induced abortions by age and previous live births of women have been shown previously in most issues of the *Demographic Yearbook* since the 1971 issue. For more information on specific topics and years for which data are reported, readers should consult the Index.

Tableau 14

Le tableau 14 présente des données sur les avortements provoqués pour des raisons légales, selon l'âge de la mère et le nombre de naissances vivantes antérieures, pour la dernière année pour laquelle ces données sont disponibles.

Descriptions des variables: Les Notes techniques au tableau 13 donnent plus de détails concernant la classification des avortements légaux.

L'âge est l'âge au dernier anniversaire, c'est-à-dire la différence entre la date de naissance et la date de l'avortement, exprimée en années solaires révolues. La classification par âge utilisée dans ce tableau est la suivante: moins de 15 ans, groupes quinquennaux jusqu'à 45 - 49 ans, 50 ans et plus, et âge inconnu.

Sauf indication contraire, les naissances vivantes antérieures sont classées dans les huit catégories suivantes: 0 à 5 naissances vivantes, 6 naissances vivantes ou plus et, le cas échéant, nombre de naissances vivantes inconnu.

Fiabilité des données: A la différence des données sur les naissances vivantes et les morts fœtales, qui proviennent généralement des registres d'état civil, les données sur l'avortement sont tirées de sources diverses. Aussi ne trouve-t-on pas ici une évaluation de la qualité des données semblable à celle qui indique, pour les autres tableaux, le degré d'exhaustivité des données de l'état civil.

Insuffisances des données: En ce qui concerne les renseignements sur l'avortement, un grand nombre de sources sont utilisées, mais les relevés hospitaliers constituent la source la plus fréquente d'information. Il s'ensuit que la plupart des cas qui ne passent pas par les hôpitaux sont ignorés. Les données du tableau 14 se limitent aux avortements provoqués pour raisons légales, dont on peut supposer, en raison de leur nature même, que les statistiques sont plus complètes que les données concernant l'ensemble des avortements provoqués.

En outre, on doit tenir compte, lorsqu'on utilise ces données, des erreurs de déclaration de l'âge de la mère et du nombre des naissances vivantes précédentes, de l'hétérogénéité des méthodes de calcul de l'âge de la mère et de la proportion d'avortements pour lesquels l'âge de la mère ou le nombre des naissances vivantes ne sont pas connus.

Portée: Ce tableau présente des données sur les avortements provoqués pour raisons légales, selon l'âge de la mère et le nombre des naissances vivantes antérieures, pour 39 pays ou zones.

Données publiées antérieurement: Des statistiques des avortements provoqués pour raisons légales, selon l'âge de la mère et le nombre de naissances vivantes antérieures, figurent déjà dans la plupart des éditions de l'Annuaire démographique depuis celle de 1971. Pour plus de précisions concernant les années et les sujets spécifiques pour lesquelles des données ont été publiées, se reporter à l'Index.

14. Legally induced abortions by age and number of previous live births of women: latest available year
Avortments provoqués légalement selon l'âge de la femme et selon le nombre des naissances vivantes précédentes: dernière année disponible

(See notes at end of table. — Voir notes à la fin du tableau.)

Continent, country or area, year and age — Continent, pays ou zone, année et âge	Total	Number of previous live births - Nombre des naissances vivantes précédentes							
		0	1	2	3	4	5	6+	Unknown Inconnu
AMERICA, NORTH — AMERIQUE DU NORD									
Canada[1]									
1995									
Total	53 567	24 747	11 894	9 443	3 439	1 214	486	368	1 976
0 - 14	301	281	9	-	-	-	-	-	11
15 - 19	10 470	8 301	1 530	311	38	6	2	3	279
20 - 24	16 060	8 907	4 103	1 878	483	137	31	18	503
25 - 29	11 553	4 167	3 044	2 518	872	278	114	69	491
30 - 34	8 426	1 918	1 943	2 518	1 027	377	150	125	368
35 - 39	5 079	896	986	1 659	770	307	137	101	223
40 - 44	1 500	224	254	506	231	101	44	45	95
45+	99	9	13	36	13	7	8	7	6
Unknown	79	44	12	17	5	1	-	-	-
1998									
Total	110 331	...	...	...	...	...	...	...	...
0 - 14	464	...	...	...	...	...	...	...	...
15 - 19	20 859	...	...	...	...	...	...	...	...
20 - 24	32 326	...	...	...	...	...	...	...	...
25 - 29	22 175	...	...	...	...	...	...	...	...
30 - 34	16 349	...	...	...	...	...	...	...	...
35 - 39	10 834	...	...	...	...	...	...	...	...
40+	3 492	...	...	...	...	...	...	...	...
Unknown	3 535	...	...	...	...	...	...	...	...
Mexico - Mexique									
2000									
Total	3 281	727	977	665	244	133	42	64	429
0 - 14	18	14	1	...	...	...	...	...	3
15 - 19	486	208	128	25	2	...	1	...	122
20 - 24	903	215	365	158	27	10	2	1	125
25 - 29	791	156	246	206	68	28	7	7	73
30 - 34	530	61	148	164	71	36	6	10	34
35 - 39	307	32	47	76	52	38	18	25	19
40 - 44	89	10	9	15	17	14	6	15	3
45 - 49	5	...	...	...	...	1	...	4	...
Unknown	152	31	33	21	7	6	2	2	50
Panama[2]									
2000									
Total	11	7	3	...	...	...	...	1	...
15 - 19	2	2	...	...	...	...	...	...	...
20 - 24	4	3	1	...	...	...	...	...	...
25 - 29	2	1	1	...	...	...	...	...	...
30 - 34	2	...	1	...	...	...	...	1	...
35+	1	1	...	...	...	...	...	...	...
ASIA — ASIE									
Azerbaijan - Azerbaïdjan									
2001									
Total	18 332	...	...	...	...	...	...	...	...
15 - 19	912	...	...	...	...	...	...	...	...
20 - 24	4 322	...	...	...	...	...	...	...	...
25 - 29	5 040	...	...	...	...	...	...	...	...
30 - 34	4 675	...	...	...	...	...	...	...	...
35 - 39	3 383	...	...	...	...	...	...	...	...
China: Hong Kong SAR - Chine: Hong Kong RAS[3]									
2000									
Total	21 372	11 298	4 066	4 835	1 173	...	...	...	...
0 - 14	25	25	...	...	...	...	...	...	...

14. Legally induced abortions by age and number of previous live births of women: latest available year
Avortments provoqués légalement selon l'âge de la femme et selon le nombre des naissances vivantes précédentes: dernière année disponible (continued — suite)

(See notes at end of table. — Voir notes à la fin du tableau.)

Continent, country or area, year and age / Continent, pays ou zone, année et âge	Total	0	1	2	3	4	5	6+	Unknown Inconnu
			Number of previous live births - Nombre des naissances vivantes précédentes						
ASIA — ASIE									
China: Hong Kong SAR - Chine: Hong Kong RAS[3]									
2000									
15 - 19	1 898	1 832	56	10	...	...	...	...	...
20 - 24	4 855	4 256	450	129	20	...	...	...	...
25 - 29	4 551	2 996	955	502	98	...	...	...	...
30 - 34	4 251	1 480	1 184	1 344	243	...	...	...	...
35 - 39	3 967	578	1 028	1 909	452	...	...	...	...
40 - 44	1 683	117	371	880	315	...	...	...	...
45 - 49	142	14	22	61	45	...	...	...	...
Georgia - Géorgie									
1995									
Total	32 016	...	...	...	...	...	...	...	...
0 - 14	177	...	...	...	...	...	...	...	...
15 - 19	2 508	...	...	...	...	...	...	...	...
20 - 34	25 510	...	...	...	...	...	...	...	...
35+	3 821	...	...	...	...	...	...	...	...
Israel - Israël[4]									
1999									
Total	17 860	...	...	...	...	...	...	...	...
0 - 14	60	...	...	...	...	...	...	...	...
15 - 19	2 365	...	...	...	...	...	...	...	...
20 - 24	3 898	...	...	...	...	...	...	...	...
25 - 29	3 754	...	...	...	...	...	...	...	...
30 - 34	3 258	...	...	...	...	...	...	...	...
35 - 39	2 831	...	...	...	...	...	...	...	...
40 - 44	1 438	...	...	...	...	...	...	...	...
45 - 49	154	...	...	...	...	...	...	...	...
50+	4	...	...	...	...	...	...	...	...
Unknown	98	...	...	...	...	...	...	...	...
Japan - Japon[5]									
1999									
Total	337 314	...	...	...	...	...	...	...	...
0 - 19	39 637	...	...	...	...	...	...	...	...
20 - 24	81 564	...	...	...	...	...	...	...	...
25 - 29	70 795	...	...	...	...	...	...	...	...
30 - 34	62 113	...	...	...	...	...	...	...	...
35 - 39	55 122	...	...	...	...	...	...	...	...
40 - 44	25 554	...	...	...	...	...	...	...	...
45 - 49	2 446	...	...	...	...	...	...	...	...
50+	39	...	...	...	...	...	...	...	...
Unknown	44	...	...	...	...	...	...	...	...
Kazakhstan									
1999									
Total	137 808	...	...	...	...	...	...	...	...
0 - 14	177	...	...	...	...	...	...	...	...
15 - 18	8 971	...	...	...	...	...	...	...	...
19 - 35	105 204	...	...	...	...	...	...	...	...
36+	23 456	...	...	...	...	...	...	...	...
Singapore - Singapour[6]									
2000									
Total	13 734	6 529	1 983	3 116	1 607	499	...	...	...
0 - 14	37	37	...	...	...	...	...	...	...
15 - 19	1 693	1 571	101	21	...	...	...	...	...
20 - 24	3 302	2 668	399	181	46	8	...	...	...
25 - 29	3 053	1 498	601	666	224	64	...	...	...
30 - 34	2 506	497	480	919	487	123	...	...	...
35 - 39	2 169	200	290	918	569	192	...	...	...
40 - 44	901	56	107	376	263	99	...	...	...

14. Legally induced abortions by age and number of previous live births of women: latest available year
Avortments provoqués légalement selon l'âge de la femme et selon le nombre des naissances vivantes précédentes: dernière année disponible (continued — suite)

(See notes at end of table. — Voir notes à la fin du tableau.)

Continent, country or area, year and age / Continent, pays ou zone, année et âge	Number of previous live births - Nombre des naissances vivantes précédentes								
	Total	0	1	2	3	4	5	6+	Unknown Inconnu
ASIA — ASIE									
Singapore - Singapour[6]									
2000									
45+	73	2	5	35	18	13	...	...	...
EUROPE									
Belarus - Bélarus									
1999									
Total	135 824	...	...	...	...	...	...	...	...
0 - 14	50	...	...	...	...	...	...	...	...
15 - 19	11 958	...	...	...	...	...	...	...	...
20 - 24	34 311	...	...	...	...	...	...	...	...
25 - 29	35 085	...	...	...	...	...	...	...	...
30 - 34	26 621	...	...	...	...	...	...	...	...
35 - 39	19 456	...	...	...	...	...	...	...	...
40 - 44	7 643	...	...	...	...	...	...	...	...
45+	700	...	...	...	...	...	...	...	...
Belgium - Belgique									
2001									
Total	14 775	...	...	...	...	...	...	...	...
0 - 14	75	...	...	...	...	...	...	...	...
15 - 19	2 133	...	...	...	...	...	...	...	...
20 - 24	3 761	...	...	...	...	...	...	...	...
25 - 29	3 332	...	...	...	...	...	...	...	...
30 - 34	2 822	...	...	...	...	...	...	...	...
35 - 39	1 936	...	...	...	...	...	...	...	...
40 - 44	656	...	...	...	...	...	...	...	...
45 - 49	54	...	...	...	...	...	...	...	...
50+	-	...	...	...	...	...	...	...	...
Bulgaria - Bulgarie[3]									
2001									
Total	51 165	...	...	...	...	...	...	...	...
0 - 14	156	...	...	...	...	...	...	...	...
15 - 19	4 506	...	...	...	...	...	...	...	...
20 - 24	14 052	...	...	...	...	...	...	...	...
25 - 29	14 294	...	...	...	...	...	...	...	...
30 - 34	10 786	...	...	...	...	...	...	...	...
35 - 39	5 348	...	...	...	...	...	...	...	...
40 - 44	1 825	...	...	...	...	...	...	...	...
45 - 49	188	...	...	...	...	...	...	...	...
50+	10	...	...	...	...	...	...	...	...
Channel Islands: Guernsey - Îles Anglo-Normandes: Guernesey									
2000									
Total	89	46	21	11	9	1	1	...	...
0 - 14	1	1	...	...	...	...	...	...	...
15 - 19	12	11	1	...	...	...	...	...	...
20 - 24	30	17	13	...	...	...	...	...	...
25 - 29	18	11	3	3	1	...	...	...	...
30 - 34	15	4	3	4	2	1	1	...	...
35 - 39	10	1	1	4	4	...	...	...	...
40 - 44	3	1	...	...	2	...	...	...	...
Croatia - Croatie[7]									
2000									
Total	7 534	1 730	1 301	2 668	839	311	...	26	...
0 - 14	4	4	...	...	...	...	...	...	...
15 - 19	422	365	23	8	1	...	...	...	...
20 - 24	1 284	788	254	126	18	1	...	...	...

14. Legally induced abortions by age and number of previous live births of women: latest available year
Avortments provoqués légalement selon l'âge de la femme et selon le nombre des naissances vivantes précédentes: dernière année disponible (continued — suite)

(See notes at end of table. — Voir notes à la fin du tableau.)

Continent, country or area, year and age / Continent, pays ou zone, année et âge	Total	0	1	2	3	4	5	6+	Unknown Inconnu
					Number of previous live births - Nombre des naissances vivantes précédentes				
EUROPE									
Croatia - Croatie[7]									
2000									
25 - 29	1 344	320	328	449	98	36	...	1	...
30 - 34	1 650	113	309	723	257	86	...	11	...
35 - 39	1 662	63	216	783	299	113	...	7	...
40 - 49	916	27	125	480	140	55	...	5	...
50+	-	...	...	...	...	...	...	...	...
Unknown	252	50	46	99	26	20	...	2	...
Czech Republic - République tchèque									
2001									
Total	32 513	8 060	8 320	11 982	3 146	705	201	99	...
0 - 14	18	17	1	...	...	...	...	...	...
15 - 19	2 816	2 474	301	38	3	...	...	...	...
20 - 24	6 802	3 543	2 290	811	117	37	4	...	...
25 - 29	8 539	1 519	2 943	3 306	581	138	38	14	...
30 - 34	6 784	331	1 619	3 556	955	206	74	43	...
35 - 39	5 120	124	826	2 921	938	220	56	35	...
40 - 44	2 155	51	296	1 199	483	92	27	7	...
45 - 49	274	1	44	147	68	12	2	...	...
50+	5	...	...	4	1	...	...	...	...
Denmark - Danemark[8]									
2000									
Total	15 681	...	...	...	...	...	...	...	...
15 - 19	1 954	...	...	...	...	...	...	...	...
20 - 24	3 258	...	...	...	...	...	...	...	...
25 - 29	3 430	...	...	...	...	...	...	...	...
30 - 34	3 552	...	...	...	...	...	...	...	...
35 - 39	2 521	...	...	...	...	...	...	...	...
40 - 44	882	...	...	...	...	...	...	...	...
45 - 49	84	...	...	...	...	...	...	...	...
50+	-	...	...	...	...	...	...	...	...
Estonia - Estonie									
2000									
Total	12 743	3 131	4 568	3 667	990	235	69	29	...
0 - 14	20	20	...	...	...	...	...	...	...
15 - 19	1 631	1 376	225	11	...	...	...	...	...
20 - 24	3 076	1 251	1 414	345	43	3	...	...	...
25 - 29	2 950	329	1 422	975	172	31	8	...	...
30 - 34	2 453	97	897	1 055	302	73	21	6	...
35 - 39	1 733	42	432	841	304	77	27	10	...
40 - 44	801	15	166	398	152	47	12	11	...
45 - 49	77	...	12	41	17	4	1	2	...
50+	1	...	...	1	...	...	...	...	...
Unknown	1	1	...	...	...	...	...	...	...
Finland - Finlande									
2001									
Total	10 696	5 472	1 955	2 005	907	249	74	33	...
0 - 14	73	73	-	-	-	-	-	-	...
15 - 19	2 406	2 265	130	11	-	-	-	-	...
20 - 24	2 394	1 655	494	211	29	5	-	-	...
25 - 29	1 980	791	509	474	168	30	7	1	...
30 - 34	1 790	394	400	615	274	77	26	4	...
35 - 39	1 397	214	293	468	284	92	29	17	...
40 - 44	608	72	122	210	143	41	12	8	...
45 - 49	47	8	7	16	9	4	-	3	...
50+	-	-	-	-	-	-	-	-	...
Unknown	1	...	...	...	...	...	...	...	...

14. Legally induced abortions by age and number of previous live births of women: latest available year
Avortments provoqués légalement selon l'âge de la femme et selon le nombre des naissances vivantes précédentes: dernière année disponible (continued — suite)

(See notes at end of table. — Voir notes à la fin du tableau.)

Continent, country or area, year and age — Continent, pays ou zone, année et âge	Total	Number of previous live births - Nombre des naissances vivantes précédentes								Unknown Inconnu
		0	1	2	3	4	5	6+	

EUROPE

France
1997

Total	163 985	...	...	...	...	...	...	...	...
15 - 19	18 695	...	...	...	...	...	...	...	...
20 - 24	38 120	...	...	...	...	...	...	...	...
25 - 29	36 510	...	...	...	...	...	...	...	...
30 - 34	32 812	...	...	...	...	...	...	...	...
35 - 39	24 846	...	...	...	...	...	...	...	...
40 - 44	10 443	...	...	...	...	...	...	...	...
45 - 49	1 171	...	...	...	...	...	...	...	...
50+	42	...	...	...	...	...	...	...	...
Unknown	1 346	...	...	...	...	...	...	...	...

Germany - Allemagne
2000

Total	134 609	...	...	...	...	...	...	...	...
0 - 14	574	...	...	...	...	...	...	...	...
15 - 19	14 930	...	...	...	...	...	...	...	...
20 - 24	28 584	...	...	...	...	...	...	...	...
25 - 29	29 212	...	...	...	...	...	...	...	...
30 - 34	30 361	...	...	...	...	...	...	...	...
35 - 39	22 359	...	...	...	...	...	...	...	...
40 - 44	7 891	...	...	...	...	...	...	...	...
45 - 49	698	...	...	...	...	...	...	...	...
50+	-	...	...	...	...	...	...	...	...

Greece - Grèce
1996

Total	12 542	...	...	...	...	...	...	...	...
0 - 14	17	...	...	...	...	...	...	...	...
15 - 19	468	...	...	...	...	...	...	...	...
20 - 29	5 460	...	...	...	...	...	...	...	...
30 - 39	5 313	...	...	...	...	...	...	...	...
40 - 49	1 007	...	...	...	...	...	...	...	...
50+	41	...	...	...	...	...	...	...	...
Unknown	236	...	...	...	...	...	...	...	...

Hungary - Hongrie
2001

Total	56 404	15 925	13 155	15 238	7 817	2 560	987	721	...
0 - 14	175	167	7	1	...	...	...	...	...
15 - 19	6 387	5 091	1 039	210	44	3	...	...	...
20 - 24	13 485	6 415	3 757	1 993	1 039	227	44	10	...
25 - 29	13 981	3 016	4 004	3 843	2 081	685	221	131	...
30 - 34	11 378	799	2 560	4 326	2 303	775	337	278	...
35 - 39	7 231	186	1 242	3 083	1 614	628	273	205	...
40 - 44	3 209	66	463	1 594	671	221	105	89	...
45 - 49	263	11	40	144	43	13	5	7	...
50+	6	1	2	2	1	...	...	...	...
Unknown	289	173	41	42	21	8	2	1	...

Iceland - Islande
2000

Total	947	...	...	...	...	...	...	...	...
0 - 14	3	...	...	...	...	...	...	...	...
15 - 19	189	...	...	...	...	...	...	...	...
20 - 24	275	...	...	...	...	...	...	...	...
25 - 29	192	...	...	...	...	...	...	...	...
30 - 34	139	...	...	...	...	...	...	...	...
35 - 39	102	...	...	...	...	...	...	...	...
40 - 44	43	...	...	...	...	...	...	...	...
45 - 49	4	...	...	...	...	...	...	...	...
50+	-	...	...	...	...	...	...	...	...

14. Legally induced abortions by age and number of previous live births of women: latest available year
Avortments provoqués légalement selon l'âge de la femme et selon le nombre des naissances vivantes précédentes: dernière année disponible (continued — suite)

(See notes at end of table. — Voir notes à la fin du tableau.)

Continent, country or area, year and age / Continent, pays ou zone, année et âge	Number of previous live births - Nombre des naissances vivantes précédentes								
	Total	0	1	2	3	4	5	6+	Unknown Inconnu
EUROPE									
Iceland - Islande									
2000									
Unknown	-	...	...	...	...	...	...	...	...
Italy - Italie									
1999									
Total	138 708	54 644	27 589	35 614	11 636	2 683	703	349	5 490
0 - 14	223	186	4	1	...	...	...	...	32
15 - 19	11 160	9 284	766	115	19	1	...	1	974
20 - 24	28 139	19 122	4 723	2 026	316	54	9	4	1 885
25 - 29	31 438	14 185	7 584	6 564	1 412	271	57	27	1 338
30 - 34	30 961	7 508	7 335	11 161	3 314	643	176	82	742
35 - 39	25 101	3 267	5 155	10 753	4 191	995	258	120	362
40 - 44	10 416	914	1 829	4 487	2 124	648	176	103	135
45 - 49	974	84	143	409	229	68	24	11	6
50+	39	5	9	13	7	...	2	...	3
Unknown	257	89	41	85	24	3	1	1	13
Latvia - Lettonie									
2001									
Total	15 647	...	...	...	...	...	...	...	...
0 - 14	9	...	...	...	...	...	...	...	...
15 - 19	1 476	...	...	...	...	...	...	...	...
20 - 24	3 678	...	...	...	...	...	...	...	...
25 - 29	3 683	...	...	...	...	...	...	...	...
30 - 34	3 318	...	...	...	...	...	...	...	...
35 - 39	2 284	...	...	...	...	...	...	...	...
40 - 44	1 076	...	...	...	...	...	...	...	...
45 - 49	116	...	...	...	...	...	...	...	...
50+	7	...	...	...	...	...	...	...	...
Lithuania - Lituanie									
2001									
Total	13 677	1 504	...	...	...	...	...	...	...
0 - 14	1	...	...	...	...	...	...	...	...
15 - 19	1 009	504	...	...	...	...	...	...	...
20 - 24	2 908	697	...	...	...	...	...	...	...
25 - 29	3 172	198	...	...	...	...	...	...	...
30 - 34	3 242	85	...	...	...	...	...	...	...
35 - 39	2 215	15	...	...	...	...	...	...	...
40 - 44	1 004	4	...	...	...	...	...	...	...
45 - 49	126	1	...	...	...	...	...	...	...
Netherlands - Pays-Bas[6]									
1992									
Total	19 422	8 420	3 168	3 392	1 464	775	...	...	...
0 - 14	52	...	...	...	...	...	...	...	...
15 - 19	1 825	...	...	...	...	...	...	...	...
20 - 24	4 063	...	...	...	...	...	...	...	...
25 - 29	4 046	...	...	...	...	...	...	...	...
30 - 34	3 616	...	...	...	...	...	...	...	...
35 - 39	2 548	...	...	...	...	...	...	...	...
40 - 44	981	...	...	...	...	...	...	...	...
45+	86	...	...	...	...	...	...	...	...
Unknown	2 205	...	...	...	...	...	...	...	...
Norway - Norvège									
2001									
Total	13 867	...	...	...	...	...	...	...	...
0 - 14	46	...	...	...	...	...	...	...	...
15 - 19	2 402	...	...	...	...	...	...	...	...
20 - 24	3 538	...	...	...	...	...	...	...	...
25 - 29	3 031	...	...	...	...	...	...	...	...
30 - 34	2 558	...	...	...	...	...	...	...	...

14. Legally induced abortions by age and number of previous live births of women: latest available year
Avortments provoqués légalement selon l'âge de la femme et selon le nombre des naissances vivantes précédentes: dernière année disponible (continued — suite)

(See notes at end of table. — Voir notes à la fin du tableau.)

Continent, country or area, year and age / Continent, pays ou zone, année et âge	Total	Number of previous live births - Nombre des naissances vivantes précédentes							
		0	1	2	3	4	5	6+	Unknown Inconnu
EUROPE									
Norway - Norvège									
2001									
35 - 39	1 676	...	...	...	...	...	...	...	...
40 - 44	571	...	...	...	...	...	...	...	...
45 - 49	40	...	...	...	...	...	...	...	...
Unknown	5	...	...	...	...	...	...	...	...
Republic of Moldova - République de Moldova									
2001									
Total	16 028	...	...	...	...	...	...	...	...
0 - 14	30	...	...	...	...	...	...	...	...
15 - 19	1 665	...	...	...	...	...	...	...	...
20 - 34	11 373	...	...	...	...	...	...	...	...
35+	2 960	...	...	...	...	...	...	...	...
Romania - Roumanie									
2001									
Total	198 086	...	...	...	...	...	...	...	...
0 - 14	951	...	...	...	...	...	...	...	...
15 - 19	15 176	...	...	...	...	...	...	...	...
20 - 24	47 522	...	...	...	...	...	...	...	...
25 - 29	53 116	...	...	...	...	...	...	...	...
30 - 34	48 072	...	...	...	...	...	...	...	...
35 - 39	23 442	...	...	...	...	...	...	...	...
40 - 44	8 764	...	...	...	...	...	...	...	...
45 - 49	1 025	...	...	...	...	...	...	...	...
50+	18	...	...	...	...	...	...	...	...
Russian Federation - Fédération de Russie[9]									
1995									
Total	2 255 797	...	...	...	...	...	...	...	...
0 - 14	2 217	...	...	...	...	...	...	...	...
15 - 19	233 166	...	...	...	...	...	...	...	...
20 - 34	1 551 440	...	...	...	...	...	...	...	...
35+	468 974	...	...	...	...	...	...	...	...
Serbia and Montenegro - Serbie-et-Montenegro[6]									
1998									
Total	58 739	6 941	10 691	31 998	7 022	2 085	...	...	2
0 - 14	10	...	...	...	...	...	...	...	...
15 - 19	9 725	...	...	...	...	...	...	...	...
20 - 24	28 223	...	...	...	...	...	...	...	...
25 - 29	19 649	...	...	...	...	...	...	...	...
30 - 34	1 121	...	...	...	...	...	...	...	...
35 - 39	4	...	...	...	...	...	...	...	...
40+	7	...	...	...	...	...	...	...	...
Slovakia - Slovaquie									
2001									
Total	18 026	4 558	4 301	6 086	2 080	612	219	170	...
0 - 14	20	19	1	...	...	...	...	...	...
15 - 19	1 707	1 432	233	38	4	...	...	...	...
20 - 24	4 043	1 942	1 313	629	120	32	7	...	...
25 - 29	4 546	768	1 455	1 714	415	140	52	2	...
30 - 34	3 630	229	762	1 754	618	174	62	31	...
35 - 39	2 720	114	406	1 314	595	167	64	60	...
40 - 44	1 229	52	120	582	304	93	31	47	...
45 - 49	128	2	11	55	23	6	3	28	...
50+	3	...	...	...	1	...	...	2	...

14. Legally induced abortions by age and number of previous live births of women: latest available year
Avortments provoqués légalement selon l'âge de la femme et selon le nombre des naissances vivantes précédentes: dernière année disponible (continued — suite)

(See notes at end of table. — Voir notes à la fin du tableau.)

Continent, country or area, year and age / Continent, pays ou zone, année et âge	Total	0	1	2	3	4	5	6+	Unknown Inconnu
EUROPE									
Slovenia - Slovénie									
2001									
Total	7 799	2 237	1 775	2 942	675	137	19	13	...
0 - 14	8	8	...	...	...	...	...	...	...
15 - 19	688	657	28	3	...	...	...	...	...
20 - 24	1 494	963	394	127	7	2	...	...	...
25 - 29	1 557	419	516	542	67	11	1	1	...
30 - 34	1 635	116	396	853	219	38	9	4	...
35 - 39	1 640	49	324	946	252	61	4	4	...
40 - 44	714	22	110	431	120	22	5	4	...
45 - 49	62	3	6	40	10	3	...	...	...
50+	1	...	1	...	...	...	...	...	...
Spain - Espagne									
2000									
Total	63 756	...	...	...	...	...	...	...	...
0 - 14	157	...	...	...	...	...	...	...	...
15 - 19	9 047	...	...	...	...	...	...	...	...
20 - 24	18 370	...	...	...	...	...	...	...	...
25 - 29	14 090	...	...	...	...	...	...	...	...
30 - 34	10 979	...	...	...	...	...	...	...	...
35 - 39	7 810	...	...	...	...	...	...	...	...
40 - 44	3 035	...	...	...	...	...	...	...	...
45+	268	...	...	...	...	...	...	...	...
45 - 49	268	...	...	...	...	...	...	...	...
50+	-	...	...	...	...	...	...	...	...
Sweden - Suède[1]									
2001									
Total	31 772	15 571	5 186	6 517	2 858	868	266	145	361
0 - 14	256	249	2	...	1	...	...	...	4
15 - 19	5 408	5 097	203	16	2	3	...	1	86
20 - 24	7 108	5 342	1 225	371	56	4	2	1	107
25 - 29	6 587	3 025	1 594	1 398	405	81	12	3	69
30 - 34	5 939	1 204	1 132	2 217	922	284	89	32	59
35 - 39	4 627	509	775	1 814	1 027	322	97	64	19
40 - 44	1 642	122	236	629	391	155	61	34	14
45 - 49	186	11	17	68	53	19	5	10	3
50+	4	...	...	3	1	...	...	...	...
Unknown	15	12	2	1	...	...	...	...	...
United Kingdom - Royaume-Uni									
2001									
Total	197 913	...	...	...	...	...	...	...	...
0 - 14	1 157	...	...	...	...	...	...	...	...
15 - 19	40 387	...	...	...	...	...	...	...	...
20 - 24	54 878	...	...	...	...	...	...	...	...
25 - 29	41 126	...	...	...	...	...	...	...	...
30 - 34	31 921	...	...	...	...	...	...	...	...
35 - 39	21 096	...	...	...	...	...	...	...	...
40 - 44	6 833	...	...	...	...	...	...	...	...
45 - 49	513	...	...	...	...	...	...	...	...
50+	-	...	...	...	...	...	...	...	...
OCEANIA — OCEANIE									
New Zealand - Nouvelle-Zélande									
1999									
Total	15 501	7 141	3 090	2 905	1 441	588	204	132	...
0 - 14	56	56	...	...	...	...	...	...	...

14. Legally induced abortions by age and number of previous live births of women: latest available year
Avortments provoqués légalement selon l'âge de la femme et selon le nombre des naissances vivantes précédentes: dernière année disponible (continued — suite)

(See notes at end of table. — Voir notes à la fin du tableau.)

Continent, country or area, year and age / Continent, pays ou zone, année et âge	Number of previous live births - Nombre des naissances vivantes précédentes								
	Total	0	1	2	3	4	5	6+	Unknown Inconnu
OCEANIA — OCEANIE									
New Zealand - Nouvelle-Zélande									
1999									
15 - 19	2 846	2 454	339	51	1	1	...	...	...
20 - 24	4 477	2 548	1 122	583	186	33	4	1	...
25 - 29	3 447	1 298	788	800	367	145	32	17	...
30 - 34	2 435	534	483	711	395	194	77	41	...
35 - 39	1 642	195	280	572	337	153	56	49	...
40 - 44	560	52	71	179	141	61	35	21	...
45 - 49	38	4	7	9	14	1	...	3	...

GENERAL NOTES - NOTES GENERALES

For method of evaluation and limitations of data, see Technical Notes for this table. — Pour la méthode d'évaluation et les insuffisances des données, voir Notes techniques pour ce tableau.

FOOTNOTES - NOTES

[1] Birth order based on number of previous deliveries rather than on live births. - La rang de naissance est déterminé par le nombre d'accouchements antérieurs plutôt que par le nombre des naissances vivantes.

[2] Data refer to abortions granted for medical reasons by the Comision Multidisciplinaria Nacional de Aborto Terapéutico. - Les données se réfèrent aux avortements autorisés pour des raisons médicales par la Comision Multidisciplinaria Nacional de Aborto Terapéutico.

[3] Column '3' including '4' and over. - Colonne '3' compris 4 plus.

[4] Including data for East Jerusalem and Israeli residents in certain other territories under occupation by Israeli military forces since June 1967. - Y compris les données pour Jérusalem-Est et les résidents israéliens dans certains autres territoires occupés depuis 1967 par les forces armées israéliennes.

[5] For Japanese nationals in Japan only. - Pour les nationaux japonais au Japon seulement.

[6] Column '4' includes also data for '5+'. - Colonne '4' comprenne aussi les données pour '5+'.

[7] Column '4' includes data for both '4' and '5'. - Colonne '4' comprenne les données pour l'ensemble de '4' et '5'.

[8] Excluding Faeroe Islands and Greenland. - Non compris les îles Féroé et Gröenland.

[9] Data as reported by national statistical authorities; they may differ from data presented in other tables. - Les données comme elles ont été déclarées par l'institut national de la statistique; elles peuvent être différentes de ceux présentées dans autre tableaux.

Table 15

Table 15 presents infant deaths and infant mortality rates by urban/rural residence for as many years as possible between 1997 and 2001.

Description of variables: Infant deaths are deaths of live-born infants under one year of age.

Statistics on the number of infant deaths are obtained from civil registers unless otherwise noted. Infant mortality rates are, in most instances, calculated from data on registered infant deaths and registered live births where civil registration is considered reliable (that is, with an estimated completeness of 90 per cent or more), except for countries or areas where civil registration of infant deaths is non-existent or considered unreliable.

The urban/rural classification of infant deaths is that provided by each country or area; it is presumed to be based on the national census definitions of urban population that have been set forth at the end of the technical notes of table 6.

Rate computation: Infant mortality rates are the annual number of deaths of infants under one year of age per 1 000 live births (as shown in table 9) in the same year.

Rates by urban/rural residence are the annual number of infant deaths, in the appropriate urban or rural category, per 1 000 corresponding live births (as shown in table 9). These rates have been calculated by the Statistics Division of the United Nations.

Rates presented in this table have been limited to those for countries or areas having at least a total of 100 infant deaths in a given year and for which the quality code is represented by a "C" or a symbol "|".

Reliability of data: Each country or area has been asked to indicate the estimated completeness of the infant deaths recorded in its civil register. These national assessments are indicated by the quality codes (C), (U) and (|) that appear in the first column of this table.

C indicates that the data are estimated to be virtually complete, that is, representing at least 90 per cent of the infant deaths occurring each year, while U indicates that data are estimated to be incomplete, that is, representing less than 90 per cent of the infant deaths occurring each year. The code (I) indicates that the source of data is not civil registration, but is still considered reliable. The code (...) indicates that no information was provided regarding completeness.

Data from civil registers which are reported as incomplete or of unknown completeness (coded U or ...) are considered unreliable. They appear in italics in this table; rates are not computed for data so coded.

Limitations: Statistics on infant deaths are subject to the same qualifications as have been set forth for vital statistics in general and death statistics in particular as discussed in section 4 of the Technical Notes.

The reliability of the data, an indication of which is described above, is an important factor in considering the limitations. In addition, some infant deaths are tabulated by date of registration and not by date of occurrence; these have been indicated by a plus sign (+). Whenever the lag between the date of occurrence and date of registration is prolonged and, therefore, a large proportion of the infant-death registrations are delayed, infant-death statistics for any given year may be seriously affected.

Another factor which limits international comparability is the practice of some countries or areas not to include in infant-death statistics infants who were born alive but died before the registration of the birth or within the first 24 hours of life, thus underestimating the total number of infant deaths. Statistics of this type are footnoted.

The method of reckoning age at death for infants may also introduce non-comparability. If year alone, rather than completed minutes, hours, days and months elapsed since birth, is used to calculate age at time of death, many of the infants who died during the eleventh month of life and some of those who died at younger ages will be classified as having completed one year of age and thus be excluded. The effect would be to underestimate the number of infant deaths. Information on this factor is given in footnotes when known. Reckoning of infant age is discussed in the technical notes for table 16.

In addition, infant mortality rates are subject to the limitations of the data on live births with which they have been calculated. These have been set forth in the technical notes for table 9.

Because the two components of the infant mortality rate, infant deaths in the numerator and live births in the denominator, are both obtained from systems of civil registration, the limitations which affect live-birth statistics are very similar to those which have been mentioned above in connection with the infant-death statistics. It is important to consider the reliability of the data (the completeness of registration) and the method of tabulation (by date of occurrence or by date of registration) of live-birth statistics as well as infant-death statistics, both of which are used to calculate infant mortality rates. The quality code and use of italics to indicate unreliable data presented in this table refer only to infant deaths. Similarly, the indication of the basis of tabulation (the use of the symbol (+) to indicate data tabulated by date of registration) presented in this table also refers only to infant deaths. Table 9 provides the corresponding information for live births.

If the registration of infant deaths is more complete than the registration of live births, then infant mortality rates would be biased upwards. If, however, the registration of live births is more complete than registration of infant deaths, infant mortality rates would be biased downwards. If both infant deaths and live births are tabulated by registration, it should be noted that deaths tend to be more promptly reported than births.

Infant mortality rates may be seriously affected by the practice of some countries or areas of not considering infants who were born alive but died before the registration of the birth or within the first 24 hours of life as live- birth and subsequently infant death. Although this practice results in both the number of infant deaths in the numerator and the number of live births in the denominator being underestimated, its impact is greater on the numerator of the infant mortality rate. As a result this practice causes infant mortality rates to be biased downwards.

Infant mortality rates will also be underestimated if the method of reckoning age at death results in an underestimation of the number of infant deaths. This point has been discussed above.

Because all of these factors are important, care should be taken in comparing and rank ordering infant mortality rates.

With respect to the method of calculating infant mortality rates used in this table, it should be noted that no adjustment was made to take account of the fact that a proportion of the infant deaths which occur during a given year are deaths of infants who were born during the preceding year and hence are not taken from the universe of births used to compute the rates. However, unless the number of live births or infant deaths is changing rapidly, the error involved is not important.

Estimated rates based directly on the results of sample surveys are subject to considerable error as a result of omissions in reporting infant deaths or as a result of erroneous reporting of those which occurred outside the period of reference. However, such rates do not have the advantage of having a "built-in" and corresponding base.

The comparability of data by urban/rural residence is affected by the national definitions of urban and rural used in tabulating these data. It is assumed, in the absence of specific information to the contrary, that the definitions of urban and rural used in connection with the national population census were also used in the compilation of the vital statistics for each country or area. However, the possibility cannot be excluded that, for a given country or area, the same definitions of urban and rural are not used for both the vital statistics data and the population census data. When known, the definitions of urban used in national population censuses are presented at the end of the technical notes for table 6. As discussed in detail in the technical notes for table 6, these definitions vary considerably from one country or area to another.

Urban/rural differentials in infant mortality rates may also be affected by whether the infant deaths and live births have been tabulated in terms of place of occurrence or place of usual residence. This problem is discussed in more detail in section 4.1.4.1 of the Technical Notes.

Coverage: Infant deaths are shown for 143 countries or areas. Data are presented by urban/rural residence for 53 countries or areas.

Earlier data: Infant deaths and infant mortality rates have been shown in previous issues of the *Demographic Yearbook*. For more information on specific topics and years for which data are reported, readers should consult the Index.

Tableau 15

Le tableau 15 présente des données sur les décès d'enfants de moins d'un an et des taux de mortalité infantile selon la résidence (urbaine/rurale) pour le plus grand nombre d'années possible entre 1997 et 2001.

Description des variables : Les chiffres se rapportent aux décès d'enfants de moins d'un an.

Sauf indication contraire, les statistiques du nombre de décès d'enfants de moins d'un an sont établies sur la base des registres de l'état civil. Dans la plupart des cas, les taux de mortalité infantile sont calculés à partir des statistiques des décès enregistrés d'enfants de moins d'un an et des naissances vivantes enregistrées où l'enregistrement de l'état civil est jugé sûr (exhaustivité estimée à 90 p. 100 ou plus), mais pas pour les pays ou zones où l'enregistrement des décès d'enfants de moins d'un an par les services de l'état civil n'existe pas ou est de qualité douteuse (exhaustivité estimée à moins de 90 p. 100 ou inconnue).

La classification des décès d'enfants de moins d'un an selon la résidence (urbaine/rurale) est celle qui a été fournie par chaque pays ou zone; il faut en conclure qu'elle repose sur les définitions de la population urbaine utilisées pour les recensements nationaux, telles qu'elles sont reproduites à la fin des notes techniques du tableau 6.

Calcul des taux : Les taux de mortalité infantile représentent le nombre annuel de décès d'enfants de moins d'un an pour 1 000 naissances vivantes (fréquences du tableau 9) survenues pendant la même année.

Les taux selon la résidence (urbaine/rurale) représentent le nombre annuel de décès d'enfants de moins d'un an, classés selon la catégorie urbaine ou rurale appropriée pour 1 000 naissances vivantes survenues dans la population correspondante (fréquences du tableau 9). Ces taux ont été calculés par la Division de statistique de l'ONU.

Les taux présentés dans ce tableau se rapportent seulement aux pays ou zones où l'on a enregistré au moins un total de 100 décès d'enfants de moins d'un an au cours d'une année donnée et où le code de qualité est indiqué avec la lettre « C » ou le symbole « | ».

Fiabilité des données : Il a été demandé à chaque pays ou zone d'indiquer le degré estimatif de complétude des données sur les décès d'enfants de moins d'un an figurant dans ses registres d'état civil. Ces évaluations nationales sont désignées par les codes de qualité (C), (U) et (|) qui apparaissent dans la première colonne du tableau.

La lettre (C) indique que les données sont jugées à peu près complètes, c'est-à-dire qu'elles représentent au moins 90 p. 100 des décès d'enfants de moins d'un an survenus chaque année; la lettre (U) indique que les données sont jugées incomplètes, c'est-à-dire qu'elles représentent moins de 90 p.100 des décès d'enfants de moins d'un an survenus chaque année. Le symbole (I) indique que la source des données n'est pas un registre de l'état civil, mais elle est quand même considérée fiable. Le signe (...) indique qu'aucun renseignement n'a été fourni quant à la complétude des données.

Les données provenant des registres de l'état civil qui sont déclarées incomplètes ou dont le degré de complétude n'est pas connu (et qui sont affectées de la lettre « U » ou du signe « ... ») sont jugées douteuses. Elles apparaissent en italique dans le présent tableau ; les taux, dans ces cas la, n'ont pas été calculés.

Insuffisance des données : Les statistiques des décès d'enfants de moins d'un an appellent toutes les réserves qui ont été faites à propos des statistiques de l'état civil en général et des statistiques des décès en particulier (voir explications à la section 4 des notes techniques).

La fiabilité des données, au sujet de laquelle des indications ont été fournies plus haut, est un facteur important. Il faut également tenir compte du fait que, dans certains cas, les données relatives aux décès d'enfants de moins d'un an sont exploitées selon la date de l'enregistrement et non la date de l'événement; ces cas ont été identifiés par le signe (+). Là où le décalage entre l'événement et son enregistrement est grand, c'est-à-dire où une forte proportion des décès d'enfants de moins d'un an fait l'objet d'un enregistrement tardif, les statistiques des décès d'enfants de moins d'un an pour une année donnée peuvent être sérieusement faussées.

Un autre facteur qui nuit à la comparabilité internationale est la pratique de certains pays ou zones qui consiste à ne pas inclure dans les statistiques des décès d'enfants de moins d'un an les enfants nés vivants mais décédés avant l'enregistrement de leur naissance ou dans les 24 heures qui ont suivi la naissance, pratique qui conduit à sous-estimer le nombre total de décès d'enfants de moins d'un an. Quand tel était le cas, on l'a signalé en note à la fin du tableau.

Les méthodes suivies pour calculer l'âge au moment du décès peuvent également nuire à la comparabilité des données. Si l'on utilise à cet effet l'année seulement, et non pas les minutes, heures, jours et mois qui se sont écoulés depuis la naissance, de nombreux enfants décédés au cours du onzième mois qui a suivi leur naissance et certains enfants décédés encore plus jeunes seront classés comme décédés à un an révolu et donc exclus des données. Cette pratique conduit à sous-estimer le nombre de décès d'enfants de moins d'un an. Les renseignements dont on dispose sur ce facteur apparaissent en note à la fin du tableau. La question du calcul de l'âge au moment du décès est examinée plus en détail dans les notes techniques se rapportant au tableau 16.

Les taux de mortalité infantile appellent en outre toutes les réserves qui ont été formulées à propos des statistiques des naissances vivantes qui ont servi à leur calcul. Voir à ce sujet les notes techniques relatives au tableau 9.

Les deux composantes du taux de mortalité infantile, décès d'enfants de moins d'un an au numérateur et naissances vivantes au dénominateur étant obtenues à partir des registres de l'état civil, les statistiques des naissances vivantes appellent des réserves presque identiques à celles qui ont été formulées plus haut à propos des statistiques des décès d'enfants de moins d'un an. Il importe de prendre en considération la fiabilité des données (complétude de l'enregistrement) et le mode d'exploitation (selon la date de l'événement ou selon la date de l'enregistrement) dans le cas des statistiques des naissances vivantes tout comme dans le cas de celles des décès d'enfants de moins d'un an, puisque les unes et les autres servent au calcul des taux de mortalité infantile. Dans le présent tableau, le code de qualité et l'emploi de caractères italiques pour signaler les données moins sûres ne concernent que les décès d'enfants de moins d'un an. L'indication du mode d'exploitation des données (emploi du signe « + » pour identifier les données exploitées selon la date de l'enregistrement) concerne aussi les décès d'enfants de moins d'un an exclusivement. Le tableau 9 fournit les renseignements correspondants pour les naissances vivantes.

Si l'enregistrement des décès d'enfants de moins d'un an est plus complet que l'enregistrement des naissances vivantes, les taux de mortalité infantile seront entachés d'une erreur par excès. En revanche, si l'enregistrement des naissances vivantes est plus complet que l'enregistrement des décès d'enfants de moins d'un an, les taux de mortalité infantile seront entachés d'une erreur par défaut. Si les décès d'enfants de moins d'un an et les naissances vivantes sont exploitées selon la date de l'enregistrement, il convient de ne pas perdre de vue que les décès sont, en règle générale, déclarés plus rapidement que les naissances.

Les taux de mortalité infantile peuvent être gravement faussés par la pratique de certains pays ou zones qui consiste à ne pas classer dans les naissances vivantes et ensuite dans les décès d'enfants de moins d'un an les enfants nés vivants mais décédés soit avant l'enregistrement de leur naissance, soit dans les 24 heures qui ont suivi la naissance. Cette pratique conduit à sous-estimer aussi bien le nombre des décès d'enfants de moins d'un an, qui constitue le numérateur, que le nombre des naissances vivantes, qui constitue le dénominateur, mais c'est pour le numérateur du taux de mortalité infantile que la distorsion est la plus marquée. Ce système a pour effet d'introduire une erreur par défaut dans les taux de mortalité infantile.

Les taux de mortalité infantile seront également sous-estimés si la méthode utilisée pour calculer l'âge au moment du décès conduit à sous-estimer le nombre de décès d'enfants de moins d'un an. Cette question a été examinée plus haut.

Tous ces facteurs sont importants et il faut donc en tenir compte lorsqu'on compare et classe les taux de mortalité infantile.

En ce qui concerne la méthode de calcul des taux de mortalité infantile utilisée dans ce tableau, il convient de noter qu'il n'a pas été tenu compte du fait qu'une partie des décès survenus pendant une année donnée sont des décès d'enfants nés l'année précédente et ne correspondent donc pas à l'univers des naissances utilisé pour le calcul des taux. Toutefois, l'erreur n'est pas grave, à moins que le nombre des naissances vivantes ou des décès d'enfants de moins d'un an ne varie rapidement.

Les taux estimatifs fondés directement sur les résultats d'enquêtes par sondage comportent des possibilités d'erreurs considérables dues soit à des omissions dans les déclarations de décès d'enfants de moins d'un an, soit au fait que l'on a déclaré à tort des décès survenus en réalité hors de la période considérée. Mais ils présentent aussi un avantage puisque le chiffre des naissances vivantes utilisé comme base est connu par définition et rigoureusement correspondant.

La comparabilité des données selon la résidence (urbaine/rurale) peut être limitée par les définitions nationales des termes "urbain" et "rural" utilisées pour la mise en tableaux de ces données. En l'absence d'indications contraires, on a supposé que les définitions des termes "urbain"et "rural" utilisées pour le recensement national de la population avaient été utilisées aussi pour l'établissement des statistiques de l'état civil pour chaque pays ou zone. Toutefois, on ne peut exclure la possibilité que, pour un pays ou zone donnée, les mêmes définitions des termes "urbain" et "rural" n'aient pas été utilisées dans les deux cas. Les définitions du terme "urbain" utilisées pour les recensements nationaux de population ont été présentées à la fin des notes techniques du tableau 6 lorsqu'elles étaient connues. Comme on l'a précisé en détail dans les Notes techniques relatives au tableau 6, ces définitions varient très sensiblement d'un pays ou d'une zone à l'autre.

La différence entre les taux de mortalité infantile pour les zones urbaines et rurales pourra aussi être faussée selon que les décès d'enfants de moins d'un an et les naissances vivantes auront été classés d'après le lieu de l'événement ou le lieu de résidence habituelle. Ce problème est examiné plus en détail à la section 4.1.4.1 des Notes techniques.

Portée : Ce tableau présente des données sur les décès d'enfants de moins d'un an pour 143 pays ou zones. Les données sont classées selon la résidence(urbaine/rurale) pour 53 pays ou zones.

Données publiées antérieurement : Des statistiques des décès d'enfants de moins d'un an et des taux de mortalité infantile ont déjà été présentées dans des éditions antérieures de l'Annuaire démographique. Pour plus de précisions concernant les sujets spécifiques et les années pour lesquelles des données ont été publiées, se reporter à l'Index.

15. Infant deaths and infant mortality rates, by urban/rural residence: 1997 - 2001
Décès d'enfants de moins d'un an et taux de mortalité infantile, selon la résidence, urbaine/rurale: 1997 - 2001

(See notes at end of table. — Voir notes à la fin du tableau.)

Continent, country or area and urban/rural residence / Continent, pays ou zone et résidence, urbaine/rurale	Code[1]	Number - Nombre					Rate - Taux				
		1997	1998	1999	2000	2001	1997	1998	1999	2000	2001
AFRICA — AFRIQUE											
Algeria - Algérie[2,3]											
Total	U	27 219	33 093	21 798	20 291	21 622	...	...	...	...	...
Benin - Bénin[4]											
Total	I	...	24 422	...	...	25 001	...	93.7	...	...	94.8
Urban-Urbaine	I	...	9 402	...	...	...	...	...	...	...	...
Rural-Rurale	I	...	15 020	...	...	...	...	...	...	...	...
Botswana[4]											
Total	I	...	...	...	...	1 576	...	...	...	...	29.3
Burundi[4]											
Total	I	...	45 684	...	...	...	...	157.0	...	...	...
Côte d'Ivoire[4]											
Total	I	...	44 045	...	47 000	...	...	71.7	...	71.7	...
Egypt - Égypte											
Total	C	50 047	49 168	49 765	...	...	30.2	29.1	29.4	...	...
Urban-Urbaine	C	19 238	18 083	19 265	...	...	26.6	26.4	29.3	...	...
Rural-Rurale	C	30 809	31 085	30 500	...	...	33.0	31.0	29.5	...	...
Ethiopia - Éthiopie											
Total	I	...	...	232 660	...	...	...	...	106.4	...	...
Libyan Arab Jamahiriya - Jamahiriya arabe libyenne											
Total	U	...	...	...	2 155	2 568	...	...	...	...	...
Malawi[5]											
Total	I	...	44 928	...	...	...	...	90.5	...	...	...
Mauritius - Maurice											
Total	+C	406	376	396	322	282	20.3	19.3	19.5	15.9	14.3
Urban-Urbaine	+C	161	145	149	127	114	19.9	18.4	18.3	15.9	14.7
Rural-Rurale	+C	245	231	247	195	168	20.6	20.0	20.3	16.0	14.1
Morocco - Maroc[6]											
Total	U	8 056	9 061	8 885	...	...	...	...	...	...	...
Urban-Urbaine	U	2 544	3 160	2 867	...	...	...	...	...	...	...
Rural-Rurale	U	5 497	5 888	5 998	...	...	...	...	...	...	...
Mozambique[4]											
Total	I	...	...	...	...	99 164	...	...	...	...	131.6
Réunion											
Total	C	89	111	84	88	89	...	8.2	...	...	...
Saint Helena ex. dep. - Sainte-Hélène sans dép.											
Total	C	-	1	-	-	-	...	...	...	...	...
Seychelles											
Total	+C	12	12	15	15	19	...	...	...	...	...
Swaziland[7]											
Total	I	1 172	...	...	...	...	37.7	...	...	...	...
Urban-Urbaine	I	270	...	...	...	...	39.0	...	...	...	...
Rural-Rurale	I	902	...	...	...	...	37.3	...	...	...	...
Tunisia - Tunisie											
Total	U	3 745	3 098	4 200	...	...	...	...	...	...	...
AMERICA, NORTH — AMÉRIQUE DU NORD											
Anguilla											
Total	+C	1	-	1	1	-	...	...	...	...	...
Aruba											
Total	+U	...	...	...	...	4	...	...	...	...	...
Bahamas											
Total	+U	...	...	86	...	...	...	...	...	...	...
Barbados - Barbade											
Total	+U	...	...	...	63	...	...	...	...	...	...
Belize											
Total	U	168	144	116	155	120	...	...	...	...	...
Bermuda - Bermudes											
Total	C	4	-	...	...	3	...	...	...	...	...

15. Infant deaths and infant mortality rates, by urban/rural residence: 1997 - 2001
Décès d'enfants de moins d'un an et taux de mortalité infantile, selon la résidence, urbaine/rurale: 1997 - 2001
(continued — suite)

(See notes at end of table. — Voir notes à la fin du tableau.)

Continent, country or area and urban/rural residence / Continent, pays ou zone et résidence, urbaine/rurale	Code[1]	Number - Nombre					Rate - Taux				
		1997	1998	1999	2000	2001	1997	1998	1999	2000	2001
AMERICA, NORTH — AMERIQUE DU NORD											
British Virgin Islands - Îles Vierges britanniques											
Total	+C	...	...	...	1	...	...	...	...	...	...
Canada[8]											
Total	C	1 928	1 811	1 776	1 737	1 739	5.5	5.3	5.3	5.3	5.2
Costa Rica											
Total	C	1 108	970	925	798	827	14.2	12.6	11.8	10.2	10.8
Cuba[6]											
Total	C	1 098	1 070	977	1 039	*861	7.2	7.1	6.5	7.2	*6.2
Urban-Urbaine	C	810	800	747	...	...	7.5	7.3	6.9	...	...
Rural-Rurale	C	287	270	230	...	...	6.4	6.4	5.5	...	...
Dominican Republic - République dominicaine											
Total	+U	1 970	1 972	1 966	2 116	...	...	...	...	...	...
El Salvador											
Total	C	2 710	2 380	1 768	1 678	1 682	16.5	15.0	11.5	11.2	12.2
Urban-Urbaine	C	1 478	1 513	1 114	1 079	1 091	15.8	14.8	11.1	11.6	13.1
Rural-Rurale	C	1 232	867	654	599	591	17.4	15.5	12.3	10.5	10.8
Greenland - Groenland											
Total	C	20	25	16	...	...	...	...	...	...	...
Urban-Urbaine	C	19	25	16	...	...	...	...	...	...	...
Rural-Rurale	C	1	-	-	...	...	...	...	...	...	...
Grenada - Grenade											
Total	+C	31	37	29	27	33	...	...	...	...	...
Guatemala											
Total	C	15 413	15 414	13 161	13 247	...	39.7	31.5	36.5	31.1	...
Jamaica - Jamaïque											
Total	+U	...	480	...	...	...	...	...	...	...	...
Mexico - Mexique[6]											
Total	+C	44 377	42 183	40 283	38 621	35 911	16.4	15.8	14.5	13.8	13.0
Urban-Urbaine	+C	32 567	30 818	29 940	29 135	27 056	18.6	17.3	16.6	16.1	15.5
Rural-Rurale	+C	11 481	11 041	10 054	9 163	8 503	14.2	14.4	12.8	12.0	11.4
Nicaragua											
Total	+U	2 474	2 552	1 768	1 649	...	...	...	...	...	...
Urban-Urbaine	+U	1 482	1 503	1 004	...	...	...	...	...	...	...
Rural-Rurale	+U	992	1 049	764	...	...	...	...	...	...	...
Panama											
Total	U	1 170	1 047	1 005	1 081	1 053	...	...	...	...	...
Urban-Urbaine	U	528	483	490	...	...	...	...	...	...	...
Rural-Rurale	U	642	564	515	...	...	...	...	...	...	...
Puerto Rico - Porto Rico											
Total	C	724	637	632	589	515	11.3	10.5	10.6	9.9	9.2
Urban-Urbaine	C	...	...	357	327	311	...	...	11.7	10.7	10.6
Rural-Rurale	C	...	...	274	262	204	...	...	9.4	9.0	7.7
Saint Kitts and Nevis - Saint-Kitts-et-Nevis											
Total	+C	20	24	...	...	...	...	...	...	...	...
Saint Lucia - Sainte-Lucie											
Total	C	58	48	42	38	*40	...	...	...	...	...
Urban-Urbaine	C	18	14	...	...	...	...	...	...	...	...
Rural-Rurale	C	42	34	...	...	...	...	...	...	...	...
Saint Vincent and the Grenadines - Saint Vincent-et-les Grenadines											
Total	+C	41	47	47	35	*38	...	...	...	...	...
Trinidad and Tobago - Trinité-et-Tobago											
Total	C	316	...	...	...	...	17.1	...	...	...	...
United States - États-Unis											
Total	C	28 045	28 371	27 937	28 035	*27 798	7.2	7.2	7.1	6.9	*6.9

15. Infant deaths and infant mortality rates, by urban/rural residence: 1997 - 2001
Décès d'enfants de moins d'un an et taux de mortalité infantile, selon la résidence, urbaine/rurale: 1997 - 2001
(continued — suite)

(See notes at end of table. — Voir notes à la fin du tableau.)

Continent, country or area and urban/rural residence / Continent, pays ou zone et résidence, urbaine/rurale	Code[1]	Number - Nombre					Rate - Taux				
		1997	1998	1999	2000	2001	1997	1998	1999	2000	2001
AMERICA, SOUTH — AMERIQUE DU SUD											
Argentina - Argentine											
Total	C	12 985	13 082	12 120	11 649	*11 111	18.8	19.1	17.6	16.6	*16.3
Bolivia - Bolivie											
Total	U	17 324	16 942	16 492	16 042	...	...	...	...	...	...
Brazil - Brésil[9]											
Total	U	...	64 702	58 767	53 097	47 171	...	...	...	...	...
Chile - Chili[10]											
Total	C	2 732	2 793	2 651	...	...	10.5	10.9	10.6	...	...
Urban-Urbaine	C	2 278	2 345	2 249	...	...	10.1	10.5	10.3	...	...
Rural-Rurale	C	454	448	402	...	...	13.3	13.6	12.5	...	...
Colombia - Colombie[6,11]											
Total	+U	11 092	14 180	14 621	*14 927		...	...	...	...	...
Urban-Urbaine	+U	10 083	13 169	13 632	*13 960		...	...	...	...	...
Rural-Rurale	+U	653	903	933	*892		...	...	...	...	...
Ecuador - Équateur[12]											
Total	U	5 463	5 186	*5 372	*5 480		...	...	...	...	...
Urban-Urbaine	U	3 927	3 740	...	...		...	...	...	...	...
Rural-Rurale	U	1 536	1 446	...	...		...	...	...	...	...
French Guiana - Guyane française											
Total	C	55	52	...	...	...	...	...	...	...	...
Peru - Pérou[9,13]											
Total	C	28 252	26 603	25 098	23 681	22 455	43.3	41.0	39.0	37.2	35.6
Suriname											
Total	C	237	163	227	156	...	22.0	15.9	22.4	15.9	...
Uruguay											
Total	C	955	901	776	742	...	16.5	16.6	14.4	14.1	...
Venezuela[9]											
Total	C	9 684	9 871	...	8 524	...	18.7	19.7	...	15.7	...
ASIA — ASIE											
Armenia - Arménie[14]											
Total	C	678	580	572	540	497	15.4	14.7	15.7	15.8	15.5
Urban-Urbaine	C	487	428	373	357	...	18.1	17.4	16.6	16.7	...
Rural-Rurale	C	191	152	199	183	...	11.2	10.2	14.2	14.2	...
Azerbaijan - Azerbaïdjan[14]											
Total	+C	2 589	2 061	1 943	1 501	1 382	19.6	16.6	16.5	12.8	12.5
Urban-Urbaine	+C	1 061	842	780	642	558	18.6	15.8	15.6	12.9	11.2
Rural-Rurale	+C	1 528	1 219	1 163	859	824	20.4	17.2	17.2	12.8	13.6
Bahrain - Bahreïn											
Total	U	108	111	129	...	*117	...	...	...	...	...
Bangladesh											
Total	U	202 000	...	...	...	...	...	...	...	...	...
Brunei Darussalam - Brunéi Darussalam											
Total	+C	55	48	44	55	...	...	...	...	...	...
China: Hong Kong SAR - Chine: Hong Kong RAS											
Total	C	229	167	157	162	124	3.9	3.2	3.1	3.0	2.6
China: Macao SAR - Chine: Macao RAS											
Total	C	27	27	17	11	14	...	...	...	...	...
Cyprus - Chypre[15]											
Total	C	74	62	51	47	...	...	...	...	...	...
Georgia - Géorgie[14]											
Total	C	849	710	714	600	478	16.3	15.2	17.5	14.9	11.8
Urban-Urbaine	C	...	...	642	550	439	...	...	24.8	21.6	17.5
Rural-Rurale	C	...	...	72	50	39	...	...	...	...	...

15. Infant deaths and infant mortality rates, by urban/rural residence: 1997 - 2001
Décès d'enfants de moins d'un an et taux de mortalité infantile, selon la résidence, urbaine/rurale: 1997 - 2001
(continued — suite)

(See notes at end of table. — Voir notes à la fin du tableau.)

Continent, country or area and urban/rural residence / Continent, pays ou zone et résidence, urbaine/rurale	Code[1]	Number - Nombre					Rate - Taux				
		1997	1998	1999	2000	2001	1997	1998	1999	2000	2001
ASIA — ASIE											
Iran (Islamic Republic of) - Iran (République islamique d')											
Total	C	...	...	39 183	...	...	...	...	33.3	...	...
Israel - Israël[16]											
Total	C	802	774	*769	*745	*694	6.4	6.0	*5.8	*5.5	*5.1
Urban-Urbaine	C	716	681	*677	*659	*610	6.4	5.8	...	*5.4	*4.9
Rural-Rurale	C	85	93	*92	*86	*83	6.6	6.9	...	*5.9	*6.9
Japan - Japon[6,17]											
Total	C	4 403	4 380	4 010	3 830	3 599	3.7	3.6	3.4	3.2	3.1
Urban-Urbaine	C	3 502	3 491	3 144	3 075	2 896	3.7	3.6	3.3	3.2	3.1
Rural-Rurale	C	892	882	857	747	698	3.8	3.8	3.8	3.3	3.1
Kazakhstan[14]											
Total	C	5 889	4 843	4 423	*4 148	*4 233	25.3	21.8	20.9	*19.1	*19.2
Urban-Urbaine	C	3 188	2 701	2 435	...	...	28.3	24.1	22.9	...	...
Rural-Rurale	C	2 701	2 142	1 988	...	...	22.5	19.4	18.9	...	...
Korea (Republic of) - Corée (République de)[18]											
Total	C	1 716	1 460	2 776	2 885	3 008	2.5	2.3	4.5	4.5	5.4
Kuwait - Koweït											
Total	C	537	450	386	379	*420	12.5	10.9	9.4	9.1	*10.2
Kyrgyzstan - Kirghizistan[14]											
Total	C	2 920	2 708	2 360	2 225	2 123	28.6	26.0	22.7	23.0	21.6
Urban-Urbaine	C	847	821	756	836	785	32.7	28.8	26.7	29.7	27.6
Rural-Rurale	C	2 073	1 887	1 604	1 389	1 338	27.2	24.9	21.2	20.3	19.2
Malaysia - Malaisie											
Total	C	5 086	4 483	*4 400	*4 500	...	9.4	8.5	*7.9	*7.9	...
Maldives											
Total	C	165	115	104	113	85	26.7	20.2	19.9	21.3	17.4
Urban-Urbaine	C	23	31	19	27	22	14.7	21.1	12.8	17.2	13.4
Rural-Rurale	C	142	84	85	86	63	30.7	19.9	22.7	23.0	19.4
Mongolia - Mongolie											
Total	C	1 962	1 741	1 846	1 596	1 464	39.6	35.3	37.3	32.8	29.5
Urban-Urbaine	C	777	936	903	808	...	35.5	41.8	37.3	33.9	...
Rural-Rurale	C	1 185	805	943	788	...	42.9	30.0	37.4	31.7	...
Nepal - Népal[19]											
Total	I	...	...	...	...	13 037	...	...	...	...	...
Occupied Palestinian Territory - Territoire palestinien occupé											
Total	U	*1 353*	*1 332*	*1 066*	*1 033*	*1 087*	...	...	...	...	...
Oman[20]											
Total	...	*368*	*374*	*386*	...	...	...	...	...	...	...
Pakistan[21,22]											
Total	I	349 746	...	...	...	...	84.4	...	...	...	...
Urban-Urbaine	I	87 087	...	...	...	...	72.7	...	...	...	...
Rural-Rurale	I	262 659	...	...	...	...	89.2	...	...	...	...
Philippines											
Total	C	28 061	28 196	25 168	27 714	...	17.0	17.3	15.6	15.7	...
Qatar											
Total	C	130	141	112	*132	111	12.4	13.1	10.3	*11.7	9.2
Saudi Arabia - Arabie saoudite											
Total	...	...	...	*11 344*	*11 071*	...	...	...	...	...	...
Singapore - Singapour[23]											
Total	+C	179	183	150	137	100	3.8	4.2	3.5	2.9	2.4
Sri Lanka											
Total	+C	...	...	...	...	*4 323	...	...	...	...	...
Tajikistan - Tadjikistan[14]											
Total	C	...	...	*2 200	...	...	...	...	*19.9	...	...
Thailand - Thaïlande											
Total	+U	*5 172*	*4 062*	*5 003*	*4 822*	*5 105	...	...	...	...	...
Urban-Urbaine	+U	...	...	*711*	*801*	...	...	...	...	...	...
Rural-Rurale	+U	...	...	*4 292*	*4 021*	...	...	...	...	...	...

404

15. Infant deaths and infant mortality rates, by urban/rural residence: 1997 - 2001
Décès d'enfants de moins d'un an et taux de mortalité infantile, selon la résidence, urbaine/rurale: 1997 - 2001
(continued — suite)

(See notes at end of table. — Voir notes à la fin du tableau.)

Continent, country or area and urban/rural residence / Continent, pays ou zone et résidence, urbaine/rurale	Code[1]	Number - Nombre					Rate - Taux				
		1997	1998	1999	2000	2001	1997	1998	1999	2000	2001
ASIA — ASIE											
Turkey - Turquie[24]											
Total	I	62 625	61 347	60 369	59 709	58 205	42.4	41.2	40.3	39.6	38.6
Urban-Urbaine	I	16 862	17 704	15 870	...	...	...	...	...	...	...
Rural-Rurale	I	45 763	43 643	44 499	...	...	...	...	...	...	...
Turkmenistan - Turkménistan[14]											
Total	C	...	*3 265	...	...	...	...	*33.2	...	...	...
Uzbekistan - Ouzbékistan[14]											
Total	C	13 908	...	12 358	10 091	9 427	23.1	...	22.3	19.1	18.4
Urban-Urbaine	C	4 759	...	4 293	3 703	3 399	25.4	...	24.8	22.6	21.3
Rural-Rurale	C	9 149	...	8 065	6 388	6 028	22.0	...	21.2	17.6	17.1
EUROPE											
Albania - Albanie											
Total	C	1 368	903	...	...	...	22.2	15.0	...	...	...
Andorra - Andorre											
Total	C	1	5	2	2	3	...	...	...	...	...
Austria - Autriche											
Total	C	398	400	341	378	365	4.7	4.9	4.4	4.8	4.8
Urban-Urbaine	C	220	233	...	...	...	...	...	...	...	...
Rural-Rurale	C	178	167	...	...	...	...	...	...	...	...
Belarus - Bélarus[14]											
Total	C	1 127	1 041	1 064	...	...	12.6	11.2	11.4	...	...
Urban-Urbaine	C	675	644	651	...	...	11.0	9.9	9.8	...	...
Rural-Rurale	C	452	397	413	...	...	16.1	14.3	15.5	...	...
Belgium - Belgique[25]											
Total	C	623	591	556	554	*583	5.4	5.2	4.9	4.8	*5.1
Bosnia and Herzegovina - Bosnie-Herzégovine											
Total	C	601	494	...	...	...	12.4	11.0	...	...	...
Bulgaria - Bulgarie											
Total	C	1 123	*943	*1 057	981	982	17.5	*14.4	*14.6	13.3	14.4
Urban-Urbaine	C	719	...	...	657	625	15.7	...	...	12.4	12.9
Rural-Rurale	C	404	...	...	324	357	22.0	...	...	15.5	18.2
Channel Islands: Guernsey - Îles Anglo-Normandes: Guernesey											
Total	C	3	2	2	4	...	...	...	...	...	...
Croatia - Croatie											
Total	C	457	388	*350	324	315	8.2	8.2	*7.7	7.4	7.7
Urban-Urbaine	C	271	223	...	194	179	8.2	8.3	...	7.8	7.8
Rural-Rurale	C	186	165	...	130	136	8.3	8.1	...	6.9	7.5
Czech Republic - République tchèque											
Total	C	531	472	413	373	360	5.9	5.2	4.6	4.1	4.0
Urban-Urbaine	C	397	340	307	272	266	6.0	5.1	4.7	4.1	4.0
Rural-Rurale	C	134	132	106	101	94	5.5	5.5	4.4	4.2	...
Denmark - Danemark[26]											
Total	C	351	309	281	358	*320	5.2	4.7	4.2	5.3	*4.9
Estonia - Estonie[6,14]											
Total	C	127	108	119	110	*111	10.1	8.9	9.5	8.4	*8.8
Urban-Urbaine	C	78	...	...	73	...	9.6	...	...	8.4	...
Rural-Rurale	C	49	...	...	36	...	11.0	...	...	8.2	...
Finland - Finlande[27]											
Total	C	232	239	...	213	181	3.9	4.2	...	3.8	3.2
Urban-Urbaine	C	136	141	...	...	112	3.6	3.9	...	...	3.1
Rural-Rurale	C	96	98	...	...	69	4.4	4.7	...	...	3.5
France[28]											
Total	C	3 439	3 399	3 221	3 543	*3 444	4.7	4.6	4.3	4.6	*4.4
Urban-Urbaine	C	2 682	2 610	2 551	...	...	4.8	4.6	4.5	...	...
Rural-Rurale	C	702	752	644	...	...	4.3	4.5	3.7	...	...

15. Infant deaths and infant mortality rates, by urban/rural residence: 1997 - 2001
Décès d'enfants de moins d'un an et taux de mortalité infantile, selon la résidence, urbaine/rurale: 1997 - 2001
(continued — suite)

(See notes at end of table. — Voir notes à la fin du tableau.)

Continent, country or area and urban/rural residence / Continent, pays ou zone et résidence, urbaine/rurale	Code[1]	Number - Nombre					Rate - Taux				
		1997	1998	1999	2000	2001	1997	1998	1999	2000	2001
EUROPE											
Germany - Allemagne											
Total	C	3 951	3 667	3 496	3 362	*3 300	4.9	4.6	4.5	4.4	*4.4
Greece - Grèce											
Total	C	657	674	*619	*610	*522	6.4	6.7	*5.3	*5.2	*5.1
Urban-Urbaine	C	464	467	...	...	...	6.6	6.7	...	...	...
Rural-Rurale	C	193	207	...	...	...	6.0	6.6	...	...	...
Hungary - Hongrie[6]											
Total	C	989	944	798	900	789	9.9	9.7	8.4	9.2	8.1
Urban-Urbaine	C	578	537	480	532	471	9.7	9.2	8.4	9.0	8.0
Rural-Rurale	C	406	391	312	359	311	10.0	10.2	8.5	9.5	8.4
Iceland - Islande											
Total	C	23	11	10	13	11	...	...	...	...	...
Ireland - Irlande[6,29]											
Total	+C	321	330	293	*322	*337	6.1	6.2	5.5	*5.9	*5.8
Urban-Urbaine	+C	212	202	195	...	...	7.4	7.0	6.3	...	...
Rural-Rurale	+C	109	128	98	...	...	4.5	5.2	4.4	...	...
Isle of Man - Îles de Man											
Total	+C	...	...	6			...	...	...	...	...
Italy - Italie											
Total	C	2 973	...	2 723	2 461	2 514	5.6	...	5.2	4.5	4.7
Latvia - Lettonie[14]											
Total	C	289	276	219	210	217	15.3	15.0	11.3	10.4	11.0
Urban-Urbaine	C	182	157	144	124	139	15.6	13.9	11.9	9.7	11.1
Rural-Rurale	C	107	119	75	86	78	15.0	16.8	...	...	...
Liechtenstein											
Total	C	8	...	...	...	...	...	...	...	...	...
Lithuania - Lituanie[14]											
Total	C	391	343	315	294	250	10.3	9.3	8.7	8.6	7.9
Urban-Urbaine	C	210	188	174	172	148	8.8	8.2	...	8.2	7.5
Rural-Rurale	C	181	155	141	122	102	12.9	11.1	...	9.3	8.6
Luxembourg											
Total	C	23	27	26	29	32	...	...	...	...	...
Malta - Malte											
Total	C	31	24	31	26	39	...	...	...	...	...
Netherlands - Pays-Bas[30]											
Total	C	968	1 035	1 048	1 059	1 088	5.0	5.2	5.2	5.1	5.4
Norway - Norvège[31]											
Total	C	247	232	232	225	223	4.1	4.0	3.9	3.8	3.9
Poland - Pologne											
Total	C	4 194	3 771	3 381	*3 068	*2 823	10.2	9.5	8.9	*8.1	*7.7
Urban-Urbaine	C	2 332	2 062	1 908	...	...	10.5	9.6	9.2	...	...
Rural-Rurale	C	1 862	1 709	1 473	...	...	9.7	9.4	8.5	...	...
Portugal											
Total	C	727	950	651	664	567	6.4	8.4	5.6	5.6	5.0
Republic of Moldova - République de Moldova[14]											
Total	C	...	738	714	681	728	...	17.9	18.5	18.4	20.0
Urban-Urbaine	C	...	294	277	236	...	...	20.7	20.9	18.6	...
Rural-Rurale	C	...	444	437	445	...	...	16.4	17.3	18.4	...
Romania - Roumanie											
Total	C	5 209	4 868	4 360	4 370	4 057	22.0	20.5	18.6	18.6	18.4
Urban-Urbaine	C	2 036	1 907	...	1 744	1 594	18.5	17.3	...	16.1	15.6
Rural-Rurale	C	3 173	2 961	...	2 626	2 463	25.0	23.3	...	20.8	20.9
Russian Federation - Fédération de Russie[14]											
Total	C	21 735	21 097	20 731	19 286	*19 124	17.3	16.4	17.1	15.2	*14.6
Urban-Urbaine	C	...	...	13 657	...	...	...	...	16.2	...	...
Rural-Rurale	C	...	...	7 074	...	...	...	...	19.0	...	...
San Marino - Saint-Marin											
Total	+C	-	4	1	-	...	...	...	...	...	...

15. Infant deaths and infant mortality rates, by urban/rural residence: 1997 - 2001
Décès d'enfants de moins d'un an et taux de mortalité infantile, selon la résidence, urbaine/rurale: 1997 - 2001
(continued — suite)

(See notes at end of table. — Voir notes à la fin du tableau.)

Continent, country or area and urban/rural residence / Continent, pays ou zone et résidence, urbaine/rurale	Code[1]	Number - Nombre					Rate - Taux				
		1997	1998	1999	2000	2001	1997	1998	1999	2000	2001
EUROPE											
Serbia and Montenegro - Serbie-et-Montenegro											
Total	C	1 876	1 791	1 691	1 668	*1 662*	14.3	13.9	13.6	13.3	...
Urban-Urbaine	C	1 052	1 016	939	962	...	15.5	15.2	14.6	14.5	...
Rural-Rurale	C	824	775	752	706	...	13.0	12.6	12.6	11.9	...
Slovakia - Slovaquie											
Total	C	...	506	467	*458	319	...	8.8	8.3	*8.3	6.2
Urban-Urbaine	C	...	234	235	...	147	...	7.9	8.2	...	5.6
Rural-Rurale	C	...	272	232	...	172	...	9.8	8.4	...	6.9
Slovenia - Slovénie											
Total	C	...	93	79	89	74	...	...	...	...	...
Urban-Urbaine	C	...	39	31	34	33	...	...	...	...	...
Rural-Rurale	C	...	54	48	55	41	...	...	...	...	...
Spain - Espagne											
Total	C	1 856	1 774	*1 700	*1 535	...	5.0	4.9	*4.5	*4.0	...
Sweden - Suède											
Total	C	328	316	297	292	334	3.6	3.5	3.4	3.2	3.7
Switzerland - Suisse											
Total	C	387	376	361	386	365	4.8	4.8	4.6	4.9	5.0
Urban-Urbaine	C	241	230	237	262	248	4.6	4.5	4.6	5.0	5.0
Rural-Rurale	C	146	146	124	124	117	5.2	5.4	4.7	4.8	4.8
The Former Yugoslav Rep. of Macedonia - L'ex-République yougoslave de Macédoine											
Total	C	463	...	406	346	321	15.7	...	14.9	11.8	11.9
Urban-Urbaine	C	248	...	201	185	182	16.1	...	14.0	11.9	12.3
Rural-Rurale	C	215	...	205	161	139	15.3	...	15.8	11.7	11.3
Ukraine[14]											
Total	C	6 282	5 423	...	4 606	4 283	14.2	12.9	...	12.0	11.4
Urban-Urbaine	C	3 947	3 361	...	...	2 690	14.4	13.0	...	...	11.3
Rural-Rurale	C	2 335	2 062	...	...	1 593	13.9	12.8	...	...	11.4
United Kingdom - Royaume-Uni											
Total	C	4 252	4 079	4 045	3 791	3 664	5.9	5.7	5.8	5.6	5.5
OCEANIA — OCEANIE											
American Samoa - Samoa américaines											
Total	C	17	27	22	11		...	...	...	...	...
Australia - Australie											
Total	+C	1 341	1 252	1 408	1 290	*1 294	5.3	5.0	5.7	5.2	*5.3
Cook Islands - Îles Cook											
Total	+C	15	8	5	...	...	...	...	...	...	...
Fiji - Fidji											
Total	+C	...	212	275	...	...	...	11.8	16.3	...	...
French Polynesia - Polynésie française											
Total	U	*36*	*32*	*31*	...	...	...	...	...	...	...
Guam[32]											
Total	C	37	34	35	*24	...	...	...	...	...	...
Marshall Islands - Îles Marshall											
Total	+U	*49*	...	...	...	*40*	...	...	...	...	...
Micronesia, Federated States of - Micronésie, États Fédérés de La											
Total	U	*69*	...	...	...		...	...	...	...	...
New Caledonia - Nouvelle-Calédonie											
Total	C	24	30	27	...	...	...	...	...	...	...

15. Infant deaths and infant mortality rates, by urban/rural residence: 1997 - 2001
Décès d'enfants de moins d'un an et taux de mortalité infantile, selon la résidence, urbaine/rurale: 1997 - 2001
(continued — suite)

(See notes at end of table. — Voir notes à la fin du tableau.)

Continent, country or area and urban/rural residence Continent, pays ou zone et résidence, urbaine/rurale	Code[1]	Number - Nombre					Rate - Taux				
		1997	1998	1999	2000	2001	1997	1998	1999	2000	2001
OCEANIA — OCEANIE											
New Zealand - Nouvelle-Zélande											
Total	+C	377	305	317	346	...	6.5	5.5	5.6	6.1	...
Urban-Urbaine	+C	343	259	261	289	...	6.8	5.4	5.3	5.9	...
Rural-Rurale	+C	34	39	33	32	...	4.5	5.8	4.5	4.5	...
Northern Mariana Islands - Îles Mariannes septentrionales											
Total	U	*8*	*15*	*11*	...	...	...	...	...	...	...
Palau - Palaos											
Total	C	4	3	5	...	...	...	...	...	...	...
Samoa											
Total	U	...	**17*	...	...	...	...	...	...	...	...
Tonga											
Total	+C	21	29	48	28	...	...	...	...	...	...

GENERAL NOTES - NOTES GENERALES

Data exclude foetal deaths. Rates are the number of deaths of infants under one year of age per 1 000 live births. Rates are shown only for countries or areas having at least a total of 100 infant deaths in a given year. For definitions of 'urban', see end of Technical Notes for table 6. For method of evaluation and limitations of data, see Technical Notes for this table. — Les données ne comprennent pas les morts foetales. Les taux représentent le nombre de décès d'enfants de moins d'un an pour 1 000 naissances vivantes. Les taux présentés ne se rapportent qu'aux pays ou zones où l'on a enregistré un total d'au moins 100 décès d'enfants de moins d'un an dans un année donnée. Pour les définitions des 'régions urbaines', se reporter à la fin des Notes techniques du tableau 6. Pour la méthode d'évaluation et les insuffisances des données, voir Notes techniques pour ce tableau.

Italics: data from civil registers which are incomplete or of unknown completeness. — *Italiques:* données incomplètes ou dont le degré d'exactitude n'est pas connu provenant des registres de l'état civil.

FOOTNOTES - NOTES

* Provisional. — Données provisoires.
[1] 'Code' indicates the source of data, as follows:
C - Civil registration, estimated over 90% complete
U - Civil registration, estimated less than 90% complete
I - Other source, estimated reliable
+ - Data tabulated by date of registration rather than occurence.
... - Information not available

Le 'Code' indique la source des données, comme suit:
C - Registres de l'état civil considérés complèts à 90 p. 100 au moins.
U - Registres de l'état civil qui ne sont pas considérés complèts à 90 p. 100 au moins.
I - Autre source, considérée pas douteuses.
+ - Données exploitées selon la date de l'enregistrement et non la date de l'événement.
... - Information pas disponible.

[2] Excluding live-born infants dying before registration of birth. — Non compris les enfants nés vivants décédés avant l'enregistrement de leur naissance.
[3] For Algerian population only. — Pour la population algérienne seulement.

[4] Data refer to national projections. — Les données se referent au projections nationales.
[5] For 1998, based on the results of the population census. — Pour 1998, d'après les résultats du recensement de la population.
[6] Data for urban and rural areas exclude infant deaths of unknown residence. — Les données urbaines/rurales ne comprennent pas les décès d'enfants de moins d'un an pour lesquels le lieu de résidence n'est pas connu.
[7] Data for 1997 refer to last twelve months preceding population and housing census of 1997. — Les données pour 1997 se réfèrent au douze mois précédant le recensement de population et de l'habitat de 1997.
[8] Including Canadian residents temporarily in the United States, but excluding United States residents temporarily in Canada. — Y compris les résidents canadiens se trouvant temporairement aux Etats-Unis, mais ne comprennent pas les résidents des Etats-Unis se trouvant temporairement au Canada.
[9] Excluding Indian jungle population. — Non compris les Indiens de la jungle.
[10] Data as reported by national statistical authorities; they may differ from data presented in other tables. — Les donées comme ils ont été déclarés par l'institut national de la statistique; ils peuvent etre different de ceux presentésdans autre tableaux.
[11] Data on live births and deaths are based on a civil registration system put in place in January 1998. - Les données sur les naissances et les décès sont basées sur un système d'enregistrement des faits d'état civil mis en place en janvier 1998.
[12] Excluding nomadic Indian tribes. — Non compris les tribus d'Indiens nomades.
[13] Including an upward adjustment for under-registration. — Y compris un ajustement pour sous-enregistrement.
[14] Excluding infants born alive with less than 28 weeks gestation, less than 1 000 grams in weight and 35 centimeters in length, who die within seven days of birth. — Non compris les enfants nés vivants avant 28 semaines de gestation, pesant moins de 1 000 grammes, mesurant moins de 35 centimètres et décédés dans les sept jours qui ont suivi leur naissance.
[15] Data refer to government controlled areas. — Les données se raportent aux zones contrôlées par le Gouvernement.
[16] Including data for East Jerusalem and Israeli residents in certain other territories under occupation by Israeli military forces since June 1967. — Y compris les données pour Jérusalem-Est et les résidents israéliens dans certains autres territoires occupés depuis 1967 par les forces armées israéliennes.
[17] For Japanese nationals in Japan only. — Pour les nationaux japonais au Japon seulement.
[18] Excluding alien armed forces, civilian aliens employed by armed forces, and foreign diplomatic personnel and their dependants. — Non compris les militaires étrangers, les civils étrangers employés par les

forces armées ni le personnel diplomatique étranger et les membres de leur famille les accompagnant.

[19] For 2001, data refer to last twelve months preceding census on June 2001. — Pour 2001, les données se rapportent pour la dernière fois à douze mois précédant le recensement juin 2001.

[20] Published by the United Nations Economic and Social Commission for Western Asia. — Edité par les Nations Unies économiques et la Commission sociale pour l'Asie occidentale.

[21] Based on the results of the Population Growth Survey. — D'après les résultats de la 'Population Growth Survey.'

[22] Excluding data for the Pakistan-held part of Jammu and Kashmir, the final status of which has not yet been determined. — Non compris les données concernant la partie du Jammu et Cachemire occupée par le Pakistan dont le statut définitif n'a pas été déterminé.

[23] Infant deaths prior to 2000 were tabulated by date of registration. Consequently, this should be taken into account when interpreting rates per 1 000 live births, tabulated by date of occurence. — Antérieurement à l'année 2000, les données sur les décès d'enfants ont été présentées selon la date d'enregistrement. Par contre, les données sur les naissances vivantes, qui ont été utilisées pour calculer les taux de mortalité infantile, sont présentées selon la date de l'événement. Les lecteurs doivent tenir compte des ces différences dans l'interprétation des taux de mortalité infantile.

[24] Based on the results of the Population Demographic Survey. — - D'après les résultats de la Population Demographic Survey.

[25] Including armed forces stationed outside the country, but excluding alien armed forces stationed in the area. — Y compris les militaires nationaux hors du pays, mais non compris les militaires étrangers en garnison sur le territoire.

[26] Excluding Faeroe Islands and Greenland. — Non compris les îles Féroé et Gröenland.

[27] Including nationals temporarily outside the country. — Y compris les nationaux se trouvant temporairement hors du pays.

[28] Urban/rural figures, excluding nationals outside the country. — Les chiffres urbaine/rurale, non compris les nationaux hors du pays.

[29] Events registered within one year of occurrence. — Evénements enregistrés dans l'année qui suit l'événement.

[30] Including residents outside the country if listed in a Netherlands population register. — Y compris les résidents hors du pays, s'ils sont inscrits sur un registre de population néerlandais.

[31] Including residents temporarily outside the country. — Y compris les résidents se trouvant temporairement hors du pays.

[32] Including United States military personnel, their dependants and contract employees. — Y compris les militaires des Etats-Unis, les membres de leur famille les accompagnant et les agents contractuels des Etats-Unis.

Table 16

Table 16 presents infant deaths and infant mortality rates by age and sex for latest available year.

Description of variables: Age is defined as hours, days and months of life completed, based on the difference between the hour, day, month and year of birth and the hour, day, month and year of death. The age classification used in this table is the following: under 1 day, 1-6 days, 7-27 days and 28-364 days. For some countries or areas the statistics presented are for several years, and include those years for which data only recently become available and were therefore not published in pervious issues of the *Demographic Yearbook*.

Rate computation: Infant mortality rates are the annual number of deaths of infants under one year of age per 1 000 live births (as shown in table 9) in the same year.

Infant mortality rates by age and sex are the annual number of infant deaths that occurred in a specific age-sex group per 1 000 live births in the corresponding sex group (as shown in table 9). These rates have been calculated by the Statistics Division of the United Nations.

The denominator for all these rates, regardless of age of infant at death, is the number of live births by sex.

Infant deaths of unknown age are included only in the rate for under one year of age. Deaths under the category of sex "unknown" are included in the rate for the total and hence these rates, shown in the first column of the table, should agree with the infant mortality rates shown in table 15. Discrepancies are explained in footnotes.

Rates presented in this table have been limited to those for countries or areas having at least a total of 1 000 deaths in a given year. Moreover, rates specific for individual sub-categories based on 30 or fewer infant deaths are identified by the symbol (♦).

Reliability of data: Data from civil registers of infant deaths which are reported as incomplete (less than 90 percent completeness) or of unknown completeness are considered unreliable and are set in italics rather than in roman type. Rates on these data are not computed. Tables 9 and 15 and the technical notes for these tables provide more detailed information on the completeness of infant death registration. For more information about the quality of vital statistics data in general, and the information available on the basis of the completeness of estimates in particular, see section 4.2 of the Technical Notes.

Limitations: Statistics on infant deaths by age and sex are subject to the same qualifications as have been set forth for vital statistics in general and death statistics in particular as discussed in section 4 of the Technical Notes.

The reliability of the data, an indication of which is described above, is an important factor in considering the limitations. In addition, some infant deaths are tabulated by date of registration and not by date of occurrence; these have been indicated by a plus sign (+). Whenever the lag between the date of occurrence and date of registration is prolonged and, therefore, a large proportion of the infant-death registrations are delayed, infant-death statistics for any given year may be seriously affected.

Another factor which limits international comparability is the practice of some countries or areas of not including in infant-death statistics infants who were born alive but died before the registration of the birth or within the first 24 hours of life, thus underestimating the total number of infant deaths. Statistics of this type are footnoted. In this table in particular, this practice may contribute to the lack of comparability among deaths under one year, under 28 days, under one week and under one day.

Variation in the method of reckoning age at the time of death may also introduce non-comparability. Although it is to some degree a limiting factor throughout the age span, it is an especially important consideration with respect to deaths at ages under one day and under one week (early neonatal deaths) and under 28 days (neonatal deaths). As noted above, the recommended method of reckoning infant age at death is to calculate duration of life in minutes, hours and days, as appropriate. This gives age in completed units of time. In some countries or areas, however, infant age is calculated to the nearest day only, that is, age at death for an infant is the difference between the day, month and year of birth and the day, month and year of death. The result of this procedure is to classify as deaths at age one day, many deaths of infants that occurred before the infants had completed 24 hours of life. The under-one-day class is thus understated while the frequency in the 1-6-day age group is inflated.

A special limitation on comparability of neonatal (under 28 days) deaths is the variation in the classification of infant age used. It is evident from the footnotes in the tables that some countries or areas continue to report infant age in calendar, rather than lunar month (4-week or 28- day) periods.

Failure to tabulate infant deaths under 4 weeks of age in terms of completed days introduces another source of variation between countries or areas. Deaths classified as occurring under one month usually connote deaths within any one calendar month; these frequencies are not strictly comparable with those referring to deaths within 4 weeks or 27 completed days. Other differences in-age classification will be evident from the table.

In addition, infant mortality rates by age and sex are subject to the limitations of the data on live births with which they have been calculated. These have been set forth in the technical notes for table 9. These limitations have also been discussed in the technical notes for table 15.

In addition, it should be noted that infant mortality rates by age are affected by the problems related to the practice of excluding infants who were born alive but died before the registration of the birth or within the first 24 hours of life from both infant-death and live-birth statistics and the problems related to the reckoning of infant age at death. These factors, which have been described above, may affect certain age groups more than others. In so far as the numbers of infant deaths for the various age groups are underestimated or overestimated, the corresponding rates for the various age groups will also be underestimated or overestimated. The youngest age groups are more likely to be underestimated than other age groups; the youngest age group (under one day) is likely to be the most seriously affected.

Coverage: Infant mortality by age and sex are shown for 113 countries or areas.

Earlier data: Infant deaths and infant mortality rates by age and sex have been shown in previous issues of the *Demographic Yearbook*. For information on specific years covered, readers should consult the Index.

Tableau 16

Le tableau 16 présente des données sur des décès d'enfants de moins d'un an et des taux de mortalité infantile selon l'âge et le sexe pour la dernière année disponible.

Description des variables: L'âge est exprimé en heures, jours et mois révolus et est calculé en retranchant la date de la naissance (heure, jour, mois et année) de celle du décès (heure, jour, mois et année). La classification par âge utilisée dans ce tableau est la suivante: moins d'un jour, 1 à 6 jours, 7 à 27 jours et 28 à 364 jours. Pour certaines pays et zones, les statistiques pour plusieurs années sont présentées, étant donné qu'elles sont devenues disponible récemment et qu'elles n'ont pas été publiées dans les Annuaires démographiques précédents.

Calcul des taux: Les taux de mortalité infantile selon l'âge et le sexe représentent le nombre annuel de décès d'enfants de moins d'un an selon l'âge et le sexe pour 1 000 naissances vivantes d'enfants du même sexe (fréquences du tableau 9) survenues au cours de l'année considérée.

Les taux de mortalité infantile selon l'âge et le sexe représentent le nombre annuel de décès d'enfants de moins d'un an intervenu dans un groupe d'âge donné dans la population du sexe masculin ou féminin (fréquences du tableau 9) pour 1 000 naissances vivantes intervenues dans la population du même sexe. Ces taux ont été calculés par la Division de statistique de l'ONU.

Le dénominateur de tous ces taux, quel que soit l'âge de l'enfant au moment du décès, est le nombre de naissances vivantes selon le sexe.

Il n'est tenu compte des décès d'enfants d'âge "inconnu" que pour le calcul du taux relatif à l'ensemble des décès de moins d'un an. Etant les décès d'enfants de sexe inconnu compris dans le numérateur des taux concernant le total qui figurent dans la première colonne du tableau 16, ces taux devraient concorder avec les taux de mortalité infantile du tableau 15. Les divergences sont expliquées en note.

Les taux présentés dans ce tableau ne concernent que les pays ou zones où l'on a enregistre un total d'au moins 1000 décès au cours d'une année donnée. Les taux relatifs à des sous-categories qui sont fondés sur un nombre égal ou inférieur à 30 décès d'enfants âgés de moins d'un an sont identifiés par le signe (♦).

Fiabilité des données: Les données sur les décès d'enfants de moins d'un an provenant des registres de l'état civil qui sont déclarés incomplets (degré de complétude inférieur à 90 p.100) ou dont le degré de complétude n'est pas connu sont jugées douteuses et apparaissent en italique et not en caractères romains. Les taux à partir de ces données n'ont pas été calculés. Les tableaux 9 et 15 et les Notes techniques se rapportant à ces tableaux présentent des renseignements plus détaillés sur le degré de complétude de l'enregistrement des décès d'enfants de moins d'un an. Pour plus de précisions sur la qualité des données reposant sur les statistiques de l'état civil en général, voir la section 4.2 des notes techniques, qui fournit aussi des renseignements fondés sur les estimations de complétude.

Insuffisance des données: Les statistiques des décès d'enfants de moins d'un an selon l'âge et le sexe appellent toutes les réserves qui ont été formulées à propos des statistiques de l'état civil en général et des statistiques des décès en particulier (voir explications à la section 4 des Notes techniques).

La fiabilité des données, au sujet de laquelle des indications ont été fournies plus haut, est un facteur important. Il faut également tenir compte du fait que, dans certains cas, les données relatives aux décès d'enfants de moins d'un an sont exploitées selon la date de l'enregistrement et non la date de l'événement; ces cas ont été identifiés par le signe (+). Là où le décalage entre l'événement et son enregistrement est grand, c'est-à-dire où une forte proportion des décès d'enfants de moins d'un an fait l'objet d'un enregistrement tardif, les statistiques des décès d'enfants de moins d'un an pour une année donnée peuvent être sérieusement faussées.

Un autre facteur qui nuit à la comparabilité internationale est la pratique de certains pays ou zones qui consiste à ne pas inclure dans les statistiques des décès d'enfants de moins d'un an les enfants nés vivants mais décédés soit avant l'enregistrement de leur naissance, soit dans les 24 heures qui ont suivi la naissance, pratique qui conduit à sous-estimer le nombre total de décès d'enfants de moins d'un an. Lorsqu'on savait que ce facteur était intervenu, on l'a signalé en note. Dans ce tableau en particulier, ce système peut contribuer au défaut de comparabilité des données concernant les décès d'enfants de moins d'un an, de moins de 28 jours, de moins d'une semaine et de moins d'un jour.

Le manque d'uniformité des méthodes suivies pour calculer l'âge au moment du décès nuit également à la comparabilité des données. Ce facteur influe dans une certaine mesure sur les données relatives à la mortalité à tous les âges, mais il a des répercussions particulièrement marquées sur les statistiques des décès de moins d'un jour et de moins d'une semaine (mortalité néo-natale précoce) et de moins de 28 jours ((mortalité néo-natale). Comme on l'a dit, l'âge d'un enfant de moins d'un an à sont décès est calculé, selon la méthode recommandée, en évaluant la durée de vie en minutes, heures et jours, selon le cas. L'âge est ainsi exprimé en unités de temps révolues. Toutefois, dans certains pays ou zones, l'âge de ces enfants n'est calculé en retranchant la date de la naissance (jour, mois et année) de celle du décès (jour, mois et année). Il s'ensuit que de nombreux décès survenus dans les vingt-quatre heures qui suivent la naissance sont classés comme décès d'un jour. Dans ces conditions, les données concernant les décès de moins d'un jour sont entachées d'une erreur par défaut et celles qui se rapportent aux décès de 1 à 6 jours d'une erreur par excès.

La comparabilité des données relatives à la mortalité néo-natale (moins de 28 jours) est influencée par un facteur spécial: l'hétérogénéité de la classification par âge utilisée pour les enfants de moins d'un an. Les notes figurant au bas des tableaux montrent que, dans un certain nombre de pays ou zones, on continue d'utiliser le mois civil au lieu du mois lunaire (4 semaines ou 28 jours).

Lorsque les données relatives aux décès de moins de 4 semaines ne sont pas exploitées sur la base de l'âge en jours révolus, il existe une nouvelle cause de non-comparabilité internationale. Les décès de "moins de 1 mois sont généralement ceux qui se produisent au cours d'un mois civil; les taux calculés sur la base de ces données ne sont pas strictement comparables à ceux qui sont établis à partir des données concernant les décès survenus pendant 4 semaines ou 27 jours révolus. Le tableau montre que la classification des âges présente d'autres différences.

Les taux de mortalité infantile selon l'âge et le sexe appellent en outre toutes les réserves qui ont été formulées à propos des statistiques des naissances vivantes qui ont servi à leur calcul. Voir à ce sujet les notes techniques relatives aux tableaux 9. Ces insuffisances ont également été examinées dans les notes techniques relatives au tableau 15.

Il convient de signaler aussi que les taux de mortalité infantile selon l'âge se ressentent des problèmes dus à la pratique qui consiste à n'inscrire ni dans les statistiques des décès d'enfants de moins d'un an ni dans celles des naissances vivantes des enfants nés vivants mais décédés soit avant l'enregistrement de leur naissance, soit dans les 24 heures qui ont suivi la naissance, et des problèmes que pose le calcul de l'âge de l'enfant au moment du décès. Ces facteurs, qui ont été décris plus haut, peuvent fausser plus les statistiques pour certains groupes d'âge que pour d'autres. Si le nombre des décès d'enfants de moins d'un an pour chaque groupe d'âge est sous-estimé (ou surestimé), les taux correspondants pour chacun de ces groupes d'âge seront eux aussi sous-estimé (ou surestimés). Les risques de sous-estimation sont plus grands pour les groupes les plus jeunes; c'est pour le groupe d'âge le plus jeune de tous (moins d'un jour) que les données risquent de présenter les plus grosses erreurs.

Portée: Ce tableau présente des donnés sur les décès d'enfants de moins d'un an selon l'âge et le sexe pour 113 pays ou zones.

Données publiées antérieurement: Des statistiques des décès d'enfants de moins d'un an et des taux de mortalité infantile selon l'âge et le sexe ont déjà été présentées dans des éditions antérieures de l'Annuaire démographique. Pour plus de précisions concernant les années pour lesquelles ces données ont été publiées, on se reportera à l'Index.

16. Infant deaths and infant mortality rates by age and sex: latest available year
Décès d'enfants de moins d'un an et taux de mortalité infantile selon l'âge et le sexe: dernière année disponible

(See notes at end of table. — Voir notes à la fin du tableau.)

Continent, country or area, year, age (in days) and urban/rural residence Continent, pays ou zone, année, âge (en jours) et résidence, urbaine/rurale	Number - Nombre			Rate - Taux		
	Both sexes Les deux sexes	Male Masculin	Female Féminin	Both sexes Les deux sexes	Male Masculin	Female Féminin
AFRICA — AFRIQUE						
Egypt - Égypte						
1999						
Total	49 765	26 263	23 502	29.4	30.2	28.6
Under 1 day - Moins d'un jour	7 992	4 418	3 574	4.7	5.1	4.3
1-6	8 352	5 127	3 225	4.9	5.9	3.9
7-27	6 028	3 488	2 540	3.6	4.0	3.1
28-364	27 393	13 230	14 163	16.2	15.2	17.2
Mauritius - Maurice[+]						
2000						
Total	322	206	116	...	...	...
Under 1 day - Moins d'un jour	62	38	24	...	...	...
1-6	120	71	49	...	...	...
7-27	73	52	21	...	...	...
28-364	67	45	22	...	...	...
Morocco - Maroc						
1999						
Total	8 885	4 711	4 174	...	...	...
0-27	1 781	1 039	742	...	...	...
28-364	7 076	3 661	3 415	...	...	...
Réunion[1]						
1990						
Total	94	58	36	...	...	...
Under 1 day - Moins d'un jour	-	-	-	...	...	...
1-6	38	26	12	...	...	...
7-27	18	9	9	...	...	...
28-364	38	23	15	...	...	...
Saint Helena ex. dep. - Sainte-Hélène sans dép.						
1998						
Total	1	1	-	...	...	...
Under 1 day - Moins d'un jour	1	1	-	...	...	...
1-6	-	-	-	...	...	...
7-27	-	-	-	...	...	...
28-364	-	-	-	...	...	...
South Africa - Afrique du Sud						
1996						
Total	24 560	12 979	11 581	...	...	...
Under 1 day - Moins d'un jour	3 795	2 098	1 697	...	...	...
1-6	4 542	2 427	2 115	...	...	...
7-27	2 415	1 288	1 127	...	...	...
28-364	13 808	7 166	6 642	...	...	...
Tunisia - Tunisie						
1998						
Total	3 098	1 775	1 323	...	...	...
Under 1 day - Moins d'un jour	464	281	183	...	...	...
1-6	847	485	362	...	...	...
7-27	559	332	227	...	...	...
28-364	1 227	677	550	...	...	...
Unknown - Inconnu	1	...	1	...	...	...
AMERICA, NORTH — AMERIQUE DU NORD						
Antigua and Barbuda - Antigua-et-Barbuda[+]						
1995						
Total	23	11	12	...	...	...
Under 1 day - Moins d'un jour	6	3	3	...	...	...
1-6	10	5	5	...	...	...
7-27	3	1	2	...	...	...
28-364	4	2	2	...	...	...
Bahamas[+]						
1996						
Total	74	42	32	...	...	...
0-6	29	19	10	...	...	...

16. Infant deaths and infant mortality rates by age and sex: latest available year
Décès d'enfants de moins d'un an et taux de mortalité infantile selon l'âge et le sexe: dernière année disponible (continued — suite)

(See notes at end of table. — Voir notes à la fin du tableau.)

Continent, country or area, year, age (in days) and urban/rural residence / Continent, pays ou zone, année, âge (en jours) et résidence,urbaine/rurale	Number - Nombre			Rate - Taux		
	Both sexes Les deux sexes	Male Masculin	Female Féminin	Both sexes Les deux sexes	Male Masculin	Female Féminin
AMERICA, NORTH — AMERIQUE DU NORD						
Bahamas+						
1996						
7-27	8	3	5	...	...	...
28-364	37	20	17	...	...	...
Barbados - Barbade+						
1991						
Total	53	40	13	...	...	...
Under 1 day - Moins d'un jour	14	11	3	...	...	...
1-6	8	7	1	...	...	...
7-27	8	8	-	...	...	...
28-364	23	14	9	...	...	...
Belize						
1993						
Total	113	58	55	...	...	...
Under 1 day - Moins d'un jour	18	9	9	...	...	...
1-6	22	15	7	...	...	...
7-27	12	5	7	...	...	...
28-364	51	25	26	...	...	...
Unknown - Inconnu	10	4	6	...	...	...
Bermuda - Bermudes						
1996						
Total	3	1	2	...	...	...
Under 1 day - Moins d'un jour	1	1	-	...	...	...
1-6	1	-	1	...	...	...
7-27	-	-	-	...	...	...
28-364	1	-	1	...	...	...
Canada[2]						
1998						
Total	1 811	1 002	809	5.3	...	...
Under 1 day - Moins d'un jour	707	377	330	2.1	...	...
1-6	335	187	148	1.0	...	...
7-27	221	117	104	0.6	...	...
28-364	548	321	227	1.6	...	...
1999						
Total	1 776	985	791	5.3	5.7	4.8
Under 1 day - Moins d'un jour	740	394	346	2.2	2.3	2.1
1-6	282	160	122	0.8	0.9	0.7
7-27	200	122	78	0.6	0.7	0.5
28-364	624	348	276	1.9	2.0	1.7
2000						
Total	1 737	986	751	5.3	5.9	4.7
Under 1 day - Moins d'un jour	722	412	310	2.2	2.4	1.9
1-6	240	129	111	0.7	0.8	0.7
7-27	231	134	97	0.7	0.8	0.6
28-364	640	363	277	2.0	2.2	1.7
Cayman Islands - Îles Caïmanes						
1996						
Total	6	3	3	...	...	...
Under 1 day - Moins d'un jour	4	1	3	...	...	...
1-6	-	-	-	...	...	...
7-27	-	-	-	...	...	...
28-364	2	2	-	...	...	...
Costa Rica						
1999						
Total	925	535	390	...	...	...
Under 1 day - Moins d'un jour	254	148	106	...	...	...
1-6	245	134	111	...	...	...
7-27	136	79	57	...	...	...
28-364	290	174	116	...	...	...

16. Infant deaths and infant mortality rates by age and sex: latest available year
Décès d'enfants de moins d'un an et taux de mortalité infantile selon l'âge et le sexe: dernière année disponible (continued — suite)

(See notes at end of table. — Voir notes à la fin du tableau.)

Continent, country or area, year, age (in days) and urban/rural residence — Continent, pays ou zone, année, âge (en jours) et résidence,urbaine/rurale	Number - Nombre			Rate - Taux		
	Both sexes Les deux sexes	Male Masculin	Female Féminin	Both sexes Les deux sexes	Male Masculin	Female Féminin
AMERICA, NORTH — AMERIQUE DU NORD						
Cuba						
1999						
Total	977	561	416	...	...	...
Under 1 day - Moins d'un jour	101	44	57	...	...	...
1-6	339	203	136	...	...	...
7-27	157	88	69	...	...	...
28-364	380	226	154	...	...	...
El Salvador						
1999						
Total	1 768	987	781	11.5	12.4	10.5
Under 1 day - Moins d'un jour	189	115	74	1.2	1.4	1.0
1-6	281	166	115	1.8	2.1	1.5
7-27	207	115	92	1.3	1.4	1.2
28-364	1 091	591	500	7.1	7.5	6.7
Greenland - Groenland						
2000						
Total	16	11	5	...	...	...
Under 1 day - Moins d'un jour	7	6	1	...	...	...
1-6	4	3	1	...	...	...
7-27	1	1	-	...	...	...
28-364	4	1	3	...	...	...
Guadeloupe[1]						
1991						
Total	61	36	25	...	...	...
Under 1 day - Moins d'un jour	3	2	1	...	...	...
1-6	21	12	9	...	...	...
7-27	11	6	5	...	...	...
28-364	26	16	10	...	...	...
Guatemala						
1999						
Total	13 161	7 349	5 812	36.5	40.0	32.8
Under 1 day - Moins d'un jour	999	570	429	2.8	3.1	2.4
1-6	2 180	1 286	894	6.0	7.0	5.0
7-27	1 741	949	792	4.8	5.2	4.5
28-364	8 241	4 544	3 697	22.8	24.7	20.9
Martinique[1]						
1992						
Total	40	23	17	...	...	...
Under 1 day - Moins d'un jour	5	3	2	...	...	...
1-6	9	3	6	...	...	...
7-27	8	6	2	...	...	...
28-364	18	11	7	...	...	...
Mexico - Mexique+,3						
2000						
Total	38 621	21 793	16 769	...	...	...
Under 1 day - Moins d'un jour	8 190	4 628	3 527	...	...	...
1-6	18 686	10 840	7 830	...	...	...
7-27	6 273	3 551	2 717	...	...	...
28-364	14 413	7 954	6 450	...	...	...
Unknown - Inconnu	402	240	160	...	...	...
Nicaragua+						
1999						
Total	1 768	1 034	734	...	...	...
Under 1 day - Moins d'un jour	281	154	127	...	...	...
1-6	608	368	240	...	...	...
7-27	226	132	94	...	...	...
28-364	645	375	270	...	...	...
Unknown - Inconnu	8	5	3	...	...	...
Panama						
1999						
Total	1 005	571	434	...	...	...

16. Infant deaths and infant mortality rates by age and sex: latest available year
Décès d'enfants de moins d'un an et taux de mortalité infantile selon l'âge et le sexe: dernière année disponible (continued — suite)

(See notes at end of table. — Voir notes à la fin du tableau.)

Continent, country or area, year, age (in days) and urban/rural residence / Continent, pays ou zone, année, âge (en jours) et résidence,urbaine/rurale	Number - Nombre			Rate - Taux		
	Both sexes Les deux sexes	Male Masculin	Female Féminin	Both sexes Les deux sexes	Male Masculin	Female Féminin
AMERICA, NORTH — AMERIQUE DU NORD						
Panama						
1999						
Under 1 day - Moins d'un jour	147	78	69	...	...	...
1-6	253	145	108	...	...	...
7-27	207	127	80	...	...	...
28-364	398	221	177	...	...	...
Urban - Urbaine						
Total	490	284	206	...	...	...
Under 1 day - Moins d'un jour	88	46	42	...	...	...
1-6	143	86	57	...	...	...
7-27	117	69	48	...	...	...
28-364	142	83	59	...	...	...
Rural - Rurale						
Total	515	287	228	...	...	...
Under 1 day - Moins d'un jour	59	32	27	...	...	...
1-6	110	59	51	...	...	...
7-27	90	58	32	...	...	...
28-364	256	138	118	...	...	...
Puerto Rico - Porto Rico						
2000						
Total	589	328	261	...	...	...
Under 1 day - Moins d'un jour	138	80	58	...	...	...
1-6	166	94	72	...	...	...
7-27	144	88	56	...	...	...
28-364	140	65	75	...	...	...
Unknown - Inconnu	1	1	...	...	...	...
Saint Lucia - Sainte-Lucie						
1998						
Total	48	26	22	...	...	...
Under 1 day - Moins d'un jour	13	11	2	...	...	...
1-6	13	7	6	...	...	...
7-27	7	2	5	...	...	...
28-364	15	6	9	...	...	...
Saint Vincent and the Grenadines - Saint Vincent-et-les Grenadines+						
2000						
Total	35	24	11	...	...	...
Under 1 day - Moins d'un jour	13	9	4	...	...	...
1-6	7	4	3	...	...	...
7-27	2	2	...	...	...	...
28-364	13	9	4	...	...	...
Trinidad and Tobago - Trinité-et-Tobago						
1997						
Total	316	170	146	...	...	...
Under 1 day - Moins d'un jour	76	45	31	...	...	...
1-6	118	62	56	...	...	...
7-27	48	22	26	...	...	...
28-364	74	41	33	...	...	...
United States - États-Unis						
1999						
Total	27 937	15 646	12 291	7.1	7.7	6.4
Under 1 day - Moins d'un jour	11 161	6 116	5 045	2.8	3.0	2.6
1-6	4 007	2 300	1 707	1.0	1.1	0.9
7-27	5 630	2 568	2 135	1.4	1.3	1.1
28-364	9 209	5 291	3 918	2.3	2.6	2.0
2000						
Total	28 035	15 718	12 317	6.9	7.6	6.2
Under 1 day - Moins d'un jour	11 103	6 118	4 985	2.7	2.9	2.5
1-6	3 810	2 243	1 567	0.9	1.1	0.8
7-27	3 863	2 150	1 713	1.0	1.0	0.9
28-364	9 259	5 207	4 052	2.3	2.5	2.0

16. Infant deaths and infant mortality rates by age and sex: latest available year
Décès d'enfants de moins d'un an et taux de mortalité infantile selon l'âge et le sexe: dernière année disponible (continued — suite)

(See notes at end of table. — Voir notes à la fin du tableau.)

Continent, country or area, year, age (in days) and urban/rural residence / Continent, pays ou zone, année, âge (en jours) et résidence,urbaine/rurale	Number - Nombre			Rate - Taux		
	Both sexes Les deux sexes	Male Masculin	Female Féminin	Both sexes Les deux sexes	Male Masculin	Female Féminin
AMERICA, NORTH — AMERIQUE DU NORD						
United States Virgin Islands - Îles Vierges américaines						
1993						
Total	31	18	13	...	...	...
Under 1 day - Moins d'un jour	19	11	8	...	...	...
1-6	6	4	2	...	...	...
7-27	4	1	3	...	...	...
28-364	2	2	-	...	...	...
AMERICA, SOUTH — AMERIQUE DU SUD						
Argentina - Argentine[3]						
1998						
Total	13 082	7 472	5 576	19.1	21.2	16.8
0-6	6 084	3 531	2 546	8.9	10.0	7.7
7-27	1 881	1 073	807	2.8	3.0	2.4
28-364	5 117	2 868	2 223	7.5	8.2	6.7
Brazil - Brésil[4]						
1998						
Total	64 702	36 729	27 973	...	...	...
Under 1 day - Moins d'un jour	14 114	8 042	6 072	...	...	...
1-6	16 159	9 472	6 687	...	...	...
7-27	8 279	4 644	3 635	...	...	...
28-364	26 150	14 571	11 579	...	...	...
Chile - Chili						
1999						
Total	2 654	1 486	1 168	10.6	11.6	9.5
Under 1 day - Moins d'un jour	657	378	279	2.6	2.9	2.3
1-6	520	308	212	2.1	2.4	1.7
7-27	370	195	175	1.5	1.5	1.4
28-364	1 107	605	502	4.4	4.7	4.1
Colombia - Colombie[3]						
1999						
Total	14 621	8 267	6 351	...	...	...
Under 1 day - Moins d'un jour	3 612	2 018	1 592	...	...	...
1-6	3 160	1 886	1 274	...	...	...
7-27	2 314	1 333	981	...	...	...
28-364	5 518	3 016	2 501	...	...	...
Unknown - Inconnu	17	14	3	...	...	...
2000						
Total	14 927	8 412	6 506	...	...	...
Under 1 day - Moins d'un jour	3 595	2 073	1 518	...	...	...
1-6	3 198	1 875	1 323	...	...	...
7-27	2 354	1 331	1 023	...	...	...
28-364	5 749	3 116	2 630	...	...	...
Unknown - Inconnu	31	17	12	...	...	...
Ecuador - Équateur[5]						
1998						
Total	5 186	2 883	2 303	...	...	...
Under 1 day - Moins d'un jour	810	470	340	...	...	...
1-6	992	573	419	...	...	...
7-27	637	359	278	...	...	...
28-364	2 747	1 481	1 266	...	...	...
French Guiana - Guyane française						
1998						
Total	52	33	19	...	...	...
0-6	29	16	13	...	...	...
7-27	6	4	2	...	...	...
28-364	17	13	4	...	...	...

16. Infant deaths and infant mortality rates by age and sex: latest available year
Décès d'enfants de moins d'un an et taux de mortalité infantile selon l'âge et le sexe: dernière année disponible (continued — suite)

(See notes at end of table. — Voir notes à la fin du tableau.)

Continent, country or area, year, age (in days) and urban/rural residence Continent, pays ou zone, année, âge (en jours) et résidence,urbaine/rurale	Number - Nombre			Rate - Taux		
	Both sexes Les deux sexes	Male Masculin	Female Féminin	Both sexes Les deux sexes	Male Masculin	Female Féminin
AMERICA, SOUTH — AMERIQUE DU SUD						
Paraguay						
1992						
Total	758	411	344	...	...	...
0-6	123	66	54	...	...	...
7-27	210	129	81	...	...	...
28-364	425	216	209	...	...	...
Suriname						
1994						
Total	211	...	...	...	...	...
Under 1 day - Moins d'un jour	16	...	...	...	...	...
1-6	85	...	...	...	...	...
7-27	28	...	...	...	...	...
28-364	82	...	...	...	...	...
Uruguay[3]						
1999						
Total	776	436	334	...	...	...
Under 1 day - Moins d'un jour	165	98	63	...	...	...
1-6	151	74	76	...	...	...
7-27	141	84	56	...	...	...
28-364	319	180	139	...	...	...
2000						
Total	742	434	304	...	...	...
Under 1 day - Moins d'un jour	152	87	61	...	...	...
1-6	124	74	50	...	...	...
7-27	142	90	52	...	...	...
28-364	324	183	141	...	...	...
Venezuela[4]						
2000						
Total	8 524	4 919	3 605	15.7	16.9	14.2
0-27	5 255	3 110	2 145	9.7	10.7	8.5
28-364	3 269	1 809	1 460	6.0	6.2	5.8
ASIA — ASIE						
Armenia - Arménie[6]						
1999						
Total	572	343	229	...	...	...
Under 1 day - Moins d'un jour	83	51	32	...	...	...
1-6	199	128	71	...	...	...
7-27	51	36	15	...	...	...
28-364	239	128	111	...	...	...
2000						
Total	540	348	192	...	...	...
Under 1 day - Moins d'un jour	106	69	37	...	...	...
1-6	185	120	65	...	...	...
7-27	34	23	11	...	...	...
28-364	215	136	79	...	...	...
Azerbaijan - Azerbaïdjan+,[6]						
2000						
Total	1 501	846	655	12.8	13.5	12.0
Under 1 day - Moins d'un jour	138	91	47	1.2	1.5	0.9
1-6	207	141	66	1.8	2.3	1.2
7-27	34	21	13	0.3	♦0.3	♦0.2
28-364	1 122	593	529	9.6	9.5	9.7
Bahrain - Bahreïn						
1995						
Total	254	138	116	...	...	...
0-6	186	104	82	...	...	...
7-27	17	7	10	...	...	...
28-364	51	27	24	...	...	...

16. Infant deaths and infant mortality rates by age and sex: latest available year
Décès d'enfants de moins d'un an et taux de mortalité infantile selon l'âge et le sexe: dernière année disponible (continued — suite)

(See notes at end of table. — Voir notes à la fin du tableau.)

Continent, country or area, year, age (in days) and urban/rural residence / Continent, pays ou zone, année, âge (en jours) et résidence,urbaine/rurale	Number - Nombre			Rate - Taux		
	Both sexes Les deux sexes	Male Masculin	Female Féminin	Both sexes Les deux sexes	Male Masculin	Female Féminin
ASIA — ASIE						
Brunei Darussalam - Brunéi Darussalam+						
1992						
Total	70	41	29	...	...	...
Under 1 day - Moins d'un jour	11	8	3	...	...	...
1-6	21	13	8	...	...	...
7-27	17	10	7	...	...	...
28-364	21	10	11	...	...	...
China: Hong Kong SAR - Chine: Hong Kong RAS						
2000						
Total	162	90	72	...	...	...
Under 1 day - Moins d'un jour	18	9	9	...	...	...
1-6	52	31	21	...	...	...
7-27	25	16	9	...	...	...
28-364	67	34	33	...	...	...
China: Macao SAR - Chine: Macao RAS						
2000						
Total	11	6	5	...	...	...
Under 1 day - Moins d'un jour	3	1	2	...	...	...
1-6	4	2	2	...	...	...
7-27	1	-	1	...	...	...
28-364	3	3	-	...	...	...
Georgia - Géorgie						
1999						
Total	714	430	284	...	...	...
Under 1 day - Moins d'un jour	209	121	88	...	...	...
1-6	276	173	103	...	...	...
7-27	72	41	31	...	...	...
28-364	156	95	61	...	...	...
2000						
Total	600	364	236	...	...	...
Under 1 day - Moins d'un jour	163	90	73	...	...	...
1-6	254	167	87	...	...	...
7-27	53	33	20	...	...	...
28-364	130	74	55	...	...	...
2001						
Total	478	301	177	...	...	...
Under 1 day - Moins d'un jour	149	101	48	...	...	...
1-6	183	111	72	...	...	...
7-27	35	16	19	...	...	...
28-364	111	73	38	...	...	...
Israel - Israël[7]						
1998						
Total	773	442	330	...	...	...
Under 1 day - Moins d'un jour	168	106	61	...	...	...
1-6	217	130	87	...	...	...
7-27	131	75	56	...	...	...
28-364	257	131	126	...	...	...
Japan - Japon[8]						
2000						
Total	3 830	2 107	1 723	3.2	3.4	3.0
Under 1 day - Moins d'un jour	900	497	403	0.8	0.8	0.7
1-6	619	342	277	0.5	0.6	0.5
7-27	587	310	277	0.5	0.5	0.5
28-364	1 724	958	766	1.4	1.6	1.3
Kazakhstan[6]						
1999						
Total	4 423	2 600	1 823	20.9	23.7	17.8
Under 1 day - Moins d'un jour	415	237	178	2.0	2.2	1.7
1-6	1 493	924	569	7.0	8.4	5.6
7-27	478	292	186	2.3	2.7	1.8

16. Infant deaths and infant mortality rates by age and sex: latest available year
Décès d'enfants de moins d'un an et taux de mortalité infantile selon l'âge et le sexe: dernière année disponible (continued — suite)

(See notes at end of table. — Voir notes à la fin du tableau.)

Continent, country or area, year, age (in days) and urban/rural residence / Continent, pays ou zone, année, âge (en jours) et résidence, urbaine/rurale	Number - Nombre			Rate - Taux		
	Both sexes Les deux sexes	Male Masculin	Female Féminin	Both sexes Les deux sexes	Male Masculin	Female Féminin
ASIA — ASIE						
Kazakhstan[6]						
1999						
28-364	2 035	1 146	889	9.6	10.5	8.7
Unknown - Inconnu	2	1	1	0.0	0.0	0.0
Kuwait - Koweït						
1999						
Total	386	196	190	...	...	...
Under 1 day - Moins d'un jour	108	60	48	...	...	...
1-6	72	39	33	...	...	...
7-27	61	28	33	...	...	...
28-364	145	69	76	...	...	...
2000						
Total	379	219	160	...	...	...
Under 1 day - Moins d'un jour	111	62	49	...	...	...
1-6	92	53	39	...	...	...
7-27	53	33	20	...	...	...
28-364	123	71	52	...	...	...
Kyrgyzstan - Kirghizistan[6]						
2000						
Total	2 225	1 313	912	23.0	26.5	19.3
Under 1 day - Moins d'un jour	170	98	72	1.8	2.0	1.5
1-6	498	301	197	5.1	6.1	4.2
7-27	234	145	89	2.4	2.9	1.9
28-364	1 323	769	554	13.7	15.5	11.7
Malaysia - Malaisie						
1998						
Total	4 481	2 533	1 948	8.5	9.3	7.7
Under 1 day - Moins d'un jour	689	386	303	1.3	1.4	1.2
1-6	2 116	1 234	882	4.0	4.5	3.5
7-27	636	359	277	1.2	1.3	1.1
28-364	1 040	554	486	2.0	2.0	1.9
Maldives						
1996						
Total	193	112	81	...	...	...
Under 1 day - Moins d'un jour	32	17	15	...	...	...
1-6	66	44	22	...	...	...
7-27	20	8	12	...	...	...
28-364	75	43	32	...	...	...
Myanmar[9]						
1994						
Urban - Urbaine						
Total	12 395	6 685	6 685	...	...	...
Under 1 day - Moins d'un jour	419	228	191	...	...	...
1-6	3 492	1 862	1 630	...	...	...
7-27	2 548	1 308	1 240	...	...	...
28-364	5 764	3 184	2 580	...	...	...
Unknown - Inconnu	172	103	69	...	...	...
Occupied Palestinian Territory - Territoire palestinien occupé						
1999						
Total	1 060	516	544	...	...	...
Under 1 day - Moins d'un jour	53	28	25	...	...	...
1-6	218	135	83	...	...	...
7-27	179	87	92	...	...	...
28-364	612	278	334	...	...	...
2000						
Total	1 025	524	501	...	...	...
Under 1 day - Moins d'un jour	47	24	23	...	...	...
1-6	216	120	96	...	...	...
7-27	230	113	117	...	...	...
28-364	532	272	260	...	...	...

(See notes at end of table. — Voir notes à la fin du tableau.)

Continent, country or area, year, age (in days) and urban/rural residence — Continent, pays ou zone, année, âge (en jours) et résidence,urbaine/rurale	Number - Nombre			Rate - Taux		
	Both sexes Les deux sexes	Male Masculin	Female Féminin	Both sexes Les deux sexes	Male Masculin	Female Féminin
ASIA — ASIE						
Pakistan[10,11]						
1997						
Total	349 744	195 063	154 681	84.4	90.8	77.6
Under 1 day - Moins d'un jour	21 217	14 373	6 844	5.1	6.7	3.4
1-6	141 679	86 239	55 440	34.2	40.1	27.8
7-27	56 123	26 693	29 430	13.5	12.4	14.8
28-364	130 725	67 758	62 967	31.5	31.5	31.6
Philippines						
1997						
Total	28 061	16 455	11 606	17.0	19.1	14.6
Under 1 day - Moins d'un jour	5 262	3 070	2 192	3.2	3.6	2.8
1-6	7 306	4 451	2 855	4.4	5.2	3.6
7-27	3 192	1 848	1 344	1.9	2.1	1.7
28-364	12 301	7 086	5 215	7.4	8.2	6.6
1998						
Total	28 196	16 655	11 541	17.3	19.5	14.8
Under 1 day - Moins d'un jour	5 248	3 050	2 198	3.2	3.6	2.8
1-6	7 130	4 385	2 745	4.4	5.1	3.5
7-27	3 076	1 850	1 226	1.9	2.2	1.6
28-364	12 742	7 370	5 372	7.8	8.6	6.9
Qatar						
1999						
Total	112	58	54	...	...	...
1-6	55	26	29	...	...	...
7-27	19	11	8	...	...	...
28-364	38	21	17	...	...	...
Singapore - Singapour[12]						
1999						
Total	150	78	72	...	...	...
Under 1 day - Moins d'un jour	26	9	17	...	...	...
1-6	32	16	16	...	...	...
7-27	28	16	12	...	...	...
28-364	64	37	27	...	...	...
Sri Lanka+						
1996						
Total	5 879	3 271	2 608	17.3	18.8	15.6
Under 1 day - Moins d'un jour	1 630	899	731	4.8	5.2	4.4
1-6	1 818	1 072	746	5.3	6.2	4.5
7-27	952	526	426	2.8	3.0	2.6
28-364	1 479	774	705	4.3	4.5	4.2
Tajikistan - Tadjikistan[6]						
1994						
Total	6 880	3 896	2 984	42.4	46.4	38.2
Under 1 day - Moins d'un jour	251	153	98	1.5	1.8	1.3
1-6	1 006	617	389	6.2	7.3	5.0
7-27	526	293	233	3.2	3.5	3.0
28-364	5 099	2 827	2 272	31.4	33.6	29.1
Unknown - Inconnu	13	6	7	♦0.1	♦0.1	♦0.1
Thailand - Thaïlande+						
1999						
Total	5 003	2 765	2 238	...	...	...
Under 1 day - Moins d'un jour	287	135	152	...	...	...
1-6	764	439	325	...	...	...
7-27	760	434	326	...	...	...
28-364	3 192	1 757	1 435	...	...	...
Turkey - Turquie						
1997						
Urban - Urbaine						
Total	16 862	9 694	7 168	...	...	...
1-6	9 072	5 367	3 705	...	...	...
7-27	2 178	1 269	909	...	...	...

16. Infant deaths and infant mortality rates by age and sex: latest available year
Décès d'enfants de moins d'un an et taux de mortalité infantile selon l'âge et le sexe: dernière année disponible (continued — suite)

(See notes at end of table. — Voir notes à la fin du tableau.)

Continent, country or area, year, age (in days) and urban/rural residence Continent, pays ou zone, année, âge (en jours) et résidence,urbaine/rurale	Number - Nombre			Rate - Taux		
	Both sexes Les deux sexes	Male Masculin	Female Féminin	Both sexes Les deux sexes	Male Masculin	Female Féminin
ASIA — ASIE						
Turkey - Turquie						
1997						
Urban - Urbaine						
28-364	5 606	3 057	2 549	...	...	...
Unknown - Inconnu	6	1	5	...	...	...
1998						
Urban - Urbaine						
Total	17 704	10 181	7 523	...	...	...
1-6	8 532	5 683	3 702	...	...	...
7-27	2 236	1 272	968	...	...	...
28-364	5 707	3 151	2 575	...	...	...
Uzbekistan - Ouzbékistan[6]						
2000						
Total	10 091	5 805	4 286	19.1	21.4	16.7
Under 1 day - Moins d'un jour	607	355	252	1.2	1.3	1.0
1-6	2 179	1 352	827	4.1	5.0	3.2
7-27	1 279	731	548	2.4	2.7	2.1
28-364	6 026	3 367	2 659	11.4	12.4	10.4
EUROPE						
Albania - Albanie						
1991						
Total	2 547	...	...	32.9	...	...
Under 1 day - Moins d'un jour	87	...	...	1.1	...	...
1-6	394	...	...	5.1	...	...
7-27	299	...	...	3.9	...	...
28-364	1 767	...	...	22.8	...	...
Austria - Autriche						
2000						
Total	378	216	162	...	...	...
Under 1 day - Moins d'un jour	145	83	62	...	...	...
1-6	50	31	19	...	...	...
7-27	60	33	27	...	...	...
28-364	123	69	54	...	...	...
2001						
Total	365	230	135	...	...	...
Under 1 day - Moins d'un jour	143	89	54	...	...	...
1-6	50	31	19	...	...	...
7-27	57	41	16	...	...	...
28-364	115	69	46	...	...	...
Belarus - Bélarus[6]						
1999						
Total	1 064	645	419	11.4	13.5	9.3
Under 1 day - Moins d'un jour	106	67	39	1.1	1.4	0.9
1-6	245	154	91	2.6	3.2	2.0
7-27	191	118	73	2.1	2.5	1.6
28-364	522	306	216	5.6	6.4	4.8
Belgium - Belgique						
1999						
Total	556	...	...	...	...	...
0-6	268	...	...	...	...	...
7-27	84	...	...	...	...	...
28-364	204	...	...	...	...	...
2000						
Total	554	305	249	...	...	...
Under 1 day - Moins d'un jour	91	46	45	...	...	...
1-6	153	85	68	...	...	...
7-27	90	56	34	...	...	...
28-364	220	118	102	...	...	...

(See notes at end of table. — Voir notes à la fin du tableau.)

Continent, country or area, year, age (in days) and urban/rural residence / Continent, pays ou zone, année, âge (en jours) et résidence,urbaine/rurale	Number - Nombre			Rate - Taux		
	Both sexes Les deux sexes	Male Masculin	Female Féminin	Both sexes Les deux sexes	Male Masculin	Female Féminin
EUROPE						
Bosnia and Herzegovina - Bosnie-Herzégovine						
1990						
Total	1 022	578	444	15.3	16.7	13.7
Under 1 day - Moins d'un jour	234	129	105	3.5	3.7	3.2
1-6	361	215	146	5.4	6.2	4.5
7-27	114	66	48	1.7	1.9	1.5
28-364	313	168	145	4.7	4.9	4.5
Bulgaria - Bulgarie						
1999						
Total	1 057	...	...	14.6	...	...
0-6	403	...	...	5.6	...	...
7-27	197	...	...	2.7	...	...
28-364	457	...	...	6.3	...	...
2000						
Total	981	550	431	...	...	...
Under 1 day - Moins d'un jour	130	72	58	...	...	...
1-6	218	130	88	...	...	...
7-27	201	108	93	...	...	...
28-364	432	240	192	...	...	...
2001						
Total	982	548	434	...	...	...
Under 1 day - Moins d'un jour	137	77	60	...	...	...
1-6	209	132	77	...	...	...
7-27	184	102	82	...	...	...
28-364	452	237	215	...	...	...
Channel Islands: Guernsey - Îles Anglo-Normandes: Guernesey						
1995						
Total	2	...	...	...	...	...
Under 1 day - Moins d'un jour	-	...	...	...	...	...
1-6	-	...	...	...	...	...
7-27	1	...	...	...	...	...
28-364	1	...	...	...	...	...
Channel Islands: Jersey - Îles Anglo-Normandes: Jersey+						
1994						
Total	2	-	2	...	...	...
Under 1 day - Moins d'un jour	-	-	-	...	...	...
1-6	1	-	1	...	...	...
7-27	-	-	-	...	...	...
28-364	1	-	1	...	...	...
Croatia - Croatie						
2000						
Total	324	173	151	...	...	...
Under 1 day - Moins d'un jour	88	38	50	...	...	...
1-6	95	55	40	...	...	...
7-27	64	33	31	...	...	...
28-364	77	47	30	...	...	...
2001						
Total	315	167	148	...	...	...
Under 1 day - Moins d'un jour	86	42	44	...	...	...
1-6	100	59	41	...	...	...
7-27	41	23	18	...	...	...
28-364	88	43	45	...	...	...
Czech Republic - République tchèque						
2000						
Total	373	218	155	...	...	...
Under 1 day - Moins d'un jour	48	30	18	...	...	...
1-6	102	58	44	...	...	...
7-27	81	41	40	...	...	...
28-364	142	89	53	...	...	...

16. Infant deaths and infant mortality rates by age and sex: latest available year
Décès d'enfants de moins d'un an et taux de mortalité infantile selon l'âge et le sexe: dernière année disponible (continued — suite)

(See notes at end of table. — Voir notes à la fin du tableau.)

Continent, country or area, year, age (in days) and urban/rural residence / Continent, pays ou zone, année, âge (en jours) et résidence,urbaine/rurale	Number - Nombre			Rate - Taux		
	Both sexes Les deux sexes	Male Masculin	Female Féminin	Both sexes Les deux sexes	Male Masculin	Female Féminin
EUROPE						
Czech Republic - République tchèque						
2001						
Total	360	212	148	...	...	...
Under 1 day - Moins d'un jour	47	25	22	...	...	...
1-6	85	48	37	...	...	...
7-27	80	47	33	...	...	...
28-364	148	92	56	...	...	...
Denmark - Danemark[13]						
2001						
Total	320	...	...	...	...	...
0-6	171	...	...	...	...	...
7-27	56	...	...	...	...	...
28-364	93	...	...	...	...	...
Estonia - Estonie[6]						
1999						
Total	119	...	...	...	...	...
0-6	51	...	...	...	...	...
7-27	24	...	...	...	...	...
28-364	44	...	...	...	...	...
2000						
Total	110	65	45	...	...	...
Under 1 day - Moins d'un jour	19	9	10	...	...	...
0-6	50	...	...	...	...	...
1-6	31	24	7	...	...	...
7-27	52	14	12	...	...	...
28-364	68	18	16	...	...	...
Faeroe Islands - Îles Féroé						
1990						
Total	6	2	4	...	...	...
Under 1 day - Moins d'un jour	1	1	-	...	...	...
1-6	2	-	2	...	...	...
7-27	1	-	1	...	...	...
28-364	2	1	1	...	...	...
Finland - Finlande[14]						
2000						
Total	213	124	89	...	...	...
Under 1 day - Moins d'un jour	60	36	24	...	...	...
1-6	41	21	20	...	...	...
7-27	40	22	18	...	...	...
28-364	72	45	27	...	...	...
2001						
Total	181	118	63	...	...	...
Under 1 day - Moins d'un jour	61	42	19	...	...	...
1-6	37	25	12	...	...	...
7-27	24	13	11	...	...	...
28-364	59	38	21	...	...	...
France						
1998						
Total	3 399	1 911	1 488	4.6	5.1	4.1
Under 1 day - Moins d'un jour	733	386	347	1.0	1.0	1.0
1-6	783	444	339	1.1	1.2	0.9
7-27	631	362	269	0.9	1.0	0.7
28-364	1 252	719	533	1.7	1.9	1.5
1999						
Total	3 221	1 844	1 377	4.3	4.8	3.8
Under 1 day - Moins d'un jour	697	380	317	0.9	1.0	0.9
1-6	760	441	319	1.0	1.2	0.9
7-27	588	325	263	0.8	0.9	0.7
28-364	1 176	698	478	1.6	1.8	1.3

16. Infant deaths and infant mortality rates by age and sex: latest available year
Décès d'enfants de moins d'un an et taux de mortalité infantile selon l'âge et le sexe: dernière année
disponible (continued — suite)

(See notes at end of table. — Voir notes à la fin du tableau.)

Continent, country or area, year, age (in days) and urban/rural residence / Continent, pays ou zone, année, âge (en jours) et résidence,urbaine/rurale	Number - Nombre			Rate - Taux		
	Both sexes Les deux sexes	Male Masculin	Female Féminin	Both sexes Les deux sexes	Male Masculin	Female Féminin
EUROPE						
Germany - Allemagne						
1999						
Total	3 496	...	...	4.5	...	...
0-6	1 685	...	...	2.2	...	...
7-27	523	...	...	0.7	...	...
28-364	1 288	...	...	1.7	...	...
2000						
Total	3 362	...	...	4.4	...	...
0-6	1 594	...	...	2.1	...	...
7-27	498	...	...	0.6	...	...
28-364	1 270	...	...	1.7	...	...
Greece - Grèce						
1999						
Total	619	...	...	...	...	...
0-6	300	...	...	...	...	...
7-27	140	...	...	...	...	...
28-364	179	...	...	...	...	...
2000						
Total	610	...	...	...	...	...
0-6	296	...	...	...	...	...
7-27	136	...	...	...	...	...
28-364	178	...	...	...	...	...
2001						
Total	522	...	...	...	...	...
0-6	235	...	...	...	...	...
7-27	129	...	...	...	...	...
28-364	158	...	...	...	...	...
Hungary - Hongrie						
2000						
Total	900	492	408	...	...	...
Under 1 day - Moins d'un jour	225	133	92	...	...	...
1-6	222	120	102	...	...	...
7-27	155	90	65	...	...	...
28-364	298	149	149	...	...	...
2001						
Total	789	435	354	...	...	...
Under 1 day - Moins d'un jour	171	106	65	...	...	...
1-6	210	119	91	...	...	...
7-27	134	74	60	...	...	...
28-364	274	136	138	...	...	...
Iceland - Islande						
1999						
Total	10	...	...	...	...	...
0-6	5	...	...	...	...	...
7-27	1	...	...	...	...	...
28-364	4	...	...	...	...	...
2000						
Total	13	10	3	...	...	...
Under 1 day - Moins d'un jour	6	5	1	...	...	...
0-6	8	...	...	...	...	...
1-6	2	2	...	...	...	...
7-27	6	1	2	...	...	...
28-364	4	2	...	...	...	...
2001						
Total	11	...	...	...	...	...
0-6	7	...	...	...	...	...
7-27	-	...	...	...	...	...
28-364	4	...	...	...	...	...
Ireland - Irlande[+,15]						
2000						
Total	322	...	...	...	...	...

16. Infant deaths and infant mortality rates by age and sex: latest available year
Décès d'enfants de moins d'un an et taux de mortalité infantile selon l'âge et le sexe: dernière année disponible (continued — suite)

(See notes at end of table. — Voir notes à la fin du tableau.)

Continent, country or area, year, age (in days) and urban/rural residence / Continent, pays ou zone, année, âge (en jours) et résidence,urbaine/rurale	Number - Nombre			Rate - Taux		
	Both sexes Les deux sexes	Male Masculin	Female Féminin	Both sexes Les deux sexes	Male Masculin	Female Féminin
EUROPE						
Ireland - Irlande+,15						
2000						
0-6	160	...	...	...	...	...
7-27	58	...	...	...	...	...
28-364	104	...	...	...	...	...
2001						
Total	337	...	...	...	...	...
0-6	180	...	...	...	...	...
7-27	55	...	...	...	...	...
28-364	102	...	...	...	...	...
Isle of Man - Îles de Man+						
1996						
Total	2	1	1	...	...	...
Under 1 day - Moins d'un jour	1	-	1	...	...	...
1-6	1	1	-	...	...	...
7-27	-	-	-	...	...	...
28-364	-	-	-	...	...	...
Italy - Italie						
1997						
Total	2 973	1 638	1 335	5.6	5.9	5.2
Under 1 day - Moins d'un jour	842	449	393	1.6	1.6	1.5
1-6	822	471	351	1.5	1.7	1.4
7-27	598	329	269	1.1	1.2	1.0
28-364	711	389	322	1.3	1.4	1.2
Latvia - Lettonie6						
2000						
Total	210	122	88	...	...	...
Under 1 day - Moins d'un jour	20	9	11	...	...	...
1-6	71	45	26	...	...	...
7-27	41	25	16	...	...	...
28-364	78	43	35	...	...	...
2001						
Total	217	115	102	...	...	...
Under 1 day - Moins d'un jour	29	14	15	...	...	...
1-6	74	41	33	...	...	...
7-27	40	20	20	...	...	...
28-364	74	40	34	...	...	...
Lithuania - Lituanie6						
2000						
Total	294	147	147	...	...	...
Under 1 day - Moins d'un jour	44	26	18	...	...	...
1-6	73	33	40	...	...	...
7-27	47	26	21	...	...	...
28-364	130	62	68	...	...	...
2001						
Total	250	158	92	...	...	...
Under 1 day - Moins d'un jour	41	27	14	...	...	...
1-6	48	30	18	...	...	...
7-27	42	30	12	...	...	...
28-364	119	71	48	...	...	...
Luxembourg						
2001						
Total	32	18	14	...	...	...
Under 1 day - Moins d'un jour	3	2	1	...	...	...
1-6	11	6	5	...	...	...
7-27	4	3	1	...	...	...
28-364	14	7	7	...	...	...
Malta - Malte						
1999						
Total	31	18	13	...	...	...
7-27	21	11	10	...	...	...

16. Infant deaths and infant mortality rates by age and sex: latest available year
Décès d'enfants de moins d'un an et taux de mortalité infantile selon l'âge et le sexe: dernière année disponible (continued — suite)

(See notes at end of table. — Voir notes à la fin du tableau.)

Continent, country or area, year, age (in days) and urban/rural residence / Continent, pays ou zone, année, âge (en jours) et résidence, urbaine/rurale	Number - Nombre			Rate - Taux		
	Both sexes Les deux sexes	Male Masculin	Female Féminin	Both sexes Les deux sexes	Male Masculin	Female Féminin
EUROPE						
Malta - Malte						
1999						
28-364	10	7	3	...	...	...
2000						
Total	26	13	13	...	...	...
7-27	16	9	7	...	...	...
28-364	10	4	6	...	...	...
Netherlands - Pays-Bas[16]						
2000						
Total	1 059	582	477	5.1	5.5	4.7
Under 1 day - Moins d'un jour	317	173	144	1.5	1.6	1.4
1-6	306	178	128	1.5	1.7	1.3
7-27	179	87	92	0.9	0.8	0.9
28-364	257	144	113	1.2	1.4	1.1
2001						
Total	1 088	615	473	5.4	5.9	4.8
Under 1 day - Moins d'un jour	332	200	132	1.6	1.9	1.3
1-6	284	155	129	1.4	1.5	1.3
7-27	168	86	82	0.8	0.8	0.8
28-364	304	174	130	1.5	1.7	1.3
Norway - Norvège[17]						
2000						
Total	225	130	95	...	...	...
Under 1 day - Moins d'un jour	61	34	27	...	...	...
1-6	63	38	25	...	...	...
7-27	31	21	10	...	...	...
28-364	70	37	33	...	...	...
2001						
Total	223	126	97	...	...	...
Under 1 day - Moins d'un jour	68	35	33	...	...	...
1-6	60	34	26	...	...	...
7-27	33	22	11	...	...	...
28-364	73	43	32	...	...	...
Poland - Pologne						
2000						
Total	3 068	...	...	8.1	...	...
0-6	1 565	...	...	4.1	...	...
7-27	551	...	...	1.5	...	...
28-364	952	...	...	2.5	...	...
2001						
Total	2 823	...	...	7.7	...	...
0-6	1 439	...	...	3.9	...	...
7-27	535	...	...	1.5	...	...
28-364	849	...	...	2.3	...	...
Portugal						
2001						
Total	567	333	234	...	...	...
Under 1 day - Moins d'un jour	140	80	60	...	...	...
1-6	100	55	45	...	...	...
7-27	92	58	34	...	...	...
28-364	235	140	95	...	...	...
Republic of Moldova - République de Moldova[6]						
2000						
Total	681	412	269	...	...	...
Under 1 day - Moins d'un jour	83	53	30	...	...	...
1-6	229	141	88	...	...	...
7-27	83	48	35	...	...	...
28-364	286	170	116	...	...	...
2001						
Total	597	334	263	...	...	...
Under 1 day - Moins d'un jour	76	48	28	...	...	...

16. Infant deaths and infant mortality rates by age and sex: latest available year
Décès d'enfants de moins d'un an et taux de mortalité infantile selon l'âge et le sexe: dernière année disponible (continued — suite)

(See notes at end of table. — Voir notes à la fin du tableau.)

Continent, country or area, year, age (in days) and urban/rural residence Continent, pays ou zone, année, âge (en jours) et résidence,urbaine/rurale	Number - Nombre			Rate - Taux		
	Both sexes Les deux sexes	Male Masculin	Female Féminin	Both sexes Les deux sexes	Male Masculin	Female Féminin
EUROPE						
Republic of Moldova - République de Moldova[6]						
2001						
1-6	178	83	95	...	...	...
7-27	61	35	26	...	...	...
28-364	385	230	155	...	...	...
Unknown - Inconnu	28	20	8	...	...	...
Romania - Roumanie						
2000						
Total	4 370	2 485	1 885	18.6	20.6	16.6
Under 1 day - Moins d'un jour	306	168	138	1.3	1.4	1.2
1-6	1 151	703	448	4.9	5.8	3.9
7-27	695	416	279	3.0	3.4	2.5
28-364	2 218	1 198	1 020	9.5	9.9	9.0
2001						
Total	4 057	2 328	1 729	18.4	20.5	16.2
Under 1 day - Moins d'un jour	266	158	108	1.2	1.4	1.0
1-6	1 082	657	425	4.9	5.8	4.0
7-27	682	377	305	3.1	3.3	2.9
28-364	2 027	1 136	891	9.2	10.0	8.3
Russian Federation - Fédération de Russie[6]						
1999						
Total	20 731	12 020	8 711	17.1	19.2	14.8
Under 1 day - Moins d'un jour	2 581	1 485	1 096	2.1	2.4	1.9
1-6	5 976	3 659	2 317	4.9	5.8	3.9
7-27	3 306	1 905	1 401	2.7	3.0	2.4
28-364	8 842	4 956	3 886	7.3	7.9	6.6
Unknown - Inconnu	26	15	11	0.0	0.0	0.0
San Marino - Saint-Marin+						
1998						
Total	4	2	2	...	...	...
1-6	1	-	1	...	...	...
7-27	-	-	-	...	...	...
28-364	3	2	1	...	...	...
1999						
Total	1	1	-	...	...	...
Under 1 day - Moins d'un jour	1	1	-	...	...	...
1-6	-	-	-	...	...	...
7-27	-	-	-	...	...	...
28-364	-	-	-	...	...	...
Serbia and Montenegro - Serbie-et-Montenegro						
2000						
Total	1 668	993	675	13.3	15.2	11.2
Under 1 day - Moins d'un jour	316	199	117	2.5	3.0	1.9
1-6	571	351	220	4.5	5.4	3.6
7-27	221	132	89	1.8	2.0	1.5
28-364	560	311	249	4.4	4.8	4.1
Slovakia - Slovaquie						
2001						
Total	319	185	134	...	...	...
Under 1 day - Moins d'un jour	69	39	30	...	...	...
1-6	94	52	42	...	...	...
7-27	48	34	14	...	...	...
28-364	104	59	45	...	...	...
Unknown - Inconnu	4	1	3	...	...	...
Slovenia - Slovénie						
2000						
Total	89	52	37	...	...	...
Under 1 day - Moins d'un jour	31	19	12	...	...	...
1-6	26	13	13	...	...	...
7-27	8	7	1	...	...	...
28-364	24	13	11	...	...	...

16. Infant deaths and infant mortality rates by age and sex: latest available year
Décès d'enfants de moins d'un an et taux de mortalité infantile selon l'âge et le sexe: dernière année
disponible (continued — suite)

(See notes at end of table. — Voir notes à la fin du tableau.)

Continent, country or area, year, age (in days) and urban/rural residence Continent, pays ou zone, année, âge (en jours) et résidence,urbaine/rurale	Number - Nombre			Rate - Taux		
	Both sexes Les deux sexes	Male Masculin	Female Féminin	Both sexes Les deux sexes	Male Masculin	Female Féminin
EUROPE						
Slovenia - Slovénie						
2001						
Total	74	44	30	...	...	...
Under 1 day - Moins d'un jour	27	19	8	...	...	...
1-6	15	8	7	...	...	...
7-27	10	4	6	...	...	...
28-364	22	13	9	...	...	...
Spain - Espagne						
1998						
Total	1 774	991	783	4.9	5.2	4.4
Under 1 day - Moins d'un jour	380	210	170	1.0	1.1	1.0
1-6	361	206	155	1.0	1.1	0.9
7-27	345	195	150	0.9	1.0	0.9
28-364	688	380	308	1.9	2.0	1.7
1999						
Total	1 700	...	...	4.5	...	...
0-6	703	...	...	1.8	...	...
7-27	368	...	...	1.0	...	...
28-364	629	...	...	1.7	...	...
Sweden - Suède						
2001						
Total	334	189	145	...	...	...
Under 1 day - Moins d'un jour	84	47	37	...	...	...
1-6	92	57	35	...	...	...
7-27	53	27	26	...	...	...
28-364	105	58	47	...	...	...
Switzerland - Suisse						
1999						
Total	361	215	146	...	...	...
Under 1 day - Moins d'un jour	131	82	49	...	...	...
1-6	100	59	41	...	...	...
7-27	38	18	20	...	...	...
28-364	92	56	36	...	...	...
2000						
Total	386	217	169	...	...	...
Under 1 day - Moins d'un jour	124	70	54	...	...	...
1-6	106	61	45	...	...	...
7-27	52	27	25	...	...	...
28-364	104	59	45	...	...	...
2001						
Total	365	209	156	...	...	...
Under 1 day - Moins d'un jour	127	72	55	...	...	...
1-6	102	53	49	...	...	...
7-27	33	21	12	...	...	...
28-364	101	61	40	...	...	...
The Former Yugoslav Rep. of Macedonia - **L'ex-République yougoslave de Macédoine**						
2000						
Total	346	190	156	...	...	...
Under 1 day - Moins d'un jour	103	54	49	...	...	...
1-6	99	55	44	...	...	...
7-27	49	28	21	...	...	...
28-364	95	53	42	...	...	...
2001						
Total	321	194	127	...	...	...
Under 1 day - Moins d'un jour	83	55	28	...	...	...
1-6	80	46	34	...	...	...
7-27	62	41	21	...	...	...
28-364	96	52	44	...	...	...

16. Infant deaths and infant mortality rates by age and sex: latest available year
Décès d'enfants de moins d'un an et taux de mortalité infantile selon l'âge et le sexe: dernière année disponible (continued — suite)

(See notes at end of table. — Voir notes à la fin du tableau.)

Continent, country or area, year, age (in days) and urban/rural residence / Continent, pays ou zone, année, âge (en jours) et résidence, urbaine/rurale	Number - Nombre			Rate - Taux		
	Both sexes Les deux sexes	Male Masculin	Female Féminin	Both sexes Les deux sexes	Male Masculin	Female Féminin
EUROPE						
Ukraine[6]						
2001						
Total	4 283	2 488	1 795	11.4	12.8	9.8
Under 1 day - Moins d'un jour	368	219	149	1.0	1.1	0.8
1-6	1 252	743	509	3.3	3.8	2.8
7-27	684	403	281	1.8	2.1	1.5
28-364	1 976	1 122	854	5.2	5.8	4.7
Unknown - Inconnu	3	1	2	0.0	0.0	0.0
United Kingdom - Royaume-Uni						
2000						
Total	3 791	2 120	1 671	5.6	6.1	5.0
Under 1 day - Moins d'un jour	1 006	562	444	1.5	1.6	1.3
1-6	961	541	420	1.4	1.6	1.3
7-27	662	365	297	1.0	1.0	0.9
28-364	1 159	652	510	1.7	1.9	1.5
2001						
Total	3 664	2 042	1 622	5.5	...	...
Under 1 day - Moins d'un jour	1 006	567	439	1.5	...	...
1-6	815	457	358	1.2	...	...
7-27	613	347	266	0.9	...	...
28-364	1 230	671	559	1.8	...	...
OCEANIA — OCEANIE						
Australia - Australie+						
2000						
Total	1 290	725	565	5.2	5.7	4.7
Under 1 day - Moins d'un jour	509	282	227	2.0	2.2	1.9
1-6	188	104	84	0.8	0.8	0.7
7-27	165	102	63	0.7	0.8	0.5
28-364	424	235	189	1.7	1.8	1.6
Unknown - Inconnu	4	1	3	0.0	0.0	0.0
Guam[18]						
1992						
Total	41	28	13	...	...	...
Under 1 day - Moins d'un jour	12	7	5	...	...	...
1-6	2	2	-	...	...	...
7-27	3	3	-	...	...	...
28-364	24	16	8	...	...	...
New Caledonia - Nouvelle-Calédonie						
1997						
Total	24	16	8	...	...	...
Under 1 day - Moins d'un jour	4	1	3	...	...	...
1-6	5	4	1	...	...	...
7-27	6	2	4	...	...	...
28-364	9	9	...	...	...	...
1998						
Total	30	14	16	...	...	...
Under 1 day - Moins d'un jour	5	4	1	...	...	...
1-6	4	1	3	...	...	...
7-27	1	...	1	...	...	...
28-364	20	9	11	...	...	...
1999						
Total	27	12	15	...	...	...
Under 1 day - Moins d'un jour	5	2	3	...	...	...
1-6	5	2	3	...	...	...
7-27	3	1	2	...	...	...
28-364	14	7	7	...	...	...
New Zealand - Nouvelle-Zélande+						
2000						
Total	346	190	156	...	...	...

16. Infant deaths and infant mortality rates by age and sex: latest available year
Décès d'enfants de moins d'un an et taux de mortalité infantile selon l'âge et le sexe: dernière année disponible (continued — suite)

(See notes at end of table. — Voir notes à la fin du tableau.)

Continent, country or area, year, age (in days) and urban/rural residence / Continent, pays ou zone, année, âge (en jours) et résidence,urbaine/rurale	Number - Nombre			Rate - Taux		
	Both sexes Les deux sexes	Male Masculin	Female Féminin	Both sexes Les deux sexes	Male Masculin	Female Féminin
OCEANIA — OCEANIE						
New Zealand - Nouvelle-Zélande+						
2000						
Under 1 day - Moins d'un jour	99	53	46	...	...	...
1-6	64	35	29	...	...	...
7-27	39	17	22	...	...	...
28-364	144	85	59	...	...	...
Tonga+						
1997						
Total	20	...	...	...	...	...
Under 1 day - Moins d'un jour	4	...	...	...	...	...
1-6	2	...	...	...	...	...
7-27	2	...	...	...	...	...
28-364	12	...	...	...	...	...

GENERAL NOTES - NOTES GENERALES

Data exclude foetal deaths. Rates are the number of deaths of infants of specified age by sex per 1 000 live births of same sex. Rates are shown only for countries having at least a total of 1 000 infant deaths in a given year. For definition of 'urban', see Technical Notes for table 6. For method of evaluation and limitations of data, see Technical Notes for this table. — Les données ne comprennent pas les morts foetales. Les taux représent le nombre de décès d'enfants d'âge et de sexe données pour 1 000 naissances vivantes du même sexe. Les taux présentés ne se rapportent qu'aux pays ou zones où l'on a enregistré un total d'au moins 1 000 décès d'un an dans un année donnée. Pour les définitions des 'regions urbaines', se reporter à la fin des Notes techniques du tableau 6. Pour la méthode d'évaluation et les insuffisances des données voir, Notes techniques pour ce tableau.

Italics: data from civil registers which are incomplete or of unknown completeness. — *Italiques:* données incomplètes ou dont le degré d'exactitude n'est pas connu provenant des registres de l'état civil.

FOOTNOTES - NOTES

+ Data tabulated by date of registration rather than occurrence. — Données exploitées selon la date de l'enregistrement et non la date de l'événement.

♦ Rates based on 30 or fewer infant deaths. — Taux basés sur 30 décès d'enfants ou moins.

[1] Excluding live-born infants dying before registration of birth. — Non compris les enfants nés vivants décédés avant l'enregistrement de leur naissance.

[2] Including Canadian residents temporarily in the United States, but excluding United States residents temporarily in Canada. — Y compris les résidents canadiens se trouvant temporairement aux Etats-Unis, mais ne comprennent pas les résidents des Etats-Unis se trouvant temporairement au Canada.

[3] The category 'Both sexes' includes infant deaths of unknown sex. — La catégorie 'Les deux sexes' comprenne les décès d'enfants de moins d'un an dont on ignore le sexe.

[4] Excluding Indian jungle population. — Non compris les Indiens de la jungle.

[5] Excluding nomadic Indian tribes. — Non compris les tribus d'Indiens nomades.

[6] Excluding infants born alive with less than 28 weeks gestation, less than 1 000 grams in weight and 35 centimeters in length, who die within seven days of birth. — Non compris les enfants nés vivants avant 28 semaines de gestation, pesant moins de 1 000 grammes, mesurant moins de 35 centimètres et décédés dans les sept jours qui ont suivi leur naissance.

[7] Including data for East Jerusalem and Israeli residents in certain other territories under occupation by Israeli military forces since June 1967. — Y compris les données pour Jérusalem-Est et les résidents israéliens dans certains autres territoires occupés depuis 1967 par les forces armées israéliennes.

[8] For Japanese nationals in Japan only. — Pour les nationaux japonais au Japon seulement.

[9] Data for urban refer to only 170 towns out of 254 towns. — Les données urbaines se rapportent à 170 des 254 villes seulement.

[10] Based on the results of the Population Growth Survey. — D'après les résultats de la 'Population Growth Survey.'

[11] Excluding data for the Pakistan-held part of Jammu and Kashmir, the final status of which has not yet been determined. — Non compris les données concernant la partie du Jammu et Cachemire occupée par le Pakistan dont le statut définitif n'a pas été déterminé.

[12] Excluding non-locally domiciled military and civilian services personnel and their dependants. — Non compris les militaires et agents civils non-résidents et les membres de leur famille les accompagnant.

[13] Excluding Faeroe Islands and Greenland. — Non compris les îles Féroé et Gröenland.

[14] Including nationals temporarily outside the country. — Y compris les nationaux se trouvant temporairement hors du pays.

[15] Events registered within one year of occurrence. — Evénements enregistrés dans l'année qui suit l'événement.

[16] Including residents outside the country if listed in a Netherlands population register. — Y compris les résidents hors du pays, s'ils sont inscrits sur un registre de population néerlandais.

[17] Including residents temporarily outside the country. — Y compris les résidents se trouvant temporairement hors du pays.

[18] Including United States military personnel, their dependants and contract employees. — Y compris les militaires des Etats-Unis, les membres de leur famille les accompagnant et les agents contractuels des Etats-Unis.

Table 17

Table 17 presents maternal deaths and maternal mortality rates for as many years as possible between 1991 and 2000.

Description of variables: Maternal deaths are defined for the purposes of the *Demographic Yearbook* as those caused by deliveries and complications of pregnancy, childbirth and the puerperium.

For further information on the definition of maternal mortality from the ninth and tenth revisions of the *International Statistical Classification of Diseases and Related Health Problems*[1], see section 4.3 of the Technical Notes.

Statistics on maternal death presented in this table have been limited to countries or areas which meet the following three criteria: first, that cause-of-death statistics are either classified by or convertible to the ninth or tenth lists mentioned above; secondly, that at least a total of 1 000 deaths (for all causes combined) occurred in a given year; and thirdly, that within this distribution the total number of deaths classified as due to ill-defined causes as shown in the table in section 4.3 does not exceed 25 per cent of deaths from all causes.

Rate computation: Maternal mortality rates are the annual number of maternal deaths per 100 000 live births (table 9) in the same year.

These rates have been calculated by the Statistics Division of the United Nations. Rates based on 30 or fewer maternal deaths are identified by the symbol (♦).

Reliability of data: Data from civil registers of deaths which are reported as incomplete (less than 90 per cent completeness) or of unknown completeness are considered unreliable and are set in italics rather than in roman type. Rates on these data are not computed. Table 18 and the technical notes for that table provide more detailed information on the completeness of death registration. For more information about the quality of vital statistics data in general, and the information available on the basis of estimates of the completeness, in particular, see section 4.2 of the Technical Notes.

In general the quality code for deaths shown in table 18 is used to determine whether data on deaths in other tables should appear in roman or *italic* type. However, some data on deaths by cause are shown in *italics* in this table when it is known that registration of cause of death is not as complete as of the total number of deaths. In cases when the quality code in table 18 does not correspond with the typeface used in this table, relevant information regarding the completeness of cause-of-death statistics is given in a footnote.

Limitations: Statistics on maternal deaths are subject to the same qualifications that have been set forth for vital statistics in general and death statistics in particular as discussed in section 4 of the Technical Notes.

The reliability of the data, an indication of which is described above, is an important factor in considering the limitations. In addition, some deaths are tabulated by date of registration and not by date of occurrence; these have been indicated by a plus sign (+). Whenever the lag between the date of occurrence and the date of registration is prolonged and a large proportion of the death registrations are, therefore, delayed, death statistics for any given year may be seriously affected.

In addition, maternal-death statistics are subject to all the qualifications relating to cause-of-death statistics. These have been set forth in section 4 of the Technical Notes.

Maternal mortality rates are subject to the limitations of the data on live births with which they have been calculated. These have been set forth in the technical notes for table 9.

The calculation of the maternal mortality rates based on the total number of live births approximates the risk of dying from complications of pregnancy, childbirth or puerperium. Ideally this rate should be based on the number of women exposed to the risk of pregnancy, in other words, the number of women conceiving. Since it is impossible to know how many women have conceived, the total number of live births is used in calculating this rate.

Coverage: Maternal deaths are shown for 76 countries or areas and maternal mortality rates are shown for 76 countries or areas.

Earlier data: Maternal deaths and maternal mortality rates have been shown in previous issues of the *Demographic Yearbook*. For information on specific years covered, the reader should consult the Index.

It should however be noted that in issues prior to 1975, maternal mortality rates were calculated using the female population rather than live births. Therefore maternal mortality rates published since 1975 are not comparable to the earlier maternal death rates.

---

[1] *The International Statistical Classification of Diseases and Related Health Problems,* World Health Organization, Geneva.

Tableau 17

Ce tableau présente des statistiques et des taux de mortalité liée à la maternité pour le plus grand nombre d'années possible entre 1991 et 2000.

Description des variables : Aux fins de *l'Annuaire démographique*, les décès liés à la maternité sont ceux entraînés par l'accouchement ou les complications de la grossesse, de l'accouchement et des suites de couches.

Pour plus de précisions concernant les définitions de la mortalité liée à la maternité dans la neuvième et dixième révision de la Classification statistique internationale des maladies et des problèmes de santé connexes, se reporter à la section 4.3 des Notes technique[1].

Les statistiques de mortalité liée à la maternité présentées dans ce tableau ne se rapportent qu'aux pays ou zones pour lesquels les trois critères suivants sont réunis : premièrement, le classement des statistiques des décès selon la cause doit être conforme à la liste de neuvième ou à celle de dixième, mentionnées plus haut, ou convertible aux catégories de cette liste; deuxièmement, le nombre total des décès (pour toutes les causes réunies) intervenus au cours d'une année doit être au moins égal à 1 000; troisièmement, à l'intérieur de cette répartition, le nombre total des décès dus à des causes mal définies selon le tableau de la section 4.3 ne doit pas dépasser 25 p. 100 du nombre des décès pour toutes causes.

Calcul des taux : Les taux de mortalité liée à la maternité représentent le nombre annuel de décès dus à la maternité pour 100 000 naissances vivantes (fréquences du tableau 9) de la même année.

Ces taux ont été calculés par la Division de statistique de l'ONU. Les taux fondés sur 30 décès de la maternité ou moins sont identifiés à l'aide du signe (♦).

Fiabilité des données: Les données sur les décès provenant des registres d'état civil qui sont déclarées incomplètes (degré d'exhaustivité inférieur à 90 p. 100) ou dont le degré d'exhaustivité n'est pas connu sont jugées douteuses et apparaissent en italique et non en caractères romains. Les taux à partir de ces données n'ont pas été calculés. Le tableau 18 et les notes techniques se rapportant à ce tableau présentent des renseignements plus détaillés sur le degré d'exhaustivité de l'enregistrement des décès. Pour plus de précisions sur la qualité des statistiques de l'état civil en général, et sur les estimations de l'exhaustivité en particulier, voir la section 4.2 des Notes techniques.

En général, le code de qualité des données sur les décès indiqués au tableau 18 sert à déterminer si, dans les autres tableaux, les données de mortalité apparaissent en caractères romains ou italiques. Toutefois, certaines données sur les décès selon la cause figurent en italique dans le présent tableau lorsqu'on sait que leur exhaustivité diffère grandement de celle des données sur le nombre total des décès. Dans les cas où le code de qualité du tableau 18 ne correspond pas aux caractères utilisés dans le présent tableau, les renseignements concernant le degré d'exhaustivité des statistiques des décès selon la cause sont indiqués en note à la fin du tableau.

Insuffisance des données: Les statistiques de la mortalité liée à la maternité appellent toutes les réserves qui ont été formulées à propos des statistiques de l'état civil en général et des statistiques de mortalité en particulier (voir explications à la section 4 des Notes techniques).

La fiabilité des données, au sujet de laquelle des indications ont été fournies plus haut, est un facteur important en l'occurrence. Il faut également tenir compte du fait que, dans certains cas, les données relatives aux décès sont classées par date d'enregistrement et non par date de décès; ces cas ont été identifiés par le signe(+). Lorsque le décalage entre le décès et son enregistrement est grand, c'est-à-dire qu'une forte proportion des décès fait l'objet d'un enregistrement tardif, les statistiques des décès de l'année peuvent être sérieusement faussées.

En outre, les statistiques de la mortalité à la maternité appellent les mêmes réserves que les statistiques des causes de décès exposées à la section 4 des Notes techniques.

Les taux de mortalité liée à la maternité appellent également toutes les réserves formulées à propos des statistiques des naissances vivantes qui ont servi à leur calcul. Voir à ce sujet les notes techniques relatives au tableau 9.

En prenant le nombre total des naissances vivantes comme base pour le calcul des taux de mortalité, on obtient une mesure approximative de la probabilité de décès dus aux complications de la grossesse, de l'accouchement et des suites de couches. Idéalement, ces taux devraient être calculés sur la base du nombre de femmes exposées au risque de grossesse, soit, en d'autres termes, sur la base du nombre de femmes qui conçoivent. Etant donné qu'il est impossible de connaître le nombre de femmes ayant conçu, c'est le nombre total de naissances vivantes que l'on utilise pour calculer ces taux.

Portée: Ce tableau présente des statistiques de la mortalité liée à la maternité (nombre de décès) pour 76 pays ou zones et les taux correspondants pour 66 pays ou zones.

Données publiées antérieurement: Des statistiques des décès liés à la maternité (nombre de décès et taux) figurent déjà dans des éditions antérieures de *l'Annuaire démographique*. Pour plus de précisions concernant les années pour lesquelles ces données ont été publiées, on se reportera à l'Index.

Il faut souligner que, avant 1975, les taux de mortalité liée à la maternité étaient calculés sur la base de la population féminine et non sur celle du nombre de naissances vivantes. Ils ne sont donc pas comparables à ceux qui figurent dans les éditions de l'Annuaire Démographique apparues après 1975.

NOTES

[1] Classification statistique internationale des maladies et des problèmes de santé connexes. Genève, Organisation mondiale de la Santé.

17. Maternal deaths and maternal death rates: 1991 - 2000
Mortalité liée à la maternité nombre de décès et taux: 1991 - 2000

(See notes at end of table. — Voir notes à la fin du tableau.)

Continent and country or area Continent et pays ou zone	1991	1992	1993	1994	1995	1996	1997	1998	1999	2000
AFRICA — AFRIQUE										
Egypt — Égypte										
Number — Nombre	724	718	...	...	...	...	...	...	...	...
Rate — Taux	44.2	48.0	...	...	...	...	...	...	...	...
Mauritius - Island of Mauritius — Maurice - Ile Maurice+										
Number — Nombre	15	9	6	15	12	6	10	4	7	...
Rate — Taux	♦70.0	♦40.8	...	...	...	♦30.3	...	...	...	...
South Africa — Afrique du Sud										
Number — Nombre	...	...	322	432	499	...	...	...	...	...
AMERICA, NORTH — AMERIQUE DU NORD										
Bahamas										
Number — Nombre	...	...	1	1	4	-	-	...	...	...
Rate — Taux	...	...	♦15.0	♦16.4	♦64.0	-	-	...	...	...
Barbados — Barbade+										
Number — Nombre	2	3	1	2	-	...	...	...	...	...
Rate — Taux	♦47.2	♦71.7	♦26.4	...	-	...	...	...	...	...
Canada[1]										
Number — Nombre	12	19	15	14	17	18	19	...	...	...
Rate — Taux	♦2.9	♦4.8	♦3.9	♦3.6	♦4.5	♦4.9	♦5.5	...	...	...
Costa Rica										
Number — Nombre	28	18	15	31	16	...	...	...	...	...
Rate — Taux	♦34.5	♦22.5	...	38.6	♦19.9	...	...	...	...	...
Cuba										
Number — Nombre	80	71	56	84	70	51	59	...	...	...
Rate — Taux	46.0	45.1	36.8	57.0	47.6	36.4	38.6	...	...	...
El Salvador										
Number — Nombre	77	50	61	...	...	...	...	...	...	...
Mexico — Mexique										
Number — Nombre	1 414	1 399	1 268	1 409	1 454	1 291	1 266	...	...	...
Rate — Taux	51.3	50.0	44.7	48.2	52.9	47.7	46.9	...	...	...
Nicaragua										
Number — Nombre	84	115	105	83	...	123	...	...	...	...
Puerto Rico — Porto Rico										
Number — Nombre	13	14	...	...	9	11	13	8	...	...
Rate — Taux	♦20.2	♦21.7	...	...	...	♦17.4	♦20.2	♦13.2	...	...
Trinidad and Tobago — Trinité-et-Tobago										
Number — Nombre	11	14	14	15	...	...	...	...	...	...
Rate — Taux	♦49.2	♦60.7	♦66.4	♦76.2	...	...	...	...	...	...
United States — Etats-Unis										
Number — Nombre	323	318	302	328	277	294	327	281	...	...
Rate — Taux	7.9	7.8	7.5	8.3	7.1	7.6	8.4	7.1	...	...
AMERICA, SOUTH — AMERIQUE DU SUD										
Argentina — Argentine										
Number — Nombre	334	328	309	265	290	317	...	...	...	...
Rate — Taux	48.1	48.3	46.3	39.3	44.0	46.9	...	...	...	...
Chile — Chili										
Number — Nombre	106	91	100	73	...	...	...	...	...	...
Rate — Taux	35.4	31.0	34.4	25.3	...	...	...	...	...	...
Colombia — Colombie+,[2]										
Number — Nombre	506	464	476	456	411	...	...	...	...	...
Ecuador — Equateur[3]										
Number — Nombre	320	338	348	241	170	194	...	...	...	...
Guyana+										
Number — Nombre	...	...	18	31	35	26	...	...	...	...
Paraguay										
Number — Nombre	...	...	...	111	...	...	...	...	...	...
Suriname										
Number — Nombre	...	11	...	...	...	...	...	...	...	...
Rate — Taux	...	♦111.8	...	...	...	...	...	...	...	...

(See notes at end of table. — Voir notes à la fin du tableau.)

Continent and country or area / Continent et pays ou zone	1991	1992	1993	1994	1995	1996	1997	1998	1999	2000
AMERICA, SOUTH — AMERIQUE DU SUD										
Venezuela[4]										
Number — Nombre	...	299	331	383	...	...	...	...	...	...
Rate — Taux	...	53.4	63.1	69.9	...	...	...	...	...	...
ASIA — ASIE										
Armenia — Arménie										
Number — Nombre	18	9	16	15	17	10	17	10	12	18
Rate — Taux	♦23.1	♦12.8	♦27.1	♦29.3	♦34.7	♦20.8	♦38.7	♦25.4	♦32.9	♦52.5
Azerbaijan — Azerbaïdjan										
Number — Nombre	20	32	60	70	53	56	41	51	51	44
Rate — Taux	...	17.6	34.4	43.8	37.0	43.3	31.0	41.1	43.4	37.6
China - Hong Kong SAR — Chine - Hong Kong RAS										
Number — Nombre	4	4	3	8	5	2	1	1	1	...
Rate — Taux	♦5.9	♦5.6	♦4.3	♦11.2	♦7.3	♦3.2	♦1.7	♦1.9	♦2.0	...
Georgia — Géorgie										
Number — Nombre	6	1	...	...	...	...	...	15	9	4
Rate — Taux[5]	♦6.7	♦1.4	...	...	...	...	...	♦26.2	...	...
Israel — Israël[5]										
Number — Nombre	9	6	3	6	7	9	12	...	...	...
Rate — Taux[6]	♦8.5	♦5.5	♦2.7	♦5.2	♦6.0	♦7.4	♦9.6	...	...	...
Japan — Japon[6]										
Number — Nombre	110	111	91	76	90	80	81	89	79	...
Rate — Taux	9.0	9.2	7.7	6.1	7.6	6.6	6.8	7.4	6.7	...
Korea, Republic of — Corée, Rép. de										
Number — Nombre	96	86	91	86	88	75	66	63	77	62
Rate — Taux	13.6	11.8	12.7	11.9	12.3	10.8	9.8	9.8	12.5	...
Kuwait — Koweït										
Number — Nombre	...	...	1	1	1	3	7	3	3	2
Rate — Taux	...	...	♦2.7	♦2.6	♦2.4	♦6.7	♦16.3	♦7.2	♦7.3	...
Kyrgyzstan — Kirghizistan										
Number — Nombre	72	64	52	47	52	27	64	35	44	...
Rate — Taux	55.6	49.9	44.5	42.7	44.3	♦25.0	62.7	33.6	42.3	...
Mongolia — Mongolie										
Number — Nombre	...	...	...	70	...	...	...	...	...	...
Philippines										
Number — Nombre	...	1 394	1 548	1 791	1 485	1 549	...	...	...	...
Singapore — Singapour+										
Number — Nombre	2	2	4	3	2	2	2	5	2	8
Rate — Taux	♦4.1	♦4.0	♦8.0	♦6.1	♦4.1	♦4.1	♦4.2	♦11.4	♦4.6	♦17.2
Tajikistan — Tadjikistan										
Number — Nombre	113	125	138	142	95	...	...	...	...	...
Rate — Taux	53.2	69.6	74.0	87.6	...	...	...	...	...	...
Thailand — Thaïlande+										
Number — Nombre	...	...	...	104	...	...	...	...	...	...
Turkmenistan — Turkménistan										
Number — Nombre	...	...	...	60	63	49	21	16	...	...
Rate — Taux	...	...	...	...	...	...	...	♦16.3	...	...
Uzbekistan — Ouzbékistan										
Number — Nombre	241	214	167	112	128	76	62	48	...	...
Rate — Taux	...	30.1	24.1	17.0	18.9	12.0	10.3	...	...	...
EUROPE										
Albania — Albanie										
Number — Nombre	...	10	16	13	9	8	5	8	...	...
Rate — Taux	...	...	...	♦18.0	♦12.5	♦11.7	♦8.1	♦13.3	...	...
Austria — Autriche										
Number — Nombre	7	4	4	8	1	4	2	4	1	2
Rate — Taux	♦7.4	♦4.2	♦4.2	♦8.7	♦1.1	♦4.5	♦2.4	♦4.9	♦1.3	♦2.6
Belarus — Bélarus										
Number — Nombre	41	27	24	21	14	21	23	26	19	...
Rate — Taux	31.1	♦21.1	♦20.4	♦19.0	♦13.8	♦21.9	♦25.7	♦28.1	♦20.4	...

17. Maternal deaths and maternal death rates: 1991 - 2000
Mortalité liée à la maternité nombre de décès et taux: 1991 - 2000 (continued — suite)

(See notes at end of table. — Voir notes à la fin du tableau.)

Continent and country or area / Continent et pays ou zone	1991	1992	1993	1994	1995	1996	1997	1998	1999	2000
EUROPE										
Belgium — Belgique										
Number — Nombre	5	7	6	7	11	...	...	...	...	...
Rate — Taux	♦4.0	♦5.6	♦5.0	♦6.0	♦9.5	...	...	...	...	...
Bulgaria — Bulgarie										
Number — Nombre	10	19	12	10	10	14	12	10	16	...
Rate — Taux	♦10.4	♦21.3	♦14.2	♦12.6	♦13.9	♦19.4	♦18.7	♦15.3	♦22.1	...
Croatia — Croatie										
Number — Nombre	4	2	5	5	6	1	6	3	5	3
Rate — Taux	♦7.7	♦4.3	♦10.3	♦10.3	♦12.0	♦1.9	♦10.8	♦6.4	♦11.1	♦6.9
Czech Republic — République Tchéque										
Number — Nombre	17	12	14	7	2	5	2	5	6	5
Rate — Taux	♦13.1	♦9.9	♦11.6	♦6.6	♦2.1	♦5.5	♦2.2	♦5.5	♦6.7	...
Denmark — Danemark[7]										
Number — Nombre	2	5	5	3	7	4	5	2	...	...
Rate — Taux	♦3.1	♦7.4	♦7.4	♦4.3	♦10.0	♦5.9	♦7.4	♦3.0	...	...
Estonia — Estonie										
Number — Nombre	6	4	5	8	7	-	2	2	2	...
Rate — Taux	♦31.1	♦22.2	♦33.0	♦56.4	♦51.6	-	♦15.8	♦16.4	♦15.9	...
Finland — Finlande[8]										
Number — Nombre	3	3	2	7	1	2	3	3	2	...
Rate — Taux	♦4.6	♦4.5	♦3.1	♦10.7	♦1.6	♦3.3	♦5.1	♦5.3	♦3.5	...
France[9]										
Number — Nombre	90	96	66	83	70	97	70	75	...	...
Rate — Taux	11.9	12.9	9.3	11.7	9.6	13.2	9.6	10.1	...	...
Germany — Allemagne										
Number — Nombre	72	54	44	40	41	51	49	44	37	...
Rate — Taux	8.7	6.7	5.5	5.2	5.4	6.4	6.0	5.5	4.8	...
Greece — Grèce										
Number — Nombre	3	6	1	2	-	4	-	7	...	...
Rate — Taux	♦2.9	♦5.8	♦1.0	♦1.9	-	♦4.0	-	♦6.9	...	...
Hungary — Hongrie										
Number — Nombre	16	12	22	12	17	12	21	6	4	10
Rate — Taux	♦12.6	♦9.9	♦18.8	♦10.4	♦15.2	♦11.4	♦20.9	♦6.2	♦4.2	♦10.3
Iceland — Islande										
Number — Nombre	-	-	-	-	-	-	-	...	...	...
Rate — Taux	-	-	-	-	-	-	-	...	...	...
Ireland — Irlande[+,10]										
Number — Nombre	4	2	-	1	-	3	3	2	...	...
Rate — Taux	♦7.6	♦3.9	-	♦2.1	-	♦6.0	♦5.7	♦3.7	...	...
Italy — Italie										
Number — Nombre	27	41	24	19	17	20	23	18	...	...
Rate — Taux	♦4.8	7.1	♦4.4	♦3.6	♦3.2	♦3.8	♦4.3	♦3.5	...	...
Latvia — Lettonie										
Number — Nombre	11	10	8	11	5	4	8	9	8	5
Rate — Taux	♦31.8	♦31.7	♦29.9	♦45.3	♦23.2	♦20.2	♦42.5	♦48.9	♦41.2	...
Lithuania — Lituanie										
Number — Nombre	11	11	6	7	7	5	6	5	5	3
Rate — Taux	♦19.6	♦20.5	♦12.6	♦16.5	♦17.0	♦12.8	♦15.9	♦13.5	♦13.7	♦8.8
Luxembourg										
Number — Nombre	-	-	-	1	1	-	-	1	-	1
Rate — Taux	-	-	-	♦18.3	♦18.4	-	-	♦18.6	-	♦17.5
Malta — Malte										
Number — Nombre	1	-	1	-	1	1	-	1	1	...
Rate — Taux	...	-	♦18.6	-	♦20.0	♦19.8	-	♦21.6	♦23.2	...
Netherlands — Pays-Bas[11]										
Number — Nombre	12	14	16	12	14	23	15	23	19	...
Rate — Taux	♦6.0	♦7.1	♦8.2	♦6.1	♦7.3	♦12.1	♦7.8	♦11.5	♦9.5	...
Norway — Norvège[12]										
Number — Nombre	5	4	2	-	4	1	1	4	...	...
Rate — Taux	♦8.2	♦6.7	♦3.4	-	♦6.6	♦1.6	♦1.7	♦6.9	...	...
Poland — Pologne										
Number — Nombre	70	51	58	53	43	21	...	...	20	...
Rate — Taux	12.8	9.9	11.7	11.0	9.9	♦4.9	...	...	♦5.2	...

17. Maternal deaths and maternal death rates: 1991 - 2000
Mortalité liée à la maternité nombre de décès et taux: 1991 - 2000 (continued — suite)

(See notes at end of table. — Voir notes à la fin du tableau.)

Continent and country or area Continent et pays ou zone	1991	1992	1993	1994	1995	1996	1997	1998	1999	2000
EUROPE										
Portugal										
Number — Nombre	14	11	7	10	9	6	6	9	6	3
Rate — Taux	♦12.0	♦9.6	♦6.1	♦9.2	♦8.4	♦5.4	♦5.3	♦7.9	♦5.2	♦2.5
Republic of Moldova — République de Moldova										
Number — Nombre	35	36	35	16	23	22	23	15	11	10
Rate — Taux	48.6	51.7	...	♦25.7	♦40.8	♦42.4	♦46.2	♦36.3	♦28.6	♦27.1
Romania — Roumanie										
Number — Nombre	183	157	133	149	113	95	98	96	98	75
Rate — Taux	66.5	60.3	53.2	60.4	47.8	41.1	41.4	40.5	41.8	32.2
Russian Federation — Fédération de Russie										
Number — Nombre	941	806	712	737	727	636	633	565	...	...
Rate — Taux	52.4	50.8	51.6	52.3	53.3	48.7	50.2	44.0	...	...
Slovakia — Slovaquie										
Number — Nombre	...	1	9	4	5	3	2	5	5	1
Rate — Taux	...	♦1.3	♦12.3	♦6.0	♦8.1	♦5.0	♦3.4	♦8.7	♦8.9	♦1.8
Slovenia — Slovénie										
Number — Nombre	1	1	1	-	1	3	2	-	2	...
Rate — Taux	♦4.6	♦5.0	♦5.1	-	♦5.3	♦16.0	♦11.0	-	♦11.4	...
Spain — Espagne										
Number — Nombre	13	19	12	13	11	11	8	10	...	...
Rate — Taux	♦3.3	♦4.8	♦3.1	♦3.6	♦3.0	♦3.0	♦2.2	♦2.7	...	...
Sweden — Suède										
Number — Nombre	5	-	6	1	4	5	3	7	...	...
Rate — Taux	♦4.0	-	♦5.1	♦0.9	♦3.9	♦5.3	♦3.3	♦7.9	...	...
Switzerland — Suisse										
Number — Nombre	1	4	5	3	7	3	...	...	...	...
Rate — Taux	♦1.2	♦4.6	♦6.0	♦3.6	♦8.5	♦3.6	...	...	...	...
The Former Yougoslav Rep. of Macedonia — L'ex-République yougoslave de Macédoine										
Number — Nombre	4	3	2	4	7	-	1	1	2	4
Rate — Taux	♦11.5	♦9.0	♦6.2	♦11.9	♦21.8	-	♦3.4	...	♦7.3	...
Ukraine										
Number — Nombre	188	187	183	163	159	142	111	114	98	95
Rate — Taux	29.8	31.3	32.8	31.3	32.3	30.4	25.1	27.2	...	...
United Kingdom — Royaume-Uni										
Number — Nombre	55	52	43	59	51	48	39	49	37	...
Rate — Taux	6.9	6.7	5.6	7.9	7.0	6.5	5.4	6.8	5.3	...
OCEANIA — OCEANIE										
Australia — Australie[+]										
Number — Nombre	9	9	16	18	21	13	12	5	13	...
Rate — Taux	♦3.5	♦3.4	♦6.1	♦7.0	♦8.2	♦5.1	♦4.8	♦2.0	♦5.2	...
New Zealand — Nouvelle Zélande[+]										
Number — Nombre	9	5	12	4	2	4	3	3	...	...
Rate — Taux	♦15.0	♦8.5	♦20.4	♦7.0	♦3.5	♦7.0	♦5.2	♦5.4	...	...

GENERAL NOTES - NOTES GENERALES

Rates are the number of maternal deaths per 100 000 live births. For method of evaluation and limitations of data, see Technical Notes for this table. — Les taux représentent le nombre de décès 'Affections périnatales' liés à la maternité per 100 000 naissances vivantes. Pour la méthode d'évaluation et les insuffisances des données, voir Notes techniques pour ce tableaux.

Italics: data from civil registers which are incomplete or of unknown completeness. — *Italiques:* données incomplètes ou dont le degré d'exactitude n'est pas connu provenant des registres de l'état civil.

FOOTNOTES - NOTES

+ Data tabulated by date of registration rather than occurrence. — Données exploitées selon la date de l'enregistrement et non la date de l'événement.
♦ Rates based on 30 or fewer deaths. — Taux basés sur 30 décès ou moins.

[1] Including Canadian residents temporarily in the United States, but excluding United States residents temporarily in Canada. — Y compris les résidents canadiens se trouvant temporairement aux Etats-Unis, mais non compris les résidents des Etats-Unis se trouvant temporairement au Canada.
[2] Based on burial permits. — D'après les permis d'inhumer.
[3] Excluding nomadic Indian tribes. — Non compris les tribus d'Indiens nomades.
[4] Excluding Indian jungle population. — Non compris les Indiens de la jungle.
[5] Including data for East Jerusalem and Israeli residents in certain other

territories under occupation by Israeli military forces since June 1967. — Y compris les données pour Jérusalem-Est et les résidents israéliens dans certains autres territoires occupés depuis 1967 par les forces.

[6] For Japanese nationals in Japan only. — Pour les nationaux japonais au Japon seulement.

[7] Excluding Faeroe Islands and Greenland. — Non compris les îles Féroé et le Gröenland.

[8] Including nationals temporarily outside the country. — Y compris les nationaux temporairement hors du pays.

[9] Including armed forces outside the country. — Y compris les militaires en garnison hors du pays.

[10] Deaths registered within one year of occurrence. — Décès enregistrés dans l'année que suit l'événement.

[11] Including residents outside the country if listed in a Netherlands population register. — Y compris les résidents hors du pays, s'ils sont inscrits sur un registre de population néerlandais.

[12] Including residents temporarily outside the country. — Y compris les résidents temporairement hors du pays.

Table 18

Table 18 presents deaths and crude death rates by urban/rural residence for as many years as possible between 1997 and 2001.

Description of variables: Death is defined as the permanent disappearance of all evidence of life at any time after live birth has taken place (post-natal cessation of vital functions without capability of resuscitation).

Statistics on the number of deaths are obtained from civil registers unless otherwise noted. For those countries or areas where civil registration statistics on deaths are considered reliable (estimated completeness of 90 per cent or more), the death rates shown have been calculated on the basis of registered deaths.

The urban/rural classification of deaths is that provided by each country or area; it is presumed to be based on the national census definitions of urban population that have been set forth at the end of the technical notes for table 6.

Rate computation: Crude death rates are the annual number of deaths per 1 000 mid-year population.

Rates by urban/rural residence are the annual number of deaths, in the appropriate urban or rural category, per 1 000 corresponding mid-year population. These rates are calculated by the Statistics Division of the United Nations.

Rates presented in this table are limited to those countries or areas with a minimum number of 30 deaths in a given year.

Reliability of data: Each country or area has been asked to indicate the estimated completeness of the infant deaths recorded in its civil register. These national assessments are indicated by the quality codes (C), (U) and (|) that appear in the first column of this table.

C indicates that the data are estimated to be virtually complete, that is, representing at least 90 per cent of the infant deaths occurring each year, while U indicates that data are estimated to be incomplete, that is, representing less than 90 per cent of the infant deaths occurring each year. The code (I) indicates that the source of data is different than civil registration, but still considered reliable and explained by footnote. The code (...) indicates that no information was provided regarding completeness.

Data from civil registers which are reported as incomplete or of unknown completeness (code U or ...) are considered unreliable. They appear in italics in this table; rates based on these data are not computed.

Limitations: Statistics on deaths are subject to the same qualifications as have been set forth for vital statistics in general and death statistics in particular as discussed in section 4 of the Technical Notes.

The reliability of the data, an indication of which is described above, is an important factor in considering the limitations. In addition, some deaths are tabulated by date of registration and not by date of occurrence; these have been indicated with a plus sign (+). Whenever the lag between the date of occurrence and date of registration is prolonged and, therefore, a large proportion of the death registrations are delayed, death statistics for any given year may be seriously affected.

As a rule, however, delays in the registration of deaths are less common and shorter than in the registration of live births.

International comparability in mortality statistics may also be affected by the exclusion of deaths of infants who were born alive but died before the registration of the birth or within the first 24 hours of life. Statistics of this type are footnoted.

In addition, it should be noted that rates are affected also by the quality and limitations of the population estimates that are used in their computation. The problems of under-enumeration or over-enumeration and, to some extent, the differences in definition of total population have been discussed in section 3 of the Technical Notes dealing with population data in general, and specific information pertaining to individual countries or areas is given in the footnotes to table 3.

Estimated rates based directly on the results of sample surveys are subject to considerable error as a result of omissions in reporting deaths or as a result of erroneous reporting of those that occurred outside the period of reference. However, such rates do have the advantage of having a "built-in" and corresponding base.

It should be emphasized that crude death rates -- like other crude rates, such as of birth, marriage and divorce -- may be seriously affected by the age-sex structure of the populations to which they relate. Nevertheless, they do provide a simple measure of the level and changes in mortality.

The comparability of data by urban/rural residence is affected by the national definitions of urban and rural used in tabulating these data. It is assumed, in the absence of specific information to the contrary, that the definitions of urban and rural used in connection with the national population census were also used in the compilation of the vital statistics for each country or area. However, the possibility cannot be excluded that, for a given country or area, the same definitions of urban and rural are not used for both the vital statistics data and the population census data. When known, the definitions of urban used in national population censuses are presented at the end of the technical notes for table 6. As discussed in detail in the technical notes for table 6, these definitions vary considerably from one country or area to another.

In addition to problems of comparability, vital rates classified by urban/rural residence are also subject to certain types of bias. If, when calculating vital rates, different definitions of urban are used in connection with the vital events and the population data and if this results in a net difference between the numerator and denominator of the rate in the population at risk, then the vital rates would be biased. Urban/rural differentials in vital rates may also be affected by whether the vital events have been tabulated in terms of place of occurrence or place of usual residence. This problem is discussed in more detail in section 4.1.4.1 of the Technical Notes.

Coverage: Deaths are shown for 157 countries or areas. Data are presented by urban/rural residence for 60 countries or areas.

Earlier data: Deaths and crude death rates have been shown in each issue of the Demographic Yearbook. Data included in this table update the series covering a period of years as follows :

Issue	Years Covered
Historical Supplement CD, 1997	1948 – 1997
1992	1983 – 1992
1985	1976 – 1985
1980	1971 – 1980
Historical Supplement, 1979	1948 – 1977

Tableau 18

Le tableau 18 présente le nombre des décès et les taux bruts de mortalité selon la résidence (urbaine/rurale) pour le plus grand nombre d'années possible entre 1997 et 2001.

Description des variables: Le décès est défini comme la disparition permanente de tout signe de vie à un moment quelconque postérieur à la naissance vivante (cessation des fonctions vitales après la naissance sans possibilité de réanimation)[1].

Sauf indication contraire, les statistiques du nombre de décès sont établies sur la base des registres d'état civil. Pour les pays ou zones où les données de l'enregistrement des décès par les services de l'état civil sont jugées sûres (complétude estimée à 90 p. 100 ou plus), les taux de mortalité ont été calculés d'après les décès enregistrés.

La classification (urbaine/rurale) des décès est celle qui a été fournie par chaque pays ou zone; il est donc présumé qu'elle repose sur les définitions de la population urbaine utilisées pour les recensements nationaux, qui sont reproduites à la fin des notes techniques du tableau 6.

Calcul des taux : Les taux bruts de mortalité représentent le nombre annuel de décès pour 1 000 habitants en milieu d'année.

Les taux selon la résidence (urbaine/rurale) représentent le nombre annuel de décès, classés selon la catégorie urbaine ou rurale appropriée, pour 1 000 habitants en milieu d'année. Ces taux ont été calculés par la Division de statistique de l'ONU.

Les taux présentés dans ce tableau se rapportent seulement aux pays ou zones où l'on a enregistré un nombre minimal de 30 naissances vivantes au cours d'une année donnée.

Fiabilité des données : Il a été demandé à chaque pays ou zone d'indiquer le degré estimatif de complétude des données sur les décès d'enfants de moins d'un an figurant dans ses registres d'état civil. Ces évaluations nationales sont désignées par les codes de qualité   (C), (U) et (I) qui apparaissent dans la première colonne du tableau.

La lettre (C) indique que les données sont jugées à peu près complètes, c'est-à-dire qu'elles représentent au moins 90 p. 100 des décès d'enfants de moins d'un an survenus chaque année; la lettre (U) indique que les données sont jugées incomplètes, c'est-à-dire qu'elles représentent moins de 90 p.100 des décès d'enfants de moins d'un an survenus chaque année. Le symbole (I) indique que la source des données est fiable mais n'est pas un registre de l'état civil; le symbole, dans ce cas, est accompagné pas une note explicative. Le signe (...) indique qu'aucun renseignement n'a été fourni quant à la complétude des données.

Les données provenant des registres de l'état civil qui sont déclarés incomplets ou dont le degré de complétude n'est pas connu (associées aux codes (U) ou (...)) sont jugées douteuses. Elles apparaissent en italique dans le présent tableau et leurs correspondants taux n'ont pas été calculés.

Insuffisance des données : Les statistiques de mortalité appellent toutes les réserves qui ont été faites à propos des statistiques de l'état civil en général et des statistiques des décès en particulier (voir explications à la section 4 des Notes techniques).

La fiabilité des données, au sujet de laquelle des indications ont été fournies plus haut, est un facteur important en l'occurrence.   Il faut également tenir compte du fait que, dans certains cas, les décès sont classés par date d'enregistrement et non par date d'occurrence; ces cas ont été identifiés par le signe (+). Lorsque le décalage entre le décès et son enregistrement est grand, c'est-à-dire quand qu'une forte proportion des décès fait l'objet d'un enregistrement tardif, les statistiques des décès dans l'année peuvent être sérieusement faussées.

En règle générale, toutefois, les décès sont enregistrés beaucoup plus rapidement que les naissances vivantes, et les longs retards sont rares.

Un autre facteur qui nuit à la comparabilité internationale des statistiques de la mortalité est la pratique qui consiste à ne pas y inclure les enfants nés vivants mais décédés avant l'enregistrement de leur naissance ou dans les 24 heures qui ont suivi la naissance. Quand tel était le cas, on l'a signalé en note à la fin du tableau.

Il convient de noter par ailleurs que l'exactitude des taux dépend également de la qualité et des limitations des estimations de la population qui sont utilisées pour leur calcul. Le problème des erreurs par excès ou par défaut commis lors du dénombrement et, dans une certaine mesure, le problème de l'hétérogénéité des définitions de la population totale ont été examinés dans la section 3 des Notes techniques, relative à la population en général; des indications concernant les différents pays ou zones sont données en note au bas du tableau 3.

Les taux estimatifs fondés directement sur les résultats d'enquêtes par sondage comportent des possibilités d'erreurs considérables dues soit à des omissions dans les déclarations des décès, soit au fait que l'on a déclaré à tort des décès survenus en réalité hors de la période considérée. Toutefois, ces taux présentent un avantage : le chiffre de population utilisé comme base est connu par définition et rigoureusement correspondant.

Il faut souligner que les taux bruts de mortalité, de même que les taux bruts de natalité, de nuptialité et de divortialité, peuvent varier très sensiblement selon la composition par âge et par sexe de la population à laquelle ils se rapportent. Ils offrent néanmoins un moyen simple de mesurer le niveau et l'évolution de la mortalité.

La comparabilité des données selon la résidence (urbaine/rurale) peut être limitée par les définitions nationales des termes "urbain" et "rural" utilisées pour le classement de ces données. En l'absence d'indications contraires, on a supposé que les définitions des termes "urbain" et "rural" utilisées pour le recensement national de la population lavaient aussi été utilisées pour l'établissement des statistiques de l'état civil dans chaque pays ou zone. Toutefois, on ne peut exclure la possibilité que, pour un pays ou une zone, les mêmes définitions n'aient pas été utilisées dans les deux cas. Les définitions du terme "urbain" utilisées pour les recensements nationaux de population ont été indiquées à la fin des Notes techniques du tableau 6 lorsqu'elles étaient connues. Comme on l'a précisé en détail dans les Notes techniques relatives au tableau 6, ces définitions varient très sensiblement d'un pays ou zone à l'autre.

Outre ces problèmes de comparabilité, les taux démographiques classés selon la résidence "urbaine" ou "rurale" sont également sujets à certaines distorsions particulières. Si, lors du calcul de ces taux des définitions différentes du terme "urbain" sont utilisées pour classer les faits d'état civil et les données relatives à la population, et s'il en résulte une différence nette entre le numérateur et le dénominateur pour le taux de la population exposée au risque, les taux démographiques s'en trouveront faussés. La différence entre ces taux pour les zones urbaines et rurales pourra aussi être faussée selon que les faits d'état civil auront été classés d'après le lieu où ils se sont produits ou le lieu de résidence habituelle. Ce problème est examiné plus en détail à la section 4.1.4.1 des Notes techniques.

Portée : Ce tableau présente les statistiques des décès pour 157 pays ou zones. Les répartitions selon la résidence (urbaine/rurale) concernent 60 pays ou zones.

Données publiées antérieurement : Des statistiques de décès et des taux bruts de mortalité figurent dans chaque édition de l'Annuaire démographique. Les données présentées dans ce tableau mettent à jour les périodes d'années suivantes :

Edition	Années considérées
Supplément rétrospectif (CD), 1997	1948 – 1997
1992	1983 – 1992
1985	1976 – 1985
1980	1971 – 1980
Supplément rétrospectif, 1979	1948 – 1977

NOTES

[1] *Principles and Recommendations for a Vital Statistics System Revision 2,* Sales No. E. 01.XVII.10, United Nations, New York, 2001.

18. Deaths and crude death rates, by urban/rural residence: 1997 - 2001
Décès et taux bruts de mortalité, selon la résidence, urbaine/rurale: 1997 - 2001

(See notes at end of table. — Voir notes à la fin du tableau.)

Continent, country or area, and urban/rural residence / Continent, pays ou zone et résidence, urbaine/rurale	Co-de[1]	Number - Nombre					Rate - Taux				
		1997	1998	1999	2000	2001	1997	1998	1999	2000	2001
AFRICA — AFRIQUE											
Algeria - Algérie[2,3]											
Total	U	172 431	171 775	129 686	127 951	129 092	...	...	...	...	...
Benin - Bénin[4]											
Total	I	72 520	72 130	71 680	71 540	83 417	12.9	12.4	12.0	11.6	13.0
Botswana[4]											
Total	I	10 675	16 244	16 352	...	16 570	7.0	10.3	10.2	...	...
Burundi[4]											
Total	I	120 145	115 693	...	...	...	19.4	18.4			
Chad - Tchad											
Total	...	...	...	...	...	138 025	...	...	...	...	...
Côte d'Ivoire[4]											
Total	I	...	189 010	...	201 690	...	...	12.3	...	12.3	...
Egypt - Égypte											
Total	C	389 301	399 772	401 433	...	...	6.5	6.5	6.4	...	...
Urban - Urbaine	C	178 808	177 404	181 665	...	...	7.0	6.8	6.8	...	...
Rural - Rurale	C	210 493	222 368	219 768	...	...	6.1	6.3	6.1	...	...
Ethiopia - Éthiopie											
Total	...	...	...	1 062 114	...	...	...	...	...	...	...
Urban - Urbaine	...	...	...	110 929	...	...	...	...	...	...	...
Rural - Rurale	...	...	...	951 185	...	...	...	...	...	...	...
Libyan Arab Jamahiriya - Jamahiriya arabe libyenne											
Total	U	...	...	...	17 367	18 334	...	...	...	...	...
Malawi[4,5]											
Total	I	...	208 040	234 641	228 245	221 963	...	...	...	...	19.9
Urban - Urbaine	I	...	22 186	...	...	...	...	...	...	...	...
Rural - Rurale	I	...	185 854	...	...	...	...	...	...	...	...
Mauritius - Maurice											
Total	+C	7 986	7 839	7 944	7 982	7 983	7.0	6.8	6.8	6.7	6.7
Urban - Urbaine	+C	3 721	3 583	3 711	3 685	3 634	7.5	7.2	7.4	7.3	7.1
Rural - Rurale	+C	4 265	4 256	4 233	4 297	4 349	6.5	6.4	6.3	6.3	6.3
Morocco - Maroc[6]											
Total	U	87 225	95 111	98 304	...	...	...	...	...	...	...
Urban - Urbaine	U	47 497	52 691	53 935	...	...	...	...	...	...	...
Rural - Rurale	U	39 484	42 163	44 121	...	...	...	...	...	...	...
Mozambique[4,7]											
Total	I	385 754	...	...	...	331 162	23.3	...	...	...	18.8
Urban - Urbaine	I	70 750	...	...	...	...	...	...	...	...	...
Rural - Rurale	I	315 004	...	...	...	...	...	...	...	...	...
Réunion[2]											
Total	C	3 553	3 731	3 825	*3 781	*3 740	5.2	5.3	5.4	*5.2	*5.1
Saint Helena ex. dep. - Sainte - Hélène sans dép.											
Total	C	30	39	45	53	41	...	...	...	...	...
Seychelles											
Total	+C	603	570	560	553	554	7.8	7.2	7.0	6.8	6.8
Swaziland[7]											
Total	I	8 480	...	...	...	...	...	...	...	...	...
Urban - Urbaine	I	1 370	...	...	...	...	...	...	...	...	...
Rural - Rurale	I	7 110	...	...	...	...	...	...	...	...	...
Tunisia - Tunisie											
Total	U	42 426	42 571	54 400	...	53 300	...	...	...	...	...
AMERICA, NORTH — AMERIQUE DU NORD											
Anguilla											
Total	+C	56	62	58	*69	*66	5.4	5.8	5.3	*6.1	*5.7

18. Deaths and crude death rates, by urban/rural residence: 1997 - 2001
Décès et taux bruts de mortalité, selon la résidence, urbaine/rurale: 1997 - 2001 (continued — suite)

(See notes at end of table. — Voir notes à la fin du tableau.)

Continent, country or area, and urban/rural residence / Continent, pays ou zone et résidence, urbaine/rurale	Co-de[1]	Number - Nombre					Rate - Taux				
		1997	1998	1999	2000	2001	1997	1998	1999	2000	2001
AMERICA, NORTH — AMERIQUE DU NORD											
Antigua and Barbuda - Antigua - et - Barbuda											
Total	+C	468	456	508	451	...	...	...	...	...	...
Aruba											
Total	+U	497	505	554	531	477	...	...	...	...	...
Bahamas											
Total	U	1 670	1 725	1 567	...	...	...	...	...	...	...
Barbados - Barbade											
Total	+U	...	...	...	2 367	...	...	...	...	...	...
Belize											
Total	U	1 173	1 350	1 183	1 534	1 261	...	...	...	...	...
Bermuda - Bermudes											
Total	C	437	505	...	473	442	7.2	...	...	...	7.1
British Virgin Islands - Îles Vierges britanniques											
Total	+C	...	...	...	...	*101	...	...	...	...	*4.9
Canada[8]											
Total	C	215 669	218 091	219 530	218 062	219 538	7.2	7.2	7.2	7.1	7.1
Cayman Islands - Îles Caïmanes											
Total	C	123	117	128	137	132	3.4	3.1	3.3	3.4	3.2
Costa Rica											
Total	C	14 260	14 708	15 052	14 944	15 609	4.1	4.2	4.2	3.8	3.9
Cuba[6]											
Total	C	77 316	77 565	79 499	76 463	79 395	7.0	7.0	7.1	6.8	7.1
Urban - Urbaine	C	63 268	63 354	64 362	...	...	7.6	7.6	7.7	...	...
Rural - Rurale	C	14 011	14 146	15 072	...	...	5.1	5.1	5.5	...	...
Dominica - Dominique											
Total	+C	513	595	631	503	...	6.8	7.8	...	7.0	...
Dominican Republic - République dominicaine											
Total	+U	26 301	25 278	26 956	23 776	...	...	...	...	...	...
El Salvador											
Total	C	29 118	29 919	28 056	28 154	*29 559	4.9	5.0	4.6	4.5	*4.6
Urban - Urbaine	C	18 280	20 533	18 770	19 276	*20 921	5.4	5.9	5.2	5.3	*5.6
Rural - Rurale	C	10 838	9 386	9 286	8 878	*8 638	4.3	3.7	3.6	3.4	*3.3
Greenland - Groenland											
Total	C	492	468	482	...	...	8.7	8.3	8.6	...	...
Urban - Urbaine	C	412	391	372	...	...	9.1	8.6	8.2	...	...
Rural - Rurale	C	80	77	110	...	...	7.5	7.3	10.4	...	...
Grenada - Grenade											
Total	+C	707	819	794	716	727	7.1	8.2	7.9	7.1	7.2
Guatemala											
Total	C	67 691	70 504	64 563	66 831	69 934	6.4	6.5	5.8	5.9	6.0
Jamaica - Jamaïque											
Total	+C	15 087	18 110	17 353	*16 338	*17 205	5.9	7.0	6.7	*6.3	*6.6
Mexico - Mexique[6]											
Total	C	440 437	444 665	443 950	437 667	443 127	4.6	4.6	4.5	4.4	4.4
Urban - Urbaine	C	326 253	329 170	332 434	333 980	336 551	4.6	4.6	4.5	4.5	4.4
Rural - Rurale	C	108 143	109 283	105 664	97 870	100 670	4.4	4.4	4.2	3.8	3.9
Netherlands Antilles - Antilles néerlandaises											
Total	C	1 235	1 282	1 321	...	...	5.9	6.2	6.4	...	...
Nicaragua											
Total	+U	13 916	14 804	13 771	10 603	...	...	...	...	...	...

18. Deaths and crude death rates, by urban/rural residence: 1997 - 2001
Décès et taux bruts de mortalité, selon la résidence, urbaine/rurale: 1997 - 2001 (continued — suite)

(See notes at end of table. — Voir notes à la fin du tableau.)

Continent, country or area, and urban/rural residence / Continent, pays ou zone et résidence, urbaine/rurale	Code[1]	Number - Nombre					Rate - Taux				
		1997	1998	1999	2000	2001	1997	1998	1999	2000	2001
AMERICA, NORTH — AMERIQUE DU NORD											
Nicaragua											
Urban - Urbaine	+U	9 358	9 487	9 037	6 890	...	...	...	...	...	...
Rural - Rurale	+U	4 558	5 317	4 734	3 713	...	...	...	...	...	...
Panama											
Total	U	12 179	11 824	11 938	11 841	12 442	...	...	...	...	...
Urban - Urbaine	U	6 997	6 664	7 108	...	...	...	...	...	...	...
Rural - Rurale	U	5 182	5 160	4 830	...	...	...	...	...	...	...
Puerto Rico - Porto Rico[6]											
Total	C	29 119	29 990	29 145	28 550	28 794	7.8	8.0	7.7	7.5	7.5
Urban - Urbaine	C	15 506	15 843	15 595	15 516	15 406	...	...	...	...	...
Rural - Rurale	C	13 573	14 127	13 542	12 991	13 367	...	...	...	...	...
Saint Kitts and Nevis - Saint - Kitts - et - Nevis											
Total	+C	393	390	418	357	352	9.6	9.7	9.8	8.8	7.6
Saint Lucia - Sainte - Lucie											
Total	C	976	976	981	939	*960	6.5	6.4	6.4	6.0	*6.1
Urban - Urbaine	C	290	287	...	...	...	6.6	6.4	...	...	...
Rural - Rurale	C	691	686	...	...	...	6.6	6.4	...	...	...
Saint Vincent and the Grenadines - Saint Vincent - et - les Grenadines											
Total	+C	736	830	833	697	*720	6.6	7.5	7.5	6.2	*6.6
Trinidad and Tobago - Trinité - et - Tobago											
Total	C	9 157	...	...	...	...	7.2	...	...	...	...
United States - États - Unis											
Total	C	2 314 245	2 337 256	2 391 399	2 403 351	*2417762	8.6	8.6	8.8	8.7	*8.5
AMERICA, SOUTH — AMERIQUE DU SUD											
Argentina - Argentine											
Total	C	270 910	280 180	289 543	277 148	285 941	7.6	7.8	7.9	7.5	7.6
Bolivia - Bolivie											
Total	U	71 543	71 618	71 680	71 742	...	...	...	...	...	...
Brazil - Brésil[9]											
Total	U	...	936 885	943 524	927 783	931 017	...	...	...	...	...
Chile - Chili											
Total	C	78 472	80 257	81 977	...	...	5.4	5.4	5.5	...	...
Urban - Urbaine	C	65 616	67 146	68 709	...	...	5.3	5.3	5.4	...	...
Rural - Rurale	C	12 856	13 111	13 268	...	...	5.8	6.0	6.0	...	...
Colombia - Colombie[6,10]											
Total	+U	170 753	175 442	183 553	183 865	...	...	...	...	...	...
Urban - Urbaine	+U	143 980	147 064	154 755	153 632	...	...	...	...	...	...
Rural - Rurale	+U	22 202	24 740	27 477	29 115	...	...	...	...	...	...
Ecuador - Équateur[11]											
Total	U	52 089	54 357	55 921	56 420	...	...	...	...	...	...
Urban - Urbaine	U	37 116	37 836	...	...	...	...	...	...	...	...
Rural - Rurale	U	14 973	16 521	...	...	...	...	...	...	...	...
Falkland Islands (Malvinas) - Îles Falkland (Malvinas)											
Total	+C	16	12	20	11	...	...	...	...	...	...

18. Deaths and crude death rates, by urban/rural residence: 1997 - 2001
Décès et taux bruts de mortalité, selon la résidence, urbaine/rurale: 1997 - 2001 (continued — suite)

(See notes at end of table. — Voir notes à la fin du tableau.)

Continent, country or area, and urban/rural residence / Continent, pays ou zone et résidence, urbaine/rurale	Co-de[1]	Number - Nombre					Rate - Taux				
		1997	1998	1999	2000	2001	1997	1998	1999	2000	2001
AMERICA, SOUTH — AMERIQUE DU SUD											
French Guiana - Guyane française[2]											
Total	C	562	614	...	...	...	...	...	...	...	...
Guyana											
Total	+C	5 117	4 977	4 197	...	...	6.6	6.4	5.4	...	...
Peru - Pérou[9,12]											
Total	C	157 500	158 500	159 900	161 000	164 296	6.5	6.4	6.3	6.3	6.2
Suriname											
Total	C	2 878	2 814	2 992	3 090	...	6.9	6.6	7.0	7.1	...
Urban - Urbaine	C	2 126	2 220	2 171	2 249	...	7.3	...	...	...	...
Rural - Rurale	C	752	594	821	841	...	5.8	...	...	...	...
Uruguay											
Total	C	30 459	32 082	32 430	30 456	...	9.3	9.8	9.8	9.1	...
Venezuela[9]											
Total	C	94 334	98 624	101 907	103 255	107 867	4.1	4.2	4.3	4.3	4.4
ASIA — ASIE											
Armenia - Arménie[13]											
Total	C	23 985	23 210	24 087	24 025	24 003	6.3	6.1	6.3	6.3	6.3
Urban - Urbaine	C	15 783	15 474	15 834	15 682	...	6.2	6.1	6.2	6.2	...
Rural - Rurale	C	8 202	7 736	8 253	8 343	...	6.6	6.1	6.5	6.6	...
Azerbaijan - Azerbaïdjan[13]											
Total	+C	46 962	46 299	46 295	46 701	45 284	6.0	5.9	5.8	5.8	5.6
Urban - Urbaine	+C	23 928	23 463	22 828	23 530	23 382	5.9	5.8	5.6	5.7	5.7
Rural - Rurale	+C	23 034	22 836	23 467	23 171	21 902	6.1	5.9	6.0	5.9	5.5
Bahrain - Bahreïn											
Total	U	*1 822*	*1 997*	*1 920*	*2 045*	*1 979*	...	...	...	...	...
Bangladesh											
Total	U	*958 000*	...	...	...	...	...	...	...	...	...
Brunei Darussalam - Brunéi Darussalam											
Total	+C	883	928	905	965	...	2.8	2.9	2.7	2.9	...
China - Chine[14]											
Total	...	*8 010 000*	*8 070 000*	*8 100 000*	...	...	...	...	...	...	...
China: Hong Kong SAR - Chine: Hong Kong RAS											
Total	C	31 738	32 847	33 255	33 758	33 378	4.9	5.0	5.0	5.1	5.0
China: Macao SAR - Chine: Macao RAS											
Total	C	1 293	1 356	1 374	1 338	1 327	3.1	3.2	3.2	3.1	3.1
Cyprus - Chypre[15]											
Total	C	5 173	5 432	5 070	5 355	4 827	6.8	7.1	6.5	6.9	6.1
Georgia - Géorgie[13]											
Total	C	37 679	39 400	40 378	41 320	39 339	6.9	7.2	8.8	8.2	8.0
Urban - Urbaine	C	20 394	20 800	22 044	22 440	21 600	6.8	6.9	8.3	8.6	...
Rural - Rurale	C	17 285	18 600	18 334	18 880	17 739	7.2	7.7	9.4	9.9	...
Iran (Islamic Republic of) - Iran (République islamique d')											
Total	C	...	...	374 838	...	...	...	...	6.0	...	...
Iraq[16]											
Total	U	*144 787*	*160 039*	*177 483*	*179 928*	...	...	...	...	...	...
Israel - Israël[6,17]											
Total	C	36 124	36 955	*37 289	*37 669	*37 162	6.2	6.2	*6.1	*6.0	*5.8
Urban - Urbaine	C	33 524	34 449	*34 834	*35 141	*34 570	6.3	6.4	*6.3	*6.2	*5.9
Rural - Rurale	C	2 585	2 498	*2 446	*2 524	*2 585	4.8	4.5	*4.3	*4.3	*4.8

18. Deaths and crude death rates, by urban/rural residence: 1997 - 2001
Décès et taux bruts de mortalité, selon la résidence, urbaine/rurale: 1997 - 2001 (continued — suite)

(See notes at end of table. — Voir notes à la fin du tableau.)

Continent, country or area, and urban/rural residence / Continent, pays ou zone et résidence, urbaine/rurale	Co-de[1]	Number - Nombre					Rate - Taux				
		1997	1998	1999	2000	2001	1997	1998	1999	2000	2001
ASIA — ASIE											
Japan - Japon[6,18]											
Total	C	913 402	936 484	982 031	961 653	970 331	7.2	7.4	7.8	7.6	7.6
Urban - Urbaine	C	664 984	683 357	717 456	704 610	712 639	...	...	...	...	...
Rural - Rurale	C	246 302	250 890	262 171	254 767	255 462	...	...	...	...	...
Jordan - Jordanie[19]											
Total	U	13 190	13 552	13 936	13 339		...	...	...	...	...
Kazakhstan[13]											
Total	C	160 138	154 314	145 880	*148 834	*147 587	10.2	10.2	9.8	*10.0	*10.0
Urban - Urbaine	C	99 677	96 877	91 180	...	...	11.5	11.5	10.9	...	...
Rural - Rurale	C	60 461	57 437	54 700	...	...	8.6	8.7	8.3	...	...
Korea (Republic of) - Corée (République de)[20]											
Total	C	244 763	245 597	246 539	247 346	242 730	5.3	5.3	5.3	5.3	5.1
Urban - Urbaine	C	150 616	150 941	152 121	155 754	154 230	...	...	...	...	...
Rural - Rurale	C	94 147	94 656	94 418	91 592	88 500	...	...	...	...	...
Kuwait - Koweït											
Total	C	3 895	4 216	4 187	4 227	*4 364	2.0	2.1	2.0	1.9	*1.9
Kyrgyzstan - Kirghizistan[13]											
Total	C	34 540	34 596	32 850	34 111	32 677	7.4	7.3	6.8	7.0	6.6
Urban - Urbaine	C	13 405	13 179	12 628	13 595	12 783	8.0	7.8	7.4	7.9	7.3
Rural - Rurale	C	21 135	21 417	20 222	20 516	19 894	7.0	7.0	6.5	6.5	6.2
Lebanon - Liban[16]											
Total	U	19 884	20 097	19 133	18 756		...	...	...	...	...
Malaysia - Malaisie											
Total	C	97 432	98 219	*100 900	*102 100	...	4.5	4.4	*4.4	*4.4	...
Maldives											
Total	C	1 175	1 130	1 050	1 031	1 081	4.5	4.2	3.8	3.8	3.9
Urban - Urbaine	C	268	158	301	298	288	...	...	...	...	...
Rural - Rurale	C	907	972	749	733	793	...	...	...	...	...
Mongolia - Mongolie											
Total	C	16 980	15 860	16 105	15 472	15 999	7.4	6.8	6.8	6.5	6.6
Urban - Urbaine	C	8 974	8 779	8 726	8 888	9 215	7.9	7.6	6.3	6.3	...
Rural - Rurale	C	8 006	7 081	7 379	6 584	6 784	6.9	6.0	7.6	6.7	...
Nepal - Népal[21]											
Total	I	...	...	...	...	106 789	...	...	...	...	...
Occupied Palestinian Territory - Territoire palestinien occupé											
Total	U	8 745	8 540	8 479	8 601	8 678	...	...	...	...	...
Oman[16]											
Total	...	2 354	2 297	2 440	...	...	...	...	...	...	...
Pakistan[22,23]											
Total	I	1 089 595	...	...	...	...	8.5	...	...	...	...
Urban - Urbaine	I	291 813	...	...	...	...	...	...	...	...	...
Rural - Rurale	I	797 782	...	...	...	...	...	...	...	...	...
Philippines											
Total	C	339 400	352 992	347 989	366 931	...	4.7	4.8	4.7	4.8	...
Qatar											
Total	C	1 060	1 157	1 148	1 173	1 210	...	2.1	...	...	2.0
Saudi Arabia - Arabie saoudite											
Total	...	...	...	68 521	51 614	...	...	...	...	...	...
Singapore - Singapour[24]											
Total	C	15 307	15 657	15 516	15 693	15 367	4.0	4.0	3.9	3.9	3.7
Sri Lanka											
Total	+C	113 078	*112 657	*114 392	...	...	6.1	*6.0	*6.0	...	...

(See notes at end of table. — Voir notes à la fin du tableau.)

Continent, country or area, and urban/rural residence / Continent, pays ou zone et résidence, urbaine/rurale	Co-de[1]	Number - Nombre					Rate - Taux				
		1997	1998	1999	2000	2001	1997	1998	1999	2000	2001
ASIA — ASIE											
Syrian Arab Republic - République arabe syrienne[2,25,26]											
Total	U	53 366	57 893	56 564	57 759	60 814	...	...	...	...	...
Tajikistan - Tadjikistan[13]											
Total	C	...	...	*24 900	...	...	...	...	*4.0	...	...
Thailand - Thaïlande											
Total	+U	303 918	317 793	362 593	365 741	369 493	...	...	...	...	...
Urban - Urbaine	+U	...	...	36 796	37 257	...	...	...	...	...	...
Rural - Rurale	+U	...	...	325 797	328 484	...	...	...	...	...	...
Turkey - Turquie[27]											
Total	I	424 000	430 000	439 000	453 000	463 000	6.6	6.6	6.6	6.7	6.7
Urban - Urbaine	I	168 060	175 429	174 174	...	...	4.2	4.2	4.1	...	...
Rural - Rurale	I	255 940	254 571	264 826	...	...	10.9	10.8	11.2	...	...
Turkmenistan - Turkménistan[13]											
Total	C	...	29 628	...	...	...	...	6.1	...	...	...
Uzbekistan - Ouzbékistan[13]											
Total	C	137 331	...	140 526	135 598	132 542	5.8	...	5.9	5.5	5.3
Urban - Urbaine	C	61 823	...	61 167	61 130	59 743	6.9	...	6.8	6.6	6.5
Rural - Rurale	C	75 508	...	79 359	74 468	72 799	5.2	...	5.3	4.8	4.6
EUROPE											
Albania - Albanie											
Total	C	18 237	18 250	...	...	...	4.9	4.8	...	...	...
Andorra - Andorre											
Total	C	197	235	207	259	237	3.0	3.6	3.1	3.9	3.6
Austria - Autriche											
Total	C	79 432	78 339	78 200	76 780	74 767	9.8	9.7	9.7	9.5	9.2
Urban - Urbaine	C	47 833	46 639	46 752	...	...	...	...	...	...	...
Rural - Rurale	C	31 599	31 700	31 448	...	...	...	...	...	...	...
Belarus - Bélarus[13]											
Total	C	136 653	137 296	142 027	...	...	13.4	13.5	14.2	...	...
Urban - Urbaine	C	68 251	69 796	73 654	...	...	9.6	9.8	10.6	...	...
Rural - Rurale	C	68 402	67 500	68 373	...	...	22.0	22.1	22.3	...	...
Belgium - Belgique[28]											
Total	C	103 802	104 583	104 904	104 903	*103 447	10.2	10.3	10.3	10.2	*10.1
Bosnia and Herzegovina - Bosnie - Herzégovine											
Total	C	27 875	28 679	...	...	...	7.5	7.9	...	...	...
Bulgaria - Bulgarie											
Total	C	121 861	118 193	111 786	115 087	112 368	14.7	14.3	13.6	14.1	14.2
Urban - Urbaine	C	66 206	...	...	64 184	62 778	11.8	...	...	11.5	11.5
Rural - Rurale	C	55 655	...	...	50 903	49 590	20.7	...	...	19.6	20.4
Channel Islands: Guernsey - Îles Anglo - Normandes: Guernesey											
Total	C	593	540	529	*565	...	10.0	9.1	8.8	*9.3	...
Croatia - Croatie											
Total	C	51 964	52 311	51 953	50 246	49 552	11.4	11.6	11.4	11.5	11.2
Urban - Urbaine	C	26 927	26 302	...	25 130	24 838	...	...	...	...	...
Rural - Rurale	C	25 037	26 009	...	25 116	24 714	...	...	...	...	...
Czech Republic - République tchèque											
Total	C	112 744	109 527	109 768	109 001	107 755	10.9	10.6	10.7	10.6	10.5

18. Deaths and crude death rates, by urban/rural residence: 1997 - 2001
Décès et taux bruts de mortalité, selon la résidence, urbaine/rurale: 1997 - 2001 (continued — suite)

(See notes at end of table. — Voir notes à la fin du tableau.)

Continent, country or area, and urban/rural residence — Continent, pays ou zone et résidence, urbaine/rurale	Code[1]	Number - Nombre					Rate - Taux				
		1997	1998	1999	2000	2001	1997	1998	1999	2000	2001
EUROPE											
Czech Republic - République tchèque											
Urban - Urbaine	C	80 121	78 326	78 518	78 276	77 649	10.4	10.2	10.3	10.2	10.3
Rural - Rurale	C	32 623	31 201	31 250	30 725	30 106	12.5	11.9	11.9	11.7	11.3
Denmark - Danemark[29]											
Total	C	59 898	58 442	59 156	57 986	58 338	11.3	11.0	11.1	10.9	10.9
Estonia - Estonie[6,13]											
Total	C	18 566	19 440	18 455	18 424	...	12.7	13.4	12.8	13.5	...
Urban - Urbaine	C	12 104	...	...	11 667	...	12.0	...	...	12.6	...
Rural - Rurale	C	6 311	...	...	6 520	...	14.1	...	...	14.6	...
Finland - Finlande[30]											
Total	C	49 108	49 262	49 345	49 339	48 550	9.6	9.6	9.6	9.5	9.4
Urban - Urbaine	C	26 386	26 784	...	...	26 928	8.7	8.7	...	...	8.5
Rural - Rurale	C	22 722	22 478	...	...	21 622	10.8	10.9	...	...	10.8
France[31,32]											
Total	C	530 319	534 005	537 661	536 300	530 200	9.0	9.1	9.2	9.1	9.0
Urban - Urbaine	C	373 031	376 390	378 644	...	...	...	...	...	...	...
Rural - Rurale	C	155 147	155 488	157 115	...	...	...	...	...	...	...
Germany - Allemagne											
Total	C	860 389	851 412	846 330	838 797	*823 500	10.5	10.4	10.3	10.2	*10.0
Gibraltar[33]											
Total	C	263	267	277	262	249	9.7	9.9	10.2	9.7	8.8
Greece - Grèce											
Total	C	99 738	102 668	*104 190	105 219	*102 559	9.5	9.8	*9.9	10.5	*10.2
Urban - Urbaine	C	53 893	55 464	...	...	...	...	...	...	...	...
Rural - Rurale	C	45 845	47 204	...	...	...	...	...	...	...	...
Holy See - Saint - Siège											
Total	C	...	...	...	10		...	...	...	...	...
Hungary - Hongrie[34]											
Total	C	139 434	140 870	143 210	135 601	132 183	13.7	13.9	14.2	13.5	13.0
Urban - Urbaine	C	84 165	85 084	86 726	82 209	81 673	12.8	13.0	13.3	12.7	12.3
Rural - Rurale	C	54 696	55 074	55 646	52 614	49 857	15.4	15.5	15.6	14.8	14.1
Iceland - Islande											
Total	C	1 843	1 821	1 901	1 828	1 725	6.8	6.7	6.9	6.5	6.1
Urban - Urbaine	C	1 673	1 633	...	1 683	1 555	6.7	6.5	...	6.5	5.9
Rural - Rurale	C	170	188	...	145	170	7.9	8.8	...	6.7	7.9
Ireland - Irlande[35]											
Total	+C	31 581	31 437	31 683	31 115	29 812	8.6	8.5	8.5	8.2	7.7
Urban - Urbaine	+C	17 530	17 397	17 288	...	...	...	...	...	...	...
Rural - Rurale	+C	14 051	14 040	14 395	...	...	...	...	...	...	...
Isle of Man - Îles de Man											
Total	+C	...	...	983	*900	...	...	...	...	*12.0	...
Italy - Italie											
Total	C	564 679	576 911	571 356	560 241	555 247	9.8	10.0	9.9	9.7	9.6
Latvia - Lettonie[13]											
Total	C	33 533	34 200	32 844	32 205	32 991	13.8	14.2	13.7	13.6	14.0
Urban - Urbaine	C	21 558	22 043	21 246	20 921	21 460	12.9	13.3	13.0	13.0	13.4
Rural - Rurale	C	11 975	12 157	11 598	11 284	11 531	15.7	16.0	15.3	14.9	15.3
Liechtenstein											
Total	C	230	...	...	...	...	7.4	...	...	...	...
Lithuania - Lituanie[13]											
Total	C	41 143	40 757	40 003	38 919	40 399	11.5	11.5	11.4	11.1	11.6
Urban - Urbaine	C	22 616	22 413	...	21 932	22 962	9.4	9.4	...	9.4	9.9
Rural - Rurale	C	18 527	18 344	...	16 987	17 437	16.0	15.8	...	14.7	15.1
Luxembourg											
Total	C	3 937	3 901	3 793	3 754	3 719	9.4	9.1	8.8	8.6	8.4

18. Deaths and crude death rates, by urban/rural residence: 1997 - 2001
Décès et taux bruts de mortalité, selon la résidence, urbaine/rurale: 1997 - 2001 (continued — suite)

(See notes at end of table. — Voir notes à la fin du tableau.)

Continent, country or area, and urban/rural residence / Continent, pays ou zone et résidence, urbaine/rurale	Code[1]	Number - Nombre					Rate - Taux				
		1997	1998	1999	2000	2001	1997	1998	1999	2000	2001
EUROPE											
Malta - Malte[36]											
Total	C	2 888	3 044	3 097	2 957	2 935	7.5	7.9	8.0	7.6	7.4
Monaco											
Total	C	485	538	...	547	...	15.2	...	...	16.4	...
Netherlands - Pays-Bas[37]											
Total	C	135 783	137 482	140 487	140 527	140 377	8.7	8.8	8.9	8.8	8.7
Urban - Urbaine	C	87 798	88 815	...	92 934	93 616	9.1	9.1	...	...	...
Rural - Rurale	C	47 985	48 667	...	47 593	46 761	8.1	8.2	...	...	...
Norway - Norvège[38]											
Total	C	44 595	44 112	45 170	44 002	43 981	10.1	10.0	10.1	9.8	9.7
Poland - Pologne											
Total	C	380 201	375 354	381 415	*368 100	*363 220	9.8	9.7	9.9	*9.5	*9.4
Urban - Urbaine	C	220 883	219 331	223 630	...	...	9.2	9.2	9.4	...	...
Rural - Rurale	C	159 318	156 023	157 785	...	...	10.8	10.6	10.7	...	...
Portugal											
Total	C	105 157	106 382	107 871	105 804	105 092	10.6	10.7	10.8	10.6	10.2
Republic of Moldova - République de Moldova[13]											
Total	C	50 614	39 922	41 315	41 224	40 075	13.9	10.9	11.3	11.3	11.0
Urban - Urbaine	C	...	13 180	13 512	13 266	12 844	...	8.6	8.8	8.8	8.6
Rural - Rurale	C	...	26 742	27 803	27 958	27 231	...	12.6	13.1	13.2	12.7
Romania - Roumanie											
Total	C	279 315	269 166	265 194	255 820	259 603	12.4	12.0	11.8	11.4	11.6
Urban - Urbaine	C	115 997	112 733	...	108 436	110 063	9.4	9.1	...	8.9	9.0
Rural - Rurale	C	163 318	156 433	...	147 384	149 540	16.1	15.4	...	14.5	14.7
Russian Federation - Fédération de Russie[13]											
Total	C	2 015 779	1 988 744	2 144 316	2 225 332	2 251 814	13.7	13.6	14.7	15.3	15.6
Urban - Urbaine	C	1 387 771	1 379 804	1 499 466	...	...	...	...	14.1	...	...
Rural - Rurale	C	628 008	608 940	644 850	...	...	...	...	16.3	...	...
San Marino - Saint-Marin											
Total	+C	178	190	198	188	...	6.9	7.3	7.5	7.0	...
Urban - Urbaine	+C	159	...	...	168	...	6.9	...	...	7.4	...
Rural - Rurale	+C	19	...	...	20	...	...	...	...	...	...
Serbia and Montenegro - Serbie-et-Montenegro											
Total	C	111 845	113 312	115 461	118 078	114 881	10.6	10.7	10.9	11.1	10.8
Urban - Urbaine	C	54 122	55 867	57 007	59 324	...	9.9	10.2	10.4	10.8	...
Rural - Rurale	C	57 723	57 445	58 454	58 754	...	11.2	11.2	11.3	11.4	...
Slovakia - Slovaquie											
Total	C	52 124	53 156	52 402	52 703	51 980	9.7	9.9	9.7	9.8	9.7
Urban - Urbaine	C	...	24 983	24 492	...	24 520	...	8.1	8.0	...	...
Rural - Rurale	C	...	28 173	27 910	...	27 460	...	12.1	12.0	...	...
Slovenia - Slovénie											
Total	C	18 928	19 039	18 885	18 588	18 508	9.5	9.6	9.5	9.3	9.3
Urban - Urbaine	C	...	8 429	8 409	8 345	8 277	...	...	...	...	...
Rural - Rurale	C	...	10 610	10 476	10 243	10 231	...	...	...	...	...
Spain - Espagne											
Total	C	349 521	360 511	371 102	360 391	*351 147	8.9	9.1	9.4	9.0	*8.7
Sweden - Suède											
Total	C	93 278	93 271	94 726	93 285	93 752	10.5	10.5	10.7	10.5	10.5
Switzerland - Suisse											
Total	C	62 839	62 568	62 503	62 528	61 287	8.9	8.8	8.7	8.7	8.5
Urban - Urbaine	C	43 274	42 928	42 693	42 868	42 157	9.0	8.9	8.9	8.8	8.6
Rural - Rurale	C	19 565	19 640	19 810	19 660	19 130	8.5	8.5	8.5	8.4	8.2

18. Deaths and crude death rates, by urban/rural residence: 1997 - 2001
Décès et taux bruts de mortalité, selon la résidence, urbaine/rurale: 1997 - 2001 (continued — suite)

(See notes at end of table. — Voir notes à la fin du tableau.)

Continent, country or area, and urban/rural residence / Continent, pays ou zone et résidence, urbaine/rurale	Code[1]	Number - Nombre					Rate - Taux				
		1997	1998	1999	2000	2001	1997	1998	1999	2000	2001
EUROPE											
The Former Yugoslav Rep. of Macedonia - L'ex - République yougoslave de Macédoine											
Total	C	16 596	...	16 789	17 253	16 919	8.3	...	8.3	...	8.3
Urban - Urbaine	C	9 429	...	9 539	10 013	9 939	7.9	...	...	...	...
Rural - Rurale	C	7 167	...	7 250	7 240	6 980	8.9	...	...	...	...
Ukraine[13]											
Total	C	754 151	719 954	739 170	758 082	745 952	14.8	14.3	14.8	15.2	15.2
Urban - Urbaine	C	444 446	425 521	...	...	450 329	12.9	12.4	...	...	...
Rural - Rurale	C	309 705	294 433	...	...	295 623	18.9	18.1	...	...	...
United Kingdom - Royaume - Uni											
Total	C	629 746	629 172	632 062	608 366	602 268	10.7	10.6	10.6	10.2	10.1
OCEANIA — OCEANIE											
Australia - Australie											
Total	+C	129 350	127 202	128 102	128 291	128 557	7.0	6.8	6.8	6.7	6.6
Cook Islands - Îles Cook											
Total	+C	143	107	96	...	...	7.8	6.1	5.9	...	...
Fiji - Fidji											
Total	+C	...	5 241	3 603	...	...	...	6.6	4.5	...	...
French Polynesia - Polynésie française											
Total	U	1 089	1 114	1 003	1 013	...	...	...	...	...	...
Guam[39]											
Total	C	639	651	724	667	...	4.1	4.4	4.8	4.3	...
Marshall Islands - Îles Marshall											
Total	+U	243	...	...	...	271	...	...	...	...	...
Micronesia, Federated States of - Micronésie, États Fédérés de La											
Total	U	464	...	...	...	...	...	...	...	...	...
New Caledonia - Nouvelle - Calédonie											
Total	C	1 016	982	1 095	...	...	5.1	4.8	5.3	...	...
New Zealand - Nouvelle - Zélande											
Total	+C	27 471	26 206	28 122	26 660	...	7.3	6.9	7.4	7.0	...
Urban - Urbaine	+C	24 803	23 668	25 385	24 014	...	...	...	...	...	...
Rural - Rurale	+C	2 656	2 418	2 620	2 563	...	...	...	...	...	...
Northern Mariana Islands - Îles Mariannes septentrionales											
Total	U	147	180	189	...	...	...	...	...	...	...
Palau - Palaos											
Total	C	121	125	131	...	...	6.7	6.8	6.9	...	...
Samoa											
Total	U	...	531	...	...	...	...	...	...	...	...
Tonga											
Total	+C	467	498	675	653	...	4.7	5.0	6.8	6.5	...

GENERAL NOTES - NOTES GENERALES

For certain countries, there is a discrepancy between the total number of deaths shown in this table and those shown in subsequent tables for the same year. Usually this discrepancy arises because the total number of deaths occurring in a given year is revised, although the remaining tabulations are not. Data exclude foetal deaths. Rates are the number of deaths per 1 000 mid-year population. For definitions of 'urban', see end of Technical Notes for table 6. For method of evaluation and limitations of data, see Technical Notes for this table. — Pour quelques pays il y a une discordance entre le nombre total des décès vivantes présenté dans ce tableau et ceux présentés après pour la même année. Habituellement ces différences apparaîssent lorsque le nombre total des décès pour une certaine année a été révisé; alors que les autres tabulations ne l'ont pas été. Les données ne comprennent pas les morts foetales. Les taux représentent le nombre de décès pour 1 000 personnes au milieu de l'année. Pour les définitions des 'régions urbaines', se reporter à la fin des Notes techniques du tableau 6. Pour la méthode d'évaluation et les insuffisances des données, voir Notes techniques, pour ce tableaux.

Italics: data from civil registers which are incomplete or of unknown completeness. — *Italiques:* données incomplètes ou dont le degré d'exactitude n'est pas connu, provenant des registres de l'état civil.

FOOTNOTES - NOTES

* Provisional. — Données provisoires.
[1] 'Code' indicates the source of data, as follows:
C - Civil registration, estimated over 90% complete
U - Civil registration, estimated less than 90% complete
I - Other source, estimated reliable
+ - Data tabulated by date of registration rather than occurence.
... - Information not available

Le 'Code' indique la source des données, comme suit:
C - Registres de l'état civil considérés complèts à 90 p. 100 au moins.
U - Registres de l'état civil qui ne sont pas considérés complèts à 90 p. 100 au moins.
I - Autre source, considérée pas douteuses.
+ - Données exploitées selon la date de l'enregistrement et non la date de l'événement.
... - Information pas disponible.

[2] Excluding live-born infants dying before registration of birth. - Non compris les enfants nés vivants décédés avant l'enregistrement de leur naissance.
[3] For Algerian population only. - Pour la population algérienne seulement.
[4] Data refer to national projections. - Les données se referent au projections nationales.
[5] For 1998, based on the results of the population census. - Pour 1998, d'après les résultats du recensement de la population.
[6] Data for urban and rural exclude deaths of unknown residence. - - Les données pur la résidence urbaine et rurale non comprent pas les décès dont on ignore la résidence.
[7] Data for 1997 refer to last twelve months preceding population and housing census of 1997. - Les données pour 1997 se réfèrent au douze mois précédant le recensement de population et de l'habitat de 1997.
[8] Including Canadian residents temporarily in the United States, but excluding United States residents temporarily in Canada. - Y compris les résidents canadiens se trouvant temporairement aux Etats-Unis, mais ne comprennent pas les résidents des Etats-Unis se trouvant temporairement au Canada.
[9] Excluding Indian jungle population. - Non compris les Indiens de la jungle.
[10] Data on live births and deaths are based on a civil registration system put in place in January 1998. - Les données sur les naissances et les décès sont basées sur un système d'enregistrement des faits d'état civil mis en place en janvier 1998.
[11] Excluding nomadic Indian tribes. - Non compris les tribus d'Indiens nomades.
[12] Including an upward adjustment for under-registration. - Y compris un ajustement pour sous-enregistrement.
[13] Excluding infants born alive with less than 28 weeks gestation, less than 1 000 grams in weight and 35 centimeters in length, who die within seven days of birth. - Non compris les enfants nés vivants avant 28 semaines de gestation, pesant moins de 1 000 grammes, mesurant moins de 35 centimètres et décédés dans les sept jours qui ont suivi leur naissance.
[14] For statistical purposes, the data for China do not include those for the Hong Kong Special Administrative Region (Hong Kong SAR), Macao special Adminstrative Region (Macao SAR) and Taiwan province of China. - Pour la présentation des statistiques, les données pour Chine ne comprend pas les Région Administrative Spéciale de Hong Kong (Hong Kong RAS), le Région Administrative Spéciale de Macao (Macao RAS) et Taïwan province de Chine.

[15] Data refer to government controlled areas. - Les données se raportent aux zones contrôlées par le Gouvernement.
[16] Published by the United Nations Economic and Social Commission for Western Asia. - Edité par les Nations Unies économiques et la Commission sociale pour l'Asie occidentale.
[17] Including data for East Jerusalem and Israeli residents in certain other territories under occupation by Israeli military forces since June 1967. - Y compris les données pour Jérusalem-Est et les résidents israéliens dans certains autres territoires occupés depuis 1967 par les forces armées israéliennes.
[18] For Japanese nationals in Japan only; however, rates computed on population including foreigners except foreign military and civilian personnel and their dependants stationed in the area. - Pour les nationaux japonais au Japon seulement; toutefois, les taux sont calculés sur la base d''une population comprenant les étrangers, mais ne comprenant ni les militaires et agents civils étrangers en poste sur le territoire ni les membres de leur famille les accompagnant.
[19] Excluding data for Jordanian territory under occupation since June 1967 by Israeli military forces. Excluding foreigners, including registered Palestinian refugees. - Non compris les données pour le territoire jordanien occupé depuis juin 1967 par les forces armées israéliennes. Non compris les étrangers, mais y compris les réfugiés de Palestine immatriculés.
[20] Excluding alien armed forces, civilian aliens employed by armed forces, and foreign diplomatic personnel and their dependants. - Non compris les militaires étrangers, les civils étrangers employés par les forces armées ni le personnel diplomatique étranger et les membres de leur famille les accompagnant.
[21] For 2001, data refer to last twelve months preceding census on June 2001. - Pour 2001, les données se rapportent pour la dernière fois à douze mois précédant le recensement juin 2001.
[22] Based on the results of the Population Growth Survey. - D'après les résultats de la 'Population Growth Survey.'
[23] Excluding data for the Pakistan-held part of Jammu and Kashmir, the final status of which has not yet been determined. - Non compris les données concernant la partie du Jammu et Cachemire occupée par le Pakistan dont le statut définitif n'a pas été déterminé.
[24] Excluding transients afloat and non-locally domiciled military and civilian services personnel and their dependants. - Non compris les personnes de passage þ bord de navires, ni les militaires et agents civils domiciliés hors du territoire et les membres de leur famille les accompagnant.
[25] Excluding nomad population and Palestinian refugees. - Non compris la population nomade et les réfugiés de Palestine.
[26] Including late registered deaths. - Y compris les décès enregistrés tardivement.
[27] Based on the results of the Population Demographic Survey. - - D'après les résultats de la Population Demographic Survey.
[28] Including armed forces stationed outside the country, but excluding alien armed forces stationed in the area. - Y compris les militaires nationaux hors du pays, mais non compris les militaires étrangers en garnison sur le territoire.
[29] Excluding Faeroe Islands and Greenland. - Non compris les îles Féroé et Gröenland.
[30] Including nationals temporarily outside the country. - Y compris les nationaux se trouvant temporairement hors du pays.
[31] Including armed forces stationed outside the country. - Y compris les militaires nationaux hors du pays.
[32] Data for urban/rural, excluding nationals outside the country. - Les données selon la résidence urbaine/rurale, non compris les nationaux hors du pays.
[33] Excluding armed forces. - Non compris les militaires en garnison.
[34] Data for urban/rural residence, for the de jure population. - Les données selon la résidence urbaine/rurale, pour la population de droit.
[35] Events registered within one year of occurrence. - Evénements enregistrés dans l'année qui suit l'événement.
[36] Rates computed on population including civilian nationals temporarily outside the country. - Les taux sont calculés sur la base d'un chiffre de population qui comprend les civils nationaux temporairement hors du pays.
[37] Including residents outside the country if listed in a Netherlands population register. - Y compris les résidents hors du pays, s'ils sont inscrits sur un registre de population néerlandais.
[38] Including residents temporarily outside the country. - Y compris les résidents se trouvant temporairement hors du pays.
[39] Including United States military personnel, their dependants and contract employees. - Y compris les militaires des Etats-Unis, les membres de leur famille les accompagnant et les agents contractuels des Etats-Unis.

Table 19

Table 19 presents deaths by age, sex and urban/rural residence for latest available year.

Description of variables: Age is defined as age at last birthday, that is, the difference between the date of birth and the date of the occurrence of the event, expressed in completed solar years. The age classification used in this table is the following: under 1 year, 1-4 years, 5-year age groups through 95-99 years, and 100 years or over.

The urban/rural classification of deaths is that provided by each country or area; it is presumed to be based on the national census definitions of urban population that have been set forth at the end of the technical notes for table 6.

Reliability of data: Data from civil registers of deaths which are reported as incomplete (less than 90 per cent completeness) or of unknown completeness are considered unreliable and are set in italics rather than in roman type. Table 18 and the technical notes for that table provide more detailed information on the completeness of death registration. For more information about the quality of vital statistics data in general, and the information available on the basis of the completeness estimates in particular, see section 4.2 of the Technical Notes.

Limitations: Statistics on deaths by age and sex are subject to the same qualifications as have been set forth for vital statistics in general and death statistics in particular as discussed in section 4 of the Technical Notes.

The reliability of the data is an important factor in considering the limitations. In addition, some deaths are tabulated by date of registration and not by date of occurrence; these have been indicated by a plus sign (+). Whenever the lag between the date of occurrence and date of registration is prolonged and, therefore, a large proportion of the death registrations are delayed, death statistics for any given year may be seriously affected.

As a rule, however, delays in the registration of deaths are less common and shorter than in the registration of live births.

Another factor which limits international comparability is the practice of some countries or areas of not including in death statistics infants who were born alive but died before the registration of the birth or within the first 24 hours of life, thus underestimating the number of deaths under one year of age. Statistics of this type are footnoted.

Because these statistics are classified according to age, they are subject to the limitations with respect to accuracy of age reporting similar to those already discussed in connection with section 3.1.3 of the Technical Notes. The factors influencing the accuracy of reporting may be somewhat dissimilar in vital statistics (because of the differences in the method of taking a census and registering a death) but, in general, the same errors can be observed.

The absence of frequencies in the unknown age group does not necessarily indicate completely accurate reporting and tabulation of the age item. It is often an indication that the unknowns have been eliminated by assigning ages to them before tabulation, or by proportionate distribution after tabulation.

International comparability of statistics on deaths by age is also affected by the use of different methods to determine age at death. If age is obtained from an item that simply requests age at death in completed years or is derived from information on year of birth and death rather than from information on complete date (day, month and year) of birth and death, the number of deaths classified in the under-one-year age group will tend to be reduced and the number of deaths in the next age group will tend to be somewhat increased.

A similar bias may affect other age groups but its impact is usually negligible. Information on this factor is given in the footnotes when known.

The comparability of data by urban/rural residence is affected by the national definitions of urban and rural used in tabulating these data. It is assumed, in the absence of specific information to the contrary, that the definitions of urban and rural used in connection with the national population census were also used in the compilation of the vital statistics for each country or area. However, the possibility cannot be excluded that, for a given country or area, the same definitions of urban and rural are not used for both the vital statistics data and the population census data. When known, the definitions of urban used in national population censuses are presented at the end of the technical notes for table 6. As discussed in detail in the technical notes for table 6, these definitions vary considerably from one country or area to another.

Coverage: Deaths by age and sex are shown for 132 countries or areas. Data are presented by urban/rural residence for 62 countries or areas.

Earlier data: Deaths by age and sex have been shown for the latest available year in each issue of the Yearbook since the 1955 issue. Data included in this table update the series covering a period of years as follows:

Issue	Years Covered
Historical Supplement CD, 1997	1948 – 1997
1996	1987 – 1995
1992	1983 – 1992
1985	1976 – 1984
1980	1971 – 1979
Historical Supplement, 1979	1948 - 1977

Data have been presented by urban/rural residence in each regular issue of the Yearbook since the 1967 issue.

Tableau 19

Le tableau 19 présente des données sur les décès selon l'âge, le sexe et la résidence (urbaine/rurale) pour la dernière année disponible.

Description des variables: L'âge considéré est l'âge au dernier anniversaire, c'est-à-dire la différence entre la date de naissance et la date du décès, exprimée en années solaires révolues. La classification par âge est la suivante : moins d'un an, 1 à 4 ans, groupes quinquennaux jusqu'à 95-99 ans, et 100 ans et plus.

La classification des décès selon la résidence (urbaine/rurale) est celle qui a été fournie par chaque pays ou zone; il est donc présumé qu'elle repose sur les définitions de la population urbaine utilisées pour les recensements nationaux, qui sont reproduites à la fin des notes techniques du tableau 6.

Fiabilité des données : Les données sur les décès provenant des registres d'état civil qui sont déclarés incomplets (degré d'exhaustivité inférieur à 90 p.100) ou dont le degré d'exhaustivité n'est pas connu sont jugées douteuses et apparaissent en italique et non en caractères romains. Le tableau 18 et les notes techniques s'y rapportant présentent des renseignements plus détaillés sur le degré d'exhaustivité de l'enregistrement des décès. Pour plus de précisions sur la qualité des statistiques de l'état civil en général, et l'exhaustivité en particulier, voir la section 4.2 des Notes techniques.

Insuffisance des données : Les statistiques des décès selon l'âge et le sexe appellent les mêmes réserves que les statistiques de l'état civil en général et les statistiques de mortalité en particulier (voir explications à la section 4 des Notes techniques).

La fiabilité des données, au sujet de laquelle des indications ont été fournies plus haut, est un facteur important en l'occurrence. Il faut également tenir compte du fait que, dans certains cas, les données relatives aux décès sont classées par date d'enregistrement et non par date d'occurrence; ces cas ont été identifiés par le signe (+). Lorsque le décalage entre le décès et son enregistrement est grand, c'est-à-dire quand une forte proportion des décès fait l'objet d'un enregistrement tardif, les statistiques des décès de l'année peuvent être sérieusement faussées.

En règle générale, toutefois, les décès sont enregistrés beaucoup plus rapidement que les naissances vivantes, et les longs retards sont rares.

Un autre facteur qui nuit à la comparabilité internationale est la pratique de certains pays ou zones qui consiste à ne pas inclure dans les statistiques des décès les enfants nés vivants mais décédés avant l'enregistrement de leur naissance ou dans les 24 heures qui ont suivi la naissance, pratique qui conduit à sous-évaluer le nombre de décès à moins d'un an. Quand tel était le cas, on l'a signalé en note à la fin du tableau.

Etant donné que ces statistiques sont classées selon l'âge, elles appellent les mêmes réserves concernant l'exactitude des déclarations d'âge que celles dont il a été fait mention dans la section 3.1.3 des Notes techniques. Dans le cas des données d'état civil, les facteurs qui interviennent à cet égard sont parfois un peu différents, étant donné que le recensement et l'enregistrement des décès se font par des méthodes différentes, mais, d'une manière générale, les erreurs observées sont les mêmes.

Si aucun nombre ne figure dans la colonne réservée aux âges inconnus, cela ne signifie pas nécessairement que les déclarations d'âge et le classement par âge sont tout à fait exacts. C'est souvent une indication que les personnes d'âge inconnu se sont vues attribuer un âge avant la répartition où elles ont été réparties proportionnellement aux effectifs connus après cette opération.

Le manque d'uniformité des méthodes suivies pour obtenir l'âge au moment du décès nuit également à la comparabilité internationale des données. Si l'âge est connu, soit d'après la réponse à une simple question sur l'âge du décès en années révolues, soit d'après l'année de la naissance et l'année du décès, et non d'après des renseignements concernant la date exacte (année, mois et jour) de la naissance et du décès, le nombre de décès classés dans la catégorie 'moins d'un an' sera entaché d'une erreur par défaut et le chiffre figurant dans la catégorie suivante d'une erreur par excès.

Les données pour les autres groupes d'âge pourront être entachées d'une distorsion analogue, mais ses répercussions seront généralement négligeables. Ces imperfections, lorsqu'elles étaient connues, ont été signalées en note à la fin du tableau.

La comparabilité des données selon la résidence (urbaine/rurale) peut être limitée par les définitions nationales des termes 'urbain' et 'rural' utilisées pour le classement de ces données. En l'absence d'indications contraires, on a supposé que les définitions des termes 'urbain' et 'rural' utilisées pour le recensement national de la population l'avaient été aussi pour l'établissement des statistiques de l'état civil dans chaque pays ou zone. Toutefois, on ne peut exclure la possibilité que, pour un pays ou une zone, les mêmes définitions n'aient pas été utilisées dans les deux cas. Les définitions du terme "urbain" utilisées pour les recensements nationaux de population ont été indiquées à la fin des notes techniques du tableau 6 lorsqu'elles étaient connues. Comme on l'a précisé en détail dans les notes techniques relatives au tableau 6, ces définitions varient très sensiblement d'un pays ou zone à l'autre.

Portée : Ce tableau présente des données sur les décès selon l'âge et le sexe pour 132 pays ou zones. Des données selon la résidence (urbaine/rurale) sont présentées pour 62 pays ou zones.

Données publiées antérieurement : Des statistiques des décès selon l'âge et le sexe ont été présentées, pour la dernière année où il en existait, dans chaque édition de l'Annuaire démographique depuis celle de 1955. Les données présentées dans ce tableau mettent à jour les périodes d'années suivantes :

Editions	Années considérées
Supplément rétrospectif (CD), 1997	1948 – 1997
1996	1987 – 1995
1992	1983 – 1992
1985	1976 – 1984
1980	1971 – 1979
Supplément rétrospectif, 1979	1948 - 1977

Des données selon la résidence (urbaine/rurale) ont été présentées dans toutes les éditions courantes de l'Annuaire depuis celle de 1967.

19. Deaths by age, sex and urban/rural residence: latest available year
Décès selon l'âge, le sexe et la résidence, urbaine/rurale: dernière année disponible

(See notes at end of table.— Voir notes à la fin du tableau.)

Continent, country or area, year and age (in years) / Continent, pays ou zone, année et âge (en années)	Code[1]	Total			Urban - Urbaine			Rural - Rurale		
		Both sexes - Les deux sexes	Male - Masculin	Female - Féminin	Both sexes - Les deux sexes	Male - Masculin	Female - Féminin	Both sexes - Les deux sexes	Male - Masculin	Female - Féminin
AFRICA — AFRIQUE										
Algeria - Algérie[2,3]										
1998										
Total	+U	131 708	73 352	58 356	...	...	...	...	...	...
0 - 1	+U	21 169	12 009	9 160	...	...	...	...	...	...
1 - 4	+U	4 475	2 378	2 097	...	...	...	...	...	...
5 - 9	+U	2 759	1 592	1 167	...	...	...	...	...	...
10 - 14	+U	2 272	1 373	899	...	...	...	...	...	...
15 - 19	+U	3 017	1 947	1 070	...	...	...	...	...	...
20 - 24	+U	3 425	2 335	1 090	...	...	...	...	...	...
25 - 29	+U	3 508	2 355	1 153	...	...	...	...	...	...
30 - 34	+U	3 216	1 958	1 258	...	...	...	...	...	...
35 - 39	+U	3 195	1 770	1 425	...	...	...	...	...	...
40 - 44	+U	3 468	1 959	1 509	...	...	...	...	...	...
45 - 49	+U	3 771	2 135	1 636	...	...	...	...	...	...
50 - 54	+U	3 777	2 184	1 593	...	...	...	...	...	...
55 - 59	+U	5 113	2 908	2 205	...	...	...	...	...	...
60 - 64	+U	7 616	4 227	3 389	...	...	...	...	...	...
65 - 69	+U	8 962	4 937	4 025	...	...	...	...	...	...
70 - 74	+U	10 320	5 732	4 588	...	...	...	...	...	...
75 - 79	+U	11 346	6 241	5 105	...	...	...	...	...	...
80+	+U	30 299	15 312	14 987	...	...	...	...	...	...
Egypt - Égypte										
1999										
Total	C	401 433	218 195	183 238	181 665	103 100	78 565	219 768	115 095	104 673
0 - 1	C	49 765	26 263	23 502	19 265	10 846	8 419	30 500	15 417	15 083
1 - 4	C	13 891	7 032	6 859	4 047	2 254	1 793	9 844	4 778	5 066
5 - 9	C	5 502	3 213	2 289	2 232	1 367	865	3 270	1 846	1 424
10 - 14	C	5 222	3 008	2 214	2 354	1 429	925	2 868	1 579	1 289
15 - 19	C	6 150	3 830	2 320	3 275	2 151	1 124	2 875	1 679	1 196
20 - 24	C	6 219	3 978	2 241	3 449	2 362	1 087	2 770	1 616	1 154
25 - 29	C	5 738	3 532	2 206	3 104	2 062	1 042	2 634	1 470	1 164
30 - 34	C	6 060	3 744	2 316	3 090	1 990	1 100	2 970	1 754	1 216
35 - 39	C	8 567	5 239	3 328	4 281	2 705	1 576	4 286	2 534	1 752
40 - 44	C	10 907	7 090	3 817	5 595	3 611	1 984	5 312	3 479	1 833
45 - 49	C	16 651	10 812	5 839	8 632	5 570	3 062	8 019	5 242	2 777
50 - 54	C	22 002	13 557	8 445	11 596	7 229	4 367	10 406	6 328	4 078
55 - 59	C	24 114	14 682	9 432	12 154	7 548	4 606	11 960	7 134	4 826
60 - 64	C	33 825	19 470	14 355	16 736	9 696	7 040	17 089	9 774	7 315
65 - 69	C	42 332	23 770	18 562	19 916	11 497	8 419	22 416	12 273	10 143
70 - 74	C	46 533	24 287	22 246	21 071	11 253	9 818	25 462	13 034	12 428
75+	C	97 955	44 688	53 267	40 868	19 530	21 338	57 087	25 158	31 929
Libyan Arab Jamahiriya - Jamahiriya arabe libyenne										
2000										
Total	U	17 367	10 143	7 224	...	...	...	...	...	...
0 - 1	U	2 155	1 198	957	...	...	...	...	...	...
1 - 4	U	560	317	243	...	...	...	...	...	...
5 - 9	U	270	155	115	...	...	...	...	...	...
10 - 19	U	641	397	244	...	...	...	...	...	...
20 - 29	U	996	763	233	...	...	...	...	...	...
30 - 39	U	987	655	332	...	...	...	...	...	...
40 - 49	U	1 093	607	486	...	...	...	...	...	...
50 - 59	U	1 624	895	729	...	...	...	...	...	...
60 - 69	U	2 749	1 631	1 118	...	...	...	...	...	...
70 - 79	U	3 347	2 000	1 347	...	...	...	...	...	...
80+	U	2 945	1 525	1 420	...	...	...	...	...	...
Malawi[4]										
1998										
Total	I	208 040	113 856	94 184	22 186	12 404	9 782	185 854	101 452	84 402
0 - 1	I	44 928	24 977	19 951	5 241	2 968	2 273	39 687	22 009	17 678
1 - 4	I	59 930	32 821	27 109	6 180	3 435	2 745	53 750	29 386	24 364
5 - 9	I	16 717	9 200	7 517	1 628	926	702	15 089	8 274	6 815
10 - 14	I	9 638	4 849	4 789	801	440	361	8 837	4 409	4 428

459

19. Deaths by age, sex and urban/rural residence: latest available year
Décès selon l'âge, le sexe et la résidence, urbaine/rurale: dernière année disponible (continued — suite)

(See notes at end of table.— Voir notes à la fin du tableau.)

Continent, country or area, year and age (in years) / Continent, pays ou zone, année et âge (en années)	Code[1]	Total			Urban - Urbaine			Rural - Rurale		
		Both sexes - Les deux sexes	Male - Masculin	Female - Féminin	Both sexes - Les deux sexes	Male - Masculin	Female - Féminin	Both sexes - Les deux sexes	Male - Masculin	Female - Féminin
AFRICA — AFRIQUE										
Malawi[4]										
1998										
15 - 19	I	7 130	3 427	3 703	672	336	336	6 458	3 091	3 367
20 - 24	I	11 710	6 947	4 763	1 240	629	611	10 470	6 318	4 152
25 - 29	I	9 290	4 853	4 437	1 168	548	620	8 122	4 305	3 817
30 - 34	I	8 797	4 481	4 316	1 168	621	547	7 629	3 860	3 769
35 - 39	I	7 036	3 678	3 358	969	553	416	6 067	3 125	2 942
40 - 44	I	6 338	3 713	2 625	822	527	295	5 516	3 186	2 330
45 - 49	I	5 639	3 705	1 934	587	388	199	5 052	3 317	1 735
50 - 54	I	3 677	2 160	1 517	461	310	151	3 216	1 850	1 366
55 - 59	I	3 872	1 739	2 133	335	200	135	3 537	1 539	1 998
60 - 64	I	2 921	1 620	1 301	259	152	107	2 662	1 468	1 194
65 - 69	I	2 695	1 257	1 438	156	90	66	2 539	1 167	1 372
70 - 74	I	2 228	1 358	870	131	76	55	2 097	1 282	815
75 - 79	I	1 599	942	657	104	64	40	1 495	878	617
80 - 84	I	1 516	842	674	92	52	40	1 424	790	634
85+	I	2 379	1 287	1 092	172	89	83	2 207	1 198	1 009
Mauritius - Maurice										
2000										
Total	+C	7 982	4 489	3 493	...	...	...	...	...	...
0 - 1	+C	322	206	116	...	...	...	...	...	...
1 - 4	+C	46	23	23	...	...	...	...	...	...
5 - 9	+C	26	17	9	...	...	...	...	...	...
10 - 14	+C	32	21	11	...	...	...	...	...	...
15 - 19	+C	61	37	24	...	...	...	...	...	...
20 - 24	+C	87	66	21	...	...	...	...	...	...
25 - 29	+C	124	80	44	...	...	...	...	...	...
30 - 34	+C	152	106	46	...	...	...	...	...	...
35 - 39	+C	220	162	58	...	...	...	...	...	...
40 - 44	+C	353	254	99	...	...	...	...	...	...
45 - 49	+C	424	295	129	...	...	...	...	...	...
50 - 54	+C	503	324	179	...	...	...	...	...	...
55 - 59	+C	521	310	211	...	...	...	...	...	...
60 - 64	+C	681	404	277	...	...	...	...	...	...
65 - 69	+C	840	521	319	...	...	...	...	...	...
70 - 74	+C	1 033	555	478	...	...	...	...	...	...
75 - 79	+C	991	499	492	...	...	...	...	...	...
80 - 84	+C	706	311	395	...	...	...	...	...	...
85+	+C	841	281	560	...	...	...	...	...	...
Unknown - Inconnu	+C	19	17	2	...	...	...	...	...	...
Morocco - Maroc[5]										
1999										
Total	U	98 304	63 651	34 653	53 935	33 089	20 846	44 121	30 404	13 717
0 - 1	U	8 885	4 711	4 174	2 867	1 578	1 289	5 998	3 119	2 879
1 - 4	U	4 370	2 264	2 106	1 105	610	495	3 258	1 651	1 607
5 - 9	U	1 676	985	691	596	354	242	1 080	631	449
10 - 14	U	1 559	902	657	611	358	253	946	544	402
15 - 19	U	2 098	1 249	849	1 057	679	378	1 035	567	468
20 - 24	U	2 883	1 742	1 141	1 385	884	501	1 486	853	633
25 - 29	U	2 641	1 657	984	1 491	986	505	1 142	665	477
30 - 34	U	2 685	1 587	1 098	1 505	931	574	1 173	651	522
35 - 39	U	3 086	1 857	1 229	1 884	1 156	728	1 194	695	499
40 - 44	U	3 402	2 136	1 266	2 125	1 344	781	1 264	782	482
45 - 49	U	3 585	2 354	1 231	2 281	1 469	812	1 292	877	415
50 - 54	U	3 934	2 591	1 343	2 438	1 553	885	1 487	1 033	454
55 - 59	U	5 658	3 651	2 007	3 525	2 078	1 447	2 111	1 559	552
60 - 64	U	8 267	5 483	2 784	5 254	3 207	2 047	2 990	2 261	729
65 - 69	U	10 269	6 870	3 399	6 345	3 848	2 497	3 899	3 004	895
70 - 74	U	10 259	7 127	3 132	6 276	3 903	2 373	3 970	3 217	753
75 - 79	U	9 680	6 790	2 890	5 702	3 500	2 202	3 957	3 276	681
80+	U	13 205	9 627	3 578	7 381	4 613	2 768	5 798	4 996	802
Unknown - Inconnu	U	162	68	94	107	38	69	41	23	18

19. Deaths by age, sex and urban/rural residence: latest available year
Décès selon l'âge, le sexe et la résidence, urbaine/rurale: dernière année disponible (continued — suite)

(See notes at end of table.— Voir notes à la fin du tableau.)

Continent, country or area, year and age (in years) / Continent, pays ou zone, année et âge (en années)	Code[1]	Total			Urban - Urbaine			Rural - Rurale		
		Both sexes - Les deux sexes	Male - Masculin	Female - Féminin	Both sexes - Les deux sexes	Male - Masculin	Female - Féminin	Both sexes - Les deux sexes	Male - Masculin	Female - Féminin
AFRICA — AFRIQUE										
Mozambique[6]										
1997										
Total	I	385 754	206 737	179 017	70 750	39 060	31 690	315 004	167 677	147 327
0 - 1	I	99 947	54 065	45 882	16 506	9 132	7 374	83 441	44 933	38 508
1 - 4	I	123 644	66 656	56 988	16 230	8 766	7 464	107 414	57 890	49 524
5 - 9	I	31 778	17 034	14 744	4 267	2 367	1 900	27 511	14 667	12 844
10 - 14	I	14 914	8 144	6 770	2 407	1 337	1 070	12 507	6 807	5 700
15 - 19	I	12 169	5 896	6 273	2 624	1 379	1 245	9 545	4 517	5 028
20 - 24	I	10 633	4 883	5 750	2 691	1 328	1 363	7 942	3 555	4 387
25 - 29	I	9 556	4 643	4 913	2 606	1 378	1 228	6 950	3 265	3 685
30 - 34	I	8 691	4 610	4 081	2 490	1 454	1 036	6 201	3 156	3 045
35 - 39	I	8 180	4 411	3 769	2 340	1 350	990	5 840	3 061	2 779
40 - 44	I	7 276	4 092	3 184	2 158	1 289	869	5 118	2 803	2 315
45 - 49	I	7 208	4 194	3 014	2 130	1 307	823	5 078	2 887	2 191
50 - 54	I	7 386	4 227	3 159	2 191	1 299	892	5 195	2 928	2 267
55 - 59	I	5 300	3 090	2 210	1 484	890	594	3 816	2 200	1 616
60 - 64	I	7 853	4 380	3 473	2 309	1 293	1 016	5 544	3 087	2 457
65 - 69	I	5 348	2 962	2 386	1 608	911	697	3 740	2 051	1 689
70 - 74	I	5 008	2 897	2 111	1 536	855	681	3 472	2 042	1 430
75 - 79	I	3 440	1 918	1 522	1 054	589	465	2 386	1 329	1 057
80+	I	6 610	3 512	3 098	1 751	894	857	4 859	2 618	2 241
Unknown - Inconnu	I	10 813	5 123	5 690	2 368	1 242	1 126	8 445	3 881	4 564
Réunion[2]										
1997										
Total	C	3 608	...	...	...	...	...	...	...	...
0 - 1	C	78	...	...	...	...	...	...	...	...
1 - 4	C	23	...	...	...	...	...	...	...	...
5 - 9	C	10	...	...	...	...	...	...	...	...
10 - 14	C	18	...	...	...	...	...	...	...	...
15 - 19	C	37	...	...	...	...	...	...	...	...
20 - 24	C	50	...	...	...	...	...	...	...	...
25 - 29	C	59	...	...	...	...	...	...	...	...
30 - 34	C	97	...	...	...	...	...	...	...	...
35 - 39	C	107	...	...	...	...	...	...	...	...
40 - 44	C	147	...	...	...	...	...	...	...	...
45 - 49	C	190	...	...	...	...	...	...	...	...
50 - 54	C	211	...	...	...	...	...	...	...	...
55 - 59	C	257	...	...	...	...	...	...	...	...
60 - 64	C	288	...	...	...	...	...	...	...	...
65 - 69	C	340	...	...	...	...	...	...	...	...
70 - 74	C	407	...	...	...	...	...	...	...	...
75 - 79	C	369	...	...	...	...	...	...	...	...
80 - 84	C	376	...	...	...	...	...	...	...	...
85 - 89	C	294	...	...	...	...	...	...	...	...
90 - 94	C	173	...	...	...	...	...	...	...	...
95 - 99	C	65	...	...	...	...	...	...	...	...
100+	C	12	...	...	...	...	...	...	...	...
Saint Helena ex. dep. - Sainte-Hélène sans dép.										
1999										
Total	C	45	24	21	...	...	...	...	...	...
50 - 54	C	2	1	1	...	...	...	...	...	...
55 - 59	C	3	3	-	...	...	...	...	...	...
60 - 64	C	5	3	2	...	...	...	...	...	...
65 - 69	C	2	1	1	...	...	...	...	...	...
70 - 74	C	7	3	4	...	...	...	...	...	...
75 - 79	C	9	5	4	...	...	...	...	...	...
80 - 84	C	8	5	3	...	...	...	...	...	...
85 - 89	C	5	2	3	...	...	...	...	...	...
90 - 94	C	3	-	3	...	...	...	...	...	...
95+	C	1	1	-	...	...	...	...	...	...

(See notes at end of table.— Voir notes à la fin du tableau.)

Continent, country or area, year and age (in years) / Continent, pays ou zone, année et âge (en années)	Code[1]	Total			Urban - Urbaine			Rural - Rurale		
		Both sexes - Les deux sexes	Male - Masculin	Female - Féminin	Both sexes - Les deux sexes	Male - Masculin	Female - Féminin	Both sexes - Les deux sexes	Male - Masculin	Female - Féminin
AFRICA — AFRIQUE										
Seychelles										
2001										
Total	+C	554	330	224	...	...	...	...	...	...
0 - 1	+C	19	8	11	...	...	...	...	...	...
1 - 4	+C	3	2	1	...	...	...	...	...	...
5 - 9	+C	1	-	1	...	...	...	...	...	...
10 - 14	+C	1	1	-	...	...	...	...	...	...
15 - 19	+C	2	1	1	...	...	...	...	...	...
20 - 24	+C	8	8	-	...	...	...	...	...	...
25 - 29	+C	10	10	-	...	...	...	...	...	...
30 - 34	+C	13	11	2	...	...	...	...	...	...
35 - 39	+C	17	11	6	...	...	...	...	...	...
40 - 44	+C	32	25	7	...	...	...	...	...	...
45 - 49	+C	27	21	6	...	...	...	...	...	...
50 - 54	+C	26	20	6	...	...	...	...	...	...
55 - 59	+C	28	22	6	...	...	...	...	...	...
60 - 64	+C	44	29	15	...	...	...	...	...	...
65 - 69	+C	59	33	26	...	...	...	...	...	...
70 - 74	+C	57	35	22	...	...	...	...	...	...
75 - 79	+C	61	35	26	...	...	...	...	...	...
80 - 84	+C	68	36	32	...	...	...	...	...	...
85+	+C	78	22	56	...	...	...	...	...	...
South Africa - Afrique du Sud										
1996										
Total	...	327 068	186 538	140 530	...	...	...	...	...	...
0 - 1	...	24 560	12 979	11 581	...	...	...	...	...	...
1 - 4	...	8 052	4 313	3 739	...	...	...	...	...	...
5 - 9	...	3 098	1 816	1 282	...	...	...	...	...	...
10 - 14	...	2 758	1 602	1 156	...	...	...	...	...	...
15 - 19	...	6 789	4 334	2 455	...	...	...	...	...	...
20 - 24	...	14 257	9 347	4 910	...	...	...	...	...	...
25 - 29	...	17 690	11 477	6 213	...	...	...	...	...	...
30 - 34	...	19 258	12 709	6 549	...	...	...	...	...	...
35 - 39	...	18 249	11 953	6 296	...	...	...	...	...	...
40 - 44	...	18 562	12 328	6 234	...	...	...	...	...	...
45 - 49	...	19 259	12 895	6 364	...	...	...	...	...	...
50 - 54	...	18 817	12 366	6 451	...	...	...	...	...	...
55 - 59	...	22 238	13 715	8 523	...	...	...	...	...	...
60 - 64	...	21 975	12 084	9 891	...	...	...	...	...	...
65 - 69	...	25 965	13 942	12 023	...	...	...	...	...	...
70 - 74	...	22 817	12 274	10 543	...	...	...	...	...	...
75 - 79	...	25 202	11 837	13 365	...	...	...	...	...	...
80 - 84	...	17 137	7 376	9 761	...	...	...	...	...	...
85+	...	19 193	6 443	12 750	...	...	...	...	...	...
Unknown - Inconnu	...	1 192	748	444	...	...	...	...	...	...
Swaziland[6]										
1997										
Total	I	8 480	4 714	3 766	1 370	753	617	7 110	3 961	3 149
0 - 4	I	2 043	1 068	975	301	165	136	1 742	903	839
5 - 9	I	191	104	87	29	15	14	162	89	73
10 - 14	I	143	74	69	23	12	11	120	62	58
15 - 19	I	258	123	135	42	20	22	216	103	113
20 - 24	I	455	199	256	86	39	47	369	160	209
25 - 29	I	603	317	286	112	62	50	491	255	236
30 - 34	I	577	321	256	97	54	43	480	267	213
35 - 39	I	529	315	214	95	49	46	434	266	168
40 - 44	I	489	309	180	86	54	32	403	255	148
45 - 49	I	434	287	147	81	49	32	353	238	115
50 - 54	I	439	274	165	78	48	30	361	226	135
55 - 59	I	358	235	123	64	40	24	294	195	99
60 - 64	I	365	237	128	50	25	25	315	212	103
65 - 69	I	305	195	110	43	31	12	262	164	98
70 - 74	I	315	189	126	41	22	19	274	167	107

19. Deaths by age, sex and urban/rural residence: latest available year
Décès selon l'âge, le sexe et la résidence, urbaine/rurale: dernière année disponible (continued — suite)

(See notes at end of table.— Voir notes à la fin du tableau.)

Continent, country or area, year and age (in years) / Continent, pays ou zone, année et âge (en années)	Code[1]	Total			Urban - Urbaine			Rural - Rurale		
		Both sexes - Les deux sexes	Male - Masculin	Female - Féminin	Both sexes - Les deux sexes	Male - Masculin	Female - Féminin	Both sexes - Les deux sexes	Male - Masculin	Female - Féminin
AFRICA — AFRIQUE										
Swaziland[6]										
1997										
75+	I	745	341	404	97	41	56	648	300	348
Unknown - Inconnu	I	231	126	105	45	27	18	186	99	87
Tunisia - Tunisie										
1995										
Total	U	42 601	25 213	17 388	32 359	19 003	13 356	10 242	6 210	4 032
0 - 1	U	4 248	2 434	1 814	3 538	2 063	1 475	710	371	339
1 - 4	U	1 055	574	481	718	398	320	337	176	161
5 - 9	U	533	301	232	410	227	183	123	74	49
10 - 14	U	398	238	160	319	189	130	79	49	30
15 - 19	U	529	345	184	408	261	147	121	84	37
20 - 24	U	684	457	227	555	371	184	129	86	43
25 - 29	U	698	479	219	564	397	167	134	82	52
30 - 34	U	805	511	294	646	424	222	159	87	72
35 - 39	U	797	480	317	639	386	253	158	94	64
40 - 44	U	887	520	367	726	434	292	161	86	75
45 - 49	U	991	598	393	815	498	317	176	100	76
50 - 54	U	1 154	748	406	959	636	323	195	112	83
55 - 59	U	2 093	1 341	752	1 714	1 105	609	379	236	143
60 - 64	U	3 012	1 847	1 165	2 420	1 490	930	592	357	235
65 - 69	U	3 883	2 394	1 489	3 045	1 890	1 155	838	504	334
70 - 74	U	4 227	2 503	1 724	3 243	1 923	1 320	984	580	404
75 - 79	U	5 002	2 966	2 036	3 619	2 071	1 548	1 383	895	488
80 - 84	U	4 854	2 885	1 969	3 308	1 863	1 445	1 546	1 022	524
85+	U	4 815	2 501	2 314	3 303	1 585	1 718	1 512	916	596
Unknown - Inconnu	U	1 936	1 091	845	1 410	792	618	526	299	227
1998										
Total	U	42 571	25 319	17 252	...	...	...	...	...	...
0 - 1	U	3 098	1 775	1 323	...	...	...	...	...	...
1 - 4	U	2 096	1 196	900	...	...	...	...	...	...
5 - 9	U	412	252	160	...	...	...	...	...	...
10 - 14	U	382	236	146	...	...	...	...	...	...
15 - 19	U	578	408	170	...	...	...	...	...	...
20 - 24	U	653	459	194	...	...	...	...	...	...
25 - 29	U	612	425	187	...	...	...	...	...	...
30 - 34	U	801	528	273	...	...	...	...	...	...
35 - 39	U	812	519	293	...	...	...	...	...	...
40 - 44	U	998	631	367	...	...	...	...	...	...
45 - 49	U	1 161	737	424	...	...	...	...	...	...
50 - 54	U	1 267	805	462	...	...	...	...	...	...
55 - 59	U	1 833	1 152	681	...	...	...	...	...	...
60 - 64	U	2 920	1 843	1 077	...	...	...	...	...	...
65 - 69	U	4 337	2 673	1 664	...	...	...	...	...	...
70 - 74	U	4 918	2 943	1 975	...	...	...	...	...	...
75 - 79	U	5 201	2 930	2 271	...	...	...	...	...	...
80+	U	10 199	5 681	4 518	...	...	...	...	...	...
Unknown - Inconnu	U	293	126	167	...	...	...	...	...	...
AMERICA, NORTH — AMERIQUE DU NORD										
Anguilla										
1999										
Total	+C	58	...	...	...	...	...	...	...	...
1 - 9	+C	1	...	...	...	...	...	...	...	...
10 - 19	+C	3	...	...	...	...	...	...	...	...
30 - 39	+C	1	...	...	...	...	...	...	...	...
40 - 49	+C	3	...	...	...	...	...	...	...	...
50 - 59	+C	5	...	...	...	...	...	...	...	...
60 - 69	+C	7	...	...	...	...	...	...	...	...
70+	+C	38	...	...	...	...	...	...	...	...

19. Deaths by age, sex and urban/rural residence: latest available year
Décès selon l'âge, le sexe et la résidence, urbaine/rurale: dernière année disponible (continued — suite)

(See notes at end of table.— Voir notes à la fin du tableau.)

Continent, country or area, year and age (in years) / Continent, pays ou zone, année et âge (en années)	Code[1]	Total			Urban - Urbaine			Rural - Rurale		
		Both sexes - Les deux sexes	Male - Masculin	Female - Féminin	Both sexes - Les deux sexes	Male - Masculin	Female - Féminin	Both sexes - Les deux sexes	Male - Masculin	Female - Féminin
AMERICA, NORTH — AMERIQUE DU NORD										
Antigua and Barbuda - Antigua-et-Barbuda										
1995										
Total	+C	454	233	221	...	...	...	...	...	...
0 - 1	+C	23	11	12	...	...	...	...	...	...
1 - 4	+C	4	3	1	...	...	...	...	...	...
10 - 14	+C	1	1	-	...	...	...	...	...	...
15 - 19	+C	2	1	1	...	...	...	...	...	...
20 - 24	+C	5	2	3	...	...	...	...	...	...
25 - 29	+C	3	2	1	...	...	...	...	...	...
30 - 34	+C	8	6	2	...	...	...	...	...	...
35 - 39	+C	10	5	5	...	...	...	...	...	...
40 - 44	+C	12	5	7	...	...	...	...	...	...
45 - 49	+C	7	5	2	...	...	...	...	...	...
50 - 54	+C	22	14	8	...	...	...	...	...	...
55 - 59	+C	27	22	5	...	...	...	...	...	...
60 - 64	+C	31	21	10	...	...	...	...	...	...
65 - 69	+C	46	25	21	...	...	...	...	...	...
70 - 74	+C	47	25	22	...	...	...	...	...	...
75 - 79	+C	62	24	38	...	...	...	...	...	...
80 - 84	+C	62	28	34	...	...	...	...	...	...
85+	+C	79	31	48	...	...	...	...	...	...
Unknown - Inconnu	+C	3	2	1	...	...	...	...	...	...
Bahamas										
1998										
Total	U	1 725	960	765	...	...	...	...	...	...
1 - 4	U	13	10	3	...	...	...	...	...	...
5 - 9	U	19	12	7	...	...	...	...	...	...
10 - 14	U	3	2	1	...	...	...	...	...	...
15 - 19	U	29	22	7	...	...	...	...	...	...
20 - 24	U	57	38	19	...	...	...	...	...	...
25 - 29	U	68	46	22	...	...	...	...	...	...
30 - 34	U	107	64	43	...	...	...	...	...	...
35 - 39	U	114	74	40	...	...	...	...	...	...
40 - 44	U	99	55	44	...	...	...	...	...	...
45 - 49	U	112	70	42	...	...	...	...	...	...
50 - 54	U	103	67	36	...	...	...	...	...	...
55 - 59	U	121	80	41	...	...	...	...	...	...
60 - 64	U	121	70	51	...	...	...	...	...	...
65 - 69	U	146	88	58	...	...	...	...	...	...
70 - 74	U	144	73	71	...	...	...	...	...	...
75 - 79	U	128	62	66	...	...	...	...	...	...
80 - 84	U	140	59	81	...	...	...	...	...	...
85 - 89	U	131	45	86	...	...	...	...	...	...
90 - 94	U	49	19	30	...	...	...	...	...	...
95 - 99	U	14	3	11	...	...	...	...	...	...
100+	U	4	-	4	...	...	...	...	...	...
Unknown - Inconnu	U	3	1	2	...	...	...	...	...	...
Belize										
1998										
Total	U	1 350	786	564	...	...	...	...	...	...
0 - 1	U	144	69	75	...	...	...	...	...	...
1 - 4	U	38	19	19	...	...	...	...	...	...
5 - 9	U	16	10	6	...	...	...	...	...	...
10 - 14	U	25	15	10	...	...	...	...	...	...
15 - 19	U	32	25	7	...	...	...	...	...	...
20 - 24	U	60	45	15	...	...	...	...	...	...
25 - 29	U	45	30	15	...	...	...	...	...	...
30 - 34	U	45	34	11	...	...	...	...	...	...
35 - 39	U	54	31	23	...	...	...	...	...	...
40 - 44	U	42	19	23	...	...	...	...	...	...

(See notes at end of table.— Voir notes à la fin du tableau.)

Continent, country or area, year and age (in years) / Continent, pays ou zone, année et âge (en années)	Code[1]	Total			Urban - Urbaine			Rural - Rurale		
		Both sexes - Les deux sexes	Male - Masculin	Female - Féminin	Both sexes - Les deux sexes	Male - Masculin	Female - Féminin	Both sexes - Les deux sexes	Male - Masculin	Female - Féminin
AMERICA, NORTH — AMERIQUE DU NORD										
Belize										
1998										
45 - 49	U	57	35	22	...	...	...	...	...	...
50 - 54	U	57	31	26	...	...	...	...	...	...
55 - 59	U	51	31	20	...	...	...	...	...	...
60 - 64	U	80	47	33	...	...	...	...	...	...
65 - 69	U	101	61	40	...	...	...	...	...	...
70 - 74	U	109	70	39	...	...	...	...	...	...
75 - 79	U	114	81	33	...	...	...	...	...	...
80+	U	269	126	143	...	...	...	...	...	...
Unknown - Inconnu	U	11	7	4	...	...	...	...	...	...
Bermuda - Bermudes										
1998										
Total	C	505	265	240	...	...	...	...	...	...
15 - 19	C	1	1	-	...	...	...	...	...	...
25 - 29	C	2	2	-	...	...	...	...	...	...
30 - 34	C	5	3	2	...	...	...	...	...	...
35 - 39	C	10	6	4	...	...	...	...	...	...
40 - 44	C	14	5	9	...	...	...	...	...	...
45 - 49	C	16	10	6	...	...	...	...	...	...
50 - 54	C	30	17	13	...	...	...	...	...	...
55 - 59	C	26	16	10	...	...	...	...	...	...
60 - 64	C	39	26	13	...	...	...	...	...	...
65 - 69	C	43	26	17	...	...	...	...	...	...
70 - 74	C	63	35	28	...	...	...	...	...	...
75 - 79	C	70	31	39	...	...	...	...	...	...
80 - 84	C	74	41	33	...	...	...	...	...	...
85 - 89	C	48	16	32	...	...	...	...	...	...
90 - 94	C	35	14	21	...	...	...	...	...	...
95 - 99	C	6	2	4	...	...	...	...	...	...
100+	C	4	-	4	...	...	...	...	...	...
Unknown - Inconnu	C	19	14	5	...	...	...	...	...	...
Canada[7]										
2000										
Total	C	218 062	111 742	106 320	...	...	...	...	...	...
0 - 1	C	1 737	986	751	...	...	...	...	...	...
1 - 4	C	300	170	130	...	...	...	...	...	...
5 - 9	C	254	150	104	...	...	...	...	...	...
10 - 14	C	329	190	139	...	...	...	...	...	...
15 - 19	C	1 049	712	337	...	...	...	...	...	...
20 - 24	C	1 318	958	360	...	...	...	...	...	...
25 - 29	C	1 220	860	360	...	...	...	...	...	...
30 - 34	C	1 645	1 120	525	...	...	...	...	...	...
35 - 39	C	2 681	1 740	941	...	...	...	...	...	...
40 - 44	C	3 888	2 432	1 456	...	...	...	...	...	...
45 - 49	C	5 214	3 205	2 009	...	...	...	...	...	...
50 - 54	C	7 475	4 482	2 993	...	...	...	...	...	...
55 - 59	C	9 339	5 762	3 577	...	...	...	...	...	...
60 - 64	C	12 206	7 607	4 599	...	...	...	...	...	...
65 - 69	C	17 878	11 086	6 792	...	...	...	...	...	...
70 - 74	C	25 412	15 074	10 338	...	...	...	...	...	...
75 - 79	C	32 893	17 947	14 946	...	...	...	...	...	...
80 - 84	C	33 592	16 326	17 266	...	...	...	...	...	...
85 - 89	C	31 616	12 737	18 879	...	...	...	...	...	...
90+	C	28 009	8 193	19 816	...	...	...	...	...	...
Unknown - Inconnu	C	7	5	2	...	...	...	...	...	...
Cayman Islands - Îles Caïmanes										
1994										
Total	C	149	81	68	...	...	...	...	...	...
0 - 1	C	7	1	6	...	...	...	...	...	...

(See notes at end of table.— Voir notes à la fin du tableau.)

Continent, country or area, year and age (in years) / Continent, pays ou zone, année et âge (en années)	Code[1]	Total			Urban - Urbaine			Rural - Rurale		
		Both sexes - Les deux sexes	Male - Masculin	Female - Féminin	Both sexes - Les deux sexes	Male - Masculin	Female - Féminin	Both sexes - Les deux sexes	Male - Masculin	Female - Féminin
AMERICA, NORTH — AMERIQUE DU NORD										
Cayman Islands - Îles Caïmanes										
1994										
15 - 24	C	5	5	-	...	...	...	...	...	...
25 - 44	C	11	7	4	...	...	...	...	...	...
45 - 64	C	30	24	6	...	...	...	...	...	...
65+	C	96	44	52	...	...	...	...	...	...
Costa Rica										
1999										
Total	C	15 052	8 699	6 353	...	...	...	...	...	...
0 - 1	C	925	535	390	...	...	...	...	...	...
1 - 4	C	165	95	70	...	...	...	...	...	...
5 - 9	C	95	65	30	...	...	...	...	...	...
10 - 14	C	111	72	39	...	...	...	...	...	...
15 - 19	C	250	184	66	...	...	...	...	...	...
20 - 24	C	309	240	69	...	...	...	...	...	...
25 - 29	C	300	223	77	...	...	...	...	...	...
30 - 34	C	369	258	111	...	...	...	...	...	...
35 - 39	C	447	312	135	...	...	...	...	...	...
40 - 44	C	524	356	168	...	...	...	...	...	...
45 - 49	C	567	372	195	...	...	...	...	...	...
50 - 54	C	607	371	236	...	...	...	...	...	...
55 - 59	C	753	463	290	...	...	...	...	...	...
60 - 64	C	876	540	336	...	...	...	...	...	...
65 - 69	C	1 211	718	493	...	...	...	...	...	...
70 - 74	C	1 539	893	646	...	...	...	...	...	...
75 - 79	C	1 643	898	745	...	...	...	...	...	...
80 - 84	C	1 633	813	820	...	...	...	...	...	...
85+	C	2 708	1 272	1 436	...	...	...	...	...	...
Unknown - Inconnu	C	20	19	1	...	...	...	...	...	...
Cuba[5]										
1999										
Total	C	79 499	43 804	35 695	64 362	34 700	29 662	15 072	9 056	6 016
0 - 1	C	977	561	416	747	431	316	230	130	100
1 - 4	C	292	165	127	217	119	98	75	46	29
5 - 9	C	225	129	96	160	89	71	65	40	25
10 - 14	C	300	184	116	215	130	85	85	54	31
15 - 19	C	446	262	184	329	185	144	115	76	39
20 - 24	C	660	467	193	496	353	143	164	114	50
25 - 29	C	1 182	795	387	875	580	295	306	214	92
30 - 34	C	1 429	957	472	1 101	733	368	327	223	104
35 - 39	C	1 654	1 078	576	1 283	840	443	369	237	132
40 - 44	C	1 772	1 087	685	1 398	861	537	373	225	148
45 - 49	C	2 573	1 549	1 024	2 109	1 271	838	460	274	186
50 - 54	C	3 426	2 004	1 422	2 824	1 652	1 172	596	347	249
55 - 59	C	4 402	2 649	1 753	3 619	2 202	1 417	781	445	336
60 - 64	C	5 402	3 100	2 302	4 453	2 551	1 902	946	547	399
65 - 69	C	7 018	3 981	3 037	5 768	3 245	2 523	1 244	731	513
70 - 74	C	8 850	4 945	3 905	7 232	3 976	3 256	1 612	964	648
75 - 79	C	10 369	5 732	4 637	8 501	4 567	3 934	1 863	1 163	700
80 - 84	C	10 933	5 736	5 197	8 933	4 532	4 401	1 986	1 195	791
85+	C	17 579	8 415	9 164	14 096	6 379	7 717	3 473	2 029	1 444
Unknown - Inconnu	C	10	8	2	6	4	2	2	2	-
Dominican Republic - République dominicaine										
1999										
Total	+U	26 956	15 624	11 332	...	...	...	...	...	...
0 - 1	+U	2 250	1 218	1 032	...	...	...	...	...	...
1 - 4	+U	477	273	204	...	...	...	...	...	...
5 - 9	+U	276	143	133	...	...	...	...	...	...
10 - 14	+U	259	138	121	...	...	...	...	...	...

(See notes at end of table.— Voir notes à la fin du tableau.)

Continent, country or area, year and age (in years) / Continent, pays ou zone, année et âge (en années)	Code[1]	Total			Urban - Urbaine			Rural - Rurale		
		Both sexes - Les deux sexes	Male - Masculin	Female - Féminin	Both sexes - Les deux sexes	Male - Masculin	Female - Féminin	Both sexes - Les deux sexes	Male - Masculin	Female - Féminin
AMERICA, NORTH — AMERIQUE DU NORD										
Dominican Republic - République dominicaine										
1999										
15 - 19	+U	495	330	165	...	...	...	...	...	...
20 - 24	+U	823	570	253	...	...	...	...	...	...
25 - 29	+U	945	600	345	...	...	...	...	...	...
30 - 34	+U	981	651	330	...	...	...	...	...	...
35 - 39	+U	955	619	336	...	...	...	...	...	...
40 - 44	+U	954	615	339	...	...	...	...	...	...
45 - 49	+U	994	600	394	...	...	...	...	...	...
50 - 54	+U	1 175	719	456	...	...	...	...	...	...
55 - 59	+U	1 246	765	481	...	...	...	...	...	...
60 - 64	+U	1 644	985	659	...	...	...	...	...	...
65 - 69	+U	2 065	1 192	873	...	...	...	...	...	...
70 - 74	+U	2 090	1 233	857	...	...	...	...	...	...
75 - 79	+U	2 050	1 185	865	...	...	...	...	...	...
80 - 84	+U	1 726	956	770	...	...	...	...	...	...
85+	+U	2 944	1 440	1 504	...	...	...	...	...	...
Unknown - Inconnu	+U	2 607	1 392	1 215	...	...	...	...	...	...
El Salvador										
2000										
Total	C	28 154	16 694	11 460	19 276	11 241	8 035	8 878	5 453	3 425
0 - 1	C	1 678	965	713	1 048	592	456	630	373	257
1 - 4	C	535	290	245	293	153	140	242	137	105
5 - 9	C	234	133	101	142	86	56	92	47	45
10 - 14	C	260	148	112	161	98	63	99	50	49
15 - 19	C	770	565	205	499	367	132	271	198	73
20 - 24	C	1 274	1 031	243	900	738	162	374	293	81
25 - 29	C	1 207	945	262	827	643	184	380	302	78
30 - 34	C	1 127	894	233	769	620	149	358	274	84
35 - 39	C	1 160	854	306	821	606	215	339	248	91
40 - 44	C	1 141	780	361	741	505	236	400	275	125
45 - 49	C	1 171	786	385	820	557	263	351	229	122
50 - 54	C	1 282	826	456	866	562	304	416	264	152
55 - 59	C	1 584	962	622	1 097	648	449	487	314	173
60 - 64	C	1 786	1 037	749	1 253	711	542	533	326	207
65 - 69	C	2 037	1 170	867	1 382	780	602	655	390	265
70 - 74	C	2 297	1 177	1 120	1 592	799	793	705	378	327
75 - 79	C	2 567	1 327	1 240	1 781	896	885	786	431	355
80 - 84	C	2 281	1 132	1 149	1 609	765	844	672	367	305
85+	C	3 763	1 672	2 091	2 675	1 115	1 560	1 088	557	531
Greenland - Groenland										
1999										
Total	C	482	281	201	372	220	152	110	61	49
0 - 1	C	16	11	5	16	11	5	-	-	-
1 - 4	C	5	2	3	2	-	2	3	2	1
5 - 9	C	2	1	1	1	1	-	1	-	1
10 - 14	C	3	3	-	2	2	-	1	1	-
15 - 19	C	14	10	4	10	7	3	4	3	1
20 - 24	C	13	12	1	8	7	1	5	5	-
25 - 29	C	17	10	7	10	4	6	7	6	1
30 - 34	C	15	12	3	12	9	3	3	3	-
35 - 39	C	21	15	6	17	11	6	4	4	-
40 - 44	C	26	18	8	22	15	7	4	3	1
45 - 49	C	23	10	13	18	8	10	5	2	3
50 - 54	C	30	18	12	22	17	5	8	1	7
55 - 59	C	42	32	10	35	28	7	7	4	3
60 - 64	C	54	33	21	43	29	14	11	4	7
65 - 69	C	57	32	25	38	24	14	19	8	11
70 - 74	C	64	33	31	52	25	27	12	8	4
75 - 79	C	36	16	20	27	12	15	9	4	5

19. Deaths by age, sex and urban/rural residence: latest available year
Décès selon l'âge, le sexe et la résidence, urbaine/rurale: dernière année disponible (continued — suite)

(See notes at end of table.— Voir notes à la fin du tableau.)

Continent, country or area, year and age (in years) Continent, pays ou zone, année et âge (en années)	Code[1]	Total			Urban - Urbaine			Rural - Rurale		
		Both sexes - Les deux sexes	Male - Masculin	Female - Féminin	Both sexes - Les deux sexes	Male - Masculin	Female - Féminin	Both sexes - Les deux sexes	Male - Masculin	Female - Féminin
AMERICA, NORTH — AMERIQUE DU NORD										
Greenland - Groenland										
1999										
80 - 84	C	33	10	23	29	9	20	4	1	3
85+	C	11	3	8	8	1	7	3	2	1
Grenada - Grenade										
2000										
Total	+C	716	365	351	...	...	...	...	...	...
0 - 1	+C	27	10	17	...	...	...	...	...	...
1 - 4	+C	1	1	-	...	...	...	...	...	...
5 - 9	+C	1	1	-	...	...	...	...	...	...
10 - 14	+C	4	4	-	...	...	...	...	...	...
15 - 19	+C	8	2	6	...	...	...	...	...	...
20 - 24	+C	11	9	2	...	...	...	...	...	...
25 - 29	+C	17	13	4	...	...	...	...	...	...
30 - 34	+C	21	11	10	...	...	...	...	...	...
35 - 39	+C	17	7	10	...	...	...	...	...	...
40 - 44	+C	14	9	5	...	...	...	...	...	...
45 - 49	+C	21	13	8	...	...	...	...	...	...
50 - 54	+C	27	15	12	...	...	...	...	...	...
55 - 59	+C	24	17	7	...	...	...	...	...	...
60 - 64	+C	50	30	20	...	...	...	...	...	...
65 - 69	+C	61	35	26	...	...	...	...	...	...
70 - 74	+C	81	52	29	...	...	...	...	...	...
75 - 79	+C	96	50	46	...	...	...	...	...	...
80 - 84	+C	69	27	42	...	...	...	...	...	...
85 - 89	+C	84	34	50	...	...	...	...	...	...
90 - 94	+C	52	16	36	...	...	...	...	...	...
95 - 99	+C	24	8	16	...	...	...	...	...	...
100+	+C	6	1	5	...	...	...	...	...	...
Guatemala										
1999										
Total	C	64 563	37 062	27 501	...	...	...	...	...	...
0 - 1	C	13 161	7 349	5 812	...	...	...	...	...	...
1 - 4	C	5 113	2 670	2 443	...	...	...	...	...	...
5 - 9	C	1 179	611	568	...	...	...	...	...	...
10 - 14	C	935	564	371	...	...	...	...	...	...
15 - 19	C	1 712	1 091	621	...	...	...	...	...	...
20 - 24	C	2 229	1 544	685	...	...	...	...	...	...
25 - 29	C	2 190	1 563	627	...	...	...	...	...	...
30 - 34	C	2 272	1 565	707	...	...	...	...	...	...
35 - 39	C	2 372	1 631	741	...	...	...	...	...	...
40 - 44	C	2 344	1 514	830	...	...	...	...	...	...
45 - 49	C	2 503	1 609	894	...	...	...	...	...	...
50 - 54	C	2 521	1 545	976	...	...	...	...	...	...
55 - 59	C	2 508	1 421	1 087	...	...	...	...	...	...
60 - 64	C	2 978	1 702	1 276	...	...	...	...	...	...
65 - 69	C	3 793	2 062	1 731	...	...	...	...	...	...
70 - 74	C	4 140	2 231	1 909	...	...	...	...	...	...
75 - 79	C	4 260	2 276	1 984	...	...	...	...	...	...
80 - 84	C	3 590	1 887	1 703	...	...	...	...	...	...
85 - 89	C	2 784	1 320	1 464	...	...	...	...	...	...
90 - 94	C	1 219	537	682	...	...	...	...	...	...
95+	C	541	213	328	...	...	...	...	...	...
Unknown - Inconnu	C	219	157	62	...	...	...	...	...	...
Martinique[2]										
1992										
Total	C	2 180	1 201	979	...	...	...	...	...	...
0 - 4	C	50	28	22	...	...	...	...	...	...
5 - 9	C	2	1	1	...	...	...	...	...	...
10 - 14	C	6	3	3	...	...	...	...	...	...
15 - 19	C	21	16	5	...	...	...	...	...	...

(See notes at end of table.— Voir notes à la fin du tableau.)

Continent, country or area, year and age (in years) / Continent, pays ou zone, année et âge (en années)	Code[1]	Total			Urban - Urbaine			Rural - Rurale		
		Both sexes - Les deux sexes	Male - Masculin	Female - Féminin	Both sexes - Les deux sexes	Male - Masculin	Female - Féminin	Both sexes - Les deux sexes	Male - Masculin	Female - Féminin
AMERICA, NORTH — AMERIQUE DU NORD										
Martinique[2]										
1992										
20 - 24	C	27	20	7	...	...	...	...	...	...
25 - 29	C	38	29	9	...	...	...	...	...	...
30 - 34	C	47	34	13	...	...	...	...	...	...
35 - 39	C	29	18	11	...	...	...	...	...	...
40 - 44	C	55	32	23	...	...	...	...	...	...
45 - 49	C	35	27	8	...	...	...	...	...	...
50 - 54	C	70	46	24	...	...	...	...	...	...
55 - 59	C	112	77	35	...	...	...	...	...	...
60 - 64	C	145	97	48	...	...	...	...	...	...
65 - 69	C	222	138	84	...	...	...	...	...	...
70 - 74	C	247	140	107	...	...	...	...	...	...
75 - 79	C	300	172	128	...	...	...	...	...	...
80 - 84	C	275	130	145	...	...	...	...	...	...
85+	C	494	191	303	...	...	...	...	...	...
Unknown - Inconnu	C	5	2	3	...	...	...	...	...	...
Mexico - Mexique[5,8]										
2000										
Total	C	437 667	244 302	193 253	333 980	183 172	150 745	97 870	56 633	41 225
0 - 1	C	38 621	21 793	16 769	29 135	16 451	12 635	9 163	5 164	3 991
1 - 4	C	6 963	3 726	3 236	4 480	2 424	2 055	2 445	1 275	1 170
5 - 9	C	3 457	2 025	1 432	2 378	1 376	1 002	1 048	629	419
10 - 14	C	3 718	2 252	1 466	2 554	1 542	1 012	1 119	687	432
15 - 19	C	7 389	5 106	2 282	5 355	3 735	1 619	1 912	1 271	641
20 - 24	C	9 995	7 388	2 606	7 377	5 496	1 881	2 372	1 682	690
25 - 29	C	11 291	8 380	2 911	8 355	6 199	2 156	2 511	1 820	691
30 - 34	C	12 009	8 737	3 271	9 015	6 537	2 478	2 562	1 823	738
35 - 39	C	13 956	9 848	4 107	10 416	7 297	3 118	3 037	2 109	928
40 - 44	C	15 496	10 387	5 109	11 775	7 787	3 988	3 296	2 242	1 054
45 - 49	C	18 061	11 455	6 603	13 935	8 801	5 133	3 775	2 362	1 412
50 - 54	C	21 068	12 574	8 493	16 547	9 739	6 808	4 207	2 582	1 624
55 - 59	C	25 494	14 839	10 653	19 944	11 471	8 472	5 240	3 127	2 113
60 - 64	C	30 849	17 100	13 747	24 180	13 217	10 962	6 326	3 644	2 681
65 - 69	C	35 978	19 510	16 467	28 249	15 039	13 210	7 439	4 249	3 190
70 - 74	C	39 371	20 865	18 506	30 776	15 986	14 790	8 292	4 651	3 641
75 - 79	C	40 938	21 513	19 424	31 937	16 374	15 562	8 779	5 005	3 774
80 - 84	C	34 891	17 043	17 847	26 926	12 767	14 158	7 816	4 195	3 621
85+	C	65 906	28 336	37 567	49 549	20 328	29 218	16 156	7 906	8 250
Unknown - Inconnu	C	2 216	1 425	757	1 097	606	488	375	210	165
Netherlands Antilles - Antilles néerlandaises										
1992										
Total	C	1 223	664	559	...	...	...	...	...	...
0 - 1	C	33	15	18	...	...	...	...	...	...
1 - 4	C	10	6	4	...	...	...	...	...	...
5 - 9	C	4	1	3	...	...	...	...	...	...
15 - 19	C	7	4	3	...	...	...	...	...	...
20 - 24	C	10	8	2	...	...	...	...	...	...
25 - 29	C	21	14	7	...	...	...	...	...	...
30 - 34	C	20	12	8	...	...	...	...	...	...
35 - 39	C	31	21	10	...	...	...	...	...	...
40 - 44	C	40	20	20	...	...	...	...	...	...
45 - 49	C	42	23	19	...	...	...	...	...	...
50 - 54	C	47	24	23	...	...	...	...	...	...
55 - 59	C	70	47	23	...	...	...	...	...	...
60 - 64	C	97	56	41	...	...	...	...	...	...
65 - 69	C	87	60	27	...	...	...	...	...	...
70 - 74	C	143	87	56	...	...	...	...	...	...
75 - 79	C	143	81	62	...	...	...	...	...	...
80 - 84	C	166	85	81	...	...	...	...	...	...

(See notes at end of table.— Voir notes à la fin du tableau.)

Continent, country or area, year and age (in years) Continent, pays ou zone, année et âge (en années)	Code[1]	Total			Urban - Urbaine			Rural - Rurale		
		Both sexes - Les deux sexes	Male - Masculin	Female - Féminin	Both sexes - Les deux sexes	Male - Masculin	Female - Féminin	Both sexes - Les deux sexes	Male - Masculin	Female - Féminin
AMERICA, NORTH — AMERIQUE DU NORD										
Netherlands Antilles - Antilles néerlandaises										
1992										
85+	C	252	100	152	...	...	...	...	...	...
Nicaragua										
1999										
Total	+U	13 771	7 978	5 793	9 037	5 077	3 960	4 734	2 901	1 833
0 - 1	+U	2 129	1 235	894	1 190	677	513	939	558	381
1 - 4	+U	406	213	193	184	100	84	222	113	109
5 - 9	+U	226	124	102	120	66	54	106	58	48
10 - 14	+U	197	124	73	112	72	40	85	52	33
15 - 19	+U	470	296	174	262	175	87	208	121	87
20 - 24	+U	481	342	139	288	210	78	193	132	61
25 - 29	+U	455	305	150	264	179	85	191	126	65
30 - 34	+U	432	300	132	270	189	81	162	111	51
35 - 39	+U	452	315	137	296	204	92	156	111	45
40 - 44	+U	530	334	196	361	223	138	169	111	58
45 - 49	+U	576	374	202	394	242	152	182	132	50
50 - 54	+U	528	328	200	353	215	138	175	113	62
55 - 59	+U	666	393	273	466	259	207	200	134	66
60 - 64	+U	813	486	327	535	312	223	278	174	104
65 - 69	+U	929	518	411	670	369	301	259	149	110
70 - 74	+U	941	511	430	715	377	338	226	134	92
75 - 79	+U	1 030	544	486	745	372	373	285	172	113
80 - 84	+U	832	452	380	611	318	293	221	134	87
85 - 89	+U	885	419	466	647	279	368	238	140	98
90 - 94	+U	419	192	227	289	125	164	130	67	63
95+	+U	374	173	201	265	114	151	109	59	50
Panama										
1999										
Total	U	11 938	6 978	4 960	7 108	4 042	3 066	4 830	2 936	1 894
0 - 1	U	1 005	571	434	490	284	206	515	287	228
1 - 4	U	302	157	145	81	42	39	221	115	106
5 - 9	U	122	76	46	49	25	24	73	51	22
10 - 14	U	95	58	37	30	17	13	65	41	24
15 - 19	U	222	154	68	117	84	33	105	70	35
20 - 24	U	302	224	78	159	119	40	143	105	38
25 - 29	U	332	246	86	190	139	51	142	107	35
30 - 34	U	369	261	108	225	163	62	144	98	46
35 - 39	U	329	222	107	197	128	69	132	94	38
40 - 44	U	396	260	136	239	158	81	157	102	55
45 - 49	U	411	272	139	265	178	87	146	94	52
50 - 54	U	496	329	167	301	210	91	195	119	76
55 - 59	U	514	322	192	319	198	121	195	124	71
60 - 64	U	663	405	258	413	251	162	250	154	96
65 - 69	U	817	489	328	468	268	200	349	221	128
70 - 74	U	1 012	594	418	620	360	260	392	234	158
75 - 79	U	1 255	693	562	796	415	381	459	278	181
80 - 84	U	1 324	704	620	860	449	411	464	255	209
85 - 89	U	1 066	548	518	690	328	362	376	220	156
90 - 94	U	553	241	312	376	142	234	177	99	78
95 - 99	U	210	75	135	141	45	96	69	30	39
100+	U	49	24	25	38	17	21	11	7	4
Unknown - Inconnu	U	94	53	41	44	22	22	50	31	19
Puerto Rico - Porto Rico[5]										
2000										
Total	C	28 550	16 091	12 459	15 516	8 376	7 140	12 991	7 678	5 313
0 - 1	C	588	327	261	326	184	142	262	143	119
1 - 4	C	74	43	31	49	25	24	25	18	7
5 - 9	C	57	31	26	33	18	15	24	13	11
10 - 14	C	51	25	26	32	15	17	19	10	9

(See notes at end of table.— Voir notes à la fin du tableau.)

Continent, country or area, year and age (in years) / Continent, pays ou zone, année et âge (en années)	Code[1]	Total			Urban - Urbaine			Rural - Rurale		
		Both sexes - Les deux sexes	Male - Masculin	Female - Féminin	Both sexes - Les deux sexes	Male - Masculin	Female - Féminin	Both sexes - Les deux sexes	Male - Masculin	Female - Féminin
AMERICA, NORTH — AMERIQUE DU NORD										
Puerto Rico - Porto Rico[5]										
2000										
15 - 19	C	269	214	55	148	118	30	121	96	25
20 - 24	C	432	364	68	237	201	36	195	163	32
25 - 29	C	422	339	83	243	200	43	179	139	40
30 - 34	C	466	326	140	258	175	83	206	149	57
35 - 39	C	662	491	171	363	264	99	298	227	71
40 - 44	C	762	526	236	444	298	146	317	227	90
45 - 49	C	1 008	693	315	517	339	178	489	352	137
50 - 54	C	1 286	863	423	682	439	243	602	422	180
55 - 59	C	1 530	976	554	799	491	308	730	484	246
60 - 64	C	1 853	1 165	688	975	613	362	878	552	326
65 - 69	C	2 497	1 475	1 022	1 321	763	558	1 174	710	464
70 - 74	C	3 014	1 689	1 325	1 634	887	747	1 380	802	578
75 - 79	C	3 509	1 919	1 590	1 984	1 042	942	1 525	877	648
80 - 84	C	3 638	1 781	1 857	2 018	925	1 093	1 619	855	764
85+	C	6 387	2 806	3 581	3 438	1 367	2 071	2 947	1 438	1 509
Unknown - Inconnu	C	45	38	7	15	12	3	1	1	-
Saint Kitts and Nevis - Saint-Kitts-et-Nevis										
1996										
Total	+C	472	244	228	...	...	...	...	...	...
0 - 1	+C	20	13	7	...	...	...	...	...	...
1 - 4	+C	2	1	1	...	...	...	...	...	...
10 - 14	+C	1	1	-	...	...	...	...	...	...
15 - 19	+C	2	1	1	...	...	...	...	...	...
20 - 24	+C	4	2	2	...	...	...	...	...	...
25 - 29	+C	5	3	2	...	...	...	...	...	...
30 - 34	+C	7	4	3	...	...	...	...	...	...
35 - 39	+C	14	10	4	...	...	...	...	...	...
40 - 44	+C	8	5	3	...	...	...	...	...	...
45 - 49	+C	11	5	6	...	...	...	...	...	...
50 - 54	+C	12	7	5	...	...	...	...	...	...
55 - 59	+C	15	7	8	...	...	...	...	...	...
60 - 64	+C	31	18	13	...	...	...	...	...	...
65 - 69	+C	45	23	22	...	...	...	...	...	...
70 - 74	+C	60	32	28	...	...	...	...	...	...
75 - 79	+C	68	38	30	...	...	...	...	...	...
80 - 84	+C	75	41	34	...	...	...	...	...	...
85+	+C	92	33	59	...	...	...	...	...	...
Saint Lucia - Sainte-Lucie										
2000										
Total	C	939	507	432	...	...	...	...	...	...
0 - 1	C	38	21	17	...	...	...	...	...	...
1 - 4	C	3	3	-	...	...	...	...	...	...
5 - 9	C	6	3	3	...	...	...	...	...	...
10 - 14	C	6	4	2	...	...	...	...	...	...
15 - 19	C	11	8	3	...	...	...	...	...	...
20 - 24	C	17	14	3	...	...	...	...	...	...
25 - 29	C	11	11	-	...	...	...	...	...	...
30 - 34	C	16	14	2	...	...	...	...	...	...
35 - 39	C	22	15	7	...	...	...	...	...	...
40 - 44	C	34	19	15	...	...	...	...	...	...
45 - 49	C	43	25	18	...	...	...	...	...	...
50 - 54	C	48	34	14	...	...	...	...	...	...
55 - 59	C	44	30	14	...	...	...	...	...	...
60 - 64	C	64	24	40	...	...	...	...	...	...
65 - 69	C	70	40	30	...	...	...	...	...	...
70 - 74	C	99	59	40	...	...	...	...	...	...
75 - 79	C	106	47	59	...	...	...	...	...	...
80 - 84	C	121	59	62	...	...	...	...	...	...

19. Deaths by age, sex and urban/rural residence: latest available year
Décès selon l'âge, le sexe et la résidence, urbaine/rurale: dernière année disponible (continued — suite)

(See notes at end of table.— Voir notes à la fin du tableau.)

Continent, country or area, year and age (in years) Continent, pays ou zone, année et âge (en années)	Code[1]	Total			Urban - Urbaine			Rural - Rurale		
		Both sexes - Les deux sexes	Male - Masculin	Female - Féminin	Both sexes - Les deux sexes	Male - Masculin	Female - Féminin	Both sexes - Les deux sexes	Male - Masculin	Female - Féminin
AMERICA, NORTH — AMERIQUE DU NORD										
Saint Lucia - Sainte-Lucie										
2000										
85+	C	167	74	93	...	...	...	...	...	...
Unknown - Inconnu	C	13	3	10	...	...	...	...	...	...
Saint Vincent and the Grenadines - Saint Vincent-et-les Grenadines										
1992										
Total	+C	714	361	353	326	178	148	388	183	205
0 - 1	+C	46	27	19	41	23	18	5	4	1
1 - 4	+C	11	8	3	9	7	2	2	1	1
5 - 9	+C	2	1	1	2	1	1	-	-	-
10 - 14	+C	2	1	1	2	1	1	-	-	-
15 - 19	+C	10	5	5	6	3	3	4	2	2
20 - 24	+C	11	10	1	5	5	-	6	5	1
25 - 29	+C	22	11	11	12	6	6	10	5	5
30 - 34	+C	17	10	7	3	3	-	14	7	7
35 - 39	+C	19	9	10	12	7	5	7	2	5
40 - 44	+C	15	8	7	9	5	4	6	3	3
45 - 49	+C	26	18	8	10	8	2	16	10	6
50 - 54	+C	25	10	15	12	6	6	13	4	9
55 - 59	+C	31	14	17	14	7	7	17	7	10
60 - 64	+C	44	26	18	22	14	8	22	12	10
65 - 69	+C	64	37	27	29	17	12	35	20	15
70 - 74	+C	79	38	41	27	15	12	52	23	29
75 - 79	+C	85	43	42	31	17	14	54	26	28
80 - 84	+C	87	39	48	37	14	23	50	25	25
85+	+C	103	36	67	30	9	21	73	27	46
Unknown - Inconnu	+C	15	10	5	13	10	3	2	-	2
2000										
Total	+C	697	406	291	...	...	...	...	...	...
0 - 1	+C	35	24	11	...	...	...	...	...	...
1 - 4	+C	6	5	1	...	...	...	...	...	...
5 - 9	+C	6	4	2	...	...	...	...	...	...
10 - 14	+C	3	-	3	...	...	...	...	...	...
15 - 19	+C	6	3	3	...	...	...	...	...	...
20 - 24	+C	18	14	4	...	...	...	...	...	...
25 - 29	+C	28	17	11	...	...	...	...	...	...
30 - 34	+C	18	9	9	...	...	...	...	...	...
35 - 39	+C	26	19	7	...	...	...	...	...	...
40 - 44	+C	23	19	4	...	...	...	...	...	...
45 - 49	+C	33	20	13	...	...	...	...	...	...
50 - 54	+C	27	21	6	...	...	...	...	...	...
55 - 59	+C	29	17	12	...	...	...	...	...	...
60 - 64	+C	38	18	20	...	...	...	...	...	...
65 - 69	+C	56	34	22	...	...	...	...	...	...
70 - 74	+C	70	45	25	...	...	...	...	...	...
75 - 79	+C	69	34	35	...	...	...	...	...	...
80 - 84	+C	84	44	40	...	...	...	...	...	...
85+	+C	122	59	63	...	...	...	...	...	...
Trinidad and Tobago - Trinité-et-Tobago										
1997										
Total	C	9 157	5 034	4 123	...	...	...	...	...	...
0 - 1	C	316	170	146	...	...	...	...	...	...
1 - 4	C	58	32	26	...	...	...	...	...	...
5 - 9	C	38	24	14	...	...	...	...	...	...
10 - 14	C	48	25	23	...	...	...	...	...	...
15 - 19	C	92	53	39	...	...	...	...	...	...
20 - 24	C	157	105	52	...	...	...	...	...	...
25 - 29	C	165	103	62	...	...	...	...	...	...

19. Deaths by age, sex and urban/rural residence: latest available year
Décès selon l'âge, le sexe et la résidence, urbaine/rurale: dernière année disponible (continued — suite)

(See notes at end of table.— Voir notes à la fin du tableau.)

Continent, country or area, year and age (in years) / Continent, pays ou zone, année et âge (en années)	Code[1]	Total			Urban - Urbaine			Rural - Rurale		
		Both sexes - Les deux sexes	Male - Masculin	Female - Féminin	Both sexes - Les deux sexes	Male - Masculin	Female - Féminin	Both sexes - Les deux sexes	Male - Masculin	Female - Féminin
AMERICA, NORTH — AMERIQUE DU NORD										
Trinidad and Tobago - Trinité-et-Tobago										
1997										
30 - 34	C	261	163	98	...	...	...	...	...	...
35 - 39	C	303	184	119	...	...	...	...	...	...
40 - 44	C	350	219	131	...	...	...	...	...	...
45 - 49	C	399	236	163	...	...	...	...	...	...
50 - 54	C	480	296	184	...	...	...	...	...	...
55 - 59	C	600	347	253	...	...	...	...	...	...
60 - 64	C	755	398	357	...	...	...	...	...	...
65 - 69	C	883	475	408	...	...	...	...	...	...
70 - 74	C	995	577	418	...	...	...	...	...	...
75 - 79	C	1 083	606	477	...	...	...	...	...	...
80 - 84	C	971	510	461	...	...	...	...	...	...
85 - 89	C	727	326	401	...	...	...	...	...	...
90 - 94	C	323	134	189	...	...	...	...	...	...
95 - 99	C	126	45	81	...	...	...	...	...	...
100+	C	25	5	20	...	...	...	...	...	...
Unknown - Inconnu	C	2	1	1	...	...	...	...	...	...
United States - États-Unis										
2001										
Total	C	2 417 762	1 183 721	1 234 041	...	...	...	...	...	...
0 - 1	C	27 801	15 591	12 211	...	...	...	...	...	...
1 - 4	C	5 125	2 922	2 203	...	...	...	...	...	...
5 - 14	C	7 100	4 172	2 928	...	...	...	...	...	...
15 - 24	C	32 157	23 880	8 277	...	...	...	...	...	...
25 - 34	C	41 474	28 626	12 849	...	...	...	...	...	...
35 - 44	C	91 457	58 007	33 451	...	...	...	...	...	...
45 - 54	C	167 836	104 697	63 139	...	...	...	...	...	...
55 - 64	C	244 002	144 831	99 171	...	...	...	...	...	...
65 - 74	C	431 306	241 776	189 530	...	...	...	...	...	...
75 - 84	C	702 657	341 182	361 476	...	...	...	...	...	...
85+	C	666 456	217 730	448 727	...	...	...	...	...	...
Unknown - Inconnu	C	390	309	81	...	...	...	...	...	...
United States Virgin Islands - Îles Vierges américaines										
1993										
Total	C	569	328	241	...	...	...	...	...	...
0 - 1	C	31	18	13	...	...	...	...	...	...
1 - 4	C	3	2	1	...	...	...	...	...	...
5 - 9	C	2	1	1	...	...	...	...	...	...
10 - 14	C	4	4	-	...	...	...	...	...	...
15 - 19	C	8	5	3	...	...	...	...	...	...
20 - 24	C	11	9	2	...	...	...	...	...	...
25 - 29	C	13	8	5	...	...	...	...	...	...
30 - 34	C	22	16	6	...	...	...	...	...	...
35 - 39	C	19	15	4	...	...	...	...	...	...
40 - 44	C	20	14	6	...	...	...	...	...	...
45 - 49	C	28	20	8	...	...	...	...	...	...
50 - 54	C	41	24	17	...	...	...	...	...	...
55 - 59	C	37	25	12	...	...	...	...	...	...
60 - 64	C	39	29	10	...	...	...	...	...	...
65 - 69	C	46	31	15	...	...	...	...	...	...
70 - 74	C	65	28	37	...	...	...	...	...	...
75 - 79	C	51	24	27	...	...	...	...	...	...
80 - 84	C	60	29	31	...	...	...	...	...	...
85+	C	68	25	43	...	...	...	...	...	...
Unknown - Inconnu	C	1	1	-	...	...	...	...	...	...

19. Deaths by age, sex and urban/rural residence: latest available year
Décès selon l'âge, le sexe et la résidence, urbaine/rurale: dernière année disponible (continued — suite)

(See notes at end of table.— Voir notes à la fin du tableau.)

Continent, country or area, year and age (in years) Continent, pays ou zone, année et âge (en années)	Code[1]	Total			Urban - Urbaine			Rural - Rurale		
		Both sexes - Les deux sexes	Male - Masculin	Female - Féminin	Both sexes - Les deux sexes	Male - Masculin	Female - Féminin	Both sexes - Les deux sexes	Male - Masculin	Female - Féminin
AMERICA, SOUTH — AMERIQUE DU SUD										
Argentina - Argentine[8]										
1998										
Total	C	280 180	153 747	126 319	...	...	...	...	...	...
0 - 1	C	13 082	7 472	5 576	...	...	...	...	...	...
1 - 4	C	2 285	1 287	996	...	...	...	...	...	...
5 - 9	C	1 002	604	395	...	...	...	...	...	...
10 - 14	C	1 045	627	418	...	...	...	...	...	...
15 - 19	C	2 639	1 814	823	...	...	...	...	...	...
20 - 24	C	3 225	2 344	879	...	...	...	...	...	...
25 - 29	C	3 300	2 340	959	...	...	...	...	...	...
30 - 34	C	3 479	2 349	1 129	...	...	...	...	...	...
35 - 39	C	4 053	2 609	1 442	...	...	...	...	...	...
40 - 44	C	5 719	3 703	2 013	...	...	...	...	...	...
45 - 49	C	8 581	5 504	3 076	...	...	...	...	...	...
50 - 54	C	11 692	7 710	3 976	...	...	...	...	...	...
55 - 59	C	15 084	10 079	5 002	...	...	...	...	...	...
60 - 64	C	19 791	13 010	6 773	...	...	...	...	...	...
65 - 69	C	27 471	17 604	9 862	...	...	...	...	...	...
70 - 74	C	33 324	20 030	13 287	...	...	...	...	...	...
75 - 79	C	36 600	19 638	16 957	...	...	...	...	...	...
80 - 84	C	36 107	16 553	19 552	...	...	...	...	...	...
85+	C	50 913	17 914	32 993	...	...	...	...	...	...
Unknown - Inconnu	C	788	556	211	...	...	...	...	...	...
Brazil - Brésil[9]										
1998										
Total	U	939 448	552 164	387 284	...	...	...	...	...	...
0 - 1	U	64 702	36 729	27 973	...	...	...	...	...	...
1 - 4	U	11 997	6 462	5 535	...	...	...	...	...	...
5 - 9	U	5 425	3 152	2 273	...	...	...	...	...	...
10 - 14	U	6 631	4 022	2 609	...	...	...	...	...	...
15 - 19	U	18 770	14 282	4 488	...	...	...	...	...	...
20 - 24	U	25 528	20 274	5 254	...	...	...	...	...	...
25 - 29	U	26 868	20 594	6 274	...	...	...	...	...	...
30 - 34	U	29 917	21 983	7 934	...	...	...	...	...	...
35 - 39	U	33 806	23 769	10 037	...	...	...	...	...	...
40 - 44	U	39 431	26 571	12 860	...	...	...	...	...	...
45 - 49	U	44 763	29 273	15 490	...	...	...	...	...	...
50 - 54	U	50 174	31 867	18 307	...	...	...	...	...	...
55 - 59	U	58 293	36 334	21 959	...	...	...	...	...	...
60 - 64	U	70 080	42 297	27 783	...	...	...	...	...	...
65 - 69	U	83 468	48 713	34 755	...	...	...	...	...	...
70 - 74	U	92 208	52 224	39 984	...	...	...	...	...	...
75 - 79	U	89 239	47 662	41 577	...	...	...	...	...	...
80 - 84	U	82 100	39 924	42 176	...	...	...	...	...	...
85 - 89	U	58 821	26 028	32 793	...	...	...	...	...	...
90 - 94	U	30 984	11 769	19 215	...	...	...	...	...	...
95 - 99	U	9 299	3 327	5 972	...	...	...	...	...	...
100+	U	2 443	1 380	1 063	...	...	...	...	...	...
Unknown - Inconnu	U	4 501	3 528	973	...	...	...	...	...	...
Chile - Chili										
1999										
Total	C	81 977	44 418	37 559	68 709	36 330	32 379	13 268	8 088	5 180
0 - 1	C	2 651	1 483	1 168	2 249	1 261	988	402	222	180
1 - 4	C	461	238	223	351	179	172	110	59	51
5 - 9	C	313	182	131	244	146	98	69	36	33
10 - 14	C	307	204	103	239	158	81	68	46	22
15 - 19	C	669	475	194	537	381	156	132	94	38
20 - 24	C	977	737	240	757	561	196	220	176	44
25 - 29	C	1 244	969	275	1 004	771	233	240	198	42
30 - 34	C	1 464	1 096	368	1 176	875	301	288	221	67
35 - 39	C	1 735	1 245	490	1 415	1 004	411	320	241	79

(See notes at end of table.— Voir notes à la fin du tableau.)

Continent, country or area, year and age (in years) / Continent, pays ou zone, année et âge (en années)	Code[1]	Total			Urban - Urbaine			Rural - Rurale		
		Both sexes - Les deux sexes	Male - Masculin	Female - Féminin	Both sexes - Les deux sexes	Male - Masculin	Female - Féminin	Both sexes - Les deux sexes	Male - Masculin	Female - Féminin
AMERICA, SOUTH — AMERIQUE DU SUD										
Chile - Chili										
1999										
40 - 44	C	2 177	1 463	714	1 800	1 191	609	377	272	105
45 - 49	C	2 656	1 705	951	2 191	1 396	795	465	309	156
50 - 54	C	3 391	2 114	1 277	2 862	1 760	1 102	529	354	175
55 - 59	C	4 562	2 886	1 676	3 840	2 402	1 438	722	484	238
60 - 64	C	5 345	3 315	2 030	4 507	2 771	1 736	838	544	294
65 - 69	C	7 710	4 596	3 114	6 520	3 813	2 707	1 190	783	407
70 - 74	C	9 513	5 443	4 070	8 023	4 517	3 506	1 490	926	564
75 - 79	C	10 154	5 469	4 685	8 474	4 408	4 066	1 680	1 061	619
80 - 84	C	10 713	4 948	5 765	8 987	4 014	4 973	1 726	934	792
85 - 89	C	9 167	3 675	5 492	7 704	2 926	4 778	1 463	749	714
90 - 94	C	4 847	1 629	3 218	4 169	1 342	2 827	678	287	391
95 - 99	C	1 646	482	1 164	1 423	399	1 024	223	83	140
100+	C	275	64	211	237	55	182	38	9	29
Colombia - Colombie[5,8]										
2000										
Total	U	183 865	111 190	72 640	153 632	89 641	63 967	29 115	20 747	8 359
0 - 1	U	14 926	8 412	6 505	13 960	7 873	6 080	891	496	393
1 - 4	U	3 062	1 646	1 415	2 425	1 318	1 106	621	320	301
5 - 9	U	1 413	826	587	1 109	635	474	296	188	108
10 - 14	U	1 633	994	639	1 225	723	502	396	262	134
15 - 19	U	6 570	5 232	1 337	4 997	3 980	1 016	1 500	1 197	303
20 - 24	U	9 195	7 807	1 385	6 714	5 601	1 110	2 377	2 110	267
25 - 29	U	8 452	7 137	1 310	6 013	4 942	1 069	2 346	2 113	231
30 - 34	U	7 559	6 038	1 518	5 546	4 277	1 268	1 944	1 702	240
35 - 39	U	7 313	5 577	1 734	5 500	4 006	1 494	1 744	1 507	235
40 - 44	U	6 951	4 815	2 136	5 556	3 658	1 898	1 345	1 115	230
45 - 49	U	7 191	4 688	2 503	5 782	3 583	2 199	1 363	1 066	297
50 - 54	U	7 320	4 469	2 851	6 196	3 640	2 556	1 085	803	282
55 - 59	U	8 323	4 889	3 432	7 169	4 072	3 095	1 119	793	326
60 - 64	U	11 055	6 253	4 802	9 678	5 355	4 323	1 335	874	461
65 - 69	U	13 727	7 504	6 223	12 041	6 471	5 570	1 639	1 006	633
70 - 74	U	16 520	9 028	7 491	14 444	7 727	6 716	2 011	1 264	747
75 - 79	U	16 472	8 586	7 885	14 390	7 391	6 998	2 011	1 158	853
80 - 84	U	15 007	7 430	7 575	13 057	6 391	6 664	1 890	1 001	889
85+	U	19 146	8 456	10 689	16 509	7 167	9 341	2 548	1 244	1 304
Unknown - Inconnu	U	2 030	1 403	623	1 321	831	488	654	528	125
Ecuador - Équateur[10]										
1996										
Total	U	52 300	29 551	22 749	37 349	21 236	16 113	14 951	8 315	6 636
0 - 1	U	5 351	2 931	2 420	3 896	2 149	1 747	1 455	782	673
1 - 4	U	2 338	1 237	1 101	1 292	671	621	1 046	566	480
5 - 9	U	773	429	344	521	292	229	252	137	115
10 - 14	U	723	429	294	515	308	207	208	121	87
15 - 19	U	1 421	904	517	1 019	654	365	402	250	152
20 - 24	U	1 687	1 202	485	1 260	924	336	427	278	149
25 - 29	U	1 737	1 242	495	1 319	958	361	418	284	134
30 - 34	U	1 692	1 167	525	1 313	933	380	379	234	145
35 - 39	U	1 722	1 181	541	1 287	911	376	435	270	165
40 - 44	U	1 808	1 122	686	1 343	863	480	465	259	206
45 - 49	U	1 946	1 208	738	1 427	872	555	519	336	183
50 - 54	U	2 154	1 324	830	1 568	953	615	586	371	215
55 - 59	U	2 423	1 432	991	1 764	1 026	738	659	406	253
60 - 64	U	2 839	1 647	1 192	2 043	1 191	852	796	456	340
65 - 69	U	3 516	2 035	1 481	2 571	1 475	1 096	945	560	385
70 - 74	U	3 718	2 151	1 567	2 639	1 513	1 126	1 079	638	441
75 - 79	U	4 156	2 281	1 875	2 965	1 621	1 344	1 191	660	531
80 - 84	U	4 378	2 237	2 141	3 021	1 530	1 491	1 357	707	650
85+	U	7 760	3 297	4 463	5 478	2 326	3 152	2 282	971	1 311
Unknown - Inconnu	U	158	95	63	108	66	42	50	29	21

19. Deaths by age, sex and urban/rural residence: latest available year
Décès selon l'âge, le sexe et la résidence, urbaine/rurale: dernière année disponible (continued — suite)

(See notes at end of table.— Voir notes à la fin du tableau.)

Continent, country or area, year and age (in years) Continent, pays ou zone, année et âge (en années)	Code[1]	Total			Urban - Urbaine			Rural - Rurale		
		Both sexes - Les deux sexes	Male - Masculin	Female - Féminin	Both sexes - Les deux sexes	Male - Masculin	Female - Féminin	Both sexes - Les deux sexes	Male - Masculin	Female - Féminin
AMERICA, SOUTH —										
AMERIQUE DU SUD										
Ecuador - Équateur[10]										
1998										
Total	U	54 357	30 842	23 515	...	...	...	...	...	...
0 - 1	U	5 186	2 883	2 303	...	...	...	...	...	...
1 - 4	U	2 420	1 312	1 108	...	...	...	...	...	...
5 - 9	U	751	430	321	...	...	...	...	...	...
10 - 14	U	758	427	331	...	...	...	...	...	...
15 - 19	U	1 461	927	534	...	...	...	...	...	...
20 - 24	U	1 889	1 370	519	...	...	...	...	...	...
25 - 29	U	1 830	1 337	493	...	...	...	...	...	...
30 - 34	U	1 764	1 238	526	...	...	...	...	...	...
35 - 39	U	1 862	1 257	605	...	...	...	...	...	...
40 - 44	U	1 931	1 229	702	...	...	...	...	...	...
45 - 49	U	2 042	1 263	779	...	...	...	...	...	...
50 - 54	U	2 121	1 270	851	...	...	...	...	...	...
55 - 59	U	2 410	1 441	969	...	...	...	...	...	...
60 - 64	U	3 051	1 772	1 279	...	...	...	...	...	...
65 - 69	U	3 616	2 060	1 556	...	...	...	...	...	...
70 - 74	U	3 944	2 181	1 763	...	...	...	...	...	...
75 - 79	U	4 418	2 404	2 014	...	...	...	...	...	...
80 - 84	U	4 645	2 387	2 258	...	...	...	...	...	...
85+	U	8 146	3 583	4 563	...	...	...	...	...	...
Unknown - Inconnu	U	112	71	41	...	...	...	...	...	...
Falkland Islands (Malvinas) -										
Îles Falkland (Malvinas)										
1992										
Total	+C	19	10	9	17	9	8	2	1	1
20 - 24	+C	1	-	1	1	-	1	-	-	-
40 - 44	+C	1	1	-	1	1	-	-	-	-
45 - 49	+C	1	-	1	-	-	-	1	-	1
50 - 54	+C	3	2	1	2	1	1	1	1	-
55 - 59	+C	3	2	1	3	2	1	-	-	-
60 - 64	+C	2	1	1	2	1	1	-	-	-
65 - 69	+C	1	-	1	1	-	1	-	-	-
70 - 74	+C	4	2	2	4	2	2	-	-	-
75 - 79	+C	1	1	-	1	1	-	-	-	-
85+	+C	2	1	1	2	1	1	-	-	-
French Guiana - Guyane										
française										
1998										
Total	C	614	391	223	...	...	...	...	...	...
0 - 1	C	52	33	19	...	...	...	...	...	...
1 - 4	C	23	10	13	...	...	...	...	...	...
5 - 9	C	6	1	5	...	...	...	...	...	...
10 - 14	C	6	6	-	...	...	...	...	...	...
15 - 19	C	19	11	8	...	...	...	...	...	...
20 - 24	C	15	10	5	...	...	...	...	...	...
25 - 29	C	17	15	2	...	...	...	...	...	...
30 - 34	C	24	16	8	...	...	...	...	...	...
35 - 39	C	25	20	5	...	...	...	...	...	...
40 - 44	C	31	25	6	...	...	...	...	...	...
45 - 49	C	26	23	3	...	...	...	...	...	...
50 - 54	C	33	25	8	...	...	...	...	...	...
55 - 59	C	34	26	8	...	...	...	...	...	...
60 - 64	C	36	24	12	...	...	...	...	...	...
65 - 69	C	52	38	14	...	...	...	...	...	...
70 - 74	C	49	25	24	...	...	...	...	...	...
75 - 79	C	50	35	15	...	...	...	...	...	...
80 - 84	C	67	36	31	...	...	...	...	...	...
85 - 89	C	31	12	19	...	...	...	...	...	...
90 - 94	C	8	-	8	...	...	...	...	...	...

(See notes at end of table.— Voir notes à la fin du tableau.)

Continent, country or area, year and age (in years) Continent, pays ou zone, année et âge (en années)	Code[1]	Total			Urban - Urbaine			Rural - Rurale		
		Both sexes - Les deux sexes	Male - Masculin	Female - Féminin	Both sexes - Les deux sexes	Male - Masculin	Female - Féminin	Both sexes - Les deux sexes	Male - Masculin	Female - Féminin
AMERICA, SOUTH — AMERIQUE DU SUD										
French Guiana - Guyane française										
1998										
95 - 99	C	8	-	8	...	...	...	...	...	...
100+	C	2	-	2	...	...	...	...	...	...
Paraguay										
1992										
Total	U	9 642	5 196	4 416	...	...	...	...	...	...
0 - 1	U	758	411	344	...	...	...	...	...	...
1 - 4	U	300	164	135	...	...	...	...	...	...
5 - 9	U	122	70	51	...	...	...	...	...	...
10 - 14	U	91	51	40	...	...	...	...	...	...
15 - 19	U	176	119	57	...	...	...	...	...	...
20 - 24	U	199	123	76	...	...	...	...	...	...
25 - 29	U	199	134	64	...	...	...	...	...	...
30 - 34	U	184	113	71	...	...	...	...	...	...
35 - 39	U	197	109	87	...	...	...	...	...	...
40 - 44	U	216	118	98	...	...	...	...	...	...
45 - 49	U	271	158	112	...	...	...	...	...	...
50 - 54	U	315	184	131	...	...	...	...	...	...
55 - 59	U	402	241	161	...	...	...	...	...	...
60 - 64	U	551	318	232	...	...	...	...	...	...
65 - 69	U	554	309	244	...	...	...	...	...	...
70 - 74	U	706	386	319	...	...	...	...	...	...
75 - 79	U	774	412	359	...	...	...	...	...	...
80 - 84	U	739	366	368	...	...	...	...	...	...
85+	U	1 090	454	634	...	...	...	...	...	...
Unknown - Inconnu	U	1 798	956	833	...	...	...	...	...	...
Suriname										
2000										
Total	C	3 090	1 756	1 334	2 249	...	...	841	...	...
0 - 1	C	156	83	73	117	...	...	39	...	...
1 - 4	C	73	36	37	44	...	...	29	...	...
5 - 9	C	19	13	6	11	...	...	8	...	...
10 - 14	C	23	16	7	17	...	...	6	...	...
15 - 19	C	54	33	21	29	...	...	25	...	...
20 - 24	C	68	50	18	42	...	...	26	...	...
25 - 29	C	97	57	40	72	...	...	25	...	...
30 - 34	C	118	75	43	83	...	...	35	...	...
35 - 39	C	132	89	43	95	...	...	37	...	...
40 - 44	C	128	86	42	98	...	...	30	...	...
45 - 49	C	161	92	69	134	...	...	27	...	...
50 - 54	C	170	103	67	130	...	...	40	...	...
55 - 59	C	191	111	80	137	...	...	54	...	...
60 - 64	C	264	148	116	196	...	...	68	...	...
65 - 69	C	320	186	134	238	...	...	82	...	...
70 - 74	C	312	177	135	217	...	...	95	...	...
75 - 79	C	303	172	131	218	...	...	85	...	...
80 - 84	C	211	100	111	165	...	...	46	...	...
85 - 89	C	162	76	86	104	...	...	58	...	...
90 - 94	C	80	39	41	60	...	...	20	...	...
95 - 99	C	44	12	32	38	...	...	6	...	...
100+	C	4	2	2	4	...	...	-	...	...
Uruguay[8]										
2000										
Total	C	30 456	16 407	14 043	...	...	...	...	...	...
0 - 1	C	742	434	304	...	...	...	...	...	...
1 - 4	C	127	74	53	...	...	...	...	...	...
5 - 9	C	56	37	19	...	...	...	...	...	...
10 - 14	C	56	34	22	...	...	...	...	...	...
15 - 19	C	170	118	52	...	...	...	...	...	...

(See notes at end of table.— Voir notes à la fin du tableau.)

Continent, country or area, year and age (in years) / Continent, pays ou zone, année et âge (en années)	Code[1]	Total			Urban - Urbaine			Rural - Rurale		
		Both sexes - Les deux sexes	Male - Masculin	Female - Féminin	Both sexes - Les deux sexes	Male - Masculin	Female - Féminin	Both sexes - Les deux sexes	Male - Masculin	Female - Féminin
AMERICA, SOUTH — AMERIQUE DU SUD										
Uruguay[8]										
2000										
20 - 24	C	275	213	62	...	...	...	...	...	...
25 - 29	C	239	172	67	...	...	...	...	...	...
30 - 34	C	266	182	84	...	...	...	...	...	...
35 - 39	C	368	252	116	...	...	...	...	...	...
40 - 44	C	507	289	218	...	...	...	...	...	...
45 - 49	C	766	491	275	...	...	...	...	...	...
50 - 54	C	1 105	731	374	...	...	...	...	...	...
55 - 59	C	1 543	1 031	512	...	...	...	...	...	...
60 - 64	C	2 060	1 396	664	...	...	...	...	...	...
65 - 69	C	3 023	1 967	1 056	...	...	...	...	...	...
70 - 74	C	3 750	2 293	1 457	...	...	...	...	...	...
75 - 79	C	4 281	2 316	1 965	...	...	...	...	...	...
80 - 84	C	4 186	1 950	2 235	...	...	...	...	...	...
85+	C	6 817	2 340	4 477	...	...	...	...	...	...
Unknown - Inconnu	C	119	87	31	...	...	...	...	...	...
Venezuela[9]										
2000										
Total	C	103 255	62 978	40 277	...	...	...	...	...	...
0 - 1	C	8 524	4 919	3 605	...	...	...	...	...	...
1 - 4	C	2 033	1 083	950	...	...	...	...	...	...
5 - 9	C	991	600	391	...	...	...	...	...	...
10 - 14	C	985	607	378	...	...	...	...	...	...
15 - 19	C	3 209	2 594	615	...	...	...	...	...	...
20 - 24	C	4 729	4 026	703	...	...	...	...	...	...
25 - 29	C	4 069	3 298	771	...	...	...	...	...	...
30 - 34	C	4 121	3 141	980	...	...	...	...	...	...
35 - 39	C	3 779	2 679	1 100	...	...	...	...	...	...
40 - 44	C	4 067	2 739	1 328	...	...	...	...	...	...
45 - 49	C	4 589	2 991	1 598	...	...	...	...	...	...
50 - 54	C	5 038	3 160	1 878	...	...	...	...	...	...
55 - 59	C	5 370	3 401	1 969	...	...	...	...	...	...
60 - 64	C	6 740	4 030	2 710	...	...	...	...	...	...
65 - 69	C	7 802	4 625	3 177	...	...	...	...	...	...
70 - 74	C	9 233	5 417	3 816	...	...	...	...	...	...
75 - 79	C	8 922	4 867	4 055	...	...	...	...	...	...
80 - 84	C	8 199	4 108	4 091	...	...	...	...	...	...
85 - 89	C	6 148	2 775	3 373	...	...	...	...	...	...
90 - 94	C	3 093	1 247	1 846	...	...	...	...	...	...
95 - 99	C	1 134	395	739	...	...	...	...	...	...
100+	C	244	86	158	...	...	...	...	...	...
Unknown - Inconnu	C	236	190	46	...	...	...	...	...	...
ASIA — ASIE										
Armenia - Arménie[11]										
2000										
Total	C	24 025	12 277	11 748	15 682	8 115	7 567	8 343	4 162	4 181
0 - 1	C	540	348	192	357	234	123	183	114	69
1 - 4	C	143	80	63	81	45	36	62	35	27
5 - 9	C	60	27	33	39	18	21	21	9	12
10 - 14	C	68	51	17	45	35	10	23	16	7
15 - 19	C	136	108	28	78	57	21	58	51	7
20 - 24	C	155	113	42	109	82	27	46	31	15
25 - 29	C	169	108	61	122	77	45	47	31	16
30 - 34	C	253	175	78	166	117	49	87	58	29
35 - 39	C	456	303	153	305	198	107	151	105	46
40 - 44	C	662	437	225	458	310	148	204	127	77
45 - 49	C	806	541	265	633	423	210	173	118	55
50 - 54	C	898	576	322	697	443	254	201	133	68

19. Deaths by age, sex and urban/rural residence: latest available year
Décès selon l'âge, le sexe et la résidence, urbaine/rurale: dernière année disponible (continued — suite)

(See notes at end of table.— Voir notes à la fin du tableau.)

Continent, country or area, year and age (in years) / Continent, pays ou zone, année et âge (en années)	Code[1]	Total			Urban - Urbaine			Rural - Rurale		
		Both sexes - Les deux sexes	Male - Masculin	Female - Féminin	Both sexes - Les deux sexes	Male - Masculin	Female - Féminin	Both sexes - Les deux sexes	Male - Masculin	Female - Féminin
ASIA — ASIE										
Armenia - Arménie[11]										
2000										
55 - 59	C	874	570	304	666	443	223	208	127	81
60 - 64	C	2 689	1 639	1 050	1 900	1 186	714	789	453	336
65 - 69	C	3 332	1 952	1 380	2 117	1 234	883	1 215	718	497
70 - 74	C	4 898	2 510	2 388	3 098	1 548	1 550	1 800	962	838
75 - 79	C	3 018	1 255	1 763	1 954	769	1 185	1 064	486	578
80 - 84	C	1 860	602	1 258	1 197	385	812	663	217	446
85+	C	3 008	882	2 126	1 660	511	1 149	1 348	371	977
Azerbaijan - Azerbaïdjan[11]										
2001										
Total	+C	45 284	23 725	21 559	23 382	12 655	10 727	21 902	11 070	10 832
0 - 1	+C	1 382	769	613	558	336	222	824	433	391
1 - 4	+C	1 352	740	612	362	201	161	990	539	451
5 - 9	+C	506	285	221	191	113	78	315	172	143
10 - 14	+C	356	206	150	153	90	63	203	116	87
15 - 19	+C	481	322	159	225	143	82	256	179	77
20 - 24	+C	554	363	191	261	184	77	293	179	114
25 - 29	+C	664	424	240	355	228	127	309	196	113
30 - 34	+C	937	596	341	482	340	142	455	256	199
35 - 39	÷C	1 218	816	402	666	474	192	552	342	210
40 - 44	+C	1 677	1 146	531	1 009	706	303	668	440	228
45 - 49	+C	1 794	1 225	569	1 142	809	333	652	416	236
50 - 54	+C	2 029	1 356	673	1 326	910	416	703	446	257
55 - 59	+C	1 728	1 080	648	1 055	676	379	673	404	269
60 - 64	+C	5 228	3 091	2 137	2 921	1 782	1 139	2 307	1 309	998
65 - 69	+C	6 619	3 720	2 899	3 300	1 892	1 408	3 319	1 828	1 491
70 - 74	+C	7 088	3 696	3 392	3 641	1 863	1 778	3 447	1 833	1 614
75 - 79	+C	4 365	1 917	2 448	2 460	1 015	1 445	1 905	902	1 003
80 - 84	+C	2 655	803	1 852	1 401	395	1 006	1 254	408	846
85 - 89	+C	2 203	639	1 564	1 046	315	731	1 157	324	833
90 - 94	+C	1 285	319	966	556	126	430	729	193	536
95 - 99	+C	578	128	450	146	30	116	432	98	334
100+	+C	585	84	501	126	27	99	459	57	402
Bahrain - Bahreïn										
1999										
Total	U	1 920	1 136	784	...	...	...	...	...	...
0 - 1	U	129	67	62	...	...	...	...	...	...
1 - 4	U	25	11	14	...	...	...	...	...	...
5 - 9	U	20	12	8	...	...	...	...	...	...
10 - 14	U	15	6	9	...	...	...	...	...	...
15 - 19	U	23	17	6	...	...	...	...	...	...
20 - 24	U	42	33	9	...	...	...	...	...	...
25 - 29	U	39	36	3	...	...	...	...	...	...
30 - 34	U	68	52	16	...	...	...	...	...	...
35 - 39	U	57	39	18	...	...	...	...	...	...
40 - 44	U	86	62	24	...	...	...	...	...	...
45 - 49	U	91	63	28	...	...	...	...	...	...
50 - 54	U	89	59	30	...	...	...	...	...	...
55 - 59	U	111	60	51	...	...	...	...	...	...
60 - 64	U	155	84	71	...	...	...	...	...	...
65 - 69	U	252	132	120	...	...	...	...	...	...
70 - 74	U	226	121	105	...	...	...	...	...	...
75+	U	492	282	210	...	...	...	...	...	...
Brunei Darussalam - Brunéi Darussalam										
2000										
Total	+C	965	553	412	...	...	...	...	...	...
0 - 1	+C	55	26	29	...	...	...	...	...	...
1 - 4	+C	22	15	7	...	...	...	...	...	...
5 - 9	+C	9	5	4	...	...	...	...	...	...
10 - 14	+C	11	6	5	...	...	...	...	...	...

(See notes at end of table.— Voir notes à la fin du tableau.)

Continent, country or area, year and age (in years) Continent, pays ou zone, année et âge (en années)	Code[1]	Total			Urban - Urbaine			Rural - Rurale		
		Both sexes - Les deux sexes	Male - Masculin	Female - Féminin	Both sexes - Les deux sexes	Male - Masculin	Female - Féminin	Both sexes - Les deux sexes	Male - Masculin	Female - Féminin
ASIA — ASIE										
Brunei Darussalam - Brunéi Darussalam										
2000										
15 - 19	+C	21	16	5	...	...	...	...	...	...
20 - 24	+C	25	15	10	...	...	...	...	...	...
25 - 29	+C	27	13	14	...	...	...	...	...	...
30 - 34	+C	25	18	7	...	...	...	...	...	...
35 - 39	+C	33	24	9	...	...	...	...	...	...
40 - 44	+C	39	22	17	...	...	...	...	...	...
45 - 49	+C	29	19	10	...	...	...	...	...	...
50 - 54	+C	51	22	29	...	...	...	...	...	...
55 - 59	+C	63	42	21	...	...	...	...	...	...
60 - 64	+C	61	34	27	...	...	...	...	...	...
65 - 69	+C	108	57	51	...	...	...	...	...	...
70+	+C	386	219	167	...	...	...	...	...	...
China - Chine[12]										
1999										
Total	...	7 420 000	4 140 000	3 280 000	...	...	...	...	...	...
0 - 4	...	474 000	237 000	237 000	...	...	...	...	...	...
5 - 9	...	40 000	22 000	18 000	...	...	...	...	...	...
10 - 14	...	33 000	20 000	13 000	...	...	...	...	...	...
15 - 19	...	72 000	38 000	34 000	...	...	...	...	...	...
20 - 24	...	104 000	59 000	45 000	...	...	...	...	...	...
25 - 29	...	165 000	87 000	78 000	...	...	...	...	...	...
30 - 34	...	180 000	112 000	68 000	...	...	...	...	...	...
35 - 39	...	147 000	93 000	54 000	...	...	...	...	...	...
40 - 44	...	229 000	150 000	79 000	...	...	...	...	...	...
45 - 49	...	306 000	199 000	107 000	...	...	...	...	...	...
50 - 54	...	286 000	177 000	109 000	...	...	...	...	...	...
55 - 59	...	414 000	242 000	172 000	...	...	...	...	...	...
60 - 64	...	673 000	432 000	241 000	...	...	...	...	...	...
65 - 69	...	906 000	540 000	366 000	...	...	...	...	...	...
70 - 74	...	1 028 000	594 000	434 000	...	...	...	...	...	...
75 - 79	...	947 000	528 000	419 000	...	...	...	...	...	...
80 - 84	...	799 000	381 000	418 000	...	...	...	...	...	...
85 - 89	...	423 000	174 000	249 000	...	...	...	...	...	...
90+	...	193 000	54 000	139 000	...	...	...	...	...	...
China: Hong Kong SAR - Chine: Hong Kong RAS[8]										
2000										
Total	C	33 758	19 100	14 656	...	...	...	...	...	...
0 - 1	C	162	90	72	...	...	...	...	...	...
1 - 4	C	49	28	20	...	...	...	...	...	...
5 - 9	C	40	25	15	...	...	...	...	...	...
10 - 14	C	53	33	20	...	...	...	...	...	...
15 - 19	C	81	45	36	...	...	...	...	...	...
20 - 24	C	156	111	45	...	...	...	...	...	...
25 - 29	C	259	175	84	...	...	...	...	...	...
30 - 34	C	296	186	110	...	...	...	...	...	...
35 - 39	C	512	324	188	...	...	...	...	...	...
40 - 44	C	806	514	292	...	...	...	...	...	...
45 - 49	C	1 028	678	350	...	...	...	...	...	...
50 - 54	C	1 246	857	389	...	...	...	...	...	...
55 - 59	C	1 323	946	377	...	...	...	...	...	...
60 - 64	C	2 147	1 534	613	...	...	...	...	...	...
65 - 69	C	3 582	2 426	1 156	...	...	...	...	...	...
70 - 74	C	4 753	3 001	1 752	...	...	...	...	...	...
75 - 79	C	5 439	3 098	2 341	...	...	...	...	...	...
80 - 84	C	5 123	2 626	2 497	...	...	...	...	...	...
85+	C	6 678	2 384	4 294	...	...	...	...	...	...
Unknown - Inconnu	C	25	19	5	...	...	...	...	...	...

(See notes at end of table.— Voir notes à la fin du tableau.)

Continent, country or area, year and age (in years) Continent, pays ou zone, année et âge (en années)	Code[1]	Total			Urban - Urbaine			Rural - Rurale		
		Both sexes - Les deux sexes	Male - Masculin	Female - Féminin	Both sexes - Les deux sexes	Male - Masculin	Female - Féminin	Both sexes - Les deux sexes	Male - Masculin	Female - Féminin

ASIA — ASIE

China: Macao SAR - Chine: Macao RAS

2000

Total	C	1 338	730	608	...	...	...	...	...	...
0 - 1	C	11	6	5	...	...	...	...	...	...
1 - 4	C	6	4	2	...	...	...	...	...	...
5 - 9	C	4	2	2	...	...	...	...	...	...
10 - 14	C	5	5	-	...	...	...	...	...	...
15 - 19	C	9	5	4	...	...	...	...	...	...
20 - 24	C	9	6	3	...	...	...	...	...	...
25 - 29	C	17	10	7	...	...	...	...	...	...
30 - 34	C	16	10	6	...	...	...	...	...	...
35 - 39	C	35	21	14	...	...	...	...	...	...
40 - 44	C	47	38	9	...	...	...	...	...	...
45 - 49	C	54	35	19	...	...	...	...	...	...
50 - 54	C	56	45	11	...	...	...	...	...	...
55 - 59	C	54	41	13	...	...	...	...	...	...
60 - 64	C	73	54	19	...	...	...	...	...	...
65 - 69	C	108	70	38	...	...	...	...	...	...
70 - 74	C	170	95	75	...	...	...	...	...	...
75 - 79	C	204	107	97	...	...	...	...	...	...
80 - 84	C	187	81	106	...	...	...	...	...	...
85+	C	257	83	174	...	...	...	...	...	...
Unknown - Inconnu	C	16	12	4	...	...	...	...	...	...

Cyprus - Chypre[13]

2001

Total	C	4 827	2 565	2 262	...	...	...	...	...	...
0 - 1	C	40	21	19	...	...	...	...	...	...
1 - 4	C	8	4	4	...	...	...	...	...	...
5 - 9	C	14	9	5	...	...	...	...	...	...
10 - 14	C	13	9	4	...	...	...	...	...	...
15 - 19	C	34	26	8	...	...	...	...	...	...
20 - 24	C	44	30	14	...	...	...	...	...	...
25 - 29	C	31	27	4	...	...	...	...	...	...
30 - 34	C	46	33	13	...	...	...	...	...	...
35 - 39	C	41	32	9	...	...	...	...	...	...
40 - 44	C	56	38	18	...	...	...	...	...	...
45 - 49	C	82	58	24	...	...	...	...	...	...
50 - 54	C	135	82	53	...	...	...	...	...	...
55 - 59	C	182	131	51	...	...	...	...	...	...
60 - 64	C	280	180	100	...	...	...	...	...	...
65 - 69	C	388	231	157	...	...	...	...	...	...
70 - 74	C	561	313	248	...	...	...	...	...	...
75 - 79	C	690	366	324	...	...	...	...	...	...
80 - 84	C	838	393	445	...	...	...	...	...	...
85+	C	1 344	582	762	...	...	...	...	...	...

Georgia - Géorgie[11]

2001

Total	C	39 339	19 569	19 770	21 600	11 077	10 523	17 739	8 492	9 247
0 - 1	C	478	301	177	439	280	159	39	21	18
1 - 4	C	58	26	32	29	10	19	29	16	13
5 - 9	C	40	29	11	27	21	6	13	8	5
10 - 14	C	74	53	21	50	36	14	24	17	7
15 - 19	C	183	114	69	99	66	33	84	48	36
20 - 24	C	208	137	71	134	88	46	74	49	25
25 - 29	C	370	271	99	231	169	62	139	102	37
30 - 34	C	463	350	113	270	204	66	193	146	47
35 - 39	C	668	506	162	427	327	100	241	179	62
40 - 44	C	953	711	242	629	484	145	324	227	97
45 - 49	C	1 156	857	299	778	584	194	378	273	105
50 - 54	C	1 294	924	370	890	635	255	404	289	115
55 - 59	C	1 311	877	434	823	568	255	488	309	179

19. Deaths by age, sex and urban/rural residence: latest available year
Décès selon l'âge, le sexe et la résidence, urbaine/rurale: dernière année disponible (continued — suite)

(See notes at end of table.— Voir notes à la fin du tableau.)

Continent, country or area, year and age (in years) Continent, pays ou zone, année et âge (en années)	Code[1]	Total			Urban - Urbaine			Rural - Rurale		
		Both sexes - Les deux sexes	Male - Masculin	Female - Féminin	Both sexes - Les deux sexes	Male - Masculin	Female - Féminin	Both sexes - Les deux sexes	Male - Masculin	Female - Féminin
ASIA — ASIE										
Georgia - Géorgie[11]										
2001										
60 - 64	C	3 440	1 980	1 460	2 067	1 242	825	1 373	738	635
65 - 69	C	5 046	2 936	2 110	2 693	1 560	1 133	2 353	1 376	977
70 - 74	C	7 055	3 787	3 268	3 703	1 965	1 738	3 352	1 822	1 530
75 - 79	C	6 361	2 713	3 648	3 381	1 361	2 020	2 980	1 352	1 628
80 - 84	C	4 249	1 361	2 888	2 177	676	1 501	2 072	685	1 387
85 - 89	C	3 498	997	2 501	1 775	512	1 263	1 723	485	1 238
90 - 94	C	1 558	413	1 145	636	175	461	922	238	684
95 - 99	C	487	97	390	165	37	128	322	60	262
100+	C	301	75	226	93	25	68	208	50	158
Unknown - Inconnu	C	88	54	34	84	52	32	4	2	2
Israel - Israël[5,14]										
1998										
Total	C	36 950	18 847	18 102	34 447	17 581	16 865	2 495	1 263	1 232
0 - 1	C	773	442	330	681	391	289	92	51	41
1 - 4	C	175	113	62	153	101	52	22	12	10
5 - 9	C	87	52	35	78	48	30	9	4	5
10 - 14	C	75	50	25	66	45	21	9	5	4
15 - 19	C	207	151	56	186	136	50	21	15	6
20 - 24	C	286	235	51	252	208	44	34	27	7
25 - 29	C	255	185	70	227	166	61	26	19	7
30 - 34	C	269	183	86	249	166	83	20	17	3
35 - 39	C	371	247	124	344	225	119	26	21	5
40 - 44	C	520	341	179	489	326	163	31	15	16
45 - 49	C	793	481	312	750	455	295	43	26	17
50 - 54	C	1 058	656	402	994	618	376	64	38	26
55 - 59	C	1 214	766	448	1 144	726	418	70	40	30
60 - 64	C	2 078	1 225	853	1 952	1 146	806	125	78	47
65 - 69	C	3 119	1 798	1 321	2 944	1 693	1 251	175	105	70
70 - 74	C	4 546	2 353	2 193	4 318	2 241	2 077	227	111	116
75 - 79	C	5 546	2 826	2 720	5 227	2 667	2 560	319	159	160
80 - 84	C	5 692	2 582	3 110	5 258	2 364	2 894	434	218	216
85+	C	9 886	4 161	5 725	9 135	3 859	5 276	748	302	446
Japan - Japon[15]										
2000										
Total	C	961 653	525 903	435 750	...	...	...	...	...	...
0 - 1	C	3 830	2 107	1 723	...	...	...	...	...	...
1 - 4	C	1 439	826	613	...	...	...	...	...	...
5 - 9	C	738	438	300	...	...	...	...	...	...
10 - 14	C	744	493	251	...	...	...	...	...	...
15 - 19	C	2 397	1 721	676	...	...	...	...	...	...
20 - 24	C	4 035	2 875	1 160	...	...	...	...	...	...
25 - 29	C	4 817	3 271	1 546	...	...	...	...	...	...
30 - 34	C	5 596	3 749	1 847	...	...	...	...	...	...
35 - 39	C	7 046	4 621	2 425	...	...	...	...	...	...
40 - 44	C	10 479	6 840	3 639	...	...	...	...	...	...
45 - 49	C	19 736	13 141	6 595	...	...	...	...	...	...
50 - 54	C	35 843	24 103	11 740	...	...	...	...	...	...
55 - 59	C	45 992	31 848	14 144	...	...	...	...	...	...
60 - 64	C	60 680	42 214	18 466	...	...	...	...	...	...
65 - 69	C	89 058	60 962	28 096	...	...	...	...	...	...
70 - 74	C	116 528	76 413	40 115	...	...	...	...	...	...
75 - 79	C	131 000	73 947	57 053	...	...	...	...	...	...
80 - 84	C	147 060	73 533	73 527	...	...	...	...	...	...
85 - 89	C	148 980	62 730	86 250	...	...	...	...	...	...
90 - 94	C	90 913	30 830	60 083	...	...	...	...	...	...
95 - 99	C	29 230	7 642	21 588	...	...	...	...	...	...
100+	C	4 789	975	3 814	...	...	...	...	...	...
Unknown - Inconnu	C	723	624	99	...	...	...	...	...	...

(See notes at end of table.— Voir notes à la fin du tableau.)

Continent, country or area, year and age (in years) / Continent, pays ou zone, année et âge (en années)	Code[1]	Total			Urban - Urbaine			Rural - Rurale		
		Both sexes - Les deux sexes	Male - Masculin	Female - Féminin	Both sexes - Les deux sexes	Male - Masculin	Female - Féminin	Both sexes - Les deux sexes	Male - Masculin	Female - Féminin
ASIA — ASIE										
Kazakhstan[11]										
1999										
Total	C	145 880	79 495	66 385	91 180	49 854	41 326	54 700	29 641	25 059
0 - 1	C	4 423	2 600	1 823	2 435	1 449	986	1 988	1 151	837
1 - 4	C	1 469	794	675	555	303	252	914	491	423
5 - 9	C	726	432	294	335	195	140	391	237	154
10 - 14	C	780	490	290	376	238	138	404	252	152
15 - 19	C	1 660	1 141	519	869	609	260	791	532	259
20 - 24	C	2 848	2 148	700	1 708	1 318	390	1 140	830	310
25 - 29	C	3 558	2 639	919	2 160	1 630	530	1 398	1 009	389
30 - 34	C	3 906	2 874	1 032	2 446	1 826	620	1 460	1 048	412
35 - 39	C	5 582	4 066	1 516	3 586	2 683	903	1 996	1 383	613
40 - 44	C	6 757	4 900	1 857	4 514	3 322	1 192	2 243	1 578	665
45 - 49	C	7 918	5 594	2 324	5 296	3 780	1 516	2 622	1 814	808
50 - 54	C	7 496	5 239	2 257	5 067	3 579	1 488	2 429	1 660	769
55 - 59	C	10 044	6 523	3 521	6 252	4 095	2 157	3 792	2 428	1 364
60 - 64	C	16 936	10 796	6 140	10 408	6 661	3 747	6 528	4 135	2 393
65 - 69	C	14 502	8 646	5 856	9 059	5 360	3 699	5 443	3 286	2 157
70 - 74	C	19 263	9 214	10 049	12 463	5 852	6 611	6 800	3 362	3 438
75 - 79	C	12 830	4 613	8 217	8 117	2 824	5 293	4 713	1 789	2 924
80 - 84	C	10 389	3 126	7 263	6 695	1 931	4 764	3 694	1 195	2 499
85 - 89	C	8 935	2 202	6 733	5 571	1 327	4 244	3 364	875	2 489
90 - 94	C	3 759	825	2 934	2 146	436	1 710	1 613	389	1 224
95 - 99	C	1 339	241	1 098	591	94	497	748	147	601
100+	C	328	54	274	124	18	106	204	36	168
Unknown - Inconnu	C	432	338	94	407	324	83	25	14	11
Korea (Dem. People's Republic of) - Corée (Rép. populaire dém. de)										
1993										
Total	...	115 609	62 046	53 563	64 067	...	...	51 542	...	...
0 - 4	...	11 202	5 978	5 224	5 212	...	...	5 990	...	...
5 - 9	...	1 065	636	429	562	...	...	503	...	...
10 - 14	...	532	322	210	310	...	...	222	...	...
15 - 19	...	730	399	331	432	...	...	298	...	...
20 - 24	...	1 245	596	649	773	...	...	472	...	...
25 - 29	...	1 776	1 084	692	1 083	...	...	693	...	...
30 - 34	...	1 626	1 048	578	985	...	...	641	...	...
35 - 39	...	1 564	1 057	507	993	...	...	571	...	...
40 - 44	...	1 866	1 316	550	1 211	...	...	655	...	...
45 - 49	...	3 452	2 428	1 024	2 213	...	...	1 239	...	...
50 - 54	...	5 575	3 963	1 612	3 509	...	...	2 066	...	...
55 - 59	...	9 785	7 027	2 758	5 945	...	...	3 840	...	...
60 - 64	...	13 900	9 369	4 531	8 441	...	...	5 459	...	...
65 - 69	...	14 526	8 547	5 979	8 245	...	...	6 281	...	...
70 - 74	...	16 149	7 955	8 194	8 521	...	...	7 628	...	...
75 - 79	...	14 977	5 769	9 208	7 628	...	...	7 349	...	...
80 - 84	...	10 461	3 397	7 064	5 401	...	...	5 060	...	...
85+	...	5 178	1 155	4 023	2 603	...	...	2 575	...	...
Korea (Republic of) - Corée (République de)[16]										
2000										
Total	C	247 346	137 266	110 080	...	...	...	...	...	...
0 - 1	C	2 885	1 539	1 346	...	...	...	...	...	...
1 - 4	C	1 223	696	527	...	...	...	...	...	...
5 - 9	C	933	581	352	...	...	...	...	...	...
10 - 14	C	616	386	230	...	...	...	...	...	...
15 - 19	C	1 783	1 215	568	...	...	...	...	...	...
20 - 24	C	2 539	1 785	754	...	...	...	...	...	...
25 - 29	C	3 342	2 346	996	...	...	...	...	...	...
30 - 34	C	4 410	3 035	1 375	...	...	...	...	...	...
35 - 39	C	6 629	4 791	1 838	...	...	...	...	...	...

(See notes at end of table.— Voir notes à la fin du tableau.)

Continent, country or area, year and age (in years) / Continent, pays ou zone, année et âge (en années)	Code[1]	Total			Urban - Urbaine			Rural - Rurale		
		Both sexes - Les deux sexes	Male - Masculin	Female - Féminin	Both sexes - Les deux sexes	Male - Masculin	Female - Féminin	Both sexes - Les deux sexes	Male - Masculin	Female - Féminin
ASIA — ASIE										
Korea (Republic of) - Corée (République de)[16]										
2000										
40 - 44	C	9 908	7 371	2 537	...	...	...	...	...	...
45 - 49	C	10 727	8 189	2 538	...	...	...	...	...	...
50 - 54	C	12 609	9 455	3 154	...	...	...	...	...	...
55 - 59	C	17 115	12 456	4 659	...	...	...	...	...	...
60 - 64	C	22 365	15 592	6 773	...	...	...	...	...	...
65 - 69	C	25 131	15 663	9 468	...	...	...	...	...	...
70 - 74	C	29 002	15 440	13 562	...	...	...	...	...	...
75 - 79	C	33 356	16 062	17 294	...	...	...	...	...	...
80 - 84	C	29 944	11 750	18 194	...	...	...	...	...	...
85+	C	32 822	8 914	23 908	...	...	...	...	...	...
Unknown - Inconnu	C	7	-	7	...	...	...	...	...	...
Kuwait - Koweït										
2000										
Total	C	4 227	2 690	1 537	...	...	...	...	...	...
0 - 1	C	379	219	160	...	...	...	...	...	...
1 - 4	C	113	64	49	...	...	...	...	...	...
5 - 9	C	53	28	25	...	...	...	...	...	...
10 - 14	C	41	29	12	...	...	...	...	...	...
15 - 19	C	88	68	20	...	...	...	...	...	...
20 - 24	C	113	89	24	...	...	...	...	...	...
25 - 29	C	124	96	28	...	...	...	...	...	...
30 - 34	C	146	101	45	...	...	...	...	...	...
35 - 39	C	167	128	39	...	...	...	...	...	...
40 - 44	C	233	177	56	...	...	...	...	...	...
45 - 49	C	233	186	47	...	...	...	...	...	...
50 - 54	C	241	180	61	...	...	...	...	...	...
55 - 59	C	271	195	76	...	...	...	...	...	...
60 - 64	C	334	209	125	...	...	...	...	...	...
65 - 69	C	366	220	146	...	...	...	...	...	...
70 - 74	C	378	214	164	...	...	...	...	...	...
75 - 79	C	292	162	130	...	...	...	...	...	...
80 - 84	C	216	108	108	...	...	...	...	...	...
85+	C	242	98	144	...	...	...	...	...	...
Unknown - Inconnu	C	197	119	78	...	...	...	...	...	...
Kyrgyzstan - Kirghizistan[11]										
2000										
Total	C	34 111	18 667	15 444	13 595	7 488	6 107	20 516	11 179	9 337
0 - 1	C	2 225	1 313	912	836	482	354	1 389	831	558
1 - 4	C	1 112	617	495	184	108	76	928	509	419
5 - 9	C	285	163	122	58	37	21	227	126	101
10 - 14	C	252	148	104	75	37	38	177	111	66
15 - 19	C	360	220	140	100	59	41	260	161	99
20 - 24	C	635	444	191	229	165	64	406	279	127
25 - 29	C	824	616	208	328	253	75	496	363	133
30 - 34	C	993	722	271	384	298	86	609	424	185
35 - 39	C	1 332	977	355	562	425	137	770	552	218
40 - 44	C	1 549	1 134	415	692	533	159	857	601	256
45 - 49	C	1 590	1 124	466	703	513	190	887	611	276
50 - 54	C	1 566	1 070	496	730	515	215	836	555	281
55 - 59	C	1 487	968	519	645	424	221	842	544	298
60 - 64	C	3 054	1 861	1 193	1 295	812	483	1 759	1 049	710
65 - 69	C	3 503	2 061	1 442	1 311	786	525	2 192	1 275	917
70 - 74	C	4 408	2 278	2 130	1 776	872	904	2 632	1 406	1 226
75 - 79	C	3 183	1 258	1 925	1 349	519	830	1 834	739	1 095
80 - 84	C	2 271	718	1 553	1 034	313	721	1 237	405	832
85 - 89	C	1 815	536	1 279	839	215	624	976	321	655
90 - 94	C	867	235	632	286	59	227	581	176	405
95 - 99	C	464	108	356	90	17	73	374	91	283
100+	C	273	53	220	37	8	29	236	45	191

19. Deaths by age, sex and urban/rural residence: latest available year
Décès selon l'âge, le sexe et la résidence, urbaine/rurale: dernière année disponible (continued — suite)

(See notes at end of table.— Voir notes à la fin du tableau.)

Continent, country or area, year and age (in years) / Continent, pays ou zone, année et âge (en années)	Code[1]	Total			Urban - Urbaine			Rural - Rurale		
		Both sexes - Les deux sexes	Male - Masculin	Female - Féminin	Both sexes - Les deux sexes	Male - Masculin	Female - Féminin	Both sexes - Les deux sexes	Male - Masculin	Female - Féminin
ASIA — ASIE										
Kyrgyzstan - Kirghizistan[11]										
2000										
Unknown - Inconnu	C	63	43	20	52	38	14	11	5	6
Malaysia - Malaisie										
1998										
Total	C	97 906	56 472	41 434	...	...	...	...	...	...
0 - 1	C	4 481	2 533	1 948	...	...	...	...	...	...
1 - 4	C	1 421	768	653	...	...	...	...	...	...
5 - 9	C	893	526	367	...	...	...	...	...	...
10 - 14	C	1 020	607	413	...	...	...	...	...	...
15 - 19	C	2 007	1 543	464	...	...	...	...	...	...
20 - 24	C	2 317	1 805	512	...	...	...	...	...	...
25 - 29	C	2 305	1 762	543	...	...	...	...	...	...
30 - 34	C	2 694	1 964	730	...	...	...	...	...	...
35 - 39	C	3 157	2 234	923	...	...	...	...	...	...
40 - 44	C	3 643	2 492	1 151	...	...	...	...	...	...
45 - 49	C	4 142	2 682	1 460	...	...	...	...	...	...
50 - 54	C	5 179	3 333	1 846	...	...	...	...	...	...
55 - 59	C	6 534	4 063	2 471	...	...	...	...	...	...
60 - 64	C	8 801	5 239	3 562	...	...	...	...	...	...
65 - 69	C	10 308	5 750	4 558	...	...	...	...	...	...
70 - 74	C	10 987	5 879	5 108	...	...	...	...	...	...
75 - 79	C	10 856	5 422	5 434	...	...	...	...	...	...
80 - 84	C	7 902	3 690	4 212	...	...	...	...	...	...
85+	C	8 907	3 914	4 993	...	...	...	...	...	...
Unknown - Inconnu	C	352	266	86	...	...	...	...	...	...
Maldives										
1996										
Total	C	1 213	684	529	268	172	96	945	512	433
0 - 1	C	193	112	81	30	18	12	163	94	69
1 - 4	C	65	26	39	8	6	2	57	20	37
5 - 9	C	21	10	11	5	2	3	16	8	8
10 - 14	C	13	8	5	-	-	-	13	8	5
15 - 19	C	13	7	6	8	4	4	5	3	2
20 - 24	C	11	6	5	3	3	-	8	3	5
25 - 29	C	22	11	11	7	5	2	15	6	9
30 - 34	C	12	5	7	6	3	3	6	2	4
35 - 39	C	42	23	19	12	9	3	30	14	16
40 - 44	C	27	15	12	9	6	3	18	9	9
45 - 49	C	42	24	18	16	9	7	26	15	11
50 - 54	C	46	27	19	13	10	3	33	17	16
55 - 59	C	92	58	34	34	25	9	58	33	25
60 - 64	C	125	73	52	32	21	11	93	52	41
65 - 69	C	132	75	57	22	15	7	110	60	50
70 - 74	C	129	76	53	22	16	6	107	60	47
75 - 79	C	98	54	44	16	9	7	82	45	37
80 - 84	C	56	31	25	12	6	6	44	25	19
85 - 89	C	23	16	7	6	2	4	17	14	3
90 - 94	C	12	5	7	3	1	2	9	4	5
95 - 99	C	9	7	2	3	2	1	6	5	1
100+	C	3	2	1	1	-	1	2	2	-
Unknown - Inconnu	C	27	13	14	-	-	-	27	13	14
Mongolia - Mongolie										
2000										
Total	C	15 472	8 683	6 789	8 888	...	...	6 584	...	...
0 - 1	C	1 596	861	735	808	...	...	788	...	...
1 - 4	C	634	360	274	282	...	...	352	...	...
5 - 9	C	147	85	62	63	...	...	84	...	...
10 - 14	C	119	77	42	73	...	...	46	...	...
15 - 19	C	190	130	60	114	...	...	76	...	...
20 - 24	C	327	215	112	206	...	...	121	...	...
25 - 29	C	450	305	145	291	...	...	159	...	...

(See notes at end of table.— Voir notes à la fin du tableau.)

Continent, country or area, year and age (in years) / Continent, pays ou zone, année et âge (en années)	Code[1]	Total			Urban - Urbaine			Rural - Rurale		
		Both sexes - Les deux sexes	Male - Masculin	Female - Féminin	Both sexes - Les deux sexes	Male - Masculin	Female - Féminin	Both sexes - Les deux sexes	Male - Masculin	Female - Féminin
ASIA — ASIE										
Mongolia - Mongolie										
2000										
30 - 34	C	587	410	177	373	...	...	214	...	...
35 - 39	C	685	432	253	457	...	...	228	...	...
40 - 44	C	800	540	260	546	...	...	254	...	...
45 - 49	C	755	481	274	448	...	...	307	...	...
50 - 54	C	867	532	335	541	...	...	326	...	...
55 - 59	C	1 053	627	426	615	...	...	438	...	...
60 - 64	C	1 247	723	524	699	...	...	548	...	...
65 - 69	C	1 515	827	688	846	...	...	669	...	...
70 - 74	C	1 560	817	743	760	...	...	800	...	...
75 - 79	C	1 056	488	568	600	...	...	456	...	...
80 - 84	C	863	380	483	516	...	...	347	...	...
85 - 89	C	651	266	385	412	...	...	239	...	...
90 - 94	C	276	96	180	172	...	...	104	...	...
95 - 99	C	83	26	57	58	...	...	25	...	...
100+	C	11	5	6	8	...	...	3	...	...
Myanmar[17,18]										
1994										
Total	U	...	...	...	80 421	...	...	86 579	...	...
0 - 1	U	...	...	...	12 168	...	...	13 177	...	...
1 - 4	U	...	...	...	6 543	...	...	7 399	...	...
5 - 14	U	...	...	...	5 333	...	...	5 118	...	...
15 - 24	U	...	...	...	4 812	...	...	4 978	...	...
25 - 34	U	...	...	...	5 288	...	...	6 030	...	...
35 - 44	U	...	...	...	6 202	...	...	5 701	...	...
45 - 54	U	...	...	...	8 173	...	...	6 927	...	...
55 - 64	U	...	...	...	10 256	...	...	10 187	...	...
65 - 74	U	...	...	...	10 633	...	...	12 403	...	...
75 - 84	U	...	...	...	7 846	...	...	10 713	...	...
85+	U	...	...	...	2 531	...	...	3 810	...	...
Unknown - Inconnu	U	...	...	...	636	...	...	136	...	...
Occupied Palestinian Territory - Territoire palestinien occupé										
2000										
Total	U	8 601	4 712	3 889	...	...	...	...	...	...
0 - 1	U	1 025	524	501	...	...	...	...	...	...
1 - 4	U	330	183	147	...	...	...	...	...	...
5 - 9	U	162	88	74	...	...	...	...	...	...
10 - 14	U	132	89	43	...	...	...	...	...	...
15 - 19	U	184	151	33	...	...	...	...	...	...
20 - 24	U	168	132	36	...	...	...	...	...	...
25 - 29	U	152	102	50	...	...	...	...	...	...
30 - 34	U	124	76	48	...	...	...	...	...	...
35 - 39	U	147	91	56	...	...	...	...	...	...
40 - 44	U	159	103	56	...	...	...	...	...	...
45 - 49	U	212	133	79	...	...	...	...	...	...
50 - 54	U	349	203	146	...	...	...	...	...	...
55 - 59	U	435	232	203	...	...	...	...	...	...
60 - 64	U	674	331	343	...	...	...	...	...	...
65 - 69	U	821	400	421	...	...	...	...	...	...
70 - 74	U	1 103	549	554	...	...	...	...	...	...
75 - 79	U	819	426	393	...	...	...	...	...	...
80 - 84	U	660	350	310	...	...	...	...	...	...
85+	U	945	549	396	...	...	...	...	...	...
Pakistan[19,20]										
1997										
Total	I	1 089 596	597 662	491 934	291 810	159 000	132 810	797 780	438 657	359 123
0 - 1	I	354 732	196 724	158 008	86 370	48 064	38 306	268 362	148 660	119 702
1 - 4	I	144 460	66 597	77 863	37 222	14 609	22 613	107 238	51 988	55 250
5 - 9	I	26 908	14 535	12 373	4 772	2 207	2 565	22 135	12 327	9 808
10 - 14	I	17 380	8 375	9 005	4 868	3 109	1 759	12 512	5 266	7 246

19. **Deaths by age, sex and urban/rural residence: latest available year**
Décès selon l'âge, le sexe et la résidence, urbaine/rurale: dernière année disponible (continued — suite)

(See notes at end of table.— Voir notes à la fin du tableau.)

Continent, country or area, year and age (in years) / Continent, pays ou zone, année et âge (en années)	Code[1]	Total			Urban - Urbaine			Rural - Rurale		
		Both sexes - Les deux sexes	Male - Masculin	Female - Féminin	Both sexes - Les deux sexes	Male - Masculin	Female - Féminin	Both sexes - Les deux sexes	Male - Masculin	Female - Féminin
ASIA — ASIE										
Pakistan[19,20]										
1997										
15 - 19	I	24 387	9 798	14 589	5 480	3 143	2 337	18 907	6 655	12 252
20 - 24	I	28 440	12 482	15 958	6 262	3 431	2 831	22 177	9 050	13 127
25 - 29	I	22 226	13 112	9 114	6 347	3 646	2 701	15 878	9 465	6 413
30 - 34	I	24 279	10 429	13 850	6 213	2 610	3 603	18 065	7 818	10 247
35 - 39	I	20 010	11 059	8 951	5 213	3 239	1 974	14 796	7 819	6 977
40 - 44	I	16 120	8 951	7 169	4 158	1 889	2 269	11 962	7 062	4 900
45 - 49	I	33 969	21 487	12 482	12 726	8 223	4 503	21 243	13 265	7 978
50 - 54	I	38 868	20 857	18 011	13 236	6 601	6 635	25 632	14 256	11 376
55 - 59	I	35 913	22 171	13 742	14 665	10 247	4 418	21 248	11 924	9 324
60 - 64	I	55 205	34 924	20 281	13 519	8 117	5 402	41 686	26 807	14 879
65 - 69	I	57 563	31 285	26 278	19 687	10 247	9 440	37 876	21 038	16 838
70+	I	189 136	114 876	74 260	51 072	29 618	21 454	138 063	85 257	52 806
Philippines										
1998										
Total	C	352 992	210 592	142 400	...	...	...	...	...	...
0 - 1	C	28 196	16 655	11 541	...	...	...	...	...	...
1 - 4	C	12 344	6 831	5 513	...	...	...	...	...	...
5 - 9	C	6 606	3 731	2 875	...	...	...	...	...	...
10 - 14	C	5 039	2 988	2 051	...	...	...	...	...	...
15 - 19	C	6 564	4 226	2 338	...	...	...	...	...	...
20 - 24	C	8 906	6 105	2 801	...	...	...	...	...	...
25 - 29	C	10 596	7 427	3 169	...	...	...	...	...	...
30 - 34	C	11 467	7 908	3 559	...	...	...	...	...	...
35 - 39	C	13 549	9 263	4 286	...	...	...	...	...	...
40 - 44	C	15 006	10 245	4 761	...	...	...	...	...	...
45 - 49	C	17 924	12 332	5 592	...	...	...	...	...	...
50 - 54	C	19 813	13 519	6 294	...	...	...	...	...	...
55 - 59	C	22 425	15 087	7 338	...	...	...	...	...	...
60 - 64	C	26 762	17 311	9 451	...	...	...	...	...	...
65 - 69	C	28 090	17 234	10 856	...	...	...	...	...	...
70 - 74	C	28 948	16 738	12 210	...	...	...	...	...	...
75 - 79	C	29 556	15 848	13 708	...	...	...	...	...	...
80 - 84	C	26 102	12 279	13 823	...	...	...	...	...	...
85+	C	34 448	14 470	19 978	...	...	...	...	...	...
Unknown - Inconnu	C	651	395	256	...	...	...	...	...	...
Qatar										
1999										
Total	C	1 148	796	352	...	...	...	...	...	...
0 - 1	C	112	58	54	...	...	...	...	...	...
1 - 4	C	26	16	10	...	...	...	...	...	...
5 - 9	C	10	4	6	...	...	...	...	...	...
10 - 14	C	19	14	5	...	...	...	...	...	...
15 - 19	C	21	15	6	...	...	...	...	...	...
20 - 24	C	39	30	9	...	...	...	...	...	...
25 - 29	C	44	41	3	...	...	...	...	...	...
30 - 34	C	44	38	6	...	...	...	...	...	...
35 - 39	C	55	44	11	...	...	...	...	...	...
40 - 44	C	73	61	12	...	...	...	...	...	...
45 - 49	C	70	60	10	...	...	...	...	...	...
50 - 54	C	69	55	14	...	...	...	...	...	...
55 - 59	C	99	68	31	...	...	...	...	...	...
60 - 64	C	94	60	34	...	...	...	...	...	...
65 - 69	C	94	59	35	...	...	...	...	...	...
70 - 74	C	91	57	34	...	...	...	...	...	...
75 - 79	C	67	44	23	...	...	...	...	...	...
80 - 84	C	56	36	20	...	...	...	...	...	...
85 - 89	C	33	20	13	...	...	...	...	...	...
90 - 94	C	19	10	9	...	...	...	...	...	...
95+	C	4	2	2	...	...	...	...	...	...
Unknown - Inconnu	C	9	4	5	...	...	...	...	...	...

19. Deaths by age, sex and urban/rural residence: latest available year
Décès selon l'âge, le sexe et la résidence, urbaine/rurale: dernière année disponible (continued — suite)

(See notes at end of table.— Voir notes à la fin du tableau.)

Continent, country or area, year and age (in years) / Continent, pays ou zone, année et âge (en années)	Code[1]	Total			Urban - Urbaine			Rural - Rurale		
		Both sexes - Les deux sexes	Male - Masculin	Female - Féminin	Both sexes - Les deux sexes	Male - Masculin	Female - Féminin	Both sexes - Les deux sexes	Male - Masculin	Female - Féminin
ASIA — ASIE										
Saudi Arabia - Arabie saoudite										
2000										
Total	...	51 614	28 632	22 982	...	...	...	...	...	...
0 - 1	...	11 071	5 818	5 253	...	...	...	...	...	...
1 - 4	...	1 903	525	1 378	...	...	...	...	...	...
5 - 9	...	1 173	1 173	-	...	...	...	...	...	...
10 - 14	...	1 092	980	112	...	...	...	...	...	...
15 - 19	...	1 098	1 060	38	...	...	...	...	...	...
20 - 24	...	813	813	-	...	...	...	...	...	...
25 - 29	...	1 361	1 361	-	...	...	...	...	...	...
30 - 34	...	693	476	217	...	...	...	...	...	...
35 - 39	...	646	441	205	...	...	...	...	...	...
40 - 44	...	2 547	1 528	1 019	...	...	...	...	...	...
45 - 49	...	1 011	747	264	...	...	...	...	...	...
50 - 54	...	1 919	1 025	894	...	...	...	...	...	...
55 - 59	...	3 695	1 751	1 944	...	...	...	...	...	...
60 - 64	...	3 068	1 663	1 405	...	...	...	...	...	...
65 - 69	...	2 858	1 570	1 288	...	...	...	...	...	...
70 - 74	...	4 431	1 962	2 469	...	...	...	...	...	...
75 - 79	...	2 651	1 186	1 465	...	...	...	...	...	...
80 - 84	...	1 536	851	685	...	...	...	...	...	...
85+	...	8 048	3 702	4 346	...	...	...	...	...	...
Singapore - Singapour[21]										
2000										
Total	C	15 692	8 689	7 003	...	...	...	...	...	...
0 - 1	C	137	80	57	...	...	...	...	...	...
1 - 4	C	60	30	30	...	...	...	...	...	...
5 - 9	C	37	14	23	...	...	...	...	...	...
10 - 14	C	53	35	18	...	...	...	...	...	...
15 - 19	C	78	48	30	...	...	...	...	...	...
20 - 24	C	176	131	45	...	...	...	...	...	...
25 - 29	C	217	155	62	...	...	...	...	...	...
30 - 34	C	249	166	83	...	...	...	...	...	...
35 - 39	C	368	252	116	...	...	...	...	...	...
40 - 44	C	488	323	165	...	...	...	...	...	...
45 - 49	C	618	396	222	...	...	...	...	...	...
50 - 54	C	761	470	291	...	...	...	...	...	...
55 - 59	C	818	525	293	...	...	...	...	...	...
60 - 64	C	1 304	819	485	...	...	...	...	...	...
65 - 69	C	1 799	1 081	718	...	...	...	...	...	...
70 - 74	C	2 009	1 163	846	...	...	...	...	...	...
75 - 79	C	2 069	1 108	961	...	...	...	...	...	...
80 - 84	C	1 910	932	978	...	...	...	...	...	...
85+	C	2 499	928	1 571	...	...	...	...	...	...
Unknown - Inconnu	C	42	33	9	...	...	...	...	...	...
Sri Lanka										
1996										
Total	+C	122 161	79 784	42 377	60 131	39 546	20 585	62 030	40 238	21 792
0 - 1	+C	5 879	3 271	2 608	5 062	2 816	2 246	817	455	362
1 - 4	+C	1 237	667	570	805	432	373	432	235	197
5 - 9	+C	924	514	410	551	301	250	373	213	160
10 - 14	+C	990	550	440	562	292	270	428	258	170
15 - 19	+C	3 320	2 487	833	1 512	1 015	497	1 808	1 472	336
20 - 24	+C	6 180	5 241	939	2 828	2 279	549	3 352	2 962	390
25 - 29	+C	5 875	4 966	909	2 557	2 041	516	3 318	2 925	393
30 - 34	+C	4 712	3 875	837	2 177	1 673	504	2 535	2 202	333
35 - 39	+C	4 838	3 793	1 045	2 467	1 853	614	2 371	1 940	431
40 - 44	+C	4 607	3 585	1 022	2 650	2 048	602	1 957	1 537	420
45 - 49	+C	5 819	4 309	1 510	3 514	2 649	865	2 305	1 660	645
50 - 54	+C	6 387	4 511	1 876	3 883	2 806	1 077	2 504	1 705	799
55 - 59	+C	6 904	4 867	2 037	4 015	2 896	1 119	2 889	1 971	918
60 - 64	+C	8 431	5 529	2 902	4 598	3 143	1 455	3 833	2 386	1 447

19. Deaths by age, sex and urban/rural residence: latest available year
Décès selon l'âge, le sexe et la résidence, urbaine/rurale: dernière année disponible (continued — suite)

(See notes at end of table.— Voir notes à la fin du tableau.)

Continent, country or area, year and age (in years) / Continent, pays ou zone, année et âge (en années)	Code[1]	Total			Urban - Urbaine			Rural - Rurale		
		Both sexes - Les deux sexes	Male - Masculin	Female - Féminin	Both sexes - Les deux sexes	Male - Masculin	Female - Féminin	Both sexes - Les deux sexes	Male - Masculin	Female - Féminin
ASIA — ASIE										
Sri Lanka										
1996										
65 - 69	+C	10 699	6 751	3 948	5 491	3 530	1 961	5 208	3 221	1 987
70 - 74	+C	12 549	7 424	5 125	5 884	3 538	2 346	6 665	3 886	2 779
75 - 79	+C	10 704	6 080	4 624	4 489	2 569	1 920	6 215	3 511	2 704
80 - 84	+C	10 071	5 404	4 667	3 609	1 950	1 659	6 462	3 454	3 008
85+	+C	12 035	5 960	6 075	3 477	1 715	1 762	8 558	4 245	4 313
Tajikistan - Tadjikistan[11]										
1994										
Total	C	39 943	21 339	18 604	13 068	7 083	5 985	26 875	14 256	12 619
0 - 1	C	6 880	3 896	2 984	1 930	1 136	794	4 950	2 760	2 190
1 - 4	C	5 267	2 742	2 525	745	402	343	4 522	2 340	2 182
5 - 9	C	753	416	337	145	88	57	608	328	280
10 - 14	C	522	315	207	120	82	38	402	233	169
15 - 19	C	671	440	231	204	142	62	467	298	169
20 - 24	C	902	574	328	302	203	99	600	371	229
25 - 29	C	984	626	358	310	220	90	674	406	268
30 - 34	C	1 106	668	438	381	260	121	725	408	317
35 - 39	C	983	594	389	378	264	114	605	330	275
40 - 44	C	1 035	646	389	489	327	162	546	319	227
45 - 49	C	890	546	344	405	271	134	485	275	210
50 - 54	C	1 219	795	424	556	383	173	663	412	251
55 - 59	C	2 154	1 283	871	934	612	322	1 220	671	549
60 - 64	C	2 783	1 541	1 242	1 009	578	431	1 774	963	811
65 - 69	C	3 108	1 695	1 413	1 232	660	572	1 876	1 035	841
70 - 74	C	2 803	1 254	1 549	1 038	438	600	1 765	816	949
75 - 79	C	2 264	983	1 281	917	351	566	1 347	632	715
80 - 84	C	2 380	1 013	1 367	1 013	344	669	1 367	669	698
85+	C	3 219	1 299	1 920	949	315	634	2 270	984	1 286
Unknown - Inconnu	C	20	13	7	11	7	4	9	6	3
Thailand - Thaïlande										
1999										
Total	+U	362 593	213 427	149 166	36 796	21 674	15 122	325 797	191 753	134 044
0 - 1	+U	5 003	2 765	2 238	711	359	352	4 292	2 406	1 886
1 - 4	+U	5 948	3 193	2 755	451	246	205	5 497	2 947	2 550
5 - 9	+U	3 040	1 804	1 236	184	106	78	2 856	1 698	1 158
10 - 14	+U	2 162	1 300	862	181	112	69	1 981	1 188	793
15 - 19	+U	6 504	4 861	1 643	553	408	145	5 951	4 453	1 498
20 - 24	+U	11 727	8 192	3 535	1 280	972	308	10 447	7 220	3 227
25 - 29	+U	22 108	16 139	5 969	1 860	1 447	413	20 248	14 692	5 556
30 - 34	+U	23 928	18 116	5 812	2 242	1 715	527	21 686	16 401	5 285
35 - 39	+U	20 640	15 414	5 226	2 120	1 607	513	18 520	13 807	4 713
40 - 44	+U	18 982	13 089	5 893	2 120	1 480	640	16 862	11 609	5 253
45 - 49	+U	18 489	12 071	6 418	2 107	1 380	727	16 382	10 691	5 691
50 - 54	+U	18 660	11 727	6 933	2 017	1 267	750	16 643	10 460	6 183
55 - 59	+U	21 563	13 072	8 491	2 322	1 419	903	19 241	11 653	7 588
60 - 64	+U	27 435	16 057	11 378	3 029	1 810	1 219	24 406	14 247	10 159
65 - 69	+U	31 442	17 504	13 938	3 299	1 895	1 404	28 143	15 609	12 534
70 - 74	+U	32 171	17 261	14 910	3 202	1 660	1 542	28 969	15 601	13 368
75 - 79	+U	30 537	15 485	15 052	2 971	1 449	1 522	27 566	14 036	13 530
80 - 84	+U	26 406	11 901	14 505	2 803	1 203	1 600	23 603	10 698	12 905
85+	+U	32 613	12 063	20 550	3 292	1 118	2 174	29 321	10 945	18 376
Unknown - Inconnu	+U	3 235	1 413	1 822	52	21	31	3 183	1 392	1 791
Uzbekistan - Ouzbékistan[11]										
2000										
Total	C	135 598	70 794	64 804	61 130	32 195	28 935	74 468	38 599	35 869
0 - 1	C	10 091	5 805	4 286	3 703	2 136	1 567	6 388	3 669	2 719
1 - 4	C	5 417	2 925	2 492	1 177	645	532	4 240	2 280	1 960
5 - 9	C	1 474	886	588	423	251	172	1 051	635	416
10 - 14	C	1 436	852	584	442	260	182	994	592	402
15 - 19	C	2 001	1 289	712	709	475	234	1 292	814	478
20 - 24	C	2 849	1 758	1 091	1 155	789	366	1 694	969	725

(See notes at end of table.— Voir notes à la fin du tableau.)

Continent, country or area, year and age (in years) / Continent, pays ou zone, année et âge (en années)	Code[1]	Total			Urban - Urbaine			Rural - Rurale		
		Both sexes - Les deux sexes	Male - Masculin	Female - Féminin	Both sexes - Les deux sexes	Male - Masculin	Female - Féminin	Both sexes - Les deux sexes	Male - Masculin	Female - Féminin
ASIA — ASIE										
Uzbekistan - Ouzbékistan[11]										
2000										
25 - 29	C	3 427	2 177	1 250	1 501	1 023	478	1 926	1 154	772
30 - 34	C	3 660	2 403	1 257	1 657	1 185	472	2 003	1 218	785
35 - 39	C	4 181	2 759	1 422	1 993	1 407	586	2 188	1 352	836
40 - 44	C	5 086	3 277	1 809	2 584	1 789	795	2 502	1 488	1 014
45 - 49	C	5 290	3 445	1 845	2 797	1 924	873	2 493	1 521	972
50 - 54	C	5 765	3 647	2 118	3 140	2 052	1 088	2 625	1 595	1 030
55 - 59	C	6 104	3 794	2 310	3 056	1 990	1 066	3 048	1 804	1 244
60 - 64	C	12 287	7 257	5 030	5 897	3 603	2 294	6 390	3 654	2 736
65 - 69	C	14 077	7 757	6 320	6 312	3 601	2 711	7 765	4 156	3 609
70 - 74	C	17 094	8 713	8 381	8 142	4 010	4 132	8 952	4 703	4 249
75 - 79	C	12 547	4 824	7 723	6 043	2 111	3 932	6 504	2 713	3 791
80 - 84	C	8 807	2 836	5 971	4 430	1 285	3 145	4 377	1 551	2 826
85 - 89	C	7 198	2 312	4 886	3 747	1 011	2 736	3 451	1 301	2 150
90 - 94	C	3 782	1 295	2 487	1 515	421	1 094	2 267	874	1 393
95 - 99	C	1 963	579	1 384	511	167	344	1 452	412	1 040
100+	C	1 062	204	858	196	60	136	866	144	722
EUROPE										
Andorra - Andorre										
1994										
Total	C	184	105	79	...	...	...	...	...	...
0 - 1	C	2	1	1	...	...	...	...	...	...
10 - 14	C	1	-	1	...	...	...	...	...	...
15 - 19	C	2	1	1	...	...	...	...	...	...
20 - 24	C	1	-	1	...	...	...	...	...	...
25 - 29	C	11	6	5	...	...	...	...	...	...
30 - 34	C	3	3	-	...	...	...	...	...	...
35 - 39	C	6	5	1	...	...	...	...	...	...
40 - 44	C	4	1	3	...	...	...	...	...	...
45 - 49	C	6	4	2	...	...	...	...	...	...
50 - 54	C	8	6	2	...	...	...	...	...	...
55 - 59	C	12	7	5	...	...	...	...	...	...
60 - 64	C	12	9	3	...	...	...	...	...	...
65 - 69	C	19	12	7	...	...	...	...	...	...
70 - 74	C	14	6	8	...	...	...	...	...	...
75 - 79	C	27	16	11	...	...	...	...	...	...
80 - 84	C	19	10	9	...	...	...	...	...	...
85+	C	37	18	19	...	...	...	...	...	...
Austria - Autriche										
1999										
Total	C	78 200	35 880	42 320	46 752	20 596	26 156	31 448	15 284	16 164
0 - 1	C	341	176	165	191	100	91	150	76	74
1 - 4	C	98	67	31	51	37	14	47	30	17
5 - 9	C	51	28	23	25	11	14	26	17	9
10 - 14	C	72	36	36	38	17	21	34	19	15
15 - 19	C	276	197	79	116	78	38	160	119	41
20 - 24	C	330	257	73	177	136	41	153	121	32
25 - 29	C	348	251	97	183	132	51	165	119	46
30 - 34	C	512	352	160	313	201	112	199	151	48
35 - 39	C	806	550	256	472	324	148	334	226	108
40 - 44	C	1 075	714	361	621	406	215	454	308	146
45 - 49	C	1 433	922	511	848	523	325	585	399	186
50 - 54	C	2 251	1 468	783	1 425	916	509	826	552	274
55 - 59	C	3 554	2 373	1 181	2 238	1 464	774	1 316	909	407
60 - 64	C	3 939	2 654	1 285	2 194	1 461	733	1 745	1 193	552
65 - 69	C	6 004	3 939	2 065	3 267	2 091	1 176	2 737	1 848	889
70 - 74	C	8 963	5 084	3 879	5 131	2 793	2 338	3 832	2 291	1 541
75 - 79	C	12 409	5 726	6 683	7 297	3 256	4 041	5 112	2 470	2 642
80 - 84	C	10 218	3 965	6 253	6 134	2 373	3 761	4 084	1 592	2 492

19. Deaths by age, sex and urban/rural residence: latest available year
Décès selon l'âge, le sexe et la résidence, urbaine/rurale: dernière année disponible (continued — suite)

(See notes at end of table.— Voir notes à la fin du tableau.)

Continent, country or area, year and age (in years) / Continent, pays ou zone, année et âge (en années)	Code[1]	Total			Urban - Urbaine			Rural - Rurale		
		Both sexes - Les deux sexes	Male - Masculin	Female - Féminin	Both sexes - Les deux sexes	Male - Masculin	Female - Féminin	Both sexes - Les deux sexes	Male - Masculin	Female - Féminin
EUROPE										
Austria - Autriche										
1999										
85+	C	25 520	7 121	18 399	16 031	4 277	11 754	9 489	2 844	6 645
2001										
Total	C	74 767	34 500	40 267	...	...	...	...	...	...
0 - 1	C	365	230	135	...	...	...	...	...	...
1 - 4	C	76	41	35	...	...	...	...	...	...
5 - 9	C	45	24	21	...	...	...	...	...	...
10 - 14	C	58	27	31	...	...	...	...	...	...
15 - 19	C	264	194	70	...	...	...	...	...	...
20 - 24	C	296	229	67	...	...	...	...	...	...
25 - 29	C	325	243	82	...	...	...	...	...	...
30 - 34	C	474	323	151	...	...	...	...	...	...
35 - 39	C	707	492	215	...	...	...	...	...	...
40 - 44	C	1 069	707	362	...	...	...	...	...	...
45 - 49	C	1 482	985	497	...	...	...	...	...	...
50 - 54	C	2 319	1 510	809	...	...	...	...	...	...
55 - 59	C	3 064	2 074	990	...	...	...	...	...	...
60 - 64	C	4 200	2 734	1 466	...	...	...	...	...	...
65 - 69	C	5 134	3 349	1 785	...	...	...	...	...	...
70 - 74	C	8 120	4 798	3 322	...	...	...	...	...	...
75 - 79	C	11 822	5 463	6 359	...	...	...	...	...	...
80 - 84	C	10 818	4 266	6 552	...	...	...	...	...	...
85 - 89	C	12 949	4 131	8 818	...	...	...	...	...	...
90 - 94	C	8 582	2 203	6 379	...	...	...	...	...	...
95 - 99	C	2 357	445	1 912	...	...	...	...	...	...
100+	C	241	32	209	...	...	...	...	...	...
Belarus - Bélarus[11]										
1999										
Total	C	142 027	73 892	68 135	73 654	40 872	32 782	68 373	33 020	35 353
0 - 1	C	1 064	645	419	651	395	256	413	250	163
1 - 4	C	317	188	129	150	93	57	167	95	72
5 - 9	C	188	127	61	112	77	35	76	50	26
10 - 14	C	259	168	91	157	96	61	102	72	30
15 - 19	C	701	473	228	466	300	166	235	173	62
20 - 24	C	1 364	1 100	264	869	688	181	495	412	83
25 - 29	C	1 759	1 441	318	1 110	889	221	649	552	97
30 - 34	C	2 281	1 857	424	1 474	1 184	290	807	673	134
35 - 39	C	3 507	2 779	728	2 317	1 817	500	1 190	962	228
40 - 44	C	4 849	3 750	1 099	3 233	2 448	785	1 616	1 302	314
45 - 49	C	6 047	4 611	1 436	4 117	3 062	1 055	1 930	1 549	381
50 - 54	C	6 637	4 788	1 849	4 503	3 220	1 283	2 134	1 568	566
55 - 59	C	8 631	6 074	2 557	5 388	3 792	1 596	3 243	2 282	961
60 - 64	C	14 328	9 444	4 884	8 071	5 358	2 713	6 257	4 086	2 171
65 - 69	C	16 974	10 186	6 788	8 428	5 053	3 375	8 546	5 133	3 413
70 - 74	C	21 031	10 502	10 529	10 447	5 285	5 162	10 584	5 217	5 367
75 - 79	C	17 379	6 511	10 868	7 926	2 983	4 943	9 453	3 528	5 925
80 - 84	C	12 693	3 799	8 894	5 842	1 864	3 978	6 851	1 935	4 916
85 - 89	C	13 354	3 364	9 990	5 163	1 396	3 767	8 191	1 968	6 223
90 - 94	C	6 164	1 414	4 750	2 244	486	1 758	3 920	928	2 992
95 - 99	C	1 776	338	1 438	543	106	437	1 233	232	1 001
100+	C	359	51	308	100	13	87	259	38	221
Unknown - Inconnu	C	365	282	83	343	267	76	22	15	7
Belgium - Belgique[22]										
2001										
Total	C	103 447	51 506	51 941	...	...	...	...	...	...
0 - 1	C	518	296	222	...	...	...	...	...	...
1 - 4	C	144	79	65	...	...	...	...	...	...
5 - 9	C	99	55	44	...	...	...	...	...	...
10 - 14	C	99	58	41	...	...	...	...	...	...
15 - 19	C	316	221	95	...	...	...	...	...	...
20 - 24	C	489	379	110	...	...	...	...	...	...

19. Deaths by age, sex and urban/rural residence: latest available year
Décès selon l'âge, le sexe et la résidence, urbaine/rurale: dernière année disponible (continued — suite)

(See notes at end of table.— Voir notes à la fin du tableau.)

Continent, country or area, year and age (in years) / Continent, pays ou zone, année et âge (en années)	Code[1]	Total			Urban - Urbaine			Rural - Rurale		
		Both sexes - Les deux sexes	Male - Masculin	Female - Féminin	Both sexes - Les deux sexes	Male - Masculin	Female - Féminin	Both sexes - Les deux sexes	Male - Masculin	Female - Féminin
EUROPE										
Belgium - Belgique[22]										
2001										
25 - 29	C	526	394	132	...	...	...	...	...	...
30 - 34	C	649	460	189	...	...	...	...	...	...
35 - 39	C	938	600	338	...	...	...	...	...	...
40 - 44	C	1 523	994	529	...	...	...	...	...	...
45 - 49	C	2 274	1 496	778	...	...	...	...	...	...
50 - 54	C	3 199	2 060	1 139	...	...	...	...	...	...
55 - 59	C	3 809	2 494	1 315	...	...	...	...	...	...
60 - 64	C	5 112	3 402	1 710	...	...	...	...	...	...
65 - 69	C	8 052	5 197	2 855	...	...	...	...	...	...
70 - 74	C	12 073	7 346	4 727	...	...	...	...	...	...
75 - 79	C	16 879	9 243	7 636	...	...	...	...	...	...
80 - 84	C	15 272	7 083	8 189	...	...	...	...	...	...
85 - 89	C	16 796	6 072	10 724	...	...	...	...	...	...
90 - 94	C	10 795	2 842	7 953	...	...	...	...	...	...
95 - 99	C	3 403	669	2 734	...	...	...	...	...	...
100+	C	482	66	416	...	...	...	...	...	...
Bosnia and Herzegovina - Bosnie-Herzégovine										
1998										
Total	C	28 679	15 303	13 376	...	...	...	...	...	...
0 - 1	C	483	294	189	...	...	...	...	...	...
1 - 4	C	99	62	37	...	...	...	...	...	...
5 - 9	C	62	40	22	...	...	...	...	...	...
10 - 14	C	53	34	19	...	...	...	...	...	...
15 - 19	C	108	84	24	...	...	...	...	...	...
20 - 24	C	182	126	56	...	...	...	...	...	...
25 - 29	C	193	141	52	...	...	...	...	...	...
30 - 34	C	269	189	80	...	...	...	...	...	...
35 - 39	C	409	276	133	...	...	...	...	...	...
40 - 44	C	698	485	213	...	...	...	...	...	...
45 - 49	C	931	617	314	...	...	...	...	...	...
50 - 54	C	1 164	776	388	...	...	...	...	...	...
55 - 59	C	2 012	1 332	680	...	...	...	...	...	...
60 - 64	C	3 683	2 260	1 423	...	...	...	...	...	...
65 - 69	C	4 851	2 838	2 013	...	...	...	...	...	...
70 - 74	C	4 733	2 272	2 461	...	...	...	...	...	...
75 - 79	C	3 761	1 522	2 239	...	...	...	...	...	...
80 - 84	C	2 102	797	1 305	...	...	...	...	...	...
85+	C	2 782	1 102	1 680	...	...	...	...	...	...
Unknown - Inconnu	C	104	56	48	...	...	...	...	...	...
Bulgaria - Bulgarie										
2001										
Total	C	112 368	60 145	52 223	62 778	33 964	28 814	49 590	26 181	23 409
0 - 1	C	982	548	434	625	349	276	357	199	158
1 - 4	C	180	98	82	104	56	48	76	42	34
5 - 9	C	105	58	47	63	38	25	42	20	22
10 - 14	C	135	89	46	88	57	31	47	32	15
15 - 19	C	306	206	100	212	141	71	94	65	29
20 - 24	C	490	352	138	363	271	92	127	81	46
25 - 29	C	532	378	154	373	265	108	159	113	46
30 - 34	C	701	486	215	493	345	148	208	141	67
35 - 39	C	1 018	691	327	681	458	223	337	233	104
40 - 44	C	1 768	1 252	516	1 224	853	371	544	399	145
45 - 49	C	3 013	2 118	895	2 070	1 404	666	943	714	229
50 - 54	C	4 824	3 475	1 349	3 242	2 301	941	1 582	1 174	408
55 - 59	C	6 039	4 238	1 801	3 916	2 751	1 165	2 123	1 487	636
60 - 64	C	8 231	5 521	2 710	4 890	3 272	1 618	3 341	2 249	1 092
65 - 69	C	12 579	7 701	4 878	6 976	4 216	2 760	5 603	3 485	2 118
70 - 74	C	17 342	9 527	7 815	9 615	5 284	4 331	7 727	4 243	3 484
75 - 79	C	22 016	10 516	11 500	11 727	5 556	6 171	10 289	4 960	5 329

(See notes at end of table.— Voir notes à la fin du tableau.)

Continent, country or area, year and age (in years) / Continent, pays ou zone, année et âge (en années)	Code[1]	Total			Urban - Urbaine			Rural - Rurale		
		Both sexes - Les deux sexes	Male - Masculin	Female - Féminin	Both sexes - Les deux sexes	Male - Masculin	Female - Féminin	Both sexes - Les deux sexes	Male - Masculin	Female - Féminin
EUROPE										
Bulgaria - Bulgarie										
2001										
80 - 84	C	14 790	6 377	8 413	7 506	3 184	4 322	7 284	3 193	4 091
85+	C	17 317	6 514	10 803	8 610	3 163	5 447	8 707	3 351	5 356
Channel Islands: Guernsey - Îles Anglo-Normandes: Guernesey										
2000										
Total	C	565	264	301	...	...	...	...	...	...
0 - 1	C	4	3	1	...	...	...	...	...	...
1 - 4	C	1	-	1	...	...	...	...	...	...
15 - 19	C	4	3	1	...	...	...	...	...	...
20 - 24	C	1	-	1	...	...	...	...	...	...
25 - 29	C	1	1	-	...	...	...	...	...	...
30 - 34	C	2	1	1	...	...	...	...	...	...
35 - 39	C	2	2	-	...	...	...	...	...	...
40 - 44	C	4	4	-	...	...	...	...	...	...
45 - 49	C	7	5	2	...	...	...	...	...	...
50 - 54	C	13	9	4	...	...	...	...	...	...
55 - 59	C	13	7	6	...	...	...	...	...	...
60 - 64	C	30	15	15	...	...	...	...	...	...
65 - 69	C	45	29	16	...	...	...	...	...	...
70 - 74	C	57	27	30	...	...	...	...	...	...
75 - 79	C	71	38	33	...	...	...	...	...	...
80 - 84	C	103	55	48	...	...	...	...	...	...
85 - 89	C	108	45	63	...	...	...	...	...	...
90 - 94	C	68	14	54	...	...	...	...	...	...
95 - 99	C	24	3	21	...	...	...	...	...	...
100+	C	5	2	3	...	...	...	...	...	...
Unknown - Inconnu	C	2	1	1	...	...	...	...	...	...
Channel Islands: Jersey - Îles Anglo-Normandes: Jersey										
1994										
Total	+C	803	368	435	...	...	...	...	...	...
0 - 1	+C	2	-	2	...	...	...	...	...	...
5 - 9	+C	3	2	1	...	...	...	...	...	...
15 - 19	+C	5	3	2	...	...	...	...	...	...
20 - 24	+C	1	-	1	...	...	...	...	...	...
25 - 29	+C	2	1	1	...	...	...	...	...	...
30 - 34	+C	5	4	1	...	...	...	...	...	...
35 - 39	+C	5	3	2	...	...	...	...	...	...
40 - 44	+C	9	7	2	...	...	...	...	...	...
45 - 49	+C	23	11	12	...	...	...	...	...	...
50 - 54	+C	17	8	9	...	...	...	...	...	...
55 - 59	+C	30	24	6	...	...	...	...	...	...
60 - 64	+C	48	36	12	...	...	...	...	...	...
65 - 69	+C	55	34	21	...	...	...	...	...	...
70 - 74	+C	101	47	54	...	...	...	...	...	...
75+	+C	497	188	309	...	...	...	...	...	...
Croatia - Croatie										
2001										
Total	C	49 552	25 077	24 475	24 838	12 678	12 160	24 714	12 399	12 315
0 - 1	C	315	167	148	179	95	84	136	72	64
1 - 4	C	62	40	22	28	16	12	34	24	10
5 - 9	C	43	25	18	16	11	5	27	14	13
10 - 14	C	44	30	14	18	12	6	26	18	8
15 - 19	C	158	117	41	85	57	28	73	60	13
20 - 24	C	236	191	45	144	117	27	92	74	18
25 - 29	C	203	163	40	112	86	26	91	77	14
30 - 34	C	255	177	78	147	97	50	108	80	28
35 - 39	C	446	325	121	233	161	72	213	164	49
40 - 44	C	809	588	221	389	266	123	420	322	98

493

19. Deaths by age, sex and urban/rural residence: latest available year
Décès selon l'âge, le sexe et la résidence, urbaine/rurale: dernière année disponible (continued — suite)

(See notes at end of table.— Voir notes à la fin du tableau.)

Continent, country or area, year and age (in years) / Continent, pays ou zone, année et âge (en années)	Code[1]	Total			Urban - Urbaine			Rural - Rurale		
		Both sexes - Les deux sexes	Male - Masculin	Female - Féminin	Both sexes - Les deux sexes	Male - Masculin	Female - Féminin	Both sexes - Les deux sexes	Male - Masculin	Female - Féminin
EUROPE										
Croatia - Croatie										
2001										
45 - 49	C	1 345	1 001	344	700	512	188	645	489	156
50 - 54	C	1 960	1 392	568	1 060	715	345	900	677	223
55 - 59	C	2 243	1 566	677	1 268	864	404	975	702	273
60 - 64	C	3 991	2 706	1 285	2 060	1 386	674	1 931	1 320	611
65 - 69	C	6 126	3 853	2 273	3 050	1 925	1 125	3 076	1 928	1 148
70 - 74	C	8 026	4 422	3 604	3 991	2 220	1 771	4 035	2 202	1 833
75 - 79	C	8 633	3 539	5 094	4 255	1 711	2 544	4 378	1 828	2 550
80 - 84	C	6 042	2 154	3 888	2 935	1 098	1 837	3 107	1 056	2 051
85 - 89	C	5 189	1 661	3 528	2 502	835	1 667	2 687	826	1 861
90 - 94	C	2 823	820	2 004	1 369	423	946	1 455	397	1 058
95 - 99	C	541	122	419	268	62	206	273	60	213
100+	C	51	14	35	23	5	18	25	9	16
Unknown - Inconnu	C	13	4	9	6	4	2	7	-	7
Czech Republic - République tchèque										
2001										
Total	C	107 755	53 772	53 983	77 649	38 344	39 305	30 106	15 428	14 678
0 - 1	C	360	212	148	266	156	110	94	56	38
1 - 4	C	91	52	39	67	39	28	24	13	11
5 - 9	C	76	44	32	48	29	19	28	15	13
10 - 14	C	105	61	44	81	46	35	24	15	9
15 - 19	C	321	226	95	237	169	68	84	57	27
20 - 24	C	594	464	130	422	318	104	172	146	26
25 - 29	C	584	432	152	405	293	112	179	139	40
30 - 34	C	568	415	153	428	313	115	140	102	38
35 - 39	C	856	598	258	642	442	200	214	156	58
40 - 44	C	1 549	1 064	485	1 152	768	384	397	296	101
45 - 49	C	2 987	2 064	923	2 163	1 461	702	824	603	221
50 - 54	C	5 024	3 471	1 553	3 668	2 479	1 189	1 356	992	364
55 - 59	C	6 448	4 415	2 033	4 793	3 225	1 568	1 655	1 190	465
60 - 64	C	6 944	4 620	2 324	5 025	3 289	1 736	1 919	1 331	588
65 - 69	C	9 958	6 164	3 794	7 184	4 396	2 788	2 774	1 768	1 006
70 - 74	C	14 879	8 173	6 706	10 652	5 805	4 847	4 227	2 368	1 859
75 - 79	C	19 934	9 088	10 846	14 326	6 496	7 830	5 608	2 592	3 016
80 - 84	C	13 846	5 421	8 425	9 968	3 856	6 112	3 878	1 565	2 313
85 - 89	C	13 933	4 533	9 400	9 923	3 165	6 758	4 010	1 368	2 642
90 - 94	C	7 241	1 971	5 270	5 164	1 399	3 765	2 077	572	1 505
95 - 99	C	1 349	268	1 081	954	188	766	395	80	315
100+	C	108	16	92	81	12	69	27	4	23
Denmark - Danemark[23]										
2001										
Total	C	58 338	28 404	29 934	...	...	...	...	...	...
0 - 1	C	320	164	156	...	...	...	...	...	...
1 - 4	C	71	34	37	...	...	...	...	...	...
5 - 9	C	51	30	21	...	...	...	...	...	...
10 - 14	C	51	33	18	...	...	...	...	...	...
15 - 19	C	107	80	27	...	...	...	...	...	...
20 - 24	C	150	111	39	...	...	...	...	...	...
25 - 29	C	211	155	56	...	...	...	...	...	...
30 - 34	C	286	196	90	...	...	...	...	...	...
35 - 39	C	518	336	182	...	...	...	...	...	...
40 - 44	C	706	431	275	...	...	...	...	...	...
45 - 49	C	1 199	741	458	...	...	...	...	...	...
50 - 54	C	1 891	1 150	741	...	...	...	...	...	...
55 - 59	C	2 927	1 776	1 151	...	...	...	...	...	...
60 - 64	C	3 225	1 914	1 311	...	...	...	...	...	...
65 - 69	C	4 669	2 660	2 009	...	...	...	...	...	...
70 - 74	C	6 386	3 595	2 791	...	...	...	...	...	...
75 - 79	C	8 755	4 632	4 123	...	...	...	...	...	...
80 - 84	C	9 756	4 669	5 087	...	...	...	...	...	...

19. Deaths by age, sex and urban/rural residence: latest available year
Décès selon l'âge, le sexe et la résidence, urbaine/rurale: dernière année disponible (continued — suite)

(See notes at end of table.— Voir notes à la fin du tableau.)

Continent, country or area, year and age (in years) / Continent, pays ou zone, année et âge (en années)	Code[1]	Total			Urban - Urbaine			Rural - Rurale		
		Both sexes - Les deux sexes	Male - Masculin	Female - Féminin	Both sexes - Les deux sexes	Male - Masculin	Female - Féminin	Both sexes - Les deux sexes	Male - Masculin	Female - Féminin
EUROPE										
Denmark - Danemark[23]										
2001										
85 - 89	C	9 053	3 522	5 531	...	...	...	...	...	...
90 - 94	C	5 900	1 726	4 174	...	...	...	...	...	...
95 - 99	C	1 846	407	1 439	...	...	...	...	...	...
100+	C	260	42	218	...	...	...	...	...	...
Estonia - Estonie[5,11]										
2000										
Total	C	18 187	9 084	9 103	11 667	5 886	5 781	6 520	3 198	3 322
0 - 1	C	109	64	45	73	43	30	36	21	15
1 - 4	C	30	18	12	18	9	9	12	9	3
5 - 9	C	29	17	12	16	10	6	13	7	6
10 - 14	C	28	19	9	18	13	5	10	6	4
15 - 19	C	69	48	21	41	28	13	28	20	8
20 - 24	C	138	114	24	96	82	14	42	32	10
25 - 29	C	153	122	31	114	92	22	39	30	9
30 - 34	C	194	145	49	129	98	31	65	47	18
35 - 39	C	303	222	81	197	146	51	106	76	30
40 - 44	C	552	427	125	387	301	86	165	126	39
45 - 49	C	787	569	218	583	407	176	204	162	42
50 - 54	C	918	657	261	632	445	187	286	212	74
55 - 59	C	1 103	733	370	728	476	252	375	257	118
60 - 64	C	1 646	1 137	509	1 100	742	358	546	395	151
65 - 69	C	1 953	1 202	751	1 248	740	508	705	462	243
70 - 74	C	2 631	1 349	1 282	1 780	904	876	851	445	406
75 - 79	C	2 419	881	1 538	1 528	548	980	891	333	558
80 - 84	C	1 811	589	1 222	1 101	357	744	710	232	478
85 - 89	C	2 042	522	1 520	1 170	310	860	872	212	660
90 - 94	C	994	196	798	553	104	449	441	92	349
95 - 99	C	239	46	193	132	26	106	107	20	87
100+	C	35	6	29	19	4	15	16	2	14
Unknown - Inconnu	C	4	1	3	4	1	3	-	-	-
Finland - Finlande[24]										
2001										
Total	C	48 550	23 783	24 767	26 928	12 704	14 224	21 622	11 079	10 543
0 - 1	C	181	118	63	112	68	44	69	50	19
1 - 4	C	36	19	17	27	13	14	9	6	3
5 - 9	C	45	31	14	25	19	6	20	12	8
10 - 14	C	35	22	13	20	15	5	15	7	8
15 - 19	C	155	115	40	82	57	25	73	58	15
20 - 24	C	238	188	50	166	126	40	72	62	10
25 - 29	C	256	204	52	176	139	37	80	65	15
30 - 34	C	328	252	76	214	164	50	114	88	26
35 - 39	C	496	326	170	330	222	108	166	104	62
40 - 44	C	822	568	254	502	339	163	320	229	91
45 - 49	C	1 289	906	383	778	538	240	511	368	143
50 - 54	C	1 995	1 375	620	1 212	815	397	783	560	223
55 - 59	C	2 090	1 485	605	1 270	871	399	820	614	206
60 - 64	C	2 667	1 798	869	1 545	987	558	1 122	811	311
65 - 69	C	3 479	2 272	1 207	1 882	1 186	696	1 597	1 086	511
70 - 74	C	5 501	3 386	2 115	2 943	1 733	1 210	2 558	1 653	905
75 - 79	C	7 466	3 737	3 729	4 011	1 886	2 125	3 455	1 851	1 604
80 - 84	C	7 900	3 170	4 730	4 282	1 652	2 630	3 618	1 518	2 100
85 - 89	C	7 637	2 408	5 229	4 103	1 193	2 910	3 534	1 215	2 319
90 - 94	C	4 626	1 142	3 484	2 533	556	1 977	2 093	586	1 507
95 - 99	C	1 159	241	918	648	116	532	511	125	386
100+	C	149	20	129	67	9	58	82	11	71
France[25,26,27]										
1999										
Total	C	535 759	273 616	262 143	378 644	190 271	188 373	157 115	83 345	73 770
0 - 1	C	3 195	1 828	1 367	2 551	1 453	1 098	644	375	269
1 - 4	C	692	395	297	513	292	221	179	103	76

19. Deaths by age, sex and urban/rural residence: latest available year
Décès selon l'âge, le sexe et la résidence, urbaine/rurale: dernière année disponible (continued — suite)

(See notes at end of table.— Voir notes à la fin du tableau.)

Continent, country or area, year and age (in years) / Continent, pays ou zone, année et âge (en années)	Code[1]	Total			Urban - Urbaine			Rural - Rurale		
		Both sexes - Les deux sexes	Male - Masculin	Female - Féminin	Both sexes - Les deux sexes	Male - Masculin	Female - Féminin	Both sexes - Les deux sexes	Male - Masculin	Female - Féminin
EUROPE										
France[25,26,27]										
1999										
5 - 9	C	469	255	214	337	179	158	132	76	56
10 - 14	C	574	341	233	403	244	159	171	97	74
15 - 19	C	1 964	1 434	530	1 288	923	365	676	511	165
20 - 24	C	2 775	2 088	687	1 972	1 472	500	803	616	187
25 - 29	C	3 220	2 355	865	2 383	1 728	655	837	627	210
30 - 34	C	3 948	2 757	1 191	3 008	2 081	927	940	676	264
35 - 39	C	5 848	3 932	1 916	4 375	2 927	1 448	1 473	1 005	468
40 - 44	C	9 431	6 426	3 005	6 995	4 728	2 267	2 436	1 698	738
45 - 49	C	14 202	9 849	4 353	10 572	7 311	3 261	3 630	2 538	1 092
50 - 54	C	18 326	12 853	5 473	13 730	9 560	4 170	4 596	3 293	1 303
55 - 59	C	18 164	12 818	5 346	13 478	9 470	4 008	4 686	3 348	1 338
60 - 64	C	26 635	18 577	8 058	19 091	13 182	5 909	7 544	5 395	2 149
65 - 69	C	40 631	27 672	12 959	28 533	19 088	9 445	12 098	8 584	3 514
70 - 74	C	56 335	35 808	20 527	39 009	24 310	14 699	17 326	11 498	5 828
75 - 79	C	77 544	43 773	33 771	53 673	29 573	24 100	23 871	14 200	9 671
80 - 84	C	59 109	27 964	31 145	42 097	19 532	22 565	17 012	8 432	8 580
85 - 89	C	99 118	38 022	61 096	68 681	25 568	43 113	30 437	12 454	17 983
90 - 94	C	66 686	19 217	47 469	46 649	12 976	33 673	20 037	6 241	13 796
95 - 99	C	23 136	4 737	18 399	16 538	3 316	13 222	6 598	1 421	5 177
100+	C	3 757	515	3 242	2 768	358	2 410	989	157	832
Germany - Allemagne										
2000										
Total	C	838 797	388 981	449 816	...	...	...	...	...	...
0 - 1	C	3 362	1 917	1 445	...	...	...	...	...	...
1 - 4	C	766	437	329	...	...	...	...	...	...
5 - 9	C	475	279	196	...	...	...	...	...	...
10 - 14	C	610	356	254	...	...	...	...	...	...
15 - 19	C	2 085	1 464	621	...	...	...	...	...	...
20 - 24	C	2 830	2 122	708	...	...	...	...	...	...
25 - 29	C	2 950	2 157	793	...	...	...	...	...	...
30 - 34	C	4 835	3 368	1 467	...	...	...	...	...	...
35 - 39	C	7 802	5 245	2 557	...	...	...	...	...	...
40 - 44	C	11 860	7 964	3 896	...	...	...	...	...	...
45 - 49	C	17 075	11 331	5 744	...	...	...	...	...	...
50 - 54	C	21 624	14 292	7 332	...	...	...	...	...	...
55 - 59	C	35 978	24 263	11 715	...	...	...	...	...	...
60 - 64	C	59 383	40 024	19 359	...	...	...	...	...	...
65 - 69	C	70 754	46 301	24 453	...	...	...	...	...	...
70 - 74	C	98 436	57 766	40 670	...	...	...	...	...	...
75 - 79	C	126 286	57 373	68 913	...	...	...	...	...	...
80 - 84	C	104 211	39 742	64 469	...	...	...	...	...	...
85 - 89	C	150 588	45 818	104 770	...	...	...	...	...	...
90 - 94	C	90 027	21 710	68 317	...	...	...	...	...	...
95 - 99	C	23 919	4 626	19 293	...	...	...	...	...	...
100+	C	2 941	426	2 515	...	...	...	...	...	...
Greece - Grèce										
1998										
Total	C	102 668	53 637	49 031	55 464	29 024	26 440	47 204	24 613	22 591
0 - 1	C	674	371	303	467	266	201	207	105	102
1 - 4	C	119	59	60	70	33	37	49	26	23
5 - 9	C	76	44	32	45	28	17	31	16	15
10 - 14	C	92	54	38	59	33	26	33	21	12
15 - 19	C	383	277	106	244	174	70	139	103	36
20 - 24	C	587	458	129	390	302	88	197	156	41
25 - 29	C	643	478	165	417	309	108	226	169	57
30 - 34	C	677	485	192	447	310	137	230	175	55
35 - 39	C	786	539	247	491	340	151	295	199	96
40 - 44	C	1 199	820	379	803	543	260	396	277	119
45 - 49	C	1 737	1 185	552	1 138	765	373	599	420	179
50 - 54	C	2 539	1 755	784	1 611	1 097	514	928	658	270

19. Deaths by age, sex and urban/rural residence: latest available year
Décès selon l'âge, le sexe et la résidence, urbaine/rurale: dernière année disponible (continued — suite)

(See notes at end of table.— Voir notes à la fin du tableau.)

Continent, country or area, year and age (in years) / Continent, pays ou zone, année et âge (en années)	Code[1]	Total			Urban - Urbaine			Rural - Rurale		
		Both sexes - Les deux sexes	Male - Masculin	Female - Féminin	Both sexes - Les deux sexes	Male - Masculin	Female - Féminin	Both sexes - Les deux sexes	Male - Masculin	Female - Féminin
EUROPE										
Greece - Grèce										
1998										
55 - 59	C	3 316	2 314	1 002	2 000	1 381	619	1 316	933	383
60 - 64	C	5 887	3 973	1 914	3 416	2 271	1 145	2 471	1 702	769
65 - 69	C	9 308	6 022	3 286	5 233	3 341	1 892	4 075	2 681	1 394
70 - 74	C	13 092	7 558	5 534	7 488	4 257	3 231	5 604	3 301	2 303
75 - 79	C	14 266	7 351	6 915	7 953	4 044	3 909	6 313	3 307	3 006
80 - 84	C	17 672	7 962	9 710	9 237	4 132	5 105	8 435	3 830	4 605
85 - 89	C	17 513	7 299	10 214	8 544	3 427	5 117	8 969	3 872	5 097
90 - 94	C	8 948	3 517	5 431	3 994	1 470	2 524	4 954	2 047	2 907
95 - 99	C	2 728	980	1 748	1 249	452	797	1 479	528	951
100+	C	426	136	290	168	49	119	258	87	171
2001										
Total	C	102 559	53 853	48 706	...	...	...	...	...	...
0 - 1	C	522	307	215	...	...	...	...	...	...
1 - 4	C	72	41	31	...	...	...	...	...	...
5 - 9	C	74	42	32	...	...	...	...	...	...
10 - 14	C	102	65	37	...	...	...	...	...	...
15 - 19	C	345	257	88	...	...	...	...	...	...
20 - 24	C	580	464	116	...	...	...	...	...	...
25 - 29	C	593	471	122	...	...	...	...	...	...
30 - 34	C	686	502	184	...	...	...	...	...	...
35 - 39	C	728	499	229	...	...	...	...	...	...
40 - 44	C	1 143	800	343	...	...	...	...	...	...
45 - 49	C	1 710	1 206	504	...	...	...	...	...	...
50 - 54	C	2 616	1 845	771	...	...	...	...	...	...
55 - 59	C	3 259	2 292	967	...	...	...	...	...	...
60 - 64	C	5 424	3 694	1 730	...	...	...	...	...	...
65 - 69	C	8 762	5 685	3 077	...	...	...	...	...	...
70 - 74	C	13 288	7 844	5 444	...	...	...	...	...	...
75 - 79	C	15 750	8 240	7 510	...	...	...	...	...	...
80 - 84	C	16 541	7 383	9 158	...	...	...	...	...	...
85 - 89	C	17 057	7 194	9 863	...	...	...	...	...	...
90 - 94	C	9 686	3 767	5 919	...	...	...	...	...	...
95 - 99	C	3 049	1 106	1 943	...	...	...	...	...	...
100+	C	572	149	423	...	...	...	...	...	...
Hungary - Hongrie[28]										
2001										
Total	C	132 183	68 389	63 794	81 673	41 044	40 629	49 857	26 899	22 958
0 - 1	C	789	435	354	471	270	201	311	162	149
1 - 4	C	121	76	45	74	47	27	46	29	17
5 - 9	C	87	51	36	52	29	23	33	20	13
10 - 14	C	123	77	46	74	45	29	48	31	17
15 - 19	C	262	182	80	142	101	41	111	75	36
20 - 24	C	471	363	108	302	234	68	150	113	37
25 - 29	C	592	416	176	358	242	116	208	155	53
30 - 34	C	838	615	223	481	331	150	333	264	69
35 - 39	C	1 336	946	390	731	503	228	580	422	158
40 - 44	C	3 248	2 337	911	1 805	1 260	545	1 402	1 042	360
45 - 49	C	6 037	4 246	1 791	3 604	2 430	1 174	2 388	1 779	609
50 - 54	C	7 347	5 178	2 169	4 424	3 008	1 416	2 855	2 118	737
55 - 59	C	8 323	5 676	2 647	5 180	3 452	1 728	3 081	2 174	907
60 - 64	C	10 188	6 549	3 639	6 086	3 781	2 305	4 043	2 723	1 320
65 - 69	C	13 264	8 050	5 214	7 946	4 705	3 241	5 259	3 306	1 953
70 - 74	C	17 833	9 636	8 197	10 862	5 827	5 035	6 916	3 768	3 148
75 - 79	C	21 828	10 117	11 711	13 341	6 114	7 227	8 435	3 978	4 457
80 - 84	C	16 063	6 319	9 744	10 164	3 952	6 212	5 861	2 348	3 513
85 - 89	C	14 478	4 783	9 695	9 515	3 147	6 368	4 930	1 632	3 298
90 - 94	C	7 269	1 939	5 330	4 890	1 311	3 579	2 363	625	1 738
95 - 99	C	1 526	346	1 180	1 064	224	840	458	120	338
100+	C	153	46	107	107	31	76	46	15	31
Unknown - Inconnu	C	7	6	1	-	-	-	-	-	-

19. Deaths by age, sex and urban/rural residence: latest available year
Décès selon l'âge, le sexe et la résidence, urbaine/rurale: dernière année disponible (continued — suite)

(See notes at end of table.— Voir notes à la fin du tableau.)

Continent, country or area, year and age (in years) Continent, pays ou zone, année et âge (en années)	Code[1]	Total			Urban - Urbaine			Rural - Rurale		
		Both sexes - Les deux sexes	Male - Masculin	Female - Féminin	Both sexes - Les deux sexes	Male - Masculin	Female - Féminin	Both sexes - Les deux sexes	Male - Masculin	Female - Féminin
EUROPE										
Iceland - Islande										
2000										
Total	C	1 823	906	917	1 679	829	850	144	77	67
0 - 1	C	13	10	3	13	10	3	-	-	-
1 - 4	C	4	1	3	4	1	3	-	-	-
5 - 9	C	2	2	-	2	2	-	-	-	-
10 - 14	C	1	1	-	1	1	-	-	-	-
15 - 19	C	14	9	5	13	9	4	1	-	1
20 - 24	C	21	17	4	20	16	4	1	1	-
25 - 29	C	12	12	-	11	11	-	1	1	-
30 - 34	C	15	14	1	13	12	1	2	2	-
35 - 39	C	19	14	5	18	13	5	1	1	-
40 - 44	C	25	16	9	25	16	9	-	-	-
45 - 49	C	39	23	16	34	19	15	5	4	1
50 - 54	C	56	41	15	52	38	14	4	3	1
55 - 59	C	73	35	38	71	34	37	2	1	1
60 - 64	C	84	38	46	74	36	38	10	2	8
65 - 69	C	138	80	58	126	71	55	12	9	3
70 - 74	C	198	114	84	180	102	78	18	12	6
75 - 79	C	265	134	131	244	124	120	21	10	11
80 - 84	C	286	134	152	269	125	144	17	9	8
85+	C	558	211	347	509	189	320	49	22	27
2001										
Total	C	1 725	924	801	...	...	...	...	...	...
0 - 1	C	11	5	6	...	...	...	...	...	...
1 - 4	C	3	3	-	...	...	...	...	...	...
5 - 9	C	2	-	2	...	...	...	...	...	...
10 - 14	C	4	2	2	...	...	...	...	...	...
15 - 19	C	12	10	2	...	...	...	...	...	...
20 - 24	C	18	14	4	...	...	...	...	...	...
25 - 29	C	15	11	4	...	...	...	...	...	...
30 - 34	C	11	8	3	...	...	...	...	...	...
35 - 39	C	5	4	1	...	...	...	...	...	...
40 - 44	C	34	21	13	...	...	...	...	...	...
45 - 49	C	30	16	14	...	...	...	...	...	...
50 - 54	C	49	29	20	...	...	...	...	...	...
55 - 59	C	71	42	29	...	...	...	...	...	...
60 - 64	C	73	43	30	...	...	...	...	...	...
65 - 69	C	122	72	50	...	...	...	...	...	...
70 - 74	C	212	129	83	...	...	...	...	...	...
75 - 79	C	243	143	100	...	...	...	...	...	...
80 - 84	C	285	153	132	...	...	...	...	...	...
85 - 89	C	277	119	158	...	...	...	...	...	...
90 - 94	C	174	74	100	...	...	...	...	...	...
95 - 99	C	59	19	40	...	...	...	...	...	...
100+	C	15	7	8	...	...	...	...	...	...
Ireland - Irlande[29]										
1999										
Total	+C	31 683	16 480	15 203	17 288	8 599	8 689	14 395	7 881	6 514
0 - 1	+C	293	160	133	195	108	87	98	52	46
1 - 4	+C	68	39	29	37	25	12	31	14	17
5 - 9	+C	41	28	13	20	14	6	21	14	7
10 - 14	+C	56	37	19	31	19	12	25	18	7
15 - 19	+C	171	123	48	90	64	26	81	59	22
20 - 24	+C	233	179	54	130	103	27	103	76	27
25 - 29	+C	196	149	47	109	83	26	87	66	21
30 - 34	+C	222	153	69	141	94	47	81	59	22
35 - 39	+C	279	174	105	178	111	67	101	63	38
40 - 44	+C	406	243	163	232	143	89	174	100	74
45 - 49	+C	637	392	245	409	249	160	228	143	85
50 - 54	+C	888	553	335	514	301	213	374	252	122
55 - 59	+C	1 226	777	449	747	460	287	479	317	162

19. Deaths by age, sex and urban/rural residence: latest available year
Décès selon l'âge, le sexe et la résidence, urbaine/rurale: dernière année disponible (continued — suite)

(See notes at end of table.— Voir notes à la fin du tableau.)

Continent, country or area, year and age (in years) / Continent, pays ou zone, année et âge (en années)	Code[1]	Total			Urban - Urbaine			Rural - Rurale		
		Both sexes - Les deux sexes	Male - Masculin	Female - Féminin	Both sexes - Les deux sexes	Male - Masculin	Female - Féminin	Both sexes - Les deux sexes	Male - Masculin	Female - Féminin
EUROPE										
Ireland - Irlande[29]										
1999										
60 - 64	+C	1 675	1 065	610	1 003	626	377	672	439	233
65 - 69	+C	2 606	1 630	976	1 485	897	588	1 121	733	388
70 - 74	+C	3 961	2 375	1 586	2 224	1 300	924	1 737	1 075	662
75 - 79	+C	5 492	3 005	2 487	2 877	1 499	1 378	2 615	1 506	1 109
80 - 84	+C	5 601	2 666	2 935	2 823	1 221	1 602	2 778	1 445	1 333
85+	+C	7 632	2 732	4 900	4 043	1 282	2 761	3 589	1 450	2 139
2001										
Total	+C	29 812	15 408	14 404	...	...	...	...	...	...
0 - 1	+C	337	197	140	...	...	...	...	...	...
1 - 4	+C	69	40	29	...	...	...	...	...	...
5 - 9	+C	39	24	15	...	...	...	...	...	...
10 - 14	+C	44	25	19	...	...	...	...	...	...
15 - 19	+C	163	117	46	...	...	...	...	...	...
20 - 24	+C	247	187	60	...	...	...	...	...	...
25 - 29	+C	213	168	45	...	...	...	...	...	...
30 - 34	+C	215	160	55	...	...	...	...	...	...
35 - 39	+C	317	183	134	...	...	...	...	...	...
40 - 44	+C	419	252	167	...	...	...	...	...	...
45 - 49	+C	602	356	246	...	...	...	...	...	...
50 - 54	+C	932	545	387	...	...	...	...	...	...
55 - 59	+C	1 176	757	419	...	...	...	...	...	...
60 - 64	+C	1 659	1 061	598	...	...	...	...	...	...
65 - 69	+C	2 482	1 593	889	...	...	...	...	...	...
70 - 74	+C	3 482	2 071	1 411	...	...	...	...	...	...
75 - 79	+C	4 886	2 594	2 292	...	...	...	...	...	...
80 - 84	+C	5 204	2 431	2 773	...	...	...	...	...	...
85 - 89	+C	4 455	1 777	2 678	...	...	...	...	...	...
90 - 94	+C	2 183	725	1 458	...	...	...	...	...	...
95 - 99	+C	608	127	481	...	...	...	...	...	...
100+	+C	80	18	62	...	...	...	...	...	...
Isle of Man - Îles de Man										
1999										
Total	+C	983	471	512	...	...	...	...	...	...
0 - 1	+C	6	3	3	...	...	...	...	...	...
1 - 4	+C	3	3	-	...	...	...	...	...	...
5 - 9	+C	1	-	1	...	...	...	...	...	...
10 - 14	+C	2	1	1	...	...	...	...	...	...
15 - 19	+C	2	1	1	...	...	...	...	...	...
20 - 24	+C	1	1	-	...	...	...	...	...	...
25 - 29	+C	3	1	2	...	...	...	...	...	...
30 - 34	+C	6	4	2	...	...	...	...	...	...
35 - 39	+C	10	7	3	...	...	...	...	...	...
40 - 44	+C	6	5	1	...	...	...	...	...	...
45 - 49	+C	12	7	5	...	...	...	...	...	...
50 - 54	+C	16	6	10	...	...	...	...	...	...
55 - 59	+C	27	19	8	...	...	...	...	...	...
60 - 64	+C	42	23	19	...	...	...	...	...	...
65 - 69	+C	68	33	35	...	...	...	...	...	...
70 - 74	+C	96	60	36	...	...	...	...	...	...
75 - 79	+C	166	82	84	...	...	...	...	...	...
80 - 84	+C	184	85	99	...	...	...	...	...	...
85+	+C	332	130	202	...	...	...	...	...	...
Italy - Italie										
1997										
Total	C	561 207	284 960	276 247	...	...	...	...	...	...
0 - 1	C	2 973	1 638	1 335	...	...	...	...	...	...
1 - 4	C	636	295	341	...	...	...	...	...	...
5 - 9	C	429	237	192	...	...	...	...	...	...
10 - 14	C	498	313	185	...	...	...	...	...	...
15 - 19	C	1 487	1 120	367	...	...	...	...	...	...

19. Deaths by age, sex and urban/rural residence: latest available year
Décès selon l'âge, le sexe et la résidence, urbaine/rurale: dernière année disponible (continued — suite)

(See notes at end of table.— Voir notes à la fin du tableau.)

Continent, country or area, year and age (in years) / Continent, pays ou zone, année et âge (en années)	Code[1]	Total			Urban - Urbaine			Rural - Rurale		
		Both sexes - Les deux sexes	Male - Masculin	Female - Féminin	Both sexes - Les deux sexes	Male - Masculin	Female - Féminin	Both sexes - Les deux sexes	Male - Masculin	Female - Féminin
EUROPE										
Italy - Italie										
1997										
20 - 24	C	2 592	2 020	572	...	...	...	...	...	...
25 - 29	C	3 055	2 291	764	...	...	...	...	...	...
30 - 34	C	4 150	2 963	1 187	...	...	...	...	...	...
35 - 39	C	4 567	3 114	1 453	...	...	...	...	...	...
40 - 44	C	5 580	3 666	1 914	...	...	...	...	...	...
45 - 49	C	8 750	5 604	3 146	...	...	...	...	...	...
50 - 54	C	13 132	8 609	4 523	...	...	...	...	...	...
55 - 59	C	21 043	13 974	7 069	...	...	...	...	...	...
60 - 64	C	31 912	21 315	10 597	...	...	...	...	...	...
65 - 69	C	49 398	32 313	17 085	...	...	...	...	...	...
70 - 74	C	70 582	42 833	27 749	...	...	...	...	...	...
75 - 79	C	74 446	39 968	34 478	...	...	...	...	...	...
80 - 84	C	97 920	45 252	52 668	...	...	...	...	...	...
85 - 89	C	98 879	37 919	60 960	...	...	...	...	...	...
90 - 94	C	51 802	15 448	36 354	...	...	...	...	...	...
95 - 99	C	15 193	3 594	11 599	...	...	...	...	...	...
100+	C	2 183	474	1 709	...	...	...	...	...	...
Latvia - Lettonie[11]										
2001										
Total	C	32 991	16 537	16 454	21 460	10 746	10 714	11 531	5 791	5 740
0 - 1	C	217	115	102	139	77	62	78	38	40
1 - 4	C	48	31	17	23	13	10	25	18	7
5 - 9	C	44	31	13	19	10	9	25	21	4
10 - 14	C	49	30	19	29	17	12	20	13	7
15 - 19	C	149	104	45	91	67	24	58	37	21
20 - 24	C	226	184	42	144	117	27	82	67	15
25 - 29	C	289	240	49	195	160	35	94	80	14
30 - 34	C	416	322	94	260	193	67	156	129	27
35 - 39	C	598	469	129	395	312	83	203	157	46
40 - 44	C	977	734	243	649	484	165	328	250	78
45 - 49	C	1 220	910	310	867	635	232	353	275	78
50 - 54	C	1 694	1 193	501	1 188	814	374	506	379	127
55 - 59	C	1 973	1 363	610	1 308	878	430	665	485	180
60 - 64	C	3 073	2 088	985	2 039	1 365	674	1 034	723	311
65 - 69	C	3 457	2 097	1 360	2 203	1 297	906	1 254	800	454
70 - 74	C	4 481	2 412	2 069	3 002	1 609	1 393	1 479	803	676
75 - 79	C	4 571	1 688	2 883	3 074	1 123	1 951	1 497	565	932
80 - 84	C	3 493	1 106	2 387	2 249	723	1 526	1 244	383	861
85 - 89	C	3 288	815	2 473	1 980	494	1 486	1 308	321	987
90 - 94	C	2 087	490	1 597	1 214	287	927	873	203	670
95 - 99	C	551	95	456	339	56	283	212	39	173
100+	C	83	13	70	48	10	38	35	3	32
Unknown - Inconnu	C	7	7	-	5	5	-	2	2	-
Liechtenstein										
1997										
Total	C	230	125	105	...	...	...	...	...	...
0 - 1	C	8	5	3	...	...	...	...	...	...
1 - 4	C	1	1	-	...	...	...	...	...	...
5 - 9	C	1	1	-	...	...	...	...	...	...
10 - 14	C	1	1	-	...	...	...	...	...	...
15 - 19	C	2	1	1	...	...	...	...	...	...
20 - 24	C	1	-	1	...	...	...	...	...	...
25 - 29	C	2	1	1	...	...	...	...	...	...
30 - 34	C	3	1	2	...	...	...	...	...	...
35 - 39	C	3	3	-	...	...	...	...	...	...
40 - 44	C	6	5	1	...	...	...	...	...	...
45 - 49	C	5	4	1	...	...	...	...	...	...
50 - 54	C	10	3	7	...	...	...	...	...	...
55 - 59	C	10	8	2	...	...	...	...	...	...
60 - 64	C	9	7	2	...	...	...	...	...	...

(See notes at end of table.— Voir notes à la fin du tableau.)

Continent, country or area, year and age (in years) Continent, pays ou zone, année et âge (en années)	Code[1]	Total			Urban - Urbaine			Rural - Rurale		
		Both sexes - Les deux sexes	Male - Masculin	Female - Féminin	Both sexes - Les deux sexes	Male - Masculin	Female - Féminin	Both sexes - Les deux sexes	Male - Masculin	Female - Féminin
EUROPE										
Liechtenstein										
1997										
65 - 69	C	13	9	4	...	...	...	...	...	...
70 - 74	C	26	15	11	...	...	...	...	...	...
75 - 79	C	38	26	12	...	...	...	...	...	...
80 - 84	C	27	15	12	...	...	...	...	...	...
85 - 89	C	40	10	30	...	...	...	...	...	...
90 - 94	C	18	8	10	...	...	...	...	...	...
95 - 99	C	5	1	4	...	...	...	...	...	...
100+	C	1	-	1	...	...	...	...	...	...
Lithuania - Lituanie[11]										
2001										
Total	C	40 399	21 571	18 828	22 962	12 209	10 753	17 437	9 362	8 075
0 - 1	C	250	158	92	148	95	53	102	63	39
1 - 4	C	92	55	37	46	27	19	46	28	18
5 - 9	C	57	43	14	25	16	9	32	27	5
10 - 14	C	75	56	19	34	24	10	41	32	9
15 - 19	C	262	209	53	177	136	41	85	73	12
20 - 24	C	385	306	79	233	181	52	152	125	27
25 - 29	C	436	362	74	244	200	44	192	162	30
30 - 34	C	648	527	121	387	311	76	261	216	45
35 - 39	C	877	662	215	546	398	148	331	264	67
40 - 44	C	1 285	969	316	788	588	200	497	381	116
45 - 49	C	1 577	1 154	423	1 023	728	295	554	426	128
50 - 54	C	2 091	1 510	581	1 350	945	405	741	565	176
55 - 59	C	2 572	1 811	761	1 553	1 072	481	1 019	739	280
60 - 64	C	3 302	2 276	1 026	1 993	1 333	660	1 309	943	366
65 - 69	C	4 085	2 603	1 482	2 364	1 467	897	1 721	1 136	585
70 - 74	C	5 160	2 831	2 329	3 009	1 669	1 340	2 151	1 162	989
75 - 79	C	5 623	2 404	3 219	3 092	1 264	1 828	2 531	1 140	1 391
80 - 84	C	4 228	1 497	2 731	2 192	764	1 428	2 036	733	1 303
85 - 89	C	3 929	1 111	2 818	2 030	522	1 508	1 899	589	1 310
90 - 94	C	2 582	790	1 792	1 308	370	938	1 274	420	854
95+	C	880	234	646	419	98	321	461	136	325
Unknown - Inconnu	C	3	3	-	1	1	-	2	2	-
Luxembourg										
2001										
Total	C	3 719	1 817	1 902	...	...	...	...	...	...
0 - 1	C	32	18	14	...	...	...	...	...	...
1 - 4	C	11	7	4	...	...	...	...	...	...
5 - 9	C	2	2	-	...	...	...	...	...	...
10 - 14	C	9	2	7	...	...	...	...	...	...
15 - 19	C	13	7	6	...	...	...	...	...	...
20 - 24	C	15	12	3	...	...	...	...	...	...
25 - 29	C	27	20	7	...	...	...	...	...	...
30 - 34	C	37	19	18	...	...	...	...	...	...
35 - 39	C	39	30	9	...	...	...	...	...	...
40 - 44	C	73	44	29	...	...	...	...	...	...
45 - 49	C	92	62	30	...	...	...	...	...	...
50 - 54	C	110	68	42	...	...	...	...	...	...
55 - 59	C	162	101	61	...	...	...	...	...	...
60 - 64	C	220	154	66	...	...	...	...	...	...
65 - 69	C	318	205	113	...	...	...	...	...	...
70 - 74	C	457	263	194	...	...	...	...	...	...
75 - 79	C	529	254	275	...	...	...	...	...	...
80 - 84	C	529	208	321	...	...	...	...	...	...
85 - 89	C	609	216	393	...	...	...	...	...	...
90 - 94	C	327	100	227	...	...	...	...	...	...
95 - 99	C	95	21	74	...	...	...	...	...	...
100+	C	13	4	9	...	...	...	...	...	...

19. Deaths by age, sex and urban/rural residence: latest available year
Décès selon l'âge, le sexe et la résidence, urbaine/rurale: dernière année disponible (continued — suite)

(See notes at end of table.— Voir notes à la fin du tableau.)

Continent, country or area, year and age (in years) / Continent, pays ou zone, année et âge (en années)	Code[1]	Total			Urban - Urbaine			Rural - Rurale		
		Both sexes - Les deux sexes	Male - Masculin	Female - Féminin	Both sexes - Les deux sexes	Male - Masculin	Female - Féminin	Both sexes - Les deux sexes	Male - Masculin	Female - Féminin
EUROPE										
Malta - Mâlte										
2001										
Total	C	2 935	1 496	1 439	...	...	...	...	...	...
0 - 1	C	17	12	5	...	...	...	...	...	...
1 - 4	C	9	5	4	...	...	...	...	...	...
5 - 9	C	3	2	1	...	...	...	...	...	...
10 - 14	C	1	1	-	...	...	...	...	...	...
15 - 19	C	12	10	2	...	...	...	...	...	...
20 - 24	C	15	11	4	...	...	...	...	...	...
25 - 29	C	16	15	1	...	...	...	...	...	...
30 - 34	C	12	10	2	...	...	...	...	...	...
35 - 39	C	18	12	6	...	...	...	...	...	...
40 - 44	C	23	16	7	...	...	...	...	...	...
45 - 49	C	68	40	28	...	...	...	...	...	...
50 - 54	C	93	60	33	...	...	...	...	...	...
55 - 59	C	127	78	49	...	...	...	...	...	...
60 - 64	C	141	79	62	...	...	...	...	...	...
65 - 69	C	267	165	102	...	...	...	...	...	...
70 - 74	C	390	227	163	...	...	...	...	...	...
75 - 79	C	533	278	255	...	...	...	...	...	...
80 - 84	C	482	237	245	...	...	...	...	...	...
85 - 89	C	409	149	260	...	...	...	...	...	...
90+	C	299	89	210	...	...	...	...	...	...
Netherlands - Pays-Bas[30]										
2001										
Total	C	140 377	68 319	72 058	93 616	44 445	49 171	46 761	23 874	22 887
0 - 1	C	963	544	419	640	361	279	323	183	140
1 - 4	C	320	189	131	191	115	76	129	74	55
5 - 9	C	117	75	42	75	47	28	42	28	14
10 - 14	C	152	86	66	86	44	42	66	42	24
15 - 19	C	312	206	106	176	113	63	136	93	43
20 - 24	C	413	294	119	280	197	83	133	97	36
25 - 29	C	511	357	154	359	243	116	152	114	38
30 - 34	C	798	505	293	543	330	213	255	175	80
35 - 39	C	1 148	668	480	801	460	341	347	208	139
40 - 44	C	1 739	998	741	1 184	672	512	555	326	229
45 - 49	C	2 805	1 606	1 199	1 919	1 082	837	886	524	362
50 - 54	C	4 420	2 605	1 815	2 975	1 765	1 210	1 445	840	605
55 - 59	C	5 793	3 549	2 244	3 701	2 260	1 441	2 092	1 289	803
60 - 64	C	7 176	4 496	2 680	4 639	2 874	1 765	2 537	1 622	915
65 - 69	C	10 380	6 602	3 778	6 658	4 143	2 515	3 722	2 459	1 263
70 - 74	C	15 540	9 458	6 082	10 145	6 019	4 126	5 395	3 439	1 956
75 - 79	C	21 149	11 610	9 539	14 148	7 605	6 543	7 001	4 005	2 996
80 - 84	C	23 900	11 226	12 674	16 119	7 480	8 639	7 781	3 746	4 035
85 - 89	C	22 540	8 152	14 388	15 314	5 392	9 922	7 226	2 760	4 466
90 - 94	C	14 408	3 910	10 498	9 775	2 537	7 238	4 633	1 373	3 260
95+	C	5 793	1 183	4 610	3 888	706	3 182	1 905	477	1 428
Norway - Norvège[31]										
2001										
Total	C	43 981	21 630	22 351	...	...	...	...	...	...
0 - 1	C	223	126	97	...	...	...	...	...	...
1 - 4	C	54	36	18	...	...	...	...	...	...
5 - 9	C	32	18	14	...	...	...	...	...	...
10 - 14	C	25	15	10	...	...	...	...	...	...
15 - 19	C	135	98	37	...	...	...	...	...	...
20 - 24	C	225	171	54	...	...	...	...	...	...
25 - 29	C	232	172	60	...	...	...	...	...	...
30 - 34	C	282	198	84	...	...	...	...	...	...
35 - 39	C	364	260	104	...	...	...	...	...	...
40 - 44	C	465	300	165	...	...	...	...	...	...
45 - 49	C	710	439	271	...	...	...	...	...	...
50 - 54	C	1 103	672	431	...	...	...	...	...	...

19. Deaths by age, sex and urban/rural residence: latest available year
Décès selon l'âge, le sexe et la résidence, urbaine/rurale: dernière année disponible (continued — suite)

(See notes at end of table.— Voir notes à la fin du tableau.)

Continent, country or area, year and age (in years) Continent, pays ou zone, année et âge (en années)	Code[1]	Total			Urban - Urbaine			Rural - Rurale		
		Both sexes - Les deux sexes	Male - Masculin	Female - Féminin	Both sexes - Les deux sexes	Male - Masculin	Female - Féminin	Both sexes - Les deux sexes	Male - Masculin	Female - Féminin
EUROPE										
Norway - Norvège[31]										
2001										
55 - 59	C	1 438	882	556	...	...	...	...	...	...
60 - 64	C	1 774	1 089	685	...	...	...	...	...	...
65 - 69	C	2 450	1 536	914	...	...	...	...	...	...
70 - 74	C	4 105	2 482	1 623	...	...	...	...	...	...
75 - 79	C	6 810	3 822	2 988	...	...	...	...	...	...
80 - 84	C	8 803	4 291	4 512	...	...	...	...	...	...
85 - 89	C	8 013	3 099	4 914	...	...	...	...	...	...
90 - 94	C	4 980	1 504	3 476	...	...	...	...	...	...
95 - 99	C	1 522	373	1 149	...	...	...	...	...	...
100+	C	236	47	189	...	...	...	...	...	...
Poland - Pologne										
1999										
Total	C	381 415	204 062	177 353	223 630	117 836	105 794	157 785	86 226	71 559
0 - 1	C	3 381	1 904	1 477	1 908	1 069	839	1 473	835	638
1 - 4	C	639	369	270	300	171	129	339	198	141
5 - 9	C	502	313	189	242	154	88	260	159	101
10 - 14	C	630	416	214	351	233	118	279	183	96
15 - 19	C	1 967	1 459	508	1 120	835	285	847	624	223
20 - 24	C	2 647	2 125	522	1 497	1 172	325	1 150	953	197
25 - 29	C	2 595	2 068	527	1 472	1 134	338	1 123	934	189
30 - 34	C	3 180	2 514	666	1 771	1 352	419	1 409	1 162	247
35 - 39	C	5 736	4 350	1 386	3 425	2 501	924	2 311	1 849	462
40 - 44	C	11 423	8 471	2 952	7 244	5 137	2 107	4 179	3 334	845
45 - 49	C	16 801	12 280	4 521	11 155	7 944	3 211	5 646	4 336	1 310
50 - 54	C	18 667	13 357	5 310	12 597	8 754	3 843	6 070	4 603	1 467
55 - 59	C	20 034	14 118	5 916	13 084	9 042	4 042	6 950	5 076	1 874
60 - 64	C	30 987	21 132	9 855	19 476	12 948	6 528	11 511	8 184	3 327
65 - 69	C	44 095	28 094	16 001	26 824	16 777	10 047	17 271	11 317	5 954
70 - 74	C	53 604	29 407	24 197	31 402	16 725	14 677	22 202	12 682	9 520
75 - 79	C	56 025	26 013	30 012	31 170	14 055	17 115	24 855	11 958	12 897
80 - 84	C	39 322	15 123	24 199	20 942	7 537	13 405	18 380	7 586	10 794
85+	C	69 180	20 549	48 631	37 650	10 296	27 354	31 530	10 253	21 277
2001										
Total	C	363 220	192 951	170 269	...	...	...	...	...	...
0 - 1	C	2 823	1 579	1 244	...	...	...	...	...	...
1 - 4	C	493	279	214	...	...	...	...	...	...
5 - 9	C	425	254	171	...	...	...	...	...	...
10 - 14	C	546	326	220	...	...	...	...	...	...
15 - 19	C	1 632	1 187	445	...	...	...	...	...	...
20 - 24	C	2 311	1 865	446	...	...	...	...	...	...
25 - 29	C	2 382	1 884	498	...	...	...	...	...	...
30 - 34	C	2 790	2 200	590	...	...	...	...	...	...
35 - 39	C	4 610	3 529	1 081	...	...	...	...	...	...
40 - 44	C	9 543	6 979	2 564	...	...	...	...	...	...
45 - 49	C	15 827	11 433	4 394	...	...	...	...	...	...
50 - 54	C	20 580	14 569	6 011	...	...	...	...	...	...
55 - 59	C	18 389	12 755	5 634	...	...	...	...	...	...
60 - 64	C	27 339	18 691	8 648	...	...	...	...	...	...
65 - 69	C	39 117	25 004	14 113	...	...	...	...	...	...
70 - 74	C	51 112	28 736	22 376	...	...	...	...	...	...
75 - 79	C	57 135	26 426	30 709	...	...	...	...	...	...
80 - 84	C	41 260	16 131	25 129	...	...	...	...	...	...
85 - 89	C	38 132	12 154	25 978	...	...	...	...	...	...
90 - 94	C	21 174	5 716	15 458	...	...	...	...	...	...
95 - 99	C	4 846	1 100	3 746	...	...	...	...	...	...
100+	C	754	154	600	...	...	...	...	...	...
Portugal[5]										
1993										
Total	C	106 384	55 896	50 488	31 845	16 235	15 610	55 333	29 382	25 951
0 - 1	C	996	580	416	325	189	136	484	290	194

(See notes at end of table.— Voir notes à la fin du tableau.)

Continent, country or area, year and age (in years) / Continent, pays ou zone, année et âge (en années)	Code[1]	Total			Urban - Urbaine			Rural - Rurale		
		Both sexes - Les deux sexes	Male - Masculin	Female - Féminin	Both sexes - Les deux sexes	Male - Masculin	Female - Féminin	Both sexes - Les deux sexes	Male - Masculin	Female - Féminin
EUROPE										
Portugal[5]										
1993										
1 - 4	C	317	183	134	74	37	37	179	108	71
5 - 9	C	199	129	70	50	35	15	111	68	43
10 - 14	C	229	141	88	50	28	22	135	86	49
15 - 19	C	721	551	170	187	146	41	390	307	83
20 - 24	C	950	760	190	293	226	67	468	379	89
25 - 29	C	1 025	780	245	367	279	88	455	362	93
30 - 34	C	1 126	831	295	392	302	90	493	351	142
35 - 39	C	1 307	929	378	385	285	100	641	452	189
40 - 44	C	1 687	1 131	556	571	385	186	761	506	255
45 - 49	C	2 196	1 421	775	710	462	248	1 018	657	361
50 - 54	C	3 041	1 991	1 050	1 010	685	325	1 437	908	529
55 - 59	C	4 795	3 212	1 583	1 570	1 063	507	2 305	1 533	772
60 - 64	C	7 053	4 704	2 349	2 305	1 496	809	3 449	2 306	1 143
65 - 69	C	10 171	6 440	3 731	3 120	1 946	1 174	5 122	3 292	1 830
70 - 74	C	12 751	7 405	5 346	3 756	2 127	1 629	6 634	3 910	2 724
75 - 79	C	16 405	8 513	7 892	4 797	2 406	2 391	8 791	4 661	4 130
80 - 84	C	19 263	8 690	10 573	5 419	2 209	3 210	10 514	4 932	5 582
85+	C	22 152	7 505	14 647	6 464	1 929	4 535	11 946	4 274	7 672
2001										
Total	C	105 092	54 838	50 254	...	...	...	...	...	...
0 - 1	C	567	333	234	...	...	...	...	...	...
1 - 4	C	162	97	65	...	...	...	...	...	...
5 - 9	C	114	64	50	...	...	...	...	...	...
10 - 14	C	142	86	56	...	...	...	...	...	...
15 - 19	C	400	303	97	...	...	...	...	...	...
20 - 24	C	681	550	131	...	...	...	...	...	...
25 - 29	C	941	751	190	...	...	...	...	...	...
30 - 34	C	1 049	797	252	...	...	...	...	...	...
35 - 39	C	1 395	1 040	355	...	...	...	...	...	...
40 - 44	C	1 859	1 295	564	...	...	...	...	...	...
45 - 49	C	2 354	1 580	774	...	...	...	...	...	...
50 - 54	C	2 890	1 926	964	...	...	...	...	...	...
55 - 59	C	3 737	2 508	1 229	...	...	...	...	...	...
60 - 64	C	5 546	3 648	1 898	...	...	...	...	...	...
65 - 69	C	8 559	5 496	3 063	...	...	...	...	...	...
70 - 74	C	12 763	7 535	5 228	...	...	...	...	...	...
75 - 79	C	17 046	9 123	7 923	...	...	...	...	...	...
80 - 84	C	17 228	7 945	9 283	...	...	...	...	...	...
85 - 89	C	16 330	6 394	9 936	...	...	...	...	...	...
90 - 94	C	8 745	2 793	5 952	...	...	...	...	...	...
95 - 99	C	2 288	529	1 759	...	...	...	...	...	...
100+	C	296	45	251	...	...	...	...	...	...
Republic of Moldova - République de Moldova[11]										
2001										
Total	C	40 075	20 591	19 484	12 844	6 927	5 917	27 231	13 664	13 567
0 - 1	C	597	334	263	212	121	91	385	213	172
1 - 4	C	144	90	54	36	26	10	108	64	44
5 - 9	C	123	76	47	32	15	17	91	61	30
10 - 14	C	141	100	41	40	27	13	101	73	28
15 - 19	C	223	156	67	69	52	17	154	104	50
20 - 24	C	349	281	68	151	123	28	198	158	40
25 - 29	C	387	297	90	161	117	44	226	180	46
30 - 34	C	467	324	143	191	130	61	276	194	82
35 - 39	C	871	642	229	318	240	78	553	402	151
40 - 44	C	1 514	1 090	424	563	408	155	951	682	269
45 - 49	C	2 055	1 421	634	810	554	256	1 245	867	378
50 - 54	C	2 410	1 557	853	1 011	695	316	1 399	862	537
55 - 59	C	2 368	1 370	998	835	534	301	1 533	836	697
60 - 64	C	3 974	2 250	1 724	1 393	894	499	2 581	1 356	1 225

19. Deaths by age, sex and urban/rural residence: latest available year
Décès selon l'âge, le sexe et la résidence, urbaine/rurale: dernière année disponible (continued — suite)

(See notes at end of table.— Voir notes à la fin du tableau.)

Continent, country or area, year and age (in years) / Continent, pays ou zone, année et âge (en années)	Code[1]	Total			Urban - Urbaine			Rural - Rurale		
		Both sexes - Les deux sexes	Male - Masculin	Female - Féminin	Both sexes - Les deux sexes	Male - Masculin	Female - Féminin	Both sexes - Les deux sexes	Male - Masculin	Female - Féminin
EUROPE										
Republic of Moldova - République de Moldova[11]										
2001										
65 - 69	C	4 807	2 598	2 209	1 444	798	646	3 363	1 800	1 563
70 - 74	C	6 055	2 931	3 124	1 784	869	915	4 271	2 062	2 209
75 - 79	C	5 812	2 291	3 521	1 666	632	1 034	4 146	1 659	2 487
80 - 84	C	3 908	1 499	2 409	1 024	358	666	2 884	1 141	1 743
85 - 89	C	2 636	905	1 731	759	241	518	1 877	664	1 213
90 - 94	C	968	308	660	283	76	207	685	232	453
95 - 99	C	230	61	169	53	14	39	177	47	130
100+	C	33	9	24	6	2	4	27	7	20
Unknown - Inconnu	C	3	1	2	3	1	2	-	-	-
Romania - Roumanie										
2001										
Total	C	259 603	139 549	120 054	110 063	59 815	50 248	149 540	79 734	69 806
0 - 1	C	4 057	2 328	1 729	1 594	945	649	2 463	1 383	1 080
1 - 4	C	761	413	348	269	146	123	492	267	225
5 - 9	C	456	281	175	190	107	83	266	174	92
10 - 14	C	967	589	378	472	290	182	495	299	196
15 - 19	C	881	615	266	420	274	146	461	341	120
20 - 24	C	1 353	971	382	682	484	198	671	487	184
25 - 29	C	1 640	1 201	439	736	522	214	904	679	225
30 - 34	C	2 652	1 925	727	1 292	887	405	1 360	1 038	322
35 - 39	C	2 929	2 120	809	1 424	955	469	1 505	1 165	340
40 - 44	C	6 197	4 467	1 730	3 341	2 303	1 038	2 856	2 164	692
45 - 49	C	10 207	7 298	2 909	5 951	4 128	1 823	4 256	3 170	1 086
50 - 54	C	12 683	8 840	3 843	6 974	4 844	2 130	5 709	3 996	1 713
55 - 59	C	14 088	9 565	4 523	7 017	4 736	2 281	7 071	4 829	2 242
60 - 64	C	22 898	14 816	8 082	10 499	6 888	3 611	12 399	7 928	4 471
65 - 69	C	30 616	18 460	12 156	12 840	7 695	5 145	17 776	10 765	7 011
70 - 74	C	38 573	21 023	17 550	15 484	8 330	7 154	23 089	12 693	10 396
75 - 79	C	43 827	20 529	23 298	16 529	7 522	9 007	27 298	13 007	14 291
80 - 84	C	26 989	10 546	16 443	10 173	3 817	6 356	16 816	6 729	10 087
85 - 89	C	24 793	9 028	15 765	9 206	3 322	5 884	15 587	5 706	9 881
90 - 94	C	10 823	3 774	7 049	4 129	1 350	2 779	6 694	2 424	4 270
95 - 99	C	2 034	704	1 330	761	245	516	1 273	459	814
100+	C	179	56	123	80	25	55	99	31	68
Russian Federation - Fédération de Russie[11]										
1999										
Total	C	2 144 316	1 112 521	1 031 795	1 499 466	784 807	714 659	644 850	327 714	317 136
0 - 1	C	20 731	12 020	8 711	13 657	7 957	5 700	7 074	4 063	3 011
1 - 4	C	5 426	3 067	2 359	3 012	1 718	1 294	2 414	1 349	1 065
5 - 9	C	4 283	2 670	1 613	2 618	1 644	974	1 665	1 026	639
10 - 14	C	5 576	3 735	1 841	3 557	2 351	1 206	2 019	1 384	635
15 - 19	C	16 521	11 887	4 634	11 388	8 151	3 237	5 133	3 736	1 397
20 - 24	C	30 186	24 232	5 954	21 784	17 425	4 359	8 402	6 807	1 595
25 - 29	C	33 206	26 956	6 250	24 118	19 439	4 679	9 088	7 517	1 571
30 - 34	C	39 103	31 288	7 815	27 817	22 073	5 744	11 286	9 215	2 071
35 - 39	C	63 709	50 202	13 507	45 331	35 381	9 950	18 378	14 821	3 557
40 - 44	C	90 077	69 801	20 276	65 129	49 976	15 153	24 948	19 825	5 123
45 - 49	C	114 294	86 262	28 032	85 130	63 862	21 268	29 164	22 400	6 764
50 - 54	C	108 325	79 033	29 292	82 867	60 266	22 601	25 458	18 767	6 691
55 - 59	C	126 338	87 584	38 754	91 064	63 150	27 914	35 274	24 434	10 840
60 - 64	C	222 581	147 332	75 249	155 408	102 181	53 227	67 173	45 151	22 022
65 - 69	C	240 433	141 540	98 893	161 847	93 691	68 156	78 586	47 849	30 737
70 - 74	C	317 672	153 065	164 607	220 871	105 889	114 982	96 801	47 176	49 625
75 - 79	C	219 975	71 623	148 352	154 016	49 779	104 237	65 959	21 844	44 115
80 - 84	C	195 030	50 551	144 479	135 378	36 207	99 171	59 652	14 344	45 308
85+	C	281 686	52 314	229 372	186 014	36 793	149 221	95 672	15 521	80 151
Unknown - Inconnu	C	9 164	7 359	1 805	8 460	6 874	1 586	704	485	219

19. Deaths by age, sex and urban/rural residence: latest available year
Décès selon l'âge, le sexe et la résidence, urbaine/rurale: dernière année disponible (continued — suite)

(See notes at end of table.— Voir notes à la fin du tableau.)

Continent, country or area, year and age (in years) / Continent, pays ou zone, année et âge (en années)	Code[1]	Total			Urban - Urbaine			Rural - Rurale		
		Both sexes - Les deux sexes	Male - Masculin	Female - Féminin	Both sexes - Les deux sexes	Male - Masculin	Female - Féminin	Both sexes - Les deux sexes	Male - Masculin	Female - Féminin
EUROPE										
San Marino - Saint-Marin										
2000										
Total	+C	188	105	83	...	...	...	...	...	...
15 - 19	+C	2	2	-	...	...	...	...	...	...
20 - 24	+C	2	2	-	...	...	...	...	...	...
25 - 29	+C	1	1	-	...	...	...	...	...	...
35 - 39	+C	6	4	2	...	...	...	...	...	...
45 - 49	+C	7	6	1	...	...	...	...	...	...
50 - 54	+C	5	3	2	...	...	...	...	...	...
55 - 59	+C	3	3	-	...	...	...	...	...	...
60 - 64	+C	11	6	5	...	...	...	...	...	...
65 - 69	+C	17	9	8	...	...	...	...	...	...
70 - 74	+C	17	12	5	...	...	...	...	...	...
75 - 79	+C	26	18	8	...	...	...	...	...	...
80 - 84	+C	32	15	17	...	...	...	...	...	...
85+	+C	59	24	35	...	...	...	...	...	...
Serbia and Montenegro - Serbie-et-Montenegro										
2000										
Total	C	118 078	61 656	56 422	59 324	30 965	28 359	58 754	30 691	28 063
0 - 1	C	1 668	993	675	962	571	391	706	422	284
1 - 4	C	318	174	144	154	83	71	164	91	73
5 - 9	C	157	99	58	53	31	22	104	68	36
10 - 14	C	187	110	77	91	52	39	96	58	38
15 - 19	C	358	247	111	189	129	60	169	118	51
20 - 24	C	564	407	157	332	248	84	232	159	73
25 - 29	C	564	403	161	308	224	84	256	179	77
30 - 34	C	717	450	267	402	243	159	315	207	108
35 - 39	C	1 103	729	374	624	398	226	479	331	148
40 - 44	C	1 959	1 331	628	1 162	768	394	797	563	234
45 - 49	C	3 660	2 418	1 242	2 214	1 431	783	1 446	987	459
50 - 54	C	4 932	3 324	1 608	3 015	2 002	1 013	1 917	1 322	595
55 - 59	C	6 066	3 918	2 148	3 456	2 185	1 271	2 610	1 733	877
60 - 64	C	10 562	6 547	4 015	5 838	3 574	2 264	4 724	2 973	1 751
65 - 69	C	16 955	9 984	6 971	8 696	5 085	3 611	8 259	4 899	3 360
70 - 74	C	21 041	10 931	10 110	10 311	5 302	5 009	10 730	5 629	5 101
75 - 79	C	21 185	9 399	11 786	10 002	4 379	5 623	11 183	5 020	6 163
80 - 84	C	10 787	4 382	6 405	4 741	1 835	2 906	6 046	2 547	3 499
85+	C	15 185	5 728	9 457	6 688	2 360	4 328	8 497	3 368	5 129
Unknown - Inconnu	C	110	82	28	86	65	21	24	17	7
Slovakia - Slovaquie										
2001										
Total	C	51 980	27 705	24 275	24 520	12 924	11 596	27 460	14 781	12 679
0 - 1	C	319	185	134	147	82	65	172	103	69
1 - 4	C	98	63	35	48	25	23	50	38	12
5 - 9	C	76	53	23	43	30	13	33	23	10
10 - 14	C	89	62	27	48	35	13	41	27	14
15 - 19	C	192	124	68	103	66	37	89	58	31
20 - 24	C	277	221	56	135	106	29	142	115	27
25 - 29	C	358	272	86	186	139	47	172	133	39
30 - 34	C	405	311	94	203	150	53	202	161	41
35 - 39	C	630	473	157	319	220	99	311	253	58
40 - 44	C	1 167	856	311	583	402	181	584	454	130
45 - 49	C	2 016	1 458	558	1 075	727	348	941	731	210
50 - 54	C	2 643	1 920	723	1 377	980	397	1 266	940	326
55 - 59	C	2 970	2 066	904	1 492	1 002	490	1 478	1 064	414
60 - 64	C	3 987	2 719	1 268	1 902	1 253	649	2 085	1 466	619
65 - 69	C	5 323	3 341	1 982	2 565	1 579	986	2 758	1 762	996
70 - 74	C	7 320	4 061	3 259	3 410	1 834	1 576	3 910	2 227	1 683
75 - 79	C	8 851	4 025	4 826	4 037	1 832	2 205	4 814	2 193	2 621
80 - 84	C	6 149	2 538	3 611	2 780	1 164	1 616	3 369	1 374	1 995
85 - 89	C	5 555	1 952	3 603	2 492	885	1 607	3 063	1 067	1 996

(See notes at end of table.— Voir notes à la fin du tableau.)

Continent, country or area, year and age (in years) / Continent, pays ou zone, année et âge (en années)	Code[1]	Total			Urban - Urbaine			Rural - Rurale		
		Both sexes - Les deux sexes	Male - Masculin	Female - Féminin	Both sexes - Les deux sexes	Male - Masculin	Female - Féminin	Both sexes - Les deux sexes	Male - Masculin	Female - Féminin
EUROPE										
Slovakia - Slovaquie										
2001										
90 - 94	C	2 887	849	2 038	1 260	349	911	1 627	500	1 127
95 - 99	C	614	147	467	283	60	223	331	87	244
100+	C	54	9	45	32	4	28	22	5	17
Slovenia - Slovénie										
2001										
Total	C	18 508	9 654	8 854	8 277	4 296	3 981	10 231	5 358	4 873
0 - 1	C	74	44	30	33	18	15	41	26	15
1 - 4	C	8	4	4	3	1	2	5	3	2
5 - 9	C	15	11	4	6	4	2	9	7	2
10 - 14	C	16	12	4	9	7	2	7	5	2
15 - 19	C	87	69	18	33	29	4	54	40	14
20 - 24	C	113	95	18	48	36	12	65	59	6
25 - 29	C	119	101	18	54	50	4	65	51	14
30 - 34	C	144	110	34	66	49	17	78	61	17
35 - 39	C	222	165	57	87	64	23	135	101	34
40 - 44	C	344	246	98	144	104	40	200	142	58
45 - 49	C	641	466	175	306	220	86	335	246	89
50 - 54	C	847	583	264	388	259	129	459	324	135
55 - 59	C	994	684	310	449	289	160	545	395	150
60 - 64	C	1 388	980	408	638	446	192	750	534	216
65 - 69	C	1 967	1 285	682	878	571	307	1 089	714	375
70 - 74	C	2 592	1 478	1 114	1 127	641	486	1 465	837	628
75 - 79	C	2 825	1 301	1 524	1 281	608	673	1 544	693	851
80 - 84	C	2 112	800	1 312	951	372	579	1 161	428	733
85 - 89	C	2 354	800	1 554	1 016	356	660	1 338	444	894
90 - 94	C	1 324	356	968	597	143	454	727	213	514
95 - 99	C	297	55	242	152	26	126	145	29	116
100+	C	25	9	16	11	3	8	14	6	8
Spain - Espagne										
2000										
Total	C	360 391	189 468	170 923	...	...	...	...	...	...
0 - 1	C	1 740	959	781	...	...	...	...	...	...
1 - 4	C	383	220	163	...	...	...	...	...	...
5 - 9	C	300	181	119	...	...	...	...	...	...
10 - 14	C	365	220	145	...	...	...	...	...	...
15 - 19	C	1 198	862	336	...	...	...	...	...	...
20 - 24	C	1 996	1 533	463	...	...	...	...	...	...
25 - 29	C	2 339	1 806	533	...	...	...	...	...	...
30 - 34	C	2 975	2 191	784	...	...	...	...	...	...
35 - 39	C	4 052	2 935	1 117	...	...	...	...	...	...
40 - 44	C	5 267	3 678	1 589	...	...	...	...	...	...
45 - 49	C	6 523	4 603	1 920	...	...	...	...	...	...
50 - 54	C	9 331	6 691	2 640	...	...	...	...	...	...
55 - 59	C	12 024	8 622	3 402	...	...	...	...	...	...
60 - 64	C	17 127	12 125	5 002	...	...	...	...	...	...
65 - 69	C	29 420	20 008	9 412	...	...	...	...	...	...
70 - 74	C	41 327	26 300	15 027	...	...	...	...	...	...
75 - 79	C	55 264	31 507	23 757	...	...	...	...	...	...
80 - 84	C	58 873	27 072	31 801	...	...	...	...	...	...
85 - 89	C	59 660	22 691	36 969	...	...	...	...	...	...
90 - 94	C	37 319	11 834	25 485	...	...	...	...	...	...
95 - 99	C	11 363	3 065	8 298	...	...	...	...	...	...
100+	C	1 545	365	1 180	...	...	...	...	...	...
Sweden - Suède										
2001										
Total	C	93 752	45 431	48 321	...	...	...	...	...	...
0 - 1	C	334	189	145	...	...	...	...	...	...
1 - 4	C	68	35	33	...	...	...	...	...	...
5 - 9	C	50	23	27	...	...	...	...	...	...
10 - 14	C	70	36	34	...	...	...	...	...	...

19. Deaths by age, sex and urban/rural residence: latest available year
Décès selon l'âge, le sexe et la résidence, urbaine/rurale: dernière année disponible (continued — suite)

(See notes at end of table.— Voir notes à la fin du tableau.)

Continent, country or area, year and age (in years) / Continent, pays ou zone, année et âge (en années)	Code[1]	Total			Urban - Urbaine			Rural - Rurale		
		Both sexes - Les deux sexes	Male - Masculin	Female - Féminin	Both sexes - Les deux sexes	Male - Masculin	Female - Féminin	Both sexes - Les deux sexes	Male - Masculin	Female - Féminin
EUROPE										
Sweden - Suède										
2001										
15 - 19	C	155	104	51	...	...	...	...	...	...
20 - 24	C	269	215	54	...	...	...	...	...	...
25 - 29	C	267	199	68	...	...	...	...	...	...
30 - 34	C	350	248	102	...	...	...	...	...	...
35 - 39	C	520	354	166	...	...	...	...	...	...
40 - 44	C	718	469	249	...	...	...	...	...	...
45 - 49	C	1 265	774	491	...	...	...	...	...	...
50 - 54	C	2 144	1 273	871	...	...	...	...	...	...
55 - 59	C	3 287	1 983	1 304	...	...	...	...	...	...
60 - 64	C	3 770	2 371	1 399	...	...	...	...	...	...
65 - 69	C	5 410	3 280	2 130	...	...	...	...	...	...
70 - 74	C	8 459	4 966	3 493	...	...	...	...	...	...
75 - 79	C	13 569	7 561	6 008	...	...	...	...	...	...
80 - 84	C	18 097	8 945	9 152	...	...	...	...	...	...
85 - 89	C	18 504	7 446	11 058	...	...	...	...	...	...
90 - 94	C	12 166	3 938	8 228	...	...	...	...	...	...
95 - 99	C	3 765	922	2 843	...	...	...	...	...	...
100+	C	515	100	415	...	...	...	...	...	...
Switzerland - Suisse										
2001										
Total	C	61 287	29 915	31 372	42 157	19 952	22 205	19 130	9 963	9 167
0 - 1	C	365	209	156	248	145	103	117	64	53
1 - 4	C	90	52	38	52	26	26	38	26	12
5 - 9	C	41	23	18	26	16	10	15	7	8
10 - 14	C	59	36	23	32	14	18	27	22	5
15 - 19	C	177	128	49	92	61	31	85	67	18
20 - 24	C	245	192	53	167	126	41	78	66	12
25 - 29	C	269	185	84	185	121	64	84	64	20
30 - 34	C	408	277	131	302	201	101	106	76	30
35 - 39	C	579	377	202	393	254	139	186	123	63
40 - 44	C	757	491	266	533	337	196	224	154	70
45 - 49	C	1 104	722	382	752	476	276	352	246	106
50 - 54	C	1 651	1 064	587	1 158	731	427	493	333	160
55 - 59	C	2 331	1 475	856	1 670	1 024	646	661	451	210
60 - 64	C	2 832	1 829	1 003	1 966	1 237	729	866	592	274
65 - 69	C	4 096	2 642	1 454	2 800	1 760	1 040	1 296	882	414
70 - 74	C	5 724	3 518	2 206	3 902	2 327	1 575	1 822	1 191	631
75 - 79	C	8 189	4 517	3 672	5 544	2 991	2 553	2 645	1 526	1 119
80 - 84	C	9 968	4 819	5 149	6 718	3 157	3 561	3 250	1 662	1 588
85 - 89	C	11 270	4 298	6 972	7 684	2 851	4 833	3 586	1 447	2 139
90 - 94	C	8 207	2 428	5 779	5 818	1 658	4 160	2 389	770	1 619
95 - 99	C	2 554	582	1 972	1 834	404	1 430	720	178	542
100+	C	371	51	320	281	35	246	90	16	74
The Former Yugoslav Rep. of Macedonia - L'ex-République yougoslave de Macédoine										
2001										
Total	C	16 919	9 313	7 606	9 939	5 498	4 441	6 980	3 815	3 165
0 - 1	C	321	194	127	182	112	70	139	82	57
1 - 4	C	47	24	23	27	12	15	20	12	8
5 - 9	C	38	24	14	22	16	6	16	8	8
10 - 14	C	36	20	16	25	14	11	11	6	5
15 - 19	C	65	41	24	33	20	13	32	21	11
20 - 24	C	83	69	14	50	44	6	33	25	8
25 - 29	C	106	83	23	57	45	12	49	38	11
30 - 34	C	132	95	37	72	50	22	60	45	15
35 - 39	C	206	142	64	118	84	34	88	58	30
40 - 44	C	327	221	106	204	133	71	123	88	35
45 - 49	C	553	370	183	366	231	135	187	139	48
50 - 54	C	776	529	247	541	376	165	235	153	82

19. Deaths by age, sex and urban/rural residence: latest available year
Décès selon l'âge, le sexe et la résidence, urbaine/rurale: dernière année disponible (continued — suite)

(See notes at end of table.— Voir notes à la fin du tableau.)

Continent, country or area, year and age (in years) / Continent, pays ou zone, année et âge (en années)	Code[1]	Total Both sexes - Les deux sexes	Total Male - Masculin	Total Female - Féminin	Urban - Urbaine Both sexes - Les deux sexes	Urban - Urbaine Male - Masculin	Urban - Urbaine Female - Féminin	Rural - Rurale Both sexes - Les deux sexes	Rural - Rurale Male - Masculin	Rural - Rurale Female - Féminin
EUROPE										
The Former Yugoslav Rep. of Macedonia - L'ex-République yougoslave de Macédoine										
2001										
55 - 59	C	951	600	351	648	413	235	303	187	116
60 - 64	C	1 436	925	511	914	588	326	522	337	185
65 - 69	C	2 231	1 336	895	1 347	820	527	884	516	368
70 - 74	C	2 620	1 370	1 250	1 500	780	720	1 120	590	530
75 - 79	C	3 016	1 433	1 583	1 741	822	919	1 275	611	664
80 - 84	C	1 967	927	1 040	1 036	474	562	931	453	478
85+	C	2 007	909	1 098	1 056	464	592	951	445	506
Unknown - Inconnu	C	1	1	-	-	-	-	1	1	-
Ukraine[11]										
2001										
Total	C	745 952	378 143	367 809	450 329	236 933	213 396	295 623	141 210	154 413
0 - 1	C	4 283	2 488	1 795	2 690	1 544	1 146	1 593	944	649
1 - 4	C	1 451	840	611	690	404	286	761	436	325
5 - 9	C	1 034	652	382	601	380	221	433	272	161
10 - 14	C	1 300	858	442	793	527	266	507	331	176
15 - 19	C	3 433	2 435	998	2 193	1 533	660	1 240	902	338
20 - 24	C	6 247	4 891	1 356	4 218	3 257	961	2 029	1 634	395
25 - 29	C	8 697	6 813	1 884	6 016	4 651	1 365	2 681	2 162	519
30 - 34	C	10 838	8 424	2 414	7 402	5 618	1 784	3 436	2 806	630
35 - 39	C	16 077	12 604	3 473	10 943	8 463	2 480	5 134	4 141	993
40 - 44	C	24 526	18 976	5 550	16 869	12 883	3 986	7 657	6 093	1 564
45 - 49	C	32 093	24 240	7 853	22 259	16 655	5 604	9 834	7 585	2 249
50 - 54	C	39 924	28 814	11 110	28 005	20 074	7 931	11 919	8 740	3 179
55 - 59	C	36 906	25 106	11 800	23 826	16 267	7 559	13 080	8 839	4 241
60 - 64	C	82 734	53 832	28 902	52 508	34 114	18 394	30 226	19 718	10 508
65 - 69	C	71 796	42 458	29 338	43 133	25 525	17 608	28 663	16 933	11 730
70 - 74	C	114 616	58 287	56 329	68 074	34 819	33 255	46 542	23 468	23 074
75 - 79	C	109 002	39 760	69 242	61 689	22 535	39 154	47 313	17 225	30 088
80 - 84	C	71 800	20 640	51 160	40 009	11 992	28 017	31 791	8 648	23 143
85+	C	105 627	23 129	82 498	55 011	12 932	42 079	50 616	10 197	40 419
Unknown - Inconnu	C	3 568	2 896	672	3 400	2 760	640	168	136	32
United Kingdom - Royaume-Uni										
2001										
Total	C	602 268	286 757	315 511	...	...	...	...	...	...
0 - 1	C	3 664	2 042	1 622	...	...	...	...	...	...
1 - 4	C	642	347	295	...	...	...	...	...	...
5 - 9	C	429	220	209	...	...	...	...	...	...
10 - 14	C	534	328	206	...	...	...	...	...	...
15 - 19	C	1 489	1 049	440	...	...	...	...	...	...
20 - 24	C	2 070	1 519	551	...	...	...	...	...	...
25 - 29	C	2 402	1 725	677	...	...	...	...	...	...
30 - 34	C	3 676	2 531	1 145	...	...	...	...	...	...
35 - 39	C	4 925	3 156	1 769	...	...	...	...	...	...
40 - 44	C	6 622	4 006	2 616	...	...	...	...	...	...
45 - 49	C	9 663	5 859	3 804	...	...	...	...	...	...
50 - 54	C	16 128	9 643	6 485	...	...	...	...	...	...
55 - 59	C	21 893	13 338	8 555	...	...	...	...	...	...
60 - 64	C	30 600	18 677	11 923	...	...	...	...	...	...
65 - 69	C	44 618	26 915	17 703	...	...	...	...	...	...
70 - 74	C	68 453	39 190	29 263	...	...	...	...	...	...
75 - 79	C	95 919	50 762	45 157	...	...	...	...	...	...
80 - 84	C	102 813	47 062	55 751	...	...	...	...	...	...
85 - 89	C	98 946	36 788	62 158	...	...	...	...	...	...
90 - 94	C	62 472	17 325	45 147	...	...	...	...	...	...
95 - 99	C	20 927	3 906	17 021	...	...	...	...	...	...
100+	C	3 382	368	3 014	...	...	...	...	...	...

19. Deaths by age, sex and urban/rural residence: latest available year
Décès selon l'âge, le sexe et la résidence, urbaine/rurale: dernière année disponible (continued — suite)

(See notes at end of table.— Voir notes à la fin du tableau.)

Continent, country or area, year and age (in years) / Continent, pays ou zone, année et âge (en années)	Code[1]	Total			Urban - Urbaine			Rural - Rurale		
		Both sexes - Les deux sexes	Male - Masculin	Female - Féminin	Both sexes - Les deux sexes	Male - Masculin	Female - Féminin	Both sexes - Les deux sexes	Male - Masculin	Female - Féminin
OCEANIA — OCEANIE										
American Samoa - Samoas américaines										
1993										
Total	C	223	128	95	...	...	...	...	...	...
0 - 1	C	23	12	11	...	...	...	...	...	...
1 - 4	C	4	2	2	...	...	...	...	...	...
5 - 9	C	4	3	1	...	...	...	...	...	...
10 - 14	C	1	1	-	...	...	...	...	...	...
15 - 19	C	6	4	2	...	...	...	...	...	...
20 - 24	C	2	2	-	...	...	...	...	...	...
25 - 29	C	6	5	1	...	...	...	...	...	...
30 - 34	C	7	4	3	...	...	...	...	...	...
35 - 39	C	8	3	5	...	...	...	...	...	...
40 - 44	C	2	1	1	...	...	...	...	...	...
45 - 49	C	9	8	1	...	...	...	...	...	...
50 - 54	C	15	8	7	...	...	...	...	...	...
55 - 59	C	13	9	4	...	...	...	...	...	...
60 - 64	C	25	16	9	...	...	...	...	...	...
65 - 69	C	19	11	8	...	...	...	...	...	...
70 - 74	C	25	11	14	...	...	...	...	...	...
75 - 79	C	25	13	12	...	...	...	...	...	...
80 - 84	C	14	6	8	...	...	...	...	...	...
85+	C	15	9	6	...	...	...	...	...	...
Australia - Australie										
2000										
Total	+C	128 291	66 817	61 474	...	...	...	...	...	...
0 - 1	+C	1 290	725	565	...	...	...	...	...	...
1 - 4	+C	268	156	112	...	...	...	...	...	...
5 - 9	+C	174	100	74	...	...	...	...	...	...
10 - 14	+C	199	121	78	...	...	...	...	...	...
15 - 19	+C	717	501	216	...	...	...	...	...	...
20 - 24	+C	947	700	247	...	...	...	...	...	...
25 - 29	+C	1 244	920	324	...	...	...	...	...	...
30 - 34	+C	1 306	932	374	...	...	...	...	...	...
35 - 39	+C	1 687	1 117	570	...	...	...	...	...	...
40 - 44	+C	2 080	1 342	738	...	...	...	...	...	...
45 - 49	+C	2 679	1 619	1 060	...	...	...	...	...	...
50 - 54	+C	3 901	2 417	1 484	...	...	...	...	...	...
55 - 59	+C	4 929	3 055	1 874	...	...	...	...	...	...
60 - 64	+C	6 376	4 082	2 294	...	...	...	...	...	...
65 - 69	+C	9 363	5 922	3 441	...	...	...	...	...	...
70 - 74	+C	14 757	9 120	5 637	...	...	...	...	...	...
75 - 79	+C	19 563	11 233	8 330	...	...	...	...	...	...
80 - 84	+C	20 418	10 028	10 390	...	...	...	...	...	...
85+	+C	36 373	12 709	23 664	...	...	...	...	...	...
Unknown - Inconnu	+C	20	18	3	...	...	...	...	...	...
Guam[32]										
1992										
Total	C	585	346	239	486	284	202	99	62	37
0 - 1	C	43	28	15	36	23	13	7	5	2
1 - 4	C	3	1	2	3	1	2	-	-	-
5 - 9	C	3	3	-	3	3	-	-	-	-
10 - 14	C	6	3	3	6	3	3	-	-	-
15 - 19	C	16	11	5	15	11	4	1	-	1
20 - 24	C	20	16	4	16	12	4	4	4	-
25 - 29	C	16	14	2	10	8	2	6	6	-
30 - 34	C	25	20	5	21	17	4	4	3	1
35 - 39	C	28	20	8	23	16	7	5	4	1
40 - 44	C	28	20	8	22	16	6	6	4	2
45 - 49	C	28	17	11	20	10	10	8	7	1
50 - 54	C	25	13	12	19	9	10	6	4	2
55 - 59	C	49	30	19	39	24	15	10	6	4

(See notes at end of table.— Voir notes à la fin du tableau.)

Continent, country or area, year and age (in years) Continent, pays ou zone, année et âge (en années)	Code[1]	Total			Urban - Urbaine			Rural - Rurale		
		Both sexes - Les deux sexes	Male - Masculin	Female - Féminin	Both sexes - Les deux sexes	Male - Masculin	Female - Féminin	Both sexes - Les deux sexes	Male - Masculin	Female - Féminin
OCEANIA — OCEANIE										
Guam[32]										
1992										
60 - 64	C	56	32	24	49	29	20	7	3	4
65 - 69	C	66	40	26	59	34	25	7	6	1
70 - 74	C	63	31	32	54	27	27	9	4	5
75 - 79	C	38	22	16	34	19	15	4	3	1
80 - 84	C	38	11	27	30	10	20	8	1	7
85+	C	34	14	20	27	12	15	7	2	5
Marshall Islands - Îles Marshall										
1997										
Total	+U	243	135	108	...	...	...	...	...	...
0 - 1	+U	49	17	32	...	...	...	...	...	...
1 - 4	+U	7	1	6	...	...	...	...	...	...
5 - 9	+U	2	1	1	...	...	...	...	...	...
10 - 14	+U	2	1	1	...	...	...	...	...	...
15 - 19	+U	8	6	2	...	...	...	...	...	...
20 - 24	+U	10	9	1	...	...	...	...	...	...
25 - 29	+U	9	6	3	...	...	...	...	...	...
30 - 34	+U	8	2	6	...	...	...	...	...	...
35 - 39	+U	6	5	1	...	...	...	...	...	...
40 - 44	+U	10	5	5	...	...	...	...	...	...
45 - 49	+U	18	12	6	...	...	...	...	...	...
50 - 54	+U	13	9	4	...	...	...	...	...	...
55 - 59	+U	17	10	7	...	...	...	...	...	...
60 - 64	+U	17	13	4	...	...	...	...	...	...
65 - 69	+U	19	12	7	...	...	...	...	...	...
70 - 74	+U	13	6	7	...	...	...	...	...	...
75+	+U	35	20	15	...	...	...	...	...	...
New Caledonia - Nouvelle-Calédonie										
1999										
Total	C	1 095	649	446	...	...	...	...	...	...
0 - 1	C	27	12	15	...	...	...	...	...	...
1 - 4	C	9	3	6	...	...	...	...	...	...
5 - 9	C	2	-	2	...	...	...	...	...	...
10 - 14	C	2	1	1	...	...	...	...	...	...
15 - 19	C	20	14	6	...	...	...	...	...	...
20 - 24	C	25	19	6	...	...	...	...	...	...
25 - 29	C	30	24	6	...	...	...	...	...	...
30 - 34	C	28	22	6	...	...	...	...	...	...
35 - 39	C	35	24	11	...	...	...	...	...	...
40 - 44	C	38	25	13	...	...	...	...	...	...
45 - 49	C	50	33	17	...	...	...	...	...	...
50 - 54	C	66	42	24	...	...	...	...	...	...
55 - 59	C	85	54	31	...	...	...	...	...	...
60 - 64	C	99	73	26	...	...	...	...	...	...
65 - 69	C	108	68	40	...	...	...	...	...	...
70 - 74	C	120	67	53	...	...	...	...	...	...
75 - 79	C	116	65	51	...	...	...	...	...	...
80 - 84	C	103	47	56	...	...	...	...	...	...
85 - 89	C	78	36	42	...	...	...	...	...	...
90 - 94	C	41	15	26	...	...	...	...	...	...
95+	C	13	5	8	...	...	...	...	...	...
New Zealand - Nouvelle-Zélande[5]										
2000										
Total	+C	26 660	13 750	12 910	24 014	12 136	11 878	2 563	1 563	1 000
0 - 1	+C	346	190	156	289	163	126	32	15	17
1 - 4	+C	86	52	34	72	43	29	12	7	5
5 - 9	+C	49	22	27	38	15	23	10	6	4
10 - 14	+C	61	44	17	57	43	14	4	1	3
15 - 19	+C	168	121	47	133	98	35	34	22	12

19. Deaths by age, sex and urban/rural residence: latest available year
Décès selon l'âge, le sexe et la résidence, urbaine/rurale: dernière année disponible (continued — suite)

(See notes at end of table.— Voir notes à la fin du tableau.)

Continent, country or area, year and age (in years) Continent, pays ou zone, année et âge (en années)	Code[1]	Total			Urban - Urbaine			Rural - Rurale		
		Both sexes - Les deux sexes	Male - Masculin	Female - Féminin	Both sexes - Les deux sexes	Male - Masculin	Female - Féminin	Both sexes - Les deux sexes	Male - Masculin	Female - Féminin
OCEANIA — OCEANIE										
New Zealand - Nouvelle-Zélande[5]										
2000										
20 - 24	+C	190	149	41	161	125	36	29	24	5
25 - 29	+C	236	165	71	200	139	61	34	24	10
30 - 34	+C	267	189	78	222	155	67	40	29	11
35 - 39	+C	308	196	112	261	162	99	47	34	13
40 - 44	+C	444	263	181	382	223	159	61	39	22
45 - 49	+C	609	357	252	518	303	215	90	53	37
50 - 54	+C	872	501	371	739	420	319	131	79	52
55 - 59	+C	1 138	659	479	964	552	412	170	104	66
60 - 64	+C	1 461	855	606	1 206	693	513	251	159	92
65 - 69	+C	2 157	1 336	821	1 866	1 146	720	289	188	101
70 - 74	+C	3 094	1 870	1 224	2 761	1 636	1 125	323	226	97
75 - 79	+C	4 043	2 302	1 741	3 680	2 065	1 615	356	234	122
80 - 84	+C	4 180	2 033	2 147	3 887	1 870	2 017	284	159	125
85+	+C	...	...	...	6 578	2 285	4 293	...	...	...
85 - 89	+C	3 865	1 561	2 304	...	...	...	213	105	108
90 - 94	+C	2 220	694	1 526	...	...	...	121	49	72
95 - 99	+C	729	176	553	...	...	...	26	5	21
100+	+C	137	15	122	...	...	...	6	1	5
Northern Mariana Islands - Îles Mariannes septentrionales										
1999										
Total	U	189	99	91	...	...	...	...	...	...
0 - 4	U	16	8	8	...	...	...	...	...	...
5 - 9	U	1	-	1	...	...	...	...	...	...
15 - 19	U	6	4	3	...	...	...	...	...	...
20 - 24	U	9	6	3	...	...	...	...	...	...
25 - 29	U	7	6	1	...	...	...	...	...	...
30 - 34	U	5	4	1	...	...	...	...	...	...
35 - 39	U	10	4	6	...	...	...	...	...	...
40 - 44	U	7	6	1	...	...	...	...	...	...
45 - 49	U	16	4	12	...	...	...	...	...	...
50 - 54	U	16	8	8	...	...	...	...	...	...
55 - 59	U	9	3	6	...	...	...	...	...	...
60 - 64	U	15	8	7	...	...	...	...	...	...
65 - 69	U	15	9	6	...	...	...	...	...	...
70 - 74	U	20	13	7	...	...	...	...	...	...
75 - 79	U	12	5	7	...	...	...	...	...	...
80 - 84	U	13	7	6	...	...	...	...	...	...
85+	U	12	4	8	...	...	...	...	...	...
Palau - Palaos										
1999										
Total	C	131	78	53	...	...	...	...	...	...
0 - 1	C	5	3	2	...	...	...	...	...	...
1 - 14	C	4	2	2	...	...	...	...	...	...
15 - 24	C	3	3	-	...	...	...	...	...	...
25 - 44	C	22	16	6	...	...	...	...	...	...
45 - 64	C	41	27	14	...	...	...	...	...	...
65+	C	56	27	29	...	...	...	...	...	...
Tonga										
2000										
Total	+C	653	334	319	...	...	...	...	...	...
0 - 1	+C	28	12	16	...	...	...	...	...	...
1 - 9	+C	23	10	13	...	...	...	...	...	...
10 - 19	+C	14	10	4	...	...	...	...	...	...
20 - 29	+C	21	10	11	...	...	...	...	...	...
30 - 39	+C	16	5	11	...	...	...	...	...	...
40 - 49	+C	33	20	13	...	...	...	...	...	...
50 - 59	+C	78	37	41	...	...	...	...	...	...
60 - 69	+C	116	67	49	...	...	...	...	...	...

19. Deaths by age, sex and urban/rural residence: latest available year
Décès selon l'âge, le sexe et la résidence, urbaine/rurale: dernière année disponible (continued — suite)

(See notes at end of table.— Voir notes à la fin du tableau.)

Continent, country or area, year and age (in years) Continent, pays ou zone, année et âge (en années)	Code[1]	Total			Urban - Urbaine			Rural - Rurale		
		Both sexes - Les deux sexes	Male - Masculin	Female - Féminin	Both sexes - Les deux sexes	Male - Masculin	Female - Féminin	Both sexes - Les deux sexes	Male - Masculin	Female - Féminin
OCEANIA — OCEANIE										
Tonga										
2000										
70+	+C	299	151	148	...	...	...	...	...	...
Unknown - Inconnu	+C	25	12	13	...	...	...	...	...	...

GENERAL NOTES - NOTES GENERALES

Data exclude foetal deaths. For definition 'urban', see end of Technical Notes for table 6. For method of evaluation and limitations of data, see Technical Notes, for this table. — Les données ne comprennent pas les morts foetales. Pour les définitions des 'régions urbaines', se reporter à la fin des Notes techniques du tableau 6. Pour la méthode d'evaluations et les insuffisances des données, voir Notes techniques, pour ce tableau.

Italics: data from civil registers which are incomplete or of unknown completeness. — Italiques: données incomplètes ou dont le degré d'exactitude n'est pas connu provenant des registres de l'état civil.

FOOTNOTES - NOTES

* Provisional. — Données provisoires.
[1] 'Code' indicates the source of data, as follows:
C - Civil registration, estimated over 90% complete
U - Civil registration, estimated less than 90% complete
I - Other source, estimated reliable
+ - Data tabulated by date of registration rather than occurence.
... - Information not available

Le 'Code' indique la source des données, comme suit:
C - Registres de l'état civil considérés complèts à 90 p. 100 au moins.
U - Registres de l'état civil qui ne sont pas considérés complèts à 90 p. 100 au moins.
I - Autre source, considérée pas douteuses.
+ - Données exploitées selon la date de l'enregistrement et non la date de l'événement.
... - Information pas disponible.

[2] Excluding live-born infants dying before registration of birth. — Non compris les enfants nés vivants décédés avant l'enregistrement de leur naissance.
[3] For Algerian population only. — Pour la population algérienne seulement.
[4] Based on the results of the population census. — D'après les résultats du recensement de la population.
[5] Data for urban and rural exclude deaths of unknown residence and thus do not add up to the total. — Les données pur la résidence urbaine et rurale ne comprennent pas les décès dont on ignore la résidence et ne s'ajoute pas au total .
[6] Data for 1997 refer to last twelve months preceding population and housing census of 1997. — Les données pour 1997 se réfèrent au douze mois précédant le recensement de population et de l'habitat de 1997.
[7] Including Canadian residents temporarily in the United States, but excluding United States residents temporarily in Canada. — Y compris les résidents canadiens se trouvant temporairement aux Etats-Unis, mais ne comprennent pas les résidents des Etats-Unis se trouvant temporairement au Canada.
[8] Data for male and female categories exclude deaths of unknown sex. — - Les données pour le sexe masculin et féminin ne comprennent pas les décès ou on ignore le sexe.
[9] Excluding Indian jungle population. — Non compris les Indiens de la jungle.
[10] Excluding nomadic Indian tribes. — Non compris les tribus d'Indiens nomades.

[11] Excluding infants born alive with less than 28 weeks gestation, less than 1 000 grams in weight and 35 centimeters in length, who die within seven days of birth. — Non compris les enfants nés vivants avant 28 semaines de gestation, pesant moins de 1 000 grammes, mesurant moins de 35 centimètres et décédés dans les sept jours qui ont suivi leur naissance.
[12] For statistical purposes, the data for China do not include those for the Hong Kong Special Administrative Region (Hong Kong SAR), Macao special Adminstrative Region (Macao SAR) and Taiwan province of China. — Pour la présentation des statistiques, les données pour Chine ne comprend pas les Région Administrative Spéciale de Hong Kong (Hong Kong RAS), le Région Administrative Spéciale de Macao (Macao RAS) et Taïwan province de Chine.
[13] Data refer to government controlled areas. — Les données se raportent aux zones contrôlées par le Gouvernement.
[14] Including data for East Jerusalem and Israeli residents in certain other territories under occupation by Israeli military forces since June 1967. — Y compris les données pour Jérusalem-Est et les résidents israéliens dans certains autres territoires occupés depuis 1967 par les forces armées israéliennes.
[15] For Japanese nationals in Japan only. — Pour les nationaux japonais au Japon seulement.
[16] Excluding alien armed forces, civilian aliens employed by armed forces, and foreign diplomatic personnel and their dependants. — Non compris les militaires étrangers, les civils étrangers employés par les forces armées ni le personnel diplomatique étranger et les membres de leur famille les accompagnant.
[17] Data for urban refer to 170 towns out of 254 towns. — Les données urbaines se rapportent à 170 des 254 villes.
[18] Data for rural refer to 62 townships out of 158 townships. — Les données rurales se rapportent à 62 des 158 municipalités.
[19] Based on the results of the Population Growth Survey. — D'après les résultats de la 'Population Growth Survey.'
[20] Excluding data for the Pakistan-held part of Jammu and Kashmir, the final status of which has not yet been determined. — Non compris les données concernant la partie du Jammu et Cachemire occupée par le Pakistan dont le statut définitif n'a pas été déterminé.
[21] Excluding transients afloat and non-locally domiciled military and civilian services personnel and their dependants. — Non compris les personnes de passage þ bord de navires, ni les militaires et agents civils domiciliés hors du territoire et les membres de leur famille les accompagnant.
[22] Including armed forces stationed outside the country, but excluding alien armed forces stationed in the area. — Y compris les militaires nationaux hors du pays, mais non compris les militaires étrangers en garnison sur le territoire.
[23] Excluding Faeroe Islands and Greenland. — Non compris les îles Féroé et Gröenland.
[24] Including nationals temporarily outside the country. — Y compris les nationaux se trouvant temporairement hors du pays.
[25] Including armed forces stationed outside the country. — Y compris les militaires nationaux hors du pays.
[26] For ages five years and over, age classification based on year of birth rather than on exact date of birth. — A partir de cinq ans, le classement selon l'âge est basé sur l'année de naissances et non sur la date exacte de naissance.
[27] Excluding nationals outside the country. — Non compris les nationaux hors du pays.
[28] Data for urban/rural residence, for the de jure population. — Les données selon la résidence urbaine/rurale, pour la population de droit.
[29] Events registered within one year of occurrence. — Evénements enregistrés dans l'année qui suit l'événement.
[30] Including residents outside the country if listed in a Netherlands

population register. — Y compris les résidents hors du pays, s'ils sont inscrits sur un registre de population néerlandais.

[31] Including residents temporarily outside the country. — Y compris les résidents se trouvant temporairement hors du pays.

[32] Including United States military personnel, their dependants and contract employees. — Y compris les militaires des Etats-Unis, les membres de leur famille les accompagnant et les agents contractuels des Etats-Unis.

Table 20

Table 20 presents death rates by age, sex and urban/rural residence for the latest available year.

Description of variables: Age is defined as age at last birthday, that is, the difference between the date of birth and the date of the occurrence of the event, expressed in completed solar years. The age classification used in this table is the following: under 1 year, 1-4 years, 5-year age groups through 95-99, and 100 years or over.

The urban/rural classification of deaths is that provided by each country or area; it is presumed to be based on the national census definition of urban population that have been set forth at the end of the technical notes for table 6.

Rate computation: Death rates specific for age and sex are the annual number of deaths in each age-sex group (as shown in table 19) per 1 000 population in the same age-sex group.

Death rates by age, sex and urban/rural residence are the annual number of deaths that occurred in a specific age-sex-urban/rural group (as shown in table 19) per 1 000 population in the corresponding age-sex-urban/rural group. These rates are calculated by the Statistics Division of the United Nations.

Deaths at unknown age and the population of unknown age are excluded from age-specific rate calculations but are part of the death rate for all ages combined.

It should be noted that the death rates for infants under one year of age in this table differ from the infant mortality rates shown elsewhere, because the latter are computed per 1 000 live births rather than per 1 000 population.

The population used in computing the rates is estimated or enumerated distributions by age and sex. First priority was given to an estimate for the mid-point of the same year (as shown in table 7), second priority to census returns of the year to which the deaths referred and third priority to an estimate for some other point of time in the year.

Rates presented in this table have been limited to those for countries or areas having at least a total of 1 000 deaths in a given year. Moreover, rates specific for individual sub-categories that are based on 30 or fewer deaths are identified by the symbol (♦).

Reliability of data: Rates are not computed if data from civil registers of deaths are reported as incomplete (less than 90 per cent completeness) or of unknown completeness, and therefore deemed unreliable. Table 18 and the technical notes for that table provide more detailed information on the completeness of death registration. For more information about the quality of vital statistics, see section 4.2 of the Technical Notes.

Limitations: Rates shown in this table are subject to all the same limitations which affect the corresponding frequencies and are set forth in the technical notes for table 19.

These include differences in the completeness of registration, the treatment of infants who were born alive but died before the registration of the birth or within the first 24 hours of life, the method used to determine age at death and the quality of the reported information relating to age at death. In addition, some rates are based on deaths tabulated by date of registration and not by date of occurrence; these have been indicated with a plus sign (+).

The problem of obtaining precise correspondence between deaths (numerator) and population (denominator) as regards the inclusion or exclusion of armed forces, refugees, displaced persons and other special groups is particularly difficult where age-specific death rates are concerned. In cases where it was not possible to achieve strict correspondence, the differences in coverage are noted. Male rates in the age range 20 to 40 years may be especially affected by this non-correspondence, and care should be exercised in using these rates for comparative purposes. Even when deaths and population do correspond conceptually, comparability of the rates may be affected by abnormal conditions such as absence from the country or area of large numbers of young men in the military forces or working abroad as temporary workers. Death rates may appear high in the younger ages, simply because a large section of the able-bodied members of the age group, whose death rates under normal conditions might be less than the average for persons of their age, is not included.

Also, in a number of cases the rates shown here for all ages combined differ from crude death rates shown elsewhere, because in this table they are computed on the population for which an appropriate age-sex distribution was available, while the crude death rates shown elsewhere may utilize a different total population. The population by age and sex might refer to a census date within the year rather than to the mid-point, or it might be more or less inclusive as regards ethnic groups, armed forces and so forth. In a few instances, the difference is attributable to the fact that the rates in this table were computed on the mean population whereas the corresponding rates in other tables were computed on an estimate for 1 July. Differences of these types are insignificant but, for convenience, they are not in the table.

The comparability of data by urban/rural residence is affected by the national definitions of urban and rural used in tabulating these data. It is assumed, in the absence of specific information to the contrary, that the definitions of urban and rural used in connection with the national population census were also used in the compilation of the vital statistics for each country or area. However, the possibility cannot be excluded that, for a given country or area, the same definitions of urban and rural are not used for both the vital statistics data and the population census data. When known, the definitions of urban used in national population censuses are presented at the end of the technical notes for table 6. As discussed in detail in the technical notes for table 6, these definitions vary considerably from one country or area to another.

In addition to problems of comparability, vital rates classified by urban/rural residence are also subject to certain special types of bias. If, when calculating vital rates, different definitions of urban are used in connection with the vital events and the population data and if this results in a net difference between the numerator and denominator of the rate in the population at risk, then the vital rates would be biased. Urban/rural differentials in vital rates may also be affected by whether the vital events have been tabulated in terms of place of occurrence or place of usual residence.

This problem is discussed in more detail in section 4.1.4.1 of the Technical Notes.

Coverage: Death rates specific for age and sex are shown for 81 countries or areas. Rates are presented by urban/rural residence for 34 countries or areas.

Earlier data: Death rates specific for age and sex have been shown for the latest available year in many of the issues of the Yearbook since the 1955 issue. Data included in this table update the series shown in the Yearbook and in the Special Supplements covering a period of years as follows:

Issue	Years Covered
Historical Supplement CD, 1997	1948 – 1997
1996	1987 - 1995
1992	1983 – 1992
1985	1976 – 1984
1980	1971 – 1979
Historical Supplement, 1979	1948 - 1977

Tableau 20

Le tableau 20 présente des taux de mortalité selon l'âge et le sexe et selon la résidence (urbaine/rurale) pour la dernière année disponible.

Description des variables: L'âge est l'âge au dernier anniversaire, c'est-à-dire la différence entre la date de naissance et la date du décès, exprimée en années solaires révolues. La classification par âge est la suivante : moins d'un an, 1 à 4 ans, groupes quinquennaux jusqu'à 95 - 99 ans, et 100 ans et plus.

La classification des décès selon la résidence (urbaine/rurale) est celle qui a été fournie par chaque pays ou zone; il est donc présumé qu'elle repose sur les définitions de la population urbaine utilisées pour les recensements nationaux, qui sont reproduites à la fin des notes techniques du tableau 6.

Calcul des taux : Les taux de mortalité selon l'âge et le sexe représentent le nombre annuel de décès survenus pour chaque sexe et chaque groupe d'âge (fréquences du tableau 19) pour 1 000 personnes du même groupe.

Les taux de mortalité selon l'âge, le sexe et la résidence (urbaine/rurale) représentent le nombre annuel de décès intervenus dans un groupe d'âge et de sexe donnés dans la population urbaine ou rurale (fréquences du tableau 19) pour 1 000 personnes du même groupe dans la population urbaine ou rurale. Ces taux ont été calculés par la Division de statistique de l'ONU.

On n'a pas tenu compte des décès à un âge inconnu ni de la population d'âge inconnu, sauf dans les taux de mortalité pour tous les âges combinés.

Il convient de noter que, dans ce tableau, les taux de mortalité des groupes de moins d'un an sont différents des taux de mortalité infantile qui figurent dans d'autres tableaux, ces derniers ayant été établis pour 1 000 naissances vivantes et non pour 1 000 habitants.

Les chiffres de population utilisés pour le calcul des taux proviennent de dénombrements ou de répartitions estimatives de la population selon l'âge et le sexe. On a utilisé de préférence les estimations de la population en milieu d'année selon les indications du tableau 7; à défaut, on s'est contenté des données censitaires se rapportant à l'année du décès et, si ces données manquaient également, d'estimations établies pour une autre date de l'année.

Les taux présentés dans le tableau 20 ne se rapportent qu'aux pays ou zones où l'on a enregistré un total d'au moins 1 000 décès dans l'année. Les taux relatifs à des sous-catégories, qui sont fondés sur 30 décès ou moins, sont identifiés à l'aide du signe (♦).

Fiabilité des données : Les taux à partir de données sur les décès provenant des registres d'état civil qui sont déclarés incomplets (degré d'exhaustivité inférieur à 90 p. 100) ou dont le degré d'exhaustivité n'est pas connu sont jugés douteux et ne sont pas calculés et présentés. Le tableau 18 et les notes techniques s'y rapportant présentent des renseignements plus détaillés sur le degré d'exhaustivité de l'enregistrement des décès. Pour plus de précisions sur la qualité des statistiques de l'état civil, voir la section 4.2 des notes techniques.

Insuffisance des données : Les taux de ce tableau appellent les mêmes réserves que les fréquences correspondantes; voir à ce sujet les explications données dans les notes techniques se rapportant au tableau 19.

Leurs imperfections tiennent notamment aux différences d'exhaustivité de l'enregistrement, au classement des enfants nés vivants mais décédés avant l'enregistrement de leur naissance ou dans les 24 heures qui ont suivi la naissance, à la méthode utilisée pour obtenir l'âge au moment du décès, et à la qualité des déclarations concernant l'âge au moment du décès. En outre, dans certains cas, les données relatives aux décès sont classées par date d'enregistrement et non par date de l'événement; ces cas ont été identifiés par le signe (+).

S'agissant des taux de mortalité par âge, il est particulièrement difficile d'établir une correspondance exacte entre les décès (numérateur) et la population (dénominateur) du fait de l'inclusion ou de l'exclusion des militaires, des réfugiés, des personnes déplacées et d'autres groupes spéciaux. Dans les cas où il n'a pas été possible de parvenir à une correspondance exacte, des notes ont été ajoutées indiquant les différences de portée des données de base. Les taux de mortalité pour le sexe masculin dans les groupes d'âge de 20 à 40 ans peuvent être tout particulièrement influencés par ce manque de correspondance, et il importe d'être prudent lorsqu'on les utilise dans des comparaisons. Il convient d'ajouter que, même lorsque population et décès correspondent, la comparabilité des taux peut être compromise par des conditions anormales telles que l'absence du pays ou de la zone d'un grand nombre de jeunes gens qui sont sous les drapeaux ou qui travaillent à l'étranger comme travailleurs temporaires. Il arrive ainsi que les taux de mortalité paraissent élevés parmi les ages les plus jeunes simplement parce qu'on a laissé de côté un grand nombre d'individus de ces groupes d'âge pour lesquels le taux de mortalité pourrait être, dans des conditions normales, inférieur à la moyenne observée pour les personnes du même âge.

De même, les taux indiqués pour tous les âges combinés diffèrent dans plusieurs cas des taux bruts de mortalité qui figurent dans d'autres tableaux, parce qu'ils se rapportent à une population pour laquelle on disposait d'une répartition par âge et par sexe appropriée, tandis que les taux bruts de mortalité indiqués ailleurs peuvent avoir été calculés sur la base d'un chiffre de population totale différent. Ainsi, il est possible que les chiffres de population par âge et par sexe proviennent d'un recensement effectué dans l'année et non au milieu de l'année, et qu'ils se différencient des autres chiffres de population en excluant ou incluant certains groupes ethniques, les militaires, etc. Quelquefois, la différence tient à ce que les taux de ce tableau ont été calculés sur la base de la population moyenne, alors que les taux correspondants des autres tableaux reposent sur une estimation au 1er juillet. Les écarts de cet ordre sont insignifiants, mais ils n'ont pas été insérés dans le tableau.

La comparabilité des données selon la résidence (urbaine/rurale) peut être limitée par les définitions nationales des termes 'urbain' et 'rural' utilisées pour le classement de ces données. En l'absence d'indications contraires, on a supposé que les définitions des termes "urbain" et 'rural' utilisées pour le recensement national de la population l'avaient été aussi pour l'établissement des statistiques de l'état civil dans chaque pays ou zone. Toutefois, on ne peut exclure la possibilité que, pour un pays ou une zone, les mêmes définitions n'aient pas été utilisées dans les deux cas. Les définitions du terme 'urbain' pour les recensements nationaux de population ont été indiquées à la fin des notes techniques du tableau 6 lorsqu'elles étaient connues. Comme on l'a précisé en détail dans les notes techniques relatives au tableau 6, ces définitions varient très sensiblement d'un pays ou zone à l'autre.

Outre ces problèmes de comparabilité, les taux démographiques classés selon la résidence urbaine ou rurale sont également sujets à certaines distorsions particulières. Si, lors du calcul de ces taux, des définitions différentes du terme 'urbain' sont utilisées pour classer les faits d'état civil et les données relatives à la population, et s'il en résulte une différence nette entre le numérateur et le dénominateur pour le taux de la population considérée, les taux démographiques s'en trouveront faussés. La différence entre ces taux pour les zones urbaines et rurales pourra aussi être faussée selon que les faits d'état civil auront été classés d'après le lieu où ils se sont produits ou le lieu de résidence habituelle.

Ce problème est examiné plus en détail à la section 4.1.4.1 des Notes techniques.

Portée : Ce tableau présente des taux de mortalité selon l'âge et le sexe pour 81 pays ou zones. Des taux selon la résidence (urbaine/rurale) sont présentés pour 34 pays ou zones.

Données publiées antérieurement : Des taux de mortalité selon l'âge et le sexe pour la dernière année où ils étaient connus figurent dans beaucoup d'éditions de l'Annuaire depuis celle de 1955. Les données présentées dans ce tableau mettent à jour les séries présentées dans l'Annuaire démographique et dans les Suppléments Spéciaux qui couvrent les périodes d'années suivantes :

Editions	Années considérées
Supplément rétrospectif (CD), 1997	1948 – 1997
1996	1987 - 1995
1992	1983 – 1992
1985	1976 – 1984
1980	1971 – 1979
Supplément rétrospectif, 1979	1948 - 1977

20. Death rates specific for age, sex and urban/rural residence: latest available year
Taux de mortalité selon l'âge, le sexe et la résidence, urbaine/rurale: dernière année disponible

(See notes at end of table. — Voir notes à la fin du tableau.)

Continent, country or area, year and age (in years) Continent, pays ou zone, année et âge (en années)	Total			Urban - Urbaine			Rural - Rurale		
	Both sexes Les deux sexes	Male Masculin	Female Féminin	Both sexes Les deux sexes	Male Masculin	Female Féminin	Both sexes Les deux sexes	Male Masculin	Female Féminin
AFRICA — AFRIQUE									
Egypt - Égypte									
1999									
Total	6.4	6.8	6.0	...	...	...	...	...	...
0-1	34.3	35.4	33.2	...	...	...	...	...	...
1-4	2.4	2.4	2.4	...	...	...	...	...	...
5-9	0.7	0.8	0.6	...	...	...	...	...	...
10-14	0.6	0.7	0.6	...	...	...	...	...	...
15-19	0.8	1.0	0.7	...	...	...	...	...	...
20-24	1.2	1.4	0.9	...	...	...	...	...	...
25-29	1.2	1.6	0.9	...	...	...	...	...	...
30-34	1.4	1.8	1.1	...	...	...	...	...	...
35-39	2.1	2.6	1.6	...	...	...	...	...	...
40-44	3.3	4.2	2.3	...	...	...	...	...	...
45-49	5.8	7.3	4.3	...	...	...	...	...	...
50-54	10.3	12.9	7.8	...	...	...	...	...	...
55-59	15.5	17.9	12.7	...	...	...	...	...	...
60-64	22.9	26.1	19.6	...	...	...	...	...	...
65-69	43.1	44.4	41.5	...	...	...	...	...	...
70-74	71.3	72.7	69.7	...	...	...	...	...	...
75+	199.5	175.9	224.8	...	...	...	...	...	...
Malawi[1]									
1998									
Total	20.9	23.4	18.6	15.5	16.7	14.1	21.9	24.6	19.3
0-1	122.0	136.9	107.4	106.9	120.9	92.9	124.3	139.3	109.6
1-4	46.4	51.2	41.6	37.2	41.4	33.1	47.7	52.7	42.9
5-9	11.6	12.9	10.4	8.9	10.3	7.5	12.0	13.2	10.8
10-14	7.8	7.9	7.8	4.4	5.2	3.8	8.4	8.3	8.5
15-19	6.6	6.5	6.6	3.7	3.8	3.7	7.1	7.0	7.2
20-24	12.0	16.0	8.8	6.7	7.0	6.4	13.2	18.3	9.3
25-29	11.7	12.3	11.1	7.7	6.4	9.3	12.7	14.0	11.5
30-34	14.6	14.8	14.5	11.1	10.2	12.3	15.4	15.9	14.9
35-39	14.5	15.4	13.7	12.9	12.9	12.9	14.8	15.9	13.8
40-44	17.6	20.6	14.5	16.3	17.5	14.6	17.8	21.2	14.5
45-49	16.9	22.3	11.6	15.2	16.7	12.9	17.2	23.2	11.5
50-54	15.4	18.0	12.8	18.6	20.4	15.8	15.0	17.6	12.5
55-59	22.1	19.3	25.0	22.5	21.8	23.5	22.1	19.1	25.1
60-64	19.1	22.4	16.1	24.9	25.4	24.1	18.7	22.1	15.6
65-69	19.3	19.1	19.5	20.0	21.3	18.4	19.3	19.0	19.6
70-74	22.7	30.0	16.5	26.5	31.6	21.7	22.5	29.9	16.2
75-79	24.4	29.3	19.7	35.4	43.0	27.6	23.9	28.6	19.3
80-84	33.2	41.1	26.8	46.7	59.6	36.5	32.6	40.3	26.4
85+	51.7	60.6	44.1	89.6	104.8	77.6	50.1	58.8	42.6
Mauritius - Maurice[+]									
2000									
Total	6.7	7.6	5.9	...	...	...	...	...	...
0-1	16.3	20.4	12.0	...	...	...	...	...	...
1-4	0.6	◆0.6	◆0.6	...	...	...	...	...	...
5-9	◆0.2	◆0.3	◆0.2	...	...	...	...	...	...
10-14	0.3	◆0.4	◆0.2	...	...	...	...	...	...
15-19	0.6	0.7	◆0.5	...	...	...	...	...	...
20-24	0.8	1.2	◆0.4	...	...	...	...	...	...
25-29	1.3	1.6	0.9	...	...	...	...	...	...
30-34	1.5	2.1	1.0	...	...	...	...	...	...
35-39	2.2	3.1	1.2	...	...	...	...	...	...
40-44	3.9	5.6	2.2	...	...	...	...	...	...
45-49	5.5	7.6	3.3	...	...	...	...	...	...
50-54	8.9	11.8	6.2	...	...	...	...	...	...
55-59	12.9	16.3	9.9	...	...	...	...	...	...
60-64	20.9	27.1	15.7	...	...	...	...	...	...
65-69	33.3	45.5	23.1	...	...	...	...	...	...
70-74	47.2	59.2	38.1	...	...	...	...	...	...

20. Death rates specific for age, sex and urban/rural residence: latest available year
Taux de mortalité selon l'âge, le sexe et la résidence, urbaine/rurale: dernière année disponible
(continued — suite)

(See notes at end of table. — Voir notes à la fin du tableau.)

Continent, country or area, year and age (in years) / Continent, pays ou zone, année et âge (en années)	Total			Urban - Urbaine			Rural - Rurale		
	Both sexes Les deux sexes	Male Masculin	Female Féminin	Both sexes Les deux sexes	Male Masculin	Female Féminin	Both sexes Les deux sexes	Male Masculin	Female Féminin
AFRICA — AFRIQUE									
Mauritius - Maurice+									
2000									
75-79	68.5	85.7	57.0	...	...	...	...	...	...
80-84	102.9	127.1	89.4	...	...	...	...	...	...
85+	200.3	245.6	183.3	...	...	...	...	...	...
Mozambique[2]									
1997									
Total	23.3	26.4	20.5	...	...	...	...	...	...
0-4	73.8	81.5	66.5	...	...	...	...	...	...
5-9	13.2	14.5	12.0	...	...	...	...	...	...
10-14	7.0	7.9	6.2	...	...	...	...	...	...
15-19	6.8	6.8	6.8	...	...	...	...	...	...
20-24	7.3	7.1	7.4	...	...	...	...	...	...
25-29	8.1	8.8	7.6	...	...	...	...	...	...
30-34	9.2	11.3	7.6	...	...	...	...	...	...
35-39	9.9	11.6	8.4	...	...	...	...	...	...
40-44	10.3	12.3	8.5	...	...	...	...	...	...
45-49	12.4	15.4	9.8	...	...	...	...	...	...
50-54	15.9	19.6	12.6	...	...	...	...	...	...
55-59	14.6	18.8	11.1	...	...	...	...	...	...
60-64	29.0	36.2	23.2	...	...	...	...	...	...
65-69	28.7	36.7	22.6	...	...	...	...	...	...
70-74	43.4	60.5	31.3	...	...	...	...	...	...
75-79	55.6	77.6	41.0	...	...	...	...	...	...
80+	167.9	233.8	127.3	...	...	...	...	...	...
Réunion[3]									
1993									
Total	5.1	...	...	...	...	...	...	...	...
0-1	5.6	...	...	...	...	...	...	...	...
1-4	0.6	...	...	...	...	...	...	...	...
5-9	♦0.3	...	...	...	...	...	...	...	...
10-14	♦0.2	...	...	...	...	...	...	...	...
15-19	0.7	...	...	...	...	...	...	...	...
20-24	0.9	...	...	...	...	...	...	...	...
25-29	0.9	...	...	...	...	...	...	...	...
30-34	2.0	...	...	...	...	...	...	...	...
35-39	2.6	...	...	...	...	...	...	...	...
40-44	3.9	...	...	...	...	...	...	...	...
45-49	6.2	...	...	...	...	...	...	...	...
50-54	8.4	...	...	...	...	...	...	...	...
55-59	11.2	...	...	...	...	...	...	...	...
60-64	15.2	...	...	...	...	...	...	...	...
65-69	19.9	...	...	...	...	...	...	...	...
70-74	33.5	...	...	...	...	...	...	...	...
75-79	50.9	...	...	...	...	...	...	...	...
80+	118.5	...	...	...	...	...	...	...	...
Swaziland[2]									
1997									
Total	9.1	10.7	7.7	6.4	7.1	5.7	9.9	11.9	8.3
0-4	15.0	15.8	14.2	12.1	13.5	10.8	15.6	16.3	14.9
5-9	1.4	1.5	1.2	♦1.3	♦1.4	♦1.2	1.4	1.5	1.2
10-14	1.0	1.1	1.0	♦1.0	♦1.2	♦0.9	1.0	1.1	1.0
15-19	2.3	2.2	2.3	1.7	♦1.9	♦1.6	2.5	2.3	2.6
20-24	5.3	5.1	5.5	3.2	3.0	3.3	6.4	6.2	6.6
25-29	8.9	10.5	7.5	4.5	4.9	4.1	11.3	14.5	9.2
30-34	11.1	14.6	8.5	5.4	5.8	4.9	14.1	21.0	10.0
35-39	11.5	16.0	8.2	6.3	6.2	6.4	14.1	22.5	8.9
40-44	13.8	19.1	9.3	7.8	8.8	6.4	16.5	25.4	10.3
45-49	14.3	19.8	9.2	9.4	9.7	9.0	16.2	25.3	9.3
50-54	18.8	25.4	13.2	13.6	14.1	♦12.8	20.6	30.6	13.3
55-59	20.0	26.8	13.4	17.0	17.6	♦16.2	20.8	30.1	12.9

20. Death rates specific for age, sex and urban/rural residence: latest available year
Taux de mortalité selon l'âge, le sexe et la résidence, urbaine/rurale: dernière année disponible
(continued — suite)

(See notes at end of table. — Voir notes à la fin du tableau.)

Continent, country or area, year and age (in years) Continent, pays ou zone, année et âge (en années)	Total			Urban - Urbaine			Rural - Rurale		
	Both sexes Les deux sexes	Male Masculin	Female Féminin	Both sexes Les deux sexes	Male Masculin	Female Féminin	Both sexes Les deux sexes	Male Masculin	Female Féminin
AFRICA — AFRIQUE									
Swaziland[2]									
1997									
60-64	26.3	37.5	17.0	21.3	♦19.3	♦23.8	27.4	42.2	15.9
65-69	30.0	42.0	20.0	32.1	43.7	♦19.0	29.7	41.7	20.1
70-74	43.1	64.6	28.8	53.5	♦64.1	♦44.9	41.9	64.7	27.1
75+	68.7	79.2	61.7	97.1	90.1	102.9	65.8	77.9	58.0
AMERICA, NORTH — **AMERIQUE DU NORD**									
Canada[4]									
1998									
Total	7.2	7.5	6.9	...	...	...	...	...	...
0-1	5.2	5.6	4.8	...	...	...	...	...	...
1-4	0.3	0.3	0.2	...	...	...	...	...	...
5-9	0.1	0.1	0.1	...	...	...	...	...	...
10-14	0.2	0.2	0.1	...	...	...	...	...	...
15-19	0.5	0.7	0.3	...	...	...	...	...	...
20-24	0.6	1.0	0.3	...	...	...	...	...	...
25-29	0.6	0.9	0.3	...	...	...	...	...	...
30-34	0.8	1.1	0.5	...	...	...	...	...	...
35-39	1.1	1.4	0.7	...	...	...	...	...	...
40-44	1.6	1.9	1.2	...	...	...	...	...	...
45-49	2.3	2.8	1.8	...	...	...	...	...	...
50-54	3.7	4.5	2.9	...	...	...	...	...	...
55-59	6.2	7.7	4.7	...	...	...	...	...	...
60-64	10.1	12.7	7.5	...	...	...	...	...	...
65-69	16.8	22.0	12.0	...	...	...	...	...	...
70-74	26.9	35.6	19.8	...	...	...	...	...	...
75-79	42.9	57.3	32.9	...	...	...	...	...	...
80-84	72.5	96.0	58.6	...	...	...	...	...	...
85-89	118.3	149.4	103.3	...	...	...	...	...	...
90+	215.2	246.4	204.6	...	...	...	...	...	...
Costa Rica									
1997									
Total	4.4	5.1	3.7	...	...	...	...	...	...
0-4	3.9	4.3	3.4	...	...	...	...	...	...
5-9	0.3	0.3	0.2	...	...	...	...	...	...
10-14	0.3	0.4	0.3	...	...	...	...	...	...
15-19	0.7	1.0	0.4	...	...	...	...	...	...
20-24	1.0	1.6	0.5	...	...	...	...	...	...
25-29	1.4	2.0	0.7	...	...	...	...	...	...
30-39	1.6	2.4	0.9	...	...	...	...	...	...
40-49	2.7	3.6	1.9	...	...	...	...	...	...
50-59	5.6	6.9	4.3	...	...	...	...	...	...
60-69	13.2	16.4	10.3	...	...	...	...	...	...
70+	53.2	57.0	49.5	...	...	...	...	...	...
Cuba[5]									
1999									
Total	7.1	7.8	6.4	7.7	8.4	6.9	5.5	6.2	4.6
0-1	6.5	7.3	5.7	6.9	7.7	6.0	5.5	6.0	4.9
1-4	0.5	0.5	0.4	0.5	0.5	0.5	0.5	0.6	♦0.4
5-9	0.3	0.3	0.2	0.3	0.3	0.2	0.3	0.3	♦0.2
10-14	0.3	0.4	0.3	0.3	0.4	0.3	0.4	0.5	0.3
15-19	0.6	0.7	0.5	0.6	0.7	0.6	0.6	0.8	0.4
20-24	0.8	1.2	0.5	0.9	1.2	0.5	0.7	1.0	0.5
25-29	1.1	1.5	0.7	1.1	1.5	0.7	1.1	1.4	0.7
30-34	1.3	1.7	0.8	1.3	1.8	0.9	1.2	1.5	0.8
35-39	1.7	2.2	1.2	1.7	2.3	1.1	1.7	2.0	1.3
40-44	2.6	3.3	2.0	2.7	3.5	2.0	2.4	2.7	2.0
45-49	3.7	4.5	2.9	3.9	4.9	3.0	3.0	3.3	2.6

20. Death rates specific for age, sex and urban/rural residence: latest available year
Taux de mortalité selon l'âge, le sexe et la résidence, urbaine/rurale: dernière année disponible
(continued — suite)

(See notes at end of table. — Voir notes à la fin du tableau.)

Continent, country or area, year and age (in years) Continent, pays ou zone, année et âge (en années)	Total			Urban - Urbaine			Rural - Rurale		
	Both sexes Les deux sexes	Male Masculin	Female Féminin	Both sexes Les deux sexes	Male Masculin	Female Féminin	Both sexes Les deux sexes	Male Masculin	Female Féminin
AMERICA, NORTH — AMERIQUE DU NORD									
Cuba[5]									
1999									
50-54	5.5	6.6	4.5	5.8	7.1	4.6	4.4	4.9	3.9
55-59	8.3	10.1	6.6	8.8	11.0	6.7	6.7	7.0	6.3
60-64	12.4	14.4	10.4	13.1	15.8	10.7	9.7	10.1	9.1
65-74	25.4	29.2	21.8	26.9	32.1	22.4	20.1	20.9	19.1
75-84	86.2	99.9	74.0	90.3	109.2	75.6	71.0	74.4	66.3
85+	146.9	160.1	136.6	152.3	171.6	139.4	128.1	131.7	123.4
El Salvador									
2000									
Total	4.5	5.4	3.6	5.3	6.4	4.2	3.4	4.1	2.7
0-1	10.3	11.6	9.0	12.8	14.2	11.4	7.8	9.0	6.5
1-4	0.8	0.9	0.8	0.8	0.9	0.8	0.8	0.9	0.7
5-9	0.3	0.3	0.3	0.3	0.4	0.3	0.3	0.3	0.3
10-14	0.4	0.4	0.3	0.4	0.5	0.4	0.3	0.3	0.3
15-19	1.2	1.7	0.6	1.4	2.1	0.7	0.9	1.3	0.5
20-24	1.9	3.0	0.7	2.4	4.0	0.8	1.3	1.9	0.6
25-29	2.1	3.4	0.9	2.4	3.9	1.0	1.7	2.6	0.7
30-34	2.6	4.3	1.0	2.7	4.8	1.0	2.3	3.6	1.1
35-39	3.5	5.6	1.7	3.6	5.9	1.7	3.1	4.8	1.5
40-44	3.9	5.8	2.3	3.9	5.8	2.3	4.0	5.7	2.3
45-49	4.8	6.8	3.0	5.3	7.8	3.1	3.9	5.3	2.7
50-54	6.1	8.3	4.1	6.6	9.2	4.4	5.2	6.8	3.7
55-59	9.6	12.3	7.2	10.9	13.9	8.3	7.6	9.9	5.3
60-64	12.8	15.9	10.1	14.8	18.6	11.7	9.8	12.0	7.5
65-69	17.3	21.6	13.7	19.2	24.7	14.9	14.4	17.4	11.5
70-74	25.9	29.7	22.8	28.6	33.5	24.9	21.3	24.1	18.9
75-79	56.9	69.8	47.5	60.7	74.9	50.9	21.5	26.3	17.6
80+	128.5	161.5	109.1	113.2	135.2	100.3	191.7	267.4	146.0
Guatemala									
1999									
Total	5.8	6.6	5.0	...	...	...	...	...	...
0-1	34.9	38.1	31.4	...	...	...	...	...	...
1-4	3.6	3.6	3.5	...	...	...	...	...	...
5-9	0.7	0.7	0.7	...	...	...	...	...	...
10-14	0.7	0.8	0.5	...	...	...	...	...	...
15-19	1.4	1.7	1.0	...	...	...	...	...	...
20-24	2.1	2.9	1.3	...	...	...	...	...	...
25-29	2.6	3.8	1.5	...	...	...	...	...	...
30-34	3.4	4.8	2.1	...	...	...	...	...	...
35-39	4.4	6.2	2.7	...	...	...	...	...	...
40-44	5.4	7.1	3.7	...	...	...	...	...	...
45-49	6.9	9.0	4.9	...	...	...	...	...	...
50-54	8.8	10.9	6.8	...	...	...	...	...	...
55-59	10.8	12.2	9.3	...	...	...	...	...	...
60-64	15.2	17.5	12.9	...	...	...	...	...	...
65+	9.8	11.1	8.6	...	...	...	...	...	...
Martinique[3]									
1992									
Total	5.9	6.7	5.1	...	...	...	...	...	...
0-4	1.6	♦1.8	♦1.4	...	...	...	...	...	...
5-9	♦0.1	♦0.1	♦0.1	...	...	...	...	...	...
10-14	♦0.2	♦0.2	♦0.2	...	...	...	...	...	...
15-19	♦0.6	♦1.0	♦0.3	...	...	...	...	...	...
20-24	♦0.8	♦1.2	♦0.4	...	...	...	...	...	...
25-29	1.1	♦1.7	♦0.5	...	...	...	...	...	...
30-34	1.5	2.2	♦0.8	...	...	...	...	...	...
35-39	♦1.1	♦1.5	♦0.8	...	...	...	...	...	...
40-44	2.5	3.1	♦2.0	...	...	...	...	...	...

20. Death rates specific for age, sex and urban/rural residence: latest available year
Taux de mortalité selon l'âge, le sexe et la résidence, urbaine/rurale: dernière année disponible
(continued — suite)

(See notes at end of table. — Voir notes à la fin du tableau.)

Continent, country or area, year and age (in years) Continent, pays ou zone, année et âge (en années)	Total			Urban - Urbaine			Rural - Rurale		
	Both sexes Les deux sexes	Male Masculin	Female Féminin	Both sexes Les deux sexes	Male Masculin	Female Féminin	Both sexes Les deux sexes	Male Masculin	Female Féminin
AMERICA, NORTH —									
AMERIQUE DU NORD									
Martinique[3]									
1992									
45-49	1.9	♦3.1	♦0.8	...	...	...	...	...	...
50-54	4.3	6.1	♦2.8	...	...	...	...	...	...
55-59	7.1	10.3	4.2	...	...	...	...	...	...
60-64	10.2	14.6	6.4	...	...	...	...	...	...
65-69	18.1	24.8	12.6	...	...	...	...	...	...
70-74	26.7	34.2	20.8	...	...	...	...	...	...
75-79	43.0	59.2	31.5	...	...	...	...	...	...
80-84	60.7	77.4	50.8	...	...	...	...	...	...
85+	135.7	171.3	120.0	...	...	...	...	...	...
Mexico - Mexique[5,6]									
2000									
Total	4.5	5.1	3.9	4.6	5.2	4.0	4.0	4.6	3.3
0-1	18.7	20.8	16.6	19.6	21.8	17.4	15.9	17.6	14.1
1-4	0.8	0.9	0.8	0.7	0.8	0.7	1.0	1.0	1.0
5-9	0.3	0.4	0.3	0.3	0.3	0.3	0.3	0.4	0.3
10-14	0.3	0.4	0.3	0.3	0.4	0.3	0.3	0.4	0.3
15-19	0.7	1.0	0.4	0.7	1.0	0.4	0.7	1.0	0.5
20-24	1.1	1.7	0.5	1.1	1.6	0.5	1.2	1.7	0.6
25-29	1.4	2.2	0.7	1.3	2.0	0.6	1.5	2.3	0.8
30-34	1.7	2.6	0.9	1.6	2.4	0.8	1.7	2.6	1.0
35-39	2.2	3.3	1.2	2.1	3.1	1.2	2.3	3.3	1.4
40-44	3.0	4.2	1.9	2.9	4.0	1.9	3.1	4.2	1.9
45-49	4.4	5.9	3.1	4.4	5.8	3.1	4.1	5.2	3.0
50-54	6.3	7.7	4.9	6.4	7.9	5.1	5.4	6.5	4.2
55-59	10.0	12.0	8.0	10.5	12.8	8.5	7.9	9.3	6.4
60-64	14.0	16.4	11.9	15.2	18.0	12.8	10.4	11.8	9.0
65-69	21.7	25.0	18.7	23.6	27.7	20.3	16.0	18.0	13.9
70-74	31.6	35.4	28.2	34.6	39.7	30.4	23.3	24.9	21.4
75-79	47.3	52.3	42.8	51.9	58.6	46.3	35.1	38.0	31.9
80-84	72.1	78.4	67.0	79.1	88.0	72.4	54.5	58.0	50.9
85+	133.2	135.2	131.8	144.7	149.5	141.5	106.1	107.4	104.9
Netherlands Antilles - Antilles néerlandaises									
1992									
Total	6.5	7.3	5.7	...	...	...	...	...	...
0-1	8.9	♦8.2	♦9.7	...	...	...	...	...	...
1-4	♦0.7	♦0.9	♦0.6	...	...	...	...	...	...
5-9	♦0.2	♦0.1	♦0.4	...	...	...	...	...	...
15-19	♦0.5	♦0.5	♦0.4	...	...	...	...	...	...
20-24	♦0.7	♦1.2	♦0.3	...	...	...	...	...	...
25-29	♦1.2	♦1.7	♦0.8	...	...	...	...	...	...
30-34	♦1.1	♦1.4	♦0.8	...	...	...	...	...	...
35-39	1.9	♦2.8	♦1.2	...	...	...	...	...	...
40-44	2.8	♦3.0	♦2.7	...	...	...	...	...	...
45-49	3.7	♦4.4	♦3.1	...	...	...	...	...	...
50-54	5.5	♦6.0	♦5.0	...	...	...	...	...	...
55-59	9.6	13.5	♦6.0	...	...	...	...	...	...
60-64	16.9	20.5	13.6	...	...	...	...	...	...
65-69	19.0	28.6	♦10.9	...	...	...	...	...	...
70-74	40.2	54.5	28.5	...	...	...	...	...	...
75-79	57.6	80.7	41.9	...	...	...	...	...	...
80-84	90.3	125.7	69.6	...	...	...	...	...	...
85+	186.9	222.7	169.1	...	...	...	...	...	...
Puerto Rico - Porto Rico[5]									
2000									
Total	7.5	8.8	6.3	...	...	...	...	...	...
0-1	10.3	11.2	9.3	...	...	...	...	...	...

20. Death rates specific for age, sex and urban/rural residence: latest available year
Taux de mortalité selon l'âge, le sexe et la résidence, urbaine/rurale: dernière année disponible
(continued — suite)

(See notes at end of table. — Voir notes à la fin du tableau.)

Continent, country or area, year and age (in years) / Continent, pays ou zone, année et âge (en années)	Total			Urban - Urbaine			Rural - Rurale		
	Both sexes Les deux sexes	Male Masculin	Female Féminin	Both sexes Les deux sexes	Male Masculin	Female Féminin	Both sexes Les deux sexes	Male Masculin	Female Féminin
AMERICA, NORTH — AMERIQUE DU NORD									
Puerto Rico - Porto Rico[5]									
2000									
1-4	0.3	0.4	0.3	...	...	...	...	...	...
5-9	0.2	0.2	♦0.2	...	...	...	...	...	...
10-14	0.2	♦0.2	♦0.2	...	...	...	...	...	...
15-19	0.9	1.3	0.4	...	...	...	...	...	...
20-24	1.4	2.4	0.4	...	...	...	...	...	...
25-29	1.6	2.5	0.6	...	...	...	...	...	...
30-34	1.8	2.6	1.0	...	...	...	...	...	...
35-39	2.5	3.9	1.2	...	...	...	...	...	...
40-44	3.0	4.5	1.7	...	...	...	...	...	...
45-49	4.3	6.4	2.5	...	...	...	...	...	...
50-54	5.5	8.1	3.4	...	...	...	...	...	...
55-59	8.0	11.1	5.4	...	...	...	...	...	...
60-64	11.5	15.6	7.9	...	...	...	...	...	...
65-69	18.5	24.1	13.9	...	...	...	...	...	...
70-74	28.1	35.4	22.2	...	...	...	...	...	...
75-79	42.0	53.1	33.5	...	...	...	...	...	...
80-84	67.7	78.0	60.0	...	...	...	...	...	...
85+	132.6	145.9	123.8	...	...	...	...	...	...
Trinidad and Tobago - Trinité-et-Tobago									
1997									
Total	7.2	7.9	6.5	...	...	...	...	...	...
0-1	19.8	21.4	18.2	...	...	...	...	...	...
1-4	0.8	0.8	♦0.7	...	...	...	...	...	...
5-9	0.3	♦0.4	♦0.2	...	...	...	...	...	...
10-14	0.4	♦0.4	♦0.3	...	...	...	...	...	...
15-19	0.7	0.8	0.6	...	...	...	...	...	...
20-24	1.4	1.8	0.9	...	...	...	...	...	...
25-29	1.6	1.9	1.2	...	...	...	...	...	...
30-34	2.5	3.2	1.9	...	...	...	...	...	...
35-39	3.0	3.7	2.3	...	...	...	...	...	...
40-44	3.9	4.8	2.9	...	...	...	...	...	...
45-49	5.4	6.6	4.3	...	...	...	...	...	...
50-54	8.3	10.3	6.3	...	...	...	...	...	...
55-59	13.6	16.6	10.9	...	...	...	...	...	...
60-64	22.1	24.2	20.2	...	...	...	...	...	...
65-69	31.7	36.0	27.8	...	...	...	...	...	...
70-74	44.7	60.6	32.8	...	...	...	...	...	...
75-79	62.6	82.7	47.8	...	...	...	...	...	...
80+	146.2	154.8	139.3	...	...	...	...	...	...
United States - États-Unis									
2000									
Total	8.7	8.8	8.7	...	...	...	...	...	...
0-4	1.8	1.9	1.6	...	...	...	...	...	...
5-9	0.2	0.2	0.1	...	...	...	...	...	...
10-14	0.2	0.3	0.2	...	...	...	...	...	...
15-19	0.7	0.9	0.4	...	...	...	...	...	...
20-24	1.0	1.4	0.5	...	...	...	...	...	...
25-29	1.0	1.4	0.6	...	...	...	...	...	...
30-34	1.2	1.6	0.8	...	...	...	...	...	...
35-39	1.6	2.1	1.2	...	...	...	...	...	...
40-44	2.4	3.0	1.7	...	...	...	...	...	...
45-49	3.6	4.6	2.5	...	...	...	...	...	...
50-54	5.2	6.6	3.9	...	...	...	...	...	...
55-59	8.0	10.1	6.1	...	...	...	...	...	...
60-64	12.6	15.6	9.8	...	...	...	...	...	...
65-69	19.3	24.0	15.2	...	...	...	...	...	...

20. Death rates specific for age, sex and urban/rural residence: latest available year
Taux de mortalité selon l'âge, le sexe et la résidence, urbaine/rurale: dernière année disponible
(continued — suite)

(See notes at end of table. — Voir notes à la fin du tableau.)

Continent, country or area, year and age (in years) / Continent, pays ou zone, année et âge (en années)	Total			Urban - Urbaine			Rural - Rurale		
	Both sexes Les deux sexes	Male Masculin	Female Féminin	Both sexes Les deux sexes	Male Masculin	Female Féminin	Both sexes Les deux sexes	Male Masculin	Female Féminin
AMERICA, NORTH — AMERIQUE DU NORD									
United States - États-Unis									
2000									
70-74	29.6	37.0	23.8	...	...	...	...	...	...
75-79	45.5	55.9	38.1	...	...	...	...	...	...
80-84	73.8	89.4	64.3	...	...	...	...	...	...
85+	152.6	165.8	146.9	...	...	...	...	...	...
AMERICA, SOUTH — AMERIQUE DU SUD									
Argentina - Argentine[6]									
1995									
Total	7.7	8.7	6.8	...	...	...	...	...	...
0-4	4.9	5.5	4.5	...	...	...	...	...	...
5-9	0.3	0.3	0.2	...	...	...	...	...	...
10-14	0.3	0.4	0.3	...	...	...	...	...	...
15-19	0.7	1.0	0.5	...	...	...	...	...	...
20-24	1.1	1.5	0.6	...	...	...	...	...	...
25-29	1.3	1.8	0.8	...	...	...	...	...	...
30-34	1.4	1.9	1.0	...	...	...	...	...	...
35-39	1.9	2.5	1.3	...	...	...	...	...	...
40-44	2.8	3.6	2.0	...	...	...	...	...	...
45-49	4.5	5.8	3.1	...	...	...	...	...	...
50-54	6.9	9.3	4.5	...	...	...	...	...	...
55-59	10.3	14.4	6.3	...	...	...	...	...	...
60-64	15.6	22.4	9.4	...	...	...	...	...	...
65-69	23.0	32.5	14.9	...	...	...	...	...	...
70-74	35.0	48.3	24.5	...	...	...	...	...	...
75-79	52.8	70.3	40.7	...	...	...	...	...	...
80+	146.1	170.7	131.4	...	...	...	...	...	...
Chile - Chili									
1998									
Total	5.4	6.0	4.9	5.3	5.8	4.8	6.0	6.7	5.1
0-1	9.7	10.6	8.7	...	...	...	...	...	...
0-4	...	...	...	2.3	2.5	2.0	2.7	2.9	2.5
1-4	0.5	0.6	0.4	...	...	...	...	...	...
5-9	0.2	0.3	0.2	0.2	0.2	0.2	0.4	0.5	♦0.2
10-14	0.2	0.3	0.2	0.2	0.2	0.2	0.3	0.4	♦0.2
15-19	0.6	0.8	0.3	0.5	0.8	0.3	0.8	1.0	0.5
20-24	0.8	1.3	0.3	0.8	1.2	0.3	1.2	1.9	0.5
25-29	1.0	1.6	0.4	0.9	1.5	0.4	1.5	2.2	0.7
30-34	1.2	1.9	0.6	1.2	1.8	0.6	1.7	2.5	0.8
35-39	1.5	2.1	0.9	1.4	2.0	0.9	2.1	2.9	1.2
40-44	2.1	2.9	1.3	2.1	2.9	1.3	2.6	3.3	1.6
45-49	3.2	4.1	2.3	3.1	4.0	2.3	3.5	4.3	2.6
50-54	5.1	6.6	3.7	5.1	6.7	3.6	5.1	6.1	3.9
55-59	8.3	11.0	5.8	8.3	11.2	5.8	8.3	10.1	6.0
60-64	12.4	16.3	9.0	12.5	17.0	8.9	11.6	13.3	9.6
65-69	20.8	28.0	15.0	21.0	29.0	14.9	20.2	23.8	15.9
70-74	32.8	43.9	24.5	33.4	46.4	24.6	29.6	34.6	23.8
75-79	50.7	66.4	40.4	51.0	69.0	40.3	49.3	57.2	40.9
80+	134.7	157.5	122.5	136.8	165.5	123.2	124.3	131.1	118.1
1999									
Total	5.5	6.0	5.0	...	...	...	...	...	...
0-1	9.2	10.1	8.3	...	...	...	...	...	...
1-4	0.4	0.4	0.4	...	...	...	...	...	...
5-9	0.2	0.2	0.2	...	...	...	...	...	...
10-14	0.2	0.3	0.1	...	...	...	...	...	...
15-19	0.5	0.7	0.3	...	...	...	...	...	...

20. Death rates specific for age, sex and urban/rural residence: latest available year
Taux de mortalité selon l'âge, le sexe et la résidence, urbaine/rurale: dernière année disponible
(continued — suite)

(See notes at end of table. — Voir notes à la fin du tableau.)

Continent, country or area, year and age (in years) / Continent, pays ou zone, année et âge (en années)	Total			Urban - Urbaine			Rural - Rurale		
	Both sexes Les deux sexes	Male Masculin	Female Féminin	Both sexes Les deux sexes	Male Masculin	Female Féminin	Both sexes Les deux sexes	Male Masculin	Female Féminin
AMERICA, SOUTH — AMERIQUE DU SUD									
Chile - Chili									
1999									
20-24	0.8	1.2	0.4	...	...	...	...	...	...
25-29	1.0	1.6	0.5	...	...	...	...	...	...
30-34	1.2	1.8	0.6	...	...	...	...	...	...
35-39	1.5	2.1	0.8	...	...	...	...	...	...
40-44	2.1	2.9	1.4	...	...	...	...	...	...
45-49	3.2	4.1	2.2	...	...	...	...	...	...
50-54	4.9	6.3	3.6	...	...	...	...	...	...
55-59	7.9	10.5	5.6	...	...	...	...	...	...
60-64	11.8	15.7	8.4	...	...	...	...	...	...
65-69	20.4	27.1	14.9	...	...	...	...	...	...
70-74	32.5	43.4	24.3	...	...	...	...	...	...
75-79	51.2	69.2	39.3	...	...	...	...	...	...
80+	138.6	161.8	126.3	...	...	...	...	...	...
Suriname									
2000									
Total	7.1	8.0	6.1	...	...	...	...	...	...
0-4	4.3	4.2	4.5	...	...	...	...	...	...
5-9	♦0.4	♦0.5	♦0.3	...	...	...	...	...	...
10-14	♦0.5	♦0.7	♦0.3	...	...	...	...	...	...
15-19	1.2	1.5	♦0.9	...	...	...	...	...	...
20-24	1.9	2.8	♦1.0	...	...	...	...	...	...
25-29	2.9	3.5	2.4	...	...	...	...	...	...
30-34	3.4	4.4	2.5	...	...	...	...	...	...
35-39	4.1	5.4	2.8	...	...	...	...	...	...
40-44	5.1	6.8	3.4	...	...	...	...	...	...
45-49	8.1	9.9	6.5	...	...	...	...	...	...
50-54	11.6	14.3	8.9	...	...	...	...	...	...
55-59	15.4	20.1	11.6	...	...	...	...	...	...
60-64	22.3	26.4	18.6	...	...	...	...	...	...
65-69	30.0	36.8	23.9	...	...	...	...	...	...
70-74	45.5	50.4	40.4	...	...	...	...	...	...
75-79	72.7	93.3	56.4	...	...	...	...	...	...
80+	149.8	160.5	141.8	...	...	...	...	...	...
Uruguay[6]									
2000									
Total	9.2	10.2	8.2	...	...	...	...	...	...
0-1	13.9	16.0	11.6	...	...	...	...	...	...
1-4	0.6	0.7	0.5	...	...	...	...	...	...
5-9	0.2	0.3	♦0.1	...	...	...	...	...	...
10-14	0.2	0.2	♦0.2	...	...	...	...	...	...
15-19	0.6	0.9	0.4	...	...	...	...	...	...
20-24	1.1	1.7	0.5	...	...	...	...	...	...
25-29	1.0	1.5	0.6	...	...	...	...	...	...
30-34	1.2	1.6	0.7	...	...	...	...	...	...
35-39	1.7	2.3	1.0	...	...	...	...	...	...
40-44	2.5	2.9	2.1	...	...	...	...	...	...
45-49	4.1	5.4	2.9	...	...	...	...	...	...
50-54	6.5	8.9	4.2	...	...	...	...	...	...
55-59	10.1	14.2	6.4	...	...	...	...	...	...
60-64	14.5	21.2	8.7	...	...	...	...	...	...
65-69	22.4	32.7	14.1	...	...	...	...	...	...
70-74	31.6	45.5	21.3	...	...	...	...	...	...
75-79	50.6	68.9	38.5	...	...	...	...	...	...
80-84	77.6	101.2	64.5	...	...	...	...	...	...
85+	152.4	173.0	143.4	...	...	...	...	...	...

20. Death rates specific for age, sex and urban/rural residence: latest available year
Taux de mortalité selon l'âge, le sexe et la résidence, urbaine/rurale: dernière année disponible
(continued — suite)

(See notes at end of table. — Voir notes à la fin du tableau.)

Continent, country or area, year and age (in years) Continent, pays ou zone, année et âge (en années)	Total			Urban - Urbaine			Rural - Rurale		
	Both sexes Les deux sexes	Male Masculin	Female Féminin	Both sexes Les deux sexes	Male Masculin	Female Féminin	Both sexes Les deux sexes	Male Masculin	Female Féminin
AMERICA, SOUTH — AMERIQUE DU SUD									
Venezuela[7]									
2000									
Total	4.3	5.2	3.4	...	...	...	...	...	...
0-4	3.8	4.2	3.3	...	...	...	...	...	...
5-9	0.4	0.4	0.3	...	...	...	...	...	...
10-14	0.4	0.4	0.3	...	...	...	...	...	...
15-19	1.3	2.1	0.5	...	...	...	...	...	...
20-24	2.1	3.5	0.6	...	...	...	...	...	...
25-29	2.1	3.4	0.8	...	...	...	...	...	...
30-34	2.3	3.4	1.1	...	...	...	...	...	...
35-39	2.3	3.2	1.3	...	...	...	...	...	...
40-44	2.9	4.0	1.9	...	...	...	...	...	...
45-49	3.9	5.1	2.7	...	...	...	...	...	...
50-54	5.3	6.7	4.0	...	...	...	...	...	...
55-59	7.7	9.9	5.5	...	...	...	...	...	...
60-64	13.0	16.1	10.1	...	...	...	...	...	...
65-69	19.0	23.7	14.7	...	...	...	...	...	...
70-74	29.3	37.3	22.4	...	...	...	...	...	...
75-79	45.0	55.9	36.4	...	...	...	...	...	...
80+	125.2	143.9	112.9	...	...	...	...	...	...
ASIA — ASIE									
Armenia - Arménie[8]									
2000									
Total	6.3	6.6	6.0	6.2	6.7	5.7	6.6	6.5	6.6
0-1	15.5	18.4	12.0	16.5	20.1	12.3	13.8	15.6	11.5
1-4	0.8	0.9	0.8	0.8	0.8	0.7	0.9	1.0	◆0.9
5-9	0.2	◆0.2	0.2	0.2	◆0.2	◆0.2	◆0.2	◆0.1	◆0.2
10-14	0.2	0.3	◆0.1	0.2	0.3	◆0.1	◆0.2	◆0.2	◆0.1
15-19	0.4	0.6	◆0.2	0.3	0.5	◆0.2	0.5	0.8	◆0.1
20-24	0.5	0.7	0.3	0.5	0.7	◆0.2	0.5	0.6	◆0.3
25-29	0.6	0.7	0.4	0.6	0.8	0.5	0.5	0.6	◆0.3
30-34	0.9	1.3	0.6	0.9	1.4	0.5	0.9	1.1	◆0.6
35-39	1.4	2.0	0.9	1.5	2.1	0.9	1.4	1.9	0.8
40-44	2.1	2.9	1.3	2.1	3.1	1.2	2.1	2.6	1.7
45-49	3.4	5.0	2.1	3.7	5.5	2.2	2.8	3.7	1.8
50-54	5.7	8.1	3.8	5.9	8.3	3.9	5.2	7.3	3.4
55-59	8.1	11.8	5.1	8.5	12.5	5.2	7.1	9.7	5.0
60-64	15.6	21.2	11.1	16.4	23.0	11.0	14.1	17.7	11.1
65-69	26.0	34.2	19.4	26.4	35.5	19.5	25.3	32.3	19.3
70-74	41.0	48.3	35.4	40.8	46.5	36.3	41.5	51.6	33.9
75-79	58.9	66.4	54.5	55.6	57.7	54.4	66.0	87.2	54.8
80-84	78.1	76.9	78.6	69.0	65.7	70.7	102.3	110.4	98.8
85+	125.8	95.4	144.9	96.9	76.6	109.9	198.6	144.1	231.9
Azerbaijan - Azerbaïdjan+,[8]									
2001									
Total	5.6	6.0	5.2	5.7	6.3	5.1	5.5	5.6	5.3
0-1	12.2	12.6	11.7	11.2	12.5	9.8	12.9	12.7	13.1
1-4	2.3	2.4	2.2	1.4	1.5	1.4	2.9	3.0	2.8
5-9	0.6	0.7	0.5	0.5	0.6	0.4	0.7	0.7	0.6
10-14	0.4	0.4	0.3	0.3	0.4	0.3	0.4	0.5	0.4
15-19	0.6	0.8	0.4	0.5	0.7	0.4	0.6	0.9	0.4
20-24	0.8	1.1	0.5	0.7	1.0	0.4	0.9	1.1	0.7
25-29	1.1	1.5	0.7	1.2	1.6	0.8	1.0	1.3	0.7
30-34	1.4	1.9	1.0	1.5	2.3	0.8	1.4	1.6	1.2
35-39	1.8	2.5	1.1	1.8	2.8	1.0	1.7	2.1	1.2
40-44	2.6	3.7	1.6	2.8	4.1	1.7	2.4	3.2	1.6
45-49	4.3	6.1	2.7	4.7	6.8	2.7	3.8	5.1	2.7

20. Death rates specific for age, sex and urban/rural residence: latest available year
Taux de mortalité selon l'âge, le sexe et la résidence, urbaine/rurale: dernière année disponible
(continued — suite)

(See notes at end of table. — Voir notes à la fin du tableau.)

Continent, country or area, year and age (in years) Continent, pays ou zone, année et âge (en années)	Total			Urban - Urbaine			Rural - Rurale		
	Both sexes Les deux sexes	Male Masculin	Female Féminin	Both sexes Les deux sexes	Male Masculin	Female Féminin	Both sexes Les deux sexes	Male Masculin	Female Féminin
ASIA — ASIE									
Azerbaijan - Azerbaïdjan+,8									
2001									
50-54	7.2	10.0	4.6	7.8	10.9	4.8	6.4	8.5	4.4
55-59	11.4	15.3	8.0	11.8	16.1	8.0	11.0	14.2	8.2
60-64	19.4	25.3	14.5	21.1	28.0	15.2	17.6	22.4	13.8
65-69	30.4	37.8	24.4	32.4	41.5	25.0	28.8	34.6	23.9
70-74	47.0	55.7	40.1	50.2	60.1	42.8	44.0	51.9	37.4
75-79	63.6	74.0	57.3	69.9	79.3	64.5	57.0	68.9	49.4
80-84	87.0	91.2	85.3	98.7	89.8	102.7	76.9	92.7	71.1
85-89	145.9	155.9	142.2	156.1	165.8	152.3	137.7	147.3	134.4
90-94	164.7	177.2	161.0	198.6	157.5	215.0	145.8	193.0	134.0
95-99	165.1	182.9	160.7	121.7	♦100.0	128.9	187.8	245.0	175.8
100+	265.9	210.0	278.3	252.0	♦270.0	247.5	270.0	190.0	287.1
China: Hong Kong SAR - Chine: Hong Kong RAS6									
2000									
Total	5.0	5.8	4.2	...	...	...	...	...	...
0-1	3.1	3.4	2.9	...	...	...	...	...	...
1-4	0.2	♦0.2	♦0.2	...	...	...	...	...	...
5-9	0.1	♦0.1	♦0.1	...	...	...	...	...	...
10-14	0.1	0.1	♦0.1	...	...	...	...	...	...
15-19	0.2	0.2	0.2	...	...	...	...	...	...
20-24	0.4	0.5	0.2	...	...	...	...	...	...
25-29	0.5	0.7	0.3	...	...	...	...	...	...
30-34	0.5	0.7	0.3	...	...	...	...	...	...
35-39	0.7	1.0	0.5	...	...	...	...	...	...
40-44	1.2	1.6	0.8	...	...	...	...	...	...
45-49	1.9	2.5	1.3	...	...	...	...	...	...
50-54	3.0	4.1	1.9	...	...	...	...	...	...
55-59	4.9	6.6	3.0	...	...	...	...	...	...
60-64	8.3	11.4	4.9	...	...	...	...	...	...
65-69	14.1	19.0	9.1	...	...	...	...	...	...
70-74	22.9	30.4	16.1	...	...	...	...	...	...
75-79	37.3	48.2	28.7	...	...	...	...	...	...
80-84	59.4	75.5	48.6	...	...	...	...	...	...
85+	101.3	109.4	97.4	...	...	...	...	...	...
China: Macao SAR - Chine: Macao RAS									
2000									
Total	3.1	3.5	2.6	...	...	...	...	...	...
0-4	♦0.7	♦0.8	♦0.6	...	...	...	...	...	...
5-9	♦0.1	♦0.1	♦0.1	...	...	...	...	...	...
10-14	♦0.1	♦0.2	...	...	...	...	...	...	...
15-19	♦0.3	♦0.3	♦0.2	...	...	...	...	...	...
20-24	♦0.3	♦0.5	♦0.2	...	...	...	...	...	...
25-29	♦0.5	♦0.7	♦0.3	...	...	...	...	...	...
30-34	♦0.4	♦0.7	♦0.3	...	...	...	...	...	...
35-39	0.8	♦1.1	♦0.6	...	...	...	...	...	...
40-44	1.0	1.7	♦0.4	...	...	...	...	...	...
45-49	1.6	2.0	♦1.2	...	...	...	...	...	...
50-54	2.5	3.6	♦1.1	...	...	...	...	...	...
55-59	4.5	6.4	♦2.3	...	...	...	...	...	...
60-64	7.5	10.6	♦4.1	...	...	...	...	...	...
65-69	11.1	15.4	7.3	...	...	...	...	...	...
70-74	18.0	23.9	13.8	...	...	...	...	...	...
75+	42.6	49.3	38.9	...	...	...	...	...	...
Cyprus - Chypre9									
1999									
Total	6.7	6.9	6.5	...	...	...	...	...	...
0-4	1.2	1.2	♦1.2	...	...	...	...	...	...

20. Death rates specific for age, sex and urban/rural residence: latest available year
Taux de mortalité selon l'âge, le sexe et la résidence, urbaine/rurale: dernière année disponible
(continued — suite)

(See notes at end of table. — Voir notes à la fin du tableau.)

Continent, country or area, year and age (in years) / Continent, pays ou zone, année et âge (en années)	Total			Urban - Urbaine			Rural - Rurale		
	Both sexes Les deux sexes	Male Masculin	Female Féminin	Both sexes Les deux sexes	Male Masculin	Female Féminin	Both sexes Les deux sexes	Male Masculin	Female Féminin
ASIA — ASIE									
Cyprus - Chypre[9]									
1999									
5-9	♦0.2	♦0.1	♦0.3	...	...	...	...	...	...
10-14	♦0.2	♦0.3	♦0.2	...	...	...	...	...	...
15-19	0.6	♦0.8	♦0.4	...	...	...	...	...	...
20-24	0.7	♦0.8	♦0.5	...	...	...	...	...	...
25-29	♦0.5	♦0.8	♦0.2	...	...	...	...	...	...
30-34	1.1	♦1.1	♦1.1	...	...	...	...	...	...
35-39	1.5	2.2	♦0.8	...	...	...	...	...	...
40-44	1.1	1.4	♦0.8	...	...	...	...	...	...
45-49	1.5	1.9	♦1.1	...	...	...	...	...	...
50-54	3.4	4.1	2.7	...	...	...	...	...	...
55-59	4.9	7.1	2.8	...	...	...	...	...	...
60-64	8.9	11.6	6.4	...	...	...	...	...	...
65-69	15.3	19.7	11.8	...	...	...	...	...	...
70-74	24.3	27.6	21.6	...	...	...	...	...	...
75-79	41.0	49.0	34.7	...	...	...	...	...	...
80+	125.6	134.9	119.0	...	...	...	...	...	...
Georgia - Géorgie[8]									
2000									
Total	8.4	8.6	8.1	7.8	8.4	7.3	9.1	8.8	9.3
0-1	14.2	15.9	12.2	21.0	23.7	17.8	3.1	♦3.2	♦3.0
1-4	0.4	0.4	♦0.3	0.4	♦0.4	♦0.3	♦0.3	♦0.4	♦0.3
5-9	0.1	♦0.2	♦0.1	♦0.1	♦0.2	♦0.1	♦0.1	♦0.1	♦0.1
10-14	0.1	0.2	♦0.1	0.1	♦0.2	♦0.1	♦0.1	♦0.1	♦0.1
15-19	0.4	0.4	0.3	0.3	0.4	♦0.2	0.4	0.5	0.4
20-24	0.6	0.9	0.3	0.7	1.1	0.3	0.5	0.7	♦0.4
25-29	1.0	1.4	0.4	1.0	1.6	0.4	0.9	1.2	0.6
30-34	1.2	1.9	0.6	1.3	2.1	0.6	1.1	1.7	0.6
35-39	1.8	2.8	0.9	1.9	3.1	0.9	1.6	2.3	0.9
40-44	2.6	4.2	1.2	2.7	4.6	1.2	2.5	3.7	1.2
45-49	3.8	6.0	1.8	4.1	6.7	2.0	3.1	4.8	1.4
50-54	5.6	8.5	3.1	6.0	9.3	3.2	4.9	7.2	2.9
55-59	6.8	10.2	4.1	7.5	11.8	4.3	5.7	8.1	3.7
60-64	13.4	17.9	9.7	14.2	20.2	9.5	12.3	15.2	9.9
65-69	21.6	30.3	15.2	22.2	32.1	15.2	21.0	28.5	15.1
70-74	35.2	46.6	27.8	36.5	50.2	28.4	33.8	43.3	27.1
75-79	54.1	68.8	47.5	55.5	67.5	50.4	52.6	70.1	44.6
80-84	77.9	57.6	92.5	79.6	54.3	99.0	76.3	61.1	86.5
85+	164.4	109.3	204.4	146.4	96.7	181.0	182.6	121.3	228.9
Israel - Israël[5,10]									
1998									
Total	6.2	6.4	6.0	...	...	...	...	...	...
0-1	6.1	6.8	5.3	...	...	...	...	...	...
1-4	0.4	0.5	0.3	...	...	...	...	...	...
5-9	0.2	0.2	0.1	...	...	...	...	...	...
10-14	0.1	0.2	♦0.1	...	...	...	...	...	...
15-19	0.4	0.6	0.2	...	...	...	...	...	...
20-24	0.6	0.9	0.2	...	...	...	...	...	...
25-29	0.6	0.8	0.3	...	...	...	...	...	...
30-34	0.7	1.0	0.4	...	...	...	...	...	...
35-39	1.0	1.4	0.7	...	...	...	...	...	...
40-44	1.4	1.9	1.0	...	...	...	...	...	...
45-49	2.2	2.8	1.7	...	...	...	...	...	...
50-54	3.8	4.8	2.8	...	...	...	...	...	...
55-59	6.2	8.2	4.4	...	...	...	...	...	...
60-64	10.4	13.4	7.9	...	...	...	...	...	...
65-69	17.6	22.7	13.5	...	...	...	...	...	...
70-74	27.8	34.3	23.1	...	...	...	...	...	...
75-79	46.4	54.6	40.3	...	...	...	...	...	...

20. Death rates specific for age, sex and urban/rural residence: latest available year
Taux de mortalité selon l'âge, le sexe et la résidence, urbaine/rurale: dernière année disponible
(continued — suite)

(See notes at end of table. — Voir notes à la fin du tableau.)

Continent, country or area, year and age (in years) / Continent, pays ou zone, année et âge (en années)	Total			Urban - Urbaine			Rural - Rurale		
	Both sexes Les deux sexes	Male Masculin	Female Féminin	Both sexes Les deux sexes	Male Masculin	Female Féminin	Both sexes Les deux sexes	Male Masculin	Female Féminin
ASIA — ASIE									
Israel - Israël[5,10]									
1998									
80-84	83.6	93.6	77.0	...	...	...	...	...	...
85+	165.6	174.1	159.9	...	...	...	...	...	...
Japan - Japon[11]									
2000									
Total	7.6	8.5	6.7	...	...	...	...	...	...
0-1	3.3	3.5	3.0	...	...	...	...	...	...
1-4	0.3	0.3	0.3	...	...	...	...	...	...
5-9	0.1	0.1	0.1	...	...	...	...	...	...
10-14	0.1	0.1	0.1	...	...	...	...	...	...
15-19	0.3	0.4	0.2	...	...	...	...	...	...
20-24	0.5	0.7	0.3	...	...	...	...	...	...
25-29	0.5	0.7	0.3	...	...	...	...	...	...
30-34	0.6	0.8	0.4	...	...	...	...	...	...
35-39	0.9	1.1	0.6	...	...	...	...	...	...
40-44	1.3	1.7	0.9	...	...	...	...	...	...
45-49	2.2	2.9	1.5	...	...	...	...	...	...
50-54	3.4	4.6	2.2	...	...	...	...	...	...
55-59	5.3	7.4	3.2	...	...	...	...	...	...
60-64	7.8	11.3	4.6	...	...	...	...	...	...
65-69	12.5	18.2	7.5	...	...	...	...	...	...
70-74	19.7	28.6	12.4	...	...	...	...	...	...
75-79	31.6	45.5	22.6	...	...	...	...	...	...
80-84	56.2	80.3	43.3	...	...	...	...	...	...
85-89	97.2	131.5	81.7	...	...	...	...	...	...
90-94	159.4	206.5	142.7	...	...	...	...	...	...
95-99	246.7	304.8	231.1	...	...	...	...	...	...
100+	390.7	481.0	372.9	...	...	...	...	...	...
Kazakhstan[8]									
1999									
Total	9.8	11.1	8.6	10.9	12.8	9.3	8.3	9.0	7.6
0-1	20.9	23.8	17.8	23.0	26.5	19.2	18.9	21.2	16.4
1-4	1.6	1.7	1.5	1.2	1.3	1.1	1.9	1.9	1.8
5-9	0.5	0.6	0.4	0.5	0.5	0.4	0.5	0.6	0.4
10-14	0.5	0.6	0.4	0.5	0.6	0.3	0.5	0.6	0.4
15-19	1.2	1.6	0.7	1.2	1.8	0.7	1.1	1.5	0.8
20-24	2.2	3.3	1.1	2.4	3.9	1.0	2.0	2.7	1.1
25-29	3.1	4.4	1.6	2.9	4.6	1.4	3.3	4.1	2.1
30-34	3.7	5.4	1.9	3.8	5.8	1.9	3.5	4.8	2.1
35-39	4.7	7.0	2.5	5.1	7.9	2.4	4.2	5.7	2.6
40-44	6.4	9.6	3.4	7.0	10.9	3.5	5.5	7.7	3.3
45-49	9.2	13.7	5.1	9.8	15.2	5.3	8.1	11.5	4.9
50-54	13.2	19.8	7.4	14.2	22.1	7.6	11.4	16.2	6.9
55-59	19.8	29.0	12.5	21.5	32.9	13.0	17.6	24.1	11.9
60-64	29.0	42.7	18.5	30.5	47.1	18.7	26.9	37.1	18.3
65-69	41.9	62.7	28.1	44.2	69.6	28.9	38.6	54.1	26.9
70-74	57.3	82.1	44.9	61.1	89.9	47.6	51.4	71.4	40.4
75-79	80.2	110.1	69.6	85.6	119.0	74.5	72.4	98.6	62.3
80-84	123.2	162.2	111.7	138.2	180.3	126.3	103.0	139.6	91.5
85-89	170.7	220.9	158.9	205.7	255.7	193.8	133.2	183.1	121.6
90-94	191.0	256.3	178.2	243.4	310.5	230.7	148.5	214.3	135.2
95+	312.6	293.5	317.1	275.6	235.3	284.7	347.7	345.9	348.1
Korea (Republic of) - Corée (République de)[12]									
2000									
Total	5.2	5.8	4.7	...	...	...	...	...	...
0-1	4.1	4.1	4.1	...	...	...	...	...	...
1-4	0.4	0.5	0.4	...	...	...	...	...	...
5-9	0.3	0.3	0.2	...	...	...	...	...	...

20. Death rates specific for age, sex and urban/rural residence: latest available year
Taux de mortalité selon l'âge, le sexe et la résidence, urbaine/rurale: dernière année disponible
(continued — suite)

(See notes at end of table. — Voir notes à la fin du tableau.)

Continent, country or area, year and age (in years) / Continent, pays ou zone, année et âge (en années)	Total			Urban - Urbaine			Rural - Rurale		
	Both sexes Les deux sexes	Male Masculin	Female Féminin	Both sexes Les deux sexes	Male Masculin	Female Féminin	Both sexes Les deux sexes	Male Masculin	Female Féminin
ASIA — ASIE									
Korea (Republic of) - Corée (République de)[12]									
2000									
10-14	0.2	0.2	0.2	...	...	...	...	...	...
15-19	0.5	0.6	0.3	...	...	...	...	...	...
20-24	0.7	0.9	0.4	...	...	...	...	...	...
25-29	0.8	1.1	0.5	...	...	...	...	...	...
30-34	1.0	1.4	0.7	...	...	...	...	...	...
35-39	1.6	2.2	0.9	...	...	...	...	...	...
40-44	2.5	3.6	1.3	...	...	...	...	...	...
45-49	3.6	5.5	1.7	...	...	...	...	...	...
50-54	5.4	8.0	2.7	...	...	...	...	...	...
55-59	8.5	12.6	4.6	...	...	...	...	...	...
60-64	12.3	18.1	7.0	...	...	...	...	...	...
65-69	18.4	26.4	12.3	...	...	...	...	...	...
70-74	31.8	44.3	24.1	...	...	...	...	...	...
75-79	54.3	73.5	43.7	...	...	...	...	...	...
80+	130.9	153.6	122.0	...	...	...	...	...	...
Kuwait - Koweït									
1998									
Total	2.1	2.2	1.9	...	...	...	...	...	...
0-1	11.6	12.6	10.6	...	...	...	...	...	...
1-4	0.6	0.6	0.5	...	...	...	...	...	...
5-9	0.3	♦0.3	♦0.3	...	...	...	...	...	...
10-14	0.2	♦0.3	♦0.2	...	...	...	...	...	...
15-19	0.6	0.9	♦0.3	...	...	...	...	...	...
20-24	0.7	1.0	0.4	...	...	...	...	...	...
25-29	0.5	0.6	0.4	...	...	...	...	...	...
30-34	0.6	0.7	0.4	...	...	...	...	...	...
35-39	0.8	0.9	0.7	...	...	...	...	...	...
40-44	1.3	1.5	0.8	...	...	...	...	...	...
45-49	2.0	2.1	1.5	...	...	...	...	...	...
50-54	3.9	4.3	3.1	...	...	...	...	...	...
55-59	7.0	7.0	6.9	...	...	...	...	...	...
60-64	13.5	12.8	14.7	...	...	...	...	...	...
65-69	25.9	27.3	24.1	...	...	...	...	...	...
70-74	46.3	47.0	45.5	...	...	...	...	...	...
75-79	69.7	77.6	62.1	...	...	...	...	...	...
80-84	120.8	119.3	122.4	...	...	...	...	...	...
85+	172.8	181.2	165.1	...	...	...	...	...	...
Kyrgyzstan - Kirghizistan[8]									
2000									
Total	7.0	7.8	6.3	8.0	9.3	6.9	6.5	7.0	5.9
0-1	21.8	25.1	18.3	30.2	34.0	26.3	18.6	21.8	15.3
1-4	2.6	2.8	2.4	1.6	1.9	1.4	3.0	3.2	2.7
5-9	0.5	0.5	0.4	0.3	0.4	♦0.3	0.5	0.6	0.5
10-14	0.4	0.5	0.4	0.4	0.4	0.4	0.4	0.5	0.3
15-19	0.7	0.9	0.6	0.6	0.7	0.5	0.8	0.9	0.6
20-24	1.4	2.0	0.9	1.3	1.9	0.7	1.6	2.1	1.0
25-29	2.1	3.1	1.1	2.2	3.4	1.0	2.1	2.9	1.1
30-34	2.8	4.1	1.5	2.8	4.4	1.2	2.8	3.9	1.8
35-39	3.9	5.7	2.0	4.2	6.7	2.0	3.6	5.2	2.1
40-44	5.4	8.0	2.8	6.1	10.0	2.7	4.9	6.8	2.9
45-49	7.6	11.1	4.3	8.3	13.0	4.2	7.1	9.9	4.4
50-54	11.5	16.5	6.9	12.3	19.0	6.7	10.8	14.8	7.1
55-59	16.4	22.5	10.9	18.1	26.6	11.2	15.3	20.1	10.7
60-64	23.8	31.9	17.0	25.5	37.2	16.7	22.6	28.7	17.2
65-69	35.9	47.9	26.4	38.1	56.1	25.8	34.7	43.9	26.8
70-74	50.3	62.8	41.4	53.7	74.1	42.4	48.2	57.3	40.7
75-79	72.5	85.3	66.0	79.6	105.5	69.0	68.0	75.2	63.8

20. Death rates specific for age, sex and urban/rural residence: latest available year
Taux de mortalité selon l'âge, le sexe et la résidence, urbaine/rurale: dernière année disponible
(continued — suite)

(See notes at end of table. — Voir notes à la fin du tableau.)

Continent, country or area, year and age (in years) Continent, pays ou zone, année et âge (en années)	Total			Urban - Urbaine			Rural - Rurale		
	Both sexes Les deux sexes	Male Masculin	Female Féminin	Both sexes Les deux sexes	Male Masculin	Female Féminin	Both sexes Les deux sexes	Male Masculin	Female Féminin
ASIA — ASIE									
Kyrgyzstan - Kirghizistan[8]									
2000									
80-84	117.7	132.3	112.0	131.9	151.4	125.0	108.0	120.5	102.8
85-89	172.8	194.7	165.0	201.0	211.8	197.5	154.2	184.7	142.6
90-94	226.0	238.8	221.6	261.2	221.8	273.8	212.0	245.1	200.2
95+	304.9	394.6	286.7	325.6	♦446.4	305.4	300.9	386.4	283.0
Malaysia - Malaisie									
1998									
Total	4.4	5.0	3.8	...	...	...	...	...	...
0-1	8.6	9.4	7.7	...	...	...	...	...	...
1-4	0.7	0.7	0.7	...	...	...	...	...	...
5-9	0.4	0.4	0.3	...	...	...	...	...	...
10-14	0.4	0.5	0.3	...	...	...	...	...	...
15-19	0.9	1.3	0.4	...	...	...	...	...	...
20-24	1.1	1.7	0.5	...	...	...	...	...	...
25-29	1.2	1.8	0.6	...	...	...	...	...	...
30-34	1.6	2.2	0.9	...	...	...	...	...	...
35-39	2.0	2.8	1.2	...	...	...	...	...	...
40-44	2.7	3.7	1.8	...	...	...	...	...	...
45-49	3.9	5.0	2.8	...	...	...	...	...	...
50-54	6.6	8.3	4.8	...	...	...	...	...	...
55-59	10.7	13.2	8.2	...	...	...	...	...	...
60-64	18.2	22.1	14.5	...	...	...	...	...	...
65-69	29.6	35.0	24.8	...	...	...	...	...	...
70-74	48.0	56.6	40.8	...	...	...	...	...	...
75+	109.8	121.6	101.0	...	...	...	...	...	...
Maldives									
1996									
Total	4.7	5.2	4.2	...	...	...	...	...	...
0-4	6.3	6.6	6.1	...	...	...	...	...	...
5-9	♦0.5	♦0.5	♦0.6	...	...	...	...	...	...
10-14	♦0.4	♦0.4	♦0.3	...	...	...	...	...	...
15-19	♦0.5	♦0.5	♦0.5	...	...	...	...	...	...
20-24	♦0.5	♦0.5	♦0.4	...	...	...	...	...	...
25-29	♦1.1	♦1.2	♦1.1	...	...	...	...	...	...
30-34	♦0.7	♦0.6	♦0.9	...	...	...	...	...	...
35-39	3.4	♦3.7	♦3.0	...	...	...	...	...	...
40-44	♦3.1	♦3.3	♦2.8	...	...	...	...	...	...
45-49	7.0	♦7.7	♦6.4	...	...	...	...	...	...
50-54	6.7	♦7.7	♦5.7	...	...	...	...	...	...
55-59	14.3	17.2	11.0	...	...	...	...	...	...
60-64	25.5	26.0	24.8	...	...	...	...	...	...
65-69	33.8	32.6	35.5	...	...	...	...	...	...
70-74	57.0	56.9	57.2	...	...	...	...	...	...
75+	91.1	87.2	96.8	...	...	...	...	...	...
Mongolia - Mongolie									
2000									
Total	6.5	7.4	5.7	6.6	...	...	6.4	...	...
0-1	32.0	34.0	30.1	34.0	...	...	30.3	...	...
1-4	3.2	3.6	2.8	3.1	...	...	3.4	...	...
5-9	0.5	0.6	0.4	0.4	...	...	0.6	...	...
10-14	0.4	0.5	0.3	0.4	...	...	0.3	...	...
15-19	0.7	1.0	0.5	0.7	...	...	0.7	...	...
20-24	1.4	1.8	1.0	1.5	...	...	1.2	...	...
25-29	2.1	2.8	1.3	2.3	...	...	1.7	...	...
30-34	3.1	4.4	1.9	3.3	...	...	2.9	...	...
35-39	4.0	5.1	2.9	4.2	...	...	3.5	...	...
40-44	6.3	8.6	4.0	6.9	...	...	5.3	...	...
45-49	9.1	11.9	6.5	8.8	...	...	9.6	...	...
50-54	15.0	19.2	11.1	15.5	...	...	14.3	...	...

20. Death rates specific for age, sex and urban/rural residence: latest available year
Taux de mortalité selon l'âge, le sexe et la résidence, urbaine/rurale: dernière année disponible
(continued — suite)

(See notes at end of table. — Voir notes à la fin du tableau.)

Continent, country or area, year and age (in years) / Continent, pays ou zone, année et âge (en années)	Total			Urban - Urbaine			Rural - Rurale		
	Both sexes Les deux sexes	Male Masculin	Female Féminin	Both sexes Les deux sexes	Male Masculin	Female Féminin	Both sexes Les deux sexes	Male Masculin	Female Féminin
ASIA — ASIE									
Mongolia - Mongolie									
2000									
55-59	18.8	22.9	14.9	20.2	...	...	17.2	...	...
60-64	29.5	34.8	24.4	31.9	...	...	26.9	...	...
65-69	42.8	51.7	35.4	45.8	...	...	39.5	...	...
70-74	77.1	93.2	64.8	69.4	...	...	86.1	...	...
75-79	71.1	83.7	63.0	75.3	...	...	66.3	...	...
80-84	122.7	163.2	102.6	136.6	...	...	106.5	...	...
85-89	192.8	268.4	161.4	236.0	...	...	146.6	...	...
90-94	317.6	373.5	294.1	390.0	...	...	243.0	...	...
95+	417.8	543.9	375.0	554.6	...	...	♦264.2	...	...
Pakistan[13,14]									
1997									
Total	8.9	9.5	8.3	7.3	7.7	6.9	9.6	10.3	8.9
0-4	26.9	28.0	25.8	22.0	21.9	22.0	29.0	30.6	27.4
5-9	1.4	1.4	1.3	0.8	0.7	0.9	1.6	1.7	1.5
10-14	1.0	1.0	1.1	0.9	1.1	0.7	1.1	0.9	1.3
15-19	1.8	1.4	2.3	1.2	1.3	1.1	2.2	1.5	2.9
20-24	2.7	2.4	3.0	1.7	1.9	1.6	3.3	2.7	3.7
25-29	2.6	3.1	2.1	2.2	2.5	1.8	2.9	3.5	2.3
30-34	3.5	3.1	4.0	2.6	2.1	3.1	4.1	3.7	4.4
35-39	3.2	3.5	2.8	2.3	2.8	1.9	3.6	3.8	3.3
40-44	3.2	3.5	3.0	2.5	2.1	3.0	3.6	4.2	3.0
45-49	7.7	9.6	5.8	8.8	10.8	6.5	7.2	9.0	5.4
50-54	11.0	10.9	11.0	12.0	10.9	13.4	10.5	10.9	10.0
55-59	13.8	16.6	10.8	17.3	23.8	10.6	12.1	13.1	11.0
60-64	21.9	24.8	18.1	18.1	19.9	16.0	23.4	26.8	19.1
65-69	35.7	36.3	35.1	40.4	38.3	42.9	33.7	35.3	31.9
70+	80.2	85.0	73.6	77.6	82.0	72.2	81.1	86.1	74.2
Singapore - Singapour[15]									
2000									
Total	4.8	5.3	4.3	...	...	...	...	...	...
0-4	0.9	1.0	0.8	...	...	...	...	...	...
5-9	0.1	♦0.1	♦0.2	...	...	...	...	...	...
10-14	0.2	0.3	♦0.2	...	...	...	...	...	...
15-19	0.4	0.4	♦0.3	...	...	...	...	...	...
20-24	0.8	1.2	0.4	...	...	...	...	...	...
25-29	0.8	1.2	0.4	...	...	...	...	...	...
30-34	0.9	1.2	0.6	...	...	...	...	...	...
35-39	1.1	1.6	0.7	...	...	...	...	...	...
40-44	1.6	2.0	1.1	...	...	...	...	...	...
45-49	2.4	3.0	1.7	...	...	...	...	...	...
50-54	3.7	4.5	2.8	...	...	...	...	...	...
55-59	6.5	8.4	4.6	...	...	...	...	...	...
60-64	11.7	15.1	8.6	...	...	...	...	...	...
65-69	20.2	25.3	15.5	...	...	...	...	...	...
70-74	29.5	36.5	23.4	...	...	...	...	...	...
75-79	51.6	61.9	43.3	...	...	...	...	...	...
80+	109.1	124.8	100.0	...	...	...	...	...	...
Sri Lanka+									
1996									
Total	6.7	8.5	4.7	...	...	...	...	...	...
0-4	3.1	3.4	2.8	...	...	...	...	...	...
5-9	0.4	0.5	0.4	...	...	...	...	...	...
10-14	0.5	0.5	0.4	...	...	...	...	...	...
15-19	1.7	2.5	0.9	...	...	...	...	...	...
20-24	3.3	5.5	1.0	...	...	...	...	...	...
25-29	3.7	6.3	1.2	...	...	...	...	...	...
30-34	3.4	5.5	1.2	...	...	...	...	...	...
35-39	4.7	7.3	2.0	...	...	...	...	...	...

20. Death rates specific for age, sex and urban/rural residence: latest available year
Taux de mortalité selon l'âge, le sexe et la résidence, urbaine/rurale: dernière année disponible
(continued — suite)

(See notes at end of table. — Voir notes à la fin du tableau.)

Continent, country or area, year and age (in years) Continent, pays ou zone, année et âge (en années)	Total			Urban - Urbaine			Rural - Rurale		
	Both sexes Les deux sexes	Male Masculin	Female Féminin	Both sexes Les deux sexes	Male Masculin	Female Féminin	Both sexes Les deux sexes	Male Masculin	Female Féminin
ASIA — ASIE									
Sri Lanka+									
1996									
40-44	5.3	8.1	2.4	...	...	...	...	...	...
45-49	7.7	11.3	4.1	...	...	...	...	...	...
50-54	9.6	12.9	6.0	...	...	...	...	...	...
55-59	13.2	17.7	8.2	...	...	...	...	...	...
60-64	20.1	24.5	15.0	...	...	...	...	...	...
65-69	34.5	41.2	27.0	...	...	...	...	...	...
70-74	56.3	61.9	49.8	...	...	...	...	...	...
75-79	81.7	88.1	74.6	...	...	...	...	...	...
80+	176.8	177.6	176.1	...	...	...	...	...	...
Tajikistan - Tadjikistan[8]									
1993									
Total	8.8	10.6	6.9	9.2	11.1	7.4	8.6	10.4	6.7
0-1	47.0	52.2	41.4	54.6	62.9	45.8	44.8	49.2	40.2
1-4	8.7	9.0	8.5	5.5	5.7	5.2	9.7	10.0	9.4
5-9	1.0	1.1	0.8	0.7	0.9	0.5	1.0	1.1	0.9
10-14	0.8	0.9	0.6	0.6	0.8	0.4	0.8	1.0	0.6
15-19	1.4	2.1	0.8	1.4	2.1	0.6	1.5	2.0	0.9
20-24	3.0	4.7	1.4	2.8	4.0	1.2	3.1	5.0	1.4
25-29	4.8	8.3	1.6	4.7	8.6	1.1	4.8	8.1	1.8
30-34	5.8	9.4	2.3	5.9	10.3	1.9	5.8	9.1	2.5
35-39	6.8	10.7	3.0	6.3	10.8	2.2	7.1	10.7	3.4
40-44	7.9	12.2	3.8	7.3	11.5	3.5	8.3	12.6	4.0
45-49	10.3	15.1	5.1	9.5	14.4	4.7	10.8	15.5	5.4
50-54	13.2	18.5	7.4	12.5	18.7	6.8	13.6	18.4	7.9
55-59	17.3	23.8	10.9	17.6	25.8	10.3	17.1	22.7	11.3
60-64	24.8	33.2	17.1	26.2	36.8	17.9	24.1	31.5	16.7
65-69	34.3	43.1	27.1	36.7	51.0	27.8	32.9	39.4	26.6
70-74	47.0	59.8	39.4	50.5	66.0	43.0	45.1	57.0	37.2
75-79	71.8	89.9	61.7	79.8	104.7	69.2	66.4	82.5	55.9
80-84	105.7	125.7	94.2	128.0	148.3	119.2	93.0	115.9	77.7
85+	174.2	185.2	167.2	191.7	221.3	179.6	167.6	176.0	161.3
Uzbekistan - Ouzbékistan[8]									
2000									
Total	5.5	5.8	5.2	6.6	7.1	6.2	4.8	5.0	4.6
0-1	19.1	21.4	16.6	22.6	25.4	19.6	17.5	19.6	15.3
1-4	2.3	2.4	2.2	1.6	1.7	1.5	2.6	2.8	2.5
5-9	0.4	0.5	0.4	0.4	0.5	0.3	0.5	0.6	0.4
10-14	0.5	0.5	0.4	0.4	0.5	0.4	0.5	0.6	0.4
15-19	0.7	0.9	0.5	0.7	1.0	0.5	0.7	0.9	0.5
20-24	1.3	1.6	1.0	1.4	1.9	0.9	1.2	1.4	1.0
25-29	1.7	2.2	1.3	1.9	2.5	1.2	1.6	1.9	1.3
30-34	2.1	2.9	1.4	2.4	3.3	1.4	2.0	2.5	1.5
35-39	2.5	3.4	1.7	3.0	4.3	1.7	2.2	2.7	1.6
40-44	3.6	4.8	2.6	4.4	6.3	2.6	3.1	3.7	2.5
45-49	5.4	7.2	3.7	6.2	8.9	3.7	4.7	5.8	3.6
50-54	9.4	12.2	6.7	10.2	14.1	6.7	8.5	10.4	6.6
55-59	14.2	17.6	10.8	15.3	20.9	10.2	13.2	15.0	11.3
60-64	22.3	27.5	17.5	23.3	31.4	16.5	21.5	24.5	18.4
65-69	35.9	43.2	29.7	37.2	49.2	28.2	34.8	39.0	30.9
70-74	52.7	61.0	46.2	54.6	69.8	45.0	51.2	55.1	47.4
75-79	72.9	80.3	68.9	73.8	84.7	69.0	72.1	77.2	68.8
80-84	114.2	129.9	108.1	115.6	127.9	111.3	112.9	131.6	104.7
85-89	164.0	194.7	152.6	166.2	183.1	160.8	161.7	204.8	143.4
90-94	195.5	192.3	197.2	171.3	152.4	179.9	215.8	219.9	213.3
95+	316.6	202.4	394.2	156.3	168.0	151.3	460.7	220.9	700.6

20. Death rates specific for age, sex and urban/rural residence: latest available year
Taux de mortalité selon l'âge, le sexe et la résidence, urbaine/rurale: dernière année disponible
(continued — suite)

(See notes at end of table. — Voir notes à la fin du tableau.)

Continent, country or area, year and age (in years) Continent, pays ou zone, année et âge (en années)	Total			Urban - Urbaine			Rural - Rurale		
	Both sexes Les deux sexes	Male Masculin	Female Féminin	Both sexes Les deux sexes	Male Masculin	Female Féminin	Both sexes Les deux sexes	Male Masculin	Female Féminin
EUROPE									
Austria - Autriche									
2001									
Total	9.2	8.7	9.6	...	...	...	...	...	...
0-4	1.1	1.3	0.9	...	...	...	...	...	...
5-9	0.1	♦0.1	♦0.1	...	...	...	...	...	...
10-14	0.1	♦0.1	0.1	...	...	...	...	...	...
15-19	0.5	0.8	0.3	...	...	...	...	...	...
20-24	0.6	0.9	0.3	...	...	...	...	...	...
25-29	0.6	0.9	0.3	...	...	...	...	...	...
30-34	0.7	0.9	0.4	...	...	...	...	...	...
35-39	1.0	1.3	0.6	...	...	...	...	...	...
40-44	1.7	2.2	1.2	...	...	...	...	...	...
45-49	2.8	3.7	1.9	...	...	...	...	...	...
50-54	4.5	5.8	3.2	...	...	...	...	...	...
55-59	6.7	9.2	4.2	...	...	...	...	...	...
60-64	9.1	12.3	6.2	...	...	...	...	...	...
65-69	15.3	21.6	9.8	...	...	...	...	...	...
70-74	24.6	33.7	17.7	...	...	...	...	...	...
75-79	40.3	54.4	33.0	...	...	...	...	...	...
80-84	68.1	87.2	59.6	...	...	...	...	...	...
85+	166.4	179.3	161.9	...	...	...	...	...	...
Belarus - Bélarus[8]									
1999									
Total	14.1	15.7	12.8	10.6	12.5	8.9	22.2	23.0	21.5
0-1	11.7	13.7	9.5	10.3	12.1	8.4	14.6	17.2	11.9
1-4	0.8	1.0	0.7	0.6	0.7	0.4	1.4	1.5	1.2
5-9	0.3	0.4	0.2	0.2	0.3	0.2	0.4	0.5	♦0.3
10-14	0.3	0.4	0.2	0.3	0.3	0.2	0.4	0.6	♦0.3
15-19	0.9	1.2	0.6	0.8	0.9	0.5	1.4	1.9	0.8
20-24	1.9	3.1	0.8	1.6	2.5	0.7	3.1	4.8	1.1
25-29	2.6	4.2	0.9	2.2	3.5	0.8	3.7	6.0	1.2
30-34	3.2	5.3	1.2	2.8	4.7	1.1	4.4	6.8	1.6
35-39	4.2	6.7	1.7	3.7	6.1	1.5	5.7	8.3	2.4
40-44	6.0	9.5	2.6	5.3	8.5	2.4	8.2	12.1	3.5
45-49	8.9	14.1	4.1	8.0	12.8	3.8	11.8	17.9	5.0
50-54	13.6	20.8	7.1	12.6	19.4	6.7	16.3	24.4	8.4
55-59	18.2	28.9	9.7	17.8	27.9	9.6	19.1	30.7	10.0
60-64	25.5	40.0	14.9	25.1	39.4	14.6	26.0	40.9	15.4
65-69	34.4	52.6	22.6	35.5	54.8	23.2	33.4	50.6	22.1
70-74	50.1	74.8	37.7	51.2	75.1	38.7	49.0	74.5	36.8
75-79	77.7	105.3	67.1	76.6	103.1	66.3	78.7	107.2	67.9
80-84	123.3	154.9	113.5	121.2	152.2	110.7	125.2	157.5	115.8
85-89	197.3	233.5	187.5	185.1	226.1	173.4	205.8	239.0	197.2
90-94	292.2	329.2	282.8	272.1	294.5	266.5	305.1	350.9	293.3
95+	373.9	429.4	363.4	342.0	383.9	333.8	389.6	453.0	377.9
Belgium - Belgique[16]									
2001									
Total	10.1	10.2	9.9	...	...	...	...	...	...
0-4	1.1	1.3	1.0	...	...	...	...	...	...
5-9	0.2	0.2	0.1	...	...	...	...	...	...
10-14	0.2	0.2	0.1	...	...	...	...	...	...
15-19	0.5	0.7	0.3	...	...	...	...	...	...
20-24	0.8	1.2	0.3	...	...	...	...	...	...
25-29	0.8	1.2	0.4	...	...	...	...	...	...
30-34	0.9	1.2	0.5	...	...	...	...	...	...
35-39	1.2	1.5	0.8	...	...	...	...	...	...
40-44	1.9	2.5	1.4	...	...	...	...	...	...
45-49	3.1	4.1	2.1	...	...	...	...	...	...
50-54	4.6	5.9	3.3	...	...	...	...	...	...
55-59	6.9	9.1	4.7	...	...	...	...	...	...

20. Death rates specific for age, sex and urban/rural residence: latest available year
Taux de mortalité selon l'âge, le sexe et la résidence, urbaine/rurale: dernière année disponible
(continued — suite)

(See notes at end of table. — Voir notes à la fin du tableau.)

Continent, country or area, year and age (in years) / Continent, pays ou zone, année et âge (en années)	Total			Urban - Urbaine			Rural - Rurale		
	Both sexes Les deux sexes	Male Masculin	Female Féminin	Both sexes Les deux sexes	Male Masculin	Female Féminin	Both sexes Les deux sexes	Male Masculin	Female Féminin
EUROPE									
Belgium - Belgique[16]									
2001									
60-64	10.0	13.8	6.5	...	...	...	...	...	...
65-69	15.9	22.0	10.6	...	...	...	...	...	...
70-74	25.9	36.0	18.1	...	...	...	...	...	...
75-79	44.1	60.3	33.3	...	...	...	...	...	...
80-84	75.0	99.1	62.0	...	...	...	...	...	...
85+	173.2	205.5	161.9	...	...	...	...	...	...
Bulgaria - Bulgarie									
2001									
Total	14.2	15.6	12.9	11.5	12.8	10.2	20.4	21.8	19.0
0-1	14.7	16.0	13.4	13.3	14.5	12.1	18.1	19.7	16.4
1-4	0.7	0.7	0.7	0.6	0.6	0.6	1.0	1.0	0.9
5-9	0.3	0.3	0.3	0.2	0.3	◆0.2	0.4	◆0.3	◆0.4
10-14	0.3	0.3	0.2	0.2	0.3	0.2	0.3	0.4	◆0.2
15-19	0.6	0.7	0.4	0.5	0.7	0.4	0.7	1.0	◆0.5
20-24	0.9	1.2	0.5	0.8	1.2	0.4	0.9	1.1	0.7
25-29	0.9	1.3	0.5	0.9	1.2	0.5	1.1	1.5	0.7
30-34	1.3	1.8	0.8	1.2	1.7	0.7	1.5	1.9	1.0
35-39	1.9	2.6	1.3	1.8	2.4	1.1	2.5	3.2	1.7
40-44	3.2	4.6	1.9	3.0	4.3	1.8	3.9	5.4	2.3
45-49	5.3	7.6	3.1	4.9	6.9	3.1	6.6	9.5	3.3
50-54	8.2	12.2	4.5	7.6	11.3	4.3	9.7	14.3	5.0
55-59	12.3	18.2	7.0	12.1	17.9	6.9	12.6	18.8	7.2
60-64	18.8	27.3	11.5	18.8	27.3	11.6	18.8	27.4	11.4
65-69	27.6	37.6	19.4	27.5	38.0	19.4	27.6	37.2	19.4
70-74	45.1	57.5	35.7	45.2	58.5	35.4	45.0	56.2	36.2
75-79	74.9	88.6	65.7	75.4	89.7	65.9	74.4	87.4	65.4
80-84	120.2	134.1	111.5	117.7	131.4	109.3	123.0	136.9	113.9
85+	233.4	244.9	227.0	226.0	238.1	219.6	241.1	251.6	235.0
Croatia - Croatie									
2001									
Total	11.2	11.7	10.6	...	...	...	...	...	...
0-1	7.3	7.6	7.1	...	...	...	...	...	...
1-4	0.3	0.4	◆0.2	...	...	...	...	...	...
5-9	0.2	◆0.2	◆0.1	...	...	...	...	...	...
10-14	0.2	◆0.2	◆0.1	...	...	...	...	...	...
15-19	0.5	0.8	0.3	...	...	...	...	...	...
20-24	0.8	1.2	0.3	...	...	...	...	...	...
25-29	0.7	1.1	0.3	...	...	...	...	...	...
30-34	0.9	1.2	0.5	...	...	...	...	...	...
35-39	1.4	2.1	0.8	...	...	...	...	...	...
40-44	2.4	3.5	1.3	...	...	...	...	...	...
45-49	4.0	5.9	2.1	...	...	...	...	...	...
50-54	6.5	9.4	3.7	...	...	...	...	...	...
55-59	9.8	14.4	5.6	...	...	...	...	...	...
60-64	15.2	22.4	9.1	...	...	...	...	...	...
65-69	24.2	34.9	16.0	...	...	...	...	...	...
70-74	39.4	54.0	29.5	...	...	...	...	...	...
75-79	62.9	80.2	54.7	...	...	...	...	...	...
80-84	106.1	126.4	97.4	...	...	...	...	...	...
85-89	168.3	191.3	159.3	...	...	...	...	...	...
90-94	275.0	318.9	260.5	...	...	...	...	...	...
95-99	394.6	404.0	392.0	...	...	...	...	...	...
100+	607.1	◆666.7	555.6	...	...	...	...	...	...
Czech Republic - République tchèque									
2000									
Total	10.6	11.0	10.3	10.3	10.6	9.9	11.7	12.0	11.3
0-1	4.1	4.6	3.5	4.1	4.7	3.4	4.2	4.5	3.9

20. Death rates specific for age, sex and urban/rural residence: latest available year
Taux de mortalité selon l'âge, le sexe et la résidence, urbaine/rurale: dernière année disponible
(continued — suite)

(See notes at end of table. — Voir notes à la fin du tableau.)

Continent, country or area, year and age (in years) / Continent, pays ou zone, année et âge (en années)	Total			Urban - Urbaine			Rural - Rurale		
	Both sexes Les deux sexes	Male Masculin	Female Féminin	Both sexes Les deux sexes	Male Masculin	Female Féminin	Both sexes Les deux sexes	Male Masculin	Female Féminin
EUROPE									
Czech Republic - République tchèque									
2000									
1-4	0.3	0.3	0.3	0.3	0.3	0.2	♦0.3	♦0.3	♦0.3
5-9	0.2	0.2	0.1	0.2	0.2	♦0.1	♦0.2	♦0.2	♦0.1
10-14	0.2	0.2	0.2	0.2	0.2	0.2	0.2	♦0.3	♦0.2
15-19	0.5	0.7	0.3	0.4	0.6	0.3	0.7	0.9	0.4
20-24	0.7	1.0	0.3	0.7	1.0	0.3	0.7	1.0	0.3
25-29	0.7	1.0	0.3	0.6	0.9	0.3	0.7	1.1	0.4
30-34	0.8	1.2	0.4	0.8	1.2	0.5	0.9	1.4	♦0.3
35-39	1.2	1.7	0.7	1.2	1.7	0.7	1.4	2.0	0.7
40-44	2.4	3.3	1.4	2.4	3.2	1.5	2.4	3.6	1.1
45-49	4.0	5.6	2.5	4.0	5.5	2.5	4.2	5.9	2.3
50-54	6.3	9.0	3.8	6.2	8.7	3.8	6.8	9.7	3.8
55-59	9.7	13.9	5.8	9.4	13.5	5.8	10.5	15.2	5.9
60-64	14.9	21.7	9.0	14.6	21.1	9.1	15.6	23.2	8.9
65-69	24.4	34.7	16.5	24.2	34.0	16.6	25.2	36.5	16.2
70-74	37.3	51.0	28.1	36.7	50.2	27.5	39.1	52.9	29.7
75-79	61.2	79.6	51.1	60.0	77.9	50.2	64.5	84.1	53.6
80-84	94.6	117.1	83.9	93.8	116.5	83.1	96.8	118.7	86.0
85-89	181.6	206.6	171.7	179.8	207.8	169.1	185.9	203.8	178.2
90-94	253.1	267.7	248.2	268.0	302.8	257.4	222.8	208.7	228.4
95-99	237.8	192.0	252.8	291.6	245.8	305.6	166.7	128.9	180.3
100+	113.2	♦100.0	116.5	158.5	♦121.5	169.4	69.8	♦72.3	♦69.3
2001									
Total	10.5	10.8	10.2	...	...	...	...	...	...
0-4	1.0	1.1	0.9	...	...	...	...	...	...
5-9	0.1	0.2	0.1	...	...	...	...	...	...
10-14	0.2	0.2	0.1	...	...	...	...	...	...
15-19	0.5	0.6	0.3	...	...	...	...	...	...
20-24	0.7	1.1	0.3	...	...	...	...	...	...
25-29	0.7	1.0	0.4	...	...	...	...	...	...
30-34	0.8	1.2	0.4	...	...	...	...	...	...
35-39	1.2	1.7	0.8	...	...	...	...	...	...
40-44	2.3	3.1	1.5	...	...	...	...	...	...
45-49	3.8	5.3	2.3	...	...	...	...	...	...
50-54	6.2	8.7	3.8	...	...	...	...	...	...
55-59	9.8	13.9	6.0	...	...	...	...	...	...
60-64	14.4	20.6	9.0	...	...	...	...	...	...
65-69	23.0	32.4	15.7	...	...	...	...	...	...
70-74	36.5	49.5	27.7	...	...	...	...	...	...
75-79	61.2	78.3	51.8	...	...	...	...	...	...
80-84	96.7	117.5	86.9	...	...	...	...	...	...
85+	199.6	221.6	191.5	...	...	...	...	...	...
Denmark - Danemark[17]									
2001									
Total	10.9	10.7	11.0	...	...	...	...	...	...
0-4	1.2	1.1	1.2	...	...	...	...	...	...
5-9	0.1	♦0.2	♦0.1	...	...	...	...	...	...
10-14	0.2	0.2	♦0.1	...	...	...	...	...	...
15-19	0.4	0.6	♦0.2	...	...	...	...	...	...
20-24	0.5	0.7	0.2	...	...	...	...	...	...
25-29	0.6	0.8	0.3	...	...	...	...	...	...
30-34	0.7	1.0	0.5	...	...	...	...	...	...
35-39	1.2	1.6	0.9	...	...	...	...	...	...
40-44	1.9	2.2	1.5	...	...	...	...	...	...
45-49	3.3	4.0	2.5	...	...	...	...	...	...
50-54	4.9	5.9	3.9	...	...	...	...	...	...
55-59	8.0	9.6	6.3	...	...	...	...	...	...
60-64	11.9	14.4	9.6	...	...	...	...	...	...

20. Death rates specific for age, sex and urban/rural residence: latest available year
Taux de mortalité selon l'âge, le sexe et la résidence, urbaine/rurale: dernière année disponible
(continued — suite)

(See notes at end of table. — Voir notes à la fin du tableau.)

Continent, country or area, year and age (in years) Continent, pays ou zone, année et âge (en années)	Total			Urban - Urbaine			Rural - Rurale		
	Both sexes Les deux sexes	Male Masculin	Female Féminin	Both sexes Les deux sexes	Male Masculin	Female Féminin	Both sexes Les deux sexes	Male Masculin	Female Féminin
EUROPE									
Denmark - Danemark[17]									
2001									
65-69	21.0	25.2	17.3	...	...	...	...	...	...
70-74	33.2	41.1	26.6	...	...	...	...	...	...
75-79	53.4	68.0	43.0	...	...	...	...	...	...
80-84	83.8	108.7	69.3	...	...	...	...	...	...
85+	172.8	200.3	161.6	...	...	...	...	...	...
Estonia - Estonie[5,8]									
2000									
Total	13.3	14.4	12.3	12.6	14.2	11.4	14.6	14.8	14.4
0-1	8.7	9.9	7.4	8.8	10.0	♦7.6	8.4	♦9.6	♦7.2
1-4	♦0.6	♦0.7	♦0.5	♦0.6	♦0.6	♦0.6	♦0.7	♦1.0	♦0.3
5-9	♦0.4	♦0.4	♦0.3	♦0.3	♦0.4	♦0.3	♦0.4	♦0.4	♦0.4
10-14	♦0.3	♦0.3	♦0.2	♦0.3	♦0.4	♦0.2	♦0.3	♦0.3	♦0.2
15-19	0.7	0.9	♦0.4	0.6	♦0.8	♦0.4	♦0.8	♦1.1	♦0.5
20-24	1.5	2.4	♦0.5	1.4	2.4	♦0.4	1.7	2.3	♦0.9
25-29	1.6	2.6	0.7	1.7	2.8	♦0.6	1.5	♦2.1	♦0.7
30-34	2.2	3.3	1.1	2.1	3.3	1.0	2.3	3.2	♦1.3
35-39	3.2	4.8	1.6	3.0	4.8	1.5	3.4	4.7	♦2.0
40-44	5.6	9.0	2.4	5.7	9.7	2.3	5.3	7.8	2.6
45-49	8.3	12.8	4.3	8.8	13.7	4.8	7.1	10.9	3.0
50-54	10.6	16.7	5.5	10.6	17.2	5.6	10.6	15.8	5.4
55-59	15.0	22.6	9.0	15.2	23.7	9.1	14.6	20.7	8.9
60-64	20.0	33.0	10.6	19.7	32.9	10.7	20.7	33.2	10.4
65-69	28.1	44.1	17.8	27.2	42.4	17.8	30.0	47.1	17.8
70-74	43.0	63.4	32.1	42.6	63.0	32.0	43.8	64.4	32.4
75-79	60.9	82.5	52.9	59.4	81.0	51.6	63.7	85.0	55.4
80-84	98.1	127.4	88.4	95.3	121.8	86.3	102.9	137.0	91.8
85-89	162.2	188.5	154.8	155.0	189.0	145.6	172.9	187.8	168.6
90-94	236.6	255.5	232.3	225.3	250.0	220.3	252.3	262.1	249.8
95+	359.1	426.2	346.3	330.4	♦405.4	315.9	402.0	♦458.3	391.5
Finland - Finlande[18]									
1998									
Total	9.6	9.7	9.4	8.7	8.7	8.6	10.9	11.2	10.6
0-1	4.1	4.5	3.7	3.9	4.3	3.5	4.5	4.9	4.1
1-4	0.2	♦0.2	♦0.1	♦0.2	♦0.2	♦0.1	♦0.2	♦0.2	♦0.1
5-9	0.1	♦0.1	♦0.1	♦0.1	♦0.1	♦0.1	♦0.1	♦0.2	♦0.1
10-14	0.2	♦0.2	♦0.1	♦0.1	♦0.1	♦0.1	♦0.2	♦0.2	♦0.1
15-19	0.5	0.7	0.3	0.4	0.6	♦0.3	0.5	0.7	♦0.3
20-24	0.7	0.9	0.4	0.6	0.8	0.4	0.8	1.1	♦0.5
25-29	0.7	1.1	0.3	0.7	1.1	0.4	0.8	1.2	♦0.3
30-34	1.0	1.4	0.6	1.1	1.5	0.7	0.9	1.3	♦0.3
35-39	1.5	2.1	0.8	1.4	2.1	0.8	1.5	2.2	0.7
40-44	2.3	3.3	1.2	2.3	3.3	1.3	2.3	3.3	1.1
45-49	3.5	5.0	2.1	3.6	5.1	2.2	3.4	4.7	1.9
50-54	5.2	7.4	3.1	5.2	7.2	3.2	5.3	7.5	2.8
55-59	7.1	10.2	4.0	7.3	10.8	4.1	6.7	9.4	3.9
60-64	10.9	15.9	6.3	10.8	15.9	6.4	11.1	16.0	6.2
65-69	17.8	26.5	10.6	17.1	25.7	10.6	18.6	27.4	10.6
70-74	29.6	42.4	20.7	28.8	42.2	20.5	30.4	42.5	21.0
75-79	48.5	69.0	37.8	46.9	68.8	36.5	50.3	69.3	39.5
80-84	83.7	113.6	71.3	81.0	111.2	69.5	87.1	116.1	73.6
85-89	142.2	179.0	129.7	140.1	176.2	129.1	144.8	181.9	130.5
90-94	236.3	267.4	227.6	235.2	273.9	225.7	237.6	261.5	230.0
95+	397.8	422.1	392.6	390.7	375.0	394.0	405.7	463.2	391.0
2001									
Total	9.4	9.4	9.3	...	...	...	...	...	...
0-4	0.8	0.9	0.6	...	...	...	...	...	...
5-9	0.1	0.2	♦0.1	...	...	...	...	...	...
10-14	0.1	♦0.1	♦0.1	...	...	...	...	...	...

20. Death rates specific for age, sex and urban/rural residence: latest available year
Taux de mortalité selon l'âge, le sexe et la résidence, urbaine/rurale: dernière année disponible
(continued — suite)

(See notes at end of table. — Voir notes à la fin du tableau.)

Continent, country or area, year and age (in years) / Continent, pays ou zone, année et âge (en années)	Total			Urban - Urbaine			Rural - Rurale		
	Both sexes Les deux sexes	Male Masculin	Female Féminin	Both sexes Les deux sexes	Male Masculin	Female Féminin	Both sexes Les deux sexes	Male Masculin	Female Féminin
EUROPE									
Finland - Finlande[18]									
2001									
15-19	0.5	0.7	0.2	...	...	...	...	...	...
20-24	0.7	1.1	0.3	...	...	...	...	...	...
25-29	0.8	1.3	0.3	...	...	...	...	...	...
30-34	1.0	1.5	0.5	...	...	...	...	...	...
35-39	1.3	1.7	0.9	...	...	...	...	...	...
40-44	2.2	2.9	1.4	...	...	...	...	...	...
45-49	3.2	4.5	1.9	...	...	...	...	...	...
50-54	4.7	6.4	2.9	...	...	...	...	...	...
55-59	6.6	9.4	3.8	...	...	...	...	...	...
60-64	10.0	14.1	6.3	...	...	...	...	...	...
65-69	15.4	21.9	9.9	...	...	...	...	...	...
70-74	26.0	37.8	17.3	...	...	...	...	...	...
75-79	45.3	62.7	35.4	...	...	...	...	...	...
80-84	78.1	104.5	66.7	...	...	...	...	...	...
85+	171.7	201.3	162.4	...	...	...	...	...	...
France[19,20,21]									
1999									
Total	9.1	9.5	8.7	...	...	...	...	...	...
0-1	4.4	4.9	3.8	...	...	...	...	...	...
1-4	0.2	0.3	0.2	...	...	...	...	...	...
5-9	0.1	0.1	0.1	...	...	...	...	...	...
10-14	0.1	0.2	0.1	...	...	...	...	...	...
15-19	0.5	0.7	0.3	...	...	...	...	...	...
20-24	0.7	1.1	0.4	...	...	...	...	...	...
25-29	0.7	1.1	0.4	...	...	...	...	...	...
30-34	0.9	1.3	0.5	...	...	...	...	...	...
35-39	1.3	1.8	0.9	...	...	...	...	...	...
40-44	2.2	3.1	1.4	...	...	...	...	...	...
45-49	3.3	4.6	2.0	...	...	...	...	...	...
50-54	4.9	6.9	2.9	...	...	...	...	...	...
55-59	6.7	9.5	3.9	...	...	...	...	...	...
60-64	9.7	14.0	5.6	...	...	...	...	...	...
65-69	14.8	21.9	8.7	...	...	...	...	...	...
70-74	23.1	34.0	14.8	...	...	...	...	...	...
75-79	39.5	55.6	28.7	...	...	...	...	...	...
80-84	64.4	86.5	52.4	...	...	...	...	...	...
85-89	119.9	152.7	105.8	...	...	...	...	...	...
90-94	206.8	245.3	194.4	...	...	...	...	...	...
95+	327.3	331.0	326.4	...	...	...	...	...	...
Germany - Allemagne									
1999									
Total	10.3	9.8	10.8	...	...	...	...	...	...
0-4	1.1	1.2	1.0	...	...	...	...	...	...
5-9	0.1	0.1	0.1	...	...	...	...	...	...
10-14	0.1	0.2	0.1	...	...	...	...	...	...
15-19	0.5	0.7	0.3	...	...	...	...	...	...
20-24	0.6	0.9	0.3	...	...	...	...	...	...
25-29	0.6	0.8	0.3	...	...	...	...	...	...
30-34	0.7	0.9	0.4	...	...	...	...	...	...
35-39	1.1	1.5	0.8	...	...	...	...	...	...
40-44	1.9	2.5	1.3	...	...	...	...	...	...
45-49	3.0	4.0	2.1	...	...	...	...	...	...
50-54	4.6	6.1	3.1	...	...	...	...	...	...
55-59	6.9	9.2	4.6	...	...	...	...	...	...
60-64	11.0	15.4	6.9	...	...	...	...	...	...
65-69	18.2	25.5	11.8	...	...	...	...	...	...
70-74	28.3	40.0	20.4	...	...	...	...	...	...
75-79	46.7	65.0	37.9	...	...	...	...	...	...

20. Death rates specific for age, sex and urban/rural residence: latest available year
Taux de mortalité selon l'âge, le sexe et la résidence, urbaine/rurale: dernière année disponible
(continued — suite)

(See notes at end of table. — Voir notes à la fin du tableau.)

Continent, country or area, year and age (in years) Continent, pays ou zone, année et âge (en années)	Total			Urban - Urbaine			Rural - Rurale		
	Both sexes Les deux sexes	Male Masculin	Female Féminin	Both sexes Les deux sexes	Male Masculin	Female Féminin	Both sexes Les deux sexes	Male Masculin	Female Féminin
EUROPE									
Germany - Allemagne									
1999									
80-84	79.8	103.7	70.1	...	...	...	...	...	...
85+	166.4	190.7	158.8	...	...	...	...	...	...
Greece - Grèce									
1998									
Total	9.8	10.3	9.2	...	...	...	...	...	...
0-1	6.7	7.1	6.2	...	...	...	...	...	...
1-4	0.3	0.3	0.3	...	...	...	...	...	...
5-9	0.1	0.2	0.1	...	...	...	...	...	...
10-14	0.2	0.2	0.1	...	...	...	...	...	...
15-19	0.5	0.7	0.3	...	...	...	...	...	...
20-24	0.7	1.1	0.3	...	...	...	...	...	...
25-29	0.8	1.2	0.4	...	...	...	...	...	...
30-34	0.9	1.2	0.5	...	...	...	...	...	...
35-39	1.0	1.4	0.7	...	...	...	...	...	...
40-44	1.7	2.3	1.1	...	...	...	...	...	...
45-49	2.6	3.5	1.6	...	...	...	...	...	...
50-54	4.0	5.5	2.4	...	...	...	...	...	...
55-59	5.6	8.1	3.3	...	...	...	...	...	...
60-64	9.3	13.2	5.8	...	...	...	...	...	...
65-69	15.6	21.4	10.4	...	...	...	...	...	...
70-74	27.1	34.8	20.8	...	...	...	...	...	...
75-79	45.8	55.1	38.8	...	...	...	...	...	...
80-84	91.8	101.2	85.3	...	...	...	...	...	...
85-89	145.4	149.4	142.6	...	...	...	...	...	...
90-94	217.5	196.1	234.0	...	...	...	...	...	...
95-99	216.9	178.6	246.4	...	...	...	...	...	...
100+	180.4	117.1	241.7	...	...	...	...	...	...
Hungary - Hongrie[22]									
2001									
Total	13.0	14.1	11.9	12.3	13.1	11.5	14.1	15.6	12.6
0-1	8.2	8.8	7.6	7.9	8.8	6.9	8.6	8.7	8.4
1-4	0.3	0.4	0.2	0.3	0.4	♦0.2	0.3	♦0.4	♦0.2
5-9	0.2	0.2	0.1	0.1	♦0.2	♦0.1	0.1	♦0.2	♦0.1
10-14	0.2	0.2	0.2	0.2	0.2	♦0.2	0.2	0.3	♦0.1
15-19	0.4	0.5	0.2	0.3	0.5	0.2	0.5	0.7	0.3
20-24	0.6	0.9	0.3	0.6	0.9	0.3	0.6	0.8	0.3
25-29	0.7	1.0	0.4	0.7	0.9	0.4	0.8	1.2	0.4
30-34	1.2	1.7	0.6	1.0	1.4	0.6	1.4	2.1	0.6
35-39	2.2	3.1	1.3	1.9	2.6	1.1	2.6	3.7	1.5
40-44	4.7	6.9	2.6	4.1	6.0	2.4	5.5	7.9	2.9
45-49	7.3	10.5	4.2	6.5	9.4	4.0	8.6	12.4	4.5
50-54	10.3	15.2	5.8	9.2	13.5	5.5	12.2	18.0	6.3
55-59	13.7	20.3	8.0	12.5	18.4	7.7	15.7	23.7	8.7
60-64	19.0	28.4	11.9	17.5	25.3	11.6	21.4	33.3	12.3
65-69	27.2	40.1	18.1	25.7	37.0	17.8	29.4	45.1	18.5
70-74	41.0	57.4	30.7	39.2	54.0	29.7	43.9	62.7	32.3
75-79	64.5	85.7	53.1	61.7	81.7	51.1	69.1	92.2	56.5
80-84	97.8	120.1	87.3	93.5	113.7	84.1	105.4	131.5	93.0
85-89	169.2	192.9	159.5	162.2	184.0	153.2	183.1	212.4	171.4
90+	242.0	234.2	244.8	238.1	231.7	240.5	248.7	237.9	252.8
Iceland - Islande									
2000									
Total	6.5	6.4	6.5	6.5	6.4	6.5	6.7	6.7	6.7
0-1	♦5.9	♦8.9	♦2.8	♦6.4	♦9.7	♦3.0	...	...	...
1-4	♦0.2	♦0.1	♦0.4	♦0.3	♦0.1	♦0.4	...	...	...
5-9	♦0.1	♦0.2	...	♦0.1	♦0.2	...	...	...	...
10-14	-	♦0.1	...	♦0.1	♦0.1	...	...	...	...
15-19	♦0.7	♦0.8	♦0.5	♦0.7	♦0.9	♦0.4	♦0.5	...	♦1.1

20. Death rates specific for age, sex and urban/rural residence: latest available year
Taux de mortalité selon l'âge, le sexe et la résidence, urbaine/rurale: dernière année disponible
(continued — suite)

(See notes at end of table. — Voir notes à la fin du tableau.)

Continent, country or area, year and age (in years) / Continent, pays ou zone, année et âge (en années)	Total			Urban - Urbaine			Rural - Rurale		
	Both sexes Les deux sexes	Male Masculin	Female Féminin	Both sexes Les deux sexes	Male Masculin	Female Féminin	Both sexes Les deux sexes	Male Masculin	Female Féminin
EUROPE									
Iceland - Islande									
2000									
20-24	♦1.0	♦1.6	♦0.4	♦1.0	♦1.6	♦0.4	♦0.6	♦1.2	...
25-29	♦0.6	♦1.1	...	♦0.5	♦1.1	...	♦0.8	♦1.5	...
30-34	♦0.7	♦1.4	♦0.1	♦0.7	♦1.3	♦0.1	♦1.6	♦3.0	...
35-39	♦0.9	♦1.3	♦0.5	♦0.9	♦1.3	♦0.5	♦0.6	♦1.2	...
40-44	♦1.2	♦1.5	♦0.9	♦1.3	♦1.6	♦0.9	...	...	...
45-49	2.1	♦2.4	♦1.7	2.0	♦2.2	♦1.7	♦3.5	♦5.1	♦1.6
50-54	3.4	4.9	♦1.9	3.4	4.9	♦1.9	♦3.2	♦4.3	♦1.8
55-59	5.7	5.4	6.0	6.0	5.8	6.3	♦1.9	♦1.8	♦2.0
60-64	8.6	7.9	9.3	8.4	8.3	8.4	♦10.8	♦4.1	♦18.5
65-69	14.4	17.2	11.7	14.5	17.1	12.1	♦13.6	♦18.1	♦7.7
70-74	22.2	27.1	17.8	22.2	27.4	17.8	♦22.2	♦25.2	♦18.0
75-79	38.7	43.2	34.9	38.8	44.7	34.2	♦36.8	♦31.0	♦44.5
80-84	64.5	72.6	58.7	66.9	76.8	60.3	♦40.7	♦41.3	♦40.0
85+	150.2	159.0	145.2	153.3	164.2	147.5	123.7	♦125.0	♦122.7
2001									
Total	6.1	6.5	5.6	...	...	...	...	...	...
0-4	♦0.7	♦0.7	♦0.6	...	...	...	...	...	...
5-9	♦0.1	...	♦0.2	...	...	...	...	...	...
10-14	♦0.2	♦0.2	♦0.2	...	...	...	...	...	...
15-19	♦0.6	♦0.9	♦0.2	...	...	...	...	...	...
20-24	♦0.8	♦1.3	♦0.4	...	...	...	...	...	...
25-29	♦0.7	♦1.0	♦0.4	...	...	...	...	...	...
30-34	♦0.5	♦0.8	♦0.3	...	...	...	...	...	...
35-39	♦0.2	♦0.4	♦0.1	...	...	...	...	...	...
40-44	1.6	♦1.9	♦1.2	...	...	...	...	...	...
45-49	♦1.6	♦1.6	♦1.5	...	...	...	...	...	...
50-54	2.9	♦3.4	♦2.5	...	...	...	...	...	...
55-59	5.4	6.3	♦4.5	...	...	...	...	...	...
60-64	7.5	8.9	♦6.1	...	...	...	...	...	...
65-69	12.9	15.8	10.2	...	...	...	...	...	...
70-74	23.9	30.7	17.7	...	...	...	...	...	...
75-79	35.8	47.0	26.7	...	...	...	...	...	...
80-84	64.1	82.3	51.0	...	...	...	...	...	...
85+	150.4	177.9	135.3	...	...	...	...	...	...
Ireland - Irlande+,23									
1996									
Total	8.8	9.2	8.3	8.1	8.4	7.8	9.7	10.4	9.0
0-1	5.7	6.2	5.2	6.1	6.6	5.5	5.2	5.6	4.9
1-4	0.3	0.3	0.3	0.3	♦0.3	♦0.3	0.4	♦0.4	♦0.4
5-9	0.1	♦0.2	♦0.1	♦0.1	♦0.2	♦0.1	♦0.1	♦0.2	-
10-14	0.2	0.2	♦0.1	0.2	♦0.2	♦0.1	♦0.2	♦0.2	♦0.1
15-19	0.5	0.6	0.3	0.4	0.5	♦0.2	0.6	0.8	♦0.4
20-24	0.8	1.3	0.3	0.6	1.0	♦0.2	1.3	1.9	♦0.5
25-29	0.8	1.2	0.4	0.7	1.1	♦0.3	1.0	1.5	♦0.6
30-34	0.8	1.1	0.5	0.8	1.1	0.5	0.8	1.2	♦0.5
35-39	1.0	1.4	0.6	1.0	1.3	0.7	1.1	1.5	0.6
40-44	1.6	2.0	1.2	1.5	2.0	1.1	1.7	2.0	1.4
45-49	2.5	3.0	1.9	2.8	3.5	2.1	2.1	2.5	1.6
50-54	4.6	5.5	3.6	4.6	5.7	3.5	4.5	5.2	3.7
55-59	7.4	9.5	5.3	8.1	10.7	5.6	6.5	8.0	4.8
60-64	13.2	17.1	9.3	14.0	18.6	9.8	12.2	15.3	8.7
65-69	23.1	30.9	16.1	24.1	32.9	17.0	21.9	28.8	14.8
70-74	38.2	49.6	29.0	40.6	54.6	30.8	35.5	45.0	26.8
75-79	63.2	81.2	50.3	66.1	89.6	52.0	60.3	74.4	48.3
80-84	106.1	135.3	88.3	103.3	140.5	85.2	108.8	131.3	92.0
85+	202.3	239.5	185.9	196.8	247.4	179.4	208.6	233.2	194.7
2001									
Total	7.7	8.0	7.4	...	...	...	...	...	...

20. Death rates specific for age, sex and urban/rural residence: latest available year
Taux de mortalité selon l'âge, le sexe et la résidence, urbaine/rurale: dernière année disponible
(continued — suite)

(See notes at end of table. — Voir notes à la fin du tableau.)

Continent, country or area, year and age (in years) / Continent, pays ou zone, année et âge (en années)	Total			Urban - Urbaine			Rural - Rurale		
	Both sexes Les deux sexes	Male Masculin	Female Féminin	Both sexes Les deux sexes	Male Masculin	Female Féminin	Both sexes Les deux sexes	Male Masculin	Female Féminin
EUROPE									
Ireland - Irlande[+,23]									
2001									
0-4	1.5	1.7	1.3	...	...	...	...	...	...
5-9	0.1	♦0.2	♦0.1	...	...	...	...	...	...
10-14	0.2	♦0.2	♦0.1	...	...	...	...	...	...
15-19	0.5	0.7	0.3	...	...	...	...	...	...
20-24	0.7	1.1	0.4	...	...	...	...	...	...
25-29	0.7	1.0	0.3	...	...	...	...	...	...
30-34	0.8	1.1	0.4	...	...	...	...	...	...
35-39	1.2	1.4	1.0	...	...	...	...	...	...
40-44	1.6	1.9	1.3	...	...	...	...	...	...
45-49	2.5	2.9	2.0	...	...	...	...	...	...
50-54	4.1	4.8	3.4	...	...	...	...	...	...
55-59	6.3	8.0	4.5	...	...	...	...	...	...
60-64	11.1	14.2	8.0	...	...	...	...	...	...
65-69	19.1	25.2	13.3	...	...	...	...	...	...
70-74	31.4	40.7	23.5	...	...	...	...	...	...
75-79	54.9	70.0	44.2	...	...	...	...	...	...
80-84	90.8	111.9	78.0	...	...	...	...	...	...
85+	167.7	192.3	156.4	...	...	...	...	...	...
Italy - Italie									
1995									
Total	9.7	10.3	9.2	...	...	...	...	...	...
0-1	6.2	6.9	5.3	...	...	...	...	...	...
1-4	0.3	0.3	0.3	...	...	...	...	...	...
5-9	0.2	0.2	0.2	...	...	...	...	...	...
10-14	0.2	0.3	0.1	...	...	...	...	...	...
15-19	0.5	0.8	0.2	...	...	...	...	...	...
20-24	0.7	1.0	0.3	...	...	...	...	...	...
25-29	0.8	1.1	0.4	...	...	...	...	...	...
30-34	1.2	1.7	0.6	...	...	...	...	...	...
35-39	1.3	1.8	0.8	...	...	...	...	...	...
40-44	1.6	2.0	1.1	...	...	...	...	...	...
45-49	2.4	3.1	1.7	...	...	...	...	...	...
50-54	3.9	5.1	2.7	...	...	...	...	...	...
55-59	6.2	8.6	4.0	...	...	...	...	...	...
60-64	10.3	14.6	6.4	...	...	...	...	...	...
65-69	17.0	24.3	10.9	...	...	...	...	...	...
70-74	27.1	38.2	18.9	...	...	...	...	...	...
75-79	45.3	61.1	35.0	...	...	...	...	...	...
80-84	77.3	98.2	65.2	...	...	...	...	...	...
85-89	132.2	157.8	120.2	...	...	...	...	...	...
90+	235.9	252.5	230.0	...	...	...	...	...	...
Latvia - Lettonie[8]									
2001									
Total	14.0	15.2	13.0	13.4	14.9	12.2	15.3	15.9	14.7
0-1	10.9	11.3	10.4	11.1	12.0	10.1	10.6	10.2	11.0
1-4	0.6	0.8	♦0.5	♦0.5	♦0.5	♦0.4	♦0.9	♦1.2	♦0.5
5-9	0.4	0.5	♦0.2	♦0.2	♦0.3	♦0.2	♦0.5	♦0.8	♦0.2
10-14	0.3	♦0.3	♦0.2	♦0.3	♦0.3	♦0.2	♦0.3	♦0.4	♦0.2
15-19	0.8	1.1	0.5	0.8	1.1	♦0.4	0.9	1.2	♦0.7
20-24	1.4	2.2	0.5	1.3	2.1	♦0.5	1.6	2.5	♦0.6
25-29	1.8	2.9	0.6	1.7	2.9	0.6	1.9	3.0	♦0.6
30-34	2.6	4.1	1.2	2.4	3.6	1.2	3.1	4.9	♦1.1
35-39	3.6	5.7	1.5	3.5	5.8	1.4	3.8	5.6	1.8
40-44	5.5	8.6	2.6	5.2	8.4	2.5	6.1	8.8	3.1
45-49	7.8	12.3	3.7	7.7	12.5	3.7	8.0	11.9	3.7
50-54	11.6	17.9	6.3	11.2	17.5	6.3	12.8	18.9	6.5
55-59	15.2	24.0	8.4	14.6	23.2	8.3	16.5	25.6	8.5
60-64	20.7	33.7	11.4	19.5	32.1	10.9	23.5	37.1	12.7

20. Death rates specific for age, sex and urban/rural residence: latest available year
Taux de mortalité selon l'âge, le sexe et la résidence, urbaine/rurale: dernière année disponible
(continued — suite)

(See notes at end of table. — Voir notes à la fin du tableau.)

Continent, country or area, year and age (in years) Continent, pays ou zone, année et âge (en années)	Total			Urban - Urbaine			Rural - Rurale		
	Both sexes Les deux sexes	Male Masculin	Female Féminin	Both sexes Les deux sexes	Male Masculin	Female Féminin	Both sexes Les deux sexes	Male Masculin	Female Féminin
EUROPE									
Latvia - Lettonie[8]									
2001									
65-69	29.1	45.7	18.6	27.3	42.4	18.1	32.9	52.4	19.8
70-74	41.6	63.9	29.5	39.9	61.0	28.5	45.4	70.8	31.8
75-79	62.5	92.5	52.5	61.2	88.5	51.9	65.4	101.7	53.7
80-84	105.3	133.4	96.0	103.0	128.2	94.2	109.8	144.3	99.3
85-89	164.7	187.9	158.3	157.7	172.2	153.4	176.7	218.7	166.3
90-94	274.2	308.4	265.2	259.0	290.5	250.5	298.6	337.8	288.4
95-99	388.8	364.0	394.5	383.9	359.0	389.3	397.0	371.4	403.3
100+	576.4	♦684.2	560.0	539.3	♦909.1	487.2	636.4	♦375.0	680.9
Lithuania - Lituanie[8]									
2001									
Total	11.6	13.3	10.2	9.9	11.4	8.5	15.1	16.8	13.6
0-1	7.7	9.5	5.9	7.2	9.0	5.3	8.6	10.3	6.8
1-4	0.6	0.7	0.5	0.5	♦0.6	♦0.4	0.9	♦1.1	♦0.7
5-9	0.3	0.4	♦0.1	♦0.2	♦0.2	♦0.1	0.4	♦0.6	♦0.1
10-14	0.3	0.4	♦0.1	0.2	♦0.3	♦0.1	0.4	0.6	♦0.2
15-19	1.0	1.5	0.4	1.0	1.5	0.5	1.0	1.6	♦0.3
20-24	1.6	2.6	0.7	1.4	2.2	0.6	2.3	3.5	♦0.9
25-29	1.8	3.0	0.6	1.4	2.4	0.5	2.9	4.6	♦1.0
30-34	2.5	4.2	0.9	2.2	3.6	0.8	3.4	5.4	1.2
35-39	3.3	5.0	1.6	2.9	4.4	1.5	4.1	6.2	1.8
40-44	4.8	7.5	2.3	4.2	6.7	2.0	6.3	9.1	3.1
45-49	7.2	11.1	3.7	6.6	10.3	3.5	8.7	12.8	4.2
50-54	10.6	16.8	5.4	9.8	15.7	5.2	12.4	18.9	5.9
55-59	14.0	22.5	7.4	12.8	20.7	6.9	16.5	25.8	8.4
60-64	18.0	29.6	9.6	17.0	27.7	9.5	19.8	32.6	9.8
65-69	24.5	39.5	14.6	23.6	37.6	14.7	25.7	42.3	14.6
70-74	36.0	54.6	25.4	35.4	53.9	24.8	36.8	55.6	26.3
75-79	57.5	83.4	46.7	55.6	79.1	46.2	60.0	88.8	47.4
80-84	96.4	121.6	86.5	91.3	116.8	81.8	102.5	127.0	92.4
85-89	160.6	182.4	153.3	150.3	160.7	147.1	173.2	207.2	161.3
90-94	248.7	256.0	245.6	228.6	240.4	224.3	273.3	271.5	274.2
95+	345.0	315.4	357.1	324.8	289.1	337.5	365.6	337.5	378.8
Luxembourg									
2001									
Total	8.4	8.3	8.5	...	...	...	...	...	...
0-4	1.5	♦1.7	♦1.3	...	...	...	...	...	...
5-9	♦0.1	♦0.1	...	...	...	...	...	...	...
10-14	♦0.3	♦0.1	♦0.5	...	...	...	...	...	...
15-19	♦0.5	♦0.6	♦0.5	...	...	...	...	...	...
20-24	♦0.6	♦0.9	♦0.2	...	...	...	...	...	...
25-29	♦0.9	♦1.3	♦0.5	...	...	...	...	...	...
30-34	1.0	♦1.0	♦1.0	...	...	...	...	...	...
35-39	1.0	♦1.5	♦0.5	...	...	...	...	...	...
40-44	2.0	2.4	♦1.6	...	...	...	...	...	...
45-49	2.9	3.9	♦1.9	...	...	...	...	...	...
50-54	4.0	4.7	3.1	...	...	...	...	...	...
55-59	7.1	8.7	5.4	...	...	...	...	...	...
60-64	10.7	15.5	6.3	...	...	...	...	...	...
65-69	17.2	23.6	11.6	...	...	...	...	...	...
70-74	25.8	33.1	19.8	...	...	...	...	...	...
75-79	43.3	57.9	35.1	...	...	...	...	...	...
80-84	74.2	91.0	66.3	...	...	...	...	...	...
85+	167.4	208.2	152.8	...	...	...	...	...	...
Malta - Malte									
2001									
Total	7.5	7.7	7.2	...	...	...	...	...	...
0-4	♦1.2	♦1.5	♦0.8	...	...	...	...	...	...
5-9	♦0.1	♦0.2	♦0.1	...	...	...	...	...	...

20. Death rates specific for age, sex and urban/rural residence: latest available year
Taux de mortalité selon l'âge, le sexe et la résidence, urbaine/rurale: dernière année disponible
(continued — suite)

(See notes at end of table. — Voir notes à la fin du tableau.)

Continent, country or area, year and age (in years) / Continent, pays ou zone, année et âge (en années)	Total			Urban - Urbaine			Rural - Rurale		
	Both sexes Les deux sexes	Male Masculin	Female Féminin	Both sexes Les deux sexes	Male Masculin	Female Féminin	Both sexes Les deux sexes	Male Masculin	Female Féminin
EUROPE									
Malta - Malte									
2001									
10-14	-	♦0.1	...	...	...	...	...	...	...
15-19	♦0.4	♦0.7	♦0.1	...	...	...	...	...	...
20-24	♦0.5	♦0.7	♦0.3	...	...	...	...	...	...
25-29	♦0.6	♦1.1	♦0.1	...	...	...	...	...	...
30-34	♦0.5	♦0.8	♦0.2	...	...	...	...	...	...
35-39	♦0.7	♦0.9	♦0.5	...	...	...	...	...	...
40-44	♦0.8	♦1.1	♦0.5	...	...	...	...	...	...
45-49	2.4	2.8	♦2.0	...	...	...	...	...	...
50-54	3.1	4.0	2.2	...	...	...	...	...	...
55-59	5.5	6.9	4.1	...	...	...	...	...	...
60-64	7.9	9.5	6.6	...	...	...	...	...	...
65-69	16.5	22.9	11.4	...	...	...	...	...	...
70-74	30.3	41.5	22.0	...	...	...	...	...	...
75-79	53.0	66.5	43.4	...	...	...	...	...	...
80-84	81.6	98.4	70.0	...	...	...	...	...	...
85+	179.5	181.8	178.4	...	...	...	...	...	...
Netherlands - Pays-Bas[24]									
2001									
Total	8.8	8.6	8.9	9.1	8.8	9.4	8.3	8.4	8.1
0-1	4.6	5.1	4.1	4.8	5.3	4.3	4.4	4.9	3.9
1-4	0.4	0.5	0.3	0.4	0.4	0.3	0.4	0.5	0.4
5-9	0.1	0.1	0.1	0.1	0.1	♦0.1	0.1	♦0.1	♦0.1
10-14	0.2	0.2	0.1	0.1	0.1	0.1	0.2	0.2	♦0.1
15-19	0.3	0.4	0.2	0.3	0.4	0.2	0.4	0.5	0.3
20-24	0.4	0.6	0.3	0.4	0.6	0.2	0.5	0.6	0.3
25-29	0.5	0.6	0.3	0.5	0.6	0.3	0.5	0.7	0.2
30-34	0.6	0.8	0.5	0.6	0.7	0.5	0.6	0.8	0.4
35-39	0.9	1.0	0.7	0.9	1.0	0.8	0.8	0.9	0.6
40-44	1.4	1.6	1.2	1.5	1.7	1.3	1.3	1.4	1.1
45-49	2.5	2.8	2.1	2.6	3.0	2.3	2.1	2.5	1.8
50-54	3.7	4.3	3.1	4.0	4.7	3.3	3.3	3.7	2.8
55-59	6.6	8.0	5.2	7.0	8.4	5.4	6.1	7.3	4.8
60-64	9.7	12.2	7.2	10.1	12.8	7.6	8.9	11.3	6.5
65-69	16.1	21.5	11.2	16.6	22.1	11.8	15.4	20.7	10.2
70-74	27.8	38.1	19.6	28.2	38.3	20.4	27.1	37.8	18.1
75-79	46.4	64.2	34.7	46.9	64.7	35.5	45.5	63.4	33.1
80-84	82.9	113.5	66.9	83.5	115.4	67.3	81.8	109.9	66.1
85-89	142.7	184.0	126.6	143.5	187.5	127.3	140.9	177.5	124.9
90-94	250.4	312.4	233.2	251.1	319.6	233.6	249.0	300.0	232.3
95+	452.6	504.0	441.0	450.5	503.6	440.2	456.9	504.8	442.9
Norway - Norvège[25]									
2001									
Total	9.7	9.7	9.8	...	...	...	...	...	...
0-4	0.9	1.1	0.8	...	...	...	...	...	...
5-9	0.1	♦0.1	♦0.1	...	...	...	...	...	...
10-14	♦0.1	♦0.1	♦0.1	...	...	...	...	...	...
15-19	0.5	0.7	0.3	...	...	...	...	...	...
20-24	0.8	1.2	0.4	...	...	...	...	...	...
25-29	0.7	1.1	0.4	...	...	...	...	...	...
30-34	0.8	1.1	0.5	...	...	...	...	...	...
35-39	1.1	1.5	0.6	...	...	...	...	...	...
40-44	1.5	1.8	1.1	...	...	...	...	...	...
45-49	2.3	2.8	1.8	...	...	...	...	...	...
50-54	3.6	4.3	2.9	...	...	...	...	...	...
55-59	5.5	6.7	4.3	...	...	...	...	...	...
60-64	9.3	11.7	7.1	...	...	...	...	...	...
65-69	14.9	19.7	10.6	...	...	...	...	...	...
70-74	25.4	33.7	18.4	...	...	...	...	...	...

20. Death rates specific for age, sex and urban/rural residence: latest available year
Taux de mortalité selon l'âge, le sexe et la résidence, urbaine/rurale: dernière année disponible
(continued — suite)

(See notes at end of table. — Voir notes à la fin du tableau.)

Continent, country or area, year and age (in years) / Continent, pays ou zone, année et âge (en années)	Total			Urban - Urbaine			Rural - Rurale		
	Both sexes Les deux sexes	Male Masculin	Female Féminin	Both sexes Les deux sexes	Male Masculin	Female Féminin	Both sexes Les deux sexes	Male Masculin	Female Féminin
EUROPE									
Norway - Norvège[25]									
2001									
75-79	44.7	60.0	33.7	...	...	...	...	...	...
80-84	77.9	103.5	63.1	...	...	...	...	...	...
85+	171.2	200.6	159.1	...	...	...	...	...	...
Poland - Pologne									
1999									
Total	9.9	10.9	8.9	9.4	10.3	8.5	10.7	11.7	9.7
0-1	8.7	9.5	7.9	9.1	9.9	8.2	8.3	9.1	7.4
1-4	0.4	0.4	0.3	0.3	0.4	0.3	0.4	0.5	0.4
5-9	0.2	0.2	0.2	0.2	0.2	0.1	0.2	0.3	0.2
10-14	0.2	0.3	0.1	0.2	0.3	0.1	0.2	0.3	0.2
15-19	0.6	0.9	0.3	0.5	0.8	0.3	0.7	1.0	0.4
20-24	0.8	1.3	0.3	0.8	1.2	0.3	1.0	1.6	0.4
25-29	1.0	1.5	0.4	0.9	1.4	0.4	1.1	1.7	0.4
30-34	1.3	2.0	0.6	1.2	1.9	0.6	1.5	2.3	0.6
35-39	2.1	3.2	1.0	2.0	3.0	1.1	2.2	3.3	1.0
40-44	3.5	5.2	1.8	3.4	5.0	1.9	3.8	5.7	1.7
45-49	5.5	8.2	2.9	5.3	8.0	2.9	5.8	8.5	2.9
50-54	8.1	12.1	4.5	8.0	11.8	4.7	8.4	12.6	4.1
55-59	12.2	18.3	6.8	12.1	18.1	6.9	12.3	18.7	6.4
60-64	17.9	27.1	10.3	17.9	26.9	10.7	17.9	27.5	9.6
65-69	26.8	39.9	17.1	27.0	39.8	17.6	26.5	39.9	16.2
70-74	39.8	56.6	29.3	40.3	56.1	30.5	39.2	57.2	27.6
75-79	62.6	82.6	51.7	62.4	82.0	52.2	62.8	83.3	51.2
80-84	102.1	123.8	92.0	99.8	120.5	91.1	104.7	127.4	93.1
85+	196.8	208.8	192.2	188.1	199.0	184.3	208.3	219.8	203.3
2001									
Total	9.4	10.3	8.6	...	...	...	...	...	...
0-4	1.7	1.9	1.5	...	...	...	...	...	...
5-9	0.2	0.2	0.1	...	...	...	...	...	...
10-14	0.2	0.2	0.2	...	...	...	...	...	...
15-19	0.5	0.7	0.3	...	...	...	...	...	...
20-24	0.7	1.1	0.3	...	...	...	...	...	...
25-29	0.8	1.3	0.3	...	...	...	...	...	...
30-34	1.1	1.8	0.5	...	...	...	...	...	...
35-39	1.8	2.8	0.9	...	...	...	...	...	...
40-44	3.1	4.5	1.7	...	...	...	...	...	...
45-49	5.0	7.4	2.8	...	...	...	...	...	...
50-54	7.6	11.2	4.3	...	...	...	...	...	...
55-59	11.1	16.4	6.4	...	...	...	...	...	...
60-64	16.3	24.7	9.4	...	...	...	...	...	...
65-69	24.4	36.5	15.4	...	...	...	...	...	...
70-74	36.6	51.9	26.5	...	...	...	...	...	...
75-79	57.5	77.0	47.2	...	...	...	...	...	...
80-84	91.4	110.0	82.5	...	...	...	...	...	...
85+	188.2	198.0	184.5	...	...	...	...	...	...
Portugal[5]									
2001									
Total	10.2	11.0	9.4	...	...	...	...	...	...
0-4	1.3	1.5	1.1	...	...	...	...	...	...
5-9	0.2	0.2	0.2	...	...	...	...	...	...
10-14	0.3	0.3	0.2	...	...	...	...	...	...
15-19	0.6	0.9	0.3	...	...	...	...	...	...
20-24	0.9	1.4	0.3	...	...	...	...	...	...
25-29	1.1	1.8	0.5	...	...	...	...	...	...
30-34	1.4	2.2	0.7	...	...	...	...	...	...
35-39	1.9	2.8	0.9	...	...	...	...	...	...
40-44	2.5	3.6	1.5	...	...	...	...	...	...
45-49	3.5	4.8	2.2	...	...	...	...	...	...

20. Death rates specific for age, sex and urban/rural residence: latest available year
Taux de mortalité selon l'âge, le sexe et la résidence, urbaine/rurale: dernière année disponible
(continued — suite)

(See notes at end of table. — Voir notes à la fin du tableau.)

Continent, country or area, year and age (in years) / Continent, pays ou zone, année et âge (en années)	Total			Urban - Urbaine			Rural - Rurale		
	Both sexes Les deux sexes	Male Masculin	Female Féminin	Both sexes Les deux sexes	Male Masculin	Female Féminin	Both sexes Les deux sexes	Male Masculin	Female Féminin
EUROPE									
Portugal[5]									
2001									
50-54	4.4	6.1	2.9	...	...	...	...	...	...
55-59	6.5	9.3	4.0	...	...	...	...	...	...
60-64	10.2	14.5	6.6	...	...	...	...	...	...
65-69	16.2	23.1	10.5	...	...	...	...	...	...
70-74	27.6	37.4	20.0	...	...	...	...	...	...
75-79	49.1	63.9	38.7	...	...	...	...	...	...
80-84	84.2	102.0	73.3	...	...	...	...	...	...
85+	183.6	192.9	178.9	...	...	...	...	...	...
Republic of Moldova - République de Moldova[8]									
2001									
Total	11.0	11.8	10.3	8.6	9.7	7.7	12.7	13.4	12.1
0-1	16.5	17.9	15.1	17.1	19.0	15.2	16.2	17.3	15.0
1-4	0.9	1.1	0.7	0.7	♦0.9	♦0.4	1.0	1.2	0.8
5-9	0.5	0.6	0.4	0.3	♦0.3	♦0.4	0.5	0.7	♦0.4
10-14	0.4	0.6	0.2	0.3	♦0.4	♦0.2	0.5	0.7	♦0.3
15-19	0.6	0.9	0.4	0.5	0.7	♦0.3	0.7	0.9	0.5
20-24	1.1	1.8	0.4	1.2	1.9	♦0.5	1.1	1.7	0.4
25-29	1.4	2.1	0.6	1.3	2.0	0.7	1.4	2.3	0.6
30-34	2.1	3.0	1.3	1.7	2.2	1.1	2.6	3.9	1.5
35-39	3.4	5.3	1.7	2.7	4.4	1.3	4.0	6.1	2.1
40-44	5.1	7.7	2.7	4.1	6.4	2.1	5.9	8.7	3.3
45-49	7.8	11.5	4.6	6.7	9.8	4.0	8.8	12.8	5.2
50-54	11.2	15.6	7.4	10.2	14.7	6.1	12.1	16.3	8.5
55-59	18.3	24.2	13.7	16.0	21.8	10.9	19.9	26.1	15.5
60-64	25.9	34.3	19.7	23.5	33.7	15.2	27.5	34.7	22.4
65-69	37.5	49.1	29.3	35.0	45.6	27.3	38.6	50.9	30.3
70-74	57.0	71.7	47.9	53.2	68.1	44.0	58.8	73.3	49.7
75-79	85.5	100.2	78.1	77.4	92.8	70.3	89.3	103.3	81.8
80-84	135.5	151.2	127.3	119.9	135.9	112.7	142.1	156.8	133.9
85+	255.6	311.7	234.7	202.1	246.3	187.5	285.8	343.7	262.7
Romania - Roumanie									
2001									
Total	11.6	12.7	10.5	9.0	10.1	7.9	14.7	15.8	13.6
0-1	18.2	20.3	15.9	15.2	17.6	12.8	20.7	22.7	18.7
1-4	0.8	0.9	0.8	0.6	0.7	0.6	1.0	1.1	0.9
5-9	0.4	0.5	0.3	0.3	0.4	0.3	0.4	0.5	0.3
10-14	0.6	0.7	0.5	0.5	0.6	0.4	0.7	0.8	0.5
15-19	0.5	0.7	0.3	0.4	0.6	0.3	0.7	1.0	0.4
20-24	0.7	1.0	0.4	0.6	0.9	0.4	0.8	1.2	0.5
25-29	0.9	1.3	0.5	0.7	1.0	0.4	1.1	1.5	0.6
30-34	1.4	2.0	0.8	1.1	1.6	0.7	1.7	2.4	0.9
35-39	2.4	3.4	1.3	1.8	2.6	1.1	3.3	4.6	1.7
40-44	4.0	5.9	2.3	3.3	4.8	2.0	5.5	7.7	2.9
45-49	6.3	9.2	3.5	5.6	7.9	3.3	7.7	11.6	3.9
50-54	9.1	13.0	5.3	8.5	11.9	5.1	9.9	14.7	5.7
55-59	13.2	19.0	8.1	13.0	18.4	8.1	13.5	19.7	8.0
60-64	19.4	27.6	12.6	19.5	27.9	12.4	19.4	27.3	12.8
65-69	27.8	37.8	19.9	28.1	38.4	20.1	27.6	37.4	19.7
70-74	42.6	54.3	33.9	42.9	55.1	34.1	42.5	53.9	33.7
75-79	69.9	83.0	61.4	69.6	84.7	60.6	70.1	82.1	61.9
80-84	109.8	122.0	103.1	106.0	121.3	98.6	112.2	122.5	106.2
85+	213.1	216.0	211.6	184.5	196.4	178.7	235.0	229.1	238.5
Russian Federation - Fédération de Russie[8]									
1999									
Total	14.7	16.3	13.3	14.1	15.8	12.6	16.3	17.4	15.3
0-1	16.6	18.7	14.4	15.9	18.0	13.7	18.1	20.3	15.8

20. **Death rates specific for age, sex and urban/rural residence: latest available year**
Taux de mortalité selon l'âge, le sexe et la résidence, urbaine/rurale: dernière année disponible
(continued — suite)

(See notes at end of table. — Voir notes à la fin du tableau.)

Continent, country or area, year and age (in years) / Continent, pays ou zone, année et âge (en années)	Total			Urban - Urbaine			Rural - Rurale		
	Both sexes Les deux sexes	Male Masculin	Female Féminin	Both sexes Les deux sexes	Male Masculin	Female Féminin	Both sexes Les deux sexes	Male Masculin	Female Féminin
EUROPE									
Russian Federation - Fédération de Russie[8]									
1999									
1-4	1.0	1.1	0.9	0.8	0.9	0.7	1.4	1.6	1.3
5-9	0.5	0.6	0.4	0.4	0.5	0.3	0.6	0.7	0.5
10-14	0.5	0.6	0.3	0.4	0.5	0.3	0.6	0.7	0.4
15-19	1.4	2.0	0.8	1.4	1.9	0.8	1.6	2.2	0.9
20-24	2.8	4.5	1.1	2.7	4.4	1.1	3.1	4.8	1.2
25-29	3.3	5.2	1.3	3.1	4.8	1.2	3.9	6.3	1.4
30-34	4.1	6.5	1.6	3.9	6.1	1.6	4.6	7.4	1.7
35-39	5.2	8.3	2.2	5.0	8.1	2.2	5.8	9.0	2.4
40-44	7.2	11.4	3.2	6.9	11.1	3.1	8.0	12.2	3.4
45-49	10.2	16.1	4.8	9.9	15.8	4.6	11.3	17.0	5.4
50-54	14.1	22.1	7.1	13.6	21.6	6.9	15.8	23.7	8.2
55-59	19.6	31.2	10.7	19.1	30.6	10.3	21.1	32.9	11.7
60-64	26.5	42.0	15.3	25.6	41.1	14.9	28.6	44.3	16.5
65-69	37.9	58.4	25.2	37.3	57.8	25.1	39.2	59.6	25.5
70-74	52.7	77.7	40.5	53.2	77.3	41.3	51.6	78.7	38.9
75-79	74.8	100.4	66.6	75.7	99.3	68.0	72.7	103.0	63.5
80-84	122.7	148.6	115.6	126.0	149.4	119.2	115.7	146.8	108.5
85+	206.3	200.1	207.8	214.3	207.2	216.2	192.3	185.0	193.8
Serbia and Montenegro - Serbie-et-Monténégro									
2000									
Total	11.1	11.7	10.5	10.8	11.6	10.1	11.4	11.8	11.0
0-1	13.4	15.3	11.3	14.7	16.8	12.4	11.9	13.6	10.0
1-4	0.6	0.6	0.6	0.6	0.6	0.5	0.7	0.7	0.6
5-9	0.2	0.3	0.2	0.1	0.2	♦0.1	0.3	0.4	0.2
10-14	0.2	0.3	0.2	0.2	0.3	0.2	0.2	0.3	0.2
15-19	0.5	0.6	0.3	0.5	0.6	0.3	0.4	0.6	0.3
20-24	0.7	1.0	0.4	0.8	1.2	0.4	0.6	0.8	0.4
25-29	0.7	1.0	0.4	0.8	1.2	0.4	0.7	0.9	0.4
30-34	1.0	1.2	0.7	1.1	1.3	0.8	0.9	1.1	0.6
35-39	1.5	2.0	1.1	1.6	2.2	1.1	1.4	1.9	0.9
40-44	2.7	3.6	1.7	2.9	3.9	1.9	2.4	3.2	1.5
45-49	4.7	6.2	3.2	5.0	6.6	3.4	4.3	5.6	2.9
50-54	7.4	10.1	4.8	7.8	10.9	5.0	6.9	9.2	4.4
55-59	12.2	16.2	8.4	12.8	17.0	9.0	11.5	15.4	7.6
60-64	18.9	24.9	13.6	19.8	25.8	14.5	17.9	23.8	12.6
65-69	31.3	40.2	23.7	33.0	41.9	25.5	29.6	38.6	22.1
70-74	47.2	56.3	40.1	51.5	60.8	44.3	43.7	52.7	36.8
75-79	75.1	81.9	70.4	81.0	83.9	78.8	70.5	80.2	64.2
80-84	104.7	108.7	102.2	120.0	107.8	129.3	95.2	109.3	87.0
85+	176.2	143.6	204.3	188.8	132.3	246.2	167.4	152.8	178.7
Slovakia - Slovaquie									
2001									
Total	9.6	10.6	8.8	...	...	...	...	...	...
0-1	13.4	15.7	11.2	...	...	...	...	...	...
1-4	0.3	0.4	0.3	...	...	...	...	...	...
5-9	0.2	0.3	♦0.1	...	...	...	...	...	...
10-14	0.2	0.3	♦0.1	...	...	...	...	...	...
15-19	0.4	0.5	0.3	...	...	...	...	...	...
20-24	0.6	0.9	0.2	...	...	...	...	...	...
25-29	0.8	1.2	0.4	...	...	...	...	...	...
30-34	1.1	1.7	0.5	...	...	...	...	...	...
35-39	1.6	2.4	0.8	...	...	...	...	...	...
40-44	2.9	4.2	1.5	...	...	...	...	...	...
45-49	4.9	7.1	2.7	...	...	...	...	...	...
50-54	7.7	11.6	4.1	...	...	...	...	...	...
55-59	11.6	17.6	6.6	...	...	...	...	...	...

20. Death rates specific for age, sex and urban/rural residence: latest available year
Taux de mortalité selon l'âge, le sexe et la résidence, urbaine/rurale: dernière année disponible
(continued — suite)

(See notes at end of table. — Voir notes à la fin du tableau.)

Continent, country or area, year and age (in years) / Continent, pays ou zone, année et âge (en années)	Total			Urban - Urbaine			Rural - Rurale		
	Both sexes Les deux sexes	Male Masculin	Female Féminin	Both sexes Les deux sexes	Male Masculin	Female Féminin	Both sexes Les deux sexes	Male Masculin	Female Féminin
EUROPE									
Slovakia - Slovaquie									
2001									
60-64	18.2	28.3	10.4	...	...	...	...	...	...
65-69	26.7	40.0	17.1	...	...	...	...	...	...
70-74	41.6	59.5	30.3	...	...	...	...	...	...
75-79	64.8	82.9	54.8	...	...	...	...	...	...
80-84	109.6	133.8	97.3	...	...	...	...	...	...
85+	193.1	205.8	187.5	...	...	...	...	...	...
Slovenia - Slovénie									
1994									
Total	9.7	10.2	9.3	8.4	8.7	8.0	11.1	11.6	10.7
0-1	6.5	6.1	6.8	6.7	6.8	◆6.7	6.3	◆5.6	7.0
1-4	0.4	◆0.5	◆0.3	◆0.4	◆0.5	◆0.4	◆0.4	◆0.5	◆0.2
5-9	0.3	◆0.3	◆0.3	◆0.3	◆0.2	◆0.3	◆0.3	◆0.3	◆0.2
10-14	◆0.2	◆0.2	◆0.1	◆0.2	◆0.2	◆0.1	◆0.2	◆0.2	◆0.1
15-19	0.8	1.3	◆0.4	0.7	1.0	◆0.4	0.9	1.5	◆0.3
20-24	1.0	1.5	0.5	1.0	1.4	◆0.5	1.0	1.6	◆0.4
25-29	1.2	1.8	0.5	1.1	1.6	◆0.5	1.3	2.0	◆0.5
30-34	1.3	1.9	0.7	1.0	1.3	◆0.7	1.6	2.5	◆0.7
35-39	1.9	2.8	1.0	1.6	2.2	1.0	2.3	3.4	1.1
40-44	3.0	4.2	1.8	2.8	3.8	1.8	3.2	4.6	1.7
45-49	4.6	6.4	2.7	3.9	5.2	2.7	5.3	7.7	2.7
50-54	7.2	10.3	4.1	6.2	8.4	4.1	8.2	12.1	4.0
55-59	10.3	14.7	6.3	9.1	12.6	5.9	11.5	16.7	6.6
60-64	16.5	25.0	9.5	14.8	22.1	8.9	18.1	27.6	10.0
65-69	23.9	35.8	16.1	22.4	33.2	15.5	25.2	38.2	16.6
70-74	35.4	52.6	26.4	32.2	47.3	24.0	38.3	57.8	28.5
75-79	64.9	82.8	55.9	62.4	78.9	54.0	67.1	86.3	57.6
80-84	103.4	128.9	91.9	95.2	120.8	83.8	109.7	135.1	98.2
85+	194.3	214.1	187.5	182.2	206.0	174.8	203.7	219.5	197.8
2001									
Total	9.3	9.9	8.7	...	...	...	...	...	...
0-4	0.9	1.0	0.8	...	...	...	...	...	...
5-9	◆0.2	◆0.2	◆0.1	...	...	...	...	...	...
10-14	◆0.1	◆0.2	◆0.1	...	...	...	...	...	...
15-19	0.6	1.0	◆0.3	...	...	...	...	...	...
20-24	0.7	1.2	◆0.2	...	...	...	...	...	...
25-29	0.8	1.3	◆0.3	...	...	...	...	...	...
30-34	1.0	1.5	0.5	...	...	...	...	...	...
35-39	1.4	2.1	0.7	...	...	...	...	...	...
40-44	2.2	3.1	1.3	...	...	...	...	...	...
45-49	4.0	5.6	2.3	...	...	...	...	...	...
50-54	6.2	8.3	3.9	...	...	...	...	...	...
55-59	9.4	13.2	5.8	...	...	...	...	...	...
60-64	13.4	19.9	7.5	...	...	...	...	...	...
65-69	20.5	30.6	12.6	...	...	...	...	...	...
70-74	31.5	46.0	22.3	...	...	...	...	...	...
75-79	48.5	72.2	37.9	...	...	...	...	...	...
80-84	81.3	107.4	70.8	...	...	...	...	...	...
85+	177.4	213.8	165.1	...	...	...	...	...	...
Spain - Espagne									
2000									
Total	9.0	9.7	8.4	...	...	...	...	...	...
0-1	4.5	4.8	4.2	...	...	...	...	...	...
1-4	0.3	0.3	0.2	...	...	...	...	...	...
5-9	0.2	0.2	0.1	...	...	...	...	...	...
10-14	0.2	0.2	0.1	...	...	...	...	...	...
15-19	0.5	0.7	0.3	...	...	...	...	...	...
20-24	0.6	0.9	0.3	...	...	...	...	...	...
25-29	0.7	1.0	0.3	...	...	...	...	...	...

20. Death rates specific for age, sex and urban/rural residence: latest available year
Taux de mortalité selon l'âge, le sexe et la résidence, urbaine/rurale: dernière année disponible
(continued — suite)

(See notes at end of table. — Voir notes à la fin du tableau.)

Continent, country or area, year and age (in years) Continent, pays ou zone, année et âge (en années)	Total			Urban - Urbaine			Rural - Rurale		
	Both sexes Les deux sexes	Male Masculin	Female Féminin	Both sexes Les deux sexes	Male Masculin	Female Féminin	Both sexes Les deux sexes	Male Masculin	Female Féminin
EUROPE									
Spain - Espagne									
2000									
30-34	0.9	1.3	0.5	...	...	...	...	...	...
35-39	1.3	1.9	0.7	...	...	...	...	...	...
40-44	1.9	2.6	1.1	...	...	...	...	...	...
45-49	2.6	3.7	1.5	...	...	...	...	...	...
50-54	3.9	5.7	2.2	...	...	...	...	...	...
55-59	5.8	8.5	3.2	...	...	...	...	...	...
60-64	9.0	13.4	5.0	...	...	...	...	...	...
65-69	14.3	21.0	8.5	...	...	...	...	...	...
70-74	23.1	33.2	15.1	...	...	...	...	...	...
75-79	40.0	55.6	29.2	...	...	...	...	...	...
80-84	69.5	89.0	58.6	...	...	...	...	...	...
85-89	129.0	155.8	116.7	...	...	...	...	...	...
90-94	229.7	252.9	220.4	...	...	...	...	...	...
95+	448.6	441.9	451.1	...	...	...	...	...	...
Sweden - Suède									
2001									
Total	10.5	10.3	10.7	...	...	...	...	...	...
0-4	0.9	1.0	0.8	...	...	...	...	...	...
5-9	0.1	◆0.1	◆0.1	...	...	...	...	...	...
10-14	0.1	0.1	0.1	...	...	...	...	...	...
15-19	0.3	0.4	0.2	...	...	...	...	...	...
20-24	0.5	0.8	0.2	...	...	...	...	...	...
25-29	0.5	0.7	0.2	...	...	...	...	...	...
30-34	0.6	0.8	0.3	...	...	...	...	...	...
35-39	0.8	1.1	0.5	...	...	...	...	...	...
40-44	1.2	1.6	0.9	...	...	...	...	...	...
45-49	2.2	2.6	1.7	...	...	...	...	...	...
50-54	3.4	4.0	2.8	...	...	...	...	...	...
55-59	5.4	6.4	4.4	...	...	...	...	...	...
60-64	8.4	10.6	6.2	...	...	...	...	...	...
65-69	14.3	18.1	10.8	...	...	...	...	...	...
70-74	23.5	30.3	17.8	...	...	...	...	...	...
75-79	40.7	52.7	31.6	...	...	...	...	...	...
80-84	71.8	90.8	59.6	...	...	...	...	...	...
85+	169.4	195.0	158.0	...	...	...	...	...	...
Switzerland - Suisse									
2001									
Total	8.5	8.5	8.5	...	...	...	...	...	...
0-4	1.2	1.3	1.0	...	...	...	...	...	...
5-9	0.1	◆0.1	◆0.1	...	...	...	...	...	...
10-14	0.1	0.2	◆0.1	...	...	...	...	...	...
15-19	0.4	0.6	0.2	...	...	...	...	...	...
20-24	0.6	0.9	0.3	...	...	...	...	...	...
25-29	0.6	0.8	0.4	...	...	...	...	...	...
30-34	0.7	1.0	0.5	...	...	...	...	...	...
35-39	0.9	1.2	0.7	...	...	...	...	...	...
40-44	1.3	1.7	1.0	...	...	...	...	...	...
45-49	2.2	2.8	1.5	...	...	...	...	...	...
50-54	3.4	4.3	2.4	...	...	...	...	...	...
55-59	5.2	6.5	3.8	...	...	...	...	...	...
60-64	7.9	10.6	5.5	...	...	...	...	...	...
65-69	13.0	18.0	8.6	...	...	...	...	...	...
70-74	20.8	29.5	14.2	...	...	...	...	...	...
75-79	35.7	49.2	26.6	...	...	...	...	...	...
80-84	64.7	85.4	52.7	...	...	...	...	...	...
85+	158.2	181.4	148.9	...	...	...	...	...	...

20. Death rates specific for age, sex and urban/rural residence: latest available year
Taux de mortalité selon l'âge, le sexe et la résidence, urbaine/rurale: dernière année disponible
(continued — suite)

(See notes at end of table. — Voir notes à la fin du tableau.)

Continent, country or area, year and age (in years) / Continent, pays ou zone, année et âge (en années)	Total			Urban - Urbaine			Rural - Rurale		
	Both sexes Les deux sexes	Male Masculin	Female Féminin	Both sexes Les deux sexes	Male Masculin	Female Féminin	Both sexes Les deux sexes	Male Masculin	Female Féminin
EUROPE									
The Former Yugoslav Rep. of Macedonia - L'ex-République yougoslave de Macédoine									
2001									
Total	8.3	9.2	7.5	...	...	...	...	...	...
0-1	12.4	14.4	10.2	...	...	...	...	...	...
1-4	0.4	♦0.4	♦0.4	...	...	...	...	...	...
5-9	0.2	♦0.3	♦0.2	...	...	...	...	...	...
10-14	0.2	♦0.2	♦0.2	...	...	...	...	...	...
15-19	0.4	0.5	♦0.3	...	...	...	...	...	...
20-24	0.5	0.8	♦0.2	...	...	...	...	...	...
25-29	0.7	1.0	♦0.3	...	...	...	...	...	...
30-34	0.9	1.2	0.5	...	...	...	...	...	...
35-39	1.4	1.9	0.9	...	...	...	...	...	...
40-44	2.8	3.7	1.8	...	...	...	...	...	...
45-49	4.0	5.3	2.7	...	...	...	...	...	...
50-54	6.6	9.2	4.1	...	...	...	...	...	...
55-59	10.1	13.3	7.2	...	...	...	...	...	...
60-64	16.0	21.6	10.8	...	...	...	...	...	...
65-69	27.1	34.9	20.3	...	...	...	...	...	...
70-74	43.6	51.1	37.6	...	...	...	...	...	...
75-79	79.2	88.0	72.6	...	...	...	...	...	...
80-84	132.5	146.4	122.2	...	...	...	...	...	...
85+	205.1	223.5	192.0	...	...	...	...	...	...
Ukraine[8]									
1998									
Total	14.3	15.2	13.6	12.5	13.8	11.4	18.1	18.3	18.0
0-1	12.4	14.5	10.2	12.4	14.5	10.1	12.4	14.5	10.3
1-4	0.9	1.0	0.8	0.7	0.8	0.6	1.3	1.4	1.2
5-9	0.4	0.5	0.3	0.3	0.4	0.3	0.5	0.6	0.4
10-14	0.4	0.5	0.3	0.4	0.5	0.3	0.4	0.5	0.3
15-19	0.9	1.2	0.6	0.8	1.1	0.5	1.1	1.4	0.7
20-24	1.6	2.5	0.7	1.5	2.3	0.7	1.8	2.8	0.7
25-29	2.1	3.3	1.0	2.0	3.1	1.0	2.4	3.7	0.9
30-34	2.9	4.5	1.2	2.7	4.4	1.2	3.1	4.8	1.3
35-39	4.0	6.3	1.7	3.7	6.0	1.7	4.6	7.2	1.8
40-44	5.8	9.3	2.6	5.4	8.8	2.4	6.9	10.6	3.1
45-49	8.5	13.5	4.1	8.0	12.6	4.0	10.1	15.9	4.6
50-54	12.3	19.4	6.4	11.9	18.7	6.2	13.2	21.0	6.8
55-59	15.9	24.9	9.0	15.6	24.1	8.8	16.6	26.2	9.3
60-64	24.8	37.5	15.2	24.8	37.1	15.4	24.9	38.2	14.9
65-69	32.7	48.6	22.4	33.4	48.6	23.3	31.7	48.5	21.2
70-74	50.1	71.5	39.8	51.6	72.0	41.4	48.0	70.8	37.7
75-79	77.4	99.6	69.1	79.3	98.6	71.6	75.3	100.9	66.6
80-84	118.3	138.9	111.9	120.3	136.4	114.7	115.9	142.6	108.7
85-89	189.9	206.2	185.3	195.8	206.6	192.4	184.2	205.6	178.6
90-94	271.9	270.4	272.3	265.5	269.3	264.5	278.2	271.6	280.0
95+	389.6	267.6	430.8	334.4	247.7	364.0	450.0	289.8	503.4
2001									
Total	15.2	16.6	14.0	...	...	...	...	...	...
0-1	11.2	12.6	9.7	...	...	...	...	...	...
1-4	0.9	1.0	0.7	...	...	...	...	...	...
5-9	0.4	0.5	0.3	...	...	...	...	...	...
10-14	0.4	0.5	0.2	...	...	...	...	...	...
15-19	0.9	1.3	0.5	...	...	...	...	...	...
20-24	1.7	2.7	0.8	...	...	...	...	...	...
25-29	2.4	3.7	1.1	...	...	...	...	...	...
30-34	3.3	5.2	1.5	...	...	...	...	...	...
35-39	4.5	7.2	1.9	...	...	...	...	...	...
40-44	6.4	10.3	2.8	...	...	...	...	...	...

20. Death rates specific for age, sex and urban/rural residence: latest available year
Taux de mortalité selon l'âge, le sexe et la résidence, urbaine/rurale: dernière année disponible
(continued — suite)

(See notes at end of table. — Voir notes à la fin du tableau.)

Continent, country or area, year and age (in years) / Continent, pays ou zone, année et âge (en années)	Total			Urban - Urbaine			Rural - Rurale		
	Both sexes Les deux sexes	Male Masculin	Female Féminin	Both sexes Les deux sexes	Male Masculin	Female Féminin	Both sexes Les deux sexes	Male Masculin	Female Féminin
EUROPE									
Ukraine[8]									
2001									
45-49	9.2	14.8	4.2	...	...	...	...	...	...
50-54	13.0	20.6	6.7	...	...	...	...	...	...
55-59	17.0	26.6	9.6	...	...	...	...	...	...
60-64	24.6	38.5	14.8	...	...	...	...	...	...
65-69	35.1	51.7	23.9	...	...	...	...	...	...
70-74	50.3	73.4	38.0	...	...	...	...	...	...
75-79	76.2	101.1	66.8	...	...	...	...	...	...
80-84	121.7	142.3	115.0	...	...	...	...	...	...
85+	210.2	208.2	210.7	...	...	...	...	...	...
United Kingdom - Royaume-Uni									
1999									
Total	10.6	10.3	11.0	...	...	...	...	...	...
0-4	1.3	1.5	1.2	...	...	...	...	...	...
5-9	0.1	0.1	0.1	...	...	...	...	...	...
10-14	0.1	0.2	0.1	...	...	...	...	...	...
15-19	0.4	0.6	0.3	...	...	...	...	...	...
20-24	0.6	0.9	0.3	...	...	...	...	...	...
25-29	0.6	0.9	0.4	...	...	...	...	...	...
30-34	0.8	1.0	0.5	...	...	...	...	...	...
35-39	1.0	1.3	0.8	...	...	...	...	...	...
40-44	1.6	1.9	1.3	...	...	...	...	...	...
45-49	2.6	3.1	2.1	...	...	...	...	...	...
50-54	4.1	5.0	3.2	...	...	...	...	...	...
55-59	6.9	8.6	5.2	...	...	...	...	...	...
60-64	11.4	14.2	8.7	...	...	...	...	...	...
65-69	19.2	24.5	14.4	...	...	...	...	...	...
70-74	32.6	41.4	25.4	...	...	...	...	...	...
75-79	52.7	67.3	42.5	...	...	...	...	...	...
80-84	86.1	109.1	73.4	...	...	...	...	...	...
85+	165.9	190.0	157.1	...	...	...	...	...	...
OCEANIA — OCEANIE									
Australia - Australie[+]									
2000									
Total	6.7	7.0	6.4	...	...	...	...	...	...
0-1	5.2	5.7	4.7	...	...	...	...	...	...
1-4	0.3	0.3	0.2	...	...	...	...	...	...
5-9	0.1	0.1	0.1	...	...	...	...	...	...
10-14	0.1	0.2	0.1	...	...	...	...	...	...
15-19	0.5	0.7	0.3	...	...	...	...	...	...
20-24	0.7	1.0	0.4	...	...	...	...	...	...
25-29	0.8	1.2	0.4	...	...	...	...	...	...
30-34	0.9	1.3	0.5	...	...	...	...	...	...
35-39	1.1	1.5	0.8	...	...	...	...	...	...
40-44	1.4	1.9	1.0	...	...	...	...	...	...
45-49	2.0	2.4	1.6	...	...	...	...	...	...
50-54	3.1	3.8	2.4	...	...	...	...	...	...
55-59	5.1	6.3	4.0	...	...	...	...	...	...
60-64	8.2	10.4	5.9	...	...	...	...	...	...
65-69	13.9	17.9	10.0	...	...	...	...	...	...
70-74	23.6	31.0	17.1	...	...	...	...	...	...
75-79	38.7	51.4	29.1	...	...	...	...	...	...
80-84	67.2	85.2	55.9	...	...	...	...	...	...
85+	144.2	162.1	136.1	...	...	...	...	...	...

20. Death rates specific for age, sex and urban/rural residence: latest available year
Taux de mortalité selon l'âge, le sexe et la résidence, urbaine/rurale: dernière année disponible
(continued — suite)

(See notes at end of table. — Voir notes à la fin du tableau.)

Continent, country or area, year and age (in years) / Continent, pays ou zone, année et âge (en années)	Total			Urban - Urbaine			Rural - Rurale		
	Both sexes Les deux sexes	Male Masculin	Female Féminin	Both sexes Les deux sexes	Male Masculin	Female Féminin	Both sexes Les deux sexes	Male Masculin	Female Féminin
OCEANIA — OCEANIE									
New Caledonia - Nouvelle-Calédonie									
1994									
Total	5.8	6.6	4.9	...	...	...	...	...	...
0-1	9.8	♦10.4	♦9.2	...	...	...	...	...	...
1-4	♦1.4	♦1.3	♦1.4	...	...	...	...	...	...
5-9	♦0.8	♦1.1	♦0.4	...	...	...	...	...	...
10-14	♦0.2	♦0.2	♦0.2	...	...	...	...	...	...
15-19	♦1.1	♦1.8	♦0.3	...	...	...	...	...	...
20-24	2.2	3.4	♦1.0	...	...	...	...	...	...
25-29	♦1.1	♦1.4	♦0.7	...	...	...	...	...	...
30-34	♦1.9	♦3.3	♦0.6	...	...	...	...	...	...
35-39	2.8	♦3.6	♦2.0	...	...	...	...	...	...
40-44	3.7	♦4.2	♦3.1	...	...	...	...	...	...
45-49	4.7	6.0	♦3.3	...	...	...	...	...	...
50-54	7.9	8.1	♦7.6	...	...	...	...	...	...
55-59	12.2	14.1	10.1	...	...	...	...	...	...
60-64	22.0	25.8	18.1	...	...	...	...	...	...
65-69	26.2	36.5	16.2	...	...	...	...	...	...
75-84	77.2	87.8	67.6	...	...	...	...	...	...
80+	108.8	118.7	101.9	...	...	...	...	...	...
New Zealand - Nouvelle-Zélande[+,5]									
1996									
Total	7.8	8.1	7.5	8.3	8.6	8.0	4.8	5.5	4.1
0-1	7.4	7.8	7.0	8.0	8.5	7.5	4.2	♦4.2	♦4.2
1-4	0.4	0.5	0.4	0.4	0.5	0.4	♦0.3	♦0.4	♦0.3
5-9	0.2	♦0.2	♦0.2	0.2	♦0.2	♦0.2	♦0.1	...	♦0.2
10-14	0.3	0.3	0.3	0.3	♦0.2	♦0.3	♦0.3	♦0.3	♦0.3
15-19	1.0	1.3	0.7	0.9	1.2	0.7	1.2	♦1.6	♦0.8
20-24	1.0	1.5	0.5	0.9	1.4	0.5	1.6	2.4	♦0.5
25-29	1.0	1.5	0.5	1.0	1.4	0.5	1.2	2.0	♦0.5
30-34	1.0	1.4	0.7	1.1	1.4	0.7	0.9	1.5	♦0.4
35-39	1.2	1.5	0.8	1.2	1.6	0.9	1.0	♦1.3	♦0.6
40-44	1.4	1.7	1.1	1.4	1.7	1.1	1.4	1.6	♦1.1
45-49	2.9	3.2	2.5	3.0	3.3	2.7	2.3	2.6	1.9
50-54	4.5	5.4	3.7	4.7	5.7	3.8	3.5	3.8	3.3
55-59	7.4	9.1	5.7	7.8	9.8	5.9	5.1	5.9	4.3
60-64	12.8	15.7	9.9	13.1	16.3	10.0	11.1	12.8	9.1
65-69	19.7	24.6	14.9	20.1	25.5	15.1	16.8	19.8	12.8
70-74	31.1	40.2	23.4	31.5	41.6	23.4	27.3	30.3	23.8
75-79	49.3	64.0	39.2	50.1	65.5	39.8	41.9	51.7	31.9
80-84	83.6	104.8	71.2	83.8	105.6	71.5	80.4	96.3	66.9
85-89	137.4	175.8	120.1	137.3	175.8	120.4	139.3	176.1	114.0
90-94	223.3	272.5	206.3	224.6	277.6	206.8	198.8	209.0	193.5
95-99	345.1	346.1	344.9	348.5	349.7	347.5	295.2	♦296.3	♦294.9
100+	475.1	♦606.1	462.2	472.2	♦545.5	467.6	♦833.3	♦666.7	♦500.0
2000									
Total	7.0	7.3	6.6	...	...	...	...	...	...
0-1	6.1	6.4	5.6	...	...	...	...	...	...
1-4	0.4	0.4	0.3	...	...	...	...	...	...
5-9	0.2	♦0.1	♦0.2	...	...	...	...	...	...
10-14	0.2	0.3	♦0.1	...	...	...	...	...	...
15-19	0.6	0.9	0.4	...	...	...	...	...	...
20-24	0.7	1.1	0.3	...	...	...	...	...	...
25-29	0.9	1.3	0.5	...	...	...	...	...	...
30-34	0.9	1.4	0.5	...	...	...	...	...	...
35-39	1.0	1.3	0.7	...	...	...	...	...	...
40-44	1.5	1.9	1.2	...	...	...	...	...	...
45-49	2.4	2.8	1.9	...	...	...	...	...	...

20. Death rates specific for age, sex and urban/rural residence: latest available year
Taux de mortalité selon l'âge, le sexe et la résidence, urbaine/rurale: dernière année disponible
(continued — suite)

(See notes at end of table. — Voir notes à la fin du tableau.)

Continent, country or area, year and age (in years) / Continent, pays ou zone, année et âge (en années)	Total			Urban - Urbaine			Rural - Rurale		
	Both sexes Les deux sexes	Male Masculin	Female Féminin	Both sexes Les deux sexes	Male Masculin	Female Féminin	Both sexes Les deux sexes	Male Masculin	Female Féminin
OCEANIA — OCEANIE									
New Zealand - Nouvelle-Zélande[+,5]									
2000									
50-54	3.7	4.2	3.1	...	...	...	...	...	...
55-59	6.2	7.2	5.2	...	...	...	...	...	...
60-64	9.7	11.6	8.0	...	...	...	...	...	...
65-69	16.7	21.0	12.5	...	...	...	...	...	...
70-74	25.9	33.0	19.5	...	...	...	...	...	...
75-79	42.6	56.9	32.0	...	...	...	...	...	...
80-84	69.7	91.4	56.9	...	...	...	...	...	...
85-89	116.1	144.0	102.5	...	...	...	...	...	...
90+	216.4	249.3	205.5	...	...	...	...	...	...

GENERAL NOTES - NOTES GENERALES

Data exclude foetal deaths. For definition of 'urban', see end of Technical Notes for table 6. For method of evaluation and limitations of data, see Technical Notes for this table. — Les données ne comprennent pas les morts foetales. Pour les définitions des 'régions urbaines', se reporter à la fin des Notes techniques du tableau 6. Pour la méthode d'evaluations et les insuffisances des données, voir Notes techniques, pour ce tableau.

Italics: data from civil registers which are incomplete or of unknown completeness. — Italiques: données incomplètes ou dont le degré d'exactitude n'est pas connu provenant des registres de l'état civil.

FOOTNOTES - NOTES

* Rates based on 30 or fewer deaths. — Taux basés sur 30 décès ou moins.

+ Data tabulated by year of registration rather than occurrence. — Données exploitées selon l'année de l'enregistrement et non l'année de l'événement.

[1] Based on the results of the population census. — D'après les résultats du recensement de la population.

[2] Data for 1997 refer to last twelve months preceding population and housing census of 1997. — Les données pour 1997 se réfèrent au douze mois précédant le recensement de population et de l'habitat de 1997.

[3] Excluding live-born infants dying before registration of birth. — Non compris les enfants nés vivants décédés avant l'enregistrement de leur naissance.

[4] Including Canadian residents temporarily in the United States, but excluding United States residents temporarily in Canada. — Y compris les résidents canadiens se trouvant temporairement aux Etats-Unis, mais ne comprennent pas les résidents des Etats-Unis se trouvant temporairement au Canada.

[5] Data for urban and rural exclude deaths of unknown residence. — Les données pur la résidence urbaine et rurale non comprent pas les décès dont on ignore la résidence.

[6] Data for male and female categories exclude deaths of unknown sex. — Les données pour le sexe masculin et féminin ne comprennent pas les décès ou on ignore le sexe.

[7] Excluding Indian jungle population. — Non compris les Indiens de la jungle.

[8] Excluding infants born alive with less than 28 weeks gestation, less than 1 000 grams in weight and 35 centimeters in length, who die within seven days of birth. — Non compris les enfants nés vivants avant 28 semaines de gestation, pesant moins de 1 000 grammes, mesurant moins de 35 centimètres et décédés dans les sept jours qui ont suivi leur naissance.

[9] Data refer to government controlled areas. — Les données se raportent aux zones contrôlées par le Gouvernement.

[10] Including data for East Jerusalem and Israeli residents in certain other territories under occupation by Israeli military forces since June 1967. — Y compris les données pour Jérusalem-Est et les résidents israéliens dans certains autres territoires occupés depuis 1967 par les forces armées israéliennes.

[11] For Japanese nationals in Japan only; however, rates computed on population including foreigners except foreign military and civilian personnel and their dependants stationed in the area. — Pour les nationaux japonais au Japon seulement; toutefois, les taux sont calculés sur la base d''une population comprenant les étrangers, mais ne comprenant ni les militaires et agents civils étrangers en poste sur le territoire ni les membres de leur famille les accompagnant.

[12] Excluding alien armed forces, civilian aliens employed by armed forces, and foreign diplomatic personnel and their dependants. — Non compris les militaires étrangers, les civils étrangers employés par les forces armées ni le personnel diplomatique étranger et les membres de leur famille les accompagnant.

[13] Based on the results of the Population Growth Survey. — D'après les résultats de la 'Population Growth Survey.'

[14] Excluding data for the Pakistan-held part of Jammu and Kashmir, the final status of which has not yet been determined. — Non compris les données concernant la partie du Jammu et Cachemire occupée par le Pakistan dont le statut définitif n'a pas été déterminé.

[15] Excluding transients afloat and non-locally domiciled military and civilian services personnel and their dependants. — Non compris les personnes de passage þ bord de navires, ni les militaires et agents civils domiciliés hors du territoire et les membres de leur famille les accompagnant.

[16] Including armed forces stationed outside the country, but excluding alien armed forces stationed in the area. — Y compris les militaires nationaux hors du pays, mais non compris les militaires étrangers en garnison sur le territoire.

[17] Excluding Faeroe Islands and Greenland. — Non compris les îles Féroé et Gröenland.

[18] Including nationals temporarily outside the country. — Y compris les nationaux se trouvant temporairement hors du pays.

[19] Including armed forces stationed outside the country. — Y compris les militaires nationaux hors du pays.

[20] For ages five years and over, age classification based on year of birth rather than exact date of birth. — A partir de cinq ans, le classement selon l'âge est basé sur l'année de naissances et non sur la date exacte de naissance.

[21] Excluding nationals outside the country. — Non compris les nationaux hors du pays.

[22] Data for urban/rural residence, for the de jure population. — Les

données selon la résidence urbaine/rurale, pour la population de droit.

[23] Events registered within one year of occurrence. — Evénements enregistrés dans l'année qui suit l'événement.

[24] Including residents outside the country if listed in a Netherlands population register. — Y compris les résidents hors du pays, s'ils sont inscrits sur un registre de population néerlandais.

[25] Including residents temporarily outside the country. — Y compris les résidents se trouvant temporairement hors du pays.

Table 21

Table 21 presents deaths by month of occurrence for as many years as possible between 1985 and 2000.

Description of variables: Death is defined as the permanent disappearance of all evidence of life at any time after live birth has taken place (post-natal cessation of vital functions without capability of resuscitation). [i]

Month of death is the calendar month when death occurred, rather than the month when the event was registered.

Statistics on the number of deaths are obtained from civil registers unless otherwise noted.

Reliability of data: Each country or area has been asked to indicate the estimated completeness of the deaths recorded in its civil register. These national assessments are indicated by the quality codes C and U that appear in the first column of this table.

C indicates that the data are estimated to be virtually complete, that is, representing at least 90 per cent of the deaths occurring each year, while U indicates that data are estimated to be incomplete, that is, representing less than 90 per cent of the deaths occurring each year. The code (...) indicates that no information was provided regarding completeness. The code (|) indicates that the source of data is not a civil register, but still reliable.

Data from civil registers which are reported as incomplete or of unknown completeness (code U or ...) are considered unreliable. They appear in italics in this table.

These quality codes apply only to data from civil registers. If a series of data for a country or area contains both data from a civil register and estimated data from, for example, a sample survey, then the code applies only to the registered data. For more information about the quality of vital statistics data in general, and the information available on the basis of the completeness estimates in particular, see section 4.2 of the Technical Notes.

Limitations: Statistics on deaths by month are subject to the same qualifications as have been set forth for vital statistics in general and death statistics in particular as discussed in section 4 of the Technical Notes.

The reliability of the data is an important factor in considering the limitations. In addition, some deaths are tabulated by date of registration and not by date of occurrence; these have been indicated by a plus sign (+). Whenever the lag between the date of occurrence and date of registration is prolonged and, therefore, a large proportion of the death registrations are delayed, death statistics for any given year may be seriously affected.

As a rule, however, delays in the registration of deaths are less common and shorter than in the registration of live births.

International comparability in mortality statistics may also be affected by the exclusion of deaths of infants who were born alive but died before the registration of the birth or within the first 24 hours of life. Statistics of this type are footnoted.

Coverage: Deaths are shown for 129 countries or areas.

Earlier data: Deaths by month have been shown in previous issues of the Demographic Yearbook featuring mortality as the special topic. Data included in this table update the series covering the period of years as follows:

Issue	Years Covered
1985	1976-1984
1980	1971-1979
1974	1965-1973
1967	1962-1966
1951	1946-1950

NOTES

[i] *Principles and Recommendations for a Vital Statistics System, Revision 2,* United Nations publication, Sales No. E.01.XVII.10, United Nations, New York, 2001.

Tableau 21

Le tableau 21 présente des statistiques des décès par mois pour le plus grand nombre d'années possible entre 1985 et 2000.

Description des variables: Le décès est défini comme la disparition permanente de tout signe de vie à un moment quelconque postérieur à la naissance vivante (cessation des fonctions vitales après la naissance sans possibilité de réanimation)[1].

Le mois du décès est le mois civil du décès effectif et non de son enregistrement.

Sauf indication contraire, les statistiques du nombre de décès sont établies sur la base des registres d'état civil.

Fiabilité des données : Il a été demandé à chaque pays ou zone d'indiquer le degré estimé d'exhaustivité des données sur les décès figurant dans ses registres d'état civil. Ces évaluations nationales sont désignées par les codes de qualité C et U qui apparaissent dans la première colonne du tableau.

La lettre C indique que les données sont jugées à peu près complètes, c'est-à-dire qu'elles représentent au moins 90 p. 100 des décès survenus chaque année; la lettre U indique que les données sont jugées incomplètes, c'est-à-dire qu'elles représentent moins de 90 p. 100 des décès survenus chaque année. Le code (...) indique qu'aucun renseignements n'a été fourni quant à l'exhaustivité des données. Le code (|) indique que les données ne proviennent pas des registres de l'état civil mais elles sont néanmoins fiables.

Les données provenant des registres d'état civil qui sont déclarées incomplètes ou dont le degré d'exhaustivité n'est pas connu (code U ou...) sont jugées douteuses. Elles apparaissent en italique dans le présent tableau

Ces codes de qualité ne s'applique qu'aux données tirées des registres d'état civil. Si une série de données pour un pays ou zone contient à la fois des données provenant de ces registres et des estimations calculées, par exemple sur la base d'enquêtes par sondage, le code s'applique uniquement aux données de l'état civil. Pour plus de précisions sur la qualité des données d'état civil en général, et sur les estimations de l'exhaustivité en particulier, voir la section 4.2 des Notes techniques.

Insuffisance des données : Les statistiques des décès par mois appellent toutes les réserves qui ont été faites à propos des statistiques de l'état civil en général et des statistiques des décès en particulier (voir explications à la section 4 des Notes techniques).

La fiabilité des données est un facteur important en l'occurrence. Il faut également tenir compte du fait que, dans certains cas, les décès sont classés par date d'enregistrement et non par date effective; ces cas ont été identifiés par le signe(+). Lorsque le décalage entre le décès et son enregistrement est grand, c'est-à-dire qu'une forte proportion des décès fait l'objet d'un enregistrement tardif, les statistiques des décès dans l'année peuvent être sérieusement faussées.

En règle générale, toutefois, les décès sont enregistrés beaucoup plus rapidement que les naissances vivantes, et les longs retards sont rares.

Un autre facteur qui nuit à la comparabilité internationale des statistiques de la mortalité est la pratique qui consiste à ne pas y inclure les enfants nés vivants mais décédés avant l'enregistrement de leur naissance ou dans les 24 heures qui ont suivi la naissance. Quand tel était le cas, on l'a signalé en note à la fin du tableau.

Portée : Ce tableau présente les statistiques des décès pour 129 pays ou zones.

Données publiées antérieurement: Des statistiques de la mortalité mensuelle figurent déjà dans des éditions antérieures de l'Annuaire présentant mortalité comme sujet spécial. Les données présentées dans ce tableau mettent à jour les périodes d'années suivantes :

Edition	Années considérées
1985	1976-1984
1980	1971-1979
1974	1965-1973
1967	1962-1966
1951	1946-1950

NOTES

[1] *Principes et recommandations pour un système de statistiques de l'état civil, deuxième révision*, Numéro de vente F. 01.XVII.10, Nations Unies, 2003.

21. Deaths by month of occurence: 1985 - 2000
Décès selon le mois de décès: 1985 - 2000

(See notes at end of table. — Voir notes à la fin du tableau.)

Continent, country or area / Continent, pays ou zone	Code[1]	Total	Jan	Feb	March	April	May	June	July	Aug	Sep	Oct	Nov	Dec
AFRICA — AFRIQUE														
Algeria - Algérie[2,3]														
1998	U	131 708	12 119	11 881	12 679	10 642	10 237	9 880	10 499	10 272	10 249	10 293	10 712	12 245
Botswana														
1986	I	1 496	127	110	148	112	122	166	153	153	116	116	98	75
Cape Verde - Cap-Vert														
1985	C	2 735	238	165	206	213	178	208	199	262	277	314	247	228
1990	C	2 498	208	197	241	151	185	181	185	224	235	245	226	220
Egypt - Égypte														
1985	C	454 450	37 382	33 134	36 229	33 092	35 492	39 267	41 951	40 671	41 166	36 588	34 372	45 106
1986	C	455 888	40 558	32 870	33 807	33 030	35 320	41 145	41 839	41 404	37 778	36 749	38 801	42 587
1987	C	466 161	36 944	34 233	40 628	40 781	39 572	35 068	37 051	39 981	40 054	42 128	40 539	39 182
1988	C	427 018	40 646	33 306	33 065	31 147	35 166	37 923	39 093	38 890	32 941	32 952	35 634	36 255
1989	C	414 214	43 623	35 957	33 786	32 457	35 377	32 568	34 174	33 538	29 361	30 420	33 998	38 955
1990	C	393 250	37 402	32 862	32 048	29 756	34 163	33 306	32 138	34 406	31 519	30 321	30 519	34 810
1991	C	391 588	33 834	31 764	30 848	28 757	30 642	31 510	35 750	34 508	32 206	31 348	31 230	39 191
1992	C	382 465	39 498	34 761	32 554	27 848	30 381	31 763	32 815	33 061	29 136	28 060	28 839	33 749
1993	C	379 800	39 153	33 491	34 322	28 862	30 485	31 657	30 977	32 867	29 073	29 013	29 245	30 655
1994	C	385 296	32 999	30 193	31 546	31 151	31 003	30 414	31 665	34 789	30 164	30 990	33 094	37 288
1995	C	384 548	40 247	29 461	27 064	27 975	28 583	30 948	34 992	33 035	30 525	33 258	35 350	33 110
1996	C	379 983	38 013	31 792	31 723	27 005	32 175	30 427	31 754	32 729	29 897	29 065	29 246	36 157
1997	C	389 301	37 136	34 137	33 844	30 503	31 797	31 241	34 067	32 415	29 392	30 241	30 122	34 406
1998	C	399 772	34 473	30 886	31 123	31 590	36 603	34 294	33 318	38 366	32 690	30 767	30 345	35 317
Mali														
1987	I	14 004	86	203	935	1 162	1 147	1 120	1 135	1 501	1 943	2 078	1 712	982
Mauritius - Maurice														
1990	+C	7 031	670	488	552	532	560	581	681	669	615	593	530	560
1991	+C	7 027	580	514	557	535	620	571	707	692	592	576	515	568
1992	+C	7 023	608	519	571	599	558	612	677	680	602	582	482	533
1994	+C	7 402	603	550	544	570	628	627	657	679	635	672	642	595
1995	+C	7 465	612	506	573	555	706	725	661	690	653	595	567	622
1996	+C	7 670	645	591	578	528	612	633	758	751	696	639	595	644
1997	+C	7 986	703	738	703	611	624	668	703	683	664	641	621	627
1998	+C	7 839	654	551	683	656	670	678	717	725	618	644	618	625
1999	+C	7 944	631	543	572	608	772	715	761	730	690	681	587	654
Réunion														
1985	C	3 018	254	251	268	219	222	239	306	280	249	263	240	227
1986	C	3 047	270	224	254	232	246	251	316	299	234	240	224	257
1989	C	3 307	274	225	264	253	276	249	297	293	268	306	300	302
1990	C	3 183	287	243	241	229	245	265	307	303	257	261	256	289
Saint Helena ex. dep. - Sainte-Hélène sans dép.														
1985	C	43	2	7	8	2	2	2	1	5	6	4	...	4
1986	C	53	5	4	4	3	2	4	11	4	2	5	4	5
1995	C	30	4	4	1	3	1	8	3	1	1	1	2	1
1996	C	44	1	4	6	2	...	3	4	5	6	5	5	3
1997	C	30	1	3	2	1	5	1	2	2	6	3	1	3
1998	C	39	2	2	1	...	3	2	9	3	4	7	4	2
1999	C	45	4	4	5	6	4	1	1	1	4	4	4	7
Seychelles														
1985	+C	468	39	40	35	42	35	32	28	45	40	40	50	42
1986	+C	498	44	31	45	55	54	41	40	45	33	27	40	43
1987	+C	505	48	53	43	39	36	40	35	38	41	47	43	42
1993	+C	597	59	48	73	55	56	40	60	42	39	42	37	46
South Africa - Afrique du Sud														
1993	...	201 273	15 263	13 637	15 586	15 897	17 952	19 080	19 876	18 970	16 341	16 912	16 089	15 670
1994	...	213 279	15 372	15 400	16 665	17 650	19 750	20 504	22 394	21 097	19 349	19 153	16 254	9 691
1995	...	268 025	17 837	17 682	21 338	20 732	21 428	24 194	26 326	14 598	21 130	24 322	24 643	33 795
1996	...	327 253	24 503	22 668	21 870	21 251	26 054	28 751	32 256	40 794	29 658	26 367	24 666	28 415
Tunisia - Tunisie														
1985	U	35 688	4 663	3 221	2 863	2 670	2 468	2 263	2 821	3 047	2 796	2 867	2 852	3 157

21. Deaths by month of occurence: 1985 - 2000
Décès selon le mois de décès: 1985 - 2000 (continued — suite)

(See notes at end of table. — Voir notes à la fin du tableau.)

Continent, country or area / Continent, pays ou zone	Code[1]	Total	Jan	Feb	March	April	May	June	July	Aug	Sep	Oct	Nov	Dec
AFRICA — AFRIQUE														
Tunisia - Tunisie														
1986	U	35 968	3 470	3 451	3 316	2 775	2 460	2 475	2 619	3 024	2 778	2 883	3 155	3 562
1987	U	35 632	4 335	3 255	3 142	2 571	2 372	2 517	2 742	2 952	2 827	2 732	2 922	3 265
1988	U	34 984	3 387	3 109	3 545	2 508	2 382	2 495	2 624	2 926	2 617	2 854	2 996	3 541
1989	U	34 921	3 633	3 371	2 904	2 458	2 593	2 402	2 715	2 982	2 639	2 805	2 900	3 519
1990	U	37 540	3 981	3 394	3 024	2 543	2 584	2 449	2 819	2 821	2 913	3 036	3 189	4 787
1991	U	37 462	4 277	3 511	3 155	2 801	2 734	2 435	2 670	2 918	2 703	3 097	3 176	3 985
1992	U	38 043	4 468	3 805	3 447	3 082	2 767	2 558	2 812	2 915	2 749	2 932	2 981	3 527
1993	U	40 865	4 242	4 113	4 843	3 210	2 786	2 692	3 029	3 099	2 813	3 075	3 203	3 760
1994	U	41 272	3 902	3 648	3 660	3 258	3 035	2 767	3 132	4 016	3 119	3 243	3 433	4 059
1995	U	42 601	5 505	4 213	3 749	3 148	3 015	2 822	3 188	3 392	3 062	3 304	3 466	3 737
1997	U	42 426	4 501	3 936	3 733	3 449	3 139	3 048	3 119	3 467	3 097	3 462	3 566	3 909
1998	U	42 571	4 061	4 020	4 098	3 261	3 078	3 000	3 390	3 201	3 029	3 158	3 560	4 715
AMERICA, NORTH — AMERIQUE DU NORD														
Bahamas														
1985	U	1 301	106	100	136	113	124	112	106	118	86	101	95	102
1986	U	1 407	106	114	143	98	123	113	125	107	118	110	121	127
1987	U	1 376	135	105	126	117	117	126	112	119	97	108	94	120
1988	U	1 319	110	104	107	107	120	113	113	122	117	99	104	103
1989	U	1 459	134	106	114	117	114	109	117	151	146	142	96	113
1990	U	1 343	102	95	122	102	103	114	113	140	122	113	99	118
1991	U	1 319	123	96	122	129	111	93	114	96	111	108	111	105
1992	U	1 383	111	117	116	89	130	133	120	143	105	99	104	116
1993	U	1 439	122	127	134	111	136	105	129	105	123	115	102	130
1994	U	1 538	117	131	131	133	124	136	126	142	144	108	128	118
1995	U	1 604	174	133	121	126	131	101	145	145	123	118	134	153
1996	U	1 503	160	155	136	123	102	125	119	130	124	124	92	114	123
Barbados - Barbade														
1985	+U	2 127	165	137	203	202	162	190	197	205	207	187	107	165
1986	+U	2 160	182	199	202	179	185	150	135	160	151	249	189	179
1987	+U	2 195	189	139	192	191	163	179	191	182	158	191	160	61
1988	+U	2 233	251	169	175	163	169	182	173	175	194	174	192	216
1989	+U	2 277	191	185	201	161	177	179	209	183	181	210	157	64
1990	+U	2 232	189	186	201	188	181	167	197	178	209	181	187	168
1991	+U	2 283	211	236	217	186	187	148	152	198	168	193	157	132
Bermuda - Bermudes														
1985	C	421	44	38	44	42	33	35	27	26	27	31	29	45
1986	C	415	29	39	42	45	39	22	28	33	35	36	27	40
1987	C	438	46	44	53	40	31	31	35	30	33	27	25	24
1988	C	399	34	32	43	37	24	28	33	32	33	26	37	32
1989	C	462	39	39	33	41	40	47	34	34	33	31	45	36
1990	C	445	38	33	40	33	41	28	40	32	28	50	32	40
1991	C	452	28	31	35	35	38	33	31	43	34	37	43	45
British Virgin Islands - Îles Vierges britanniques														
1985	+C	65	7	3	3	5	3	3	9	8	2	7	8	7
1986	+C	82	7	7	5	10	5	5	5	9	10	10	6	3
Canada[4]														
1985	C	181 323	16 499	14 711	16 263	14 900	15 016	14 489	14 361	14 365	14 169	15 152	14 923	16 475
1986	C	184 224	16 777	15 695	16 989	14 946	15 166	14 335	14 739	14 408	14 532	15 386	15 205	16 046
1987	C	184 953	16 468	14 548	15 971	15 032	15 527	14 737	15 893	14 980	14 553	15 791	15 561	15 892
1988	C	190 011	17 363	16 245	17 225	15 773	15 611	15 030	15 861	15 114	14 528	15 663	15 163	16 435
1989	C	190 965	17 268	15 110	16 718	15 801	15 718	15 029	15 517	15 192	14 611	16 167	15 570	18 264
1990	C	191 973	18 766	15 467	16 392	15 584	15 824	15 254	15 692	15 291	15 029	16 140	15 875	16 659
1992	C	196 535	18 353	16 298	16 785	15 931	16 404	15 380	15 837	15 737	15 316	16 737	16 349	17 408
1993	C	204 912	18 441	16 333	19 430	17 473	16 955	15 792	16 125	16 234	15 776	17 196	16 709	18 448
1994	C	207 077	20 954	17 035	17 860	16 589	16 930	16 609	16 569	15 919	16 119	17 274	16 981	18 238
1995	C	210 733	19 005	17 766	19 552	17 785	17 781	16 399	16 788	16 403	16 028	17 306	17 244	18 676

21. Deaths by month of occurence: 1985 - 2000
Décès selon le mois de décès: 1985 - 2000 (continued — suite)

(See notes at end of table. — Voir notes à la fin du tableau.)

Continent, country or area — Continent, pays ou zone	C-o-d-e[1]	Total	Jan	Feb	March	April	May	June	July	Aug	Sep	Oct	Nov	Dec
AMERICA, NORTH — AMERIQUE DU NORD														
Cayman Islands - Îles Caïmanes														
1985	C	126	13	7	10	7	7	7	10	11	12	15	12	15
1986	C	141	9	14	13	10	11	13	12	14	8	9	12	16
1987	C	118	7	16	8	8	6	19	4	11	6	9	14	10
1988	C	124	9	9	16	6	13	8	9	10	8	11	16	9
1989	C	122	11	15	11	9	10	17	18	6	3	8	7	7
1990	C	120	6	6	15	13	9	5	11	13	12	6	13	11
1991	C	113	9	10	11	9	13	9	6	11	4	7	13	11
1992	C	128	12	10	10	14	8	11	9	9	13	7	9	16
1993	C	133	10	11	14	9	6	13	13	12	11	14	11	9
1994	C	149	8	12	11	13	8	13	7	19	17	10	14	17
Costa Rica														
1987	C	10 687	959	894	872	843	865	888	1 014	953	825	915	754	905
1988	C	10 944	919	837	912	867	847	856	951	969	895	990	916	985
1989	C	11 272	959	884	914	895	882	883	945	941	931	995	976	1 067
1990	C	11 366	1 128	880	933	900	940	875	941	950	903	927	992	997
1991	C	11 792	1 031	888	883	976	1 019	895	1 067	1 087	951	955	965	1 075
1994	C	13 313	1 183	1 052	1 100	1 018	1 015	1 033	1 218	1 195	1 132	1 138	1 122	1 107
1995	C	14 061	1 181	1 052	1 155	1 107	1 060	1 155	1 214	1 144	1 146	1 438	1 230	1 179
1996	C	13 993	1 320	1 141	1 136	1 046	1 092	1 104	1 131	1 106	1 080	1 132	1 241	1 464
1999	C	15 052	1 307	1 068	1 342	1 245	1 197	1 310	1 301	1 217	1 178	1 282	1 224	1 381
Cuba														
1985	C	64 430	5 958	5 365	5 432	5 120	5 367	5 448	5 381	5 524	5 106	5 182	5 071	5 476
1986	C	63 145	5 869	5 105	5 767	5 226	5 148	4 968	5 451	5 184	5 108	5 150	4 912	5 257
1987	C	65 079	5 982	5 207	5 586	5 457	5 287	5 298	5 548	5 553	5 170	5 091	5 197	5 703
1988	C	67 944	5 664	5 598	6 266	5 738	5 575	5 458	6 192	5 732	5 330	5 413	5 182	5 796
1989	C	67 356	5 699	5 246	6 017	5 223	5 645	5 499	5 655	5 622	5 482	5 537	5 384	6 344
1990	C	72 144	6 381	5 400	6 216	5 645	5 794	5 601	5 942	6 311	6 054	6 386	6 014	6 400
1991	C	71 709	6 061	6 010	6 137	5 677	5 678	5 896	6 091	5 821	5 577	5 950	6 367	6 444
1992	C	75 457	6 869	6 371	6 292	5 844	6 185	5 889	6 355	6 088	5 693	6 441	6 027	7 403
1993	C	78 531	6 933	7 104	7 702	6 655	6 452	6 879	7 106	5 955	5 554	5 665	5 768	6 758
1994	C	78 648	7 136	5 786	6 620	5 854	6 182	6 163	6 999	7 345	6 804	6 535	6 269	6 955
1995	C	77 937	7 722	6 873	6 746	5 978	6 235	5 962	6 792	6 559	6 003	6 218	5 995	6 854
1996	C	79 654	7 841	7 677	7 461	6 329	6 215	6 252	6 678	6 141	5 942	5 953	6 071	7 094
1997	C	77 316	6 889	5 936	6 046	5 983	5 916	6 449	7 663	7 114	6 253	6 341	5 866	6 860
1998	C	77 565	6 900	6 774	6 780	6 132	6 296	6 966	7 039	6 348	5 826	6 046	5 946	6 512
Dominican Republic - République dominicaine														
1985	+U	27 844	2 512	2 305	2 596	2 381	2 363	1 925	2 362	2 276	2 284	2 456	2 333	2 051
1999	+U	26 956	2 391	2 176	2 528	2 119	2 302	2 524	2 439	2 138	1 991	1 981	2 238	2 129
El Salvador														
1985	C	27 225	2 455	2 134	2 112	2 126	2 202	2 237	2 243	2 298	2 101	2 311	2 447	2 559
1986	C	25 731	2 046	1 769	2 038	1 926	1 864	2 113	2 135	2 290	2 109	2 592	2 177	2 672
1987	C	27 581	2 449	2 132	2 323	2 226	2 232	2 183	2 502	2 548	2 104	2 199	2 109	2 574
1988	C	27 774	2 382	2 272	2 150	2 243	2 343	2 365	2 435	2 511	2 260	2 301	2 226	2 286
1989	C	27 768	2 289	2 063	2 369	2 310	2 378	2 412	2 489	2 354	1 999	2 236	2 542	2 327
1990	C	28 224	2 470	2 139	2 307	2 275	2 368	2 396	2 621	2 277	2 337	2 383	2 291	2 360
1991	C	27 096	2 398	2 221	2 268	2 242	2 158	2 327	2 346	2 087	2 070	2 299	2 375	2 305
1992	C	27 869	2 746	2 251	2 374	2 185	2 420	2 159	2 539	2 282	2 173	2 335	2 114	2 291
1993	C	29 203	1 831	2 729	1 592	2 492	2 811	2 950	2 506	2 551	2 284	2 149	2 423	2 885
1994	C	29 407	2 843	2 245	2 327	2 289	2 514	2 383	2 480	2 575	2 079	2 818	2 425	2 429
1995	C	29 130	2 594	2 219	2 502	2 249	2 518	2 588	2 569	2 628	2 477	2 377	2 587	1 822
1996	C	28 904	2 470	2 394	2 394	2 341	2 649	2 681	2 526	2 156	2 338	2 387	2 169	2 399
1997	C	29 118	2 389	2 178	2 047	2 590	2 427	2 431	2 709	2 419	2 334	2 608	2 341	2 645
1998	C	29 919	2 479	2 163	2 413	2 535	2 500	2 467	2 756	2 863	2 539	2 656	2 228	2 320
1999	C	28 056	2 526	2 130	2 111	2 230	2 166	2 275	2 602	2 537	2 318	2 337	2 374	2 450
Greenland - Groenland														
1985	C	436	29	26	47	43	33	34	32	22	44	51	38	37

(See notes at end of table. — Voir notes à la fin du tableau.)

Continent, country or area / Continent, pays ou zone	Code[1]	Total	Jan	Feb	March	April	May	June	July	Aug	Sep	Oct	Nov	Dec
AMERICA, NORTH — AMERIQUE DU NORD														
Greenland - Groenland														
1986	C	446	35	29	35	28	40	46	46	49	32	32	35	39
1987	C	445	51	33	39	24	24	28	49	44	52	40	26	35
1990	C	468	39	57	38	32	37	44	41	39	32	43	32	34
1993	C	436	33	30	43	35	35	35	47	35	38	23	39	43
1994	C	447	42	45	50	35	40	33	43	29	35	27	37	31
1995	C	487	38	35	42	42	42	40	54	42	44	35	27	46
1996	C	447	46	34	38	34	44	35	40	47	32	41	28	28
1997	C	492	37	33	42	44	39	36	48	45	40	39	48	41
1998	C	468	30	37	30	37	46	35	43	43	35	39	46	47
1999	C	482	34	38	48	48	43	35	38	36	41	41	39	41
Guadeloupe														
1985	C	2 309	217	185	193	179	191	168	168	226	197	206	201	178
1986	C	2 238	185	181	194	192	182	174	175	198	192	174	181	210
1991	C	2 147	180	167	180	173	167	153	199	200	178	184	160	206
Guatemala														
1985	C	68 951	5 418	4 594	5 087	5 687	6 126	6 064	6 609	6 182	5 930	5 922	5 722	5 610
1986	C	69 275	5 983	4 866	5 516	5 762	5 988	6 287	7 024	5 969	5 704	5 457	5 324	5 395
1987	C	66 703	5 837	4 855	5 569	5 531	6 249	5 829	6 328	5 785	5 465	5 083	5 102	5 070
1988	C	64 837	5 108	5 072	4 960	5 321	5 966	5 735	5 728	6 045	5 443	5 326	4 962	5 171
Martinique														
1985	C	2 157	176	179	209	166	169	188	181	201	159	157	181	191
1986	C	2 104	197	171	174	162	191	156	184	188	185	169	163	164
1987	C	2 149	189	135	177	198	200	185	150	179	176	185	179	196
1988	C	2 092	206	182	168	160	174	172	180	177	182	181	155	155
1989	C	2 162	180	170	220	184	177	165	221	182	173	205	140	145
1990	C	2 220	177	169	207	194	192	184	203	179	166	198	183	168
1991	C	2 180	174	164	177	166	188	187	190	221	193	173	165	182
1992	C	2 180	226	177	181	178	160	179	188	180	182	193	149	187
Mexico - Mexique														
1985	C	400 079	42 021	32 512	33 609	30 062	31 607	32 334	34 476	33 529	31 709	32 045	32 205	33 970
1987	C	400 280	42 202	32 825	33 044	30 412	31 599	32 305	34 415	34 517	31 962	33 418	32 677	30 904
1989	C	423 304	43 558	35 006	36 679	32 048	33 445	33 252	34 509	34 581	32 769	35 463	34 106	36 603
1990	C	422 803	46 169	37 431	37 903	33 499	34 589	32 691	33 156	33 197	31 999	32 903	33 620	34 641
1991	C	411 131	41 605	32 676	33 784	32 702	33 208	32 364	33 758	32 789	31 955	34 418	34 610	36 469
1992	C	409 814	43 975	35 841	33 340	31 271	31 933	32 385	32 808	32 538	31 440	33 639	34 652	35 226
1993	C	416 335	38 268	32 606	35 392	35 194	34 517	32 783	34 102	33 457	32 027	34 012	34 235	39 102
1994	C	419 074	42 239	34 609	35 170	32 438	33 581	32 236	33 950	33 581	32 959	34 485	34 961	38 288
1995	C	430 278	41 953	35 260	36 593	33 581	34 547	32 216	34 346	34 402	33 152	36 064	36 362	41 270
1996	C	436 321	45 642	38 071	36 655	33 707	34 024	32 017	33 979	33 874	33 268	35 240	35 613	42 867
1997	C	440 437	44 996	35 403	37 196	33 153	34 082	32 926	33 948	34 165	33 276	36 769	36 885	46 516
1999	C	443 950	45 498	39 498	37 689	34 602	34 822	31 988	33 883	34 137	33 376	36 118	36 460	43 926
Montserrat														
1985	+C	136	9	9	10	8	19	9	11	12	10	4	13	9
1986	+C	123	10	11	9	11	8	9	16	9	11	6	10	13
Nicaragua														
1985	+U	11 586	923	997	1 030	868	1 038	905	1 143	1 138	928	981	949	686
1986	+U	11 005	1 072	860	764	1 044	873	928	1 012	957	906	981	890	718
1987	+U	11 056	967	883	902	914	953	982	1 043	998	929	973	855	657
1997	+U	13 916	1 188	1 034	1 171	1 116	1 194	1 089	1 196	1 244	1 198	1 232	1 129	1 125
1998	+U	14 804	1 114	997	1 085	1 048	1 115	1 162	1 465	1 373	1 202	1 842	1 119	1 282
1999	+U	13 771	1 211	1 015	1 143	1 100	1 084	1 106	1 461	1 208	1 113	1 142	1 104	1 084
Panama														
1985	U	8 991	723	658	761	659	716	706	816	835	733	801	800	783
1986	U	8 942	747	637	720	727	759	685	745	764	722	782	795	859
1987	U	9 105	767	711	729	688	768	735	765	775	773	799	740	855
1988	U	9 382	764	724	707	720	710	790	792	798	811	898	817	851
1989	U	9 557	822	739	810	730	775	743	791	754	742	813	786	1 052
1990	U	9 799	854	716	832	741	799	723	832	829	858	852	873	890
1991	U	9 683	808	712	795	756	808	763	848	818	860	829	842	844

(See notes at end of table. — Voir notes à la fin du tableau.)

Continent, country or area Continent, pays ou zone	C-o-d-e[1]	Total	Jan	Feb	March	April	May	June	July	Aug	Sep	Oct	Nov	Dec
AMERICA, NORTH — AMERIQUE DU NORD														
Panama														
1992	U	10 143	870	762	881	811	805	823	818	877	837	878	842	939
1993	U	10 669	900	794	935	901	889	900	956	877	875	903	820	919
1994	U	10 983	934	822	951	834	870	1 047	1 039	939	876	924	890	857
1995	U	11 032	895	831	897	877	944	974	981	858	882	1 015	931	947
1996	U	11 161	964	869	950	871	893	928	940	978	910	936	877	1 045
1998	U	11 824	974	922	980	950	956	1 113	1 171	975	956	920	925	982
Puerto Rico - Porto Rico														
1985	C	23 194	2 313	1 961	1 917	1 846	1 966	1 906	1 889	1 881	1 817	1 965	1 676	2 057
1987	C	23 954	2 116	1 866	2 036	1 948	2 037	1 912	2 024	2 121	2 015	1 931	1 922	2 024
1988	C	25 123	2 184	2 087	2 229	2 047	2 217	2 114	2 104	2 028	1 960	2 031	1 943	2 175
1989	C	25 987	2 406	2 028	2 326	2 144	2 121	2 107	2 082	2 036	2 186	2 150	2 091	2 310
1991	C	26 328	2 315	2 003	2 264	2 242	2 180	2 346	2 164	2 148	2 168	2 063	2 141	2 294
1992	C	27 397	2 431	2 429	2 305	2 164	2 244	2 171	2 212	2 276	2 093	2 287	2 312	2 471
1993	C	28 494	2 740	2 334	2 587	2 313	2 494	2 425	2 318	2 234	2 171	2 307	2 180	2 391
1994	C	28 444	2 535	2 347	2 455	2 200	2 339	2 314	2 397	2 432	2 190	2 291	2 342	2 602
1996	C	29 871	2 540	2 406	2 516	2 283	2 526	2 385	2 509	2 557	2 556	2 493	2 415	2 684
1997	C	29 119	2 671	2 469	2 728	2 559	2 441	2 379	2 460	2 307	2 298	2 205	2 238	2 363
1999	C	29 145	2 572	2 430	2 546	2 421	2 368	2 314	2 546	2 473	2 349	2 341	2 363	2 422
Saint Lucia - Sainte-Lucie														
1985	C	824	60	54	70	66	71	52	61	82	78	77	79	74
1986	C	843	65	69	65	66	74	75	70	58	79	80	69	73
Saint Vincent and the Grenadines - Saint Vincent-et-les Grenadines														
1986	+C	655	59	43	57	48	53	44	63	66	61	61	49	51
1988	+C	712	50	56	60	75	66	51	65	43	57	57	65	67
1992	+C	714	46	60	66	55	67	58	60	53	65	77	52	55
1993	+C	680	61	43	53	50	62	76	65	63	52	54	48	53
1994	+C	732	63	40	43	88	52	73	55	59	61	57	69	72
1995	+C	730	76	57	78	42	56	64	60	54	63	56	49	75
1996	+C	792	70	62	62	62	68	70	65	67	99	57	55	55
1997	+C	736	65	60	68	52	49	44	70	73	62	65	63	65
1999	+C	833	77	54	69	60	86	54	74	81	66	65	64	83
Trinidad and Tobago - Trinité-et-Tobago														
1985	C	8 026	662	629	710	673	660	633	683	718	698	623	644	693
1986	C	7 699	708	570	673	639	592	595	615	648	635	677	670	677
1987	C	8 054	649	543	689	645	672	658	682	706	693	707	652	758
1988	C	8 036	689	690	630	618	655	583	672	695	680	726	690	708
1989	C	8 213	740	658	672	673	691	597	588	710	676	777	664	767
1990	C	8 196	693	597	705	673	642	641	672	674	742	787	660	710
1991	C	8 192	688	702	705	667	654	660	647	650	732	691	687	709
1992	C	8 533	753	624	701	673	690	648	730	753	800	743	696	722
1993	C	8 807	723	690	748	744	668	695	729	782	762	758	717	791
1994	C	9 265	775	702	770	787	696	726	719	788	758	822	875	847
1995	C	9 042	769	702	749	696	749	707	781	781	824	778	719	787
Turks Caicos Islands - Îles Turques et Caïques														
1997	+C	49	3	5	2	3	2	5	5	3	5	4	4	7
1998	+C	22	2	5	5	3	1	...	...	...	1	...	3	2
1999	+C	39	5	2	2	3	4	2	5	2	1	4	2	7
2000	+C	67	1	4	5	5	4	7	5	8	8	7	6	7
United States - États-Unis														
1985	C	2086440	201 346	184 029	182 616	168 848	168 374	160 838	164 700	162 492	161 563	172 307	170 082	189 245
1986	C	2105361	194 612	178 283	189 897	172 481	172 185	163 514	169 943	165 977	163 100	172 586	174 412	188 371

21. Deaths by month of occurence: 1985 - 2000
Décès selon le mois de décès: 1985 - 2000 (continued — suite)

(See notes at end of table. — Voir notes à la fin du tableau.)

Continent, country or area — Continent, pays ou zone	C-o-d-e[1]	Total	Jan	Feb	March	April	May	June	July	Aug	Sep	Oct	Nov	Dec
AMERICA, NORTH — AMERIQUE DU NORD														
United States - États-Unis														
1987	C	2123323	196 235	170 273	186 651	175 249	174 902	167 327	171 935	170 028	164 838	180 733	175 679	189 473
1988	C	2171000	200 610	195 000	197 995	184 000	176 806	170 000	172 193	170 000	166 201	179 000	175 198	185 000
1989	C	2150466	197 780	182 374	192 680	174 682	175 422	165 174	169 048	168 135	165 225	178 722	175 827	205 397
1990	C	2162000	213 000	182 000	193 000	182 000	180 000	169 000	173 000	170 000	168 000	178 000	169 000	185 000
1991	C	2165000	195 000	179 000	191 000	185 000	183 000	168 000	178 000	172 000	165 000	180 000	176 000	191 000
1992	C	2177000	207 000	185 000	195 000	181 000	175 000	172 000	180 000	172 000	169 000	181 000	175 000	186 000
1993	C	2271947	200 803	188 018	212 568	189 985	185 450	175 530	181 405	176 532	173 199	189 198	188 012	211 247
1995	C	2312132	210 713	192 267	207 231	191 092	189 556	179 336	185 465	182 337	177 642	189 765	192 514	214 214
1996	C	2314690	221 525	193 228	203 057	191 779	188 184	178 208	181 964	178 952	175 586	190 326	190 670	221 211
1998	C	2337256	233 237	204 453	205 691	186 808	188 120	181 429	184 149	183 556	177 915	193 421	192 465	206 012
United States Virgin Islands - Îles Vierges américaines														
1985	C	547	59	50	48	54	39	33	49	37	47	48	44	39
1986	C	508	51	42	49	32	51	45	34	31	52	50	33	38
1987	C	558	34	53	51	53	48	38	48	48	57	50	34	44
1988	C	549	60	55	49	32	42	39	44	37	49	44	47	51
1989	C	548	50	56	38	56	52	40	46	36	51	47	37	39
1990	C	511	55	35	41	41	42	50	31	38	45	43	41	49
1993	C	569	51	40	44	39	52	53	50	38	50	51	41	60
AMERICA, SOUTH — AMERIQUE DU SUD														
Brazil - Brésil[5]														
1985	U	806 238	66 495	61 568	68 252	65 462	70 322	73 255	74 289	69 090	65 235	65 931	64 372	61 967
1986	U	834 927	71 679	62 155	68 822	68 620	71 601	73 192	77 598	72 664	69 564	69 512	67 387	62 133
1987	U	816 397	72 644	64 399	68 819	68 060	72 515	72 378	71 064	70 973	64 772	66 747	63 005	61 021
1988	U	844 037	73 114	65 165	69 869	70 280	75 724	78 177	80 420	74 366	66 725	65 305	63 676	61 216
1989	U	835 139	69 619	63 358	68 020	67 560	75 127	75 362	82 299	73 942	66 452	69 430	64 359	59 611
1990	U	847 639	72 154	61 342	67 297	66 820	75 512	78 136	82 629	76 990	70 948	71 649	65 684	58 478
1991	U	823 438	68 062	61 765	68 041	68 303	71 478	70 372	76 848	73 641	69 023	71 328	64 377	60 200
1992	U	840 648	68 694	65 754	70 974	67 958	70 494	71 522	77 425	75 774	70 023	71 997	66 858	63 175
1994	U	912 110	75 567	70 085	75 516	75 467	79 213	83 539	89 315	80 201	73 422	73 040	69 775	66 970
1995	U	901 626	77 090	67 759	75 199	74 214	81 422	85 356	85 132	78 109	73 144	72 360	68 981	62 860
1996	U	924 171	77 339	70 239	74 648	74 213	80 249	84 031	93 429	85 879	76 329	74 976	67 976	64 871
Chile - Chili														
1985	C	73 534	5 616	5 023	5 743	5 599	6 461	7 237	7 692	6 783	6 202	5 871	5 627	5 680
1986	C	72 209	5 772	4 917	5 676	5 671	6 276	6 622	6 937	6 864	6 490	5 964	5 477	5 543
1987	C	70 559	5 514	4 766	5 313	5 465	6 294	6 471	7 023	6 993	6 296	5 665	5 488	5 271
1988	C	74 435	5 451	4 992	5 241	5 542	6 580	7 527	7 891	7 069	6 532	6 149	5 696	5 765
1989	C	75 453	6 048	5 177	5 690	5 761	6 572	7 067	7 845	6 985	6 467	5 996	5 782	6 063
1990	C	78 434	6 204	5 132	5 980	6 173	8 030	7 643	7 664	6 862	6 886	6 217	5 769	5 874
1991	C	74 862	5 848	5 218	5 712	5 737	6 479	6 637	7 506	7 248	6 444	6 464	5 855	5 714
1992	C	74 090	5 812	5 029	5 449	5 496	6 436	6 974	7 517	7 187	6 602	6 333	5 693	5 562
1993	C	76 261	6 029	5 144	5 599	5 784	6 910	8 287	7 681	7 003	6 274	6 215	5 659	5 676
1994	C	75 445	5 808	5 034	5 642	5 888	6 439	6 469	7 710	7 428	6 892	6 097	5 859	6 179
1995	C	78 531	5 996	5 327	5 662	6 014	6 789	7 185	8 650	7 869	6 670	6 311	5 801	6 257
1996	C	79 123	6 098	5 588	5 844	6 050	6 835	8 421	8 549	6 771	6 584	6 235	5 889	6 259
1997	C	78 472	6 196	5 427	6 241	6 132	6 599	7 063	7 283	7 112	6 832	6 798	6 286	6 503
1999	C	81 977	6 378	5 508	6 083	6 286	7 973	8 772	8 094	7 248	6 955	6 357	6 025	6 298
Colombia - Colombie[6,7]														
1989	U	154 694	14 105	12 046	12 864	13 022	12 598	12 669	13 339	12 516	12 372	12 812	12 908	13 443
1990	U	154 685	13 770	12 089	13 751	13 173	13 223	12 941	13 393	13 069	12 458	12 893	12 563	11 362
1991	U	163 692	14 267	12 363	13 105	13 392	14 089	13 565	14 103	13 830	13 768	13 620	13 329	14 261
1992	U	167 743	14 023	12 665	13 757	13 120	13 945	13 667	14 321	14 234	14 014	14 342	14 024	15 631
1993	U	168 647	15 030	13 128	13 959	13 273	14 519	14 013	14 451	14 251	13 673	13 968	13 562	14 820
1994	U	168 568	15 024	12 585	13 529	13 828	14 584	14 439	14 426	14 124	13 630	14 039	13 889	14 471

(See notes at end of table. — Voir notes à la fin du tableau.)

Continent, country or area / Continent, pays ou zone	Code[1]	Total	Jan	Feb	March	April	May	June	July	Aug	Sep	Oct	Nov	Dec
AMERICA, SOUTH — AMERIQUE DU SUD														
Colombia - Colombie[6,7]														
1997	U	170 753	15 025	12 785	14 188	13 878	14 682	14 386	14 694	14 414	13 515	13 595	14 219	15 372
1998	U	175 442	15 075	13 302	14 342	13 525	14 575	14 257	14 597	14 945	14 899	15 128	15 099	15 698
Ecuador - Équateur[8]														
1985	U	51 134	4 884	4 068	4 464	4 274	4 259	4 067	4 487	4 238	4 048	4 090	4 164	4 091
1986	U	50 957	5 194	4 405	4 795	4 230	4 054	4 044	4 166	4 261	3 904	3 976	3 985	3 943
1987	U	51 567	5 631	4 101	4 390	4 117	4 427	4 193	4 246	4 605	4 108	4 035	3 544	4 170
1988	U	52 732	5 167	4 200	4 722	4 294	4 691	4 487	4 469	4 569	4 190	4 372	3 621	3 950
1989	U	51 736	5 075	4 563	4 864	4 330	4 230	4 209	4 260	4 111	3 912	4 301	4 048	3 833
1990	U	50 217	4 998	3 975	4 657	4 266	4 448	3 994	4 186	4 159	4 042	3 952	3 814	3 726
1992	U	53 430	5 290	4 574	4 995	4 801	4 647	4 438	4 538	4 441	4 039	4 019	3 980	3 668
1993	U	52 453	4 770	4 217	4 912	4 836	4 670	4 320	4 284	4 345	3 977	4 123	4 057	3 942
1995	U	50 867	5 221	4 470	4 679	4 394	4 323	4 206	4 340	4 054	3 863	3 785	3 861	3 671
1996	U	52 300	5 320	4 242	4 581	4 335	4 257	4 099	4 471	4 219	4 076	4 151	4 244	4 305
French Guiana - Guyane française[2]														
1985	C	481	42	32	46	51	31	46	45	44	32	33	44	35
1986	C	491	41	39	44	38	36	32	41	42	52	37	14	45
Paraguay														
1985	U	14 094	1 354	1 135	1 054	1 035	1 167	1 094	1 308	1 349	1 174	1 086	1 193	1 145
1987	U	13 197	1 217	959	1 098	883	1 085	1 297	1 184	1 171	1 132	1 153	1 009	1 009
1988	U	12 069	1 068	920	922	902	1 040	1 301	1 260	1 095	956	900	915	790
1991	U	10 171	1 040	801	778	873	956	928	1 063	930	739	902	641	520
1992	U	9 642	876	624	749	694	730	793	1 076	929	839	783	803	746
Suriname														
1989	C	2 717	264	214	230	225	196	372	213	241	219	223	146	174
1990	C	2 792	232	227	220	240	256	250	237	228	241	212	206	243
1991	C	2 573	264	185	174	217	203	232	277	222	221	184	189	205
1992	C	2 717	254	242	229	221	194	213	231	232	202	229	215	250
1993	C	2 998	300	241	256	253	267	273	286	263	244	255	203	154
1994	C	2 842	287	239	217	209	219	211	214	310	211	251	216	258
1995	C	2 696	261	242	204	245	199	209	219	233	244	204	197	239
1996	C	2 894	318	261	262	206	209	218	246	255	245	234	232	208
1997	C	2 878	271	226	246	243	252	245	240	238	250	213	219	235
1998	C	2 814	277	212	258	281	272	217	231	246	249	194	221	156
1999	C	2 992	250	197	285	253	270	249	264	261	249	242	248	224
Uruguay														
1985	C	28 566	2 259	1 897	2 165	2 124	2 545	2 748	3 304	2 762	2 376	2 313	2 118	1 951
1986	C	28 791	2 338	2 029	2 187	2 157	2 597	2 604	2 676	2 713	2 559	2 443	2 212	2 268
1987	C	29 885	2 241	2 066	2 331	2 207	2 711	3 212	2 877	2 848	2 638	2 327	2 157	2 265
1988	C	30 912	2 201	1 991	2 143	2 388	2 661	3 522	3 474	2 919	2 608	2 540	2 226	2 230
1989	C	29 629	2 332	2 044	2 107	2 235	2 563	2 748	3 241	2 867	2 610	2 408	2 297	2 174
1990	C	30 225	2 359	1 982	2 241	2 334	2 823	3 318	3 128	2 770	2 542	2 335	2 162	2 224
1992	C	30 011	2 258	2 191	2 232	2 186	2 560	2 753	3 217	3 128	2 640	2 343	2 188	2 315
1993	C	31 616	2 530	2 008	2 314	2 305	2 935	3 314	3 370	3 153	2 644	2 603	2 372	2 062
1994	C	30 209	2 637	2 050	2 287	2 373	2 467	2 707	3 082	2 937	2 809	2 495	2 326	2 035
1995	C	31 715	2 646	2 077	2 261	2 360	2 655	3 025	3 842	3 388	2 725	2 548	2 307	1 870
1996	C	30 888	2 848	2 018	2 157	2 263	2 553	3 174	3 747	2 930	2 673	2 474	2 160	1 891
Venezuela[5]														
1985	C	78 938	7 205	6 007	6 318	6 500	6 379	6 095	6 505	6 316	6 580	7 347	6 510	7 176
1986	C	77 647	6 845	6 021	6 395	6 186	6 111	6 392	6 661	6 357	6 439	6 594	6 279	7 367
1987	C	80 322	6 783	6 115	6 877	6 538	6 400	6 856	7 052	6 965	6 671	6 689	6 551	6 825
1988	C	81 442	6 475	6 294	6 641	6 393	6 730	6 423	6 904	7 368	6 974	7 066	6 836	7 338
1989	C	84 761	6 916	6 464	7 076	6 581	7 047	6 596	7 041	7 233	6 824	7 524	7 394	8 065
1990	C	89 830	7 661	6 800	7 484	6 882	7 507	7 267	7 939	8 254	6 927	7 876	7 284	7 949
1991	C	88 634	7 812	6 654	7 004	7 732	7 159	6 691	7 325	7 259	7 266	7 818	7 409	8 505

21. Deaths by month of occurence: 1985 - 2000
Décès selon le mois de décès: 1985 - 2000 (continued — suite)

(See notes at end of table. — Voir notes à la fin du tableau.)

Continent, country or area / Continent, pays ou zone	C-o-d-e[1]	Total	Jan	Feb	March	April	May	June	July	Aug	Sep	Oct	Nov	Dec
ASIA — ASIE														
Armenia - Arménie[9]														
1987	C	19 727	1 820	1 648	1 685	1 655	1 585	1 627	1 596	1 553	1 591	1 581	1 661	1 725
1988	C	35 567	3 752	1 848	1 879	1 744	1 785	1 606	1 490	1 419	1 441	1 403	1 394	15 806
1989	C	20 853	1 641	1 556	2 001	1 773	1 803	1 709	1 573	1 597	1 485	1 678	1 717	2 320
1990	C	21 993	1 911	2 017	2 004	1 748	1 874	1 689	1 712	1 562	1 458	1 777	1 681	2 560
1991	C	23 425	1 916	1 977	2 010	2 095	1 883	1 944	1 886	1 787	1 562	1 825	2 007	2 533
1992	C	25 824	2 282	2 694	2 341	2 212	2 091	2 001	2 519	1 863	1 914	2 075	1 867	1 965
1993	C	27 500	3 337	2 822	3 114	2 689	2 408	2 117	2 042	1 777	1 721	1 820	1 870	1 783
1994	C	24 652	3 186	2 773	2 600	2 589	2 225	1 744	1 689	1 606	1 578	1 513	1 490	1 659
1995	C	24 842	2 504	2 941	2 383	2 264	2 218	1 886	1 696	1 717	1 510	1 878	1 837	2 008
1996	C	24 936	3 523	2 615	2 274	2 076	2 018	1 801	1 785	1 686	1 671	1 794	1 929	1 764
1998	C	23 210	2 329	2 051	2 280	2 099	2 015	1 888	1 724	1 635	1 654	1 684	1 845	2 006
Azerbaijan - Azerbaïdjan[9]														
1992	+C	51 258	4 594	4 653	4 479	3 864	3 858	3 856	4 208	3 926	4 005	4 271	4 255	5 289
1993	+C	52 809	4 732	4 777	5 136	5 134	4 396	3 956	3 563	3 595	3 955	3 937	4 025	5 603
1994	+C	54 921	5 254	5 278	5 743	5 527	4 642	4 246	3 902	3 666	3 609	3 745	4 237	5 072
1995	+C	50 828	5 125	4 381	4 218	4 231	4 401	3 819	3 418	3 667	3 489	3 675	4 133	6 271
1996	+C	48 242	5 516	4 519	4 321	4 570	3 828	3 726	3 578	3 324	3 271	3 475	3 857	4 257
1999	+C	46 295	3 874	4 321	4 444	4 012	3 662	3 609	3 333	3 699	3 366	3 356	4 280	4 339
Brunei Darussalam - Brunéi Darussalam														
1985	+C	794	59	57	54	84	73	58	68	70	73	72	56	70
1986	+C	723	63	48	59	50	52	72	65	61	66	67	51	69
1987	+C	765	57	47	65	58	62	60	58	59	74	66	79	80
1988	+C	777	73	53	73	59	63	56	65	78	78	57	63	59
1989	+C	827	55	65	74	69	68	65	60	108	61	77	46	79
1990	+C	770	67	55	64	62	81	71	58	57	67	61	60	67
1991	+C	852	75	72	65	65	73	81	57	65	61	91	77	70
1992	+C	887	65	74	83	76	92	64	74	82	66	71	66	74
China - Chine[10]														
1989	...	6572959	507 054	592 139	567 382	552 574	524 611	537 039	545 735	551 923	481 886	583 028	542 259	587 329
China: Hong Kong SAR - Chine: Hong Kong RAS														
1985	C	25 248	2 431	2 133	2 448	2 222	2 026	2 073	1 969	1 938	1 724	2 017	1 950	2 317
1986	C	25 902	2 501	2 175	2 554	2 181	2 176	1 953	2 079	2 065	1 842	1 984	2 034	2 358
1987	C	26 916	2 406	2 141	2 152	2 210	2 137	2 423	2 350	2 086	1 940	2 117	2 154	2 800
1988	C	27 659	2 381	2 346	2 734	2 537	2 241	2 140	2 184	2 107	2 032	2 094	2 283	2 580
1989	C	28 745	2 654	2 759	2 614	2 369	2 309	2 126	2 405	2 197	2 155	2 313	2 313	2 706
1990	C	29 136	2 798	2 452	2 877	2 418	2 286	2 285	2 430	2 451	2 101	2 254	2 170	2 614
1991	C	28 429	2 529	2 379	2 528	2 337	2 371	2 178	2 313	2 386	2 156	2 271	2 459	2 522
1992	C	30 550	3 150	2 970	2 905	2 751	2 377	2 417	2 338	2 298	2 287	2 228	2 283	2 546
1993	C	30 571	2 979	2 941	2 789	2 599	2 510	2 372	2 488	2 231	2 136	2 306	2 401	2 819
1994	C	29 905	2 842	2 444	3 012	2 647	2 363	2 260	2 503	2 381	2 214	2 463	2 338	2 438
1995	C	31 468	2 942	2 832	3 105	2 685	2 510	2 348	2 423	2 489	2 383	2 366	2 517	2 868
1996	C	32 176	2 928	2 915	3 242	2 926	2 720	2 424	2 661	2 428	2 262	2 372	2 408	2 890
1997	C	31 738	2 968	2 713	2 824	2 631	2 661	2 647	2 720	2 471	2 297	2 479	2 497	2 830
1999	C	33 258	3 268	3 087	2 985	2 712	2 639	2 498	2 717	2 627	2 505	2 508	2 558	3 154
China: Macao SAR - Chine: Macao RAS														
1985	C	1 466	136	128	171	121	108	107	132	120	89	109	121	124
1986	C	1 324	144	119	140	127	97	100	109	107	88	80	99	114
1987	C	1 321	118	86	112	113	114	134	129	88	106	103	94	124
1988	C	1 437	109	140	160	146	113	112	109	91	106	102	113	136
1989	C	1 516	162	159	141	114	112	96	117	129	102	109	143	132
1991	C	1 335	132	111	104	118	116	118	98	102	81	101	129	125
1992	C	1 432	146	128	158	115	113	123	122	121	92	110	95	109
1993	C	1 531	173	185	139	124	126	114	104	114	100	108	114	130
1994	C	1 330	123	120	151	105	98	105	110	100	89	98	117	114
1995	C	1 351	122	144	119	109	122	94	117	100	108	99	83	134
1996	C	1 413	128	139	129	150	108	117	103	103	88	107	118	123

(See notes at end of table. — Voir notes à la fin du tableau.)

Continent, country or area Continent, pays ou zone	C-o-d-e[1]	Total	Jan	Feb	March	April	May	June	July	Aug	Sep	Oct	Nov	Dec
ASIA — ASIE														
China: Macao SAR - Chine: Macao RAS														
1997	C	1 293	107	132	122	124	87	109	93	127	83	120	99	90
1999	C	1 374	162	123	101	121	114	94	130	108	100	93	105	123
2000	C	1 338	142	130	131	114	110	93	99	100	98	108	94	119
Cyprus - Chypre[11]														
1985	C	5 653	586	507	560	474	403	414	446	465	428	411	445	514
1986	C	4 579	483	415	365	315	413	303	365	323	359	343	410	485
1987	C	4 912	470	400	473	397	412	336	449	411	342	337	415	470
1988	C	4 903	505	479	486	405	318	334	456	402	372	327	365	454
1990	C	4 844	619	465	441	419	394	366	334	356	321	383	347	399
1991	C	5 075	521	449	440	423	361	406	335	400	400	396	423	521
1992	C	5 220	653	602	536	388	414	317	392	402	346	376	357	437
1993	C	4 789	515	387	413	416	384	354	387	385	333	409	371	435
1994	C	4 924	460	394	456	378	397	343	411	445	383	385	399	473
1995	C	4 935	449	405	409	399	420	310	401	382	395	389	413	563
1996	C	4 958	536	433	444	414	392	415	388	407	353	373	393	410
1997	C	5 173	503	534	487	440	429	415	483	346	351	353	388	444
1999	C	5 070	480	422	450	369	384	375	400	421	415	391	423	540
Georgia - Géorgie[9]														
1992	C	46 762	4 321	3 988	4 630	3 565	3 855	3 576	6 400	999	2 896	3 475	3 764	5 293
1994	C	41 596	3 952	3 734	4 484	3 665	3 558	3 314	3 136	2 792	2 768	2 645	3 108	4 440
1995	C	37 874	2 641	3 156	3 795	3 375	3 192	3 206	2 797	2 767	2 619	2 665	2 800	4 861
1996	C	34 414	2 667	3 525	3 189	2 995	2 985	2 566	2 570	2 283	2 118	2 429	2 616	4 471
Iran (Islamic Republic of) - Iran (République islamique d')														
1986	C	190 061	19 187	18 126	17 496	13 144	17 304	12 645	15 061	15 469	14 402	14 986	15 681	16 560
Israel - Israël[12]														
1985	C	28 093	2 695	2 492	2 983	2 231	2 093	2 072	2 086	2 290	2 052	2 225	2 299	2 575
1986	C	29 415	2 802	2 708	2 631	2 408	2 224	2 097	2 163	2 176	2 201	2 301	2 626	3 078
1987	C	29 244	2 983	2 428	2 772	2 439	2 300	2 139	2 261	2 341	2 165	2 283	2 517	2 616
1988	C	29 146	2 961	2 854	2 768	2 238	2 457	2 000	2 228	2 234	2 158	2 232	2 428	2 588
1989	C	28 580	3 060	2 888	2 633	2 373	2 084	2 020	2 169	2 121	2 041	2 172	2 385	2 634
1990	C	28 725	3 203	2 901	2 498	2 345	2 282	2 063	2 184	2 080	2 081	2 289	2 255	2 544
1991	C	31 266	3 086	2 735	2 813	2 431	2 363	2 284	2 315	2 395	2 386	2 477	2 593	3 388
1993	C	33 000	3 187	3 125	3 399	2 732	2 535	2 341	2 395	2 531	2 467	2 659	2 679	2 950
1994	C	33 535	3 079	2 984	2 996	2 745	2 622	2 373	2 417	2 689	2 588	2 809	2 879	3 354
1995	C	35 348	3 405	3 234	3 161	2 932	2 706	2 486	2 660	2 535	2 617	2 807	2 921	3 884
1996	C	34 658	3 598	3 029	3 109	2 789	2 786	2 644	2 699	2 799	2 631	2 720	2 849	3 005
1998	C	36 950	3 859	3 344	3 389	3 025	2 869	2 683	2 811	3 077	2 818	2 939	2 815	3 321
1999	C	*37 242	*3 905	*3 559	*3 591	*2 987	*2 799	*2 648	*2 670	*2 926	*2 815	*2 791	*2 864	*3 687
Japan - Japon[13]														
1985	C	752 283	71 890	62 025	66 571	60 953	59 890	55 584	58 231	58 738	54 709	61 804	63 122	78 766
1986	C	750 620	77 074	64 083	67 323	62 502	60 895	56 927	57 370	57 324	55 212	61 862	63 231	66 817
1987	C	751 172	72 123	61 262	67 186	62 561	60 944	57 571	58 765	58 124	56 651	62 149	63 456	70 380
1988	C	793 014	71 188	68 902	74 184	66 642	64 633	59 699	60 079	61 928	58 089	65 424	69 151	73 095
1989	C	788 594	76 261	64 290	69 575	64 320	64 802	60 716	61 660	60 863	59 395	66 813	65 595	74 304
1990	C	820 305	86 321	72 327	72 963	66 321	65 776	61 009	63 735	64 117	60 061	66 399	68 203	73 073
1991	C	829 797	79 568	71 133	76 077	69 379	69 460	62 706	64 337	63 451	60 903	67 236	71 485	74 062
1992	C	856 643	80 133	76 508	76 365	69 626	70 534	65 217	67 280	66 385	64 367	69 422	72 160	78 646
1993	C	878 532	90 340	80 576	80 705	72 850	70 802	64 771	67 071	65 978	63 933	71 457	71 107	78 942
1994	C	875 933	82 166	73 677	81 175	73 396	69 637	64 002	69 240	71 697	65 827	71 340	73 201	80 575
1995	C	922 139	104 324	86 085	86 986	74 787	72 093	65 931	68 778	69 268	65 904	70 587	75 284	82 112
1996	C	896 211	85 194	79 458	80 781	75 578	73 412	65 575	68 880	68 190	66 203	73 374	73 927	85 639
1997	C	913 402	102 195	80 072	81 559	75 638	72 479	67 852	68 232	68 358	65 865	74 523	75 916	80 713
1999	C	982 031	115 975	93 049	87 896	79 394	78 116	70 518	72 044	72 916	69 434	76 179	78 206	88 304
Kazakhstan[9]														
1987	C	122 835	10 633	9 591	10 275	9 724	10 466	10 306	10 805	10 714	9 724	10 026	10 045	10 526
1988	C	126 898	11 265	11 317	10 955	10 433	10 939	10 661	10 597	10 260	9 938	10 560	9 868	10 105
1989	C	126 378	10 838	10 287	11 354	10 415	10 770	10 535	11 127	10 541	10 064	10 446	9 719	10 282
1990	C	128 787	11 628	10 889	11 009	10 726	11 027	10 981	10 731	10 724	10 182	10 574	9 937	10 379

21. Deaths by month of occurence: 1985 - 2000
Décès selon le mois de décès: 1985 - 2000 (continued — suite)

(See notes at end of table. — Voir notes à la fin du tableau.)

Continent, country or area / Continent, pays ou zone	Code[1]	Total	Jan	Feb	March	April	May	June	July	Aug	Sep	Oct	Nov	Dec
ASIA — ASIE														
Kazakhstan[9]														
1991	C	134 572	11 318	10 102	11 409	11 361	11 730	11 412	12 235	11 252	10 489	11 095	10 659	11 488
1992	C	137 705	12 551	10 819	11 507	11 024	11 645	11 462	11 551	11 280	11 062	11 917	11 283	11 581
1993	C	156 317	14 133	12 717	14 070	13 132	13 672	12 946	12 773	13 411	12 831	12 869	11 492	12 231
1994	C	160 590	13 743	14 294	15 290	13 240	14 053	12 759	12 636	12 910	12 699	12 945	12 616	13 363
1995	C	168 885	15 280	13 055	15 441	14 624	14 929	13 761	13 491	13 318	12 836	13 060	12 670	16 367
1996	C	166 028	16 215	13 740	13 934	14 680	14 999	13 446	13 955	12 555	12 657	13 277	13 097	13 473
1997	C	160 138	16 764	13 404	14 452	13 278	13 591	12 770	12 733	12 677	11 905	12 433	12 691	13 440
1999	C	145 880	13 257	12 596	13 564	12 492	12 341	11 352	11 859	11 795	10 975	11 720	11 713	12 216
Korea (Republic of) - Corée (République de)[14]														
1985	C	239 091	23 459	18 672	21 029	21 137	19 328	17 846	18 566	18 508	18 395	21 239	19 165	21 747
1986	C	238 057	22 861	20 170	22 029	20 753	18 401	17 519	18 080	17 887	17 583	20 098	21 853	20 823
1987	C	242 123	20 465	19 468	22 276	21 095	19 247	18 308	18 437	20 556	20 532	20 147	20 103	21 489
1988	C	234 970	21 004	19 817	21 927	20 295	19 080	17 830	18 511	18 891	17 203	19 538	19 990	20 884
1989	C	236 017	20 598	19 552	21 433	19 972	19 245	18 848	18 930	18 763	18 233	20 081	19 202	21 160
1990	C	240 842	21 649	19 298	20 674	20 015	20 057	19 410	19 729	20 015	18 826	20 365	19 229	21 575
1991	C	242 040	23 311	19 910	22 012	20 333	19 550	18 768	19 092	19 475	18 339	20 150	19 859	21 241
1992	C	236 002	21 680	20 694	19 968	19 173	19 131	18 272	18 560	18 920	18 306	21 326	19 823	20 149
1993	C	234 953	20 866	18 562	20 714	19 996	19 542	18 791	18 525	18 876	18 193	20 501	19 303	21 084
1994	C	243 284	21 624	18 926	20 786	19 744	19 588	18 613	21 810	20 263	19 477	20 761	19 684	22 008
1995	C	243 589	20 579	19,686	22 599	20 319	20 287	19 388	19 126	19 327	19 921	20 757	20 327	21 273
1996	C	241 765	20 974	19 053	21 140	20 638	20 329	19 239	19 843	19 577	18 834	21 151	20 030	20 957
1997	C	244 069	22 371	19 182	20 823	20 169	20 736	19 652	19 512	19 494	19 045	21 386	20 089	21 610
1998	C	243 252	20 420	19 015	20 694	20 205	20 211	19 356	19 362	19 162	20 006	19 690	20 977	22 778
1999	C	246 539	23 083	18 838	21 026	20 305	20 712	19 816	19 150	19 846	19 455	21 611	20 625	22 072
Kuwait - Koweït														
1985	C	4 711	463	406	413	363	371	378	371	380	372	366	392	436
1986	C	4 390	414	382	394	347	368	328	371	328	343	334	344	437
1991	C	3 380	261	353	318	312	272	269	253	269	263	321	258	231
1992	C	3 369	331	296	267	295	247	269	257	307	265	237	291	307
1993	C	3 441	320	301	322	290	287	283	273	247	261	251	284	322
1994	C	3 464	295	258	276	282	318	278	299	271	253	287	290	357
1995	C	3 781	358	272	333	299	315	294	276	325	277	326	332	374
1996	C	3 812	368	320	349	321	284	321	253	311	288	317	332	348
1998	C	4 216	373	355	413	387	343	329	343	339	311	331	340	352
1999	C	4 187	354	320	369	366	393	350	295	330	321	328	318	443
Kyrgyzstan - Kirghizistan[9]														
1985	C	32 332	2 999	3 413	3 090	2 602	2 585	2 421	2 672	2 634	2 405	2 381	2 457	2 673
1986	C	29 083	2 364	2 408	2 447	2 369	2 438	2 216	2 465	2 362	2 344	2 365	2 393	2 912
1987	C	30 597	2 661	2 532	2 684	2 486	2 616	2 404	2 667	2 548	2 391	2 455	2 438	2 715
1988	C	31 879	2 426	2 922	2 743	2 538	2 827	2 555	2 564	2 521	2 374	2 367	2 634	3 408
1989	C	31 156	2 866	2 866	3 008	2 660	2 563	2 359	2 398	2 448	2 433	2 517	2 434	2 604
1990	C	30 580	2 794	2 766	2 746	2 473	2 491	2 646	2 499	2 506	2 279	2 480	2 319	2 581
1991	C	30 859	2 633	2 660	2 740	2 644	2 591	2 457	2 536	2 534	2 459	2 521	2 411	2 673
1992	C	32 163	3 111	3 038	2 999	2 647	2 699	2 570	2 540	2 608	2 395	2 613	2 359	2 584
1993	C	34 513	3 430	3 165	3 131	2 952	2 841	2 776	2 751	2 790	2 584	2 677	2 747	2 669
1994	C	37 109	3 570	3 418	3 482	3 252	3 108	2 862	2 978	2 831	2 852	2 826	2 927	3 003
1995	C	36 915	3 366	2 950	3 523	3 124	3 196	2 735	2 876	2 725	2 612	2 880	2 848	4 050
1996	C	34 562	3 620	2 832	2 916	2 941	3 039	2 662	2 783	2 677	2 455	2 747	2 770	3 120
1999	C	32 850	2 933	2 643	3 049	2 746	2 649	2 585	2 518	2 663	2 560	2 680	2 730	3 094
Malaysia - Malaisie														
1990	C	83 244	7 112	6 650	7 151	6 754	7 258	6 916	7 105	7 031	6 452	6 917	6 950	6 948
1991	C	83 851	7 191	6 724	7 295	6 952	6 997	6 932	6 927	6 860	6 680	7 340	7 133	6 820
1992	C	85 646	7 440	6 955	7 421	7 203	6 986	7 151	7 076	7 201	6 821	7 023	7 150	7 219
1994	C	89 702	8 070	7 123	7 879	7 799	7 695	7 570	7 420	7 054	7 217	7 412	7 226	7 237
1995	C	94 648	7 990	7 374	8 641	7 581	8 145	7 573	7 572	7 687	7 512	8 054	8 131	8 388
1996	C	95 520	8 431	8 040	8 485	7 797	7 998	8 227	8 243	7 947	7 721	7 520	7 335	7 776
1997	C	97 042	8 665	7 751	8 565	8 153	8 748	8 454	8 054	8 038	7 650	7 693	7 594	7 677

(See notes at end of table. — Voir notes à la fin du tableau.)

Continent, country or area / Continent, pays ou zone	C-o-d-e[1]	Total	Jan	Feb	March	April	May	June	July	Aug	Sep	Oct	Nov	Dec
ASIA — ASIE															
Maldives															
1985	C	1 607	132	110	141	157	139	104	131	130	137	152	137	137
1986	C	1 511	117	114	134	136	151	139	125	128	109	116	140	102
1987	C	1 525	146	117	140	123	128	114	135	110	98	155	141	118
1988	C	1 526	118	109	135	143	110	125	117	106	136	146	128	153
1989	C	1 476	181	144	133	106	115	109	126	141	119	101	105	96
1990	C	1 355	104	85	121	128	115	110	106	113	125	135	115	98
1991	C	1 366	108	86	111	99	114	98	142	135	118	122	113	120
1992	C	1 330	134	109	104	90	100	92	111	129	108	135	106	112
1993	C	1 319	114	104	122	94	119	130	116	106	101	90	104	119
1996	C	1 213	97	96	96	104	113	110	100	109	86	93	93	116
Mongolia - Mongolie															
1994	C	15 611	1 253	1 411	1 514	1 459	1 479	1 393	1 071	1 098	1 128	1 163	1 122	1 520
1995	C	16 287	1 196	1 698	1 554	1 618	1 631	1 475	1 069	1 031	1 105	1 101	1 166	1 643
1996	C	15 312	1 188	1 294	1 527	1 492	1 521	1 372	1 011	980	1 174	1 045	1 158	1 550
1997	C	16 980	986	1 115	1 416	1 661	1 417	1 488	1 080	1 024	1 216	1 099	1 611	2 867
1998	C	14 574	996	1 191	1 306	1 553	1 283	1 284	1 019	1 073	1 152	1 105	1 127	1 485
Pakistan[15]															
1985	I	839 247	64 946	73 666	61 361	55 753	76 063	84 710	52 516	81 397	84 282	59 354	62 323	82 876
1986	I	760 969	60 044	48 082	68 151	52 602	65 705	78 522	55 254	65 331	72 215	61 091	52 833	81 139
1987	I	809 163	51 504	53 096	62 040	59 963	66 898	81 147	56 588	63 446	66 015	70 566	70 262	107 638
1988	I	852 341	74 286	60 129	63 709	55 855	66 146	76 918	66 996	96 875	78 824	55 534	66 608	90 461
1989	I	884 590	42 485	52 046	66 313	80 554	82 827	86 557	68 718	77 419	83 630	74 451	77 582	92 008
1990	I	944 670	86 112	71 818	68 310	85 059	86 121	76 308	86 739	74 799	71 510	65 106	68 745	104 043
1991	I	892 570	86 059	60 507	54 415	84 061	82 721	83 042	69 343	63 266	68 769	57 019	77 807	105 561
1992	I	932 678	77 929	68 895	82 238	91 351	69 814	90 124	71 507	82 378	60 599	82 706	79 528	75 609
1993	I	932 066	88 890	70 960	75 557	72 930	72 103	101 783	60 539	75 475	77 918	81 962	56 579	97 370
1994	I	919 288	87 485	71 700	70 352	76 762	73 511	83 779	72 251	69 220	78 699	95 358	52 402	87 769
Philippines															
1985	U	*334 663*	*30 539*	*25 980*	*27 273*	*26 023*	*28 177*	*30 448*	*29 463*	*28 917*	*26 496*	*27 814*	*26 242*	*27 291*
1986	U	*326 749*	*29 078*	*24 802*	*27 565*	*25 946*	*26 796*	*26 706*	*28 132*	*28 520*	*27 647*	*27 383*	*27 502*	*26 672*
1987	U	*335 254*	*29 858*	*27 511*	*29 519*	*27 539*	*28 973*	*26 910*	*28 170*	*29 750*	*27 133*	*27 117*	*26 315*	*26 459*
1988	U	*325 098*	*27 830*	*25 970*	*26 891*	*26 267*	*28 163*	*25 545*	*27 214*	*28 672*	*26 206*	*26 214*	*26 625*	*29 501*
1989	U	*325 621*	*28 247*	*26 128*	*26 470*	*26 389*	*27 159*	*27 152*	*29 120*	*27 955*	*26 228*	*27 309*	*25 840*	*27 624*
1990	U	*313 890*	*27 504*	*23 323*	*24 733*	*25 107*	*26 640*	*26 384*	*29 286*	*27 438*	*25 935*	*25 973*	*25 847*	*25 720*
1991	U	*298 063*	*27 071*	*22 961*	*24 769*	*23 846*	*24 861*	*23 934*	*24 607*	*25 152*	*25 471*	*25 887*	*25 519*	*23 985*
1992	U	*319 579*	*27 638*	*24 133*	*25 950*	*24 451*	*26 096*	*25 911*	*28 294*	*29 256*	*27 750*	*27 847*	*26 403*	*25 850*
1993	U	*318 546*	*27 874*	*24 971*	*26 191*	*25 099*	*26 588*	*24 823*	*27 473*	*29 205*	*26 304*	*26 674*	*25 755*	*27 589*
Qatar															
1985	C	794	84	67	67	51	63	71	63	57	54	60	76	81
1986	C	784	74	55	56	74	68	71	63	63	60	58	73	69
1987	C	788	66	59	62	74	61	63	76	54	59	64	74	76
1988	C	861	91	63	61	63	77	72	59	79	65	59	78	94
1989	C	847	93	61	71	65	67	82	66	59	66	67	67	83
1990	C	871	88	79	70	63	63	65	63	76	68	70	77	89
1992	C	944	105	80	88	77	95	71	82	68	70	59	77	72
1993	C	913	77	68	78	76	80	74	75	55	70	86	71	103
1994	C	964	80	74	69	81	89	72	73	86	89	82	74	95
1996	C	1 015	99	88	85	84	98	65	74	95	70	87	82	88
Singapore - Singapour[16]															
1985	C	13 348	1 174	1 044	1 097	1 164	1 141	1 139	1 123	1 112	1 007	1 094	1 123	1 130
1986	C	12 821	1 016	950	1 163	1 132	1 132	1 094	1 038	1 069	1 002	1 096	1 041	1 088
1987	C	13 173	1 123	1 062	1 113	1 070	1 073	1 058	1 060	1 093	1 090	1 124	1 108	1 199
1988	C	13 690	1 038	1 036	1 175	1 168	1 262	1 106	1 143	1 083	1 123	1 147	1 150	1 259
1989	C	14 069	1 197	1 129	1 186	1 142	1 197	1 294	1 271	1 151	1 028	1 134	1 150	1 190
1990	C	13 891	1 154	1 080	1 125	1 113	1 270	1 211	1 198	1 120	1 125	1 092	1 148	1 255
1991	C	13 876	1 213	1 006	1 210	1 104	1 222	1 159	1 153	1 129	1 101	1 155	1 179	1 245
1992	C	14 337	1 275	1 196	1 246	1 192	1 156	1 205	1 183	1 260	1 057	1 092	1 109	1 366
1993	C	14 461	1 411	1 153	1 288	1 198	1 218	1 147	1 191	1 160	1 070	1 190	1 204	1 231
1994	C	14 946	1 301	1 171	1 310	1 280	1 254	1 311	1 250	1 272	1 146	1 231	1 159	1 261
1995	C	15 569	1 239	1 210	1 453	1 274	1 344	1 336	1 233	1 261	1 266	1 278	1 309	1 366

21. Deaths by month of occurence: 1985 - 2000
Décès selon le mois de décès: 1985 - 2000 (continued — suite)

(See notes at end of table. — Voir notes à la fin du tableau.)

Continent, country or area / Continent, pays ou zone	Code[1]	Total	Jan	Feb	March	April	May	June	July	Aug	Sep	Oct	Nov	Dec
ASIA — ASIE														
Singapore - Singapour[16]														
1996	C	15 590	1 379	1 229	1 344	1 299	1 421	1 342	1 352	1 266	1 260	1 210	1 224	1 264
1997	C	15 305	1 277	1 100	1 319	1 286	1 589	1 387	1 283	1 235	1 174	1 191	1 157	1 307
1998	C	15 657	1 356	1 330	1 394	1 357	1 518	1 332	1 247	1 237	1 195	1 250	1 197	1 244
1999	C	15 516	1 469	1 390	1 366	1 263	1 228	1 243	1 241	1 179	1 196	1 301	1 298	1 342
2000	C	15 692	1 397	1 284	1 347	1 364	1 399	1 228	1 334	1 262	1 238	1 264	1 271	1 304
Sri Lanka														
1986	+C	96 145	8 988	7 650	7 952	8 005	7 923	7 826	7 448	7 857	7 275	8 021	8 327	8 524
1987	+C	97 756	8 251	7 596	7 819	7 617	8 062	7 739	7 924	7 455	7 119	8 036	7 463	4 934
1988	+C	95 934	8 542	7 842	7 846	7 803	7 879	7 653	7 804	7 281	7 046	6 199	4 876	3 849
1989	+C	105 239	8 488	8 367	8 189	7 760	8 221	8 811	8 725	8 160	7 336	7 135	6 283	4 441
1991	+C	95 574	4 870	6 648	7 549	6 905	7 193	7 769	7 949	7 359	7 525	7 435	7 546	7 933
1995	+C	104 707	4 738	6 258	7 618	7 109	8 110	8 450	8 196	7 497	7 554	8 225	8 647	9 797
Syrian Arab Republic - République arabe syrienne[2,17,18]														
1985	U	*60 989*	*6 555*	*5 706*	*6 519*	*5 323*	*4 434*	*3 597*	*4 528*	*3 829*	*5 108*	*5 394*	*5 042*	*4 954*
1986	U	*50 711*	*4 923*	*4 565*	*4 849*	*4 291*	*3 577*	*3 611*	*4 287*	*3 608*	*3 993*	*4 046*	*4 397*	*4 564*
1987	U	*51 581*	*5 227*	*4 645*	*4 721*	*4 229*	*3 287*	*4 241*	*4 047*	*3 994*	*4 280*	*4 035*	*4 259*	*4 616*
1988	U	*44 899*	*4 211*	*3 943*	*4 089*	*3 119*	*3 051*	*3 229*	*2 676*	*4 068*	*4 121*	*4 047*	*4 103*	*4 242*
1989	U	*45 481*	*4 351*	*4 176*	*3 712*	*3 335*	*3 308*	*3 581*	*3 534*	*3 826*	*3 786*	*4 038*	*3 945*	*3 889*
1990	U	*32 966*	*3 582*	*3 038*	*2 705*	*2 174*	*2 601*	*2 272*	*2 523*	*2 632*	*2 929*	*2 560*	*2 807*	*3 143*
Tajikistan - Tadjikistan[9]														
1989	C	33 395	3 366	2 805	2 786	2 432	2 651	2 740	2 999	3 055	2 662	2 533	2 590	2 764
1990	C	33 020	3 065	2 815	2 814	2 456	2 521	2 968	2 778	2 975	2 586	2 678	2 625	2 719
1991	C	33 067	2 741	2 440	2 818	2 529	2 493	2 628	3 127	3 260	2 763	2 816	2 599	2 840
1992	C	36 718	3 627	3 105	3 082	2 591	2 858	3 009	3 681	3 667	3 070	2 839	2 467	2 703
1993	C	49 326	4 186	3 860	3 828	3 218	3 207	3 611	4 271	4 299	3 997	4 207	4 820	5 796
1994	C	39 943	3 961	3 957	3 385	3 171	2 944	3 216	3 845	3 800	3 008	2 647	2 924	3 085
Thailand - Thaïlande														
1985	+U	*202 634*	*18 568*	*16 014*	*17 360*	*17 663*	*17 551*	*17 446*	*18 125*	*16 879*	*16 189*	*15 697*	*14 828*	*16 314*
1986	+U	*218 025*	*20 466*	*18 260*	*19 069*	*18 816*	*17 685*	*18 147*	*18 201*	*16 938*	*17 268*	*17 309*	*17 169*	*18 697*
1987	+U	*232 968*	*18 165*	*18 071*	*19 007*	*19 611*	*19 863*	*19 764*	*20 103*	*18 846*	*19 605*	*19 928*	*19 309*	*20 696*
1988	+U	*231 227*	*20 090*	*18 458*	*20 222*	*19 432*	*18 467*	*19 730*	*17 856*	*19 445*	*18 189*	*18 478*	*20 090*	*20 770*
1991	+U	*264 350*	*23 098*	*21 423*	*23 071*	*23 617*	*21 881*	*21 535*	*21 503*	*21 088*	*20 553*	*22 177*	*20 970*	*23 434*
1992	+U	*275 313*	*25 154*	*22 584*	*22 754*	*23 983*	*22 491*	*22 100*	*21 642*	*22 613*	*22 061*	*22 331*	*24 807*	*22 813*
1994	+U	*305 526*	*27 798*	*24 207*	*25 499*	*26 654*	*24 800*	*25 224*	*25 563*	*25 102*	*24 246*	*24 901*	*26 267*	*25 265*
1997	+U	*303 918*	*25 200*	*22 927*	*25 544*	*26 310*	*28 150*	*26 169*	*25 494*	*25 462*	*23 371*	*24 876*	*25 681*	*24 734*
1998	+U	*317 793*	*25 408*	*23 236*	*26 927*	*27 624*	*27 369*	*25 905*	*27 804*	*27 290*	*25 712*	*26 949*	*26 436*	*27 133*
1999	+U	*362 593*	*32 784*	*29 168*	*32 593*	*31 863*	*33 000*	*31 366*	*30 715*	*29 837*	*28 468*	*28 879*	*26 152*	*27 768*
Turkey - Turquie[19]														
1994	I	163 232	15 195	14 233	14 288	12 453	13 115	12 117	12 906	13 199	12 873	13 158	14 212	15 483
1995	I	169 856	14 999	13 008	16 121	14 397	14 009	12 655	12 873	13 228	12 854	14 357	15 003	16 352
1996	I	164 534	17 473	14 561	14 691	13 645	13 435	12 439	13 442	12 335	12 123	13 114	13 410	13 866
1997	I	168 060	15 761	14 762	15 018	14 693	14 288	13 488	12 991	12 164	12 213	13 480	13 937	15 265
1998	I	175 429	19 023	15 481	14 748	13 815	13 410	13 582	14 562	14 478	13 930	13 632	13 933	14 835
Uzbekistan - Ouzbékistan[9]														
1993	C	145 294	14 281	11 811	12 896	11 925	11 825	11 903	13 294	12 111	11 258	11 827	10 859	11 304
1994	C	148 423	12 505	13 527	12 845	12 053	11 423	11 524	12 038	13 112	12 299	11 870	12 385	12 842
1995	C	145 439	12 397	10 336	11 858	11 513	11 818	11 839	12 215	12 123	11 028	11 250	12 215	16 847
1996	C	144 829	12 280	12 100	11 849	12 372	12 291	11 732	12 017	12 410	10 727	11 294	11 554	14 203
1997	C	137 331	12 552	11 931	12 380	11 259	11 170	11 456	12 485	11 175	9 873	10 601	10 591	11 858
EUROPE														
Albania - Albanie														
1985	C	17 179	1 705	1 374	1 544	1 622	1 536	1 149	1 255	1 194	1 200	1 398	1 442	1 760
1986	C	17 369	1 680	1 512	1 900	1 617	1 331	1 213	1 182	1 319	1 267	1 354	1 318	1 676
1987	C	17 119	1 754	1 362	1 774	1 640	1 446	1 287	1 294	1 160	1 137	1 196	1 444	1 625

(See notes at end of table. — Voir notes à la fin du tableau.)

Continent, country or area / Continent, pays ou zone	Code[1]	Total	Jan	Feb	March	April	May	June	July	Aug	Sep	Oct	Nov	Dec
EUROPE														
Albania - Albanie														
1988	C	17 027	1 453	1 418	1 747	1 451	1 406	1 267	1 282	1 251	1 123	1 226	1 486	1 917
1989	C	18 168	1 937	1 637	1 743	1 529	1 411	1 265	1 199	1 246	1 285	1 439	1 499	1 978
1990	C	18 193	1 690	1 957	2 297	1 418	1 393	1 206	1 235	1 274	1 163	1 359	1 484	1 717
1991	C	17 743	1 906	1 691	1 766	1 557	1 505	1 497	1 360	1 308	1 163	1 242	1 294	1 454
Andorra - Andorre														
1992	C	219	19	23	15	17	16	20	22	14	16	24	16	17
1993	C	211	16	21	18	18	12	15	19	15	14	24	16	23
1994	C	184	13	14	11	11	11	15	13	15	16	20	14	31
Austria - Autriche														
1985	C	89 578	8 824	8 279	9 142	7 124	7 497	6 640	7 074	6 620	6 406	6 902	7 417	7 653
1986	C	87 071	7 844	7 679	8 757	7 138	6 799	6 739	6 774	6 743	6 637	7 182	7 135	7 644
1987	C	84 907	8 405	6 960	7 651	6 812	7 081	6 809	6 791	6 649	6 263	7 079	6 916	7 491
1988	C	83 263	7 387	6 860	7 454	7 006	7 059	6 590	6 858	6 573	6 200	6 836	7 122	7 318
1989	C	83 407	8 505	7 712	7 229	6 348	6 624	6 193	6 756	6 432	6 288	6 914	6 906	7 500
1990	C	82 952	8 107	7 412	7 746	6 777	6 686	6 483	6 484	6 481	6 076	6 811	6 714	7 175
1991	C	83 428	7 560	7 276	7 454	6 700	6 920	6 594	6 743	6 447	6 234	6 885	7 055	7 560
1992	C	83 162	8 022	7 922	7 297	6 733	6 505	6 209	6 683	7 069	6 093	6 947	6 850	6 832
1993	C	82 517	7 458	7 294	7 684	6 637	6 614	6 152	6 406	6 228	6 278	6 674	6 726	8 366
1994	C	80 684	8 452	6 442	6 666	6 370	6 530	6 402	6 751	6 566	6 318	6 946	6 492	6 749
1995	C	81 171	7 432	6 839	7 408	6 889	6 454	6 109	6 573	6 004	6 179	6 827	6 540	7 917
1996	C	80 790	8 309	7 308	7 524	6 803	6 407	6 361	6 076	6 141	5 931	6 443	6 427	7 060
1997	C	79 432	7 836	7 334	7 025	6 494	6 441	6 218	6 067	6 112	5 870	6 807	6 514	6 714
1999	C	78 200	7 610	8 333	7 165	6 110	6 047	5 819	5 971	5 673	5 642	6 256	6 352	7 222
Belarus - Bélarus[9]														
1985	C	105 690	10 541	11 461	11 314	8 825	9 043	7 796	7 543	7 345	7 227	7 954	7 998	8 643
1986	C	97 276	8 491	8 309	8 869	8 197	8 500	7 826	7 652	6 862	7 549	8 139	8 506	8 376
1987	C	99 921	10 253	8 170	8 975	8 506	8 314	8 018	7 839	7 606	7 497	7 893	7 994	8 856
1988	C	102 671	8 862	9 443	9 899	8 648	8 515	7 691	8 043	7 714	7 689	8 319	8 750	9 098
1989	C	103 479	9 294	8 314	9 168	8 696	8 897	7 904	8 171	7 827	7 951	8 980	8 522	9 755
1990	C	109 582	11 751	9 188	9 363	8 605	9 353	8 673	8 211	8 172	8 136	9 413	9 092	9 625
1991	C	114 650	10 154	10 052	10 168	9 943	9 762	9 343	9 282	8 715	8 498	9 388	9 384	9 961
1992	C	116 674	10 993	9 907	9 761	9 314	9 765	9 055	9 260	8 927	8 724	10 330	9 988	10 650
1993	C	128 544	11 377	10 669	11 883	10 841	10 755	9 981	10 056	9 811	10 121	10 515	11 062	11 473
1994	C	130 003	11 189	11 328	12 736	11 051	11 200	10 620	10 169	10 039	9 233	10 577	10 771	11 090
1995	C	133 775	12 824	10 249	11 670	11 931	12 296	10 209	9 879	10 113	9 546	11 027	10 896	13 135
1996	C	133 422	15 463	11 671	11 028	10 804	10 902	9 729	10 326	9 603	10 020	11 446	10 714	11 716
1997	C	136 653	13 856	12 422	11 503	12 116	11 390	10 493	10 244	9 428	10 471	11 806	10 856	12 068
1998	C	137 433	12 129	10 869	12 131	11 548	11 204	10 970	10 836	10 131	11 054	12 002	11 941	12 618
1999	C	142 027	12 662	13 692	13 942	12 062	12 681	11 319	10 695	10 410	10 196	11 165	11 338	11 865
Belgium - Belgique[20]														
1985	C	110 770	11 120	9 718	10 141	9 217	9 007	8 318	8 701	8 158	8 162	8 935	9 526	9 767
1986	C	111 343	11 275	11 794	11 037	8 980	8 672	8 507	8 249	8 097	8 399	8 595	8 486	9 252
1987	C	105 426	10 112	8 569	9 202	8 719	8 707	8 263	8 145	8 304	7 827	8 927	8 918	9 733
1988	C	104 552	9 191	8 424	9 537	8 822	8 890	8 100	8 163	8 547	8 144	8 628	8 681	9 425
1989	C	107 619	9 361	8 642	9 122	8 259	9 090	8 138	8 389	8 183	7 993	8 596	8 743	13 103
1990	C	104 818	10 500	8 662	8 980	8 597	8 542	8 209	8 200	8 504	7 768	8 853	8 658	9 345
1991	C	105 150	9 477	9 465	9 182	8 795	8 598	8 044	8 626	7 984	7 861	8 707	8 655	9 756
1992	C	104 200	9 901	9 451	8 795	8 700	8 665	8 070	8 220	7 983	8 061	8 747	8 568	9 039
1993	C	108 170	9 868	8 604	10 545	9 474	8 547	8 266	8 379	7 801	8 230	8 527	9 193	10 736
1994	C	104 894	9 974	8 665	9 097	8 489	8 350	8 551	9 063	8 533	8 174	8 727	8 295	8 976
1995	C	105 933	9 617	8 183	9 946	9 025	9 014	8 441	8 566	8 321	7 778	8 660	8 416	9 966
Bosnia and Herzegovina - Bosnie-Herzégovine														
1989	C	30 383	3 438	2 637	2 576	2 419	2 491	2 337	2 430	2 353	2 272	2 523	2 238	2 669
Bulgaria - Bulgarie														
1985	C	107 485	10 711	11 026	10 969	9 301	8 900	7 921	8 160	7 605	7 296	8 231	8 480	8 885
1986	C	104 039	9 592	8 810	9 920	8 863	8 697	7 886	7 790	7 543	7 355	8 545	8 935	10 103
1987	C	107 213	10 514	8 682	9 895	9 013	9 234	8 868	9 631	7 576	7 253	8 323	8 889	9 335
1988	C	107 385	9 982	9 831	10 091	8 938	9 147	8 350	9 182	7 654	7 325	8 556	9 002	9 327
1989	C	106 902	9 786	9 545	9 794	8 887	8 985	8 409	8 333	8 021	7 413	8 874	8 740	10 115

(See notes at end of table. — Voir notes à la fin du tableau.)

Continent, country or area / Continent, pays ou zone	Code[1]	Total	Jan	Feb	March	April	May	June	July	Aug	Sep	Oct	Nov	Dec
EUROPE														
Bulgaria - Bulgarie														
1990	C	108 608	11 439	9 029	9 656	9 028	9 515	8 662	8 318	7 979	7 740	8 716	8 966	9 560
1992	C	107 998	10 646	11 256	9 737	8 950	9 000	8 168	7 940	7 994	7 456	8 569	8 605	9 677
1993	C	109 540	11 247	9 429	10 784	9 250	9 253	8 339	8 380	7 833	7 629	8 255	9 366	9 775
1994	C	111 787	10 171	10 244	10 062	9 190	9 725	8 315	8 468	8 405	7 994	9 279	9 454	10 480
1995	C	114 670	10 983	9 483	10 297	10 331	10 358	9 053	8 533	8 127	8 039	9 343	9 752	10 371
1997	C	121 861	11 045	11 263	12 197	11 396	10 122	9 612	8 597	8 366	8 061	9 875	10 035	11 292
1999	C	111 786	10 948	10 486	11 100	9 346	9 170	8 368	8 274	8 206	7 822	8 721	9 323	10 022
Channel Islands: Guernsey - Îles Anglo-Normandes: Guernesey														
1985	C	608	60	59	54	49	52	53	51	39	45	53	48	45
1986	C	614	48	76	61	61	47	38	49	41	43	41	50	59
1988	C	589	50	56	43	52	42	50	39	45	48	43	68	53
1989	C	569	46	42	71	49	61	33	32	38	52	51	50	44
1990	C	602	83	54	50	48	53	48	52	41	39	37	37	60
1992	C	552	49	74	48	37	53	41	36	30	50	53	33	48
1993	C	606	76	43	61	56	53	51	35	45	35	49	41	61
1994	C	591	52	62	57	55	52	50	40	54	44	45	38	42
1995	C	617	64	37	50	55	51	43	43	54	46	47	61	66
1996	C	611	83	56	48	51	54	39	38	44	56	49	53	40
1997	C	593	62	50	51	46	47	42	48	33	43	58	49	64
1998	C	540	51	63	46	35	41	44	49	30	52	37	39	53
1999	C	529	57	51	44	35	39	54	40	37	31	43	51	47
2000	C	565	89	46	43	37	42	37	43	50	41	48	43	46
Channel Islands: Jersey - Îles Anglo-Normandes: Jersey														
1985	+C	875	82	64	79	83	85	84	68	68	62	76	69	55
1986	+C	874	72	81	103	73	74	74	72	70	84	51	62	58
1987	+C	845	82	68	82	55	60	86	72	55	71	62	76	76
1988	+C	810	74	57	84	53	64	73	62	73	70	59	64	77
1989	+C	896	94	79	68	60	80	70	69	69	63	93	62	89
Croatia - Croatie														
1988	C	52 686	4 859	4 290	4 784	4 545	4 320	4 120	4 338	3 972	3 814	4 182	4 649	4 813
1989	C	52 569	6 089	4 424	4 429	4 004	4 226	3 976	3 904	3 878	3 909	4 377	4 421	4 932
1990	C	52 192	5 565	4 395	4 785	4 245	4 365	3 973	3 964	3 817	3 697	4 273	4 359	4 754
1991	C	54 832	4 905	4 669	4 632	4 418	4 479	4 136	4 076	3 763	4 278	5 008	5 200	5 268
1992	C	51 800	4 736	4 878	4 537	4 139	4 152	3 800	3 816	4 117	3 895	4 466	4 425	4 839
1993	C	49 482	5 063	4 676	4 291	3 948	3 909	3 852	3 851	3 980	3 509	4 146	3 925	4 332
1994	C	50 846	4 951	4 393	5 318	4 418	4 045	3 758	3 840	3 714	3 624	4 006	4 225	4 554
1995	C	50 536	4 663	3 680	4 263	4 375	4 159	3 612	3 980	4 017	3 870	4 080	4 478	5 359
1996	C	50 636	4 951	4 438	4 675	4 442	4 169	3 978	3 793	3 698	3 776	4 074	4 086	4 556
1997	C	51 964	4 913	4 775	4 778	4 600	4 141	4 085	3 820	3 905	3 798	4 211	4 362	4 576
1998	C	52 311	4 485	4 676	4 934	4 332	4 276	4 110	4 106	3 992	3 926	4 163	4 340	4 971
1999	C	51 953	4 863	5 827	4 989	4 138	4 102	3 718	3 883	3 854	3 665	4 120	4 104	4 690
Czech Republic - République tchèque														
1991	C	124 290	11 368	11 327	11 355	10 155	10 502	9 884	10 118	9 662	9 522	9 860	10 003	10 534
1992	C	120 337	10 976	11 632	10 401	9 895	9 734	9 454	9 711	9 804	8 814	9 991	9 613	10 312
1993	C	118 185	10 710	9 982	11 406	9 854	9 635	8 978	9 456	9 010	9 261	9 507	9 630	10 756
1994	C	117 373	11 578	10 057	9 905	9 647	9 604	9 764	9 672	9 267	8 954	9 883	9 246	9 796
1995	C	117 913	9 808	8 989	10 072	9 794	9 706	8 950	9 650	8 839	9 014	9 584	9 366	14 141
1996	C	112 782	11 094	9 607	9 813	9 355	9 107	8 826	9 206	8 858	8 817	9 180	9 093	9 826
1997	C	112 744	10 708	10 003	9 935	9 366	9 223	8 977	8 855	8 922	8 571	9 494	9 035	9 655
1998	C	109 527	9 408	9 000	9 779	9 174	9 043	8 749	8 887	8 616	8 630	9 122	9 179	9 940
1999	C	109 768	10 634	10 672	9 613	8 538	8 558	8 266	8 858	8 560	8 326	9 013	8 619	10 111
Denmark - Danemark[21]														
1985	C	58 378	5 573	5 469	5 407	4 665	4 765	4 387	4 590	4 593	4 517	4 717	4 802	4 893

(See notes at end of table. — Voir notes à la fin du tableau.)

Continent, country or area / Continent, pays ou zone	Code e1	Total	Jan	Feb	March	April	May	June	July	Aug	Sep	Oct	Nov	Dec
EUROPE														
Denmark - Danemark21														
1986	C	58 100	5 309	4 652	5 584	5 014	4 649	4 598	4 542	4 436	4 665	4 642	4 714	5 295
1987	C	58 136	5 540	4 470	4 961	4 729	4 724	4 683	4 647	4 699	4 595	4 910	4 803	5 375
1988	C	58 984	5 125	4 734	5 257	5 218	5 174	4 576	4 619	4 592	4 610	4 859	4 828	5 392
1989	C	59 397	5 438	4 990	5 290	4 827	4 871	4 731	4 705	4 722	4 480	4 844	4 937	5 562
1990	C	60 926	6 332	4 997	5 278	4 985	4 936	4 624	4 817	4 768	4 601	4 896	5 061	5 631
1991	C	59 581	5 457	4 816	5 223	4 805	5 109	4 704	4 839	4 645	4 711	4 931	4 869	5 472
1992	C	60 821	5 363	5 202	5 446	5 164	5 016	4 862	4 831	4 813	4 656	5 111	4 944	5 413
1993	C	62 809	5 683	5 002	5 531	5 184	4 962	4 690	4 659	4 700	4 813	5 069	5 324	7 192
1994	C	61 099	5 862	4 834	5 119	4 880	5 036	4 859	5 184	5 052	4 850	5 043	4 932	5 448
1995	C	63 127	5 680	4 838	5 440	5 247	5 190	4 905	5 024	4 854	4 752	4 998	5 179	7 020
1996	C	61 043	6 434	5 262	5 483	5 068	4 957	4 864	4 789	4 691	4 632	4 736	4 715	5 411
1997	C	59 898	5 903	5 296	5 307	4 788	4 997	4 553	4 642	4 838	4 672	4 868	4 808	5 226
1998	C	58 442	5 384	5 173	5 079	4 851	4 683	4 501	4 586	4 618	4 565	4 764	4 731	5 507
1999	C	59 156	5 649	5 782	5 768	4 597	4 707	4 437	4 611	4 600	4 427	4 665	4 564	5 349
Estonia - Estonie9														
1989	C	18 530	1 590	1 460	1 654	1 477	1 550	1 546	1 504	1 354	1 523	1 614	1 523	1 735
1990	C	19 530	1 846	1 642	1 670	1 590	1 627	1 604	1 500	1 516	1 592	1 596	1 548	1 799
1991	C	19 705	1 761	1 564	1 776	1 747	1 641	1 618	1 701	1 455	1 586	1 561	1 625	1 670
1992	C	20 115	1 829	1 682	1 699	1 597	1 702	1 586	1 519	1 508	1 532	1 823	1 717	1 921
1993	C	21 267	1 939	1 680	1 813	1 764	1 719	1 812	1 705	1 617	1 730	1 723	1 712	2 053
1994	C	22 150	1 988	1 751	1 829	1 757	1 777	1 793	1 831	1 645	1 980	1 974	1 832	1 993
1995	C	20 872	1 891	1 673	1 875	1 917	1 828	1 651	1 657	1 533	1 628	1 702	1 646	1 871
1996	C	19 019	2 104	1 767	1 532	1 612	1 553	1 526	1 504	1 431	1 407	1 502	1 430	1 651
1997	C	18 566	1 650	1 532	1 620	1 447	1 574	1 495	1 465	1 512	1 424	1 622	1 528	1 697
1999	C	18 455	1 670	1 552	1 690	1 559	1 538	1 497	1 474	1 435	1 429	1 520	1 504	1 587
Faeroe Islands - Îles Féroé														
1985	C	335	36	27	29	19	23	25	35	26	24	27	38	26
1986	C	367	32	29	32	31	33	31	34	23	24	33	32	33
1987	C	367	29	31	20	29	37	24	38	26	27	31	42	33
1989	C	371	37	24	33	26	41	28	38	22	28	25	36	33
1990	C	355	33	21	32	45	29	26	34	24	28	31	21	31
Finland - Finlande22														
1985	C	48 198	4 711	4 179	4 445	3 918	4 097	3 817	3 745	3 655	3 770	3 776	3 698	4 387
1986	C	47 135	4 315	3 999	4 220	3 878	3 917	3 890	3 670	3 719	3 747	3 837	3 722	4 221
1987	C	47 949	4 514	3 883	4 044	3 916	4 039	3 843	3 945	3 838	3 715	3 848	4 010	4 354
1988	C	49 063	4 204	3 913	4 258	4 158	4 033	4 163	4 289	3 869	3 758	3 942	3 956	4 520
1990	C	50 058	5 105	4 072	4 201	3 922	4 074	4 142	4 082	3 895	3 879	4 101	4 141	4 444
1994	C	48 000	4 663	3 899	3 991	3 876	3 868	3 943	4 220	3 763	3 800	4 018	3 786	4 173
1995	C	49 280	4 405	3 902	4 373	4 096	4 243	3 961	3 983	3 818	3 955	3 983	3 945	4 616
1996	C	49 167	5 243	4 304	4 278	3 914	4 027	3 856	3 852	3 819	3 772	3 880	3 821	4 401
1997	C	49 108	4 550	3 986	4 363	4 104	4 060	3 990	3 798	3 856	3 818	4 197	3 975	4 411
1999	C	49 345	4 473	4 711	4 672	3 890	4 001	3 850	3 902	3 948	3 775	3 821	3 798	4 504
France23														
1985	C	552 496	57 357	47 112	51 271	45 653	45 269	41 673	43 230	41 105	40 213	43 963	47 412	48 238
1986	C	546 926	51 466	52 732	53 666	45 204	43 594	43 632	42 198	40 821	41 165	42 798	42 894	46 756
1987	C	527 466	51 229	43 613	45 600	43 337	43 786	42 176	42 516	41 422	39 308	43 554	43 478	47 447
1988	C	524 600	46 740	43 408	47 762	43 770	42 715	41 272	41 457	41 105	40 145	44 085	43 970	48 171
1989	C	529 283	48 428	43 397	45 384	42 154	43 099	41 112	42 710	40 663	40 376	45 098	43 021	53 841
1991	C	524 685	47 211	46 308	45 463	42 788	42 962	40 314	41 871	41 130	39 195	44 502	44 288	48 653
1993	C	530 120	49 080	42 850	49 650	43 420	42 180	40 470	40 690	41 050	40 410	43 420	44 340	52 560
1994	C	519 965	49 932	42 613	44 356	43 104	41 841	40 573	43 940	41 822	41 050	43 503	41 833	45 398
1995	C	531 618	48 788	40 937	46 454	45 670	43 965	41 742	43 819	42 078	40 873	43 462	43 346	50 484
1996	C	535 775	51 341	46 604	47 495	44 833	43 636	41 237	42 390	39 915	40 680	42 725	43 337	51 582
1997	C	530 319	59 227	44 788	45 218	48 135	42 644	43 954	42 105	42 519	39 394	42 266	43 100	45 779
1998	C	534 005	47 361	46 023	51 720	48 135	43 961	40 956	41 368	41 319	40 016	42 846	42 928	47 372
1999	C	541 600	52 000	49 900	51 100	43 900	42 200	40 600	42 200	41 500	40 300	43 800	43 900	50 200
Germany - Allemagne														
1991	C	911 245	80 593	78 020	81 097	74 701	75 918	71 527	74 402	70 497	68 215	75 505	76 619	84 151
1992	C	885 443	81 761	75 456	77 424	74 308	72 910	68 606	70 455	71 260	68 658	75 074	73 045	76 486

21. Deaths by month of occurence: 1985 - 2000
Décès selon le mois de décès: 1985 - 2000 (continued — suite)

(See notes at end of table. — Voir notes à la fin du tableau.)

Continent, country or area / Continent, pays ou zone	Code[1]	Total	Jan	Feb	March	April	May	June	July	Aug	Sep	Oct	Nov	Dec
EUROPE														
Germany - Allemagne														
1993	C	897 270	81 535	73 271	89 611	75 661	71 199	67 576	69 470	68 081	68 731	73 481	74 935	83 719
1994	C	884 661	82 514	73 073	78 061	71 545	70 216	71 294	75 759	72 474	68 421	74 724	70 393	76 187
1995	C	884 588	79 171	69 053	83 907	77 097	72 513	67 852	71 140	68 075	67 506	71 386	72 188	84 700
1996	C	882 843	94 684	81 447	79 053	72 679	70 589	68 175	67 805	66 041	66 094	70 574	69 219	76 483
1997	C	860 389	83 490	75 162	75 100	70 517	70 228	67 290	66 489	68 917	64 862	71 914	71 538	74 882
1998	C	852 382	74 667	72 829	78 610	71 360	69 676	65 888	67 849	67 259	65 552	70 917	70 041	77 734
1999	C	846 330	70 360	77 518	85 961	67 732	66 329	65 916	65 229	66 604	64 155	65 235	71 164	80 127
Gibraltar[24]														
1985	C	276	30	21	31	27	22	21	26	18	20	19	24	17
1986	C	290	30	22	34	27	25	24	30	30	23	17	14	14
1987	C	217	24	17	17	17	15	19	17	13	16	20	22	20
1988	C	293	24	28	30	31	21	16	17	25	16	25	23	37
1989	C	219	19	19	16	19	23	12	24	20	13	20	18	16
1990	C	279	24	26	28	22	23	25	21	22	22	21	22	23
Greece - Grèce														
1985	C	92 886	8 887	8 424	9 122	7 563	7 226	6 853	7 406	7 958	6 448	7 324	7 664	8 011
1990	C	94 152	10 722	8 319	8 450	7 539	7 463	7 104	7 356	7 492	6 697	7 301	7 551	8 158
1991	C	95 498	9 061	8 476	8 186	7 861	7 716	7 712	7 867	7 439	6 715	7 307	7 918	9 240
1992	C	98 231	10 465	9 439	9 240	7 701	7 671	7 379	7 512	8 084	6 749	7 496	7 585	8 910
1993	C	97 419	9 543	8 985	9 357	7 994	8 004	7 489	7 658	7 714	6 597	7 252	7 891	8 935
1994	C	97 807	9 418	8 433	8 568	7 844	8 068	7 117	8 143	8 342	6 950	7 632	8 154	9 138
1995	C	100 158	9 013	8 535	9 323	8 839	8 413	7 820	7 900	7 566	7 025	8 030	8 780	8 914
1996	C	100 740	9 837	9 227	9 819	8 782	8 181	7 535	7 856	7 908	7 125	7 985	8 032	8 453
1997	C	99 738	9 791	9 127	8 799	8 923	8 670	8 144	7 937	7 478	6 893	7 756	7 853	8 367
1999	C	102 956	8 955	9 551	10 159	8 668	8 058	8 300	8 500	8 612	7 552	7 809	8 124	8 668
Hungary - Hongrie														
1985	C	147 614	14 582	12 800	14 261	12 939	12 486	11 599	12 061	10 940	10 516	11 547	11 614	12 269
1986	C	147 089	12 415	12 958	15 759	12 442	12 116	11 582	11 127	10 830	10 727	11 821	11 884	13 428
1987	C	142 601	13 523	11 687	12 971	11 854	12 246	11 651	11 933	11 122	10 273	11 486	11 521	12 334
1988	C	140 042	11 895	10 977	12 093	11 800	12 023	11 035	11 570	10 930	10 425	11 470	12 007	13 817
1989	C	144 695	14 513	11 398	12 307	11 576	12 219	11 423	11 630	11 276	10 944	11 748	12 053	13 608
1990	C	145 660	13 446	11 504	13 494	12 907	12 437	11 873	11 511	10 798	10 786	12 065	11 880	12 959
1991	C	144 813	12 888	12 398	13 129	12 221	12 162	11 700	11 546	11 093	10 661	11 879	11 973	13 163
1992	C	148 781	13 605	13 323	12 911	12 104	11 870	11 689	11 703	12 535	10 910	12 483	11 989	13 659
1994	C	146 889	13 888	12 825	12 516	11 753	12 328	11 839	11 848	11 722	10 968	12 542	11 743	12 917
1995	C	145 431	12 805	11 310	13 065	13 545	12 539	11 139	11 747	10 753	11 118	12 071	11 778	13 561
1996	C	143 130	14 970	13 040	13 016	11 960	11 408	11 099	10 922	10 499	10 945	11 372	11 090	12 809
1997	C	139 434	13 463	12 189	12 141	11 716	11 485	11 111	10 823	10 728	10 276	11 787	11 521	12 194
1999	C	143 210	13 693	13 664	12 856	11 384	11 310	10 416	10 852	10 485	10 293	11 163	11 247	15 847
Iceland - Islande														
1985	C	1 652	143	142	157	115	128	124	158	138	127	134	128	158
1986	C	1 598	136	134	148	153	125	124	124	128	127	138	114	147
1987	C	1 724	139	111	159	135	159	136	152	150	137	151	143	152
1988	C	1 818	169	140	146	169	219	138	127	128	160	133	130	159
1989	C	1 715	166	115	167	137	145	120	125	141	153	140	150	156
1990	C	1 704	148	124	133	145	158	137	156	140	149	117	135	162
1991	C	1 796	153	137	138	152	158	154	150	135	141	141	156	181
1992	C	1 719	153	151	172	129	135	148	124	118	141	145	130	173
1993	C	1 753	167	154	143	121	140	139	110	143	138	146	157	195
1995	C	1 923	183	158	173	170	157	142	152	141	158	159	158	172
1996	C	1 879	190	164	151	147	140	159	160	136	133	166	136	197
1997	C	1 843	175	149	166	137	143	168	140	161	170	164	122	148
1998	C	1 821	173	157	161	152	130	131	130	175	150	154	149	159
1999	C	1 901	187	165	183	144	164	146	147	168	122	155	142	178
Ireland - Irlande[25]														
1985	+C	33 210	3 303	3 095	3 382	2 832	2 582	2 529	2 406	2 350	2 360	2 462	2 780	3 129
1986	+C	33 630	3 426	3 391	3 714	2 907	2 669	2 388	2 327	2 463	2 497	2 407	2 507	2 934
1987	+C	31 413	3 202	2 779	2 799	2 664	2 554	2 374	2 314	2 382	2 365	2 540	2 479	2 961
1988	+C	31 625	2 916	2 945	3 130	2 660	2 622	2 323	2 409	2 409	2 339	2 514	2 479	2 879
1989	+C	32 111	2 765	2 530	3 030	2 763	2 616	2 455	2 360	2 381	2 266	2 496	2 518	3 931
1990	+C	31 370	3 627	2 630	2 700	2 505	2 439	2 430	2 460	2 256	2 315	2 495	2 532	2 981

21. Deaths by month of occurence: 1985 - 2000
Décès selon le mois de décès: 1985 - 2000 (continued — suite)

(See notes at end of table. — Voir notes à la fin du tableau.)

Continent, country or area / Continent, pays ou zone	Code[1]	Total	Jan	Feb	March	April	May	June	July	Aug	Sep	Oct	Nov	Dec
EUROPE														
Ireland - Irlande[25]														
1991	+C	31 544	3 110	2 928	2 914	2 632	2 542	2 398	2 303	2 280	2 216	2 556	2 588	3 077
1992	+C	30 930	2 988	3 033	2 704	2 547	2 438	2 307	2 382	2 305	2 432	2 465	2 497	2 832
1993	+C	32 148	2 961	2 398	2 886	2 733	2 583	2 422	2 431	2 400	2 433	2 672	3 166	3 063
1994	+C	30 948	3 155	2 630	2 804	2 592	2 471	2 411	2 433	2 337	2 384	2 447	2 436	2 848
1995	+C	32 259	3 096	2 710	3 250	2 685	2 626	2 429	2 434	2 286	2 303	2 504	2 605	3 331
1996	+C	31 723	3 277	2 804	2 832	2 637	2 658	2 425	2 348	2 398	2 433	2 485	2 502	2 924
1997	+C	31 581	3 722	2 763	2 762	2 634	2 601	2 396	2 369	2 294	2 287	2 433	2 436	2 884
1998	+C	31 437	2 926	2 707	3 133	2 758	2 613	2 408	2 448	2 383	2 281	2 565	2 409	2 806
1999	+C	31 683	3 740	2 991	2 944	2 558	2 453	2 405	2 306	2 331	2 319	2 491	2 351	2 794
Isle of Man - Îles de Man														
1985	+C	1 045	96	91	105	116	71	64	81	91	80	66	85	99
1986	+C	952	91	91	107	102	81	63	77	59	80	77	65	59
1987	+C	925	80	64	85	92	78	88	76	68	68	74	69	83
1988	+C	991	80	97	98	88	79	94	80	68	81	72	68	86
Italy - Italie														
1985	C	547 436	56 918	46 044	50 911	44 497	44 579	40 037	46 470	42 377	38 572	42 837	45 363	48 831
1986	C	537 453	52 586	55 006	50 559	43 190	42 517	40 361	40 413	42 278	37 864	41 481	43 577	47 621
1987	C	524 999	51 164	42 466	49 436	43 478	42 178	40 728	47 592	39 601	37 361	41 300	42 857	46 838
1988	C	539 426	47 339	44 197	51 591	44 904	42 704	40 556	47 422	42 749	39 189	42 663	45 768	50 344
1989	C	531 853	52 937	45 122	45 382	41 216	42 581	40 384	41 851	42 221	39 682	44 793	44 202	51 482
1990	C	543 708	63 648	45 521	46 584	43 465	42 945	41 310	42 750	40 564	38 833	42 702	44 654	50 732
1991	C	553 833	50 914	49 653	48 205	45 242	45 231	43 531	46 188	43 125	39 193	43 450	46 176	52 925
1992	C	546 690	55 300	45 854	47 953	44 653	43 344	40 723	45 443	47 948	39 564	44 601	44 079	47 228
1993	C	552 365	51 867	47 350	56 676	45 292	43 995	41 065	41 770	45 542	39 601	43 644	45 444	50 119
1994	C	555 325	54 077	48 469	47 800	44 607	43 823	42 354	47 078	48 666	40 404	45 262	44 552	48 233
1995	C	556 690	52 030	46 802	53 470	48 805	45 111	42 104	46 498	41 708	40 615	44 499	46 306	48 742
1996	C	554 576	51 703	49 435	53 010	45 371	44 097	43 521	42 742	41 626	41 263	45 609	44 982	51 217
1997	C	561 207	60 727	48 986	50 179	47 892	45 538	41 953	42 820	41 997	40 213	45 561	46 467	48 874
Latvia - Lettonie[9]														
1989	C	32 584	2 788	2 528	2 833	2 695	2 823	2 641	2 614	2 508	2 539	2 758	2 710	3 147
1990	C	34 812	3 595	2 874	3 013	2 833	2 968	2 832	2 658	2 563	2 775	2 792	2 889	3 020
1991	C	34 749	2 954	2 910	3 030	2 946	2 944	2 917	2 776	2 689	2 708	2 893	2 917	3 065
1992	C	35 420	3 163	2 865	2 927	2 927	2 753	3 022	2 730	2 756	2 652	2 785	3 285	3 367
1993	C	39 197	3 445	3 084	3 466	3 342	3 013	3 099	3 107	2 765	3 264	3 413	3 549	3 650
1994	C	41 757	3 536	3 653	3 653	3 340	3 374	3 328	3 444	3 216	3 230	3 736	3 426	3 821
1995	C	38 931	3 774	3 278	3 383	3 452	3 591	3 093	3 175	2 961	2 646	3 044	2 814	3 720
1996	C	34 320	3 535	3 045	2 939	2 853	2 877	2 666	2 780	2 605	2 648	2 818	2 572	2 982
1997	C	33 533	3 162	2 889	2 954	2 819	2 745	2 727	2 561	2 560	2 533	2 896	2 702	2 985
1999	C	32 844	3 065	3 043	3 156	2 686	2 811	2 540	2 467	2 404	2 453	2 755	2 642	2 822
Liechtenstein														
1985	C	171	18	12	16	16	13	17	14	12	9	12	14	18
1986	C	188	11	12	22	19	15	14	10	20	17	13	17	18
1987	C	180	16	19	30	18	13	13	7	15	11	14	7	17
1993	C	178	19	7	18	8	14	16	26	8	14	15	17	16
1994	C	206	26	13	17	15	17	12	13	21	10	25	17	20
1995	C	225	15	17	24	18	14	11	22	21	22	25	19	17
1996	C	230	20	26	17	15	19	18	18	15	17	19	20	26
1997	C	230	16	19	18	17	15	14	20	20	23	27	21	20
Lithuania - Lituanie[9]														
1987	C	36 917	3 679	3 009	3 277	3 134	3 043	3 075	2 965	2 907	2 795	2 911	3 023	3 099
1988	C	37 649	3 279	3 499	3 794	3 170	3 197	2 898	2 877	2 813	2 731	2 993	3 123	3 275
1989	C	38 150	3 308	2 949	3 362	3 283	3 214	3 075	3 063	2 891	3 030	3 268	3 211	3 496
1990	C	39 760	3 948	3 460	3 467	3 230	3 184	3 215	3 105	3 018	3 115	3 285	3 278	3 455
1991	C	41 013	3 545	3 344	3 696	3 517	3 573	3 330	3 267	3 212	3 164	3 495	3 283	3 587
1992	C	41 455	3 791	3 522	3 407	3 164	3 415	3 308	3 173	3 082	3 155	3 938	3 729	3 771
1995	C	45 306	4 071	3 488	3 882	3 892	4 021	3 367	3 451	3 382	3 215	3 928	3 899	4 710
1996	C	42 896	4 843	3 830	3 644	3 409	3 446	3 205	3 187	3 178	3 239	3 582	3 379	3 954
1997	C	41 143	3 731	3 705	3 770	3 478	3 329	3 150	3 050	2 975	2 993	3 613	3 348	4 001
1998	C	40 757	3 488	3 225	3 606	3 795	3 327	3 105	3 165	3 023	3 305	3 595	3 482	3 641
1999	C	40 003	3 620	3 587	3 801	3 513	3 476	3 181	3 024	2 987	2 895	3 189	3 210	3 520

21. Deaths by month of occurence: 1985 - 2000
Décès selon le mois de décès: 1985 - 2000 (continued — suite)

(See notes at end of table. — Voir notes à la fin du tableau.)

Continent, country or area / Continent, pays ou zone	Code[1]	Total	Jan	Feb	March	April	May	June	July	Aug	Sep	Oct	Nov	Dec
EUROPE														
Luxembourg														
1985	C	4 027	404	347	371	378	321	292	312	281	295	314	350	362
1986	C	3 970	351	411	438	345	305	304	276	279	301	333	314	313
1987	C	4 012	355	305	356	323	333	322	338	335	315	339	342	349
1988	C	3 840	336	320	376	349	303	263	317	303	293	326	335	319
1989	C	3 984	334	325	348	315	340	304	338	295	297	328	334	426
1994	C	3 800	354	327	286	306	284	307	322	325	292	348	339	310
1995	C	3 797	346	310	285	324	320	298	342	321	294	306	309	342
1996	C	3 895	368	345	361	326	312	301	315	302	322	296	302	345
1999	C	3 793	364	362	363	311	323	292	293	300	306	274	295	310
Malta - Malte														
1985	C	2 837	384	271	251	220	218	169	247	224	185	191	231	246
1986	C	2 824	285	289	235	304	226	183	209	238	208	174	223	250
1987	C	2 908	320	249	315	237	234	209	340	190	211	173	190	240
1988	C	2 708	275	224	292	197	218	175	251	192	177	181	221	305
1990	C	2 745	305	260	266	212	204	189	220	197	191	173	228	300
1992	C	2 900	426	301	288	242	233	165	208	215	246	191	178	207
1993	C	2 692	278	252	287	221	223	218	176	219	211	163	193	251
1994	C	2 698	263	241	239	224	188	183	211	290	195	196	199	269
1995	C	2 708	302	258	233	232	232	192	240	184	166	192	224	253
1996	C	2 765	271	232	306	243	226	196	220	203	206	221	220	221
1999	C	3 097	407	326	281	250	224	212	211	259	205	203	230	289
Netherlands - Pays-Bas[26]														
1985	C	122 704	11 871	10 386	11 697	9 850	9 888	9 320	9 567	9 331	9 113	10 053	10 727	10 901
1986	C	125 307	11 574	11 826	12 753	10 076	9 834	9 822	9 713	9 355	9 532	9 857	10 108	10 857
1987	C	122 199	11 385	9 938	10 735	9 804	10 027	9 862	9 822	9 502	9 354	10 267	10 199	11 304
1988	C	124 163	10 875	10 001	10 991	10 147	10 402	9 670	10 119	9 844	9 611	10 634	10 503	11 366
1990	C	128 824	13 556	9 929	10 664	10 473	10 641	10 159	9 998	10 390	9 777	10 949	10 489	11 799
1991	C	129 958	11 646	11 127	11 448	10 661	10 513	10 056	10 898	9 973	10 030	10 801	10 773	12 032
1992	C	129 887	12 018	10 707	11 138	10 535	10 905	10 312	10 588	10 236	10 165	11 016	10 770	11 497
1993	C	137 795	12 326	11 126	12 950	11 411	10 784	10 396	10 456	10 099	10 303	11 120	11 887	14 937
1994	C	133 471	12 015	10 809	11 308	10 737	10 845	10 923	12 298	11 100	10 285	11 113	10 463	11 575
1995	C	135 675	11 974	10 106	12 069	11 412	11 180	10 508	11 288	10 928	10 199	11 030	11 234	13 747
1996	C	137 561	13 912	12 376	12 264	11 675	11 271	10 672	10 933	10 379	10 187	10 747	10 970	12 175
1999	C	140 487	13 145	12 334	13 153	11 289	11 374	10 914	11 299	11 284	10 694	11 077	11 104	12 820
Norway - Norvège[27]														
1985	C	44 372	4 951	3 776	3 651	3 481	3 655	3 386	3 460	3 367	3 428	3 593	3 568	4 056
1986	C	43 560	4 024	3 489	3 873	3 563	3 612	3 522	3 500	3 378	3 469	3 572	3 500	4 058
1987	C	44 959	4 283	3 383	3 765	3 576	3 848	3 739	3 805	3 614	3 612	3 682	3 553	4 099
1990	C	46 021	4 574	3 637	3 856	3 771	3 802	3 617	3 734	3 614	3 545	3 760	3 776	4 335
1991	C	44 923	4 224	3 799	3 913	3 693	3 734	3 560	3 744	3 576	3 453	3 630	3 635	3 962
1992	C	44 731	4 571	4 078	3 727	3 623	3 582	3 471	3 517	3 486	3 496	3 728	3 431	4 021
1995	C	45 190	4 085	3 490	3 945	3 913	3 700	3 471	3 644	3 413	3 454	3 658	3 759	4 658
1996	C	43 860	4 219	3 664	3 770	3 550	3 619	3 435	3 504	3 405	3 401	3 599	3 504	4 190
1997	C	44 595	4 433	4 027	3 902	3 603	3 658	3 417	3 536	3 374	3 401	3 777	3 539	3 928
1999	C	45 170	4 178	4 050	4 548	3 686	3 552	3 370	3 497	3 414	3 312	3 541	3 558	4 464
Poland - Pologne														
1985	C	381 458	36 733	31 556	38 438	32 626	32 198	29 004	29 677	28 197	27 675	30 706	31 564	33 084
1986	C	376 316	34 459	36 717	35 352	31 791	30 140	29 866	28 749	27 417	27 979	30 279	29 985	33 582
1987	C	378 365	39 525	31 350	33 143	30 905	31 278	30 704	29 187	28 980	27 408	30 843	31 349	33 693
1988	C	370 821	32 232	30 226	32 805	31 044	31 509	29 150	30 021	28 153	28 365	31 229	32 073	34 014
1989	C	381 173	33 323	34 154	33 384	31 043	32 072	30 713	31 615	29 725	28 549	31 730	30 586	34 279
1990	C	388 440	34 558	31 620	33 056	31 901	31 694	30 914	30 046	29 956	30 442	33 129	32 743	38 381
1991	C	403 951	36 521	34 578	36 562	34 383	33 974	32 623	31 815	30 899	29 979	32 587	33 501	36 529
1992	C	393 131	35 086	34 685	34 245	32 777	32 164	30 803	31 364	31 195	29 679	33 684	32 092	35 357
1993	C	390 874	36 810	33 426	37 890	32 756	30 731	28 981	30 615	28 929	29 970	32 277	32 955	35 534
1994	C	386 398	34 207	32 775	34 695	31 798	31 694	31 826	32 007	31 541	29 024	33 043	30 638	33 150
1995	C	386 084	34 439	30 005	35 813	34 674	32 856	29 179	30 564	29 251	29 101	31 868	31 902	36 432
1996	C	385 496	40 895	34 269	32 997	31 600	30 546	29 297	29 506	28 583	29 286	31 279	30 471	36 767
1997	C	380 201	39 478	33 328	31 506	30 684	30 311	29 809	28 873	29 436	28 540	32 443	31 378	34 415
1998	C	375 354	32 324	28 863	32 601	32 860	30 782	29 270	30 142	28 569	29 725	32 612	31 612	35 994

(See notes at end of table. — Voir notes à la fin du tableau.)

Continent, country or area / Continent, pays ou zone	C-o-d-e[1]	Total	Jan	Feb	March	April	May	June	July	Aug	Sep	Oct	Nov	Dec
EUROPE														
Poland - Pologne														
1999	C	381 415	41 394	36 004	33 375	30 429	30 492	28 271	29 670	28 959	28 079	31 253	30 346	33 143
Portugal														
1985	C	97 339	11 072	8 485	8 822	7 811	7 349	6 958	7 334	6 973	6 924	6 903	8 152	10 556
1986	C	95 828	11 051	9 441	8 702	8 050	7 660	6 948	7 185	6 754	6 677	6 899	7 791	8 670
1987	C	95 423	10 172	8 171	8 316	7 944	7 272	7 148	7 430	7 351	6 961	7 631	7 983	9 044
1988	C	98 236	9 649	8 965	9 280	7 816	7 702	7 155	7 350	7 476	7 130	7 517	7 789	10 407
1989	C	96 220	10 495	8 983	8 307	7 689	7 462	7 135	7 977	7 362	6 703	7 246	7 500	9 361
1990	C	103 115	13 040	9 246	8 717	8 108	7 562	6 956	8 448	7 432	6 957	7 697	8 180	10 772
1991	C	104 361	10 045	9 941	9 753	8 482	8 842	7 297	8 389	7 678	6 981	8 183	8 427	10 343
1992	C	101 161	11 964	9 676	8 765	8 024	7 617	7 239	7 659	7 704	7 283	8 127	7 938	9 165
1993	C	106 384	10 764	9 465	9 940	8 323	8 255	7 743	7 779	7 599	7 189	8 314	9 045	11 968
1995	C	103 939	10 135	8 234	9 595	8 280	7 967	7 509	8 111	8 209	7 522	8 265	8 921	11 191
1996	C	107 259	10 042	10 074	9 938	8 322	8 614	8 286	8 148	7 577	7 608	7 913	8 866	11 871
1997	C	105 157	12 961	10 002	9 402	7 957	7 877	7 432	8 164	8 006	7 472	7 637	8 444	9 803
1999	C	107 871	14 709	11 285	9 946	8 190	8 035	7 361	7 515	7 478	7 142	7 887	8 447	9 876
Republic of Moldova - République de Moldova[9]														
1987	C	40 185	4 115	3 356	3 457	3 403	3 469	3 215	3 122	2 893	2 884	3 378	3 370	3 523
1988	C	40 912	3 476	3 620	4 020	3 410	3 630	3 184	3 179	2 941	2 901	3 299	3 675	3 577
1989	C	40 113	3 592	3 283	3 480	3 247	3 556	3 214	3 059	2 947	2 942	3 442	3 595	3 756
1990	C	42 427	4 401	3 611	3 611	3 295	3 590	3 278	2 931	2 931	3 213	3 812	3 843	3 766
1991	C	45 849	3 985	3 996	4 037	4 313	3 918	3 637	3 597	3 252	3 477	3 719	3 912	4 006
1992	C	44 522	4 219	4 088	3 714	3 527	3 837	3 351	3 278	3 028	3 155	3 777	3 859	4 689
1995	C	52 969	5 507	4 219	4 689	4 783	4 583	3 740	3 650	3 490	3 467	4 042	4 603	6 169
1999	C	41 315	3 693	3 744	4 259	3 735	3 357	3 089	2 874	2 582	3 042	3 155	3 936	3 849
Romania - Roumanie														
1986	C	242 330	21 668	18 972	21 992	20 849	19 968	18 154	17 955	17 358	17 059	20 229	21 625	26 501
1987	C	254 286	25 212	22 410	26 123	22 372	21 671	19 548	20 095	17 772	16 869	19 494	20 769	21 951
1988	C	253 370	22 347	20 980	23 353	23 440	21 898	19 257	19 391	17 184	17 038	19 982	22 672	25 828
1989	C	247 306	26 103	21 318	21 507	20 142	20 704	18 576	18 110	17 904	17 406	20 669	20 322	24 545
1990	C	247 086	23 606	19 825	23 255	22 433	21 434	19 101	18 179	17 435	17 893	20 525	21 014	22 386
1991	C	251 760	23 498	21 419	21 767	22 007	21 693	20 020	19 217	18 178	18 424	19 627	21 616	24 294
1992	C	263 855	25 790	26 374	24 098	22 627	22 260	20 568	19 162	18 846	17 804	20 907	21 290	24 129
1994	C	266 101	26 896	24 914	23 389	20 998	22 314	20 171	19 394	19 197	18 184	22 871	22 580	25 193
1995	C	271 672	25 964	21 551	23 862	23 575	23 061	21 085	20 412	19 636	18 918	22 890	23 838	25 670
1996	C	286 158	31 748	29 756	27 410	24 413	22 694	20 885	20 072	18 794	20 074	22 612	22 316	25 384
1997	C	279 315	26 800	23 897	25 735	24 118	23 061	21 959	20 575	19 636	19 804	23 804	24 160	25 766
1999	C	265 194	26 415	29 201	26 194	22 625	21 705	18 932	18 856	17 973	17 920	20 877	21 203	23 293
Russian Federation - Fédération de Russie[9]														
1992	C	1807441	164 388	137 737	144 756	141 117	151 006	145 844	147 146	146 698	146 684	159 880	154 131	168 051
1993	C	2129339	181 491	163 406	183 146	174 100	183 424	177 860	175 673	167 861	176 463	178 360	179 520	188 035
1994	C	2301366	194 488	191 950	205 555	183 654	200 520	189 333	188 720	187 135	185 952	192 261	185 015	195 474
1995	C	2203811	200 247	170 391	193 434	187 130	196 786	180 728	177 533	171 338	168 628	178 344	171 534	206 495
1999	C	2144316	186 161	180 392	184 852	172 260	184 499	173 453	173 774	169 362	174 240	179 004	178 082	187 095
San Marino - Saint-Marin														
1985	+C	188	15	12	23	18	17	9	13	20	11	22	14	14
1986	+C	171	10	10	16	19	11	15	10	16	16	20	17	11
1987	+C	154	16	15	16	9	9	20	9	6	15	17	7	15
1988	+C	187	12	13	28	13	12	20	15	16	16	13	15	14
1989	+C	173	10	15	13	26	18	15	17	11	11	10	11	16
1992	+C	172	17	12	12	14	13	12	18	13	17	12	21	11
1993	+C	145	12	13	9	13	12	10	8	14	7	14	13	20
1994	+C	184	16	17	11	12	19	17	12	11	15	18	16	20
1995	+C	186	16	8	20	15	15	14	19	21	15	16	14	13
2000	+C	188	17	21	21	15	11	18	17	19	11	12	14	12

(See notes at end of table. — Voir notes à la fin du tableau.)

Continent, country or area / Continent, pays ou zone	Code[1]	Total	Jan	Feb	March	April	May	June	July	Aug	Sep	Oct	Nov	Dec
EUROPE														
Serbia and Montenegro - Serbie-et-Montenegro														
1990	C	97 665	9 821	8 591	9 430	8 302	7 911	7 305	7 044	7 296	6 976	8 055	8 039	8 895
1991	C	101 573	9 205	8 751	8 846	7 978	8 235	7 974	7 675	7 534	7 882	8 381	9 138	9 974
1992	C	105 872	10 108	10 472	10 271	8 912	8 567	8 047	7 975	8 219	7 576	8 023	8 365	9 337
1993	C	107 396	10 734	9 123	10 517	9 395	9 058	8 068	8 142	7 834	7 633	8 367	9 091	9 434
1994	C	105 338	10 305	9 470	9 424	8 817	8 907	8 193	7 809	7 837	7 517	8 617	8 730	9 712
1995	C	107 535	10 101	8 885	10 405	9 379	9 239	7 845	8 280	7 841	8 045	8 971	9 112	9 432
1996	C	111 744	10 917	11 133	10 743	9 621	8 847	8 451	8 412	7 990	8 172	9 080	8 869	9 509
1997	C	111 845	10 522	10 180	10 414	9 742	9 229	8 792	8 248	7 894	8 203	9 421	9 292	9 908
1998	C	113 312	10 002	9 180	11 069	10 906	9 387	8 876	8 586	8 248	8 365	9 074	9 381	10 238
Slovakia - Slovaquie														
1988	C	52 475	4 636	4 214	4 532	4 474	4 428	4 235	4 358	4 067	4 056	4 329	4 462	4 684
1989	C	53 902	4 774	4 671	4 671	4 461	4 488	4 322	4 257	4 200	4 218	4 489	4 505	4 846
1990	C	54 619	5 042	4 348	4 936	4 625	4 645	4 432	4 411	4 353	4 112	4 450	4 416	4 849
1991	C	54 618	4 896	4 820	4 889	4 478	4 770	4 463	4 417	4 196	4 136	4 496	4 280	4 777
1992	C	53 423	4 729	4 967	4 731	4 340	4 331	4 223	4 294	4 462	4 064	4 331	4 340	4 611
1993	C	52 707	4 905	4 487	4 897	4 445	4 360	4 043	4 296	4 031	4 032	4 323	4 165	4 723
1994	C	51 386	4 854	4 347	4 457	4 232	4 207	4 167	4 122	4 182	3 986	4 324	4 150	4 358
1995	C	52 686	4 609	3 967	4 366	4 358	4 444	3 970	4 388	3 928	3 840	4 364	4 225	6 227
1998	C	53 156	4 325	4 113	4 619	4 422	4 456	4 314	4 429	4 284	4 222	4 531	4 524	4 917
1999	C	52 402	4 649	4 899	5 007	4 100	4 023	4 010	4 139	4 013	4 093	4 420	4 245	4 804
Slovenia - Slovénie														
1988	C	19 126	1 704	1 511	1 853	1 618	1 593	1 468	1 478	1 509	1 400	1 557	1 643	1 792
1989	C	18 669	1 900	1 683	1 568	1 477	1 528	1 463	1 450	1 400	1 345	1 635	1 547	1 673
1990	C	18 555	1 840	1 603	1 731	1 423	1 538	1 499	1 376	1 339	1 420	1 581	1 488	1 717
1991	C	19 324	1 705	1 569	1 665	1 562	1 611	1 559	1 655	1 529	1 442	1 594	1 613	1 820
1992	C	19 333	1 935	1 711	1 697	1 587	1 536	1 448	1 523	1 603	1 448	1 607	1 595	1 643
1993	C	20 012	1 873	1 819	2 032	1 648	1 688	1 418	1 513	1 512	1 460	1 607	1 594	1 848
1994	C	19 359	2 218	1 676	1 595	1 479	1 491	1 494	1 550	1 575	1 403	1 619	1 566	1 693
1995	C	18 968	1 666	1 534	1 663	1 597	1 589	1 438	1 534	1 455	1 457	1 530	1 563	1 942
1996	C	18 620	1 702	1 614	1 704	1 624	1 552	1 525	1 500	1 433	1 439	1 507	1 435	1 585
1999	C	18 885	1 775	2 039	1 746	1 474	1 497	1 382	1 458	1 373	1 443	1 496	1 584	1 618
Spain - Espagne														
1985	C	308 430	33 068	25 088	28 119	25 480	24 604	22 199	24 644	23 025	21 840	22 962	26 073	31 328
1986	C	310 413	34 835	29 453	27 248	25 696	24 858	22 689	23 935	23 151	22 087	23 267	25 390	27 804
1987	C	309 364	32 140	26 186	26 241	25 020	24 245	23 462	24 411	25 249	23 061	25 314	25 679	28 356
1988	C	318 848	28 979	26 635	30 552	25 555	24 917	23 695	25 653	25 769	23 724	24 881	25 784	32 704
1991	C	337 691	32 331	30 995	29 175	27 321	27 570	25 130	27 716	26 545	23 741	27 013	27 681	30 760
1992	C	331 515	35 324	30 351	29 175	27 123	26 214	24 339	26 827	26 364	23 512	27 181	26 302	28 803
1993	C	339 661	32 609	29 599	33 489	27 840	26 546	25 342	26 138	26 464	24 244	27 790	27 570	32 030
1994	C	338 242	35 324	29 616	28 590	26 991	26 746	25 350	29 468	27 408	24 731	27 295	26 756	29 967
1995	C	346 227	33 787	29 151	31 853	28 486	27 481	25 542	29 164	26 989	25 159	26 990	27 316	34 309
1996	C	351 449	33 783	30 515	32 510	28 092	28 249	26 829	28 140	26 483	25 872	27 876	28 994	34 106
1997	C	349 521	38 937	30 320	31 066	28 496	27 761	25 867	27 079	27 763	25 300	26 782	28 498	31 952
1998	C	360 511	35 096	34 733	33 505	28 957	28 276	26 791	28 785	28 211	25 553	28 296	27 844	34 374
1999	C	370 423	40 694	39 889	34 468	28 855	27 991	25 918	28 111	27 949	25 701	27 966	29 189	33 692
Sweden - Suède														
1985	C	94 032	9 246	8 687	8 638	7 393	7 783	7 286	7 110	7 241	7 181	7 377	7 701	8 389
1986	C	93 295	8 792	8 183	8 567	7 805	7 420	7 456	7 242	7 226	7 345	7 489	7 288	8 482
1987	C	93 307	9 051	7 478	8 291	7 655	7 854	7 557	7 629	7 460	7 294	7 344	7 445	8 249
1988	C	96 743	8 307	7 687	8 293	8 249	8 088	7 472	7 478	7 747	7 217	7 755	7 893	10 557
1989	C	92 110	9 434	7 000	7 651	7 441	7 604	7 526	7 549	7 129	7 033	7 691	7 450	8 602
1990	C	95 161	8 741	7 559	8 421	7 976	7 926	7 421	7 696	7 499	7 367	7 587	7 878	8 894
1992	C	94 710	9 402	8 390	8 330	7 751	7 535	7 535	7 601	7 219	7 247	7 705	7 727	8 280
1993	C	97 008	9 113	7 624	9 095	7 866	7 509	7 264	7 494	7 264	7 304	7 538	7 884	11 053
1994	C	91 844	9 189	7 278	7 743	7 186	7 428	7 072	7 707	7 159	7 653	7 509	7 508	8 070
1996	C	94 133	10 492	8 154	7 993	7 425	7 534	7 158	7 276	7 159	7 136	7 511	7 541	8 754
1998	C	93 271	8 439	7 860	8 629	7 984	7 420	7 006	7 381	7 357	6 982	7 637	7 846	8 730
1999	C	94 726	8 991	8 434	9 070	7 492	7 529	6 931	7 390	7 507	7 200	7 605	7 624	8 953

(See notes at end of table. — Voir notes à la fin du tableau.)

Continent, country or area / Continent, pays ou zone	Code1	Total	Jan	Feb	March	April	May	June	July	Aug	Sep	Oct	Nov	Dec
EUROPE														
Switzerland - Suisse														
1985	C	59 583	5 866	4 971	5 504	5 041	4 940	4 457	4 698	4 541	4 485	4 772	5 028	5 280
1986	C	60 105	5 613	5 841	6 095	4 702	4 702	4 589	4 543	4 517	4 618	4 849	4 835	5 201
1987	C	59 511	5 474	4 799	5 250	5 015	4 948	4 755	4 748	4 579	4 555	5 070	5 000	5 318
1988	C	60 648	5 247	4 986	5 539	5 339	4 933	4 756	4 677	4 613	4 736	5 213	4 988	5 621
1989	C	60 882	5 470	4 702	5 299	4 692	5 141	4 697	4 778	4 781	4 870	5 360	5 059	6 033
1990	C	63 739	7 748	5 462	5 452	5 112	4 938	4 758	4 841	4 687	4 684	5 295	5 175	5 587
1992	C	62 302	5 922	5 569	5 510	5 175	5 072	4 663	4 885	5 069	4 759	5 119	5 089	5 470
1994	C	61 987	6 073	4 982	5 245	5 067	5 015	4 852	5 117	4 847	4 817	5 292	5 113	5 567
1995	C	63 387	5 920	5 032	6 305	5 435	5 020	4 734	4 949	4 778	4 872	5 254	5 135	5 953
1996	C	62 637	6 206	5 674	5 644	5 215	4 882	4 778	4 803	4 639	4 835	5 108	5 169	5 684
1999	C	62 503	6 174	6 323	5 831	4 881	4 795	4 556	4 657	4 700	4 599	5 054	5 083	5 850
The Former Yugoslav Rep. of Macedonia - L'ex-République yougoslave de Macédoine														
1989	C	14 592	1 669	1 321	1 253	1 121	1 182	1 124	1 087	1 076	1 055	1 183	1 145	1 376
1990	C	14 643	1 643	1 364	1 309	1 224	1 183	1 072	1 087	1 016	1 091	1 186	1 148	1 320
1991	C	14 789	1 404	1 351	1 284	1 197	1 215	1 201	1 111	1 103	1 051	1 194	1 255	1 423
1992	C	16 022	1 741	1 517	1 430	1 323	1 262	1 207	1 127	1 202	1 207	1 262	1 337	1 407
1993	C	15 616	1 517	1 336	1 750	1 391	1 230	1 256	1 133	1 063	1 127	1 053	1 380	1 380
1995	C	16 338	1 575	1 337	1 397	1 507	1 433	1 241	1 236	1 207	1 225	1 394	1 366	1 420
1997	C	16 596	1 772	1 455	1 491	1 449	1 352	1 309	1 229	1 240	1 161	1 347	1 380	1 411
1998	C	16 870	1 482	1 414	1 677	1 568	1 325	1 220	1 343	1 261	1 272	1 391	1 399	1 518
1999	C	16 789	1 664	1 662	1 675	1 386	1 374	1 224	1 241	1 226	1 215	1 290	1 356	1 476
Ukraine[9]														
1985	C	617 548	62 881	72 916	60 306	52 676	52 109	44 374	45 479	42 733	42 306	46 883	46 420	48 465
1986	C	565 150	48 628	46 042	50 713	46 426	48 388	44 257	44 806	43 852	42 294	48 866	48 713	52 165
1987	C	586 387	56 386	48 918	52 779	48 338	51 265	47 820	46 654	44 452	44 604	47 182	47 629	50 360
1988	C	600 725	52 156	57 455	55 678	49 049	50 731	46 097	46 769	44 125	44 362	49 380	51 559	53 364
1989	C	600 590	52 752	48 908	53 983	50 465	51 019	48 576	46 190	46 039	45 031	52 124	50 217	55 286
1990	C	629 602	64 321	53 570	54 587	51 632	53 954	50 546	48 436	46 281	47 646	52 359	51 371	54 899
1991	C	669 960	57 102	56 495	60 238	56 575	56 535	54 850	53 479	49 264	51 698	54 297	57 336	62 091
1992	C	697 110	71 554	56 496	59 159	57 045	60 032	55 341	53 416	52 554	51 471	59 004	56 920	64 118
1993	C	741 662	69 996	61 417	66 449	61 420	60 894	58 236	57 464	53 567	57 455	62 599	64 825	67 266
1994	C	764 669	64 555	66 099	72 404	62 637	64 999	60 168	59 365	58 229	56 666	65 050	64 888	69 525
1995	C	792 587	73 019	61 812	69 154	68 530	72 091	61 513	59 501	57 964	56 254	66 401	66 826	79 522
United Kingdom - Royaume-Uni														
1985	C	670 656	69 320	60 947	66 969	57 006	53 064	49 287	49 575	48 540	48 012	51 315	56 601	60 020
1986	C	660 735	69 294	64 555	65 556	54 646	51 448	49 461	48 347	48 654	50 084	50 303	51 069	57 318
1987	C	644 342	63 797	53 216	57 797	52 179	51 336	50 351	49 839	48 705	47 849	54 316	53 575	61 382
1988	C	649 178	58 115	59 165	63 144	52 668	50 844	52 075	46 602	51 241	49 279	51 458	55 162	59 425
1990	C	641 799	71 182	52 867	53 704	53 271	52 452	48 598	50 876	48 360	44 201	54 669	52 755	58 864
1991	C	646 181	66 857	60 094	52 518	56 433	52 609	46 773	51 225	45 603	46 784	53 531	52 427	61 327
1993	C	657 852	62 015	51 310	59 057	54 668	51 470	48 691	48 358	49 234	48 548	54 934	63 154	66 413
1994	C	625 897	62 982	52 746	54 423	50 907	50 725	49 397	48 282	47 492	48 456	52 522	49 741	58 224
1995	C	641 712	62 851	52 343	57 158	51 749	52 556	49 186	49 078	48 236	47 184	51 809	55 333	64 229
1996	C	638 896	73 649	55 721	51 651	53 406	51 555	44 730	51 154	45 653	47 287	51 636	49 837	62 617
1997	C	629 746	77 526	53 698	51 465	50 007	49 495	47 121	47 763	46 709	46 679	50 783	51 276	57 224
1998	C	629 172	57 970	51 835	56 856	53 891	49 939	47 861	48 411	47 461	47 259	51 265	51 667	64 757
1999	C	632 062	72 974	53 820	54 727	48 416	47 791	46 604	46 490	46 962	45 682	49 790	50 063	68 743
OCEANIA — OCEANIE														
American Samoa - Samoa américaines														
1985	C	156	8	10	10	9	12	18	10	7	18	14	15	25
1986	C	170	16	9	12	18	17	13	13	14	14	13	13	18
1987	C	156	16	12	6	19	10	12	14	16	16	14	13	8
1988	C	197	19	17	22	18	12	12	22	13	14	16	11	21

(See notes at end of table. — Voir notes à la fin du tableau.)

Continent, country or area / Continent, pays ou zone	C-o-d-e[1]	Total	Jan	Feb	March	April	May	June	July	Aug	Sep	Oct	Nov	Dec
OCEANIA — OCEANIE														
American Samoa - Samoa américaines														
1989	C	175	18	15	18	9	13	16	14	15	16	10	19	12
1990	C	240	12	18	22	18	20	22	25	24	16	19	24	20
1991	C	217	19	15	21	20	13	8	16	14	27	12	18	34
1992	C	226	28	11	19	19	22	22	11	18	20	15	22	19
1993	C	223	22	20	20	20	15	22	20	16	20	14	20	14
Australia - Australie[28]														
1985	+C	117 811	8 821	7 557	8 618	9 018	10 114	10 946	12 515	11 579	10 474	9 722	9 065	9 382
1986	+C	114 336	8 717	7 806	8 945	8 779	9 509	10 406	11 121	10 742	9 842	9 823	9 104	9 542
1987	+C	118 143	9 294	8 205	9 341	9 147	9 899	10 151	11 237	11 108	10 733	10 168	9 365	9 495
1988	+C	118 973	9 222	8 516	9 311	9 233	10 222	10 841	11 545	11 304	10 198	9 883	9 257	9 441
1989	+C	125 252	9 401	8 270	9 253	9 422	10 134	11 375	12 434	13 137	12 302	10 699	9 319	9 506
1990	+C	118 939	9 148	8 328	9 160	9 115	10 242	10 452	11 413	11 122	10 653	10 248	9 360	9 698
1991	+C	118 556	9 539	8 179	9 504	9 259	10 307	9 938	11 055	11 306	10 683	9 932	9 322	9 532
1992	+C	122 946	9 397	8 527	9 386	9 473	10 549	11 676	12 089	11 432	10 833	10 188	9 604	9 792
1993	+C	120 813	9 294	8 456	9 360	9 218	10 180	10 899	11 197	11 552	10 741	10 338	9 712	9 866
1994	+C	126 996	10 001	8 610	9 913	9 769	10 832	10 972	12 567	13 057	11 069	10 659	9 827	9 720
1995	+C	125 225	9 481	8 700	9 631	9 984	10 502	11 085	12 217	11 897	10 916	10 604	10 083	10 125
1996	+C	128 271	9 836	9 127	10 006	9 856	10 553	11 364	13 281	12 552	11 216	10 427	10 056	9 997
1997	+C	128 744	9 897	8 794	9 690	9 721	10 382	11 258	13 035	13 613	11 335	11 154	9 983	9 882
1998	+C	127 358	9 847	8 862	9 733	9 878	10 640	11 247	12 949	12 417	11 028	10 675	9 873	10 209
1999	+C	122 730	9 989	8 836	9 965	10 016	10 875	11 261	12 329	12 383	11 091	10 628	10 040	5 317
Cook Islands - Îles Cook														
1985	+C	137	10	14	12	12	7	10	14	13	10	13	15	7
1986	+C	119	4	9	6	7	10	11	15	9	10	10	11	17
1987	+C	128	15	9	11	9	12	8	10	11	11	10	10	12
1988	+C	94	9	7	14	2	8	6	8	12	10	7	6	5
Fiji - Fidji														
1985	+C	3 680	345	279	308	289	290	325	320	294	252	285	267	263
1986	+C	2 656	274	244	304	273	307	265	267	287	186	133	83	33
1987	+C	3 178	360	242	294	268	241	220	212	206	269	317	269	280
French Polynesia - Polynésie française														
1985	U	993	78	73	74	79	87	95	82	97	81	85	81	81
1986	U	982	81	69	87	95	79	65	81	94	84	87	77	83
1987	U	1 055	95	82	91	94	113	79	89	89	84	81	62	96
1988	U	985	96	75	101	85	87	63	93	81	76	76	80	72
1989	U	1 088	91	90	87	87	95	80	98	91	85	102	73	109
1990	U	982	110	87	97	85	84	61	74	81	63	73	78	89
1991	U	1 021	102	75	78	89	93	78	89	89	75	79	83	91
1992	U	1 055	122	94	94	87	83	95	80	92	82	75	75	76
Guam[29]														
1985	C	441	24	34	28	46	38	39	42	48	46	30	36	30
1986	C	451	21	24	49	33	40	33	32	38	43	48	34	56
1988	C	492	45	37	40	40	46	31	40	29	43	63	41	37
1989	C	544	46	47	36	44	44	35	48	43	59	53	44	45
1990	C	557	45	44	36	47	56	41	29	47	47	52	49	64
1991	C	607	31	48	55	52	51	56	59	58	44	44	55	54
1992	C	585	68	52	44	42	38	49	37	47	57	52	46	53
New Caledonia - Nouvelle-Calédonie														
1985	C	891	72	78	68	79	67	87	86	80	75	72	57	70
1986	C	904	62	56	68	81	82	77	86	75	93	89	61	74
1987	C	913	105	61	82	63	74	75	91	63	89	55	78	77
1988	C	962	71	89	87	69	111	102	82	76	73	60	68	74
1989	C	990	101	74	91	75	64	99	81	77	111	80	62	75
1990	C	928	70	77	69	73	79	66	91	98	86	84	71	64
1991	C	978	84	79	86	76	71	78	87	85	95	82	77	78
1992	C	931	75	65	85	77	76	82	94	63	92	79	78	65
1993	C	954	78	61	88	67	78	82	93	101	85	74	71	76

(See notes at end of table. — Voir notes à la fin du tableau.)

Continent, country or area / Continent, pays ou zone	C-o-d-e[1]	Total	Jan	Feb	March	April	May	June	July	Aug	Sep	Oct	Nov	Dec
OCEANIA — OCEANIE														
New Caledonia - Nouvelle-Calédonie														
1994	C	1 060	88	77	84	86	95	94	88	85	105	90	85	82
New Zealand - Nouvelle-Zélande[28]														
1985	+C	27 480	2 056	1 746	2 106	2 147	2 422	2 759	2 760	2 538	2 387	2 201	2 107	1 350
1986	+C	27 045	2 132	1 781	2 108	2 067	2 207	2 336	2 642	2 511	2 524	2 300	2 184	1 411
1987	+C	27 419	2 058	1 934	2 130	2 236	2 377	2 455	2 637	2 543	2 433	2 327	2 098	1 400
1988	+C	27 408	2 129	1 939	2 124	2 161	2 461	2 586	2 737	2 494	2 309	2 299	2 056	1 307
1989	+C	27 042	2 045	1 900	2 233	2 136	2 242	2 261	2 629	2 786	2 503	2 218	2 052	1 163
1990	+C	26 531	2 039	1 876	1 988	2 099	2 251	2 308	2 510	2 679	2 340	2 222	2 052	1 201
1991	+C	26 389	2 003	1 796	1 959	2 060	2 273	2 341	2 493	2 456	2 411	2 290	2 115	2 192
1992	+C	27 115	1 988	1 795	2 201	2 106	2 375	2 476	2 559	2 610	2 464	2 329	2 016	2 196
1993	+C	27 100	2 018	1 879	2 091	2 082	2 327	2 354	2 654	2 545	2 539	2 252	2 150	2 209
1994	+C	26 953	1 870	1 778	1 990	2 123	2 297	2 362	2 767	2 814	2 432	2 308	2 130	2 082
1995	+C	27 813	2 069	1 793	2 233	1 998	2 287	2 443	2 721	2 794	2 609	2 352	2 224	2 290
1996	+C	28 255	2 093	1 946	2 198	2 095	2 295	2 846	3 254	2 436	2 430	2 269	2 181	2 212
1997	+C	27 471	2 082	1 824	2 156	2 181	2 293	2 316	2 616	2 754	2 547	2 358	2 126	2 218
1999	+C	28 122	2 210	1 901	2 148	2 164	2 292	2 573	2 854	2 770	2 499	2 332	2 122	2 257
2000	+C	26 660	2 155	1 921	2 061	2 125	2 259	2 296	2 377	2 427	2 405	2 293	2 136	2 205
Niue - Nioué														
1985	...	*16*	*1*	*1*	*1*	*...*	*2*	*1*	*1*	*1*	*3*	*3*	*1*	*1*
1986	...	*22*	*4*	*1*	*2*	*1*	*2*	*2*	*3*	*...*	*2*	*3*	*2*	*...*
1987	...	*13*	*2*	*2*	*2*	*1*	*...*	*2*	*2*	*...*	*...*	*...*	*1*	*1*
Norfolk Island - Île Norfolk														
1988	C	9	2	1	1	...	...	2	2	...	...	...	...	1
Northern Mariana Islands - Îles Mariannes septentrionales														
1985	U	*95*	*11*	*7*	*5*	*6*	*5*	*11*	*6*	*6*	*9*	*9*	*8*	*12*
1989	U	*122*	*8*	*9*	*11*	*10*	*11*	*9*	*13*	*14*	*10*	*11*	*9*	*7*
Tonga														
1994	+C	424	44	43	35	31	42	27	30	27	40	33	33	39
1995	+C	467	40	55	47	44	42	31	41	37	32	33	23	42
1996	+C	456	41	44	36	38	24	39	40	49	36	30	37	42
1997	+C	467	45	38	27	33	29	41	37	52	55	39	38	33
1998	+C	498	39	32	36	40	39	47	40	55	54	39	39	38

GENERAL NOTES - NOTES GENERALES

For certain countries, there is a discrepancy between the total number of deaths shown in this table and those shown in subsequent tables for the same year. Usually this discrepancy arises because the total number of deaths occurring in a given year is revised, although the remaining tabulations are not. Data exclude foetal deaths. — Pour quelques pays il y a une discordance entre le nombre total des décès vivantes présenté dans ce tableau et ceux présentés après pour la même année. Habituellement ces différences apparaîssent lorsque le nombre total des décès pour une certaine année a été révisé; alors que les autres tabulations ne l'ont pas été. Les données ne comprennent pas les morts foetales.

Italics: data from civil registers which are incomplete or of unknown completeness. — Italiques: données incomplètes ou dont le degré d'exactitude n'est pas connu, provenant des registres de l'état civil.

FOOTNOTES - NOTES

* Provisional. — Données provisoires.

[1] 'Code' indicates the source of data, as follows:

C - Civil registration, estimated over 90% complete
U - Civil registration, estimated less than 90% complete
I - Other source, estimated reliable
+ - Data tabulated by date of registration rather than occurence.
... - Information not available

Le 'Code' indique la source des données, comme suit:
C - Registres de l'état civil considérés complèts à 90 p. 100 au moins.
U - Registres de l'état civil qui ne sont pas considérés complèts à 90 p. 100 au moins.
I - Autre source, considérée pas douteuses.
+ - Données exploitées selon la date de l'enregistrement et non la date de l'événement.
... - Information pas disponible.

[2] Excluding live-born infants dying before registration of birth. — Non compris les enfants nés vivants décédés avant l'enregistrement de leur naissance.
[3] Registered data are for Algerian population only. — Les données ne sont enregistrées que pour la population algérienne seulement.
[4] Including Canadian residents temporarily in the United States, but excluding United States residents temporarily in Canada. — Y compris les résidents canadiens se trouvant temporairement aux Etats-Unis, mais ne comprennent pas les résidents des Etats-Unis se trouvant temporairement au

Canada.

⁵ Excluding Indian jungle population. — Non compris les Indiens de la jungle.

⁶ Based on burial permits. — D'après les permis d'inhumer.

⁷ Data on live births and deaths are based on a civil registration system put in place in January 1998. — Les données sur les naissances et les décès sont basées sur un système civil d'enregistrement mis en place en janvier 1998.

⁸ Excluding nomadic Indian tribes. — Non compris les tribus d'indiens nomades.

⁹ Excluding infants born alive after less than 28 weeks' gestation, of less than 1 000 grams in weight and 35 centimeters in length, who die within seven days of birth. — Non compris les enfants nés vivants après moins de 28 semaines de gestation, pesant moins de 1 000 grammes, mesurant moins de 35 centimètres et décédés dans les sept jours qui ont suivi leur naissance.

¹⁰ For statistical purposes, the data for China do not include those for the Hong Kong Special Administrative Region (Hong Kong SAR), Macao special Adminstrative Region (Macao SAR) and Taiwan province of China. — Pour la présentation des statistiques, les données pour Chine ne comprend pas les Région Administrative Spéciale de Hong-kong (Hong Kong RAS), le Région Administrative Spéciale de Macao (Macao RAS) et Taïwan province de Chine.

¹¹ For government controlled areas. — Pour les zones contrôlées par le Gouvernement.

¹² Including data for East Jerusalem and Israeli residents in certain other territories under occupation by Israeli military forces since June 1967. — Y compris les données pour Jérusalem-Est et les résidents israéliens dans certains autres territoires occupés depuis 1967 par les forces armées israéliennes.

¹³ For Japanese nationals in Japan only; however, rates are computed based on total population. — Pour les nationaux japonais au Japon seulement; toutefois, les taux sont calculés sur la base de la population totale.

¹⁴ Excluding alien armed forces, civilian aliens employed by armed forces, foreign diplomatic personnel and their dependants and Korean diplomatic personnel and their dependants outside the country. — Non compris les militaires étrangers, les civils étrangers employés par les forces armées, le personnel diplomatique étranger et les membres de leur famille les accompagnant et le personnel diplomatique coréen hors du pays et les membres de leurs familles les accompagnant.

¹⁵ Based on the results of the Population Growth Survey. — D'après les résultants de la 'Population Growth Survey'.

¹⁶ Excluding transients afloat and non-locally domiciled military and civilian services personnel and their dependants. — Non compris les personnes de passage þ bord de navires, ni les militaires et agents civils domiciliés hors du territoire et les membres de leur famille les accompagnant.

¹⁷ Excluding nomad population and Palestinian refugees. — Non compris la population nomade et les réfugiés de Palestine.

¹⁸ Including late registered deaths. — Y compris les décès enregistrés tardivement.

¹⁹ Based on the results of the Population Demographic Survey. — D'après les résultats de la Population Demographic Survey.

²⁰ Including armed forces stationed outside the country, but excluding alien armed forces stationed in the area. — Y compris les militaires nationaux hors du pays, mais non compris les militaires étrangers en garnison sur le territoire.

²¹ Excluding Faeroe Islands and Greenland. — Non compris les îles Féroé et Gröenland.

²² Including nationals temporarily outside the country. — Y compris les nationaux se trouvant temporairement hors du pays.

²³ Including armed forces stationed outside the country. — Y compris les militaires nationaux hors du pays.

²⁴ Excluding armed forces. — Non compris les militaires.

²⁵ Events registered within one year of occurrence. — Evénements enregistrés dans l'année qui suit l'événement.

²⁶ Including residents outside the country if listed in a Netherlands population register. — Y compris les résidents hors du pays, s'ils sont inscrits sur un registre de population néerlandais.

²⁷ Including residents temporarily outside the country. — Y compris les résidents se trouvant temporairement hors du pays.

²⁸ Data are tabulated by year and month of occurence of events registered up to 31 December of a given year. — Données exploitées selon la date de l'événement, registrées jusque le 31 Decembre.

²⁹ Including United States military personnel, their dependants and contract employees. — Y compris les militaires des Etats-Unis, les membres de leur famille les accompagnant et les agents contractuels des Etats-Unis.

Table 22

Table 22 presents expectation of life at specified ages for each sex for the latest available year.

Description of variables: Expectation of life at birth is defined as the average number of years of life for males and females if they continued to be subject to the same mortality experienced in the year(s) to which these life expectancies refer.

The table shows life expectancy derived from an abridged life table as reported by the country.

Male and female expectations are shown separately for selected ages beginning at birth (age 0) and proceeding with ages 5, 10, l5, 20, 25, 30, 35, 40, 45, 50, 55, 60, 65, 70, 75, 85, 90, 95 and 100 years.

Life expectancy is shown with one decimal regardless of the number of digits provided in the original computation. The data are from the official life tables of the countries or areas concerned.

Life table computation: From the demographic point of view, a life table is regarded as a theoretical model of a population that is continuously replenished by births and depleted by deaths. The model gives a complete picture of the mortality experience of a population based on the assumption that the theoretical cohort is subject, throughout its existence, to the age-specific mortality rates observed at a particular time. Thus levels of mortality prevailing at the time a life table is constructed are assumed to remain unchanged into the future until all members of the cohort have died.

Expectation of life, e_x is defined as the average number of years of life which would remain for males and females reaching age if they continued to be subjected to the same mortality experienced in the year(s) to which these life expectancies refer.

Reliability of data: The values shown in this table come from official life tables. It is assumed that, if necessary, the basic data (population and deaths classified by age and sex) have been adjusted for deficiencies before their use in constructing the life tables.

Limitations: Expectation-of-life values are subject to the same qualifications as have been set forth for population statistics in general and death statistics in particular, as discussed in sections 3 and 4, respectively, of the Technical Notes. They must be interpreted strictly using the underlying assumption that surviving cohorts are subjected to the same age-specific mortality rates of the period to which the life table refers.

Coverage: Expectation of life at specified ages for each sex is shown for 108 countries or areas.

Earlier data: Expectation of life at specified ages for each sex has been shown in previous issues of the *Demographic Yearbook*. Data included in this table update the series covering a period of years as follows:

Issue	Years Covered
Historical Supplement CD, 1997	1948 – 1997
Special Issue on Population Ageing and the Situation of Elderly Persons, 1991	1950 – 1990
Historical Supplement, 1979	1948 – 1977
1948	1896 – 1947

Tableau 22

Le tableau 22 présente les espérances de vie à des âges déterminés, pour chaque sexe, pour la dernière année disponible.

Description des variables : L'espérance de vie est le nombre moyen d'années restant à vivre aux personnes du sexe masculin et du sexe féminin atteignant les âges indiqués si elles continuent d'être soumises aux mêmes conditions de mortalité que celles qui existaient pendant les années auxquelles se rapportent les valeurs considérées.

Dans le tableau figurent les espérances de vie calculées selon une table de mortalité abrégée par le pays même.

Les chiffres sont présentés séparément pour chaque sexe à partir de la naissance (âge 0) et pour les âges suivants : 5,10, 15, 20, 25, 30, 35, 40, 45, 50, 55, 60, 65, 70, 75, 80, 85, 90, 95 et 100 ans.

Les espérances de vie sont chiffrées à une décimal, indépendamment du nombre de celles qui figurent dans le calcul initial. Ces données proviennent des tables officielles de mortalité des pays ou zones auxquels elles se rapportent.

Calcul des tables de mortalité : Du point de vue démographique, les tables de mortalité sont considérées comme des modèles théoriques représentant une population constamment reconstituée par les naissances et réduite par les décès. Ces modèles donnent un aperçu complet de la mortalité d'une population, reposant sur l'hypothèse que chaque cohorte théoriquement distinguée connaît, pendant tout son existence, la mortalité par âge observée à un moment donné. Les mortalités correspondant à l'époque à laquelle sont calculées les tables de mortalité sont ainsi censées demeurer inchangées dans l'avenir jusqu'au décès de tous les membres de la cohorte.

L'espérance de vie e_x se définit comme le nombre moyen d'années de survie des hommes et des femmes qui ont atteint les âges indiqués, au cas où leur cohorte continuerait d'être soumise à la même mortalité que dans l'année ou les années auxquelles se réfère l'espérance de vie.

Fiabilité des donnés : Etant donné que les chiffres figurant dans ce tableau proviennent de tables officielles de mortalité, elles sont toutes présumées sûres. En ce qui concerne les chiffres tirés de tables officielles de mortalité, on suppose que les données de base (effectif de la population et nombre de décès selon l'âge et le sexe) ont été ajustées, en tant que de besoin, avant de servir à l'établissement de la table de mortalité.

Insuffisance des données : Les espérances de vie appellent les mêmes réserves que celles qui ont été formulées à propos des statistiques de la population en général et des statistiques de mortalité en particulier (voir explications aux sections 3 et 4, respectivement, des Notes techniques). La principale réserve à faire au sujet des espérances de vie est peut-être que, lorsqu'on interprète les données, il ne faut jamais perdre de vue que, par hypothèse, les cohortes de survivants sont soumises, pour chaque âge, aux conditions de mortalité de la période visée par la table de mortalité.

Portée : Ce tableau présente les espérances de vie à des âges déterminés pour chaque sexe, pour 108 pays ou zones.

Données publiées antérieurement : Des espérances de vie à des âges déterminés pour chaque sexe figurent déjà dans des éditions antérieures de l'*Annuaire démographique*. Les données présentées dans ce tableau mettent à jour les périodes d'années suivantes:

Editions	Années considérées
Supplément rétrospectif (CD), 1997	1948 – 1997
Edition spéciale, Vieillissement de la population et situation des personnes âgées, 1991	1950 – 1990
Supplément rétrospectif, 1979	1948 – 1977
1948	1896 – 1947

22. Expectation of life at specified ages for each sex: latest available year
Espérance de vie à un âge donné pour chaque sexe: dernière année disponible

(See notes at end of table. — Voir notes à la fin du tableau.)

Continent, country or area and date / Continent, pays ou zone et date	0	5	10	15	20	25	30	35	40	45	50	55	60	65	70	75	80	85	90	95	100
AFRICA — AFRIQUE																					
Algeria - Algérie[1]																					
1996																					
Male	66.8	66.4	61.7	57.0	52.4	48.0	43.6	39.1	34.6	30.2	25.8	21.7	17.7	14.1	10.6	7.5	...	...	...	...	...
Female	68.4	67.8	63.1	58.3	53.6	48.9	44.2	39.6	35.0	30.5	26.2	21.9	17.8	14.1	10.5	7.1	...	...	...	...	...
Benin - Bénin																					
1992																					
Male	51.8	57.4	53.5	49.1	44.7	40.7	36.8	32.9	29.1	25.4	21.8	18.4	15.2	12.3	9.8	7.7	6.0	4.7	...	...	...
Female	56.8	61.5	57.5	53.0	48.6	44.3	40.2	36.1	32.1	28.1	24.2	20.4	16.9	13.7	10.9	8.6	6.6	5.1	...	...	...
Botswana[2]																					
1999																					
Male	65.7	...	...	...	...	...	...	...	...	...	...	...	...	...	...	...	...	...	...	...	...
Female	69.0	...	...	...	...	...	...	...	...	...	...	...	...	...	...	...	...	...	...	...	...
Cape Verde - Cap-Vert																					
1990																					
Male	63.5	62.8	58.3	53.7	49.1	44.7	40.8	37.2	33.2	29.9	26.2	22.9	19.4	16.0	12.0	9.3	7.0	...	...	...	...
Female	71.3	71.3	66.7	62.0	57.4	53.0	48.5	44.3	39.8	35.8	31.3	26.8	22.5	18.8	14.6	11.9	9.6	...	...	...	...
Egypt - Égypte																					
2001																					
Male	65.6	64.7	59.9	55.1	50.4	45.6	40.9	36.2	31.6	27.2	22.9	18.9	15.4	12.1	9.2	6.8	5.2	4.0	...	...	...
Female	67.4	66.8	62.0	57.2	52.3	47.5	42.7	37.9	33.1	28.4	23.9	19.5	15.5	11.7	8.6	5.7	4.0	2.8	...	...	...
Malawi																					
1992 - 1997																					
Male	43.5	52.1	49.5	45.7	41.9	38.4	34.8	31.2	27.6	24.0	20.6	17.3	14.1	11.2	8.6	6.3	4.4	...	...	...	...
Female	46.8	54.5	52.0	48.2	44.4	40.6	36.9	33.2	29.6	25.9	22.2	18.6	15.1	11.9	9.2	6.8	4.6	...	...	...	...
Mauritius - Maurice																					
1998 - 2000																					
Male	67.4	63.9	59.0	54.1	49.3	44.6	39.9	35.4	30.9	26.7	22.7	19.0	15.5	12.6	10.1	7.8	5.8	4.3	...	...	...
Female	74.7	71.0	66.0	61.1	56.2	51.3	46.6	41.7	37.0	32.4	27.9	23.7	19.7	16.1	12.8	9.8	7.3	5.4	...	...	...
Swaziland[3]																					
1997																					
Male	58.0	...	...	...	...	...	...	...	...	...	...	...	...	...	...	...	...	...	...	...	...
Female	63.0	...	...	...	...	...	...	...	...	...	...	...	...	...	...	...	...	...	...	...	...
Tunisia - Tunisie																					
1995																					
Male	69.6	67.5	62.7	57.9	53.1	48.4	43.8	39.2	34.6	30.1	25.8	21.6	17.7	14.1	10.8	7.9	5.2	3.5	...	...	...
Female	73.1	70.7	65.9	61.0	56.2	51.3	46.5	41.7	37.0	32.4	27.8	23.3	19.1	15.0	11.3	7.8	4.8	2.9	...	...	...
Zimbabwe																					
1990																					
Male	58.0	59.9	55.5	50.9	46.5	42.3	38.1	33.9	29.8	25.7	21.9	18.3	14.9	11.9	9.3	7.0	5.3	...	...	...	...
Female	62.0	63.0	58.5	53.9	49.5	45.2	40.9	36.7	32.5	28.3	24.3	20.4	16.7	13.3	10.3	7.8	5.8	...	...	...	...
AMERICA, NORTH — AMERIQUE DU NORD																					
Aruba																					
1991																					
Male	71.1	67.1	62.4	57.5	52.6	47.8	43.3	38.5	34.0	29.7	25.3	21.4	17.4	13.7	10.4	8.0	6.0	4.6	...	...	...
Female	77.1	72.8	68.0	63.0	58.1	53.2	48.4	43.4	38.7	33.9	29.4	24.6	20.4	16.6	12.2	8.9	6.0	2.6	...	...	...
Belize																					
1991																					
Male	70.0	67.9	63.0	58.2	53.4	48.8	44.5	40.1	35.3	30.8	26.7	22.6	18.9	15.2	12.2	9.4	6.3	...	...	...	...
Female	74.1	72.0	67.1	62.2	57.4	52.4	47.7	43.0	38.4	34.4	29.8	25.5	21.5	17.3	13.8	10.3	7.0	...	...	...	...
Bermuda - Bermudes																					
1991																					
Male	71.1	66.9	62.0	57.0	52.0	47.3	42.6	38.1	33.7	29.5	25.4	21.5	17.8	14.4	11.5	9.0	6.9	4.6	...	...	...
Female	77.8	73.4	68.4	63.5	58.5	53.6	48.7	44.0	39.3	34.7	30.1	25.7	21.5	17.5	13.7	10.4	7.5	4.9	...	...	...
Canada[4]																					
2000																					
Male	76.7	72.3	67.3	62.4	57.6	52.8	48.0	43.2	38.5	33.8	29.3	24.9	20.7	16.9	13.4	10.3	7.8	5.7	4.2	...	...
Female	82.0	77.4	72.4	67.5	62.6	57.7	52.8	47.9	43.1	38.3	33.6	29.1	24.7	20.5	16.5	12.9	9.7	7.0	5.0	...	...

22. Expectation of life at specified ages for each sex: latest available year
Espérance de vie à un âge donné pour chaque sexe: dernière année disponible (continued — suite)

(See notes at end of table. — Voir notes à la fin du tableau.)

Continent, pays ou zone et date	0	5	10	15	20	25	30	35	40	45	50	55	60	65	70	75	80	85	90	95	100
AMERICA, NORTH — AMERIQUE DU NORD																					
Costa Rica 1990 - 1995																					
Male	72.9	69.5	64.6	59.8	54.9	50.3	45.6	40.8	36.2	31.6	27.1	22.8	18.8	15.1	11.8	9.1	6.9	...	...	...	...
Female	77.6	73.9	69.0	64.1	59.2	54.3	49.4	44.6	39.9	35.2	30.6	26.2	21.9	17.9	14.1	10.7	7.8	...	...	...	...
Cuba 1994 - 1995																					
Male	72.9	69.0	64.1	59.3	54.6	50.0	45.4	40.8	36.3	31.8	27.5	23.3	19.5	15.8	12.5	9.5	7.2	5.0	...	...	...
Female	76.9	72.8	67.9	63.0	59.2	53.4	48.6	43.9	39.2	34.6	30.1	25.7	21.6	17.7	14.1	10.8	8.1	5.6	...	...	...
Dominican Republic - République dominicaine 1995 - 2000																					
Male	69.8	67.7	62.9	58.1	53.4	48.8	44.2	39.7	35.2	30.8	26.5	22.4	18.5	15.0	11.8	9.1	7.1	...	...	...	...
Female	73.1	71.2	66.4	61.6	56.8	52.0	47.3	42.7	38.1	33.5	29.1	24.8	20.7	16.9	13.3	10.3	7.9	...	...	...	...
El Salvador 1995 - 2000																					
Male	66.5	64.6	59.9	55.1	50.5	46.2	42.0	37.8	33.8	29.7	25.8	22.0	18.3	14.9	11.7	8.9	6.6	...	...	...	...
Female	72.5	70.3	65.5	60.7	56.0	51.4	46.8	42.3	37.9	33.6	29.3	25.2	21.2	17.4	13.9	10.8	8.1	...	...	...	...
Greenland - Groenland 1995 - 1999																					
Male	62.7	59.4	54.6	50.0	46.2	42.6	38.8	34.5	30.2	26.0	21.6	17.6	14.0	10.9	8.1	6.1	4.8	...	...	...	...
Female	68.0	64.9	60.0	55.2	50.6	46.0	41.3	36.6	32.1	27.7	23.3	19.3	15.7	12.4	9.5	7.1	5.3	...	...	...	...
Guatemala 1995 - 2000																					
Male	61.4	60.6	56.0	51.2	46.8	42.7	38.8	34.9	31.2	27.4	23.7	20.1	16.8	13.6	10.7	8.2	6.1	...	...	...	
Female	67.2	66.2	62.6	56.9	52.2	47.7	43.3	38.9	34.6	30.4	26.3	22.3	18.6	15.2	12.0	9.2	6.9	...	...	...	
Nicaragua 1995																					
Male	64.6	63.9	59.2	54.4	49.9	45.6	41.3	37.1	33.0	29.0	25.1	21.4	17.9	14.6	11.6	8.9	6.4	...	...	...	
Female	69.4	67.9	63.2	58.4	53.7	49.1	44.5	39.9	35.4	31.1	26.9	22.9	19.1	15.6	12.4	9.5	6.8	...	...	...	
Panama[5] 2000																					
Male	72.2	69.2	64.4	59.5	54.8	50.2	45.6	41.0	36.4	31.9	27.5	23.3	19.3	15.6	12.4	9.5	7.1	...	...	...	...
Female	76.8	73.7	68.9	64.0	59.2	54.3	49.5	44.8	40.1	35.4	30.9	26.4	22.2	18.1	14.3	10.9	7.9	...	...	...	...
Puerto Rico - Porto Rico 1997 - 1999																					
Male	71.4	71.2	67.3	62.4	57.5	52.8	48.3	43.9	39.5	35.3	31.2	27.3	23.5	19.9	16.4	13.3	10.4	8.1	6.3	5.2	...
Female	79.3	79.2	75.2	70.3	65.4	60.4	55.6	50.8	46.0	41.3	36.7	32.1	27.7	23.4	19.4	15.8	12.4	9.5	7.2	5.7	...
Saint Kitts and Nevis - Saint-Kitts-et-Nevis 1996																					
Male	68.2	65.2	60.3	55.4	50.5	45.7	41.0	36.6	32.3	28.0	23.9	20.1	16.8	13.8	10.7	7.7	5.4	4.0	2.9	1.8	...
Female	71.6	68.3	63.3	58.3	53.5	48.6	43.8	39.1	34.4	30.1	26.0	21.9	18.0	14.6	11.6	8.5	6.3	4.7	3.5	2.4	...
Saint Lucia - Sainte-Lucie 2000																					
Male	68.7	65.0	60.2	55.3	50.6	46.0	41.5	37.0	32.5	28.2	24.2	20.5	16.9	13.8	10.9	8.7	6.3	7.2	...	...	...
Female	73.6	70.1	65.3	60.3	55.5	50.7	46.0	41.3	36.7	32.4	28.2	24.1	20.3	16.9	13.5	10.7	8.2	6.2	...	...	...
Trinidad and Tobago - Trinité-et-Tobago 1990																					
Male	68.4	64.5	59.6	54.8	50.0	45.5	41.0	36.6	32.1	27.8	23.6	19.9	16.5	13.5	10.8	8.6	6.8	...	...	...	...
Female	73.2	69.1	64.2	59.3	54.5	49.7	45.0	40.2	35.6	31.1	26.9	22.9	19.3	15.9	12.8	10.2	8.0	...	...	...	...

(See notes at end of table. — Voir notes à la fin du tableau.)

Continent, country or area and date / Continent, pays ou zone et date	Age (in years) - Age (en années)																				
	0	5	10	15	20	25	30	35	40	45	50	55	60	65	70	75	80	85	90	95	100
AMERICA, NORTH — AMERIQUE DU NORD																					
United States - États-Unis																					
2001																					
Male	74.4	70.1	65.2	60.2	55.5	50.9	46.2	41.5	37.0	32.5	28.2	24.0	20.1	16.4	13.1	10.2	7.7	5.7	4.2	3.2	...
Female	79.8	75.4	70.4	65.5	60.6	55.7	50.9	46.0	41.3	36.6	32.1	27.7	23.4	19.4	15.7	12.3	9.3	6.9	5.0	3.7	...
AMERICA, SOUTH — AMERIQUE DU SUD																					
Argentina - Argentine																					
1990 - 1992																					
Male	68.4	65.6	60.8	55.9	51.2	46.5	41.8	37.2	32.6	28.2	24.1	20.2	16.7	13.5	10.6	8.1	6.0	4.5	...	...	...
Female	75.6	72.6	67.7	62.8	57.9	53.1	48.3	43.6	38.9	34.3	29.8	25.4	21.3	17.3	13.5	10.2	7.3	5.2	...	...	...
Bolivia - Bolivie																					
1995 - 2000																					
Male	59.8	60.8	56.7	52.2	48.0	43.7	39.5	35.3	31.2	27.1	23.2	19.5	15.9	12.7	9.8	7.5	5.9	...	...	...	
Female	63.2	63.8	59.7	55.2	50.8	46.5	42.1	37.8	33.6	29.4	25.3	21.4	17.6	14.0	10.8	8.3	6.5	...	...	...	
Brazil - Brésil[6]																					
2000																					
Male	64.8	62.7	57.9	53.0	48.4	44.1	39.7	35.4	31.2	27.1	23.2	19.5	16.0	12.7	9.8	7.3	5.4	...	...	...	
Female	72.6	70.0	65.2	60.3	55.4	50.6	45.8	41.1	36.5	32.0	27.6	23.4	19.4	15.7	12.2	9.2	6.7	...	...	...	
Chile - Chili																					
1999																					
Male	72.4	68.6	63.7	58.8	54.1	49.4	44.8	40.2	35.6	31.1	26.7	22.6	18.7	15.2	12.1	9.3	7.1	5.2	3.8	...	...
Female	78.4	74.5	69.6	64.6	59.7	54.8	50.0	45.1	40.3	35.6	31.1	26.6	22.4	18.5	14.9	11.7	9.0	6.7	4.9	...	...
Colombia - Colombie																					
2000 - 2005																					
Male	69.2	70.2	66.7	61.8	57.0	52.5	48.3	44.0	39.7	35.4	31.0	26.7	22.6	18.8	15.3	12.2	9.6	7.5	...	...	...
Female	75.3	76.0	72.7	67.8	62.9	58.1	53.3	48.6	43.8	39.1	34.5	30.0	25.7	21.6	17.8	14.4	11.5	9.2	...	...	...
Ecuador - Équateur[7]																					
1995																					
Male	67.3	67.0	62.3	57.6	52.9	48.4	43.9	39.5	35.1	30.9	26.7	22.7	18.9	15.4	12.1	9.3	7.0	...	...	...	
Female	72.5	71.6	66.8	62.0	57.3	52.6	47.4	43.3	38.8	34.3	29.9	25.6	21.5	17.7	14.2	11.0	8.2	...	...	...	
French Guiana - Guyane française																					
1997																					
Male	72.4	...	...	...	54.9	...	...	...	36.9	...	...	...	19.8								
Female	78.7	...	...	...	60.4	...	...	...	41.7	...	...	...	23.7								
Paraguay																					
1990 - 1995																					
Male	66.3	65.5	60.8	56.0	51.3	46.7	42.1	37.5	32.9	28.5	24.2	20.2	16.5	13.2	10.2	7.7	5.6	...	...		
Female	70.8	69.3	64.5	59.7	54.9	50.1	45.4	40.7	36.0	31.5	27.0	22.8	18.7	14.9	11.5	8.5	6.2	...	...		
Peru - Pérou[6]																					
1995 - 2000																					
Male	65.9	65.9	61.4	56.6	52.0	47.4	42.9	38.5	34.1	29.8	25.6	21.7	18.1	14.7	11.7	9.2	7.0	...	...		
Female	70.8	70.2	65.6	60.7	55.9	51.2	46.5	41.9	37.3	32.9	28.5	24.3	20.3	16.5	13.3	10.4	7.8	...	...		
Uruguay																					
1995 - 1996																					
Male	69.6	66.4	61.4	56.6	51.9	47.2	42.6	38.0	33.4	28.9	24.6	20.7	17.1	14.0	11.1	8.7	6.6	5.0	3.7	3.0	...
Female	77.6	74.0	69.0	64.1	59.3	54.4	49.6	44.8	40.1	35.5	31.0	26.6	22.4	18.4	14.7	11.4	8.4	6.2	4.6	4.0	...
Venezuela[6]																					
1995 - 2000																					
Male	68.6	66.6	61.8	56.9	52.3	47.8	43.3	38.8	34.3	29.9	25.6	21.6	17.9	14.5	11.4	8.6	5.9	...	...	...	
Female	74.4	72.1	67.2	62.3	57.4	52.6	47.8	43.1	38.4	33.7	29.2	24.9	20.8	16.9	13.3	9.9	6.9	...	...	...	

(See notes at end of table. — Voir notes à la fin du tableau.)

Continent, country or area and date / Continent, pays ou zone et date	Age (in years) - Age (en années)																				
	0	5	10	15	20	25	30	35	40	45	50	55	60	65	70	75	80	85	90	95	100
ASIA — ASIE																					
Armenia - Arménie																					
2000																					
Male	70.6	67.0	62.1	57.2	52.4	47.6	42.8	38.1	33.4	29.0	23.9	20.6	16.8	13.5	10.5	7.8	5.0	1.0	...	...	...
Female	75.5	71.7	66.8	61.8	56.9	52.0	47.1	42.2	37.4	32.6	28.0	23.4	19.1	15.1	11.4	8.0	5.0	1.0	...	...	...
Azerbaijan - Azerbaïdjan																					
2001																					
Male	68.6	66.3	61.5	56.6	51.8	47.1	42.4	37.8	33.2	28.8	24.6	20.7	17.2	14.2	11.5	9.5	7.5	5.5	4.5	3.6	...
Female	75.2	71.3	66.5	61.6	56.7	51.8	47.0	42.2	37.5	32.7	28.1	23.7	19.6	15.9	12.6	10.0	7.4	5.6	4.2	3.7	...
Bangladesh																					
1994																					
Male	58.6	61.4	57.3	53.0	48.6	44.0	40.1	34.8	30.8	26.0	22.0	18.6	15.1	12.1	9.0	6.4	4.6	...	...	...	...
Female	58.2	60.4	56.6	51.4	47.1	42.6	38.4	34.1	30.0	26.2	22.3	18.5	15.0	11.9	8.6	5.9	4.0	...	...	...	...
Bhutan - Bhoutan[8]																					
1994																					
Male	66.0	...	...	...	...	...	...	...	...	...	...	...	...	...	...	...	...	...	...	...	...
Female	66.2	...	...	...	...	...	...	...	...	...	...	...	...	...	...	...	...	...	...	...	...
China - Chine[9]																					
1990																					
Male	66.8	64.9	60.2	55.4	50.6	46.0	48.3	36.7	32.1	27.6	23.3	19.2	15.5	12.2	9.3	6.9	5.1	3.7	...	...	...
Female	70.5	68.8	64.0	59.2	54.4	49.8	45.0	40.3	35.7	31.1	26.6	22.4	18.4	14.7	11.5	8.3	6.5	4.9	...	...	...
1996																					
Male	68.7	...	...	...	...	...	...	...	...	...	...	...	...	...	...	...	...	...	...	...	...
Female	73.0	...	...	...	...	...	...	...	...	...	...	...	...	...	...	...	...	...	...	...	...
China: Hong Kong SAR - Chine: Hong Kong RAS																					
2000																					
Male	77.0	72.3	67.3	62.4	57.5	52.6	47.8	43.0	38.2	33.5	28.9	24.5	20.4	16.5	13.0	9.8	7.3	5.3	3.7	2.5	...
Female	82.2	77.6	72.6	67.6	62.7	57.8	52.8	47.9	43.1	38.3	33.6	28.9	24.4	20.1	16.1	12.4	9.4	6.8	4.7	3.1	...
China: Macao SAR - Chine: Macao RAS																					
1993 - 1996																					
Male	75.1	70.8	65.8	61.0	56.1	51.3	46.6	41.8	37.1	32.4	27.8	23.3	19.2	15.3	11.9	8.9	6.3	4.5	3.1	...	...
Female	80.0	75.6	70.7	65.7	60.8	55.9	51.0	46.2	41.3	36.5	31.8	27.2	22.7	18.6	14.7	11.3	8.4	6.0	4.2	...	...
Cyprus - Chypre[10]																					
1998 - 1999																					
Male	75.3	70.9	65.9	61.0	56.3	51.7	47.0	42.3	37.6	32.9	28.3	23.9	19.8	16.0	12.5	9.5	7.1	...	...	...	...
Female	80.4	76.0	71.0	66.1	61.2	56.3	51.4	46.7	41.8	37.0	32.3	27.7	23.2	18.9	15.1	11.6	8.8	...	...	...	...
India - Inde[11]																					
1992 - 1996																					
Male	60.1	62.1	57.7	53.0	48.5	44.0	39.5	35.0	30.7	26.4	22.5	18.8	15.3	12.5	10.0	...	...	...	...	...	...
Female	61.4	64.4	60.2	55.6	51.2	46.9	42.6	38.2	33.8	29.4	25.1	21.2	17.5	14.3	11.4	...	...	...	...	...	...
Indonesia - Indonésie																					
1990 - 1995																					
Male	61.0	...	...	...	...	...	...	...	...	...	...	...	...	...	...	...	...	...	...	...	...
Female	64.5	...	...	...	...	...	...	...	...	...	...	...	...	...	...	...	...	...	...	...	...
Iran (Islamic Republic of) - Iran (République islamique d')																					
1990 - 1995																					
Male	67.0	...	...	...	...	...	...	...	...	...	...	...	...	...	...	...	...	...	...	...	...
Female	68.0	...	...	...	...	...	...	...	...	...	...	...	...	...	...	...	...	...	...	...	...
Iraq																					
1990																					
Male	77.4	74.1	69.2	69.4	59.5	54.9	50.2	45.6	40.8	36.3	32.4	28.8	24.8	21.3	18.0	15.6	13.1	...	...	...	...
Female	78.2	74.8	69.9	65.0	60.2	55.3	50.4	45.5	40.8	36.0	31.1	26.6	22.0	17.7	12.9	8.7	4.2	...	...	...	...

22. Expectation of life at specified ages for each sex: latest available year
Espérance de vie à un âge donné pour chaque sexe: dernière année disponible (continued — suite)

(See notes at end of table. — Voir notes à la fin du tableau.)

Continent, country or area and date / Continent, pays ou zone et date	Age (in years) - Age (en années)																				
	0	5	10	15	20	25	30	35	40	45	50	55	60	65	70	75	80	85	90	95	100
ASIA — ASIE																					
Israel - Israël[12] 1998																					
Male	76.1	71.8	66.8	61.9	57.1	52.3	47.5	42.7	38.0	33.3	28.8	24.4	20.4	16.6	13.2	10.2	7.7	5.6	4.1	...	...
Female	80.6	76.1	71.2	66.2	61.2	56.3	51.4	46.5	41.6	36.8	32.1	27.5	23.1	18.9	15.1	11.6	8.7	6.3	4.4	...	...
Japan - Japon[13] 2000																					
Male	77.6	73.0	68.1	63.1	58.2	53.4	48.6	43.8	39.0	34.4	29.8	25.5	21.3	17.4	13.9	10.6	7.9	5.6	4.0	2.8	...
Female	84.6	80.0	75.0	70.0	65.1	60.2	55.3	50.4	45.5	40.7	36.0	31.4	26.9	22.4	18.2	14.2	10.6	7.6	5.4	3.8	...
Jordan - Jordanie[14] 1990 - 1995																					
Male	66.2	...	...	...	...	...	...	...	...	...	...	...	...	...	...	...	...	...	...	...	...
Female	69.8	...	...	...	...	...	...	...	...	...	...	...	...	...	...	...	...	...	...	...	...
Kazakhstan 1997																					
Male	59.0	56.3	51.4	46.6	42.0	37.7	33.5	29.5	25.6	22.0	18.6	15.7	13.0	10.8	8.7	6.9	5.4	4.2	3.2	2.4	...
Female	70.2	67.2	62.3	57.4	52.6	48.0	43.3	38.7	34.2	29.8	25.6	21.8	18.0	14.7	11.7	9.0	6.8	5.0	3.6	2.6	...
Korea (Dem. People's Republic of) - Corée (Rép. populaire dém. de) 1990 - 1995																					
Male	67.7	...	...	...	...	...	...	...	...	...	...	...	...	...	...	...	...	...	...	...	...
Female	73.9	...	...	...	...	...	...	...	...	...	...	...	...	...	...	...	...	...	...	...	...
Korea (Republic of) - Corée (République de)[15] 1999																					
Male	71.7	67.3	62.4	57.5	52.7	47.9	43.2	38.5	33.9	29.5	25.3	21.3	17.5	14.1	11.0	8.3	6.2	4.6	3.4	2.6	...
Female	79.2	74.8	69.9	65.0	60.1	55.2	50.3	45.5	40.7	35.9	31.2	26.7	22.2	18.0	14.0	10.6	7.7	5.6	3.9	2.8	...
Kuwait - Koweït 1992 - 1993																					
Male	71.8	67.9	63.0	58.2	53.6	48.9	44.2	39.4	34.7	30.0	25.6	21.4	17.3	14.1	10.8	7.8	4.4	2.5	...	...	...
Female	73.3	69.2	64.3	59.4	54.5	49.6	44.7	39.8	35.0	30.2	25.5	21.1	16.8	13.3	10.0	7.4	4.3	2.6	...	...	...
Kyrgyzstan - Kirghizistan 2000																					
Male	64.9	62.4	57.5	52.6	47.8	43.2	38.7	34.4	30.2	26.2	22.4	18.8	15.6	12.7	10.1	7.3	4.6	2.4	1.0	0.2	...
Female	72.4	69.5	64.6	59.7	54.8	50.0	45.2	40.5	35.9	31.3	26.9	22.6	18.6	14.9	11.5	8.0	4.9	2.5	1.1	0.3	...
Malaysia - Malaisie 1998																					
Male	69.6	65.6	60.8	55.9	51.3	46.7	42.2	37.6	33.1	28.6	24.3	20.2	16.5	13.1	10.2	7.7	5.6	...	...	...	...
Female	74.6	70.5	65.6	60.8	55.9	51.0	46.2	41.4	36.6	31.9	27.4	23.0	18.8	15.0	11.7	8.8	6.4	...	...	...	...
Maldives 1992																					
Male	67.2	65.7	61.0	56.2	51.5	40.8	42.2	37.5	32.9	28.7	24.3	20.4	16.8	13.5	10.5	7.9	5.6	...	...	...	...
Female	66.6	63.9	59.3	54.4	49.6	44.8	40.2	35.7	31.5	27.2	22.6	18.7	15.4	12.2	9.4	7.1	5.2	...	...	...	...
1997																					
Male	69.2	...	...	...	...	...	...	...	...	...	...	...	...	...	...	...	...	...	...	...	...
Female	70.2	...	...	...	...	...	...	...	...	...	...	...	...	...	...	...	...	...	...	...	...
Myanmar 1990																					
Male	50.2	54.6	51.6	47.2	43.1	39.1	35.2	31.5	28.0	24.5	21.0	17.5	14.3	11.5	9.1	6.5	...	...	...	...	...
Female	54.7	58.7	55.7	51.9	47.9	43.8	39.5	35.4	31.4	27.3	23.2	19.1	15.4	12.1	9.4	7.0	...	...	...	...	...
Occupied Palestinian Territory - Territoire palestinien occupé 2001																					
Male	70.4	67.5	62.7	57.8	53.1	48.4	43.6	38.9	34.2	29.6	25.2	21.1	17.2	13.8	10.7	8.1	6.1	...	...	...	...
Female	73.6	70.3	65.4	60.5	55.7	50.9	46.1	41.3	36.6	32.0	27.5	23.2	19.0	15.2	11.7	8.8	6.4	...	...	...	...

22. Expectation of life at specified ages for each sex: latest available year
Espérance de vie à un âge donné pour chaque sexe: dernière année disponible (continued — suite)

(See notes at end of table. — Voir notes à la fin du tableau.)

Continent, country or area and date / Continent, pays ou zone et date	0	5	10	15	20	25	30	35	40	45	50	55	60	65	70	75	80	85	90	95	100
ASIA — ASIE																					
Philippines 1991																					
Male	63.1	62.8	58.2	53.5	48.9	44.5	40.1	35.6	31.2	27.0	22.9	19.1	15.5	12.3	9.5	7.1	5.1	...	...	...	...
Female	66.7	65.7	61.1	56.3	51.7	47.2	42.7	38.2	33.8	29.4	25.2	21.2	17.3	13.7	10.6	7.9	5.6	...	...	...	...
Singapore - Singapour[16] 2000																					
Male	76.0	71.3	66.4	61.4	56.5	51.7	46.9	42.1	37.3	32.6	28.0	23.5	19.4	15.7	12.4	9.3	6.7	4.4	...	...	...
Female	80.0	75.3	70.4	65.4	60.5	55.6	50.6	45.7	40.9	36.1	31.4	26.7	22.3	18.1	14.3	10.7	7.6	4.6	...	...	...
Tajikistan - Tadjikistan 1992																					
Male	65.4	...	60.5	...	50.9	...	42.0	...	33.3	...	25.0	...	17.7	...	11.7	...	7.3	...	...	...	...
Female	71.1	...	65.7	...	56.0	...	46.6	...	37.4	...	28.4	...	20.4	...	13.5	...	8.5	...	...	...	...
Turkey - Turquie[17] 2000																					
Male	66.4	...	...	...	...	...	...	...	...	...	...	...	...	...	...	...	...	...	...	...	...
Female	71.0	...	...	...	...	...	...	...	...	...	...	...	...	...	...	...	...	...	...	...	...
EUROPE																					
Austria - Autriche 2001																					
Male	75.9	71.4	66.5	61.5	56.7	52.0	47.2	42.4	37.7	33.1	28.6	24.4	20.4	16.6	13.2	10.1	7.5	5.4	...	...	...
Female	81.7	77.0	72.1	67.1	62.2	57.3	52.4	47.5	42.6	37.9	33.2	28.7	24.2	19.9	15.8	12.0	8.7	6.0	...	...	...
Belarus - Bélarus 1999																					
Male	62.2	58.3	53.4	48.5	43.8	39.4	35.2	31.1	27.0	23.2	19.7	16.6	13.8	11.3	9.0	7.0	5.2	3.8	2.8	2.0	...
Female	73.9	69.8	64.9	60.0	55.1	50.3	45.5	40.8	36.1	31.6	27.2	23.0	19.1	15.4	11.9	8.8	6.4	4.5	3.1	2.1	...
Belgium - Belgique[18] 2000																					
Male	74.6	70.1	65.1	60.2	55.4	50.7	46.0	41.3	36.6	32.0	27.5	23.3	19.3	15.5	12.1	9.1	6.7	4.7	3.2	2.1	...
Female	80.8	76.3	71.3	66.3	61.4	56.6	51.7	46.8	42.0	37.3	32.7	28.2	23.8	19.5	15.4	11.7	8.4	5.8	3.7	2.3	...
Bulgaria - Bulgarie 2000																					
Male	68.5	64.7	59.8	54.9	50.1	45.3	40.6	36.0	31.4	27.1	23.0	19.3	15.9	12.8	10.0	7.6	5.7	4.1	2.9	2.0	...
Female	75.1	71.2	66.3	61.3	56.4	51.6	46.7	41.9	37.1	32.5	27.9	23.5	19.3	15.3	11.7	8.6	6.1	4.1	2.6	1.6	...
Czech Republic - République tchèque 2001																					
Male	72.1	67.5	62.6	57.7	52.8	48.1	43.3	38.6	33.9	29.3	25.0	21.0	17.4	14.0	11.0	8.4	6.2	4.5	3.2	2.2	...
Female	78.5	73.8	68.8	63.9	59.0	54.0	49.1	44.2	39.4	34.7	30.0	25.6	21.3	17.1	13.3	9.9	7.0	4.7	3.0	1.9	...
Denmark - Danemark[19] 2000																					
Male	74.5	70.0	65.0	60.1	55.3	50.5	45.7	40.9	36.2	31.6	27.2	22.9	18.9	15.2	11.9	9.1	6.8	4.9	3.4	2.3	...
Female	79.3	74.7	69.7	64.7	59.8	54.9	50.0	45.1	40.3	35.5	30.9	26.5	22.3	18.3	14.8	11.6	8.8	6.4	4.6	3.2	...
Estonia - Estonie 2000																					
Male	65.1	61.0	56.1	51.2	46.4	41.9	37.5	33.1	28.8	25.1	21.6	18.3	15.3	12.6	10.2	8.2	6.2	4.5	3.6	2.7	...
Female	76.2	71.9	67.0	62.0	57.2	52.3	47.5	42.7	38.0	33.5	29.2	24.9	20.9	17.0	13.3	10.2	7.6	5.1	3.5	2.3	...
Finland - Finlande[20] 2001																					
Male	74.6	69.9	65.0	60.0	55.2	50.5	45.8	41.1	36.5	32.0	27.6	23.4	19.5	15.7	12.2	9.2	6.8	4.8	3.4	2.3	...
Female	81.5	76.8	71.8	66.8	61.9	57.0	52.1	47.2	42.4	37.7	33.0	28.5	24.0	19.7	15.5	11.7	8.5	5.8	3.9	2.8	...
France[20] 1998																					
Male	74.8	70.2	65.3	60.4	55.5	50.8	46.1	41.4	36.8	32.4	28.1	24.0	20.0	16.4	13.0	10.0	7.4	5.3	3.7	2.5	...
Female	82.4	77.8	72.8	67.9	63.0	58.1	53.2	48.4	43.6	38.8	34.2	29.7	25.2	20.9	16.7	12.9	9.4	6.5	4.3	2.7	...

22. Expectation of life at specified ages for each sex: latest available year
Espérance de vie à un âge donné pour chaque sexe: dernière année disponible (continued — suite)

(See notes at end of table. — Voir notes à la fin du tableau.)

Continent, country or area and date / Continent, pays ou zone et date	Age (in years) - Age (en années)																					
	0	5	10	15	20	25	30	35	40	45	50	55	60	65	70	75	80	85	90	95	100
EUROPE																						
Germany - Allemagne 1999																						
Male	74.7	70.2	65.2	60.3	55.5	50.7	45.9	41.1	36.4	31.9	27.4	23.2	19.2	15.5	12.2	9.3	6.8	4.9	3.4	2.3	...
Female	80.7	76.1	71.2	66.2	61.3	56.4	51.5	46.6	41.8	37.0	32.4	27.8	23.4	19.2	15.2	11.5	8.3	5.7	3.8	2.4	...
Greece - Grèce 1998																						
Male	75.3	70.9	66.0	61.1	56.3	51.6	46.9	42.1	37.4	32.8	28.4	24.1	20.0	16.2	12.8	9.8	7.3	5.6	4.3	3.1	...
Female	80.5	76.1	71.2	66.2	61.3	56.4	51.5	46.6	41.8	37.0	32.3	27.6	23.1	18.7	14.6	10.9	7.8	5.7	4.2	3.0	...
Hungary - Hongrie 2001																						
Male	68.2	63.8	58.9	54.0	49.1	44.3	39.5	34.8	30.4	26.3	22.6	19.2	16.0	13.0	10.4	8.0	6.0	4.1	2.6	1.5	...
Female	76.5	72.1	67.2	62.2	57.3	52.3	47.4	42.6	37.9	33.3	29.0	24.8	20.6	16.7	13.1	9.8	7.0	4.7	2.8	1.6	...
Iceland - Islande 2000																						
Male	78.0	73.4	68.5	63.5	58.8	54.1	49.4	44.7	40.0	35.3	30.8	26.5	22.2	18.1	14.4	11.1	8.4	6.1	4.3	2.9	...
Female	81.4	76.6	71.7	66.7	61.8	56.9	51.9	47.0	42.1	37.3	32.6	28.0	23.7	19.6	15.7	12.0	8.8	6.2	4.1	2.6	...
Ireland - Irlande 2000																						
Male	74.2	69.8	64.8	59.9	55.1	50.4	45.6	40.8	36.1	31.4	26.8	22.5	18.3	14.6	11.2	8.4	6.2	4.5	3.0	2.0	...
Female	79.2	74.6	69.7	64.7	59.8	54.9	50.0	45.1	40.3	35.5	30.8	26.3	21.9	17.7	13.9	10.4	7.5	5.2	3.4	2.1	...
Isle of Man - Îles de Man 1996																						
Male	73.6	68.6	63.6	58.6	53.6	49.1	44.6	40.2	35.8	31.2	26.7	22.4	18.4	15.1	12.0	9.3	7.5	5.2	4.6	3.2	0.5
Female	79.9	75.1	70.1	65.1	60.1	55.1	50.1	45.1	40.2	35.4	30.6	26.2	22.0	18.3	14.4	11.3	8.6	5.9	3.6	2.0	1.5
Italy - Italie 1999																						
Male	76.0	71.5	71.5	66.5	61.6	56.8	52.0	47.3	42.5	37.8	33.1	28.5	24.2	20.0	16.2	12.7	9.7	7.1	5.2	3.7	...
Female	82.1	77.6	77.6	72.7	67.7	62.8	57.9	53.0	48.1	43.2	38.4	33.7	29.1	24.6	20.2	16.1	12.3	8.9	6.4	4.3	...
Latvia - Lettonie 2001																						
Male	65.2	61.1	56.2	51.4	46.6	41.9	37.5	33.3	29.3	25.5	21.9	18.5	15.4	12.5	9.8	7.6	5.7	4.1	3.0	...	...
Female	76.6	72.6	67.6	62.7	57.9	53.0	48.2	43.4	38.7	34.2	29.7	25.5	21.5	17.8	14.5	11.5	9.0	6.8	5.1	...	...
Lithuania - Lituanie 2001																						
Male	65.9	61.7	56.8	51.9	47.3	42.9	38.5	34.2	30.0	26.1	22.4	19.2	16.1	13.3	10.7	8.3	6.4	4.8	3.7	3.2	...
Female	77.4	73.0	68.1	63.1	58.2	53.4	48.6	43.8	39.1	34.5	30.1	25.9	21.7	17.7	13.9	10.4	7.5	5.3	3.7	2.9	...
Luxembourg 2000																						
Male	74.9	70.4	65.4	60.5	55.6	50.9	46.2	41.5	36.7	32.1	27.6	23.3	19.3	15.6	12.2	9.1	6.5	4.7	3.1	2.0	...
Female	81.3	76.8	71.8	66.8	61.9	57.0	52.1	47.2	42.3	37.6	32.8	28.3	24.1	19.8	15.7	12.0	8.8	6.3	4.2	2.7	...
Malta - Malte 2001																						
Male	76.1	71.6	66.6	61.6	56.8	52.0	47.3	42.5	37.7	32.9	28.3	23.8	19.6	15.4	12.0	9.3	7.1	5.3	...	...	...
Female	80.9	76.2	71.3	66.3	61.3	56.4	51.4	46.4	41.6	36.6	32.0	27.3	22.9	18.6	14.5	11.0	8.0	5.5	...	...	...
Netherlands - Pays-Bas[21] 2001																						
Male	75.8	71.8	66.9	61.9	57.1	52.2	47.4	42.6	37.8	33.0	28.5	24.0	19.8	15.9	12.4	9.4	6.9	4.9	3.4	2.5	...
Female	80.7	76.6	71.7	66.7	61.8	56.9	52.0	47.1	42.2	37.5	32.8	28.3	24.0	19.7	15.7	12.0	8.8	6.1	4.2	2.8	...
Norway - Norvège[22] 2001																						
Male	76.2	71.6	66.7	61.7	56.9	52.2	47.5	42.8	38.0	33.4	28.8	24.4	20.1	16.2	12.6	9.4	6.8	4.9	3.4	2.3	...
Female	81.5	76.9	71.9	66.9	62.0	57.1	52.2	47.4	42.5	37.7	33.0	28.5	24.0	19.8	15.8	12.0	8.7	6.0	4.1	2.8	...
Poland - Pologne 2000																						
Male	69.7	65.4	60.5	55.6	50.8	46.0	41.3	36.7	32.2	27.9	23.9	20.1	16.7	13.6	10.9	8.5	6.5	4.8	3.6	2.6	...
Female	77.9	73.6	68.6	63.7	58.7	53.8	48.9	44.1	39.2	34.6	30.0	25.6	21.4	17.3	13.6	10.2	7.4	5.1	3.4	2.1	...

22. Expectation of life at specified ages for each sex: latest available year
Espérance de vie à un âge donné pour chaque sexe: dernière année disponible (continued — suite)

(See notes at end of table. — Voir notes à la fin du tableau.)

Continent, country or area and date / Continent, pays ou zone et date	0	5	10	15	20	25	30	35	40	45	50	55	60	65	70	75	80	85	90	95	100
EUROPE																					
Portugal																					
2000																					
Male	72.7	68.3	63.4	58.5	53.7	49.1	44.5	39.9	35.4	31.0	26.7	22.5	18.5	14.7	11.4	8.3	5.8	3.6	2.4	1.4	...
Female	79.7	75.2	70.3	65.3	60.4	55.5	50.6	45.8	41.0	36.3	31.6	27.1	22.6	18.3	14.2	10.5	7.2	4.5	2.8	1.6	...
Republic of Moldova - République de Moldova																					
1999																					
Male	63.7	60.3	55.5	50.6	45.9	41.3	36.9	32.5	28.3	24.3	20.6	17.1	14.0	11.2	8.8	6.6	4.7	3.1	1.5	1.2	...
Female	71.0	67.5	62.7	57.8	52.9	48.0	43.2	38.5	33.8	29.3	25.0	20.9	17.1	13.6	10.4	7.7	5.4	3.7	2.0	1.2	...
Romania - Roumanie																					
2000																					
Male	67.7	64.4	59.6	54.8	50.0	45.2	40.5	35.9	31.5	27.3	23.4	19.7	16.4	13.4	10.6	8.1	6.1	4.5	3.2	2.2	...
Female	74.6	71.2	66.3	61.4	56.5	51.6	46.8	41.9	37.2	32.6	28.2	23.8	19.7	15.7	12.1	9.0	6.4	4.3	2.8	1.7	...
Russian Federation - Fédération de Russie																					
1999																					
Male	59.9	56.4	51.5	46.7	42.2	38.0	34.0	30.0	26.2	22.6	19.3	16.3	13.5	11.1	9.0	7.3	5.8	4.7	3.8	3.2	...
Female	72.4	68.7	63.8	59.0	54.2	49.5	44.8	40.1	35.5	31.0	26.7	22.6	18.6	15.0	11.8	9.0	6.8	5.0	3.7	2.9	...
San Marino - Saint-Marin																					
2000																					
Male	77.4	73.0	68.0	63.1	58.5	53.8	49.1	44.3	39.5	34.7	30.0	25.6	21.4	17.2	13.5	10.5	7.7	5.7	3.8	2.3	...
Female	84.0	79.6	74.6	69.6	64.7	59.7	54.8	49.9	45.0	40.2	35.4	30.7	26.0	21.6	17.1	13.1	9.2	6.3	4.2	2.7	...
Serbia and Montenegro - Serbie-et-Montenegro																					
2000																					
Male	69.8	66.1	61.2	56.3	51.4	46.7	41.9	37.2	32.5	28.1	23.9	20.0	16.4	13.3	10.7	8.3	6.3	5.4	4.1	3.1	...
Female	74.9	70.9	66.0	61.1	56.2	51.3	46.4	41.5	36.7	32.1	27.6	23.2	19.0	15.2	11.8	8.9	6.6	4.5	3.1	2.0	...
Slovakia - Slovaquie																					
2000																					
Male	69.2	65.0	60.1	55.1	50.3	45.5	40.8	36.1	31.5	27.2	23.1	19.4	15.9	12.9	10.3	8.1	6.2	4.6	3.4	2.5	...
Female	77.4	73.0	68.1	63.2	58.3	53.3	48.4	43.5	38.7	33.9	29.3	24.9	20.6	16.5	12.8	9.6	6.9	4.8	3.1	2.0	...
Slovenia - Slovénie																					
2000																					
Male	72.1	67.6	62.6	57.7	52.9	48.2	43.5	38.8	34.1	29.6	25.4	21.4	17.7	14.2	11.2	8.6	6.4	4.3	3.4	2.4	...
Female	79.6	74.9	70.0	65.0	60.1	55.2	50.3	45.4	40.5	35.8	31.2	26.8	22.4	18.2	14.3	10.7	7.4	4.6	3.6	2.3	...
Spain - Espagne																					
1998																					
Male	75.2	70.7	65.8	60.8	56.0	51.3	46.5	41.8	37.2	32.7	28.2	24.0	19.9	16.1	12.7	9.6	7.0	4.9	3.4	2.0	...
Female	82.2	77.6	72.6	67.7	62.8	57.9	53.0	48.1	43.2	38.5	33.8	29.1	24.5	20.1	15.8	11.9	8.5	5.7	3.6	2.0	...
Sweden - Suède																					
2001																					
Male	77.6	72.9	67.9	63.0	58.1	53.3	48.5	43.7	38.9	34.2	29.6	25.1	20.9	16.9	13.2	10.0	7.2	5.0	3.4	2.4	...
Female	82.1	77.4	72.4	67.5	62.6	57.6	52.7	47.8	42.9	38.1	33.4	28.8	24.4	20.1	16.0	12.3	8.9	6.2	4.2	2.9	...
Switzerland - Suisse																					
2000																					
Male	76.9	72.4	67.5	62.5	57.7	53.0	48.2	43.5	38.7	34.0	29.5	25.1	20.9	16.9	13.3	10.1	7.4	5.2	3.5	2.3	...
Female	82.6	78.0	73.0	68.1	63.1	58.2	53.3	48.4	43.6	38.8	34.1	29.4	25.0	20.7	16.5	12.6	9.1	6.2	4.0	2.4	...

22. Expectation of life at specified ages for each sex: latest available year
Espérance de vie à un âge donné pour chaque sexe: dernière année disponible (continued — suite)

(See notes at end of table. — Voir notes à la fin du tableau.)

Continent, country or area and date / Continent, pays ou zone et date	\multicolumn{21}{c}{Age (in years) - Age (en années)}
	0	5	10	15	20	25	30	35	40	45	50	55	60	65	70	75	80	85	90	95	100

	0	5	10	15	20	25	30	35	40	45	50	55	60	65	70	75	80	85	90	95	100
EUROPE																					
The Former Yugoslav Rep. of Macedonia - L'ex-République yougoslave de Macédoine 1998 - 2000																					
Male	70.5	66.8	62.0	57.1	52.2	47.4	42.7	37.9	33.2	28.7	24.4	20.4	16.6	13.2	10.2	7.6	5.6	3.9	3.4	3.2	...
Female	74.8	71.1	66.2	61.2	56.3	51.4	46.5	41.7	36.9	32.2	27.6	23.2	19.0	15.0	11.4	8.4	6.0	4.4	3.7	3.2	...
Ukraine 1998 - 1999																					
Male	63.0	59.2	54.3	49.4	44.7	40.3	35.9	31.7	27.7	23.9	20.4	17.2	14.3	11.7	9.4	7.4	5.6	4.0	2.7	1.6	...
Female	73.7	69.8	64.9	60.0	55.1	50.3	45.5	40.8	36.2	31.6	27.2	23.0	19.0	15.3	11.8	8.9	6.4	4.6	3.5	2.6	
United Kingdom - Royaume-Uni 2000																					
Male	75.4	71.0	66.0	61.1	56.2	51.4	46.7	41.9	37.2	32.5	27.9	23.6	19.4	15.6	12.2	9.3	6.9	4.9	3.4	2.3	...
Female	80.2	75.6	70.7	65.7	60.8	55.9	51.0	46.1	41.3	36.5	31.9	27.4	23.0	18.9	15.0	11.6	8.6	6.1	4.2	2.8	
OCEANIA — OCEANIE																					
Australia - Australie 1998 - 2000																					
Male	76.6	72.1	67.2	62.2	57.4	52.8	48.1	43.4	38.7	34.1	29.5	25.0	20.8	16.8	13.3	10.2	7.6	5.5	...	...	...
Female	82.0	77.5	72.6	67.6	62.7	57.8	53.0	48.1	43.3	38.5	33.8	29.2	24.7	20.4	16.4	12.6	9.4	6.6	...	...	...
Micronesia, Federated States of - Micronésie, États Fédérés de La 1991 - 1992																					
Male	64.4	63.6	59.0	54.2	49.6	45.2	40.7	36.2	31.8	27.4	23.3	19.4	15.9	12.7	9.9	7.5	5.6	...	...	...	...
Female	66.8	65.9	61.2	56.5	51.9	47.3	42.8	38.4	34.0	29.6	25.4	21.3	17.5	13.9	10.8	8.1	6.0	...	...	...	...
New Caledonia - Nouvelle-Calédonie 1999																					
Male	69.8	65.3	60.3	55.3	50.7	46.2	41.8	37.3	32.8	28.4	24.2	...	16.3	...	10.3						
Female	75.8	71.5	66.6	61.6	56.8	52.0	47.2	42.3	37.6	33.0	28.5	...	20.2	...	12.5						
New Zealand - Nouvelle-Zélande 1997 - 1999																					
Male	75.2	70.9	65.1	61.0	56.3	51.7	47.0	42.3	37.6	32.9	28.4	24.0	19.9	16.1	12.7	9.8	7.2	5.3	3.7	...	...
Female	80.4	75.9	71.0	66.0	61.2	56.3	51.5	46.6	41.8	37.1	32.4	27.9	23.6	19.5	15.7	12.2	9.0	6.4	4.4	...	...
Tonga 1998																					
Male	69.8	66.5	61.6	56.7	52.0	47.2	42.5	37.8	33.1	28.5	24.1	20.0	16.2	13.0	10.4	7.2	...	...	...		
Female	71.8	68.3	63.4	58.6	53.7	48.9	44.2	39.4	34.8	30.2	25.8	21.6	17.7	14.1	11.2	7.8	...	...	...		

GENERAL NOTES - NOTES GENERALES

Average number of years of life remaining to persons surviving to exact age specified, if subject to mortality conditions of the period indicated. For limitations of data, see Technical Notes for this table. — Nombre moyen d'années restant à vivre aux personnes ayant atteint l'âge donné si elles sont soumises aux conditions de mortalité de la période indiquée. Pour les insuffisances des données, voir Notes techniques pour ce tableau.

FOOTNOTES - NOTES

[1] For Algerian population only. — Pour la population algérienne seulement.

[2] Data refer to national projections. — Les données se referent aux projections nationales.

[3] Data for 1997 refer to last twelve months preceding population and housing census of 1997. — Les données pour 1997 se réfèrent au douze mois précédant le recensement de population et de l'habitat de 1997.

[4] Including Canadian residents temporarily in the United States, but excluding United States residents temporarily in Canada. — Y compris les résidents canadiens se trouvant temporairement aux Etats-Unis, mais ne comprennent pas les résidents des Etats-Unis se trouvant temporairement au Canada.

[5] Excluding tribal Indian population. — Non compris les Indiens vivant en tribus.

[6] Excluding Indian jungle population. — Non compris les Indiens de la jungle.

[7] Excluding nomadic Indian tribes. — Non compris les tribus d'Indiens nomades.

[8] Based on 1994 national health survey. — Basé sur l'enquête par

sondage de santé pour 1994.

[9] For statistical purposes, the data for China do not include those for the Hong Kong Special Administrative Region (Hong Kong SAR), Macao special Adminstrative Region (Macao SAR) and Taiwan province of China. — Pour la présentation des statistiques, les données pour Chine ne comprend pas les Région Administrative Spéciale de Hong Kong (Hong Kong RAS), le Région Administrative Spéciale de Macao (Macao RAS) et Taïwan province de Chine.

[10] Data refer to government controlled areas. — Les données se raportent aux zones contrôlées par le Gouvernement.

[11] Including data for the Indian-held part of Jammu and Kashmir, the final status of which has not yet been determined. — Y compris les données pour la partie du Jammu et du Cachemire occupée par l'Inde dont le statut définitif n'a pas encore été déterminé.

[12] Including data for East Jerusalem and Israeli residents in certain other territories under occupation by Israeli military forces since June 1967. — Y compris les données pour Jérusalem-Est et les résidents israéliens dans certains autres territoires occupés depuis 1967 par les forces armées israéliennes.

[13] For Japanese nationals in Japan only. — Pour les nationaux japonais au Japon seulement.

[14] Excluding data for Jordanian territory under occupation since June 1967 by Israeli military forces. Excluding foreigners, including registered Palestinian refugees. — Non compris les données pour le territoire jordanien occupé depuis juin 1967 par les forces armées israéliennes. Non compris les étrangers, mais y compris les réfugiés de Palestine immatriculés.

[15] Excluding alien armed forces stationed in the area. — Non compris les militaires étrangers en garnison sur le territoire.

[16] Excluding transients afloat and non-locally domiciled military and civilian services personnel and their dependants. — Non compris les personnes de passage þ bord de navires, ni les militaires et agents civils

domiciliés hors du territoire et les membres de leur famille les accompagnant.

[17] Based on the results of the Population Demographic Survey. — - D'après les résultats de la Population Demographic Survey.

[18] Including armed forces stationed outside the country, but excluding alien armed forces stationed in the area. — Y compris les militaires nationaux hors du pays, mais non compris les militaires étrangers en garnison sur le territoire.

[19] Excluding Faeroe Islands and Greenland. — Non compris les îles Féroé et Gröenland.

[20] Including nationals temporarily outside the country. — Y compris les nationaux se trouvant temporairement hors du pays.

[21] Including residents outside the country if listed in a Netherlands population register. — Y compris les résidents hors du pays, s'ils sont inscrits sur un registre de population néerlandais.

[22] Including nationals temporarily outside the country. — Y compris les nationaux se trouvant temporairement hors du pays.

Table 23

Table 23 presents number of marriages and crude marriage rates by urban/rural residence for as many years as possible between 1997 and 2001.

Description of variables: Marriage is defined as the act, ceremony or process by which the legal relationship of husband and wife is constituted[1]. The legality of the union may be established by civil, religious or other means as recognized by the laws of each country.

Marriage statistics in this table, therefore, include both first marriages and remarriages after divorce, widowhood or annulment. They do not, unless otherwise noted, include resumption of marriage ties after legal separation. These statistics refer to the number of marriages performed, and not to the number of persons marrying.

Statistics shown are obtained from civil registers of marriage. Exceptions, such as data from church registers, are identified in the footnotes.

The urban/rural classification of marriages is that provided by each country or area; it is presumed to be based on the national census definitions of urban population which have been set forth at the end of the technical notes for table 6.

Rate computation: Crude marriage rates are the annual number of marriages per 1 000 mid-year population.

Rates by urban/rural residence are the annual number of marriages, in the appropriate urban or rural category, per 1 000 corresponding mid-year population. These rates are calculated by the Statistics Division of the United Nations.

Rates presented in this table have been limited to those for countries or areas having at least a total of 100 marriages in a given year. Urban and/or rural rates based on 30 or fewer marriages are identified by the symbol (♦).

Reliability of data: Each country or area has been asked to indicate the estimated completeness of the number of marriages recorded in its civil register. These national assessments are indicated by the quality codes C and U that appear in the first column of this table.

C indicates that the data are estimated to be virtually complete, that is, representing at least 90 per cent of the marriages occurring each year, while U indicates that data are estimated to be incomplete, that is, representing less than 90 per cent of the marriages occurring each year. The code (...) indicates that no information was provided regarding completeness.

Data from civil registers which are reported as incomplete or of unknown completeness (coded U or ...) are considered unreliable. They appear in italics in this table; rates are not computed for these data.

These quality codes apply only to data from civil registers. For more information about the quality of vital statistics data in general, see section 4.2 of the Technical Notes.

Limitations: Statistics on marriages are subject to the same qualifications which have been set forth for vital statistics in general and marriage statistics in particular as discussed in section 4 of the Technical Notes.

The fact that marriage is a legal event, unlike birth and death that are biological events, has implications for international comparability of data. Marriage has been defined, for statistical purposes, in terms of the laws of individual countries or areas. These laws vary throughout the world. In addition, comparability is further limited because some countries or areas compile statistics only for civil marriages although religious marriages may also be legally recognized; in others, the only available records are church registers and, therefore, the statistics do not reflect marriages that are civil marriages only.

Because in many countries or areas marriage is a civil legal contract which, to establish its legality, must be celebrated before a civil officer, it follows that for these countries or areas registration would tend to be almost automatic at the time of, or immediately following, the marriage ceremony. This factor should be kept in mind when considering the reliability of data, described above. For this reason the practice of tabulating data by date of registration does not generally pose serious problems of comparability as it does in the case of birth and death statistics.

As indicators of family formation, the statistics on the number of marriages presented in this table are bound to be deficient to the extent that they do not include either customary unions, which are not registered even though they are considered legal and binding under customary law, or consensual unions (also known as extra-legal or de facto unions). In general, lower marriage rates over a period of years are an indication of higher incidence of customary or consensual unions.

In addition, rates are affected also by the quality and limitations of the population estimates that are used in their computation. The problems of under-enumeration or over-enumeration and, to some extent, the differences in definition of total population have been discussed in section 3 of the Technical Notes dealing with population data in general, and specific information pertaining to individual countries or areas is given in the footnotes to table 3.

Strict correspondence between the numerator of the rate and the denominator is not always obtained; for example, marriages among civilian and military segments of the population may be related to civilian population. The effect of this may be to increase the rates or, if the population is larger than that from which the marriages are drawn, to decrease them, but, in most cases, it is probably negligible.

It should be emphasized that crude marriage rates like crude birth, death and divorce rates, may be seriously affected by age-sex-marital structure of the population to which they relate. Crude marriage rates do, however, provide a simple measure of the level and changes in marriage.

The comparability of data by urban/rural residence is affected by the national definitions of urban and rural used in tabulating these data. It is assumed, in the absence of specific information to the contrary, that the definitions of urban and rural used in connection with the national population census were also used in the compilation of the vital statistics for each country or area. However, the possibility cannot be excluded that, for a given country or area, the same definitions of urban and rural are not used for both the vital statistics data and the population census data. When known, the definitions of urban in national population censuses are presented at the end of the technical notes for table 6. As discussed in detail in the notes, these definitions vary considerably from one country or area to another.

In addition to problems of comparability, marriage rates classified by urban/rural residence are also subject to certain special types of bias. If, when calculating marriage rates, different definitions of urban are used in connection with the vital events and the population data, and if this results in a net difference between the numerator and denominator of the rate in the population at risk, then the marriage rates would be biased. Urban/rural differentials in marriage rates may also be affected by whether the vital events have been tabulated in terms of place of occurrence or place of usual residence. This problem is discussed in more detail in section 4.1.4.1. of the Technical Notes.

Coverage: Marriages are shown for 129 countries or areas. Data are presented for urban/rural residence for 43 countries or areas.

Earlier data: Marriages and crude marriage rates have been shown in each issue of the *Demographic Yearbook*. For more information on specific topics, and years for which data are reported, readers should consult the Index.

NOTES

[i] *Principles and Recommendations for a Vital Statistics System Revision 2*, Sales No. E. 01.XVII.10, United Nations, New York, 2001

Tableau 23

Le tableau 23 présente des données sur les mariages et les taux bruts de nuptialité selon la résidence (urbaine/rurale) pour le plus grand nombre possible d'années entre 1997 et 2001.

Description des variables : Le mariage désigne l'acte, la cérémonie ou la procédure qui établit un rapport légal entre mari et femme[1]. L'union peut être rendue légale par une procédure civile ou religieuse, ou par toute autre procédure, conformément à la législation du pays.

Les statistiques de la nuptialité présentées dans ce tableau comprennent donc les premiers mariages et les remariages faisant suite à un divorce, un veuvage ou une annulation. Toutefois, sauf indication contraire, elles ne comprennent pas les unions reconstituées après une séparation légale. Ces statistiques se rapportent au nombre de mariages célébrés, non au nombre de personnes qui se marient.

Les statistiques présentées reposent sur l'enregistrement des mariages par les services de l'état civil. Les exceptions (données tirées des registres des églises, par exemple) font l'objet d'une note au bas du tableau.

La classification des mariages selon la résidence (urbaine/rurale) est celle qui a été fournie par chaque pays ou zone; il faut en conclure qu'elle repose sur les définitions de la population urbaine utilisées pour les recensements nationaux telles qu'elles sont reproduites à la fin des Notes techniques du tableau 6.

Calcul des taux: Les taux bruts de nuptialité représentent le nombre annuel de mariages pour 1 000 habitants au milieu de l'année. Ces taux ont été calculés par la Division de statistique de l'ONU.

Les taux selon la résidence (urbaine/rurale) représentent le nombre annuel de mariages, classés selon la catégorie urbaine ou rurale appropriée, pour 1 000 habitants au milieu de l'année.

Les taux de ce tableau ne se rapportent qu'aux pays ou zones où l'on a enregistré un total d'au moins 100 mariages dans une année donnée. Les taux par la résidence urbaine ou rurale calculés sur la base de 30 mariages ou moins, qui sont indiqués dans le tableau sont identifiés par le signe (♦).

Fiabilité des données : Il a été demandé à chaque pays ou zone d'indiquer le degré estimatif de complétude des données sur les mariages figurant dans ses registres d'état civil. Ces évaluations nationales sont désignées par les codes de qualité C et U qui apparaissent dans la première colonne du tableau.

La lettre (C) indique que les données sont jugées à peu près complètes, c'est-à-dire qu'elles représentent au moins 90 p. 100 des mariages survenus chaque année; la lettre (U) indique que les données sont jugées incomplètes, c'est-à-dire qu'elles représentent moins de 90 p. 100 des mariages survenus chaque année. Le signe(...) indique qu'aucun renseignement n'a été fourni quant à la complétude des données.

Les données provenant des registres de l'état civil qui sont déclarés incomplets ou dont le degré de complétude n'est pas connu (et qui sont affectés de la lettre (U) ou du signe (...) sont jugées douteuses et les correspondant taux ne sont pas calculés.

Ces codes de qualité ne s'appliquent qu'aux données tirées des registres de l'état civil. Pour plus de précisions sur la qualité des données reposant sur les statistiques de l'état civil en général, voir la section 4.2 des Notes techniques.

Insuffisance des données : Les statistiques des mariages appellent toutes les réserves qui ont été formulées à propos des statistiques de l'état civil en général et des statistiques de la nuptialité en particulier (voir explications figurant à la section 4 des notes techniques).

Le fait que le mariage soit un acte juridique, à la différence de la naissance et du décès, qui sont des faits biologiques, a des répercussions sur la comparabilité internationale des données. Aux fins de la statistique, le mariage est défini par la législation de chaque pays ou zone. Cette législation varie d'un pays à l'autre. La comparabilité est limitée en outre du fait que certains pays ne réunissent des statistiques que pour les mariages civils, bien que les mariages religieux y soient également reconnus par la loi; dans d'autres, les seuls relevés disponibles sont les registres des églises et, en conséquence, les statistiques ne rendent pas compte des mariages exclusivement civils.

Etant le mariage, dans de nombreux pays ou zones, un contrat juridique civil qui, pour être légal, doit être conclu devant un officier d'état civil, il s'ensuit que dans ces pays ou zones l'enregistrement se fait à peu près automatiquement au moment de la cérémonie ou immédiatement après. Il faut tenir compte de cet élément lorsqu'on étudie la fiabilité des données, dont il est question plus haut. C'est pourquoi la pratique consistant à exploiter les données selon la date de l'enregistrement ne pose généralement pas les graves problèmes de comparabilité auxquels on se heurte dans le cas des statistiques des naissances et des décès.

Les statistiques relatives au nombre des mariages présentées dans ce tableau donnent une idée forcément trompeuse de la formation des familles, dans la mesure où elles ne tiennent compte ni des mariages coutumiers, qui ne sont pas enregistrés bien qu'ils soient considérés comme légaux et créateurs d'obligations en vertu du droit coutumier, ni des unions consensuelles (appelées également unions non légalisées ou unions de fait). En général, une diminution du taux de nuptialité pendant un certain nombre d'années indique une augmentation de mariages coutumiers ou d'unions consensuelles.

L'exactitude des taux dépend également de la qualité et des insuffisances des estimations de population qui sont utilisées pour leur calcul. Le problème des erreurs par excès ou par défaut commises lors du dénombrement et, dans une certaine mesure, le problème de l'hétérogénéité des définitions de la population totale ont été examinés à la section 3 des Notes techniques relative à la population en général; des indications concernant les différents pays ou zones sont données en note au bas du tableau 3.

Il n'a pas toujours été possible, pour le calcul des taux, d'obtenir une correspondance rigoureuse entre le numérateur et le dénominateur. Par exemple, les mariages parmi la population civile et les militaires sont parfois rapportés à la population civile. Cela peut avoir pour effet d'accroître les taux; au contraire, si la population de base englobe un plus grand nombre de personnes que celle dans laquelle les mariages ont été comptés, les taux seront plus faibles, mais, dans la plupart des cas, il est probable que la différence sera négligeable.

Il faut souligner que les taux bruts de nuptialité, de même que les taux bruts de natalité, de mortalité et de divortialité, peuvent varier sensiblement selon la structure par âge et par sexe de la population à laquelle ils se rapportent. Les taux bruts de nuptialité offrent néanmoins un moyen simple de mesurer la fréquence et l'évolution des mariages.

La comparabilité des données selon la résidence (urbaine/rurale) peut être limitée par les définitions nationales des termes 'urbain' et 'rural' utilisées pour la mise en tableaux de ces données. En l'absence d'indications contraires, on a supposé que les définitions des termes 'urbain' et 'rural' utilisées pour le recensement national de la population avaient été utilisées pour l'établissement des statistiques de l'état civil pour chaque pays ou zone. Toutefois, on ne peut exclure la possibilité que, pour un pays ou zone donné les mêmes définitions des termes 'urbain' et 'rural' n'aient pas été utilisées dans les deux cas. Les définitions du terme 'urbain' pour les recensements nationaux de population ont été présentées à la fin des notes techniques du tableau 6 lorsqu'elles étaient connues. Comme on l'a précisé en détail dans cette note, ces définitions varient très sensiblement d'un pays ou d'une zone à l'autre.

Outre ces problèmes de comparabilité, les taux de nuptialité classés selon la résidence urbaine ou rurale sont également sujets à certains types particuliers d'erreurs. Si, lors du calcul de ces taux, des définitions différentes du terme "urbain" sont utilisées pour classer les faits d'état civil et les données relatives à la population, et s'il en résulte une différence nette entre le numérateur et le dénominateur pour le taux de la population exposée au risque, les taux de nuptialité s'en trouveront faussés. La différence entre ces taux pour les zones urbaines et rurales pourra aussi être faussée selon que les faits d'état civil auront été classés d'après le lieu de l'événement ou le lieu de résidence habituelle. Ce problème est examiné plus en détail à la section 4.1.4.1 des notes techniques.

Portée : Ce tableau présente des données sur le nombre des mariages pour 129 pays ou zones. Les répartitions selon la résidence (urbaine/rurale)intéressent 43 pays ou zones.

Données publiées antérieurement : Des données sur le nombre des mariages ont été présentées dans chaque édition de l'Annuaire démographique. Pour plus de précisions concernant les années et les sujets spécifiques pour lesquelles des données ont été publiées, se reporter à l'Index.

NOTES

[1] Principles and Recommendations for a Vital Statistics System Revision 2, Sales No. E. 01.XVII.10, United Nations, New York, 2001

23. Marriages and crude marriage rates, by urban/rural residence: 1997 - 2001
Mariages et taux bruts de nuptialité, selon la résidence, urbaine/rurale: 1997 - 2001

(See notes at end of table. — Voir notes à la fin du tableau.)

Continent, country or area and urban/rural residence / Continent, pays ou zone et résidence, urbaine/rurale	Code[1]	Marriages - Mariages					Rate - Taux				
		1997	1998	1999	2000	2001	1997	1998	1999	2000	2001
AFRICA — AFRIQUE											
Algeria - Algérie[2]											
Total	...	157 831	158 298	163 126	177 548	194 273	...	...	...	...	...
Djibouti											
Total	...	...	3 255	3 808	...	...	...	...	...	...	...
Egypt - Égypte[3]											
Total	+...	493 787	503 651	525 412	...	...	...	...	...	...	...
Urban-Urbaine	+...	181 185	183 976	191 224	...	...	...	...	...	...	...
Rural-Rurale	+...	312 602	319 675	334 188	...	...	...	...	...	...	...
Ethiopia - Éthiopie											
Total	...	...	...	630 290	...	...	...	...	...	...	...
Urban-Urbaine	...	...	...	24 093	...	...	...	...	...	...	...
Rural-Rurale	...	...	...	606 197	...	...	...	...	...	...	...
Libyan Arab Jamahiriya - Jamahiriya arabe libyenne[4]											
Total	U	20 089	19 051	19 348	27 655	...	...	...	...	...	...
Mauritius - Maurice											
Total	+C	10 887	10 898	11 295	10 963	10 635	9.5	9.4	9.6	9.2	8.9
Urban-Urbaine	+C	3 756	3 740	3 537	3 542	3 423	7.6	7.5	7.0	7.0	6.7
Rural-Rurale	+C	7 131	7 158	7 758	7 421	7 212	10.9	10.8	11.5	10.9	10.5
Réunion											
Total	C	3 197	3 343	3 446	3 444	*3 334	4.7	4.8	4.9	4.8	4.5
Saint Helena ex. dep. - Sainte-Hélène sans dép.											
Total	C	22	29	25	17	20	...	...	...	...	...
Seychelles											
Total	+C	859	718	883	949	790	11.1	9.1	11.0	11.7	9.7
South Africa - Afrique du Sud											
Total	...	146 729	146 741	...	...	...	...	...	...	...	...
Tunisia - Tunisie											
Total	...	57 861	56 081	60 082	...	61 800	...	...	...	...	...
AMERICA, NORTH — AMERIQUE DU NORD											
Anguilla											
Total	C	195	219	201	171	*181	18.8	20.5	18.4	15.2	15.7
Aruba											
Total	C	592	564	578	616	546	6.9	6.4	6.4	6.8	5.9
Barbados - Barbade											
Total	C	...	...	...	*3 516	...	...	...	...	13.1	...
Belize											
Total	+C	1 543	1 374	1 517	...	...	6.7	5.8	...	...	...
Bermuda - Bermudes											
Total	C	966	1 033	...	...	...	16.0	...	...	...	...
Canada											
Total	+C	153 306	152 821	155 742	157 395	*146 618	5.1	5.1	5.1	5.1	4.7
Cayman Islands - Îles Caïmanes											
Total	+C	310	300	375	...	...	8.6	8.0	9.6	...	...
Costa Rica											
Total	C	24 300	24 831	25 613	24 436	*23 790	7.0	7.0	7.1	6.2	6.0
Cuba											
Total	C	60 920	64 900	57 252	57 001	*54 345	5.5	5.8	5.1	5.1	4.8
Urban-Urbaine	C	55 486	59 009	51 645	51 762	...	6.7	7.1	6.2	6.1	...
Rural-Rurale	C	5 434	5 891	5 607	5 239	...	2.0	2.1	2.0	1.9	...
Dominica - Dominique											
Total	+C	287	336	*339	...	...	3.8	4.4	...	...	...
Dominican Republic - République dominicaine											
Total	+C	...	28 723	36 446	33 904	*24 470	...	3.5	4.4	4.0	2.9
El Salvador											
Total	C	23 519	25 923	34 306	28 231	*29 216	4.0	4.3	5.6	4.5	4.6
Urban-Urbaine	C	18 990	21 219	27 071	22 525	*23 668	5.6	6.1	7.6	6.1	6.3

23. Marriages and crude marriage rates, by urban/rural residence: 1997 - 2001
Mariages et taux bruts de nuptialité, selon la résidence, urbaine/rurale: 1997 - 2001 (continued — suite)

(See notes at end of table. — Voir notes à la fin du tableau.)

Continent, country or area and urban/rural residence / Continent, pays ou zone et résidence, urbaine/rurale	Code[1]	Marriages - Mariages					Rate - Taux				
		1997	1998	1999	2000	2001	1997	1998	1999	2000	2001
AMERICA, NORTH — AMERIQUE DU NORD											
El Salvador											
Rural-Rurale	C	4 529	4 704	7 235	5 706	*5 548	1.8	1.8	2.8	2.2	2.1
Grenada - Grenade											
Total	+C	497	563	570	616	*509	5.0	5.6	5.7	6.1	5.0
Guatemala											
Total	C	51 908	52 952	60 922	...	...	4.9	4.9	5.5	...	...
Jamaica - Jamaïque											
Total	+C	21 502	24 131	26 871	...	...	8.4	9.4	10.4	...	...
Mexico - Mexique[5]											
Total	+U	707 840	704 456	743 856	707 442	665 434	...	...	...	...	...
Urban-Urbaine	+U	521 115	521 176	...	...	...	...	...	...	...	...
Rural-Rurale	+U	174 725	163 414	...	...	...	...	...	...	...	...
Netherlands Antilles - Antilles néerlandaises											
Total	C	1 370	1 276	956	...	...	6.6	6.1	4.7	...	...
Nicaragua											
Total	+C	24 487	20 816	28 005	...	...	5.2	4.3	5.7	...	...
Panama[5,6]											
Total	C	10 357	10 415	10 388	10 430	9 767	3.8	3.8	3.7	3.7	3.4
Urban-Urbaine	C	7 312	7 209	7 506	7 499	7 416	4.8	4.7	4.8	4.7	...
Rural-Rurale	C	3 045	3 206	2 882	2 931	2 351	2.5	2.6	2.3	2.3	...
Puerto Rico - Porto Rico											
Total	C	31 493	26 760	27 255	25 980	28 598	8.5	7.1	7.2	6.8	7.4
Saint Kitts and Nevis - Saint-Kitts-et-Nevis											
Total	+...	354	315	...	...	...	...	...	...	...	...
Saint Lucia - Sainte-Lucie[7]											
Total	C	467	627	661	661	661	3.1	4.1	4.3	4.2	4.2
Urban-Urbaine	C	160	150	...	...	...	3.6	3.3	...	...	...
Rural-Rurale	C	380	359	...	...	...	3.6	3.4	...	...	...
Saint Vincent and the Grenadines - Saint Vincent-et-les Grenadines											
Total	+C	516	521	630	673	*480	4.6	4.7	5.6	6.0	4.4
Trinidad and Tobago - Trinité-et-Tobago											
Total	+C	7 418	...	...	...	...	5.8	...	...	...	...
United States - États-Unis											
Total	C	2 384 000	2 244 000	2 358 000	2 329 000	...	8.9	8.3	8.6	8.5	...
AMERICA, SOUTH — AMERIQUE DU SUD											
Argentina - Argentine											
Total	C	...	...	...	...	130 533	...	...	...	...	3.5
Brazil - Brésil[8]											
Total	U	...	698 614	788 744	732 721	710 121	...	...	...	...	...
Chile - Chili											
Total	+C	78 077	73 456	69 765	...	...	5.3	5.0	4.6	...	...
Urban-Urbaine	+C	68 268	64 073	60 636	...	...	5.5	5.1	4.7	...	...
Rural-Rurale	+C	9 809	9 383	9 129	...	...	4.5	4.3	4.2	...	...
Ecuador - Équateur[9]											
Total	U	66 967	69 867	77 597	74 875	...	...	...	...	...	...
French Guiana - Guyane française											
Total	U	671	...	...	...	...	...	...	...	...	...
Peru - Pérou											
Total	+C	78 946	60 730	...	...	...	3.2	2.4	...	...	...
Suriname											
Total	+U	2 073	1 982	2 257	2 267	...	...	...	...	...	...

23. Marriages and crude marriage rates, by urban/rural residence: 1997 - 2001
Mariages et taux bruts de nuptialité, selon la résidence, urbaine/rurale: 1997 - 2001 (continued — suite)

(See notes at end of table. — Voir notes à la fin du tableau.)

Continent, country or area and urban/rural residence / Continent, pays ou zone et résidence, urbaine/rurale	Code[1]	Marriages - Mariages					Rate - Taux				
		1997	1998	1999	2000	2001	1997	1998	1999	2000	2001
AMERICA, SOUTH — AMERIQUE DU SUD											
Uruguay											
Total	C	17 056	16 176	15 488	13 888	...	5.2	4.9	4.7	4.2	...
Venezuela[8]											
Total	C	86 423	86 152	90 220	91 088	81 516	3.8	3.7	3.8	3.8	3.3
ASIA — ASIE											
Armenia - Arménie											
Total	C	12 521	11 365	12 459	10 986	12 302	3.3	3.0	3.3	2.9	3.2
Urban-Urbaine	C	8 167	7 666	8 560	7 626	...	3.2	3.0	3.4	3.0	...
Rural-Rurale	C	4 354	3 699	3 899	3 360	...	3.5	2.9	3.1	2.6	...
Azerbaijan - Azerbaïdjan											
Total	+C	46 999	40 851	37 382	39 611	41 861	6.0	5.2	4.7	4.9	5.2
Urban-Urbaine	+C	23 293	20 322	18 799	19 994	22 927	5.7	5.0	4.6	4.9	5.6
Rural-Rurale	+C	23 706	20 529	18 583	19 617	18 934	6.3	5.3	4.8	5.0	4.7
Bahrain - Bahrein											
Total	...	3 984	3 677	3 673	3 963		...	...	...	...	...
Bangladesh											
Total	...	1 181 000	...	...	...	...	...	...	...	...	...
Brunei Darussalam - Brunéi Darussalam											
Total	...	2 207	2 039	2 318	2 184		...	...	...	...	...
China - Chine											
Total	+C	9 090 000	8 918 000	...	...	...	38.5	35.9	...	...	...
China: Hong Kong SAR - Chine: Hong Kong RAS											
Total	C	37 593	31 673	31 287	30 879	32 825	5.8	4.8	4.7	4.6	4.9
China: Macao SAR - Chine: Macao RAS											
Total	+C	1 678	1 451	1 367	1 222	1 222	4.0	3.4	3.2	2.8	2.8
Cyprus - Chypre[10]											
Total	C	7 187	7 738	9 080	9 282	*10 574	9.5	10.1	11.7	11.9	13.4
Georgia - Géorgie											
Total	C	17 100	15 300	13 845	12 870	13 336	3.1	2.8	3.0	2.6	2.7
Urban-Urbaine	C	...	...	...	7 977	8 027	...	...	...	3.0	...
Rural-Rurale	C	...	...	...	4 893	5 309	...	...	...	2.6	...
Iran (Islamic Republic of) - Iran (République islamique d')											
Total	+U	511 277	...	...	...	...	...	...	...	...	...
Urban-Urbaine	+U	387 231	...	...	...	...	...	...	...	...	...
Rural-Rurale	+U	124 046	...	...	...	...	...	...	...	...	...
Iraq[11]											
Total	C	127 901	136 149	148 963	171 134	...	5.8	6.1	6.5	7.3	...
Israel - Israël[12]											
Total	C	37 611	40 137	40 236	38 894	38 924	6.5	6.7	6.6	6.2	6.0
Japan - Japon[13]											
Total	+C	775 651	784 595	762 028	798 138	799 999	6.2	6.2	6.0	6.3	6.3
Urban-Urbaine	+C	643 761	650 738	630 726	...	663 506	...	...	...	...	...
Rural-Rurale	+C	131 890	133 857	131 302	...	136 493	...	...	...	...	...
Jordan - Jordanie[14]											
Total	+C	37 278	39 376	39 443	*45 608	...	8.1	8.3	8.0	9.1	...
Urban-Urbaine	+C	28 513	...	...	...	...	...	...	...	...	...
Rural-Rurale	+C	8 765	...	...	...	...	...	...	...	...	...
Kazakhstan											
Total	C	101 874	96 048	85 872	90 873	*92 852	6.5	6.4	5.8	6.1	6.3
Urban-Urbaine	C	58 258	54 801	50 089	...	...	6.7	6.5	6.0	...	...
Rural-Rurale	C	43 616	41 247	35 783	...	...	6.2	6.2	5.4	...	...
Korea (Republic of) - Corée (République de)											
Total	+C	388 591	375 616	362 673	334 030	320 063	8.5	8.1	7.8	3.6	6.8

23. Marriages and crude marriage rates, by urban/rural residence: 1997 - 2001
Mariages et taux bruts de nuptialité, selon la résidence, urbaine/rurale: 1997 - 2001 (continued — suite)

(See notes at end of table. — Voir notes à la fin du tableau.)

Continent, country or area and urban/rural residence Continent, pays ou zone et résidence, urbaine/rurale	Code[1]	Marriages - Mariages					Rate - Taux				
		1997	1998	1999	2000	2001	1997	1998	1999	2000	2001

ASIA — ASIE

Korea (Republic of) - Corée (République de)											
Urban-Urbaine	+C	314 962	304 318	294 612	273 040	261 575	...	...	...	7.4	...
Rural-Rurale	+C	73 629	71 298	68 061	60 990	58 488	...	...	...	6.5	...
Kuwait - Koweït											
Total	C	9 612	10 335	10 847	10 785	...	4.9	5.1	5.1	4.9	...
Kyrgyzstan - Kirghizistan											
Total	C	26 588	25 726	26 033	24 294	27 455	5.7	5.4	5.4	5.0	5.6
Urban-Urbaine	C	7 899	7 932	7 926	7 528	8 258	4.7	4.7	4.6	4.4	4.7
Rural-Rurale	C	18 689	17 794	18 107	16 766	19 197	6.2	5.8	5.8	5.3	6.0
Lebanon - Liban[11]											
Total	C	31 676	31 219	30 477	32 586	...	...	...	...	...	...
Mongolia - Mongolie											
Total	C	14 421	13 908	13 722	12 601	12 393	6.3	6.0	5.8	5.3	5.1
Urban-Urbaine	C	6 986	7 446	7 383	6 096	...	6.1	6.5	5.3	4.4	...
Rural-Rurale	C	7 435	6 462	6 339	6 505	...	6.4	5.5	6.5	6.6	...
Occupied Palestinian Territory - Territoire palestinien occupé											
Total	U	*23 492*	*24 400*	*24 874*	*23 890*	*24 635*	...	...	...	...	...
Philippines											
Total	U	*562 808*	*549 265*	*551 445*	*577 387*	...	...	...	...	...	...
Qatar											
Total	U	*1 766*	*1 851*	*1 905*	*2 096*	*2 194*	...	...	...	...	...
Saudi Arabia - Arabie saoudite											
Total	...	...	...	...	64 339	79 595	...	...	...	...	...
Singapore - Singapour[15,16,17]											
Total	C	25 667	23 106	25 648	22 561	22 280	6.8	5.9	6.5	5.6	5.4
Syrian Arab Republic - République arabe syrienne[18]											
Total	+U	*128 146*	*130 835*	*136 157*	*139 843*	*153 842*	...	...	...	...	...
Tajikistan - Tadjikistan											
Total	C	...	...	*21 600	...	...	...	...	3.5	...	...
Thailand - Thaïlande											
Total	C	...	...	*354 198	...	...	...	...	5.8	...	...
Turkey - Turquie[19]											
Total	+U	*518 856*	*485 035*	*475 613*	...	*453 213*	...	...	...	...	...
Urban-Urbaine	+U	*323 237*	*302 739*	*294 248*	...	...	...	...	...	...	...
Rural-Rurale	+U	*195 619*	*182 296*	*181 365*	...	...	...	...	...	...	...
Turkmenistan - Turkménistan											
Total	C	...	*26 361	...	...	...	...	5.4	...	...	...
Uzbekistan - Ouzbékistan											
Total	C	181 126	...	170 525	168 908	170 101	7.7	...	7.1	6.9	6.8
Urban-Urbaine	C	68 250	...	64 685	65 104	64 302	7.6	...	7.2	7.1	6.9
Rural-Rurale	C	112 876	...	105 840	103 804	105 799	7.7	...	7.1	6.7	6.7

EUROPE

Albania - Albanie											
Total	C	25 260	27 887	...	...	...	6.8	7.4	...	...	...
Andorra - Andorre											
Total	C	143	208	178	226	213	2.2	3.2	2.7	3.4	3.2
Austria - Autriche[20]											
Total	C	41 394	39 143	39 485	39 228	34 213	5.1	4.8	4.9	4.8	4.2
Belarus - Bélarus											
Total	C	69 735	71 354	72 994	...	...	6.8	7.0	7.3	...	...
Urban-Urbaine	C	53 190	55 256	57 648	...	...	7.5	7.7	8.3	...	...
Rural-Rurale	C	16 545	16 098	15 346	...	...	5.3	5.3	5.0	...	...
Belgium - Belgique[21]											
Total	C	47 759	44 393	44 171	45 123	*42 110	4.7	4.4	4.3	4.4	4.1

23. Marriages and crude marriage rates, by urban/rural residence: 1997 - 2001
Mariages et taux bruts de nuptialité, selon la résidence, urbaine/rurale: 1997 - 2001 (continued — suite)

(See notes at end of table. — Voir notes à la fin du tableau.)

Continent, country or area and urban/rural residence / Continent, pays ou zone et résidence, urbaine/rurale	Code[1]	Marriages - Mariages					Rate - Taux				
		1997	1998	1999	2000	2001	1997	1998	1999	2000	2001
EUROPE											
Bosnia and Herzegovina - Bosnie-Herzégovine											
Total	C	23 220	22 398	...	*21 216	...	6.2	6.1	...	...	...
Bulgaria - Bulgarie[22]											
Total	C	34 772	*35 591	*35 540	35 164	31 974	4.2	4.3	4.3	4.3	4.0
Urban-Urbaine	C	27 029	...	...	26 576	24 466	4.8	...	...	4.8	4.5
Rural-Rurale	C	7 743	...	...	8 588	7 508	2.9	...	...	3.3	3.1
Channel Islands: Guernsey - Îles Anglo-Normandes: Guernesey											
Total	C	318	356	385	343	...	5.4	6.0	6.4	5.7	...
Croatia - Croatie											
Total	C	24 517	24 243	23 778	22 017	22 076	5.4	5.4	5.2	5.0	5.0
Urban-Urbaine	C	14 661	14 241	...	12 439	12 380	...	...	...	...	...
Rural-Rurale	C	9 856	10 002	...	9 578	9 696	...	...	...	...	...
Czech Republic - République tchèque											
Total	C	57 804	55 027	53 523	55 321	52 374	5.6	5.3	5.2	5.4	5.1
Urban-Urbaine	C	44 024	41 476	40 370	41 763	39 666	5.7	5.4	5.3	5.5	5.2
Rural-Rurale	C	13 780	13 551	13 153	13 558	12 708	5.3	5.2	5.0	5.2	4.8
Denmark - Danemark[23]											
Total	C	34 244	34 733	35 439	38 388	*36 567	6.5	6.6	6.7	7.2	6.8
Estonia - Estonie[24]											
Total	C	5 589	5 416	5 590	5 485	5 647	3.8	3.7	3.9	4.0	4.1
Urban-Urbaine	C	3 902	...	...	3 929	...	3.9	...	...	4.3	...
Rural-Rurale	C	1 687	...	...	1 304	...	3.8	...	...	2.9	...
Finland - Finlande[25]											
Total	C	23 444	24 023	24 271	26 150	24 830	4.6	4.7	4.7	5.1	4.8
Urban-Urbaine	C	16 525	16 992	...	...	17 843	5.4	5.5	...	...	5.6
Rural-Rurale	C	6 919	7 031	...	...	6 987	3.3	3.4	...	...	3.5
France[5,26]											
Total	C	283 984	271 361	286 191	*305 000	*304 700	4.8	4.6	4.9	5.2	5.1
Urban-Urbaine	C	221 792	212 630	222 831	...	...	...	...	...	...	...
Rural-Rurale	C	59 294	53 755	59 000	...	...	...	...	...	...	...
Germany - Allemagne											
Total	C	422 776	416 281	430 585	418 550	389 000	5.2	5.1	5.2	5.1	4.7
Gibraltar[27]											
Total	C	...	141	161	149	164	...	5.2	5.9	5.5	5.8
Greece - Grèce											
Total	C	60 535	55 489	61 848	63 585	*57 000	5.8	5.3	5.9	6.4	5.7
Urban-Urbaine	C	41 131	38 197	...	...	...	...	...	...	...	...
Rural-Rurale	C	19 404	17 292	...	...	...	...	...	...	...	...
Hungary - Hongrie[5]											
Total	C	46 905	44 915	45 465	48 110	43 583	4.6	4.4	4.5	4.8	4.3
Urban-Urbaine	C	29 460	28 957	29 345	31 314	28 876	4.5	4.4	4.5	4.8	4.3
Rural-Rurale	C	16 657	15 117	15 138	15 890	13 769	4.7	4.2	4.3	4.5	3.9
Iceland - Islande[5,28]											
Total	C	1 481	1 529	1 560	1 777	1 484	5.5	5.6	5.6	6.3	5.2
Urban-Urbaine	C	1 386	1 415	...	1 668	1 406	5.6	5.6	...	6.4	5.3
Rural-Rurale	C	90	114	...	109	78	4.2	5.3	...	5.1	3.6
Ireland - Irlande											
Total	+C	15 631	16 783	18 526	19 168	*19 246	4.3	4.5	4.9	5.1	5.0
Isle of Man - Îles de Man											
Total	C	...	...	403	...	...	...	...	...	...	...
Italy - Italie											
Total	C	277 738	280 034	280 330	280 488	260 904	4.8	4.9	4.9	4.9	4.5
Latvia - Lettonie											
Total	C	9 680	9 641	9 399	9 211	9 258	4.0	4.0	3.9	3.9	3.9
Urban-Urbaine	C	7 069	7 096	6 955	...	6 755	4.2	4.3	4.3	...	4.2
Rural-Rurale	C	2 611	2 545	2 444	...	2 503	3.4	3.4	3.2	...	3.3
Liechtenstein											
Total	C	392	...	...	...	...	12.6	...	...	...	...

23. Marriages and crude marriage rates, by urban/rural residence: 1997 - 2001
Mariages et taux bruts de nuptialité, selon la résidence, urbaine/rurale: 1997 - 2001 (continued — suite)

(See notes at end of table. — Voir notes à la fin du tableau.)

Continent, country or area and urban/rural residence / Continent, pays ou zone et résidence, urbaine/rurale	Code[1]	Marriages - Mariages					Rate - Taux				
		1997	1998	1999	2000	2001	1997	1998	1999	2000	2001
EUROPE											
Lithuania - Lituanie											
Total	C	18 796	18 486	17 868	16 906	15 764	5.3	5.2	5.1	4.8	4.5
Urban-Urbaine	C	12 686	12 423	12 150	11 705	11 036	5.3	5.2	5.1	5.0	4.7
Rural-Rurale	C	6 110	6 063	5 718	5 201	4 728	5.3	5.2	4.9	4.5	4.1
Luxembourg[28]											
Total	C	2 007	2 040	2 090	2 148	1 983	4.8	4.8	4.8	4.9	4.5
Malta - Malte[29]											
Total	C	2 414	2 376	2 409	2 545	2 194	6.3	6.1	6.2	6.5	5.6
Monaco											
Total	C	208	192	...	*160	...	6.5	...	...	4.8	...
Netherlands - Pays-Bas[5,30,31]											
Total	C	85 059	86 956	*88 970	88 074	82 091	5.4	5.5	5.6	5.5	5.1
Urban-Urbaine	C	...	...	...	48 058	45 261	...	...	...	...	...
Rural-Rurale	C	...	...	...	31 380	36 830	...	...	...	...	...
Norway - Norvège[32]											
Total	C	22 933	22 349	24 889	25 356	22 967	5.2	5.0	5.6	5.6	5.1
Poland - Pologne											
Total	C	204 850	209 430	219 398	211 150	*195 122	5.3	5.4	5.7	5.5	5.0
Urban-Urbaine	C	121 598	125 194	131 990	...	...	5.1	5.2	5.5	...	...
Rural-Rurale	C	83 252	84 236	87 408	...	...	5.7	5.7	5.9	...	...
Portugal											
Total	C	65 770	66 575	68 337	63 752	58 390	6.6	6.7	6.8	6.4	5.7
Republic of Moldova - République de Moldova											
Total	C	...	21 814	23 524	21 684	21 065	...	6.0	6.5	6.0	5.8
Urban-Urbaine	C	...	9 479	9 886	9 514	9 727	...	6.2	6.5	6.3	6.5
Rural-Rurale	C	...	12 335	13 638	12 170	11 338	...	5.8	6.4	5.7	5.3
Romania - Roumanie											
Total	C	147 105	145 303	140 014	135 808	129 930	6.5	6.5	6.2	6.1	5.8
Urban-Urbaine	C	82 522	82 912	...	79 128	77 231	6.7	6.7	...	6.5	6.3
Rural-Rurale	C	64 583	62 391	...	56 680	52 699	6.4	6.1	...	5.6	5.2
Russian Federation - Fédération de Russie											
Total	C	928 411	848 691	911 162	1 266 800	*1 001 589	6.3	5.8	6.2	8.7	7.0
San Marino - Saint-Marin											
Total	C	233	214	231	193	...	9.0	8.2	8.8	7.2	...
Serbia and Montenegro - Serbie-et-Monténégro											
Total	C	56 203	54 822	53 034	58 318	*57 858	5.3	5.2	5.0	5.5	5.4
Urban-Urbaine	C	30 949	30 465	29 921	33 251	...	5.7	5.6	5.5	6.1	...
Rural-Rurale	C	25 254	24 357	23 113	25 067	...	4.9	4.7	4.5	4.9	...
Slovakia - Slovaquie											
Total	C	27 910	27 494	27 340	25 903	23 795	5.2	5.1	5.1	4.8	4.4
Urban-Urbaine	C	...	15 106	14 320	...	13 591	...	4.9	4.7	...	...
Rural-Rurale	C	...	12 388	13 020	...	10 204	...	5.3	5.6	...	...
Slovenia - Slovénie											
Total	C	7 500	7 528	7 716	7 201	6 935	3.8	3.8	3.9	3.6	3.5
Urban-Urbaine	C	...	3 764	...	3 571	3 569	...	...	...	...	...
Rural-Rurale	C	...	3 764	...	3 630	3 366	...	...	...	...	...
Spain - Espagne											
Total	C	196 499	207 041	206 048	216 451	*210 159	5.0	5.2	5.2	5.4	5.2
Sweden - Suède											
Total	C	32 313	31 598	35 628	39 895	35 778	3.7	3.6	4.0	4.5	4.0
Switzerland - Suisse											
Total	C	39 102	38 683	40 646	39 758	35 987	5.5	5.4	5.7	5.5	5.0
Urban-Urbaine	C	27 176	26 952	28 427	28 031	25 668	5.7	5.6	5.9	5.8	5.2
Rural-Rurale	C	11 926	11 731	12 219	11 727	10 319	5.2	5.1	5.3	5.0	4.4

23. Marriages and crude marriage rates, by urban/rural residence: 1997 - 2001
Mariages et taux bruts de nuptialité, selon la résidence, urbaine/rurale: 1997 - 2001 (continued — suite)

(See notes at end of table. — Voir notes à la fin du tableau.)

Continent, country or area and urban/rural residence / Continent, pays ou zone et résidence, urbaine/rurale	Code[1]	Marriages - Mariages					Rate - Taux				
		1997	1998	1999	2000	2001	1997	1998	1999	2000	2001
EUROPE											
The Former Yugoslav Rep. of Macedonia - L'ex-République yougoslave de Macédoine											
Total	C	14 072	13 993	14 172	14 255	13 267	7.0	7.0	7.0	...	6.5
Urban-Urbaine	C	7 902	...	...	7 530	7 584	6.6	...	...	...	...
Rural-Rurale	C	6 170	...	...	6 725	5 683	7.6	...	...	...	...
Ukraine											
Total	C	345 013	310 504	...	...	309 602	6.8	6.1	...	...	6.3
Urban-Urbaine	C	244 041	219 172	...	...	223 638	7.1	6.4	...	...	...
Rural-Rurale	C	100 972	91 332	...	...	85 964	6.2	5.6	...	...	...
United Kingdom - Royaume-Uni											
Total	C	310 218	304 797	301 083	305 912	...	5.3	5.1	5.1	5.1	
OCEANIA — OCEANIE											
Australia - Australie											
Total	+C	106 735	110 598	114 316	113 429	*109 071	5.8	5.9	6.0	5.9	5.6
Cook Islands - Îles Cook											
Total	+C	229	259	*387	...	...	12.5	14.9	23.6	...	
Fiji - Fidji											
Total	+C	...	8 058	...	...	...	...	10.1	...	...	
French Polynesia - Polynésie française											
Total	...	1 176	...	...	...	...	...	...	...	...	
Guam[33]											
Total	C	1 388	1 328	1 426	*1 499	...	8.9	8.9	9.4	9.7	
New Caledonia - Nouvelle-Calédonie											
Total	C	1 005	1 005	943	...	...	5.0	4.9	4.5	...	
New Zealand - Nouvelle-Zélande											
Total	+C	19 953	20 135	21 085	...	...	5.3	5.3	5.5	...	
Samoa											
Total	...	...	...	935	...	...	...	...	...	...	
Tonga											
Total	+C	679	736	770	747	...	6.9	7.4	7.7	7.4	

GENERAL NOTES - NOTES GENERALES

For certain countries, there is a discrepancy between the total number of marriages shown in this table and those shown in subsequent tables for the same year. Usually this discrepancy arises because the total number of marriages that occur in a given year is revised, although the remaining tabulations are not. Rates are the number of legal (recognized) marriages performed and registered per 1 000 mid-year population. Rates are shown only for countries or areas having a total of at least 100 marriages in a given year. For definitions of 'urban', see end of Technical Notes for table 6. For method of evaluation and limitations of data, see Technical Notes for this table. — Pour quelques pays il y a une discordance entre le nombre total des mariages présenté dans ce tableau et ceux présentés pour la même année. Habituellement ces différences apparaîssent lorsque le nombre total des mariages pour une certaine année a été révisé; alors que les autres tabulations ne l'ont pas été. Les taux représentent le nombre de mariages qui ont été célébrés et reconnus par la loi pour 1 000 personnes au milieu de l'année. Les taux présentés ne se rapportent qu'aux pays où zones où l'on a enregistré un total d'au moins 100 mariages dans une année donnée. Pour les définitions des 'régions urbaines', se reporter à la fin des Notes techniques du tableau 6. Pour la méthode d'évaluation et les insuffisances des données, voir Notes techniques, pour ce tableau.

Italics: data from civil registers which are incomplete or of unknown completeness. — *Italiques:* données incomplètes ou dont le degré d'exactitude n'est pas connu, provenant des registres de l'état civil.

FOOTNOTES - NOTES

* Provisional. — Données provisoires.

[1] 'Code' indicates the source of data, as follows:
C - Civil registration, estimated over 90% complete
U - Civil registration, estimated less than 90% complete
+ - Data tabulated by date of registration rather than occurence.
... - Information not available

Le 'Code' indique la source des données, comme suit:
C - Registres de l'état civil considérés complèts à 90 p. 100 au moins.
U - Registres de l'état civil qui ne sont pas considérés complèts à 90 p. 100 au moins.
+ - Données exploitées selon la date de l'enregistrement et non la date de l'événement.
... - Information pas disponible.

[2] For Algerian population only. - Pour la population algérienne seulement.
[3] Including marriages resumed after 'revocable divorce' (among Moslem population), which approximates legal separation. - Y compris les unions

reconstituées après un 'divorce révocable' (parmi la population musulmane), qui est à peu près l'équivalent d'une séparation légale.
  [4] For Libyan nationals only. - Pour les nationaux libyens seulement.
  [5] The difference between 'Total' and the sum of 'urban' and 'rural' is due to the cases of unknown place of residence or residence abroad. - La différence entre le 'Total' et la somme des données selon la résidence urbaine/rurale se rapporte à la situation ou on ignore la résidence ou si la résidence est à l'étranger.
  [6] Excluding tribal Indian population. - Non compris les Indiens vivant en tribus.
  [7] Data for urban and rural areas were not revised, as opposed to data for the whole. - Les données selon la résidence urbaine/rurale n'ont pas été révisées, ce qui a été le cas avec les données pour l'ensemble du pays.
  [8] Excluding Indian jungle population. - Non compris les Indiens de la jungle.
  [9] Excluding nomadic Indian tribes. - Non compris les tribus d'Indiens nomades.
  [10] Data refer to government controlled areas. - Les données se raportent aux zones contrôlées par le Gouvernement.
[11] Published by the United Nations Economic and Social Commission for Western Asia. - Publié par la Commission économique et sociale des Nations Unies pour l'Asie occidentale.
[12] Including data for East Jerusalem and Israeli residents in certain other territories under occupation by Israeli military forces since June 1967. - Y compris les données pour Jérusalem-Est et les résidents israéliens dans certains autres territoires occupés depuis 1967 par les forces armées israéliennes.
[13] For Japanese nationals in Japan only; however, rates computed using total population. - Pour les nationaux japonais au Japon seulement; toutefois, les taux sont calculés sur la base de la population totale.
[14] Excluding data for Jordanian territory under occupation since June 1967 by Israeli military forces. Excluding foreigners, including registered Palestinian refugees. - Non compris les données pour le territoire jordanien occupé depuis juin 1967 par les forces armées israéliennes. Non compris les étrangers, mais y compris les réfugiés de Palestine enregistrés.
[15] Registration of Kandyan marriages is complete; registration of Moslem and general marriages is incomplete. - Tous les mariages des Kandyens sont enregistrés; l'enregistrement des mariages musulmans et des autres mariages est incomplet.
[16] Rates computed on population excluding transients afloat and non-locally domiciled military and civilian services personnel and their dependants. - Taux calculés sur la base d'un chiffre de population qui ne comprend pas les personnes de passage à bord de navires, ni les militaires et agents civils domiciliés hors du territoire et les membres de leur famille les accompagnant.
[17] Figures exclude marriages previously officiated outside Singapore or under religious and customary rites. - Les figures excluent les mariages célébrés précédemment au dehors de Singapoure ou sous les rites réligieuse ou accoutumés.
[18] Excluding nomads. - Non compris les nomades.
[19] Data refer to provincial capitals and district centres only. - Les données se rapportent aux capitales des provinces et les chefs-lieux de districts seulement.
[20] Excluding aliens temporarily in the area. - Non compris les étrangers se trouvant temporairement le territoire.
[21] Including armed forces stationed outside the country, but excluding alien armed forces in the area unless marriage performed by local foreign authority. - Y compris les militaires nationaux hors du pays et les militaires étrangers en garnison sur le territoire, sauf si le mariage a été célébré pour l'autorité locale.
[22] Including Bulgarian nationals outside the country, but excluding aliens in the area. - Y compris les nationaux bulgares à l'étranger, mais non compris les étrangers sur le territoire.

[23] Excluding Faeroe Islands and Greenland. - Non compris les îles Féroé et Gröenland.
[24] Urban and rural distribution of marriages and divorces is displayed by place of residence of groom/husband. The difference between 'Total' and the sum of urban and rural is due to the unknown place of residence of grooms/husbands and to grooms/husbands living outside Estonia. - Les mariages et divorces sont classés par rapport à la résidence urbaine/rurale de l'époux. La somme des mariages et divorces par résidence urbaine/rurale est différente du « total » car elle ne tient pas compte ni des résidences inconnues de l'époux ni des mariages et divorces d'époux vivant à l'étranger.
[25] Marriages in which the bride was resident in Finland only. - Mariages où l'épouse a la résidence en Finlande seulement.
[26] Including armed forces stationed outside the country.- Y compris les militaires nationaux hors du pays.
[27] Rates computed on population excluding armed forces. - Taux calculés sur la base d'un chiffre de population qui ne comprend pas les militaires.
[28] For de jure population. - Pour la population de droit.
[29] Computed on population including civilian nationals temporarily outside the country. - Les taux sont calculés sur la base d'un chiffre de population qui comprend les civils nationaux temporairement hors du pays.
[30] Including residents outside the country if listed in a Netherlands population register. - Y compris les résidents hors du pays, s'ils sont inscrits sur un registre de population néerlandais.
[31] Including same sex marriages. - Y compris les mariages entre personnes du même sexe.
[32] Marriages in which the groom was resident in Norway only. - Mariages où l'époux a la résidence en Norvège seulement.
[33] Including United States military personnel, their dependants and contract employees. - Y compris les militaires des Etats-Unis, les membres de leur famille les accompagnant et les agents contractuels des Etats-Unis.

Table 24

Table 24 presents the marriages by age of groom and age of bride for as many years as possible between 1997 and 2001.

Description of variables: Marriage is defined as the act, ceremony or process by which the legal relationship of husband and wife is constituted[i]. Marriages include both first marriages and remarriages after divorce, widowhood or annulment. They do not, unless otherwise noted, include resumption of marriage ties after legal separation.

Age is defined as age at last birthday, that is, the difference between the date of birth and the date of the occurrence of the event, expressed in completed solar years. The age classification used in this table is the following: under 15 years, 5-year age groups through 70-74, and 75 years and over. The same classification is used for both grooms and brides.

To aid in the interpretation of data this table also provides information on the legal minimum age for marriage for grooms and the corresponding age for brides. Information is not available for all countries and, even for those for which data are at hand, there is confusion as to what is meant by "minimum age for marriage". In some cases, it appears to mean "age below which marriage is not valid without consent of parents or other specified persons"; in others, it is the "age below which valid marriage cannot be performed, irrespective of consent". Beginning in 1986, the countries or areas providing data on marriages by age of bride and groom were requested to specify "the minimum legal age at which marriage with parental consent can occur". The minimum age shown in this table comes primarily from responses to this request.

Reliability of data: Data from civil registers of marriages which are reported as incomplete (less than 90 per cent completeness) or of unknown completeness are considered unreliable and are set in *italics* rather than in roman type. Table 23 and the technical notes for that table provide more detailed information on the completeness of marriage registration. For more information about the quality of vital statistics data in general, see section 4.2 of the Technical Notes.

Limitations: Statistics on marriages by age of groom and age of bride are subject to the same qualifications as have been set forth for vital statistics in general and marriage statistics in particular as discussed in Section 4 of the Technical Notes.

The fact that marriage is a legal event, unlike birth and death that are biological events, has implications for international comparability of data. Marriage has been defined, for statistical purposes, in terms of the laws of individual countries or areas. These laws vary throughout the world. In addition, comparability is further limited because some countries or areas compile statistics only for civil marriages although religious marriages may also be legally recognized; in others, the only available records are church registers and, therefore, the statistics do not reflect to marriages which are civil marriages only.

Because in many countries or areas marriage is a civil legal contract which, to establish its legality, must be celebrated before a civil officer, it follows that for these countries or areas registration would tend to be almost automatic at the time of, or immediately following, the marriage ceremony. This factor should be kept in mind when considering the reliability of data, described above. For this reason the practice of tabulating data by date of registration does not generally pose serious problems of comparability as it does in the case of birth and death statistics.

Because these statistics are classified according to age, they are subject to the limitations with respect to accuracy of age reporting similar to those already discussed in connection with Section 3.1.3 of the Technical Notes. It is probable that biases are less pronounced in marriage statistics, because information is obtained from the persons concerned and since marriage is a legal act, the participants are likely to give correct information. However, in some countries or areas, there appears to be an abnormal concentration of marriages at the legal minimum age for marriage and at the age at which valid marriage may be contracted without parental consent, indicating perhaps an overstatement in some cases to comply with the law.

Aside from the possibility of age misreporting, it should be noted that marriage patterns at younger ages, that is, for ages up to 24 years, are indeed influenced to a large extent by laws regarding the minimum age for marriage. Information on legal minimum age for both grooms and brides is included in this table.

Factors which may influence age reporting, particularly at older ages include an inclination to understate the age of bride in order that it may be equal to or less than that of the groom.

The absence of frequencies in the unknown age group does not necessarily indicate completely accurate reporting and tabulation of the age item. It is sometimes an indication that the unknowns have been eliminated by assigning ages to them before tabulation, or by proportionate distribution after tabulation.

Another age-reporting factor, which must be kept in mind in using these data, is the variation that may result from calculating age at marriage from year of birth rather than from day, month and year of birth. Information on this factor is given in footnotes when known.

Coverage: Marriages by age of groom and age of bride are shown for 90 countries or areas.

Earlier data: Marriages by age of groom and age of bride have been shown for the latest available year in most issues of the *Demographic Yearbook*. In addition, issues, including those featuring marriage and divorce statistics, have presented data covering a period of years. For information on the specific topics and the years covered, readers should consult the Index.

NOTES

[i] *Principles and Recommendations for a Vital Statistics System Revision 2,* Sales No. E. 01.XVII.10, United Nations, New York, 2001

Tableau 24

Le tableau 24 tableau présente des statistiques des mariages classés selon l'âge de l'époux et selon l'âge de l'épouse pour le plus grand nombre possible d'années entre 1997 et 2001.

Description des variables : Le mariage désigne l'acte, la cérémonie ou la procédure qui établit un rapport légal entre mari et femme. L'union peut être rendue légale par une procédure civile ou religieuse ou par toute autre procédure, conformément à la législation du pays[1]. La notion de mariage recouvre les premiers mariages et les remariages faisant suite à un divorce, un veuvage ou une annulation. Toutefois, sauf indication contraire, elle ne comprend pas les unions reconstituées après une séparation légale.

L'âge désigne l'âge au dernier anniversaire, c'est-à-dire la différence entre la date de naissance et la date de l'événement, exprimée en années solaires révolues. Le classement par âge utilisé dans le tableau 24 comprend les groupes suivants: moins de 15 ans, groupes quinquennaux jusqu'à 70 à 74 ans, 75 ans et plus. On a adopté la même classification pour les deux sexes.

Pour faciliter l'interprétation des données, ce tableau indique aussi l'âge minimal légal de nubilité pour le sexe masculin et pour le sexe féminin. On n'a pas à ce sujet de données pour tous les pays et, même lorsqu'on en possède, une certaine confusion subsiste sur ce qu'il faut entendre par "âge minimum du mariage". Dans certains cas, il semble qu'il s'agisse de « l'âge au-dessous duquel le mariage n'est pas valide sans le consentement des parents ou d'autres personnes autorisées »; dans d'autres, ce serait « l'âge au-dessous duquel le mariage ne peut pas être valide, même avec le consentement des personnes responsables ». A partir de 1986, il a été demandé aux pays ou zones qui fournissent des données sur les mariages selon l'âge de l'épouse et de l'époux de préciser l'âge de nubilité, à savoir « l'âge minimum auquel le mariage peut avoir lieu avec le consentement des parents ». Les chiffres d'âge minimum qui apparaissent dans le tableau proviennent principalement de renseignements communiqués en réponse à cette demande.

Fiabilité des données: Les données sur les mariages provenant des registres de l'état civil qui sont déclarés incomplets (degré de complétude inférieur à 90 p. 100) ou dont le degré de complétude n'est pas connu sont jugées douteuses et apparaissent en italique et non en caractères romains. Le tableau 23 et les notes techniques s'y rapportant présentent des renseignements plus détaillés sur le degré de complétude de l'enregistrement des mariages. Pour plus de précisions sur la qualité des données reposant sur les statistiques de l'état civil en général, voir la section 4.2 des notes techniques.

Insuffisance des données : Les statistiques des mariages selon l'âge de l'époux et selon l'âge de l'épouse appellent toutes les réserves qui ont été faites à propos des statistiques de l'état civil en général et des statistiques de la nuptialité en particulier (voir explications à la section 4 des Notes techniques).

Le fait que le mariage soit un acte juridique, à la différence de la naissance et du décès, qui sont des faits biologiques, a des répercussions sur la comparabilité internationale des données. Aux fins de la statistique, le mariage est défini par la législation de chaque pays ou zone. Cette législation varie d'un pays à l'autre. La comparabilité est limitée en outre du fait que certains pays ne réunissent des statistiques que pour les mariages civils, bien que les mariages religieux y soient également reconnus par la loi; dans d'autres, les seuls relevés disponibles sont les registres des églises et, en conséquence, les statistiques ne rendent pas compte des mariages exclusivement civils.

Le mariage étant, dans de nombreux pays ou zones, un contrat juridique civil qui, pour être légal, doit être conclu devant un officier d'état civil, il s'ensuit que, dans ces pays ou zones, l'enregistrement se fait à peu près automatiquement au moment de la cérémonie ou immédiatement après. Il faut tenir compte de cet élément lorsqu'on étudie la fiabilité des données, dont il est question plus haut. C'est pourquoi la pratique consistant à exploiter les données selon la date de l'enregistrement ne pose généralement pas les graves problèmes de comparabilité auxquels on se heurte dans le cas des statistiques des naissances et des décès.

Etant donné que ces statistiques sont classées selon l'âge, elles appellent les mêmes réserves concernant l'exactitude des déclarations d'âge que celles dont il a déjà été fait mention dans la section 3.1.3 des Notes techniques. Il est probable que les statistiques de la nuptialité sont moins faussées par ce genre d'erreur, car les renseignements sont donnés par les intéressés eux-mêmes, et, comme le mariage et un acte juridique, il y a toutes chances pour que leurs déclarations soient exactes. Toutefois, dans certains pays ou zones, il semble y avoir une concentration anormale des mariages à l'âge minimal légal de nubilité ainsi qu'à l'âge auquel le mariage peut être valablement contracté sans le consentement des parents, ce qui peut indiquer que certains déclarants se vieillissent pour se conformer à la loi.

Outre la possibilité d'erreurs dans les déclarations d'âge, il convient de noter que la législation fixant l'âge minimal de nubilité influe notablement sur les caractéristiques de la nuptialité pour les premiers âges, c'est-à-dire jusqu'à 24 ans. Le tableau 24 indique l'âge minimal légal de nubilité pour les époux et les épouses.

Parmi les facteurs pouvant exercer une influence sur les déclarations d'âge, en particulier celles qui sont faites par des personnes plus âgées, il faut citer la tendance à diminuer l'âge de l'épouse de façon qu'il soit égal ou inférieur à celui de l'époux.

Si aucun nombre ne figure dans la colonne réservée aux âges inconnus, cela ne signifie pas nécessairement que les déclarations d'âge et l'exploitation des données par âge aient été tout à fait exactes. C'est parfois une indication que l'on a attribué un âge aux personnes d'âge inconnu avant l'exploitation des données ou que celles-ci ont été réparties proportionnellement entre les différents groupes après cette opération.

Il importe de ne pas oublier non plus, lorsqu'on utilisera ces données, que l'on calcule parfois l'âge des conjoints au moment du mariage sur la base de l'année de naissance seulement et non d'après la date exacte (jour, mois et année) de naissance. Des renseignements à ce sujet sont fournis en note chaque fois que possible.

Portée : Ce tableau présente des statistiques des mariages selon l'âge de l'époux et selon l'âge de l'épouse pour 90 pays ou zones.

Donnés publiées antérieurement: Des statistiques des mariages selon l'âge de l'époux et selon l'âge de l'épouse ont été présentées pour la dernière année disponible dans la plupart des éditions de l'Annuaire démographique. En outre, des éditions, y compris celles dont le sujet spécial était les statistiques de la nuptialité et de la divortialité, ont présenté des données qui portaient sur des périodes d'années. Pour plus de précisions concernant les années pour lesquelles ces données ont été publiées, on se reportera à l'Index.

NOTES

[1] *Principles and Recommendations for a Vital Statistics System Revision 2,* Sales No. E. 01.XVII.10, United Nations, New York, 2001

24. Marriages by age of bridegroom and by age of bride: 1997 - 2001
Mariages selon l'âge de l'époux et selon l'âge de l'épouse: 1997 - 2001

(See notes at end of table. — Voir notes à la fin du tableau.)

Continent, country or area and age / Continent, pays ou zone et âge	1997 Groom Epoux	1997 Bride Epouse	1998 Groom Epoux	1998 Bride Epouse	1999 Groom Epoux	1999 Bride Epouse	2000 Groom Epoux	2000 Bride Epouse	2001 Groom Epoux	2001 Bride Epouse
AFRICA — AFRIQUE										
Egypt - Égypte[+,1]										
Groom — Epoux 18 ⊗										
Bride — Epouse 16 ⊗										
All ages - Tous âges	493 787	493 787	503 651	503 651	525 412	525 412	...	...	...	...
0-19	17 159	64 682	15 724	63 838	14 982	64 422	...	...	...	...
20-24	106 981	141 912	106 970	141 655	115 939	152 234	...	...	...	...
25-29	180 573	136 892	183 211	137 177	192 784	143 382	...	...	...	...
30-34	106 879	120 286	110 462	130 581	111 874	134 280	...	...	...	...
35-39	37 673	13 748	40 594	14 116	42 038	14 515	...	...	...	...
40-44	15 514	7 138	16 337	7 259	16 707	7 500	...	...	...	...
45-49	9 666	4 269	11 067	4 424	11 422	4 447	...	...	...	...
50-54	6 020	2 066	6 152	2 044	6 527	2 185	...	...	...	...
55-59	4 393	1 117	4 412	1 029	4 296	987	...	...	...	...
60-64	3 557	607	3 471	584	3 514	617	...	...	...	...
65-69	2 580	376	2 545	354	2 549	333	...	...	...	...
70-74	1 653	254	1 546	241	1 555	178	...	...	...	...
75+	1 003	306	1 021	345	1 045	329	...	...	...	...
Unknown - Inconnu	136	134	139	4	180	3	...	...	...	...
Mauritius - Maurice[+]										
Groom — Epoux 16 ⊗										
Bride — Epouse 16 ⊗										
All ages - Tous âges	10 887	10 887	10 898	10 898	11 295	11 295	10 963	10 963	...	...
15-19	183	2 594	198	2 522	172	2 442	163	2 054	...	...
20-24	2 148	3 860	2 268	4 110	2 402	4 356	2 243	4 132	...	...
25-29	3 795	1 964	3 741	1 927	3 879	2 009	3 663	2 180	...	...
30-34	2 511	1 148	2 435	1 111	2 405	1 142	2 297	1 148	...	...
35-39	1 021	630	1 068	593	1 115	673	1 152	689	...	...
40-44	528	333	517	298	573	318	631	362	...	...
45-49	306	185	306	194	342	195	381	208	...	...
50-54	149	95	145	76	174	98	172	99	...	...
55-59	122	35	103	32	115	25	136	44	...	...
60-64	55	21	56	18	54	19	66	23	...	...
65-69	39	14	24	5	39	11	26	12	...	...
70-74	20	5	19	8	13	3	17	9	...	...
75+	10	3	18	4	12	4	16	3	...	...
Seychelles										
All ages - Tous âges	...	...	718	718	...	...	...	...	790	790
15-19	...	...	4	26	...	...	...	...	7	26
20-24	...	...	73	121	...	...	...	...	66	136
25-29	...	...	177	208	...	...	...	...	149	198
30-34	...	...	188	176	...	...	...	...	210	196
35-39	...	...	120	100	...	...	...	...	156	103
40-44	...	...	65	33	...	...	...	...	92	62
45-49	...	...	23	24	...	...	...	...	43	35
50-54	...	...	30	11	...	...	...	...	27	19
55+	...	...	38	19	...	...	...	...	40	15
South Africa - Afrique du Sud										
All ages - Tous âges	...	...	146 741	146 741	...	...	...	...	...	...
0-19	...	...	262	2 971	...	...	...	...	...	...
20-24	...	...	13 300	31 036	...	...	...	...	...	...
25-29	...	...	35 387	42 166	...	...	...	...	...	...
30-34	...	...	32 840	27 640	...	...	...	...	...	...
35-39	...	...	22 694	16 720	...	...	...	...	...	...
40-44	...	...	14 501	9 922	...	...	...	...	...	...
45-49	...	...	9 810	6 274	...	...	...	...	...	...
50-54	...	...	6 075	3 563	...	...	...	...	...	...
55-59	...	...	4 400	2 436	...	...	...	...	...	...
60-64	...	...	2 760	1 693	...	...	...	...	...	...
65-69	...	...	2 174	1 049	...	...	...	...	...	...
70-74	...	...	1 297	442	...	...	...	...	...	...
75+	...	...	1 241	829	...	...	...	...	...	...

24. Marriages by age of bridegroom and by age of bride: 1997 - 2001
Mariages selon l'âge de l'époux et selon l'âge de l'épouse: 1997 - 2001 (continued — suite)

(See notes at end of table. — Voir notes à la fin du tableau.)

Continent, country or area and age / Continent, pays ou zone et âge	1997 Groom Epoux	1997 Bride Epouse	1998 Groom Epoux	1998 Bride Epouse	1999 Groom Epoux	1999 Bride Epouse	2000 Groom Epoux	2000 Bride Epouse	2001 Groom Epoux	2001 Bride Epouse
AFRICA — AFRIQUE										
Tunisia - Tunisie										
Groom — Epoux 20 ⊗										
Bride — Epouse 17 ⊗										
All ages - Tous âges	57 861	57 861	56 081	56 081	...	...	...	...	...	...
15-19	-	8 109	-	7 411	...	...	...	...	...	...
20-24	6 671	22 142	5 960	21 217	...	...	...	...	...	...
25-29	19 396	15 691	18 259	15 689	...	...	...	...	...	...
30-34	19 525	6 586	19 332	6 496	...	...	...	...	...	...
35-39	6 340	2 437	6 628	2 515	...	...	...	...	...	...
40-44	2 072	1 194	2 162	1 159	...	...	...	...	...	...
45+	...	880	...	918	...	...	...	...	...	...
45-49	879	...	961	...	...	...	...	...	...	...
50-54	552	...	507	...	...	...	...	...	...	...
55+	1 895	...	1 798	...	...	...	...	...	...	...
Unknown - Inconnu	531	822	474	676	...	...	...	...	...	...
AMERICA, NORTH — AMERIQUE DU NORD										
Belize+										
All ages - Tous âges	1 515	1 515	1 374	1 374	...	...	...	...	...	...
0-14	-	12	-	13	...	...	...	...	...	...
15-19	106	349	97	329	...	...	...	...	...	...
20-24	504	470	443	434	...	...	...	...	...	...
25-29	342	298	332	273	...	...	...	...	...	...
30-34	210	149	198	142	...	...	...	...	...	...
35-39	127	90	99	64	...	...	...	...	...	...
40-44	66	59	62	31	...	...	...	...	...	...
45-49	47	35	41	35	...	...	...	...	...	...
50-54	30	12	25	13	...	...	...	...	...	...
55-59	21	6	21	14	...	...	...	...	...	...
60+	51	22	43	15	...	...	...	...	...	...
Unknown - Inconnu	11	13	13	11	...	...	...	...	...	...
Bermuda - Bermudes										
All ages - Tous âges	...	...	1 033	1 033	...	...	...	...	...	...
15-19	...	...	1	5	...	...	...	...	...	...
20-24	...	...	72	110	...	...	...	...	...	...
25-29	...	...	222	298	...	...	...	...	...	...
30-34	...	...	261	251	...	...	...	...	...	...
35-39	...	...	159	153	...	...	...	...	...	...
40-44	...	...	126	104	...	...	...	...	...	...
45-49	...	...	77	56	...	...	...	...	...	...
50-54	...	...	57	34	...	...	...	...	...	...
55-59	...	...	28	13	...	...	...	...	...	...
60-64	...	...	16	5	...	...	...	...	...	...
65-69	...	...	11	2	...	...	...	...	...	...
70-74	...	...	2	-	...	...	...	...	...	...
75+	...	...	1	2	...	...	...	...	...	...
Canada										
Groom — Epoux 16 ⊗										
Bride — Epouse 16 ⊗										
All ages - Tous âges	153 306	153 306	...	...	...	...	...	...	...	...
0-14	-	1	...	...	...	...	...	...	...	...
15-19	1 213	4 800	...	...	...	...	...	...	...	...
20-24	24 165	38 933	...	...	...	...	...	...	...	...
25-29	48 050	47 314	...	...	...	...	...	...	...	...
30-34	32 000	25 394	...	...	...	...	...	...	...	...
35-39	17 822	14 439	...	...	...	...	...	...	...	...
40-44	10 338	8 662	...	...	...	...	...	...	...	...
45-49	6 971	5 721	...	...	...	...	...	...	...	...
50-54	4 776	3 513	...	...	...	...	...	...	...	...
55-59	2 846	1 785	...	...	...	...	...	...	...	...
60-64	1 846	1 009	...	...	...	...	...	...	...	...
65-69	1 365	795	...	...	...	...	...	...	...	...

24. Marriages by age of bridegroom and by age of bride: 1997 - 2001
Mariages selon l'âge de l'époux et selon l'âge de l'épouse: 1997 - 2001 (continued — suite)

(See notes at end of table. — Voir notes à la fin du tableau.)

Continent, country or area and age / Continent, pays ou zone et âge	1997 Groom Epoux	1997 Bride Epouse	1998 Groom Epoux	1998 Bride Epouse	1999 Groom Epoux	1999 Bride Epouse	2000 Groom Epoux	2000 Bride Epouse	2001 Groom Epoux	2001 Bride Epouse
AMERICA, NORTH — AMERIQUE DU NORD										
Canada										
Groom — Epoux 16 ⊗										
Bride — Epouse 16 ⊗										
70-74	955	563	...	...	...	...	...	...	...	...
75+	877	339	...	...	...	...	...	...	...	...
Unknown - Inconnu	82	38	...	...	...	...	...	...	...	...
Costa Rica										
Groom — Epoux 15 ⊗										
Bride — Epouse 15 ⊗										
All ages - Tous âges	24 300	24 300	...	...	...	...	...	...	...	...
0-14	3	145	...	...	...	...	...	...	...	...
15-19	1 713	6 105	...	...	...	...	...	...	...	...
20-24	7 535	7 590	...	...	...	...	...	...	...	...
25-29	6 544	4 647	...	...	...	...	...	...	...	...
30-34	3 641	2 344	...	...	...	...	...	...	...	...
35-39	1 812	1 303	...	...	...	...	...	...	...	...
40-44	1 044	758	...	...	...	...	...	...	...	...
45-49	582	482	...	...	...	...	...	...	...	...
50+	1 136	580	...	...	...	...	...	...	...	...
Unknown - Inconnu	290	346	...	...	...	...	...	...	...	...
Cuba										
Groom — Epoux 16 ⊗										
Bride — Epouse 14 ⊗										
All ages - Tous âges	60 920	60 920	64 900	64 900	57 252	57 252	57 001	57 001	...	...
0-14	1	396	4	324	2	318	5	282	...	...
15-19	2 293	8 977	1 860	8 423	1 608	7 629	1 509	7 141	...	...
20-24	13 981	16 565	12 826	16 434	10 239	13 212	9 384	12 143	...	...
25-29	15 206	12 895	16 446	14 719	13 724	12 174	13 332	11 956	...	...
30-34	11 021	8 693	12 519	10 099	10 420	8 552	10 127	8 527	...	...
35-39	5 709	4 659	7 532	5 870	6 955	5 802	7 587	6 409	...	...
40-44	3 541	2 856	4 033	3 165	4 021	3 080	4 158	3 398	...	...
45-49	2 797	2 143	3 126	2 233	3 100	2 379	3 139	2 566	...	...
50-54	2 074	1 517	2 236	1 559	2 367	1 653	2 515	1 861	...	...
55-59	1 497	917	1 611	837	1 738	1 040	1 918	1 159	...	...
60-64	1 040	500	1 060	520	1 250	648	1 362	721	...	...
65-69	700	312	660	282	785	320	798	360	...	...
70-74	453	186	435	196	484	213	539	222	...	...
75+	520	208	472	177	507	176	572	202	...	...
Unknown - Inconnu	87	96	80	62	52	56	56	54	...	...
El Salvador[2]										
Groom — Epoux 16 ⊗										
Bride — Epouse 14 ⊗										
All ages - Tous âges	23 561	23 561	25 937	25 937	34 346	34 346	28 275	28 275	...	...
0-14	-	84	-	66	-	105	-	80	...	...
15-19	1 466	4 405	1 469	4 622	1 717	5 613	1 366	4 343	...	...
20-24	7 032	7 649	7 707	8 502	9 792	10 981	7 831	8 997	...	...
25-29	5 811	4 869	6 536	5 530	8 849	7 383	6 999	6 005	...	...
30-34	3 450	2 643	3 756	2 771	5 099	4 126	4 287	3 327	...	...
35-39	1 899	1 421	2 167	1 707	3 001	2 344	2 544	2 034	...	...
40-44	1 253	894	1 333	1 014	1 918	1 384	1 583	1 273	...	...
45-49	796	617	965	693	1 293	972	1 126	890	...	...
50-54	550	401	632	407	897	625	838	526	...	...
55-59	408	196	493	257	660	325	581	361	...	...
60-64	355	174	351	168	456	239	471	207	...	...
65+	533	195	526	196	664	249	649	232	...	...
Unknown - Inconnu	8	13	2	4	...	...	...	...	...	...
Grenada - Grenade										
All ages - Tous âges	497	497	563	563	570	570	616	616	...	...
15-19	1	7	...	8	2	10	2	16	...	...
20-24	36	85	23	82	34	92	44	91	...	...
25-29	113	143	146	162	131	160	132	163	...	...
30-34	130	111	148	132	143	114	149	122	...	...

(See notes at end of table. — Voir notes à la fin du tableau.)

Continent, country or area and age / Continent, pays ou zone et âge	1997		1998		1999		2000		2001	
	Groom Epoux	Bride Epouse	Groom Epoux	Bride Epouse	Groom Epoux	Bride Epouse	Groom Epoux	Bride Epouse	Groom Epoux	Bride Epouse
AMERICA, NORTH — AMERIQUE DU NORD										
Grenada - Grenade										
35-39	85	66	93	80	102	88	112	93	...	...
40-44	50	27	50	38	51	37	70	58	...	...
45-49	21	22	38	26	40	23	50	38	...	...
50-54	23	19	29	14	20	21	18	13	...	...
55-59	12	4	10	4	18	5	14	9	...	...
60-64	10	4	11	6	13	9	13	8	...	...
65+	10	2	13	9	13	8	11	4	...	...
Unknown - Inconnu	6	7	2	2	...	3	1	1	...	...
Guatemala										
Groom — Epoux 16 ⊗										
Bride — Epouse 14 ⊗										
All ages - Tous âges	51 526	51 526	51 709	51 709	60 922	60 922	...	...	...	...
0-14	25	1 317	22	1 258	25	1 414	...	...	...	...
15-19	9 416	19 861	9 346	19 924	10 622	22 362	...	...	...	...
20-24	19 426	14 857	19 495	14 881	22	17 716	...	...	...	...
25-29	9 476	6 172	9 416	6 226	320	7 775	...	...	...	...
30-34	4 516	3 125	4 573	3 102	11 515	3 948	...	...	...	...
35-39	2 611	1 957	2 693	2 012	5 637	2 454	...	...	...	...
40-44	1 758	1 345	1 737	1 372	3 323	1 708	...	...	...	...
45-49	1 253	978	1 240	977	2 171	1 269	...	...	...	...
50-54	858	680	912	649	1 541	862	...	...	...	...
55-59	648	456	699	467	1 166	527	...	...	...	...
60-64	611	330	586	337	852	383	...	...	...	...
65-69	401	191	429	204	697	207	...	...	...	...
70-74	249	90	248	115	443	117	...	...	...	...
75+	168	55	204	76	302	85	...	...	...	...
Unknown - Inconnu	110	112	109	109	224	95	...	...	...	...
Mexico - Mexique+										
Groom — Epoux 17 ⊗										
Bride — Epouse 15 ⊗										
All ages - Tous âges	707 840	707 840	704 456	704 456	743 856	743 856	707 422	707 422	...	...
0-14	617	9 493	571	9 100	432	9 005	684	8 345	...	...
15-19	98 356	218 142	97 762	216 809	100 317	221 571	95 878	208 090	...	...
20-24	277 415	256 777	275 221	255 541	279 710	262 171	257 844	243 353	...	...
25-29	178 417	127 326	182 025	130 411	194 658	142 456	186 990	140 046	...	...
30-34	72 786	45 619	72 583	45 423	79 061	51 580	77 951	51 131	...	...
35-39	31 839	20 869	31 232	19 848	35 831	23 587	34 904	23 276	...	...
40-44	16 517	11 181	15 557	10 383	18 654	12 724	18 056	12 392	...	...
45-49	9 734	6 580	8 826	6 094	10 605	7 475	11 030	7 740	...	...
50+	22 159	11 853	20 679	10 847	24 588	13 287	24 085	13 049	...	...
Panama3										
Groom — Epoux 16 ⊗										
Bride — Epouse 14 ⊗										
All ages - Tous âges	10 357	10 357	10 415	10 415	10 388	10 388	...	...	...	...
0-14	-	40	-	32	-	20	...	...	...	...
15-19	198	907	170	873	192	832	...	...	...	...
20-24	1 929	2 702	1 832	2 775	1 828	2 626	...	...	...	...
25-29	2 928	2 799	3 017	2 793	3 000	2 904	...	...	...	...
30-34	1 951	1 549	1 970	1 511	2 015	1 551	...	...	...	...
35-39	1 080	793	1 075	805	1 146	817	...	...	...	...
40-44	598	441	614	516	...	...	...	...	...	...
40-49					1 099	866	...	...	...	...
45-49	450	365	468	340	...	...	...	...	...	...
50-54	312	237	357	228	...	...	...	...	...	...
50-59					520	383	...	...	...	...
55-59	223	148	259	173	...	...	...	...	...	...
60-64	247	85	252	102	...	...	...	...	...	...
60-69					316	131	...	...	...	...
65-69	104	48	108	68	...	...	...	...	...	...
70+	...	...	...	...	129	34	...	...	...	...
70-74	77	44	77	37	...	...	...	...	...	...

(See notes at end of table. — Voir notes à la fin du tableau.)

Continent, country or area and age / Continent, pays ou zone et âge	1997 Groom Epoux	1997 Bride Epouse	1998 Groom Epoux	1998 Bride Epouse	1999 Groom Epoux	1999 Bride Epouse	2000 Groom Epoux	2000 Bride Epouse	2001 Groom Epoux	2001 Bride Epouse
AMERICA, NORTH — AMERIQUE DU NORD										
Panama[3]										
Groom — Epoux 16 ⊗										
Bride — Epouse 14 ⊗										
75+	105	20	89	22	...	...	...	...	...	...
Unknown - Inconnu	155	179	127	140	143	224	...	...	...	...
Puerto Rico - Porto Rico										
Groom — Epoux 16 ⊗										
Bride — Epouse 14 ⊗										
All ages - Tous âges	31 480	31 480	26 760	26 760	27 255	27 255	25 980	25 980	...	...
0-14	-	182	-	144	-	133	-	117	...	...
15-19	2 600	5 920	2 209	4 862	2 115	4 721	1 921	4 281	...	...
20-24	9 629	9 380	8 285	8 464	8 298	8 420	7 705	8 016	...	...
25-29	7 410	6 290	6 477	5 380	6 538	5 547	6 190	5 378	...	...
30-34	3 891	3 470	3 189	2 764	3 370	2 929	3 298	2 759	...	...
35-39	2 413	2 139	2 014	1 753	2 090	1 897	2 044	1 771	...	...
40-44	1 675	1 450	1 346	1 115	1 416	1 247	1 360	1 245	...	...
45-49	1 244	1 002	976	838	988	851	1 022	874	...	...
50-54	836	678	700	567	808	600	812	621	...	...
55+	1 780	969	1 563	872	1 632	910	1 628	917	...	...
Unknown - Inconnu	2	-	1	1	...	...	-	1	...	...
Saint Kitts and Nevis - Saint-Kitts-et-Nevis+										
All ages - Tous âges	354	354	315	315	...	...	...	...	...	...
15-19	2	5	3	5	...	...	...	...	...	...
20-24	25	45	28	44	...	...	...	...	...	...
25-29	66	106	72	84	...	...	...	...	...	...
30-34	87	83	62	76	...	...	...	...	...	...
35-39	72	55	57	47	...	...	...	...	...	...
40-44	32	21	36	28	...	...	...	...	...	...
45-49	29	17	21	13	...	...	...	...	...	...
50-54	20	12	19	8	...	...	...	...	...	...
55-59	9	7	6	3	...	...	...	...	...	...
60-64	6	1	2	...	...	...	...	...	...	...
65+	5	1	4	3	...	...	...	...	...	...
Unknown - Inconnu	1	1	5	4	...	...	...	...	...	...
Saint Lucia - Sainte-Lucie										
All ages - Tous âges	...	...	509	509	...	...	...	...	...	...
0-14	...	...	-	-	...	...	...	...	...	...
15-19	...	...	3	12	...	...	...	...	...	...
20-24	...	...	55	100	...	...	...	...	...	...
25-29	...	...	134	149	...	...	...	...	...	...
30-34	...	...	109	102	...	...	...	...	...	...
35-39	...	...	91	63	...	...	...	...	...	...
40-44	...	...	46	32	...	...	...	...	...	...
45-49	...	...	19	19	...	...	...	...	...	...
50-54	...	...	20	8	...	...	...	...	...	...
55-59	...	...	7	9	...	...	...	...	...	...
60-64	...	...	9	6	...	...	...	...	...	...
65+	...	...	16	7	...	...	...	...	...	...
Unknown - Inconnu	...	...	-	2	...	...	...	...	...	...
Trinidad and Tobago - Trinité-et-Tobago+										
All ages - Tous âges	7 418	7 418	...	...	...	...	...	...	...	...
0-14	-	15	...	...	...	...	...	...	...	...
15-19	145	954	...	...	...	...	...	...	...	...
20-24	1 464	2 230	...	...	...	...	...	...	...	...
25-29	2 165	1 789	...	...	...	...	...	...	...	...
30-34	1 492	1 082	...	...	...	...	...	*	...	...
35-39	877	587	...	...	...	...	...	...	...	...
40-44	451	313	...	...	...	...	...	...	...	...
45-49	291	188	...	...	...	...	...	...	...	...
50-54	180	110	...	...	...	...	...	...	...	...

24. Marriages by age of bridegroom and by age of bride: 1997 - 2001
Mariages selon l'âge de l'époux et selon l'âge de l'épouse: 1997 - 2001 (continued — suite)

(See notes at end of table. — Voir notes à la fin du tableau.)

Continent, country or area and age / Continent, pays ou zone et âge	1997		1998		1999		2000		2001	
	Groom Epoux	Bride Epouse	Groom Epoux	Bride Epouse	Groom Epoux	Bride Epouse	Groom Epoux	Bride Epouse	Groom Epoux	Bride Epouse
AMERICA, NORTH — AMERIQUE DU NORD										
Trinidad and Tobago - Trinité-et-Tobago+										
55-59	115	68	...	...	...	...	...	...	...	...
60-64	92	38	...	...	...	...	...	...	...	...
65+	144	37	...	...	...	...	...	...	...	...
Unknown - Inconnu	2	7	...	...	...	...	...	...	...	...
AMERICA, SOUTH — AMERIQUE DU SUD										
Brazil - Brésil[4]										
Groom — Epoux 14 ⊗										
Bride — Epouse 12 ⊗										
All ages - Tous âges	...	...	698 614	698 614	...	...	...	...	...	...
0-14	...	...	8	2 024	...	...	...	...	...	...
15-19	...	...	41 022	193 967	...	...	...	...	...	...
20-24	...	...	246 436	239 035	...	...	...	...	...	...
25-29	...	...	206 529	136 968	...	...	...	...	...	...
30-34	...	...	100 957	61 355	...	...	...	...	...	...
35-39	...	...	43 271	27 860	...	...	...	...	...	...
40-44	...	...	20 264	14 510	...	...	...	...	...	...
45-49	...	...	11 748	8 682	...	...	...	...	...	...
50-54	...	...	7 742	5 386	...	...	...	...	...	...
55-59	...	...	5 981	3 621	...	...	...	...	...	...
60-64	...	...	4 703	2 044	...	...	...	...	...	...
65+	...	...	9 266	2 369	...	...	...	...	...	...
Unknown - Inconnu	...	...	687	793	...	...	...	...	...	...
Chile - Chili+										
Groom — Epoux 14 ⊗										
Bride — Epouse 12 ⊗										
All ages - Tous âges	78 077	78 077	73 456	73 456	69 765	69 765	...	...	...	...
0-14	1	259	1	210	2	178	...	...	...	...
15-19	3 477	13 392	3 076	12 042	2 687	10 607	...	...	...	...
20-24	25 943	29 120	22 874	26 043	20 200	23 817	...	...	...	...
25-29	25 978	19 932	24 867	19 772	24 430	19 675	...	...	...	...
30-34	12 296	7 860	11 977	7 832	11 648	7 712	...	...	...	...
35-39	4 527	3 424	4 784	3 468	4 748	3 493	...	...	...	...
40-44	2 055	1 579	2 100	1 558	2 165	1 670	...	...	...	...
45-49	1 068	842	1 037	898	1 067	905	...	...	...	...
50-54	717	596	703	573	743	603	...	...	...	...
55-59	552	378	557	384	547	414	...	...	...	...
60-64	419	277	437	288	443	291	...	...	...	...
65-69	418	203	417	210	417	184	...	...	...	...
70-74	279	123	289	90	288	118	...	...	...	...
75+	347	92	337	88	380	98	...	...	...	...
Ecuador - Équateur[5]										
Groom — Epoux 14 ⊗										
Bride — Epouse 12 ⊗										
All ages - Tous âges	66 967	66 967	69 867	69 867	...	...	...	...	...	...
0-14	15	839	30	884	...	...	...	...	...	...
15-19	8 322	20 216	8 421	20 577	...	...	...	...	...	...
20-24	24 148	23 170	25 480	24 604	...	...	...	...	...	...
25-29	16 751	11 775	17 426	12 250	...	...	...	...	...	...
30-34	8 513	5 276	8 620	5 578	...	...	...	...	...	...
35-39	3 835	2 463	4 176	2 636	...	...	...	...	...	...
40-44	1 972	1 378	2 218	1 426	...	...	...	...	...	...
45-49	1 146	739	1 239	820	...	...	...	...	...	...
50-54	754	434	790	438	...	...	...	...	...	...
55-59	502	260	507	248	...	...	...	...	...	...
60-64	338	178	334	168	...	...	...	...	...	...
65-69	291	116	263	120	...	...	...	...	...	...
70+	380	123	360	106	...	...	...	...	...	...

24. Marriages by age of bridegroom and by age of bride: 1997 - 2001
Mariages selon l'âge de l'époux et selon l'âge de l'épouse: 1997 - 2001 (continued — suite)

(See notes at end of table. — Voir notes à la fin du tableau.)

Continent, country or area and age / Continent, pays ou zone et âge	1997 Groom Epoux	1997 Bride Epouse	1998 Groom Epoux	1998 Bride Epouse	1999 Groom Epoux	1999 Bride Epouse	2000 Groom Epoux	2000 Bride Epouse	2001 Groom Epoux	2001 Bride Epouse
AMERICA, SOUTH — AMERIQUE DU SUD										
Ecuador - Équateur[5]										
Groom — Epoux 14[⊗]										
Bride — Epouse 12[⊗]										
Unknown - Inconnu	-	-	3	12	...	...	...	...	...	...
Suriname+										
All ages - Tous âges	...	...	1 982	1 982	2 257	2 257	2 267	2 267	...	...
0-14	...	...	-	1	-	11	-	2	...	...
15-19	...	...	40	387	32	415	34	378	...	...
20-24	...	...	406	588	441	635	409	586	...	...
25-29	...	...	627	409	642	455	618	459	...	...
30-34	...	...	316	245	412	286	386	327	...	...
35-39	...	...	233	152	246	190	269	207	...	...
40-44	...	...	127	66	150	113	181	130	...	...
45-49	...	...	71	54	118	78	141	63	...	...
50-54	...	...	63	34	75	35	77	55	...	...
55+	...	...	99	46	141	39	152	60	...	...
Uruguay										
Groom — Epoux 14[⊗]										
Bride — Epouse 12[⊗]										
All ages - Tous âges	17 056	17 056	...	...	...	...	13 888	13 888	...	...
0-19	524	2 304	...	...	...	...	360	1 536	...	...
20-24	4 268	5 096	...	...	...	...	2 856	3 752	...	...
25-29	4 860	4 284	...	...	...	...	4 292	3 940	...	...
30-34	2 868	2 136	...	...	...	...	2 524	1 860	...	...
35-39	1 492	1 004	...	...	...	...	1 260	920	...	...
40-49	1 276	1 152	...	...	...	...	1 144	932	...	...
50+	1 768	1 080	...	...	...	...	1 444	940	...	...
Unknown - Inconnu	...	...	...	...	...	...	8	8	...	...
Venezuela[4]										
Groom — Epoux 21[⊗]										
Bride — Epouse 18[⊗]										
All ages - Tous âges	...	...	86 152	86 152	...	...	91 088	91 088	...	...
0-14	...	...	19	1 382	...	...	54	1 061	...	...
15-19	...	...	7 654	21 245	...	...	6 282	18 749	...	...
20-24	...	...	27 401	27 210	...	...	26 750	28 925	...	...
25-29	...	...	23 004	18 039	...	...	25 569	20 833	...	...
30-34	...	...	12 529	8 612	...	...	14 152	10 016	...	...
35-39	...	...	6 507	4 298	...	...	7 488	5 160	...	...
40-44	...	...	3 537	2 252	...	...	4 195	2 781	...	...
45-49	...	...	2 206	1 396	...	...	2 618	1 617	...	...
50-54	...	...	1 226	690	...	...	1 597	862	...	...
55-59	...	...	727	354	...	...	844	440	...	...
60+	...	...	1 342	674	...	...	1 539	644	...	...
ASIA — ASIE										
Armenia - Arménie										
Groom — Epoux 18[⊗]										
Bride — Epouse 17[⊗]										
All ages - Tous âges	12 521	12 521	11 365	11 365	12 459	12 459	10 986	10 986	...	...
15-19	235	3 812	243	3 177	202	3 088	104	1 865	...	...
20-24	4 444	5 933	4 020	5 635	4 460	6 548	3 603	6 349	...	...
25-29	4 434	1 411	4 077	1 413	4 528	1 625	4 342	1 709	...	...
30-34	1 887	512	1 697	423	1 845	473	1 607	404	...	...
35-39	742	333	634	298	710	264	624	222	...	...
40-44	263	221	255	181	257	199	272	177	...	...
45-49	121	111	135	93	130	114	137	112	...	...
50-54	81	45	61	48	99	60	83	63	...	...
55-59	106	49	79	28	67	29	43	21	...	...
60+	208	94	164	69	161	59	171	64	...	...
Azerbaijan - Azerbaïdjan+										
All ages - Tous âges	46 999	46 999	40 851	40 851	37 382	37 382	39 611	39 611	41 861	41 861

(See notes at end of table. — Voir notes à la fin du tableau.)

Continent, country or area and age / Continent, pays ou zone et âge	1997		1998		1999		2000		2001	
	Groom Epoux	Bride Epouse	Groom Epoux	Bride Epouse	Groom Epoux	Bride Epouse	Groom Epoux	Bride Epouse	Groom Epoux	Bride Epouse

ASIA — ASIE

Azerbaijan - Azerbaïdjan+

0-17	50	3 963	38	3 410	22	2 649	11	2 473	15	2 348
18-19	1 387	10 134	1 222	8 553	802	7 417	539	7 331	470	7 661
20-24	12 774	19 981	11 624	17 474	10 172	16 523	10 393	18 010	11 123	19 299
25-29	19 613	7 103	16 272	6 270	15 015	5 977	16 361	6 741	17 230	7 334
30-34	8 242	2 869	7 158	2 495	6 986	2 339	7 721	2 399	8 162	2 656
35-39	2 303	1 558	2 112	1 337	2 144	1 260	2 245	1 378	2 525	1 306
40-44	831	725	818	701	766	674	907	728	952	727
45-49	482	299	396	284	387	252	413	283	404	281
50-54	249	124	255	129	235	108	284	119	276	112
55-59	360	101	285	78	199	47	155	43	136	54
60+	708	142	671	120	654	136	582	106	568	83

Bahrain — Bahreïn
Groom — Epoux 15 ⊗

All ages - Tous âges	3 984	3 984	...	...	3 673	3 673	...	...	...	...
0-14	-	22	...	...	-	32	...	...	...	...
15-19	145	1 145	...	...	99	897	...	...	...	...
20-24	1 358	1 569	...	...	1 176	1 509	...	...	...	...
25-29	1 317	647	...	...	1 198	603	...	...	...	...
30-34	568	305	...	...	543	340	...	...	...	...
35-39	268	181	...	...	278	165	...	...	...	...
40-44	145	66	...	...	162	86	...	...	...	...
45-49	57	29	...	...	83	28	...	...	...	...
50+	125	14	...	...	133	12	...	...	...	...
Unknown - Inconnu	1	6	...	...	1	1	...	...	...	...

Brunei Darussalam - Brunéi Darussalam

All ages - Tous âges	...	...	...	...	...	...	2 184	2 184	...	...
0-14	...	...	...	...	...	...	11	15	...	...
15-19	...	...	...	...	...	...	125	412	...	...
20-24	...	...	...	...	...	...	688	834	...	...
25-29	...	...	...	...	...	...	733	551	...	...
30-34	...	...	...	...	...	...	313	192	...	...
35-39	...	...	...	...	...	...	137	87	...	...
40-44	...	...	...	...	...	...	70	48	...	...
45-49	...	...	...	...	...	...	44	22	...	...
50-54	...	...	...	...	...	...	31	13	...	...
55-59	...	...	...	...	...	...	10	5	...	...
60-64	...	...	...	...	...	...	10	5	...	...
65-69	...	...	...	...	...	...	7	-	...	...
70+	...	...	...	...	...	...	5	-	...	...

China: Hong Kong SAR - Chine: Hong Kong RAS
Groom — Epoux 16 ⊗
Bride — Epouse 12 ⊗

All ages - Tous âges	37 593	37 593	31 673	31 673	31 287	31 287	30 879	30 879	...	...
15-19	279	1 173	295	1 103	250	1 061	232	966	...	...
20-24	4 842	9 898	3 828	8 084	3 519	7 578	3 091	6 728	...	...
25-29	12 566	14 958	10 215	12 350	10 078	12 379	9 997	12 566	...	...
30-34	10 385	6 860	8 404	5 814	8 242	5 965	8 027	6 101	...	...
35-39	4 840	2 304	4 411	2 267	4 534	2 328	4 609	2 489	...	...
40-44	1 805	889	1 912	867	2 029	802	2 047	923	...	...
45-49	942	418	934	415	903	374	1 077	439	...	...
50-54	480	294	486	217	506	223	593	206	...	...
55-59	383	201	309	135	308	150	333	116	...	...
60-64	349	257	311	177	324	165	299	121	...	...
65-69	356	214	266	130	264	146	257	117	...	...
70-74	225	85	161	79	194	87	185	71	...	...
75+	141	42	141	35	136	29	132	36	...	...

China: Macao SAR - Chine: Macao RAS

All ages - Tous âges	1 678	1 678	1 451	1 451	1 367	1 367	1 222	1 222	...	...

24. Marriages by age of bridegroom and by age of bride: 1997 - 2001
Mariages selon l'âge de l'époux et selon l'âge de l'épouse: 1997 - 2001 (continued — suite)

(See notes at end of table. — Voir notes à la fin du tableau.)

Continent, country or area and age / Continent, pays ou zone et âge	1997 Groom Epoux	1997 Bride Epouse	1998 Groom Epoux	1998 Bride Epouse	1999 Groom Epoux	1999 Bride Epouse	2000 Groom Epoux	2000 Bride Epouse	2001 Groom Epoux	2001 Bride Epouse
ASIA — ASIE										
China: Macao SAR - Chine: Macao RAS										
15-19	4	36	11	45	11	54	7	43	...	...
20-24	163	340	162	327	140	267	142	223	...	...
25-29	490	642	477	618	484	613	411	509	...	...
30-34	416	327	390	263	357	224	271	227	...	...
35-39	297	167	228	91	200	110	175	102	...	...
40-44	159	98	82	58	73	43	99	54	...	...
45-49	74	36	42	16	28	18	42	20	...	...
50-54	33	18	19	14	26	10	24	11	...	...
55-59	11	5	14	5	8	4	13	9	...	...
60-64	15	3	5	7	13	10	9	8	...	...
65-69	6	2	8	5	8	9	11	10	...	...
70+	10	4	...	...	...	...	...	...	...	...
70-74	...	...	10	2	12	4	13	6	...	...
75+	...	...	3	-	7	1	5	-	...	...
Cyprus - Chypre[6]										
Groom — Epoux •										
Bride — Epouse •										
All ages - Tous âges	7 187	7 187	7 738	7 738	9 080	9 080	9 282	9 282	...	...
15-19	49	552	66	572	69	630	84	572	...	...
20-24	1 462	2 516	1 476	2 494	1 632	2 883	1 479	2 627	...	...
25-29	2 570	2 143	2 582	2 380	3 150	2 844	3 087	2 974	...	...
30-34	1 456	951	1 643	1 075	1 924	1 328	2 091	1 505	...	...
35-39	706	457	829	516	1 013	637	1 033	696	...	...
40-44	335	222	403	283	477	324	541	390	...	...
45-49	225	159	277	156	316	194	372	250	...	...
50-54	150	94	172	126	221	139	260	148	...	...
55-59	90	40	90	51	109	48	133	62	...	...
60+	134	40	169	54	166	53	194	50	...	...
Unknown - Inconnu	10	13	31	31	3	...	8	8	...	...
Georgia - Géorgie										
All ages - Tous âges	...	...	...	...	...	...	12 870	12 870	...	...
0-15	...	...	...	...	...	...	3	233	...	...
16-19	...	...	...	...	...	...	747	2 582	...	...
20-24	...	...	...	...	...	...	4 055	5 200	...	...
25-29	...	...	...	...	...	...	3 459	2 505	...	...
30-34	...	...	...	...	...	...	2 152	1 059	...	...
35-39	...	...	...	...	...	...	1 141	580	...	...
40-44	...	...	...	...	...	...	551	291	...	...
45-49	...	...	...	...	...	...	272	165	...	...
50-54	...	...	...	...	...	...	173	99	...	...
55-59	...	...	...	...	...	...	71	41	...	...
60+	...	...	...	...	...	...	241	108	...	...
Unknown - Inconnu	...	...	...	...	...	...	5	7	...	...
Israel - Israël[7]										
Groom — Epoux ≡										
Bride — Epouse 17 ⊗										
All ages - Tous âges	37 611	37 611	40 137	40 137	40 236	40 236	...	...	...	...
0-19	1 143	7 015	1 241	7 463	1 305	7 337	...	...	...	...
20-24	11 919	17 037	12 572	17 704	12 066	17 335	...	...	...	...
25-29	15 197	9 153	16 667	10 499	16 469	10 556	...	...	...	...
30-34	5 208	2 221	5 575	2 420	5 873	2 542	...	...	...	...
35-39	1 811	860	1 956	933	1 994	960	...	...	...	...
40-44	787	394	853	473	895	480	...	...	...	...
45-49	430	245	438	241	502	299	...	...	...	...
50-54	255	139	268	137	306	139	...	...	...	...
55-59	156	64	162	90	188	85	...	...	...	...
60-64	131	68	120	51	139	65	...	...	...	...
65-69	118	55	109	53	101	58	...	...	...	...
70-74	103	71	72	29	96	38	...	...	...	...
75+	191	142	73	12	80	19	...	...	...	...
Unknown - Inconnu	162	147	31	32	222	323	...	...	...	...

(See notes at end of table. — Voir notes à la fin du tableau.)

Continent, country or area and age / Continent, pays ou zone et âge	1997		1998		1999		2000		2001	
	Groom Epoux	Bride Epouse	Groom Epoux	Bride Epouse	Groom Epoux	Bride Epouse	Groom Epoux	Bride Epouse	Groom Epoux	Bride Epouse
ASIA — ASIE										
Japan - Japon[+,8]										
Groom — Epoux 18 ⊗										
Bride — Epouse 18 ⊗										
All ages - Tous âges	698 857	698 857	709 087	709 087	685 626	685 626	708 159	708 159	...	...
0-19	9 207	19 128	9 972	20 181	9 836	20 075	10 772	21 607	...	...
20-24	132 917	213 468	130 922	204 356	120 702	184 703	119 706	179 410	...	...
25-29	296 961	318 239	301 426	326 866	290 946	318 464	296 363	326 418	...	...
30-34	147 140	91 438	151 013	98 603	148 177	102 291	155 381	113 693	...	...
35-39	56 405	27 023	57 959	28 917	57 572	30 029	62 382	34 542	...	...
40-44	23 128	10 553	23 274	10 759	23 290	10 785	24 912	11 800	...	...
45-49	15 755	9 117	15 363	8 685	14 587	7 907	15 031	7 858	...	...
50-54	7 671	4 861	8 739	5 519	9 394	5 760	11 179	6 564	...	...
55-59	4 861	2 856	5 274	2 968	5 576	3 150	6 221	3 430	...	...
60-64	2 539	1 323	2 721	1 326	2 889	1 462	3 229	1 669	...	...
65-69	1 252	536	1 403	582	1 471	631	1 608	743	...	...
70-74	582	196	594	214	712	251	828	286	...	...
75+	427	111	418	102	468	114	541	137	...	...
Unknown - Inconnu	12	8	9	9	6	4	6	2	...	...
Jordan - Jordanie[9]										
Groom — Epoux 18 ⊗										
Bride — Epouse 16 ⊗										
All ages - Tous âges	37 278	37 278	...	...	39 443	39 443	...	...	...	...
0-14	-	22	...	...	5	36	...	...	...	...
15-19	1 337	13 412	...	...	1 095	12 991	...	...	...	...
20-24	11 250	14 480	...	...	10 920	15 789	...	...	...	...
25-29	14 457	5 996	...	...	15 384	6 517	...	...	...	...
30-34	5 727	2 004	...	...	6 781	2 414	...	...	...	...
35-39	1 895	767	...	...	2 378	990	...	...	...	...
40-44	890	322	...	...	1 017	414	...	...	...	...
45-49	524	148	...	...	621	163	...	...	...	...
50+	...	...	...	...	...	129	...	...	...	...
50-54	368	74	...	...	361	...	...	...	...	...
55-59	321	25	...	...	345	...	...	...	...	...
60-64	209	18	...	...	231	...	...	...	...	...
65+	...	...	...	...	305	...	...	...	...	...
65-69	150	3	...	...	...	...	...	...	...	...
70-74	83	3	...	...	...	...	...	...	...	...
75+	67	4	...	...	...	...	...	...	...	...
Kazakhstan										
Groom — Epoux 18 ⊗										
Bride — Epouse 17 ⊗										
All ages - Tous âges	101 874	101 874	96 048	96 048	85 872	85 872	...	...	...	...
0-14	-	2	-	1	1	1	...	...	...	...
15-19	6 053	26 531	5 424	22 697	4 214	18 629	...	...	...	...
20-24	45 757	45 493	40 346	43 521	36 288	40 975	...	...	...	...
25-29	26 982	14 156	27 195	14 577	25 026	13 429	...	...	...	...
30-34	9 691	5 739	9 857	5 602	9 047	4 960	...	...	...	...
35-39	5 125	3 596	5 098	3 623	4 372	2 849	...	...	...	...
40-44	2 632	2 034	2 573	1 898	2 391	1 641	...	...	...	...
45-49	1 753	1 459	1 824	1 455	1 409	1 136	...	...	...	...
50-54	802	708	942	733	854	751	...	...	...	...
55-59	1 138	901	906	743	590	467	...	...	...	...
60+	1 926	1 240	1 876	1 182	1 660	1 015	...	...	...	...
Unknown - Inconnu	15	15	7	16	20	19	...	...	...	...
Korea (Republic of) - Corée République de)[+]										
Groom — Epoux 18 ⊗										
Bride — Epouse 16 ⊗										
All ages - Tous âges	310 536	310 536	306 853	306 853	362 673	362 673	334 030	334 030	...	...
0-14	1	1	-	3	11	83	1	65	...	...
15-19	736	4 448	663	4 119	2 340	9 301	2 096	8 255	...	...
20-24	28 059	109 882	23 830	94 903	28 989	99 688	25 062	86 319	...	...
25-29	177 926	154 272	169 404	157 722	182 337	178 029	163 203	164 887	...	...

(See notes at end of table. — Voir notes à la fin du tableau.)

Continent, country or area and age / Continent, pays ou zone et âge	1997		1998		1999		2000		2001	
	Groom Epoux	Bride Epouse	Groom Epoux	Bride Epouse	Groom Epoux	Bride Epouse	Groom Epoux	Bride Epouse	Groom Epoux	Bride Epouse
ASIA — ASIE										
Korea (Republic of) - Corée (République de)+										
Groom — Epoux 18 ⊗										
Bride — Epouse 16 ⊗										
30-34	70 744	22 181	74 165	25 718	91 889	36 928	89 551	38 294	...	...
35-39	17 152	9 827	19 329	11 601	26 929	18 206	25 481	16 924	...	...
40-44	6 878	5 031	8 354	6 594	13 272	10 602	12 791	10 131	...	...
45-49	3 764	2 490	4 452	3 081	6 835	4 960	6 731	4 921	...	...
50-54	2 278	1 249	2 817	1 609	4 332	2 566	4 155	2 303	...	...
55+	2 903	1 069	3 720	1 423	5 590	2 247	4 959	1 931	...	...
Unknown - Inconnu	95	86	119	80	149	63	...	...		
Kuwait - Koweït										
All ages - Tous âges	...	...	...	...	...	...	10 785	10 785	...	...
15-19	...	...	...	...	...	...	416	2 832	...	...
20-24	...	...	...	...	...	...	3 806	3 941	...	...
25-29	...	...	...	...	...	...	3 096	1 931	...	...
30-34	...	...	...	...	...	...	1 596	1 021	...	...
35-44	...	...	...	...	...	...	1 320	894	...	...
45+	...	...	...	...	...	...	551	166	...	...
Kyrgyzstan - Kirghizistan										
Groom — Epoux 18 ⊗										
Bride — Epouse 18 ⊗										
All ages - Tous âges	26 588	26 588	25 726	25 726	26 033	26 033	24 294	24 294	...	...
15-19	1 226	8 795	999	7 709	833	7 010	760	6 417	...	...
20-24	12 795	12 401	11 759	12 276	11 019	12 585	9 966	11 863	...	...
25-29	8 217	2 878	8 355	3 124	8 950	3 565	8 587	3 353	...	...
30-34	2 063	969	2 227	1 100	2 603	1 144	2 543	1 149	...	...
35-39	854	582	944	592	1 033	682	963	585	...	...
40-44	472	313	518	328	522	384	560	349	...	...
45-49	301	229	284	212	351	241	265	188	...	...
50-54	134	108	150	107	204	158	209	146	...	...
55-59	201	126	161	100	150	66	93	65	...	...
60-64	136	76	139	77	167	111	150	94	...	...
65-69	107	60	77	38	94	43	86	37	...	...
70-74	50	34	65	39	72	28	77	31	...	...
75+	32	13	45	19	32	15	35	17	...	...
Unknown - Inconnu	-	4	3	5	3	1	...	...		
Mongolia - Mongolie										
All ages - Tous âges	14 421	14 421	...	...	...	...	...	...		
0-17	29	193	...	...	...	...	...	...		
18-19	518	1 468	...	...	...	...	...	...		
20-24	6 593	7 474	...	...	...	...	...	...		
25-29	4 910	3 656	...	...	...	...	...	...		
30-34	1 506	992	...	...	...	...	...	...		
35-39	559	422	...	...	...	...	...	...		
40-44	169	125	...	...	...	...	...	...		
45-49	75	58	...	...	...	...	...	...		
50+	62	33	...	...	...	...	...	...		
Occupied Palestinian Territory - Territoire palestinien occupé										
All ages - Tous âges	...	...	24 400	24 400	24 874	24 874	23 890	23 890	...	...
0-14	...	...	-	346	5	743	1	682	...	...
15-19	...	...	2 629	14 310	2 363	13 817	2 332	13 163	...	...
20-24	...	...	10 485	6 399	10 705	6 816	9 961	6 641	...	...
25-29	...	...	7 000	1 915	7 280	1 965	7 190	1 991	...	...
30-34	...	...	2 116	776	2 234	818	2 207	757	...	...
35-39	...	...	774	393	850	426	799	401	...	...
40-44	...	...	399	173	400	175	443	165	...	...
45-49	...	...	267	52	293	69	264	54	...	...
50-54	...	...	200	18	216	19	206	22	...	...
55+	...	...	530	16	526	23	...	...	...	...
55-59	...	...	...	...	...	...	176	10	...	...
60-64	...	...	...	...	...	...	119	3	...	...

(See notes at end of table. — Voir notes à la fin du tableau.)

Continent, country or area and age / Continent, pays ou zone et âge	1997 Groom Epoux	1997 Bride Epouse	1998 Groom Epoux	1998 Bride Epouse	1999 Groom Epoux	1999 Bride Epouse	2000 Groom Epoux	2000 Bride Epouse	2001 Groom Epoux	2001 Bride Epouse
ASIA — ASIE										
Occupied Palestinian Territory - Territoire palestinien occupé										
65-69	...	...	...	...	...	...	91	1	...	...
70-74	...	...	...	...	...	...	55	...	...	...
75+	...	...	...	...	...	...	45	...	...	...
Unknown - Inconnu	...	...	-	2	2	3	1	...	...	...
Philippines										
All ages - Tous âges	...	...	549 265	549 265	...	...	...	...	...	...
0-19	...	...	23 982	86 200	...	...	...	...	...	...
20-24	...	...	176 179	212 909	...	...	...	...	...	...
25-29	...	...	179 105	139 749	...	...	...	...	...	...
30-34	...	...	84 409	56 587	...	...	...	...	...	...
35-39	...	...	38 033	25 738	...	...	...	...	...	...
40-44	...	...	18 937	12 666	...	...	...	...	...	...
45-49	...	...	10 832	6 542	...	...	...	...	...	...
50+	...	...	17 542	8 607	...	...	...	...	...	...
Unknown - Inconnu	...	...	246	267	...	...	...	...	...	...
Qatar										
All ages - Tous âges	1 766	1 766	...	...	1 905	1 905	...	...	...	...
0-19	60	399	...	...	54	382	...	...	...	...
20-24	466	769	...	...	514	815	...	...	...	...
25-29	704	379	...	...	726	419	...	...	...	...
30-34	303	122	...	...	315	179	...	...	...	...
35-39	114	62	...	...	162	67	...	...	...	...
40-44	60	26	...	...	51	30	...	...	...	...
45-49	23	6	...	...	38	5	...	...	...	...
50-54	20	1	...	...	12	5	...	...	...	...
55-59	9	-	...	...	14	3	...	...	...	...
60-64	4	2	...	...	11	-	...	...	...	...
65-69	1	-	...	...	4	-	...	...	...	...
70-74	2	-	...	...	3	-	...	...	...	...
75+	-	-	...	...	1	-	...	...	...	...
Singapore - Singapour[10,11]										
Groom — Epoux 18 ⊗										
Bride — Epouse 18 ⊗										
All ages - Tous âges	25 667	25 667	23 106	23 106	22 561	22 561	...	...	...	...
0-14	1	...	-	1	...	...	...	...	...	...
15-19	126	784	136	934	188	883	...	...	...	...
20-24	3 726	8 850	2 978	7 366	2 577	6 486	...	...	...	...
25-29	10 978	10 281	9 813	9 453	9 504	9 648	...	...	...	...
30-34	5 929	3 396	5 321	3 105	5 144	3 125	...	...	...	...
35-39	2 754	1 358	2 558	1 295	2 563	1 330	...	...	...	...
40-44	1 168	589	1 237	555	1 367	645	...	...	...	...
45-49	528	256	528	256	641	270	...	...	...	...
50-54	218	93	251	93	295	109	...	...	...	...
55-59	120	31	160	25	132	33	...	...	...	...
60+	119	29	124	23	150	32	...	...	...	...
Turkey - Turquie[+,12]										
Groom — Epoux 17 ⊗										
Bride — Epouse 15 ⊗										
All ages - Tous âges	518 856	518 856	485 035	485 035	475 613	475 613	...	...	...	...
0-14	-	1 526	-	1 283	-	1 044	...	...	...	...
15-19	28 883	156 350	25 768	144 015	23 958	134 599	...	...	...	...
20-24	194 867	222 340	181 810	209 339	166 893	202 235	...	...	...	...
25-29	191 934	85 193	182 760	81 863	190 673	89 314	...	...	...	...
30-34	59 610	28 951	54 082	25 967	53 441	25 684	...	...	...	...
35-39	19 056	11 272	17 640	10 783	18 481	11 481	...	...	...	...
40-44	9 084	6 333	8 027	5 063	7 733	4 833	...	...	...	...
45-49	4 460	2 744	4 634	2 580	4 406	2 680	...	...	...	...
50-54	2 956	1 505	3 303	1 407	2 737	1 384	...	...	...	...
55-59	2 593	1 092	2 615	1 122	2 165	939	...	...	...	...
60+	5 413	1 550	4 396	1 613	5 126	1 420	...	...	...	...

24. Marriages by age of bridegroom and by age of bride: 1997 - 2001
Mariages selon l'âge de l'époux et selon l'âge de l'épouse: 1997 - 2001 (continued — suite)

(See notes at end of table. — Voir notes à la fin du tableau.)

Continent, country or area and age / Continent, pays ou zone et âge	1997 Groom Epoux	1997 Bride Epouse	1998 Groom Epoux	1998 Bride Epouse	1999 Groom Epoux	1999 Bride Epouse	2000 Groom Epoux	2000 Bride Epouse	2001 Groom Epoux	2001 Bride Epouse
ASIA — ASIE										
Uzbekistan - Ouzbékistan										
Groom — Epoux 17 ⊗										
Bride — Epouse 17 ⊗										
All ages - Tous âges	181 126	181 126	...	...	170 525	170 525	168 908	168 908	...	...
0-17	230	12 689	...	...	183	10 847	158	9 606	...	...
18-19	14 016	69 225	...	...	12 058	61 917	8 625	52 422	...	...
20-24	115 380	77 416	...	...	106 637	77 044	102 113	84 289	...	...
25-29	36 226	12 444	...	...	36 733	12 092	41 332	13 386	...	...
30-34	6 866	4 184	...	...	7 074	4 026	8 139	4 351	...	...
35-39	3 389	2 363	...	...	3 114	2 077	3 369	2 103	...	...
40-44	1 758	1 035	...	...	1 645	932	1 911	1 134	...	...
45-49	1 123	638	...	...	1 101	556	1 118	626	...	...
50-54	471	318	...	...	536	363	684	440	...	...
55-59	680	362	...	...	581	278	454	194	...	...
60+	986	451	...	...	863	393	1 005	354	...	...
Unknown - Inconnu	1	1	...	...	-	-	-	3	...	...
EUROPE										
Austria - Autriche										
Groom — Epoux 18 ⊗										
Bride — Epouse 16 ⊗										
All ages - Tous âges	41 394	41 394	39 143	39 143	39 485	39 485	39 228	39 228	34 213	34 213
15-19	430	1 704	363	1 540	398	1 469	360	1 507	389	1 334
20-24	5 527	10 423	4 861	9 458	4 597	8 840	4 386	8 227	3 852	7 261
25-29	13 882	13 996	12 642	13 008	11 600	12 528	11 118	12 369	9 019	10 063
30-34	10 222	7 619	10 069	7 473	10 388	7 857	10 346	8 071	8 795	7 063
35-39	4 827	3 459	4 772	3 409	5 239	3 870	5 579	4 103	5 118	3 740
40-44	2 290	1 740	2 314	1 839	2 628	2 068	2 872	2 248	2 704	2 151
45-49	1 497	1 137	1 405	1 063	1 534	1 284	1 610	1 234	1 527	1 233
50-54	1 147	689	1 185	721	1 238	795	1 191	785	1 148	740
55-59	888	425	901	423	1 014	524	951	424	823	365
60-64	278	103	276	108	414	127	446	157	478	165
65-69	207	48	145	67	194	70	176	55	169	46
70-74	102	38	128	19	127	34	100	30	94	30
75+	97	13	82	15	114	19	93	18	97	22
Belarus - Bélarus										
Groom — Epoux 18 ⊗										
Bride — Epouse 18 ⊗										
All ages - Tous âges	69 735	69 735	71 354	71 354	72 994	72 994	...	...	...	...
0-14	231	2 676	...	...	...	...	...	...	...	...
0-17	...	...	194	2 352	207	2 234	...	...	...	...
15-19	2 937	14 001	...	...	...	...	...	...	...	...
18-19	...	...	2 849	13 482	2 821	13 130	...	...	...	...
20-24	32 781	28 781	32 853	30 106	32 986	31 399	...	...	...	...
25-29	15 723	10 104	16 415	10 810	17 337	11 159	...	...	...	...
30-34	6 645	5 003	7 084	5 192	7 097	5 164	...	...	...	...
35-39	4 249	3 336	4 419	3 383	4 611	3 527	...	...	...	...
40-44	2 436	2 040	2 652	2 122	2 837	2 325	...	...	...	...
45-49	1 606	1 410	1 732	1 474	1 768	1 496	...	...	...	...
50-54	820	651	923	815	1 114	942	...	...	...	...
55-59	850	691	781	619	694	560	...	...	...	...
60+	1 457	1 042	1 452	999	1 522	1 058	...	...	...	...
Unknown - Inconnu	-	...	...	...	...	...	...	...	...	...
Belgium - Belgique[13]										
Groom — Epoux 18 ⊗										
Bride — Epouse 15 ⊗										
All ages - Tous âges	...	...	...	...	...	...	45 123	45 123	...	...
15-19	...	...	...	...	...	...	217	1 410	...	...
20-24	...	...	...	...	...	...	6 944	13 112	...	...
25-29	...	...	...	...	...	...	16 216	14 485	...	...
30-34	...	...	...	...	...	...	8 374	6 169	...	...
35-39	...	...	...	...	...	...	4 795	3 702	...	...

24. Marriages by age of bridegroom and by age of bride: 1997 - 2001
Mariages selon l'âge de l'époux et selon l'âge de l'épouse: 1997 - 2001 (continued — suite)

(See notes at end of table. — Voir notes à la fin du tableau.)

Continent, country or area and age / Continent, pays ou zone et âge	1997 Groom Epoux	1997 Bride Epouse	1998 Groom Epoux	1998 Bride Epouse	1999 Groom Epoux	1999 Bride Epouse	2000 Groom Epoux	2000 Bride Epouse	2001 Groom Epoux	2001 Bride Epouse
EUROPE										
Belgium - Belgique[13]										
Groom — Epoux 18 ⊗										
Bride — Epouse 15 ⊗										
40-44	...	...	...	...	...	...	2 963	2 556	...	...
45-49	...	...	...	...	...	...	2 138	1 805	...	...
50-54	...	...	...	...	...	...	1 599	1 065	...	...
55-59	...	...	...	...	...	...	831	437	...	...
60-64	...	...	...	...	...	...	494	195	...	...
65-69	...	...	...	...	...	...	255	106	...	...
70-74	...	...	...	...	...	...	159	45	...	...
75+	...	...	...	...	...	...	138	36	...	...
Bulgaria - Bulgarie[14]										
Groom — Epoux 18 ⊗										
Bride — Epouse 18 ⊗										
All ages - Tous âges	34 772	34 772	...	...	...	...	35 164	35 164	31 974	31 974
0-14	29	1 299	...	...	...	...	...	...	...	...
15-19	818	5 900	...	...	...	...	...	...	...	...
16-17	...	...	...	...	...	...	15	745	...	...
16-19	...	...	...	...	...	...	...	...	473	3 523
18-19	...	...	...	...	...	...	518	4 312	...	...
20-24	13 354	16 327	...	...	...	...	9 941	14 706	8 292	13 287
25-29	11 647	6 477	...	...	...	...	12 931	8 896	12 363	8 848
30-34	4 066	2 076	...	...	...	...	5 431	2 733	5 387	2 654
35-39	1 974	1 086	...	...	...	...	2 330	1 296	2 128	1 068
40-44	1 143	658	...	...	...	...	1 286	835	1 147	690
45-49	695	419	...	...	...	...	929	595	748	469
50-54	394	217	...	...	...	...	603	383	528	360
55-59	238	136	...	...	...	...	330	212	320	194
60-64	180	74	...	...	...	...	297	173	209	134
65-69	109	61	...	...	...	...	229	129	180	87
70-74	63	32	...	...	...	...	176	100	98	33
75+	62	10	...	...	...	...	148	49	101	31
Croatia - Croatie										
Groom — Epoux 16 ⊗										
Bride — Epouse 16 ⊗										
All ages - Tous âges	24 517	24 517	24 243	24 243	...	...	22 017	22 017	22 076	22 076
15-19	272	3 116	239	3 006	...	...	205	2 438	224	2 456
20-24	6 559	9 974	6 357	9 737	...	...	5 289	8 667	5 251	8 414
25-29	9 108	6 454	9 101	6 528	...	...	8 475	6 355	8 529	6 558
30-34	4 406	2 344	4 421	2 417	...	...	4 150	2 205	4 117	2 230
35-39	1 690	995	1 698	984	...	...	1 717	906	1 677	907
40-44	849	540	808	526	...	...	774	492	781	478
45-49	535	375	543	351	...	...	465	346	459	329
50-54	304	186	278	195	...	...	278	217	309	265
55-59	213	167	225	172	...	...	190	135	196	170
60-64	182	146	198	117	...	...	154	108	157	136
65-69	150	69	152	88	...	...	137	76	145	79
70-74	87	36	87	36	...	...	103	41	127	28
75+	77	12	83	21	...	...	72	10	94	14
Unknown - Inconnu	85	103	53	65	...	...	8	21	10	12
Czech Republic - République tchèque										
Groom — Epoux 16 ⊗										
Bride — Epouse 16 ⊗										
All ages - Tous âges	57 804	57 804	55 027	55 027	53 523	53 523	55 321	55 321	52 374	52 374
15-19	1 591	6 696	1 200	5 269	913	4 037	701	3 014	482	2 404
20-24	21 352	27 777	19 031	26 628	16 183	24 214	14 462	23 523	11 569	19 971
25-29	15 875	10 726	16 787	11 568	17 987	13 484	20 368	16 164	20 343	17 486
30-34	7 094	4 123	6 911	3 930	7 041	4 061	7 732	4 497	8 195	4 717
35-39	3 397	2 256	3 328	2 099	3 443	2 125	3 834	2 375	4 053	2 356
40-44	2 691	2 137	2 494	1 901	2 355	1 810	2 356	1 845	2 234	1 699
45-49	2 281	1 908	2 061	1 662	2 038	1 713	2 220	1 786	1 973	1 662
50-54	1 657	1 236	1 466	1 123	1 675	1 162	1 668	1 145	1 651	1 144

623

24. Marriages by age of bridegroom and by age of bride: 1997 - 2001
Mariages selon l'âge de l'époux et selon l'âge de l'épouse: 1997 - 2001 (continued — suite)

(See notes at end of table. — Voir notes à la fin du tableau.)

Continent, country or area and age / Continent, pays ou zone et âge	1997 Groom Epoux	1997 Bride Epouse	1998 Groom Epoux	1998 Bride Epouse	1999 Groom Epoux	1999 Bride Epouse	2000 Groom Epoux	2000 Bride Epouse	2001 Groom Epoux	2001 Bride Epouse
EUROPE										
Czech Republic - République tchèque										
Groom — Epoux 16 ⊗										
Bride — Epouse 16 ⊗										
55-59	806	495	784	424	901	474	1 014	563	929	560
60-64	480	212	388	212	430	212	443	206	444	189
65-69	292	142	281	122	285	125	266	116	227	85
70-74	166	69	157	61	142	67	142	55	129	61
75+	122	27	139	28	130	39	115	32	145	40
Denmark - Danemark[15]										
Groom — Epoux 18 ⊗										
Bride — Epouse 15 ⊗										
All ages - Tous âges	34 244	34 244	34 733	34 733	...	...	38 388	38 388	...	...
0-14	...	...	-	1	...	...	...	...	...	...
0-19	136	494	...	...	...	...	...	...	...	...
15-19	...	...	106	467	...	...	203	753	...	...
20-24	2 065	4 396	1 907	4 178	...	...	2 195	4 458	...	...
25-29	9 292	10 683	9 138	10 712	...	...	9 821	12 002	...	...
30-34	8 372	7 311	8 593	7 321	...	...	9 214	7 922	...	...
35-39	4 797	3 708	5 051	3 932	...	...	5 988	4 593	...	...
40-44	2 929	2 258	3 008	2 446	...	...	3 326	2 749	...	...
45-49	2 070	1 650	2 102	1 652	...	...	2 360	1 810	...	...
50-54	1 634	1 184	1 723	1 231	...	...	1 825	1 363	...	...
55-59	863	509	964	555	...	...	1 203	732	...	...
60-64	425	243	466	282	...	...	582	328	...	...
65-69	237	124	228	144	...	...	272	171	...	...
70+	205	110	...	...	...	...	...	...	...	...
70-74	...	...	128	77	...	...	131	72	...	...
75+	...	...	115	61	...	...	117	54	...	...
Unknown - Inconnu	1 219	1 574	1 204	1 674	...	...	1 151	1 381	...	...
Estonia - Estonie										
Groom — Epoux 18 ⊗										
Bride — Epouse 18 ⊗										
All ages - Tous âges	5 589	5 589	...	...	...	...	5 485	5 485	...	...
15-19	194	723	...	...	...	...	110	492	...	...
20-24	1 647	1 938	...	...	...	...	1 293	1 773	...	...
25-29	1 457	1 095	...	...	...	...	1 569	1 327	...	...
30-34	667	535	...	...	...	...	898	672	...	...
35-39	473	408	...	...	...	...	472	375	...	...
40-44	334	277	...	...	...	...	382	264	...	...
45-49	269	239	...	...	...	...	255	233	...	...
50-54	174	139	...	...	...	...	191	155	...	...
55-59	160	99	...	...	...	...	116	67	...	...
60-64	86	57	...	...	...	...	88	66	...	...
65-69	60	50	...	...	...	...	53	34	...	...
70-74	37	20	...	...	...	...	39	19	...	...
75+	31	9	...	...	...	...	19	8	...	...
Finland - Finlande[16]										
Groom — Epoux 18 ⊗										
Bride — Epouse 18 ⊗										
All ages - Tous âges	23 444	23 444	24 023	24 023	...	...	...	...	24 830	24 830
15-19	269	820	251	815	...	...	...	...	275	813
20-24	3 210	5 400	3 348	5 443	...	...	...	...	3 130	5 100
25-29	7 624	7 620	7 233	7 334	...	...	...	...	7 088	7 340
30-34	5 385	4 256	5 591	4 459	...	...	...	...	5 382	4 518
35-39	2 710	2 056	2 926	2 329	...	...	...	...	3 356	2 614
40-44	1 563	1 332	1 708	1 422	...	...	...	...	2 027	1 673
45-49	1 163	984	1 310	1 091	...	...	...	...	1 437	1 308
50-54	731	488	822	644	...	...	...	...	1 027	791
55-59	386	237	410	270	...	...	...	...	548	361
60-64	167	123	213	106	...	...	...	...	298	178
65-69	115	61	115	58	...	...	...	...	136	71
70-74	56	48	48	31	...	...	...	...	72	38

(See notes at end of table. — Voir notes à la fin du tableau.)

Continent, country or area and age / Continent, pays ou zone et âge	1997 Groom Epoux	1997 Bride Epouse	1998 Groom Epoux	1998 Bride Epouse	1999 Groom Epoux	1999 Bride Epouse	2000 Groom Epoux	2000 Bride Epouse	2001 Groom Epoux	2001 Bride Epouse
EUROPE										
Finland - Finlande[16]										
Groom — Epoux 18 ⊗										
Bride — Epouse 18 ⊗										
75+	65	19	48	21	...	...	...	...	54	25
France[17,18]										
Groom — Epoux 18 ⊗										
Bride — Epouse 18 ⊗										
All ages - Tous âges	283 984	283 984	...	...	286 191	286 191	...	...	...	...
0-14	...	...	...	...	-	3	...	...	...	...
0-19	419	3 202	...	...	...	...	...	...	...	...
15-19	...	...	...	...	407	3 509	...	...	...	...
20-24	27 698	60 134	...	...	22 455	53 482	...	...	...	...
25-29	104 283	105 604	...	...	106 040	110 711	...	...	...	...
30-34	65 678	51 566	...	...	67 503	51 868	...	...	...	...
35-39	34 489	27 079	...	...	35 368	27 928	...	...	...	...
40-44	...	...	...	...	20 575	16 302	...	...	...	...
40-49	33 101	25 825	...	...	...	...	...	...	...	...
45-49	...	...	...	...	13 420	10 429	...	...	...	...
50-54	...	...	...	...	9 861	6 818	...	...	...	...
50-59	12 600	8 003	...	...	...	...	...	...	...	...
55-59	...	...	...	...	4 689	2 633	...	...	...	...
60-64	...	...	...	...	2 722	1 210	...	...	...	...
60+	5 716	2 571	...	...	...	...	...	...	...	...
65-69	...	...	...	...	1 473	691	...	...	...	...
70-74	...	...	...	...	828	344	...	...	...	...
75+	...	...	...	...	850	263	...	...	...	...
Germany - Allemagne										
Groom — Epoux 18 ⊗										
Bride — Epouse 18 ⊗										
All ages - Tous âges	422 776	422 776	...	...	...	...	...	...	...	...
0-14	-	1	...	...	...	...	...	...	...	...
15-19	3 078	16 211	...	...	...	...	...	...	...	...
20-24	45 765	85 967	...	...	...	...	...	...	...	...
25-29	132 058	141 360	...	...	...	...	...	...	...	...
30-34	112 617	85 427	...	...	...	...	...	...	...	...
35-39	51 433	38 297	...	...	...	...	...	...	...	...
40-44	26 072	20 854	...	...	...	...	...	...	...	...
45-49	17 889	14 601	...	...	...	...	...	...	...	...
50-54	12 241	8 529	...	...	...	...	...	...	...	...
55-59	10 513	6 399	...	...	...	...	...	...	...	...
60-64	5 330	3 009	...	...	...	...	...	...	...	...
65-69	2 689	1 195	...	...	...	...	...	...	...	...
70+	3 091	926	...	...	...	...	...	...	...	...
Greece - Grèce										
Groom — Epoux 18 ⊗										
Bride — Epouse 18 ⊗										
All ages - Tous âges	60 535	60 535	55 489	55 489	...	...	...	...	...	...
0-14	-	85	5	83	...	...	...	...	...	...
15-19	505	4 541	461	3 826	...	...	...	...	...	...
20-24	7 021	18 676	6 025	16 261	...	...	...	...	...	...
25-29	22 388	21 788	19 640	20 016	...	...	...	...	...	...
30-34	16 543	8 835	16 082	8 834	...	...	...	...	...	...
35-39	7 024	3 119	6 466	3 123	...	...	...	...	...	...
40-44	2 962	1 452	2 830	1 437	...	...	...	...	...	...
45-49	1 470	810	1 423	751	...	...	...	...	...	...
50-54	884	542	900	553	...	...	...	...	...	...
55-59	526	320	527	262	...	...	...	...	...	...
60-64	493	190	434	193	...	...	...	...	...	...
65-69	366	107	322	94	...	...	...	...	...	...
70-74	207	47	208	44	...	...	...	...	...	...
75+	146	23	166	12	...	...	...	...	...	...

24. Marriages by age of bridegroom and by age of bride: 1997 - 2001
Mariages selon l'âge de l'époux et selon l'âge de l'épouse: 1997 - 2001 (continued — suite)

(See notes at end of table. — Voir notes à la fin du tableau.)

Continent, country or area and age / Continent, pays ou zone et âge	1997 Groom Epoux	1997 Bride Epouse	1998 Groom Epoux	1998 Bride Epouse	1999 Groom Epoux	1999 Bride Epouse	2000 Groom Epoux	2000 Bride Epouse	2001 Groom Epoux	2001 Bride Epouse
EUROPE										
Hungary - Hongrie										
Groom — Epoux 16 ⊗										
Bride — Epouse 16 ⊗										
All ages - Tous âges	46 905	46 905	44 915	44 915	45 465	45 465	48 110	48 110	43 583	43 583
15-19	1 318	6 671	1 072	5 239	887	4 495	769	3 821	...	...
16-19	...	...	...	...	...	...	...	...	667	2 978
20-24	16 862	21 426	15 570	20 750	14 143	19 910	12 651	19 345	9 409	15 230
25-29	14 620	9 699	14 582	10 204	15 301	11 426	17 853	14 203	16 383	14 216
30-34	5 229	3 028	5 577	3 202	6 408	3 793	7 662	4 746	7 629	4 959
35-39	2 661	1 619	2 420	1 590	2 690	1 772	2 906	1 922	3 158	2 074
40-44	2 128	1 635	1 956	1 417	1 969	1 434	2 040	1 335	2 028	1 337
45-49	1 374	1 134	1 372	1 121	1 521	1 171	1 633	1 254	1 663	1 236
50-54	941	721	958	700	977	689	1 046	723	1 089	769
55-59	632	422	588	345	658	375	657	365	663	392
60-64	389	256	305	162	371	191	357	202	371	216
65-69	337	169	251	94	242	116	228	111	233	102
70-74	216	85	117	64	161	59	168	57	153	49
75+	198	40	147	27	137	34	140	26	137	25
Iceland - Islande[19]										
Groom — Epoux 18 ⊗										
Bride — Epouse 18 ⊗										
All ages - Tous âges	1 481	1 481	1 529	1 529	...	...	1 777	1 777	...	...
15-19	3	20	4	23	...	...	5	30	...	...
20-24	124	220	115	216	...	...	117	259	...	...
25-29	371	438	420	503	...	...	477	590	...	...
30-34	382	350	385	356	...	...	459	361	...	...
35-39	268	210	277	224	...	...	300	244	...	...
40-44	116	116	132	92	...	...	167	136	...	...
45-49	97	60	84	46	...	...	108	79	...	...
50-54	64	33	53	33	...	...	77	37	...	...
55-59	16	14	30	21	...	...	29	23	...	...
60-64	17	11	12	6	...	...	18	13	...	...
65-69	15	4	11	4	...	...	14	3	...	...
70-74	2	3	2	2	...	...	3	1	...	...
75+	6	1	4	3	...	...	2	1	...	...
Unknown - Inconnu	-	1	...	...	...	...	1	...	...	...
Isle of Man - Îles de Man										
All ages - Tous âges	...	...	...	...	403	403	...	...	...	...
15-19	...	...	...	...	1	7	...	...	...	...
20-24	...	...	...	...	37	64	...	...	...	...
25-29	...	...	...	...	99	119	...	...	...	...
30-34	...	...	...	...	103	79	...	...	...	...
35-39	...	...	...	...	59	47	...	...	...	...
40-44	...	...	...	...	30	34	...	...	...	...
45-49	...	...	...	...	22	23	...	...	...	...
50-54	...	...	...	...	21	16	...	...	...	...
55-59	...	...	...	...	12	5	...	...	...	...
60-64	...	...	...	...	8	3	...	...	...	...
65-69	...	...	...	...	2	5	...	...	...	...
70-74	...	...	...	...	6	1	...	...	...	...
75+	...	...	...	...	3	...	...	...	...	...
Italy - Italie										
Groom — Epoux 16 ⊗										
Bride — Epouse 16 ⊗										
All ages - Tous âges	277 738	277 738	280 034	280 034	280 330	280 330	...	...	...	...
15-19	1 251	10 759	1 129	10 034	1 180	9 520	...	...	...	...
20-24	29 616	77 177	28 085	73 550	26 384	68 763	...	...	...	...
25-29	113 170	113 814	111 893	116 597	107 180	115 570	...	...	...	...
30-34	83 249	49 637	85 912	51 639	87 563	54 787	...	...	...	...
35-39	26 735	13 958	28 209	15 179	31 034	17 270	...	...	...	...
40-44	9 838	5 302	10 535	5 744	11 210	6 277	...	...	...	...
45-49	5 114	2 925	5 289	3 021	5 606	3 317	...	...	...	...
50-54	3 159	1 827	3 350	1 948	3 758	2 192	...	...	...	...

See notes at end of table. — Voir notes à la fin du tableau.)

Continent, country or area and age / Continent, pays ou zone et âge	1997 Groom Epoux	1997 Bride Epouse	1998 Groom Epoux	1998 Bride Epouse	1999 Groom Epoux	1999 Bride Epouse	2000 Groom Epoux	2000 Bride Epouse	2001 Groom Epoux	2001 Bride Epouse
EUROPE										
Italy - Italie										
Groom — Epoux 16 ⊗										
Bride — Epouse 16 ⊗										
55-59	2 227	1 095	2 161	1 110	2 514	1 239	...	...	...	...
60-64	1 435	629	1 464	625	1 656	703	...	...	...	...
65-69	899	353	949	315	1 021	371	...	...	...	...
70-74	565	178	569	183	655	215	...	...	...	...
75+	480	84	489	89	569	106	...	...	...	...
Latvia - Lettonie										
Groom — Epoux 18 ⊗										
Bride — Epouse 18 ⊗										
All ages - Tous âges	9 680	9 680	9 641	9 641	9 399	9 399	9 211	9 211	9 258	9 258
15-19	312	1 173	287	1 025	222	859	217	787	174	719
20-24	3 258	3 765	3 016	3 546	2 758	3 503	2 588	3 351	2 585	3 407
25-29	2 524	1 861	2 642	2 082	2 673	2 114	2 719	2 171	2 843	2 326
30-34	1 127	899	1 148	941	1 215	940	1 272	1 049	1 387	1 069
35-39	737	609	718	595	743	572	679	541	689	558
40-44	443	336	467	400	526	401	520	394	504	394
45-49	317	312	369	294	317	285	342	279	327	275
50-54	233	197	269	244	269	251	301	237	268	210
55-59	226	192	236	195	210	165	177	134	161	103
60-64	198	158	202	160	184	166	148	136	149	103
65-69	153	83	149	86	142	71	119	58	66	47
70-74	84	69	83	54	82	50	79	53	67	32
75+	68	26	55	19	58	22	50	21	38	15
Liechtenstein										
All ages - Tous âges	203	203	...	...	...	...	...	...	...	...
0-20	5	10	...	...	...	...	...	...	...	...
21-25	28	50	...	...	...	...	...	...	...	...
26-30	64	77	...	...	...	...	...	...	...	...
31-35	51	31	...	...	...	...	...	...	...	...
36-40	29	19	...	...	...	...	...	...	...	...
41-45	13	8	...	...	...	...	...	...	...	...
46-50	7	6	...	...	...	...	...	...	...	...
51+	6	2	...	...	...	...	...	...	...	...
Unknown - Inconnu	-	-	...	...	...	...	...	...	...	...
Lithuania - Lituanie										
Groom — Epoux 18 ⊗										
Bride — Epouse 18 ⊗										
All ages - Tous âges	18 796	18 796	18 486	18 486	...	...	16 906	16 906	15 764	15 764
0-14	-	5	..	..	...	...	-	1	-	2
15-19	1 225	3 968	961	3 624	...	...	667	2 455	459	1 976
20-24	8 181	8 126	7 820	8 137	...	...	6 251	7 279	5 460	6 759
25-29	4 672	3 044	4 998	3 105	...	...	4 750	3 466	4 694	3 472
30-34	1 729	1 252	1 749	1 267	...	...	2 035	1 405	1 991	1 396
35-39	928	799	966	792	...	...	1 064	765	1 060	744
40-44	564	424	580	491	...	...	689	525	682	470
45-49	431	365	410	350	...	...	447	363	455	350
50-54	265	244	283	255	...	...	328	253	335	254
55-59	247	216	249	170	...	...	226	167	247	134
60-64	203	152	204	140	...	...	203	110	147	96
65-69	162	114	137	98	...	...	116	72	117	58
70-74	93	61	65	34	...	...	70	31	61	38
75+	96	26	64	17	...	...	60	14	56	15
Luxembourg[19]										
Groom — Epoux 18 ⊗										
Bride — Epouse 15 ⊗										
All ages - Tous âges	...	...	...	...	...	...	...	...	1 983	1 983
15-19	...	...	...	...	...	...	...	...	6	59
20-24	...	...	...	...	...	...	...	...	206	346
25-29	...	...	...	...	...	...	...	...	521	660
30-34	...	...	...	...	...	...	...	...	541	452
35-39	...	...	...	...	...	...	...	...	284	203

(See notes at end of table. — Voir notes à la fin du tableau.)

Continent, country or area and age / Continent, pays ou zone et âge	1997 Groom Epoux	1997 Bride Epouse	1998 Groom Epoux	1998 Bride Epouse	1999 Groom Epoux	1999 Bride Epouse	2000 Groom Epoux	2000 Bride Epouse	2001 Groom Epoux	2001 Bride Epouse
EUROPE										
Luxembourg[19]										
Groom — Epoux 18 ⊗										
Bride — Epouse 15 ⊗										
40-44	...	...	...	...	...	...	...	...	161	115
45-49	...	...	...	...	...	...	...	...	130	81
50-54	...	...	...	...	...	...	...	...	69	39
55-59	...	...	...	...	...	...	...	...	36	13
60-64	...	...	...	...	...	...	...	...	11	10
65-69	...	...	...	...	...	...	...	...	10	2
70-74	...	...	...	...	...	...	...	...	5	1
75+	...	...	...	...	...	...	...	...	3	1
Malta - Malte										
Groom — Epoux 16 ⊗										
Bride — Epouse 16 ⊗										
All ages - Tous âges	2 414	2 414	...	...	...	...	2 545	2 545	...	...
15-19	60	247	...	...	...	...	...	...	...	...
16-19	...	...	...	...	...	...	41	169	...	...
20-24	763	1 224	...	...	...	...	724	1 230	...	...
25-29	1 029	643	...	...	...	...	1 123	776	...	...
30-34	290	130	...	...	...	...	379	210	...	...
35-39	123	64	...	...	...	...	132	67	...	...
40-44	55	47	...	...	...	...	61	43	...	...
45-49	36	23	...	...	...	...	30	27	...	...
50-54	21	23	...	...	...	...	28	10	...	...
55-59	18	3	...	...	...	...	15	5	...	...
60-64	12	5	...	...	...	...	5	2	...	...
65+	7	5	...	...	...	...	7	6	...	...
Netherlands - Pays-Bas										
Groom — Epoux 18 ⊗										
Bride — Epouse 18 ⊗										
All ages - Tous âges	85 059	85 059	86 956	86 956	...	...	88 074	88 074	79 677	79 677
0-19	399	2 462	415	2 588	...	...	492	2 788	...	...
15-19	...	...	...	...	...	...	...	...	321	2 073
20-24	8 162	17 815	7 669	16 798	...	...	7 607	16 663	6 351	13 982
25-29	30 292	32 451	29 921	33 076	...	...	26 834	30 821	21 217	25 922
30-34	22 851	16 453	23 779	17 176	...	...	25 122	18 739	24 441	18 785
35-39	9 665	6 520	10 336	7 052	...	...	11 759	7 911	11 410	7 840
40-44	4 859	3 568	5 050	3 740	...	...	5 805	4 195	5 789	4 280
45-49	3 283	2 526	3 398	2 732	...	...	3 681	2 855	3 523	2 759
50-54	2 369	1 581	2 818	1 931	...	...	3 011	2 115	2 736	1 983
55-59	1 328	823	1 540	908	...	...	1 657	1 027	1 744	1 031
60-64	897	400	1 029	507	...	...	1 113	529	1 001	513
65+	954	460	1 001	448	...	...	993	431	...	...
65-69	...	...	...	...	...	...	...	...	606	297
70-74	...	...	...	...	...	...	...	...	305	122
75+	...	...	...	...	...	...	...	...	233	90
Norway - Norvège[18,20]										
Groom — Epoux 16 ⊗										
Bride — Epouse 16 ⊗										
All ages - Tous âges	23 815	23 815	23 354	23 354	23 456	23 456	25 356	25 356	22 967	22 967
15-19	106	527	133	605	90	516	110	501	114	551
20-24	2 263	4 935	2 138	4 300	1 796	4 004	1 800	4 101	1 641	3 706
25-29	7 728	8 684	7 210	8 456	6 754	8 145	7 010	8 666	5 932	7 459
30-34	6 132	4 669	6 041	4 860	6 105	5 014	6 845	5 696	6 114	5 149
35-39	3 078	2 241	3 155	2 184	3 414	2 504	3 827	2 793	3 565	2 622
40-44	1 756	1 244	1 818	1 309	1 953	1 385	2 115	1 526	2 028	1 413
45-49	1 162	767	1 229	812	1 331	893	1 466	993	1 417	1 025
50-54	882	450	870	477	1 024	570	1 121	661	1 087	574
55-59	400	188	390	211	547	255	583	265	578	282
60-64	160	55	213	73	244	84	281	82	309	97
65-69	73	32	83	38	106	44	111	37	99	52
70+	75	23	...	...	...	...	...	...	...	...
70-74	...	...	44	14	57	20	45	20	42	22

(See notes at end of table. — Voir notes à la fin du tableau.)

Continent, country or area and age / Continent, pays ou zone et âge	1997 Groom Epoux	1997 Bride Epouse	1998 Groom Epoux	1998 Bride Epouse	1999 Groom Epoux	1999 Bride Epouse	2000 Groom Epoux	2000 Bride Epouse	2001 Groom Epoux	2001 Bride Epouse
EUROPE										
Norway - Norvège[18,20]										
Groom — Epoux 16 ⊗										
Bride — Epouse 16 ⊗										
75+	...	...	30	15	35	21	42	14	41	15
Unknown - Inconnu	-	-	-	-	-	1	...	1	...	...
Poland - Pologne										
Groom — Epoux 18 ⊗										
Bride — Epouse 16 ⊗										
All ages - Tous âges	204 850	204 850	209 430	209 430	219 398	219 398	...	...	...	...
15-19	4 971	30 475	5 007	29 046	6 746	29 583	...	...	...	...
20-24	95 795	113 612	94 680	114 776	95 243	118 358	...	...	...	...
25-29	61 962	33 841	65 977	37 654	71 636	42 483	...	...	...	...
30-34	17 497	8 653	17 933	9 119	19 143	9 708	...	...	...	...
35-39	7 990	4 944	8 086	4 972	8 100	4 762	...	...	...	...
40-44	4 731	3 886	5 119	4 100	5 206	4 094	...	...	...	...
45-49	3 292	3 188	3 657	3 390	3 815	3 416	...	...	...	...
50-54	2 026	2 031	2 429	2 195	2 639	2 530	...	...	...	...
55-59	1 637	1 572	1 688	1 524	1 677	1 492	...	...	...	...
60-64	1 689	1 240	1 617	1 231	1 693	1 410	...	...	...	...
65-69	1 450	852	1 461	886	1 532	928	...	...	...	...
70-74	997	396	1 006	381	1 081	438	...	...	...	...
75+	813	160	770	156	887	196	...	...	...	...
Portugal										
Groom — Epoux 16 ⊗										
Bride — Epouse 16 ⊗										
All ages - Tous âges	65 770	65 770	...	...	...	...	...	...	58 390	58 390
0-14	20	689	...	...	...	...	...	...	...	...
0-16	...	...	...	...	...	...	...	...	24	492
15-19	1 879	7 550	...	...	...	...	...	...	...	...
17-19	...	...	...	...	...	...	...	...	1 256	5 234
20-24	21 463	26 651	...	...	...	...	...	...	15 079	19 551
25-29	24 589	18 976	...	...	...	...	...	...	23 394	20 079
30-34	9 054	5 764	...	...	...	...	...	...	9 488	6 519
35-39	3 320	2 422	...	...	...	...	...	...	3 495	2 559
40-44	1 702	1 259	...	...	...	...	...	...	1 797	1 378
45-49	1 011	820	...	...	...	...	...	...	1 140	956
50-54	714	590	...	...	...	...	...	...	806	591
55-59	574	391	...	...	...	...	...	...	609	400
60-64	513	272	...	...	...	...	...	...	437	282
65-69	401	204	...	...	...	...	...	...	399	175
70-74	276	115	...	...	...	...	...	...	235	108
75+	254	67	...	...	...	...	...	...	231	66
Republic of Moldova - République Moldova[21]										
Groom — Epoux 18 ⊗										
Bride — Epouse 16 ⊗										
All ages - Tous âges	...	...	16 644	16 644	18 221	18 221	16 554	16 554	16 076	16 076
0-15	...	...	-	77	-	67	-	53	-	28
16-19	...	...	1 093	6 777	1 058	7 170	1 026	6 118	838	5 572
20-24	...	...	10 457	7 956	11 199	8 883	9 669	8 302	9 176	8 344
25-29	...	...	3 903	1 331	4 639	1 553	4 480	1 500	4 676	1 619
30-34	...	...	772	242	849	281	844	285	887	267
35-39	...	...	222	101	245	94	251	76	251	80
40-44	...	...	61	41	71	41	76	33	90	38
45-49	...	...	31	23	42	29	29	29	26	13
50-54	...	...	13	11	22	11	13	11	19	9
55-59	...	...	14	17	10	7	16	8	8	9
60-64	...	...	15	13	14	18	13	12	14	10
65-69	...	...	15	8	12	16	16	18	9	13
70-74	...	...	16	18	16	24	20	40	7	15
75+	...	...	27	22	39	19	101	69	72	56
Unknown - Inconnu	...	...	5	7	5	8	...	...	3	3

(See notes at end of table. — Voir notes à la fin du tableau.)

Continent, country or area and age / Continent, pays ou zone et âge	1997 Groom Epoux	1997 Bride Epouse	1998 Groom Epoux	1998 Bride Epouse	1999 Groom Epoux	1999 Bride Epouse	2000 Groom Epoux	2000 Bride Epouse	2001 Groom Epoux	2001 Bride Epouse
EUROPE										
Romania - Roumanie										
Groom — Epoux 18 ⊗										
Bride — Epouse 16 ⊗										
All ages - Tous âges	147 105	147 105	145 303	145 303	...	...	135 808	135 808	129 930	129 930
15-19	3 480	34 638	2 882	31 639	...	...	1 993	24 646	1 604	21 434
20-24	60 069	65 495	57 734	65 116	...	...	47 311	60 585	41 940	56 394
25-29	51 084	28 055	48 513	26 965	...	...	47 973	27 792	47 305	28 671
30-34	13 276	7 213	16 601	9 693	...	...	19 580	11 571	20 085	12 196
35-39	7 152	3 963	7 003	3 916	...	...	6 494	3 692	6 179	3 485
40-44	4 690	3 023	4 937	3 051	...	...	4 530	2 865	4 561	2 781
45-49	2 824	2 080	3 111	2 277	...	...	3 156	2 015	3 191	2 168
50-54	1 491	1 026	1 590	1 080	...	...	1 831	1 204	1 990	1 273
55-59	1 203	725	1 095	684	...	...	1 029	619	1 143	616
60-64	...	...	...	...	...	...	943	409	...	...
60+	1 836	887	1 837	882	...	...	...	...	1 932	912
65-69	...	...	...	...	...	...	485	257	...	...
70-74	...	...	...	...	...	...	288	107	...	...
75+	...	...	...	...	...	...	195	46	...	...
Russian Federation - Fédération de Russie										
Groom — Epoux 18 ⊗										
Bride — Epouse 18 ⊗										
All ages - Tous âges	928 411	928 411	848 691	848 691	911 162	911 162	...	...	...	...
0-17	5 906	43 815	4 851	37 016	3 773	32 945	...	...	...	...
18-24	456 025	540 549	406 962	493 365	425 864	530 779	...	...	...	...
25-34	279 800	188 873	264 497	178 447	297 276	202 142	...	...	...	...
35+	186 531	155 055	172 250	139 743	184 148	145 226	...	...	...	...
Unknown - Inconnu	149	119	131	120	101	70	...	...	...	...
San Marino - Saint-Marin										
All ages - Tous âges	233	233	...	...	...	...	193	193	...	...
15-19	-	4	...	...	...	...	1	2	...	...
20-24	28	55	...	...	...	...	14	41	...	...
25-29	88	94	...	...	...	...	70	90	...	...
30-34	70	52	...	...	...	...	59	34	...	...
35-39	19	14	...	...	...	...	20	15	...	...
40-44	11	7	...	...	...	...	14	5	...	...
45-49	9	6	...	...	...	...	4	2	...	...
50-54	2	1	...	...	...	...	3	3	...	...
55-59	1	-	...	...	...	...	1	1	...	...
60-64	1	-	...	...	...	...	3	-	...	...
65-69	3	-	...	...	...	...	1	-	...	...
70-74	-	...	...	...	...	...	1	-	...	...
75+	1	-	...	...	...	...	1	-	...	...
Unknown - Inconnu	-	-	...	...	...	...	1	-	...	...
Serbia and Montenegro - Serbie-et-Montenegro										
Groom — Epoux 18 ⊗										
Bride — Epouse 18 ⊗										
All ages - Tous âges	...	...	54 822	54 822	...	...	58 318	58 318	...	...
15-19	...	...	1 029	8 503	...	...	1 060	8 356	...	...
20-24	...	...	15 220	22 122	...	...	14 740	22 784	...	...
25-29	...	...	18 977	13 170	...	...	20 743	14 859	...	...
30-34	...	...	9 305	4 753	...	...	10 463	5 389	...	...
35-39	...	...	4 097	2 145	...	...	4 332	2 288	...	...
40-44	...	...	1 981	1 269	...	...	2 176	1 411	...	...
45-49	...	...	1 242	993	...	...	1 417	1 112	...	...
50-54	...	...	741	564	...	...	929	759	...	...
55-59	...	...	525	431	...	...	586	402	...	...
60-64	...	...	541	285	...	...	528	314	...	...
65-69	...	...	436	208	...	...	456	215	...	...
70-74	...	...	297	136	...	...	320	113	...	...
75+	...	...	293	117	...	...	291	114	...	...
Unknown - Inconnu	...	...	138	126	...	...	277	202	...	...

24. Marriages by age of bridegroom and by age of bride: 1997 - 2001
Mariages selon l'âge de l'époux et selon l'âge de l'épouse: 1997 - 2001 (continued — suite)

(See notes at end of table. — Voir notes à la fin du tableau.)

Continent, country or area and age / Continent, pays ou zone et âge	1997 Groom Epoux	1997 Bride Epouse	1998 Groom Epoux	1998 Bride Epouse	1999 Groom Epoux	1999 Bride Epouse	2000 Groom Epoux	2000 Bride Epouse	2001 Groom Epoux	2001 Bride Epouse
EUROPE										
Slovakia - Slovaquie										
Groom — Epoux 16 ⊗										
Bride — Epouse 16 ⊗										
All ages - Tous âges	...	...	27 494	27 494	27 340	27 340	...	...	23 795	23 795
15-19	...	...	1 084	5 043	933	4 368	...	...	614	2 830
20-24	...	...	12 280	14 269	11 285	14 035	...	...	7 949	11 251
25-29	...	...	8 333	5 023	9 013	5 580	...	...	9 078	6 331
30-34	...	...	2 687	1 382	2 776	1 487	...	...	2 950	1 545
35-39	...	...	1 287	656	1 317	712	...	...	1 282	666
40-44	...	...	686	455	762	431	...	...	668	438
45-49	...	...	462	340	517	366	...	...	469	368
50-54	...	...	294	178	328	191	...	...	343	179
55-59	...	...	161	64	176	81	...	...	171	87
60-64	...	...	93	48	86	49	...	...	124	51
65-69	...	...	61	21	79	22	...	...	81	35
70-74	...	...	34	11	39	15	...	...	38	11
75+	...	...	32	4	29	3	...	...	28	3
Slovenia - Slovénie										
Groom — Epoux 18 ⊗										
Bride — Epouse 18 ⊗										
All ages - Tous âges	...	...	7 528	7 528	7 716	7 716	7 201	7 201	6 935	6 935
0-14	...	...	...	...	...	1	...	...	...	1
15-19	...	...	42	308	42	334	32	226	34	225
20-24	...	...	1 316	2 777	1 318	2 656	1 076	2 279	976	1 988
25-29	...	...	3 080	2 686	3 092	2 768	2 894	2 820	2 770	2 799
30-34	...	...	1 681	910	1 693	995	1 724	976	1 646	997
35-39	...	...	588	357	695	384	633	392	683	380
40-44	...	...	327	172	314	216	316	171	281	194
45-49	...	...	168	141	184	166	205	165	200	127
50-54	...	...	119	73	140	85	118	71	129	97
55-59	...	...	74	41	80	44	70	42	78	53
60-64	...	...	48	35	51	29	46	33	42	33
65-69	...	...	40	12	52	23	40	16	38	25
70-74	...	...	21	9	22	10	33	8	30	11
75+	...	...	24	7	33	5	14	2	28	5
Spain - Espagne[22]										
Groom — Epoux 14 ⊗										
Bride — Epouse 12 ⊗										
All ages - Tous âges	196 499	196 499	207 041	207 041	...	...	...	...	...	...
0-14	1	16	...	19	...	...	...	...	...	...
15-19	1 778	7 274	1 518	6 302	...	...	...	...	...	...
20-24	25 072	48 775	24 432	48 589	...	...	...	...	...	...
25-29	89 221	89 858	92 989	96 350	...	...	...	...	...	...
30-34	51 429	32 927	56 526	36 434	...	...	...	...	...	...
35-39	14 881	9 564	16 291	10 420	...	...	...	...	...	...
40-44	5 689	3 596	6 169	4 074	...	...	...	...	...	...
45-49	3 097	1 892	3 361	2 059	...	...	...	...	...	...
50-54	1 942	1 136	2 109	1 224	...	...	...	...	...	...
55-59	1 153	580	1 243	678	...	...	...	...	...	...
60-64	876	407	952	409	...	...	...	...	...	...
65-69	623	239	651	215	...	...	...	...	...	...
70-74	363	140	368	156	...	...	...	...	...	...
75+	374	95	432	112	...	...	...	...	...	...
Sweden - Suède[2]										
Groom — Epoux 18 ⊗										
Bride — Epouse 18 ⊗										
All ages - Tous âges	30 328	30 328	29 585	29 585	...	...	...	...	33 077	33 077
0-19	...	...	72	369	...	...	...	...	...	...
15-19	72	384	...	...	...	...	...	...	70	359
20-24	1 909	4 086	1 655	3 520	...	...	...	...	1 519	3 118
25-29	8 141	9 972	7 671	9 712	...	...	...	...	7 699	10 240
30-34	8 528	7 105	8 356	7 089	...	...	...	...	9 267	8 314
35-39	4 159	3 355	4 254	3 304	...	...	...	...	5 595	4 468

24. Marriages by age of bridegroom and by age of bride: 1997 - 2001
Mariages selon l'âge de l'époux et selon l'âge de l'épouse: 1997 - 2001 (continued — suite)

(See notes at end of table. — Voir notes à la fin du tableau.)

Continent, country or area and age / Continent, pays ou zone et âge	1997 Groom Epoux	1997 Bride Epouse	1998 Groom Epoux	1998 Bride Epouse	1999 Groom Epoux	1999 Bride Epouse	2000 Groom Epoux	2000 Bride Epouse	2001 Groom Epoux	2001 Bride Epouse
EUROPE										
Sweden - Suède[2]										
Groom — Epoux 18 ⊗										
Bride — Epouse 18 ⊗										
40-44	2 485	1 936	2 527	1 962	...	...	...	...	3 050	2 345
45-49	1 934	1 574	1 871	1 588	...	...	...	...	2 095	1 763
50-54	1 562	1 121	1 550	1 205	...	...	...	...	1 694	1 309
55-59	800	419	871	499	...	...	...	...	1 183	698
60-64	360	190	420	170	...	...	...	...	514	250
65-69	193	84	168	85	...	...	...	...	186	113
70-74	95	55	81	47	...	...	...	...	111	58
75+	90	47	89	35	...	...	...	...	94	42
Switzerland - Suisse										
Groom — Epoux 18 ⊗										
Bride — Epouse 17 ⊗										
All ages - Tous âges	...	...	38 683	38 683	...	...	39 758	39 758	35 987	35 987
0-14	...	...	-	1	...	...	...	3	...	1
15-19	...	...	169	982	...	...	229	1 112	189	950
20-24	...	...	3 505	7 702	...	...	3 628	7 357	3 040	6 486
25-29	...	...	11 674	13 508	...	...	10 574	13 047	8 939	11 398
30-34	...	...	10 799	8 430	...	...	10 962	9 051	10 100	8 476
35-39	...	...	5 126	3 592	...	...	5 756	4 059	5 641	4 035
40-44	...	...	2 547	1 764	...	...	3 071	2 039	2 905	1 883
45-49	...	...	1 723	1 249	...	...	1 962	1 413	1 812	1 208
50-54	...	...	1 440	838	...	...	1 605	938	1 425	851
55-59	...	...	868	370	...	...	1 045	470	1 041	457
60-64	...	...	442	150	...	...	501	158	479	149
65-69	...	...	204	47	...	...	218	59	230	47
70-74	...	...	94	30	...	...	97	31	102	26
75+	...	...	92	20	...	...	110	21	84	20
The Former Yugoslav Rep. of Macedonia - L'ex-République yougoslave de Macédoine										
Groom — Epoux 18 ⊗										
Bride — Epouse 18 ⊗										
All ages - Tous âges	14 072	14 072	...	...	14 172	14 172	14 255	14 255	13 267	13 267
15-19	574	3 534	...	...	539	3 314	551	3 151	458	2 759
20-24	5 481	6 311	...	...	5 258	6 292	5 059	6 241	4 397	5 719
25-29	5 056	2 710	...	...	5 214	3 057	5 205	3 166	5 109	3 152
30-34	1 792	763	...	...	1 877	772	2 032	848	1 946	869
35-39	573	274	...	...	666	331	715	376	674	319
40-44	221	161	...	...	274	153	307	179	270	172
45-49	110	108	...	...	117	99	131	107	153	114
50-54	71	60	...	...	74	47	75	65	84	71
55-59	62	31	...	...	44	35	56	29	45	23
60-64	37	22	...	...	39	20	47	19	42	33
65-69	31	18	...	...	33	12	29	14	33	16
70-74	37	7	...	...	17	6	24	6	32	6
75+	20	5	...	...	20	5	24	5	24	4
Unknown - Inconnu	7	68	...	...	...	29	...	49	...	10
Ukraine										
Groom — Epoux 18 ⊗										
Bride — Epouse 17 ⊗										
All ages - Tous âges	...	...	310 504	310 504	...	...	...	...	309 602	309 602
0-15	...	...	17	1 163	...	...	...	...	14	807
16-19	...	...	17 979	88 821	...	...	...	...	13 624	71 888
20-24	...	...	140 318	115 474	...	...	...	...	127 627	124 256
25-29	...	...	65 934	38 437	...	...	...	...	76 809	45 768
30-34	...	...	26 992	18 959	...	...	...	...	31 069	20 755
35-39	...	...	17 758	13 437	...	...	...	...	17 747	12 487
40-44	...	...	11 415	9 756	...	...	...	...	12 662	9 876
45-49	...	...	8 797	7 999	...	...	...	...	8 662	7 514
50-54	...	...	5 176	4 688	...	...	...	...	6 798	5 820
55-59	...	...	5 140	4 389	...	...	...	...	3 486	2 811

24. Marriages by age of bridegroom and by age of bride: 1997 - 2001
Mariages selon l'âge de l'époux et selon l'âge de l'épouse: 1997 - 2001 (continued — suite)

(See notes at end of table. — Voir notes à la fin du tableau.)

Continent, country or area and age / Continent, pays ou zone et âge	1997 Groom Epoux	1997 Bride Epouse	1998 Groom Epoux	1998 Bride Epouse	1999 Groom Epoux	1999 Bride Epouse	2000 Groom Epoux	2000 Bride Epouse	2001 Groom Epoux	2001 Bride Epouse
EUROPE										
Ukraine										
Groom — Epoux 18 ⊗										
Bride — Epouse 17 ⊗										
60+	...	...	10 978	7 381	...	...	...	...	11 104	7 620
United Kingdom - Royaume-Uni										
Groom — Epoux 16 ⊗										
Bride — Epouse 16 ⊗										
All ages - Tous âges	310 218	310 218	304 796	304 796	301 083	301 083	305 912	305 912	...	...
15-19	3 232	9 283	3 187	9 225	2 528	9 250	2 390	8 870	...	...
20-24	42 847	63 445	38 737	58 185	32 096	57 182	31 096	55 646	...	...
25-29	97 224	98 058	94 917	96 960	90 412	94 703	85 870	92 753	...	...
30-34	69 449	60 058	69 690	60 754	72 129	60 446	73 809	62 478	...	...
35-39	36 560	30 922	37 860	31 592	40 244	31 981	43 653	34 891	...	...
40-44	20 523	17 656	20 428	17 679	21 870	18 155	24 366	19 806	...	...
45-49	14 929	13 145	14 345	12 550	14 753	12 176	15 919	13 230	...	...
50-54	10 859	8 574	11 173	8 758	11 828	8 646	12 872	9 391	...	...
55-59	5 863	3 728	5 912	3 895	6 463	3 781	6 939	4 121	...	...
60-64	3 798	2 438	3 739	2 453	3 822	2 302	4 075	2 321	...	...
65-69	2 268	1 374	2 276	1 382	2 406	1 249	2 410	1 247	...	...
70-74	1 400	888	1 341	775	1 312	670	1 319	683	...	...
75+	1 266	649	1 191	588	1 220	542	1 194	475	...	...
OCEANIA — OCEANIE										
Australia - Australie+										
Groom — Epoux 16 ⊗										
Bride — Epouse 16 ⊗										
All ages - Tous âges	...	...	...	...	114 316	114 316	113 429	113 429	...	...
15-19	...	...	...	...	756	3 291	702	3 221	...	...
20-24	...	...	...	...	17 966	29 220	16 752	27 332	...	...
25-29	...	...	...	...	38 122	38 375	37 293	37 723	...	...
30-34	...	...	...	...	23 233	18 584	23 818	19 438	...	...
35-39	...	...	...	...	13 155	9 787	12 923	9 953	...	...
40-44	...	...	...	...	7 145	5 720	7 562	5 901	...	...
45-49	...	...	...	...	5 076	4 026	5 080	4 194	...	...
50-54	...	...	...	...	3 708	2 469	3 944	2 727	...	...
55-59	...	...	...	...	2 096	1 227	2 242	1 347	...	...
60-64	...	...	...	...	1 231	677	1 341	725	...	...
65-69	...	...	...	...	770	424	787	424	...	...
70-74	...	...	...	...	560	309	513	257	...	...
75+	...	...	...	...	498	207	472	187	...	...
New Caledonia - Nouvelle-Calédonie										
All ages - Tous âges	...	...	...	...	943	943	...	...	...	...
0-19	...	...	...	...	4	27	...	...	...	...
20-24	...	...	...	...	78	230	...	...	...	...
25-29	...	...	...	...	300	289	...	...	...	...
30-34	...	...	...	...	213	182	...	...	...	...
35-39	...	...	...	...	142	104	...	...	...	...
40-49	...	...	...	...	136	79	...	...	...	...
50-59	...	...	...	...	52	27	...	...	...	...
60+	...	...	...	...	18	5	...	...	...	...
New Zealand - Nouvelle-Zélande										
Groom — Epoux 16 ⊗										
Bride — Epouse 16 ⊗										
All ages - Tous âges	19 953	19 953	20 135	20 135	21 085	21 085	...	...	...	...
15-19	176	575	182	644	199	665	...	...	...	...
20-24	3 136	4 921	3 022	4 677	3 033	4 692	...	...	...	...
25-29	6 036	6 115	5 951	6 254	6 200	6 585	...	...	...	...
30-34	4 100	3 471	4 295	3 580	4 539	3 820	...	...	...	...
35-39	2 307	1 895	2 531	1 958	2 637	2 095	...	...	...	...
40-44	1 410	1 111	1 377	1 135	1 580	1 291	...	...	...	...
45-49	1 022	780	1 026	843	1 019	821	...	...	...	...

24. Marriages by age of bridegroom and by age of bride: 1997 - 2001
Mariages selon l'âge de l'époux et selon l'âge de l'épouse: 1997 - 2001 (continued — suite)

(See notes at end of table. — Voir notes à la fin du tableau.)

Continent, country or area and age / Continent, pays ou zone et âge	1997		1998		1999		2000		2001	
	Groom Epoux	Bride Epouse	Groom Epoux	Bride Epouse	Groom Epoux	Bride Epouse	Groom Epoux	Bride Epouse	Groom Epoux	Bride Epouse
OCEANIA — OCEANIE										
New Zealand - Nouvelle-Zélande										
Groom — Epoux 16 ⊗										
Bride — Epouse 16 ⊗										
50-54	670	499	713	505	783	542	...	...	...	...
55-59	451	270	430	233	465	255	...	...	...	...
60-64	256	131	226	118	261	141	...	...	...	...
65-69	192	82	177	79	168	91	...	...	...	...
70-74	113	62	114	65	106	42	...	...	...	...
75+	84	41	91	44	95	45	...	...	...	...
Tonga										
All ages - Tous âges	688	688	736	736	...	...	747	747	...	...
15-19	35	154	52	139	...	...	62	169	...	...
20-24	252	268	234	290	...	...	257	278	...	...
25-29	230	167	241	171	...	...	217	163	...	...
30-34	80	50	106	70	...	...	106	82	...	...
35-39	41	27	42	30	...	...	36	27	...	...
40-44	16	6	25	20	...	...	28	9	...	...
45-49	11	9	11	9	...	...	12	10	...	...
50+	23	7	25	7	...	...	29	9	...	...

GENERAL NOTES - NOTES GENERALES

Data refer to legal (recognized) marriages performed and registered. For method of evaluation and limitations of data, see Technical Notes, for this table. — Les données représentent le nombre de mariages qui ont été célébrés et reconnus par la loi. Pour la méthode d'évaluation et les insuffisances des données, voir Notes techniques pour ce tableau.

Italics: data from civil registers which are incomplete or of unknown completeness. — *Italiques:* données incomplètes ou dont le degré d'exactitude n'est pas connu, provenant des registres de l'état civil.

FOOTNOTES - NOTES

* Provisional. — Données provisoires.

+ Data tabulated by date of registration rather than occurrence. — Données exploitées selon la date de l'enregistrement et non la date de l'événement.

⊗ Age below which marriage is unlawful or invalid without dispensation by competent authority. — Age en-dessous duquel le mariage est illégal ou nul sans une dispense de l'autorité compétente.

• Varies among major civil divisions, or ethnic or religious groups. — Varie selon les grandes divisions administratives ou selon les groups ethniques ou religieux.

≡ No minimum age has been fixed for males. — Il n'y a pas d'âge minimal pour les hommes.

1 Including marriages resumed after 'revocable divorce' (among Moslem population), which approximates legal separation. — Y compris les unions reconstituées après un 'divorce révocable' (parmi la population musulmane), qui est à peu près l'équivalent d'une séparation légale.

2 Including residents outside the country. — Y compris les résidents hors du pays.

3 Excluding tribal Indian population. — Non compris les Indiens vivant en tribus.

4 Excluding Indian jungle population. — Non compris les Indiens de la jungle.

5 Excluding nomadic Indian tribes. — Non compris les tribus d'Indiens nomades.

6 Data refer to government controlled areas. — Les données se raportent aux zones contrôlées par le Gouvernement.

7 Including data for East Jerusalem and Israeli residents in certain other territories under occupation by Israeli military forces since June 1967. — Y compris les données pour Jérusalem-Est et les résidents israéliens dans certains autres territoires occupés depuis 1967 par les forces armées israéliennes.

8 Data refer to Japanese nationals in Japan only; and to grooms and brides married for the first time whose marriages occurred and were registered in the same year. — Les données se raportent aux nationaux japonais au Japon seulement; et aux époux et épouses mariés pour la première fois, dont le mariage a été célébré et enregistré la même année.

9 Excluding data for Jordanian territory under occupation since June 1967 by Israeli military forces. Excluding foreigners, including registered Palestinian refugees. — Non compris les données pour le territoire jordanien occupé depuis juin 1967 par les forces armées israéliennes. Non compris les étrangers, mais y compris les réfugiés de Palestine enregistrés.

10 Figures exclude marriages previously officiated outside Singapore or under religious and customary rites. — Les figures excluent les mariages célébrés précédemment au dehors de Singapoure ou sous les rites réligieuse ou accoutumés.

11 Minimum age of marriage for men and women with parental consent is 16 years in case of Muslim marriage and 18 for civil marriage. Without parental consent, that age is 21 for both Muslim and civil marriages. — L'âge minimum du mariage pour les hommes et les femmes avec le consentement parental est de 16 ans en cas de mariage musulman et de 18 ans pour le mariage civil. Sans consentement parental, cet âge est 21 pour les mariages musulmans et civils.

12 Data refer to provincial capitals and district centres only. - Les données se rapportent aux capitales des provinces et les chefs-lieux de districts seulement.

13 Including armed forces stationed outside the country, but excluding alien armed forces in the area unless marriage performed by local foreign authority. — Y compris les militaires nationaux hors du pays et les militaires étrangers en garnison sur le territoire, sauf si le mariage a été célébré pour l'autorité locale.

14 Including Bulgarian nationals outside the country, but excluding aliens in the area. — Y compris les nationaux bulgares à l'étranger, mais non compris les étrangers sur le territoire.

15 Excluding Faeroe Islands and Greenland. — Non compris les îles Féroé et Gröenland.

16 Marriages in which the bride was domiciled in Finland only. — Mariages où l'épouse était domicilié en Finlande seulement.

17 Including armed forces stationed outside the country. — Y compris les militaires nationaux hors du pays.

18 Age classification based on year of birth rather than exact date of birth. — Le classement selon l'âge est basé sur l'année de naissances et non sur la date exacte de naissance.

19 For de jure population. — Pour la population de droit.

20 Marriages in which the groom was domiciled in Norway only. — Mariages où l'époux était domicilié en Norvège seulement.

21 Beginning with year 1998 data refer to first marriages only. — Après 1998 des données se rapportent aux premiers mariages seulement.

22 Civil marriages only. Canonical marriages are void for males under 16 years of age and for females under 14 years of age. — Mariages civils seulement. Les mariages religieux sont nuls pour les hommes ayant moins de 16 ans et pour les femmes ayant moins de 14 ans.

Table 25

Table 25 presents number of divorces and crude divorce rates for as many years as possible between 1997 and 2001.

Description of variables: Divorce is defined as a final legal dissolution of a marriage, that is, that separation of husband and wife which confers on the parties the right to remarriage under civil, religious and/or other provisions, according to the laws of each country[i].

Unless otherwise noted, divorce statistics exclude legal separations that do not allow remarriage. These statistics refer to the number of divorces granted, and not to the number of persons divorcing.

Divorce statistics are obtained from court records and/or civil registers according to national practice. The actual compilation of these statistics may be the responsibility of the civil registrar, the national statistical office or other government offices.

Rate computation: Crude divorce rates are the annual number of divorces per 1 000 mid-year population.

Rates presented in this table have been limited to those countries or areas having at least a total of 100 divorces in a given year. These rates have been calculated by the Statistics Division of the United Nations.

Reliability of data: Each country or area has been asked to indicate the estimated completeness of the divorces recorded in its civil register. These national assessments are indicated by the quality codes C and U that appear in the first column of this table.

C indicates that the data are estimated to be virtually complete, that is, representing at least 90 per cent of the divorces that occur each year, while U indicates that data are estimated to be incomplete, that is, representing less than 90 per cent of the divorces occurring each year. The code (...) indicates that no information was provided regarding completeness.

Data from civil registers which are reported as incomplete or of unknown completeness (coded U or ...) are considered unreliable. They appear in *italics* in this table and the rates were not computed on data so coded. These quality codes apply only to data from civil registers. For more information about the quality of vital statistics data in general, see section 4.2 of the Technical Notes.

Limitations: Statistics on divorces are subject to the same qualifications as have been set forth for vital statistics in general and divorce statistics in particular as discussed in section 4 of the Technical Notes.

Divorce, like marriage, is a legal event, and this has implications for international comparability of data. Divorce has been defined, for statistical purposes, in terms of the laws of individual countries or areas. The laws pertaining to divorce vary considerably from one country or area to another. This variation in the legal provision for divorce also affects the incidence of divorce, which is relatively low in countries or areas where divorce decrees are difficult to obtain.

Since divorces are granted by courts and statistics on divorce refer to the actual divorce decree, effective as of the date of the decree, marked year-to-year fluctuations may reflect court delays and clearances rather than trends in the incidence of divorce. The comparability of divorce statistics may also be affected by tabulation procedures. In some countries or areas annulments and/or legal separations may be included. This practice is more common for countries or areas in which the number of divorces is small. Information on this practice is given in the footnotes when known.

Because the registration of a divorce in many countries or areas is the responsibility solely of the court or the authority which granted it, and since the registration recording such cases is part of the records of the court proceedings, it follows that divorces are likely to be registered soon after the decree is granted. For this reason the practice of tabulating data by date of registration does not generally pose serious problems of comparability as it does in the case of birth and death statistics.

As noted briefly above, the incidence of divorce is affected by the relative ease or difficulty of obtaining a divorce according to the laws of individual countries or areas. The incidence of divorce is also affected by the ability of individuals to meet financial and other costs of the court procedures. Connected with this aspect is the influence of certain religious faiths on the incidence of divorce. For all these reasons, divorce statistics are not strictly comparable as measures of family dissolution by legal means. Furthermore, family dissolution by other than legal means, such as separation, is not measured in statistics for divorce.

For certain countries or areas there is or was no legal provision for divorce in the sense used here, and therefore no data for these countries or areas appear in this table.

In addition, it should be noted that rates are affected also by the quality and limitations of the population estimates which are used in their computation. The problems of under-enumeration or over-enumeration, and to some extent, the differences in definition of total population, have been discussed in section 3 of the Technical Notes dealing with population data in general, and specific information pertaining to individual countries or areas is given in the footnotes to table 3.

As will be seen from the footnotes, strict correspondence between the numerator of the rate and the denominator is not always obtained; for example, divorces among civilian plus military segments of the population may be related to civilian population. The effect of this may be to increase the rates or, if the population is larger than that from which the divorces are drawn, to decrease them but, in most cases, the effect is probably negligible.

As mentioned above, data for some countries or areas may include annulments and/or legal separations. This practice will affect the comparability of the crude divorce rates. For example, inclusion of annulments in the numerator of the rates produces a negligible effect on the rates, but inclusion of legal separations may have a measurable effect on the level.

It should be emphasized that crude divorce rates like crude birth, death and marriage rates may be seriously affected by age-sex structure of the populations to which they relate. Like crude marriage rates, they also affected by the existing distribution of the population by marital status. Nevertheless, crude divorce rates provide a simple measure of the level and changes in divorce.

Coverage: Divorces are shown for 115 countries or areas.

Earlier data: Divorces have been shown in previous issues of the Demographic Yearbook. The earliest data, which were for 1935, appeared in the 1951 issue. For more information on specific topics and years for which data are reported, readers should consult the Index.

NOTES

[i] For definition, please see section 4.1.1.4 of the Technical Notes.

Tableau 25

Le tableau 25 présente des statistiques des divorces et des taux bruts de divortialité pour le plus grand nombre d'années possible entre 1997 et 2001.

Description des variables: Le divorce est la dissolution légale et définitive des liens du mariage, c'est-à-dire la séparation de l'époux et de l'épouse qui confère aux parties le droit de se remarier civilement ou religieusement, ou selon toute autre procédure, conformément à la législation du pays[1].

Sauf indication contraire, les statistiques de la divortialité n'englobent pas les séparations légales qui excluent un remariage. Ces statistiques se rapportent aux jugements de divorce prononcés, non aux personnes divorcées.

Les statistiques de la divortialité sont tirées, selon la pratique suivie par chaque pays, des actes des tribunaux et/ou des registres de l'état civil. L'officier d'état civil, les services nationaux de statistique ou d'autres services gouvernementaux peuvent être chargés d'établir ces statistiques.

Calcul des taux : Les taux bruts de divortialité représentent le nombre annuel de divorces enregistrés pour 1 000 habitants au milieu de l'année.

Les taux de ce tableau ne se rapportent qu'aux pays ou zones où l'on a enregistré un total d'au moins 100 divorces dans une année donnée. Ces taux ont été calculés par la Division de statistique de l'ONU.

Fiabilité des données : Il a été demandé à chaque pays ou zone d'indiquer le degré estimatif de complétude des données sur les divorces figurant dans ses registres d'état civil. Ces évaluations nationales sont désignées par les codes de qualité (C) et (U) qui apparaissent dans la première colonne du tableau.

La lettre (C) indique que les données sont jugées à peu près complètes, c'est-à-dire qu'elles représentent au moins 90 p. 100 des divorces survenus chaque année; la lettre (U) indique que les données sont jugées incomplètes, c'est-à-dire qu'elles représentent moins de 90 p. 100 des divorces survenus chaque année. Le signe (...) indique qu'aucun renseignement n'a été fourni quant à la complétude des données.

Les données provenant des registres de l'état civil qui sont déclarées incomplètes ou dont le degré de complétude n'est pas connu (et qui sont affectées de la lettre (U) ou du signe (...) sont jugées douteuses. Elles apparaissent en *italique* dans le présent tableau. Les taux ne sont pas calculés sur ces données. Ces codes de qualité ne s'appliquent qu'aux données tirées des registres de l'état civil. Pour plus de précision sur la qualité des données reposant sur les statistiques de l'état civil en général, voir la section 4.2 des notes techniques.

Insuffisance des données : Les statistiques des divorces appellent toutes les réserves qui ont été formulées à propos des statistiques de l'état civil en général et des statistiques de divortialité en particulier (voir explications figurant à la section 4 des notes techniques).

Le divorce est, comme le mariage, un acte juridique, et ce fait influe sur la comparabilité internationale des données. Aux fins de la statistique, le divorce est défini par la législation de chaque pays ou zone. La législation sur le divorce varie considérablement d'un pays ou d'une zone à l'autre, ce qui influe aussi sur la fréquence des divorces qui est relativement faible dans les pays ou zones où le jugement de divorce est difficile à obtenir.

Comme les divorces sont prononcés par les tribunaux et que les statistiques de la divortialité se rapportent aux jugements de divorce proprement dits qui prennent effet à la date où ces jugements sont rendus, il se peut que des fluctuations annuelles accusées traduisent le rythme plus ou moins rapide auquel les affaires sont jugées plutôt que l'évolution de la fréquence des divorces. Les méthodes d'exploitation des données peuvent aussi influer sur la comparabilité des statistiques de la divortialité. Dans certains pays ou zones, ces statistiques peuvent comprendre les annulations et ou les séparations légales. C'est fréquemment le cas, en particulier dans les pays ou zones où les divorces sont peu nombreux. Lorsqu'ils sont connus, des renseignements à ce propos sont indiqués dans une note au bas du tableau.

Comme dans de nombreux pays ou zones, le tribunal ou l'autorité qui a prononcé le divorce est seul habilité à enregistrer cet acte, et, comme l'acte d'enregistrement figure alors sur les registres du tribunal, l'enregistrement suit généralement de peu le jugement. C'est pourquoi la pratique consistant à exploiter les données selon la date de l'enregistrement ne pose généralement pas les graves problèmes de comparabilité auxquels on se heurte dans le cas des statistiques des naissances et des décès.

Comme on l'a brièvement mentionné ci-dessus, la fréquence des divorces est fonction notamment de la facilité relative avec laquelle la législation de chaque pays ou zone permet d'obtenir le divorce. La fréquence des divorces dépend également de la capacité des intéressées à supporter les frais de procédure. A cet égard, il convient de citer aussi l'influence de certaines religions sur la fréquence des divorces. Pour toutes ces raisons, les statistiques de divortialité ne sont pas rigoureusement comparables et ne permettent pas de mesurer exactement la fréquence des dissolutions légales de mariages. De plus, les statistiques de la divortialité ne rendent pas compte des cas de dissolution extrajudiciaire du mariage, comme la séparation.

Dans certains pays ou zones, il n'existe ou il n'existait pas de législation sur le divorce selon l'acceptation retenue aux fins du présent tableau, si bien qu'on n'y trouve aucune indication pour ces pays ou zones.

Il convient de noter par ailleurs que l'exactitude des taux dépend également de la qualité et des insuffisances des estimations de population qui sont utilisées pour leur calcul. Le problème des erreurs par excès ou par défaut commises lors du dénombrement et, dans une certain mesure, le problème de l'hétérogénéité des définitions de la population totale ont été examinés à la section 3 des Notes techniques relatives à la population en général; des indications concernant les différents pays ou zones sont données en note au bas du tableau 3.

Comme on le verra dans les notes, il n'a pas toujours été possible pour le calcul des taux, d'obtenir une correspondance rigoureuse entre le numérateur et le dénominateur. Par exemple, les divorces parmi la population civile et les militaires sont parfois rapportés à la population civile. Cela peut avoir pour effet d'accroître les taux; au contraire, si la population de base englobe un plus grand nombre de personnes que celle dans laquelle les divorces ont été comptés, les taux seront plus faibles, mais, dans la plupart des cas, il est probable que la différence sera négligeable.

Comme il est indiqué plus haut, les données fournies pour certains pays ou zones peuvent comprendre les annulations et/ou les séparations légales. Cette pratique influe sur la comparabilité des taux bruts de divortialité. Par exemple, l'inclusion des annulations dans le numérateur a une influence négligeable, mais l'inclusion des séparations légales peut avoir un effet appréciable sur le niveau du taux.

Il faut souligner que les taux bruts de divortialité, de même que les taux bruts de natalité, de mortalité et de nuptialité, peuvent varier sensiblement selon la structure par âge et par sexe. Comme les taux bruts de nuptialité, ils peuvent également varier du fait de la répartition de la population selon l'état matrimonial. Les taux bruts de divortialité offrent néanmoins un moyen simple de mesurer la fréquence et l'évolution des divorces.

Portée: Ce tableau présente des statistiques des divorces pour 115 pays ou zones.

Données publiées antérieurement : Des statistiques des divorces ont déjà été présentées dans des éditions antérieures de l'Annuaire démographique. Les plus anciennes qui portaient sur 1935 ont été publiées dans l'édition de 1951. Pour plus de précisions concernant les sujets spécifiques et les années pour lesquelles des données ont été publiées, se reporter à l'Index.

NOTES

[1] Pour la définition, voir la section 4.1.1.4 des Notes techniques.

(See notes at end of table. — Voir notes à la fin du tableau.)

Continent and country or area Continent et pays ou zone	Code[1]	Divorces					Rate - Taux				
		1997	1998	1999	2000	2001	1997	1998	1999	2000	2001
AFRICA — AFRIQUE											
Côte d'Ivoire	...	...	52 083	...	...	...	...	...	...	...	...
Djibouti	C	...	1 327	1 207	...	...	...	...	...	...	...
Egypt - Égypte[2]	U	70 899	71 792	73 414	...	...	...	...	...	...	...
Ethiopia - Éthiopie	...	...	...	161 390	...	...	...	...	...	...	...
Libyan Arab Jamahiriya - Jamahiriya arabe libyenne[3]	C	1 174	1 279	1 095	1 444	1 662	0.25	0.27	0.22	0.28	0.31
Mauritius - Maurice	+C	891	1 012	1 150	1 191	1 512	0.78	0.87	0.98	1.00	1.26
Réunion	C	967	1 121	1 057	934	*904	1.41	1.61	1.49	1.29	*1.23
Saint Helena ex. dep. - Sainte-Hélène sans dép.	C	7	5	8	9	...	...	...	...	...	...
Seychelles	+C	89	79	102	88	109	...	...	1.27	...	1.34
South Africa - Afrique du Sud	...	34 231	35 792	...	...	...	...	...	...	...	...
Tunisia - Tunisie	...	9 546	...	8 915	...	...	...	...	...	...	...
AMERICA, NORTH — AMERIQUE DU NORD											
Anguilla	+C	...	...	...	10	*11	...	...	...	...	...
Aruba	C	305	331	292	329	332	3.53	3.74	3.26	3.63	3.61
Belize	+C	39	35	72	43	36	...	...	...	...	...
Bermuda - Bermudes	C	183	186	...	...	...	3.03	...	...	...	...
Canada	C	67 408	69 088	70 910	71 144	...	2.25	2.29	2.33	2.32	...
Cayman Islands - Îles Caïmanes	C	40	76	64	...	...	...	...	...	...	...
Costa Rica	C	4 355	7 188	...	...	...	1.26	2.04	...	...	...
Cuba	C	41 195	39 798	40 068	37 937	37 260	3.72	3.58	3.59	3.39	3.32
Dominica - Dominique	...	51	71	61	...	...	...	...	...	...	...
Dominican Republic - République dominicaine	C	...	7 813	9 639	...	8 358	...	0.96	1.16	...	0.98
El Salvador	C	3 067	2 931	3 146	3 430	*2 662	0.52	0.49	0.51	0.55	*0.42
Grenada - Grenade	C	131	127	120	102	*114	1.32	1.27	1.19	1.01	*1.13
Guatemala	...	1 403	1 275	1 373	...	...	...	...	...	...	...
Jamaica - Jamaïque	C	1 266	1 420	1 131	...	...	0.50	0.55	0.44	...	...
Mexico - Mexique	+C	40 792	45 889	49 271	52 358	*57 370	0.43	0.47	0.50	0.52	*0.56
Netherlands Antilles - Antilles néerlandaises	+C	604	547	532	...	...	2.90	2.63	2.59	...	...
Nicaragua[4]	...	2 789	2 775	2 903	...	...	...	...	...	...	...
Panama[4]	C	1 756	2 126	2 135	2 189	2 309	0.65	0.77	0.76	0.77	0.80
Puerto Rico - Porto Rico	C	13 737	14 636	15 550	17 829	13 870	3.70	3.90	4.11	4.67	3.61
Saint Lucia - Sainte-Lucie	C	37	43	26	26	26	...	...	...	...	...
Saint Vincent and the Grenadines - Saint Vincent-et-les Grenadines	C	66	71	64	57	56	...	...	...	...	...
Trinidad and Tobago - Trinité-et-Tobago	C	1 278	...	...	...	...	1.00	...	...	...	...
United States - États-Unis[5]	...	1 163 000	1 135 000	...	...	...	...	...	...	...	...
AMERICA, SOUTH — AMERIQUE DU SUD											
Brazil - Brésil[6]	...	...	...	121 333	121 417	122 791	...	...	...	...	...
Chile - Chili	...	6 302	6 269	...	...	...	...	...	...	...	...
Ecuador - Équateur[7]	...	8 557	8 907	...	10 796	...	...	...	...	...	...
French Guiana - Guyane française	...	167	...	...	...	...	...	...	...	...	...
Peru - Pérou	...	...	2 108	...	...	...	...	...	...	...	...
Suriname	...	517	357	384	392	...	...	...	...	...	...
Uruguay	+C	8 347	6 598	7 002	6 822	...	2.56	2.01	2.11	2.04	...
Venezuela[6]	...	20 341	21 334	20 544	19 062	16 939	...	...	...	...	...
ASIA — ASIE											
Armenia - Arménie	C	2 317	1 612	1 253	1 343	1 776	0.61	0.42	0.33	0.35	0.47
Azerbaijan - Azerbaïdjan	+C	5 806	5 657	5 013	5 478	5 382	0.74	0.71	0.63	0.68	0.66
Bahrain - Bahreïn	...	814	790	834	769	...	...	...	...	...	...

(See notes at end of table. — Voir notes à la fin du tableau.)

Continent and country or area	Code[1]	Divorces					Rate - Taux				
Continent et pays ou zone		1997	1998	1999	2000	2001	1997	1998	1999	2000	2001

ASIA — ASIE

Brunei Darussalam - Brunéi Darussalam	...	...	376	389	369	...	...	...	...	...	...
China - Chine	+C	1 198 000	1 191 000	...	...	...	0.97	0.95	...	...	...
China: Hong Kong SAR - Chine: Hong Kong RAS	...	10 492	13 129	13 408	13 247	13 425	...	...	...	...	...
China: Macao SAR - Chine: Macao RAS	C	304	260	283	369	348	0.73	0.62	0.66	0.86	0.80
Cyprus - Chypre[8]	C	851	852	1 193	1 182	1 197	1.12	1.11	1.54	1.51	1.52
Georgia - Géorgie	C	2 300	1 800	1 622	1 854	1 987	0.42	0.33	0.35	0.37	0.40
Iran (Islamic Republic of) - Iran (République islamique d')	...	41 816	42 391	51 044	...	...	...	...	...	...	...
Iraq[9]	U	28 800									
Israel - Israël[10]	C	9 099	9 886	10 683	10 723	11 164	1.56	1.66	1.74	1.70	1.73
Japan - Japon[11]	+C	222 635	243 183	250 529	264 246	285 911	1.77	1.92	1.98	2.08	2.25
Jordan - Jordanie[12]	+C	6 535	7 671	7 885	6 317	...	1.42	1.61	1.61	1.25	*...
Kazakhstan	C	35 736	35 460	25 583	...	*29 599	2.27	2.35	1.71	...	*2.00
Korea (Republic of) - Corée (République de)[13]	+C	91 159	116 727	118 014	119 982	135 014	1.98	2.52	2.53	2.55	2.85
Kuwait - Koweït	C	3 128	3 428	3 412	3 649	...	1.58	1.69	1.62	1.67	...
Kyrgyzstan - Kirghizistan	C	6 541	6 216	6 287	5 348	5 861	1.39	1.31	1.30	1.09	1.19
Lebanon - Liban[9]	+C	3 795	3 925	2 292	4 220	...	...	...	...	...	...
Mongolia - Mongolie	C	1 027	917	941	815	650	0.45	0.39	0.40	0.34	0.27
Occupied Palestinian Territory - Territoire palestinien occupé	U	3 449	3 465	3 761	3 546	3 687	...	...	...	...	...
Qatar	U	551	458	496	615	566	...	...	...	...	...
Saudi Arabia - Arabie saoudite	...	...	...	15 697	18 583	...	...	...	...	...	...
Singapore - Singapour	+C	4 687	5 389	5 084	4 943	4 838	1.24	1.37	1.29	1.23	1.17
Syrian Arab Republic - République arabe syrienne[14]	U	11 673	11 363	12 453	11 863	13 077	...	...	...	...	...
Turkey - Turquie	U	32 717	32 167	31 540	34 862	...	...	...	...	...	...
Turkmenistan - Turkménistan	C	...	5 346	...	...	...	...	1.10	...	...	...
Uzbekistan - Ouzbékistan	C	21 545	...	14 608	19 903	15 646	0.91	...	0.61	0.81	0.63

EUROPE

Austria - Autriche	C	18 027	17 884	18 512	19 552	20 582	2.23	2.21	2.29	2.41	2.53
Belarus - Bélarus	C	47 301	47 127	47 254	43 512	...	4.63	4.62	4.71	4.35	...
Belgium - Belgique[15]	C	26 748	26 503	26 423	27 002	*29 314	2.63	2.60	2.58	2.63	*2.85
Bosnia and Herzegovina - Bosnie-Herzégovine	C	1 835	1 964	...	1 436	...	0.49	0.54	...	...	...
Bulgaria - Bulgarie[16]	C	9 368	10 390	9 781	10 575	10 268	1.13	1.26	1.19	1.29	1.30
Channel Islands: Guernsey - Îles Anglo-Normandes: Guernesey	C	175	143	142	173	...	2.96	2.42	2.36	2.86	...
Croatia - Croatie	C	3 899	3 962	3 721	4 419	4 670	0.85	0.88	0.82	1.01	1.05
Czech Republic - République tchèque	C	32 465	32 363	23 657	29 704	*31 586	3.15	3.14	2.30	2.89	3.09
Denmark - Danemark[17]	C	12 774	13 164	13 537	14 381	*14 597	2.42	2.48	2.54	2.70	*2.72
Estonia - Estonie	C	5 281	4 491	4 561	4 230	4 312	3.62	3.10	3.16	3.09	3.17
Finland - Finlande[18]	C	13 507	13 848	14 030	13 913	13 568	2.63	2.69	2.72	2.69	2.62
France[19]	C	116 158	116 515	116 813	114 003	...	1.98	2.00	1.99	1.94	...
Germany - Allemagne	C	187 802	...	190 590	194 408	...	2.29	...	2.32	2.37	...
Greece - Grèce	C	9 422	9 500	...	11 119	*9 500	0.90	0.90	...	1.11	*0.95
Hungary - Hongrie	C	24 992	25 763	25 584	23 987	24 379	2.46	2.55	2.54	2.39	2.39
Iceland - Islande[20]	C	514	484	473	545	551	1.90	1.77	1.71	1.94	1.93
Ireland - Irlande	...	...	...	...	2 623	...	...	...	...	...	...
Isle of Man - Îles de Man	+C	443	372	388	394	353	6.11	5.04	...	5.26	...
Italy - Italie	C	33 342	33 540	34 341	37 573	...	0.58	0.58	0.60	0.65	...
Latvia - Lettonie	C	6 103	6 211	6 010	6 134	5 740	2.51	2.58	2.51	2.58	2.44
Liechtenstein	C	64	...	...	...	...	...	...	...	...	...
Lithuania - Lituanie	C	11 371	11 752	11 390	10 882	11 024	3.18	3.31	3.23	3.11	3.17
Luxembourg	C	1 001	1 017	1 043	1 030	1 029	2.38	2.38	2.41	2.36	2.33

25. Divorces and crude divorce rates: 1997 - 2001
Divorces et taux bruts de divortialité: 1997 - 2001 (continued — suite)

(See notes at end of table. — Voir notes à la fin du tableau.)

Continent and country or area / Continent et pays ou zone	Code[1]	Divorces					Rate - Taux				
		1997	1998	1999	2000	2001	1997	1998	1999	2000	2001
EUROPE											
Monaco	C	66	62	...	82	...	...	...	...	...	...
Netherlands - Pays-Bas	C	33 740	32 459	33 571	34 650	37 104	2.16	2.07	2.12	2.18	2.31
Norway - Norvège	C	9 961	9 346	9 124	10 053	10 308	2.26	2.11	2.04	2.24	2.28
Poland - Pologne	C	42 549	45 230	42 020	42 770	45 308	1.10	1.17	1.09	1.11	1.17
Portugal	C	14 078	...	17 881	19 104	18 851	1.42	...	1.79	1.91	1.83
Republic of Moldova - République de Moldova	C	10 156	10 156	8 913	9 707	10 808	2.78	2.78	2.44	2.67	2.98
Romania - Roumanie	C	34 752	39 985	34 408	30 725	31 135	1.54	1.78	1.53	1.37	1.39
Russian Federation - Fédération de Russie	C	555 160	501 654	532 533	627 703	*763 493	3.77	3.42	3.65	4.31	*5.30
San Marino - Saint-Marin	+C	34	36	51	38	...	...	...	...	...	...
Serbia and Montenegro - Serbie-et-Montenegro	C	7 947	7 874	7 211	8 520	8 511	0.75	0.74	0.68	0.80	0.80
Slovakia - Slovaquie	C	...	9 312	9 664	9 273	9 817	...	1.73	1.79	1.72	1.82
Slovenia - Slovénie	C	1 996	2 074	2 074	2 125	2 274	1.00	1.05	1.04	1.07	1.14
Spain - Espagne	C	34 147	36 072	36 900	38 973	...	0.87	0.91	0.93	0.98	...
Sweden - Suède	C	21 009	20 761	21 000	21 502	21 022	2.37	2.35	2.37	2.42	2.36
Switzerland - Suisse	C	17 073	17 868	20 809	10 511	15 778	2.41	2.51	2.91	1.46	2.18
The Former Yugoslav Rep. of Macedonia - L'ex-République yougoslave de Macédoine	C	1 021	...	1 045	1 325	1 448	0.51	...	0.52	...	0.71
Ukraine	C	188 232	179 688	...	...	181 334	3.70	3.56	...	...	3.70
United Kingdom - Royaume-Uni	C	160 733	159 688	158 418	154 273	...	2.72	2.70	2.66	2.58	...
OCEANIA — OCEANIE											
Australia - Australie[21]	C	51 288	51 370	52 566	49 906	*55 330	2.77	2.74	2.78	2.61	*2.85
New Caledonia - Nouvelle-Calédonie	C	179	196	161	159	*230	0.89	0.96	0.78	0.75	*1.07
New Zealand - Nouvelle-Zélande	+C	9 754	10 037	9 936	...	9 683	2.59	2.65	2.61	...	2.52
Tonga[22]	+C	66	86	91	113	...	...	...	...	1.13	...

GENERAL NOTES - NOTES GENERALES

Data exclude annulments and legal separations unless otherwise specified. Rates are the number of final divorce decrees granted under civil law per 1 000 mid-year population. Rates are shown only for countries or areas having at least a total of 100 divorces in a given year. For method of evaluation and limitations of data, see Technical Notes for this table. — Sauf indications contraires, il n'est pas tenu compte des annulations et des séparations légales. Les taux représentent le nombre de jugements de divorce définitifs prononcés par les tribunaux pour 1 000 personnes au milieu de l'année. Les taux présentés ne se rapportent qu'aux pays ou zones où l'on a enregistré un total d'au moins 100 divorces dans une année donnée. Pour la méthode d'évaluation et les insuffisances des données, voir Notes techniques pour ce tableau.

Italics: data from civil registers which are incomplete or of unknown completeness. — *Italiques:* données incomplètes ou dont le degré d'exactitude n'est pas connu, provenant des registres de l'état civil.

FOOTNOTES - NOTES

* Provisional. — Données provisoires.
+ Data tabulated by date of registration rather than occurrence. — Données exploitées selon la date de l'enregistrement et non la date de l'événement.

[1] 'Code' indicates the source of data, as follows:
C - Civil registration, estimated over 90% complete
U - Civil registration, estimated less than 90% complete
+ - Data tabulated by date of registration rather than occurence.

... - Information not available

Le 'Code' indique la source des données, comme suit:
C - Registres de l'état civil considérés complèts à 90 p. 100 au moins.
U - Registres de l'état civil qui ne sont pas considérés complèts à 90 p. 100 au moins.
+ - Données exploitées selon la date de l'enregistrement et non la date de l'événement.
... - Information pas disponible.

[2] Including 'revocable divorces' (among Moslem population), which approximate legal separations. — Y compris les 'divorces révocables' (parmi la population musulmane), qui sont à peu près l'équivalent des séparations légales.
[3] Data refer to Libyan nationals only. — Les données se raportent aux nationaux libyens seulement.
[4] Excluding tribal Indian population. — Non compris les Indiens vivant en tribus.
[5] Estimates based on divorces and annulments reported by varying number of states from year to year. — Estimations fondées sur les chiffres (divorces et annulations) communiqués par un nombre variable d'Etats d'une année a l'autre.
[6] Excluding Indian jungle population. — Non compris les Indiens de la jungle.
[7] Excluding nomadic Indian tribes. — Non compris les tribus d'Indiens nomades.
[8] Data refer to government controlled areas. — Les données se raportent aux zones contrôlées par le Gouvernement.
[9] Published by the United Nations Economic and Social Commission for Western Asia. — Edité par les Nations Unies économiques et la Commission sociale pour l'Asie occidentale.
[10] Including data for East Jerusalem and Israeli residents in certain other

territories under occupation by Israeli military forces since June 1967. — Y compris les données pour Jérusalem-Est et les résidents israéliens dans certains autres territoires occupés depuis 1967 par les forces armées israéliennes.

[11] Data refer to Japanese nationals in Japan only. — Les données se raportent aux nationaux japonais au Japon seulement.

[12] Excluding data for Jordanian territory under occupation since June 1967 by Israeli military forces. Excluding foreigners, including registered Palestinian refugees. — Non compris les données pour le territoire jordanien occupé depuis juin 1967 par les forces armées israéliennes. Non compris les étrangers, mais y compris les réfugiés de Palestine immatriculés.

[13] Excluding alien armed forces, civilian aliens employed by armed forces, and foreign diplomatic personnel and their dependants. — Non compris les militaires étrangers, les civils étrangers employés par les forces armées ni le personnel diplomatique étranger et les membres de leur famille les accompagnant.

[14] Excluding nomads. — Non compris les nomades.

[15] Including divorces among armed forces stationed outside the country and alien armed forces in the area. — Y compris les divorces de militaires nationaux hors du pays et les militaires étrangers en garnison sur le territoire.

[16] Including Bulgarian nationals outside the country, but excluding foreigners in the country. — Y compris les nationaux bulgares à l'étranger, mais non compris les étrangers sur le territoire.

[17] Excluding Faeroe Islands and Greenland. — Non compris les îles Féroé et Gröenland.

[18] Including nationals temporarily outside the country. — Y compris les nationaux se trouvant temporairement hors du pays.

[19] Rates computed on population including armed forces stationed outside the country, but excluding alien armed forces living in military camps within the country. — Taux calculés sur la base de la population qui comprend les militaires nationaux hors du pays, mais pas les militaires étrangers en garnison sur le territoire.

[20] Data refer to de jure population. — Les données se raportent a la population de droit.

[21] Excluding full-blooded aborigines estimated at 49 036 in June 1966. — - Non compris les aborig-nes purs, estimés à 49 036 personnes en juin 1966.

[22] Including annulments. — Y compris les annulations.

Annex I: United Nations Projections - Annual interpolated mid-year population, estimates 1992-2000 and medium variant projections 2001
Annexe I: Projections de la population de l'ONU 2002 - Population au milieu de l'année interpolée, estimations 1992 - 2000 et projections de variante moyenne 2001

(See notes at end of table. — Voir notes à la fin du tableau.)

Continent and country or area / Continent et pays ou zone	Population estimates and projections (in thousands) - Estimations et projections (en milliers)[1]									
	1992	1993	1994	1995	1996	1997	1998	1999	2000	2001
AFRICA — AFRIQUE										
Algeria - Algérie	26 216	26 794	27 350	27 878	28 376	28 847	29 304	29 766	30 245	30 746
Angola	9 915	10 236	10 558	10 868	11 162	11 447	11 734	12 043	12 386	12 768
Benin - Bénin	4 969	5 139	5 307	5 470	5 624	5 772	5 917	6 066	6 222	6 387
Botswana	1 433	1 472	1 511	1 550	1 589	1 627	1 663	1 697	1 725	1 750
Burkina Faso	9 451	9 726	10 010	10 302	10 603	10 913	11 233	11 563	11 905	12 259
Burundi	5 819	5 903	5 970	6 024	6 060	6 085	6 114	6 169	6 267	6 412
Cameroon - Cameroun	12 354	12 706	13 060	13 414	13 766	14 115	14 458	14 793	15 117	15 429
Cape Verde - Cap-Vert	365	374	383	391	400	409	418	427	436	445
Central African Republic - République centrafricaine	3 100	3 186	3 271	3 354	3 434	3 511	3 585	3 653	3 715	3 770
Chad - Tchad	6 167	6 346	6 533	6 731	6 941	7 161	7 389	7 623	7 861	8 103
Comoros - Comores	558	575	592	609	627	646	665	685	705	726
Congo	2 662	2 750	2 841	2 936	3 035	3 139	3 244	3 348	3 447	3 542
Côte d'Ivoire	13 287	13 663	14 023	14 365	14 685	14 987	15 275	15 553	15 827	16 098
Democratic Republic of the Congo - République démocratique du Congo	40 239	41 759	43 170	44 383	45 353	46 128	46 821	47 596	48 571	49 785
Djibouti	550	554	559	568	584	604	626	648	666	681
Egypt - Égypte	58 132	59 297	60 463	61 638	62 823	64 019	65 237	66 489	67 784	69 124
Equatorial Guinea - Guinée équatoriale	371	381	391	401	411	422	433	444	456	468
Eritrea - Érythrée	3 149	3 154	3 169	3 207	3 271	3 358	3 464	3 584	3 712	3 847
Ethiopia - Éthiopie	52 202	53 925	55 648	57 349	59 020	60 667	62 299	63 936	65 590	67 266
Gabon	1 015	1 046	1 078	1 109	1 141	1 171	1 202	1 230	1 258	1 283
Gambia - Gambie	1 006	1 041	1 077	1 115	1 153	1 193	1 233	1 273	1 312	1 351
Ghana	16 165	16 620	17 071	17 510	17 935	18 349	18 758	19 171	19 593	20 028
Guinea - Guinée	6 593	6 850	7 098	7 321	7 518	7 691	7 844	7 984	8 117	8 242
Guinea-Bissau - Guinée-Bissau	1 082	1 118	1 154	1 190	1 224	1 259	1 293	1 329	1 367	1 407
Kenya	25 146	25 915	26 665	27 390	28 088	28 757	29 392	29 991	30 549	31 065
Lesotho	1 616	1 638	1 660	1 683	1 706	1 729	1 751	1 770	1 785	1 794
Liberia - Libéria	2 075	2 057	2 070	2 129	2 239	2 395	2 580	2 768	2 943	3 099
Libyan Arab Jamahiriya - Jamahiriya arabe libyenne	4 485	4 572	4 661	4 751	4 843	4 939	5 036	5 136	5 237	5 340
Madagascar	12 650	13 016	13 395	13 789	14 199	14 623	15 062	15 511	15 970	16 439
Malawi	9 797	9 854	9 921	10 047	10 245	10 501	10 793	11 091	11 370	11 627
Mali	9 543	9 806	10 077	10 356	10 643	10 940	11 248	11 568	11 904	12 256
Mauritania - Mauritanie	2 130	2 184	2 241	2 300	2 362	2 428	2 496	2 569	2 645	2 724
Mauritius - Maurice[2]	1 082	1 096	1 111	1 125	1 138	1 150	1 162	1 174	1 186	1 198
Morocco - Maroc	25 500	25 949	26 394	26 839	27 285	27 732	28 183	28 641	29 108	29 585
Mozambique	14 290	14 855	15 428	15 949	16 404	16 808	17 172	17 517	17 861	18 204
Namibia - Namibie	1 507	1 552	1 598	1 646	1 697	1 750	1 802	1 851	1 894	1 930
Niger	8 169	8 447	8 735	9 036	9 348	9 674	10 013	10 369	10 742	11 134
Nigeria - Nigéria	91 310	94 050	96 853	99 717	102 640	105 616	108 635	111 681	114 746	117 823
Réunion	627	639	652	664	676	688	700	711	723	734
Rwanda	6 057	5 567	5 217	5 136	5 378	5 890	6 557	7 209	7 724	8 066
Saint Helena - Sainte-Hélène[3]	5	5	5	5	5	5	5	5	5	5
Sao Tome and Principe - Sao Tomé-et-Principe	122	125	128	131	134	138	142	145	149	153
Senegal - Sénégal	7 740	7 937	8 137	8 338	8 542	8 748	8 957	9 172	9 393	9 621
Seychelles	73	73	74	75	76	77	77	78	79	80
Sierra Leone	4 091	4 081	4 074	4 081	4 105	4 144	4 205	4 294	4 415	4 573
Somalia - Somalie	7 209	7 215	7 254	7 356	7 528	7 762	8 050	8 373	8 720	9 088
South Africa - Afrique du Sud	38 507	39 343	40 157	40 930	41 657	42 334	42 956	43 513	44 000	44 416
Sudan - Soudan	26 105	26 752	27 415	28 077	28 736	29 397	30 062	30 741	31 437	32 151
Swaziland	887	904	920	939	960	983	1 006	1 027	1 044	1 058
Togo	3 609	3 683	3 767	3 869	3 991	4 130	4 278	4 425	4 562	4 686
Tunisia - Tunisie	8 522	8 672	8 815	8 950	9 075	9 193	9 305	9 412	9 519	9 624

Annex I: United Nations Projections - Annual interpolated mid-year population, estimates 1992-2000 and medium variant projections 2001
Annexe I: Projections de la population de l'ONU 2002 - Population au milieu de l'année interpolée, estimations 1992 - 2000 et projections de variante moyenne 2001
(continued — suite)

(See notes at end of table. — Voir notes à la fin du tableau.)

Continent and country or area Continent et pays ou zone	Population estimates and projections (in thousands) - Estimations et projections (en milliers)[1]									
	1992	1993	1994	1995	1996	1997	1998	1999	2000	2001
AFRICA — AFRIQUE										
Uganda - Ouganda	18 518	19 097	19 681	20 274	20 877	21 491	22 125	22 788	23 487	24 225
United Republic of Tanzania - République Unie de Tanzanie	27 960	28 949	29 921	30 849	31 723	32 549	33 335	34 094	34 837	35 565
Western Sahara - Sahara occidental	223	231	239	247	254	262	270	277	285	293
Zambia - Zambie	8 673	8 908	9 140	9 371	9 600	9 827	10 044	10 243	10 419	10 570
Zimbabwe	11 025	11 272	11 506	11 731	11 948	12 155	12 346	12 512	12 650	12 756
AMERICA, NORTH — AMERIQUE DU NORD										
Anguilla	10	10	10	10	10	11	11	11	11	11
Antigua and Barbuda - Antigua-et-Barbuda	64	65	66	67	68	69	70	71	72	72
Aruba	70	73	76	79	82	85	88	91	93	96
Bahamas	266	272	278	283	288	292	296	299	303	307
Barbados - Barbade	259	260	262	263	264	265	266	267	267	268
Belize	196	202	208	213	219	224	230	235	240	245
Bermuda - Bermudes	75	76	77	77	78	78	79	79	80	80
British Virgin Islands - Îles Vierges britanniques	18	18	18	19	19	19	19	20	20	20
Canada	28 399	28 726	29 044	29 354	29 656	29 949	30 232	30 505	30 769	31 025
Cayman Islands - Îles Caïmanes	28	29	30	31	32	33	34	36	37	38
Costa Rica	3 230	3 309	3 390	3 475	3 564	3 655	3 748	3 840	3 929	4 013
Cuba	10 784	10 848	10 908	10 964	11 019	11 070	11 118	11 162	11 202	11 238
Dominica - Dominique	73	74	74	75	76	76	77	77	78	78
Dominican Republic - République dominicaine	7 304	7 429	7 556	7 685	7 817	7 950	8 085	8 220	8 353	8 485
El Salvador	5 318	5 435	5 553	5 669	5 781	5 891	5 998	6 104	6 209	6 313
Greenland - Groenland	56	56	56	56	56	56	56	56	56	56
Grenada - Grenade	85	84	84	83	83	82	82	81	81	81
Guadeloupe	400	403	406	409	413	416	420	424	428	432
Guatemala	9 211	9 456	9 711	9 976	10 250	10 533	10 825	11 121	11 423	11 728
Haiti - Haïti	7 165	7 275	7 381	7 485	7 590	7 693	7 797	7 901	8 005	8 111
Honduras	5 166	5 320	5 476	5 636	5 797	5 962	6 127	6 292	6 457	6 619
Jamaica - Jamaïque	2 406	2 428	2 450	2 472	2 493	2 514	2 536	2 558	2 580	2 603
Martinique	366	369	371	373	376	378	381	383	386	388
Mexico - Mexique	86 382	87 971	89 560	91 143	92 718	94 287	95 846	97 395	98 933	100 456
Montserrat	11	11	11	10	9	8	6	5	4	3
Netherlands Antilles - Antilles néerlandaises	194	198	202	205	208	210	212	213	215	217
Nicaragua	4 047	4 171	4 298	4 426	4 555	4 683	4 813	4 943	5 073	5 204
Panama	2 512	2 564	2 617	2 670	2 725	2 781	2 837	2 893	2 950	3 007
Puerto Rico - Porto Rico	3 590	3 622	3 653	3 683	3 712	3 740	3 767	3 792	3 816	3 838
Saint Kitts and Nevis - Saint-Kitts-et-Nevis	42	43	43	44	44	43	43	43	42	42
Saint Lucia - Sainte-Lucie	135	137	139	140	141	143	144	145	146	147
Saint Pierre and Miquelon - Saint Pierre-et-Miquelon	6	6	6	6	6	6	6	6	6	6
Saint Vincent and the Grenadines - Saint Vincent-et-les Grenadines ..	112	113	113	114	115	116	116	117	118	118
Trinidad and Tobago - Trinité-et-Tobago	1 233	1 243	1 252	1 261	1 268	1 274	1 279	1 284	1 289	1 294
Turks Caicos Islands - Îles Turques et Caïques	13	14	15	15	16	16	17	18	19	19
United States - États-Unis	261 192	264 065	266 991	269 945	272 924	275 928	278 948	281 975	285 003	288 025
United States Virgin Islands - Îles Vierges américaines	103	104	104	105	106	107	107	108	109	110

Annex I: United Nations Projections - Annual interpolated mid-year population, estimates 1992-2000 and medium variant projections 2001
Annexe I: Projections de la population de l'ONU 2002 - Population au milieu de l'année interpolée, estimations 1992 - 2000 et projections de variante moyenne 2001
(continued — suite)

(See notes at end of table. — Voir notes à la fin du tableau.)

Continent and country or area / Continent et pays ou zone	Population estimates and projections (in thousands) - Estimations et projections (en milliers)[1]									
	1992	1993	1994	1995	1996	1997	1998	1999	2000	2001
AMERICA, SOUTH — AMERIQUE DU SUD										
Argentina - Argentine	33 418	33 865	34 314	34 768	35 227	35 689	36 153	36 615	37 074	37 529
Bolivia - Bolivie	6 985	7 149	7 315	7 482	7 649	7 816	7 984	8 150	8 317	8 481
Brazil - Brésil	153 632	155 962	158 261	160 545	162 816	165 073	167 321	169 561	171 796	174 029
Chile - Chili	13 547	13 771	13 993	14 210	14 422	14 628	14 829	15 027	15 224	15 419
Colombia - Colombie	36 377	37 096	37 819	38 542	39 262	39 981	40 697	41 410	42 120	42 826
Ecuador - Équateur	10 729	10 959	11 184	11 404	11 617	11 823	12 025	12 223	12 420	12 616
Falkland Islands (Malvinas) - Îles Falkland (Malvinas)	2	2	2	2	3	3	3	3	3	3
French Guiana - Guyane française	126	130	134	139	143	149	154	159	164	169
Guyana	732	734	738	741	745	749	752	756	759	762
Paraguay	4 463	4 584	4 705	4 829	4 954	5 080	5 208	5 338	5 470	5 604
Peru - Pérou	22 597	23 009	23 421	23 837	24 259	24 684	25 111	25 535	25 952	26 362
Suriname	405	406	407	409	412	415	418	422	425	429
Uruguay	3 149	3 171	3 195	3 218	3 242	3 267	3 292	3 317	3 342	3 366
Venezuela	20 458	20 935	21 411	21 888	22 367	22 845	23 323	23 800	24 277	24 752
ASIA — ASIE										
Afghanistan	15 780	17 060	18 257	19 217	19 875	20 287	20 570	20 896	21 391	22 083
Armenia - Arménie	3 492	3 439	3 380	3 324	3 273	3 225	3 181	3 144	3 112	3 088
Azerbaijan - Azerbaïdjan	7 439	7 565	7 684	7 790	7 880	7 957	8 025	8 090	8 157	8 226
Bahrain - Bahreïn	527	547	567	587	606	624	642	660	677	693
Bangladesh	114 885	117 697	120 541	123 406	126 290	129 191	132 103	135 025	137 952	140 880
Bhutan - Bhoutan	1 745	1 763	1 785	1 814	1 851	1 896	1 948	2 004	2 063	2 125
Brunei Darussalam - Brunéi Darussalam	272	280	288	295	303	311	318	326	334	342
Cambodia - Cambodge	10 437	10 789	11 140	11 485	11 824	12 158	12 488	12 817	13 147	13 478
China - Chine[4]	1 183 306	1 195 728	1 207 658	1 219 435	1 231 131	1 242 632	1 253 879	1 264 764	1 275 215	1 285 229
China - Hong Kong SAR - Chine - Hong Kong RAS[5]	5 864	5 961	6 068	6 183	6 307	6 439	6 571	6 696	6 807	6 901
China - Macao SAR - Chine - Macao RAS[6]	390	398	405	412	420	428	436	443	450	455
Cyprus - Chypre	705	719	732	744	754	762	770	776	783	789
Timor-Leste	795	823	839	840	821	787	747	715	702	711
Georgia - Géorgie	5 437	5 408	5 378	5 352	5 334	5 320	5 307	5 289	5 262	5 224
India - Inde	880 166	897 140	914 200	931 351	948 591	965 878	983 110	1 000 161	1 016 938	1 033 395
Indonesia - Indonésie	188 260	191 279	194 265	197 221	200 145	203 038	205 902	208 741	211 559	214 356
Iran (Islamic Republic of) - Iran (République islamique d')	59 275	60 394	61 424	62 382	63 273	64 100	64 887	65 661	66 443	67 245
Iraq	18 415	19 005	19 606	20 206	20 801	21 396	21 994	22 602	23 224	23 860
Israel - Israël	4 822	5 002	5 181	5 349	5 504	5 646	5 780	5 911	6 042	6 174
Japan - Japon	124 373	124 754	125 119	125 472	125 816	126 151	126 470	126 767	127 034	127 271
Jordan - Jordanie	3 628	3 841	4 052	4 249	4 428	4 591	4 742	4 889	5 035	5 183
Kazakhstan	16 849	16 790	16 690	16 556	16 388	16 190	15 983	15 793	15 640	15 533
Korea (Dem. People's Republic of) - Corée (Rép. populaire dém. de)	20 554	20 847	21 123	21 373	21 595	21 790	21 962	22 120	22 268	22 409
Korea (Republic of) - Corée (République de)	43 739	44 185	44 623	45 041	45 437	45 814	46 172	46 512	46 835	47 142
Kuwait - Koweït	1 976	1 843	1 738	1 696	1 730	1 829	1 969	2 117	2 247	2 353
Kyrgyzstan - Kirghizistan	4 468	4 492	4 521	4 562	4 619	4 687	4 764	4 844	4 921	4 995
Lao People's Democratic Republic - République démocratique populaire lao	4 350	4 460	4 572	4 686	4 801	4 918	5 036	5 156	5 279	5 403
Lebanon - Liban	2 861	2 960	3 059	3 150	3 229	3 298	3 360	3 419	3 478	3 537
Malaysia - Malaisie	18 817	19 323	19 839	20 363	20 894	21 431	21 966	22 492	23 001	23 492

Annex I: United Nations Projections - Annual interpolated mid-year population, estimates 1992-2000 and medium variant projections 2001

Annexe I: Projections de la population de l'ONU 2002 - Population au milieu de l'année interpolée, estimations 1992 - 2000 et projections de variante moyenne 2001

(continued — suite)

(See notes at end of table. — Voir notes à la fin du tableau.)

Continent and country or area / Continent et pays ou zone	Population estimates and projections (in thousands) - Estimations et projections (en milliers)[1]									
	1992	1993	1994	1995	1996	1997	1998	1999	2000	2001
ASIA — ASIE										
Maldives	229	236	243	250	258	266	274	282	291	300
Mongolia - Mongolie	2 303	2 336	2 366	2 392	2 415	2 436	2 455	2 476	2 500	2 528
Myanmar	41 927	42 652	43 376	44 094	44 803	45 502	46 193	46 874	47 544	48 205
Nepal - Népal	19 518	19 980	20 453	20 938	21 434	21 941	22 457	22 983	23 518	24 060
Oman	1 998	2 079	2 160	2 239	2 314	2 388	2 460	2 533	2 609	2 688
Pakistan	116 545	119 277	122 107	125 125	128 367	131 803	135 381	139 018	142 654	146 277
Philippines	63 989	65 453	66 924	68 396	69 867	71 337	72 802	74 261	75 711	77 151
Qatar	493	503	513	523	534	546	558	570	581	591
Saudi Arabia - Arabie saoudite	17 583	18 020	18 470	18 969	19 531	20 143	20 796	21 469	22 147	22 829
Singapore - Singapour	3 182	3 275	3 374	3 478	3 586	3 698	3 811	3 918	4 016	4 105
Sri Lanka	17 242	17 428	17 607	17 781	17 951	18 116	18 277	18 437	18 595	18 752
Syrian Arab Republic - République arabe syrienne	13 472	13 844	14 218	14 596	14 979	15 367	15 759	16 157	16 560	16 968
Tajikistan - Tadjikistan	5 509	5 591	5 667	5 741	5 816	5 889	5 961	6 028	6 089	6 144
Thailand - Thaïlande	55 806	56 497	57 171	57 828	58 465	59 084	59 695	60 306	60 925	61 555
Turkey - Turquie	59 820	60 914	61 998	63 070	64 131	65 181	66 221	67 254	68 281	69 303
Turkmenistan - Turkménistan	3 883	3 996	4 106	4 210	4 307	4 398	4 483	4 564	4 643	4 720
United Arab Emirates - Émirats arabes unis	2 229	2 324	2 414	2 497	2 572	2 639	2 701	2 761	2 820	2 879
Uzbekistan - Ouzbékistan	21 438	21 892	22 341	22 785	23 224	23 657	24 084	24 502	24 913	25 313
Viet Nam	68 901	70 279	71 598	72 841	73 995	75 070	76 093	77 106	78 137	79 197
Occupied Palestinian Territory - Territoire palestinien occupé	2 334	2 431	2 531	2 635	2 740	2 849	2 960	3 074	3 191	3 310
Yemen - Yémen	13 156	13 824	14 488	15 124	15 722	16 291	16 849	17 418	18 017	18 651
EUROPE										
Albania - Albanie	3 284	3 253	3 217	3 185	3 159	3 137	3 122	3 113	3 113	3 122
Andorra - Andorre	58	60	62	64	65	65	65	66	66	67
Austria - Autriche	7 859	7 932	7 997	8 047	8 078	8 094	8 099	8 100	8 102	8 106
Belarus - Bélarus	10 295	10 291	10 276	10 252	10 220	10 179	10 132	10 083	10 034	9 986
Belgium - Belgique	10 035	10 071	10 105	10 137	10 164	10 188	10 209	10 229	10 251	10 273
Bosnia and Herzegovina - Bosnie-Herzégovine	3 952	3 715	3 522	3 420	3 427	3 527	3 683	3 846	3 977	4 067
Bulgaria - Bulgarie	8 594	8 531	8 469	8 406	8 344	8 284	8 223	8 162	8 099	8 033
Channel Islands - Îles Anglo-Normandes	143	143	144	144	144	144	144	144	144	145
Croatia - Croatie	4 730	4 624	4 524	4 453	4 417	4 410	4 422	4 438	4 446	4 445
Czech Republic - République tchèque	10 319	10 327	10 331	10 331	10 324	10 313	10 298	10 283	10 269	10 257
Denmark - Danemark	5 170	5 188	5 208	5 228	5 248	5 268	5 287	5 305	5 322	5 338
Estonia - Estonie	1 542	1 508	1 475	1 446	1 424	1 407	1 393	1 380	1 367	1 353
Faeroe Islands - Îles Féroé	46	45	44	44	44	44	45	45	46	46
Finland - Finlande	5 034	5 061	5 086	5 108	5 126	5 142	5 154	5 166	5 177	5 188
France	57 318	57 605	57 880	58 139	58 380	58 604	58 823	59 051	59 296	59 564
Germany - Allemagne	80 410	80 890	81 316	81 661	81 909	82 067	82 159	82 221	82 282	82 349
Gibraltar	27	27	27	27	27	27	27	27	27	27
Greece - Grèce	10 259	10 314	10 378	10 454	10 543	10 644	10 745	10 834	10 903	10 947
Holy See - Saint-Siège[7]	1	1	1	1	1	1	1	1	1	1
Hungary - Hongrie	10 301	10 274	10 245	10 214	10 179	10 140	10 099	10 056	10 012	9 968
Iceland - Islande	260	262	265	267	270	273	276	279	282	285
Ireland - Irlande	3 533	3 553	3 579	3 609	3 644	3 684	3 728	3 773	3 819	3 865
Isle of Man - Îles de Man	70	71	71	71	72	72	73	73	74	74
Italy - Italie	56 930	57 062	57 191	57 301	57 390	57 458	57 504	57 530	57 536	57 521
Latvia - Lettonie	2 652	2 598	2 544	2 498	2 462	2 434	2 413	2 393	2 373	2 351
Liechtenstein	30	30	30	31	31	32	32	32	33	33

Annex I: United Nations Projections - Annual interpolated mid-year population, estimates 1992-2000 and medium variant projections 2001
Annexe I: Projections de la population de l'ONU 2002 - Population au milieu de l'année interpolée, estimations 1992 - 2000 et projections de variante moyenne 2001
(continued — suite)

(See notes at end of table. — Voir notes à la fin du tableau.)

Continent and country or area Continent et pays ou zone	Population estimates and projections (in thousands) - Estimations et projections (en milliers)[1]									
	1992	1993	1994	1995	1996	1997	1998	1999	2000	2001
EUROPE										
Lithuania - Lituanie	3 693	3 647	3 600	3 563	3 540	3 526	3 519	3 512	3 501	3 484
Luxembourg	387	393	399	405	411	417	423	429	435	441
Malta - Malte	367	371	375	378	381	383	385	387	389	391
Monaco	31	31	31	32	32	32	33	33	33	34
Netherlands - Pays-Bas	15 156	15 259	15 361	15 459	15 553	15 642	15 728	15 813	15 898	15 982
Norway - Norvège	4 287	4 311	4 335	4 359	4 383	4 406	4 429	4 451	4 473	4 494
Poland - Pologne	38 352	38 451	38 532	38 595	38 639	38 667	38 681	38 681	38 671	38 651
Portugal	9 885	9 891	9 903	9 916	9 933	9 953	9 974	9 996	10 016	10 033
Republic of Moldova - République de Moldova	4 370	4 362	4 351	4 339	4 327	4 315	4 303	4 292	4 283	4 276
Romania - Roumanie	23 059	22 924	22 789	22 681	22 608	22 563	22 536	22 512	22 480	22 437
Russian Federation - Fédération de Russie	148 787	148 685	148 449	148 141	147 778	147 348	146 848	146 270	145 612	144 877
San Marino - Saint-Marin	24	24	25	25	25	26	26	26	27	27
Serbia and Montenegro - Serbie-et-Montenegro	10 328	10 417	10 493	10 548	10 579	10 587	10 581	10 568	10 555	10 545
Slovakia - Slovaquie	5 304	5 327	5 348	5 364	5 375	5 381	5 385	5 388	5 391	5 394
Slovenia - Slovénie	1 948	1 965	1 979	1 990	1 996	1 997	1 995	1 992	1 990	1 988
Spain - Espagne	39 556	39 672	39 796	39 935	40 092	40 264	40 440	40 606	40 752	40 875
Sweden - Suède	8 678	8 737	8 789	8 827	8 850	8 859	8 859	8 856	8 856	8 860
Switzerland - Suisse	6 963	7 024	7 077	7 118	7 147	7 163	7 170	7 172	7 173	7 173
The Former Yugoslav Rep. of Macedonia - L'ex-République yougoslave de Macédoine ..	1 933	1 943	1 953	1 963	1 975	1 987	2 000	2 012	2 024	2 035
Ukraine	51 944	51 876	51 738	51 531	51 251	50 904	50 510	50 097	49 688	49 290
United Kingdom - Royaume-Uni	57 120	57 309	57 502	57 698	57 896	58 096	58 296	58 494	58 689	58 881
OCEANIA — OCEANIE										
American Samoa - Samoas américaines	49	50	51	52	53	54	55	56	58	59
Australia - Australie[8]	17 374	17 610	17 842	18 072	18 298	18 520	18 737	18 948	19 153	19 352
Cook Islands - Îles Cook	19	19	19	19	19	19	19	18	18	18
Fiji - Fidji	738	748	758	768	777	787	796	805	814	822
French Polynesia - Polynésie française	203	207	211	215	218	222	226	230	233	237
Guam	139	141	143	145	147	149	151	153	155	158
Kiribati	74	75	77	78	79	80	81	83	84	85
Marshall Islands - Îles Marshall	46	47	47	48	48	49	50	50	51	52
Micronesia, Federated States of - Micronésie, États Fédérés de La	101	104	106	107	108	108	107	107	107	107
Nauru	10	10	10	11	11	11	12	12	12	12
New Caledonia - Nouvelle-Calédonie	179	184	189	193	198	202	206	211	215	220
New Zealand - Nouvelle-Zélande	3 450	3 504	3 556	3 604	3 647	3 685	3 719	3 752	3 784	3 815
Niue - Nioué	2	2	2	2	2	2	2	2	2	2
Northern Mariana Islands - Îles Mariannes septentrionales	49	51	53	55	58	61	64	67	70	73
Palau - Palaos	16	16	17	17	18	18	18	19	19	20
Papua New Guinea - Papouasie-Nouvelle-Guin- ée	4 336	4 456	4 578	4 702	4 827	4 953	5 080	5 207	5 334	5 460
Pitcairn[9]	-	-	-	-	-	-	-	-	-	-
Samoa	162	163	164	166	167	168	170	171	173	175

Annex I: United Nations Projections - Annual interpolated mid-year population, estimates 1992-2000 and medium variant projections 2001

Annexe I: Projections de la population de l'ONU 2002 - Population au milieu de l'année interpolée, estimations 1992 - 2000 et projections de variante moyenne 2001

(continued — suite)

(See notes at end of table. — Voir notes à la fin du tableau.)

Continent and country or area Continent et pays ou zone	Population estimates and projections (in thousands) - Estimations et projections (en milliers)[1]									
	1992	1993	1994	1995	1996	1997	1998	1999	2000	2001
OCEANIA — OCEANIE										
Solomon Islands - Îles Salomon	340	351	362	374	386	398	411	424	437	450
Tokelau - Tokélaou	2	2	2	2	2	2	2	2	2	2
Tonga	99	99	99	99	99	100	100	100	101	102
Tuvalu	9	9	9	10	10	10	10	10	10	10
Vanuatu	158	163	167	172	177	182	187	192	197	202
Wallis and Futuna Islands - Îles Wallis et Futuna	14	14	14	14	14	14	14	14	14	15

FOOTNOTES - NOTES

[1] For 1992-2000 all data refer to annual interpolated estimates of mid-year population. For 2001 data refer to medium variant projections of the mid-year population. Both the estimates and the projections are produced by the Population Division of the Department for Economic and Social Affairs of the UN Secretariat and published in *World Population Prospects - The 2002 Revision,* United Nations publication, Sales no. E/03.XIII.6, Volume I, Table A.20, New York, 2003. — Les données pour 1992-2000 sont des estimations de population au milieu de l'année interpolée et ceux pour 2001 sont des projections de la population au milieu de l'année de variante moyenne. Toutes ces données sont produites par la Division pour la population de Département des affaires économiques et sociales du Secrétariat de l'Organisation des Nations Unies et ont été publiées dans *World Population Prospects - The 2002 Revision,* United Nations publication, Sales no. E/03.XIII.6, Volume I, Table A.20, New York, 2003.

[2] Including Agalega, Rodrigues and Saint Brandon. — Y compris Agalega, Rodrigues et Saint Brandon.

[3] Including Ascension and Tristan da Cunha. — Y compris Ascension et Tristan da Cunha.

[4] For statistical purposes, the data for China do not include Hong Kong and Macao Special Administrative Regions (SAR) of China. — A des fins statistiques, les données pour la Chine ne comprennent pas les Régions Administratives Spéciales (SAR) de Hong Kong et Macao.

[5] As of 1 July 1997, Hong Kong became a Special Administrative Region (SAR) of China. — A partir du 1 juillet 1997, Hong Kong est devenue une Région Administrative Spéciale (SAR) de la Chine.

[6] As of 20 December 1999, Macao became a Special Administrative Region (SAR) of China. — A partir du 20 décembre 1999, Macao est devenue une Région Administrative Spéciale (SAR) de la Chine.

[7] Refers to the Vatican City State. — Ce rapport à l'état du Vatican.

[8] Including Christmas Island, Cocos (Keeling) Islands and Norfolk Island. — Y compris Christmas Island, Cocos (Keeling) Islands et Norfolk Island.

[9] The population of Pitcairn is projected to be 68 persons from 2000 to 2050. — La population de Pitcairn a été estimée à 68 personnes pour la période 2000 - 2050.

Annex II: United Nations Medium Variant Population Projections - Vital statistics summary and expectation of life at birth: 2000 - 2005
Annexe II: Projections de la population de variante moyenne de l'ONU - Aperçu des statistiques de l'état civil et espérance de vie à la naissance: 2000 - 2005

(See notes at end of table. — Voir notes à la fin du tableau.)

Continent, country or area / Continent, pays ou zone	Crude birth rate — Taux bruts de natalité[1]	Crude death rate — Taux bruts de mortalité[1]	Infant mortality rate — Décès d'enfants de moins d'un an[1]	Expectation of life at birth — Espérance de vie à la naissance[1] Male — Masculin	Female — Féminin	Total fertilty rate — Indice synthétique de fécondité[1]	Natural increase — Accroissement naturel[1]
AFRICA — AFRIQUE							
Algeria - Algérie	22.8	5.5	43.9	68.1	71.3	2.80	1.67
Angola	52.3	23.6	140.3	38.8	41.5	7.20	3.20
Benin - Bénin	41.5	14.3	92.7	48.4	53.0	5.66	2.65
Botswana	30.6	21.4	56.6	38.9	40.5	3.70	0.85
Burkina Faso	47.8	17.4	93.2	45.2	46.2	6.68	2.95
Burundi	44.2	20.6	107.4	40.4	41.4	6.80	3.10
Cameroon - Cameroun	35.4	16.9	88.1	45.1	47.4	4.61	1.83
Cape Verde - Cap-Vert	27.7	5.4	29.7	67.0	72.8	3.30	2.01
Central African Republic - République centrafricaine	37.7	22.1	100.4	38.5	40.6	4.92	1.29
Chad - Tchad	48.4	19.5	115.3	43.7	45.7	6.65	2.96
Comoros - Comores	36.7	8.4	67.0	59.4	62.2	4.90	2.83
Congo	44.2	15.4	84.0	46.6	49.7	6.29	2.57
Côte d'Ivoire	35.5	20.0	101.3	40.8	41.2	4.73	1.62
Democratic Republic of the Congo - République démocratique du Congo	50.2	21.4	119.6	40.8	42.8	6.70	2.88
Djibouti	39.5	17.7	102.4	44.7	46.8	5.70	1.58
Egypt - Égypte	26.6	6.2	40.6	66.7	71.0	3.29	1.99
Equatorial Guinea - Guinée équatoriale	43.1	16.7	100.9	47.8	50.5	5.89	2.65
Eritrea - Érythrée	39.7	11.9	73.0	51.2	54.2	5.43	3.65
Ethiopia - Éthiopie	42.5	17.7	100.4	44.6	46.3	6.14	2.46
Gabon	31.6	11.5	56.8	55.8	57.5	3.99	1.79
Gambia - Gambie	35.8	12.7	80.5	52.7	55.5	4.70	2.66
Ghana	31.9	10.0	57.8	56.5	59.3	4.11	2.17
Guinea - Guinée	42.9	16.1	101.7	48.8	49.5	5.82	1.59
Guinea-Bissau - Guinée-Bissau	49.9	19.6	120.0	43.8	46.9	7.10	2.95
Kenya	32.5	16.7	69.3	43.5	45.6	4.00	1.45
Lesotho	31.1	25.7	92.1	32.3	37.7	3.84	0.14
Liberia - Libéria	50.0	21.5	147.4	40.7	42.2	6.80	4.05
Libyan Arab Jamahiriya - Jamahiriya arabe libyenne	23.2	4.2	20.7	70.8	75.4	3.02	1.93
Madagascar	41.6	13.2	91.5	52.5	54.8	5.70	2.84
Malawi	44.6	24.1	115.4	37.3	37.7	6.10	2.01
Mali	49.9	16.2	118.7	48.0	49.1	7.00	3.00
Mauritania - Mauritanie	41.8	14.2	96.7	50.9	54.1	5.79	2.98
Mauritius - Maurice[2]	16.2	6.7	16.0	68.4	75.8	1.95	0.96
Morocco - Maroc	23.2	6.0	42.1	66.8	70.5	2.75	1.62
Mozambique	41.2	23.5	122.0	36.6	39.6	5.63	1.75
Namibia - Namibie	33.4	17.9	59.8	42.9	45.6	4.56	1.42
Niger	55.2	19.1	125.7	45.9	46.5	8.00	3.62
Nigeria - Nigéria	39.1	13.7	78.8	51.1	51.8	5.42	2.53
Réunion	18.6	5.5	7.9	71.2	79.3	2.30	1.45
Rwanda	44.0	21.8	111.5	38.8	39.7	5.74	2.16
Sao Tome and Principe - Sao Tomé-et-Principe	33.2	5.8	31.6	67.0	72.8	3.99	2.49
Senegal - Sénégal	37.1	12.2	60.7	50.8	55.1	4.97	2.39
Sierra Leone	49.6	29.3	177.2	33.1	35.5	6.50	3.80
Somalia - Somalie	52.1	17.7	117.7	46.4	49.5	7.25	4.17
South Africa - Afrique du Sud	22.6	16.9	47.9	45.1	50.7	2.61	0.59
Sudan - Soudan	33.0	11.7	77.0	54.1	57.1	4.39	2.17
Swaziland	34.5	25.4	78.3	33.3	35.4	4.54	0.80
Togo	38.5	14.7	81.5	48.2	51.1	5.33	2.34
Tunisia - Tunisie	17.0	5.5	23.3	70.8	74.9	2.01	1.07
Uganda - Ouganda	50.7	16.7	86.1	45.4	46.9	7.10	3.24
United Republic of Tanzania - République Unie de Tanzanie	39.3	18.1	99.8	42.5	44.1	5.11	1.93
Western Sahara - Sahara occidental	27.5	7.9	53.6	62.3	65.6	3.89	2.55
Zambia - Zambie	42.2	28.0	104.8	32.7	32.1	5.64	1.16

Annex II: United Nations Medium Variant Population Projections - Vital statistics summary and expectation of life at birth: 2000 - 2005

Annexe II: Projections de la population de variante moyenne de l'ONU - Aperçu des statistiques de l'état civil et espérance de vie à la naissance: 2000 - 2005

(continued — suite)

(See notes at end of table. — Voir notes à la fin du tableau.)

Continent, country or area / Continent, pays ou zone	Crude birth rate — Taux bruts de natalité[1]	Crude death rate — Taux bruts de mortalité[1]	Infant mortality rate — Décès d'enfants de moins d'un an[1]	Expectation of life at birth — Espérance de vie à la naissance[1]		Total fertility rate— Indice synthétique de fécondité[1]	Natural increase — Accroissement naturel[1]
				Male — Masculin	Female — Féminin		
AFRICA — AFRIQUE							
Zimbabwe	32.1	27.0	58.4	33.7	32.6	3.90	0.49
AMERICA, NORTH — AMERIQUE DU NORD							
Bahamas	19.4	8.2	17.7	63.9	70.3	2.29	1.13
Barbados - Barbade	12.2	7.8	10.9	74.5	79.5	1.50	0.35
Belize	27.0	5.3	31.1	69.9	73.0	3.15	2.06
Canada	10.3	7.5	5.3	76.7	81.9	1.48	0.77
Costa Rica	19.1	3.9	10.5	75.8	80.6	2.28	1.93
Cuba	11.6	7.2	7.3	74.8	78.7	1.55	0.27
Dominican Republic - République dominicaine	23.3	7.0	35.7	64.4	69.2	2.71	1.49
El Salvador	25.1	5.9	26.4	67.7	73.7	2.88	1.55
Guadeloupe	16.1	6.2	7.4	74.8	81.7	2.10	0.84
Guatemala	34.2	6.7	41.2	63.0	68.9	4.41	2.55
Haiti - Haïti	30.3	14.6	63.2	49.0	50.0	3.98	1.32
Honduras	30.0	5.7	32.1	66.5	71.4	3.72	2.34
Jamaica - Jamaïque	20.5	5.7	19.9	73.7	77.8	2.36	0.92
Martinique	13.7	6.9	6.8	75.8	82.3	1.90	0.56
Mexico - Mexique	22.4	5.0	28.2	70.4	76.4	2.50	1.45
Netherlands Antilles - Antilles néerlandaises	15.0	6.2	12.6	73.3	79.2	2.05	0.83
Nicaragua	31.6	5.1	35.7	67.2	71.9	3.75	2.43
Panama	22.7	5.0	20.6	72.3	77.4	2.70	1.84
Puerto Rico - Porto Rico	14.3	8.3	10.3	71.2	80.1	1.89	0.52
Saint Lucia - Sainte-Lucie	20.4	5.9	14.8	70.8	74.1	2.27	0.78
Saint Vincent and the Grenadines - Saint Vincent-et-les Grenadines	20.0	5.8	15.7	72.6	75.6	2.23	0.58
Trinidad and Tobago - Trinité-et-Tobago	13.7	7.3	14.1	68.4	74.4	1.55	0.34
United States - États-Unis	14.5	8.3	6.7	74.3	79.9	2.11	1.03
United States Virgin Islands - Îles Vierges américaines	14.4	5.7	10.1	74.2	82.0	2.15	0.87
AMERICA, SOUTH — AMERIQUE DU SUD							
Argentina - Argentine	19.0	7.6	20.0	70.6	77.7	2.44	1.17
Bolivia - Bolivie	29.3	8.1	55.6	61.8	66.0	3.82	1.89
Brazil - Brésil	19.7	7.1	38.4	64.0	72.6	2.21	1.24
Chile - Chili	18.2	5.6	11.6	73.0	79.0	2.35	1.23
Colombia - Colombie	22.2	5.4	25.6	69.2	75.3	2.62	1.59
Ecuador - Équateur	23.0	5.8	41.5	68.3	73.5	2.76	1.49
French Guiana - Guyane française	24.5	3.7	14.3	72.5	78.3	3.33	2.53
Guyana	21.9	9.0	51.2	60.1	66.3	2.31	0.24
Paraguay	29.6	5.1	37.0	68.6	73.1	3.84	2.37
Peru - Pérou	23.3	6.1	33.4	67.3	72.4	2.86	1.50
Suriname	21.7	5.9	25.7	68.5	73.7	2.45	0.80
Uruguay	16.8	9.1	13.1	71.6	78.9	2.30	0.72
Venezuela	22.8	4.6	18.9	70.9	76.7	2.72	1.86
ASIA — ASIE							
Afghanistan	47.4	21.5	161.7	43.0	43.3	6.80	3.88
Armenia - Arménie	9.7	7.7	17.3	69.0	75.6	1.15	...
Azerbaijan - Azerbaïdjan	17.8	5.6	29.3	68.7	75.5	2.10	0.89
Bahrain - Bahreïn	19.9	3.1	14.2	72.5	75.9	2.66	2.17
Bangladesh	28.9	8.3	64.0	61.0	61.8	3.46	2.02
Bhutan - Bhoutan	34.5	8.6	53.6	62.0	64.5	5.02	2.96

Annex II: United Nations Medium Variant Population Projections - Vital statistics summary and expectation of life at birth: 2000 - 2005

Annexe II: Projections de la population de variante moyenne de l'ONU - Aperçu des statistiques de l'état civil et espérance de vie à la naissance: 2000 - 2005

(continued — suite)

(See notes at end of table. — Voir notes à la fin du tableau.)

Continent, country or area — Continent, pays ou zone	Crude birth rate — Taux bruts de natalité[1]	Crude death rate — Taux bruts de mortalité[1]	Infant mortality rate — Décès d'enfants de moins d'un an[1]	Expectation of life at birth — Espérance de vie à la naissance[1]		Total fertility rate— Indice synthétique de fécondité[1]	Natural increase — Accroissement naturel[1]
				Male — Masculin	Female — Féminin		
ASIA — ASIE							
Brunei Darussalam - Brunéi Darussalam ...	23.5	2.8	6.1	74.2	78.9	2.48	2.27
Cambodia - Cambodge	33.9	10.0	73.2	55.2	59.5	4.77	2.40
China - Chine[3]	14.5	7.0	36.6	68.9	73.3	1.83	0.73
China - Hong Kong SAR - Chine - Hong Kong RAS[4]	8.5	5.9	4.1	77.3	82.8	1.00	1.07
China - Macao SAR - Chine - Macao RAS[5]	9.7	4.7	8.6	76.5	81.2	1.10	0.94
Cyprus - Chypre	13.2	7.5	7.7	76.0	80.5	1.90	0.76
Timor-Leste	23.8	13.2	123.7	48.7	50.4	3.85	4.00
Georgia - Géorgie	10.4	9.9	17.6	69.5	77.6	1.40	...
India - Inde	23.8	8.5	64.5	63.2	64.6	3.01	1.51
Indonesia - Indonésie	20.7	7.3	41.6	64.8	68.8	2.35	1.26
Iran (Islamic Republic of) - Iran (République islamique d')	20.3	5.3	33.3	68.9	71.9	2.33	1.24
Iraq	35.1	8.8	83.3	59.2	62.3	4.77	2.68
Israel - Israël	19.8	6.0	5.9	77.1	81.0	2.70	2.02
Japan - Japon	9.2	8.2	3.2	77.9	85.1	1.32	0.14
Jordan - Jordanie	28.0	4.3	23.9	69.7	72.5	3.57	2.66
Kazakhstan	16.2	9.5	51.7	60.9	71.9	1.95	...
Korea (Dem. People's Republic of) - Corée (Rép. populaire dém. de)	16.3	11.0	45.1	60.5	66.0	2.02	0.54
Korea (Republic of) - Corée (République de)	11.9	5.9	5.0	71.8	79.3	1.41	0.57
Kuwait - Koweït	20.2	1.9	10.8	74.9	79.0	2.66	3.46
Kyrgyzstan - Kirghizistan	21.9	7.1	37.0	64.8	72.3	2.64	1.40
Lao People's Democratic Republic - République démocratique populaire lao	35.6	12.6	88.0	53.3	55.8	4.78	2.29
Lebanon - Liban	19.1	5.4	17.2	71.9	75.1	2.18	1.56
Malaysia - Malaisie	22.6	4.6	10.1	70.8	75.7	2.90	1.93
Maldives	35.8	6.1	38.3	67.8	67.0	5.33	2.98
Mongolia - Mongolie	22.5	7.2	58.2	61.9	65.9	2.42	1.29
Myanmar	23.9	11.2	83.5	54.6	60.2	2.86	1.28
Nepal - Népal	32.9	9.7	70.9	60.1	59.6	4.26	2.23
Oman	31.8	3.3	19.7	71.0	74.4	4.96	2.93
Pakistan	35.9	9.6	86.5	61.2	60.9	5.08	2.44
Philippines	25.3	5.1	29.0	68.0	72.0	3.18	1.79
Qatar	17.4	3.7	12.3	70.5	75.4	3.22	1.54
Saudi Arabia - Arabie saoudite	31.5	3.7	20.6	71.1	73.7	4.53	2.92
Singapore - Singapour	10.2	5.2	2.9	75.9	80.3	1.36	1.69
Sri Lanka	16.4	6.6	20.1	69.9	75.9	2.01	0.81
Syrian Arab Republic - République arabe syrienne	27.7	3.9	22.3	70.6	73.1	3.32	2.38
Tajikistan - Tadjikistan	24.5	6.0	50.0	66.2	71.4	3.06	0.86
Thailand - Thaïlande	17.3	7.1	19.8	65.3	73.5	1.93	1.01
Turkey - Turquie	20.9	6.0	39.5	68.0	73.2	2.43	1.42
Turkmenistan - Turkménistan	22.2	6.5	48.6	63.9	70.4	2.70	1.54
United Arab Emirates - Émirats arabes unis	16.7	2.4	13.6	73.3	77.4	2.82	1.94
Uzbekistan - Ouzbékistan	21.7	5.8	36.7	66.8	72.5	2.44	1.51
Viet Nam	20.2	6.4	33.6	66.9	71.6	2.30	1.35
Occupied Palestinian Territory - Territoire palestinien occupé	38.8	4.3	20.7	70.8	74.0	5.57	3.57
Yemen - Yémen	45.0	9.2	70.6	58.9	61.1	7.01	3.52

651

Annex II: United Nations Medium Variant Population Projections - Vital statistics summary and expectation of life at birth: 2000 - 2005

Annexe II: Projections de la population de variante moyenne de l'ONU - Aperçu des statistiques de l'état civil et espérance de vie à la naissance: 2000 - 2005

(continued — suite)

(See notes at end of table. — Voir notes à la fin du tableau.)

Continent, country or area Continent, pays ou zone	Crude birth rate — Taux bruts de natalité[1]	Crude death rate — Taux bruts de mortalité[1]	Infant mortality rate — Décès d'enfants de moins d'un an[1]	Expectation of life at birth — Espérance de vie à la naissance[1]		Total fertility rate— Indice synthétique de fécondité[1]	Natural increase — Accroissement naturel[1]
				Male — Masculin	Female — Féminin		
EUROPE							
Albania - Albanie	18.2	5.4	25.0	70.9	76.7	2.28	0.68
Austria - Autriche	8.6	9.9	4.7	75.4	81.5	1.28	0.05
Belarus - Bélarus	8.8	13.2	11.3	64.9	75.3	1.20	...
Belgium - Belgique	10.8	10.0	4.2	75.7	81.9	1.66	0.21
Bosnia and Herzegovina - Bosnie-Herzégovine	9.7	8.1	13.5	71.3	76.7	1.30	1.13
Bulgaria - Bulgarie	7.9	15.1	15.2	67.4	74.6	1.10	...
Channel Islands - Îles Anglo-Normandes	10.9	10.1	5.5	75.7	80.7	1.54	0.08
Croatia - Croatie	11.1	11.8	8.1	70.3	78.1	1.65	...
Czech Republic - République tchèque	8.8	10.8	5.6	72.1	78.7	1.16	...
Denmark - Danemark	11.8	11.3	5.0	74.2	79.1	1.77	0.24
Estonia - Estonie	8.7	13.6	9.4	66.5	76.8	1.22	...
Finland - Finlande	10.8	9.8	4.0	74.4	81.5	1.73	0.18
France	12.8	9.3	5.0	75.2	82.8	1.89	0.47
Germany - Allemagne	8.7	10.6	4.5	75.2	81.2	1.35	0.07
Greece - Grèce	9.1	10.5	6.4	75.7	80.9	1.27	0.14
Hungary - Hongrie	8.8	13.5	8.8	67.7	76.0	1.20	...
Iceland - Islande	14.1	6.9	3.4	77.6	81.9	1.95	0.79
Ireland - Irlande	14.4	8.3	5.8	74.4	79.6	1.90	1.12
Italy - Italie	8.8	10.9	5.4	75.5	81.9	1.23	...
Latvia - Lettonie	7.8	13.6	14.2	65.6	76.2	1.10	...
Lithuania - Lituanie	8.8	11.6	8.7	67.5	77.6	1.25	...
Luxembourg	12.6	8.2	5.4	75.1	81.4	1.73	1.32
Malta - Malte	11.8	7.9	7.1	75.9	80.7	1.77	0.42
Netherlands - Pays-Bas	12.1	8.9	4.5	75.6	81.0	1.72	0.50
Norway - Norvège	12.0	9.9	4.5	76.0	81.9	1.80	0.43
Poland - Pologne	9.6	10.0	9.1	69.8	78.0	1.26	...
Portugal	11.0	10.8	6.1	72.6	79.6	1.45	0.13
Republic of Moldova - République de Moldova	11.5	10.7	18.1	65.5	72.2	1.40	...
Romania - Roumanie	10.4	12.5	20.0	67.0	74.2	1.32	...
Russian Federation - Fédération de Russie	8.6	14.6	15.9	60.8	73.1	1.14	...
Serbia and Montenegro - Serbie-et-Montenegro	11.7	10.6	13.0	70.9	75.6	1.65	...
Slovakia - Slovaquie	10.2	9.8	8.0	69.8	77.6	1.28	0.08
Slovenia - Slovénie	8.3	9.8	5.5	72.6	79.8	1.14	...
Spain - Espagne	9.3	9.1	5.1	75.9	82.8	1.15	0.21
Sweden - Suède	10.3	10.6	3.4	77.6	82.6	1.64	0.09
Switzerland - Suisse	8.7	9.8	4.8	75.9	82.3	1.41	...
The Former Yugoslav Rep. of Macedonia - L'ex-République yougoslave de Macédoine	14.5	8.4	16.0	71.4	75.8	1.90	0.51
Ukraine	8.4	14.2	13.8	64.7	74.7	1.15	...
United Kingdom - Royaume-Uni	11.0	10.4	5.4	75.7	80.7	1.60	0.31
OCEANIA — OCEANIE							
Australia - Australie[6]	12.3	7.4	5.5	76.4	82.0	1.70	0.96
Fiji - Fidji	23.6	5.5	17.8	68.1	71.5	2.88	0.98
French Polynesia - Polynésie française	20.0	4.8	8.7	70.7	75.8	2.44	1.52
Guam	20.4	4.9	9.8	72.4	77.0	2.88	1.54
Micronesia, Federated States of - Micronésie, États Fédérés de La	28.0	5.9	33.9	68.0	69.1	3.80	0.81
New Caledonia - Nouvelle-Calédonie	19.4	4.9	6.6	72.5	77.7	2.45	1.92
New Zealand - Nouvelle-Zélande	14.0	7.6	5.8	75.8	80.7	2.01	0.77

Annex II: United Nations Medium Variant Population Projections - Vital statistics summary and expectation of life at birth: 2000 - 2005

Annexe II: Projections de la population de variante moyenne de l'ONU - Aperçu des statistiques de l'état civil et espérance de vie à la naissance: 2000 - 2005

(continued — suite)

(See notes at end of table. — Voir notes à la fin du tableau.)

Continent, country or area Continent, pays ou zone	Crude birth rate — Taux bruts de natalité[1]	Crude death rate — Taux bruts de mortalité[1]	Infant mortality rate — Décès d'enfants de moins d'un an[1]	Expectation of life at birth — Espérance de vie à la naissance[1]		Total fertilty rate— Indice synthétique de fécondité[1]	Natural increase — Accroissement naturel[1]
				Male — Masculin	Female — Féminin		
OCEANIA — OCEANIE							
Papua New Guinea - Papouasie-Nouvelle-Guinée	31.6	9.4	62.1	56.8	58.7	4.09	2.22
Samoa	28.8	5.5	26.1	66.9	73.4	4.12	0.97
Solomon Islands - Îles Salomon	33.3	4.6	20.7	67.9	70.7	4.42	2.88
Tonga	26.5	7.2	33.9	68.0	69.1	3.71	0.97
Vanuatu	30.5	5.4	28.5	67.5	70.5	4.13	2.43

FOOTNOTES - NOTES

[1] All data are medium variant projections, produced by the Population Division of the Department for Economic and Social Affairs of the UN Secretariat and published in *World Population Prospects - The 2002 Revision,* United Nations publication, Sales no. E/03.XIII.6, Volume I, Tables , New York, 2003. — Toutes ces données sont des projections de la population au milieu de l'année de variante moyenne; elles sont produites par la Division pour la population de Département des affaires économiques et sociales du Secrétariat de l'Organisation des Nations Unies et ont été publiées dans *World Population Prospects - The 2002 Revision,* United Nations publication, Sales no. E/03.XIII.6, Volume I, Tables A.15, A.21, A.24, A.27, A.30 et A.31, New York, 2003.

[2] Including Agalega, Rodrigues and Saint Brandon. — Y compris Agalega, Rodrigues et Saint Brandon.

[3] For statistical purposes, the data for China do not include Hong Kong and Macao Special Administrative Regions (SAR) of China. — A des fins statistiques, les données pour la Chine ne comprennent pas les Régions Administratives Spéciales (SAR) de Hong Kong et Macao.

[4] As of 1 July 1997, Hong Kong became a Special Administrative Region (SAR) of China. — A partir du 1 juillet 1997, Hong Kong est devenue une Région Administrative Spéciale (SAR) de la Chine.

[5] As of 20 December 1999, Macao became a Special Administrative Region (SAR) of China. — A partir du 20 décembre 1999, Macao est devenue une Région Administrative Spéciale (SAR) de la Chine.

[6] Including Christmas Island, Cocos (Keeling) Islands and Norfolk Island. — Y compris Christmas Island, Cocos (Keeling) Islands et Norfolk Island.

Index
Detailed guide to the subject-matter in the current Yearbook

Index
Detailed guide to the subject-matter in the current Yearbook

Index
Detailed guide to the subject-matter in the current Yearbook

Index
Detailed guide to the subject-matter in the current Yearbook

Index
Detailed guide to the subject-matter in the current Yearbook

Index
Detailed guide to the subject-matter in the current Yearbook

Index
Detailed guide to the subject-matter in the current Yearbook

Subject-matter	Year of issue	Time coverage		Subject-matter	Year of issue	Time coverage
A					1955	1900-55[i]
Abortions, Legal	1971	Latest		**Births**	1948	1932-47
	1972	1964-72			1949/50	1934-49
	1973	1965-73			1951	1935-50
	1974	1965-74			1952	1936-51
	1975	1965-74			1953	1950-52
	1976	1966-75			1954	1938-53
	1977	1967-76			1955	1946-54
	1978	1968-77			1956	1947-55
	1979	1969-78			1957	1948-56
	1980	1971-79			1958	1948-57
	1981	1972-80			1959	1949-58
	1982	1973-81			1960	1950-59
	1983	1974-82			1961	1952-61
	1984	1975-83			1962	1953-62
	1985	1976-84			1963	1954-63
	1986	1977-85			1964	1960-64
	1987	1978-86			1965	1946-65
	1988	1979-87			1966	1957-66
	1989	1980-88			1967	1963-67
	1990	1981-89			1968	1964-68
	1991	1982-90			1969	1950-69
	1992	1983-91			1970	1966-70
	1993	1984-92			1971	1967-71
	1994	1985-93			1972	1968-72
	1995	1986-94			1973	1969-73
	1996	1987-95			1974	1970-74
	1997	1988-96			1975	1956-75
	1998	1989-97			1976	1972-76
	1999	1990-98			1977	1973-77
	2000	1991-99			1978	1974-78
	2001	1993-01			1978HS[ii]	1948-78
- by age of mother and number of previous live births of mother	1971-1975	Latest			1979	1975-79
	1977-1981	Latest			1980	1976-80
	1983-2001	Latest			1981	1962-81
Ageing (see: Population)					1982	1978-82
Annulments	1958	1948-57			1983	1979-83
	1968	1958-67			1984	1980-84
	1976	1966-75			1985	1981-85
					1986	1967-86
Annulment rates	1958	1948-57			1987	1983-87
	1968	1958-67			1988	1984-88
	1976	1966-75			1989	1985-89
					1990	1986-90
B					1991	1987-91
					1992	1983-92
Bibliography	1948	1930-48			1993	1989-93
	1949/50	1930-50			1994	1990-94
	1951-1952	1930-51[i]			1995	1991-95
	1953	1900-53			1996	1992-96
	1954	1900-54[i]			1997	1993-97
					1997HS[iii]	1948-97
					1998	1994-98

Subject-matter	Year of issue	Time coverage	Subject-matter	Year of issue	Time coverage
	1999	1995-99		1981	1972-80
	1999CD[iv]	1980-99		1986	1977-85
	2000	1996-00		1999CD[iv]	1990-98
	2001	1997-01	- by age of mother and sex		
- by age of father	1949/50	1942-49		1965-1968	Latest
	1954	1936-53		1969	1963-68
	1959	1949-58		1970-1974	Latest
	1965	1955-64		1975	1966-74
	1969	1963-68		1976-1978	Latest
	1975	1966-74		1978HS[ii]	1948-77
	1981	1972-80		1979-1980	Latest
	1999CD[iv]	1990-98		1981	1972-80
				1982-1985	Latest
- by age of mother	1948	1936-47		1986	1977-85
	1949/50	1936-49		1987-1991	Latest
	1954	1936-53		1992	1983-92
	1955-1956	Latest		1993-1997	Latest
	1958	Latest		1997HS[iii]	1948-96
	1959	1949-58		1998-99	Latest
	1960-1964	Latest		1999CD[iv]	1990-98
	1965	1955-64		2000-2001	Latest
	1966-1968	Latest	- by age of mother and urban/rural residence (see: by urban/rural residence, below)		
	1969	1963-68			
	1970-1974	Latest			
	1975	1966-74			
	1976-1978	Latest	- by birth order	1948	1936-47
	1978HS[ii]	1948-77		1949/50	1936-49
	1979-1980	Latest		1954	1936-53
	1981	1972-80		1955	Latest
	1982-1985	Latest		1959	1949-58
	1986	1977-85		1965	1955-64
	1987-1991	Latest		1969	1963-68
	1992	1983-92		1975	1966-74
	1993-1997	Latest		1981	1972-80
	1997HS[iii] [3]	1948-96		1986	1977-85
	1998-99	Latest		1999CD[iv]	1990-98
	1999CD[iv]	1990-98			
	2000-2001	Latest	- by birth weight	1975	Latest
- by age of mother and birth order	1949/50	1936-47		1981	1972-80
	1954	Latest		1986	1977-85
	1959	1949-58		1999CD[iv]	1990-98
	1965	1955-64			
	1969	1963-68	- by gestational age	1975	Latest
	1975	1966-74		1981	1972-80
				1986	1977-85
				1999CD[iv]	1990-98

Index
Historical index
(See notes at end of index)

Subject-matter	Year of issue	Time coverage	Subject-matter	Year of issue	Time coverage
	1999	1995-99		1999CD[iv]	1990-98
	1999CD[iv]	1985-99	- by age of mother and urban/rural residence (see: by urban/rural residence, below)		
	2000	1996-00			
	2001	1997-01			
- by age of father	1949/50	1942-49	- by birth order	1951	1936-49
	1954	1936-53		1952	1936-50
	1959	1949-58		1953	1936-52
	1965	1955-64		1954	1936-53
	1969	1963-68		1955	Latest
	1975	1966-74		1959	1949-58
	1981	1972-80		1965	1955-64
	1986	1977-85		1969	1963-68
	1999CD[iv]	1990-98		1975	1966-74
- by age of mother	1948	1936-47		1981	1972-80
	1949/50	1936-49		1986	1977-85
	1951	1936-50		1999CD[iv]	1990-98
	1952	1936-50	- by urban/rural residence	1965	Latest
	1953	1936-52		1967	Latest
	1954	1936-53		1968	1964-68
	1955-1956	Latest		1969	1964-68
	1959	1949-58		1970	1966-70
	1965	1955-64		1971	1967-71
	1969	1963-68		1972	1968-72
	1975	1966-74		1973	1969-73
	1976-1978	Latest		1974	1970-74
	1978HS[ii]	1948-77		1975	1956-75
	1979-1980	Latest		1976	1972-76
	1981	1972-80		1977	1973-77
	1982-1985	Latest		1978	1974-78
	1986	1977-85		1979	1975-79
	1987-1991	Latest		1980	1976-80
	1992	1983-92		1981	1962-81
	1993-1997	Latest		1982	1978-82
	1997HS[iii]	1948-96		1983	1979-83
	1998-1999	Latest		1984	1980-84
	1999CD[iv]	1990-98		1985	1981-85
	2000-2001	Latest		1986	1967-86
- by age of mother and birth order	1954	1948 and 1951		1987	1983-87
	1959	1949-58		1988	1984-88
	1965	1955-64		1989	1985-89
	1969	1963-68		1990	1986-90
	1975	1966-74		1991	1987-91
	1981	1972-80		1992	1983-92
	1986	1977-85		1993	1989-93
				1994	1990-94
				1995	1991-95

Subject-matter	Year of issue	Time coverage	Subject-matter	Year of issue	Time coverage
	1968	1964-68		1993-1995	Latest
	1969	1965-69		1996	1987-95
	1970	1966-70		1997	Latest
	1971	1967-71		1997HS[iii]	1948-96
	1972	1968-72		1998-2001	Latest
	1973	1969-73	- by age and sex and urban/rural residence		
	1974	1965-74		1967-1973	Latest
	1975	1971-75		1974	1965-73
	1976	1972-76		1975-1979	Latest
	1977	1973-77		1980	1971-79
	1978	1974-78		1981-1984	Latest
	1978HS[ii]	1948-78		1985	1976-84
	1979	1975-79		1986-1991	Latest
	1980	1971-80		1992	1983-92
	1981	1977-81		1993-1995	Latest
	1982	1978-82		1996	1987-95
	1983	1979-83		1997	Latest
	1984	1980-84		1997HS[iii]	1948-96
	1985	1976-85		1998-2001	Latest
	1986	1982-86	- by cause	1951	1947-50
	1987	1983-87		1952	1947-51[vi]
	1988	1984-88		1953	Latest
	1989	1985-89		1954	1945-53
	1990	1986-90		1955-1956	Latest
	1991	1987-91		1957	1952-56
	1992	1983-92		1958-1960	Latest
	1993	1989-93		1961	1955-60
	1994	1990-94		1962-1965	Latest
	1995	1991-95		1966	1960-65
	1996	1987-96		1967-1973	Latest
	1997	1993-97		1974	1965-73
	1997HS[iii]	1948-97		1975-1979	Latest
	1998	1994-98		1980	1971-79
	1999	1995-99		1981-1984	Latest
	2000	1996-00		1985	1976-84
	2001	1997-01		1986-1991	Latest
- by age and sex	1948	1936-47		1991PA[vii]	1960-90
	1951	1936-50		1992-1995	Latest
	1955-1956	Latest		1996	1987-95
	1957	1948-56		1997-2000	Latest
	1958-1960	Latest	- by cause, age and sex	1951	Latest
	1961	1955-60		1952	Latest
	1962-1965	Latest		1957	Latest
	1966	1961-65		1961	Latest
	1967-1973	Latest		1967	Latest
	1974	1965-73		1974	Latest
	1975-1979	Latest		1980	Latest
	1978HS[ii]	1948-77		1985	Latest
	1980	1971-79		1991PA[vii]	1960-90
	1981-1984	Latest		1996	Latest
	1985	1976-84	- by cause, age	1967	Latest
	1986-1991	Latest			
	1992	1983-92			

674

Index
Historical index
(See notes at end of index)

Subject-matter	Year of issue	Time coverage	Subject-matter	Year of issue	Time coverage
	1985	Latest		1993	1989-93
	1996	Latest		1994	1990-94
- by marital status, age and sex	1961	Latest		1995	1991-95
	1967	Latest		1996	1987-96
	1974	Latest		1997	1993-97
	1980	Latest		1998	1994-98
	1985	Latest		1999	1995-99
	1996	Latest		2000	1996-00
- by occupation, age and sex	1957	Latest		2001	1997-01
			- estimated		
- by occupation and age, males	1961	Latest	for continents	1949/50	1947
	1967	Latest		1956-1977	Latest
- by urban/rural residence	1967	Latest		1978-1979	1970-75
	1968	1964-68		1980-1983	1975-80
	1969	1965-69		1984-1986	1980-85
	1970	1966-70		1984-1986	1980-85
	1971	1967-71		1987-1992	1985-90
	1972	1968-72		1993-1997	1990-95
	1973	1969-73		1998-2000	1995-00
	1974	1965-74		2001	2000-05
	1975	1971-75	for macro regions	1964-1977	Latest
	1976	1972-76		1978-1979	1970-75
	1977	1973-77		1980-1983	1975-80
	1978	1974-78		1984-1986	1980-85
	1979	1975-79		1987-1992	1985-90
	1980	1971-80		1993-1997	1990-95
	1981	1977-81		1998-2000	1995-00
	1982	1978-82		2001	2000-05
	1983	1979-83	for regions	1949/50	1947
	1984	1980-84		1956-1977	Latest
	1985	1976-85		1978-1979	1970-75
	1986	1982-86		1980-1983	1975-80
	1987	1983-87		1984-1986	1980-85
	1988	1984-88		1987-1992	1985-90
	1989	1985-89		1993-1997	1990-95
	1990	1986-90		1998-2000	1995-00
	1991	1987-91		2001	2000-05
	1992	1983-92	for the world	1949/50	1947
	1993	1989-93		1956-1977	Latest
	1994	1990-94		1978-1979	1970-75
	1995	1991-95		1980-1983	1975-80
	1996	1987-96		1984-1986	1980-85
	1997	1993-97		1987-1992	1985-90
	1998	1994-98		1993-1997	1990-95
	1999	1995-99		1998-2000	1995-00
	1987	1983-87		2001	2000-05
	1988	1984-88	- of infants (see: Infant deaths)		
	1989	1985-89			
	1990	1986-90	**Density of population**:		
	1991	1987-91	- of continents	1949/50	1920-49
	1992	1983-92		1951-1999	Latest

Index
Historical index
(See notes at end of index)

Subject-matter	Year of issue	Time coverage	Subject-matter	Year of issue	Time coverage
	2000	2000		1982	1963-82
	2001	2001		1983	1979-83
- of countries	1948-1999	Latest		1984	1980-84
	2000	2000		1985	1981-85
	2001	2001		1986	1982-86
- of major areas	1964-1999	Latest		1987	1983-87
	2000	2000		1988	1984-88
	2001	2001		1989	1985-89
- of regions	1949/50	1920-49		1990	1971-90
	1952-1999	Latest		1991	1987-91
	2000	2000		1992	1988-92
	2001	2001		1993	1989-93
- of the world	1949/50	1920-49		1994	1990-94
	1952-1999	Latest		1995	1991-95
	2000	2000		1996	1992-96
	2001	2001		1997	1993-97
				1998	1994-98
				1999	1995-99
				2000	1996-00
				2001	1997-01
Disability (see: Population)			- by age of husband	1968	1958-67
				1976	1966-75
Divorces	1951	1935-50		1982	1972-81
	1952	1936-51		1987	1975-86
	1953	1950-52		1990	1980-89
	1954	1946-53			
	1955	1946-54	- by age of wife	1968	1958-67
	1956	1947-55		1976	1966-75
	1957	1948-56		1982	1972-81
	1958	1940-57		1987	1975-86
	1959	1949-58		1990	1980-89
	1960	1950-59	- by age of wife classified by age of husband	1958	1946-57
	1961	1952-61		1968	Latest
	1962	1953-62		1976	Latest
	1963	1954-63		1982	Latest
	1964	1960-64		1982	Latest
	1965	1961-65		1990	Latest
	1966	1962-66	- by duration of marriage	1958	1948-57
	1967	1963-67		1968	1958-67
	1968	1949-68		1976	1966-75
	1969	1965-69		1982	1972-81
	1970	1966-70		1990	1980-89
	1971	1967-71	- by duration of marriage and age of husband, wife	1958	1946-57
	1972	1968-72		1968	Latest
	1973	1969-73		1976	Latest
	1974	1970-74		1982	Latest
	1975	1971-75		1990	Latest
	1976	1957-76	- by number of children involved	1958	1948-57
	1977	1973-77			
	1978	1974-78			
	1979	1975-79			
	1980	1976-80			
	1981	1977-81			

Subject-matter	Year of issue	Time coverage	Subject-matter	Year of issue	Time coverage
	1991	1986-90		1974	1965-73
	1992	1987-91		1975	1966-74
	1993	1988-92		1976	1971-75
	1994	1989-93		1977	1972-76
	1995	1990-94		1978	1973-77
	1996	1987-95		1979	1974-78
	1997	1992-96		1980	1971-79
	1998	1993-97		1981	1972-80
	1999	1994-98		1982	1977-81
	1999CD[iv]	1990-98		1983	1978-82
	2000	1995-99		1984	1979-83
	2001	1997-01		1985	1975-84
				1986	1977-85
- by age of mother	1954	1936-53		1987	1982-86
	1959	1949-58		1988	1983-87
	1965	1955-64		1989	1984-88
	1969	1963-68		1990	1985-89
	1975	1966-74		1991	1986-90
	1981	1972-80		1992	1987-91
	1986	1977-85		1993	1988-92
	1996	1987-95		1994	1989-93
	1999CD[iv]	1990-98		1995	1990-94
- by age of mother and birth order	1954	Latest		1996	1987-95
	1959	1949-58		1997	1992-96
	1965	3-Latest		1998	1993-97
	1969	1963-68		1999	1994-98
	1975	1966-74		1999CD[iv]	1990-98
	1981	1972-80		2000	1995-99
	1986	1977-85		2001	1997-01
	1999CD[iv]	1990-98	- illegitimate	1961	1952-60
- by period of gestation	1957	1950-56		1965	5-Latest
	1959	1949-58			
	1961	1952-60	- legitimate	1959	1949-58
	1965	5-Latest		1965	1955-64
	1966	1956-65		1969	1963-68
	1967-1968	Latest		1975	1966-74
	1969	1963-68		1981	1972-80
	1974	1965-73		1986	1977-85
	1975	1966-74			
	1980	1971-79	- legitimate by age of mother	1959	1949-58
	1981	1972-80		1965	1955-64
	1985	1976-84		1969	1963-68
	1986	1977-85		1975	1966-74
- by urban/rural residence	1971	1966-70		1981	1972-80
	1972	1967-71		1986	1977-85
	1973	1968-72			

Subject-matter	Year of issue	Time coverage	Subject-matter	Year of issue	Time coverage
	1978	1974-78		1996	1987-95
	1978HS[ii]	1948-78		1997-1999	Latest
	1979	1975-79	- by urban/rural residence	1967	Latest
	1980	1971-80		1968	1964-68
	1981	1977-81		1969	1965-69
	1982	1978-82		1970	1966-70
	1983	1979-83		1971	1967-71
	1984	1980-84		1972	1968-72
	1985	1976-85		1973	1969-73
	1986	1982-86		1974	1965-74
	1987	1983-87		1975	1971-75
	1988	1984-88		1976	1972-76
	1989	1985-89		1977	1973-77
	1990	1986-90		1978	1974-78
	1991	1987-91		1979	1975-79
	1992	1983-92		1980	1971-80
	1993	1989-93		1981	1977-81
	1994	1990-94		1982	1978-82
	1995	1991-95		1983	1979-83
	1996	1987-96		1984	1980-84
	1997	1993-97		1985	1976-85
	1997HS[iii]	1948-97		1986	1982-86
	1998	1994-98		1987	1983-87
	1999	1995-99		1988	1984-88
	2000	1996-00		1989	1985-89
	2001	1997-01		1990	1986-90
				1991	1987-91
- by age and sex	1948	1936-47		1992	1983-92
	1951	1936-49		1993	1989-93
	1957	1948-56		1994	1990-94
	1961	1952-60		1995	1991-95
	1966	1956-65		1996	1987-96
	1967	1962-66		1997	1993-97
	1971-1973	Latest		1998	1994-98
	1974	1965-73		1999	1995-99
	1975-1979	Latest		2000	1996-00
	1980	1971-79		2001	1997-01
	1981-1984	Latest			
	1985	1976-84	Intercensal rates of population increase	1948	1900-48
	1986-1991	Latest		1949/50	1900-50
	1992	1983-92		1951	1900-51
	1993-1995	Latest		1952	1850-1952
	1996	1987-95		1953	1850-1953
	1997-2001	Latest		1955	1850-1954
- by age and sex and urban/rural residence				1960	1900-61
	1971-1973	Latest		1962	1900-62
	1974	1965-73		1964	1955-64
	1975-1979	Latest		1970	1900-70
	1980	1971-79		1978HS[ii]	1948-78
	1981-1984	Latest		1997HS[iii]	1948-97
	1985	1976-84			
	1986-1991	Latest			
	1992	1983-92			
	1993-1995	Latest			

Subject-matter	Year of issue	Time coverage	Subject-matter	Year of issue	Time coverage
International migration (see: Migration)				1996	2-Latest
				1997	Latest
				1997HS[iii]	1948-96
L				1998-2001	Latest
Late foetal deaths(see: Foetal deaths, late)			- mortality rates at specified ages, by sex	1948	1891-1945
				1951	1891-1950
Life tables				1952	1891-1951[vi]
- expectation of life at birth, by sex	1959-1973	Latest		1953	1891-1952
	1974	2-Latest		1954	1891-1953[vi]
	1975-1978	Latest		1957	1900-56
	1978HS[ii]	1948-77		1961	1940-60
	1979	Latest		1966	2-Latest
	1980	2-Latest		1974	2-Latest
	1981-1984	Latest		1980	2-Latest
	1985	2-Latest		1985	2-Latest
	1986-1991	Latest		1996	2-Latest
	1991PA[vii]	1950-90	- survivors at specified ages, by sex		
	1992-1995	Latest		1948	1891-1945
	1996	2-Latest		1951	1891-1950
	1997	Latest		1952	1891-1951[vi]
	1997HS[iii]	1948-96		1953	1891-1952
	1998-2001	Latest		1954	1891-1953[vi]
- expectation of life at specified ages, by sex				1957	1900-56
	1948	1891-1945		1961	1940-60
	1951	1891-1950		1966	2-Latest
	1952	1891-1951[vi]		1974	2-Latest
	1953	1891-1952		1980	2-Latest
	1954	1891-1953[vi]		1985	2-Latest
	1955-1956	Latest		1996	2-Latest
	1957	1900-56	**Literacy** (see: Population)		
	1958-1960	Latest			
	1961	1940-60	**Localities** (see: Population)		
	1962-1964	Latest			
	1966	2-Latest	**M**		
	1967	1900-66			
	1968-1973	Latest	**Major civil divisions** (see: Population)		
	1974	2-Latest			
	1975-1978	Latest	**Marriages**	1948	1932-47
	1978HS[ii]	1948-77		1949/50	1934-49
	1979	Latest		1951	1935-50
	1980	2-Latest		1952	1936-51
	1981-1984	Latest		1953	1950-52
	1985	2-Latest		1954	1946-53
	1986-1991	Latest		1955	1946-54
	1991PA[vii]	1950-90		1956	1947-55
	1992-1995	Latest		1957	1948-56
				1958	1940-57
				1959	1949-58
				1960	1950-59
				1961	1952-61

Subject-matter	Year of issue	Time coverage	Subject-matter	Year of issue	Time coverage
	1962	1953-62		1991-1997	Latest
	1963	1954-63		1998	1993-97
	1964	1960-64		1999	1994-98
	1965	1956-65		2000	1995-99
	1966	1962-66		2001	1997-01
	1967	1963-67	- by age of bride classified by age of groom		
	1968	1949-68		1958	1948-57
	1969	1965-69		1968	Latest
	1970	1966-70		1976	Latest
	1971	1967-71		1982	Latest
	1972	1968-72		1990	Latest
	1973	1969-73	- by age of bride and previous marital status		
	1974	1970-74		1958	1948-57
	1975	1971-75		1968	Latest
	1976	1957-76		1976	Latest
	1977	1973-77		1982	Latest
	1978	1974-78		1990	Latest
	1979	1975-79	- by age of groom	1948	1936-47
	1980	1976-80		1949/50	1936-49
	1981	1977-81		1958	1948-57
	1982	1963-82		1959-1967	Latest
	1983	1979-83		1968	1958-67
	1984	1980-84		1969-1975	Latest
	1985	1981-85		1976	1966-75
	1986	1982-86		1977-1981	Latest
	1987	1983-87		1982	1972-81
	1988	1984-88		1983-1986	Latest
	1989	1985-89		1987	1975-86
	1990	1971-90		1988-1989	Latest
	1991	1987-91		1990	1980-1989
	1992	1988-92		1990-1997	Latest
	1993	1989-93		1998	1993-97
	1994	1990-94		1999	1994-98
	1995	1991-95		2000	1995-99
	1996	1992-96		2001	1997-01
	1997	1993-97	- by age of groom classified by age of bride		
	1998	1994-98		1958	1948-57
	1999	1995-99		1968	Latest
	2000	1996-00		1976	Latest
	2001	1997-01		1982	Latest
- by age of bride	1948	1936-47		1990	Latest
	1949/50	1936-49	- by age of groom and previous marital status	1958	1948-57
	1958	1948-57			
	1959-1967	Latest		1968	Latest
	1968	1958-67		1976	Latest
	1969-1975	Latest		1982	Latest
	1976	1966-75		1990	Latest
	1977-1981	Latest			
	1982	1972-81			
	1983-1986	Latest			
	1987	1975-86			
	1988-1989	Latest	- by month	1968	1963-67
	1990	1980-1989			

Index
Historical index
(See notes at end of index)

Subject-matter	Year of issue	Time coverage	Subject-matter	Year of issue	Time coverage
	1951-1952	Latest		1983	1974-83
				1988	1980-88[vi]
- by country or area of birth and sex (see also: foreign-born, below)				1993	1985-93
			- by level of education, age and sex		
	1956	1945-55		1956	1945-55
	1963	1955-63		1963	1955-63
	1964	1955-64[vi]		1964	1955-64[vi]
	1971	1962-71		1971	1962-71
	1973	1965-73[vi]		1973	1965-73[vi]
- by country or area of birth and sex and age (see also: foreign-born, below)				1979	1970-79[vi]
				1983	1974-83
	1977	Latest		1988	1980-88[vi]
	1983	1974-83		1993	1985-93
	1989	1980-88[vi]	- by literacy, age and sex (see also: illiteracy, below)		
				1948	Latest
- by citizenship	1956	1945-55		1955	1945-54
	1963	1955-63		1963	1955-63
	1964	1955-64[vi]		1964	1955-64[vi]
	1971	1962-71		1971	1962-71
	1973	1965-73[vi]	- by literacy, age and sex and urban/rural residence		
- by citizenship, sex and age	1977	Latest			
	1983	1974-83		1973	1965-73[vi]
	1989	Latest		1979	1970-79[vi]
- by ethnic composition and sex				1983	1974-83
				1988	1980-88[vi]
	1956	1945-55		1993	1985-93
	1963	1955-63	- by localities of: 100000+ inhabitants		
	1964	1955-64[vi]		1948	Latest
	1971	1962-71		1952	Latest
	1973	1965-73[vi]		1955	1945-54
	1979	1970-79[vi]		1960	1920-61
	1983	1974-83		1962	1955-62
	1993	1985-93		1963	1955-63[vi]
- by households, number and size (see also: Households)				1970	1950-70
				1971	1962-71
	1955	1945-54		1973	1965-73[vi]
	1962	1955-62		1979	1970-79[vi]
	1963	1955-63[vi]		1983	1974-83
	1968	Latest		1988	1980-88[vi]
	1971	1962-71		1993	1985-93
	1973	1965-73[vi]	20000+ inhabitants		
	1976	Latest		1948	Latest
	1982	Latest		1952	Latest
	1987	1975-86		1955	1945-54
	1990	1980-89		1960	1920-61
	1995	1985-95		1962	1955-62
- by language and sex				1963	1955-63[vi]
	1956	1945-55		1970	1950-70
	1963	1955-63		1971	1962-71
	1964	1955-64[vi]		1973	1965-73[vi]
	1971	1962-71		1979	1970-79[vi]
	1973	1965-73[vi]		1983	1974-83
	1979	1970-79[vi]			

Subject-matter	Year of issue	Time coverage	Subject-matter	Year of issue	Time coverage
				1994	1985-94
by sex	1948	Latest	female, by marital status and age		
	1949/50	1926-48			
	1955	1945-54			
	1956	1945-55		1956	1945-55
	1960	1920-60		1964	1955-64
	1963	1955-63		1968	Latest
	1964	1955-64		1972	1962-72
	1970	1950-70	female, by marital status and age and urban/rural residence		
	1972	1962-72			
	1973	1965-73[vi]			
	1979	1970-79[vi]			
	1984	1974-84		1973	1965-73[vi]
	1994	1985-94		1979	1970-79[vi]
by status, age and sex				1984	1974-84
	1956	1945-55		1988	1980-88[vi]
	1964	1955-64		1994	1985-94
	1972	1962-72	foreign-born by occupation, age and sex (see also: country of birth above)	1984	1974-84
by status, age and sex and urban/rural residence					1980-88
				1994	1985-94
	1973	1965-73[vi]	foreign-born by occupation and sex (see also: country of birth above)	1977	Latest
	1979	1970-79[vi]	unemployed, by age and sex	1949/50	1946-49
	1984	1974-84	- economically inactive by sub-groups and sex		
	1988	1980-88[vi]			
	1994	1985-94			
by status, industry and sex	1948	Latest		1956	1945-54
	1949/50	Latest		1964	1955-64
	1955	1945-54		1972	1962-72
	1964	1955-64		1973	1965-73[vi]
	1972	1962-72		1979	1970-79[vi]
by status, industry, and sex and urban/rural residence				1984	1974-84[vi]
				1988	1980-88[vi]
				1994	1985-94
	1973	1965-73[vi]	- Elderly		
	1979	1970-79[vi]	- by economic, socio-demographic and urban/rural	1991PA[vii]	1950-90
	1984	1974-84			
	1988	1980-88[vi]			
	1994	1985-94	-female:		
by status, occupation and sex			by age and duration of marriage	1968	Latest
	1956	1945-55			
	1964	1955-64			
	1972	1962-72	by number of children born alive and age	1949/50	Latest
by status, occupation and sex and urban/rural residence					
	1973	1965-73[vi]			
	1979	1970-79[vi]			
	1984	1974-84			
	1988	1980-88[vi]		1954	1930-53

Subject-matter	Year of issue	Time coverage	Subject-matter	Year of issue	Time coverage
	1955	1945-54		1962	1958-61
	1959	1949-58		1963	1958-62
	1963	1955-63		1964	1958-63
	1965	1955-65		1965	1958-64
	1969	Latest		1966	1958-66
	1971	1962-71		1967	1963-67
	1973	1965-73[vi]		1968	1963-68
	1975	1965-74		1969	1963-69
	1978HS[ii]	1948-77		1970	1963-70
	1981	1972-80		1971	1963-71
	1986	1977-85		1972	1963-72
	1997HS[iii]	1948-96		1973	1970-73
by number of children living and age				1974	1970-74
				1975	1970-75
	1949/50	Latest		1976	1970-76
	1954	1930-53		1977	1970-77
	1955	1945-54		1978	1975-78
	1959	1949-58		1979	1975-79
	1963	1955-63		1980	1975-80
	1965	1955-65		1981	1975-81
	1968-1969	Latest		1982	1975-82
	1971	1962-71		1983	1980-83
	1973	1965-73[vi]		1984	1980-84
	1975	1965-74		1985	1980-85
	1978HS[ii]	1948-77		1986	1980-86
	1981	1972-80		1987	1980-87
	1986	1977-85		1988	1985-88
	1997HS[iii]	1948-96		1989	1985-89
in households by age, sex of householder, size and relationship to householder and urban/rural residence				1990	1985-90
				1991	1985-91
				1992	1985-92
				1993	1990-93
				1994	1990-94
				1995	1990-95
				1996	1990-96
				1997	1990-97
				1998	1993-98
	1987	1975-86		1999	1995-99
	1995	1991-95		2000	1995-00
institutional, by age, sex and urban/rural residence				2001	2000-05
			average annual for the world, macro-regions (continents) and regions		
	1987	1875-86			
	1995	1991-95		1957	1950-56
-growth rates:				1958	1950-57
average annual for countries or areas				1959	1950-58
				1960	1950-59
	1957	1953-56		1961	1950-60
	1958	1953-57		1962	1950-61
	1959	1953-58		1963	1958-62
	1960	1953-59			1960-62
	1961	1953-60		1964	1958-63

Subject-matter	Year of issue	Time coverage
		1960-63
	1965	1958-64
		1960-64
	1966	1958-66
		1960-66
	1967	1960-67
		1963-67
	1968	1960-68
		1963-68
	1969	1960-69
		1963-69
	1970	1963-70
		1965-70
	1971	1963-71
		1965-71
	1972	1963-72
		1965-72
	1973	1965-73
		1970-73
	1974	1965-74
		1970-74
	1975	1965-75
		1970-75
	1976	1965-76
		1970-76
	1977	1965-77
		1970-77
	1978-1979	1970-75
	1980-1983	1975-80
	1984-1986	1980-85
	1987-1992	1985-90
	1993-1997	1990-95
	1998-2000	1995-00
	2001	2000-05
- Homeless by age and sex	1991PA[vii]	Latest
- illiteracy rates by sex	1948	Latest
	1955	1945-54
	1960	1920-60
	1963	1955-63[vi]
	1964	1955-64[vi]
	1970	1950-70
- illiteracy rates by sex and urban/rural residence	1973	1965-73
	1979	1970-79[vi]
	1983	1974-83
	1988	1980-88[vi]
	1993	1985-93
- illiterate, by sex	1948	Latest
	1955	1945-54
	1960	1920-60

Subject-matter	Year of issue	Time coverage
	1963	1955-63
	1964	1955-64
	1970	1950-70
- illiterate, by sex and age	1948	Latest
	1955	1945-54
	1963	1955-63
	1964	1955-64[vi]
	1970	1950-70
- illiterate, by sex and age and urban/rural residence	1973	1965-73
	1979	1970-79[vi]
	1983	1974-83
	1988	1980-88[vi]
	1993	1985-93
- illiterate, by sex and urban/rural residence	1973	1965-73
	1979	1970-79[vi]
	1983	1974-83
	1988	1980-88[vi]
	1993	1985-93
- in collective living quarters and homeless	1991PA[vii]	Latest
- in households (see: by household type, above, also: Households)		
- in localities (see: by localities and by locality size-classes, above)		
- increase rates (see: growth rates, above)		
- literacy rates: by sex (see also: illiteracy rates, above)	1955	1945-54
- literacy rates, by sex and age	1955	1945-54
- literate, by sex and age (see also: illiterate, above)	1948	Latest
	1955	1945-54
	1963	1955-63
	1964	1955-64[vi]
- literate, by sex and age by urban/rural	1971	1962-71

Index
Historical index
(See notes at end of index)

Subject-matter	Year of issue	Time coverage
residence		
	1973	1965-73[vi]
	1979	1970-74[vi]
	1983	1974-83
	1988	1980-88[vi]
	1993	1985-93
	1987	1975-86
- living arrangements	1991PA[vii]	1950-90
	1995	1985-95
- localities (see: by localities, above)		
- major civil divisions (see: by major civil divisions, above)		
- married by age and sex (see also: by marital status, above): numbers and percent	1954	1926-52
	1960	1920-60
	1970	1950-70
- married female by percentage and duration of marriage	1968	Latest
- never married proportion by sex, selected ages	1976	1966-75
	1978HS[ii]	1948-77
	1982	1972-81
	1990	1980-89
- not economically active	1972	1962-72
- not economically active by urban/rural residence	1973	1965-73[vi]
	1979	1970-79[vi]
	1984	1974-84
	1988	1980-88[vi]
	1994	1985-94
- of cities:		
capital city	1952	Latest
	1955	1945-54
	1957	Latest
	1960	1939-61
	1962	1955-62
	1963	1955-63
	1964-1969	Latest
	1970	1950-70
	1971	1962-71
	1972	Latest
	1973	1965-73

Subject-matter	Year of issue	Time coverage
	1974-2001	Latest
of 100000+ inhabitants	1952	Latest
	1955	1945-54
	1957	Latest
	1960	1939-61
	1962	1955-62
	1963	1955-63
	1964-1969	Latest
	1970	1950-70
	1971	1962-71
	1972	Latest
	1973	1965-73
	1974-2001	Latest
- of continents (see: of macro regions, below)		
- of countries or areas (totals):		
enumerated	1948	1900-48
	1949/50	1900-50
	1951	1900-51
	1952	1850-1952
	1953	1850-1953
	1954	Latest
	1955	1850-1954
	1956-1961	Latest
	1962	1900-62
	1963	Latest
	1964	1955-64
	1965-1978	Latest
	1978HS[ii]	1948-78
	1979-1997	Latest
	1997HS[iii]	1948-97
	1998-2001	Latest
estimated	1948	1932-47
	1949/50	1932-49
	1951	1930-50
	1952	1920-51
	1953	1920-53
	1954	1920-54
	1955	1920-55
	1956	1920-56
	1957	1940-57
	1958	1939-58
	1959	1940-59
	1960	1920-60
	1961	1941-61
	1962	1942-62
	1963	1943-63
	1964	1955-64
	1965	1946-65
	1966	1947-66
	1967	1958-67

Subject-matter	Year of issue	Time coverage	Subject-matter	Year of issue	Time coverage
	1968	1959-68		1967	1930-67
	1969	1960-69		1968	1930-68
	1970	1950-70		1969	1930-69
	1971	1962-71		1970	1950-70
	1972	1963-72		1971	1950-71
	1973	1964-73		1972	1950-72
	1974	1965-74		1973	1950-73
	1975	1966-75		1974	1950-74
	1976	1967-76		1975	1950-75
	1977	1968-77		1976	1950-76
	1978	1969-78		1977	1950-77
	1978HS[ii]	1948-78		1978	1950-78
	1979	1970-79		1979	1950-79
	1980	1971-80		1980	1950-80
	1981	1972-81		1981	1950-81
	1982	1973-82		1982	1950-82
	1983	1974-83		1983	1950-83
	1984	1975-84		1984	1950-84
	1985	1976-85		1985	1950-85
	1986	1977-86		1986	1950-86
	1987	1978-87		1987	1950-87
	1988	1979-88		1988	1950-88
	1989	1980-89		1989	1950-89
	1990	1981-90		1990	1950-90
	1991	1982-91		1991	1950-91
	1992	1983-92		1992	1950-92
	1993	1984-93		1993	1950-93
	1994	1985-94		1994	1950-94
	1995	1986-95		1995	1950-95
	1996	1987-96		1996	1950-96
	1997	1988-97		1997	1950-97
	1997HS[iii]	1948-97		1998-1999	1950-00
	1998	1989-98		2000	1950-00
	1999	1990-99		2001	1950-01
	2000	1991-00			
	2001	1992-01	- of regions	1949/50	1920-49
				1952	1920-51
- of major regions	1949/50	1920-49		1953	1920-52
	1951	1950		1954	1920-53
	1952	1920-51		1955	1920-54
	1953	1920-52		1956	1920-55
	1954	1920-53		1957	1920-56
	1955	1920-54		1958	1920-57
	1956	1920-55		1959	1920-58
	1957	1920-56		1960	1920-59
	1958	1920-57		1961	1920-60
	1959	1920-58		1962	1920-61
	1960	1920-59		1963	1930-62
	1961	1920-60		1964	1930-63
	1962	1920-61		1965	1930-65
	1963	1930-62		1966	1930-66
	1964	1930-63		1967	1930-67
	1965	1930-65		1968	1930-68
	1966	1930-66		1969	1930-69

Subject-matter	Year of issue	Time coverage	Subject-matter	Year of issue	Time coverage
	1970	1950-70		1972	1950-72
	1971	1950-71		1973	1950-73
	1972	1950-72		1974	1950-74
	1973	1950-73		1975	1950-75
	1974	1950-74		1976	1950-76
	1975	1950-75		1977	1950-77
	1976	1950-76		1978	1950-78
	1977	1950-77		1979	1950-79
	1978	1950-78		1980	1950-80
	1979	1950-79		1981	1950-81
	1980	1950-80		1982	1950-82
	1981	1950-81		1983	1950-83
	1982	1950-82		1984	1950-84
	1983	1950-83		1985	1950-85
	1984	1950-84		1986	1950-86
	1985	1950-85		1987	1950-87
	1986	1950-86		1988	1950-88
	1987	1950-87		1989	1950-89
	1988	1950-88		1990	1950-90
	1989	1950-89		1991	1950-91
	1990	1950-90		1992	1950-92
	1991	1950-91		1993	1950-93
	1992	1950-92		1994	1950-94
	1993	1950-93		1995	1950-95
	1994	1950-94		1996	1950-96
	1995	1950-95		1997	1950-97
	1996	1950-96		1998-1999	1950-00
	1997	1950-97		2000	1950-00
	1998-1999	1950-00		2001	1950-01
	2000	1950-00	- rural residence (see: urban/rural residence, below)		
	2001	1950-01			
- of the world	1949/50	1920-49	- single, by age and sex (see also: by marital status, above):		
	1951	1950			
	1952	1920-51			
	1953	1920-52			
	1954	1920-53	numbers	1960	1920-60
	1955	1920-54		1970	1950-70
	1956	1920-55	percent	1949/50	1926-48
	1957	1920-56		1960	1920-60
	1958	1920-57		1970	1950-70
	1959	1920-58	- urban/rural residence	1968	1964-68
	1960	1920-59		1969	1965-69
	1961	1920-60		1970	1950-70
	1962	1920-61		1971	1962-71
	1963	1930-62		1972	1968-72
	1964	1930-63		1973	1965-73
	1965	1930-65		1974	1966-74
	1966	1930-66		1975	1967-75
	1967	1930-67		1976	1967-76
	1968	1930-68		1977	1968-77
	1969	1930-69		1978	1969-78
	1970	1950-70		1979	1970-79
	1971	1950-71		1980	1971-80

APPENDIX

Special text of each Demographic Yearbook:

Divorce:
'Uses of Marriage and Divorce Statistics', 1958.

Marriage:
'Uses of Marriage and Divorce Statistics', 1958.

Households:
'Concepts and definitions of households, householder and institutional population', 1987.

Migration:
'Statistics of International Migration', 1977.

Mortality:
'Recent Mortality Trends', 1951.
'Development of Statistics of Causes of Death', 1951.
'Factors in Declining Mortality', 1957.
'Notes on Methods of Evaluating the Reliability of Conventional Mortality Statistics', 1961.
'Recent Trends of Mortality', 1966.
'Mortality Trends among Elderly Persons', 1991PA[vii].

Natality:
'Graphic Presentation of Trends in Fertility', 1959.
'Recent Trends in Birth Rates', 1965.
'Recent Changes in World Fertility', 1969.

Population
'World Population Trends, 1920-1949', 1949/50.
'Urban Trends and Characteristics', 1952.
'Background to the1950 Censuses of Population', 1955.
'The World Demographic Situation', 1956.
'How Well Do We Know the Present Size and Trend of the World's Population?', 1960.
'Notes on Availability of National Population Census Data and Methods of Estimating their Reliability', 1962.
'Availability and Adequacy of Selected Data Obtained from Population Censuses Taken 1955-1963', 1963.
'Availability of Selected Population Census Statistics: 1955-1964', 1964.
'Statistical Concepts and Definitions of Urban and Rural Population', 1967.
'Statistical Concepts and Definitions of Household', 1968.
'How Well Do We Know the Present Size and Trend of the World's Population?', 1970.
'United Nations Recommendations on Topics to be Investigated in a Population Census
Compared with Country Practice in National Censuses taken 1965-1971', 1971.
'Statistical Definitions of Urban Population and their Use in Applied Demography', 1972.
'Dates of National Population and Housing Census carried out during the decade1965-1974', 1974.
'Dates of National Population and/or Housing Censuses taken or anticipated during the decade 1975-1984', 1979.
'Dates of National Population and/or Housing Censuses taken during the decade1965-1974 and
taken or anticipated during the decade 1975-1984', 1983.
'Dates of National Population and/or Housing Censuses taken during the decade1975-1984 and taken or anticipated
during the decade 1985-1994', 1988 and 1993.
'Statistics Concerning the Economically Active Population: An Overview', 1984.
'Disability', 1991PA[vii].
'Population Ageing', 1991PA[vii].
'Special Needs for the Study of Population Ageing and Elderly Persons', 1991PA[vii].

Index
Historical index
(See notes at end of index)

General Notes

This cumulative index covers the contents of each of the 52 issues of the Demographic Yearbook. 'Year of issue' stands for the particular issue in which the indicated subject-matter appears. Unless otherwise specified, 'Time coverage' designates the years for which annual statistics are shown in the Demographic Yearbook referred to in 'Year of issue' column. 'Latest' or '2-Latest' indicates that data are for latest available year(s) only.

[i] Only titles not available for preceding bibliography.

[ii] Historical Supplement to the 30th DYB published in a separate volume in year 1979.

[iii] Historical Supplement to the 49th DYB published in a separate volume (CD-ROM) in year 2000.

[iv] Supplement to the 51st DYB focusing on natality published in a separate volume (CD-ROM) in year 2002.

[v] Five-year average rates.

[vi] Only data not available for preceding issue.

[vii] Population ageing published in separate volume.

Index
Index historique (suite)
(Voir notes à la fin de l'index)

Index
Index historique (suite)
(Voir notes à la fin de l'index)

Index
Index historique (suite)
(Voir notes à la fin de l'index)

Index
Index historique (suite)
(Voir notes à la fin de l'index)

Sujet	Année de l'édition	Période considérée
	1984	1980-84
	1985	1976-85
	1986	1982-86
	1987	1983-87
	1988	1984-88
	1989	1985-89
	1990	1986-90
	1991	1987-91
	1992	1983-92
	1993	1989-93
	1994	1990-94
	1995	1991-95
	1996	1987-96
	1997	1993-97
	1997SR [ii]	1948-97
	1998	1994-98
	1999	1995-99
	2000	1996-00
	2001	1997-01
-d'enfants de moins d'un an (voir: Mortalités infantile)		
-estimatifs:		
pour les continents	1949/50	1947
	1956-1977	Dernière
	1978-1979	1970-75
	1980-1983	1975-80
	1984-1986	1980-85
	1987-1992	1985-90
	1993-1997	1990-95
	1998-2000	1995-00
	2001	2000-05
pour les grandes régions (continentales)	1964-1977	Dernière
	1978-1979	1970-75
	1980-1983	1975-80
	1984-1986	1980-85
	1987-1992	1985-90
	1993-1997	1990-95
	1998-2000	1995-00
	2001	2000-05
pour les régions	1949/50	1947
	1956-1977	Dernière
	1978-1979	1970-75
	1980-1983	1975-80
	1984-1986	1980-85
	1987-1992	1985-90
	1993-1997	1990-95
	1998-2000	1995-00
	2001	2000-05
pour l'ensemble du monde	1949/50	1947
	1956-1977	Dernière
	1978-1979	1970-75
	1980-1983	1975-80
	1984-1986	1980-85
	1987-1992	1985-90
	1993-1997	1990-95
	1998-2000	1995-00
	2001	2000-05

Sujet	Année de l'édition	Période considérée
-selon l'âge et le sexe	1948	1935-47
	1949/50	1936-49
	1951	1936-50
	1952	1936-51
	1953	1940-52
	1954	1946-53
	1955-1956	Dernière
	1957	1948-56
	1961	1952-60
	1966	1950-65
	1967	Dernière
	1972	Dernière
	1974	1965-73
	1975-1978	Dernière
	1978SR [i]	1948-77
	1979	Dernière
	1980	1971-79
	1981-1984	Dernière
	1985	1976-84
	1986-1991	Dernière
	1991 VP [v]	1950-90
	1992	1983-92
	1993-1995	Dernière
	1996	1987-95
	1997	Dernière
	1997SR [ii]	1948-96
	1998-2001	Dernière
-selon la cause	1951	1947-49
	1952	1947-51
	1953	1947-52
	1954	1945-53
	1955-1956	Dernière
	1957	1952-56
	1958-1960	Dernière
	1961	1955-60
	1962-1965	Dernière
	1966	1960-65
	1967-1973	Dernière
	1974	1965-73
	1975-1979	Dernière
	1980	1971-79 [vi]
	1981-1984	Dernière
	1985	1976-84
	1986-1995	Dernière
	1996	1987-95
	1997-2000	Dernière
-selon la cause, l'âge et le sexe	1957	Dernière
	1961	Dernière
	1991 VP [v]	1960-90
-selon la cause et le sexe	1967	Dernière
	1974	Dernière
	1980	Dernière
	1985	Dernière
	1991 VP [v]	1960-90
	1996	Dernière
-selon l'état matrimonial, l'âge et le sexe	1961	Dernière
	1967	Dernière
	1974	Dernière
	1980	Dernière

Index
Index historique (suite)
(Voir notes à la fin de l'index)

Index
Index historique (suite)
(Voir notes à la fin de l'index)

Index
Index historique (suite)
(Voir notes à la fin de l'index)

Index
Index historique (suite)
(Voir notes à la fin de l'index)

Index
Index historique (suite)
(Voir notes à la fin de l'index)

Sujet	Année de l'édition	Période considérée	Sujet	Année de l'édition	Période considérée
	1998	1993-97		1983	1979-83
	1999	1994-98		1984	1980-84
	2000	1995-99		1985	1981-85
	2001	1997-01		1986	1982-86
-selon l'âge de l'époux et				1987	1983-87
l'âge de l'épouse	1958	1948-57		1988	1984-88
	1968	Dernière		1989	1985-89
	1976	Dernière		1990	1971-90
	1982	Dernière		1991	1987-91
	1990	Dernière		1992	1988-92
-selon l'âge de l'époux et				1993	1989-93
l'état matrimonial Antérieur	1958	1946-57		1994	1990-94
	1968	Dernière		1995	1991-95
	1976	Dernière		1996	1992-96
	1982	Dernière		1997	1993-97
	1990	Dernière		1998	1994-98
-selon l'état matrimonial				1999	1995-99
antérieur de l'épouse: et				2000	1996-00
l'âge	1958	1946-57		2001	1997-01
	1968	Dernière	-selon le mois	1968	1963-67
	1976	Dernière			
	1982	Dernière	**Mariages, premiers:**		
	1990	Dernière	-classification détaillé selon		
-selon l'état matrimonial			l'âge de l'épouse et de		
antérieur de l'épouse			l'époux	1976	Dernière
(suite): et l'état matrimonial				1982	1972-81
antérieur de l'époux	1949/50	Dernière		1990	1980-89
	1958	1948-57			
	1968	1958-67	**Mariages, taux de** (voir:		
	1976	1966-75	Nuptialité, taux de)		
	1982	1972-81			
	1990	1980-89	**Ménages:**		
-selon l'état matrimonial			-dimension moyenne des	1962	1955-62
antérieur de l'époux				1963	1955-63 [iii]
et l'âge	1958	1946-57		1968	Dernière
	1968	Dernière		1971	1962-71
	1976	Dernière		1973	1965-73 [iii]
	1982	Dernière		1976	Dernière
	1990	Dernière		1982	Dernière
et l'état matrimonial				1987	1975-86
antérieur de l'épouse	1949/50	Dernière		1990	1980-89
	1958	1948-57		1995	1985-95
	1968	1958-67	-le lien avec le chef de		
	1976	1966-75	ménage et la résidence		
	1982	1972-81	urbaine/rurale	1987	1975-86
	1990	1980-89		1995	1985-95
-selon la résidence			-nombre de	1955	1945-54
(urbaine/rurale)	1968	Dernière		1962	1955-62
	1969	1965-69		1963	1955-63 [iii]
	1970	1966-70		1968	Dernière
	1971	1967-71		1971	1962-71
	1972	1968-72		1973	1965-73 [iii]
	1973	1969-73		1976	Dernière
	1974	1970-74		1982	Dernière
	1975	1971-75		1987	1975-86
	1976	1957-76		1990	1980-89
	1977	1973-77		1995	1985-95
	1978	1974-78	-personnes 60+	1991 VP [v]	Dernière
	1979	1975-79	-nombre de noyaux		
	1980	1976-80	familiaux, selon la		
	1981	1977-81	dimension des	1973	1965-73
	1982	1963-82		1976	Dernière

Index
Index historique (suite)
(Voir notes à la fin de l'index)

Index
Index historique (suite)
(Voir notes à la fin de l'index)

Index
Index historique (suite)
(Voir notes à la fin de l'index)

Index
Index historique (suite)
(Voir notes à la fin de l'index)

Sujet	Année de l'édition	Période considérée
	1963	1954-63
	1964	1960-64
	1965	1961-65
	1966	1947-66
	1967	1963-67
	1968	1964-68
	1969	1965-69
	1970	1966-70
	1971	1967-71
	1972	1968-72
	1973	1969-73
	1974	1965-74
	1975	1971-75
	1976	1972-76
	1977	1973-77
	1978	1974-78
	1978SR [i]	1948-78
	1979	1975-79
	1980	1971-80
	1981	1977-81
	1982	1978-82
	1983	1979-83
	1984	1980-84
	1985	1976-85
	1986	1982-86
	1987	1983-87
	1988	1984-88
	1989	1985-89
	1990	1986-90
	1991	1987-91
	1992	1983-92
	1993	1989-93
	1994	1990-94
	1995	1991-95
	1996	1987-96
	1997	1993-97
	1997SR [ii]	1948-97
	1998	1994-98
	1999	1995-99
	2000	1996-00
	2001	1997-01
-selon l'âge et le sexe	1948	1936-47
	1951	1936-49
	1957	1948-56
	1961	1952-60
	1962-1965	Dernière
	1966	1961-65
	1967	1962-66
-selon l'âge et le sexe et la résidence (urbaine/rurale)	1968-1973	Dernière
	1974	1965-73
	1975-1979	Dernière
	1980	1971-79
	1981-1984	Dernière
	1985	1976-84
	1986-1991	Dernière
	1992	1983-92
	1993-1995	Dernière
	1996	1987-95
	1998-2001	Dernière
-selon la résidence (urbaine/rurale)	1967	Dernière
	1968	1964-68

Sujet	Année de l'édition	Période considérée
	1969	1965-69
	1970	1966-70
	1971	1967-71
	1972	1968-72
	1973	1969-73
	1974	1965-74
	1975	1971-75
	1976	1972-76
	1977	1973-77
	1978	1974-78
	1979	1975-79
	1980	1971-80
	1981	1977-81
	1982	1978-82
	1983	1979-83
	1984	1980-84
	1985	1976-85
	1986	1982-86
	1987	1983-87
	1988	1984-88
	1989	1985-89
	1990	1986-90
	1991	1987-91
	1992	1983-92
	1993	1989-93
	1994	1990-94
	1995	1991-95
	1996	1987-96
	1997	1993-97
	1998	1994-98
	1999	1995-99
	2000	1996-00
	2001	1997-01
-selon le mois	1967	1962-66
	1974	1965-73
	1980	1971-79
	1985	1976-84
Mortalité infantile, taux de .,	1948	1932-47
	1949/50	1932-49
	1951	1930-50
	1952	1920-34 [vi]
		1934-51
	1953	1920-39 [vi]
		1940-52
	1954	1920-39 [vi]
		1946-53
	1955	1920-34 [vi]
		1946-54
	1956	1947-55
	1957	1948-56
	1958	1948-57
	1959	1949-58
	1960	1950-59
	1961	1945-59 [vi]
		1952-61
	1962	1945-59 [vi]
		1952-62
	1963	1945-59 [vi]
		1954-63
	1964	1960-64
	1965	1961-65

Index
Index historique (suite)
(Voir notes à la fin de l'index)

Index
Index historique (suite)
(Voir notes à la fin de l'index)

Sujet	Année de l'édition	Période considérée	Sujet	Année de l'édition	Période considérée
	1978	1968-77		1967-1973	Dernière
	1979	1969-78		1974	1965-73
	1980	1971-79		1975	1966-74
	1981	1972-80		1976	1966-75
	1982	1972-81		1977	1967-76
				1978	1968-77
Mortalité maternelle				1979	1969-78
(nombres)	1951	1947-50		1980	1971-79
	1952	1947-51		1981	1972-80
	1953	Dernière		1982	1972-81
	1954	1945-53		1983	1973-82
	1955-1956	Dernière		1984	1974-83
	1957	1952-56		1985	1975-84
	1958-1960	Dernière		1986	1976-85
	1961	1955-60		1987	1977-86
	1962-1965	Dernière		1988	1978-87
	1966	1960-65		1989	1979-88
	1967-1973	Dernière		1990	1980-89
	1974	1965-73		1991	1981-90
	1975-1979	Dernière		1992	1982-91
	1980	1971-79		1993	1983-92
	1981	1972-80		1994	1984-93
	1982	1972-81		1995	1985-94
	1983	1973-82		1996	1986-95
	1984	1974-83		1997	1987-96
	1985	1975-84		1998	1988-97
	1986	1976-85		1999	1989-98
	1987	1977-86		2000	1991-00
	1988	1978-87		2001	1991-00
	1989	1979-88	-selon l'âge	1957	Dernière
	1990	1980-89		1961	Dernière
	1991	1981-90			
	1992	1982-91	**Mortalité néonatale:**		
	1993	1983-92	-selon le sexe (nombres)	1948	1936-47
	1994	1984-93		1951	1936-50
	1995	1985-94		1957	1948-56
	1996	1986-95		1961	1952-60
	1997	1987-96		1963-1965	Dernière
	1998	1988-97		1966	1961-65
	1999	1989-98		1967	1962-66
	2000	1991-00	-selon le sexe et la		
	2001	1991-00	résidence (urbaine/rurale)	1968-1973	Dernière
-selon l'âge	1951	Dernière		1974	1965-73
	1952	Dernière		1975-1979	Dernière
	1957	Dernière		1980	1971-79
	1961	Dernière		1981-1984	Dernière
	1967	Dernière		1985	1976-84
	1974	Dernière		1986-1991	Dernière
	1980	Dernière		1992	1983-92
	1985	Dernière		1993-1995	Dernière
	1996	Dernière		1996	1987-95
				1997	Dernière
Mortalité maternelle, taux de	1951	1947-50		1997SR[ii]	1948-96
	1952	1947-51		1998-2001	Dernière
	1953	Dernière			
	1954	1945-53	**Mortalité néonatale, taux de**		
	1955-1956	Dernière	-selon le sexe	1948	1936-47
	1957	1952-56		1951	1936-50
	1958-1960	Dernière		1957	1948-56
	1961	1955-60		1961	1952-60
	1962-1965	Dernière		1966	1956-65
	1966	1960-65		1967	1962-66

Index
Index historique (suite)
(Voir notes à la fin de l'index)

Index
Index historique (suite)
(Voir notes à la fin de l'index)

Sujet	Année de l'édition	Période considérée	Sujet	Année de l'édition	Période considérée
	1979	Dernière		1980	2-Dernières
	1980	2-Dernières		1985	2-Dernières
	1981-1984	Dernière		1996	2-Dernières
	1985	2-Dernières			
	1986-1991	Dernière	**Mortalité, taux de**.......................	1948	1932-47
	1991 VP [v]	1950-90		1949/50	1932-49
	1992-1995	Dernière		1951	1905-30 [vi]
	1996	2-Dernières			1930-50
	1997	Dernière		1952	1920-34 [vi]
	1997SR [ii]	1948-1996			1934-51
	1998-2001	Dernière		1953	1920-39 [vi]
-espérance de vie à un âge donné selon le sexe	1948	1891-1945			1940-52
	1951	1891-1950		1954	1920-39 [vi]
	1952	1891-1951 [iii]			1946-53
	1953	1891-1952		1955	1920-34 [vi]
	1954	1891-1953 [iii]			1946-54
	1955-1956	Dernière		1956	1947-55
	1957	1900-56		1957	1930-56
	1958-1960	Dernière		1958	1948-57
	1961	1940-60		1959	1949-58
	1962-64	Dernière		1960	1950-59
	1966	2-Dernières		1961	1945-59 [vi]
	1967	1900-66			1952-61
	1968-1973	Dernière		1962	1945-54 [vi]
	1974	2-Dernières			1952-62
	1975-1978	Dernière		1963	1945-59 [vi]
	1978HS [i]	1948-77			1954-63
	1979	Dernière		1964	1960-64
	1980	2-Dernières		1965	1961-65
	1981-1984	Dernière		1966	1920-64 [vi]
	1985	2-Dernières			1951-66
	1986-1991	Dernière		1967	1963-67
	1991 VP [v]	1950-90		1968	1964-68
	1992-1994	Dernière		1969	1965-69
	1996	2-Dernières		1970	1966-70
	1997	Dernière		1971	1967-71
	1997SR [ii]	1948-96		1972	1968-72
	1998-2001	Dernière		1973	1969-73
-taux de mortalité à un âge donné selon le sexe	1948	1891-1945		1974	1965-74
	1951	1891-1950		1975	1971-75
	1952	1891-1951 [iii]		1976	1972-76
	1953	1891-1952		1977	1973-77
	1954	1891-1953 [iii]		1978	1974-78
	1957	1900-56		1978SR [i]	1948-78
	1961	1940-60		1979	1975-79
	1966	2-Dernières		1980	1971-80
	1974	2-Dernières		1981	1977-81
	1980	2-Dernières		1982	1978-82
	1985	2-Dernières		1983	1979-83
	1996	2-Dernières		1984	1980-84
-survivants à un âge donné selon le sexe	1948	1891-1945		1985	1976-85
	1951	1891-1950		1986	1982-86
	1952	1891-1951 [iii]		1987	1983-87
	1953	1891-1952		1988	1984-88
	1954	1891-1953 [iii]		1989	1985-89
	1957	1900-56		1990	1986-90
	1961	1940-60		1991	1987-91
	1966	2-Dernières		1992	1983-92
	1974	2-Dernières		1993	1989-93
				1994	1990-94
				1995	1991-95
				1996	1987-96

Index
Index historique (suite)
(Voir notes à la fin de l'index)

Index historique (suite)

(Voir notes à la fin de l'index)

Index
Index historique (suite)
(Voir notes à la fin de l'index)

Index
Index historique (suite)
(Voir notes à la fin de l'index)

Index
Index historique (suite)
(Voir notes à la fin de l'index)

Sujet	Année de l'édition	Période considérée
	1959	1949-58
	1965	1955-64
	1969	1963-68
	1975	1966-74
	1981	1972-80
	1986	1977-85
	1999CD [vii]	1990-98
-selon la durée de gestation	1975	Dernière
	1981	1972-80
	1986	1977-85
	1999CD [vii]	1990-98
-selon la durée du mariage (voir: légitimes selon la durée du mariage)		
-selon la profession du père	1965	Dernière
	1969	Dernière
-selon la résidence (urbaine/rurale)	1965	Dernière
	1967	Dernière
	1968	1964-68
	1969	1964-68
	1970	1966-70
	1971	1967-71
	1972	1968-72
	1973	1969-73
	1974	1970-74
	1975	1956-75
	1976	1972-76
	1977	1973-77
	1978	1974-78
	1979	1975-79
	1980	1976-80
	1981	1962-81
	1982	1978-82
	1983	1979-83
	1984	1980-84
	1985	1981-85
	1986	1967-86
	1987	1983-87
	1988	1984-88
	1989	1985-89
	1990	1986-90
	1991	1987-91
	1992	1983-92
	1993	1989-93
	1994	1990-94
	1995	1991-95
	1996	1992-96
	1997	1993-97
	1998	1994-98
	1999	1995-99
	1999CD [vii]	1980-99
	2000	1996-00
	2001	1997-01
-selon la résidence (urbaine/rurale) et l'âge de la mère	1965	Dernière
	1969-1974	Dernière
	1975	1966-74
	1976-1980	Dernière

Sujet	Année de l'édition	Période considérée
	1981	1972-80
	1982-1985	Dernière
	1986	1977-85
	1987-1991	Dernière
	1992	1983-92
	1993-1997	Dernière
	1997SR [ii]	1948-96
	1998-1999	Dernière
	1999CD [vii]	1990-98
	2000-2001	Dernière
-selon le poids à la naissance	1975	Dernière
	1981	1972-80
	1986	1977-85
	1999CD [vii]	1990-98
-selon le rang de naissance	1948	1936-47
	1949/50	1936-49
	1954	1936-53
	1955	Dernière
	1959	1949-58
	1965	1955-64
	1969	1963-68
	1975	1966-74
	1981	1972-80
	1986	1977-85
	1999CD [vii]	1990-98
-selon le sexe	1959	1949-58
	1965	1955-64
	1967-1968	Dernière
	1969	1963-68
	1970-1974	Dernière
	1975	1956-75
	1976-1980	Dernière
	1981	1962-81
	1982-1985	Dernière
	1986	1967-86
	1987-1991	Dernière
	1992	1983-92
	1993-1997	Dernière
	1997SR [ii]	1948-96
	1998-1999	Dernière
	1999CD [vii]	1980-1999
	2000-2001	Dernière
-selon les naissances multiples	1965	Dernière
	1969	Dernière
	1975	Dernière
	1981	1972-80
	1986	1977-85
	1999CD [vii]	1990-98
Naissances des femmes de moins de 20 ans selon l'âge de la mère: -et la résidence (urbaine/rurale)	1986	1970-85
Natalité proportionnelle: -fécondité	1949/50	Dernière
	1954	Dernière
	1959	1949-58
	1965	1955-65
	1969	1963-68

Index
Index historique (suite)
(Voir notes à la fin de l'index)

Index
Index historique (suite)
(Voir notes à la fin de l'index)

Index
Index historique (suite)
(Voir notes à la fin de l'index)

Index
Index historique (suite)
(Voir notes à la fin de l'index)

Sujet	Année de l'édition	Période considérée
	1978	1974-78
	1979	1975-79
	1980	1976-80
	1981	1977-81
	1982	1963-82
	1983	1979-83
	1984	1980-84
	1985	1981-85
	1986	1982-86
	1987	1983-87
	1988	1984-88
	1989	1985-89
	1990	1971-90
	1991	1987-91
	1992	1988-92
	1993	1989-93
	1994	1990-94
	1995	1991-95
	1996	1992-96
	1997	1993-97
	1998	1994-98
	1999	1995-99
	2000	1996-00
	2001	1997-01
-selon le sexe et la population mariable	1958	1935-56
	1968	1935-67
	1976	1966-75
	1982	1972-81
	1990	1980-89
Nuptialité au premier mariage, taux de, classification détaillée selon l'âge de l'épouse et de l'époux	1982	1972-81
	1990	1980-89

P

Sujet	Année de l'édition	Période considérée
Population:		
-accroissement, taux d'......: annuels moyens pour les pays ou zones	1957	1953-56
	1958	1953-57
	1959	1953-58
	1960	1953-59
	1961	1953-60
	1962	1958-61
	1963	1958-62
	1964	1958-63
	1965	1958-64
	1966	1958-66
	1967	1963-67
	1968	1963-68
	1969	1963-69
	1970	1963-70
	1971	1963-71
	1972	1963-72
	1973	1970-73
	1974	1970-74
	1975	1970-75

Sujet	Année de l'édition	Période considérée
	1976	1970-76
	1977	1970-77
	1978	1975-78
	1979	1975-79
	1980	1975-80
	1981	1975-81
	1982	1975-82
	1983	1980-83
	1984	1980-84
	1985	1980-85
	1986	1980-86
	1987	1980-87
	1988	1985-88
	1989	1985-89
	1990	1985-90
	1991	1985-91
	1992	1985-92
	1993	1990-93
	1994	1990-94
	1995	1990-95
	1996	1990-96
	1997	1990-97
	1998	1993-98
	1999	1995-99
	2000	1996-00
	2001	1997-01
annuels moyens pour le monde, les grandes régions (continentes) et les régions géographiques	1957	1950-56
	1958	1950-57
	1959	1950-58
	1960	1950-59
	1961	1950-60
	1962	1950-61
	1963	1958-62
		1960-62
	1964	1958-63
		1960-63
	1965	1958-64
		1960-64
	1966	1958-66
		1960-66
	1967	1960-67
		1963-67
	1968	1960-68
		1963-68
	1969	1960-69
		1963-69
	1970	1963-70
		1965-70
	1971	1963-71
		1965-71
	1972	1963-72
		1965-72
	1973	1965-73
		1970-73
	1974	1965-74
		1970-74
	1975	1965-75

Index
Index historique (suite)
(Voir notes à la fin de l'index)

Index
Index historique (suite)
(Voir notes à la fin de l'index)

Index
Index historique (suite)
(Voir notes à la fin de l'index)

Sujet	Année de l'édition	Période considérée	Sujet	Année de l'édition	Période considérée
	1993	1985-93 [iii]		1979	1950-79
-célibataire selon l'âge et le sexe (voir également: selon l'état matrimonial, ci-dessous):				1980	1950-80
				1981	1950-81
				1982	1950-82
				1983	1950-83
nombres	1960	1920-60		1984	1950-84
	1970	1950-70		1985	1950-85
pourcentages	1949/50	1926-48		1986	1950-86
	1960	1920-60		1987	1950-87
	1970	1950-70		1988	1950-88
-chômeurs selon l'âge et le sexe				1989	1950-89
	1949/50	1946-49		1990	1950-90
-dans les localités (voir: selon l'importance des localités, ci-dessous)				1991	1950-91
				1992	1950-92
				1993	1950-93
des collectivités, âge et sexe et résidence urbaine/rurale				1994	1950-94
				1995	1950-95
	1987	1975-86		1996	1950-96
	1995	1985-95		1997	1950-97
-dans les ménages selon le type et la dimension des ménages privés (voir également: Ménages)				1998-2000	1950-00
				2001	1950-01
			-des pays ou zones (total):		
			dénombrée	1948	1900-48
	1955	1945-54		1949/50	1900-50
	1962	1955-62		1951	1900-51
	1963	1955-63 [iii]		1952	1850-1952
-dans les logements collectifs et sans abri	1991VP [v]	Dernière		1953	1850-1953
-dans les villes (voir: des grandes régions)				1954	Dernière
				1955	1850-1954
-des continents (voir: des grandes régions (continentales))				1956-1961	Dernière
				1962	1900-62
				1963	Dernière
-des grandes régions (continentales)				1964	1955-64
	1949/50	1920-49		1965-1978	Dernière
	1951	1950		1978SR [i]	1948-78
	1952	1920-51		1979-1997	Dernière
	1953	1920-52		1979SR [ii]	1948-78
	1954	1920-53		1998-2001	Dernière
	1955	1920-54	estimée	1948	1932-47
	1956	1920-55		1949/50	1932-49
	1957	1920-56		1951	1930-50
	1958	1920-57		1952	1920-51
	1959	1920-58		1953	1920-53
	1960	1920-59		1954	1920-54
	1961	1920-60		1955	1920-55
	1962	1920-61		1956	1920-56
	1963	1930-62		1957	1940-57
	1964	1930-63		1958	1939-58
	1965	1930-65		1959	1940-59
	1966	1930-66		1960	1920-60
	1967	1930-67		1961	1941-61
	1968	1930-68		1962	1942-62
	1969	1930-69		1963	1943-63
	1970	1950-70		1964	1955-64
	1971	1950-71		1965	1946-65
	1972	1950-72		1966	1947-66
	1973	1950-73		1967	1958-67
	1974	1950-74		1968	1959-68
	1975	1950-75		1969	1960-69
	1976	1950-76		1970	1950-70
	1977	1950-77		1971	1962-71
	1978	1950-78		1972	1963-72

Index
Index historique (suite)
(Voir notes à la fin de l'index)

Index
Index historique (suite)
(Voir notes à la fin de l'index)

Sujet	Année de l'édition	Période considérée	Sujet	Année de l'édition	Période considérée
	1957	1920-56		1978SR [i]	1948-77
	1958	1920-57		1981	1972-80
	1959	1920-58		1986	1977-85
	1960	1920-59		1997SR [ii]	1948-96
	1961	1920-60	selon le nombre total		
	1962	1920-61	d'enfants vivants et l'âge	1949/50	Dernière
	1963	1930-62		1954	1930-53
	1964	1930-63		1955	1945-54
	1965	1930-65		1959	1949-58
	1966	1930-66		1963	1955-63
	1967	1930-67		1965	1955-65
	1968	1930-68		1968-1969	Dernière
	1969	1930-69		1971	1962-71
	1970	1950-70		1973	1965-73 [iii]
	1971	1950-71		1975	1965-74
	1972	1950-72		1978SR [i]	1948-77
	1973	1950-73		1981	1972-80
	1974	1950-74		1986	1977-85
	1975	1950-75		1997SR [ii]	1948-96
	1976	1950-76	-féminine mariée: selon		
	1977	1950-77	l'âge actuel et la durée du		
	1978	1950-78	présent mariage	1968	Dernière
	1979	1950-79	-fréquentant l'école selon		
	1980	1950-80	l'âge et le sexe	1956	1945-55
	1981	1950-81		1963	1955-63
	1982	1950-82		1964	1955-64 [iii]
	1983	1950-83		1971	1962-71
	1984	1950-84		1973	1965-73 [iii]
	1985	1950-85		1979	1970-79
	1986	1950-86		1983	1974-83
	1987	1950-87		1988	1980-88 [iii]
	1988	1950-88		1993	1985-93 [iii]
	1989	1950-89	-indicateurs divers de		
	1990	1950-90	conditions d'habitation	1991 VP [v]	Dernière
	1991	1950-91	-inactive par sous-groupes,		
	1992	1950-92	âge et sexe	1956	1945-55
	1993	1950-93		1964	1955-64
	1994	1950-94		1972	1962-72
	1995	1950-95		1973	1965-73 [iii]
	1996	1950-96		1979	1970-79 [iii]
	1997	1950-97		1984	1974-84
	1998-2000	1950-00		1988	1980-88 [iii]
	2001	1950-01		1994	1985-94
-effectifs des ménages, âge, sexe et résidence urbaine/rurale	1987	1975-86	-mariée selon l'âge et le sexe (voir également: Population selon l'état matrimonial) nombres et pourcentages	1954	1926-52
	1995	1950-95		1960	1920-60
-féminine:				1970	1950-70
selon l'âge et selon l'âge et la durée du mariage	1968	Dernière	-par année d'âge et par sexe	1955	1945-54
selon le nombre total d'enfants nés vivants et l'âge	1949/50	Dernière		1962	1955-62
	1954	1930-53		1963	1955-63 [iii]
	1955	1945-54		1971	1962-71
	1959	1949-58		1973	1965-73 [iii]
	1963	1955-63		1979	1970-79 [iii]
	1965	1955-65		1983	1974-83
	1969	Dernière		1988	1980-88 [iii]
	1971	1962-71		1993	1985-93
	1973	1965-73 [iii]	-par groupes d'âge et par sexe:		
	1975	1965-74			

Index
Index historique (suite)
(Voir notes à la fin de l'index)

Sujet	Année de l'édition	Période considérée	Sujet	Année de l'édition	Période considérée
dénombrée	1948-1952	Dernière	-selon la composition ethnique et le sexe		
	1953	1950-52		1956	1945-55
	1954-1959	Dernière		1963	1955-63
	1960	1940-60		1964	1955-64 [iii]
	1961	Dernière		1971	1962-71
	1962	1955-62		1973	1965-73 [iii]
	1963	1955-63		1979	1970-79 [iii]
	1964	1955-64 [iii]		1983	1974-83
	1965-1969	Dernière		1988	1980-88 [iii]
	1970	1950-70		1993	1985-93
	1971	1962-71			
	1972	Dernière	-selon l'état matrimonial, l'âge et le sexe (voir également: Population mariée et célibataire)		
	1973	1965-73		1948	Dernière
	1974-1978	Dernière		1949/50	1926-48
	1978SR [i]	1948-77		1955	1945-54
	1979-1991	Dernière		1958	1945-57
	1991 VP [v]	1950-90		1962	1955-62
	1992-1997	Dernière		1963	1955-63 [iii]
	1997SR [ii]	1948-97		1965	1955-65
	1998-2001	Dernière		1968	1955-67
estimée	1948-			1971	1962-71
	1949/50	1945 et Dernière		1973	1965-73 [iii]
	1951-1954	Dernière		1976	1966-75
	1955-1959	Dernière		1978 SR [i]	1948-77
	1960	1940-60		1982	1972-81
	1961-1969	Dernière		1987	1975-86
	1970	1950-70		1990	1980-89
	1971-1997	Dernière		1997SR [ii]	1948-96
	1997SR [ii]	1948-97	répartition en pourcentage	1948	Dernière
	1998-2001	Dernière	-selon le type de ménage et la résidence urbaine/rurale		
pourcentage	1948-			1987	1975-86
	1949/50	1945 et Dernière		1995	1985-95
	1951-1952	Dernière	-selon l'importance des localités:		
-par ménages, nombres et dimension moyenne selon la résidence (urbaine/rurale)(voir aussi: Ménages)			de 100 000 habitants et plus		
				1948	Dernière
				1952	Dernière
	1955	1945-54		1955	1945-54
	1962	1955-62		1960	1920-61
	1963	1955-63 [iii]		1962	1955-62
	1968	Dernière		1963	1955-63 [iii]
	1971	1962-71		1970	1950-70
	1973	1965-72 [iii]		1971	1962-71
	1976	1ernière		1973	1965-73 [iii]
	1982	Dernière		1979	1970-79 [iii]
	1987	1975-86		1983	1974-83
	1990	1980-89		1988	1980-88 [iii]
	1995	1985-95		1993	1985-93
-personnes âgées selon caractéristique socio-démographique			de 20 000 habitants et plus		
	1991VP [v]	1950-90		1948	Dernière
selon caractéristique				1952	Dernière
économique	1991VP [v]	1950-90		1955	1945-54
personnes atteintes d'incapacités	1991VP [v]	Dernière		1960	1920-61
-rurale (voir: urbaine/rurale (résidence), ci-dessous)				1962	1955-62
-selon l'âge et le sexe (voir: par groupes d'âge et par sexe, ci-dessous)				1963	1955-63 [iii]
				1970	1950-70
				1971	1962-71
				1973	1965-73 [iii]
				1979	1970-79 [iii]
				1983	1974-83
				1988	1980-88 [iii]

Index
Index historique (suite)
(Voir notes à la fin de l'index)

Sujet	Année de l'édition	Période considérée
	1993	1985-93
-selon l'importance des localités et le sexe	1948	Dernière
	1952	Dernière
	1955	1945-54
	1962	1955-62
	1963	1955-63 [iii]
	1971	1962-71
	1973	1965-73 [iii]
	1979	1970-79 [iii]
	1983	1974-83
	1988	1980-88 [iii]
	1993	1985-93
-selon la langue et le sexe	1956	1945-55
	1963	1955-63
	1964	1955-64 [iii]
	1971	1962-71
	1973	1965-73 [iii]
	1979	1970-79 [iii]
	1983	1974-83
	1988	1980-88 [iii]
	1993	1985-93
-selon le niveau d'instruction, l'âge et le sexe	1956	1945-55
	1963	1955-63
	1964	1955-64 [iii]
	1971	1962-71
	1973	1965-73 [iii]
	1979	1970-79 [iii]
	1983	1974-83
	1988	1980-88 [iii]
	1993	1985-93
-selon le pays ou zone de naissance et le sexe	1956	1945-55
	1963	1955-63
	1964	1955-64 [iii]
	1971	1962-71
	1973	1965-73 [iii]
-selon le pays ou zone de naissance et le sexe et l'âge	1977	Dernière
	1983	1974-83
	1989	1980-88
-selon la nationalité juridique et le sexe	1956	1945-55
	1963	1955-63
	1964	1955-64 [iii]
	1971	1962-71
	1973	1965-73 [iii]
-selon la nationalité juridique et le sexe et l'âge	1977	Dernière
	1983	1974-83
	1989	1980-88
-selon les principales divisions administratives (voir: des principales divisions administratives, ci-dessus)		
-selon la religion et le sexe	1956	1945-55
	1963	1955-63
	1964	1955-64 [iii]
	1971	1962-71
	1973	1965-73 [iii]

Sujet	Année de l'édition	Période considérée
	1979	1970-79 [iii]
	1983	1974-83
	1988	1980-88 [iii]
	1993	1985-93
-selon la résidence (urbaine/rurale) (voir: urbaine/rurale (résidence), ci-dessous)		
-selon le sexe (voir: également: par année d'âge et par sexe, et aussi par groupes d'âge et par sexe, ci-dessus):		
dénombrée	1948-1952	Dernière
	1953	1950-52
	1954-1959	Dernière
	1960	1900-61
	1961	Dernière
	1962	1900-62
	1963	1955-63
	1964	1955-64
	1965-1969	Dernière
	1970	1950-70
	1971	1962-71
	1972	Dernière
	1973	1965-73
	1974-1978	Dernière
	1978SR [i]	1948-78
	1979-1982	Dernière
	1983	1974-83
	1984-1991	Dernière
	1991 VP [v]	1950-90
	1992-1997	Dernière
	1997SR [ii]	1948-97
	1998-2001	Dernière
estimée	1948-	
	1949/50	1945 et Dernière
	1951-1954	Dernière [iii]
	1955-1959	Dernière
	1960	1940-60
	1961-1969	Dernière
	1970	1950-70
	1971	1962-71
	1972	Dernière
	1973	1965-73
	1974-1997	Dernière
	1997SR [ii]	1948-97
	1998-2001	Dernière
-urbaine/rurale (résidence)	1968	1964-68
	1969	1965-69
	1970	1950-70
	1971	1962-71
	1972	1968-72
	1973	1965-73
	1974	1966-74
	1975	1967-75
	1976	1967-76
	1977	1968-77
	1978	1969-78
	1979	1970-79
	1980	1971-80

Index
Index historique (suite)
(Voir notes à la fin de l'index)

Sujet	Année de l'édition	Période considérée
	1981	1972-81
	1982	1973-82
	1983	1974-83
	1984	1975-84
	1985	1976-85
	1986	1977-86
	1987	1978-87
	1988	1979-88
	1989	1980-89
	1990	1981-90
	1991	1982-91
	1992	1983-92
	1993	1984-93
	1994	1985-94
	1995	1986-95
	1996	1987-96
	1997	1988-97
	1998	1989-98
	1999	1990-99
	2000	1991-00
	2001	1992-01
féminine: selon le nombre total d'enfants nés vivants et l'âge		
	1971	1962-71
	1973	1965-73 [iii]
	1975	1965-74
	1978SR [i]	1948-77
	1981	1972-80
	1986	1977-85
	1997SR [ii]	1948-96
féminine: selon le nombre total d'enfants vivants et l'âge		
	1971	1962-71
	1973	1965-73 [iii]
	1975	1965-74
	1978SR [i]	1948-77
	1981	1972-80
	1986	1977-85
	1997SR [ii]	1948-96
fréquentant l'école selon l'âge et le sexe		
	1971	1962-71
	1973	1965-73 [iii]
	1979	1970-79 [iii]
	1983	1974-83
	1988	1980-88 [iii]
	1988	1980-88 [iii]
	1993	1985-93
par année d'âge et par sexe		
	1971	1962-71
	1973	1965-73 [iii]
	1979	1970-79 [iii]
	1983	1974-83
	1993	1985-93
selon la situation familiale	1991 VP [v]	Dernière
selon l'âge et le sexe: dénombrée		
	1963	1955-63
	1964	1955-64 [iii]
	1967	Dernière
	1970	1950-70
	1971	1962-71
	1972	Dernière
	1973	1965-73

Sujet	Année de l'édition	Période considérée
	1974-1978	Dernière
	1978SR [i]	1948-77
	1979-1991	Dernière
	1991VP [v]	1950-90
	1992-1997	Dernière
	1997SR [ii]	1948-97
	1998-2001	Dernière
selon l'âge et le sexe: estimée		
	1963	Dernière
	1967	Dernière
	1970	1950-70
	1971-1997	Dernière
	1997SR [ii]	1948-97
	1998-1999	Dernière
selon l'alphabétisme, l'âge et le sexe		
	1971	1962-71
	1973	1965-73 [iii]
	1979	1970-79 [iii]
	1983	1974-83
	1988	1980-88 [iii]
	1993	1985-93
selon la composition ethnique et le sexe		
	1971	1962-71
	1973	1965-73 [iii]
	1979	1970-79 [iii]
	1983	1974-83
	1988	1980-88 [iii]
	1993	1985-93
	1971	1962-71
selon l'état matrimonial, l'âge et le sexe		
	1971	1962-71
	1973	1965-73 [iii]
selon la langue et le sexe	1971	1962-71
	1973	1965-73 [iii]
	1979	1970-79 [iii]
	1983	1974-83
	1988	1980-88 [iii]
	1993	1985-93
selon la nationalité juridique et le sexe		
	1971	1962-71
	1973	1965-73 [iii]
selon la nationalité juridique et le sexe et l'âge		
	1977	Dernière
	1983	1974-83
	1989	1980-88
selon le niveau d'instruction, l'âge et le sexe		
	1971	1962-71
	1973	1965-73 [iii]
	1979	1970-79 [iii]
	1983	1974-83
	1988	1980-88 [iii]
	1993	1985-93
selon le pays ou zone de naissance et le sexe		
	1971	1962-71
	1973	1965-73 [iii]
selon le pays ou zone de naissance et le sexe et l'âge		
	1977	Dernière
	1983	1974-83
	1989	1980-88

Index
Index historique (suite)
(Voir notes à la fin de l'index)

Sujet	Année de l'édition	Période considérée	Sujet	Année de l'édition	Période considérée
selon les principales divisions administratives	1971	1962-71		1973	1965-73
	1973	1965-73 [iii]		1974	1966-74
	1979	1970-79 [iii]		1975	1967-75
	1983	1974-83		1976	1967-76
	1988	1980-88 [iii]		1977	1968-77
	1993	1985-93		1978	1969-78
selon la religion et le sexe	1971	1962-71		1979	1970-79
	1973	1965-73 [iii]		1980	1971-80
	1979	1970-79 [iii]		1981	1972-81
	1983	1974-83		1982	1973-82
	1988	1980-88 [iii]		1983	1974-83
	1993	1985-93		1984	1975-84
selon le sexe: nombres	1948	Dernière		1985	1976-85
	1952	1900-51		1986	1977-86
	1955	1945-54		1987	1978-87
	1960	1920-60		1988	1979-88
	1962	1955-62		1989	1980-89
	1963	1955-63		1990	1981-90
	1964	1955-64 [iii]		1991	1982-91
	1967	Dernière		1992	1983-92
	1970	1950-70		1993	1984-93
	1971	1962-71		1994	1985-94
	1972	Dernière		1995	1986-95
	1973	1965-73		1996	1987-96
	1974	1966-74		1997	1988-97
	1975	1967-75		1998	1989-98
	1976	1967-76		1999	1990-99
	1977	1968-77		2000	1991-00
	1978	1969-78		2001	1992-01
	1979	1970-79	-Vieillissement indicateurs divers	1991 VP [v]	1950-90
	1980	1971-80	-Villes (voir: des villes, ci-dessus)		
	1981	1972-81			
	1982	1973-82			
	1983	1974-83			
	1984	1975-84			
	1985	1976-85	**R**		
	1986	1977-86			
	1987	1978-87	**Rapports** (voir: Fécondité proportionnelle; Mortalité fœtale (tardive), rapports de; Mortalité périnatale, rapports de; Natalité proportionnelle; Rapports enfants-femmes)		
	1988	1979-88			
	1989	1980-89			
	1990	1981-90			
	1991	1982-91			
	1992	1983-92			
	1993	1984-93	**Rapports enfants-femmes**	1949/50	1900-50
	1994	1985-94		1954	1900-52
	1995	1986-95		1955	1945-54
	1996	1987-96		1959	1935-59
	1997	1988-97		1963	1955-63
	1998	1989-98		1965	1945-65
	1999	1990-99		1969	Dernière
	2000	1991-00		1975	1966-74
	2001	1992-01		1978SR [i]	1948-77
pourcentage	1948	Dernière		1981	1962-80
	1952	1900-51		1986	1967-85
	1955	1945-54		1997SR [ii]	1948-96
	1960	1920-60		1999CD [vii]	1980-1999
	1962	1955-62	-dans les zones (urbaines/rurales)	1965	Dernière
	1970	1950-70		1969	Dernière
	1971	1962-71			

Index
Index historique (suite)
(Voir notes à la fin de l'index)

Index
Index historique (suite)
(Voir notes à la fin de l'index)

Sujet	Année de l'édition	Période considérée
Caractéristiques relatives aux ménages	1955	1945-54
	1962	1955-62
	1963	1955-63 [iii]
	1971	1962-71
	1973	1965-73 [iii]
	1976	1966-75
	1983	1974-83
	1987	1975-86
	1995	1985-95
Caractéristiques relatives à la fécondité	1949/50	1900-50
	1954	1900-53
	1955	1945-54
	1959	1935-59
	1963	1955-63
	1965	1955-65
	1969	Dernière
	1971	1962-71
	1973	1965-73 [iii]
	1975	1965-75
	1981	1972-81
	1986	1977-86
	1992	1983-92
	1999CD [vii]	1980-99
-Evolution de la population	1960	1920-60
	1970	1950-70
-Supplément historique	1978SR [i]	1948-78
	1997SR [ii]	1948-97
Superficie		
-des continents	1949/50- 1992-2001	Dernière
-des grandes régions(continentales)	1964-2001	Dernière
-des pays ou zones	1948-2001	Dernière
-des régions	1952-2001	Dernière
-du monde	1949/50- 2001	Dernière
-Vieillissement de la population et situation des personnes âgées	1991VP [v]	1950-90

Survivants (voir: Mortalité, tables de)

T

Tables de mortalité (voir: Mortalité, tables de)

Sujet	Année de l'édition	Période considérée
Taux (voir: Accroissement intercensitaire de la population; Accroissement naturel; Alphabétisme; Analphabétisme; Annulation; Divortialité; Fécondité Intercensitaire; Mortalité Infantile, Mortalité maternelle; Mortalité néonatale; Mortalité post-néonatale; Mortalité, tables de; Mortalité; Natalité; Nuptialité; Reproduction; taux bruts et nets de)		

Taux bruts de reproduction (voir: Reproduction)

Taux nets de reproduction (voir: Reproduction)

Texte spécial (voir liste détaillée dans l'Appendice de cet index)

U

Urbaine/rurale (décès) (voir: Décès)

Urbaine/rurale (ménages: dimension moyenne des) (voir: Ménages)

Urbaine/rurale (mortalité infantile) (voir: Mortalité infantile)

Urbaine/rurale(naissances) (voir: Naissances)

Urbaine/rurale(population) (voir: Population selon la résidence (urbaine/rurale))

V

Vieillissement (voir: Population)

Villes (voir: Population)

Index
Index historique (suite)
(Voir notes à la fin de l'index)

APPENDICE

Texte spécial de chaque Annuaire démographique

Divorce:

"Application des statistiques de la nuptialité et de la divortialité", 1958.

Mariage:

"Application des statistiques de la nuptialité et de la divortialité", 1958.

Ménages:

"Concepts et définitions des ménages, du chef de ménage et de la population des collectivités", 1987.

Migration:

"'Statistiques des migrations internationales",1977.

Mortalité:

"Tendances récentes de la mortalité", 1951.
"Développement des statistiques des causes de décès",1951.
"Les facteurs du fléchissement de la mortalité",1957.
"Notes sur les méthodes d'évaluation de la fiabilité des statistiques classiques de la mortalité",1961.
"Mortalité: Tendances récentes",1966.
"Tendances de la mortalité chez les personnes âgées",1991VP [v].

Natalité:

"Présentation graphiques des tendances de la fécondité",1959.

"Taux de natalité: Tendances récentes",1965.

Population:

"Tendances démo-graphiques mondiales,1920-1949",1949/50.
"Mouvements d'urbanisation et ses caractéristiques",1952.
"Les recensements de population de 1950",1955.
"Situation démographique mondiale",1956.
"Ce que nous savons de l'état et de l'évolution de la population mondiale",1960.
"Notes sur les statistiques disponibles des recensements nationaux de population et méthodes d'évaluation de leur exactitude",1962.
"Disponibilité et qualité de certaines données statistiques fondées sur les recensements de population effectués entre 1955 et 1963",1963.
"Disponibilité de certaines statistiques fondées sur les recensements de population: 1955-1964",1964.
"Définitions et concepts statistiques de la population urbaine et de la population rurale",1967.
"Application des statistiques de la nuptialité et de la divortialité",1958.
"Ce que nous savons de l'état et de l'évolution de la population mondiale",1970.
"Recommandations de l'Organisation des Nations Unies quant aux sujets sur lesquels doit porter un recensement de population, en regard de la pratique adoptée par les différents pays dans les recensements nationaux effectués de 1965 à 1971",1971.
"Les définitions statistiques de la population urbaine et leurs usages en démographie appliquée",1972.
"Evolution récente de la fécondité dans le monde",1969.
"Dates des recensements nationaux de la population et de l'habitation effectués au cours de la décennie 1965-1974", 1974.
"Dates des recensements nationaux de la population et de l'habitation effectués ou prévus, au cours de la décennie 1975-1984",1979.
"Dates des recensements nationaux de la population et/ou de l'habitation effectués au cours de la décennie 1965-1974 et effectués ou prévus au cours de la décennie1975-1984",1983.
"Définitions et concepts statistiques du ménage",1968.
"Dates des recensements nationaux de la population et/ou de l'habitation effectués au cours de la décennie 1975-1984 et effectués ou prévus au cours de la décennie1985-1994", 1988, 1993.
"Statistiques concernant la population active: un aperçu",1984.

Index
Index historique (suite)
(Voir notes à la fin de l'index)

"'Etude du vieillissement et de la situation des personnes âgées: Besoins particuliers",1991VP [v].
"Les incapacités", 1991VP [v].
"Le vieillissement", 1991VP [v].

Notes générales

Cet index alphabétique donne la liste des sujets traités dans chacune de 51 éditions de l'Annuaire démographique. La colonne "Année de l'édition" indique l'édition spécifique dans laquelle le sujet a été traité. Sauf indication contraire, la colonne "Période considérée" désigne les années pour lesquelles les statistiques annuelles apparaissant dans l'Annuaire démographique sont indiquées sous la colonne "Année de l'édition". La rubrique "Dernière" ou " 2-Dernières" indique que les données représentent la ou les dernières années disponibles seulement.

---

[i] Le Supplément rétrospectif du 30ème Annuaire Démographique fait l'objet d'un tirage spécial publié en 1979.

[ii] Le Supplément rétrospectif du 49ème Annuaire Démographique fait l'objet d'un tirage spécial (CD-ROM) publié en 2000

[iii] Données non disponibles dans l'édition précédente seulement.

[iv] Titres non disponibles dans la bibliographie précédente seulement.

[v] Taux moyens pour 5 ans.

[vi] Vieillissement de la population.

[vii] Le Supplément du 51 Annuaire Démographique, ayant comme suject la natalité, fait l'objet d'un tirage spécial (CD-ROM) publié en 2002.

كيفيـة الحصـول على منشـورات الأمـم المتحـدة

يمكـن الحصول على منشـورات الأمم المتحـدة من المكتبات ودور التوزيع في جميع أنحـاء العالـم . استعلم عنها من المكتبة
التي تتعامـل معها أو اكتـب إلى : الأمـم المتحـدة ، قسم البيع في نيويورك أو في جنيف .

如何购取联合国出版物

联合国出版物在全世界各地的书店和经售处均有发售。请向书店询问或写信到纽约或日内瓦的
联合国销售组。

HOW TO OBTAIN UNITED NATIONS PUBLICATIONS

United Nations publications may be obtained from bookstores and distributors throughout the
world. Consult your bookstore or write to: United Nations, Sales Section, New York or Geneva.

COMMENT SE PROCURER LES PUBLICATIONS DES NATIONS UNIES

Les publications des Nations Unies sont en vente dans les librairies et les agences dépositaires
du monde entier. Informez-vous auprès de votre libraire ou adressez-vous à : Nations Unies,
Section des ventes, New York ou Genève.

КАК ПОЛУЧИТЬ ИЗДАНИЯ ОРГАНИЗАЦИИ ОБЪЕДИНЕННЫХ НАЦИЙ

Издания Организации Объединенных Наций можно купить в книжных магазинах
и агентствах во всех районах мира. Наводите справки об изданиях в вашем книжном
магазине или пишите по адресу: Организация Объединенных Наций, Секция по
продаже изданий, Нью-Йорк или Женева.

COMO CONSEGUIR PUBLICACIONES DE LAS NACIONES UNIDAS

Las publicaciones de las Naciones Unidas están en venta en librerías y casas distribuidoras en
todas partes del mundo. Consulte a su librero o diríjase a: Naciones Unidas, Sección de Ventas,
Nueva York o Ginebra.

Litho in United Nations, New York
37854—December 2003—4,660
ISBN 92-1-051094-1

ISSN 0082-8041

United Nations publication
Sales No. E/F.03.XIII.1
ST/ESA/STAT/SER.R/32